The **profit margin** shows the percentage of each sales dollar that results in net income.

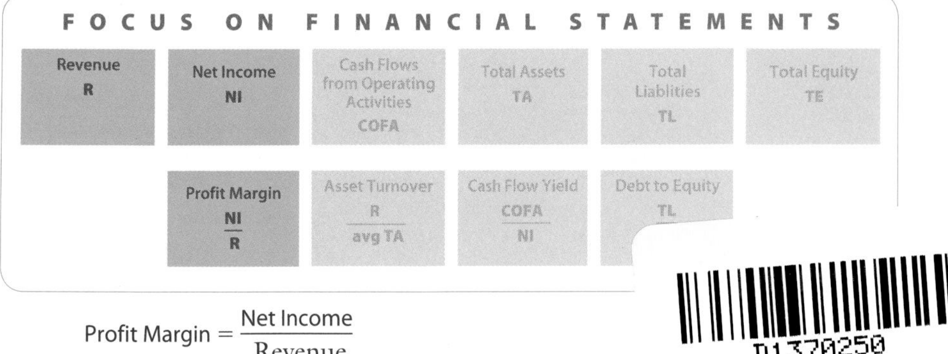

$$\text{Profit Margin} = \frac{\text{Net Income}}{\text{Revenue}}$$

The **asset turnover** ratio measures how efficiently assets ar

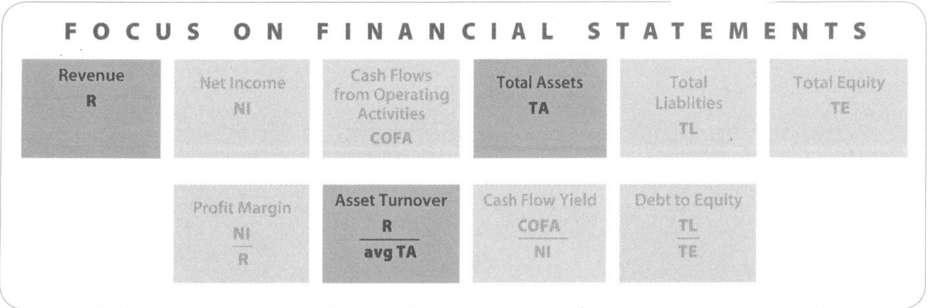

$$\text{Asset Turnover} = \frac{\text{Revenue}}{\text{Average Total Assets}}$$

The **cash flow yield** ratio measures how much cash a company's operations generate in relation to its net income.

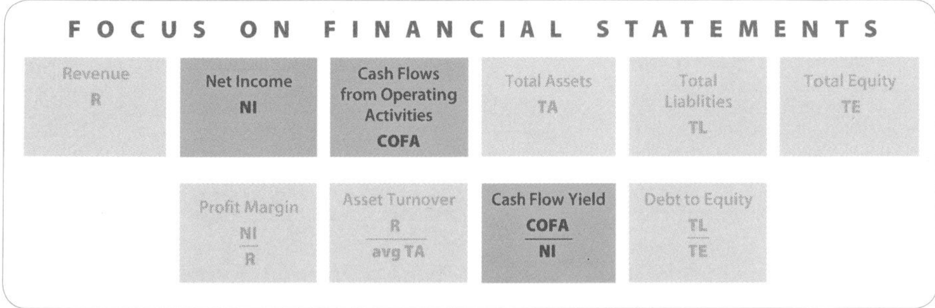

$$\text{Cash Flow Yield} = \frac{\text{Cash Flows from Operating Activities}}{\text{Net Income}}$$

The **debt to equity ratio** reflects a company's strategy for financing its operations.

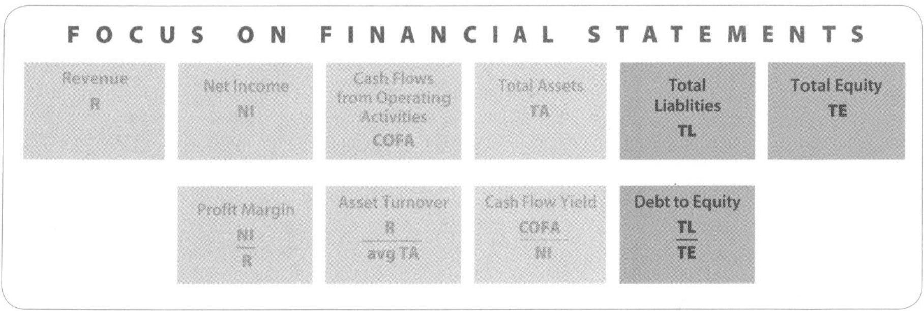

$$\text{Debt to Equity} = \frac{\text{Total Liabilities}}{\text{Total Equity}}$$

Simply understanding how to find these six elements on the financial statements and how to compute these four ratios will allow you to analyze financial statements and determine how well or poorly a company is performing, which, in turn, is the basis for making good business decisions.

Financial Accounting

ELEVENTH EDITION

Belverd E. Needles, Jr., Ph.D., C.P.A., C.M.A.
DePaul University

Marian Powers, Ph.D.
Northwestern University

Australia • Brazil • Canada • Mexico • Singapore • Spain • United Kingdom • United States

SOUTH-WESTERN
CENGAGE Learning™

Financial Accounting, 11th Edition

Belverd E. Needles, Jr.
Marian Powers

Vice President of Editorial, Business: Jack W. Calhoun
Editor-in-Chief: Rob Dewey
Senior Acquisitions Editor: Sharon Oblinger
Developmental Editor: Krista Kellman
Editorial Assistant: Courtney Doyle
Senior Marketing Manager: Kristen Hurd
Marketing Coordinator: Nicole Parsons
Content Project Manager: Corey Geissler
Media Editor: Bryan England
Senior Frontlist Buyer, Manufacturing: Doug Wilke
Production Service: Cadmus Communications
Senior Art Director: Stacy Jenkins Shirley
Internal Designer: Craig Ramsdell
Cover Designer: Craig Ramsdell
Cover Image: © Mike Grandmaison/All Canada Photos/ Corbis
Rights Acquisitions Specialist: John Hill

Library of Congress Control Number: 2010940446

Package ISBN-13: 978-0-538-47601-0
Package ISBN-10: 0-538-47601-X

Student Edition ISBN 13: 978-1-111-82094-7
Student Edition ISBN 10: 1-111-82094-5

South-Western
5191 Natorp Boulevard
Mason, OH 45040
USA

Cengage Learning products are represented in Canada by Nelson Education, Ltd.

For your course and learning solutions, visit www.cengage.com
Purchase any of our products at your local college store or at our preferred online store **www.CengageBrain.com**

Printed in Canada
1 2 3 4 5 6 7 14 13 12 11 10

BRIEF CONTENTS

1 Uses of Accounting Information and the Financial Statements 3

SUPPLEMENT TO CHAPTER 1 How to Read an Annual Report 46

2 Analyzing Business Transactions 89

3 Measuring Business Income 137

SUPPLEMENT TO CHAPTER 3 Closing Entries and the Work Sheet 184

4 Financial Reporting and Analysis 197

SUPPLEMENT TO CHAPTER 4 The Annual Report Project 242

5 The Operating Cycle and Merchandising Operations 245

6 Inventories 291

7 Cash and Receivables 327

8 Current Liabilities and Fair Value Accounting 363

9 Long-Term Assets 401

10 Long-Term Liabilities 443

11 Stockholders' Equity 487

12 The Statement of Cash Flows 537

13 Financial Performance Measurement 585

14 Investments 635

APPENDIX A Accounting for Unincorporated Businesses 674

APPENDIX B Present Value Tables 684

CONTENTS

Preface xii
About the Authors xxv

CHAPTER 1 **Uses of Accounting Information and the Financial Statements** 3

DECISION POINT **A USER'S FOCUS CVS CAREMARK** 2
Accounting as an Information System 4
Business Goals and Activities 4
Financial and Management Accounting 6
Ethical Financial Reporting 7
Decision Makers: The Users of Accounting Information 8
Management 9
Users with a Direct Financial Interest 9
Users with an Indirect Financial Interest 10
Governmental and Not-for-Profit Organizations 10
Accounting Measurement 11
Business Transactions 11
Money Measure 12
Separate Entity 12
The Corporate Form of Business 13
Forms of Business 13
Formation and Organization of a Corporation 14
The Financial Statements and Their Elements 15
Income Statement 15
Statement of Retained Earnings 16
Balance Sheet 16
Statement of Cash Flows 18
Relationships Among the Financial Statements 19
Focus on Financial Statement Elements: Financial Ratios 19
Generally Accepted Accounting Principles 22
GAAP and the Independent CPA's Report 23
Organizations That Issue Accounting Standards 24
Other Organizations That Influence GAAP 24
Professional Conduct 25
A LOOK BACK AT **CVS CAREMARK** 27
STOP & REVIEW 29
CHAPTER ASSIGNMENTS 30

SUPPLEMENT TO CHAPTER 1 HOW TO READ AN ANNUAL REPORT 46

The Components of an Annual Report 46
Letter to the Stockholders 46
Financial Highlights 47
Description of the Company 47
Management's Discussion and Analysis 47
Financial Statements 47
Notes to the Financial Statements 50
Reports of Management's Responsibilities 53
Reports of Certified Public Accountants 53

CHAPTER 2 **Analyzing Business Transactions** 89

DECISION POINT **A USER'S FOCUS THE BOEING COMPANY** 88
Measurement Issues 90
Recognition 90
Valuation 91
Classification 92
Ethics and Measurement Issues 92
Double-Entry System 93
Accounts 93
The T Account 94
The T Account Illustrated 94
Rules of Double-Entry Accounting 94
Normal Balance 95
Stockholders' Equity Accounts 96

The Accounting Cycle 96
Business Transaction Analysis 98
Owner's Investment in the Business 98
Economic Event That Is Not a Business Transaction 99
Prepayment of Expenses in Cash 99
Purchase of an Asset on Credit 100
Purchase of an Asset Partly in Cash and Partly on Credit 100
Payment of a Liability 101
Revenue in Cash 101
Revenue on Credit 102
Revenue Received in Advance 102
Collection on Account 102
Expense Paid in Cash 103
Expense to Be Paid Later 103
Dividends 104
Summary of Transactions 104
The Trial Balance 106
Preparation and Use of a Trial Balance 106
Finding Trial Balance Errors 107
Recording and Posting Transactions 108
Chart of Accounts 108
General Journal 108
General Ledger 110
Some Notes on Presentation 111
Cash Flows and the Timing of Transactions 112
A LOOK BACK AT **THE BOEING COMPANY** 114
STOP & REVIEW 118
CHAPTER ASSIGNMENTS 119

CHAPTER 3 **Measuring Business Income** 137

DECISION POINT **A USER'S FOCUS NETFLIX, INC.** 136
Profitability Measurement Issues and Ethics 138
Net Income 138
Income Measurement Assumptions 138
Ethics and the Matching Rule 140
Accrual Accounting 141
Recognizing Revenues 142
Recognizing Expenses 142
Adjusting the Accounts 143
Adjustments and Ethics 143
The Adjustment Process 144
Type 1 Adjustment: Allocating Recorded Costs (Deferred Expenses) 145
Type 2 Adjustment: Recognizing Unrecorded Expenses (Accrued Expenses) 148
Type 3 Adjustment: Allocating Recorded, Unearned Revenues (Deferred Revenues) 150
Type 4 Adjustment: Recognizing Unrecorded, Earned Revenues (Accrued Revenues) 151
A Note About Journal Entries 152
Using the Adjusted Trial Balance to Prepare Financial Statements 152
Closing Entries 154
Cash Flows from Accrual-Based Information 156
A LOOK BACK AT **NETFLIX, INC.** 158
STOP & REVIEW 163
CHAPTER ASSIGNMENTS 164

SUPPLEMENT TO CHAPTER 3 CLOSING ENTRIES AND THE WORK SHEET 184

Preparing Closing Entries 184
Step 1: Closing the Credit Balances 184
Step 2: Closing the Debit Balances 184
Step 3: Closing the Income Summary Account Balance 187
Step 4: Closing the Dividends Account Balance 187
The Accounts After Closing 187
The Work Sheet: An Accountant's Tool 188
Preparing the Work Sheet 188
Using the Work Sheet 191
SUPPLEMENT ASSIGNMENTS 192

CHAPTER 4 Financial Reporting and Analysis 197

DECISION POINT **A USER'S FOCUS DELL COMPUTER CORPORATION 196**

Foundations of Financial Reporting 198

Objective of Financial Reporting 198

Qualitative Characteristics of Accounting Information 199

Accounting Conventions 200

Ethical Financial Reporting 200

Accounting Conventions for Preparing Financial Statements 201

Consistency 202

Full Disclosure (Transparency) 202

Materiality 202

Conservatism 203

Cost-Benefit 203

Classified Balance Sheet 204

Assets 206

Liabilities 207

Stockholders' Equity 207

Owner's Equity and Partners' Equity 207

Dell's Balance Sheets 208

Forms of the Income Statement 210

Multistep Income Statement 210

Dell's Income Statements 213

Single-Step Income Statement 214

Using Financial Ratios for Performance Evaluation 215

Critical Financial Ratios and Financial Statement Elements 215

Beyond the Basics: Additional Financial Ratios 219

A LOOK BACK AT **DELL COMPUTER CORPORATION** 223

STOP & REVIEW 226

CHAPTER ASSIGNMENTS 228

SUPPLEMENT TO CHAPTER 4 THE ANNUAL REPORT PROJECT 242

Instructions 242

CHAPTER 5 The Operating Cycle and Merchandising Operations 245

DECISION POINT **A USER'S FOCUS BEST BUY CO., INC.** 244

Managing Merchandising Businesses 246

Evaluation of Liquidity 246

Operating Cycle 247

Choice of Inventory System 248

Foreign Business Transactions 249

The Need for Internal Controls 250

Management's Responsibility for Internal Control 251

Terms of Sale 252

Sales and Purchases Discounts 252

Transportation Costs 253

Terms of Debit and Credit Card Sales 253

Perpetual Inventory System 254

Purchases of Merchandise 254

Sales of Merchandise 256

Periodic Inventory System 258

Purchases of Merchandise 259

Sales of Merchandise 261

Internal Control: Components, Activities, and Limitations 263

Components of Internal Control 263

Control Activities 263

Limitations on Internal Control 264

Internal Control over Merchandising Transactions 265

Internal Control and Management Goals 265

Control of Cash Receipts 266

Control of Purchases and Cash Disbursements 267

A LOOK BACK AT **BEST BUY CO., INC.** 270

STOP & REVIEW 272

CHAPTER ASSIGNMENTS 274

CHAPTER 6 Inventories 291

DECISION POINT A USER'S FOCUS CISCO SYSTEMS, INC. 290
Managing Inventories 292
Inventory Decisions 292
Financial Ratios: Inventory Turnover and Days' Inventory on Hand 293
Inventory Management 294
Effects of Inventory Misstatements on Income Measurement 295
Inventory Misstatements and Fraud 295
Inventory Cost and Valuation 297
Goods Flows and Cost Flows 297
Lower-of-Cost-or-Market (LCM) Rule 298
Disclosure of Inventory Methods 299
Inventory Cost Under the Periodic Inventory System 299
Specific Identification Method 300
Average-Cost Method 300
First-In, First-Out (FIFO) Method 301
Last-In, First-Out (LIFO) Method 301
Summary of Inventory Costing Methods 302
Impact of Inventory Decisions 302
Effects on the Financial Statements 303
Effects on Income Taxes 304
Effects on Cash Flows 305
Inventory Cost Under the Perpetual Inventory System 305
Valuing Inventory by Estimation 308
Retail Method 308
Gross Profit Method 308
A LOOK BACK AT CISCO SYSTEMS, INC. 310
STOP & REVIEW 313
CHAPTER ASSIGNMENTS 314

CHAPTER 7 Cash and Receivables 327

DECISION POINT A USER'S FOCUS HEWLETT-PACKARD COMPANY 326
Management Issues Related to Cash and Receivables 328
Cash Management 328
Accounts Receivable and Credit Policies 329
Evaluating the Level of Accounts Receivable 330
Financing Receivables 331
Ethics and Estimates in Accounting for Receivables 333
Cash Equivalents and Cash Control 334
Cash Equivalents 334
Cash Control Methods 334
Uncollectible Accounts 337
The Allowance Method 338
Disclosure of Uncollectible Accounts 338
Estimating Uncollectible Accounts Expense 339
Writing Off Uncollectible Accounts 342
Notes Receivable 343
Maturity Date 344
Duration of a Note 344
Interest and Interest Rate 345
Maturity Value 345
Accrued Interest 346
Dishonored Note 346
A LOOK BACK AT HEWLETT-PACKARD COMPANY (HP) 347
STOP & REVIEW 348
CHAPTER ASSIGNMENTS 350

CHAPTER 8 Current Liabilities and Fair Value Accounting 363

DECISION POINT A USER'S FOCUS MICROSOFT 362
Management Issues Related to Current Liabilities 364
Managing Liquidity and Cash Flows 364
Evaluating Accounts Payable 365
Reporting Liabilities 366
Common Types of Current Liabilities 368
Definitely Determinable Liabilities 368
Estimated Liabilities 373
Contingent Liabilities and Commitments 376
Valuation Approaches to Fair Value Accounting 377
Interest, the Time Value of Money, and Future Value 378

Calculating Present Value 379
Applications Using Present Value 382
Valuing an Asset 382
Deferred Payment 383
Other Applications 383
A LOOK BACK AT **MICROSOFT** 384
STOP & REVIEW 387
CHAPTER ASSIGNMENTS 388

CHAPTER 9 **Long-Term Assets** 401

DECISION POINT **A USER'S FOCUS APPLE COMPUTER, INC.** 400
Management Issues Related to Long-Term Assets 402
Acquiring Long-Term Assets 404
Financing Long-Term Assets 405
Applying the Matching Rule 406
Acquisition Cost of Property, Plant, and Equipment 407
General Approach to Acquisition Costs 408
Specific Applications 408
Depreciation 411
Factors in Computing Depreciation 411
Methods of Computing Depreciation 412
Special Issues in Depreciation 415
Disposal of Depreciable Assets 417
Discarded Plant Assets 417
Plant Assets Sold for Cash 418
Exchanges of Plant Assets 419
Natural Resources 419
Depletion 419
Depreciation of Related Plant Assets 420
Development and Exploration Costs in the Oil and Gas Industry 421
Intangible Assets 422
Research and Development Costs 424
Computer Software Costs 425
Goodwill 425
A LOOK BACK AT **APPLE COMPUTER, INC.** 426
STOP & REVIEW 428
CHAPTER ASSIGNMENTS 429

CHAPTER 10 **Long-Term Liabilities** 443

DECISION POINT **A USER'S FOCUS MCDONALD'S CORPORATION** 442
Management Issues Related to Long-Term Debt Financing 444
Deciding to Issue Long-Term Debt 444
Evaluating Long-Term Debt 445
Types of Long-Term Debt 446
Cash Flow Information 451
The Nature of Bonds 452
Bond Issue: Prices and Interest Rates 452
Characteristics of Bonds 453
Accounting for the Issuance of Bonds 455
Bonds Issued at Face Value 455
Bonds Issued at a Discount 455
Bonds Issued at a Premium 456
Bond Issue Costs 457
Using Present Value to Value a Bond 457
Market Rate Above Face Rate 458
Market Rate Below Face Rate 458
Amortization of Bond Discounts and Premiums 459
Amortizing a Bond Discount 459
Amortizing a Bond Premium 464
Retirement and Conversion of Bonds 468
Retirement of Bonds 468
Conversion of Bonds 469
A LOOK BACK AT **MCDONALD'S CORPORATION** 470
STOP & REVIEW 472
CHAPTER ASSIGNMENTS 474

CHAPTER 11 **Stockholders' Equity** 487

DECISION POINT **A USER'S FOCUS GOOGLE, INC.** 486

Management Issues Related to Contributed Capital 488

The Corporate Form of Business 488

Equity Financing 490

Dividend Policies 491

Measuring Performance Using Financial Ratios 493

Stock Options as Compensation 495

Cash Flow Information 496

Components of Stockholders' Equity 497

Characteristics of Preferred Stock 498

Issuance of Stock for Cash and Other Assets 501

Par Value Stock 501

No-Par Stock 502

Issuance of Stock for Noncash Assets 503

Accounting for Treasury Stock 505

Purchase of Treasury Stock 505

Sale of Treasury Stock 506

Retirement of Treasury Stock 507

Stock Dividends and Stock Splits 508

Stock Dividends 508

Stock Splits 510

The Statement of Stockholders' Equity and Book Value per Share 512

Statement of Stockholders' Equity 512

Book Value per Share 514

A LOOK BACK AT **GOOGLE, INC.** 515

STOP & REVIEW 519

CHAPTER ASSIGNMENTS 521

CHAPTER 12 **The Statement of Cash Flows** 537

DECISION POINT **A USER'S FOCUS AMAZON.COM, INC.** 536

Overview of the Statement of Cash Flows 538

Purposes and Uses of the Statement of Cash Flows 538

Classification of Cash Flows 538

Required Disclosure of Noncash Investing and Financing Transactions 541

Ethical Considerations and the Statement of Cash Flows 541

Analyzing Cash Flows 542

Cash Flow Ratios 542

Free Cash Flow 544

Asking the Right Questions About the Statement of Cash Flows 545

Step One: Determining Cash Flows from Operating Activities 546

Depreciation, Amortization, and Depletion 549

Gains and Losses 550

Changes in Current Assets 550

Changes in Current Liabilities 551

Schedule of Cash Flows from Operating Activities 552

Step Two: Determining Cash Flows from Investing Activities 553

Investments 554

Plant Assets 554

Step Three: Determining Cash Flows from Financing Activities 556

Bonds Payable 557

Common Stock 557

Retained Earnings 558

Treasury Stock 558

Step Four: Preparing the Statement of Cash Flows 559

A LOOK BACK AT **AMAZON.COM, INC.** 560

STOP & REVIEW 564

CHAPTER ASSIGNMENTS 565

CHAPTER 13 **Financial Performance Measurement** 585

DECISION POINT **A USER'S FOCUS STARBUCKS CORPORATION** 584

Foundations of Financial Performance Measurement 586

Financial Performance Measurement: Management's Objectives 586

Management Compensation 586

Financial Performance Measurement: Creditors' and Investors' Objectives 587

Standards of Comparison 587

Sources of Information 589

Evaluating Quality of Earnings 590
Accounting Methods 590
Accounting Estimates 591
One-Time Items 592
Tools and Techniques of Financial Analysis 594
Horizontal Analysis 594
Trend Analysis 597
Vertical Analysis 598
Financial Ratio Analysis 600
Comprehensive Illustration of Financial Ratio Analysis 600
Evaluating Profitability and Total Asset Management 601
Evaluating Liquidity 604
Evaluating Financial Risk 605
Evaluating Operating Asset Management 607
Supplemental Financial Ratios for Assessing Operating Asset Management and Liquidity 609
Evaluating Market Strength with Financial Ratios 610
A LOOK BACK AT **STARBUCKS CORPORATION** 612
STOP & REVIEW 616
CHAPTER ASSIGNMENTS 617

CHAPTER 14 **Investments** 635

DECISION POINT **A USER'S FOCUS INTEL CORPORATION** 634
Management Issues Related to Investments 636
Recognition 636
Valuation 636
Classification 636
Disclosure 638
Ethics of Investing 638
Short-Term Investments in Equity Securities 639
Trading Securities 639
Available-for-Sale Securities 642
Long-Term Investments in Equity Securities 643
Noninfluential and Noncontrolling Investment 643
An Influential but Noncontrolling Investment 646
A Controlling Investment 648
Consolidated Financial Statements 649
Consolidated Balance Sheet 649
Consolidated Income Statement 654
Restatement of Foreign Subsidiary Financial Statements 654
Investments in Debt Securities 656
Held-to-Maturity Securities 656
Long-Term Investments in Bonds 657
A LOOK BACK AT **INTEL CORPORATION** 658
STOP & REVIEW 660
CHAPTER ASSIGNMENTS 662

APPENDIX A **Accounting for Unincorporated Businesses** 674

Accounting for Sole Proprietorships 674
Accounting for Partnerships 675
Accounting for Partners' Equity 676
Distribution of Partnership Income and Losses 676
Dissolution of a Partnership 679
Liquidation of a Partnership 681

APPENDIX B **Present Value Tables** 684

Endnotes 689
Company Name Index 693
Subject Index 695

PREFACE

Making the Complex Simple!

Financial Accounting, 11th edition, continues a distinguished tradition of combining academic needs with professional thought to prepare students for a dynamic business world. Through market-leading integration of International Financial Reporting Standards coverage and real-world data, trusted pedagogy, and a clear writing style that simplifies complex concepts, *Financial Accounting*, develops the judgment and critical-thinking skills students will need to succeed.

NEW

Superior Readability and Clarity for Complex Topics through Enhanced Presentation The revised and refocused content makes this edition accessible to a broad range of interests and levels of reading ability. Building on its proven strength of making the complex simple, extra care has been taken to clarify the topics with which students traditionally struggle most—including the accounting cycle, long-term liabilities, contributed capital, and the statement of cash flows—to make them easy to comprehend. Whenever possible, detailed information has been made more concise by shortening paragraphs and breaking sentences into bulleted lists and additional headers have been added to help students navigate the content.

NEW

Streamlined Coverage To make *Financial Accounting* more manageable for one-term courses, this edition now includes 14 chapters instead of 15. All topics related to stockholders' equity (previously split between Chapters 11 and 12) have been combined into a single chapter. Other topics previously covered in these chapters (corporate income statement, deferred income taxes, comprehensive income, etc.) have been made more concise and are included in chapters covering related topics.

Accounting Equation Relationships To help students understand how accounting works and how business transactions impact the financial statements, accounting equations are shown next to important journal entries.

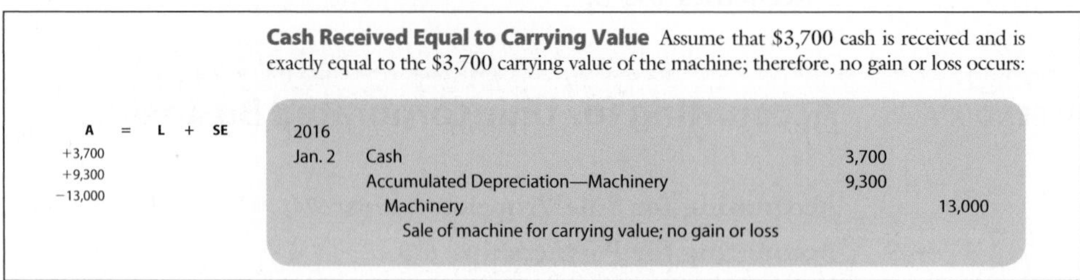

Cash Received Equal to Carrying Value Assume that $3,700 cash is received and is exactly equal to the $3,700 carrying value of the machine; therefore, no gain or loss occurs:

A = L + SE				
+3,700	2016 Jan. 2	Cash	3,700	
+9,300		Accumulated Depreciation—Machinery	9,300	
−13,000		Machinery		13,000
		Sale of machine for carrying value; no gain or loss		

NEW

Strengthened Transaction Analysis Using Walk-Through Method Maintaining a solid foundation in double-entry accounting is critical in the first financial accounting course. This edition logically guides students step-by-step through accounting for business transactions as follows:

- Statement of the transaction
- Analysis of the effect on the accounts
- Application of double-entry accounting in T accounts
- Illustration of the journal entry (linked to the T account in a way that allows students to see the relationships between the methods)
- Comments that offer supporting explanations regarding the significance of the transaction

This walk-through method is continued in future chapters where transaction analysis is critical, such as merchandising accounting, long-term liabilities, contributed capital, and investments. In every case where it will help student comprehension, more in-text journal entries have been included.

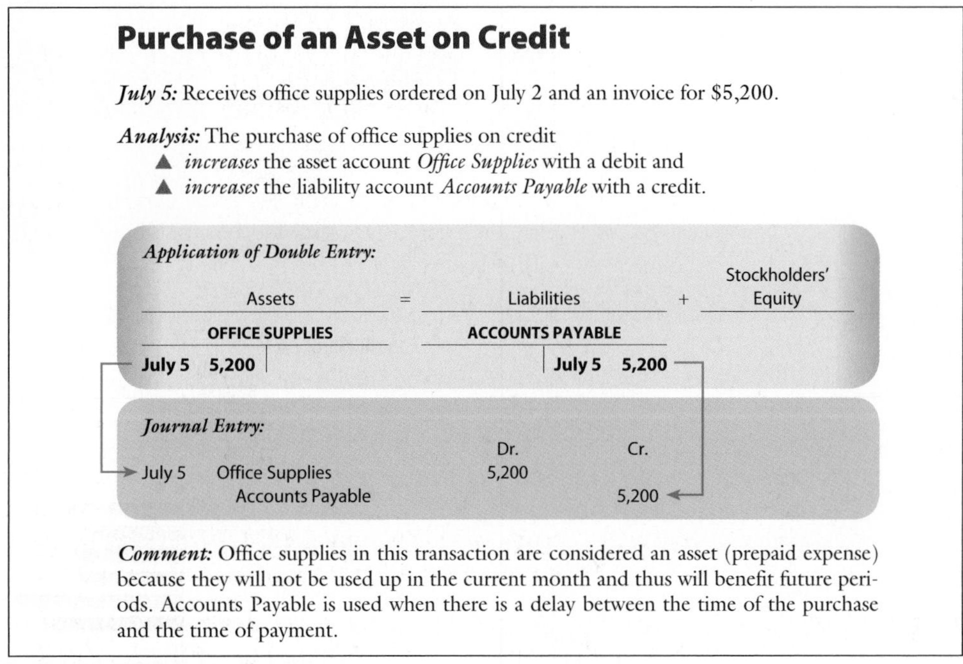

Purchase of an Asset on Credit

July 5: Receives office supplies ordered on July 2 and an invoice for $5,200.

Analysis: The purchase of office supplies on credit

▲ *increases* the asset account *Office Supplies* with a debit and

▲ *increases* the liability account *Accounts Payable* with a credit.

Application of Double Entry:
Assets = Liabilities + Stockholders' Equity
OFFICE SUPPLIES
July 5 5,200
ACCOUNTS PAYABLE
July 5 5,200
Journal Entry:
Dr.
Cr.
July 5 Office Supplies 5,200
Accounts Payable 5,200

Comment: Office supplies in this transaction are considered an asset (prepaid expense) because they will not be used up in the current month and thus will benefit future periods. Accounts Payable is used when there is a delay between the time of the purchase and the time of payment.

Highlighting the Importance of the Financial Statements

Highlighting financial statements allows students to hone their decision-making skills to provide them with real-world experience.

Organizing Chapter Content with Focus on Financial Statements The **Focus on Financial Statements** graphic found at the beginning of each chapter reinforces the connection between the financial statements and each chapter's topics.

Introducing and Integrating Financial Statements In *Financial Accounting*, students are introduced to financial statements in Chapter 1. This early introduction emphasizes the importance of studying accounting while it also provides students with the big picture in which to frame the remaining chapters. Beginning with the **How to Read an Annual Report** Supplement to Chapter 1, students compare and examine the **CVS** financial statements with the **Southwest Airlines** annual report. **The Annual Report Project** after Chapter 4 solidifies this critical skill. In addition, students can practice using these annual reports with the **Annual Report** and **Comparison Analysis** cases, which require students to reference major portions of the reports.

NEW

Teaching Ratios with Focus on Financial Statement Elements In this edition of *Financial Accounting*, the authors present an exciting new framework for teaching how to analyze company information and make informed decisions using ratio analysis. In a simplified approach based on extensive research regarding high-performing companies, students learn that finding just six elements on the financial statements and computing four strategic financial ratios will allow them to determine how well or poorly a company is performing. Comprehensive coverage of all ratios related to evaluating liquidity, financial risk, operating asset management, and market strength is included as a way of further analyzing why one of the four strategic ratios may be good or bad. In addition, all end-of-chapter assignments involving ratio analysis are identified with a ratio icon.

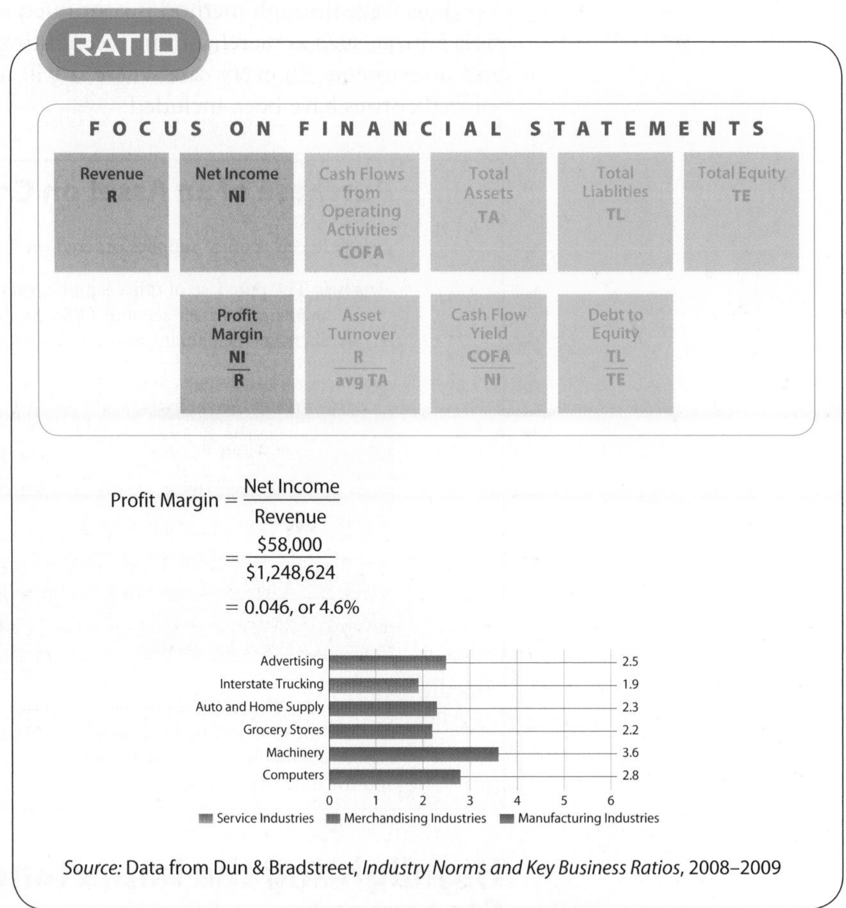

Source: Data from Dun & Bradstreet, *Industry Norms and Key Business Ratios*, 2008–2009

Demonstrating Relevance in Today's Business World

Students need context to understand the importance and relevance of accounting in the real world. That's why *Financial Accounting* offers a variety of ways to relate core accounting concepts to real life.

Prominent Real-World Examples from Start to Finish Each chapter begins with a **Decision Point** that shows how a real, easily recognizable company uses accounting information to make decisions. Excerpts from the company's financial statements are included in the **Financial Highlights** section. At the end of each chapter, **A Look Back At** revisits the Decision Point company and prompts students to refine their critical-thinking skills by examining the impact of the chapter concepts on the company. These Decision Point and Look Back features create real-world bookends for the chapter concepts. In addition, examples from the Decision Point company are integrated throughout the chapter.

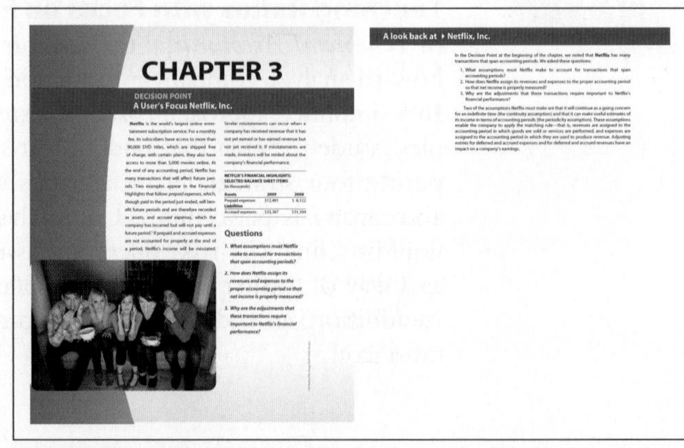

Seeing Accounting in Motion with Focus on Business Practice Boxes Each chapter includes several **Focus on Business Practice** boxes, which illustrate accounting concepts and practices in the context of the general business world.

Focus on Business Practice
A Whirlwind Inventory Turnover—How Does Dell Do It?

Dell Computer Corporation turns its inventory over every five days. How can it do this when other computer companies have inventory on hand for 60 days or even longer? Technology and good inventory management are a big part of the answer.

Dell's speed from order to delivery sets the standard for the computer industry. Consider that a computer ordered by 9 A.M. can be delivered the next day by 9 P.M. How can Dell do this when it does not start ordering components and assembling computers until a customer places an order? First, Dell's suppliers keep components warehoused just minutes from Dell's factories, making efficient, just-in-time (JIT) operations possible. Further, computer monitors are no longer shipped first to Dell and then on to buyers. Dell sends an email message to a shipper, such as **United Parcel Service**, and the shipper picks up a monitor from a supplier and schedules it to arrive with the PC. In addition to contributing to a high inventory turnover, this practice saves Dell about $30 per monitor in freight costs. Dell is showing the world how to run a business in the cyber age by selling more than $1 million worth of computers a day on its website.[3]

iStock Photo

Engaging Students with Numerous In-Chapter Examples More than 230 publicly held companies as well as international, governmental, and not-for-profit organizations are used as illustrative examples. All companies were carefully selected from one of the following rankings: Top 100 Brands, the 25 Most Innovative Companies, The Infotech 100, World's Most Ethical Companies, Top 50 Companies to Work for, Most Admired Companies, or Customer Service Champs. This selection process ensures that students will be able to immediately recognize the companies used as examples.

Keeping Up-to-Date with Integrated International Coverage

The growing acceptance of International Financial Reporting Standards (IFRS) presents challenges for current and future U.S. accountants. Every business student needs some basic knowledge and awareness of IFRS. This edition provides three ways to cover this current issue, so instructors can select the coverage that is right for the course.

Extensive International Financial Reporting Standards Coverage In this edition of *Financial Accounting*, every chapter includes at least one feature that highlights the differences between U.S. GAAP and IFRS.

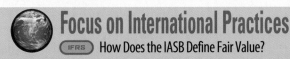

Focus on International Practices
IFRS
How Does the IASB Define Fair Value?

In contrast to U.S. GAAP, the IASB defines *fair value* as a single concept based on exit value. Specifically, fair value is the amount an asset may be exchanged for, or a liability settled, between knowledgeable parties in an arm's length transaction. The best evidence of fair value is quoted prices in an active market. If the market for a financial instrument is not active, a valuation technique must be used. The objective of a valuation technique is to establish what the transaction price is on the measurement date in an arm's length exchange motivated by normal business considerations. Valuation techniques include using arm's length market transactions between knowledgeable, willing parties, if available; reference to the current fair value of another instrument that is substantially the same; discounted cash flow analysis; and options pricing models.[14]

iStock Photo

Added Coverage with *International Financial Reporting Standards: An Overview* Automatically bundled with every new book and available on the product website, supplementary material provides an overview of IFRS and the proposed presentation of financial statements.

In-Depth Treatment in *International Financial Reporting Standards: An Introduction, 2e* (ISBN: 978-0-538-47680-5) For instructors who want more thorough coverage, this separate 64-page booklet delivers the basics of IFRS coverage in a few hours of study. It offers review questions for students and an Instructor's Resource CD-ROM with solutions, a Test Bank, and PowerPoint slides. *International Financial Reporting Standards* introduces accounting students to the status of IFRS and the impact on the financial reporting environment. In addition, a new section on IFRS for small to medium-sized entities (SMEs) has been added. IFRS for SMEs, a complete set of accounting standards, are now acceptable for use in the United States by private entities as an alternative to U.S. GAAP or full IFRS. The AICPA endorses the use of IFRS for SMEs. This booklet delivers the relevant content, trusted authorship, and appropriate scope for learners new to the subject.

Solid Student Pedagogy

The pedagogical features in *Financial Accounting* reflect the authors' active teaching and researching experience.

Clear Learning Objectives Refined over many editions, clearly presented learning objectives guide students through mastering the chapter's material. Based on Bloom's taxonomy, the learning objectives that structure each chapter teach concepts before proceeding to applications, ensuring that readers have a solid understanding of the accounting concept and its importance before they attempt calculations.

Stop & Apply Revised and enhanced **Stop & Apply** features follow each learning objective section and review key concepts and information by providing discussion questions or solved exercises. These features provide students with an effective framework they can use to apply to similar examples and homework assignments.

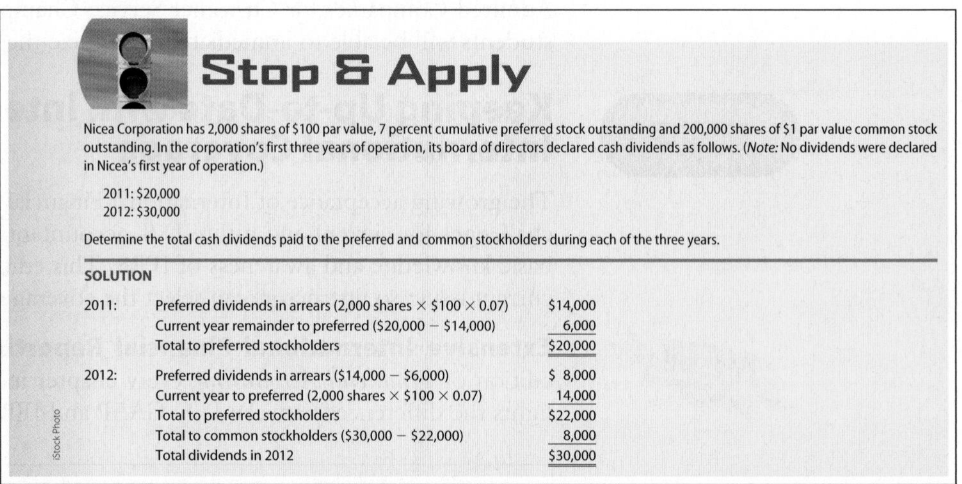

Stop & Apply

Nicea Corporation has 2,000 shares of $100 par value, 7 percent cumulative preferred stock outstanding and 200,000 shares of $1 par value common stock outstanding. In the corporation's first three years of operation, its board of directors declared cash dividends as follows. (*Note:* No dividends were declared in Nicea's first year of operation.)

2011: $20,000
2012: $30,000

Determine the total cash dividends paid to the preferred and common stockholders during each of the three years.

SOLUTION

2011:	Preferred dividends in arrears (2,000 shares × $100 × 0.07)	$14,000
	Current year remainder to preferred ($20,000 − $14,000)	6,000
	Total to preferred stockholders	$20,000
2012:	Preferred dividends in arrears ($14,000 − $6,000)	$ 8,000
	Current year to preferred (2,000 shares × $100 × 0.07)	14,000
	Total to preferred stockholders	$22,000
	Total to common stockholders ($30,000 − $22,000)	8,000
	Total dividends in 2012	$30,000

iStock Photo

STUDY NOTE: *On the income statement, freight-in is included as part of cost of goods sold, and delivery expense (freight-out) is included as an operating (selling) expense.*

Study Notes Marginal **Study Note** features highlight important information and provide useful tips on ways to avoid common mistakes.

Developing Ethical Business Leaders The need for students to analyze business situations and make informed, ethical decisions is essential in today's world. *Financial Accounting* weaves ethical considerations throughout the chapter so that students learn to consistently think of the ethical implications of their actions. In addition, **Ethical Dilemma** cases at the end of the chapters ask students to consider issues they may encounter in their future careers.

Ensuring Comprehension with End-of-Chapter Review Materials The end-of-chapter Review Problems, Stop & Review, and Key Terms and Ratios allow students to check their understanding of core chapter concepts before attempting the homework assignments. The **Review Problems** and solutions provide students with a model for how to work through problems before they are required to complete similar assignments on their own. **Stop & Review** provides an overview of the learning objectives covered in the chapter to help students identify critical concepts. In addition, the **Key Terms and Ratios** section lists important terms and financial ratios, including page references, to make sure students are comfortable with essential terminology.

Developing Decision-Making and Critical-Thinking Skills

Trusted end-of-chapter short exercises, exercises, problems, and cases provide a rich variety to satisfy any approach.

Enhanced End-of-Chapter Assignments

NEW

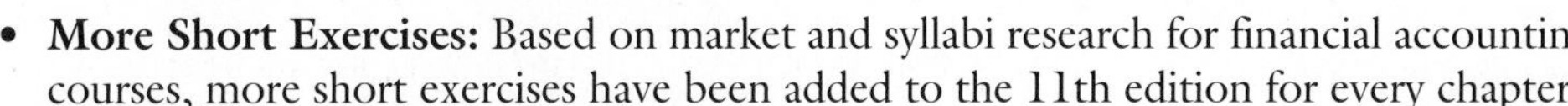

- **More Short Exercises:** Based on market and syllabi research for financial accounting courses, more short exercises have been added to the 11th edition for every chapter.
- **Exercises, Problems, and Alternate Problems:** End-of-chapter assignments have been updated throughout with new numbers and current data where applicable.
- **Market-Leading Case Material:** The rich assortment of case material offers plenty of opportunities to engage and challenge students. The following types of cases appear in this edition:
  - *Conceptual Understanding*
  - *Interpreting Financial Reports*
  - *Annual Report Case*
  - *Comparison Analysis*
  - *Ethical Dilemma*
  - *Business Communication*
  - *Decision Analysis Using Excel*

LO 1 **Ethical Dilemma: Recognition Point and Ethical Considerations**

C 7. Robert Shah, a sales representative for Quality Office Supplies Corporation, will receive a substantial bonus if he meets his annual sales goal. The company's recognition point for sales is the day of shipment. On December 31, Shah realizes he needs sales of $2,000 to reach his sales goal and receive the bonus. He calls a purchaser for a local insurance company, whom he knows well, and asks him to buy $2,000 worth of copier paper today. The purchaser says, "But Bob, that's more than a year's supply for us." Shah says, "Buy it today. If you decide it's too much, you can return however much you want for full credit next month." The purchaser says, "Okay, ship it." The paper is shipped on December 31 and recorded as a sale. On January 15, the purchaser returns $1,750 worth of paper for full credit (approved by Shah) against the bill. Should the shipment on December 31 be recorded as a sale? Discuss the ethics of Shah's action.

Easily Identify Assignments You Want to Cover

Assignments that involve using financial ratios to measure a company's performance are highlighted with a ratio icon.

CASH FLOW

Assignments that assess a company's profitability and liquidity are noted with a cash flow icon.

Assignments that can be completed using General Ledger software are marked with a GL icon. This software is available in an online format in CengageNOW (see p. xx for more information) and as a CD-ROM to bundle with the textbook.

The User Insight requirements of select items develop students' abilities to make sound business decisions based on financial information.

Cases that require students to work in Excel with preformatted templates are noted with an Excel icon. In addition, all electronic working papers for students are provided in an Excel format (without formula functionality).

✔ Uncollectible accounts expense: percentage of net sales method, $4,488; accounts receivable aging method, $3,925

New to this edition, Check Figures for problems have been added to the margins where applicable.

ONLINE SOLUTIONS FOR EVERY LEARNING STYLE

South-Western, a division of Cengage Learning, offers a vast array of online solutions to suit your course and your students' learning styles. Choose the product that best meets your classroom needs and course goals. Please check with your sales representative for more details and ordering information.

CENGAGENOW™

CengageNOW for Needles/Powers' *Financial Accounting, 11th edition,* is a powerful and fully integrated online teaching and learning system that provides you with flexibility and control. This complete digital solution offers a comprehensive set of digital tools to power your course. CengageNOW offers:

- **Homework**, including algorithmic variations.
- **Integrated E-book**.
- **Personalized Study Plans**, which include a pre- and post-test for each chapter and a variety of multimedia assets (from author demonstration videos to QuizBowl). These help students master the chapter materials.
- Assessment options which include the **full test bank**.
- **Reporting capability** based on AACSB, AICPA, and ACBSP-APC competencies and standards.
- **Course Management tools**, including grade book.
- **WebCT and Blackboard Integration**.

CengageNOW Upgrades

New Design CengageNOW has been redesigned to enhance your experience.

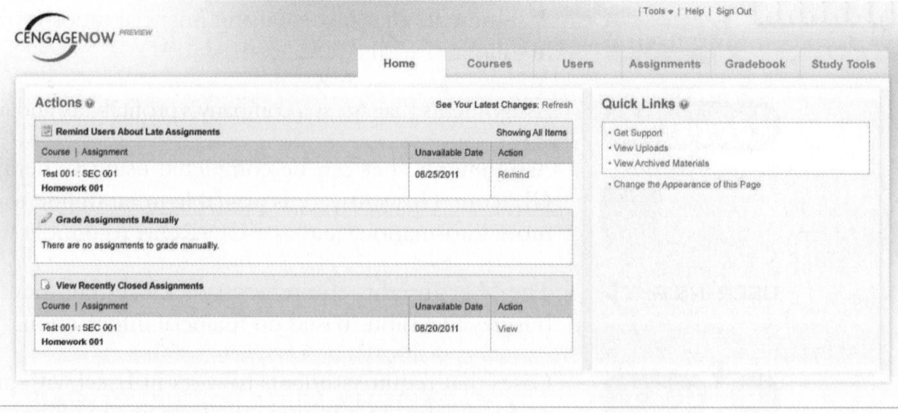

New Cengage Online General Ledger (CLGL) CLGL offers the best general ledger educational product in a new online format. Your students can solve selected end-of-chapter and practice set assignments in a format that emulates commercial general ledger software. Students make entries into the general journal or special journals, track the posting of the entries to the general ledger, and create financial statements or reports. This gives students important exposure to similar commercial accounting software, yet in a manner that is more forgiving of student errors. Assignments are automatically graded online and included in the CNOW grade book.

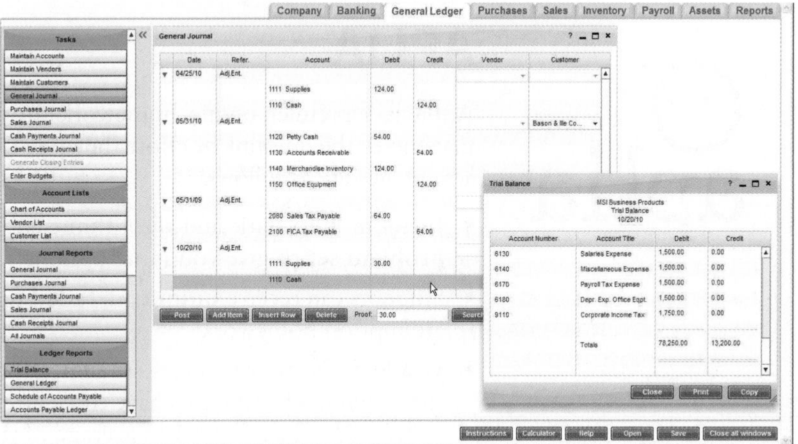

Improved Smart Entry **Smart Entry** challenges students to enter an account title without the guidance of drop-down menus. Instructors can change the setting to turn Smart Entry on or off depending on the preference.

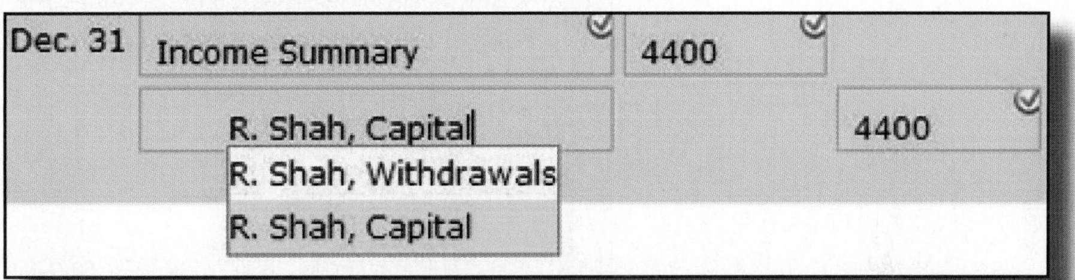

Enhanced Feedback More **robust feedback** is included with selected questions to help students complete homework assignments. Instructors can customize how much feedback students receive.

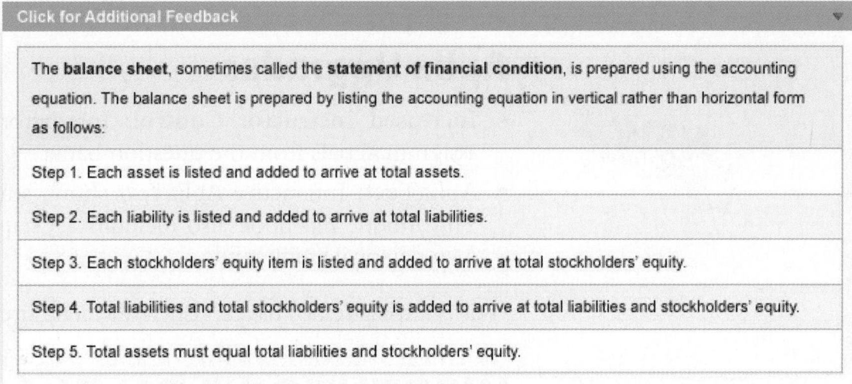

Click for Additional Feedback

The **balance sheet**, sometimes called the **statement of financial condition**, is prepared using the accounting equation. The balance sheet is prepared by listing the accounting equation in vertical rather than horizontal form as follows:

Step 1. Each asset is listed and added to arrive at total assets.

Step 2. Each liability is listed and added to arrive at total liabilities.

Step 3. Each stockholders' equity item is listed and added to arrive at total stockholders' equity.

Step 4. Total liabilities and total stockholders' equity is added to arrive at total liabilities and stockholders' equity.

Step 5. Total assets must equal total liabilities and stockholders' equity.

- A **boarding pass** on the homepage allows the instructor to provide CengageNOW login instructions to the entire class by printing off a flyer or emailing students.
- **Study tools** are more prominent for students to use when taking homework assignments. The instructor can turn these on or off!
- **Longer problems have been sequenced** in parts to help students move at an easier pace, offering better feedback and navigation.

- Students can highlight, take notes, and search the textbook easily and efficiently in the **enhanced eBook**.

For a CengageNOW demo, visit **www.cengage.com/community/needles**

APLIA

Aplia is a premier online homework product that successfully engages students and maximizes the amount of effort they put forth, creating more efficient learners. Aplia's advantages are as follows:

- In addition to static and algorithmic end-of-chapter homework, Aplia offers an **extra problem set** to give you more options!
- Students can receive **unique, detailed feedback** and the complete solution after each attempt on homework.
- **Grade It Now** maximizes student effort on each attempt and ensures students do their own work. Students have three attempts. Each attempt produces an algorithmic variety. The final score is an average of the three attempts.
- **Smart Entry** helps eliminate common data entry errors and prevents students from guessing their way through the homework. It challenges students to enter an account title without the guidance of drop-down menus.

JOURNAL

	Date		Description	Post. Ref.	Debit	Credit	
1	Apr	3	Raw and In Process Inventory				1
2			Raw and In Process Inventory				2
3			Raw Materials				3
4			Rent Expense				4
5			Rent Revenue				5
6			Repairs and Maintenance Expense				6
7			Repairs Expense				7
8			Restructuring Charge				8
9			Retained Earnings				9
10			Retirement Savings Deductions Payable				10
11							11
12							12
13							13
14							14
15							15

< Aplia's Smart Entry system auto-formats answer entries to ensure accurate grading.

< Smart Entry works on both numeric and text fields.

Aplia Upgrades

- **Increased Instructor Control:** Instructors now have more options in how they assign materials from the question banks.
- **ApliaText:** Interactive ApliaText shows students how to use eBooks in a new way. This unique flip-book also includes a Chapter Recap that helps students craft their own personal study guide.

For an Aplia demo, please visit **www.cengage.com/community/needles**

WEBTUTOR™ ON BLACKBOARD® AND WEBCT™

WebTutor™ is available packaged with Needles/Powers' *Financial Accounting, 11th edition,* or for individual student purchase. **Improve students' grades with online review and test preparation tools in an easy-to-use course cartridge.**

Visit **www.cengage.com/webtutor** for more information.

TEACHING TOOLS FOR INSTRUCTORS

Instructor's Resource CD (ISBN: 1-111-52702-4) Place all of the key teaching resources you need at your fingertips with this all-in-one source. Find everything you need to plan, teach, grade, and assess student understanding and progress. This CD includes the Solutions Manual, a Test Bank in Word and ExamView®, PowerPoint® slides, and Spreadsheet Solutions.

- ***Solutions Manual:*** Author-written and carefully verified multiple times to ensure accuracy and consistency with the text, the Solutions Manual contains answers to all short exercises, exercises, problems, and cases that appear in the text. These solutions help you plan, assign, and grade assignments.

- ***Test Bank:*** New to this edition, a matching problem type has been added for each chapter and the short answer and problem question types have been reclassified and expanded when appropriate. Also, new difficulty level ratings, AICPA tagging, and ABCSP-APO tagging have been added (in addition to AACSB tagging). This is particularly valuable during the accreditation process or when your school wants to standardize assessment.
- ***ExamView:*** This easy-to-use test-creation program for Microsoft® Windows or Macintosh contains all questions from the printed Test Bank, including true/false, multiple choice, short answer, and problem questions. Each question provides an answer, a learning objective, a key concept, a level of difficulty, a learning type, and AACSB, AICPA, and ACBSP-APC standards. It's simple to customize tests to your specific class needs as you edit or create questions and store customized exams. This is an ideal tool for online testing.
- ***PowerPoint Slides:*** Bring your lectures to life and clarify difficult concepts with concise slides designed to capture and keep your students' attention. Ideal as guides for student note taking and study, print the slides or simply use with a projector.

Companion Website This robust companion website provides immediate access to a rich array of teaching and interactive learning resources—including chapter-by-chapter online tutorial quizzes, a final exam, online learning games, and flashcards. Easily download the instructor resources you need from the password-protected, instructor-only section of the site. Visit **www.cengage.com/accounting/needles**.

Peachtree CD-ROM (ISBN: 1-111-52881-0) Teach your students how to use leading commercial software with Peachtree. Students will gain experience working with real computerized accounting software, an employable skill.

LEARNING RESOURCES FOR STUDENTS

Companion Website This robust companion website provides immediate access to a rich array of teaching and interactive learning resources—including chapter-by-chapter online tutorial quizzes, a final exam, online learning games, and flashcards. Visit **www.cengage.com/accounting/needles**.

Electronic Working Papers Verified to ensure accuracy and quality consistent with the text, the working papers for the problems are provided in Excel® format to provide students with a starting point for completing end-of-chapter problems and journal entries from the textbook.

ACKNOWLEDGEMENTS

A successful textbook is a collaborative effort. We are grateful to the many professors, other professional colleagues, and students who have taught and studied from our book, and we thank all of them for their constructive comments. In the space available, we cannot possibly mention everyone who has been helpful, but we do want to recognize those who made special contributions to our efforts in preparing the eleventh edition of *Financial Accounting*.

We wish to express deep appreciation to our colleagues at DePaul University, who have been extremely supportive and encouraging. We also wish to thank our Editorial Assistant, Joanna Dabrowska, for her thorough, diligent, and timely work with the manuscript and Mary Roth for her unwavering professionalism in managing our office.

Very important to the quality of this book are our Developmental Editor, Krista Kellman; Senior Acquisitions Editor, Sharon Oblinger; and Senior Marketing Manager, Kristen Hurd.

Others who have had a major impact on this book through their reviews, suggestions, and participation in surveys and reviews are listed below. We cannot begin to say how grateful we are for the feedback from the many instructors who have generously shared their responses and teaching experiences with us.

Arinola O. Adebayo
University of South Carolina Aiken

Jay Ballantine
University of Colorado at Boulder

Benjamin W. Bean
Utah Valley University

John Bedient
Albion College

Chris Bjornson
Indiana University Southeast

Cynthia Bolt-Lee
The Citadel

Michael Bootsma
Kirkwood Community College

Kevin Bosner
Medaille College

Rada Brooks
University of California, Berkeley

Amy Browning
Ivy Tech Community College

Sandra Byrd
Missouri State University

Kevin Carduff
Case Western Reserve University

Bea Chiang
The College of New Jersey

Linda Christiansen
Indiana University Southeast

Robin D'Agati
Palm Beach Community College

Rosemond Desir
Colorado State University

Austin Emeagwai
LeMoyne-Owen College

Harlan Etheridge
University of Louisiana at Lafayette

Sara Fernandez
The Citadel

Marvin Gordon
University of Illinois at Chicago

Cynthia Beier Greeson
Ivy Tech Community College

Philip M. Hanley
University of Southern Indiana

Rhonda Harbeson
Lone Star College University Park

Florence W. Harrison
Becker College

Sueann Hely
West Kentucky Community & Technical College

Yongtao Hong
North Dakota State University

Kathy Hsiao Yu Hsu
University of Louisiana at Lafayette

Laura Ilcisin
University of Nebraska at Omaha

Ronald Jastzrebski
Penn State Berks

Raymond Johnson
Guilford College

Edward H. Julius
California Lutheran University

Christine H. Kloezeman
Glendale Community College

C. Andrew Lafond
The College of New Jersey

Jennifer Lesure
Ivy Tech Community College

Joseph LiPari
Montclair State University

Joseph F. Lupino
St. Mary's College of California

Nancy P. Lynch
West Virginia University

Amarjeet Kaur Malhotra
North Dakota State University

Paul McKillop
Salve Regina University

Birendra Mishra
University of California, Riverside

Adam Myers, III
Texas A&M University

Michelle Nickla
Ivy Tech Community College

Betty Nolen
Georgia Highlands College

Tim Nygaard
Madisonville Community College

Gary Olsen
Carroll University

Glenn Pate
Palm Beach Community College

Simon R. Pearlman
California State University—Long Beach

John C. Purisky
Salem State University

Delvan Roehling
Ivy Tech Community College

Miles Romney
University of San Diego

Robert Russ
Northern Kentucky University

Michael Scott
Glendale Community College

Gabrielle Serrano
Elgin Community College

Andreas Simon
California Polytechnic State University—San Luis Obispo

Vic Stanton
University of California, Berkeley

Jenny Staskey
Northern Arizona University

Demelece Stewart
Ivy Tech Community College

Steve Teeter
Utah Valley University

Yanfeng Xue
George Washington University

Judith Zander
Grossmont College

ABOUT THE AUTHORS

Belverd E. Needles, Jr., received B.B.A. and M.B.A. degrees from Texas Tech University and a Ph.D. degree from the University of Illinois at Urbana-Champaign. He teaches financial accounting, managerial accounting, and auditing at DePaul University, where he is an internationally recognized expert in international accounting and education. He has published in leading journals and is the author or editor of more than 20 books and monographs. His current research relates to international financial reporting, performance measurement, and corporate governance of high-performance companies in the United States, Europe, India, and Australia. His textbooks are used throughout the world and have received many awards, including (in 2008) the McGuffey Award from the Text and Academic Authors Association. Active in many academic and professional organizations, he is currently Vice President-Education of the American Accounting Association. He has received the Distinguished Alumni Award from Texas Tech University, the Illinois CPA Society Outstanding Educator Award and its Life-Time Achievement Award, the Joseph A. Silvoso Faculty Award of Merit from the Federation of Schools of Accountancy, the Ledger & Quill Award of Merit, and the Ledger & Quill Teaching Excellence Award. He was named Educator of the Year by the American Institute of CPAs, Accountant of the Year for Education by the national honorary society Beta Alpha Psi, and Outstanding International Accounting Educator by the American Accounting Association. He has received the Excellence in Teaching Award from DePaul University.

Marian Powers received a B.S. degree from Chicago State University and a Ph.D. degree from the University of Illinois at Urbana-Champaign. In addition to the Kellogg Graduate School of Management at Northwestern University, she has taught financial accounting at the University of Illinois, Chicago, and at the Lake Forest Graduate School of Management. Internationally recognized as a dynamic teacher in executive education, she specializes in teaching nonfinancial managers how to read and understand internal and external financial reports, including the impact of international financial reporting standards (IFRS). Dr. Powers' current research relates to international financial reporting, performance measurement, and corporate governance of high-performance companies in the United States, Europe, India, and Australia. Her research has been published in leading journals. Her textbooks, co-authored with Belverd E. Needles, Jr., are used throughout the world and have received many awards, including the Textbook Excellence Award and the McGuffey Award from the Text and Academic Authors Association. She has also co-authored three interactive multimedia software products. Dr. Powers currently serves on the board of the CPA Endowment Fund of Illinois and on the board of governors of the Winnetka Community House. She is a member of the International Association of Accounting Education and Research and the Illinois CPA Society. She has served on the board of directors of the Illinois CPA Society, the Educational Foundation of Women in Accounting, and both the national and Chicago chapters of ASWA.

Financial Accounting

CHAPTER 1

DECISION POINT
A User's Focus CVS Caremark

CVS Caremark operates a chain of more than 7,000 stores. Its pharmacies fill more than 1 billion prescriptions each year. Over the last five years, CVS has opened or purchased 2,600 new stores and more than doubled its sales and profits. This performance places it among the fastest-growing retail companies.

Why is CVS considered successful? Customers give the company high marks because of the quality of the products that it sells and the large selection and good service that its stores offer. Investment firms and others with a stake in CVS evaluate the company's success in financial terms.

Whether a company is large or small, the same financial measures are used to evaluate its management and to compare it with other companies. In this chapter, as you learn more about accounting and the business environment, you will become familiar with these financial measures.

CVS'S Financial Highlights (In millions)

	2009	2008	2007
Net sales	$98,729	$87,472	$76,330
Net earnings	3,696	3,212	2,637
Total assets	61,641	60,960	54,722
Stockholders' equity	35,768	31,574	31,322

STUDY NOTE: *Most companies list the most recent year of information in the first column, as shown here.*

Questions

1. ***As a manager at CVS, what financial knowledge would you need to measure progress toward the company's goals?***
2. ***As a potential investor or creditor, what financial knowledge would you need to evaluate CVS's financial performance?***
3. ***Is CVS meeting its goal of profitability?***

Scott Olson/Staff/Getty Images News/Getty Images

Uses of Accounting Information and the Financial Statements

LEARNING OBJECTIVES

LO 1 Define *accounting* and describe its role in making informed decisions, identify business goals and activities, and explain the importance of ethics in accounting. (pp. 4–8)

LO 2 Identify the users of accounting information. (pp. 8–11)

LO 3 Explain the importance of business transactions, money measure, and separate entity. (pp. 11–12)

LO 4 Describe the characteristics of a corporation. (pp. 13–15)

LO 5 Identify the four basic financial statements and define their elements. (pp. 15–22)

LO 6 Explain how generally accepted accounting principles (GAAP) relate to financial statements and the independent CPA's report and identify the organizations that influence GAAP. (pp. 22–25)

Today, more people than ever before recognize the importance of accounting information to a business, its owners, its employees, its lenders, and the financial markets. In this chapter, we discuss the importance of ethical financial reporting, the uses and users of accounting information, and the financial statements that accountants prepare. We end the chapter with a discussion of generally accepted accounting principles.

FOCUS ON FINANCIAL STATEMENTS

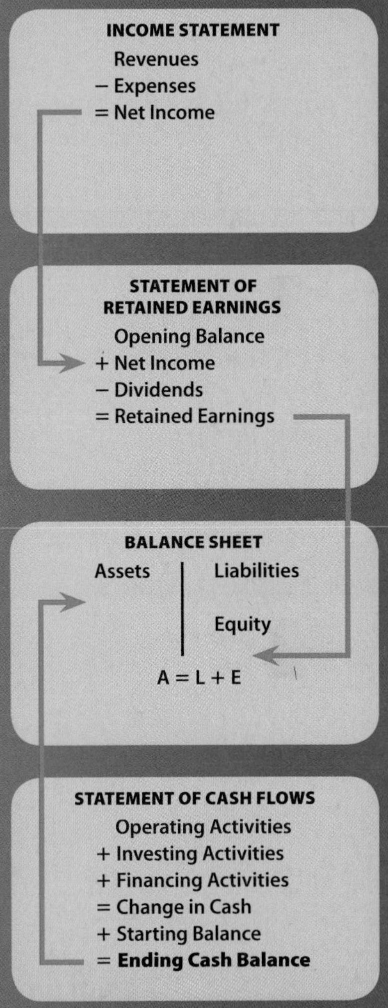

INCOME STATEMENT
Revenues
− Expenses
= Net Income

STATEMENT OF RETAINED EARNINGS
Opening Balance
+ Net Income
− Dividends
= Retained Earnings

BALANCE SHEET
Assets | Liabilities
Equity
A = L + E

STATEMENT OF CASH FLOWS
Operating Activities
+ Investing Activities
+ Financing Activities
= Change in Cash
+ Starting Balance
= **Ending Cash Balance**

Although each financial statement gives a unique view of a company's results, all four are interrelated.

ACCOUNTING AS AN INFORMATION SYSTEM

LO 1 Define *accounting* and describe its role in making informed decisions, identify business goals and activities, and explain the importance of ethics in accounting.

Accounting is an information system that measures, processes, and communicates financial information about an economic entity.[1] An economic entity is a unit that exists independently, such as a business, a hospital, or a governmental body. Although the central focus of this book is on business entities, we include other economic units at appropriate points in the text and in the end-of-chapter assignments.

Accountants focus on the needs of decision makers who use financial information, whether those decision makers are inside or outside a business or another economic entity. Accountants provide a vital service by supplying the information decision makers need to make "reasoned choices among alternative uses of scarce resources in the conduct of business and economic activities."[2] As shown in Exhibit 1.1, accounting is a link between business activities and decision makers.

- Accounting measures business activities by recording data about them for future use.
- The data are stored until needed and then processed to become useful information.
- The information is communicated through reports to decision makers.
- Based on information from accounting, decision makers take actions that affect subsequent business activities.

In other words, data about business activities are the input to the accounting system, and useful information for decision makers is the output.

Business Goals and Activities

A **business** is an economic unit that aims to sell goods and services to customers at prices that will provide an adequate return to its owners. The list that follows contains the names of some well-known businesses and the principal goods or services that they sell.

Costco Wholesale Corp.	Comprehensive discount goods
Nike, Inc.	Athletic footwear and clothing
Best Buy Co.	Consumer electronics, personal computers
Burger King Holdings, Inc.	Food service
Starbucks Corp.	Coffee and related service
UAL (United Airlines) Corp.	Passenger airline service

EXHIBIT 1.1
Accounting as an Information System

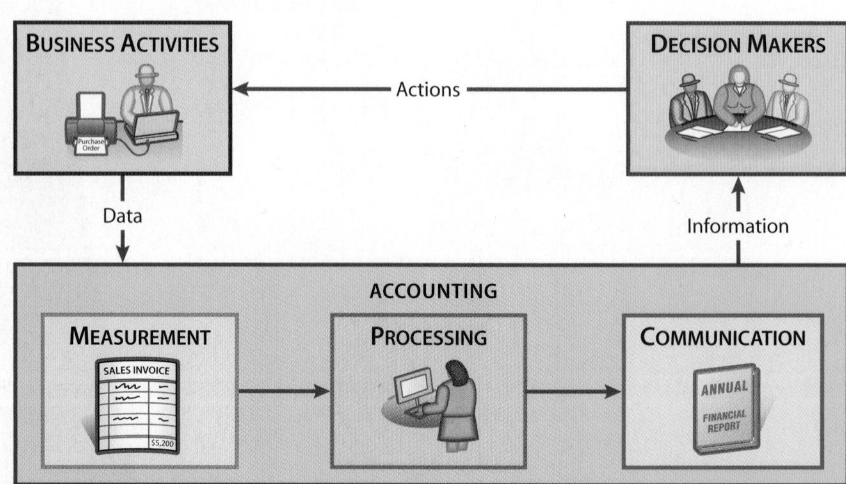

Despite their differences, these businesses have similar goals and engage in similar activities, as shown in Exhibit 1.2.

The two major goals of all businesses are profitability and liquidity.

- **Profitability** is the ability to earn enough income to attract and hold investment capital.
- **Liquidity** is the ability to have enough cash to pay debts when they are due.

To succeed and even to survive, a company must meet both goals. For example, **Honda** may meet the goal of profitability by selling many cars at a price that earns a profit, but if its customers do not pay for their cars quickly enough to enable Honda to pay its suppliers and employees, the company may fail to meet the goal of liquidity, which could force it into bankruptcy.

All companies, whether they are retailers, manufacturers, or service providers, pursue their goals by engaging in operating, investing, and financing activities.

- **Operating activities** include buying, producing, and selling goods and services; hiring managers and other employees; and paying taxes.
- **Investing activities** involve spending a company's capital in ways that will help it achieve its goals. They include buying the resources needed to operate the business, such as land, buildings, and equipment, and selling those resources when they are no longer needed.
- **Financing activities** involve obtaining adequate funds to begin operating the business and to continue operating it. They include obtaining capital from creditors, such as banks and suppliers, and from the company's owners. They also include repaying creditors and paying a return to the owners.

Financial Analysis **Financial analysis** is the use of financial statements to determine that a business is well managed and is achieving its goals. The effectiveness of financial analysis depends on the use of relevant performance measures and financial ratios.

To be relevant, **performance measures** must be well aligned with the two major goals of business—profitability and liquidity. Profitability is commonly measured in terms of net income, and cash flows are a common measure of liquidity. For example, in 2009, **CVS** had net income of $3,696 million and cash flows from operating activities of $4,035 million. These figures indicate that CVS was achieving both profitability

EXHIBIT 1.2
Business Goals and Activities

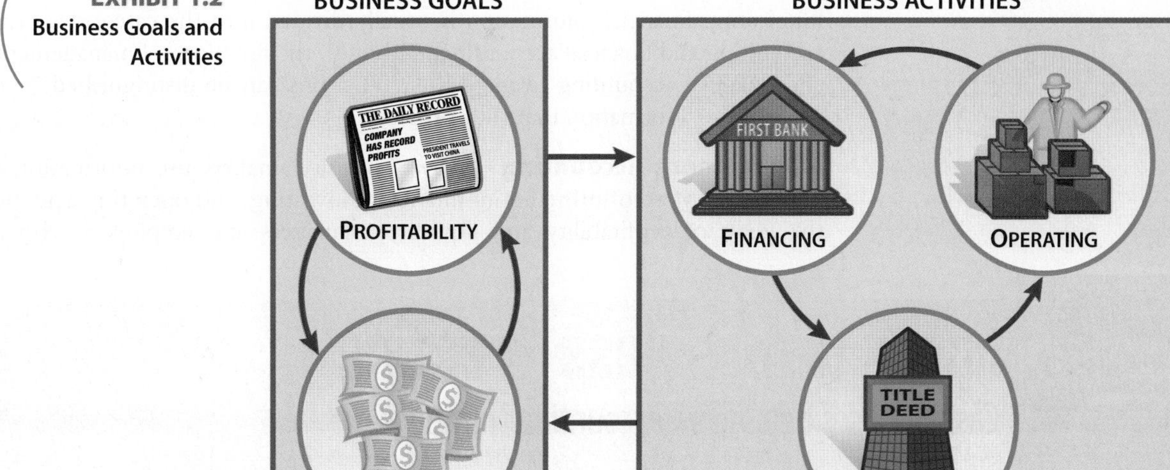

Focus on Business Practice

What Does CVS Have to Say About Itself?

In its annual report, **CVS**'s management describes the company's goals in meeting the major business objectives:

- **Liquidity:** "We maintain a level of liquidity sufficient to allow us to cover our cash needs in the short-term. . . . We believe our operating cash flows, commercial paper program, sale-leaseback program, as well as any potential future borrowings, will be sufficient to fund these future payments and long-term initiatives."
- **Profitability:** "The profitability of retail and mail order pharmacy businesses is dependent upon the utilization of prescription drug products. . . . The Company evaluates . . . segment performance based on net revenues, gross profit and operating profit before the effect of non-recurring charges and gains and certain intersegment activities and charges."[3]

CVS's main business activities are shown at the right.

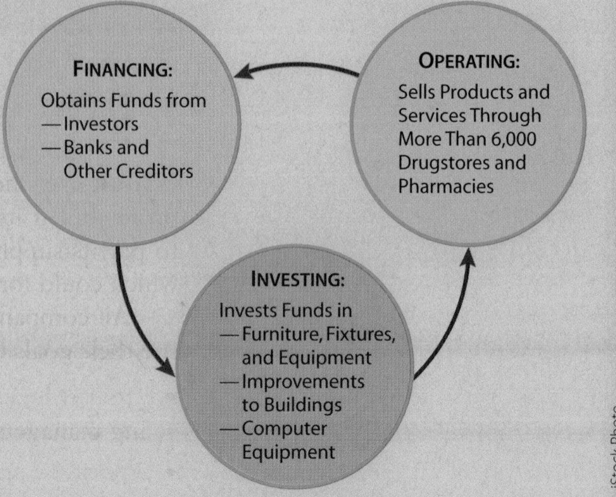

STUDY NOTE: Users of accounting information focus on different measures of performance. For example, lenders are concerned primarily with cash flow, and owners are concerned with earnings and dividends.

and liquidity. Not all companies were so fortunate in 2009. For instance, a year earlier, **General Motors** reported that it would have to curtail spending on new auto and truck models because its earnings were negative and, even worse, its cash flows were negative. Its cash flow problem led to its bankruptcy and a government bailout in 2009. Clearly, General Motors was not meeting either its profitability or liquidity goals.

RATIO

Financial ratios show how the elements of financial statements relate to each other. They allow for comparisons from one period to another and from one company to another. For example, to assess CVS's profitability, it would be helpful to consider the ratio of its earnings to total assets as well as its profit margin, and for liquidity, the ratio of its cash flows to total assets.

The most important elements of financial statements are introduced later in this chapter, and financial ratios are introduced beginning in this chapter and continued in subsequent chapters.

Financial and Management Accounting

Accounting's role of assisting decision makers by measuring, processing, and communicating financial information is usually divided into the categories of management accounting and financial accounting. Although the functions of management accounting and financial accounting overlap, their functions can be distinguished by the principal users of the information that they provide.

Management Accounting *Internal* decision makers use information provided by **management accounting** about financing, investing, and operating activities to achieve the goals of profitability and liquidity. Managers and employees who conduct the

Focus on Business Practice

Cash Bonuses Depend on Accounting Numbers!

Most businesses use the amounts reported in their financial statements as a basis for rewarding management. Because managers act to achieve these accounting measures, selecting measures that are not easily manipulated is important. Equally important is maintaining a balance of measures that reflect the goals of profitability and liquidity.

iStock Photo

activities of the business need information about how they have done in the past and what they can expect in the future. For example, **Gap Inc.**, a retail clothing business, needs an operating report on each outlet that tells how much was sold at that outlet and what costs were incurred, and it needs a budget for each outlet that projects the sales and costs for the next year.

Financial Accounting *External* decision makers use **financial accounting** reports to evaluate how well the business has achieved its goals. These reports are called **financial statements**. **CVS**, whose stock is traded on the New York Stock Exchange, sends its financial statements to its owners (called *stockholders*), its banks and other creditors, and government regulators. Financial statements report directly on the goals of profitability and liquidity and are used extensively both inside and outside a business to evaluate the business's success. Every person involved with a business should have an understanding of financial statements. They are a central feature of accounting and a primary focus of this book.

It is important to distinguish accounting from the ways in which accounting information is processed by bookkeeping and management information systems.

- **Bookkeeping** is mechanical and repetitive; it is the process, usually through the use of computers, of recording financial transactions and keeping financial records. It is a small—but important—part of accounting.
- **Management information systems (MIS)** consist of the interconnected subsystems, including accounting, that provide the information needed to run a business.

Ethical Financial Reporting

Ethics is a code of conduct that applies to everyday life. It addresses the question of whether actions are right or wrong. Actions—whether ethical or unethical, right or wrong—are the product of individual decisions. Thus, when an organization acts unethically by using false advertising, cheating customers, polluting the environment, or treating employees unfairly, it is not the organization that is responsible—it is the members of management and other employees who have made a conscious decision to act in this manner.

Ethics is especially important in preparing financial reports because users of these reports must depend on the good faith of the people involved in their preparation. Users have no other assurance that the reports are accurate and fully disclose all relevant facts.

The intentional preparation of misleading financial statements is called **fraudulent financial reporting**.[4] It can result from the distortion of records (e.g., the manipulation of inventory records), falsified transactions (e.g., fictitious sales), or the misapplication of various accounting principles. There are a number of motives for fraudulent reporting—for instance, to cover up financial weakness in order to obtain a higher price when a company is sold, to meet the expectations of stockholders and financial analysts, or to obtain a loan. The incentive can also be personal gain, such as additional compensation, promotion, or avoidance of penalties for poor performance.

Whatever the motive for fraudulent financial reporting, it can have dire consequences, as the accounting scandals that erupted at **Enron Corporation** and **WorldCom** in 2001 and 2002, respectively, attest. Unethical financial reporting and accounting practices at

Focus on Business Practice

How Did Accounting Develop?

Accounting is a very old discipline. Forms of it have been essential to commerce for more than 5,000 years. Accounting, in a version close to what we know today, gained widespread use in the 1400s, especially in Italy, where it was instrumental in the development of shipping, trade, construction, and other forms of commerce. This system of double-entry bookkeeping was documented by the famous Italian mathematician, scholar, and philosopher Fra Luca Pacioli. In 1494, Pacioli published his most important work, *Summa de Arithmetica, Geometrica, Proportioni et Proportionalita*, which contained a detailed description of accounting as practiced in that age. This book became the most widely read book on mathematics in Italy and firmly established Pacioli as the "Father of Accounting."

iStock Photo

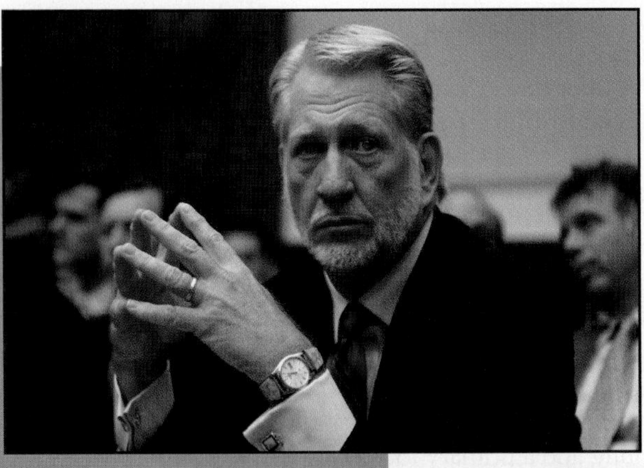

Bernard Ebbers, the founder and former CEO of WorldCom, was sentenced to 25 years in prison for his role in an accounting fraud that cost investors $11 billion dollars. The charges included conspiracy, securities fraud, and filing false financial statements.

those two major corporations caused thousands of people to lose their jobs, their investment incomes, and their pensions. They also resulted in prison sentences and fines for the corporate executives who were involved.

Passed in response to these scandals, the **Sarbanes-Oxley Act** of 2002 regulates financial reporting and the accounting profession, among other things. This legislation ordered the Securities and Exchange Commission (SEC) to draw up rules requiring the chief executives and chief financial officers of all publicly traded U.S. companies to swear that, based on their knowledge, the quarterly statements and annual reports that their companies file with the SEC are accurate and complete. Violation can result in criminal penalties.

A company's management expresses its duty to ensure that financial reports are not false or misleading in the management report that appears in the company's annual report. For example, in its management report, **Target Corporation** makes the following statement:

> Management is responsible for the consistency, integrity and presentation of the information in the Annual Report.[5]

However, it is accountants, not management, who physically prepare and audit financial reports. To meet the high ethical standards of the accounting profession, they must apply accounting concepts in such a way as to present a fair view of a company's operations and financial position and to avoid misleading readers of their reports. Like the conduct of a company, the ethical conduct of a profession is a collection of individual actions. As a member of a profession, each accountant has a responsibility—not only to the profession but also to employers, clients, and society as a whole—to ensure that any report he or she prepares or audits provides accurate, reliable information. The high regard that the public has historically had for the accounting profession is evidence that an overwhelming number of accountants have upheld the ethics of the profession.

Stop & Apply

Match each term with one of the four definitions that follow:

_____ 1. Management accounting
_____ 2. Liquidity
_____ 3. Financial accounting
_____ 4. Investing activities
_____ 5. Operating activities
_____ 6. Financing activities
_____ 7. Profitability
_____ 8. Fraudulent financial reporting

a. An unethical practice
b. A business goal
c. Engaged in by all businesses
d. A major branch of accounting

SOLUTION 1. d; 2. b; 3. d; 4. c; 5. c; 6. c; 7. b; 8. a

DECISION MAKERS: THE USERS OF ACCOUNTING INFORMATION

Identify the users of accounting information. 

As shown in Exhibit 1.3, the people who use accounting information to make decisions fall into three categories:

- Those who manage a business
- Those outside a business enterprise who have a direct financial interest in the business
- Those who have an indirect financial interest in a business

Harry Hamburg/NY Daily News Archive /Getty Images iStock Photo

EXHIBIT 1.3
The Users of Accounting Information

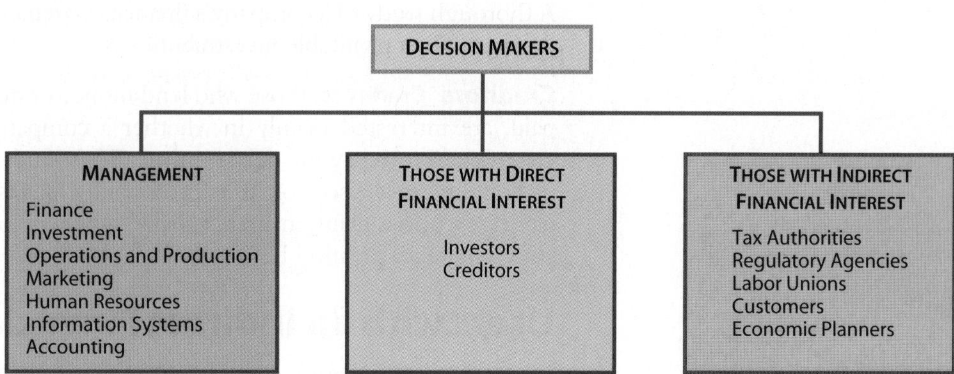

These categories apply to governmental and not-for-profit organizations as well as to profit-oriented ventures.

Management

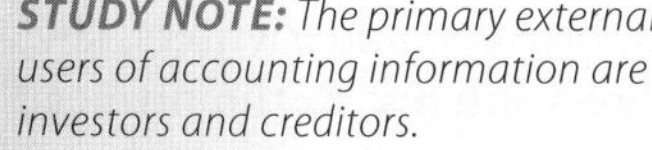

STUDY NOTE: Managers are internal users of accounting information.

Management refers to the people who are responsible for ensuring that a company meet its goals of profitability and liquidity As we noted earlier, all companies pursue these goals by engaging in operating, investing, and financing activities. Making decisions about these activities is the basic function of managers, and to make good decisions, they must have timely and valid accounting information.

For example, managers at **CVS** and other companies need answers to such questions as:

- What were the company's earnings during the past quarter?
- Is the rate of return to the owners adequate?
- Does the company have enough cash?
- Which products or services are most profitable?

Because so many key decisions are based on accounting data, management is one of the most important users of accounting information.

Users with a Direct Financial Interest

STUDY NOTE: The primary external users of accounting information are investors and creditors.

Most companies periodically publish financial statements that report their success in meeting the goals of profitability and liquidity. These statements, which we discuss later in this chapter, show what has happened in the past and are important indicators of what will happen in the future. Many people outside a company, particularly investors and creditors and potential investors and creditors, study these statements carefully.

Investors **Investors**, such as **CVS**'s stockholders, who have invested capital in a company and thus acquired part ownership in it have a direct financial interest in its success, and they depend on the financial statements to evaluate how the business has performed. Potential investors are interested in a company's past success and its future earnings.

iStock Photo

Focus on Business Practice

What Do CFOs Do?

According to a business survey, the chief financial officer (CFO) is the "new business partner of the chief executive officer" (CEO). CFOs (most of whom have an accounting or finance background) are increasingly required to take on responsibilities for strategic planning, mergers and acquisitions, and tasks involving international operations, and many of them are becoming CEOs of their companies. Those who do become CEOs are finding that "a financial background is invaluable when they're saddled with the responsibility of making big calls."[6]

A thorough study of a company's financial statements helps potential investors judge the prospects for a profitable investment.

Creditors **Creditors**, those who lend money or deliver goods and services before being paid, are interested mainly in whether a company will have the cash to pay interest charges and to repay the debt on time. They study a company's cash flow to determine its liquidity; they also look at its profitability. Banks, finance companies, mortgage companies, securities firms, insurance firms, suppliers, and other lenders must analyze a company's financial position before they make a loan.

Users with an Indirect Financial Interest

In recent years, society as a whole, through governmental and public groups, has become one of the largest and most important users of accounting information. Users who need accounting information to make decisions on public issues include tax authorities, regulatory agencies, and various other groups.

Tax Authorities Government at every level is financed through the collection of taxes. Companies and individuals pay many kinds of taxes, including federal, state, and city income taxes; Social Security and other payroll taxes; excise taxes; and sales taxes. Each tax requires special tax returns and often a complex set of records as well. Proper reporting is generally a matter of law and can be very complicated. The Internal Revenue Code, for instance, contains thousands of rules governing the preparation of the accounting information used in computing federal income taxes.

Regulatory Agencies Most companies must report periodically to one or more regulatory agencies at the federal, state, and local levels. For example, all publicly traded corporations must report periodically to the **Securities and Exchange Commission (SEC)**. This body, set up by Congress to protect the public, regulates the issuing, buying, and selling of stocks in the United States. Companies listed on a stock exchange also must meet the special reporting requirements of their exchange.

Other Groups Other groups with an indirect financial interest in accounting information include the following:

- **Labor Unions:** As they prepare for contract negotiations with a company, labor unions study the company's financial statements. A company's income and expenses often play an important role in these negotiations.
- **Advisors of Investors and Creditors:** Financial analysts, brokers, underwriters, lawyers, economists, and the financial press all have an indirect interest in the financial performance and prospects of a business.
- **Consumer Groups, Customers, and the General Public:** The public has become more concerned about the financing and earnings of corporations as well as about the effects that corporations have on inflation, the environment, social issues, and the quality of life.
- **Economic Planners:** The President's Council of Economic Advisers and the Federal Reserve Board use aggregated accounting information to set and evaluate economic policies and programs.

Governmental and Not-for-Profit Organizations

More than 30 percent of the U.S. economy is generated by governmental and not-for-profit organizations (hospitals, universities, professional organizations, and charities). The managers of these diverse entities perform the same functions as managers of businesses, and they therefore have the same need for accounting information and a knowledge of how to use it. Their functions include raising funds from investors, creditors, taxpayers, and donors and deploying scarce resources. They must also plan how to pay for operations and to repay creditors on a timely basis. In addition, they have an obligation to report their financial performance to legislators, boards, and donors, as well as to deal with tax authorities, regulators, and labor unions.

Although most of the examples that we present in this text focus on business enterprises, the same basic principles apply to governmental and not-for-profit organizations.

Stop & Apply

Match each term with one of the three types of users of accounting information that follow:

_____ 1. Tax authorities
_____ 2. Investors
_____ 3. Management
_____ 4. Creditors
_____ 5. Regulatory agencies
_____ 6. Labor unions and consumer groups

a. Internal user
b. Direct external user
c. Indirect user

iStock Photo

SOLUTION 1. c; 2. b; 3. a; 4. b; 5. c; 6. c

ACCOUNTING MEASUREMENT

LO 3 Explain the importance of business transactions, money measure, and separate entity.

In this section, we begin the study of the measurement aspects of accounting—that is, what accounting actually measures. To make an accounting measurement, the accountant must answer four basic questions:

- What is measured?
- When should the measurement be made?
- What value should be placed on what is measured?
- How should what is measured be classified?

Accountants debate the answers to these questions constantly, and the answers change as new knowledge and practice require. But the basis of today's accounting practice rests on a number of widely accepted concepts and conventions, which we describe in this book. We begin by focusing on the first question: What is measured? We discuss the other three questions (recognition, valuation, and classification) in the next chapter.

Every system must define what it measures, and accounting is no exception. Basically, financial accounting uses money to gauge the impact of business transactions on business entities.

Business Transactions

Business transactions are economic events that affect a business's financial position. Businesses can have hundreds or even thousands of transactions every day. These transactions are the raw material of accounting reports.

A transaction can be an exchange of value (a purchase, sale, payment, collection, or loan) between two or more parties. A transaction also can be an economic event that has the same effect as an exchange transaction but that does not involve an exchange. Some examples of these nonexchange transactions are losses from fire, flood, explosion, and theft; physical wear and tear on machinery and equipment; and the day-by-day accumulation of interest.

To be recorded, a transaction must relate directly to a business entity. Suppose a customer buys toothpaste from **CVS** but has to buy shampoo from a competing store because CVS is out of shampoo. The transaction in which the toothpaste was sold is entered in CVS's records. However, the purchase of the shampoo from the competitor is not entered in CVS's records because even though it indirectly affects CVS economically (in that the company lost a sale), it does not involve a direct exchange of value between CVS and the customer.

Money Measure

STUDY NOTE: The common unit of measurement used in the United States for financial reporting purposes is the dollar.

All business transactions are recorded in terms of money. This concept is called **money measure**. Of course, nonfinancial information may also be recorded, but it is through the recording of monetary amounts that a business's transactions and activities are measured. Money is the only factor common to all business transactions, and thus it is the only unit of measure capable of producing financial data that can be compared.

The monetary unit a business uses depends on the country in which the business resides. For example, in the United States, the basic unit of money is the dollar. In China, it is the yuan; in Japan, the yen; in Europe, the euro; and in the United Kingdom, the pound. In international transactions, exchange rates must be used to translate from one currency to another. An **exchange rate** is the value of one currency in terms of another. For example, a British person purchasing goods from a U.S. company like **CVS** and paying in U.S. dollars must exchange British pounds for U.S. dollars before making payment. In effect, currencies are goods that can be bought and sold.

Exhibit 1.4 illustrates the exchange rates for several currencies in dollars. It shows the exchange rate for British pounds as $1.63 per pound on a particular date. Like the prices of many goods, currency prices change daily according to supply and demand. For example, a year and a half earlier, the exchange rate for British pounds was $1.98. Although our discussion in this book focuses on dollars, some examples and assignments involve foreign currencies.

Separate Entity

STUDY NOTE: For accounting purposes, a business is always separate and distinct from its owners, creditors, and customers.

For accounting purposes, a business is a **separate entity**, distinct not only from its creditors and customers but also from its owners. It should have its own set of financial records, and its records and reports should refer only to its own affairs.

For example, Just Because Flowers Company should have a bank account separate from the account of Holly Sapp, the owner. Holly Sapp may own a home, a car, and other property, and she may have personal debts, but these are not the resources or debts of Just Because Flowers. Holly Sapp may own another business, say a stationery shop. If she does, she should have a completely separate set of records for each business.

EXHIBIT 1.4
Examples of Foreign Exchange Rates

Country	Price in $ U.S.	Country	Price in $ U.S
Australia (dollar)	0.93	Europe (euro)	1.43
Brazil (real)	0.57	Hong Kong (dollar)	0.13
Britain (pound)	1.63	Japan (yen)	0.011
Canada (dollar)	0.97	Mexico (peso)	0.08
China (yuan)	0.147	Russia (ruble)	0.03

Source: *The Wall Street Journal*, January 18, 2010.

Stop & Apply

Match each description with one of the terms that follow:

____ 1. An exchange of value between two or more parties
____ 2. Requires a separate set of records for a business
____ 3. An amount associated with a business transaction

a. Business transaction
b. Money measure
c. Separate entity

iStock Photo

SOLUTION 1. a; 2. c; 3. b

THE CORPORATE FORM OF BUSINESS

Describe the characteristics of a corporation. LO4

The three basic forms of business enterprise are the sole proprietorship, the partnership, and the corporation. The characteristics of corporations make them very efficient in amassing capital, which enables them to grow extremely large. As Exhibit 1.5 shows, even though corporations are fewer in number than sole proprietorships and partnerships, they contribute much more to the U.S. economy in monetary terms. For example, in 2009, **ExxonMobil** generated more revenues than all but 30 of the world's countries. Because of the economic significance of corporations, this book emphasizes accounting for the corporate form of business.

Forms of Business

There are three basic forms of business: sole proprietorship, partnership, and corporation.

Sole Proprietorship In a **sole proprietorship**, one person is the owner, takes all the profits or losses of the business, and is liable for all its obligations. Sole proprietorships represent the largest number of businesses in the United States, but typically they are the smallest in size.

STUDY NOTE: A key disadvantage of a partnership is the unlimited liability of its owners. Unlimited liability can be avoided by organizing the business as a corporation or, in some states, by forming what is known as a limited liability partnership.

Partnership Similar in most ways to a sole proprietorship, a **partnership** has two or more owners. The partners share the profits and losses of the business according to a prearranged formula. Generally, any partner can obligate the business to another party, and the personal resources of each partner can be called on to pay the obligations. A partnership must be dissolved if the ownership changes, as when a partner leaves or dies. If the business is to continue as a partnership after this occurs, a new partnership must be formed.

Both the sole proprietorship and the partnership are convenient ways of separating the owners' commercial activities from their personal activities. Legally, however, there is no economic separation between the owners and the businesses.

Corporation A **corporation** is a business unit chartered by the state and that is legally separate from its owners (the *stockholders*). The stockholders, whose ownership is represented by shares of stock, do not directly control the corporation's operations. Instead, they elect a board of directors to run the corporation for their benefit. In exchange for their limited involvement in the corporation's operations, stockholders enjoy limited liability; that is, their risk of loss is limited to the amount they paid for their shares. Thus, stockholders are often willing to invest in risky, but potentially profitable, activities. Also, because stockholders can sell their shares without dissolving the corporation, the life of a corporation is unlimited and not subject to the whims or health of a proprietor or a partner.

EXHIBIT 1.5
Number and Receipts of U.S. Proprietorships, Partnerships, and Corporations

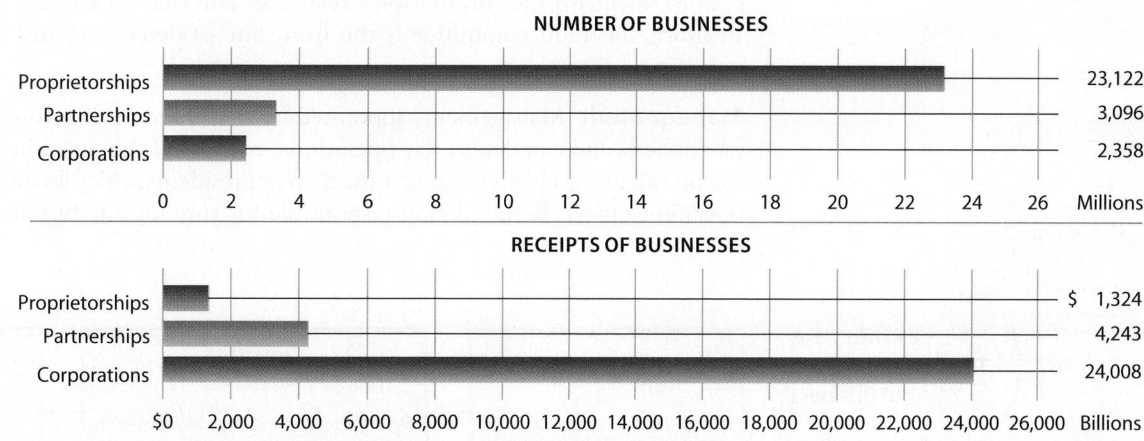

Source: U.S.Treasury Department, Internal Revenue Service, *Statistics of Income Bulletin*, Winter 2009.

Because this surf shop is a partnership, the owners share the profits and losses of the business, and their personal resources can be called on to pay the obligations of the business.

AP Photo/Chris Carlson

Formation and Organization of a Corporation

To form a corporation, most states require individuals, called incorporators, to sign an application and file it with the proper state official. This application contains the **articles of incorporation**. If approved by the state, these articles, which form the company charter, become a contract between the state and the incorporators. The company is then authorized to do business as a corporation.

The authority to manage a corporation is delegated by its stockholders to a board of directors and by the board of directors to the corporation's officers (see Exhibit 1.6 below). That is, the stockholders elect a board of directors, which sets corporate policies and chooses the corporation's officers, who in turn carry out the corporate policies in their management of the business.

Stockholders A unit of ownership in a corporation is called a **share of stock**. The articles of incorporation state the maximum number of shares that a corporation is authorized to issue. The number of shares held by stockholders is the outstanding stock; this may be less than the number authorized in the articles of incorporation. To invest in a corporation, a stockholder transfers cash or other resources to the corporation. In return, the stockholder receives shares of stock representing a proportionate share of ownership in the corporation. Afterward, the stockholder may transfer the shares at will. Corporations may have more than one kind of stock, but in the first part of this book, we refer only to **common stock**—the most universal form of stock.

Board of Directors A corporation's board of directors decides on major business policies. Among the board's specific duties are authorizing contracts, setting executive salaries, and arranging major loans with banks. The financial scandals at **Enron**, **WorldCom**, and other companies highlighted the importance of **corporate governance**, which is the oversight of a corporation's management and ethics by its board of directors. The composition of the board of directors varies from company to company, but generally corporate governance is strengthened when it includes several officers of the corporation and several outsiders. The outsiders are called *independent directors* because they do not directly participate in managing the business.

To strengthen corporate governance, the Sarbanes-Oxley Act requires boards of directors to establish an **audit committee** made up of the independent directors who have financial expertise. The purpose of this provision is to ensure that boards of directors are objective in evaluating management's performance. The audit committee is also responsible for engaging the corporation's independent auditors and reviewing their work. Another of the committee's functions is to ensure that adequate systems exist to safeguard the corporation's resources and that accounting records are reliable. In short, the audit committee is the front line of defense against fraudulent financial reporting.

Management Management, appointed by the board of directors to carry out corporate policies and run day-to-day operations, consists of the operating officers—generally the president, or chief executive officer; vice presidents; chief financial officer; and chief operating officer. Besides being responsible for running the business, management has

EXHIBIT 1.6
The Corporate Form of Business

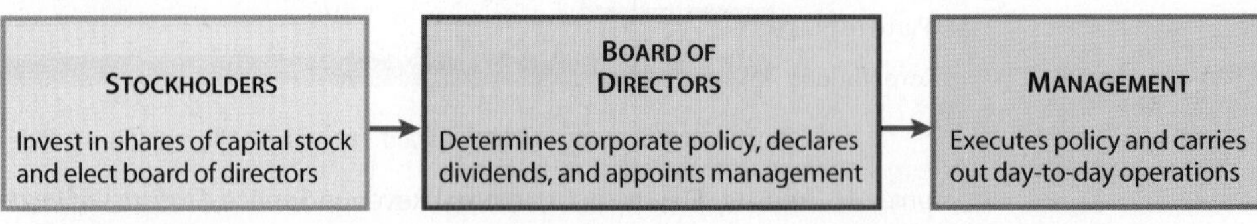
STOCKHOLDERS
Invest in shares of capital stock and elect board of directors
BOARD OF DIRECTORS
Determines corporate policy, declares dividends, and appoints management
MANAGEMENT
Executes policy and carries out day-to-day operations

Focus on Business Practice

Are Most Corporations Big or Small Businesses?

Most people think of corporations as large national or global companies whose shares of stock are held by thousands of people and institutions. Indeed, corporations can be huge and have many stockholders. However, of the approximately 4 million corporations in the United States, only about 15,000 have stock that is publicly bought and sold. The vast majority of corporations are small businesses privately held by a few stockholders. Illinois alone has more than 250,000 corporations. Thus, the study of corporations is just as relevant to small businesses as it is to large ones.

iStock Photo

the duty of reporting the financial results of its administration to the board of directors and the stockholders. Though management must, at a minimum, make a comprehensive annual report, it generally reports more often. The annual reports of large public corporations are available to the public. Excerpts from many of them appear throughout this book.

Stop & Apply

Match each of the descriptions with the terms that follow:

_____ 1. Issues stock		a. Sole proprietorship
_____ 2. Owned by only one person		b. Partnership
_____ 3. Multiple co-owners		c. Corporation
_____ 4. Management appointed by board of directors		
_____ 5. Most numerous but usually small in size		
_____ 6. Biggest segment of the economy		

iStock Photo

SOLUTION 1. c; 2. a; 3. b; 4. c; 5. a; 6. c

THE FINANCIAL STATEMENTS AND THEIR ELEMENTS

LO 5 Identify the four basic financial statements and define their elements.

Financial statements are the primary means of communicating important accounting information about a business to those who have an interest in the business. These statements are models of the business enterprise in that they show the business in financial terms. As is true of all models, however, financial statements are not perfect pictures of the real thing. Rather, they are the accountant's best effort to represent what is real. Four major financial statements are used to communicate accounting information about a business: the income statement, the statement of retained earnings, the balance sheet, and the statement of cash flows.

Income Statement

Many people consider the **income statement**, also referred to as the *statement of operations*, the most important financial report because it shows whether a business achieved its profitability goal through its operating activities—that is, whether it earned an acceptable income over a period of time. The basic elements of an income statement are revenues, expenses, and net income.

Revenues **Revenues** are the increases in stockholders' equity that result from operating a business. For example, the amount a customer pays (or agrees to pay in the future) to **CVS** in return for a product or service is revenue to CVS.

Expenses **Expenses** are the decreases in stockholders' equity that result from operating a business. Generally, a company is successful if its revenues exceed its expenses. For example, the amount CVS must pay out (or agree to pay out) so that it can provide a product or service is an expense.

Net Income When revenues exceed expenses, the difference is called **net income**. When expenses exceed revenues, the difference is called **net loss**.

Exhibit 1.7 shows an income statement for Inglot Consultancy, Inc. The company had revenues of $10,000 earned from consulting fees. From this amount, total expenses of $5,600 were deducted (equipment rental expense of $2,800, wages expense of $1,600, and utilities expense of $1,200) to arrive at income before income taxes of $4,400. Income taxes of $1,200 were deducted to arrive at net income of $3,200. To show the period to which it applies, the statement is labeled "For the Month Ended December 31, 2011."

Statement of Retained Earnings

Retained earnings represent the accumulated earnings generated by a business's income-producing activities less amounts that have been paid out to the stockholders. The **statement of retained earnings** shows the changes in retained earnings over an accounting period. The elements of the statement of retained earnings are net income (shown on the income statement) and dividends.

STUDY NOTE: *It is important not to confuse expenses and dividends, both of which reduce retained earnings.*

Dividends **Dividends** are distributions of resources, generally in the form of cash, to stockholders, and only the board of directors has the authority to declare them. Paying dividends is one way of rewarding stockholders for their investment when the corporation has been successful in earning a profit. (The other way is through an increase in the market value of the stock.) Although there is usually a delay of two or three weeks between the time the board declares a dividend and the date of the actual payment, we assume in the early chapters of this book that declaration and payment are made on the same day.

In Exhibit 1.8 (p. 17), beginning retained earnings are zero because Inglot began operations in this accounting period. During the month, the company earned an income (as shown on the income statement) of $3,200. Deducted from this amount are the dividends for the month of $2,400, leaving an ending balance of $800 of earnings retained in the business.

Balance Sheet

The purpose of a **balance sheet** is to show the financial position of a business on a certain date, usually the end of the month or year. For this reason, it often is called the *statement of financial position* and is dated as of a specific date.

EXHIBIT 1.7
Income Statement for Inglot Consultancy, Inc.

Inglot Consultancy, Inc.
Income Statement
For the Month Ended December 31, 2011

Revenues		
Consulting fees		$10,000
Expenses		
Equipment rental expense	$2,800	
Wages expense	1,600	
Utilities expense	1,200	
Total expenses		5,600
Income before income taxes		**$ 4,400**
Income taxes expense		1,200
Net income		**$ 3,200**

EXHIBIT 1.8
Statement of Retained Earnings for Inglot Consultancy, Inc.

Inglot Consultancy, Inc. Statement of Retained Earnings For the Month Ended December 31, 2011	
Retained earnings, December 1, 2011	$ 0
Net income for the month	3,200
Subtotal	$3,200
Less dividends	2,400
Retained earnings, December 31, 2011	$ 800

STUDY NOTE: *The date on the balance sheet is a single date, whereas the dates on the other three statements cover a period of time, such as a month, quarter, or year.*

The balance sheet presents a view of the business as the holder of resources, or assets, that are equal to the claims against those assets. It has three elements: assets, liabilities (also called *creditors' equities*), and stockholders' equity. (In the case of sole proprietorships and partnerships, which do not have stockholders, stockholders' equity is called *owner's equity*.) The assets equal the sum of the liabilities and stockholders' equities:

Assets = Liabilities + Stockholders' Equity

This equation is known as the **accounting equation**. The two sides of the equation must always be equal, or be "in balance," as shown in Exhibit 1.9.

Assets **Assets** are the economic resources of a company that are expected to benefit the company's future operations. Certain kinds of assets—for example, cash and money that customers owe to the company (called *accounts receivable*)—are monetary items. Other assets—inventories (goods held for sale), land, buildings, and equipment—are nonmonetary physical items. Still other assets—the rights granted by patents, trademarks, and copyrights—are nonphysical.

Liabilities **Liabilities** are a business's present obligations to pay cash, transfer assets, or provide services to other entities in the future. Among these obligations are amounts owed to suppliers for goods or services bought on credit (called *accounts payable*), borrowed money (e.g., money owed on bank loans), salaries and wages owed to employees, taxes owed to the government, and services to be performed.

As debts, liabilities are claims recognized by law. That is, the law gives creditors the right to force the sale of a company's assets if the company fails to pay its debts. Creditors have rights over stockholders and must be paid in full before the stockholders receive anything, even if payment of the debt uses up all the assets of the business.

Stockholders' Equity **Stockholders' equity** (also called *shareholders' equity*) represents the claims of the owners of a corporation (the stockholders) to the assets of the business. Theoretically, it is what would be left over if all liabilities were paid, and it is sometimes said to equal **net assets** (also called *net worth*).

EXHIBIT 1.9
The Accounting Equation

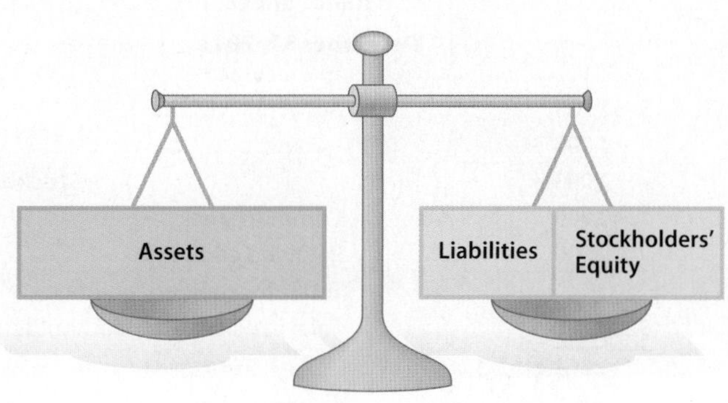

By rearranging the accounting equation, we can define stockholders' equity this way:

Stockholders' Equity = Assets − Liabilities

Stockholders' equity has two parts, contributed capital and retained earnings:

Stockholders' Equity = Contributed Capital + Retained Earnings

Contributed capital is the amount that stockholders invest in the business. As noted earlier, their ownership in the business is represented by shares of capital stock.

Typically, contributed capital is divided between par value and additional paid-in capital. **Par value** is an amount per share that when multiplied by the number of common shares becomes the corporation's common stock amount; it is the minimum amount that can be reported as contributed capital. When the value received is greater than par value, the amount over par value is called **additional paid-in capital.*** As noted earlier, retained earnings represent the accumulated income of the business less distributions to the stockholders.

The balance sheet for Inglot Consultancy in Exhibit 1.10 shows several categories of assets, which total $207,200. These assets equal the total liabilities of $6,400 (accounts payable) plus the ending balance of stockholders' equity of $200,800. Notice that the amount of retained earnings on the balance sheet comes from the ending balance on the statement of retained earnings.

Statement of Cash Flows

CASH FLOW

STUDY NOTE: The statement of cash flows provides valuable information about the change in cash flows from operating, investing, and financing activities over an accounting period, This information cannot be determined in an examination of the other financial statements.

Whereas the income statement focuses on a company's profitability, the **statement of cash flows** focuses on its liquidity (see Exhibit 1.11 on p. 19). **Cash flows** are the inflows and outflows of cash into and out of a business. Net cash flows are the difference between the inflows and outflows. As you can see in Exhibit 1.11, the statement of cash flows is organized according to the three major business activities described earlier in the chapter.

- **Cash Flows from Operating Activities** The first section of Exhibit 1.11 shows the cash produced by business operations. Inglot's operating activities produced cash flows of $3,600 (liquidity) compared with net income of $3,200 (profitability). The increase in accounts receivable is a use of cash because it represents sales included in net income that were not yet collected. Also, cash was used to increase supplies. However, by borrowing funds, it increased accounts payable. This is not a good trend, and Inglot should try to reverse it in future months.
- **Cash Flows from Investing Activities** Inglot used cash to expand by purchasing land and a building.
- **Cash Flows from Financing Activities** Inglot obtained most of its cash from stockholders and paid a small dividend.

EXHIBIT 1.10
Balance Sheet for Inglot Consultancy, Inc.

Inglot Consultancy, Inc.
Balance Sheet
December 31, 2011

Assets		**Liabilities**		
Cash	$ 61,200	Accounts payable		$ 6,400
Accounts receivable	4,000			
Supplies	2,000	**Stockholders' Equity**		
Land	40,000	Common stock	$200,000	
Building	100,000	Retained earnings	800	
		Total stockholders' equity		200,800
Total assets	$207,200	Total liabilities and stockholders' equity		$207,200

*We assume in the early chapters of this book that common stock is listed at par value.

EXHIBIT 1.11
Statement of Cash Flows for Inglot Consultancy, Inc.

Inglot Consultancy, Inc.
Statement of Cash Flows
For the Month Ended December 31, 2011

Cash flows from operating activities		
Net income		$ 3,200
Adjustments to reconcile net income to net cash flows from operating activities		
(Increase) in accounts receivable	$ (4,000)	
(Increase) in supplies	(2,000)	
Increase in accounts payable	6,400	400
Net cash flows from operating activities		$ 3,600
Cash flows from investing activities		
Purchase of land	$ (40,000)	
Purchase of building	(100,000)	
Net cash flows from investing activities		(140,000)
Cash flows from financing activities		
Issued common stock	$200,000	
Paid dividends	(2,400)	
Net cash flows from financing activities		197,600
Net increase (decrease) in cash		$ 61,200
Cash at beginning of month		0
Cash at end of month		$ 61,200

Note: Parentheses indicate a negative amount.

Overall, Inglot had a net increase in cash of $61,200, due in large part to the investment by stockholders. In future months, Inglot must generate more cash through operations.

The statement of cash flows is related directly to the other three financial statements. Notice that net income comes from the income statement and that dividends come from the statement of retained earnings. The other items in the statement represent changes in the balance sheet accounts: accounts receivable, supplies, accounts payable, land, building, and common stock.

Relationships Among the Financial Statements

Exhibit 1.12 (p. 20) illustrates the relationships among the four financial statements by showing how they would appear for Inglot Consultancy, Inc. The period covered is the month of December 2011. Notice the similarity of the headings at the top of each statement. Each identifies the company and the kind of statement. The income statement, the statement of retained earnings, and the statement of cash flows indicate the period to which they apply; the balance sheet gives the specific date to which it applies.

Focus on Financial Statement Elements: Financial Ratios

A company's overall performance is important not only to managers but also to investors and creditors. Managers want to know if they are achieving their financial goals. Investors and creditors want to evaluate a firm's past and potential financial performance before deciding whether to invest in the company or extend credit to it. In order to do

EXHIBIT 1.12
Income Statement, Statement of Retained Earnings, Balance Sheet, and Statement of Cash Flows for Inglot Consultancy, Inc.

Inglot Consultancy, Inc.
Statement of Cash Flows
For the Month Ended December 31, 2011

Cash flows from operating activities		
Net income		$ 3,200
Adjustments to reconcile net income to net cash flows from operating activities		
(Increase) in accounts receivable	($ 4,000)	
(Increase) in supplies	(2,000)	
Increase in accounts payable	6,400	400
Net cash flows from operating activities		$ 3,600
Cash flows from investing activities		
Purchase of land	($ 40,000)	
Purchase of building	(100,000)	
Net cash flows from investing activities		(140,000)
Cash flows from financing activities		
Issued common stock	$200,000	
Paid dividends	(2,400)	
Net cash flows from financing activities		197,600
Net increase (decrease) in cash		$ 61,200
Cash at beginning of month		0
Cash at end of month		$ 61,200

Inglot Consultancy, Inc.
Income Statement
For the Month Ended December 31, 2011

Revenues		
Consulting fees		$10,000
Expenses		
Equipment rental expense	$2,800	
Wages expense	1,600	
Utilities expense	1,200	
Total expenses		5,600
Income before income taxes		$ 4,400
Income taxes expense		1,200
Net income		$ 3,200

Inglot Consultancy, Inc.
Statement of Retained Earnings
For the Month Ended December 31, 2011

Retained earnings, December 1, 2011	$ 0
Net income for the month	3,200
Subtotal	$3,200
Less dividends	2,400
Retained earnings, December 31, 2011	$ 800

Inglot Consultancy, Inc.
Balance Sheet
December 31, 2011

Assets		**Liabilities**		
Cash	$ 61,200	Accounts payable		$ 6,400
Accounts receivable	4,000			
Supplies	2,000	**Stockholders' Equity**		
Land	40,000	Common stock	$200,000	
Building	100,000	Retained earnings	800	
		Total stockholders' equity		$200,800
Total assets	$207,200	Total liabilities and stockholders' equity		$207,200

__STUDY NOTE:__ Notice the sequence in which these financial statements must be prepared. The statement of retained earnings is a link between the income statement and the balance sheet, and the statement of cash flows is prepared last.

so, all three groups need to understand the financial statements and the relationships between them.

Data from specific elements of the financial statements is very important to overall company performance. These include:

- Revenues (from the income statement)
- Net income (from the income statement)

- Cash flows from operating activities (from the statement of cash flows)
- Total assets (from the balance sheet)
- Total liabilities (from the balance sheet)
- Total equity (from the balance sheet)

These key elements of the financial statements provide us with high-level information about important activities. For instance, the CEO of Inglot Consultancy will want to know if revenues and net income increased or decreased from month to month. But this does not tell the whole story. Is the company more profitable when net income increases? Quantitatively, net income may be higher, but what is the relationship to revenues? Is Inglot Consultancy controlling its costs per dollar of revenue more effectively?

In order to answer this question, users of financial statements rely on *financial ratios*. Financial ratios show important relationships among the elements of the financial statements. They can be used to assess a company's performance and compare it relative to its past performance as well as to those of other companies in the same industry. The following financial ratios have been shown to be most predictive of company performance:

- Profit margin
- Asset turnover
- Cash flow yield
- Debt to equity ratio

Each time a financial ratio is introduced in this textbook, we will highlight which elements of the financial statements are needed to compute the ratio, as shown in the top row of Exhibit 1.13. The ratio to be discussed will be highlighted as well, as shown in the bottom row of the exhibit.

These elements and ratios have been chosen because research shows they are critical for companies achieving their strategic objectives.[7] In other words, simply understanding how to find these six elements on the financial statements and how to compute these four ratios will allow you to analyze financial statements and determine how well or poorly a company is performing, which, in turn, is the basis for making good business decisions. When companies perform well on these ratios, other financial ratios either derived from these ratios or underlying them are also likely to be performing well. When any these four ratios are underperforming, further ratio analysis is warranted. We discuss all of the financial ratios in the chapters that follow and introduce the derived and underlying ratios beginning in Chapter 4.

EXHIBIT 1.13
Focus on Financial Statement Elements

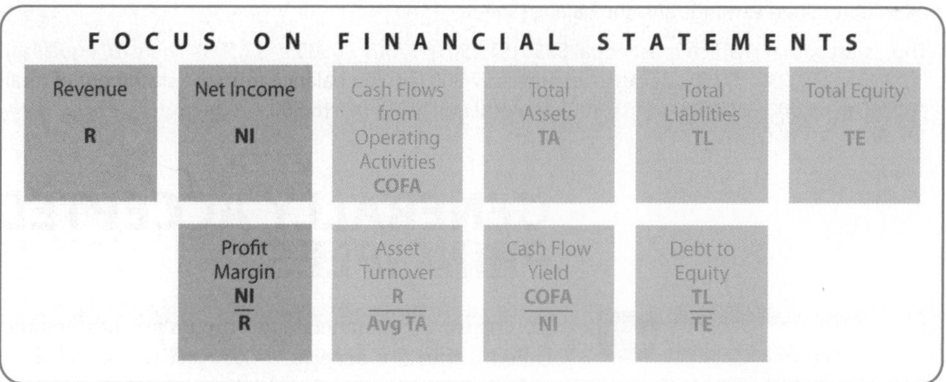

RATIO

Profit margin is calculated by dividing net income by revenues. By using the net income and revenues that appear on Inglot Consultancy's income statement, we can calculate Inglot's profit margin as follows:

$$\text{Profit Margin} = \frac{\text{Net Income}}{\text{Revenues}}$$

$$\text{Profit Margin} = \frac{\$3{,}200}{\$10{,}000}$$

$$= 0.320, \text{ or } 32.0\%$$

Thus, on each dollar of sales, Inglot earns $.32. By paying close attention to a company's profit margin, managers, investors, and creditors can assess how well the company is controlling its expenses in relation to its revenues.

Stop & Apply

Complete the financial statements that appear below by determining the amounts that correspond to the letters. (Assume no new investments by stockholders.)

Income Statement	
Revenues	$2,775
Expenses	(a)
Net income	$ (b)
Statement of Retained Earnings	
Beginning balance	$7,250
Net income	(c)
Less dividends	500
Ending balance	$7,500
Balance Sheet	
Total assets	$ (d)
Liabilities	$4,000
Stockholders' equity	
Common stock	5,000
Retained earnings	(e)
Total liabilities and stockholders' equity	$ (f)

SOLUTION

Net income links the income statement and the statement of retained earnings. The ending balance of retained earnings links the statement of retained earnings and the balance sheet.

Thus, start with (c), which must equal $750 ($7,250 + $750 − $500 = $7,500). Then, (b) equals (c), or $750. Thus, (a) must equal $2,025 ($2,775 − $2,025 = $750). Because (e) equals $7,500 (ending balance from the statement of retained earnings), (f) must equal $16,500 ($4,000 + $5,000 + $7,500 = $16,500). Now, (d) equals (f), or $16,500.

iStock Photo

GENERALLY ACCEPTED ACCOUNTING PRINCIPLES

LO 6 Explain how generally accepted accounting principles (GAAP) relate to financial statements and the independent CPA's report, and identify the organizations that influence GAAP.

To ensure that financial statements are understandable to their users, a set of practices, called **generally accepted accounting principles (GAAP)**, has been developed to provide guidelines for financial accounting. "Generally accepted accounting principles encompass the conventions, rules, and procedures necessary to define accepted accounting practice at a particular time."[8] In other words, GAAP arise from wide agreement on the theory and practice of accounting at a particular time. These "principles" are not like

Focus on International Practices

IFRS The Arrival of International Financial Reporting Standards in the United States

Over the next few years, international financial reporting standards (IFRS) will become much more important in the United States and globally. The International Accounting Standards Board (IASB) has been working with the Financial Accounting Standards Board (FASB) and similar boards in other nations to achieve identical or nearly identical standards worldwide. IFRS are now required in many parts of the world, including Europe, Canada, and most of Asia. The Securities and Exchange Commission (SEC) recently voted to allow foreign registrants in the United States to use IFRS. This is a major development because in the past, the SEC required foreign registrants to explain how the standards used in their statements differed from U.S. standards. This change affects approximately 10 percent of all public U.S. companies. In addition, the SEC may in the near future allow U.S. public companies to use IFRS.[9]

the unchangeable laws of nature in chemistry or physics. They evolve to meet the needs of decision makers, and they change as circumstances change or as better methods are developed.

In this book, we present accounting practice, or GAAP, as it is today, and we try to explain the reasons or theory on which the practice is based. However, accounting is a discipline that is always growing, changing, and improving. Just as years of research are necessary before a new surgical method or lifesaving drug can be introduced, it may take years for new accounting practices to be implemented. Your instructor may mention certain weaknesses in current theory or practice, and at various times in the text, we point out new directions in accounting that may overcome these weaknesses.

GAAP and the Independent CPA's Report

Because financial statements are prepared by management and could be falsified for personal gain, all companies that sell shares of their stock to the public and many companies that apply for sizable loans have their financial statements audited by an independent **certified public accountant (CPA)**. *Independent* means that the CPA is not an employee of the company being audited and has no financial or other compromising ties with it. CPAs are licensed by all states for the same reason that lawyers and doctors are—to protect the public by ensuring the quality of professional service. The firms listed in Exhibit 1.14 employ about 25 percent of all CPAs in the United States.

An **audit** is an examination of a company's financial statements and the accounting systems, controls, and records that produced them. The purpose of the audit is to ascertain that the financial statements have been prepared in accordance with generally accepted accounting principles. If the independent CPA is satisfied that this standard has been met, his or her report contains the following language:

> In our opinion, the financial statements . . . present fairly, in all material respects . . . in conformity with generally accepted accounting principles. . . .

This wording emphasizes that accounting and auditing are not exact sciences. Because the framework of GAAP provides room for interpretation and the application of GAAP necessitates the making of estimates, the auditor can render only an opinion about whether the financial statements *present fairly* or conform *in all material respects* to GAAP. The auditor's report does not preclude minor or immaterial errors in the financial statements. However, a favorable report from the auditor does imply that on

EXHIBIT 1.14
Large International Certified Public Accounting Firms

Firm	Home Office	Some Major Clients
Deloitte & Touche	New York	General Motors, Procter & Gamble
Ernst & Young	New York	Coca-Cola, McDonald's
KPMG	New York	General Electric, Xerox
PricewaterhouseCoopers	New York	ExxonMobil, IBM, Ford

the whole, investors and creditors can rely on the financial statements. In other words, the audit lends credibility to a set of financial statements. Auditors offer opinions, based on testing, about the fairness of the presentation of a company's financial information, but they cannot attest to the absolute accuracy of such information.

Historically, auditors have enjoyed a strong reputation for competence and independence. The independent audit has been an important factor in the worldwide growth of financial markets.

Organizations That Issue Accounting Standards

Two organizations issue accounting standards that are used in the United States: the FASB and the IASB.

- The **Financial Accounting Standards Board (FASB)** is the most important body for developing rules on accounting practice. This independent body has been designated by the Securities and Exchange Commission to issue the *Statements of Financial Accounting Standards.* The FASB organizes these statements including any amendments, interpretations, or other references to them into a topical U.S. GAAP compendium called an American Standard Codification (ASC). This codification, which is available through the FASB website, makes it easy to find all references to a particular topic, such as revenues, in one place.

- The **International Accounting Standards Board (IASB)**, which issues **international financial reporting standards (IFRS)**, is becoming increasingly important because of the acceptance of its standards in many financial markets throughout the world. The SEC now allows foreign companies to use these standards in the United States rather than having to convert their statements to U.S. GAAP. The SEC is also presently considering allowing U.S. public companies to use IFRS.

Other Organizations That Influence GAAP

Many other organizations directly or indirectly influence GAAP and so influence much of what is in this book.

- The **Public Company Accounting Oversight Board (PCAOB)**, a governmental body created by the Sarbanes-Oxley Act, regulates the accounting profession and has wide powers to determine the standards that auditors must follow and to discipline them if they do not. The PCAOB regulates audits of public companies registered with the SEC.
- The **American Institute of Certified Public Accountants (AICPA)**, the professional association of certified public accountants, influences accounting practice through the activities of its senior technical committees. In addition to endorsing standards issued by the FASB, the AICPA has determined that standards issued by the IASB are also of high quality and are thus acceptable for use in the United States.*
- The **Securities and Exchange Commission (SEC)** is an agency of the federal government that has the legal power to set and enforce accounting practices for companies whose securities are offered for sale to the general public. As such, it has enormous influence on accounting practice.
- The **Governmental Accounting Standards Board (GASB)**, which is a separate but related body to the FASB, issues accounting standards for state and local governments.

---

*Established in January 2007, the Private Company Financial Reporting Committee of the AICPA is charged with amending FASB accounting standards so that they better suit the needs of private companies, especially as they relate to the cost or benefit of implementing certain standards. A Blue-Ribbon Committee established by the FASB, AICPA, and other organizations is currently studying this issue. Its recommendations could ultimately result in two sets of standards, one for private companies and one for public companies.

- The **Internal Revenue Service (IRS)** interprets and enforces the tax laws that specify the rules for determining taxable income also influence accounting practice. In some cases, the rules conflict with good accounting practice, but they are nonetheless an important influence on practice. Cases in which the tax laws affect accounting practice are noted throughout this book.

Professional Conduct

The code of professional ethics of the American Institute of Certified Public Accountants (adopted, with variations, by each state) governs the conduct of CPAs. Fundamental to this code is responsibility to clients, creditors, investors, and anyone else who relies on the work of a CPA. The code requires CPAs to act with integrity, objectivity, and independence. Research shows that these are the attributes that business decision makers and the investing public most closely associate with CPAs.[10]

- **Integrity** means the accountant is honest and candid and subordinates personal gain to service and the public trust.
- **Objectivity** means the accountant is impartial and intellectually honest.
- **Independence** means the accountant avoids all relationships that impair or even appear to impair his or her objectivity.

The accountant must also exercise **due care** in all activities, carrying out professional responsibilities with competence and diligence. For example, an accountant must not accept a job for which he or she is not qualified, even at the risk of losing a client to another firm, and careless work is unacceptable. These broad principles are supported by more specific rules that public accountants must follow; for instance, with certain exceptions, client information must be kept strictly confidential. Accountants who violate the rules can be disciplined or even suspended from practice.

The **Institute of Management Accountants (IMA)**, the primary professional association of management accountants, also has a code of professional conduct. It emphasizes that management accountants have a responsibility to be competent in their jobs, to keep information confidential except when authorized or legally required to disclose it, to maintain integrity and avoid conflicts of interest, and to communicate information objectively and without bias.[11]

Stop & Apply

Match the following acronyms with the descriptions that follow:

____ 1. GAAP	a. Sets U.S. accounting standards
____ 2. IFRS	b. Audits financial statements
____ 3. CPA	c. Established by the Sarbanes-Oxley Act
____ 4. FASB	d. Sets international accounting standards
____ 5. IASB	e. Established by the FASB
____ 6. PCAOB	f. Established by the IASB
____ 7. AICPA	g. Influences accounting standards through member CPAs
____ 8. SEC	h. Receives audited financial statements of public companies

SOLUTION 1. e; 2. f; 3. b; 4. a; 5. d; 6. c; 7. g; 8. h

A look back at ▸ CVS Caremark

The Decision Point at the beginning of this chapter focuses on **CVS** Caremark, a successful nationwide chain of more than 7,000 drugstores. It poses these questions:

1. As a manager at CVS, what financial knowledge would you need to measure progress toward the company's goals?
2. As a potential investor or creditor, what financial knowledge would you need to evaluate CVS's financial performance?
3. Is CVS meeting its goal of profitability?

As you've learned in this chapter, measuring a company's progress toward achieving its goals requires a knowledge of key elements of the financial statements. To evaluate a company's profitability, managers and others with an interest in the company look at its net sales, net earnings, total assets, and stockholders' equity. These important performance measures are the starting point for the analysis of financial statements.

The highlights from CVS's financial statements presented at the beginning of the chapter show that the company's net sales, net earnings (net income), total assets, and stockholders' equity have increased over the years. But how can these data be used to determine if CVS is meeting its goal of profitability? As we noted earlier, financial ratios, which show the relationships among elements of the financial statements, provide a way of doing this. They allow for comparisons of a company's financial performance from one period to the next and for comparisons among companies.

Financial Ratio: Profit Margin

One way to tell if CVS is meeting its goal of profitability is to compute its profit margin by comparing two elements of the income statement: net income (called net earnings by CVS) and revenues (called net sales by CVS).

Using the data from CVS's Financial Highlights at the beginning of the chapter, the company's profit margin in 2009 is calculated as follows (amounts are in millions):

	2009	2008
$\frac{\text{Net income}}{\text{Net sales}}$	$\frac{\$3,696}{\$98,729}$	$\frac{\$3,212}{\$87,472}$
Profit margin	$0.037 \times 100 = 3.7\%$	$0.037 \times 100 = 3.7\%$

We can draw several conclusions from this ratio. First, CVS earned 3.7 cents on each dollar of net sales. Second, from 2008 to 2009, its profitability was the same at 3.7 percent. These amounts indicate that CVS has been able to earn an income from the sale of its products and services, but more information is needed to further evaluate its profitability. You will learn much more about financial ratios in the chapters that follow.

Review Problem

Preparation and Interpretation of Financial Statements 

The following accounts and amounts are from the records of Orion Realty for the year ended April 30, 2011, the company's first year of operations:

Accounts payable	$ 19,000
Accounts receivable	104,000
Cash	90,000
Commissions earned	375,000
Common stock	100,000
Dividends	10,000
Equipment	47,000
Income taxes expense	27,000
Income taxes payable	6,000
Marketing expense	18,000
Office and equipment rent expense	91,000
Salaries and commission expense	178,000
Salaries payable	78,000
Supplies	2,000
Utilities expense	11,000

Required

1. Prepare an income statement, statement of retained earnings, and balance sheet for Orion Realty. For examples, refer to Exhibit 1.12.
2. What is the difference between Income Taxes Expense and Income Taxes Payable? (USER INSIGHT)
3. How are the statements related to each other?

ANSWERS TO REVIEW PROBLEM

1.

	A	B	C	D
1		**Orion Realty**		
2		**Income Statement**		
3		**For the Year Ended April 30, 2011**		
4				
5	**Revenues**			
6		Commissions earned		$375,000
7	**Expenses**			
8		Marketing expense	$ 18,000	
9		Office and equipment rent expense	91,000	
10		Salaries and commission expense	178,000	
11		Utilities expense	11,000	
12		Total expenses		298,000
13	Income before income taxes			$ 77,000
14	Income taxes expense			27,000
15	**Net income**			$ 50,000
16				

	A	B	C
1		Orion Realty	
2		Statement of Retained Earnings	
3		For the Year Ended April 30, 2011	
4			
5	Retained earnings, April 30, 2010		$ —
6	Net income for the year		50,000
7	Subtotal		$50,000
8	Less dividends		10,000
9	Retained earnings, April 30, 2011		$40,000
10			

	A	B	C	D	E
1			Orion Realty		
2			Balance Sheet		
3			April 30, 2011		
4					
5	Assets		Liabilities		
6	Cash	$ 90,000	Accounts payable	$ 19,000	
7	Accounts receivable	104,000	Salaries payable	78,000	
8	Supplies	2,000	Income taxes payable	6,000	
9	Equipment	47,000	Total liabilities		$103,000
10					
11			Stockholders' Equity		
12			Common stock	$100,000	
13			Retained earnings	40,000	
14			Total stockholders' equity		140,000
15			Total liabilities and		
16	Total assets	$243,000	stockholders' equity		$243,000
17					

2. Income Taxes Expense is the total expense for the accounting period. Income Taxes Payable is the amount that has not yet been paid to the government.
3. Net income from the income statement appears on the statement of retained earnings. The ending balance (on April 30, 2011) on the statement of retained earnings appears on the balance sheet.

Stop & Review

LO1 Define *accounting* and describe its role in making informed decisions, identify business goals and activities, and explain the importance of ethics in accounting.

Accounting is an information system that measures, processes, and communicates financial information about an economic entity. It provides the information necessary to make reasoned choices among alternative uses of scarce resources in the conduct of business and economic activities. A business is an economic entity that engages in operating, investing, and financing activities to achieve the goals of profitability and liquidity.

Management accounting focuses on the preparation of information primarily for internal use by management. Financial accounting is concerned with the development and use of reports that are communicated to those outside the business as well as to management. Ethical financial reporting is important to the well-being of a company; fraudulent financial reports can have serious consequences for many people.

LO2 Identify the users of accounting information.

Accounting plays a significant role in society by providing information to managers of all institutions and to individuals with a direct financial interest in those institutions, including present and potential investors and creditors. Accounting information is also important to those with an indirect financial interest in the business—for example, tax authorities, regulatory agencies, and economic planners.

LO3 Explain the importance of business transactions, money measure, and separate entity.

To make an accounting measurement, the accountant must determine what is measured, when the measurement should be made, what value should be placed on what is measured, and how to classify what is measured. The objects of accounting measurement are business transactions. Financial accounting uses money measure to gauge the impact of these transactions on a separate business entity.

LO4 Describe the characteristics of a corporation.

Corporations, whose ownership is represented by shares of stock, are separate entities for both legal and accounting purposes. The stockholders own the corporation and elect the board of directors. The board is responsible for determining corporate policies and appointing corporate officers, or top managers, to operate the business in accordance with the policies that it sets. The board is also responsible for corporate governance, the oversight of a corporation's management and ethics. The audit committee, which is appointed by the board and is made up of independent directors, is an important factor in corporate governance.

LO5 Identify the four basic financial statements and define their elements.

The four basic financial statements are the income statement, the statement of retained earnings, the balance sheet, and the statement of cash flows. They are the primary means by which accountants communicate the financial condition and activities of a business to those who have an interest in the business.

The elements of the income statement are revenues, expenses, and net income. The elements of the statement of retained earnings are net income (shown on the income statement) and dividends. The elements of the balance sheet reflect the accounting equation: Assets = Liabilities + Stockholders' Equity. (In the case of sole proprietorships and partnerships, stockholders' equity is called owner's equity.) The elements of the statement of cash flows are cash flows from operating activities, cash flows from investing activities, and cash flows from financing activities

LO6 Explain how generally accepted accounting principles (GAAP) relate to financial statements and the independent CPA's report and identify the organizations that influence GAAP.

Acceptable accounting practice consists of the conventions, rules, and procedures that make up generally accepted accounting principles at a particular time. GAAP are essential to the preparation and interpretation of financial statements and the independent CPA's report. Foreign companies registered in the United States may use international financial reporting standards (IFRS).

Among the organizations that influence the formulation of GAAP are the Public Company Accounting Oversight Board, the Financial Accounting Standards Board, the American Institute of Certified Public Accountants, the Securities and Exchange Commission, and the Internal Revenue Service.

All accountants must follow a code of professional ethics, which is based on responsibility to the public. Accountants must act with integrity, objectivity, and independence, and they must exercise due care in all their activities.

Key Terms and Ratios

Accounting 4 (LO1)
Accounting equation 17 (LO5)
Additional paid-in capital 18 (LO5)
American Institute of Certified Public Accountants (AICPA) 24 (LO6)
Articles of incorporation 14 (LO4)
Assets 17 (LO5)
Audit 23 (LO6)
Audit committee 14 (LO4)
Balance sheet 16 (LO5)
Bookkeeping 7 (LO1)
Business 4 (LO1)
Business transactions 11 (LO3)
Cash flows 18 (LO5)
Certified public accountant (CPA) 23 (LO6)
Common stock 14 (LO4)
Contributed capital 18 (LO5)
Corporate governance 14 (LO4)
Corporation 13 (LO4)
Creditors 10 (LO2)
Dividends 16 (LO5)
Due care 25 (LO6)
Ethics 7 (LO1)
Exchange rate 12 (LO3)
Expenses 16 (LO5)
Financial accounting 7 (LO1)
Financial Accounting Standards Board (FASB) 24 (LO6)
Financial analysis 5 (LO1)
Financial ratios 6 (LO1)
Financial statements 7 (LO1)
Financing activities 5 (LO1)
Fraudulent financial reporting 7 (LO1)
Generally accepted accounting principles (GAAP) 22 (LO6)
Governmental Accounting Standards Board (GASB) 24 (LO6)
Income statement 15 (LO5)
Independence 25 (LO6)
Institute of Management Accountants (IMA) 25 (LO6)
Integrity 25 (LO6)
Internal Revenue Service (IRS) 25 (LO6)
International Accounting Standards Board (IASB) 24 (LO6)
International financial reporting standards (IFRS) 24 (LO6)
Investors 9 (LO2)
Investing activities 5 (LO1)
Liabilities 17 (LO5)
Liquidity 5 (LO1)
Management 9 (LO2)
Management accounting 6 (LO1)
Management information systems (MIS) 7 (LO1)
Money measure 12 (LO3)
Net assets 17 (LO5)
Net income 16 (LO5)
Net loss 16 (LO5)
Objectivity 25 (LO6)
Operating activities 5 (LO1)
Partnership 13 (LO4)
Par value 18 (LO5)
Performance measures 5 (LO1)
Profitability 5 (LO1)
Public Company Accounting Oversight Board (PCAOB) 24 (LO6)
Retained earnings 16 (LO5)
Revenues 15 (LO5)
Sarbanes-Oxley Act 8 (LO1)
Securities and Exchange Commission (SEC) 10, 24 (LO2, LO6)
Separate entity 12 (LO3)
Share of stock 14 (LO4)
Sole proprietorship 13 (LO4)
Statement of cash flows 18 (LO5)
Statement of retained earnings 16 (LO5)
Stockholders' equity 17 (LO5)

FINANCIAL RATIO
Profit margin 22 (LO5)

Chapter Assignments Building Your Basic Knowledge and Skills

Short Exercises

LO 1 **Accounting and Business Enterprises**

SE 1. Match the terms on the left with the definitions on the right:

____ 1. Accounting	a. The process of producing accounting information for the internal use of a company's management
____ 2. Profitability	b. Having enough cash available to pay debts when they are due
____ 3. Liquidity	c. Activities management engages in to obtain adequate funds for beginning and continuing to operate a business
____ 4. Financing activities	d. The process of generating and communicating accounting information in the form of financial statements to decision makers outside the organization
____ 5. Investing activities	e. Activities management engages in to spend capital in ways that are productive and will help a business achieve its objectives
____ 6. Operating activities	
____ 7. Financial accounting	

____ 8.	Management accounting	f. The ability to earn enough income to attract and hold investment capital
____ 9.	Ethics	g. An information system that measures, processes, and communicates financial information about an identifiable economic entity
____ 10.	Fraudulent financial reporting	h. The intentional preparation of misleading financial statements
		i. Activities management engages in to operate the business
		j. A code of conduct that applies to everyday life

LO 3, 4

Accounting Concepts

SE 2. Indicate whether each of the following words or phrases relates most closely to (a) a business transaction, (b) a separate entity, or (c) a money measure:

1. Partnership
2. U.S. dollar
3. Payment of an expense
4. Corporation
5. Sale of an asset

LO 4

Forms of Business Enterprise

SE 3. Indicate whether each of the following most accurately describes (a) a sole proprietorship, (b) a partnership, or (c) a corporation.

____ 1. Most numerous
____ 2. Commands most revenues
____ 3. Two or more co-owners
____ 4. Has stockholders
____ 5. Owned by only one person
____ 6. Has a board of directors

LO 5

The Accounting Equation

SE 4. Determine the amount missing from each accounting equation below.

	Assets	=	Liabilities	+	Stockholders' Equity
1.	?		$50,000		$ 70,000
2.	$156,000		$84,000		?
3.	$292,000		?		$192,000

LO 5

The Accounting Equation

SE 5. Use the accounting equation to answer each question below.

1. The assets of Tiller Company are $480,000, and the liabilities are $180,000. What is the amount of the stockholders' equity?
2. The liabilities of Elm Company equal one-fifth of the total assets. The stockholders' equity is $80,000. What is the amount of the liabilities?

LO 5

The Accounting Equation

SE 6. Use the accounting equation to answer each question below.

1. At the beginning of the year, Helena Company's assets were $90,000 and its stockholders' equity was $50,000. During the year, assets increased by $60,000 and liabilities increased by $10,000. What was the stockholders' equity at the end of the year?
2. At the beginning of the year, Alfredo Company had liabilities of $100,000 and stockholders' equity of $192,000. If assets increased by $80,000 and liabilities decreased by $60,000, what was the stockholders' equity at the end of the year?

LO 5

The Accounting Equation and Net Income

SE 7. Carlton Company had assets of $280,000 and liabilities of $120,000 at the beginning of the year and assets of $400,000 and liabilities of $140,000 at the end of the year. During the year, there was an investment of $40,000 in the business and the company paid dividends of $48,000. What amount of net income did the company earn during the year?

LO 5

Preparation and Completion of a Balance Sheet

SE 8. Use the following accounts and balances to prepare a balance sheet with the accounts in proper order for Globe Company at June 30, 2011. (*Note:* Use Exhibit 1.10 on p. 18 as a model.)

Accounts Receivable	$1,600	Common Stock	$24,000
Wages Payable	700	Building	22,000
Retained Earnings	4,700	Cash	?

LO 5

Preparation of Financial Statements

SE 9. Tarech Corporation engaged in activities during the first year of its operations that resulted in the following: Service Revenue, $4,800; Total Expenses, $2,450; and Dividends, $410. In addition, the year-end balances of selected accounts were as follows: Cash, $1,890; Other Assets, $1,000; Accounts Payable, $450; and Common Stock, $500. In proper format, prepare the income statement, statement of retained earnings, and balance sheet for Tarech (assume the year ends on December 31, 2011). (*Hint:* You must solve for the beginning and ending balances of retained earnings for 2011.)

LO 5

Preparation and Completion of a Balance Sheet

SE 10. Use the following accounts and balances to prepare a balance sheet with the accounts in proper order for Anatole Company at April 30, 2011, using Exhibit 1.10 (p. 18) as a model:

Accounts Receivable	$3,200	Common Stock	$48,000
Wages Payable	1,000	Building	40,000
Retained Earnings	7,000	Cash	?

LO 5

Preparation of Financial Statements

SE 11. Patel Corporation engaged in activities during the first year of its operations that resulted in the following: Service Revenue, $9,600; Total Expenses, $4,900; and Dividends, $820. In addition, the year-end balances of selected accounts were as follows: Cash, $3,780; Other Assets, $2,000; Accounts Payable, $900; and Common Stock, $1,000. In proper format, prepare the income statement, statement of retained earnings, and balance sheet for Patel (assume the year ends on December 31, 2011). (*Hint:* You must solve for the beginning and ending balances of retained earnings for 2011.)

LO 6

Accounting Abbreviations

SE 12. Identify the accounting meaning of each of the following abbreviations: AICPA, SEC, PCAOB, GAAP, FASB, IFRS, IRS, GASB, IASB, IMA, and CPA.

LO 5

Financial Ratio: Profit Margin

SE 13. Orbit Company had net income of $30,000 in 2010. Revenues during the year were $220,000. Calculate profit margin. (*Note*: Round to three decimal places.)

Exercises

LO 1, 2, 3, 4

Discussion Questions

E 1. Develop a brief answer to each of the following questions.

1. What makes accounting a valuable discipline?
2. Why do managers in governmental and not-for-profit organizations need to understand financial information as much as managers in profit-seeking businesses?

3. Are all economic events business transactions?
4. Sole proprietorships, partnerships, and corporations differ legally; how and why does accounting treat them alike?

LO 5, 6

Discussion Questions

E 2. Develop a brief answer to each of the following questions.

1. How are expenses and dividends similar, and how are they different?
2. In what ways are **CVS** and **Southwest Airlines** comparable? Not comparable?
3. How do generally accepted accounting principles (GAAP) differ from the laws of science?
4. What are some unethical ways in which a business may do its accounting or prepare its financial statements?

LO 1, 2, 3, 6

The Nature of Accounting

E 3. Match the terms below with the descriptions in the list that follows:

____ 1. Bookkeeping
____ 2. Creditors
____ 3. Money measure
____ 4. Financial Accounting Standards Board (FASB)
____ 5. Business transactions
____ 6. Audit
____ 7. Communication
____ 8. Securities and Exchange Commission (SEC)
____ 9. Investors
____ 10. Sarbanes-Oxley Act
____ 11. Management
____ 12. Management information system

a. The recording of all business transactions in terms of money
b. A process by which information is exchanged between individuals through a common system of symbols, signs, or behavior
c. The process of identifying and assigning values to business transactions
d. Legislation ordering CEOs and CFOs to swear that any reports they file with the SEC are accurate and complete
e. An examination of a company's financial statements and the accounting system, controls, and records that produced them
f. Collectively, the people who have overall responsibility for operating a business and meeting its goals
g. People who commit money to earn a financial return
h. The interconnected subsystems that provide the information needed to run a business
i. The most important body for developing and issuing rules on accounting practice, called *Statements of Financial Accounting Standards*
j. An agency set up by Congress to protect the public by regulating the issuing, buying, and selling of stocks
k. Economic events that affect a business's financial position
l. People to whom money is due

LO 2, 4

Users of Accounting Information and Forms of Business Enterprise

E 4. Cellhealth Pharmacy has recently been formed to develop a new type of drug treatment for cancer. Previously a partnership, Cellhealth has now become a corporation. List the various groups that will have an interest in the financial statements of Cellhealth. What is the difference between a partnership and a corporation? What advantages does the corporate form have over the partnership form of business organization?

LO 3

Business Transactions

E 5. Tom owns and operates a minimart. Which of Tom's actions described below are business transactions? Explain why any other actions are not considered transactions.

1. Tom reduces the price of a gallon of milk in order to match the price offered by a competitor.
2. Tom pays a high school student cash for cleaning up the driveway behind the market.

3. Tom fills his son's car with gasoline in payment for his son's restocking the vending machines and the snack food shelves.
4. Tom pays interest to himself on a loan he made to the business three years ago.

LO 3, 4

Accounting Concepts

E 6. Financial accounting uses money measures to gauge the impact of business transactions on a separate business entity. Tell whether each of the following words or phrases relates most closely to (a) a business transaction, (b) a separate entity, or (c) a money measure:

1. Corporation
2. Euro
3. Sales of products
4. Receipt of cash
5. Sole proprietorship
6. U.S. dollar
7. Partnership
8. Stockholders' investments
9. Japanese yen
10. Purchase of supplies

LO 3

Money Measure

E 7. You have been asked to compare the sales and assets of four companies that make computer chips to determine which company is the largest in each category. You have gathered the following data, but they cannot be used for direct comparison because each company's sales and assets are in its own currency:

Company (Currency)	Sales	Assets
US.Chip (U.S. dollar)	2,750,000	1,300,000
Nanhai (Hong Kong dollar)	5,000,000	2,800,000
Tova (Japanese yen)	350,000,000	290,000,000
Holstein (euro)	3,500,000	3,900,000

Assuming that the exchange rates in Exhibit 1.4 (p. 12) are current and appropriate, convert all the figures to U.S. dollars and determine which company is the largest in sales and which is the largest in assets.

LO 5

The Accounting Equation

E 8. Use the accounting equation to answer each question that follows. Show any calculations you make.

1. The assets of Dusan Corporation are $760,000, and the stockholders' equity is $310,000. What is the amount of the liabilities?
2. The liabilities and stockholders' equity of Bem Corporation are $130,000 and $159,000, respectively. What is the amount of the assets?
3. The liabilities of Acosta Corporation equal one-third of the total assets, and stockholders' equity is $90,000. What is the amount of the liabilities?
4. At the beginning of the year, Larry Corporation's assets were $620,000, and its stockholders' equity was $300,000. During the year, assets increased $90,000 and liabilities decreased $45,000. What is the stockholders' equity at the end of the year?

LO 5

Identification of Accounts

E 9. 1. Indicate whether each of the following accounts is an asset (A), a liability (L), or a part of stockholders' equity (SE):

a. Cash
b. Salaries Payable
c. Accounts Receivable
d. Common Stock
e. Land
f. Accounts Payable
g. Supplies

2. Indicate whether each account below would be shown on the income statement (IS), the statement of retained earnings (RE), or the balance sheet (BS).

a. Repair Revenue
b. Automobile
c. Fuel Expense
d. Cash
e. Rent Expense
f. Accounts Payable
g. Dividends

LO 5 **Preparation of a Balance Sheet**

E 10. Listed in random order are some of the account balances for Rojas Services Company as of December 31, 2011.

Accounts Payable	$ 50,000	Accounts Receivable	$62,500
Building	112,500	Cash	25,000
Common Stock	125,000	Equipment	50,000
Supplies	12,500	Retained Earnings	87,500

Place the balances in proper order and prepare a balance sheet similar to the one in Exhibit 1.10 (p. 18).

LO 5 **Preparation and Integration of Financial Statements**

E 11. Kaisha Corporation had the following account balances at the end of 2011: Service Revenue, $13,200; Rent Expense, $1,200; Wages Expense, $8,340; Advertising Expense, $1,350; Utilities Expense, $900; Income Taxes Expense, $200; and Dividends, $700. In addition, the year-end balances of selected accounts were as follows: Cash, $1,550; Accounts Receivable, $750; Supplies, $100; Land, $1,000; Accounts Payable, $450; and Common Stock, $1,000.

In proper format, prepare the income statement, statement of retained earnings, and balance sheet for Kaisha (assume the year ends on December 31, 2011). (*Hint:* You must solve for the beginning and ending balances of retained earnings for 2011.)

LO 5 **Stockholders' Equity and the Accounting Equation**

E 12. The total assets and liabilities at the beginning and end of the year for Luther Company are listed below.

	Assets	Liabilities
Beginning of the year	$360,000	$137,500
End of the year	550,000	301,000

Determine Luther's net income or net loss for the year under each of the following alternatives:

1. The stockholders made no investments in the business, and no dividends were paid during the year.
2. The stockholders made no investments in the business, but dividends of $55,000 were paid during the year.
3. The stockholders invested $32,500 in the business, but no dividends were paid during the year.
4. The stockholders invested $25,000 in the business, and dividends of $58,000 were paid during the year.

LO 5 **Statement of Cash Flows**

E 13. Primorsk Corporation began the year 2011 with cash of $27,950. In addition to earning a net income of $19,000 and paying a cash dividend of $9,750, Primorsk borrowed $39,000 from the bank and purchased equipment with $62,500 of cash. Also, Accounts Receivable increased by $3,900, and Accounts Payable increased by $5,850.

Determine the amount of cash on hand at December 31, 2011, by preparing a statement of cash flows similar to the one in Exhibit 1.11 (p. 19).

LO 5 **Statement of Retained Earnings**

E 14. Below is information from the statement of retained earnings of Mrs. Bell's Pastry, Inc.

Dividends	$ 0
Net income	?
Retained earnings, January 31, 2011	159,490
Retained earnings, January 31, 2010	105,000

Prepare the statement of retained earnings for Mrs. Bell's Pastry in good form. You will need to solve for the amount of net income. What are retained earnings? Why would the company's board of directors decide not to pay any dividends to its owners?

Financial Ratio: Profit Margin

E 15. Max wants to know if his company's profitability performance has increased from 2010 to 2011. Specifically, he wants to know if the company is maintaining its margin on revenues. The company had net income of $24,000 in 2010 and $25,000 in 2011. Total revenues were $200,000 in 2010 and $240,000 in 2011. Calculate profit margin for 2010 and 2011 and comment on the results. (*Note*: Round your answer to three decimal places.)

Problems

LO 5

Preparation and Interpretation of the Financial Statements

P 1. Below is a list of financial statement items.

a. Utilities expense	g. Revenues	m. Fees earned
b. Building	h. Accounts receivable	n. Cash
c. Common stock	i. Accounts payable	o. Supplies
d. Net income	j. Rent expense	p. Wages expense
e. Land	k. Dividends	
f. Equipment	l. Income taxes expense	

REQUIRED

1. Indicate whether each item is found on the income statement (IS), statement of retained earnings (RE), and/or balance sheet (BS).
2. USER INSIGHT ▶ Which of the financial statements is most closely associated with the goal of profitability?

LO 5

Interrelationship of Financial Statements

✔ (f) $6,600; (l) $31,000; (q) $580

P 2. The following three independent sets of financial statements have several amounts missing:

	Set A	Set B	Set C
Income Statement			
Revenue	$1,100	$ g	$240
Expenses	a	5,200	m
Net income	$ b	$ h	$ 80
Statement of Retained Earnings			
Beginning balance	$2,900	$15,400	$200
Net income	c	1,600	n
Less dividends	200	i	o
Ending balance	$3,000	$ j	$ p
Balance Sheet			
Total assets	$ d	$31,000	$ q
Liabilities	$1,600	$ 5,000	$ r
Stockholders' equity			
Common stock	2,000	10,000	100
Retained earnings	e	k	280
Total liabilities and stockholders' equity	$ f	$ l	$580

REQUIRED

1. Complete each set of financial statements by determining the amounts that correspond to the letters. (*Hint:* Amounts are not necessarily solved in alphabetical order.)

USER INSIGHT ▶

2. In what order is it necessary to prepare the financial statements? Why is that order necessary?

LO 1, 5

Preparation and Interpretation of the Income Statement, Statement of Retained Earnings, and Balance Sheet

P 3. Below are the financial accounts of Landscape Design, Inc. The company has just completed its third year of operations ended November 30, 2011.

✔ Total assets: $125,650

Accounts Payable	$ 7,400	Marketing Expense	$19,700
Accounts Receivable	9,100	Office Rent Expense	18,200
Cash	115,750	Retained Earnings, November 30, 2010	55,400
Common Stock	15,000	Salaries Expense	96,000
Design Service Revenue	248,000	Salaries Payable	2,700
Dividends	40,000	Supplies	800
Income Taxes Expense	38,850	Utilities Expense	3,100
Income Taxes Payable	13,000		

REQUIRED

1. Prepare the income statement, statement of retained earnings, and balance sheet for Landscape Design.

USER INSIGHT ▶

2. Explain the difference between Salaries Expense and Salaries Payable.
3. Evaluate the company's ability to meet its bills when they come due.

LO 1, 5

Preparation and Interpretation of Financial Statements

P 4. Below are the accounts of Collegiate Painters, Inc. The company has just completed its first year of operations ended September 30, 2011.

✔ Total assets: $20,900

Accounts Payable	$10,500	Income Taxes Payable	$ 3,000
Accounts Receivable	13,200	Marketing Expense	1,500
Cash	2,600	Painting Service Revenue	78,800
Common Stock	2,000	Salaries Expense	56,000
Dividends	1,000	Salaries Payable	700
Equipment	4,700	Supplies	400
Equipment Rental Expense	1,300	Truck Rent Expense	7,200
Income Taxes Expense	3,000	Utilities Expense	4,100

REQUIRED

1. Prepare the income statement, statement of retained earnings, and balance sheet for Collegiate Painters.

USER INSIGHT ▶

2. Why would the owners of Collegiate Painters set their business up as a corporation and not a partnership?

LO 1, 5 LO 6

Use and Interpretation of Financial Statements

P 5. The financial statements for Wichita Riding Club, Inc., follow.

Wichita Riding Club, Inc.
Income Statement
For the Month Ended November 30, 2011

Revenues		
Riding lesson revenue	$4,650	
Locker rental revenue	1,275	
Total revenues		$5,925
Expenses		
Salaries expense	$1,125	
Feed expense	750	
Utilities expense	450	
Total expenses		2,325
Income before income taxes		$3,600
Income taxes expense		600
Net income		$3,000

Wichita Riding Club, Inc.
Statement of Retained Earnings
For the Month Ended November 30, 2011

Retained earnings, October 31, 2011	$5,475
Net income for the month	3,000
Subtotal	$8,475
Less dividends	2,400
Retained earnings, November 30, 2011	$6,075

Wichita Riding Club, Inc.
Balance Sheet
November 30, 2011

Assets		**Liabilities**		
Cash	$ 6,525	Accounts payable		$13,350
Accounts receivable	900			
Supplies	750	**Stockholders' Equity**		
Land	15,750	Common stock	$34,500	
Building	22,500	Retained earnings	6,075	
Horses	7,500	Total stockholders' equity		40,575
Total assets	$53,925	Total liabilities and stockholders' equity		$53,925

Wichita Riding Club, Inc.
Statement of Cash Flows
For the Month Ended November 30, 2011

Cash flows from operating activities		
Net income		$3,000
Adjustments to reconcile net income to net cash flows from operating activities		
(Increase) in accounts receivable	$ (400)	
(Increase) in supplies	(550)	
Increase in accounts payable	400	(550)
Net cash flows from operating activities		$2,450
Cash flows from investing activities		
Purchase of horses	$(1,000)	
Sale of horses	2,000	
Net cash flows from investing activities		1,000
Cash flows from financing activities		
Issue of common stock	$ 5,000	
Payment of cash dividends	(2,400)	
Net cash flows from financing activities		2,600
Net increase in cash		$6,050
Cash at beginning of month		475
Cash at end of month		$6,525

REQUIRED

USER INSIGHT ▶ 1. Explain how the four statements for Wichita Riding Club are related to each other.

USER INSIGHT ▶ 2. Which statements are most closely associated with the goals of liquidity and profitability? Why?

USER INSIGHT ▶ 3. If you were the owner of this business, how would you evaluate the company's performance? Give specific examples.

USER INSIGHT ▶ 4. If you were a banker considering Wichita Riding Club for a loan, why might you want the company to get an audit by an independent CPA? What would the audit tell you?

Alternate Problems

LO 5 Interrelationship of Financial Statements

✔ (e) $2,700; (l) $26,000; (r) $1,900

P 6. The following three independent sets of financial statements have several amounts missing.

	Set A	Set B	Set C
Income Statement			
Revenue	$5,320	$ 8,600	$ m
Expenses	a	g	2,010
Net income	$ 510	$ h	$ n
Statement of Retained Earnings			
Beginning balance	$1,780	$15,400	$ 200
Net income	b	i	450
Less dividends	c	1,000	o
Ending balance	$ d	$16,000	$ p
Balance Sheet			
Total assets	$ e	$ j	$1,900
Liabilities	$ f	$ 2,000	$1,300
Stockholders' equity			
Common stock	200	8,000	50
Retained earnings	2,100	k	q
Total liabilities and stockholders' equity	$2,700	$ l	$ r

REQUIRED

1. Complete each set of financial statements by determining the amounts that correspond to the letters. (*Hint*: Amounts are not necessarily solved in alphabetical order.)

USER INSIGHT ▶ 2. Why is it necessary to prepare the income statement before preparing the balance sheet?

LO 1, 5

Preparation and Interpretation of the Income Statement, Statement of Retained Earnings, and Balance Sheet

✔ Total assets: $122,800

P 7. The accounts of Real Deal, Inc., follow. The company completed its 10th year of operations on December 31, 2011.

Accounts Payable	$ 3,600	Income Taxes Payable	$13,000
Accounts Receivable	4,500	Marketing Expense	20,100
Cash	57,700	Office Rent Expense	36,000
Commission Sales Revenue	400,000	Retained Earnings,	
Commissions Expense	225,000	December 31, 2010	35,300
Commissions Payable	22,700	Supplies	700
Common Stock	29,000	Telephone and	
Dividends	33,000	Computer Expenses	5,100
Equipment	59,900	Utilities Expense	2,600
Income Taxes Expense	27,000	Wages Expense	32,000

REQUIRED

1. Prepare the income statement, statement of retained earnings, and balance sheet for Real Deal.

USER INSIGHT ▶ 2. The owners of Real Deal are considering expansion. What other statement would be useful to the owners in assessing whether the company's operations are generating sufficient funds to support the expenses? Why would it be useful?

LO 5

Preparation and Interpretation of Financial Statements

✔ Total assets: $28,300

P 8. Following are the accounts of Creative Ads, Inc., an agency that develops marketing materials for print, radio, and television. The agency's first year of operations ended on January 31, 2011.

Accounts Payable	$ 19,400	Income Taxes Payable	$ 560
Accounts Receivable	24,900	Marketing Expense	6,800
Advertising Service Revenue	165,200	Office Rent Expense	13,500
Cash	1,800	Salaries Expense	86,000
Common Stock	5,000	Salaries Payable	1,300
Dividends	0	Supplies	1,600
Equipment Rental Expense	37,200	Utilities Expense	19,100
Income Taxes Expense	560		

REQUIRED

1. Prepare the income statement, statement of retained earnings, and balance sheet for Creative Ads.

USER INSIGHT ▶ 2. Explain the difference between Income Taxes Expense and Income Taxes Payable.

3. Review the financial statements and comment on the financial challenges that Creative Ads faces.

LO 5

Integration of Financial Statements

✔ (d) $6,400; (l) $27,600; (q) $880

P 9. Below are three independent sets of financial statements with several amounts missing.

Income Statement	**Set A**	**Set B**	**Set C**
Revenue	$1,100	$ g	$210
Expenses	a	5,200	m
Net income	$ b	$ h	$ 80
Statement of Retained Earnings			
Beginning balance	$2,700	$11,400	$340
Net income	c	1,700	n
Less dividends	200	i	o
Ending balance	$3,000	$ j	$ p
Balance Sheet			
Total assets	$ d	$27,600	$ q
Liabilities	$1,500	$ 7,000	$ r
Stockholders' equity			
Common stock	$1,900	$ 8,500	$280
Retained earnings	e	k	400
Total liabilities and stockholders' equity	$ f	$ l	$880

REQUIRED

1. Complete each set of financial statements by determining the amounts that correspond to the letters. (*Hint:* Amounts are not necessarily solved in alphabetical order.)

USER INSIGHT ▶

2. In what order is it necessary to prepare the financial statements? Why is that order necessary?

LO 1, 5

Preparation and Interpretation of Financial Statements

✔ Total assets: $115,300

P 10. Below are the financial accounts of Bradford Realty, Inc. The company has just completed its 5th year of operations ended October 31, 2011.

Accounts Payable	$ 3,500	Income Taxes Payable	$12,500
Accounts Receivable	12,700	Office Rent Expense	40,000
Cash	57,500	Retained Earnings, October 31, 2010	15,700
Commission Sales Revenue	415,000	Supplies	900
Commissions Expense	230,000	Utilities Expense	2,700
Commissions Payable	21,500	Telephone and Computer Expenses	6,300
Common Stock	31,000	Wages Expense	29,400
Dividends	40,000		
Equipment	44,200		
Income Taxes Expense	35,700		

REQUIRED

1. Prepare the income statement, statement of retained earnings, and balance sheet for Bradford Realty.

USER INSIGHT ▶

2. Explain the difference between Commissions Expense and Commissions Payable.
3. Evaluate the company's ability to meet its bills when they come due.

Cases

LO 1, 2

Conceptual Understanding: Business Activities and Management Functions

C 1. Costco Wholesale Corporation is America's largest membership retail company. According to its letter to stockholders:

> Since we opened our doors twenty-six years ago, our Company mission has been "to continually provide our members with quality goods and services at the lowest possible prices." This commitment has never been more relevant than today, and nearly 60 million card-carrying members have benefited from this promise every time they shop at any of Costco's 566 warehouses around the globe or at our Ecommerce web sites.[12]

To achieve its strategy, Costco must organize its management by functions that relate to the principal activities of a business. Discuss the three basic activities Costco will engage in to achieve its goals and suggest some examples of each. What is the role of Costco's management? What functions must its management perform to carry out these activities?

LO 3

Conceptual Understanding: Concept of an Asset

C 2. Southwest Airlines Co. is one of the most successful airlines in the United States. One of its annual reports contains this statement: "We are a company of People, not Planes. That is what distinguishes us from other airlines and other companies. At Southwest Airlines, People are our most important asset."[13] Are employees considered assets in the financial statements? Why or why not? Discuss in what sense Southwest considers its employees to be assets.

LO 6

Conceptual Understanding: Generally Accepted Accounting Principles

C 3. Fidelity Investments Company is a well-known mutual fund investment company. It makes investments worth billions of dollars in companies listed on the New York Stock Exchange and other stock markets. Generally accepted accounting principles (GAAP) are very important for Fidelity's investment analysts. What are generally accepted accounting principles? Why are financial statements that have been prepared in accordance with GAAP and audited by an independent CPA useful for Fidelity's investment analysts? What organizations influence GAAP? Explain how they do so.

LO 1

Conceptual Understanding: Operating Cash

C 4. In May 2001, unable to get credit from enough of its lenders, housewares retailer **Lechters, Inc.**, filed for Chapter 11 bankruptcy. It then secured new bank financing in the amount of $86 million. Suppliers, however, remained concerned about Lechters' ability to meet future obligations. Many suppliers took back their terms of sale specifying the number of days the company had to pay for its merchandise and instead asked for cash in advance or on delivery. Smaller home-furnishing retailers like Lechters struggle against big rivals, such as **Bed Bath & Beyond**, which are more valuable to suppliers and thus can demand better terms and pricing. In spite of these problems and an annual net loss of $101.8 million on sales of $405 million, management believed the company could eventually succeed with its strategy under the bankruptcy.[14]

Which is more critical to the short-term survival of a company faced with Lechters' problems: liquidity or profitability? Which is more important in the long term? Explain your answers.

LO 5

Interpreting Financial Reports: Nature of Cash, Assets, and Net Income

C 5. Research in Motion Limited (RIM) is not well known, but it produces a well-known product: the Blackberry mobile phone. Information for 2009 and 2008 from the company's annual report appears below.[15] (All numbers are in thousands.) Three students who were looking at RIM's annual report were overheard making the following comments:

Student A: What a great year RIM had in 2009! The company earned income of $2,590,185 because its total assets increased from $5,511,187 to $8,101,372.

Student B: But the company didn't do that well because the change in total assets isn't the same as net income! The company had a net loss of $348,852 because its cash decreased from $1,184,398 to $835,546.

Student C: I see that retained earnings went from $1,653,094 to $3,545,710. Don't you have to take that into consideration when analyzing the company's performance?

USER INSIGHT ▶

1. Comment on the interpretations of Students A and B and then answer Student C's questions.
2. Estimate RIM's net income for the year ended February 28, 2009. (*Note:* RIM did not pay any cash dividends.)

RIM Limited
Condensed Balance Sheets
February 28, 2009 and March 1, 2008
(In thousands)

	2009	2008
Assets		
Cash	$ 835,546	$1,184,398
Other assets	7,265,826	4,326,789
Total assets	$8,101,372	$5,511,187
Liabilities		
Total liabilities	$2,227,244	$1,577,621
Stockholders' Equity		
Common stock and other	2,328,418	2,280,472
Retained earnings	3,545,710	1,653,094
Total liabilities and stockholders' equity	$8,101,372	$5,511,187

LO 5

Annual Report Case: Analysis of Four Basic Financial Statements

C 6. Refer to the **CVS** annual report in the Supplement to Chapter 1 to answer the questions below. Keep in mind that every company, while following basic principles, adapts financial statements and terminology to its own special needs. Therefore, the complexity of CVS's financial statements and the terminology in them will differ somewhat from the financial statements in the text.

1. What names does CVS give to its four basic financial statements? (*Note*: The word *consolidated* in the names of the financial statements means that these statements combine those of several companies owned by CVS.)
2. Prove that the accounting equation works for CVS on December 31, 2009 by finding the amounts for the following equation: Assets = Liabilities + Stockholders' Equity.
3. What were the total revenues of CVS for the year ended December 31, 2009?
4. Was CVS profitable in the year ended December 31, 2009? How much was net income (loss) in that year, and did it increase or decrease from the year ended December 31, 2008?
5. Did the company's cash and cash equivalents increase from December 31, 2008 to December 31, 2009? If so, by how much? In what two places in the statements can this number be found or computed?
6. Did cash flows from operating activities, cash flows from investing activities, and cash flows from financing activities increase or decrease from 2008 to 2009?
7. Who is the auditor for the company? Why is the auditor's report that accompanies the financial statements important?

LO 1, 5

Comparison: Performance Measures, Financial Ratio, and Financial Statements

LO 6

C 7. Refer to the **CVS** annual report and the financial statements of **Southwest Airlines Co.** in the Supplement to Chapter 1 to answer these questions:

1. Which company is larger in terms of assets and in terms of revenues? What do you think is the best way to measure the size of a company?
2. Which company is more profitable in terms of net income? What is the trend of profitability over the past three years for both companies?

3. Compute the profit margin for each company for 2009. By this measure, which company is more profitable? Is this a better measure than simply comparing the net income of the two companies? Explain your answer.

4. Which company has more cash? Which increased its cash the most in the last year? Which has more liquidity as measured by cash flows from operating activities?

LO 6

Ethical Dilemma: Professional Ethics

C 8. Discuss the ethical choices in the situations below. In each instance, describe the ethical dilemma, determine the alternative courses of action, and tell what you would do.

1. You are the payroll accountant for a small business. A friend asks you how much another employee is paid per hour.
2. As an accountant for the branch office of a wholesale supplier, you discover that several of the receipts the branch manager has submitted for reimbursement as selling expenses actually stem from nights out with his spouse.
3. You are an accountant in the purchasing department of a construction company. When you arrive home from work on December 22, you find a large ham in a box marked "Happy Holidays—It's a pleasure to work with you." The gift is from a supplier who has bid on a contract your employer plans to award next week.
4. As an auditor with one year's experience at a local CPA firm, you are expected to complete a certain part of an audit in 20 hours. Because of your lack of experience, you know you cannot finish the job within that time. Rather than admit this, you are thinking about working late to finish the job and not telling anyone.
5. You are a tax accountant at a local CPA firm. You help your neighbor fill out her tax return, and she pays you $200 in cash. Because there is no record of this transaction, you are considering not reporting it on your tax return.
6. The accounting firm for which you work as a CPA has just won a new client, a firm in which you own 200 shares of stock that you received as an inheritance from your grandmother. Because it is only a small number of shares and you think the company will be very successful, you are considering not disclosing the investment.

LO 5

Decision Analysis Using Excel: Effect of Transactions on the Balance Sheet

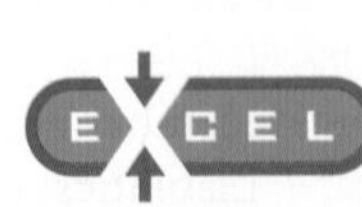

C 9. The summer after finishing her junior year in college, Beth Murphy started a lawn service business in her neighborhood. On June 1, she deposited $2,700 in a new bank account in the name of her corporation. The $2,700 consisted of a $1,000 loan from her father and $1,700 of her own money. In return for her investment, Murphy issued 1,700 shares of $1 par value common stock to herself.

Using the money in this checking account, Murphy rented lawn equipment, purchased supplies, and hired local high school students to mow and trim the lawns of neighbors who had agreed to pay her for the service. At the end of each month, she mailed bills to her customers.

On August 31, Murphy was ready to dissolve her business and go back to school for the fall term. Because she had been so busy, she had not kept any records other than her checkbook and a list of amounts owed by customers.

Her checkbook had a balance of $3,520, and her customers owed her $875. She expected these customers to pay her during September. She planned to return unused supplies to the Lawn Care Center for a full credit of $50. When she brought back the rented lawn equipment, the Lawn Care Center also would return a deposit of $200 she had made in June. She owed the Lawn Care Center $525 for equipment rentals and supplies. In addition, she owed the students who had worked for her $100, and she still owed her father $700. Although Murphy feels she did quite well, she is not sure just how successful she was. You have agreed to help her find out.

1. Prepare one balance sheet dated June 1, 2011 and another dated August 31, 2011 for Murphy Lawn Services, Inc.
2. Using information that can be inferred from comparing the balance sheets, write a memorandum to Murphy commenting on her company's performance in achieving profitability and liquidity. (Assume that she used none of the company's assets for personal purposes.) Also, mention the other two financial statements that would be helpful to her in evaluating these business goals.

SUPPLEMENT TO CHAPTER 1

How to Read an Annual Report

More than 4 million corporations are chartered in the United States. Most of them are small, family-owned businesses. They are called *private* or *closely held corporations* because their common stock is held by only a few people and is not for sale to the public. Larger companies usually find it desirable to raise investment funds from many investors by issuing common stock to the public. These companies are called *public companies.* Although they are fewer in number than private companies, their total economic impact is much greater.

Public companies must register their common stock with the Securities and Exchange Commission (SEC), which regulates the issuance and subsequent trading of the stock of public companies. The SEC requires the management of public companies to report each year to stockholders on their companies' financial performance. This report, called an *annual report*, contains the company's annual financial statements and other pertinent data. Annual reports are a primary source of financial information about public companies and are distributed to all of a company's stockholders. They must also be filed with the SEC on a Form 10-K.

The general public may obtain an annual report by calling or writing the company or accessing the report online at the company's website. If a company has filed its 10-K electronically with the SEC, it can be accessed at www.sec.gov/edgar.shtml. Many libraries also maintain files of annual reports or have them available on electronic media, such as *Compact Disclosure*.

This supplement describes the major components of the typical annual report. We have included many of these components in the annual report of **CVS Caremark Corporation**, one of the country's most successful retailers. Case assignments in many chapters refer to this annual report. For purposes of comparison, the supplement also includes the financial statements and summary of significant accounting policies of **Southwest Airlines Co.**, one of the largest and most successful airlines in the United States.

The Components of an Annual Report

In addition to listing the corporation's directors and officers, an annual report usually contains a letter to the stockholders (also called *shareholders*), a multiyear summary of financial highlights, a description of the company, management's discussion and analysis of the company's operating results and financial condition, the financial statements, notes to the financial statements, a statement about management's responsibilities, and the auditors' report.

Letter to the Stockholders

Traditionally, an annual report begins with a letter in which the top officers of the corporation tell stockholders about the company's performance and prospects. In CVS's 2009 annual report, the chairman and chief executive officer wrote to the stockholders about the highlights of the past year, the key priorities for the new year, and other aspects of the business. He reported as follows:

> Today we're the nation's largest pharmacy health care company in the United States . . . let me provide a quick review of our solid financial performance in 2009. In the midst of a challenging economic environment, CVS Caremark reported record revenue and earnings. Total revenue rose 13 percent to $98.7 billion, with income from continuing operations up 11 percent to $3.7 billion.

Financial Highlights

The financial highlights section of an annual report presents key statistics for at least a 5-year period but often for a 10-year period. It is often accompanied by graphs. CVS's annual report, for example, gives critical figures for sales, operating profits, and other key measures. Note that the financial highlights section often includes nonfinancial data and graphs, such as the number of stores in CVS's case.

Description of the Company

An annual report contains a detailed description of the company's products and divisions. Some analysts tend to scoff at this section of the annual report because it often contains glossy photographs and other image-building material, but it should not be overlooked because it may provide useful information about past results and future plans.

Management's Discussion and Analysis

In this section, management describes the company's financial condition and results of operations and explains the difference in results from one year to the next. For example, CVS's management explains the effects of an acquisition and the length of its 2009 fiscal year on its net revenues:

> Net revenues increased $11.3 billion and $11.1 billion during 2009 and 2008, respectively.
>
> - During 2009, the Longs Acquisition increased net revenues by $6.6 billion, compared to 2008.
> - Three fewer days in the 2009 fiscal year negatively impacted net revenues by $671 million, compared to 2008.

This kind of detail is invaluable to understanding CVS's financial performance.

Financial Statements

All companies present the same four basic financial statements in their annual reports, but the names they use may vary. As you can see in Exhibits S1.1 to S1.4 (pp. 48–53), CVS presents statements of operations (income statements), balance sheets, statements of cash flows, and statements of shareholders' equity (includes retained earnings). (Note that the numbers given in the statements are in millions, but the last six digits are omitted. For example, $6,046,200,000 is shown as $6,046.2.)

The headings of CVS's financial statements are preceded by the word *consolidated.* A corporation issues *consolidated* financial statements when it consists of more than one company and has combined the companies' data for reporting purposes.

CVS provides several years of data for each financial statement: two years for the balance sheet and three years for the others. Financial statements presented in this fashion are called *comparative financial statements.* Such statements are in accordance with generally accepted accounting principles and help readers assess the company's performance over several years.

CVS's fiscal year ends on the Saturday nearest the end of December (December 31, 2009 in the latest year). Retailers commonly end their fiscal years during a slow period, usually the end of January, which is in contrast to CVS's choosing the end of December.

Income Statements CVS uses a multistep form of the income statement in that results are shown in several steps (in contrast to the single-step form illustrated in the chapter). The steps are gross profit, operating profit, earnings before income tax provision, and net earnings (see Exhibit S1.1). The company also shows net earnings available to common shareholders, and it discloses the basic earnings per share and diluted earnings per share. Basic earnings per share is used for most analysis. Diluted earnings per share assumes that all rights that could be exchanged for common shares, such as stock options, are in fact exchanged. The weighted average number of shares of common stock, used in calculating the per share figures, are shown at the bottom of the income statement.

Balance Sheets CVS has a typical balance sheet for a retail company (see Exhibit S1.2). In the assets and liabilities sections, the company separates out the current assets and the current liabilities. Current assets will become available as cash or will be used up in the next year; current liabilities will have to be paid or satisfied in the next year. These groupings are useful in assessing a company's liquidity.

Several items in the shareholders' equity section of the balance sheet may need explanation. Common stock represents the number of shares outstanding at par value. Capital surplus (additional paid-in capital) represents amounts invested by stockholders in excess of the par value of the common stock. Preferred stock is capital stock that has certain features that distinguish it from common stock. Treasury stock represents shares of common stock the company repurchased.

EXHIBIT S1.1
CVS's Income Statements

Consolidated means that data from all companies owned by CVS are combined.

CVS Caremark Corporation
Consolidated Statements of Operations

CVS's fiscal year ends on the Saturday closest to December 31.

		Fiscal Year Ended	
(In millions, except per share amounts)	**Dec. 31, 2009**	**Dec. 31, 2008**	**Dec. 29, 2007**
Net revenues	$ 98,729	$ 87,472	$ 76,330
Cost of revenues	78,349	69,182	60,222
Gross profit	20,380	18,290	16,108
Operating expenses	13,942	12,244	11,314
Operating profit[1]	6,438	6,046	4,794
Interest expense, net[2]	525	509	435
Income before income tax provision	5,913	5,537	4,359
Income tax provision	2,205	2,193	1,722
Loss from continuing operations	3,708	3,344	2,637
Loss from discontinued operations, net of income tax benefit	(12)	(132)	—
Net income[3]	3,696	3,212	2,637
Preference dividends, net of income tax benefit[4]	—	14	14
Net income available to common shareholders	$ 3,696	$ 3,198	$ 2,623
BASIC EARNINGS PER COMMON SHARE:[5]			
Income from continuing operations	$ 2.59	$ 2.32	$ 1.97
Loss from discontinued operations	(0.01)	(0.09)	—
Net income	$ 2.58	$ 2.23	$ 1.97
Weighted average common shares outstanding	1,434	1,434	1,328
DILUTED EARNINGS PER COMMON SHARE:			
Income from continuing operations	$ 2.56	$ 2.27	$ 1.92
Loss from discontinued operations	(0.01)	(0.09)	—
Net income	$ 2.55	$ 2.18	$ 1.92
Weighted average common shares outstanding	1,450	1,469	1,372
DIVIDENDS DECLARED PER COMMON SHARE	$0.30500	$0.25800	$0.22875

[1] This section shows earnings from ongoing operations
[2] CVS shows interest expense and income taxes separately
[3] The net income figure moves to the statements of shareholders' equity
[4] CVS shows the dividends distributed to preferred shareholders. This distribution is not an expense
[5] CVS discloses various breakdowns of earnings per share

EXHIBIT S1.2
CVS's Balance Sheets

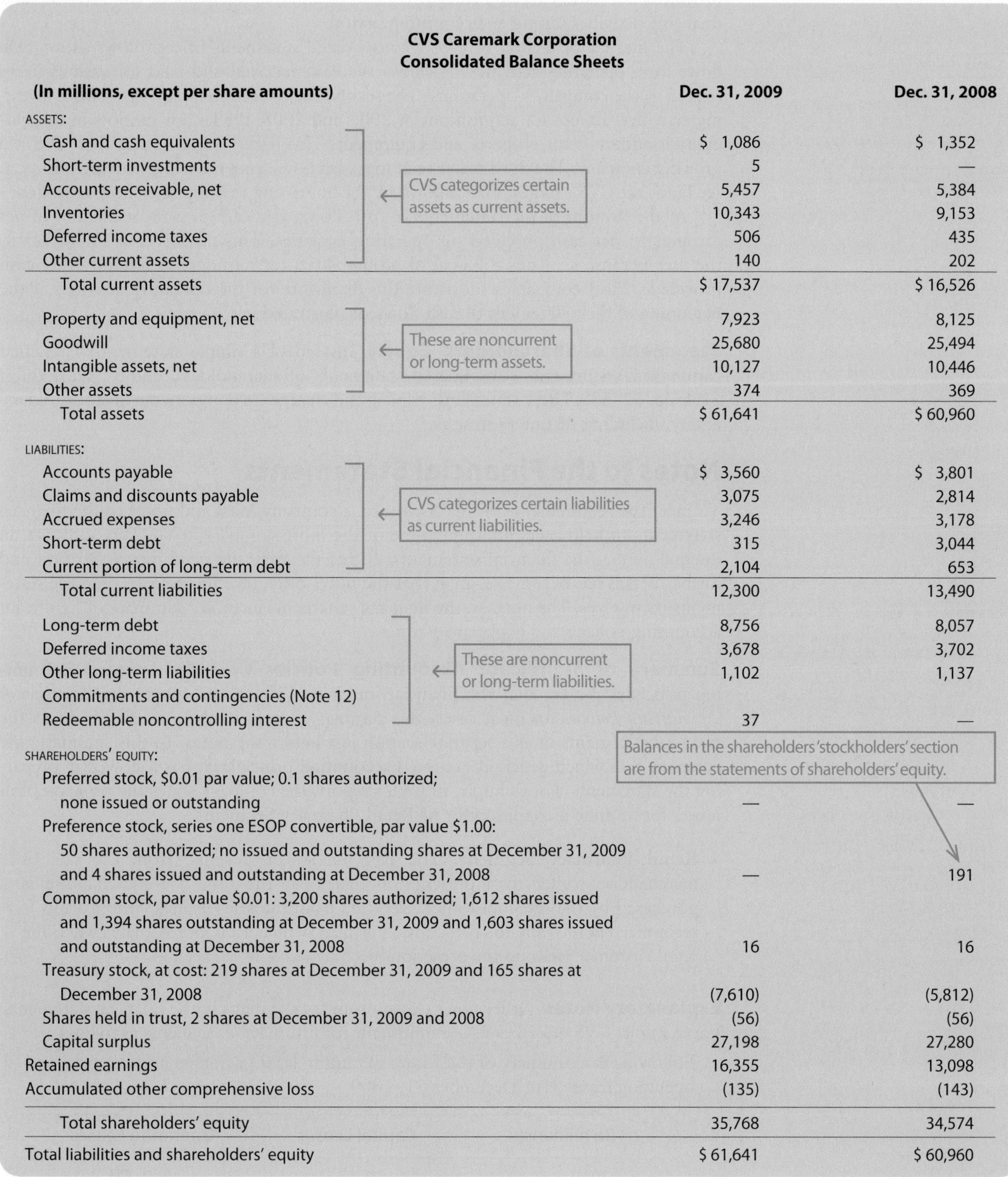

CVS Caremark Corporation
Consolidated Balance Sheets

(In millions, except per share amounts)	Dec. 31, 2009	Dec. 31, 2008
ASSETS:		
Cash and cash equivalents	$ 1,086	$ 1,352
Short-term investments	5	—
Accounts receivable, net	5,457	5,384
Inventories	10,343	9,153
Deferred income taxes	506	435
Other current assets	140	202
Total current assets	$ 17,537	$ 16,526
Property and equipment, net	7,923	8,125
Goodwill	25,680	25,494
Intangible assets, net	10,127	10,446
Other assets	374	369
Total assets	$ 61,641	$ 60,960
LIABILITIES:		
Accounts payable	$ 3,560	$ 3,801
Claims and discounts payable	3,075	2,814
Accrued expenses	3,246	3,178
Short-term debt	315	3,044
Current portion of long-term debt	2,104	653
Total current liabilities	12,300	13,490
Long-term debt	8,756	8,057
Deferred income taxes	3,678	3,702
Other long-term liabilities	1,102	1,137
Commitments and contingencies (Note 12)		
Redeemable noncontrolling interest	37	—
SHAREHOLDERS' EQUITY:		
Preferred stock, $0.01 par value; 0.1 shares authorized; none issued or outstanding	—	—
Preference stock, series one ESOP convertible, par value $1.00: 50 shares authorized; no issued and outstanding shares at December 31, 2009 and 4 shares issued and outstanding at December 31, 2008	—	191
Common stock, par value $0.01: 3,200 shares authorized; 1,612 shares issued and 1,394 shares outstanding at December 31, 2009 and 1,603 shares issued and outstanding at December 31, 2008	16	16
Treasury stock, at cost: 219 shares at December 31, 2009 and 165 shares at December 31, 2008	(7,610)	(5,812)
Shares held in trust, 2 shares at December 31, 2009 and 2008	(56)	(56)
Capital surplus	27,198	27,280
Retained earnings	16,355	13,098
Accumulated other comprehensive loss	(135)	(143)
Total shareholders' equity	35,768	34,574
Total liabilities and shareholders' equity	$ 61,641	$ 60,960

CVS categorizes certain assets as current assets.
These are noncurrent or long-term assets.
CVS categorizes certain liabilities as current liabilities.
These are noncurrent or long-term liabilities.
Balances in the shareholders 'stockholders' section are from the statements of shareholders' equity.

Statements of Cash Flows Whereas the income statement reflects CVS's profitability, the statement of cash flows reflects its liquidity (see Exhibit S1.3). This statement provides information about a company's cash receipts, cash payments, and investing and financing activities during an accounting period.

The first major section of CVS's consolidated statements of cash flows shows cash flows from operating activities. It shows the cash received and paid for various items related to the company's operations. The second major section is cash flows from investing activities. Except for acquisitions in 2007 and 2008, the largest outflow in this category is additions for property and equipment. This figure demonstrates that CVS is a growing company. The third major section is cash flows from financing activities. You can see here that CVS's largest cash inflows are for borrowing of long- and short-term debt.

At the bottom of the statements of cash flows, you can see a reconciliation of net earnings to net cash provided by operating activities. This disclosure is important to the user because it relates the goal of profitability (net earnings) to liquidity (net cash provided). Most companies substitute this disclosure for the operating activities at the beginning of their statement of cash flows, as illustrated in Chapter 1.

Statements of Shareholders' Equity Instead of a simple statement of retained earnings, CVS presents consolidated statements of shareholders' equity (see Exhibit S1.4, pp. 52–53). These statements explain the changes in components of stockholders' equity, including retained earnings.

Notes to the Financial Statements

To meet the requirements of full disclosure, a company must add notes to the financial statements to help users interpret some of the more complex items. The notes are an integral part of the financial statements. In recent years, the need for explanation and further details has become so great that the notes often take more space than the statements themselves. The notes to the financial statements include a summary of significant accounting policies and explanatory notes.

Summary of Significant Accounting Policies Generally accepted accounting principles require that the financial statements include a *Summary of Significant Accounting Policies.* In most cases, this summary is presented in the first note to the financial statements or as a separate section just before the notes. In this summary, the company tells which generally accepted accounting principles it has followed in preparing the statements. For example, in CVS's report, the company states the principles followed for revenue recognition for its Retail Pharmacy Segment:

> **Retail Pharmacy Segment.** The RPS recognizes revenue from the sale of merchandise (other than prescription drugs) at the time the merchandise is purchased by the retail customer. Revenue from the sale of prescription drugs is recognized at the time the prescription is filled, which is or approximates when the retail customer picks up the prescription.

Explanatory Notes Other notes explain some of the items in the financial statements. For example, CVS describes its commitments for future lease payments as follows:

> Following is a summary of the future minimum lease payments under capital and operating leases as of December 31, 2009:

(In millions)	Capital Leases	Operating Leases
2010	$ 17	$ 2,094
2011	17	1,877
2012	18	1,953
2013	18	1,855
2014	18	1,657
Thereafter	236	17,477
	$324	$26,913

EXHIBIT S1.3
CVS's Statements of Cash Flows

Cash flows are shown for operating activities, investing activities, and financing activities.

CVS Caremark Corporation
Consolidated Statements of Cash Flows

		Fiscal Year Ended	
(In millions)	**Dec. 31, 2009**	**Dec. 31, 2008**	**Dec. 29, 2007**
CASH FLOWS FROM OPERATING ACTIVITIES:			
Cash receipts from revenues	$ 93,568	$ 82,250	$ 72,533
Cash paid for inventory and prescriptions dispensed by retail network pharmacies	(73,536)	(64,131)	(56,319)
Cash paid to other suppliers and employees	(13,121)	(11,832)	(10,769)
Interest and dividends received	5	20	34
Interest paid	(542)	(574)	(468)
Income taxes paid	(2,339)	(1,786)	(1,781)
NET CASH PROVIDED BY OPERATING ACTIVITIES	4,035	3,947	3,230
CASH FLOWS FROM INVESTING ACTIVITIES:			
Additions to property and equipment	(2,548)	(2,180)	(1,805)
Proceeds from sale-leaseback transactions	1,562	204	601
Acquisitions (net of cash acquired) and other investments	(101)	(2,651)	(1,984)
Purchase of short-term investments	(5)	—	—
Sale of short-term investments	—	28	—
Proceeds from sale or disposal of assets	23	19	106
NET CASH USED IN INVESTING ACTIVITIES	(1,069)	(4,580)	(3,082)
CASH FLOWS FROM FINANCING ACTIVITIES:			
Increase (decrease) in short-term debt	(2,729)	959	242
Repayment of debt assumed in acquisition	—	(353)	—
Issuance of long-term debt	2,800	350	6,000
Repayments of long-term debt	(653)	(2)	(822)
Dividends paid	(439)	(383)	(323)
Derivative settlements	(3)	—	—
Proceeds from exercise of stock options	250	328	553
Excess tax benefits from stock-based compensation	19	53	98
Repurchase of common stock	(2,477)	(23)	(5,370)
NET CASH PROVIDED BY (USED IN) FINANCING ACTIVITIES	(3,232)	929	378
Net increase (decrease) in cash and cash equivalents	(266)	296	526
Cash and cash equivalents at beginning of year	1,352	1,056	530
CASH AND CASH EQUIVALENTS AT END OF YEAR	$ 1,086	$ 1,352	$ 1,056
RECONCILIATION OF NET INCOME TO NET CASH PROVIDED BY OPERATING ACTIVITIES:			
Net income	$ 3,696	$ 3,212	$ 2,637
Adjustments required to reconcile net income to net cash provided by operating activities:			
Depreciation and amortization	1,389	1,274	1,095
Stock-based compensation	165	92	78
Deferred income taxes and other non-cash items	48	(3)	39
Change in operating assets and liabilities, net of effects from acquisitions:			
Accounts receivable, net	(86)	(291)	280
Inventories	(1,199)	(488)	(448)
Other current assets	48	12	(59)
Other assets	(2)	19	(26)
Accounts payable	4	(64)	(181)
Accrued expenses	(66)	183	(168)
Other long-term liabilities	38	1	(17)
NET CASH PROVIDED BY OPERATING ACTIVITIES	$ 4,035	$ 3,947	$ 3,230

Cash and cash equivalents move to balance sheets.

This section explains the difference between net earnings and net cash provided by operating activities.

EXHIBIT S1.4
CVS's Statements of Stockholders' Equity

Each component of shareholders' equity is explained.

CVS Caremark Corporation
Consolidated Statements of Shareholders' Equity

(In millions)	Shares Dec. 31, 2009	Shares Dec. 31, 2008	Shares Dec. 29, 2007	Dollars Dec. 31, 2009	Dollars Dec. 31, 2008	Dollars Dec. 29, 2007
PREFERENCE STOCK:						
Beginning of year	4	4	4	$ 191	$ 202	$ 212
Conversion to common stock	(4)	—	—	(191)	(11)	(10)
End of year	—	4	4	—	191	202
COMMON STOCK:						
Beginning of year	1,603	1,590	847	16	16	9
Common stock issued for Caremark Merger	—	—	713	—	—	7
Stock options exercised and stock awards	9	13	30	—	—	—
End of year	1,612	1,603	1,590	16	16	16
TREASURY STOCK:						
Beginning of year	(165)	(154)	(22)	(5,812)	(5,620)	(314)
Purchase of treasury shares	(73)	(7)	(135)	(2,477)	(33)	(5,379)
Conversion of preference stock	17	1	1	583	35	25
Transfer from shares held in trust	—	(7)	—	—	(272)	—
Employee stock purchase plan issuances	2	2	2	96	78	48
End of year	(219)	(165)	(154)	(7,610)	(5,812)	(5,620)
GUARANTEED ESOP OBLIGATION:						
Beginning of year				—	(44)	(82)
Reduction of guaranteed ESOP obligation				—	44	38
End of year				—	—	(44)
SHARES HELD IN TRUST:						
Beginning of year	(2)	(9)	—	(56)	(301)	—
Transfer to treasury stock	—	7	—	—	245	—
Shares acquired through Caremark Merger	—	—	(9)	—	—	(301)
End of year	(2)	(2)	(9)	(56)	(56)	(301)
CAPITAL SURPLUS:						
Beginning of year				27,280	26,832	2,198
Common stock issued for Caremark Merger, net of issuance costs				—	—	23,942
Conversion of shares held in Trust to treasury stock				—	27	—
Stock option activity and awards				291	392	608
Tax benefit on stock options and awards				19	53	98
Conversion of preference stock				(392)	(24)	(14)
End of year				$ 27,198	$ 27,280	$ 26,832
ACCUMULATED OTHER COMPREHENSIVE LOSS:						
Beginning of year				(143)	(50)	(73)
Net cash flow hedges, net of income tax				1	3	3
Pension liability adjustment, net of income tax				7	(96)	20
End of year				(135)	(143)	(50)

RETAINED EARNINGS:			
Beginning of year	$13,098	$10,287	$ 7,966
Net income	3,696	3,212	2,637
Common stock dividends	(439)	(370)	(308)
Preference stock dividends	—	(14)	(15)
Tax benefit on preference stock dividends	—	1	1
Adoption of ASC 715-60 (formerly EITF 06-04 and 06-10)	—	(18)	—
Adoption of ASC 740 (formerly FIN 48)	—	—	6
End of year	16,355	13,098	10,287
TOTAL SHAREHOLDERS' EQUITY	$35,768	$34,574	$31,322
COMPREHENSIVE INCOME:			
Net income	$ 3,696	$ 3,212	$ 2,637
Net cash flow hedges, net of income tax	1	3	3
Pension liability adjustment, net of income tax	7	(96)	20
COMPREHENSIVE INCOME	$ 3,704	$ 3,119	$ 2,660

Net income is from the income statement.

Information like this is very useful in determining the full scope of a company's liabilities and other commitments.

Supplementary Information Notes In recent years, the FASB and the SEC have ruled that certain supplemental information must be presented with financial statements. Examples are the quarterly reports that most companies present to their stockholders and to the SEC. These quarterly reports, called *interim financial statements*, are in most cases reviewed but not audited by a company's independent CPA firm. In its annual report, CVS presents unaudited quarterly financial data from its 2008 quarterly statements. The quarterly data also include the high and low price for the company's common stock during each quarter.

Reports of Management's Responsibilities

Separate statements of management's responsibility for the financial statements and for internal control structure accompany the financial statements as required by the Sarbanes-Oxley Act of 2002. In its reports, CVS's management acknowledges its responsibility for the consistency, integrity, and presentation of the financial information and for the system of internal controls.

Reports of Certified Public Accountants

The *registered independent auditors' report* deals with the credibility of the financial statements. This report, prepared by independent certified public accountants, gives the accountants' opinion about how fairly the statements have been presented. Because management is responsible for preparing the financial statements, issuing statements that have not been independently audited would be like having a judge hear a case in which he or she was personally involved. The certified public accountants add the necessary credibility to management's figures for interested third parties. They report to the board of directors and the stockholders rather than to the company's management.

In form and language, most auditors' reports are like the one shown in Exhibit S1.5. Usually, such a report is short, but its language is very important. It normally has four parts, but it can have a fifth part if an explanation is needed.

1. The first paragraph identifies the financial statements that have been audited. It also identifies responsibilities. The company's management is responsible for the financial statements, and the auditor is responsible for expressing an opinion on the financial statements based on the audit.

2. The second paragraph, or *scope section*, states that the examination was made in accordance with standards of the Public Company Accounting Oversight Board (PCAOB). This paragraph also contains a brief description of the objectives and nature of the audit.
3. The third paragraph, or *opinion section*, states the results of the auditors' examination. The use of the word *opinion* is very important because the auditor does not certify or guarantee that the statements are absolutely correct. To do so would go beyond the truth, because many items, such as depreciation, are based on estimates. Instead, the auditors simply give an opinion about whether, overall, the financial statements "present fairly," in all material respects, the company's financial position, results of operations, and cash flows. This means that the statements are prepared in accordance with generally accepted accounting principles. If, in the auditors' opinion, the statements do not meet accepted standards, the auditors must explain why and to what extent.
4. The fourth paragraph identifies a new accounting standard adopted by the company.
5. The fifth paragraph says the company's internal controls are effective.

EXHIBIT S1.5
Auditor's Report for CVS

Report of Independent Registered Public Accounting Firm
The Board of Directors and Shareholders
CVS Caremark Corporation

① We have audited the accompanying consolidated balance sheets of CVS Caremark Corporation as of December 31, 2009 and 2008, and the related consolidated statements of operations, shareholders' equity, and cash flows for each of the three fiscal years in the period ended December 31, 2009. These financial statements are the responsibility of the Company's management. Our responsibility is to express an opinion on these financial statements based on our audits.

② We conducted our audits in accordance with auditing standards of the Public Company Accounting Oversight Board (United States). Those standards require that we plan and perform the audit to obtain reasonable assurance about whether the financial statements are free of material misstatement. An audit includes examining, on a test basis, evidence supporting the amounts and disclosures in the financial statements. An audit also includes assessing the accounting principles used and significant estimates made by management, and evaluating the overall financial statement presentation. We believe that our audits provide a reasonable basis for our opinion.

③ In our opinion, the financial statements referred to above present fairly, in all material respects, the consolidated financial position of CVS Caremark Corporation at December 31, 2009 and 2008, and the consolidated results of its operations and its cash fows for each of the three fiscal years in the period ended December 31, 2009, in conformity with U.S. generally accepted accounting principles.

④ As discussed in Note 1 to the consolidated financial statements, effective December 30, 2007, CVS Caremark Corporation adopted Accounting Standards Codification (ASC) 715-60, *Defined Benefit Plans – Other Postretirement* (formerly Emerging Issues Task Force (EITF) Issue No. 06-4, *Accounting for Deferred Compensation and Postretirement Benefit Aspects of Endorsement Split-Dollar Life Insurance Arrangements* and EITF 06-10, *Accounting for Collateral Assignment Split-Dollar Life Insurance Agreements)*, and effective January 1, 2009 CVS Caremark Corporation adopted ASC 805, *Business Combinations* (formerly Statement of Financial Accounting Standards No. 141(R), *Business Combinations)*.

⑤ We also have audited, in accordance with the standards of the Public Company Accounting Oversight Board (United States), CVS Caremark Corporation's internal control over financial reporting as of December 31, 2009, based on criteria established in Internal Control – Integrated Framework issued by the Committee of Sponsoring Organizations of the Treadway Commission and our report dated February 26, 2010 expressed an unqualified opinion thereon.

Ernst + Young LLP

Boston, Massachusetts

February 26, 2010

2009 ANNUAL REPORT

Pharmacy Innovation In a Changing Health Care Environment

FINANCIAL HIGHLIGHTS

(in millions, except per share figures)		FISCAL YEAR 2009		FISCAL YEAR 2008	% change
Revenues	$	**98,729**	$	87,472	12.9%
Operating profit	$	**6,438**	$	6,046	6.5%
Net income	$	**3,696**	$	3,212	15.1%
Diluted EPS from continuing operations	$	**2.56**	$	2.27	12.5%
Stock price at year-end	$	**32.21**	$	28.74	12.1%
Market capitalization at year-end	$	**44,841**	$	41,301	8.6%

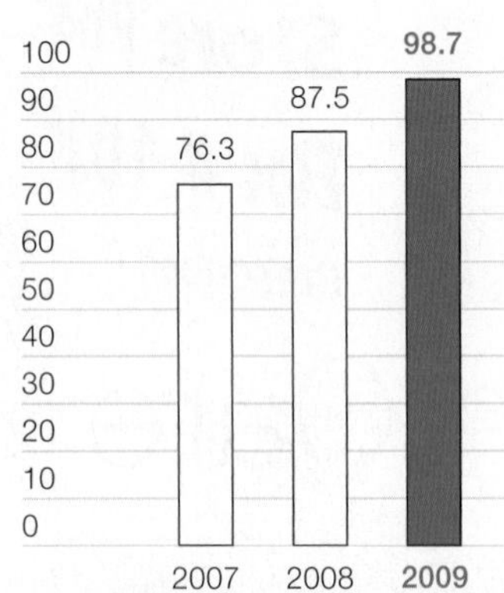

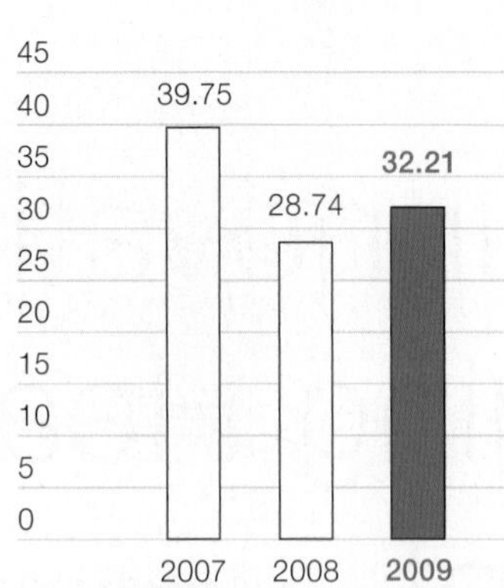

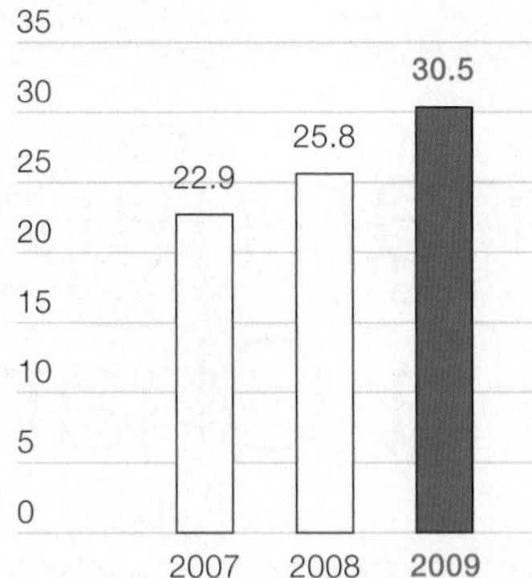

Health care in the United States is in flux today as never before. Although no one can predict with certainty its direction in the coming years, it's clear that companies experienced in delivering savings and improving the plan member experience will be among the winners. CVS Caremark already has programs in place that do an outstanding job of controlling costs for payors and patients while promoting better health outcomes. Moreover, we are well positioned to take our efforts to the next level. Our pharmacy benefits management business enjoys a long-standing reputation for excellence. Add to that our nearly unmatched retail presence, clinical strengths, and specialty leadership, and you can see why CVS Caremark is ready for the changes – and challenges – that lie ahead…whatever they may be.

Dear Fellow Shareholder,

Health care delivery in the United States is slowly evolving to a new model, and we believe that companies best positioned to promote better outcomes and lower costs will be among the winners. That thinking guided the 2007 merger of CVS and Caremark. Today we're the largest pharmacy health care company in the United States, and our strengths across the spectrum of pharmacy care are helping us deliver savings and improve the plan member experience for PBM clients.

I'll have more to say about the success of our differentiated approach as well as the core strengths of our PBM and retail businesses. First, let me provide a quick review of our solid financial performance in 2009. In the midst of a challenging economic environment, CVS Caremark reported record revenue and earnings. Total revenue rose 13 percent to $98.7 billion, with income from continuing operations up 11 percent to $3.7 billion. We generated approximately $3 billion in free cash flow, deploying part of it to complete a $2 billion share repurchase program. Furthermore, the board of directors authorized an additional $2 billion share repurchase program, which we began in 2009 and intend to complete in the first half of 2010. Our strong free cash flow also allowed us to raise the dividend by 15 percent for 2010. This marks our seventh consecutive annual dividend increase. Over this period, our dividend has risen at an 18 percent compound annual growth rate.

CVS Caremark shares produced a total return of 13 percent for 2009, although we trailed the broad market averages due largely to some concerns over our PBM's near-term growth outlook. However, over the past five years, CVS Caremark delivered a total return to shareholders of 48 percent, while the S&P 500 and the Dow Jones Industrial Average returned 2 percent and 10 percent, respectively, over the same period.

OUR INTEGRATED MODEL BUILDS ON EXISTING PBM STRENGTHS

Building on Caremark's long-standing reputation for customer service, clinical excellence, and an ability to control payor costs, our integrated approach to pharmacy care is yielding substantial benefits. Our more than 26,000 pharmacists, nurse practitioners, and physician assistants drive our efforts every day. Based on internal surveys, colleague engagement stands at an all-time high. Their commitment is clearly reflected in our outstanding performance across a number of measures.

I'm pleased to report that we have done an outstanding job of controlling costs for our PBM clients. We've done this by driving generic utilization through unique plan designs, by controlling specialty pharmacy trend through our specialty guideline management programs, and by improving adherence to prescribed medications through our multiple points of contact with plan members. For many people, a face-to-face interaction with their pharmacist results in a significantly higher adherence rate.

We have a broad research effort underway to learn more about why patients do not take prescriptions that are prescribed or drop medications in the middle of therapy. The research includes continuing internal analysis of CVS Caremark client utilization and an external partnership with Harvard and Brigham and Women's Hospital. Separately, a recent study by the New England Healthcare

THOMAS M. RYAN
Chairman of the Board, President, and Chief Executive Officer

Institute found that not taking medications as prescribed leads to poorer health, more frequent hospitalization, a higher risk of death, and as much as $290 billion annually in increased medical costs across the U.S. health care system. As the health care debate continues, one thing is clear: We all have to find ways to make health care more affordable. CVS Caremark is focusing on adherence to impact the health of our customers and help take costs out of the health care system.

In 2010, we expect adherence rates to be further enhanced when our Consumer Engagement Engine (CEE) goes live across our major channels during the second half of the year. Powered by clinical rules, the CEE will identify opportunities to promote better health outcomes and to achieve costs savings across our unparalleled points of contact.

The marketplace has enthusiastically embraced our innovative Maintenance Choice® offering, which gives eligible plan members access to 90-day mail pricing whether they receive their prescriptions through the mail or choose to pick them up at one of our approximately 7,000 conveniently located retail locations. This offering eliminates the plan member disruption that many payors face when they consider mandatory mail programs for cost savings. Furthermore, clients that switched from a voluntary mail program to Maintenance Choice saw their generic dispensing rates (GDR) improve and achieved savings of up to 6 percent of their pharmacy costs.

We currently serve 2,200 PBM clients, and more than 480 have signed up for Maintenance Choice to date. That leaves significant upside as more existing and prospective clients begin to appreciate its benefits.

WE ANTICIPATE HIGHER RETENTION LEVELS AND MORE NEW BUSINESS OPPORTUNITIES FOR 2011

Obviously, we've faced some headwinds as well in our PBM business. We won $11 billion dollars in new PBM revenues over the past two years, but we also lost a similar amount of existing business over this same time-frame as a result of some unique circumstances affecting a handful of accounts. Client renewals for 2011 are looking strong, though, and I'm confident that retention will return to Caremark's historically high levels.

On the new business front, we took steps to reposition our sales message to focus first on our industry-leading PBM capabilities. We're talking to clients about how we are able to lower their costs and improve the plan member experience. That is resonating well during the 2011 selling season, and there are a significant number of large prospects out to bid.

With Howard McLure's retirement, I'm delighted that we were able to hire Per Lofberg as our new PBM president. Per, who joined us in January 2010, brings more than 30 years of experience in the health care and PBM industries. Formerly chairman of Merck-Medco Managed Care LLC, which later became Medco Health Solutions, he

> "We generated approximately $3 billion in free cash flow, deploying part of it to complete a $2 billion share repurchase program."

most recently served as president and CEO of our strategic partner, Generation Health, Inc. Per is widely respected in the industry, and his expertise, along with his demonstrated ability to execute growth strategies, makes him the perfect person to guide our PBM in this evolving health care environment.

OUR SAME-STORE SALES GROWTH LEADS ALL PHARMACY RETAILERS

Despite the recession, our retail stores put up outstanding numbers. Same-store sales rose 5.0 percent, while pharmacy same-store sales increased 6.9 percent. These results led our industry throughout 2009, and we gained significant market share. Organic growth continued apace as we opened 287 new or relocated stores. Factoring in closings, net unit growth was 102 stores. Today, approximately 75 percent of the U.S. population lives within three miles of a CVS store. Our stores fill nearly one in five prescriptions nationwide, and we have the #1 or #2 market share in 14 of the top 15 U.S. drugstore markets.

Our industry-leading customer service and the use of advanced technology, combined with the increasing adoption of Maintenance Choice by PBM clients, all contributed to our pharmacy growth.

In the front of the store, we gained share in 82 percent of our core categories. Moreover, sales of private-label and CVS-exclusive brands rose faster than they have historically to account for nearly 17 percent of our front-end total. These lower-cost products offer excellent value, which clearly appealed to cost-conscious consumers in the midst of a recession. We, in turn, benefited from the higher margins these products provide compared with national brands. Our private-label program is ambitious, and we added more than 900 offerings to our shelves during the year.

The Longs Drugs® stores we acquired in October 2008 were integrated on schedule and are on track to be accretive to earnings in 2010. Profitability is already on the rise as we've begun to leverage our systems, our focus on private label, our category mix, and the ExtraCare® card. We have a solid track record at making the most of our acquisitions, roughly doubling the profitability of the drugstores we acquired from JCPenney in 2004 and from Albertsons in 2006.

EXTRACARE AND OTHER LONG-TERM INVESTMENTS HAVE HELPED DRIVE PROFITABILITY

We can trace our industry-leading performance in no small part to the many investments we have made over the past decade in technology, in enhancing the layout and "shopability" of our stores, and in driving customer loyalty. The ExtraCare loyalty program, which we rolled out in 2001, is today the most popular among all retailers.

More than 64 million active cardholders take advantage of sales in the store and at CVS.com, and they received $1.9 billion in ExtraCare savings and Extra Bucks rewards throughout 2009. ExtraCare represents a significant competitive advantage for us, and CVS Caremark has a huge head start over any drug retailer contemplating its own loyalty program.

More recent investments position CVS Caremark for greater profitability in the coming years. For example, our proprietary RxConnect™ computer system, whose rollout will be completed during 2010, should improve both efficiency and customer service in our pharmacies. We've also opened call centers that allow us to redirect much of the telephone call volume from our busiest stores. That frees up retail pharmacists to spend more time counseling patients face-to-face.

WE'VE EXPANDED MINUTECLINIC'S OFFERINGS AND FORGED NEW ALLIANCES

At MinuteClinic, our retail-based health clinics, we expanded the services offered, further integrated MinuteClinic into our PBM offerings, and forged a number of strategic alliances with highly regarded health care providers such as Humana, Inc., and the Cleveland Clinic. Today we have approximately 570 clinics in 56 markets across the country.

> "We will continue to offer new and innovative services that help attract and retain PBM and retail customers."

In 2010, a key focus will be adding protocol-driven monitoring services for common chronic illnesses, such as diabetes, hypertension, and high cholesterol. That will be done in coordination with a patient's treating physician and is designed to improve adherence and outcomes. We also expect to offer additional acute care services and improved point of service lab tests. Under its new president, Andrew Sussman, M.D., this business is moving in the right direction.

CVS CAREMARK WILL CONTINUE TO BENEFIT FROM NEW PRODUCTS AND BROAD INDUSTRY TRENDS

Looking ahead, we will continue to offer new and innovative services that help attract and retain PBM and retail customers. For example, we plan to expand pharmacogenomic clinical and testing services for CVS Caremark PBM clients through our ownership stake in Generation Health. We want to improve care for patients who are either non-responsive to their medications or who experience adverse reactions as a result of their genomic makeup. We expect to begin offering these services during 2010.

We are currently in the process of transitioning our iScribe® clients to Allscripts, the largest provider of e-prescribing and electronic health record solutions. E-prescribing can significantly reduce medication errors. With this partnership, we hope to accelerate the adoption of e-prescribing across our client base.

Broad industry trends will work in our favor as well, from potential health care reform and an aging population to new blockbuster and generic drug introductions. CVS Caremark has been participating in the national debate over legislation to reform the U.S. health care system. We believe the right combination of reform and expansion will be good for the nation. As the largest provider of cost-effective pharmacy care in this country, we stand ready to support this effort.

Looking at demographics, the number of people in the United States who are 65 or older will jump to roughly 47 million by 2015 and to 55 million by 2020. This age group fills an average of more than 25 prescriptions per person annually – 30 percent more than people between the ages of 55 and 64. That will increase utilization dramatically for years to come and will help drive the growth of both our PBM and retail businesses.

Of course, the opportunity in generics is enormous. Nearly $100 billion in branded drug sales will lose patent protection over the next six years. As a result, our GDR could eventually approach 80 percent. That is expected to further reduce costs for health plans, plan sponsors, and their members while expanding our pharmacy margins. We are also hopeful that Congress will pass legislation that finally paves the way for a biogeneric approval process.

As you can see, we're very optimistic about our prospects, both in the short-term and long-term. Pharmacy health care in this country has a bright future, and we believe our combined assets will lead to a bright future for our company for years to come. On behalf of our board of directors and our 211,000 colleagues across the country, thank you for investing in CVS Caremark.

Thomas M. Ryan
Chairman of the Board,
President, and Chief Executive Officer

February 26, 2010

Consolidated Statements of Operations

in millions, except per share amounts	Dec. 31, 2009	Dec. 31, 2008	Dec. 29, 2007
		Fiscal Year Ended	
Net revenues	$ 98,729	$ 87,472	$ 76,330
Cost of revenues	78,349	69,182	60,222
Gross profit	20,380	18,290	16,108
Operating expenses	13,942	12,244	11,314
Operating profit	6,438	6,046	4,794
Interest expense, net	525	509	435
Income before income tax provision	5,913	5,537	4,359
Income tax provision	2,205	2,193	1,722
Income from continuing operations	3,708	3,344	2,637
Loss from discontinued operations, net of income tax benefit	(12)	(132)	–
Net income	3,696	3,212	2,637
Preference dividends, net of income tax benefit	–	14	14
Net income available to common shareholders	$ 3,696	$ 3,198	$ 2,623
BASIC EARNINGS PER COMMON SHARE:			
Income from continuing operations	$ 2.59	$ 2.32	$ 1.97
Loss from discontinued operations	(0.01)	(0.09)	–
Net income	$ 2.58	$ 2.23	$ 1.97
Weighted average common shares outstanding	1,434	1,434	1,328
DILUTED EARNINGS PER COMMON SHARE:			
Income from continuing operations	$ 2.56	$ 2.27	$ 1.92
Loss from discontinued operations	(0.01)	(0.09)	–
Net income	$ 2.55	$ 2.18	$ 1.92
Weighted average common shares outstanding	1,450	1,469	1,372
Dividends declared per common share	$ 0.30500	$ 0.25800	$ 0.22875

See accompanying notes to consolidated financial statements.

Consolidated Balance Sheets

in millions, except per share amounts	December 31, 2009	2008
ASSETS:		
Cash and cash equivalents	$ 1,086	$ 1,352
Short-term investments	5	–
Accounts receivable, net	5,457	5,384
Inventories	10,343	9,153
Deferred income taxes	506	435
Other current assets	140	202
Total current assets	17,537	16,526
Property and equipment, net	7,923	8,125
Goodwill	25,680	25,494
Intangible assets, net	10,127	10,446
Other assets	374	369
Total assets	$ 61,641	$ 60,960
LIABILITIES:		
Accounts payable	$ 3,560	$ 3,801
Claims and discounts payable	3,075	2,814
Accrued expenses	3,246	3,178
Short-term debt	315	3,044
Current portion of long-term debt	2,104	653
Total current liabilities	12,300	13,490
Long-term debt	8,756	8,057
Deferred income taxes	3,678	3,702
Other long-term liabilities	1,102	1,137
Commitments and contingencies (Note 12)		
Redeemable noncontrolling interest	37	–
SHAREHOLDERS' EQUITY:		
Preferred stock, par value $0.01: 0.1 shares authorized; none issued or outstanding	–	–
Preference stock, series one ESOP convertible, par value $1.00: 50 shares authorized; no issued and outstanding shares at December 31, 2009 and 4 shares issued and outstanding at December 31, 2008	–	191
Common stock, par value $0.01: 3,200 shares authorized; 1,612 shares issued and 1,391 shares outstanding at December 31, 2009 and 1,603 shares issued and 1,436 shares outstanding at December 31, 2008	16	16
Treasury stock, at cost: 219 shares at December 31, 2009 and 165 shares at December 31, 2008	(7,610)	(5,812)
Shares held in trust: 2 shares at December 31, 2009 and 2008	(56)	(56)
Capital surplus	27,198	27,280
Retained earnings	16,355	13,098
Accumulated other comprehensive loss	(135)	(143)
Total shareholders' equity	35,768	34,574
Total liabilities and shareholders' equity	$ 61,641	$ 60,960

See accompanying notes to consolidated financial statements.

Consolidated Statements of Cash Flows

		Fiscal Year Ended	
in millions	Dec. 31, 2009	Dec. 31, 2008	Dec. 29, 2007
CASH FLOWS FROM OPERATING ACTIVITIES:			
Cash receipts from revenues	$ 93,568	$ 82,250	$ 72,533
Cash paid for inventory and prescriptions dispensed by retail network pharmacies	(73,536)	(64,131)	(56,319)
Cash paid to other suppliers and employees	(13,121)	(11,832)	(10,769)
Interest and dividends received	5	20	34
Interest paid	(542)	(574)	(468)
Income taxes paid	(2,339)	(1,786)	(1,781)
Net cash provided by operating activities	4,035	3,947	3,230
CASH FLOWS FROM INVESTING ACTIVITIES:			
Additions to property and equipment	(2,548)	(2,180)	(1,805)
Proceeds from sale-leaseback transactions	1,562	204	601
Acquisitions (net of cash acquired) and other investments	(101)	(2,651)	(1,984)
Purchase of short-term investments	(5)	–	–
Sale of short-term investments	–	28	–
Proceeds from sale or disposal of assets	23	19	106
Net cash used in investing activities	(1,069)	(4,580)	(3,082)
CASH FLOWS FROM FINANCING ACTIVITIES:			
Increase (decrease) in short-term debt	(2,729)	959	242
Repayment of debt assumed in acquisition	–	(353)	–
Issuance of long-term debt	2,800	350	6,000
Repayments of long-term debt	(653)	(2)	(822)
Dividends paid	(439)	(383)	(323)
Derivative settlements	(3)	–	–
Proceeds from exercise of stock options	250	328	553
Excess tax benefits from stock-based compensation	19	53	98
Repurchase of common stock	(2,477)	(23)	(5,370)
Net cash provided by (used in) financing activities	(3,232)	929	378
Net increase (decrease) in cash and cash equivalents	(266)	296	526
Cash and cash equivalents at beginning of year	1,352	1,056	530
Cash and cash equivalents at end of year	$ 1,086	$ 1,352	$ 1,056
RECONCILIATION OF NET INCOME TO NET CASH PROVIDED BY OPERATING ACTIVITIES:			
Net income	$ 3,696	$ 3,212	$ 2,637
Adjustments required to reconcile net income to net cash provided by operating activities:			
Depreciation and amortization	1,389	1,274	1,095
Stock-based compensation	165	92	78
Deferred income taxes and other non-cash items	48	(3)	39
Change in operating assets and liabilities, net of effects from acquisitions:			
Accounts receivable, net	(86)	(291)	280
Inventories	(1,199)	(488)	(448)
Other current assets	48	12	(59)
Other assets	(2)	19	(26)
Accounts payable	4	(64)	(181)
Accrued expenses	(66)	183	(168)
Other long-term liabilities	38	1	(17)
Net cash provided by operating activities	$ 4,035	$ 3,947	$ 3,230

See accompanying notes to consolidated financial statements.

Consolidated Statements of Shareholders' Equity

	Shares			Dollars		
in millions	**Dec. 31, 2009**	Dec. 31, 2008	Dec. 29, 2007	**Dec. 31, 2009**	Dec. 31, 2008	Dec. 29, 2007
PREFERENCE STOCK:						
Beginning of year	**4**	4	4	**$ 191**	$ 202	$ 212
Conversion to common stock	**(4)**	–	–	**(191)**	(11)	(10)
End of year	**–**	4	4	**–**	191	202
COMMON STOCK:						
Beginning of year	**1,603**	1,590	847	**16**	16	9
Common stock issued for Caremark Merger	**–**	–	713	**–**	–	7
Stock options exercised and stock awards	**9**	13	30	**–**	–	–
End of year	**1,612**	1,603	1,590	**16**	16	16
TREASURY STOCK:						
Beginning of year	**(165)**	(154)	(22)	**(5,812)**	(5,620)	(314)
Purchase of treasury shares	**(73)**	(7)	(135)	**(2,477)**	(33)	(5,379)
Conversion of preference stock	**17**	1	1	**583**	35	25
Transfer from shares held in trust	**–**	(7)	–	**–**	(272)	–
Employee stock purchase plan issuances	**2**	2	2	**96**	78	48
End of year	**(219)**	(165)	(154)	**(7,610)**	(5,812)	(5,620)
GUARANTEED ESOP OBLIGATION:						
Beginning of year				**–**	(44)	(82)
Reduction of guaranteed ESOP obligation				**–**	44	38
End of year				**–**	–	(44)
SHARES HELD IN TRUST:						
Beginning of year	**(2)**	(9)	–	**(56)**	(301)	–
Transfer to treasury stock	**–**	7	–	**–**	245	–
Shares acquired through Caremark Merger	**–**	–	(9)	**–**	–	(301)
End of year	**(2)**	(2)	(9)	**(56)**	(56)	(301)
CAPITAL SURPLUS:						
Beginning of year				**27,280**	26,832	2,198
Common stock issued for Caremark Merger, net of issuance costs				**–**	–	23,942
Conversion of shares held in Trust to treasury stock				**–**	27	–
Stock option activity and stock awards				**291**	392	608
Tax benefit on stock options and stock awards				**19**	53	98
Conversion of preference stock				**(392)**	(24)	(14)
End of year				**$ 27,198**	$ 27,280	$ 26,832

See accompanying notes to consolidated financial statements.

Consolidated Statements of Shareholders' Equity

	Shares			Dollars		
in millions	**Dec. 31, 2009**	Dec. 31, 2008	Dec. 29, 2007	**Dec. 31, 2009**	Dec. 31, 2008	Dec. 29, 2007
ACCUMULATED OTHER COMPREHENSIVE LOSS:						
Beginning of year				**$ (143)**	$ (50)	$ (73)
Net cash flow hedges, net of income tax				**1**	3	3
Pension liability adjustment, net of income tax				**7**	(96)	20
End of year				**(135)**	(143)	(50)
RETAINED EARNINGS:						
Beginning of year				**13,098**	10,287	7,966
Net income				**3,696**	3,212	2,637
Common stock dividends				**(439)**	(370)	(308)
Preference stock dividends				**–**	(14)	(15)
Tax benefit on preference stock dividends				**–**	1	1
Adoption of ASC 715-60 (formerly EITF 06-04 and 06-10)				**–**	(18)	–
Adoption of ASC 740 (formerly FIN 48)				**–**	–	6
End of year				**16,355**	13,098	10,287
Total shareholders' equity				**$ 35,768**	$ 34,574	$ 31,322
COMPREHENSIVE INCOME:						
Net income				**$ 3,696**	$ 3,212	$ 2,637
Net cash flow hedges, net of income tax				**1**	3	3
Pension liability adjustment, net of income tax				**7**	(96)	20
Comprehensive income				**$ 3,704**	$ 3,119	$ 2,660

See accompanying notes to consolidated financial statements.

Notes to Consolidated Financial Statements

Note 1 Significant Accounting Policies

Description of business. CVS Caremark Corporation ("Company") is the largest pharmacy health care provider (based on revenues and prescriptions filled) in the United States.

Pharmacy Services Segment (the "PSS"). The PSS provides a full range of prescription benefit management services including mail order pharmacy services, specialty pharmacy services, plan design and administration, formulary management and claims processing. The Company's clients are primarily employers, insurance companies, unions, government employee groups, managed care organizations and other sponsors of health benefit plans and individuals throughout the United States.

As a pharmacy benefits manager, the PSS manages the dispensing of pharmaceuticals through our mail order pharmacies and national network of approximately 64,000 retail pharmacies to eligible members in the benefits plans maintained by our clients and utilizes its information systems to perform, among other things, safety checks, drug interaction screenings and brand to generic substitutions.

The PSS's specialty pharmacies support individuals that require complex and expensive drug therapies. The specialty pharmacy business includes mail order and retail specialty pharmacies that operate under the Caremark® and CarePlus CVS/pharmacy™ names.

The PSS also provides health management programs, which include integrated disease management for 27 conditions, through Alere® and our Accordant® health management offering.

In addition, through our SilverScript Insurance Company ("SilverScript") and Accendo Insurance Company ("Accendo") subsidiaries, the PSS is a national provider of drug benefits to eligible beneficiaries under the Federal Government's Medicare Part D program. The PSS acquired Accendo in the Longs Acquisition (defined later in Note 2), and, effective January 1, 2009, Accendo replaced RxAmerica® as the Medicare-approved prescription drug plan for the RxAmerica Medicare Part D drug benefit plans.

The pharmacy services business generates net revenues primarily by contracting with clients to provide prescription drugs to plan members. Prescription drugs are dispensed by the mail order pharmacies, specialty pharmacies and national network of retail pharmacies. Net revenues are also generated by providing additional services to clients, including administrative services such as claims processing and formulary management, as well as health care related services such as disease management.

The pharmacy services business operates under the Caremark Pharmacy Services®, Caremark, CVS Caremark™, CarePlus CVS/pharmacy, CarePlus™, RxAmerica, Accordant Care™ and TheraCom® names. As of December 31, 2009, the Pharmacy Services segment operated 49 retail specialty pharmacy stores, 18 specialty mail order pharmacies and six mail service pharmacies located in 25 states, Puerto Rico and the District of Columbia.

Retail Pharmacy Segment (the "RPS"). The RPS sells prescription drugs and a wide assortment of general merchandise, including over-the-counter drugs, beauty products and cosmetics, photo finishing, seasonal merchandise, greeting cards and convenience foods, through our CVS/pharmacy and Longs Drug retail stores and online through CVS.com®.

The RPS also provides health care services through its MinuteClinic® health care clinics. MinuteClinics are staffed by nurse practitioners and physician assistants who utilize nationally recognized protocols to diagnose and treat minor health conditions, perform health screenings and deliver vaccinations.

As of December 31, 2009, the retail pharmacy business included 7,025 retail drugstores (of which 6,964 operated a pharmacy) located in 41 states and the District of Columbia operating primarily under the CVS/pharmacy® name, the online retail website, CVS.com® and 569 retail health care clinics operating under the MinuteClinic name (of which 557 were located in CVS/pharmacy stores).

Corporate Segment. The Corporate segment provides management and administrative services to support the Company. The Corporate segment consists of certain aspects of our executive management, corporate relations, legal, compliance, human resources, corporate information technology and finance departments.

Principles of Consolidation. The consolidated financial statements include the accounts of the Company and its majority owned subsidiaries. All intercompany balances and transactions have been eliminated.

Fiscal Year Change. On December 23, 2008, the Board of Directors of the Company approved a change in the Company's fiscal year-end from the Saturday nearest December 31 of each year to December 31 of each year to better reflect the Company's position in the health care, rather than the retail, industry. The fiscal year change was effective beginning with the fourth quarter of fiscal 2008.

Notes to Consolidated Financial Statements

Following is a summary of the impact of the fiscal year change:

Fiscal Year	Fiscal Year-End	Fiscal Period	Fiscal Period Includes
2009	December 31, 2009	January 1, 2009 - December 31, 2009	365 days
2008	December 31, 2008	December 30, 2007 - December 31, 2008	368 days
2007	December 29, 2007	December 31, 2006 - December 29, 2007	364 days

Unless otherwise noted, all references to years relate to the above fiscal years.

Reclassifications. Certain reclassifications have been made to the 2008 and 2007 consolidated financial statements to conform to the current year presentation.

Use of estimates. The preparation of financial statements in conformity with accounting principles generally accepted in the United States of America requires management to make estimates and assumptions that affect the reported amounts in the consolidated financial statements and accompanying notes. Actual results could differ from those estimates.

Fair Value Hierarchy. The Company utilizes the three-level valuation hierarchy for the recognition and disclosure of fair value measurements. The categorization of assets and liabilities within this hierarchy is based upon the lowest level of input that is significant to the measurement of fair value. The three levels of the hierarchy consist of the following:

- Level 1 – Inputs to the valuation methodology are unadjusted quoted prices in active markets for identical assets or liabilities that the Company has the ability to access at the measurement date.
- Level 2 – Inputs to the valuation methodology are quoted prices for similar assets and liabilities in active markets, quoted prices in markets that are not active or inputs that are observable for the asset or liability, either directly or indirectly, for substantially the full term of the instrument.
- Level 3 – Inputs to the valuation methodology are unobservable inputs based upon management's best estimate of inputs market participants could use in pricing the asset or liability at the measurement date, including assumptions about risk.

Cash and cash equivalents. Cash and cash equivalents consist of cash and temporary investments with maturities of three months or less when purchased. The Company invests in short-term money market funds, commercial paper, time deposits, as well as other available-for-sale debt securities that are classified as cash and cash equivalents within the accompanying consolidated balance sheets, as these funds are highly liquid and readily convertible to known amounts of cash. These investments are classified within Level 1 of the fair value hierarchy because they are valued using quoted market prices.

Short-term investments. The Company's short-term investments consist of certificate of deposits with initial maturities of greater than three months when purchased. These investments, which were classified as available-for-sale within Level 1 of the fair value hierarchy, were carried at historical cost, which approximated fair value at December 31, 2009. The Company had no short-term investments at December 31, 2008.

Fair value of financial instruments. As of December 31, 2009, the Company's financial instruments include cash and cash equivalents, accounts receivable, accounts payable, short-term debt and current portion of short-term debt. Due to the short-term nature of these instruments, the Company's carrying value approximates fair value. The carrying amount and estimated fair value of long-term debt was $8.6 billion and $8.8 billion, respectively, as of December 31, 2009. The fair value of long-term debt was estimated based on rates currently offered to the Company for debt with similar terms and maturities. The Company had outstanding letters of credit, which guaranteed foreign trade purchases, with a fair value of $9 million and $7 million as of December 31, 2009 and 2008, respectively. There were no outstanding investments in derivative financial instruments as of December 31, 2009 and 2008.

Accounts receivable. Accounts receivable are stated net of an allowance for doubtful accounts of $272 million and $189 million as of December 31, 2009 and 2008, respectively. The balance primarily includes amounts due from third-party providers (e.g., pharmacy benefit managers, insurance companies and governmental agencies) and vendors as well as clients, members and manufacturers.

Inventories. Inventories are stated at the lower of cost or market on a first-in, first-out basis using the retail method of accounting to determine cost of sales and inventory in our CVS/pharmacy stores, average cost to determine cost of sales and inventory in our mail service and specialty pharmacies and the cost method of accounting to determine inventory in our distribution centers. Physical inventory counts are taken on a regular basis in each store and a continuous cycle count process is the primary procedure used to validate the inventory balances on hand in each distribution center to ensure that the amounts reflected in the accompanying consolidated financial statements are properly stated. During the interim period between physical inventory counts, the Company accrues for anticipated physical inventory losses on a location-by-location basis based on historical results and current trends.

The cost method of accounting was used to determine inventory in the Longs Drug Stores as of December 31, 2008. The Longs Drug Stores began using the retail method of accounting beginning in the second quarter of 2009.

Property and equipment. Property, equipment and improvements to leased premises are depreciated using the straight-line method over the estimated useful lives of the assets, or when applicable, the term of the lease, whichever is shorter. Estimated useful lives generally range from 10 to 40 years for buildings, building improvements and leasehold improvements and 3 to 10 years for fixtures and equipment. Repair and maintenance costs are charged directly to expense as incurred. Major renewals or replacements that substantially extend the useful life of an asset are capitalized and depreciated.

The following are the components of property and equipment at December 31:

in millions	2009	2008
Land	$ 1,076	$ 1,304
Building and improvements	2,020	1,525
Fixtures and equipment	6,322	6,216
Leasehold improvements	2,673	2,581
Software	853	666
	12,944	12,292
Accumulated depreciation and amortization	(5,021)	(4,167)
	$ 7,923	$ 8,125

The gross amount of property and equipment under capital leases was $191 million and $182 million as of December 31, 2009 and 2008, respectively.

The Company capitalizes application development stage costs for significant internally developed software projects. These costs are amortized over the estimated useful lives of the software, which generally range from 3 to 5 years.

Goodwill. Goodwill and other indefinite-lived assets are not amortized, but are subject to impairment reviews annually, or more frequently if necessary. See Note 3 for additional information on goodwill.

Intangible assets. Purchased customer contracts and relationships are amortized on a straight-line basis over their estimated useful lives between 10 and 20 years. Purchased customer lists are amortized on a straight-line basis over their estimated useful lives of up to 10 years. Purchased leases are amortized on a straight-line basis over the remaining life of the lease. See Note 3 for additional information about intangible assets.

Impairment of long-lived assets. The Company groups and evaluates fixed and finite-lived intangible assets, excluding goodwill, for impairment at the lowest level at which individual cash flows can be identified. When evaluating assets for potential impairment, the Company first compares the carrying amount of the asset group to the individual store's estimated future cash flows (undiscounted and without interest charges). If the estimated future cash flows used in this analysis are less than the carrying amount of the asset group, an impairment loss calculation is prepared. The impairment loss calculation compares the carrying amount of the asset group to the asset group's estimated future cash flows (discounted and with interest charges). If required, an impairment loss is recorded for the portion of the asset group's carrying value that exceeds the asset group's estimated future cash flows (discounted and with interest charges).

Redeemable noncontrolling interest. The Company has an approximately 60% ownership interest in Generation Health, Inc. ("Generation Health") and consolidates Generation Health in its consolidated financial statements. The noncontrolling shareholders of Generation Health hold put rights for the remaining interest in Generation Health that if exercised would require the Company to purchase the remaining interest in Generation Health in 2015 for a minimum of $27 million and a maximum of $159 million, depending on certain financial metrics of Generation Health in 2014. Since the noncontrolling shareholders of Generation Health have a redemption feature as a result of the put right, the Company has classified the redeemable noncontrolling interest in Generation Health in the mezzanine section of the consolidated balance sheet outside of shareholders' equity. The Company initially recorded the redeemable noncontrolling interest at a fair value of $37 million on the date of acquisition. At the end of each reporting period, if the estimated accreted redemption value exceeds the carrying value of the noncontrolling interest, the difference is recorded as a reduction of retained earnings. Any such reductions in retained earnings would also reduce income available to common shareholders in the Company's earnings per share calculations.

REVENUE RECOGNITION:

Pharmacy Services Segment. The PSS sells prescription drugs directly through its mail service pharmacies and indirectly through its national retail pharmacy network. The PSS recognizes revenues from prescription drugs sold by its mail service pharmacies and under national retail pharmacy network contracts where the PSS is the principal using the gross method at the contract prices negotiated with its clients. Net revenue from the PSS includes: (i) the portion of the price the client pays directly to the PSS, net of any volume-related

Notes to Consolidated Financial Statements

or other discounts paid back to the client (see "Drug Discounts" later in this document), (ii) the price paid to the PSS ("Mail Co-Payments") or a third-party pharmacy in the PSS' national retail pharmacy network ("Retail Co-Payments") by individuals included in its clients' benefit plans and (iii) administrative fees for national retail pharmacy network contracts where the PSS is not the principal as discussed later in this document.

The PSS recognizes revenue when: (i) persuasive evidence of an arrangement exists, (ii) delivery has occurred or services have been rendered, (iii) the seller's price to the buyer is fixed or determinable and (iv) collectability is reasonably assured. The Company has established the following revenue recognition policies for the PSS:

- Revenues generated from prescription drugs sold by mail service pharmacies are recognized when the prescription is shipped. At the time of shipment, the Company has performed substantially all of its obligations under its client contracts and does not experience a significant level of reshipments.
- Revenues generated from prescription drugs sold by third-party pharmacies in the PSS' national retail pharmacy network and associated administrative fees are recognized at the PSS' point-of-sale, which is when the claim is adjudicated by the PSS' online claims processing system.

The PSS determines whether it is the principal or agent for its national retail pharmacy network transactions on a contract by contract basis. In the majority of its contracts, the PSS has determined it is the principal due to it: (i) being the primary obligor in the arrangement, (ii) having latitude in establishing the price, changing the product or performing part of the service, (iii) having discretion in supplier selection, (iv) having involvement in the determination of product or service specifications and (v) having credit risk. The PSS' obligations under its client contracts for which revenues are reported using the gross method are separate and distinct from its obligations to the third-party pharmacies included in its national retail pharmacy network contracts. Pursuant to these contracts, the PSS is contractually required to pay the third-party pharmacies in its national retail pharmacy network for products sold, regardless of whether the PSS is paid by its clients. The PSS' responsibilities under its client contracts typically include validating eligibility and coverage levels, communicating the prescription price and the co-payments due to the third-party retail pharmacy, identifying possible adverse drug interactions for the pharmacist to address with the physician prior to dispensing, suggesting clinically appropriate generic alternatives where appropriate and approving the prescription for dispensing. Although the PSS does not have credit risk with respect to Retail Co-Payments, management believes that all of the other indicators of gross revenue reporting are present. For contracts under which the PSS acts as an agent, the PSS records revenues using the net method.

Drug Discounts – The PSS deducts from its revenues any discounts paid to its clients. The PSS pays discounts to its clients in accordance with the terms of its client contracts, which are normally based on a fixed discount per prescription for specific products dispensed or a percentage of manufacturer discounts received for specific products dispensed. The liability for discounts due to the PSS' clients is included in "Claims and discounts payable" in the accompanying consolidated balance sheets.

Medicare Part D – The PSS participates in the Federal Government's Medicare Part D program as a Prescription Drug Plan ("PDP"). The PSS' net revenues include insurance premiums earned by the PDP, which are determined based on the PDP's annual bid and related contractual arrangements with the Centers for Medicare and Medicaid Services ("CMS"). The insurance premiums include a beneficiary premium, which is the responsibility of the PDP member, but is subsidized by CMS in the case of low-income members, and a direct premium paid by CMS. Premiums collected in advance are initially deferred in accrued expenses and are then recognized in net revenues over the period in which members are entitled to receive benefits.

In addition to these premiums, the PSS' net revenues include co-payments, deductibles and co-insurance (collectively, the "Member Co-Payments") related to PDP members' actual prescription claims in its net revenues. In certain cases, CMS subsidizes a portion of these Member Co-Payments and pays the PSS an estimated prospective Member Co-Payment subsidy amount each month. The prospective Member Co-Payment subsidy amounts received from CMS are also included in the PSS' net revenues. The Company assumes no risk for these amounts, which represented 3.5%, 1.3% and 0.8% of consolidated net revenues in 2009, 2008 and 2007, respectively. If the prospective Member Co-Payment subsidies received differ from the amounts based on actual prescription claims, the difference is recorded in either accounts receivable or accrued expenses.

The PSS accounts for CMS obligations and Member Co-Payments (including the amounts subsidized by CMS) using the gross method consistent with its revenue recognition policies for Mail Co-Payments and Retail Co-Payments (discussed previously in this document). See Note 7 for additional information about Medicare Part D.

Retail Pharmacy Segment. The RPS recognizes revenue from the sale of merchandise (other than prescription drugs) at the time the merchandise is purchased by the retail customer. Revenue from the sale of prescription drugs is recognized at the time the prescription is filled, which is or approximates when the retail customer picks up the prescription. Customer returns are not material. Revenue generated from the performance of services in the RPS' health care clinics is recognized at the time the services are performed. See Note 13 for additional information about the revenues of the Company's business segments.

COST OF REVENUES:

Pharmacy Services Segment. The PSS' cost of revenues includes: (i) the cost of prescription drugs sold during the reporting period directly through its mail service pharmacies and indirectly through its national retail pharmacy network, (ii) shipping and handling costs and (iii) the operating costs of its mail service pharmacies and client service operations and related information technology support costs including depreciation and amortization. The cost of prescription drugs sold component of cost of revenues includes: (i) the cost of the prescription drugs purchased from manufacturers or distributors and shipped to members in clients' benefit plans from the PSS' mail service pharmacies, net of any volume-related or other discounts (see "Drug Discounts" previously in this document) and (ii) the cost of prescription drugs sold (including Retail Co-Payments) through the PSS' national retail pharmacy network under contracts where it is the principal, net of any volume-related or other discounts.

Retail Pharmacy Segment. The RPS' cost of revenues includes: the cost of merchandise sold during the reporting period and the related purchasing costs, warehousing and delivery costs (including depreciation and amortization) and actual and estimated inventory losses. See Note 13 for additional information about the cost of revenues of the Company's business segments.

VENDOR ALLOWANCES AND PURCHASE DISCOUNTS:

The Company accounts for vendor allowances and purchase discounts as follows:

Pharmacy Services Segment. The PSS receives purchase discounts on products purchased. The PSS' contractual arrangements with vendors, including manufacturers, wholesalers and retail pharmacies, normally provide for the PSS to receive purchase discounts from established list prices in one, or a combination of, the following forms: (i) a direct discount at the time of purchase, (ii) a discount for the prompt payment of invoices or (iii) when products are purchased indirectly from a manufacturer (e.g., through a wholesaler or retail pharmacy), a discount (or rebate) paid subsequent to dispensing. These rebates are recognized when prescriptions are dispensed and are generally calculated and billed to manufacturers within 30 days of the end of each completed quarter. Historically, the effect of adjustments resulting from the reconciliation of rebates recognized to the amounts billed and collected has not been material to the PSS' results of operations. The PSS accounts for the effect of any such differences as a change in accounting estimate in the period the reconciliation is completed. The PSS also receives additional discounts under its wholesaler contract if it exceeds contractually defined annual purchase volumes.

The PSS earns purchase discounts at various points in its business cycle (e.g., when the product is purchased, when the vendor is paid or when the product is dispensed) for products sold through its mail service pharmacies and third-party pharmacies included in its national retail pharmacy network. In addition, the PSS receives fees from pharmaceutical manufacturers for administrative services. Purchase discounts and administrative service fees are recorded as a reduction of "Cost of revenues".

Retail Pharmacy Segment. Vendor allowances received by the RPS reduce the carrying cost of inventory and are recognized in cost of revenues when the related inventory is sold, unless they are specifically identified as a reimbursement of incremental costs for promotional programs and/or other services provided. Funds that are directly linked to advertising commitments are recognized as a reduction of advertising expense (included in operating expenses) when the related advertising commitment is satisfied. Any such allowances received in excess of the actual cost incurred also reduce the carrying cost of inventory. The total value of any upfront payments received from vendors that are linked to purchase commitments is initially deferred. The deferred amounts are then amortized to reduce cost of revenues over the life of the contract based upon purchase volume. The total value of any upfront payments received from vendors that are not linked to purchase commitments is also initially deferred. The deferred amounts are then amortized to reduce cost of revenues on a straight-line basis over the life of the related contract. The total amortization of these upfront payments was not material to the accompanying consolidated financial statements.

Insurance. The Company is self-insured for certain losses related to general liability, workers' compensation and auto liability. The Company obtains third-party insurance coverage to limit exposure from these claims. The Company is also

Notes to Consolidated Financial Statements

self-insured for certain losses related to health and medical liabilities. The Company's self-insurance accruals, which include reported claims and claims incurred but not reported, are calculated using standard insurance industry actuarial assumptions and the Company's historical claims experience.

Store opening and closing costs. New store opening costs, other than capital expenditures, are charged directly to expense when incurred. When the Company closes a store, the present value of estimated unrecoverable costs, including the remaining lease obligation less estimated sublease income and the book value of abandoned property and equipment, are charged to expense. The long-term portion of the lease obligations associated with store closings was $424 million and $399 million in 2009 and 2008, respectively.

Advertising costs. Advertising costs are expensed when the related advertising takes place. Advertising costs, net of vendor funding (included in operating expenses), were $317 million in 2009, $324 million in 2008 and $291 million in 2007.

Interest expense, net. Interest expense was $530 million, $530 million and $468 million, and interest income was $5 million, $21 million and $33 million in 2009, 2008 and 2007, respectively. Capitalized interest totaled $39 million in 2009, $28 million in 2008 and $24 million in 2007.

Shares held in trust. As a result of the Caremark Merger (see Note 2), the Company maintains grantor trusts, which held approximately 2 million shares of its common stock at December 31, 2009 and 2008. These shares are designated for use under various employee compensation plans. Since the Company holds these shares, they are excluded from the computation of basic and diluted shares outstanding.

Accumulated other comprehensive loss. Accumulated other comprehensive loss consists of changes in the net actuarial gains and losses associated with pension and other postretirement benefit plans, and unrealized losses on derivatives. The amount included in accumulated other comprehensive income related to the Company's pension and postretirement plans was $203 million pre-tax ($125 million after-tax) as of December 31, 2009 and $217 million pre-tax ($132 million after-tax) as of December 31, 2008. The net impact on cash flow hedges totaled $15 million pre-tax ($10 million after-tax) and $17 million pre-tax ($11 million after-tax) as of December 31, 2009 and 2008, respectively.

Stock-based compensation. Stock-based compensation expense is measured at the grant date based on the fair value of the award and is recognized as expense over the applicable requisite service period of the stock award (generally 3 to 5 years) using the straight-line method. Stock-based compensation costs are included in selling, general and administrative expenses.

Income taxes. The Company provides for federal and state income taxes currently payable, as well as for those deferred because of timing differences between reported income and expenses for financial statement purposes versus tax purposes. Federal and state tax credits are recorded as a reduction of income taxes. Deferred tax assets and liabilities are recognized for the future tax consequences attributable to differences between the carrying amount of assets and liabilities for financial reporting purposes and the amounts used for income tax purposes. Deferred tax assets and liabilities are measured using the enacted tax rates expected to apply to taxable income in the years in which those temporary differences are expected to be recoverable or settled. The effect of a change in tax rates is recognized as income or expense in the period of the change.

Loss from discontinued operations. In connection with certain business dispositions completed between 1991 and 1997, the Company continues to guarantee store lease obligations for a number of former subsidiaries, including Linens 'n Things. On May 2, 2008, Linens Holding Co. and certain affiliates, which operate Linens 'n Things, filed voluntary petitions under Chapter 11 of the United States Bankruptcy Code in the United States Bankruptcy Court for the District of Delaware. The Company's loss from discontinued operations includes $12 million of lease-related costs ($19 million, net of a $7 million income tax benefit) and $132 million of lease-related costs ($214 million, net of an $82 million income tax benefit) as of December 31, 2009 and 2008, respectively, which the Company believes is likely required to satisfy the lease guarantees associated with Linens 'n Things.

Earnings per common share. Basic earnings per common share is computed by dividing: (i) net earnings, after deducting the after-tax Employee Stock Ownership Plan ("ESOP") preference dividends, by (ii) the weighted average number of common shares outstanding during the year (the "Basic Shares").

When computing diluted earnings per common share for fiscal years 2008 and 2007, the Company assumed that the ESOP preference stock was converted into common stock and all dilutive stock awards were exercised. After the assumed ESOP preference stock conversion, the ESOP Trust would hold common stock rather than ESOP preference stock and would receive common stock dividends ($0.25800 per share in 2008 and $0.22875 per share in 2007) rather than ESOP preference stock dividends ($3.90 per share). Since the ESOP Trust used the dividends it received to service its debt, the Company had to increase its contribution to the ESOP Trust to compensate it for the lower dividends. This additional contribution reduced the Company's net earnings, which in turn, reduced the amounts that would be accrued under the Company's incentive compensation plans.

Diluted earnings per common share is computed by dividing: (i) net earnings, after accounting for the difference between the dividends on the ESOP preference stock and common stock and after making adjustments for the incentive compensation plans, by (ii) Basic Shares plus the additional shares that would be issued assuming that all dilutive stock awards are exercised and the ESOP preference stock is converted into common stock. Options to purchase 37.7 million, 20.9 million and 10.7 million shares of common stock were outstanding as of December 31, 2009, December 31, 2008 and December 29, 2007, respectively, but were not included in the calculation of diluted earnings per share because the options' exercise prices were greater than the average market price of the common shares and, therefore, the effect would be antidilutive. See Note 8 for additional information about the ESOP.

Note 15 Quarterly Financial Information (Unaudited)

in millions, except per share amounts	First Quarter	Second Quarter	Third Quarter	Fourth Quarter	Fiscal Year
2009:					
Net revenues	**$ 23,394**	**$ 24,871**	**$ 24,642**	**$ 25,822**	**$ 98,729**
Gross profit	**4,748**	**5,052**	**5,012**	**5,568**	**20,380**
Operating profit	**1,377**	**1,600**	**1,566**	**1,895**	**6,438**
Income from continuing operations	**743**	**889**	**1,023**	**1,053**	**3,708**
Loss from discontinued operations, net of income tax benefit	**(5)**	**(3)**	**(2)**	**(2)**	**(12)**
Net income	**738**	**886**	**1,021**	**1,051**	**3,696**
Earnings per share from continuing operations, basic	**$ 0.51**	**$ 0.61**	**$ 0.72**	**$ 0.75**	**$ 2.59**
Loss per common share from discontinued operations	**–**	**–**	**(0.01)**	**–**	**(0.01)**
Net earnings per common share, basic	**$ 0.51**	**$ 0.61**	**$ 0.71**	**$ 0.75**	**$ 2.58**
Earnings per common share from continuing operations, diluted	**$ 0.51**	**$ 0.60**	**$ 0.71**	**$ 0.74**	**$ 2.56**
Loss per common share from discontinued operations	**(0.01)**	**–**	**–**	**–**	**(0.01)**
Net earnings per common share, diluted	**$ 0.50**	**$ 0.60**	**$ 0.71**	**$ 0.74**	**$ 2.55**
Dividends per common share	**$ 0.07625**	**$ 0.07625**	**$ 0.07625**	**$ 0.07625**	**$ 0.30500**
Stock price: (New York Stock Exchange)					
High	**$ 30.47**	**$ 34.22**	**$ 37.75**	**$ 38.27**	**$ 38.27**
Low	**$ 23.74**	**$ 27.08**	**$ 30.58**	**$ 27.38**	**$ 23.74**
2008 (1):					
Net revenues	$ 21,326	$ 21,140	$ 20,863	$ 24,143	$ 87,472
Gross profit	4,293	4,373	4,401	5,223	18,290
Operating profit	1,370	1,478	1,466	1,732	6,046
Income from continuing operations	749	824	819	952	3,344
Loss from discontinued operations, net of income tax benefit	–	(49)	(83)	–	(132)
Net income	749	775	736	952	3,212
Earnings per share from continuing operations, basic	$ 0.52	$ 0.57	$ 0.57	$ 0.66	$ 2.32
Loss per common share from discontinued operations	–	(0.03)	(0.06)	–	(0.09)
Net earnings per common share, basic	$ 0.52	$ 0.54	$ 0.51	$ 0.66	$ 2.23
Earnings per common share from continuing operations, diluted	$ 0.51	$ 0.56	$ 0.56	$ 0.65	$ 2.27
Loss per common share from discontinued operations	–	(0.03)	(0.06)	–	(0.09)
Net earnings per common share, diluted	$ 0.51	$ 0.53	$ 0.50	$ 0.65	$ 2.18
Dividends per common share	$ 0.06000	$ 0.06000	$ 0.06900	$ 0.06900	$ 0.25800
Stock price: (New York Stock Exchange)					
High	$ 41.53	$ 44.29	$ 40.14	$ 34.90	$ 44.29
Low	$ 34.91	$ 39.02	$ 31.81	$ 23.19	$ 23.19

(1) On December 23, 2008, our Board of Directors approved a change in our fiscal year-end from the Saturday nearest December 31 of each year to December 31 of each year to better reflect our position in the health care, rather than the retail, industry. The fiscal year change was effective beginning with the fourth of fiscal 2008.

Five-Year Financial Summary

In millions, except per share amounts	2009	2008 (1)	2007 (2)	2006	2005
Statement of operations data:					
Net revenues	**$ 98,729**	$ 87,472	$ 76,330	$ 43,821	$ 37,007
Gross profit	**20,380**	18,290	16,108	11,742	9,695
Operating expenses (3)	**13,942**	12,244	11,314	9,300	7,675
Operating profit (4)	**6,438**	6,046	4,794	2,442	2,020
Interest expense, net	**525**	509	435	216	111
Income tax provision (5)	**2,205**	2,193	1,722	857	684
Income from continuing operations	**3,708**	3,344	2,637	1,369	1,225
Loss from discontinued operations, net of tax benefit (6)	**(12)**	(132)	–	–	–
Net income	**$ 3,696**	$ 3,212	$ 2,637	$ 1,369	$ 1,225
Per common share data:					
Basic earnings per common share:					
Income from continuing operations	**$ 2.59**	$ 2.32	$ 1.97	$ 1.65	$ 1.49
Loss from discontinued operations	**(0.01)**	(0.09)	–	–	–
Net income	**$ 2.58**	$ 2.23	$ 1.97	$ 1.65	$ 1.49
Diluted earnings per common share:					
Income from continuing operations	**$ 2.56**	$ 2.27	$ 1.92	$ 1.60	$ 1.45
Loss from discontinued operations	**(0.01)**	(0.09)	–	–	–
Net income	**$ 2.55**	$ 2.18	$ 1.92	$ 1.60	$ 1.45
Cash dividends per common share	**$ 0.30500**	$ 0.25800	$ 0.22875	$ 0.15500	$ 0.14500
Balance sheet and other data:					
Total assets	**$ 61,641**	$ 60,960	$ 54,722	$ 20,574	$ 15,247
Long-term debt	**$ 8,756**	$ 8,057	$ 8,350	$ 2,870	$ 1,594
Total shareholders' equity	**$ 35,768**	$ 34,574	$ 31,322	$ 9,918	$ 8,331
Number of stores (at end of year)	**7,074**	6,981	6,301	6,205	5,474

(1) On December 23, 2008, our Board of Directors approved a change in our fiscal year-end from the Saturday nearest December 31 of each year to December 31 of each year to better reflect our position in the health care, rather than the retail, industry. The fiscal year change is effective beginning with the fourth quarter of fiscal 2008. As you review our operating performance, please consider that fiscal 2008 includes 368 days, compared to each of the remaining fiscal years presented, which include 364 days.

(2) Effective March 22, 2007, pursuant to the Agreement and Plan of Merger dated as of November 1, 2006, as amended (the "Merger Agreement"), Caremark Rx, Inc. was merged with a newly formed subsidiary of CVS Corporation, with Caremark Rx, L.L.C., continuing as the surviving entity (the "Caremark Merger"). Following the Caremark Merger, the name of the Company was changed to "CVS Caremark Corporation." By virtue of the Caremark Merger, each issued and outstanding share of Caremark common stock, par value $0.001 per share, was converted into the right to receive 1.67 shares of CVS Caremark's common stock, par value $0.01 per share. Cash was paid in lieu of fractional shares.

(3) In 2006, the Company adopted the Securities and Exchange Commission (SEC) Staff Accounting Bulletin ("SAB") No. 108, "Considering the Effects of Prior Year Misstatements when Qualifying Misstatements in Current Year Financial Statements." The adoption of this statement resulted in a $40 million pre-tax ($25 million after-tax) decrease in operating expenses for 2006.

(4) Operating profit includes the pre-tax effect of the charge discussed in Note (3) above.

(5) Income tax provision includes the effect of the following: (i) in 2009, the recognition of $167 million of previously unrecognized tax benefits, including interest, relating to the expiration of various statutes of limitation and settlements with tax authorities, (ii) in 2006, a $11 million reversal of previously recorded tax reserves through the tax provision principally based on resolving certain state tax matters, and (iii) in 2005, a $53 million reversal of previously recorded tax reserves through the tax provision principally based on resolving certain state tax matters.

(6) In connection with certain business dispositions completed between 1991 and 1997, the Company continues to guarantee store lease obligations for a number of former subsidiaries, including Linens 'n Things. On May 2, 2008, Linens Holding Co. and certain affiliates, which operate Linens 'n Things, filed voluntary petitions under Chapter 11 of the United States Bankruptcy Code in the United States Bankruptcy Court for the District of Delaware. Pursuant to the court order entered on October 16, 2008, Linens Holding Co. is in the process of liquidating the entire Linens 'n Things retail chain. The loss from discontinued operations includes $12 million of lease-related costs ($19 million, net of a $7 million income tax benefit), and $132 million ($214 million, net of an $82 million income tax benefit) for 2009 and 2008 respectively, which the Company believes it will likely be required to satisfy pursuant to its Linens 'n Things lease guarantees.

Report of Independent Registered Public Accounting Firm

The Board of Directors and Shareholders
CVS Caremark Corporation

We have audited the accompanying consolidated balance sheets of CVS Caremark Corporation as of December 31, 2009 and 2008, and the related consolidated statements of operations, shareholders' equity, and cash flows for each of the three fiscal years in the period ended December 31, 2009. These financial statements are the responsibility of the Company's management. Our responsibility is to express an opinion on these financial statements based on our audits.

We conducted our audits in accordance with auditing standards of the Public Company Accounting Oversight Board (United States). Those standards require that we plan and perform the audit to obtain reasonable assurance about whether the financial statements are free of material misstatement. An audit includes examining, on a test basis, evidence supporting the amounts and disclosures in the financial statements. An audit also includes assessing the accounting principles used and significant estimates made by management, and evaluating the overall financial statement presentation. We believe that our audits provide a reasonable basis for our opinion.

In our opinion, the financial statements referred to above present fairly, in all material respects, the consolidated financial position of CVS Caremark Corporation at December 31, 2009 and 2008, and the consolidated results of its operations and its cash flows for each of the three fiscal years in the period ended December 31, 2009, in conformity with U.S. generally accepted accounting principles.

As discussed in Note 1 to the consolidated financial statements, effective December 30, 2007, CVS Caremark Corporation adopted Accounting Standards Codification (ASC) 715-60, *Defined Benefit Plans – Other Postretirement* (formerly Emerging Issues Task Force (EITF) Issue No. 06-4, *Accounting for Deferred Compensation and Postretirement Benefit Aspects of Endorsement Split-Dollar Life Insurance Arrangements* and EITF 06-10, *Accounting for Collateral Assignment Split-Dollar Life Insurance Agreements*), and effective January 1, 2009 CVS Caremark Corporation adopted ASC 805, *Business Combinations* (formerly Statement of Financial Accounting Standards No. 141(R), *Business Combinations*).

We also have audited, in accordance with the standards of the Public Company Accounting Oversight Board (United States), CVS Caremark Corporation's internal control over financial reporting as of December 31, 2009, based on criteria established in *Internal Control – Integrated Framework* issued by the Committee of Sponsoring Organizations of the Treadway Commission and our report dated February 26, 2010 expressed an unqualified opinion thereon.

Ernst + Young LLP

Boston, Massachusetts
February 26, 2010

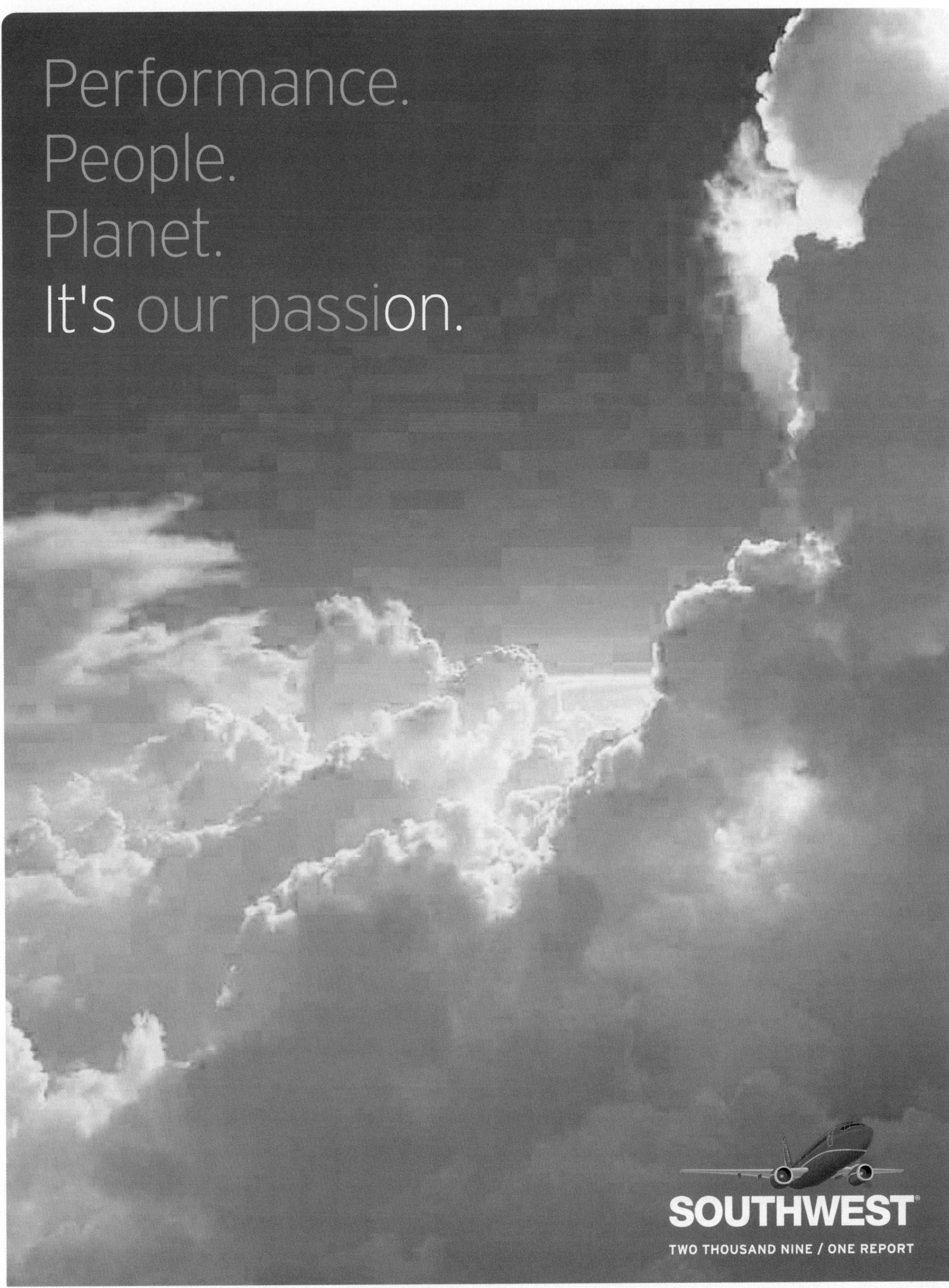
Performance.
People.
Planet.
It's our passion.
SOUTHWEST
TWO THOUSAND NINE / ONE REPORT

Item 8. ***Financial Statements and Supplementary Data***

SOUTHWEST AIRLINES CO.

CONSOLIDATED BALANCE SHEET

(In millions, except share data)

	DECEMBER 31, 2009	DECEMBER 31, 2008
ASSETS		
Current assets:		
Cash and cash equivalents	$ 1,114	$ 1,368
Short-term investments	1,479	435
Accounts and other receivables	169	209
Inventories of parts and supplies, at cost	221	203
Deferred income taxes	291	365
Prepaid expenses and other current assets	84	73
Total current assets	3,358	2,653
Property and equipment, at cost:		
Flight equipment	13,719	13,722
Ground property and equipment	1,922	1,769
Deposits on flight equipment purchase contracts	247	380
	15,888	15,871
Less allowance for depreciation and amortization	5,254	4,831
	10,634	11,040
Other assets	277	375
	$14,269	$14,068
LIABILITIES AND STOCKHOLDERS' EQUITY		
Current liabilities:		
Accounts payable	$ 746	$ 668
Accrued liabilities	696	1,012
Air traffic liability	1,044	963
Current maturities of long-term debt	190	163
Total current liabilities	2,676	2,806
Long-term debt less current maturities	3,325	3,498
Deferred income taxes	2,207	1,904
Deferred gains from sale and leaseback of aircraft	102	105
Other non-current liabilities	493	802
Commitments and contingencies		
Stockholders' equity:		
Common stock, $1.00 par value: 2,000,000,000 shares authorized; 807,611,634 shares issued in 2009 and 2008	808	808
Capital in excess of par value	1,216	1,215
Retained earnings	4,983	4,919
Accumulated other comprehensive loss	(578)	(984)
Treasury stock, at cost: 64,820,703 and 67,619,062 shares in 2009 and 2008, respectively	(963)	(1,005)
Total stockholders' equity	5,466	4,953
	$14,269	$14,068

See accompanying notes.

SOUTHWEST AIRLINES CO.

CONSOLIDATED STATEMENT OF INCOME

(In millions, except per share amounts)

	YEARS ENDED DECEMBER 31,		
	2009	2008	2007
OPERATING REVENUES:			
Passenger	$ 9,892	$10,549	$9,457
Freight	118	145	130
Other	340	329	274
Total operating revenues	10,350	11,023	9,861
OPERATING EXPENSES:			
Salaries, wages, and benefits	3,468	3,340	3,213
Fuel and oil	3,044	3,713	2,690
Maintenance materials and repairs	719	721	616
Aircraft rentals	186	154	156
Landing fees and other rentals	718	662	560
Depreciation and amortization	616	599	555
Other operating expenses	1,337	1,385	1,280
Total operating expenses	10,088	10,574	9,070
OPERATING INCOME	262	449	791
OTHER EXPENSES (INCOME):			
Interest expense	186	130	119
Capitalized interest	(21)	(25)	(50)
Interest income	(13)	(26)	(44)
Other (gains) losses, net	(54)	92	(292)
Total other expenses (income)	98	171	(267)
INCOME BEFORE INCOME TAXES	164	278	1,058
PROVISION FOR INCOME TAXES	65	100	413
NET INCOME	$ 99	$ 178	$ 645
NET INCOME PER SHARE, BASIC	$ .13	$ .24	$ .85
NET INCOME PER SHARE, DILUTED	$ .13	$ .24	$ .84

See accompanying notes.

SOUTHWEST AIRLINES CO.

CONSOLIDATED STATEMENT OF STOCKHOLDERS' EQUITY

	YEARS ENDED DECEMBER 31, 2009, 2008, AND 2007					
(In millions, except per share amounts)	**Common Stock**	**Capital in excess of par value**	**Retained earnings**	**Accumulated other comprehensive income (loss)**	**Treasury stock**	**Total**
Balance at December 31, 2006	$808	$1,142	$4,307	$ 582	$ (390)	$ 6,449
Purchase of shares of treasury stock	—	—	—	—	(1,001)	(1,001)
Issuance of common and treasury stock pursuant to Employee stock plans	—	—	(150)	—	288	138
Tax benefit of options exercised	—	28	—	—	—	28
Share-based compensation	—	37	—	—	—	37
Cash dividends, $.018 per share	—	—	(14)	—	—	(14)
Comprehensive income (loss)						
Net income	—	—	645	—	—	645
Unrealized gain on derivative instruments	—	—	—	636	—	636
Other	—	—	—	23	—	23
Total comprehensive income						1,304
Balance at December 31, 2007	$808	$1,207	$4,788	$ 1,241	$(1,103)	$ 6,941
Purchase of shares of treasury stock	—	—	—	—	(54)	(54)
Issuance of common and treasury stock pursuant to Employee stock plans	—	—	(34)	—	152	118
Tax benefit of options exercised	—	(10)	—	—	—	(10)
Share-based compensation	—	18	—	—	—	18
Cash dividends, $.018 per share	—	—	(13)	—	—	(13)
Comprehensive income (loss)						
Net income	—	—	178	—	—	178
Unrealized (loss) on derivative instruments	—	—	—	(2,166)	—	(2,166)
Other	—	—	—	(59)	—	(59)
Total comprehensive income (loss)						(2,047)
Balance at December 31, 2008	$808	$1,215	$4,919	$ (984)	$(1,005)	$ 4,953
Issuance of common and treasury stock pursuant to Employee stock plans	—	—	(22)	—	42	20
Tax benefit of options exercised	—	(13)	—	—	—	(13)
Share-based compensation	—	14	—	—	—	14
Cash dividends, $.018 per share	—	—	(13)	—	—	(13)
Comprehensive income (loss)						
Net income	—	—	99	—	—	99
Unrealized gain on derivative instruments	—	—	—	366	—	366
Other	—	—	—	40	—	40
Total comprehensive income (loss)						505
Balance at December 31, 2009	$808	$1,216	$4,983	$ (578)	$ (963)	$ 5,466

See accompanying notes.

SOUTHWEST AIRLINES CO.

CONSOLIDATED STATEMENT OF CASH FLOWS

(In millions)	YEARS ENDED DECEMBER 31, 2009	2008	2007
CASH FLOWS FROM OPERATING ACTIVITIES:			
Net income	$ 99	$ 178	$ 645
Adjustments to reconcile net income to cash provided by operating activities:			
Depreciation and amortization	616	599	555
Unrealized loss on fuel derivative instruments	14	206	(353)
Deferred income taxes	72	56	328
Amortization of deferred gains on sale and leaseback of aircraft	(12)	(12)	(14)
Share-based compensation expense	13	18	37
Excess tax benefits from share-based compensation arrangements	(1)	—	(28)
Changes in certain assets and liabilities:			
Accounts and other receivables	40	71	(38)
Other current assets	(27)	(21)	(73)
Accounts payable and accrued liabilities	59	(98)	149
Air traffic liability	81	32	131
Cash collateral received from (provided to) fuel derivative counterparties	(90)	(2,240)	1,460
Other, net	121	(310)	46
Net cash provided by (used in) operating activities	985	(1,521)	2,845
CASH FLOWS FROM INVESTING ACTIVITIES:			
Purchases of property and equipment, net	(585)	(923)	(1,331)
Purchases of short-term investments	(6,106)	(5,886)	(5,086)
Proceeds from sales of short-term investments	5,120	5,831	4,888
Other, net	2	—	—
Net cash used in investing activities	(1,569)	(978)	(1,529)
CASH FLOWS FROM FINANCING ACTIVITIES:			
Issuance of long-term debt	455	1,000	500
Proceeds from credit line borrowing	83	91	—
Proceeds from revolving credit facility	—	400	—
Proceeds from sale leaseback transactions	381	173	—
Proceeds from Employee stock plans	20	117	139
Payments of long-term debt and capital lease obligations	(86)	(55)	(122)
Payments of revolving credit facility	(400)	—	—
Payment of credit line borrowing	(97)	—	—
Payments of cash dividends	(13)	(13)	(14)
Repurchase of common stock	—	(54)	(1,001)
Excess tax benefits from share-based compensation arrangements	1	—	28
Other, net	(14)	(5)	(23)
Net cash provided by (used in) financing activities	330	1,654	(493)
NET CHANGE IN CASH AND CASH EQUIVALENTS	(254)	(845)	823
CASH AND CASH EQUIVALENTS AT BEGINNING OF PERIOD	1,368	2,213	1,390
CASH AND CASH EQUIVALENTS AT END OF PERIOD	$ 1,114	$ 1,368	$ 2,213
SUPPLEMENTAL DISCLOSURES			
Cash payments for:			
Interest, net of amount capitalized	$ 152	$ 100	$ 63
Income taxes	$ 5	$ 71	$ 94

See accompanying notes.

NOTES TO CONSOLIDATED FINANCIAL STATEMENTS
December 31, 2009

1. SUMMARY OF SIGNIFICANT ACCOUNTING POLICIES

Basis of Presentation

Southwest Airlines Co. (the Company) is a major domestic airline that provides point-to-point, low-fare service. The Consolidated Financial Statements include the accounts of the Company and its wholly owned subsidiaries. All significant inter-entity balances and transactions have been eliminated. The preparation of financial statements in conformity with generally accepted accounting principles in the United States (GAAP) requires management to make estimates and assumptions that affect the amounts reported in the financial statements and accompanying notes. Actual results could differ from these estimates.

Certain prior period amounts have been reclassified to conform to the current presentation. In the Consolidated Balance Sheet as of December 31, 2008, the Company's cash collateral deposits related to fuel derivatives that have been provided to a counterparty have been adjusted to show a "net" presentation against the fair value of the Company's fuel derivative instruments. The entire portion of cash collateral deposits as of December 31, 2008, $240 million, has been reclassified to reduce "Other deferred liabilities." In the Company's 2008 Form 10-K filing, these cash collateral deposits were presented "gross" and all were included as an increase to "Prepaid expenses and other current assets." This change in presentation was made in order to comply with the requirements of Accounting Standards Codification ("ASC") Subtopic 210-20 (originally issued as part of FIN 39-1, "Amendment of FASB Interpretation No. 39"), which was required to be adopted by the Company effective January 1, 2008. Following the Company's 2008 Form 10-K filing on February 2, 2009, the Company became aware that the requirements of ASC Subtopic 210-20 had not been properly applied to its financial derivative instruments within the financial statements. The Company determined that the effect of this error was not material to its financial statements and disclosures taken as a whole, and decided to apply ASC Subtopic 210-20 prospectively beginning with its first quarter 2009 Form 10-Q. Also, in the Consolidated Statement of Cash Flows for the years ended December 31, 2008, and 2007, the Company has reclassified certain unrealized noncash gains and/or losses recorded on fuel derivative instruments and the cash collateral received from counterparties to its fuel hedging program, in order to conform to the current year presentation. The current presentation now displays these items as separate captions, rather than netting them within other line items as in prior periods. These reclassifications had no impact on net cash flows provided by operations.

In preparing the accompanying consolidated financial statements, the Company has reviewed, as determined necessary by the Company's management, events that have occurred after December 31, 2009, up until the issuance of the financial statements, which occurred on January 29, 2010.

Cash and cash equivalents

Cash in excess of that necessary for operating requirements is invested in short-term, highly liquid, income-producing investments. Investments with maturities of three months or less are classified as cash and cash equivalents, which primarily consist of certificates of deposit, money market funds, and investment grade commercial paper issued by major corporations and financial institutions. Cash and cash equivalents are stated at cost, which approximates market value.

Short-term and noncurrent investments

Short-term investments consist of investments with maturities of greater than three months but less than twelve months. These are primarily investment grade commercial paper issued by major corporations and financial institutions, short-term securities issued by the U.S. Government, certificates of deposit issued by domestic banks, and certain auction rate securities that will be redeemed during 2010. All of these investments are classified as available-for-sale securities and are stated at fair value, which approximates costs, except for

NOTES TO CONSOLIDATED FINANCIAL STATEMENTS—(Continued)
December 31, 2009

$75 million in auction rate securities that are classified as trading securities as discussed in Note 11. For all short-term investments, at each reset period, the Company accounts for the transaction as "Proceeds from sales of short-term investments" for the security relinquished, and a "Purchase of short-investments" for the security purchased, in the accompanying Consolidated Statement of Cash Flows. Unrealized gains and losses, net of tax, are recognized in "Accumulated other comprehensive income (loss)" in the accompanying Consolidated Balance Sheet. Realized net gains on specific investments, which totaled $3 million in 2009, $13 million in 2008, and $17 million in 2007, are reflected in "Interest income" in the accompanying Consolidated Statement of Income.

Noncurrent investments consist of investments with maturities of greater than twelve months. At December 31, 2009, these primarily consisted of the Company's auction rate security instruments that it expects will not be redeemed during 2010. See Note 11 for further information. Noncurrent investments are included as a component of "Other assets" in the Consolidated Balance Sheet.

As of December 31, 2009 and 2008, the Company had provided cash collateral deposits to its fuel hedge counterparties totaling $330 million and $240 million, respectively. Although cash collateral amounts provided or held associated with fuel derivative instruments are not restricted in any way, investment earnings from these deposits generally must be remitted back to the entity that provided the deposit. Depending on the fair value of the Company's fuel derivative instruments, the amounts of collateral deposits held or provided at any point in time can fluctuate significantly. See Note 10 for further information on these collateral deposits and fuel derivative instruments.

Accounts and other receivables

Accounts and other receivables are carried at cost. They primarily consist of amounts due from credit card companies associated with sales of tickets for future travel and amounts due from counterparties associated with fuel derivative instruments that have settled. The amount of allowance for doubtful accounts as of December 31, 2009, 2008, and 2007 was immaterial. In addition, the provision for doubtful accounts and write-offs for 2009, 2008, and 2007 were immaterial.

Inventories

Inventories primarily consist of flight equipment expendable parts, materials, aircraft fuel, and supplies. All of these items are carried at average cost, less an allowance for obsolescence. These items are generally charged to expense when issued for use. The reserve for obsolescence was immaterial at December 31, 2009, 2008, and 2007. In addition, the Company's provision for obsolescence and write-offs for 2009, 2008, and 2007 was immaterial.

Property and equipment

Property and equipment is stated at cost. Depreciation is provided by the straight-line method to estimated residual values over periods generally ranging from 23 to 25 years for flight equipment and 5 to 30 years for ground property and equipment once the asset is placed in service. Residual values estimated for aircraft are generally 10 to 15 percent and for ground property and equipment range from zero to 10 percent. Property under capital leases and related obligations is recorded at an amount equal to the present value of future minimum lease payments computed on the basis of the Company's incremental borrowing rate or, when known, the interest rate implicit in the lease. Amortization of property under capital leases is on a straight-line basis over the lease term and is included in depreciation expense. Leasehold improvements generally are amortized on a straight-line basis over the shorter of the estimated useful life of the improvement or the remaining term of the lease.

NOTES TO CONSOLIDATED FINANCIAL STATEMENTS—(Continued)
December 31, 2009

When appropriate, the Company evaluates its long-lived assets used in operations for impairment. Impairment losses would be recorded when events and circumstances indicate that an asset might be impaired and the undiscounted cash flows to be generated by that asset are less than the carrying amounts of the asset. Factors that would indicate potential impairment include, but are not limited to, significant decreases in the market value of the long-lived asset(s), a significant change in the long-lived asset's physical condition, and operating or cash flow losses associated with the use of the long-lived asset. Excluding the impact of cash collateral deposits with counterparties, the Company continues to experience positive cash flow associated with its aircraft fleet, and there have been no impairments of long-lived assets recorded during 2009, 2008, or 2007.

Aircraft and engine maintenance

The cost of scheduled inspections and repairs and routine maintenance costs for all aircraft and engines are charged to maintenance expense as incurred. The Company has "power-by-the-hour" agreements related to virtually all of its aircraft engines with an external service provider. Under these agreements, which the Company has determined effectively transfer the risks associated with the maintenance on such engines to the counterparty, expense is recorded commensurate with each hour flown on an engine. Modifications that significantly enhance the operating performance or extend the useful lives of aircraft or engines are capitalized and amortized over the remaining life of the asset.

Intangible assets

Intangible assets primarily consist of acquired leasehold rights to certain airport owned gates at Chicago's Midway International Airport and take-off and landing slots at New York's LaGuardia International Airport. The rights to gates, which have a cost basis of approximately $60 million, are amortized on a straight-line basis over the expected useful life of the lease, approximately 20 years. The take-off and landing slots, which have a cost basis of approximately $7 million, are being amortized over the expected useful life of approximately 12 years. The accumulated amortization related to both the rights to gates and take-off and landing slots at December 31, 2009, and 2008, was $15 million and $12 million, respectively. The Company periodically assesses its intangible assets for impairment; however, no impairments have been noted.

Revenue recognition

Tickets sold are initially deferred as "Air traffic liability". Passenger revenue is recognized when transportation is provided. "Air traffic liability" primarily represents tickets sold for future travel dates and estimated refunds and exchanges of tickets sold for past travel dates. The majority of the Company's tickets sold are nonrefundable. Tickets that are sold but not flown on the travel date (whether refundable or nonrefundable) can be reused for another flight, up to a year from the date of sale, or refunded (if the ticket is refundable). A small percentage of tickets (or partial tickets) expire unused. The Company estimates the amount of future refunds and exchanges, net of forfeitures, for all unused tickets once the flight date has passed.

The Company is also required to collect certain taxes and fees from Customers on behalf of government agencies and remit these back to the applicable governmental entity on a periodic basis. These taxes and fees include U.S. federal transportation taxes, federal security charges, and airport passenger facility charges. These items are collected from Customers at the time they purchase their tickets, but are not included in Passenger revenue. The Company records a liability upon collection from the Customer and relieves the liability when payments are remitted to the applicable governmental agency.

Frequent flyer program

The Company records a liability for the estimated incremental cost of providing free travel under its Rapid Rewards frequent flyer program at the time an award is earned. The estimated incremental cost includes direct

NOTES TO CONSOLIDATED FINANCIAL STATEMENTS—(Continued)
December 31, 2009

passenger costs such as fuel, food, and other operational costs, but does not include any contribution to overhead or profit. The Company does not accrue for partially earned frequent flyer awards. Due to the expected expiration of a portion of frequent flyer credits making up partial awards, not all of them will turn into useable award tickets. Likewise, not all award tickets will be redeemed for future travel.

The Company also sells frequent flyer credits and related services to companies participating in its Rapid Rewards frequent flyer program. Funds received from the sale of flight segment credits are accounted for using the residual method. Under this method, the Company has determined the portion of funds received for sale of flight segment credits that relate to free travel, currently estimated at 75 percent of the amount received per flight segment credit sold. These amounts are deferred and recognized as "Passenger revenue" when the ultimate free travel awards are flown or the credits expire unused. The remaining 25 percent of the amount received per flight segment credit sold (the residual), which is assumed not to be associated with future travel, includes items such as access to the Company's frequent flyer program population for marketing/solicitation purposes on a monthly or quarterly basis, use of the Company's logo on co-branded credit cards, and other trademarks, designs, images, etc. of the Company for use in marketing materials. This residual portion is recognized in "Other revenue" in the period earned, which the Company has determined is the period in which it has fulfilled its obligation under the contract signed with the particular business partner, which is on a monthly or quarterly basis, upon sale, as the related marketing services are performed or provided.

Advertising

The Company expenses the costs of advertising as incurred. Advertising expense for the years ended December 31, 2009, 2008, and 2007 was $204 million, $199 million, and $191 million, respectively.

Share-based Employee compensation

The Company has share-based compensation plans covering the majority of its Employee groups, including a plan covering the Company's Board of Directors and plans related to employment contracts with the Chairman Emeritus of the Company. The Company accounts for share-based compensation based on its grant date fair value. See Note 14.

Financial derivative instruments

The Company accounts for financial derivative instruments at fair value and applies special hedge accounting rules where appropriate. The Company utilizes various derivative instruments, including crude oil, unleaded gasoline, and heating oil-based derivatives, to attempt to reduce the risk of its exposure to jet fuel price increases. These instruments primarily consist of purchased call options, collar structures, and fixed-price swap agreements, and upon proper qualification are accounted for as cash-flow hedges. The Company has also entered into interest rate swap agreements to convert a portion of its fixed-rate debt to floating rates and one floating-rate debt issuance to a fixed-rate. These interest rate hedges are accounted for as fair value hedges or as cash flow hedges.

Since the majority of the Company's financial derivative instruments are not traded on a market exchange, the Company estimates their fair values. Depending on the type of instrument, the values are determined by the use of present value methods or standard option value models with assumptions about commodity prices based on those observed in underlying markets. Also, since there is not a reliable forward market for jet fuel, the Company must estimate the future prices of jet fuel in order to measure the effectiveness of the hedging instruments in offsetting changes to those prices. Forward jet fuel prices are estimated through utilization of a statistical-based regression equation with data from market forward prices of like commodities. This equation is then adjusted for certain items, such as transportation costs, that are stated in the Company's fuel purchasing contracts with its vendors.

NOTES TO CONSOLIDATED FINANCIAL STATEMENTS—(Continued)
December 31, 2009

For the effective portion of settled hedges, the Company records the associated gains or losses as a component of "Fuel and oil" expense in the Consolidated Statement of Income. For amounts representing ineffectiveness, as defined, or changes in fair value of derivative instruments for which hedge accounting is not applied, the Company records any gains or losses as a component of "Other (gains) losses, net", in the Consolidated Statement of Income. Amounts that are paid or received associated with the purchase or sale of financial derivative instruments (i.e., premium costs of option contracts) are classified as a component of "Other (gains) losses, net", in the Consolidated Statement of Income in the period in which the instrument settles or expires. All cash flows associated with purchasing and selling derivatives are classified as operating cash flows in the Consolidated Statement of Cash Flows, within "Changes in certain assets and liabilities." See Note 10 for further information on hedge accounting and financial derivative instruments.

The Company classifies its cash collateral provided to or held from counterparties in a "net" presentation on the Consolidated Balance Sheet against the fair value of the derivative positions with those counterparties. See Note 10 for further information.

Software capitalization

The Company capitalizes certain internal and external costs related to the acquisition and development of internal use software during the application development stages of projects. The Company amortizes these costs using the straight-line method over the estimated useful life of the software which ranges from five to ten years. Costs incurred during the preliminary project or the post-implementation/operation stages of the project are expensed as incurred.

Income taxes

The Company accounts for deferred income taxes utilizing an asset and liability method, whereby deferred tax assets and liabilities are recognized based on the tax effects of temporary differences between the financial statements and the tax bases of assets and liabilities, as measured by current enacted tax rates. When appropriate, the Company evaluates the need for a valuation allowance to reduce deferred tax assets to estimated recoverable amounts.

The Company's policy for recording interest and penalties associated with uncertain tax positions is to record such items as a component of income before taxes. Penalties are recorded in "Other (gains) losses, net," and interest paid or received is recorded in interest expense or interest income, respectively, in the statement of income. For the year ended December 31, 2009, the Company recorded no interest related to uncertain tax positions.

Concentration Risk

Approximately 82 percent of the Company's Employees are unionized and are covered by collective bargaining agreements. Historically, the Company has managed this risk by maintaining positive relationships with its Employees and its Employee's Representatives. Employee groups that are under agreements that have become amendable and are currently in negotiations include its Aircraft Appearance Technicians and its Flight Dispatchers. The Company recently negotiated a Tentative Agreement with its Stock Clerks that will be voted on during 2010. The Company has no Employee group subject to agreements that become amendable during 2010.

The Company attempts to minimize its concentration risk with regards to its cash, cash equivalents, and its investment portfolio. This is accomplished by diversifying and limiting amounts among different counterparties, the type of investment, and the amount invested in any individual security or money market fund.

NOTES TO CONSOLIDATED FINANCIAL STATEMENTS—(Continued)
December 31, 2009

To manage risk associated with financial derivative instruments held, the Company selects and will periodically review counterparties based on credit ratings, limits its exposure to a single counterparty, and monitors the market position of the program and its relative market position with each counterparty. The Company also has agreements with counterparties containing early termination rights and/or bilateral collateral provisions whereby security is required if market risk exposure exceeds a specified threshold amount or credit ratings fall below certain levels. At December 31, 2009, the Company had provided $330 million in cash collateral deposits to its counterparties under these bilateral collateral provisions. Cash collateral deposits serve to decrease, but not totally eliminate, the credit risk associated with the Company's hedging program. See Note 10 for further information.

The Company operates an all-Boeing 737 fleet of aircraft. If the Company was unable to acquire additional aircraft or associated aircraft parts from Boeing, or Boeing was unable or unwilling to provide adequate support for its products, the Company's operations would be adversely impacted. In addition, the Company would be adversely impacted in the event of a mechanical or regulatory issue associated with the Boeing 737 aircraft type, whether as a result of downtime for part or all of the Company's fleet or because of a negative perception by the flying public. The Company is also dependent on a sole supplier for aircraft engines and would therefore also be materially adversely impacted in the event of a mechanical or regulatory issue associated with its engines. The Company considers its relationship with Boeing and other suppliers to be excellent and believes the advantages of operating a single fleet type outweigh the risks of such a strategy.

CHAPTER 2

DECISION POINT
A User's Focus The Boeing Company

In December 2009, **Boeing** received an order from **United Airlines** for 25 of **Boeing**'s long-awaited 787 wide-body jetliners. Valued at about $4 billion, the order was an important economic event for both Boeing and United.[1]

Typically, it takes Boeing two years to manufacture a plane, but there have been a series of delays in the production of the fuel-efficient and environmentally friendly 787s. Even for "firm" orders, such as the one from United, Boeing cautions its customers that various factors, such as an economic downturn and a delay in receiving parts from suppliers, could result in the rescheduling or cancellation of orders.[2]

Questions

1. *Is there a difference between an economic event and a business transaction that should be recorded in the accounting records?*
2. *Should Boeing record the order in its accounting records?*
3. *How important are cash flows and liquidity to Boeing?*

Mikael Damkier/Shutterstock.com

Analyzing Business Transactions

LEARNING OBJECTIVES

LO1 Explain how the concepts of recognition, valuation, and classification apply to business transactions and why they are important factors in ethical financial reporting. (pp. 90–93)

LO2 Explain the double-entry system and the usefulness of T accounts in analyzing business transactions. (pp. 93–98)

LO3 Demonstrate how the double-entry system is applied to common business transactions. (pp. 98–105)

LO4 Prepare a trial balance, and describe its value and limitations. (pp. 106–107)

LO5 Define the *chart of accounts*, record transactions in the general journal, and post transactions to the ledger. (pp. 108–112)

LO6 Show how the timing of transactions affects cash flows and liquidity. (pp. 112–114)

All business transactions require the application of three basic accounting concepts: recording a transaction at the right time, placing the right value on it, and calling it by the right name. Most accounting frauds and mistakes violate one or more of these basic accounting concepts. What you learn in this chapter will help you avoid making such mistakes. It will also help you recognize correct accounting practices.

FOCUS ON FINANCIAL STATEMENTS

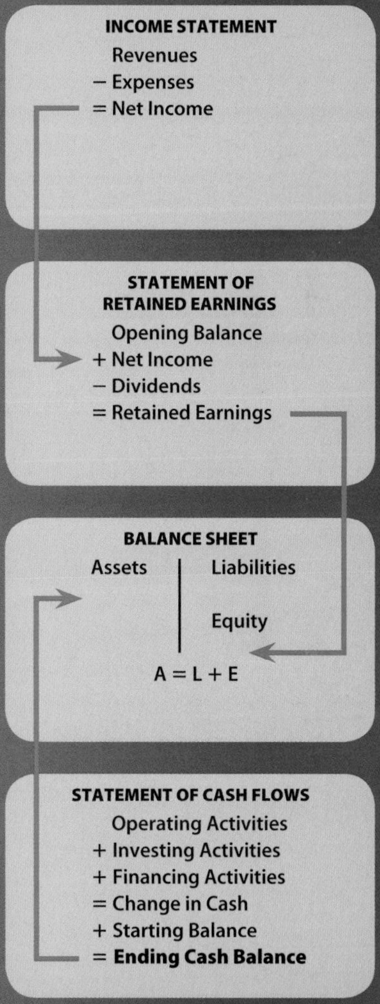

INCOME STATEMENT
Revenues
− Expenses
= Net Income

STATEMENT OF RETAINED EARNINGS
Opening Balance
+ Net Income
− Dividends
= Retained Earnings

BALANCE SHEET
Assets | Liabilities
Equity
A = L + E

STATEMENT OF CASH FLOWS
Operating Activities
+ Investing Activities
+ Financing Activities
= Change in Cash
+ Starting Balance
= **Ending Cash Balance**

Business transactions affect all the financial statements.

MEASUREMENT ISSUES

LO 1 Explain how the concepts of recognition, valuation, and classification apply to business transactions and why they are important factors in ethical financial reporting.

Business transactions are economic events that affect a company's financial position. As shown in Exhibit 2.1, to measure a business transaction, you must decide

- **The recognition issue:** when the transaction occurred
- **The valuation issue:** what value to place on the transaction
- **The classification issue:** how the components of the transaction should be categorized

These three issues—recognition, valuation, and classification—underlie almost every major decision in financial accounting today. They are at the heart of accounting for pension plans, mergers of giant companies, and international transactions. In discussing these issues, we follow generally accepted accounting principles (GAAP) and use an approach that promotes an understanding of basic accounting concepts. Keep in mind, however, that measurement issues can be controversial, and resolutions to them are not always as cut-and-dried as the ones presented here.

Recognition

STUDY NOTE: *In accounting, recognize means to record a transaction or event.*

The **recognition** issue refers to the difficulty of deciding *when* a business transaction should be recorded. The resolution of this issue is important because the date on which a transaction is recorded affects amounts in the financial statements.

To illustrate some of the factors involved in the recognition issue, suppose a company wants to purchase an office desk. The following events take place:

Event 1: An employee sends a purchase requisition for the desk to the purchasing department.

Event 2: The purchasing department sends a purchase order to the supplier.

Event 3: The supplier ships the desk.

Event 4: The company receives the desk.

Event 5: The company receives the bill from the supplier.

Event 6: The company pays the bill.

STUDY NOTE: *A purchase should usually not be recognized (recorded) before title is transferred because until that point, the vendor has not fulfilled its contractual obligation and the buyer has no liability.*

According to accounting tradition, a transaction should be recorded when title to merchandise passes from the supplier to the purchaser and creates an obligation to pay. Thus, depending on the details of the shipping agreement for the desk, the transaction should be recognized (recorded) at the time of either Event 3 or 4. We generally use this guideline in this book. However, many small businesses that have simple accounting systems do not record a transaction until they receive a bill (Event 5) or pay it (Event 6)

EXHIBIT 2.1
The Role of Measurement Issues

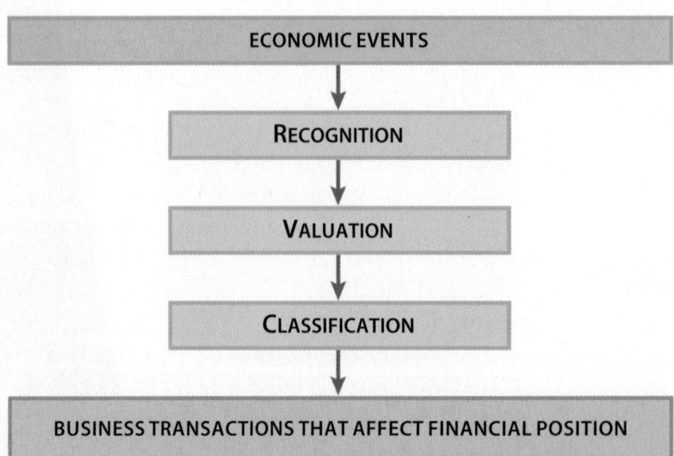

Focus on Business Practice

Accounting Policies: Where Do You Find Them?

iStock Photo

As the text explains, **United Airlines'** order of 25 **Boeing** jetliners was not an event that either the buyer or the seller should have recorded as a transaction. But when do companies record sales or purchase transactions? The answer to this question and others about companies' accounting policies can be found in the Summary of Significant Accounting Policies in their annual reports. For example, in that section of its annual report, Boeing states: "We recognize sales for commercial airplane deliveries as each unit is completed and accepted by the customer."[3]

because these are the implied points of title transfer. The predetermined time at which a transaction should be recorded is the **recognition point**.

Although purchase requisitions and purchase orders (Events 1 and 2) are economic events, they do not affect a company's financial position, and they are not recognized in the accounting records. Even the most important economic events may not be recognized in the accounting records. For example, the order of 25 jetliners described in the Decision Point was a very important economic event for both **Boeing** and **United**, but the recognition point for the transaction for both the buyer and the seller is several years in the future—that is, when the planes are delivered and title to them transfers from Boeing to United.

Here are some more examples of economic events that should and should not be recorded as business transactions:

Events That Are *Not* Recorded as Transactions	Events That *Are* Recorded as Transactions
A customer inquires about the availability of a service.	A customer buys a service.
A company hires a new employee for work to be performed.	A company pays an employee
A company signs a contract to provide a service in the future.	A company performs a service.

The recognition issue can be a difficult one to resolve. For example, consider an advertising agency that is planning a major advertising campaign for one of its clients. Employees may work on the plan several hours a day for a number of weeks. They add value to the plan as they develop it. Should this added value be recognized as the plan is being developed or at the time it is completed? In most cases, the increase in value is recorded at the time the plan is finished and the client is billed for it. However, if a plan is going to take several months to develop, the agency and the client may agree that the client will be billed at key points during its development. In that case, a transaction is recorded at each billing.

Valuation

STUDY NOTE: *The value of a transaction usually is based on a business document—a contract, a canceled check, or an invoice.*

The **valuation** issue focuses on assigning a monetary value to business transactions and the resulting assets and liabilities. Generally accepted accounting principles state that all business transactions should be valued at *fair value* when they occur. **Fair value** is the *exchange price* of an actual or potential business transaction between market participants.[4] This practice of recording transactions at exchange price at the point of recognition is referred to as the **cost principle**. The cost, or exchange price, is used because it is verifiable. For example, when the aircraft referred to in the Decision Point is finally complete and **Boeing** delivers the planes to **United**, the two entities will record the transaction in their respective records at the agreed-upon price.

Normally, an asset's value remains at its initial fair value or cost until the asset is sold, expires, or is consumed. However, if evidence of a change in the fair value of the

Focus on International Practices

IFRS The Challenge of Fair Value Accounting

The measurement of fair value is a major challenge in merging international financial reporting standards (IFRS) with U.S. GAAP. Both the International Accounting Standards Board (IASB) and the Financial Accounting Standards Board (FASB) are committed to this effort. Fair value is the price at which an asset *could* be sold or a liability settled in a current transaction between independent parties. It is not the actual, or historical, price at which the asset was acquired or the liability assumed. Because it represents the price in a hypothetical transaction, fair value is often difficult to measure. For example, when there is no ready market for an asset—as might be the case for an investment in a private company or for used factory equipment—the potential selling price may not be easy to determine.

iStock Photo

asset (or of a liability) occurs, an adjustment may be required. Different fair-value rules apply to different classes of assets. For example, a building or equipment remains at cost unless convincing evidence exists that the fair value is less than cost. In this case, a loss is recorded to reduce the value from its cost to fair value. Investments, on the other hand, are often accounted for at fair value, regardless of whether fair value is greater or less than cost.

Classification

Barter transactions, in which exchanges are made but no cash changes hands, can make valuation complicated. For example, if an office supply company provides a year's supply of computer paper to a local newspaper in exchange for an advertisement in the weekly paper, the value of the transactions equals the fair value of the items being traded.

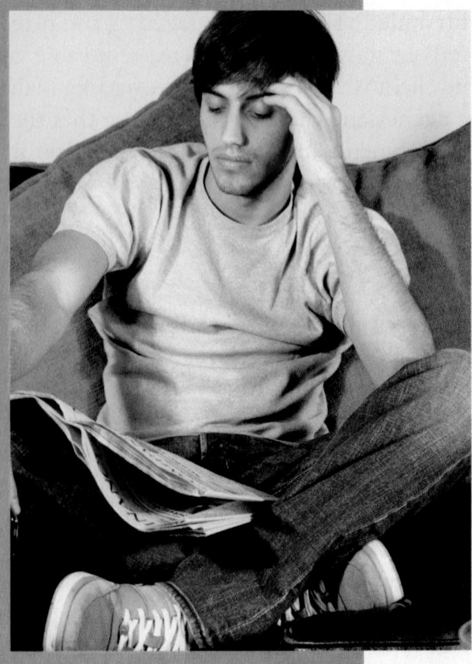

Martin Lee/mediablitzimages (uk) Limited/Alamy

The **classification** issue has to do with assigning all the transactions in which a business engages to appropriate categories, or accounts. Classification of debts can affect a company's ability to borrow money, and classification of purchases can affect its income. For example, if **CVS** buys paper towels to resell to customers, the cost would be recorded as an asset in the Inventory account. If the paper towels are used for cleaning in the store, the cost is an expense (a component of stockholders' equity).

As noted in the Decision Point, it will take **Boeing** several years to manufacture the 25 jetliners ordered by **United**. Over those years, many classification issues will arise. One of the most important is how to classify the numerous costs that Boeing will incur in building the planes. As you will see, generally accepted accounting principles require that these costs be classified as assets until the sale is recorded at the time the planes are delivered. At that time, they will be reclassified as expenses. In this way, the costs will offset the revenues from the sale. It will then be possible to tell whether Boeing made a profit or loss on the transaction.

As we explain later in the chapter, proper classification depends not only on correctly analyzing the effect of each transaction on a business, but also on maintaining a system of accounts that reflects that effect.

Ethics and Measurement Issues

Recognition, valuation, and classification are important factors in ethical financial reporting, and generally accepted accounting principles provide direction about their treatment. These guidelines are intended to help managers meet their obligation to their company's owners and to the public. Many of the most egregious financial reporting frauds that occurred in the last decade resulted from violations of these guidelines.

- **Computer Associates** violated the guidelines for recognition when it kept its books open a few days after the end of a reporting period so revenues could be counted a quarter earlier than they should have been. In all, the company prematurely reported $3.3 billion in revenues from 363 software contracts. When the SEC ordered the company to stop the practice, Computer Associates' stock price dropped by 43 percent in a single day.

- Among its many other transgressions, **Enron Corporation** violated the guidelines for valuation when it valued assets that it transferred to related companies at far more than their actual value.
- By a simple violation of the guidelines for classification, **WorldCom** (now **MCI**) perpetrated the largest financial fraud in history, which, until the recent financial crisis, resulted in the largest bankruptcy in history. Over a period of several years, the company recorded as assets expenditures that should have been classified as expenses; this had the effect of understating the company's expenses and overstating its income by more than $10 billion.

Stop & Apply

Four major issues underlie every accounting transaction: recognition, valuation, classification, and ethics. Match each of these issues to the statements below that are most closely associated with the issue. A company

1. records a piece of equipment at the price paid for it.
2. records the purchase of the equipment on the day on which it takes ownership.
3. records the equipment as an expense in order to show lower earnings.
4. records the equipment as an asset because it will benefit future periods.

iStock Photo

SOLUTION 1. valuation; 2. recognition; 3. ethics; 4. classification

DOUBLE-ENTRY SYSTEM

LO2 Explain the double-entry system and the usefulness of T accounts in analyzing business transactions.

The double-entry system, the backbone of accounting, evolved during the Renaissance. The first systematic description of double-entry bookkeeping appeared in 1494, two years after Columbus discovered America, in a mathematics book by Fra Luca Pacioli. Goethe, the famous German poet and dramatist, referred to double-entry bookkeeping as "one of the finest discoveries of the human intellect." Werner Sombart, an eminent economist-sociologist, believed that "double-entry bookkeeping is born of the same spirit as the system of Galileo and Newton."

__STUDY NOTE:__ Each transaction must include at least one debit and one credit, and the debit totals must equal the credit totals.

What is the significance of the double-entry system? The system is based on the *principle of duality*, which means that every economic event has two aspects—effort and reward, sacrifice and benefit, source and use—that offset, or balance, each other. In the **double-entry system**, each transaction must be recorded with at least one debit and one credit, and the total amount of the debits must equal the total amount of the credits. Because of the way it is designed, the whole system is always in balance. All accounting systems, no matter how sophisticated, are based on the principle of duality.

Accounts

Accounts are the basic storage units for accounting data and are used to accumulate amounts from similar transactions. An accounting system has a separate account for each asset, each liability, and each component of stockholders' equity, including revenues and expenses. Whether a company keeps records by hand or by computer, managers must be able to refer to accounts so that they can study their company's financial history and plan for the future. A very small company may need only a few dozen accounts; a multinational corporation may need thousands.

An account title should describe what is recorded in the account. However, account titles can be rather confusing. For example, *Fixed Assets, Plant and Equipment, Capital*

Assets, and *Long-Lived Assets* are all titles for long-term assets. Moreover, many account titles change over time as preferences and practices change.

STUDY NOTE: *When you come across an account title that you don't recognize, examine the context of the name—whether it is classified in the financial statements as an asset, a liability, or a component of stockholders' equity—and look for the kind of transaction that gave rise to the account.*

The T Account

The **T account** is a good place to begin the study of the double-entry system. Such an account has three parts: a title, which identifies the asset, liability, or stockholders' equity account; a left side, which is called the **debit** side; and a right side, which is called the **credit** side. The T account, so called because it resembles the letter *T*, is used to analyze transactions. It looks like this:

TITLE OF ACCOUNT	
Debit (left) side	Credit (right) side

STUDY NOTE: *It is important to realize that debit simply means "left side" and credit simply means "right side." Do not let preconceived ideas about what debit and credit mean affect your understanding.*

Any entry made on the left side of the account is a debit, and any entry made on the right side is a credit. The terms *debit* (abbreviated Dr., from the Latin *debere*) and *credit* (abbreviated Cr., from the Latin *credere*) are simply the accountant's words for "left" and "right" (*not* for "increase" or "decrease"). We present a more formal version of the T account, the ledger account form, later in this chapter.

The T Account Illustrated

Suppose a company had several transactions that involved the receipt or payment of cash. These transactions can be summarized in the Cash account by recording receipts on the left (debit) side of a T account and payments on the right (credit) side.

	CASH	
	50,000	35,000
	1,500	200
		600
	51,500	**35,800**
Bal.	**15,700**	

The cash receipts on the left total $51,500. (The total is written in smaller, blue color figures so that it cannot be confused with an actual debit entry.) The cash payments on the right side total $35,800. These totals are simply working totals, or **footings**. Footings, which are calculated at the end of each month, are an easy way to determine cash on hand. The difference in dollars between the total debit footing and the total credit footing is called the **balance**, or *account balance*. If the balance is a debit, it is written on the left side. If it is a credit, it is written on the right side. Notice that the Cash account has a debit balance of $15,700 ($51,500 – $35,800). This is the amount of cash the business has on hand at the end of the month.

Rules of Double-Entry Accounting

The two rules of the double-entry system are as follows:

- Every transaction affects at least two accounts.
- Total debits must equal total credits.

In other words, for every transaction, one or more accounts must be debited, or entered on the left side of the T account, and one or more accounts must be credited, or entered on the right side of the T account, and the total dollar amount of the debits must equal the total dollar amount of the credits.

Look again at the accounting equation:

Assets = Liabilities + Stockholders' Equity

You can see that if a debit increases assets, then a credit must be used to increase liabilities or stockholders' equity because they are on opposite sides of the equal sign. Likewise, if a credit decreases assets, then a debit must be used to decrease liabilities or stockholders' equity. These rules can be shown as follows:

ASSETS		=	LIABILITIES		+	STOCKHOLDERS' EQUITY	
Debit for increases (+)	Credit for decreases (−)		Debit for decreases (−)	Credit for increases (+)		Debit for decreases (−)	Credit for increases (+)

▲ Debit asset accounts to *increase* them.
▼ Credit asset accounts to *decrease* them.
▲ Credit liabilities and stockholders' equity accounts to *increase* them.
▼ Debit liabilities and stockholders' equity accounts to *decrease* them.

One of the more difficult points to understand is the application of double-entry rules to the components of stockholders' equity. The key is to remember that dividends and expenses are deductions from stockholders' equity. Thus, transactions that *increase* dividends or expenses *decrease* stockholders' equity. Consider this expanded version of the accounting equation:

Stockholders' Equity

Assets = Liabilities + Common Stock + Retained Earnings − Dividends + Revenues − Expenses

ASSETS		LIABILITIES		COMMON STOCK		RETAINED EARNINGS		DIVIDENDS		REVENUES		EXPENSES	
+	−	−	+	−	+	−	+	+	−	−	+	+	−
(Dr.)	(Cr.)	(Dr.)	(Cr.)	(Dr.)	(Cr.)	(Dr.)	(Cr.)	(Dr.)	(Cr.)	(Dr.)	(Cr.)	(Dr.)	(Cr.)

STUDY NOTE: *To remember the normal balances and the rules of debit and credit, use the acronym ADE: Asset accounts, Dividends, and Expenses are always increased by debits. All other accounts are increased by credits.*

Normal Balance

The **normal balance** of an account is its usual balance and is the side (debit or credit) that increases the account. Exhibit 2.2 summarizes the normal account balances of the major account categories.

EXHIBIT 2.2
Normal Account Balances of Major Account Categories

	Increases Recorded by		Normal Balance	
Account Category	**Debit**	**Credit**	**Debit**	**Credit**
Assets	x		x	
Liabilities		x		x
Stockholders' Equity:				
Common Stock		x		x
Retained Earnings		x		x
Dividends	x		x	
Revenues		x		x
Expenses	x		x	

EXHIBIT 2.3
Relationships of Stockholders' Equity Accounts

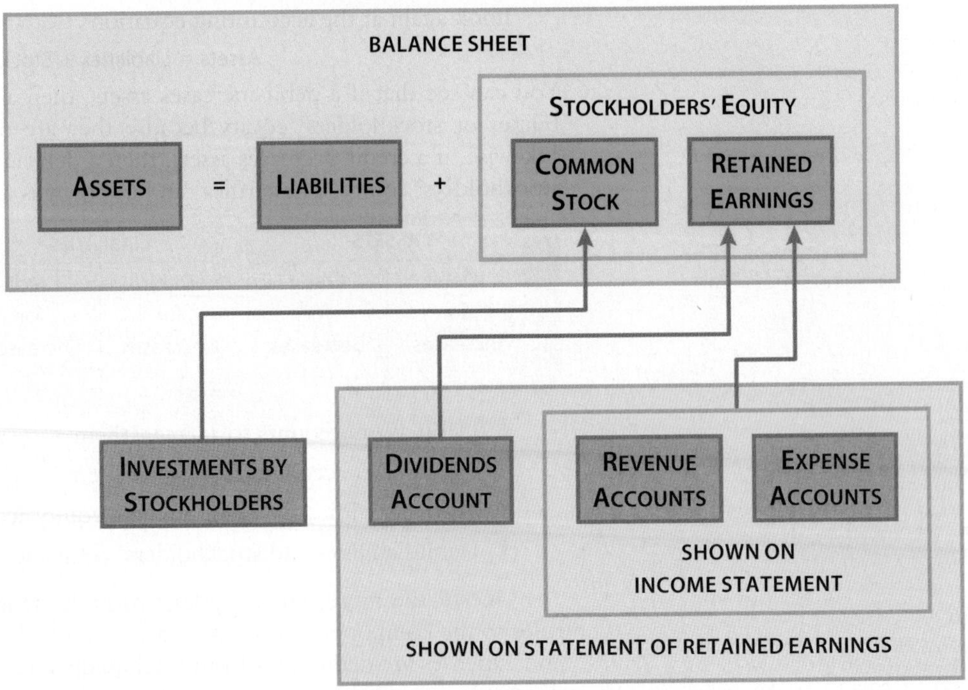

STUDY NOTE: *Although revenues and expenses are components of stockholders' equity, they appear on the income statement, not in the stockholders' equity section of the balance sheet (as shown here).*

Stockholders' Equity Accounts

Exhibit 2.3 illustrates how stockholders' equity accounts relate to each other and to the financial statements. The distinctions among these accounts are important for both legal purposes and financial reporting.

STUDY NOTE: *Although dividends are a component of stockholders' equity, they normally appear only in the statement of retained earnings. They do not appear in the stockholders' equity section of the balance sheet.*

- Stockholders' equity accounts represent the legal claims of stockholders to the assets of a corporation. The Common Stock account represents stockholders' claims arising from their investments in the business, and the Retained Earnings account represents stockholders' claims arising from profitable operations. Both are claims against the general assets of the company, not against specific assets. Dividends are deducted from the stockholders' claims on retained earnings and are shown on the statement of retained earnings.
- By law, investments by stockholders and dividends must be separated from revenues and expenses for both income tax purposes and financial reporting purposes.
- Managers need a detailed breakdown of revenues and expenses for budgeting and operating purposes. From the Revenue and Expense accounts on the income statement, they can identify the sources of all revenues and the nature of all expenses. In this way, accounting gives managers information about whether they have achieved a primary business goal—that is, whether they have enabled their company to earn a net income.

The Accounting Cycle

As Exhibit 2.4 shows, the **accounting cycle** is a series of six steps whose basic purpose is to produce financial statements for decision makers. It is called a "cycle" because the steps are repeated in the same order in every period in which financial statements are prepared. The steps are as follows:

Step 1: *Analyze* business transactions from source documents.

Step 2: *Record* the transactions by entering them in the general journal.

EXHIBIT 2.4
Overview of the Accounting Cycle

BUSINESS ACTIVITIES

Decisions and Actions

DECISION MAKERS

THE ACCOUNTING CYCLE

MEASUREMENT
1. Analyze business transactions from source documents.

COMMUNICATION
5. Prepare financial statements.

PROCESSING

2. Record the entries in the journal.

3. Post the entries to the ledger and prepare a trial balance.

4. Adjust the accounts and prepare an adjusted trial balance.

6. Close the accounts and prepare a post-closing trial balance.

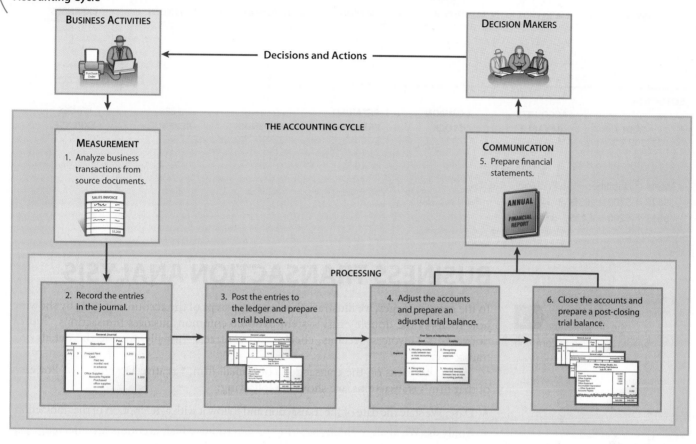

Step 3: *Post* the journal entries to the ledger and prepare a trial balance.

Step 4: *Adjust* the accounts and prepare an adjusted trial balance.

Step 5: *Prepare* financial statements to communicate to decision makers.

Step 6: *Close* the accounts and prepare a post-closing trial balance.

Note that Steps 3, 4, and 6 entail the preparation of trial balances. As explained later in this chapter, a trial balance is a device used to ensure that the accounts are in balance. The remainder of this chapter examines Steps 1–3 in detail.

Stop & Apply

You are given the following list of accounts with dollar amounts:

Dividends	$ 75	Common Stock	$300
Accounts Payable	200	Fees Revenue	250
Wages Expense	150	Retained Earnings	100
Cash	625		

Insert the account title at the top of its corresponding T account and enter the dollar amount as a normal balance in the account. Then show that the accounting equation is in balance.

iStock Photo

(continued)

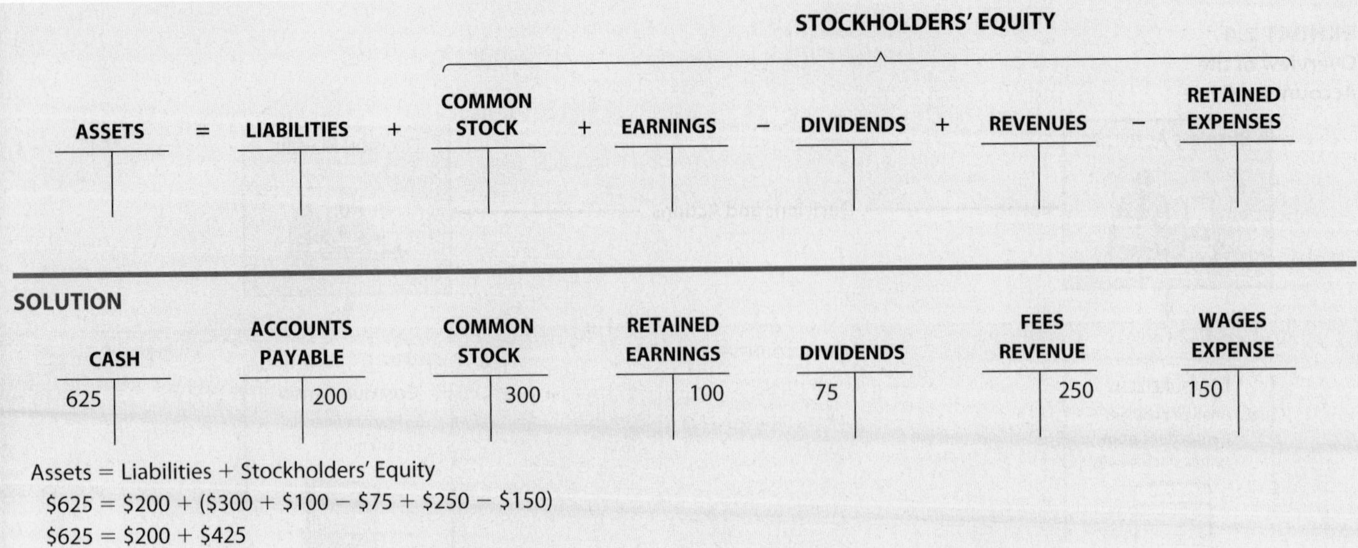

BUSINESS TRANSACTION ANALYSIS

LO 3 Demonstrate how the double-entry system is applied to common business transactions.

In the next few pages, we illustrate the first three steps of the accounting cycle by showing how to apply the double-entry system to some common business transactions. **Source documents**—invoices, receipts, checks, and contracts—usually provide the details of a transaction.

Here, we focus on the transactions of a small firm, Creative Designs, Inc. For each of that firm's transactions, we show the following:

- **Date:** We state the date of the transaction and follow it with a description of the transaction.
- **Analysis:** We analyze the transaction to determine which accounts are affected.
- **Application of Double-Entry:** We apply the rules of double-entry accounting by using T accounts to show how the transaction affects the accounting equation. Note that this is *not* part of the accounting records but is undertaken *before* recording a transaction in order to understand the effects of the transaction on the accounts.
- **Journal Entry:** A **journal entry** is a notation that records a single transaction in the chronological accounting record known as a **journal** (also sometimes called the *book of original entry* because it is where transactions first enter the accounting records). Each entry must be in proper journal form, which, as illustrated in the sections that follow, is a way of recording a transaction with the date, debit account, and debit amount shown on one line, and the credit account (indented) and credit amount shown on the next line. The amounts are shown in their respective debit and credit columns. (We discuss journals in more detail later in the chapter.)
- **Comment:** We provide a comment that will help you apply the rules of double entry.

Owner's Investment in the Business

July 1: To begin the business, Toni Ross files articles of incorporation with the state to receive her charter and invests $40,000 in Creative Designs, Inc., in exchange for 40,000 shares of $1 par value common stock.

Analysis: An owner's investment in the business

▲ *increases* the asset account *Cash* with a debit and

▲ *increases* the stockholders' equity account *Common Stock* with a credit.

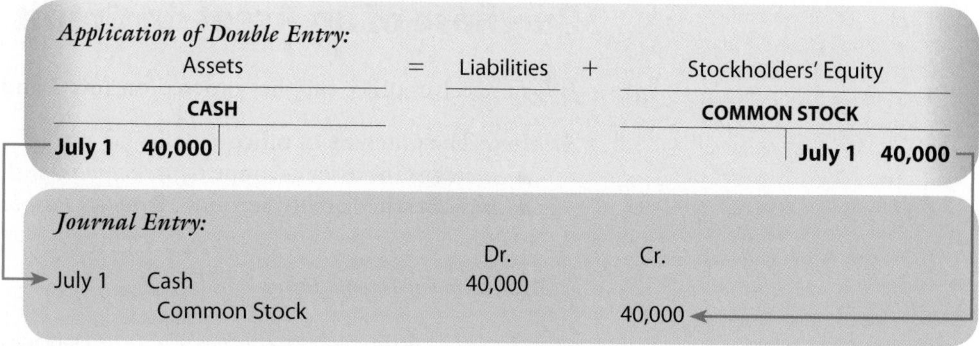

Comment: If Toni Ross had invested assets other than cash in the business, the appropriate asset accounts would be increased with a debit.

Economic Event That Is Not a Business Transaction

July 2: Orders office supplies, $5,200.

Comment: When an economic event does not constitute a business transaction, no entry is made. In this case, there is no confirmation that the supplies have been shipped or that title has passed.

Prepayment of Expenses in Cash

July 3: Rents an office; pays two months' rent in advance, $3,200.

Analysis: The prepayment of office rent in cash
- ▲ *increases* the asset account *Prepaid Rent* with a debit and
- ▼ *decreases* the asset account *Cash* with a credit.

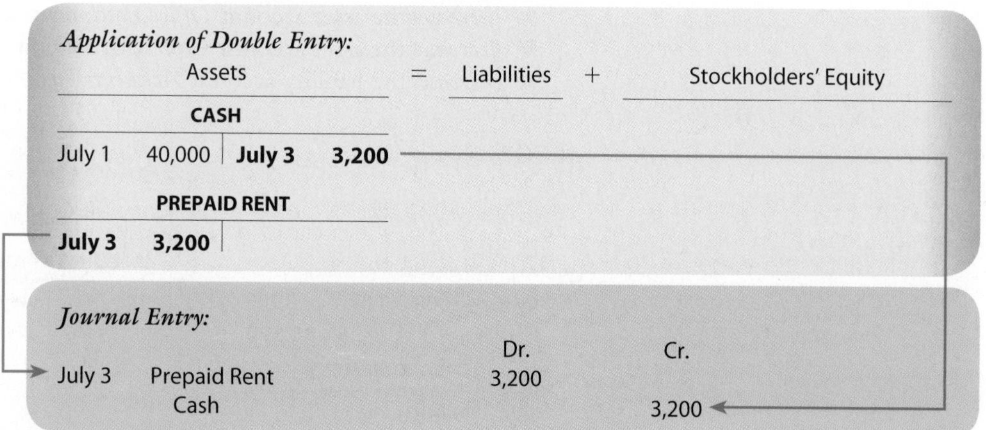

Comment: A prepaid expense is an asset because the expenditure will benefit future operations. This transaction does not affect the totals of assets, liabilities, or stockholders' equity because it simply trades one asset for another. If the company had paid only July's rent, the stockholders' equity account *Rent Expense* would be debited because the total benefit of the expenditure would be used up in the current month.

Purchase of an Asset on Credit

July 5: Receives office supplies ordered on July 2 and an invoice for $5,200.

Analysis: The purchase of office supplies on credit
- ▲ *increases* the asset account *Office Supplies* with a debit and
- ▲ *increases* the liability account *Accounts Payable* with a credit.

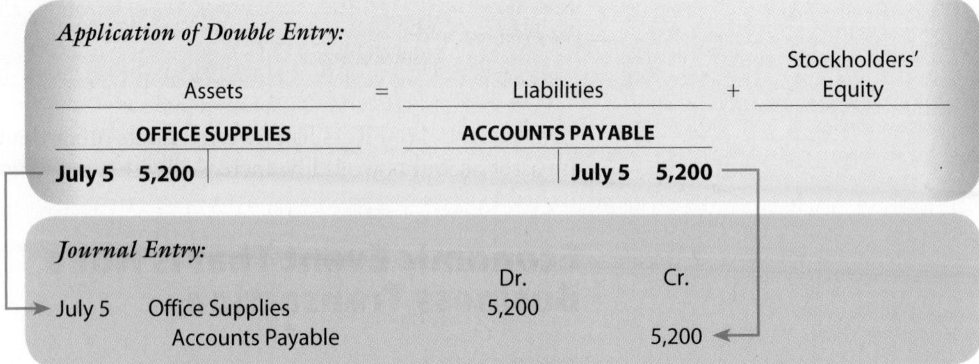

Comment: Office supplies in this transaction are considered an asset (prepaid expense) because they will not be used up in the current month and thus will benefit future periods. Accounts Payable is used when there is a delay between the time of the purchase and the time of payment.

Purchase of an Asset Partly in Cash and Partly on Credit

July 6: Purchases office equipment, $16,320; pays $13,320 in cash and agrees to pay the rest next month.

Analysis: The purchase of office equipment in cash and on credit
- ▲ *increases* the asset account *Office Equipment* with a debit,
- ▼ *decreases* the asset account *Cash* with a credit, and
- ▲ *increases* the liability account *Accounts Payable* with a credit.

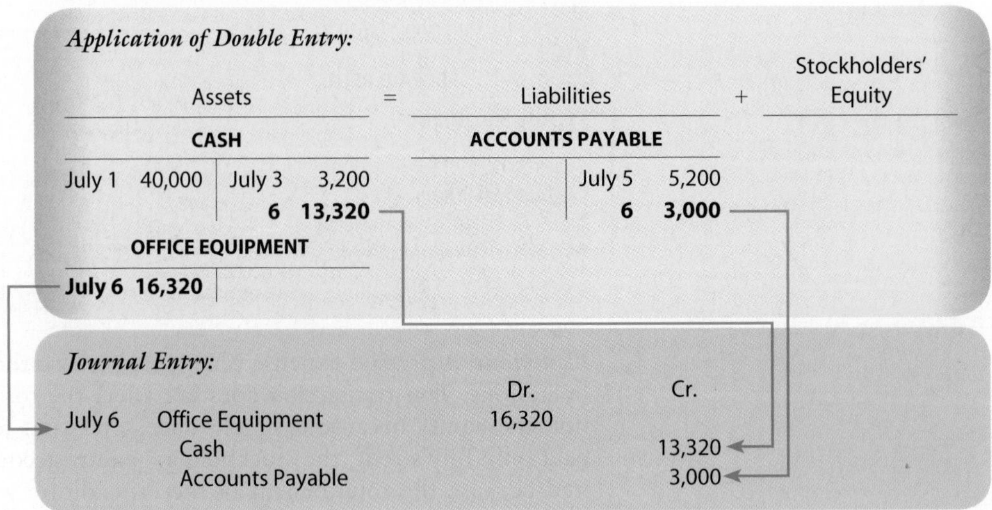

Comment: As this transaction illustrates, assets may be paid for partly in cash and partly on credit. When more than two accounts are involved in a journal entry, as they are in this one, it is called a **compound entry**.

Payment of a Liability

July 9: Makes a partial payment of the amount owed for the office supplies received on July 5, $2,600.

Analysis: A payment of a liability

- ▼ *decreases* the liability account *Accounts Payable* with a debit and
- ▼ *decreases* the asset account *Cash* with a credit.

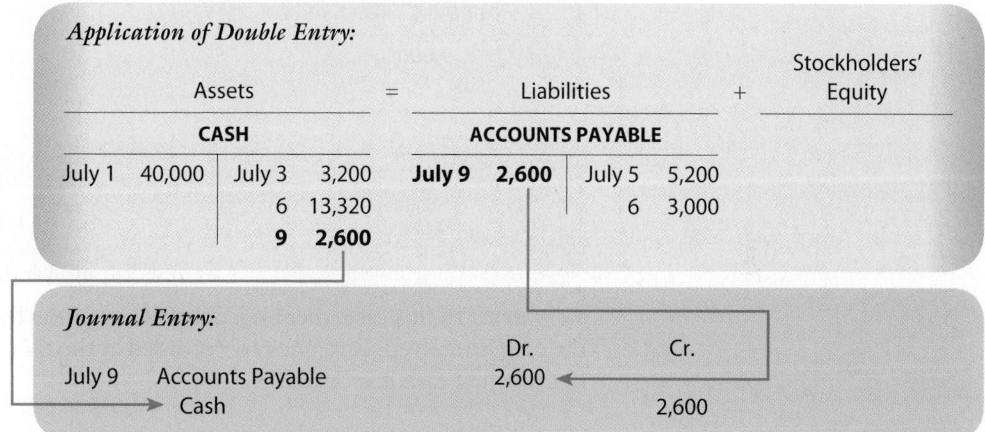

Comment: Note that the office supplies were recorded when they were purchased on July 5.

Revenue in Cash

July 10: Performs a service for an investment advisor by designing a series of brochures and collects a fee in cash, $2,800.

Analysis: A revenue received in cash

- ▲ *increases* the asset account *Cash* with a debit and
- ▲ *increases* the stockholders' equity account *Design Revenue* with a credit.

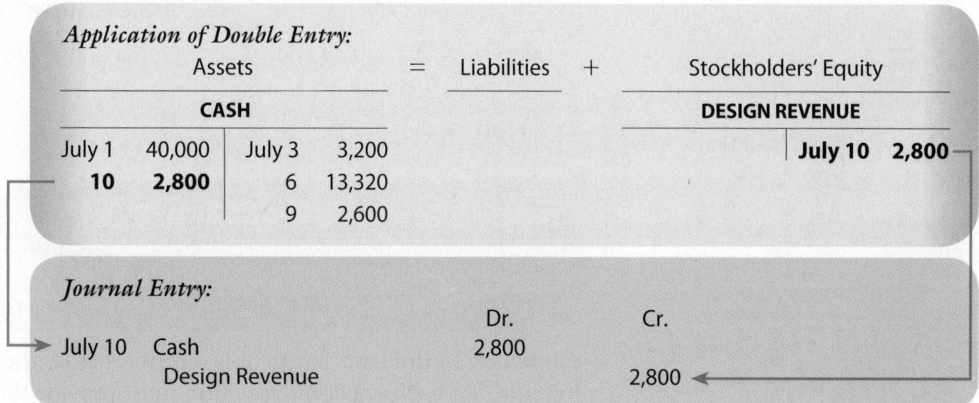

Comment: For this transaction, revenue is recognized when the service is provided and the cash is received.

Revenue on Credit

July 15: Performs a service for a department store by designing a TV commercial; bills for the fee now but will be paid later, $9,600.

Analysis: A revenue billed to a customer
- ▲ *increases* the asset account *Accounts Receivable* with a debit and
- ▲ *increases* the stockholders' equity account *Design Revenue* with a credit.

Accounts Receivable is used to indicate the customer's obligation until it is paid.

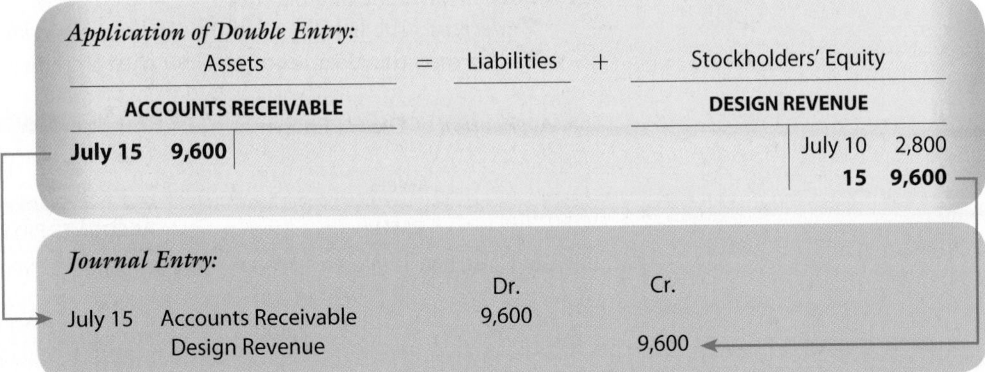

Comment: In this case, there is a delay between the time revenue is earned and the time the cash is received. Revenues are recorded at the time they are earned and billed regardless of when cash is received.

Revenue Received in Advance

July 19: Accepts an advance fee as a deposit on a series of brochures to be designed, $1,400.

Analysis: A revenue received in advance
- ▲ *increases* the asset account *Cash* with a debit and
- ▲ *increases* the liability account *Unearned Design Revenue* with a credit.

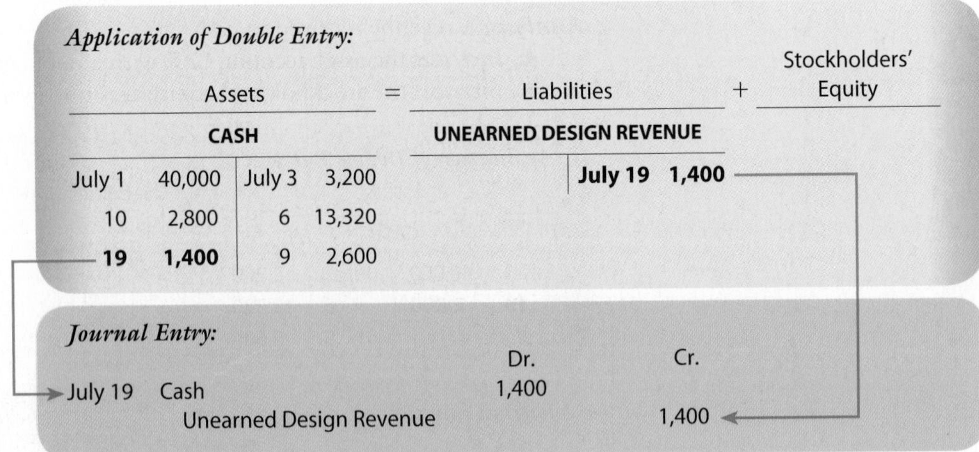

Comment: In this case, payment is received before the fees are earned. Unearned Design Revenue is a liability because the firm must provide the service or return the deposit.

Collection on Account

July 22: Receives partial payment from customer billed on July 15, $5,000.

Analysis: Collection of an account receivable from a customer previously billed

▲ *increases* the asset account *Cash* with a debit and
▼ *decreases* the asset account *Accounts Receivable* with a credit.

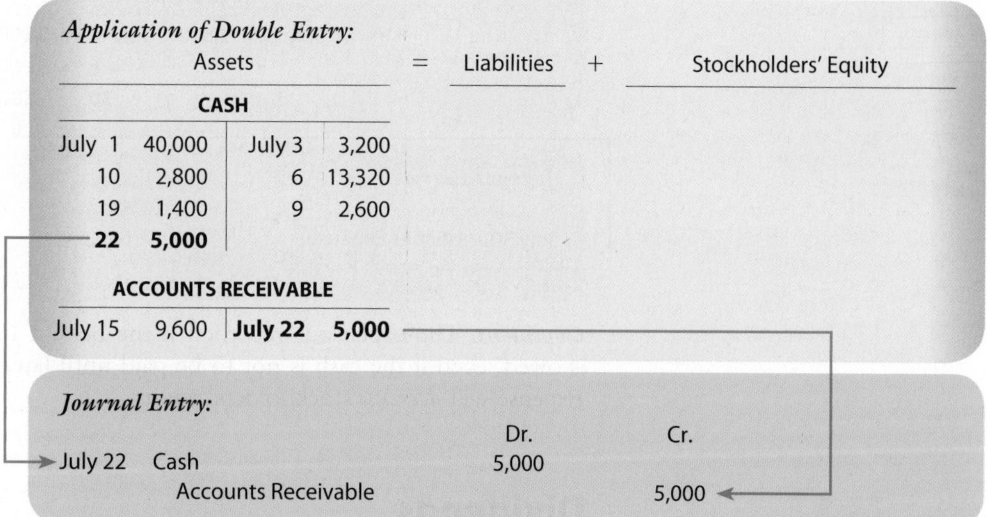

Comment: Note that the revenue related to this transaction was recorded on July 15. Thus, no revenue is recorded at this time.

Expense Paid in Cash

July 26: Pays employees four weeks' wages, $4,800.

Analysis: This cash expense

▲ *increases* the stockholders' equity account *Wages Expense* with a debit and
▼ *decreases* the asset account *Cash* with a credit.

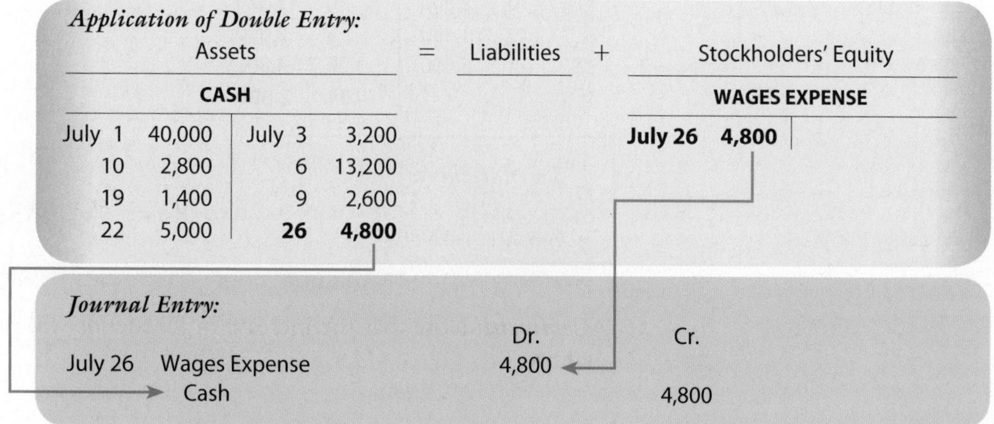

Comment: The increase in Wages Expense will *decrease* stockholders' equity.

Expense to Be Paid Later

July 30: Receives, but does not pay, the utility bill, which is due next month, $680.

Analysis: This cash expense

▲ *increases* the stockholders' equity account *Utilities Expense* with a debit and
▲ *increases* the liability account *Accounts Payable* with a credit.

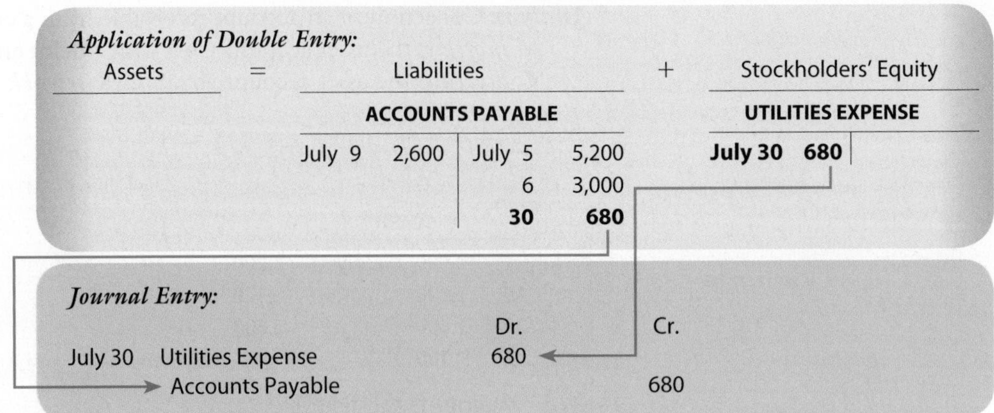

Comment: The expense is recorded if the benefit has been received and the amount is owed, even if the cash is not to be paid until later. Note that the increase in Utility Expense will *decrease* stockholders' equity.

Dividends

July 31: Declares and pays a dividend, $2,800.

Analysis: Payment of a cash dividend

▲ *increases* the stockholders' equity account *Dividends* with a debit and

▼ *decreases* the asset account *Cash* with a credit.

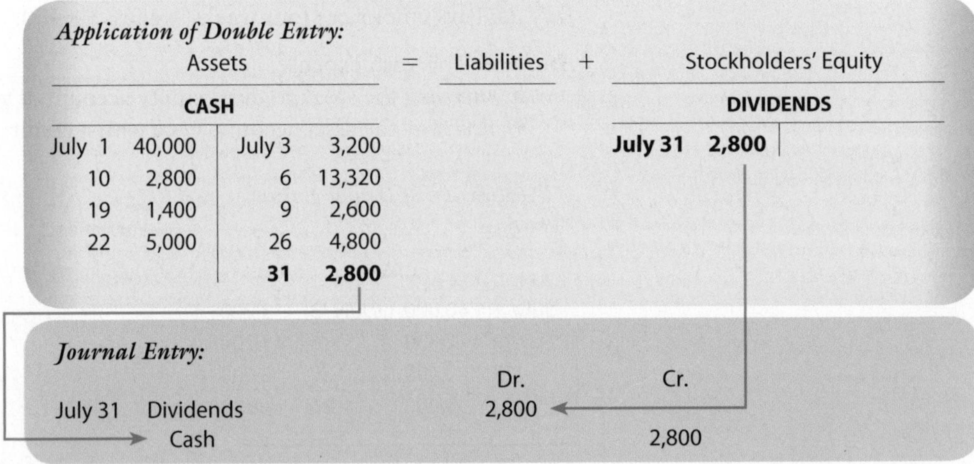

Comment: Note that the increase in Dividends will result in a *decrease* in stockholders' equity.

Summary of Transactions

Exhibit 2.5 uses the accounting equation to summarize the transactions of Creative Designs, Inc. Note that the income statement accounts appear under stockholders' equity and that the transactions in the Cash account will be reflected on the statement of cash flows. No Retained Earnings account appears under stockholders' equity because this is the company's first month of operation.

EXHIBIT 2.5
Summary of Transactions of Creative Designs, Inc.

Assets = Liabilities + Stockholders' Equity

CASH

July 1	40,000	July 3	3,200
10	2,800	6	13,320
19	1,400	9	2,600
22	5,000	26	4,800
		31	2,800
	49,200		26,720
Bal.	22,480		

This account links to the statement of cash flows.

ACCOUNTS RECEIVABLE

July 15	9,600	July 22	5,000
Bal.	4,600		

OFFICE SUPPLIES

July 5	5,200		

PREPAID RENT

July 3	3,200		

OFFICE EQUIPMENT

July 6	16,320		

ACCOUNTS PAYABLE

July 9	2,600	July 5	5,200
		6	3,000
		30	680
	2,600		8,880
		Bal.	6,280

UNEARNED DESIGN REVENUE

		July 19	1,400

COMMON STOCK

		July 1	40,000

DIVIDENDS

July 31	2,800		

DESIGN REVENUE

		July 10	2,800
		15	9,600
		Bal.	12,400

WAGES EXPENSE

July 26	4,800		

UTILITIES EXPENSE

July 30	680		

These accounts link to the income statement.

Assets	=	**Liabilities**	+	**Stockholders' Equity**
$51,800	=	$7,680	+	$44,120

Stop & Apply

Eva's Nail Salon, a company that provides manicures and pedicures, has the following accounts:

1. Cash
2. Accounts Receivable
3. Supplies
4. Equipment
5. Accounts Payable
6. Services Revenue
7. Wages Expense
8. Rent Expense

In the transaction list that follows, enter the account number in the appropriate debit or credit column.

	Debit	Credit
a. Made a rent payment for the current month.	____	____
b. Received cash from customers for current services.	____	____
c. Agreed to accept payment next month from a client for current services.	____	____
d. Purchased supplies on credit.	____	____
e. Purchased a new chair and table for cash.	____	____
f. Made a payment on accounts payable.	____	____

SOLUTION

	Debit	Credit
a. Made a rent payment for the current month.	8	1
b. Received cash from customers for current services.	1	6
c. Agreed to accept payment next month from a client for current services.	2	6
d. Purchased supplies on credit.	3	5
e. Purchased a new chair and table for cash.	4	1
f. Made a payment on accounts payable.	5	1

iStock Photo

THE TRIAL BALANCE

Prepare a trial balance and describe its value and limitations. LO 4

At the end of each step in the accounting cycle in which transactions have been recorded, the accountant prepares a trial balance. The **trial balance** tests that the total of debits and credits in the accounts are equal. Exhibit 2.6 shows a trial balance for Creative Designs, Inc., at the end of Step 3 in the accounting cycle. It was prepared from the accounts in Exhibit 2.5.

Preparation and Use of a Trial Balance

STUDY NOTE: *A trial balance is usually prepared at the end of an accounting period. It is an initial check that the accounts are in balance.*

Although a trial balance may be prepared at any time, it is usually prepared on the last day of an accounting period. These are the steps involved in preparing a trial balance:

Step 1: List each account that has a balance, with debit balances in the left column and credit balances in the right column. Accounts are listed in the order in which they appear on the financial statements.

Step 2: Add each column.

Step 3: Compare the totals of the columns.

Once in a while, a transaction leaves an account with a balance that isn't "normal." For example, when a company overdraws its bank account, its Cash account (an asset) will show a credit balance instead of a debit balance. The "abnormal" balance should be copied into the trial balance columns as it stands, as a debit or a credit.

The trial balance proves whether the accounts are in balance. *In balance* means that the total of all debits recorded equals the total of all credits recorded. But the trial balance does not prove that the transactions were analyzed correctly or recorded in the proper accounts. For example, there is no way of determining from a trial balance that a debit should have been made in the Office Supplies account rather than in the Office Equipment account. And the trial balance does not detect whether transactions have been omitted because equal debits and credits will have been omitted. Also, if an error of the same amount is made in both a debit and a credit, it will not be evident in the trial balance. The trial balance proves only that the debits and credits in the accounts are in balance.

EXHIBIT 2.6
Trial Balance

Creative Designs, Inc.
Trial Balance
July 31, 2011

Cash	$22,480	
Accounts Receivable	4,600	
Office Supplies	5,200	
Prepaid Rent	3,200	
Office Equipment	16,320	
Accounts Payable		$ 6,280
Unearned Design Revenue		1,400
Common Stock		40,000
Dividends	2,800	
Design Revenue		12,400
Wages Expense	4,800	
Utilities Expense	680	
	$60,080	$60,080

In computerized accounting systems, posting is done automatically and the trial balance can be easily prepared as often as needed. Any accounts with abnormal balances are highlighted for investigation.

Finding Trial Balance Errors

If the debit and credit balances in a trial balance are not equal, look for one or more of the following errors:

- A debit was entered in an account as a credit, or vice versa.
- The balance of an account was computed incorrectly.
- An error was made in carrying the account balance to the trial balance.
- The trial balance was summed incorrectly.

Other than simply adding the columns incorrectly, the two most common mistakes in preparing a trial balance are as follows:

- Recording an account as a credit when it usually carries a debit balance, or vice versa. This mistake causes the trial balance to be out of balance by an amount divisible by 2.
- Transposing two digits when transferring an amount to the trial balance (e.g., entering \$23,459 as \$23,549). This error causes the trial balance to be out of balance by a number divisible by 9.

So, if a trial balance is out of balance and the addition of the columns is correct, determine the amount by which the trial balance is out of balance and divide it first by 2 and then by 9. If the amount is divisible by 2, look in the trial balance for an amount that is equal to the quotient. If you find such an amount, chances are it is in the wrong column. If the amount is divisible by 9, trace each amount back to the T account balance, checking carefully for a transposition error. If neither of these techniques is successful in identifying the error, first recompute the balance of each T account. Then, if you still have not found the error, retrace each posting to the journal or the T account.

Stop & Apply

Prepare a trial balance from the following list of Ringo Company's accounts as of March 31, 2011. Compute the balance of cash.

Accounts Payable	\$ 9	Equipment	\$2
Accounts Receivable	5	Land	6
Building	10	Retained Earnings	8
Cash	?	Supplies	3
Common Stock	13		

SOLUTION

Ringo Company
Trial Balance
March 31, 2011

Cash	\$ 4	
Accounts Receivable	5	
Supplies	3	
Land	6	
Building	10	
Equipment	2	
Accounts Payable		\$ 9
Common Stock		13
Retained Earnings		8
	\$30	\$30

iStock Photo

RECORDING AND POSTING TRANSACTIONS

LO 5 Define the *chart of accounts*, record transactions in the general journal, and post transactions to the ledger.

Earlier in the chapter, we described how transactions are analyzed according to the rules of double entry and how a trial balance is prepared. In this section, we use a manual accounting system to demonstrate steps 1–3 of the accounting cycle.

Chart of Accounts

In a manual accounting system, each account is kept on a separate page or card. These pages or cards are placed together in a book or file called the general ledger. In the computerized systems that most companies have today, accounts are maintained electronically. However, accountants still refer to the group of company accounts as the *general ledger*, or simply the *ledger*.

STUDY NOTE: *A chart of accounts is a table of contents for the ledger. Typically, it lists accounts in the order in which they appear in the ledger, which is usually the order in which they appear on the financial statements. The numbering scheme allows some flexibility.*

To help identify accounts in the ledger and make them easy to find, accountants assign them numbers. A list of these numbers with the corresponding account titles is called a **chart of accounts**. A very simple chart of accounts appears in Exhibit 2.7. The first digit in the account number identifies the major financial statement classification—that is, an account number that begins with the digit 1 means that the account is an asset account, an account number that begins with a 2 means that the account is a liability account, and so forth. The second and third digits identify individual accounts. The gaps in the sequence of numbers allow the accountant to expand the number of accounts.

General Journal

STUDY NOTE: *The journal is a chronological record of events.*

Although transactions can be entered directly into the ledger accounts, this method makes identifying individual transactions or finding errors very difficult because the debit is recorded in one account and the credit in another. The solution is to record all transactions chronologically in a *journal*, which, as we noted earlier, is where transactions first enter the accounting records. Later, the debit and credit portions of each transaction are transferred to the appropriate accounts in the ledger.

Most businesses have more than one kind of journal. The simplest and most flexible kind is the **general journal**, the one we focus on here. Businesses may also have several special-purpose journals, each for recording a common transaction, such as credit sales, credit purchases, cash receipts, and cash disbursements. At this point, we cover only the general journal. Exhibit 2.8, which displays two of the transactions of Creative Designs that we discussed earlier, shows the format for recording entries in a general journal.

As you can see in Exhibit 2.8 (p. 110), the entries in a general journal include the following information about each transaction:

- **Date:** The year appears on the first line of the first column, the month appears on the next line of the first column, and the day appears in the second column opposite the month. For subsequent entries on the same page for the same month and year, the month and year can be omitted.
- **Accounts:** The names of the accounts debited and credited appear in the Description column. The names of the accounts that are debited are placed next to the left margin opposite the month and day; on the line below, the names of the accounts that are credited are indented.
- **Amounts:** The debit amounts appear in the Debit column opposite the accounts that are debited, and the credit amounts appear in the Credit column opposite the accounts that are credited.
- **Explanation:** An explanation of each transaction appears in the Description column below the account names. An explanation should be brief but sufficient to explain and identify the transaction.
- **Account numbers:** The account numbers appear in the Post. Ref. (posting reference) column, if they apply.

EXHIBIT 2.7
Chart of Accounts for a Small Business

Account Number	Account Name	Description
		Assets
111	Cash	Money and any medium of exchange (coins, currency, checks, money orders, and money on deposit in a bank)
112	Notes Receivable	Promissory notes due from others (written promises to pay definite sums of money at fixed future dates)
113	Accounts Receivable	Amounts due from others for revenues or sales on credit (sales on account)
116	Office Supplies	Prepaid expense; office supplies purchased and not used
117	Prepaid Rent	Prepaid expense; rent paid in advance and not used
118	Prepaid Insurance	Prepaid expense; insurance purchased and not expired
141	Land	Property owned for use in the business
142	Buildings	Structures owned for use in the business
143	Accumulated Depreciation—Buildings	Periodic allocation of the cost of buildings to expense; deducted from Buildings
146	Office Equipment	Office equipment owned for use in the business
147	Accumulated Depreciation—Office Equipment	Periodic allocation of the cost of office equipment to expense; deducted from Office Equipment
		Liabilities
211	Notes Payable	Promissory notes due to others
212	Accounts Payable	Amounts due to others for purchases on credit
213	Unearned Design Revenue	Unearned revenue; advance deposits for website design to be provided in the future
214	Wages Payable	Amounts due to employees for wages earned and not paid
215	Income Taxes Payable	Amounts due to government for income taxes owed and not paid
		Stockholders' Equity
311	Common Stock	Stockholders' investments in a corporation for which they receive shares of stock
312	Retained Earnings	Stockholders' claims against company assets derived from profitable operations
313	Dividends	Distributions of assets (usually cash) that reduce retained earnings
314	Income Summary	Temporary account used at the end of the accounting period to summarize the revenues and expenses for the period
		Revenues
411	Design Revenue	Revenues derived from website design services
		Expenses
511	Wages Expense	Amounts earned by employees
512	Utilities Expense	Amounts for utilities used, such as water, electricity, and gas
513	Telephone Expense	Amounts of telephone services used
514	Rent Expense	Amounts of rent on property and buildings used
515	Insurance Expense	Amounts for insurance expired
517	Office Supplies Expense	Amounts for office supplies used
518	Depreciation Expense—Buildings	Amount of buildings' cost allocated to expense
520	Depreciation Expense—Office Equipment	Amount of office equipment cost allocated to expense
521	Income Taxes Expense	Amount of tax on income

EXHIBIT 2.8
The General Journal

A	=	L	+	SE
+ 3,200				
− 3,200				

A	=	L	+	SE
+ 5,200		+ 5,200		

General Journal **Page 1**

Date		Description	Post. Ref.	Debit	Credit
2011					
July	3	Prepaid Rent		3,200	
		Cash			3,200
		Paid two months' rent in advance			
	5	Office Supplies		5,200	
		Accounts Payable			5,200
		Purchased office supplies on credit			

At the time the transactions are recorded, nothing is placed in the Post. Ref. column. (This column is sometimes called *LP* or *Folio.*) Later, if the company uses account numbers to identify accounts in the ledger, the account numbers are filled in. They provide a convenient cross-reference from the general journal to the ledger and indicate that the entry has been posted to the ledger. If the accounts are not numbered, the accountant uses a checkmark (✓) to signify that the entry has been posted.

General Ledger

The general journal is used to record the details of each transaction. The **general ledger** is used to update each account.

Ledger Account Form The T account is a simple, direct means of recording transactions. In practice, a somewhat more complicated form of the account is needed to record more information. The **ledger account form**, which contains four columns for dollar amounts, is illustrated in Exhibit 2.9.

STUDY NOTE: *A T account is a means of quickly analyzing a set of transactions. It is an abbreviated version of a ledger account. Ledger accounts, which provide more information, are used in the accounting records.*

The account title and number appear at the top of the account form. As in the journal, the transaction date appears in the first two columns. The Item column is rarely used to identify transactions because explanations already appear in the journal. The Post. Ref. column is used to note the journal page on which the original entry for the transaction can be found. The dollar amount is entered in the appropriate Debit or Credit column, and a new account balance is computed in the last two columns opposite each entry. The advantage of this account form over the T account is that the current balance of the account is readily available.

Posting After transactions have been entered in the journal, they must be transferred to the ledger. The process of transferring information from the journal to the ledger is called **posting**. Posting is usually done after several entries have been made. It could be done at the end of each day or less often, depending on the volume of transactions. As Exhibit 2.10 shows, in posting, each amount in the Debit column of the journal

EXHIBIT 2.9
Accounts Payable in the General Ledger

General Ledger

Accounts Payable **Account No. 212**

Date		Item	Post. Ref.	Debit	Credit	Balance Debit	Balance Credit
2011							
July	5		J1		5,200		5,200
	6		J1		3,000		8,200
	9		J1	2,600			5,600
	30		J2		680		6,280

EXHIBIT 2.10
Posting from the General Journal to the Ledger

A = L + SE
+ 680 − 680

General Journal — Page 2

Date		Description	Post. Ref.	Debit	Credit
2011					
July	30	Utilities Expense	512	680	
		Accounts Payable	212		680
		Received bill from utility company			

General Ledger

Accounts Payable — Account No. 212

Date		Item	Post. Ref.	Debit	Credit	Balance Debit	Balance Credit
2011							
July	5		J1		5,200		5,200
	6		J1		3,000		8,200
	9		J1	2,600			5,600
	30		J2		680		6,280

Utilities Expense — Account No. 512

Date		Item	Post. Ref.	Debit	Credit	Balance Debit	Balance Credit
2011							
July	30		J2	680		680	

is transferred to the Debit column of the appropriate account in the ledger, and each amount in the Credit column of the journal is transferred to the Credit column of the appropriate account in the ledger.

The steps in the posting process are as follows:

Step 1: In the ledger, locate the debit account named in the journal entry.

Step 2: Enter the date of the transaction in the ledger and in the Post. Ref. column, enter the journal page number from which the entry comes.

Step 3: In the Debit column of the ledger account, enter the amount of the debit as it appears in the journal.

Step 4: Calculate the account balance and enter it in the appropriate Balance column.

Step 5: Enter in the Post. Ref. column of the journal the account number to which the amount has been posted.

Step 6: Repeat the same five steps for the credit side of the journal entry.

Notice that Step 5 is the last step in the posting process for each debit and credit. As noted earlier, in addition to serving as an easy reference between the journal entry and the ledger account, this entry in the Post. Ref. column of the journal indicates that the entry has been posted to the ledger.

Some Notes on Presentation

Exhibit 2.11 (p. 112) offers some guidance on how to format financial statements, trial balances, journals, and ledgers in accordance with common accounting conventions.

EXHIBIT 2.11
Formatting Guidelines

MCDONALD'S FINANCIAL HIGHLIGHTS (in millions)*

	2009	2008
Cash	$ 1,796.0	$ 2,063.4
Accounts receivable	1,060.4	931.2
Inventories	106.2	111.5
Prepaid expenses	453.7	411.5
Total current assets	$ 3,416.3	$ 3,517.6
Property and equipment (net)	21,531.5	20,254.5
Other assets	5,277.1	4,689.4
Total assets	$30,224.9	$28,461.5

*Adapted from 2009 Annual Report

❶ A ruled line appears in financial reports before each subtotal and total to indicate that the amounts above are added or subtracted. It is common practice to use a double line under a final total to show that it has been verified.

❷ Dollar signs ($) are required in all financial statements and in the trial balance and other schedules. On these reports, a dollar sign should be placed before the first amount in each column and before the first amount in a column following a ruled line. Dollar signs in the same column are aligned. Dollar signs are not used in journals and ledgers.

❸ On normal unruled paper, commas and decimal points are used when recording dollar amonts. On the paper used in journals and ledgers, commas and decimal points are unnecessary because ruled columns are provided to properly align dollars and cents. Comas, dollar signs, and decimal points are also unnecessary in electronic spreadsheets. In this book, because most problems and illustrations are in whole dollar amounts, the cents column usually is omitted. When accountants deal with whole dollars, they often use a dash in the cents column to indicate whole dollars rather than taking the time to write zeros.

❹ Account names are capitalized when referenced in text or listed in work documents like the journal or ledger. In financial statement, however, only the first word of an account name is capitalized.

Stop & Apply

Prepare journal entries for the transactions described below. Use these account numbers—Cash (111), Supplies (114), and Accounts Payable (212)—to show in the Post. Ref. column that the entries have been posted:

June 4 Purchased supplies for $40 on credit
8 Paid for the supplies purchased on June 4

SOLUTION

Date		Description	Post. Ref.	Debit	Credit
June	4	Supplies	114	40	
		Accounts Payable	212		40
		Purchased supplies on credit			
	8	Accounts Payable	212	40	
		Cash	111		40
		Paid amount due for supplies			

iStock Photo

CASH FLOWS AND THE TIMING OF TRANSACTIONS

Show how the timing of transactions affects cash flows and liquidity. 

To avoid financial distress, a company must be able to pay its bills on time. Because the timing of cash flows is critical to maintaining adequate liquidity to pay bills, managers and other users of financial information must understand the difference between transactions that generate immediate cash and those that do not. Consider the transactions of Creative Designs, Inc., shown in Exhibit 2.12. Most of them involve either an inflow or outflow of cash.

As you can see in Exhibit 2.12, Creative Designs' Cash account has more transactions than any of its other accounts. Look at the transactions of July 10, 15, and 22:

- July 10: Creative Designs received a cash payment of $2,800.
- July 15: The firm billed a customer $9,600 for a service it had already performed.
- July 22: The firm received a partial payment of $5,000 from the customer, but it had not received the remaining $4,600 by the end of the month.

EXHIBIT 2.12
Transactions of Creative Designs, Inc.

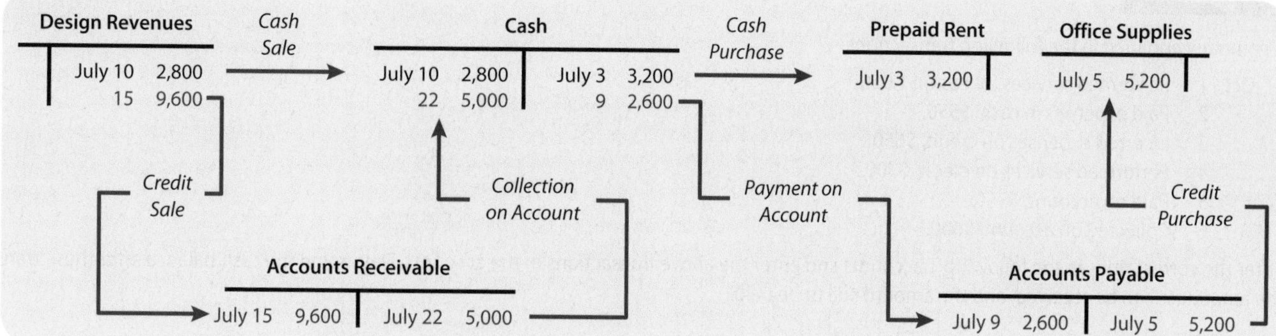

Because Creative Designs incurred expenses in providing this service, it must pay careful attention to its cash flows and liquidity.

One way Creative Designs can manage its expenditures is to rely on its creditors to give it time to pay. Compare the transactions of July 3, 5, and 9 in Exhibit 2.12.

- July 3: Creative Designs prepaid rent of $3,200. That immediate cash outlay may have caused a strain on the business.
- July 5: The firm received an invoice for office supplies in the amount of $5,200. In this case, it took advantage of the opportunity to defer payment.
- July 9: The firm paid $2,600, but it deferred paying the remaining $2,600 until after the end of the month.

STUDY NOTE: *Recording revenues and expenses when they occur will provide a clear picture of a company's profitability on the income statement. The change in cash flows will provide a clear picture of the company's liquidity on the statement of cash flows.*

Of course, Creative Designs expects to receive the rest of the cash from the customer that it billed on July 15, and it must eventually pay the rest of what it owes on the office supplies. In the meantime, the firm must perform a delicate balancing act with its cash flows to ensure that it achieves the goal of liquidity so that it can grow and be profitable.

Large companies face the same challenge, but often on a much greater scale. Recall from the Decision Point that **Boeing** takes years to plan and make the aircraft that the Chinese government and other customers order. At the end of 2009, Boeing had orders for 8,888 airplanes totaling $250.5 billion, or about $28 million per plane.[5] Think of the cash outlays that Boeing must make before it delivers the planes and collects payment for them. To maintain liquidity so that Boeing can eventually reap the rewards of delivering the planes, Boeing's management must carefully plan the company's needs for cash.

iStock Photo

Focus on Business Practice

Should Earnings Be Aligned with Cash Flows?

When **Electronic Data Systems Corporation (EDS)**, the large computer services company, announced that it was reducing past earnings by $2.24 billion to implement a new accounting rule that would more closely align its earnings with cash flows, financial analysts responded very positively. They had previously been critical of EDS for recording revenue from its long-term contracts when the contracts were signed rather than when the cash was received. In fact, about 40 percent of EDS's revenue had been recognized well before the cash was to be received. "Finally," said one analyst, "maybe, we'll see cash flows moving in line with earnings."[6] Although there are natural and unavoidable differences between earnings and cash flows, it is best if accounting rules do not exaggerate these differences.

Stop & Apply

A company engaged in the following transactions:

Oct. 1 Performed services for cash, $1,050.
2 Paid expenses in cash, $550.
3 Incurred expenses on credit, $650.
4 Performed services on credit, $900.
5 Paid on account, $350.
6 Collected on account, $600.

Enter the correct titles in the following T accounts and enter the above transactions in the accounts. Determine the cash balance after these transactions, the amount still to be received, and the amount still to be paid.

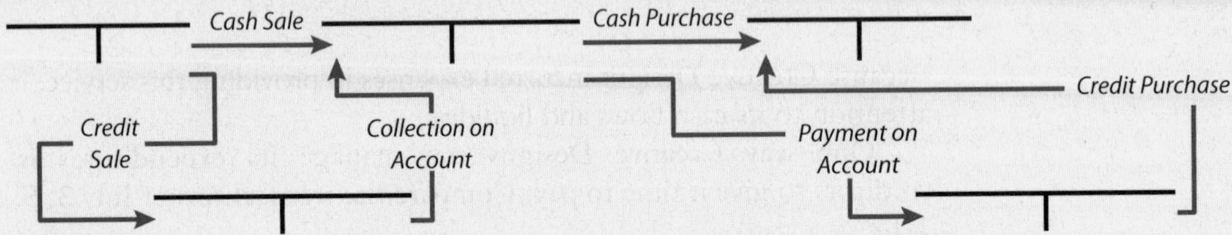

SOLUTION

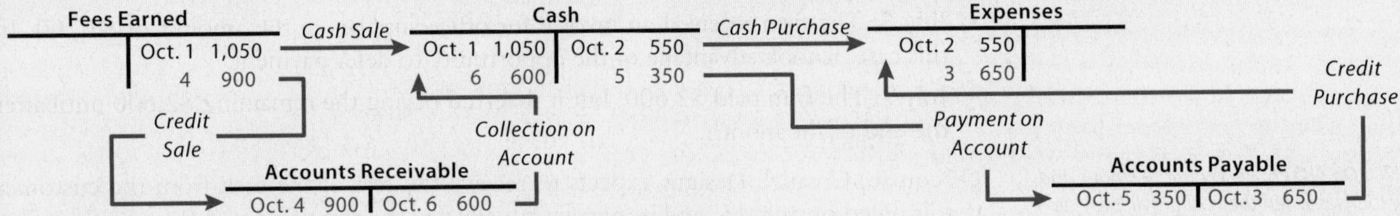

Cash balance after transactions: $1,050 + $600 – $550 – $350 = $750
Amount still to be received: $900 – $600 = $300
Amount still to be paid: $650 – $350 = $300

iStock Photo

A look back at ▸ The Boeing Company

The Decision Point at the beginning of the chapter described the order that **United Airlines** placed with **Boeing** for 25 jetliners. It posed the following questions:

1. Is there a difference between an economic event and a business transaction that should be recorded in the accounting records?
2. Should Boeing record the order in its accounting records?
3. How important are cash flows and liquidity to Boeing?

Despite its importance, the order did not constitute a business transaction, and neither the buyer nor the seller should have recognized it in its accounting records. At the time **United** placed the order, Boeing had not yet built the planes. Until it delivers them and title to them shifts to United, Boeing cannot record any revenue.

Even for "firm" orders like this one, Boeing cautions that "[c]hanges in the economic environment and the financial condition of the airline industry and our customers could result in customer requests to reschedule or cancel contractual orders."[7] In fact, in the period following the 9/11 attacks on the World Trade Center and the war in Iraq, many airlines canceled or renegotiated orders they had placed with Boeing. The ongoing energy crisis is also causing airlines to rethink their orders.

RATIO

Financial Ratio: Asset Turnover

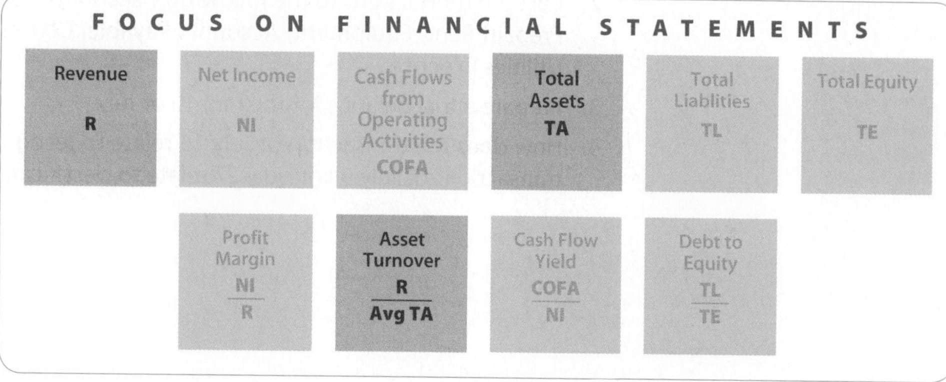

Because it takes almost two years to manufacture an airplane, Boeing must pay close attention to its liquidity and profitability. One measure related to both these goals is the **asset turnover** ratio, which shows how productive assets are in generating revenues. In other words, it shows how much revenue is generated by each dollar of assets invested in operations. This ratio is different from the profit margin ratio, a profitability measure that we introduced in Chapter 1, in that it uses important elements from two financial statements: the income statement and the balance sheet. Since the income statement represents a period of time and the balance sheet is a "snapshot" at the end of the period, average total assets (ending balance plus beginning balance divided by 2) from the balance sheet must be computed to put the measures on a more comparable basis. Using amounts (in millions) from Boeing's income statement and balance sheet in its annual report, we can calculate the company's cash return on assets as follows:[8]

		2009	2008
Asset Turnover =	$\frac{\text{Revenue}}{\text{Average Total Assets}}$	$\frac{\$68{,}281}{(\$62{,}053 + \$53{,}779) \div 2}$	$\frac{\$60{,}909}{(\$53{,}779 + \$58{,}986) \div 2}$
		$\frac{\$68{,}281}{\$57{,}916}$	$\frac{\$60{,}909}{\$56{,}383}$
		1.2 times	1.1 times

What do these results tell us? First, in 2009, Boeing produced about $1.2 of revenue for each dollar invested in assets compared with $1.1 per dollar of assets generated a year earlier. Second, revenues increase from $60,909 million to $68,281 million, while average total assets increased slightly from $56,383 to $57,916. This trend indicates a weak revenue-generating ability and will weaken Boeing's profitability and liquidity.

Review Problem

Transaction Analysis, T Accounts, Journal Entries, and the Trial Balance

After completing yoga school, John Lee started a private practice. The transactions of his company in July are as follows:

2011

July	1	John Lee invested $4,000 in 4,000 shares of $1 par value common stock of his newly chartered company, Yoga Center, Inc.
	3	Paid $600 in advance for two months' rent of a studio.
	9	Purchased supplies for $400 in cash.
	12	Purchased $800 of equipment on credit; made a 25 percent down payment.
	15	Gave a private yoga lesson for a fee of $70 on credit.
	18	Made a payment of $100 on the equipment purchased on July 12.
	27	Paid a utility bill of $80.

Required

1. Prepare a journal entry for each of the company's transactions.
2. Post the transactions to the following T accounts: Cash, Accounts Receivable, Supplies, Prepaid Rent, Equipment, Accounts Payable, Common Stock, Yoga Fees Earned, and Utilities Expense.
3. Prepare a trial balance for the month of July.
4. How does the transaction of July 15 relate to recognition and cash flows? How do the transactions of July 9 and July 27 relate to classification?

ANSWERS TO REVIEW PROBLEM

1. Journal entries:

	A	B	C	D	E	F	G	H
1	July	1		Cash			4,000	
2					Common Stock			4,000
3						Issued 4,000 shares of $1 par		
4						value common stock		
5		3		Prepaid Rent			600	
6					Cash			600
7						Paid two months' rent in advance		
8						for a studio		
9		9		Supplies			400	
10					Cash			400
11						Purchased supplies for cash		
12		12		Equipment			800	
13					Accounts Payable			600
14					Cash			200
15						Purchased equipment on credit,		
16						paying 25 percent down		
17		15		Accounts Receivable			70	
18					Yoga Fees Earned			70
19						Fee on credit for private yoga lesson		
20		18		Accounts Payable			100	
21					Cash			100
22						Partial payment for equipment		
23						purchased July 12		
24		27		Utilities Expense			80	
25					Cash			80
26						Paid utility bill		
27								

2. Transactions posted to T accounts

	A	B	C	D	E	F	G	H	I	J	K	L	M
1			**Cash**							**Accounts Payable**			
2	July	1	4,000	July	3	600		July	18	100	July	12	600
3					9	400					*Bal.*		*500*
4					12	200							
5					18	100				**Common Stock**			
6					27	80					July	1	4,000
7			*4,000*			*1,380*							
8	*Bal.*		*2,620*							**Yoga Fees Earned**			
9											July	15	70
10			**Accounts Receivable**										
11	July	15	70							**Utilities Expense**			
12								July	27	80			
13			**Supplies**										
14	July	9	400										
15													
16			**Prepaid Rent**										
17	July	3	600										
18													
19			**Equipment**										
20	July	12	800										
21													

3. Trial balance:

	A	B	C	D	E
1			**Yoga Center, Inc.**		
2			**Trial Balance**		
3			**July 31, 2011**		
4					
5	Cash			$2,620	
6	Accounts Receivable			70	
7	Supplies			400	
8	Prepaid Rent			600	
9	Equipment			800	
10	Accounts Payable				$ 500
11	Common Stock				4,000
12	Yoga Fees Earned				70
13	Utilities Expense			80	
14				$4,570	$4,570
15					

4. The transaction of July 15 is recorded, or recognized, on that date even though the company received no cash. The company earned the revenue by providing the service, and the customer accepted the service and now has an obligation to pay for it. The transaction is recorded as an account receivable because the company allowed the customer to pay for the service later. The transaction of July 9 is classified as an asset, Supplies, because these supplies will benefit the company in the future. The transaction of July 27 is classified as an expense, Utilities Expense, because the utilities have already been used and will not benefit the company in the future.

Stop & Review

LO 1 Explain how the concepts of recognition, valuation, and classification apply to business transactions and why they are important factors in ethical financial reporting.

To measure a business transaction, you must determine when the transaction occurred (the recognition issue), what value to place on the transaction (the valuation issue), and how the components of the transaction should be categorized (the classification issue). In general, recognition should occur when title passes, and a transaction should be valued at the exchange price—the fair value or cost at the time the transaction is recognized. Classification refers to assigning transactions to the appropriate accounts. Generally accepted accounting principles provide guidance about the treatment of these three basic measurement issues. Failure to follow these guidelines is a major reason some companies issue unethical financial statements.

LO 2 Explain the double-entry system and the usefulness of T accounts in analyzing business transactions.

In the double-entry system, each transaction must be recorded with at least one debit and one credit, and the total amount of the debits must equal the total amount of the credits. Each asset, liability, and component of stockholders' equity, including revenues and expenses, has a separate account, which is a device for storing transaction data. The T account is a useful tool for quickly analyzing the effects of transactions. It shows how increases and decreases in assets, liabilities, and stockholders' equity are debited and credited to the appropriate accounts. The accounting cycle is a series of steps whose basic purpose is to produce financial statements for decision makers.

LO 3 Demonstrate how the double-entry system is applied to common business transactions.

The double-entry system is applied by analyzing transactions to determine which accounts are affected and by using T accounts to show how the transactions affect the accounting equation. The transactions are recorded in journal form with the date, debit account, and debit amount shown on one line, and the credit account (indented) and credit amount on the next line. The amounts are shown in their respective debit and credit columns.

LO 4 Prepare a trial balance and describe its value and limitations.

A trial balance is used to check that the debit and credit balances are equal. It is prepared by listing each account balance in the appropriate Debit or Credit column. The two columns are then added, and the totals are compared. The major limitation of a trial balance is that even when it shows that debit and credit balances are equal, it does not guarantee that the transactions were analyzed correctly or recorded in the proper accounts.

LO 5 Define the *chart of accounts*, record transactions in the general journal, and post transactions to the ledger.

The chart of accounts is a list of account numbers and titles; it serves as a table of contents for the ledger. The general journal is a chronological record of all transactions; it contains the date of each transaction, the titles of the accounts involved, the amounts debited and credited, and an explanation of each entry. After transactions have been entered in the general journal, they are posted to the ledger. Posting is done by transferring the amounts in the Debit and Credit columns of the general journal to the Debit and Credit columns of the corresponding account in the ledger. After each entry is posted, a new balance is entered in the appropriate Balance column.

LO 6 Show how the timing of transactions affects cash flows and liquidity.

Some transactions generate immediate cash. For those that do not, there is a holding period in either Accounts Receivable or Accounts Payable before the cash is received or paid. The timing of cash flows is critical to a company's ability to maintain adequate liquidity.

Key Terms and Ratios

Accounting cycle 96 (LO2)
Accounts 93 (LO2)
Balance 94 (LO2)
Chart of accounts 108 (LO5)
Classification 92 (LO1)
Compound entry 101 (LO3)
Cost principle 91 (LO1)
Credit 94 (LO2)
Debit 94 (LO2)
Double-entry system 93 (LO2)
Fair value 91 (LO1)
Footings 94 (LO2)
General journal 108 (LO5)
General ledger 110 (LO5)
Journal 98 (LO3)
Journal entry 98 (LO3)
Ledger account form 110 (LO5)
Normal balance 95 (LO2)
Posting 110 (LO5)
Recognition 90 (LO1)
Recognition point 91 (LO1)
Source documents 98 (LO3)
T account 94 (LO2)
Trial balance 106 (LO4)
Valuation 91 (LO1)

RATIO
Asset turnover 115 (LO6)

Chapter Assignments Building Your Basic Knowledge and Skills

Short Exercises

LO 1 **Recognition**

SE 1. Which of the following events would be recognized and entered in the accounting records of Tania Corporation? Why?

Jan. 10 Tania Corporation places an order for office supplies.
Feb. 15 Tania Corporation receives the office supplies and a bill for them.
Mar. 1 Tania Corporation pays for the office supplies.

LO 1, 3 **Recognition, Valuation, and Classification**

SE 2. Tell how the concepts of recognition, valuation, and classification apply to this transaction:

CASH			SUPPLIES		
	June 1	2,000	June 1	2,000	

LO 1, 5 **Classification of Accounts**

SE 3. Tell whether each of the following accounts is (a) an asset, (b) a liability, (c) a revenue, (d) an expense, or (e) none of these:

1. Accounts Payable
2. Supplies
3. Dividends
4. Fees Earned
5. Rent Expense
6. Accounts Receivable
7. Unearned Revenue
8. Equipment

LO 2 **Normal Balances**

SE 4. Tell whether the normal balance of each account in **SE 3** is a debit or a credit.

LO 3 **Transaction Analysis**

SE 5. For each transaction that follows, indicate which account is debited and which account is credited.

Mar. 2 Robert Smile started a recording business, Smile's Recordings, Inc., by investing $10,000 in exchange for common stock.
5 Purchased equipment for $5,000 in cash.

Mar. 7 Purchased supplies on credit for $600.
19 Received cash for recording services performed, $1,000.
22 Received cash for recording services to be performed, $1,200.
25 Paid the rent for March, $1,300.
31 Billed a customer for recording services performed, $500.

LO 3 **Recording Transactions in T Accounts**

SE 6. Set up T accounts and record each transaction in **SE 5.** Determine the balance of each account.

LO 4 **Preparing a Trial Balance**

SE 7. From the T accounts created in **SE 6,** prepare a trial balance dated March 31, 2011.

LO 3 **Transaction Analysis**

SE 8. For each transaction that follows, indicate which account is debited and which account is credited.

May 2 Leon Bear started a computer programming business, Bear's Programming Service, Inc., by investing $5,000 in exchange for common stock.
5 Purchased a computer for $2,500 in cash.
7 Purchased supplies on credit for $300.
19 Received cash for programming services performed, $500.
22 Received cash for programming services to be performed, $600.
25 Paid the rent for May, $650.
31 Billed a customer for programming services performed, $250.

LO 3 **Recording Transactions in T Accounts**

SE 9. Set up T accounts and record each transaction in **SE 8.** Determine the balance of each account.

LO 4 **Preparing a Trial Balance**

SE 10. From the T accounts created in **SE 8,** prepare a trial balance dated May 31, 2011.

LO 5 **Recording Transactions in the General Journal**

SE 11. Prepare a general journal form like the one in Exhibit 2.8 and label it Page 4. Record the following transactions in the journal:

Sept. 6 Billed a customer for services performed, $3,800.
16 Received partial payment from the customer billed on September 6, $1,800.

LO 5 **Posting to the Ledger Accounts**

SE 12. Prepare ledger account forms like the ones in Exhibit 2.9 for the following accounts: Cash (111), Accounts Receivable (113), and Service Revenue (411). Post the transactions that are recorded in **SE 11** to the ledger accounts, at the same time making the proper posting references. Also prepare a trial balance.

LO 5 **Recording Transactions in the General Journal**

SE 13. Record the transactions in **SE 5** in the general journal.

LO 6 **Timing and Cash Flows**

SE 14. Set up a T account for Cash and record the portion of each of the following transactions, if any, that affect cash. How do these transactions affect the company's liquidity?

CASH

Jan.	2	Provided services for cash, $1,200
	4	Paid expenses in cash, $700
	8	Provided services on credit, $1,100
	9	Incurred expenses on credit, $800

Financial Ratio: Asset Turnover

RATIO

SE 15. In 2011, a company had revenues of $29,700, beginning total assets of $26,000, and ending total assets of $28,000. Calculate the company's asset turnover ratio for 2011. (*Note:* Round answer to one decimal place.)

Exercises

Discussion Questions

LO 1, 2, 3

E 1. Develop a brief answer to each of the following questions.

1. Which is the most important issue in recording a transaction: recognition, valuation, or classification?
2. What is an example of how a company can make false financial statements through a violation of the recognition concept?
3. How are assets and expenses related, and why are the debit and credit effects for assets and expenses the same?
4. In what way are unearned revenues the opposite of prepaid expenses?

LO 4, 5, 6

E 2. Develop a brief answer to each of the following questions.

1. Which account would be most likely to have an account balance that is not normal?
2. A company incurs a cost for a part that is needed to repair a piece of equipment. Is the cost an asset or an expense? Explain.
3. If a company's cash flows for expenses temporarily exceed its cash flows from revenues, how might it make up the difference so that it can maintain liquidity?
4. How would the asset accounts in the chart of accounts for Creative Designs, Inc., differ if it were a retail company that sold advertising products instead of a service company that designs ads?

LO 1

Recognition

E 3. Which of the following events would be recognized and recorded in the accounting records of Villa Corporation on the date indicated?

Jan.	15	Villa Corporation offers to purchase a tract of land for $140,000. There is a high likelihood that the offer will be accepted.
Feb.	2	Villa Corporation receives notice that its rent will increase from $500 to $600 per month effective March 1.
Mar.	29	Villa Corporation receives its utility bill for the month of March. The bill is not due until April 9.
June	10	Villa Corporation places an order for new office equipment costing $21,000.
July	6	The office equipment Villa Corporation ordered on June 10 arrives. Payment is not due until August 1.

LO 1

Application of Recognition Point

E 4. Davis Parts Shop, Inc., uses a large amount of supplies in its business. The following table summarizes selected transaction data for supplies that Davis Parts Shop purchased:

Order	Date Shipped	Date Received	Amount
a	June 26	July 5	$ 600
b	July 10	15	1,500
c	16	22	900
d	23	30	1,200
e	27	Aug. 1	1,400
f	Aug. 3	7	1,000

Determine the total purchases of supplies for July alone under each of the following assumptions:

1. Davis Parts Shop, Inc., recognizes purchases when orders are shipped.
2. Davis Parts Shop, Inc., recognizes purchases when orders are received.

LO 2 **T Accounts, Normal Balance, and the Accounting Equation**

E 5. You are given the following list of accounts with dollar amounts:

Rent Expense	$ 450	Dividends	$375
Cash	1,725	Accounts Payable	600
Service Revenue	750	Common Stock	900
Retained Earnings	300		

Insert each account name at the top of its corresponding T account and enter the dollar amount as a normal balance in the account. Then show that the accounting equation is in balance.

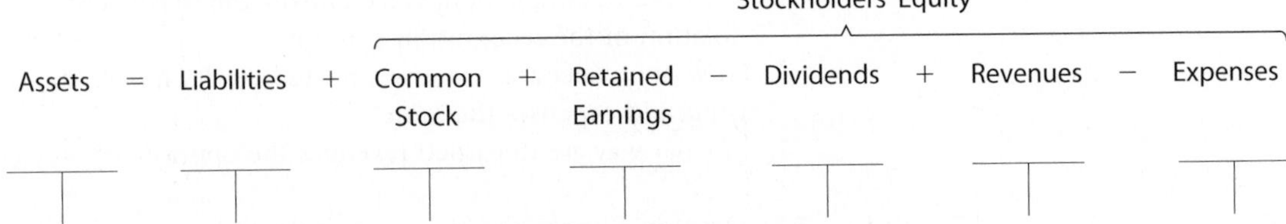

LO 2 **Classification of Accounts**

E 6. The following ledger accounts are for the Tuner Service Corporation:

a. Cash
b. Wages Expense
c. Accounts Receivable
d. Common Stock
e. Service Revenue
f. Prepaid Rent
g. Accounts Payable
h. Investments in Securities
i. Income Taxes Payable
j. Income Taxes Expense
k. Land
l. Advertising Expense
m. Prepaid Insurance
n. Utilities Expense
o. Fees Earned
p. Dividends
q. Wages Payable
r. Unearned Revenue
s. Office Equipment
t. Rent Payable
u. Notes Receivable
v. Interest Expense
w. Notes Payable
x. Supplies
y. Interest Receivable
z. Rent Expense

Complete the following table, using Xs to indicate each account's classification and normal balance (whether a debit or a credit increases the account).

	Type of Account							Normal Balance (increases balance)	
			Stockholders' Equity						
				Retained Earnings					
Item	**Asset**	**Liability**	**Common Stock**	**Dividends**	**Revenue**	**Expense**		**Debit**	**Credit**
a.	X							X	

LO 3 **Transaction Analysis**

E 7. Using the example given for transaction (a) below, analyze each transaction that follows.

EXAMPLE:

a. The asset account Cash was increased. Increases in assets are recorded by debits. Debit Cash $5,000. A component of stockholders' equity, Common Stock, was increased. Increases in stockholders' equity are recorded by credits. Credit Common Stock $5,000.

a. Jenny Wu established Jenny's Beauty Parlor, Inc., by incorporating and investing $5,000 in exchange for 500 shares of $10 par value common stock.
b. Paid two months' rent in advance, $3,360.
c. Purchased supplies on credit, $240.
d. Received cash for hair cutting services, $1,400.
e. Paid for supplies purchased in **c**.
f. Paid utility bill, $144.
g. Declared and paid a dividend of $200.

LO 3

Transaction Analysis

E 8. The following accounts are applicable to Dale's Lawn Service, Inc., a company that maintains condominium grounds:

1. Cash
2. Accounts Receivable
3. Supplies
4. Equipment
5. Accounts Payable
6. Lawn Services Revenue
7. Wages Expense
8. Rent Expense

Dale's Lawn Service, Inc., completed the following transactions:

	Debit	Credit
a. Paid for supplies purchased on credit last month.	5	1
b. Received cash from customers billed last month.	___	___
c. Made a payment on accounts payable.	___	___
d. Purchased supplies on credit.	___	___
e. Billed a client for lawn services.	___	___
f. Made a rent payment for the current month.	___	___
g. Received cash from customers for current lawn services.	___	___
h. Paid employee wages.	___	___
i. Ordered equipment.	___	___
j. Received and paid for the equipment ordered in **i**.	___	___

Analyze each transaction and show the accounts affected by entering the corresponding numbers in the appropriate debit or credit columns as shown in transaction **a.** Indicate no entry, if appropriate.

LO 3

Recording Transactions in T Accounts

E 9. Open the following T accounts: Cash, Repair Supplies, Repair Equipment, Accounts Payable, Common Stock, Dividends, Repair Fees Earned, Salaries Expense, and Rent Expense. Record the following transactions for the month of June directly in the T accounts; use the letters to identify the transactions in your T accounts. Determine the balance in each account.

a. Michael Change opened Change Repair Service, Inc., by investing $8,600 in cash and $3,200 in repair equipment in return for 11,800 shares of the company's $1 par value common stock.
b. Paid $1,600 for the current month's rent.
c. Purchased repair supplies on credit, $2,200.
d. Purchased additional repair equipment for cash, $1,200.
e. Paid salary to a helper, $1,800.
f. Paid $800 of amount purchased on credit in **c**.
g. Accepted cash for repairs completed, $7,440.
h. Declared and paid a dividend of $2,000.

LO 4

Trial Balance

E 10. After recording the transactions in **E 9,** prepare a trial balance for Change Repair Service, Inc., as of June 30, 2011.

LO 3

Analysis of Transactions

E 11. Explain each transaction **a–h** in the following T accounts:

CASH

a.	40,000	b.	15,000
g.	1,500	e.	3,600
h.	900	f.	4,500

ACCOUNTS RECEIVABLE

c.	8,000	g.	1,500

EQUIPMENT

b.	15,000	h.	900
d.	9,000		

ACCOUNTS PAYABLE

f.	4,500	d.	9,000

COMMON STOCK

		a.	40,000

SERVICE REVENUE

		c.	8,000

WAGES EXPENSE

e.	3,600		

LO 4

Preparing a Trial Balance

E 12. The list that follows presents the accounts (in alphabetical order) of the Chapla Corporation as of March 31, 2011.

Accounts Payable	?	Equipment	$14,400
Accounts Receivable	$ 5,600	Land	6,240
Building	40,800	Notes Payable	20,000
Cash	10,800	Prepaid Insurance	1,320
Common Stock	24,000	Retained Earnings	13,740

Prepare a trial balance with the proper heading (see Exhibit 2.6) and with the accounts listed in the sequence of the chart of accounts (see Exhibit 2.7). Compute the balance of Accounts Payable.

LO 4

Effects of Errors on a Trial Balance

E 13. Which of the following errors would cause a trial balance to have unequal totals? Explain your answers.

a. A payment to a creditor was recorded as a debit to Accounts Payable for $129 and as a credit to Cash for $102.
b. A payment of $150 to a creditor for an account payable was debited to Accounts Receivable and credited to Cash.
c. A purchase of office supplies of $420 was recorded as a debit to Office Supplies for $42 and as a credit to Cash for $42.
d. A purchase of equipment for $450 was recorded as a debit to Supplies for $450 and as a credit to Cash for $450.

LO 4

Correcting Errors in a Trial Balance

E 14. The trial balance for Kilda Services, Inc., at the end of July follows. It does not balance because of a number of errors. Kilda's accountant compared the amounts in the trial balance with the ledger, recomputed the account balances, and compared the postings. She found the following errors:

a. The balance of Cash was understated by $1,600.
b. A cash payment of $840 was credited to Cash for $480.
c. A debit of $240 to Accounts Receivable was not posted.
d. Supplies purchased for $120 were posted as a credit to Supplies.
e. A debit of $360 to Prepaid Insurance was not posted.
f. The Accounts Payable account had debits of $10,640 and credits of $18,360.
g. The Notes Payable account, with a credit balance of $4,800, was not included on the trial balance.
h. The debit balance of Dividends was listed in the trial balance as a credit.
i. A $400 debit to Dividends was posted as a credit.
j. The actual balance of Utilities Expense, $520, was listed as $52 in the trial balance.

Kilda Services, Inc. Trial Balance July 31, 2011		
Cash	$ 6,880	
Accounts Receivable	11,320	
Supplies	240	
Prepaid Insurance	360	
Equipment	14,800	
Accounts Payable		$ 9,080
Common Stock		6,000
Retained Earnings		15,120
Dividends		1,400
Revenues		11,840
Salaries Expense	5,200	
Rent Expense	1,200	
Advertising Expense	680	
Utilities Expense	52	
	$40,732	$43,440

Prepare a corrected trial balance.

LO 6

Cash Flow Analysis

E 15. A company engaged in the following transactions:

Dec.	1	Performed services for cash, $1,500
	1	Paid expenses in cash, $1,100
	2	Performed services on credit, $1,800
	3	Collected on account, $1,200
	4	Incurred expenses on credit, $1,300
	5	Paid on account, $700

Enter the correct titles on the following T accounts and enter the above transactions in the accounts. Determine the cash balance after these transactions, the amount still to be received, and the amount still to be paid.

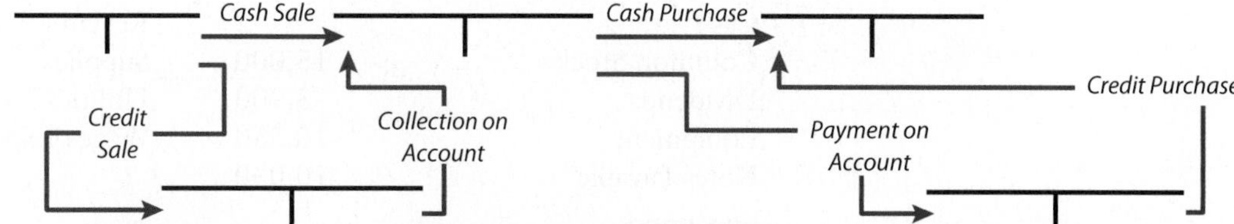

LO 5

Recording Transactions in the General Journal

E 16. Record the transactions in E 9 in the general journal.

LO 3, 5

Analysis of Unfamiliar Transactions

E 17. Managers and accountants often encounter transactions with which they are unfamiliar. Use your analytical skills to analyze and prepare journal entries for the following transactions, which have not yet been discussed in the text.

May	1	Purchased merchandise inventory on account, $2,400.
	2	Purchased marketable securities for cash, $6,000.
	3	Returned part of merchandise inventory for full credit, $500.
	4	Sold merchandise inventory on account, $1,600 (record sale only).
	5	Purchased land and a building for $600,000. Payment is $120,000 cash, and there is a 30-year mortgage for the remainder. The purchase price is allocated as follows: $200,000 to the land and $400,000 to the building.
	6	Received an order for $24,000 in services to be provided. With the order was a deposit of $7,000.

LO 5

Recording Transactions in the General Journal and Posting to the Ledger Accounts

E 18. Open a general journal form like the one in Exhibit 2.8 and label it Page 10. After opening the form, record the following transactions in the journal:

Dec. 14 Purchased equipment for $12,000, paying $4,000 as a cash down payment.
28 Paid $6,000 of the amount owed on the equipment.

Prepare three ledger account forms like the one shown in Exhibit 2.9. Use the following account numbers: Cash, 111; Equipment, 144; and Accounts Payable, 212. Post the two transactions from the general journal to the ledger accounts, being sure to make proper posting references. The Cash account has a debit balance of $16,000 on the day prior to the first transaction.

Financial Ratio: Asset Turnover

RATIO

E 19. Senior Company knows revenues have increased but wonders if they are keeping up with its growing investment in assets. Calculate asset turnover for 2011 and 2012 using the following data (*Note:* Round to one decimal place.):

Revenues, 2011	$ 80,000
Revenues, 2012	88,000
Total assets, 2010	72,000
Total assets, 2011	80,000
Total assets, 2012	102,000

By this measure has the company improved? Why is it important to use average total assets in the calculation?

Problems

LO 2

T Accounts, Normal Balance, and the Accounting Equation

✔ Total assets: $28,540

P 1. Anderson Construction Corporation builds foundations for buildings and parking lots. The following alphabetical list shows Anderson Construction's account balances as of April 30, 2011:

Accounts Payable	$ 1,950	Rent Expense	$3,600
Accounts Receivable	5,060	Retained Earnings	5,000
Cash	?	Revenue Earned	8,700
Common Stock	15,000	Supplies	3,250
Dividends	3,900	Utilities Expense	210
Equipment	13,350	Wages Expense	4,400
Notes Payable	10,000		

REQUIRED

Insert the account title at the top of its corresponding T account and enter the dollar amount as a normal balance in the account. Determine the balance of Cash and then show that the accounting equation is in balance.

Stockholders' Equity

Assets = Liabilities + Common Stock + Retained Earnings − Dividends + Revenues − Expenses

LO 3

Transaction Analysis

P 2. The following accounts are applicable to Walter's Chimney Sweeps, Inc.:

1. Cash
2. Accounts Receivable
3. Supplies
4. Prepaid Insurance
5. Equipment
6. Notes Payable
7. Accounts Payable
8. Common Stock
9. Retained Earnings
10. Dividends
11. Service Revenue
12. Rent Expense
13. Repair Expense

Walter's Chimney Sweeps, Inc., completed the following transactions:

	Debit	Credit
a. Paid for supplies purchased on credit last month.	7	1
b. Billed customers for services performed.	____	____
c. Paid the current month's rent.	____	____
d. Purchased supplies on credit.	____	____
e. Received cash from customers for services performed but not yet billed.	____	____
f. Purchased equipment on account.	____	____
g. Received a bill for repairs.	____	____
h. Returned part of equipment purchased in **f** for a credit.	____	____
i. Received payments from customers previously billed.	____	____
j. Paid the bill received in **g.**	____	____
k. Received an order for services to be performed.	____	____
l. Paid for repairs with cash.	____	____
m. Made a payment to reduce the principal of the note payable.	____	____
n. Declared and paid a dividend.	____	____

REQUIRED

Analyze each transaction and show the accounts affected by entering the corresponding numbers in the appropriate debit or credit column as shown in transaction **a.** Indicate no entry, if appropriate.

LO 3, 4

✔ Trial balance: $34,400

Transaction Analysis, T Accounts, and Trial Balance

P 3. Sharon Potamitis opened a secretarial school called Best Secretarial Training, Inc.

a. Potamitis contributed the following assets to the business in exchange for 28,600 shares of $1 par value common stock:

Cash	$11,400
Computers	10,000
Office Equipment	7,200

b. Found a location for the business and paid the first month's rent, $520.
c. Paid for an advertisement announcing the opening of the school, $380.
d. Received applications from three students for a four-week secretarial program and two students for a 10-day keyboarding course. The students will be billed a total of $2,600.
e. Purchased supplies on credit, $660.
f. Billed the enrolled students, $4,080.
g. Purchased a secondhand computer, $960, and office equipment, $760, on credit.
h. Paid for the supplies purchased on credit in **e**, $660.
i. Paid cash to repair a broken computer, $80.
j. Received partial payment from students previously billed, $2,760.
k. Paid the utility bill for the current month, $180.
l. Paid an assistant one week's salary, $880.
m. Declared and paid a dividend of $600.

REQUIRED

1. Set up the following T accounts: Cash, Accounts Receivable, Supplies, Computers, Office Equipment, Accounts Payable, Common Stock, Dividends, Tuition Revenue, Salaries Expense, Utilities Expense, Rent Expense, Repair Expense, and Advertising Expense.
2. Record the transactions directly in the T accounts, using the transaction letter to identify each debit and credit.
3. Prepare a trial balance using today's date.
4. USER INSIGHT ▶ Examine transactions **f** and **j**. What were the revenues, and how much cash was received from the revenues? What business issues might you see arising from the differences in these numbers?

LO 1, 3, 4

Transaction Analysis, T Accounts, and Trial Balance

✔ Trial balance: $14,800

P 4. Hiroshi Mori began an upholstery cleaning business on October 1 and engaged in the following transactions during the month:

Oct.	1	Began business by depositing $12,000 in a bank account in the name of the corporation in exchange for 12,000 shares of $1 par value common stock.
	2	Ordered cleaning supplies, $1,000.
	3	Purchased cleaning equipment for cash, $2,800.
	4	Made two months' van lease payment in advance, $1,200.
	7	Received the cleaning supplies ordered on October 2 and agreed to pay half the amount in 10 days and the rest in 30 days.
	9	Paid for repairs on the van with cash, $80.
	12	Received cash for cleaning upholstery, $960.
	17	Paid half the amount owed on supplies purchased on October 7, $500.
	21	Billed customers for cleaning upholstery, $1,340.
	24	Paid cash for additional repairs on the van, $80.
	27	Received $600 from the customers billed on October 21.
	31	Declared and paid a dividend of $700.

REQUIRED

1. Set up the following T accounts: Cash, Accounts Receivable, Cleaning Supplies, Prepaid Lease, Cleaning Equipment, Accounts Payable, Common Stock, Dividends, Cleaning Revenue, and Repair Expense.
2. Record transactions directly in the T accounts. Identify each entry by date.
3. Prepare a trial balance for Mori Upholstery Cleaning, Inc., as of October 31, 2011.
4. USER INSIGHT ▶ Compare and contrast how the issues of recognition, valuation, and classification are settled in the transactions of October 7 and 9.

LO 3, 4, 5, 6

Transaction Analysis, General Journal, Ledger Accounts, and Trial Balance

✔ Trial balance: $23,805

P 5. Acorn Nursery School Corporation provides baby-sitting and child-care programs. On January 31, 2011, it had the following trial balance:

Acorn Nursery School Corporation
Trial Balance
January 31, 2011

Cash (111)	$ 1,870	
Accounts Receivable (113)	1,700	
Equipment (141)	1,040	
Buses (143)	17,400	
Notes Payable (211)		$15,000
Accounts Payable (212)		1,640
Common Stock (311)		4,000
Retained Earnings (312)		1,370
	$22,010	$22,010

During the month of February, the company completed the following transactions:

Feb.	2	Paid this month's rent, $270.
	3	Received fees for this month's services, $650.
	4	Purchased supplies on account, $85.
	5	Reimbursed the bus driver for gas expenses, $40.
	6	Ordered playground equipment, $1,000.
	8	Made a payment on account, $170.
	9	Received payments from customers on account, $1,200.
	10	Billed customers who had not yet paid for this month's services, $700.
	11	Paid for the supplies purchased on February 4.
	13	Received and paid cash for playground equipment ordered on February 6, $1,000.
	17	Purchased equipment on account, $290.
	19	Paid this month's utility bill, $145.
	22	Received payment for one month's services from customers previously billed, $500.
	26	Paid part-time assistants for services, $460.
	27	Purchased gas and oil for the bus on account, $325.
	28	Declared and paid a dividend of $110.

REQUIRED

1. Open accounts in the ledger for the accounts in the trial balance plus the following ones: Supplies (115), Dividends (313), Service Revenue (411), Rent Expense (511), Gas and Oil Expense (512), Wages Expense (513), and Utilities Expense (514).
2. Enter the January 31, 2011, account balances from the trial balance.
3. Enter the above transactions in the general journal (Pages 17 and 18).
4. Post the entries to the ledger accounts. Be sure to make the appropriate posting references in the journal and ledger as you post.
5. Prepare a trial balance as of February 28, 2011.

USER INSIGHT ▶

6. Examine the transactions for February 3, 9, 10, and 22. What were the revenues, and how much cash was received from the revenues? What business issue might you see arising from the differences in these numbers?

Alternate Problems

LO 2

T Accounts, Normal Balance, and the Accounting Equation

✔ Total assets: $72,790

P 6. Smart Design Corporation creates radio and television advertising for local businesses in the twin cities. The following alphabetical list shows Smart Design's account balances as of January 31, 2011:

Accounts Payable	$ 2,710	Loans Payable	$ 5,000
Accounts Receivable	35,000	Rent Expense	6,440
Cash	6,200	Retained Earnings	22,000
Common Stock	15,000	Telephone Expense	480
Design Revenue	103,000	Unearned Revenue	9,000
Dividends	18,000	Wages Expense	59,000
Equipment	?		

REQUIRED

Insert the account at the top of its corresponding T account and enter the dollar amount as a normal balance in the account. Determine the balance of equipment and then show that the accounting equation is in balance.

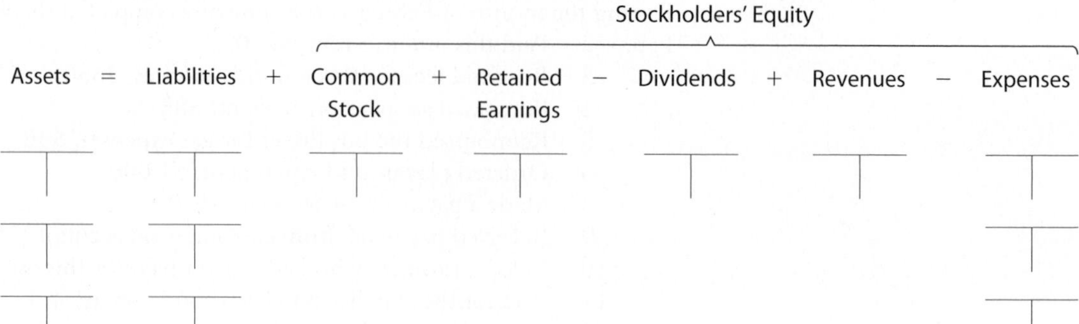

LO 1, 3, 4

Transaction Analysis, Journal Entries, T Accounts, and Trial Balance

✔ Trial balance: $21,080

P 7. Norman Kluz bid for and won a concession to rent bicycles in the local park during the summer. During June, he completed the following transactions for his business:

June	2	Began business by placing $14,400 in a business checking account in the name of the corporation in exchange for 14,400 shares of $1 par value common stock.
	3	Purchased supplies on account for $300.
	4	Purchased 10 bicycles for $5,000, paying $2,400 down and agreeing to pay the rest in 30 days.
	5	Paid $5,800 in cash for a small shed to store the bicycles and to use for other operations.
	8	Paid $800 in cash for shipping and installation costs (considered an addition to the cost of the shed) to place the shed at the park entrance.
	9	Hired a part-time assistant to help out on weekends at $7 per hour.
	10	Paid a maintenance person $150 to clean the grounds.
	13	Received $1,940 in cash for rentals.
	17	Paid $300 for the supplies purchased on June 3.
	18	Paid a $110 repair bill on bicycles.
	23	Billed a company $220 for bicycle rentals for an employee outing.
	25	Paid the $200 fee for June to the Park District for the right to operate the bicycle concession.
	27	Received $1,920 in cash for rentals.
	29	Paid the assistant wages of $480.
	30	Declared and paid a dividend of $1,000.

REQUIRED

1. Prepare journal entries for Kluz's transactions in June.
2. Set up the following T accounts and post all the journal entries: Cash, Accounts Receivable, Supplies, Shed, Bicycles, Accounts Payable, Common Stock, Dividends, Rental Revenue, Wages Expense, Maintenance Expense, Repair Expense, and Concession Fee Expense.
3. Prepare a trial balance for Kluz Rentals, Inc., as of June 30, 2011.
4. Compare and contrast how the issues of recognition, valuation, and classification are settled in the transactions of June 3 and 10. (USER INSIGHT ▶)

LO 3, 4, 5

Transaction Analysis, General Journal, Ledger Accounts, and Trial Balance

✔ Trial balance: $30,710

P 8. Brilliant Ads Corporation is a marketing firm. The company's trial balance on July 31, 2011, appears at the top of the next page.

Brilliant Ads Corporation
Trial Balance
July 31, 2011

Cash (111)	$10,200	
Accounts Receivable (113)	5,500	
Supplies (115)	610	
Office Equipment (141)	4,200	
Accounts Payable (212)		$ 2,600
Common Stock (311)		12,000
Retained Earnings (312)		5,910
	$20,510	$20,510

During August, the company completed the following transactions:

Aug. 2 Paid rent for August, $650.
3 Received cash from customers on account, $2,300.
7 Ordered supplies, $380.
10 Billed customers for services provided, $2,800.
12 Made a payment on accounts payable, $1,100.
14 Received the supplies ordered on August 7 and agreed to pay for them in 30 days, $380.
17 Discovered some of the supplies were not as ordered and returned them for full credit, $80.
19 Received cash from a customer for services provided, $4,800.
24 Paid the utility bill for August, $280.
26 Received a bill, to be paid in September, for advertisements placed in the local newspaper during August to promote Brilliant Ads Corporation, $700.
29 Billed a customer for services provided, $2,700.
30 Paid salaries for August, $3,800.
31 Declared and paid a dividend of $1,200.

REQUIRED

1. Open accounts in the ledger for the accounts in the trial balance plus the following accounts: Dividends (313), Marketing Fees (411), Salaries Expense (511), Rent Expense (512), Utilities Expense (513), and Advertising Expense (515).
2. Enter the July 31, 2011, account balances from the trial balance.
3. Enter the above transactions in the general journal (Pages 22 and 23).
4. Post the journal entries to the ledger accounts. Be sure to make the appropriate posting references in the journal and ledger as you post.
5. Prepare a trial balance as of August 31, 2011.

USER INSIGHT ▶

6. Examine the transactions for August 3, 10, 19, and 29. How much were revenues, and how much cash was received from the revenues? What business issues might you see arising from the differences in these numbers?

LO 3

Transaction Analysis

P 9. The following accounts are applicable to Sasha Cleaning, Inc.:

1. Cash
2. Accounts Receivable
3. Supplies
4. Prepaid Insurance
5. Equipment
6. Notes Payable
7. Accounts Payable
8. Common Stock
9. Retained Earnings
10. Dividends
11. Service Revenue
12. Rent Expense
13. Repair Expense

Sasha Cleaning, Inc., completed the following transactions:

	Debit	Credit
a. Paid for supplies purchased on credit last month.	7	1
b. Billed customers for services performed.	____	____
c. Paid the current month's rent.	____	____
d. Purchased supplies with cash.	____	____
e. Received cash from customers for services performed but not yet billed.	____	____
f. Purchased equipment on account.	____	____
g. Received a bill for repairs.	____	____
h. Returned part of equipment purchased in **f** for a credit.	____	____
i. Received payments from customers previously billed.	____	____
j. Paid the bill received in **g.**	____	____
k. Received an order for services to be performed.	____	____
l. Paid for repairs with cash.	____	____
m. Made a payment to reduce the principal of the note payable.	____	____
n. Declared and paid a dividend.	____	____

REQUIRED

Analyze each transaction and show the accounts affected by entering the corresponding numbers in the appropriate debit or credit column as shown in transaction **a**. Indicate no entry, if appropriate.

LO **3, 4**

Transaction Analysis, T Accounts, and Trial Balance

✔ **Trial balance: $18,634**

P 10. Bob Lutz opened a design school called Creative Training, Inc.

a. Lutz contributed the following assets to the business in exchange for 15,800 shares of $1 par value common stock:

Cash	$6,100
Computers	4,300
Office Equipment	5,400

b. Found a location for his business and paid the first month's rent, $700.
c. Paid for an advertisement announcing the opening of the school, $220.
d. Received applications from three students for a four-week secretarial program and two students for a 10-day keyboarding course. The students will be billed a total of $1,500.
e. Purchased supplies on credit, $270.
f. Billed the enrolled students, $1,910.
g. Purchased a secondhand computer, $499, and office equipment, $425, on credit.
h. Paid for the supplies purchased on credit in **e,** $270.
i. Paid cash to repair a broken computer, $80.
j. Received partial payment from students previously billed, $1,060.
k. Paid the utility bill for the current month, $110.
l. Paid an assistant one week's salary, $530.
m. Declared and paid a dividend of $250.

REQUIRED

1. Set up the following T accounts: Cash, Accounts Receivable, Supplies, Computers, Office Equipment, Accounts Payable, Common Stock, Dividends, Tuition Revenue, Salaries Expense, Utilities Expense, Rent Expense, Repair Expense, and Advertising Expense.
2. Record the transactions directly in the T accounts, using the transaction letter to identify each debit and credit.
3. Prepare a trial balance using today's date.

USER INSIGHT ▶

4. Examine transactions **f** and **j**. What were the revenues, and how much cash was received from the revenues? What business issues might you see arising from the differences in these numbers?

Cases

LO 1, 3

Conceptual Understanding: Valuation and Classification of Business Transactions

C 1. Tower Garden Center purchased two pre-owned trucks at a cash-only auction for 15 percent below current market value. The owners have asked you to record this purchase at current market value. You don't think that is correct. Write the owners a brief business memorandum in good form based on your knowledge of Chapter 2. Explain how the purchase of the pre-owned trucks will affect the balance sheet, include the entry to record the transaction, and explain why the amount must be at the price paid for the trucks.

LO 3

Conceptual Understanding: Recording of Rebates

C 2. Is it revenue or a reduction of an expense? That is the question companies that receive manufacturers' rebates for purchasing a large quantity of product must answer. Food companies like **Sara Lee**, **Kraft Foods**, and **Nestlé** give supermarkets special manufacturers' rebates of up to 45 percent, depending on the quantities purchased. Some firms recorded these rebates as revenue, and others recorded them as a reduction of the cost until the SEC said that only one way is correct. What, then, is the correct way for supermarkets to record these rebates? Does your answer change net income?

LO 2, 3

Interpreting Financial Statements: Interpreting a Bank's Financial Statements

C 3. **Mellon Bank** is a large bank holding company. Selected accounts from the company's 2009 annual report are as follows (in millions):[9]

Cash and Due from Banks	$ 3,732
Loans to Customers	36,186
Securities Available for Sale	51,632
Deposits by Customers	135,050

1. Indicate whether each of these accounts is an asset, a liability, or a component of stockholders' equity on Mellon Bank's balance sheet.
2. Assume that you are in a position to do business with Mellon. Show how Mellon Bank's accountants would prepare the entry in T account form to record each of the following transactions:
   a. You sell securities in the amount of $2,000 to the bank.
   b. You deposit in the bank the $2,000 received from selling the securities.
   c. You borrow $5,000 from the bank.

LO 6

Interpreting Financial Statements: Cash Flows

C 4. Having been promoted recently, you now have access to your firm's monthly financial statements. You notice that revenues are increasing rapidly and that income is at an all-time high. The balance sheet shows growth in receivables, and accounts payable have declined. However, the chief financial officer is concerned because the firm's cash flows from operating activities are decreasing. What are some reasons a company with a positive net income may fall short of cash from its operating activities? What could be done to improve this situation?

LO 1

Annual Report Case: Recognition, Valuation, and Classification

C 5. Refer to the Summary of Significant Accounting Policies in the notes to the financial statements in the **CVS** annual report in the Supplement to Chapter 1.

1. How does the concept of recognition apply to advertising costs?
2. How does the concept of valuation apply to inventories?
3. How does the concept of classification apply to cash and cash equivalents?

Comparison Analysis: Financial Ratio: Asset Turnover

RATIO

C 6. Refer to the financial statements of **CVS** and **Southwest Airlines Co.** in the Supplement to Chapter 1. Compute asset turnover for the past two years for both companies and comment on the results. (*Note:* Round to one decimal place.) Total assets in fiscal 2007 were $54,722 million for CVS and $16,772 million for Southwest.

LO 1

Ethical Dilemma: Recognition Point and Ethical Considerations

C 7. Robert Shah, a sales representative for Quality Office Supplies Corporation, will receive a substantial bonus if he meets his annual sales goal. The company's recognition point for sales is the day of shipment. On December 31, Shah realizes he needs sales of $2,000 to reach his sales goal and receive the bonus. He calls a purchaser for a local insurance company, whom he knows well, and asks him to buy $2,000 worth of copier paper today. The purchaser says, "But Jerry, that's more than a year's supply for us." Shah says, "Buy it today. If you decide it's too much, you can return however much you want for full credit next month." The purchaser says, "Okay, ship it." The paper is shipped on December 31 and recorded as a sale. On January 15, the purchaser returns $1,750 worth of paper for full credit (approved by Shah) against the bill. Should the shipment on December 31 be recorded as a sale? Discuss the ethics of Shah's action.

LO 1, 2, 3, 4

Decision Analysis Using Excel: Transaction Analysis and Evaluation of a Trial Balance

C 8. Irena Takla hired an attorney to help her start Takla Delivery Service Corporation. On March 1, Takla deposited $14,375 cash in a bank account in the name of the corporation in exchange for 575 shares of $25 par value common stock. When she paid the attorney's bill of $875, the attorney advised her to hire an accountant to keep her records. Takla was so busy that it was March 31 before she hired you to straighten out her records.

After investing in her business and paying her attorney, Takla borrowed $6,250 from the bank. She later paid $325, including interest of $75, on this loan. She also purchased a used pickup truck in the company's name, paying $3,125 down and financing $9,250. The first payment on the truck is due April 15. Takla then rented an office and paid three months' rent, $1,125, in advance. Credit purchases of office equipment of $1,000 and material handling equipment of $625 must be paid by April 10.

In March, Takla Delivery Service completed deliveries of $1,625, of which $500 were cash transactions. Of the credit transactions, $375 was collected during March, and $750 remained to be collected at the end of March. The company paid wages of $562 to its employees. On March 31, the company received a $93 bill for the March utilities expense and a $62 check from a customer for deliveries to be made in April. A customer requested a delivery on March 31 for the following week and agreed to pay $250. Takla is considering recording this agreement as revenue in March to make the business look better.

1. Prepare journal entries for all of the transactions for March that are described in the three paragraphs above. Label each of the entries alphabetically.
2. Set up T accounts. Then post the entries to the T accounts. Identify each posting with the letter corresponding to the transaction.
3. Determine the balance of each account.
4. Prepare a trial balance for Takla Delivery Service Corporation as of March 31, 2011. (*Hint:* Trial Balance total is $33,030.)
5. Irena Takla is unsure how to evaluate the trial balance. The Cash account balance is $15,550, which exceeds the original investment of $14,375 by $1,175. Did the company make a profit of $1,175? Explain why the Cash account is not an indicator of business earnings. Cite specific examples to show why it is difficult to determine net income by looking solely at figures in the trial balance.
6. What are the ethical implications of recording the delivery order received on March 31 as revenue in March?

CHAPTER 3

DECISION POINT
A User's Focus Netflix, Inc.

Netflix is the world's largest online entertainment subscription service. For a monthly fee, its subscribers have access to more than 90,000 DVD titles, which are shipped free of charge; with certain plans, they also have access to more than 5,000 movies online. At the end of any accounting period, Netflix has many transactions that will affect future periods. Two examples appear in the Financial Highlights that follow: *prepaid expenses*, which, though paid in the period just ended, will benefit future periods and are therefore recorded as assets, and *accrued expenses*, which the company has incurred but will not pay until a future period.[1] If prepaid and accrued expenses are not accounted for properly at the end of a period, Netflix's income will be misstated. Similar misstatements can occur when a company has received revenue that it has not yet earned or has earned revenue but not yet received it. If misstatements are made, investors will be misled about the company's financial performance.

CW Hanley/The Image Bank/Getty Images

NETFLIX'S FINANCIAL HIGHLIGHTS: SELECTED BALANCE SHEET ITEMS
(in thousands)

Assets	**2009**	**2008**
Prepaid expenses	$12,491	$ 8,122
Liabilities		
Accrued expenses	$33,387	$31,394

Questions

1. *What assumptions must Netflix make to account for transactions that span accounting periods?*
2. *How does Netflix assign its revenues and expenses to the proper accounting period so that net income is properly measured?*
3. *Why are the adjustments that these transactions require important to Netflix's financial performance?*

Measuring Business Income

LEARNING OBJECTIVES

LO 1 Define *net income* and explain the assumptions underlying income measurement and their ethical application. (pp. 138–141)

LO 2 Define *accrual accounting* and explain how it is accomplished. (pp. 141–144)

LO 3 Identify the four situations that require adjusting entries and illustrate typical adjusting entries. (pp. 144–152)

LO 4 Prepare financial statements from an adjusted trial balance. (pp. 152–154)

LO 5 Explain and prepare closing entries. (pp. 154–156)

LO 6 Use accrual-based information to analyze cash flows. (pp. 156–157)

In the previous chapter, we examined the recording of business transactions and the preparation of the trial balance, which constitute the first three steps of the accounting cycle. In this chapter, we will consider the next steps in the accounting cycle, which include the measurement of income, or earnings, the most important measure of a company's success or failure. The incentive to manage, or misstate, earnings by manipulating the numbers can be powerful, and because earnings are based on estimates, manipulation can be easy. For these reasons, ethical behavior is extremely important when measuring business income.

FOCUS ON FINANCIAL STATEMENTS

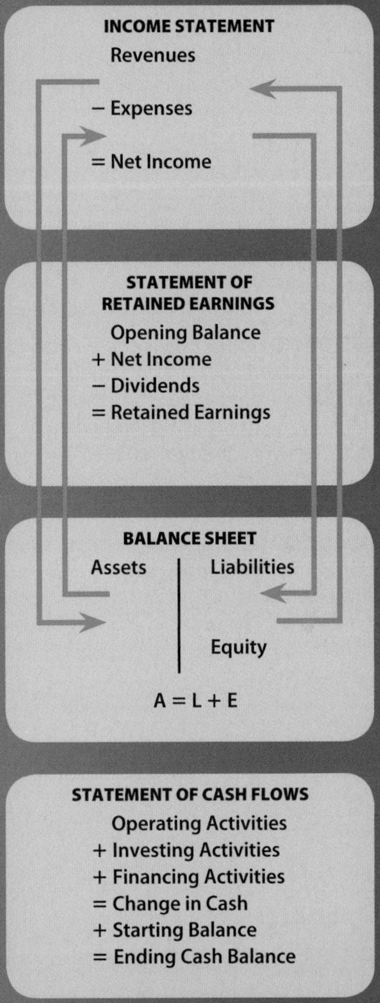

INCOME STATEMENT
Revenues
− Expenses
= Net Income

STATEMENT OF RETAINED EARNINGS
Opening Balance
+ Net Income
− Dividends
= Retained Earnings

BALANCE SHEET
Assets | Liabilities
Equity
A = L + E

STATEMENT OF CASH FLOWS
Operating Activities
+ Investing Activities
+ Financing Activities
= Change in Cash
+ Starting Balance
= Ending Cash Balance

Adjusting entries bring balance sheet and income statement accounts up to date at end of period.

PROFITABILITY MEASUREMENT ISSUES AND ETHICS

Define *net income* and explain the assumptions underlying income measurement and their ethical application. LO 1

As you know, profitability and liquidity are the two major goals of a business. For a business to succeed, or even to survive, it must earn a profit. **Profit**, however, means different things to different people. Accountants prefer to use the term **net income** because it can be precisely defined from an accounting point of view as the *net increase in stockholders' equity that results from a company's operations.*

Net Income

Net income is accumulated in the Retained Earnings account and reported on the income statement. Management, stockholders, and others use it to assess a company's progress in meeting the goal of profitability. Readers of income statements need to understand what net income means and be aware of its strengths and weaknesses as an indicator of a company's performance.

In its simplest form, net income is measured as the difference between revenues and expenses when revenues exceed expenses:

$$\text{Net Income} = \text{Revenues} - \text{Expenses}$$

When expenses exceed revenues, a **net loss** occurs.

STUDY NOTE: *The essence of revenue is that something has been earned through the sale of goods or services. That is why cash received through a loan does not constitute revenue.*

Revenues are *increases in stockholders' equity* resulting from selling goods, rendering services, or performing other business activities. When a business delivers a product or provides a service to a customer, it usually receives cash or a promise from the customer to pay cash in the near future. The promise to pay is recorded in either Accounts Receivable or Notes Receivable. The total of these accounts and the total cash received from customers in an accounting period are the company's revenues for that period.

STUDY NOTE: *The primary purpose of an expense is to generate revenue.*

Expenses are *decreases in stockholders' equity* resulting from the cost of selling goods or rendering services and the cost of the activities necessary to carry on a business, such as attracting and serving customers. In other words, expenses are the cost of the goods and services used in the course of earning revenues. Examples include salaries expense, rent expense, advertising expense, utilities expense, and depreciation (allocation of cost) of a building or office equipment. These expenses are often called the *cost of doing business or expired costs.*

Not all increases in stockholders' equity arise from revenues, nor do all decreases in stockholders' equity arise from expenses. Stockholders' investments increase stockholders' equity but are not revenues, and dividends decrease stockholders' equity but are not expenses.

Income Measurement Assumptions

Users of financial reports should be aware that estimates and assumptions play a major role in the measurement of net income and other key indicators of performance. **Netflix**'s management acknowledges this in its annual report, as follows:

> The preparation of financial statements in conformity with accounting principles generally accepted in the United States requires . . . estimates and assumptions that affect the reported amounts of assets and liabilities, disclosure of contingent assets and liabilities at the date of the financial statements, and the reported amounts of revenues and expenses during the reported periods.[2]

The major assumptions made in measuring business income have to do with continuity, periodicity, and matching.

Continuity Measuring business income requires that certain expense and revenue transactions be allocated over several accounting periods. Choosing the number of accounting periods raises the issue of **continuity**. What is the expected life of the business? Many businesses last less than five years, and in any given year, thousands of businesses go bankrupt. The majority of companies present annual financial statements on the assumption that the business will continue to operate indefinitely—that is, that the company is a **going concern**. The continuity assumption is as follows:

> Unless there is evidence to the contrary, the accountant assumes that the business will continue to operate indefinitely.

Justification for all the techniques of income measurement rests on the assumption of continuity. Consider, for example, the value of assets on the balance sheet. The continuity assumption allows the cost of certain assets to be held on the balance sheet until a future accounting period, when the cost will become an expense on the income statement. When a firm is facing bankruptcy, the accountant may set aside the assumption of continuity and prepare financial statements based on the assumption that the firm will go out of business and sell all of its assets at liquidation value—that is, for what they will bring in cash.

Periodicity Measuring business income requires assigning revenues and expenses to a specific accounting period. However, not all transactions can be easily assigned to specific periods. For example, when a company purchases a building, it must estimate the number of years the building will be in use. The portion of the cost of the building assigned to each period depends on this estimate and requires an assumption about **periodicity**. The assumption is as follows:

> Although the lifetime of a business is uncertain, it is nonetheless useful to estimate the business's net income in terms of accounting periods.

STUDY NOTE: *Accounting periods are of equal length so that one period can be compared with the next.*

Financial statements may be prepared for any time period, but to make comparisons easier, the periods are generally of equal length. A 12-month accounting period is called a **fiscal year**; accounting periods of less than a year are called **interim periods**. The fiscal year of many organizations is the calendar year, January 1 to December 31. However, retailers often end their fiscal years during a slack season, and in this case, the fiscal year corresponds to the yearly cycle of business activity.

iStock Photo

Focus on Business Practice

Fiscal Years Vary

The fiscal years of many schools and governmental agencies end on June 30 or September 30. The table at the right shows the last month of the fiscal year of some well-known companies.

Company	*Last Month of Fiscal Year*
Apple Computer	September
Caesars World	July
Fleetwood Enterprises	April
H.J. Heinz	March
Kelly Services	December
MGM-UA Communications	August
Toys "R" Us	January

Matching Rule To measure net income adequately, revenues and expenses must be assigned to the accounting period in which they occur, regardless of when cash is received or paid. This is an application of the **matching rule**:

> Revenues must be assigned to the accounting period in which the goods are sold or the services performed, and expenses must be assigned to the accounting period in which they are used to produce revenue.

In other words, expenses should be recognized in the same accounting period as the revenues to which they are related. However, a direct cause-and-effect relationship between expenses and revenues is often difficult to identify. When there is no direct means of connecting expenses and revenues, costs are allocated in a systematic way among the accounting periods that benefit from the costs. For example, a building's cost is expensed over the building's expected useful life, and interest on investments is recorded as income even though it may not have been received.

The **cash basis of accounting** is the practice of accounting for revenues in the period in which cash is received and for expenses in the period in which cash is paid. With this method, taxable income is calculated as the difference between cash receipts from revenues and cash payments for expenses. Although this method works well for some small businesses and many individuals, it does not fit the needs of most businesses.

Ethics and the Matching Rule

As shown in Exhibit 3.1, applying the matching rule involves making assumptions. It also involves exercising judgment. Consider the assumptions and judgment involved in estimating the useful life of a building. The estimate should be based on realistic assumptions, but management has latitude in making that estimate, and its judgment will affect the final net income that is reported.

The manipulation of revenues and expenses to achieve a specific outcome is called **earnings management**. Research has shown that companies that manage their earnings are much more likely to exceed projected earnings targets by a little than to fall short by a little. Why would management want to manage earnings to keep them from falling short? It may want to

- Meet a previously announced goal and thus meet the expectations of the market.
- Keep the company's stock price from dropping.
- Meet a goal that will enable it to earn bonuses.
- Avoid embarrassment.

Earnings management, though not the best practice, is not illegal. However, when the estimates involved in earnings management begin moving outside a reasonable range, the financial statements become misleading. For instance, net income is misleading when revenue is overstated by a significant amount or when expenses are

EXHIBIT 3.1
Assumptions and the Matching Rule

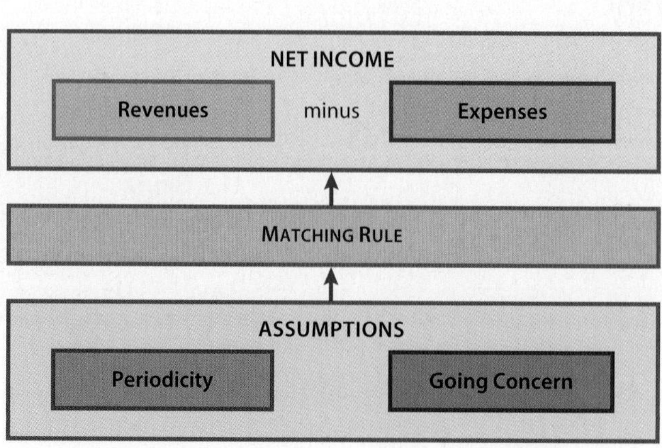

Focus on Business Practice

Are Misstatements of Earnings Always Overstatements?

Not all misstatements of earnings are overstatements. For instance, privately held companies, which do not have to be concerned about the effect of their earnings announcements on stockholders or investors, may understate income to reduce or avoid income taxes. In an unusual case involving a public company, the SEC cited and fined **Microsoft** for understating its income. Microsoft, a very successful company, accomplished this by overstating its unearned revenue on the balance sheet. The company's motive in trying to appear less successful than it actually was may have been that it was facing government charges of being a monopoly.[3]

iStock Photo

understated by a significant amount. As noted earlier in the text, the preparation of financial statements that are intentionally misleading constitutes fraudulent financial reporting.

Most of the enforcement actions that the Securities and Exchange Commission (SEC) has brought against companies in recent years involve misapplications of the matching rule resulting from improper accrual accounting. For example, **Dell Computer** had to restate four years of its financial results because senior executives improperly applied accrual accounting to give the impression that the company was meeting quarterly earnings targets. After the SEC action, the company conducted an internal investigation that resulted in many changes in its accounting controls.[4] In the rest of this chapter, we focus on accrual accounting and its proper application.

Stop & Apply

Match the concepts on the right with the assumptions or actions on the left:

_____ 1. Increases in stockholders' equity resulting from selling goods, rendering services, or performing other business activities	a. Net income
_____ 2. Manipulation of revenues and expenses to achieve a specific change in stockholders' equity	b. Revenues
_____ 3. Increase in stockholders' equity that results from a company's operations	c. Expenses
_____ 4. Decreases in stockholders' equity resulting from the cost of selling goods, rendering services, and performing other business activities	d. Earnings management

SOLUTION

1. b; 2. d; 3. a; 4. c

iStock Photo

ACCRUAL ACCOUNTING

Define *accrual accounting* and explain how it is accomplished.

Accrual accounting encompasses all the techniques accountants use to apply the matching rule. In accrual accounting, revenues and expenses are recorded in the periods in which they occur rather than in the periods in which they are received or paid.

Accrual accounting is accomplished in the following ways:

- Recognizing revenues when they are earned.
- Recognizing expenses when they are incurred.
- Adjusting the accounts.

Certain revenues and expenses, like those associated with business travel, change during the period, but there usually is no need to adjust them until the end of the period, when preparing the financial statements.

Recognizing Revenues

As you may recall, the process of determining when revenue should be recorded is called **revenue recognition**. The Securities and Exchange Commission requires that all the following conditions be met before revenue is recognized:[5]

- Persuasive evidence of an arrangement exists.
- A product or service has been delivered.
- The seller's price to the buyer is fixed or determinable.
- Collectability is reasonably assured.

For example, suppose Creative Designs, Inc., has created a website for a customer and that the transaction meets the SEC's four criteria:

- The company and the customer agree that the customer owes for the service.
- The service has been rendered.
- Both parties understand the price.
- There is a reasonable expectation that the customer will pay the bill.

When Creative Designs bills the customer, it records the transaction as revenue by debiting Accounts Receivable and crediting Design Revenue. Note that revenue can be recorded even though cash has not been collected; all that is required is a reasonable expectation that cash will be paid.

Recognizing Expenses

Expenses are recorded when there is an agreement to purchase goods or services, the goods have been delivered or the services rendered, a price has been established or can be determined, and the goods or services have been used to produce revenue. For example, when Creative Designs receives its utility bill, it recognizes the expense as having been incurred and as having helped produce revenue. The company records this transaction by debiting Utilities Expense and crediting Accounts Payable. Until the bill is paid, Accounts Payable serves as a holding account. Note that recognition of the expense does not depend on the payment of cash.

Alexander/iStockphoto.com

Focus on International Practices

Revenue Recognition: Principles Versus Rules

Revenue recognition highlights the differences between international and U.S. accounting standards. Although U.S. standards are referred to as generally accepted accounting *principles*, the FASB has issued extensive *rules*, that is, specific guidance for revenue recognition in various situations and industries. The IASB, on the other hand, generally has a few broad IFRS for revenue recognition and leaves it to companies and their auditors to determine how to apply the broad *principle* in specific situations. As a result, revenue recognition is an issue that will provide a challenge to achieving international convergence of accounting practice.

iStock Photo

Adjusting the Accounts

Accrual accounting also involves adjusting the accounts. Adjustments are necessary because an accounting period, by definition, ends on a particular day. The balance sheet must list all assets and liabilities as of the end of that day, and the income statement must contain all revenues and expenses applicable to the period ending on that day. Although operating a business is a continuous process, there must be a cutoff point for the periodic reports. Some transactions invariably span the cutoff point, and some accounts therefore need adjustment.

As you can see in Exhibit 3.2, some of the accounts in Creative Designs' trial balance as of July 31 do not show the correct balances for preparing the financial statements. The trial balance lists prepaid rent of $3,200. At $1,600 per month, this represents rent for the months of July and August. So, on July 31, one-half of the $3,200 represents rent expense for July, and the remaining $1,600 represents an asset that will be used in August. An adjustment is needed to reflect the $1,600 balance in the Prepaid Rent account on the balance sheet and the $1,600 rent expense on the income statement.

As you will see, several other accounts in Creative Designs' trial balance do not reflect their correct balances. Like the Prepaid Rent account, they need to be adjusted.

Adjustments and Ethics

Accrual accounting can be difficult to understand. The account adjustments take time to calculate and enter in the records. Also, adjusting entries do not affect cash flows in the current period because they never involve the Cash account. You might ask, "Why go to all the trouble of making them? Why worry about them?" For one thing, the SEC has identified issues related to accrual accounting and adjustments as an area of utmost importance because of the potential for abuse and misrepresentation.[6]

All adjustments are important because of their effect on performance measures of profitability and liquidity. Adjusting entries affect net income on the income statement, and they affect profitability comparisons from one accounting period to the next. They also affect assets and liabilities on the balance sheet and thus provide information about a company's *future* cash inflows and outflows. This information is needed to assess management's performance in achieving sufficient liquidity to meet the need for cash to pay ongoing obligations. The potential for abuse arises because considerable judgment underlies the application of adjusting entries. When this judgment is misused, performance measures can be misleading.

EXHIBIT 3.2
Trial Balance for Creative Designs, Inc.

Creative Designs, Inc.
Trial Balance
July 31, 2011

Cash	$22,480	
Accounts Receivable	4,600	
Office Supplies	5,200	
Prepaid Rent	3,200	
Office Equipment	16,320	
Accounts Payable		$ 6,280
Unearned Design Revenue		1,400
Common Stock		40,000
Dividends	2,800	
Design Revenue		12,400
Wages Expense	4,800	
Utilities Expense	680	
	$60,080	$60,080

Stop & Apply

Four conditions must be met before revenue should be recognized. Identify which of these conditions applies to the following actions of Hasting Corporation in reference to a client:

a. Determines that the client has a good credit rating.
b. Agrees to a price for services before it performs them.
c. Performs services.
d. Signs a contract to perform services.

SOLUTION

a. Collectibility is reasonably assured.
b. The seller's price to the buyer is fixed or determinable.
c. A product or service has been delivered.
d. Persuasive evidence of an arrangement exists.

iStock Photo

THE ADJUSTMENT PROCESS

Identify the four situations that require adjusting entries and illustrate typical adjusting entries. **LO 3**

When transactions span more than one accounting period, accrual accounting requires the use of **adjusting entries**. Exhibit 3.3 shows the four situations in which adjusting entries must be made. Each adjusting entry affects one balance sheet account and one income statement account. As we have already noted, adjusting entries never affect the Cash account.

STUDY NOTE: *Adjusting entries provide information about past or future cash flows but never involve an entry to the Cash account.*

The four types of adjusting entries are as follows:

Type 1: Allocating recorded costs between two or more accounting periods: Examples of these costs are prepayments of rent, insurance, and supplies and the depreciation of plant and equipment. The adjusting entry in this case involves an asset account and an expense account.

Type 2: Recognizing unrecorded expenses: Examples of these expenses are wages, interest, and income taxes that have been incurred but are not recorded during an accounting period. The adjusting entry involves an expense account and a liability account.

Type 3: Allocating recorded, unearned revenues between two or more accounting periods: Examples include payments received in advance and deposits made on goods or services. The adjusting entry involves a liability account and a revenue account.

Type 4: Recognizing unrecorded, earned revenues: An example is revenue that a company has earned for providing a service but for which it has not billed or been paid by the end of the accounting period. The adjusting entry involves an asset account and a revenue account.

EXHIBIT 3.3
The Four Types of Adjustments

INCOME STATEMENT	BALANCE SHEET: Asset	BALANCE SHEET: Liability
Expense	1. Allocating recorded costs between two or more accounting periods.	2. Recognizing unrecorded expenses.
Revenue	4. Recognizing unrecorded, earned revenues.	3. Allocating recorded, unearned revenues between two or more accounting periods.

Adjusting entries are either deferrals or accruals.

- A **deferral** is the postponement of the recognition of an expense already paid (Type 1 adjustment) or of revenue received in advance (Type 3 adjustment). The cash receipt or payment is recorded before the adjusting entry is made.
- An **accrual** is the recognition of a revenue (Type 4 adjustment) or expense (Type 2 adjustment) that has arisen but not been recorded during the accounting period. The cash receipt or payment occurs in a future accounting period, after the adjusting entry has been made.

Type 1 Adjustment: Allocating Recorded Costs (Deferred Expenses)

Companies often make expenditures that benefit more than one period. These costs are debited to an asset account. At the end of an accounting period, the amount of the asset that has been used is transferred from the asset account to an expense account. Two important adjustments of this type are for prepaid expenses and the depreciation of plant and equipment.

STUDY NOTE: The expired portion of a prepayment is converted to an expense; the unexpired portion remains an asset.

Prepaid Expenses Companies customarily pay some expenses, including those for rent, supplies, and insurance, in advance. These costs are called **prepaid expenses**. By the end of an accounting period, a portion or all of prepaid services or goods will have been used or have expired. The required adjusting entry reduces the asset and increases the expense, as shown in Exhibit 3.4. The amount of the adjustment equals the cost of the goods or services used or expired.

If adjusting entries for prepaid expenses are not made at the end of an accounting period, both the balance sheet and the income statement will present incorrect information. The company's assets will be overstated, and its expenses will be understated. Thus, stockholders' equity on the balance sheet and net income on the income statement will be overstated.

To illustrate this type of adjusting entry and the others discussed below, we refer again to the transactions of Creative Designs, Inc.

At the beginning of July, Creative Designs paid two months' rent in advance. The advance payment resulted in an asset consisting of the right to occupy the office for two months. As each day in the month passed, part of the asset's cost expired and became an

EXHIBIT 3.4
Adjustment for Prepaid (Deferred) Expenses

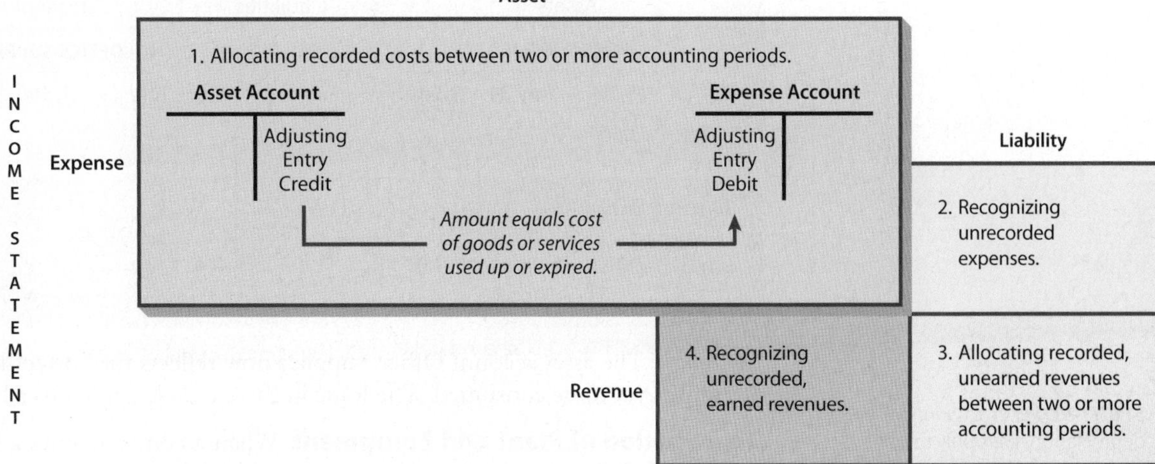

expense. By July 31, one-half of the asset's cost had expired and had to be treated as an expense. The adjustment is as follows:

Adjustment for Prepaid Rent

July 31: Expiration of one month's rent, $1,600

Analysis: Expiration of prepaid rent

- ▼ *decreases* the asset account *Prepaid Rent* with a credit and
- ▲ *increases* the expense account *Rent Expense* with a debit.

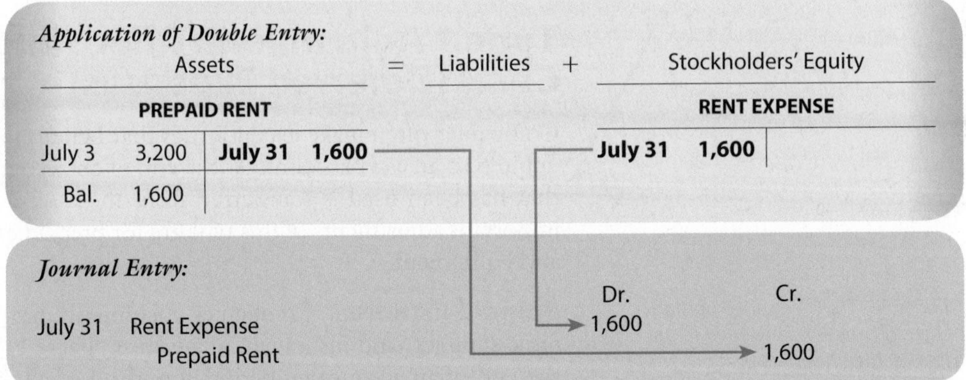

Comment: The Prepaid Rent account now has a balance of $1,600, which represents one month's rent that will be expensed during August. The logic in this analysis applies to all prepaid expenses.

Creative Designs purchased $5,200 of office supplies in early July. An inventory of supplies made at the end of July records the number and cost of supplies that have not yet been consumed and are thus still assets of the company. Suppose the inventory shows that office supplies costing $3,660 are still on hand. This means that of the $5,200 of supplies originally purchased, $1,540 worth were used (became an expense) in July. The adjustment is as follows:

Adjustment for Supplies

July 31: Consumption of supplies, $1,540

Analysis: Consumption of office supplies

- ▼ *decreases* the asset account *Office Supplies* with a credit and
- ▲ *increases* the expense account *Office Supplies Expense* with a debit.

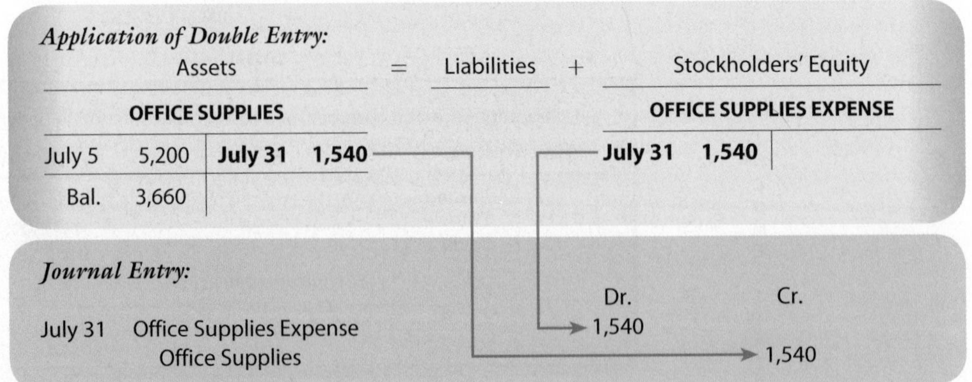

Comment: The asset account Office Supplies now reflects the correct balance of $3,660 of supplies yet to be consumed. The logic in this example applies to all kinds of supplies.

STUDY NOTE: *In accounting, depreciation refers only to the allocation of an asset's cost, not to any decline in the asset's value.*

Depreciation of Plant and Equipment When a company buys a long-term asset—such as a building, truck, computer, or store fixture—it is, in effect, prepaying for the usefulness of that asset for as long as it benefits the company. Because a long-term asset is a

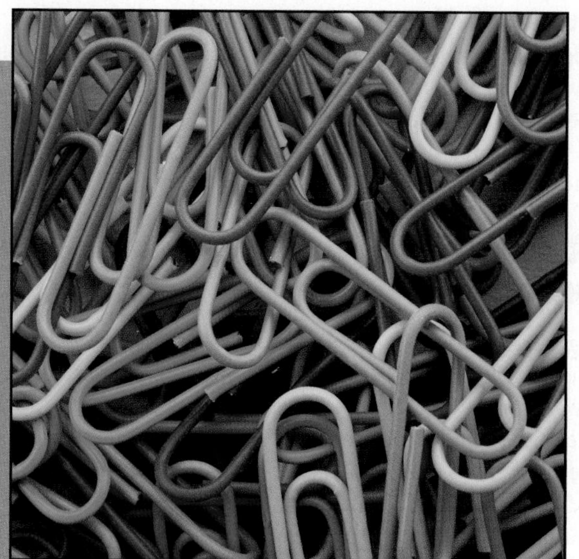

Noam Armonn/iStockphoto.com

Think of accounting for supplies as using a storage cabinet in an office: supplies are put in the cabinet when purchased (assets); employees take some out and use them during the accounting period (expenses); and at the end of the accounting period, the supplies left over in the cabinet can be used in the next period (assets).

deferral of an expense, the accountant must allocate the cost of the asset over its estimated useful life. The amount allocated to any one accounting period is called **depreciation**, or *depreciation expense*. Depreciation, like other expenses, is incurred during the accounting period during which the related long-term asset is used to produce revenue.

It is often impossible to tell exactly how long an asset will last or how much of the asset has been used in any one period. For this reason, depreciation must be estimated. Accountants have developed a number of methods for estimating depreciation and for dealing with the related complex problems. (In the discussion that follows, we assume that the amount of depreciation has been established.)

To maintain historical cost in specific long-term asset accounts, separate accounts—**Accumulated Depreciation accounts**—are used to accumulate the depreciation on each long-term asset. These accounts, which are deducted from their related asset accounts on the balance sheet, are called *contra accounts*. A **contra account** is a separate account that is paired with a related account—in our example, an asset account. The balance of the contra account is shown on the financial statement as a deduction from its related account. The net amount is called the **carrying value**, or *book value*, of the asset. As the months pass, the amount of the accumulated depreciation grows, and the carrying value shown as an asset declines.

Adjustment for Plant and Equipment

July 31: Depreciation of office equipment, $300

Analysis: Depreciation

decreases the asset account *Office Equipment*,

▲ *increases* the contra account *Accumulated Depreciation—Office Equipment* with a credit, and

▲ *increases* the expense account *Depreciation Expense—Office Equipment* with a debit.

STUDY NOTE: The difficulty in estimating an asset's useful life is further evidence that the net income figure is, at best, an estimate.

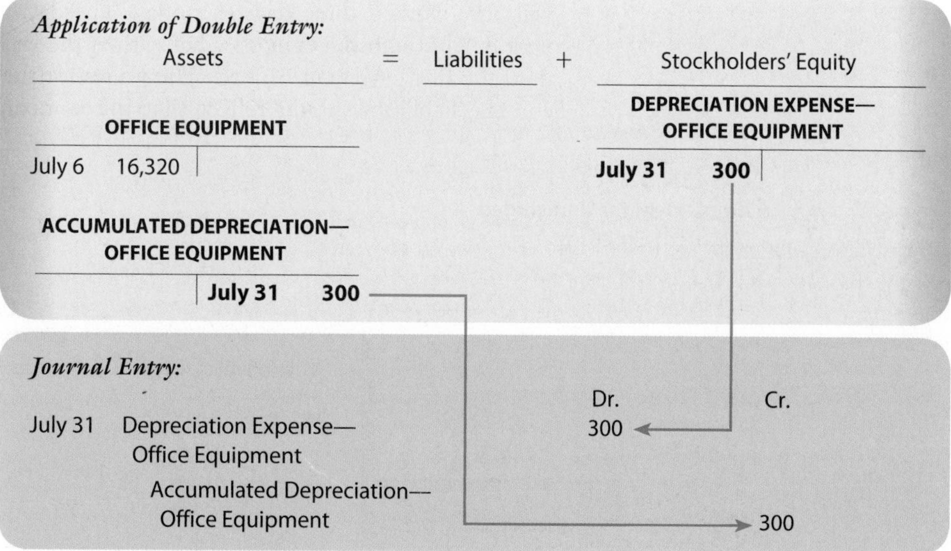

Application of Double Entry:

Assets = Liabilities + Stockholders' Equity

OFFICE EQUIPMENT	
July 6 16,320	

ACCUMULATED DEPRECIATION—OFFICE EQUIPMENT	
	July 31 300

DEPRECIATION EXPENSE—OFFICE EQUIPMENT	
July 31 300	

Journal Entry:

		Dr.	Cr.
July 31	Depreciation Expense—Office Equipment	300	
	Accumulated Depreciation—Office Equipment		300

Comment: The carrying value of Office Equipment is $16,020 ($16,320 – $300) and is presented on the balance sheet as follows:

PROPERTY, PLANT, AND EQUIPMENT		
Office equipment	$16,320	
Less accumulated depreciation	300	$16,020

Application to Netflix, Inc. Netflix has prepaid expenses and property and equipment similar to those in the examples we have presented. Among Netflix's prepaid expenses are payments made in advance to movie companies for rights to DVDs. By paying in advance, Netflix is able to negotiate lower prices. These fixed payments are debited to Prepaid Expense. When the movies produce revenue, the prepaid amounts are transferred to expense through adjusting entries.[7]

Type 2 Adjustment: Recognizing Unrecorded Expenses (Accrued Expenses)

STUDY NOTE: In accrual accounting, an expense must be recorded in the period in which it is incurred, regardless of when payment is made.

Usually, at the end of an accounting period, some expenses incurred during the period have not been recorded in the accounts. These expenses require adjusting entries. One such expense is interest on borrowed money. Each day, interest accumulates on the debt. As shown in Exhibit 3.5, at the end of the accounting period, an adjusting entry is made to record the accumulated interest, which is an expense of the period, and the corresponding liability to pay the interest. Other common unrecorded expenses are wages, taxes, and utilities. As the expense and the corresponding liability accumulate, they are said to *accrue*—hence, the term **accrued expenses**.

To illustrate how an adjustment is made for unrecorded wages, suppose Creative Designs has two pay periods a month. In July, its pay periods end on the 12th and the 26th, as indicated in this calendar:

July

Sun	M	T	W	Th	F	Sa
	1	2	3	4	5	6
7	8	9	10	11	12	13
14	15	16	17	18	19	20
21	22	23	24	25	26	27
28	29	30	31			

By the end of business on July 31, the assistant to Toni Ross, Creative Designs' CEO, will have worked three days (Monday, Tuesday, and Wednesday) beyond the last pay period. Although the employee has earned the wages for those days, he will not be paid until the first payday in August. The wages for these three days are an expense for July, and the liabilities should reflect that the company owes the assistant for those days.

EXHIBIT 3.5
Adjustment for Unrecorded (Accrued) Expenses

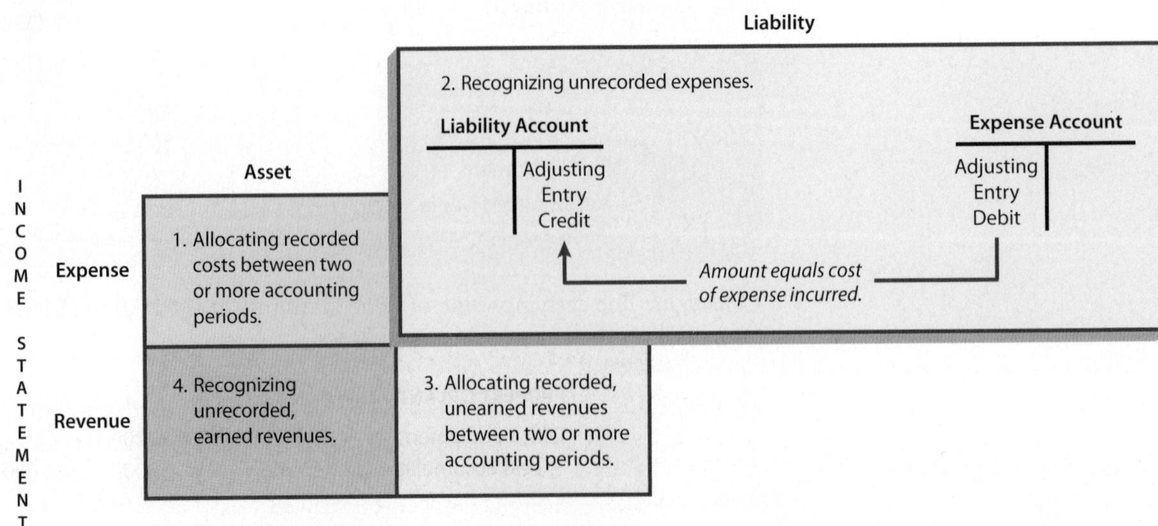

Because the assistant's wage rate is $2,400 every two weeks, or $240 per day ($2,400 ÷ 10 working days), the expense is $720 ($240 × 3 days).

Adjustment for Unrecorded Wages

July 31: Accrual of unrecorded wages, $720

Analysis: Accrual of wages
▲ *increases* the stockholders' equity account *Wages Expense* with a debit and
▲ *increases* the liability account *Wages Payable* with a credit.

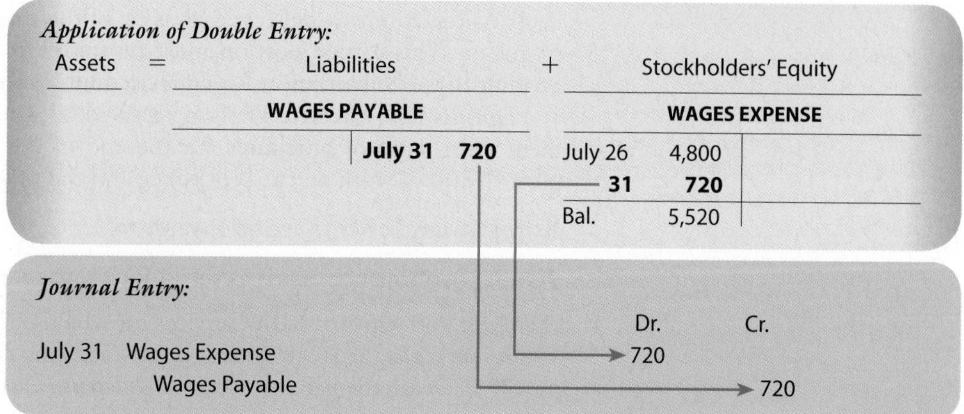

Journal Entry:

		Dr.	Cr.
July 31	Wages Expense	720	
	Wages Payable		720

Comment: Note that the increase in Wages Expense will *decrease* stockholders' equity and that total wages for the month are $5,520, of which $720 will be paid next month.

As a corporation, Creative Designs is subject to federal income taxes. The actual amount owed for taxes cannot be determined until net income has been computed at the end of the fiscal year. However, to be in accordance with the matching rule, each month should bear its part of the total year's expense. Therefore, the amount of income taxes expense for the current month must be estimated. Assume that after analyzing the firm's operations in its first month of business and conferring with her CPA, Toni Ross estimates July's share of income taxes for the year to be $800.

Adjustment for Estimated Income Taxes

July 31: Accrual of estimated income taxes, $800

Analysis: Accrual of income taxes
▲ *increases* the stockholders' equity account *Income Taxes Expense* with a debit and
▲ *increases* the liability account *Income Taxes Payable* with a credit.

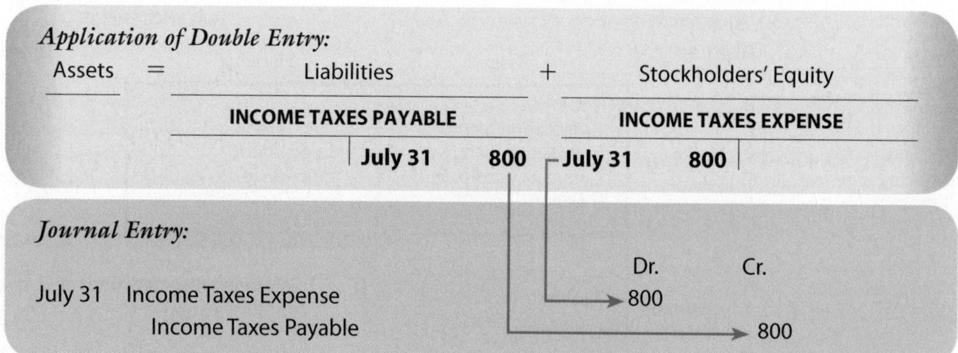

Journal Entry:

		Dr.	Cr.
July 31	Income Taxes Expense	800	
	Income Taxes Payable		800

Comment: Note that the increase in Income Taxes Expense will *decrease* stockholders' equity. There are many types of accrued expenses, and the adjustments made for all of them follow the same procedure as the one used for accrued wages and accrued income taxes.

Application to Netflix Inc. In 2009, **Netflix** had accrued expenses of $33,387,000.[8] If the expenses had not been accrued, Netflix's liabilities would be significantly understated, as would the corresponding expenses on Netflix's income statement. The end result would be an overstatement of the company's earnings.

Type 3 Adjustment: Allocating Recorded, Unearned Revenues (Deferred Revenues)

STUDY NOTE: *Unearned revenue is a liability because there is an obligation to deliver goods or perform a service, or to return a payment. Once the goods have been delivered or the service performed, the liability is transferred to revenue.*

Just as expenses can be paid before they are used, revenues can be received before they are earned. When a company receives revenues in advance, it has an obligation to deliver goods or perform services. **Unearned revenues** are therefore shown in a liability account.

For example, publishing companies usually receive payment in advance for magazine subscriptions. These receipts are recorded in a liability account, Unearned Subscriptions. If the company fails to deliver the magazines, subscribers are entitled to their money back. As the company delivers each issue of the magazine, it earns a part of the advance payments. This earned portion must be transferred from the Unearned Subscriptions account to the Subscription Revenue account, as shown in Exhibit 3.6.

During July, Creative Designs received $1,400 from another firm as advance payment for a series of brochures. By the end of the month, Creative Designs had completed $800 of work on the brochures, and the other firm had accepted the work.

Adjustment for Unearned Revenue

July 31: Performance of services paid for in advance, $800

Analysis: Performance of the services for which payment had been received in advance
▲ *increases* the stockholders' equity account *Design Revenue* with a credit and
▼ *decreases* the liability account *Unearned Design Revenue* with a debit.

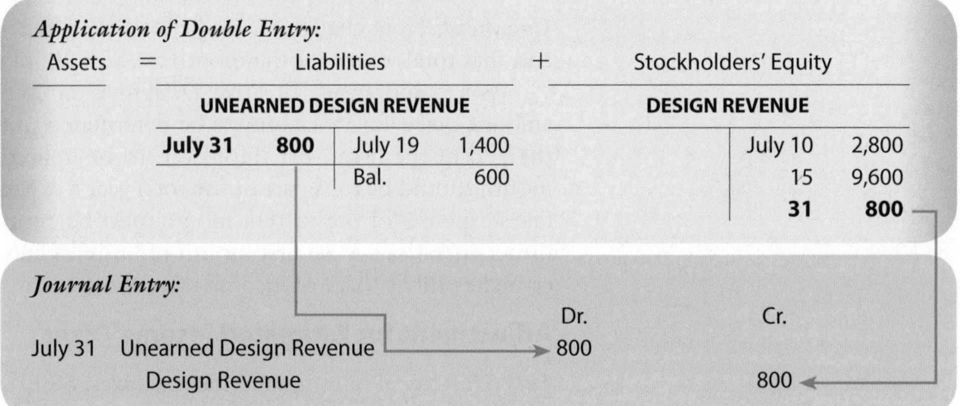

EXHIBIT 3.6
Adjustment for Unearned (Deferred) Revenues

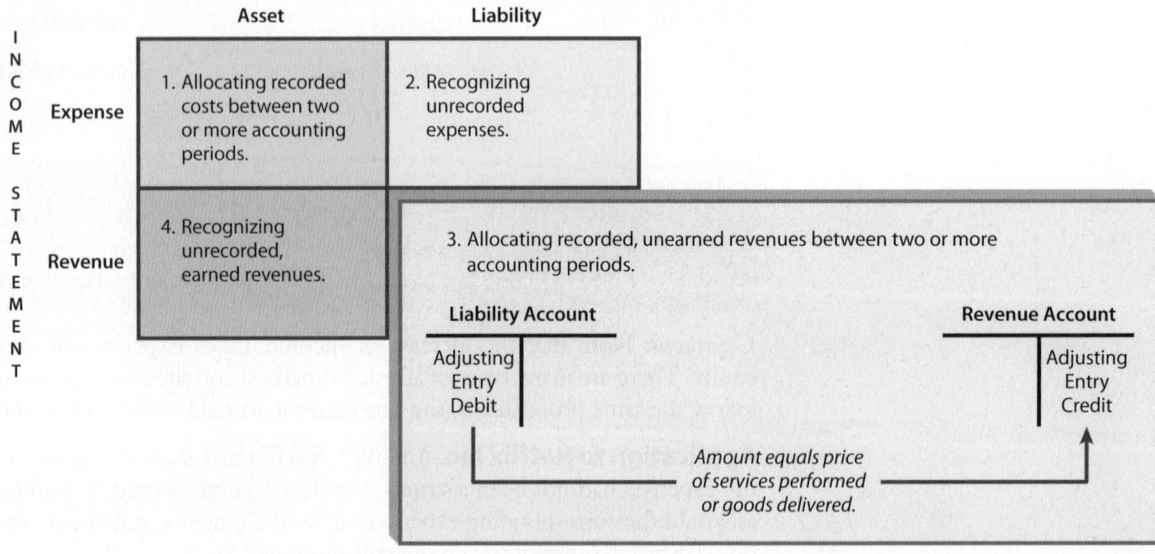

Comment: Unearned Design Revenue now reflects the amount of work still to be performed, $600.

Application to Netflix, Inc. Netflix has a current liability account called Deferred (Unearned) Revenue. Deferred revenue consists of subscriptions (monthly payments) billed in advance to customers, for which revenues have not yet been earned. Subscription revenues are pro-rated over each subscriber's monthly subscription period. As time passes and customers use the service, the revenue is transferred from Netflix's Deferred Revenue account to its Subscription Revenue account.

Type 4 Adjustment: Recognizing Unrecorded, Earned Revenues (Accrued Revenues)

Accrued revenues are revenues that a company has earned by performing a service or delivering goods but for which no entry has been made in the accounting records. Any revenues earned but not recorded during an accounting period require an adjusting entry that debits an asset account and credits a revenue account, as shown in Exhibit 3.7. For example, the interest on a note receivable is earned day by day but may not be received until another accounting period. In this case, Interest Receivable should be debited and Interest Income should be credited for the interest accrued at the end of the current period.

When a company earns revenue by performing a service—such as designing a website or developing marketing plans—but will not receive the revenue for the service until a future accounting period, it must make an adjusting entry. This type of adjusting entry involves an asset account and a revenue account.

Suppose Creative Designs agrees to create two advertisements for Maggio's Pizza Company and to finish the first advertisement by July 31. By the end of July, Creative Designs has earned $400 for completing the first advertisement, but it will not bill Maggio's Pizza until the entire project has been completed.

Adjustment for Design Revenue

July 31: Accrual of unrecorded revenue, $400

Analysis: Accrual of unrecorded revenue

▲ *increases* the stockholders' equity account *Design Revenue* with a credit and
▲ *increases* the asset account *Accounts Receivable* with a debit.

EXHIBIT 3.7
Adjustment for Unrecorded (Accrued) Revenues

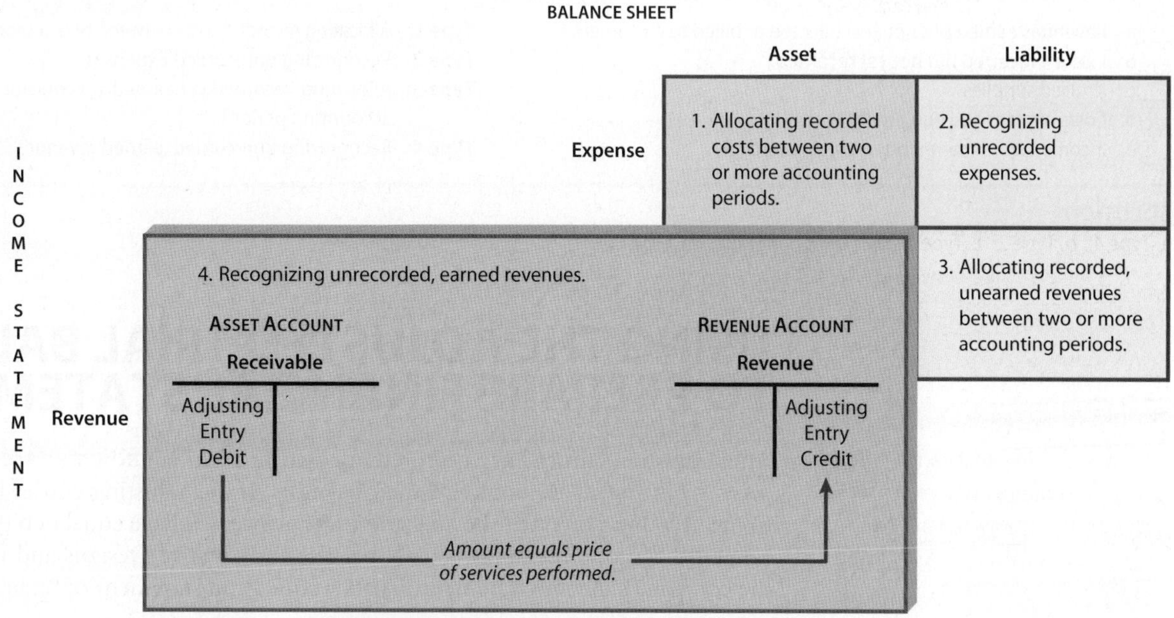

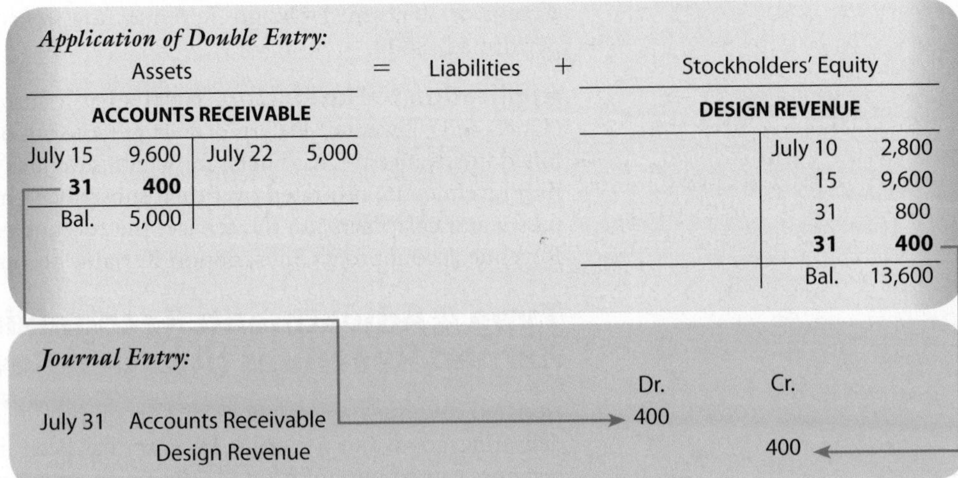

Application of Double Entry:

Assets = Liabilities + Stockholders' Equity

ACCOUNTS RECEIVABLE

July 15	9,600	July 22	5,000
31	**400**		
Bal.	5,000		

DESIGN REVENUE

		July 10	2,800
		15	9,600
		31	800
		31	**400**
		Bal.	13,600

Journal Entry:

		Dr.	Cr.
July 31	Accounts Receivable	400	
	Design Revenue		400

Comment: Design Revenue now reflects the total revenue earned during July: $13,600. On the balance sheet, revenues that have been earned but not recorded are usually combined with accounts receivable. However, some companies prefer to debit an account called Unbilled Accounts Receivable, and others simply flag the transactions in Accounts Receivable as "unbilled."

Application to Netflix, Inc. Because **Netflix**'s subscribers pay their subscriptions in advance by credit card, Netflix does not need to bill customers for services provided but not paid. The company is in the enviable position of having no accounts receivable and thus a high degree of liquidity.

A Note About Journal Entries

Thus far, we have presented a full analysis of each journal entry and showed the thought process behind each entry. Because you should now be fully aware of the effects of transactions on the accounting equation and the rules of debit and credit, we present journal entries without full analysis in the rest of the book.

Stop & Apply

For each of the items on the left, identify the type of adjusting entry required:

___a. Revenues earned but not yet collected or billed to customers
___b. Interest incurred but not yet recorded
___c. Unused supplies
___d. Costs of plant and equipment
___e. Income taxes incurred but not yet recorded

Type 1: Allocating recorded costs between two or more accounting periods
Type 2: Recognizing unrecorded expenses
Type 3: Allocating recorded, unearned revenue between two or more accounting periods
Type 4: Recognizing unrecorded, earned revenues

SOLUTION
a. Type 4; b. Type 2; c. Type 1; d. Type 1; e. Type 2

USING THE ADJUSTED TRIAL BALANCE TO PREPARE FINANCIAL STATEMENTS

Prepare financial statements from an adjusted trial balance. LO 4

After adjusting entries have been recorded and posted, an **adjusted trial balance** is prepared by listing all accounts and their balances. If the adjusting entries have been posted to the accounts correctly, the adjusted trial balance will have equal debit and credit totals. Exhibit 3.8 shows the adjusted trial balance for Creative Designs and its relationship to the company's income statement, balance sheet, and statement of retained earnings.

EXHIBIT 3.8
Relationship of the Adjusted Trial Balance to the Income Statement, Balance Sheet, and Statement of Retained Earnings

Creative Designs, Inc.
Adjusted Trial Balance
July 31, 2011

Cash	$22,480	
Accounts Receivable	5,000	
Office Supplies	3,660	
Prepaid Rent	1,600	
Office Equipment	16,320	
Accumulated Depreciation—Office Equipment		$ 300
Accounts Payable		6,280
Unearned Design Revenue		600
Wages Payable		720
Income Taxes Payable		800
Common Stock		40,000
Dividends	2,800	
Design Revenue		13,600
Wages Expense	5,520	
Utilities Expense	680	
Rent Expense	1,600	
Office Supplies Expense	1,540	
Depreciation Expense—Office Equipment	300	
Income Taxes Expense	800	
	$62,300	$62,300

Creative Designs, Inc.
Income Statement
For the Month Ended July 31, 2011

Revenues		
Design revenue		$13,600
Expenses		
Wages expense	$5,520	
Rent expense	1,600	
Office supplies expense	1,540	
Income taxes expense	800	
Utilities expense	680	
Depreciation expense—office equipment	300	
Total expenses		10,440
Net income		$ 3,160

Creative Designs, Inc.
Statement of Retained Earnings
For the Month Ended July 31, 2011

Retained earnings, July 1, 2011	—
Net income	$3,160
Subtotal	$3,160
Less dividends	2,800
Retained earnings, July 31, 2011	$ 360

Creative Designs, Inc.
Balance Sheet
July 31, 2011

Assets		
Cash		$22,480
Accounts receivable		5,000
Office supplies		3,660
Prepaid rent		1,600
Office equipment	$16,320	
Less accumulated depreciation	300	16,020
Total assets		$48,760
Liabilities		
Accounts payable		$ 6,280
Unearned design revenue		600
Wages payable		720
Income taxes payable		800
Total liabilities		$ 8,400
Stockholders' Equity		
Common stock	$40,000	
Retained earnings	360	
Total stockholders' equity		40,360
Total liabilities and stockholders' equity		$48,760

STUDY NOTE: *The figure for Retained Earnings does not appear on the adjusted trial balance. The balance is updated when the closing entries (explained beginning on the next page) are prepared.*

STUDY NOTE: *Note the order in which the statements must be prepared: Income statement—statement of retained earnings—balance sheet. This sequence is required because the statement of retained earnings needs the net income from the income statement and the balance sheet needs the ending retained earnings balance from the statement of retained earnings.*

Notice that some accounts in the adjusted trial balance, such as Cash and Accounts Payable, have the same balances as the trial balance in Exhibit 3.2 because no adjusting entries affected them. The balances of other accounts, such as Office Supplies and Prepaid Rent, differ from those in the trial balance because adjusting entries did affect them. The adjusted trial balance also includes accounts that do not appear in the trial balance—for example, depreciation accounts and Wages Payable.

***STUDY NOTE:** As is done after any step in the accounting cycle in which journal entries are recorded and posted, the adjusted trial balance is prepared to determine that the ledger is still in balance after adjustments have been made.*

The adjusted trial balance facilitates the preparation of the income statement, the balance sheet, and the statement of retained earnings. As shown in Exhibit 3.8, the balances of the revenue and expense accounts in the adjusted trial balance are used to prepare the income statement, and the balances of the asset and liability accounts are used to prepare the balance sheet.

The balance of the Dividends account appears in the statement of retained earnings. Notice that net income from the income statement is combined with dividends on the statement of retained earnings to give the net change in the Retained Earnings account. Also notice that the resulting balance of Retained Earnings at July 31 is used to prepare the stockholders' equity portion of the balance sheet.

Stop & Apply

The adjusted trial balance for Carroll Corporation on December 31, 2011, contains the following accounts and balances: Common Stock, $180; Retained Earnings, $120; Dividends, $100; Service Revenue, $1,100; Rent Expense, $300; Wages Expense, $400; Telephone Expense, $100; and Income Tax Expense, $50. Compute net income and prepare a statement of retained earnings for the month of December.

SOLUTION

Net income = $1,100 − $300 − $400 − $100 − $50
= $1,100 − $850
= $250

Carroll Corporation
Statement of Retained Earnings
For the Month Ended December 31, 2011

Retained Earnings November 30, 2011	$120
Net income	250
Subtotal	$370
Less dividends	100
Retained Earnings, December 31, 2011	$270

iStock Photo

CLOSING ENTRIES

Explain and prepare closing entries. LO 5

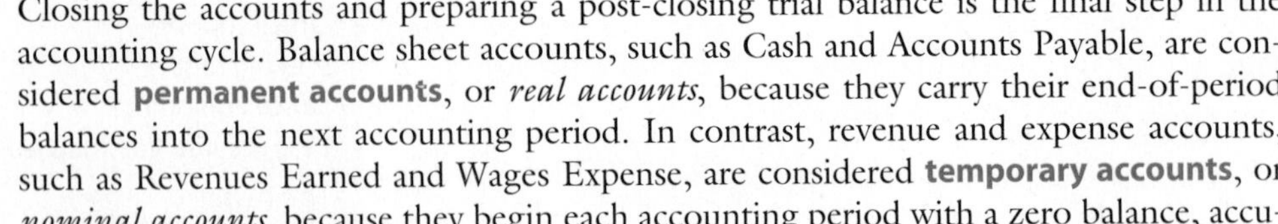

Closing the accounts and preparing a post-closing trial balance is the final step in the accounting cycle. Balance sheet accounts, such as Cash and Accounts Payable, are considered **permanent accounts**, or *real accounts*, because they carry their end-of-period balances into the next accounting period. In contrast, revenue and expense accounts, such as Revenues Earned and Wages Expense, are considered **temporary accounts**, or *nominal accounts*, because they begin each accounting period with a zero balance, accumulate a balance during the period, and are then cleared by means of closing entries.

Closing entries are journal entries made at the end of an accounting period. They serve two purposes:

- **Setting the stage for the next accounting period:** Since the income statement reports net income (or loss) for a single accounting period and shows revenues and expenses for the period only, it is necessary to clear revenue and expense accounts and the Dividends accounts of their balances. This step enables them to start over with a zero balance in the next accounting period.
- **Summarizing a period's revenues and expenses:** The **Income Summary account** is a temporary account that summarizes all revenues and expenses for the period. It is used only in the closing process—never in the financial statements. Its balance equals the net income or loss reported on the income statement. The net income or loss is then transferred to the Retained Earnings account.

EXHIBIT 3.9
Overview of the Closing Process*

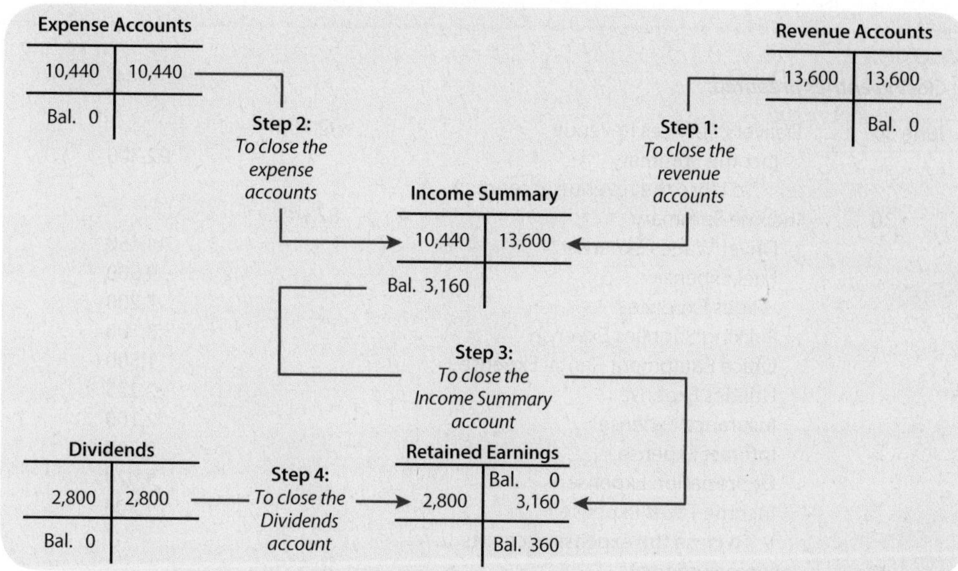

*Amounts are for Creative Designs, Inc. See Exhibit S3.1 in the Supplement to Chapter 3.

The net income or loss is transferred from the Income Summary account to Retained Earnings because even though revenues and expenses are recorded in revenue and expense accounts, they actually represent increases and decreases in stockholders' equity. Closing entries transfer the net effect of increases (revenues) and decreases (expenses) to stockholders' equity. Exhibit 3.9 shows an overview of the closing process.

Closing entries are required at the end of any period for which financial statements are prepared. **Netflix** prepares financial statements each quarter, and when it does, it must close its books and make closing entries. Many companies close their books monthly to give management a more timely view of ongoing operations.

As is done in any step in the accounting cycle in which entries are posted to the ledger accounts, a trial balance is prepared after closing entries have been posted. The purpose of a **post-closing trial balance** is to determine that all temporary accounts have zero balances and to double-check that total debits equal total credits. This final trial balance contains only balance sheet accounts because the income statement accounts and the Dividends account have all been closed and now have zero balances.

We explain the preparation of closing entries and the post-closing trial balance further in the Supplement to Chapter 3.

Stop & Apply

Prepare the necessary closing entries from the following partial adjusted trial balance for MGC Delivery Service, Inc. (except for Retained Earnings, balance sheet accounts have been omitted) and compute the ending balance of Retained Earnings.

MGC Delivery Service, Inc.
Partial Adjusted Trial Balance
June 30, 2011

Retained Earnings		$12,370
Dividends	$ 9,000	
Delivery Services Revenue		92,700
Driver Wages Expense	44,450	
Fuel Expense	9,500	
Wages Expense	7,200	
Packing Supplies Expense	3,100	
Office Equipment Rental Expense	1,500	
Utilities Expense	2,225	
Insurance Expense	2,100	
Interest Expense	2,550	
Depreciation Expense	5,020	
Income Taxes Expense	4,500	

iStock Photo

(continued)

SOLUTION

Closing entries prepared:

June 30	Delivery Services Revenue	92,700	
	Income Summary		92,700
	To close the revenue account		
30	Income Summary	82,145	
	Driver Wages Expense		44,450
	Fuel Expense		9,500
	Wages Expense		7,200
	Packing Supplies Expense		3,100
	Office Equipment Rental Expense		1,500
	Utilities Expense		2,225
	Insurance Expense		2,100
	Interest Expense		2,550
	Depreciation Expense		5,020
	Income Taxes Expense		4,500
	To close the expense accounts		
30	Income Summary	10,555	
	Retained Earnings		10,555
	To close the Income Summary account $92,700 – $82,145 = $10,555		
30	Retained Earnings	9,000	
	Dividends		9,000
	To close the Dividends account		

Ending balance of Retained Earnings computed:

RETAINED EARNINGS			
June 30	9,000	Beg. Bal.	12,370
		June 30	10,555
		End. Bal.	13,925

CASH FLOWS FROM ACCRUAL-BASED INFORMATION

LO 6 Use accrual-based information to analyze cash flows.

Management has the short-range goal of ensuring that its company has sufficient cash to pay ongoing obligations—in other words, management must ensure the company's liquidity. To plan payments to creditors and assess the need for short-term borrowing, managers must know how to use accrual-based information to analyze cash flows.

Almost every revenue or expense account on the income statement has one or more related accounts on the balance sheet. For instance, Supplies Expense is related to Supplies, Wages Expense is related to Wages Payable, and Design Revenue is related to Unearned Design Revenue. As we have shown, these accounts are related by making adjusting entries, the purpose of which is to apply the matching rule to the measurement of net income.

The cash inflows that a company's operations generate and the cash outflows that they require can also be determined by analyzing these relationships. For example, suppose that after receiving the financial statements in Exhibit 3.8 (p. 153), management wants to know how much cash was expended for office supplies. On the income statement, Office Supplies Expense is $1,540, and on the balance sheet, Office Supplies is $3,660. Because July was the company's first month of operation, there was no prior balance of office supplies, so the amount of cash expended for office supplies during the month was $5,200 ($1,540 + $3,660 = $5,200).

EXHIBIT 3.10
Determination of Cash Flows from Accrual-Based Information

Type of Account	*Potential Payment or Receipt Not Paid or Received*				*Result*
Prepaid Expense	Ending Balance	+ Expense for the Period	− Beginning Balance	=	Cash Payments for Expenses
Unearned Revenue	Ending Balance	+ Revenue for the Period	− Beginning Balance	=	Cash Receipts from Revenues
Accrued Payable	Beginning Balance	+ Expense for the Period	− Ending Balance	=	Cash Payments for Expenses
Accrued Receivable	Beginning Balance	+ Revenue for the Period	− Ending Balance	=	Cash Receipts from Revenues

Thus, the cash flow used in purchasing office supplies—$5,200—was much greater than the amount expensed in determining income—$1,540. In planning for August, management can anticipate that the cash needed may be less than the amount expensed because, given the large inventory of office supplies, the company will probably not have to buy office supplies in the coming month. Understanding these cash flow effects enables management to better predict the business's need for cash in August.

The general rule for determining the cash flow received from any revenue or paid for any expense (except depreciation, which is a special case not covered here) is to determine the potential cash payments or cash receipts and deduct the amount not paid or received. As shown in Exhibit 3.10, the application of the general rule varies with the type of asset or liability account.

For instance, suppose that on May 31, a company had a balance of $480 in Prepaid Insurance and that on June 30, the balance was $670. If the insurance expense during June was $120, the amount of cash expended on insurance during June can be computed as follows:

Prepaid Insurance at June 30	$670
Insurance Expense during June	120
Potential cash payments for insurance	$790
Less Prepaid Insurance at May 31	480
Cash payments for insurance during June	$310

The beginning balance is deducted because it was paid in a prior accounting period. Note that the cash payments equal the expense plus the increase in the balance of the Prepaid Insurance account [$120 + ($670 − $480) = $310]. In this case, the cash paid was almost three times the amount of insurance expense. In future months, cash payments are likely to be less than the expense.

Stop & Apply

Supplies had a balance of $400 at the end of May and $360 at the end of June. Supplies Expense was $550 for the month of June. How much cash was paid for supplies during June? Assume all purchases are for cash.

SOLUTION

Supplies at June 30	$360
Supplies Expense during June	550
Potential cash payments for supplies	$910
Less Supplies at May 31	400
Cash payments for supplies during June	$510

iStock Photo

A look back at ▸ Netflix, Inc.

In the Decision Point at the beginning of the chapter, we noted that **Netflix** has many transactions that span accounting periods. We asked these questions:

1. What assumptions must Netflix make to account for transactions that span accounting periods?
2. How does Netflix assign its revenues and expenses to the proper accounting period so that net income is properly measured?
3. Why are the adjustments that these transactions require important to Netflix's financial performance?

Two of the assumptions Netflix must make are that it will continue as a going concern for an indefinite time (the continuity assumption) and that it can make useful estimates of its income in terms of accounting periods (the periodicity assumption). These assumptions enable the company to apply the matching rule—that is, revenues are assigned to the accounting period in which goods are sold or services are performed, and expenses are assigned to the accounting period in which they are used to produce revenue. Adjusting entries for deferred and accrued expenses and for deferred and accrued revenues have an impact on a company's earnings.

RATIO

Financial Ratio: Cash Flow Yield

Netflix's earnings are an important measure of performance, but more can be learned about a company's profitability by calculating **cash flow yield**. This ratio helps to evaluate whether or not the company's income-producing operations are also generating sufficient cash to maintain the company's liquidity. For example, if a company is not successful in collecting its receivables, its liquidity will be adversely affected. A rule of thumb is that a company should generate at least $1 dollar of cash flows from operating activities for each $1 of net income—a cash flow yield of 1.0 times. To calculate Netflix's cash flow yield, we use the following data (in thousands) from the company's 2009 annual report:

	2009	2008
Net Income	$ 115,860	$ 83,026
Cash Flows from Operations	$ 325,063	$ 284,037

The company's cash flow yield is computed as follows:

	2009	2008
	$ 115,860 / **$325,063**	$ 83,026 / **$284,037**
Cash Flows from Operating Activities / Net Income	$ 325,063 / **$115,860**	$ 284,037 / **$ 83,026**
Cash Flow Yield:	**2.8 times**	**3.4 times**

These are very strong results for Netflix. Even though there was a decrease from 3.4 times in 2008 to 2.8 times in 2009, Netflix far exceeds the minimum benchmark of 1.0 times. Not only is Netflix profitable, it achieves a high level of liquidity.

Review Problem

Posting to T Accounts, Determining Adjusting Entries, and Using an Adjusted Trial Balance to Prepare Financial Statements

The following is the unadjusted trial balance for Reliable Lawn Care, Inc., on December 31, 2011:

Reliable Lawn Care, Inc.		
Trial Balance		
December 31, 2011		
Cash	$ 4,320	
Accounts Receivable	2,500	
Office Supplies	360	
Prepaid Insurance	480	
Office Equipment	6,800	
Accumulated Depreciation—Office Equipment		$ 1,200
Accounts Payable		1,400
Unearned Revenue		920
Common Stock		4,000
Retained Earnings		5,740
Dividends	800	
Service Revenue		5,800
Wages Expense	3,000	
Rent Expense	800	
	$19,060	$19,060

The following information is also available:

a. Insurance that expired during December, $80.
b. Office supplies on hand on December 31, $150.
c. Depreciation for December, $200.
d. Accrued wages on December 31, $240.
e. Revenues earned for services performed in December but not billed by the end of the month, $600.
f. Performance of services paid for in advance, $320.
g. Estimated income taxes for December, $500.

Required

1. Prepare T accounts for the accounts in the trial balance and enter the balances.
2. Determine the required adjusting entries and record them directly in the T accounts. Open new T accounts as needed.
3. Prepare an adjusted trial balance.
4. Prepare an income statement, statement of retained earnings, and balance sheet for the month ended December 31, 2011.

ANSWERS TO REVIEW PROBLEM

1. T accounts set up and amounts from trial balance entered
2. Adjusting entries recorded

	A	B	C	D	E	F	G	H	I	J	K	L	M	N
1		**Cash**					**Accounts Receivable**					**Office Supplies**		
2	Bal.	4,320				Bal.	2,500				Bal.	360	(b)	210
3						(e)	600				*Bal.*	*150*		
4						*Bal.*	*3,100*							
5														
6												**Accumulated Depreciation—**		
7		**Prepaid Insurance**					**Office Equipment**					**Office Equipment**		
8	Bal.	480	(a)	80		Bal.	6,800						Bal.	1,200
9	*Bal.*	*400*											(c)	200
10													*Bal.*	*1,400*
11														
12		**Accounts Payable**					**Unearned Revenue**					**Wages Payable**		
13			Bal.	1,400		(f)	320	Bal.	920				(d)	240
14								*Bal.*	*600*					
15														
16		**Income Taxes Payable**					**Common Stock**					**Retained Earnings**		
17			(g)	500				Bal.	4,000				Bal.	5,740
18														
19		**Dividends**					**Service Revenue**					**Wages Expense**		
20	Bal.	800						Bal.	5,800		Bal.	3,000		
21								(e)	600		(d)	240		
22								(f)	320		*Bal.*	*3,240*		
23								*Bal.*	*6,720*					
24														
25		**Rent Expense**					**Insurance Expense**					**Office Supplies Expense**		
26	Bal.	800				(a)	80				(b)	210		
27														
28		**Depreciation Expense—**												
29		**Office Equipment**					**Income Taxes Expense**							
30	(c)	200				(g)	500							
31														

3. Adjusted trial balance prepared

	A	B	C	D	E
1	Reliable Lawn Care, Inc.				
2	Adjusted Trial Balance				
3	December 31, 2011				
4					
5	Cash			$ 4,320	
6	Accounts Receivable			3,100	
7	Office Supplies			150	
8	Prepaid Insurance			400	
9	Office Equipment			6,800	
10	Accumulated Depreciation—Office Equipment				$ 1,400
11	Accounts Payable				1,400
12	Unearned Revenue				600
13	Wages Payable				240
14	Income Taxes Payable				500
15	Common Stock				4,000
16	Retained Earnings				5,740
17	Dividends			800	
18	Service Revenue				6,720
19	Wages Expense			3,240	
20	Rent Expense			800	
21	Insurance Expense			80	
22	Office Supplies Expense			210	
23	Depreciation Expense—Office Equipment			200	
24	Income Taxes Expense			500	
25				$20,600	$20,600
26					

4. Financial statements prepared

	A	B	C	D	E
1	Reliable Lawn Care, Inc.				
2	Income Statement				
3	For the Month Ended December 31, 2011				
4					
5	**Revenue**				
6		Service revenue			$6,720
7					
8	**Expenses**				
9		Wages expense		$3,240	
10		Rent expense		800	
11		Insurance expense		80	
12		Office supplies expense		210	
13		Depreciation expense--office equipment		200	
14		Income taxes expense		500	
15		Total expenses			5,030
16	**Net income**				$1,690
17					

	A	B	C	D
1	Reliable Lawn Care, Inc.			
2	Statement of Retained Earnings			
3	For the Month Ended December 31, 2011			
4				
5	Retained earnings, November 30, 2011			$5,740
6	Net income			1,690
7	Subtotal			$7,430
8	Less dividends			800
9	Retained earnings, December 31, 2011			$6,630
10				

	A	B	C	D	E
1	Reliable Lawn Care, Inc.				
2	Balance Sheet				
3	December 31, 2011				
4					
5	Assets				
6	Cash				$ 4,320
7	Accounts receivable				3,100
8	Office supplies				150
9	Prepaid insurance				400
10	Office equipment			$6,800	
11		Less accumulated depreciation		1,400	5,400
12	Total assets				$13,370
13					
14	Liabilities				
15	Accounts payable				$ 1,400
16	Unearned revenue				600
17	Wages payable				240
18	Income taxes payable				500
19	Total liabilities				$ 2,740
20					
21	Stockholders' Equity				
22	Common stock			$4,000	
23	Retained earnings			6,630	
24	Total stockholders' equity				10,630
25	Total liabilities and stockholders' equity				$13,370
26					

Stop & Review

LO1 Define *net income* and explain the assumptions underlying income measurement and their ethical application.

Net income is the net increase in stockholders' equity that results from a company's operations. Net income equals revenues minus expenses; when expenses exceed revenues, a net loss results. Revenues equal the price of goods sold or services rendered during a specific period. Expenses are the costs of goods and services used in the process of producing revenues.

The continuity assumption recognizes that even though businesses face an uncertain future, without evidence to the contrary, accountants must assume that a business will continue to operate indefinitely. The periodicity assumption recognizes that although the lifetime of a business is uncertain, it is nonetheless useful to estimate the business's net income in terms of accounting periods. The matching rule holds that revenues must be assigned to the accounting period in which the goods are sold or the services performed and that expenses must be assigned to the accounting period in which they are used to produce revenue.

Because applying the matching rule involves making assumptions and exercising judgment, it can lead to earnings management, which is the manipulation of revenues and expenses to achieve a specific outcome. When the estimates involved in earnings management move outside a reasonable range, financial statements become misleading. Financial statements that are intentionally misleading constitute fraudulent financial reporting.

LO2 Define *accrual accounting* and explain how it is accomplished.

Accrual accounting consists of all the techniques accountants use to apply the matching rule. It is accomplished by recognizing revenues when they are earned, by recognizing expenses when they are incurred, and by adjusting the accounts.

LO3 Identify the four situations that require adjusting entries and illustrate typical adjusting entries.

Adjusting entries are required when (1) recorded costs must be allocated between two or more accounting periods; (2) unrecorded expenses exist; (3) recorded, unearned revenues must be allocated between two or more accounting periods; and (4) unrecorded, earned revenues exist. The preparation of adjusting entries is summarized as follows:

	Type of Account		
Type of Adjusting Entry	**Debited**	**Credited**	**Examples of Balance Sheet Accounts**
1. Allocating recorded costs (previously paid, expired)	Expense	Asset (or contra-asset)	Prepaid Rent Prepaid Insurance Office Supplies Accumulated Depreciation—Office Equipment
2. Accrued expenses (incurred, not paid)	Expense	Liability	Wages Payable Income Taxes Payable
3. Allocating recorded, unearned revenues (previously received, earned)	Liability	Revenue	Unearned Design Revenue
4. Accrued revenues (earned, not received)	Asset	Revenue	Accounts Receivable Interest Receivable

LO4 Prepare financial statements from an adjusted trial balance.

An adjusted trial balance is prepared after adjusting entries have been posted to the accounts. Its purpose is to test whether the adjusting entries have been posted correctly before the financial statements are prepared. The balances in the revenue and expense accounts in the adjusted trial balance are used to prepare the income statement. The balances in the asset and liability accounts in the adjusted trial balance and in the statement of retained earnings are used to prepare the balance sheet.

Explain and prepare closing entries. 

Closing entries have two purposes: (1) they clear the balances of all temporary accounts (revenue, expense, and Dividends accounts) so that they have zero balances at the beginning of the next accounting period, and (2) they summarize a period's revenues and expenses in the Income Summary account so that the net income or net loss for the period can be transferred as a total to Retained Earnings. As a final check on the balance of the ledger and to ensure that all temporary accounts have been closed, a post-closing trial balance is prepared after the closing entries have been posted to the ledger accounts.

Use accrual-based information to analyze cash flows. LO 6

To ensure a company's liquidity, managers must know how to use accrual-based information to analyze cash flows. The general rule for determining the cash flow received from any revenue or paid for any expense (except depreciation) is to determine the potential cash payments or cash receipts and deduct the amount not paid or received.

Key Terms and Ratios

Accrual 145 (LO3)
Accrual accounting 141 (LO2)
Accrued expenses 148 (LO3)
Accrued revenues 151 (LO3)
Accumulated Depreciation accounts 147 (LO3)
Adjusted trial balance 152 (LO4)
Adjusting entries 144 (LO3)
Carrying value 147 (LO3)
Cash basis of accounting 140 (LO1)
Closing entries 154 (LO5)
Continuity 139 (LO1)
Contra account 147 (LO3)
Deferral 145 (LO3)
Depreciation 147 (LO3)
Earnings management 140 (LO1)
Expenses 138 (LO1)
Fiscal year 139 (LO1)
Going concern 139 (LO1)
Income Summary account 154 (LO5)
Interim periods 139 (LO1)
Matching rule 140 (LO1)
Net income 138 (LO1)
Net loss 138 (LO1)
Periodicity 139 (LO1)
Permanent accounts 154 (LO5)
Post-closing trial balance 155 (LO5)
Prepaid expenses 145 (LO3)
Profit 138 (LO1)
Revenue recognition 142 (LO2)
Revenues 138 (LO1)
Temporary accounts 154 (LO5)
Unearned revenues 150 (LO3)

FINANCIAL RATIO
Cash flow yield 158 (LO6)

Chapter Assignments Building Your Basic Knowledge and Skills

Short Exercises

LO 1, 2

Accrual Accounting Concepts

SE 1. Match the concepts of accrual accounting on the right with the assumptions on the left:

___1. Assumes expenses should be assigned to the accounting period in which they are used to produce revenues
___2. Assumes a business will last indefinitely
___3. Assumes revenues are earned at a certain point in time
___4. Assumes net income that is measured for a short period of time, such as one quarter, is a useful measure

a. Periodicity
b. Going concern
c. Matching rule
d. Revenue recognition

LO 3 **Adjustment for Prepaid Insurance**

SE 2. The Prepaid Insurance account began the year with a balance of $460. During the year, insurance in the amount of $1,040 was purchased. At the end of the year (December 31), the amount of insurance still unexpired was $700. Prepare the year-end journal entry to record the adjustment for Insurance Expense for the year.

LO 3 **Adjustment for Supplies**

SE 3. The Supplies account began the year with a balance of $380. During the year, supplies in the amount of $980 were purchased. At the end of the year (December 31), the inventory of supplies on hand was $440. Prepare the year-end journal entry to record the adjustment for Supplies Expense for the year.

LO 3 **Adjustment for Depreciation**

SE 4. The depreciation expense on office equipment for the month of March is $100. This is the third month that the office equipment, which cost $1,900, has been owned. Prepare the adjusting entry to record depreciation for March and show the balance sheet presentation for office equipment and related accounts after the March 31 adjustment.

LO 3 **Adjustment for Accrued Wages**

SE 5. Wages are paid each Saturday for a six-day workweek. Wages are currently running $1,380 per week. Prepare the adjusting entry required on June 30, assuming July 1 falls on a Tuesday.

LO 3 **Adjustment for Unearned Revenue**

SE 6. During the month of August, deposits in the amount of $1,100 were received for services to be performed. By the end of the month, services in the amount of $760 had been performed. Prepare the necessary adjustment for Service Revenue at the end of the month.

LO 4 **Preparation of an Income Statement and Statement of Retained Earnings from an Adjusted Trial Balance**

SE 7. The adjusted trial balance for Shimura Company on December 31, 2011, contains the following accounts and balances: Retained Earnings, $4,300; Dividends, $175; Service Revenue, $1,300; Rent Expense, $200; Wages Expense, $450; Utilities Expense, $100; Telephone Expense, $25; and Income Taxes Expense, $175. Prepare an income statement and statement of retained earnings for the month of December.

LO 5 **Preparation of Closing Entries**

SE 8. Using the data in **SE 7**, prepare required closing entries for Shimura Company.

LO 4 **Preparation of an Income Statement and Statement of Retained Earnings from an Adjusted Trial Balance**

SE 9. The adjusted trial balance for Cloud Company on October 31, 2011, contains the following accounts and balances: Retained Earnings, $6,450; Dividends, $263; Service Revenue, $1,950; Rent Expense, $300; Wages Expense, $675; Utilities Expense, $150; Telephone Expense, $38; and Income Taxes Expense, $263. Prepare an income statement and statement of retained earnings for the month of October.

LO 5 **Preparation of Closing Entries**

SE 10. Using the data in **SE 9**, prepare required closing entries for Cloud Company.

LO 6 **Determination of Cash Flows**

SE 11. Unearned Revenue had a balance of $650 at the end of November and $450 at the end of December. Service Revenue was $2,550 for the month of December. How much cash was received in December for services to be provided?

Financial Ratio: Cash Flow Yield

SE 12. Calculate cash flow yield for 2011 using the following data. A company has net income of $7,000 and cash flow from operations of $8,750. (*Note:* Round to one decimal place.)

Exercises

LO 1, 2, 3

Discussion Questions

E 1. Develop a brief answer to each of the following questions:

1. When a company has net income, what happens to its assets and/or to its liabilities?
2. Why must a company that gives a guaranty or warranty with its product or service show an expense in the year of sale rather than in a later year when a repair or replacement is made?
3. Is accrual accounting more closely related to a company's goal of profitability or liquidity?
4. Under normal circumstances, will the carrying value of a long-term asset be equal to its market value? Explain your answers.

Discussion Questions

LO 4

E 2. Develop a brief answer to each of the following questions:

1. Why is Retained Earnings not listed on the trial balance for Creative Designs, Inc., in Exhibits 3.2 and 3.8?
2. If, at the end of the accounting period, you were looking at the T account for a prepaid expense like supplies, would you look for the amounts expended in cash on the debit or credit side? On which side would you find the amount expensed during the period?
3. Would you expect cash flow yield to be a good measure of a company's liquidity? Why or why not?

RATIO

LO 1, 2, 3

Applications of Accounting Concepts Related to Accrual Accounting

E 3. The accountant for Statos Company makes the assumptions or performs the activities in the list that follows. Tell which of these concepts of accrual accounting most directly relates to each assumption or action: (a) periodicity, (b) going concern, (c) matching rule, (d) revenue recognition, (e) deferral, and (f) accrual.

1. In estimating the life of a building, assumes that the business will last indefinitely
2. Records a sale when the customer is billed
3. Postpones the recognition of a one-year insurance policy as an expense by initially recording the expenditure as an asset
4. Recognizes the usefulness of financial statements prepared on a monthly basis even though they are based on estimates
5. Recognizes, by making an adjusting entry, wages expense that has been incurred but not yet recorded
6. Prepares an income statement that shows the revenues earned and the expenses incurred during the accounting period

LO 2

Application of Conditions for Revenue Recognition

E 4. Four conditions must be met before revenue should be recognized. In each of the following cases, tell which condition has *not* been met:

1. Kellman Company accepts a contract from another company to perform services in the future for $2,000.
2. Oblinger Company ships products worth $3,000 to another company without an order from the other company but tells the company it can return the products if it does not sell them.

3. Kearney Company performs services for $10,000 for a company that is in financial difficulty.
4. Evans Company agrees to work out a price later for services that it performs for another company.

LO 3 **Adjusting Entry for Unearned Revenue**

E 5. City Life, Inc. of Fargo, North Dakota, publishes a monthly magazine featuring local restaurant reviews and upcoming social, cultural, and sporting events. Subscribers pay for subscriptions either one year or two years in advance. Cash received from subscribers is credited to an account called Magazine Subscriptions Received in Advance. On December 31, 2011, the end of the company's fiscal year, the balance of Magazine Subscriptions Received in Advance is $420,000. Expiration of subscriptions revenue is as follows:

During 2011	$ 87,500
During 2012	207,500
During 2013	125,000

Record the adjusting entry for December 31, 2011.

LO 3 **Adjusting Entries for Prepaid Insurance**

E 6. An examination of the Prepaid Insurance account shows a balance of $33,690 at the end of an accounting period, before adjustment. Prepare journal entries to record the insurance expense for the period under the following independent assumptions:

1. An examination of the insurance policies shows unexpired insurance that cost $16,540 at the end of the period.
2. An examination of the insurance policies shows insurance that cost $4,300 has expired during the period.

LO 3 **Adjusting Entries for Supplies: Missing Data**

E 7. Each of the following columns represents a Supplies account:

	a	b	c	d
Supplies on hand at July 1	$264	$217	$196	$?
Supplies purchased during the month	52	?	174	1,928
Supplies consumed during the month	194	972	?	1,632
Supplies on hand at July 31	?	436	56	1,118

1. Determine the amounts indicated by the question marks.
2. Make the adjusting entry for column **a**, assuming supplies purchased are debited to an asset account.

LO 3 **Adjusting Entry for Accrued Salaries**

E 8. Oscar Incorporated has a five-day workweek and pays salaries of $70,000 each Friday.

1. Prepare the adjusting entry required on May 31, assuming that June 1 falls on a Wednesday.
2. Prepare the journal entry to pay the salaries on June 3, including the amount of salaries payable from requirement **1**.

LO 3 **Revenue and Expense Recognition**

E 9. Regina Company produces computer software that Bit Comp, Inc., sells. Regina receives a royalty of 15 percent of sales. Bit Comp pays royalties to Regina Company semiannually—on May 1 for sales made in July through December of the previous year and on November 1 for sales made in January through June of the current year. Royalty expense for Bit Comp and royalty income for Regina Company in the amount of

$12,000 were accrued on December 31, 2010. Cash in the amounts of $12,000 and $20,000 was paid and received on May 1 and November 1, 2011, respectively. Software sales during the July to December 2011 period totaled $430,000.

1. Calculate the amount of royalty expense for Bit Comp and royalty income for Regina during 2011.
2. Record the adjusting entry that each company made on December 31, 2011.

LO 4 **Preparation of Financial Statements**

E 10. Prepare the monthly income statement, statement of retained earnings, and balance sheet for Spark Cleaning Company, Inc., from the data provided in the adjusted trial balance presented below.

Spark Cleaning Company, Inc.
Adjusted Trial Balance
August 31, 2011

Cash	$ 4,590	
Accounts Receivable	2,592	
Prepaid Insurance	380	
Prepaid Rent	200	
Cleaning Supplies	152	
Cleaning Equipment	3,200	
Accumulated Depreciation—Cleaning Equipment		$ 320
Truck	7,200	
Accumulated Depreciation—Truck		720
Accounts Payable		420
Wages Payable		80
Unearned Janitorial Revenue		920
Income Taxes Payable		800
Common Stock		4,000
Retained Earnings		11,034
Dividends	2,000	
Janitorial Revenue		14,620
Wages Expense	5,680	
Rent Expense	1,200	
Gas, Oil, and Other Truck Expenses	580	
Insurance Expense	380	
Supplies Expense	2,920	
Depreciation Expense—Cleaning Equipment	320	
Depreciation Expense—Truck	720	
Income Taxes Expense	800	
	$32,914	$32,914

LO 5 **Preparation of Closing Entries**

E 11. From the adjusted trial balance in **E 10**, prepare the required closing entries for Spark Cleaning Company, Inc.

LO 3 **Adjusting Entries**

E 12. Prepare year-end adjusting entries for each of the following:

1. Office Supplies has a balance of $168 on January 1. Purchases debited to Office Supplies during the year amount to $830. A year-end inventory reveals supplies of $570 on hand.
2. Depreciation of office equipment is estimated to be $1,065 for the year.

3. Property taxes for six months, estimated at $900, have accrued but have not been recorded.
4. Unrecorded interest receivable on U.S. government bonds is $425.
5. Unearned Revenue has a balance of $900. Services for $375 received in advance have now been performed.
6. Services totaling $400 have been performed; the customer has not yet been billed.

LO 3

Accounting for Revenue Received in Advanced

E 13. Edward Papa, a lawyer, was paid $42,000 on October 1 to represent a client in real estate negotiations over the next 12 months.

1. Record the journal entries required in Papa's records on October 1 and at the end of the fiscal year, December 31.
2. How would this transaction be reflected on the income statement and balance sheet on December 31?

LO 5

Preparation of Closing Entries

E 14. The adjusted trial balance for Gott Consultant Corporation at the end of its fiscal year is presented below. Prepare the required closing entries.

Gott Consultant Corporation
Trial Balance
December 31, 2011

Cash	$ 7,275	
Accounts Receivable	2,325	
Prepaid Insurance	585	
Office Supplies	440	
Office Equipment	6,300	
Accumulated Depreciation—Office Equipment		$ 765
Automobile	6,750	
Accumulated Depreciation—Automobile		750
Accounts Payable		1,700
Unearned Consulting Fees		1,500
Income Taxes Payable		3,000
Common Stock		10,000
Retained Earnings		4,535
Dividends	7,000	
Consulting Fees Earned		31,700
Office Salaries Expense	13,500	
Advertising Expense	2,525	
Rent Expense	2,650	
Telephone Expense	1,600	
Income Taxes Expense	3,000	
	$53,950	$53,950

LO 4, 5

Preparation of a Statement of Retained Earnings

E 15. The Retained Earnings, Dividends, and Income Summary accounts for Cindy's Beauty Salon, Inc., are shown in T account forms (p. 170). The closing entries have been recorded for the year ended December 31, 2011. Prepare a statement of retained earnings for Cindy's Beauty Salon, Inc.

RETAINED EARNINGS

12/31/11	19,000	12/31/10	52,000
		12/31/11	44,000
		Bal.	**77,000**

INCOME SUMMARY

12/31/11	86,000	12/31/11	130,000
12/31/11	44,000		
Bal.	—		

DIVIDENDS

4/1/11	6,000	12/31/11	19,000
7/1/11	7,000		
10/1/11	6,000		
Bal.	—		

LO 6

Determination of Cash Flows

E 16. After adjusting entries, the balance sheets of Tukan Company showed the following asset and liability amounts at the end of 2011 and 2010:

	2011	2010
Prepaid insurance	$1,200	$1,450
Wages payable	600	1,100
Unearned revenue	2,100	950

The following amounts were taken from the 2011 income statement:

Insurance expense	$1,900
Wages expense	9,750
Fees earned	4,450

Calculate the amount of cash paid for insurance and wages and the amount of cash received for fees during 2011.

LO 6

Relationship of Expenses to Cash Paid

E 17. The income statement for Popov Company included the following expenses for 2011:

Rent expense	$150,000
Interest expense	23,400
Salaries expense	242,000

Listed below are the related balance sheet account balances at year-end for this year and last year.

	This Year	Last Year
Prepaid rent	$ 2,700	—
Interest payable	—	$ 3,000
Salaries payable	28,000	15,000

1. Compute the cash paid for rent during the year.
2. Compute the cash paid for interest during the year.
3. Compute the cash paid for salaries during the year.

Financial Ratio: Cash Flow Yield

E 18. Zenon Company wants to know if its liquidity has improved. Calculate its cash flow yield for 2011 and 2010 using the following data. (*Note:* Round to one decimal place.)

Net Income, 2011	$5,000
Net Income, 2010	4,300
Cash Flows from Operating Activities, 2011	6,000
Cash Flows from Operating Activities, 2010	5,500

By this measure, has liquidity improved? Explain your answer.

Problems

Determining Adjustments

LO 2, 3

P 1. At the end of its fiscal year, Dickens Cleaners, Inc., had the following trial balance:

Dickens Cleaners, Inc.
Trial Balance
September 30, 2011

Cash	$ 23,576	
Accounts Receivable	52,988	
Prepaid Insurance	6,800	
Cleaning Supplies	14,748	
Land	36,000	
Building	372,000	
Accumulated Depreciation—Building		$ 91,200
Accounts Payable		36,800
Unearned Cleaning Revenue		3,400
Mortgage Payable		220,000
Common Stock		80,000
Retained Earnings		33,120
Dividends	18,000	
Cleaning Revenue		319,268
Wages Expense	202,660	
Cleaning Equipment Rental Expense	12,200	
Delivery Truck Expense	8,748	
Interest Expense	22,000	
Other Expenses	14,068	
	$783,788	$783,788

The following information is also available:

a. A study of the company's insurance policies shows that $1,360 is unexpired at the end of the year.
b. An inventory of cleaning supplies shows $2,300 on hand.
c. Estimated depreciation on the building for the year is $25,600.
d. Accrued interest on the mortgage payable is $2,000.
e. On September 1, the company signed a contract, effective immediately, with Kings County Hospital to dry-clean, for a fixed monthly charge of $850, the uniforms used by doctors in surgery. The hospital paid for four months' service in advance.
f. The company pays sales and delivery wages on Saturday. The weekly payroll is $6,120. September 30 falls on a Thursday, and the company has a six-day pay week.
g. Estimated federal income taxes for the period are $4,600.

REQUIRED

All adjustments affect one balance sheet account and one income statement account. For each of the above situations, show the accounts affected, the amount of the adjustment (using a + or – to indicate an increase or a decrease, respectively), and the balance of the account after the adjustment in the following format:

Balance Sheet Account	Amount of Adjustment (+ or –)	Balance after Adjustment	Income Statement Account	Amount of Adjustment (+ or –)	Balance after Adjustment

LO 2, 3

Preparing Adjusting Entries

P 2. On June 30, the end of the current fiscal year, the following information is available to Heart Company's accountants for making adjusting entries:

a. One of the company's liabilities is a mortgage payable in the amount of $520,000. On June 30, the accrued interest on this mortgage was $26,000.
b. On Friday, July 2, the company, which is on a five-day workweek and pays employees weekly, will pay its regular salaried employees $37,400.
c. On June 29, the company completed negotiations and signed a contract to provide services to a new client at an annual rate of $14,400.
d. The Supplies account shows a beginning balance of $3,230 and purchases during the year of $8,230. The end-of-year inventory reveals supplies on hand of $2,636.
e. The Prepaid Insurance account shows the following entries on June 30:

Beginning Balance	$3,240
January 1	5,800
May 1	6,732

The beginning balance represents the unexpired portion of a one-year policy purchased a year ago. The January 1 entry represents a new one-year policy; the May 1 entry represents the additional coverage of a three-year policy.

f. The following table contains the cost and annual depreciation for buildings and equipment, all of which were purchased before the current year:

Account	Cost	Annual Depreciation
Buildings	$340,000	$14,600
Equipment	436,000	41,300

g. On June 1, the company completed negotiations with another client and accepted a payment of $43,200, representing one year's services paid in advance. The $43,200 was credited to Services Collected in Advance.
h. The company calculates that as of June 30, it had earned $9,000 on a $15,000 contract that will be completed and billed in August.
i. Federal income taxes for the year are estimated to be $12,600.

REQUIRED

1. Prepare adjusting entries for each item listed above.

USER INSIGHT ▶ 2. Explain how the conditions for revenue recognition are applied to transactions **c** and **h**.

LO 3, 4

Determining Adjusting Entries, Posting to T Accounts, and Preparing an Adjusted Trial Balance

✔ Adjusted trial balance: $64,389

P 3. The trial balance for Financial Service, Inc., on December 31 follows.

Financial Service, Inc.
Trial Balance
December 31, 2011

Cash	$ 9,250	
Accounts Receivable	4,125	
Office Supplies	1,331	
Prepaid Rent	660	
Office Equipment	4,620	
Accumulated Depreciation—Office Equipment		$ 770
Accounts Payable		2,970
Notes Payable		5,500
Unearned Service Revenue		1,485
Common Stock		6,000
Retained Earnings		7,001
Dividends	11,000	
Service Revenue		36,300
Salaries Expense	24,700	
Rent Expense	2,200	
Utilities Expense	2,140	
	$60,026	$60,026

The following information is also available:

a. Ending inventory of office supplies, $150.
b. Prepaid rent expired, $305.
c. Depreciation of office equipment for the period, $263.
d. Accrued interest expense at the end of the period, $285.
e. Accrued salaries at the end of the period, $165.
f. Service revenue still unearned at the end of the period, $583.
g. Service revenue earned but unrecorded, $1,550.
h. Estimated income taxes for the period, $2,100.

REQUIRED

1. Open T accounts for the accounts in the trial balance plus the following: Interest Payable, Salaries Payable, Income Taxes Payable, Office Supplies Expense, Depreciation Expense—Office Equipment, Interest Expense, and Income Taxes Expense. Enter the balances shown on the trial balance.
2. Determine the adjusting entries and post them directly to the T accounts.
3. Prepare an adjusted trial balance.

USER INSIGHT ▶

4. What financial statements does each of the above adjustments affect? What financial statement is *not* affected by the adjustments?

LO 3, 4

Determining Adjusting Entries and Tracing Their Effects to Financial Statements

✔ Adjusted trial balance: $67,470

P 4. Randy Kazai opened a small tax-preparation service. At the end of its second year of operation, Kazai Tax Service, Inc., had the trial balance shown below.

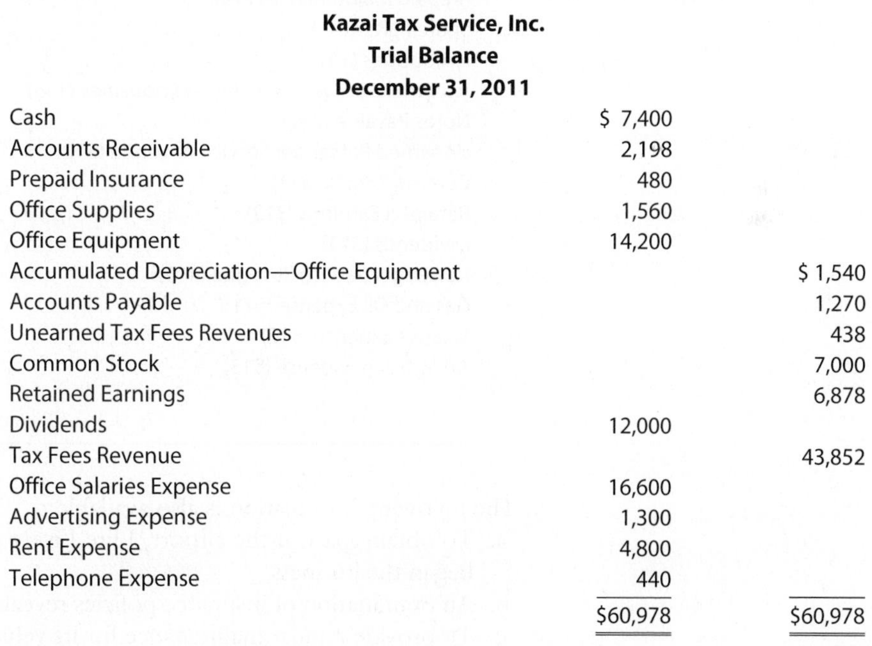

Kazai Tax Service, Inc.
Trial Balance
December 31, 2011

Cash	$ 7,400	
Accounts Receivable	2,198	
Prepaid Insurance	480	
Office Supplies	1,560	
Office Equipment	14,200	
Accumulated Depreciation—Office Equipment		$ 1,540
Accounts Payable		1,270
Unearned Tax Fees Revenues		438
Common Stock		7,000
Retained Earnings		6,878
Dividends	12,000	
Tax Fees Revenue		43,852
Office Salaries Expense	16,600	
Advertising Expense	1,300	
Rent Expense	4,800	
Telephone Expense	440	
	$60,978	$60,978

The following information is also available:

a. Office supplies on hand, December 31, 2011, $450.
b. Insurance still unexpired, $200.
c. Estimated depreciation of office equipment, $1,590.
d. Telephone expense for December, $42; the bill was received but not recorded.
e. The services for all unearned tax fees revenue had been performed by the end of the year.
f. Estimated federal income taxes for the year, $4,860.

REQUIRED

1. Open T accounts for the accounts in the trial balance plus the following: Income Taxes Payable, Insurance Expense, Office Supplies Expense, Depreciation Expense—Office Equipment, and Income Taxes Expense. Record the balances shown in the trial balance.
2. Determine the adjusting entries and post them directly to the T accounts.
3. Prepare an adjusted trial balance, an income statement, a statement of retained earnings, and a balance sheet.

USER INSIGHT ▶ 4. Why is it not necessary to show the effects of the above transactions on the statement of cash flows?

LO 3, 4

Determining Adjusting Entries and Tracing Their Effects to Financial Statements

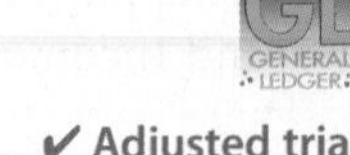

✔ Adjusted trial balance: $339,380

P 5. Elite Livery, Inc., was organized to provide limousine service between the airport and various suburban locations. It has just completed its second year of business. Its trial balance appears below.

Elite Livery, Inc.
Trial Balance
June 30, 2011

Account	Debit	Credit
Cash (111)	$ 4,906	
Accounts Receivable (112)	7,114	
Prepaid Rent (117)	6,000	
Prepaid Insurance (118)	2,450	
Prepaid Maintenance (119)	6,000	
Spare Parts (141)	5,655	
Limousines (142)	110,000	
Accumulated Depreciation—Limousines (143)		$ 17,500
Notes Payable (211)		22,500
Unearned Passenger Service Revenue (212)		15,000
Common Stock (311)		20,000
Retained Earnings (312)		24,106
Dividends (313)	10,000	
Passenger Service Revenue (411)		214,249
Gas and Oil Expense (511)	44,650	
Salaries Expense (512)	103,180	
Advertising Expense (513)	13,400	
	$313,355	$313,355

The following information is also available:

a. To obtain space at the airport, Elite Livery paid two years' rent in advance when it began the business.
b. An examination of insurance policies reveals that $900 expired during the year.
c. To provide regular maintenance for its vehicles, Elite Livery deposited $6,000 with a local garage. An examination of maintenance invoices reveals charges of $5,472 against the deposit.
d. An inventory of spare parts shows $1,008 on hand.
e. Elite Livery depreciates all of its limousines at the rate of 12.5 percent per year. No limousines were purchased during the year.
f. A payment of $5,650 for one full year's interest on notes payable is now due.
g. Unearned Passenger Service Revenue on June 30 includes $8,908 for tickets that employers purchased for use by their executives but that have not yet been redeemed.
h. Federal income taxes for the year are estimated to be $6,625.

REQUIRED

1. Determine adjusting entries and enter them in the general journal (Page 14).
2. Open ledger accounts for the accounts in the trial balance plus the following: Interest Payable (213), Income Taxes Payable (214), Rent Expense (514), Insurance Expense (515), Spare Parts Expense (516), Depreciation Expense—Limousines (517), Maintenance Expense (518), Interest Expense (519), and Income Taxes Expense (520). Record the balances shown in the trial balance.
3. Post the adjusting entries from the general journal to the ledger accounts, showing proper references.
4. Prepare an adjusted trial balance, an income statement, a statement of retained earnings, and a balance sheet.

USER INSIGHT ▶

5. Do adjustments affect the cash flow yield? After the adjustments, is the cash flow yield for the year more or less than it would have been if the adjustments had not been made?

Alternate Problems

LO 3

Determining Adjustments

P 6. At the end of its first three months of operation, Metropolitan Answering Service, Inc., had the following trial balance.

Metropolitan Answering Service, Inc.
Trial Balance
March 31, 2011

Cash	$ 3,582	
Accounts Receivable	4,236	
Office Supplies	933	
Prepaid Rent	800	
Equipment	4,700	
Accounts Payable		$ 2,673
Unearned Answering Service Revenue		888
Common Stock		5,933
Dividends	2,100	
Answering Service Revenue		9,102
Wages Expense	1,900	
Office Cleaning Expense	345	
	$18,596	$18,596

Dan Arrow, the owner of Metropolitan Answering Service, has hired an accountant to prepare financial statements to determine how well the company is doing after three months. Upon examining the accounting records, the accountant finds the following items of interest:

a. An inventory of office supplies reveals supplies on hand of $150.
b. The Prepaid Rent account includes the rent for the first three months plus a deposit for April's rent.
c. Depreciation on the equipment for the first three months is $416.
d. The balance of the Unearned Answering Service Revenue account represents a 12-month service contract paid in advance on February 1.
e. On March 31, accrued wages total $105.
f. Federal income taxes for the three months are estimated to be $1,110.

REQUIRED

All adjustments affect one balance sheet account and one income statement account. For each of the preceding situations, show the accounts affected, the amount of the adjustment (using a + or – to indicate an increase or a decrease, respectively), and the balance of the account after the adjustment in the following format:

Balance Sheet Account	Amount of Adjustment (+ or –)	Balance after Adjustment	Income Statement Account	Amount of Adjustment (+ or –)	Balance after Adjustment

LO 2, 3

Preparing Adjusting Entries

P 7. On November 30, the end of the current fiscal year, the following information is available to assist Rosatti Corporation's accountants in making adjusting entries:

a. Rosatti Corporation's Supplies account shows a beginning balance of $2,350. Purchases during the year were $4,218. The end-of-year inventory reveals supplies on hand of $1,397.

b. The Prepaid Insurance account shows the following on November 30:

Beginning balance	$4,720
July 1	4,200
October 1	7,272

The beginning balance represents the unexpired portion of a one-year policy purchased the previous year. The July 1 entry represents a new one-year policy, and the October 1 entry represents additional coverage in the form of a three-year policy.

c. The following table contains the cost and annual depreciation for buildings and equipment, all of which Rosatti Corporation purchased before the current year:

Account	Cost	Annual Depreciation
Buildings	$298,000	$16,000
Equipment	374,000	40,000

d. On September 1, the company completed negotiations with a client and accepted an advance payment of $18,600 for services to be performed in the next year. The $18,600 was credited to the Unearned Service Revenue account.

e. The company calculated that as of November 30, it had earned $7,000 on an $11,000 contract that would be completed and billed in January.

f. Among the liabilities of the company is a note payable in the amount of $300,000. On November 30, the accrued interest on this note amounted to $18,000.

g. On Saturday, December 2, the company, which is on a six-day workweek, will pay its regular salaried employees $15,000.

h. On November 29, the company completed negotiations and signed a contract to provide services to a new client at an annual rate of $17,500.

i. Management estimates income taxes for the year to be $23,000.

REQUIRED

1. Prepare adjusting entries for each item listed above.
2. Explain how the conditions for revenue recognition are applied to transactions **e** and **h**. (USER INSIGHT)

LO 3, 4

Determining Adjusting Entries, Posting to T Accounts, and Preparing an Adjusted Trial Balance

✔ Adjusted trial balance: $111,412

P 8. The trial balance for Sigma Consultants Corporation on December 31, 2011, follows.

Sigma Consultants Corporation
Trial Balance
December 31, 2011

Cash	$ 13,786	
Accounts Receivable	24,840	
Office Supplies	991	
Prepaid Rent	1,400	
Office Equipment	7,300	
Accumulated Depreciation—Office Equipment		$ 2,600
Accounts Payable		1,820
Notes Payable		10,000
Unearned Service Revenue		2,860
Common Stock		11,000
Retained Earnings		19,387
Dividends	15,000	
Service Revenue		58,500
Salaries Expense	33,400	
Utilities Expense	1,750	
Rent Expense	7,700	
	$106,167	$106,167

The following information is also available:

a. Ending inventory of office supplies, $97.
b. Prepaid rent expired, $500.
c. Depreciation of office equipment for the period, $720.
d. Interest accrued on the note payable, $600.
e. Salaries accrued at the end of the period, $230.
f. Service revenue still unearned at the end of the period, $1,410.
g. Service revenue earned but not billed, $915.
h. Estimated federal income taxes for the period, $2,780.

REQUIRED

1. Open T accounts for the accounts in the trial balance plus the following: Interest Payable, Salaries Payable, Income Taxes Payable, Office Supplies Expense, Depreciation Expense—Office Equipment, Interest Expense, and Income Taxes Expense. Enter the account balances.
2. Determine the adjusting entries and post them directly to the T accounts.
3. Prepare an adjusted trial balance.

USER INSIGHT ▶

4. What financial statements does each of the above adjustments affect? What financial statement is *not* affected by the adjustments?

LO 3, 4

✔ Adjusted trial balance: $31,151

Determining Adjusting Entries and Tracing Their Effects to Financial Statements

P 9. Tim Angel opened a small travel agency. At the end of its second year of operation, Angel Travel, Inc., had the trial balance shown below.

Angel Travel, Inc.
Trial Balance
December 31, 2011

Cash	$ 3,650	
Accounts Receivable	970	
Prepaid Insurance	195	
Office Supplies	610	
Office Equipment	6,800	
Accumulated Depreciation—Office Equipment		$ 670
Accounts Payable		590
Unearned Travel Fees Revenues		315
Common Stock		3,300
Retained Earnings		3,117
Dividends	4,200	
Travel Fees Revenue		20,079
Office Salaries Expense	8,300	
Advertising Expense	585	
Rent Expense	2,350	
Telephone Expense	411	
	$28,071	$28,071

The following information is also available:

a. Office supplies on hand, December 31, 2011, $180.
b. Insurance still unexpired, $65.
c. Estimated depreciation of office equipment, $650.
d. Telephone expense for December, $45; the bill was received but not recorded.
e. The services for all unearned travel fees revenue had been performed by the end of the year.
f. Estimated federal income taxes for the year, $2,385.

REQUIRED

1. Open T accounts for the accounts in the trial balance plus the following: Income Taxes Payable, Insurance Expense, Office Supplies Expense, Depreciation Expense—Office Equipment, and Income Taxes Expense. Record the balances shown in the trial balance.
2. Determine the adjusting entries and post them directly to the T accounts.
3. Prepare an adjusted trial balance, an income statement, a statement of retained earnings, and a balance sheet.

USER INSIGHT ▶

4. Why is it not necessary to show the effects of the above transactions on the statement of cash flows?

LO 3, 4

✔ Adjusted trial balance: $650,840

Determining Adjusting Entries and Tracing Their Effects to Financial Statements

P 10. Ray Heating & Cooling, Inc., was organized to provide heating and cooling service. It has just completed its second year of business. Its trial balance appears below.

Ray Heating & Cooling, Inc.
Trial Balance
June 30, 2011

Cash (111)	$ 8,120	
Accounts Receivable (112)	13,270	
Prepaid Rent (117)	11,000	
Prepaid Insurance (118)	3,700	
Prepaid Maintenance (119)	11,000	
Spare Parts (141)	15,100	
Vehicles (142)	190,000	
Accumulated Depreciation—Vehicles (143)		$ 25,000
Notes Payable (211)		48,000
Unearned Service Revenue (212)		29,500
Common Stock (311)		27,000
Retained Earnings (312)		53,650
Dividends (313)	19,000	
Service Revenue (411)		419,160
Gas and Oil Expense (511)	95,600	
Salaries Expense (512)	214,320	
Advertising Expense (513)	21,200	
	$602,310	$602,310

The following information is also available:

a. To obtain space at the airport, Ray Heating & Cooling paid two years' rent in advance when it began the business.
b. An examination of insurance policies reveals that $1,400 expired during the year.
c. To provide regular maintenance for the vehicles, Ray Heating & Cooling deposited $11,000 with a local garage. An examination of maintenance invoices reveals charges of $9,879 against the deposit.
d. An inventory of spare parts shows $2,580 on hand.
e. Ray Heating & Cooling depreciates its service vehicles at the rate of 12.5 percent per year. No vehicles were purchased during the year.
f. A payment of $11,800 for one full year's interest on notes payable is now due.
g. Unearned Service Revenue on June 30 includes $13,535 for contracts with local restaurants, but the service has not been provided yet.
h. Federal income taxes for the year are estimated to be $12,980.

REQUIRED

1. Determine adjusting entries and enter them in the general journal (Page 14).
2. Open ledger accounts for the accounts in the trial balance plus the following: Interest Payable (213), Income Taxes Payable (214), Rent Expense (514), Insurance Expense (515), Spare Parts Expense (516), Depreciation Expense—Vehicles (517), Maintenance Expense (518), Interest Expense (519), and Income Taxes Expense (520). Record the balances shown in the trial balance.

3. Post the adjusting entries from the general journal to the ledger accounts, showing proper references.
4. Prepare an adjusted trial balance, an income statement, a statement of retained earnings, and a balance sheet.

USER INSIGHT ▶

5. Do adjustments affect the cash flow yield? After the adjustments, is the cash flow yield for the year more or less than it would have been if the adjustments had not been made?

Cases

LO 1, 2, 3

Conceptual Understanding: Importance of Adjustments

C 1. Never Flake Company provided a rust-prevention coating for the underside of new automobiles. The company advertised widely and offered its services through new-car dealers. When a dealer sold a new car, the salesperson attempted to sell the rust-prevention coating as an option. A key selling point was Never Flake's warranty, which stated that it would repair any damage due to rust at no charge for as long as the buyer owned the car.

For several years, Never Flake had been very successful, but in 2011, the company suddenly declared bankruptcy. Company officials said that the firm had only $5.5 million in assets against liabilities of $32.9 million. Most of the liabilities represented potential claims under the company's lifetime warranty. It seemed that owners were keeping their cars longer than they had previously. Therefore, more damage was being attributed to rust.

Discuss what accounting decisions could have helped Never Flake to survive under these circumstances.

LO 1

Conceptual Understanding: Earnings Management and Fraudulent Financial Reporting

C 2. In recent years, the Securities and Exchange Commission (SEC) has been waging a public campaign against corporate accounting practices that manage or manipulate earnings to meet the expectations of Wall Street analysts. Corporations engage in such practices in the hope of avoiding shortfalls that might cause serious declines in their stock price.

For each of the following cases that the Securities and Exchange Commission challenged, explain why each was a violation of the matching rule and how it should have been accounted for:

a. **Lucent Technologies** sold telecommunications equipment to companies from which there was no reasonable expectation of payment because of the companies' poor financial condition.
b. **America Online (AOL)** recorded advertising as an asset rather than as an expense.
c. **Eclipsys** recorded software contracts as revenue even though it had not yet rendered the services.
d. **Xerox Corporation** recorded revenue from lease agreements at the time the leases were signed rather than over the lease term.
e. **KnowledgeWare** recorded revenue from sales of software even though it told customers they did not have to pay until they had the software.

LO 2, 3

Interpreting Financial Reports: Application of Accrual Accounting

C 3. The **Lyric Opera of Chicago** is one of the largest and best-managed opera companies in the United States. Managing opera productions requires advance planning, including the development of scenery, costumes, and stage properties and the sale of tickets. To measure how well the company is operating in any given year, management must apply accrual accounting to these and other transactions. At year-end, April 30, 2009, Lyric Opera's balance sheet showed deferred production costs and other assets of $1,794,804 and deferred ticket and other revenue of $13,102,512.[9] What accounting policies and adjusting entries are applicable to these accounts? Why are they important to Lyric Opera's management?

LO 2, 3

Interpreting Financial Reports: Analysis of an Asset Account

C 4. The Walt Disney Company is engaged in the financing, production, and distribution of motion pictures and television programming. In Disney's 2009 annual report, the balance sheet contains an asset called "film and television costs." Film and television costs, which consist of the costs associated with producing films and television programs less the amount expensed, were $5,125 million. The notes reveal that the amount of film and television costs expensed (amortized) during the year was $3,486 million. The amount spent for new film productions was $3,421 million.[10]

1. What are film and television costs, and why would they be classified as an asset?
2. Prepare an entry in T account form to record the amount the company spent on new film and television production during the year (assume all expenditures are paid for in cash).
3. Prepare an adjusting entry in T account form to record the expense for film and television productions.
4. Suggest a method by which The Walt Disney Company might have determined the amount of the expense in **3** in accordance with the matching rule.

LO 3

Annual Report Case: Analysis of Balance Sheet and Adjusting Entries

C 5. In the **CVS** annual report in the Supplement to Chapter 1, refer to the balance sheet and the Summary of Significant Accounting Policies in the notes to the financial statements.

1. Examine the accounts in the current assets, property and equipment, and current liabilities sections of CVS's balance sheet. Which are most likely to have had year-end adjusting entries? Describe the nature of the adjusting entries. For more information about the property and equipment section, refer to the notes to the financial statements.
2. Where is depreciation (and amortization) expense disclosed in CVS's financial statements?
3. CVS has a statement on the "Use of Estimates" in its Summary of Significant Accounting Policies. Read this statement and tell how important estimates are in determining depreciation expense. What assumptions do accountants use in estimating depreciation?

Comparison: Financial Ratio: Cash Flow Yield

RATIO

C 6. Cash flow yield is an important measure of liquidity. Use data from **CVS**'s income statement and the financial statements of **Southwest Airlines Co.** in the Supplement to Chapter 1 to calculate each company's cash flow yield for the past two years. (*Note:* Round to one decimal place.) By this measure, which company produces more cash from its operations?

LO 1, 2, 3

Ethical Dilemma: Importance of Adjustments

C 7. Central Appliance Service Co., Inc., has achieved fast growth by selling service contracts on large appliances, such as washers, dryers, and refrigerators. For a fee, the company agrees to provide all parts and labor on an appliance after the regular warranty runs out. For example, by paying a fee of $200, a person who buys a dishwasher can add two years to the regular one-year warranty on the appliance. In 2011, the company sold service contracts in the amount of $1.8 million, all of which applied to future years. Management wanted all the sales recorded as revenues in 2011, contending that the amount of the contracts could be determined and the cash had been received. Do you agree with this logic? How would you record the cash receipts? What assumptions do you think Central Appliance should make? Would you consider it unethical to follow management's recommendation? Who might be hurt or helped by this action?

LO 1, 3

Decision Analysis Using Excel: Adjusting Entries, Performance Evaluation, and Dividend Policy

C 8. Martin Rak, the owner of a newsletter for managers of hotels and restaurants, has prepared the following condensed figures from his company's financial statements for 2011:

Revenues	$432,500
Expenses	352,500
Net income	$ 80,000
Total assets	$215,000
Liabilities	$ 60,000
Stockholders' equity	155,000
Total liabilities and stockholders' equity	$215,000

Given these figures, Rak is planning a cash dividend of $62,500. However, Rak's accountant has found that the following items were overlooked:

a. Although the balance of the Printing Supplies account is $40,000, only $17,500 worth of supplies is on hand at the end of the year.
b. Depreciation of $25,000 on equipment has not been recorded.
c. Rak's employees have earned wages of $11,750, but that amount has not been recognized in the accounts.
d. No provision has been made for estimated income taxes payable of $13,500.
e. A liability account called Unearned Subscriptions Revenue has a balance of $20,250, but one-third of these subscriptions have already been mailed to subscribers.

REQUIRED

1. Prepare the necessary adjusting entries.
2. Recast the condensed figures from the financial statements after you have made the necessary adjustments.
3. Discuss the performance of Rak's business after the adjustments have been made. (*Hint*: Compare net income to revenues and to total assets before and after the adjustments.) Do you think that paying the dividend is advisable? Why or why not?

USER INSIGHT ▶

SUPPLEMENT TO CHAPTER 3

Closing Entries and the Work Sheet

PREPARING CLOSING ENTRIES

As you know, closing entries have two purposes:

- They clear the balances of all temporary accounts (revenue, expense, and Dividends accounts) so that they have zero balances at the beginning of the next accounting period.
- They summarize a period's revenues and expenses in the Income Summary account so that the net income or net loss for the period can be transferred as a total to Retained Earnings.

The steps involved in making closing entries are as follows:

Step 1. Close the credit balance accounts on the income statement to the Income Summary account.

Step 2. Close the debit balance accounts on the income statement to the Income Summary account.

Step 3. Close the Income Summary account balance to the Retained Earnings account.

Step 4. Close the Dividends account balance to the Retained Earnings account.

You will learn in later chapters that not all credit balance accounts are revenues and not all debit balance accounts are expenses. For that reason, when referring to closing entries, we often use the term *credit balances* instead of *revenue accounts* and the term *debit balances* instead of *expense accounts.*

An adjusted trial balance provides all the data needed to record the closing entries. Exhibit S3.1 shows the relationships of the four kinds of closing entries to Creative Designs, Inc.'s adjusted trial balance.

Step 1: Closing the Credit Balances

STUDY NOTE: *While it is not necessary to use the Income Summary account when preparing closing entries, it does simplify the procedure.*

On the credit side of the adjusted trial balance in Exhibit S3.1, Design Revenue shows a balance of $13,600. To close this account, an entry must be made debiting the account in the amount of its balance and crediting it to the Income Summary account. Exhibit S3.2 (p. 186) shows how the entry is posted. Notice that the entry sets the balance of the revenue account to zero and transfers the total revenues to the credit side of the Income Summary account.

Step 2: Closing the Debit Balances

STUDY NOTE: *The Income Summary account now reflects the account balance of the revenue account before it was closed.*

Several expense accounts show balances on the debit side of the adjusted trial balance in Exhibit S3.1. A compound entry is needed to credit each of these expense accounts for its balance and to debit the Income Summary account for the total. Exhibit S3.3 (p. 186) shows the effect of posting the closing entry. Notice how the entry reduces the expense account balances to zero and transfers the total of the account balances to the debit side of the Income Summary account.

EXHIBIT S3.1
Preparing Closing Entries from the Adjusted Trial Balance

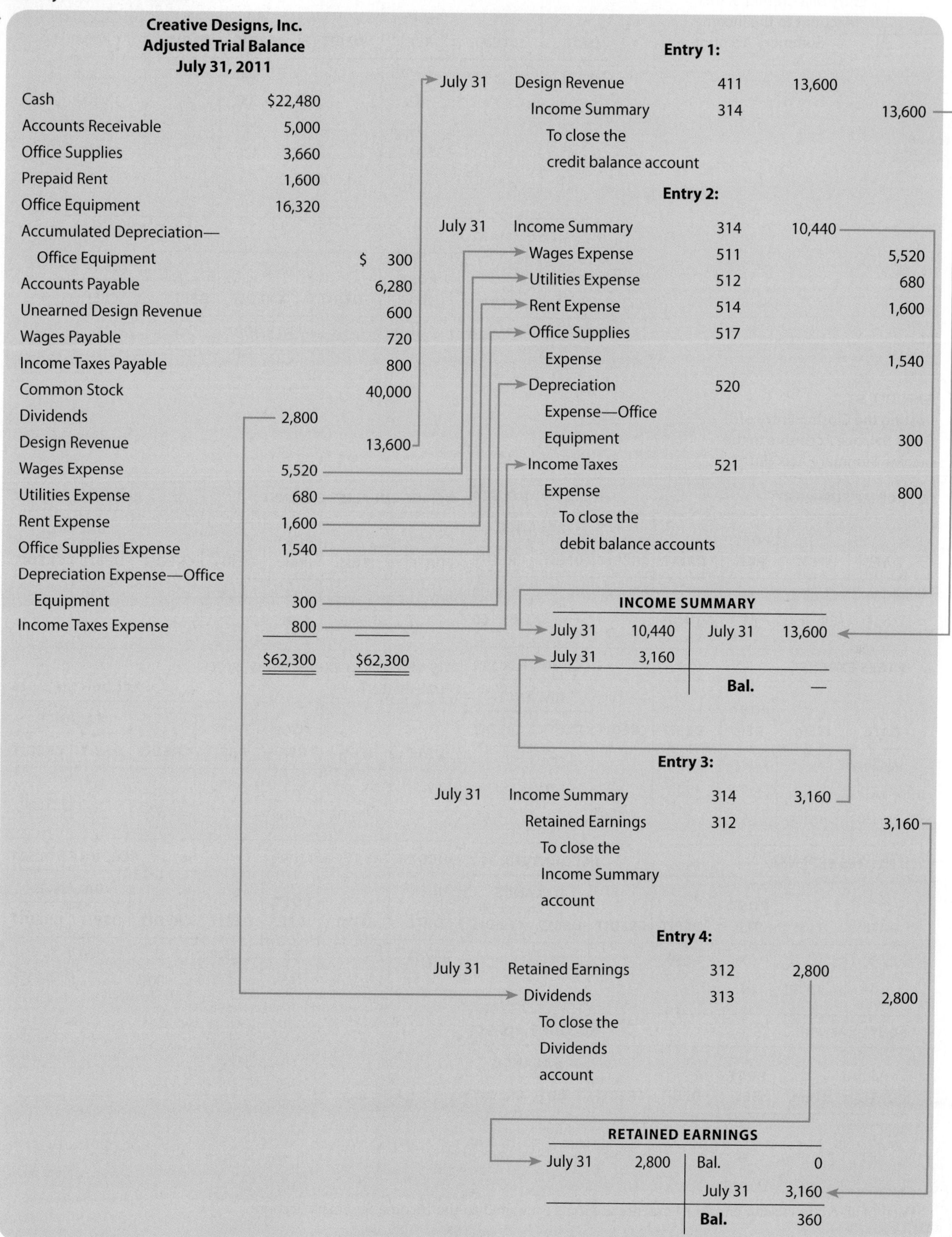

Creative Designs, Inc.
Adjusted Trial Balance
July 31, 2011

Cash	$22,480	
Accounts Receivable	5,000	
Office Supplies	3,660	
Prepaid Rent	1,600	
Office Equipment	16,320	
Accumulated Depreciation—Office Equipment		$ 300
Accounts Payable		6,280
Unearned Design Revenue		600
Wages Payable		720
Income Taxes Payable		800
Common Stock		40,000
Dividends	2,800	
Design Revenue		13,600
Wages Expense	5,520	
Utilities Expense	680	
Rent Expense	1,600	
Office Supplies Expense	1,540	
Depreciation Expense—Office Equipment	300	
Income Taxes Expense	800	
	$62,300	$62,300

Entry 1:

July 31	Design Revenue	411	13,600	
	Income Summary	314		13,600
	To close the credit balance account			

Entry 2:

July 31	Income Summary	314	10,440	
	Wages Expense	511		5,520
	Utilities Expense	512		680
	Rent Expense	514		1,600
	Office Supplies Expense	517		1,540
	Depreciation Expense—Office Equipment	520		300
	Income Taxes Expense	521		800
	To close the debit balance accounts			

INCOME SUMMARY

July 31	10,440	July 31	13,600
July 31	3,160		
		Bal.	—

Entry 3:

July 31	Income Summary	314	3,160	
	Retained Earnings	312		3,160
	To close the Income Summary account			

Entry 4:

July 31	Retained Earnings	312	2,800	
	Dividends	313		2,800
	To close the Dividends account			

RETAINED EARNINGS

July 31	2,800	Bal.	0
		July 31	3,160
		Bal.	360

EXHIBIT S3.2
Posting the Closing Entry of a Credit Balance Account to the Income Summary Account

DESIGN REVENUE — ACCOUNT NO. 411

DATE	ITEM	POST. REF.	DEBIT	CREDIT	BALANCE DEBIT	BALANCE CREDIT
July 10		J2		2,800		2,800
15		J2		9,600		12,400
31		J3		800		13,200
31		J3		400		13,600
31	Closing	J4	13,600			—

INCOME SUMMARY — ACCOUNT NO. 314

DATE	ITEM	POST. REF.	DEBIT	CREDIT	BALANCE DEBIT	BALANCE CREDIT
July 31	Closing	J4		13,600		13,600

EXHIBIT S3.3
Posting the Closing Entry of Debit Balance Accounts to the Income Summary Account

INCOME SUMMARY — ACCOUNT NO. 314

DATE	ITEM	POST. REF.	DEBIT	CREDIT	BALANCE DEBIT	BALANCE CREDIT
July 31	Closing	J4		13,600		13,600
31	Closing	J4	10,440*			3,160

WAGES EXPENSE — ACCOUNT NO. 511

DATE	ITEM	POST. REF.	DEBIT	CREDIT	BALANCE DEBIT	BALANCE CREDIT
July 26		J2	4,800		4,800	
31		J3	720		5,520	
31	Closing	J4		5,520	—	

UTILITIES EXPENSE — ACCOUNT NO. 512

DATE	ITEM	POST. REF.	DEBIT	CREDIT	BALANCE DEBIT	BALANCE CREDIT
July 30		J2	680		680	
31	Closing	J4		680	—	

RENT EXPENSE — ACCOUNT NO. 514

DATE	ITEM	POST. REF.	DEBIT	CREDIT	BALANCE DEBIT	BALANCE CREDIT
July 31		J3	1,600		1,600	
31	Closing	J4		1,600	—	

OFFICE SUPPLIES EXPENSE — ACCOUNT NO. 517

DATE	ITEM	POST. REF.	DEBIT	CREDIT	BALANCE DEBIT	BALANCE CREDIT
July 31		J3	1,540		1,540	
31	Closing	J4		1,540	—	

DEPRECIATION EXPENSE—OFFICE EQUIPMENT — ACCOUNT NO. 520

DATE	ITEM	POST. REF.	DEBIT	CREDIT	BALANCE DEBIT	BALANCE CREDIT
July 31		J3	300		300	
31	Closing	J4		300	—	

INCOME TAXES EXPENSE — ACCOUNT NO. 521

DATE	ITEM	POST. REF.	DEBIT	CREDIT	BALANCE DEBIT	BALANCE CREDIT
July 31		J3	800		800	
31	Closing	J4		800	—	

*Total of all credit closing entries to expense accounts is debited to the Income Summary account.

EXHIBIT S3.4
Posting the Closing Entry of the Income Summary Account Balance to the Retained Earnings Account

INCOME SUMMARY — ACCOUNT NO. 314

DATE	ITEM	POST. REF.	DEBIT	CREDIT	BALANCE DEBIT	BALANCE CREDIT
July 31	Closing	J4		13,600		13,600
31	Closing	J4	10,440			3,160
31	Closing	J4	3,160			—

RETAINED EARNINGS — ACCOUNT NO. 312

DATE	ITEM	POST. REF.	DEBIT	CREDIT	BALANCE DEBIT	BALANCE CREDIT
July 31	Closing	J4		3,160		3,160

Step 3: Closing the Income Summary Account Balance

STUDY NOTE: The credit balance of the Income Summary account at this point ($3,160) represents net income—the key measure of performance. When a net loss occurs, debit the Retained Earnings account (to reduce it) and credit the Income Summary account (to close it).

After the entries closing the revenue and expense accounts have been posted, the balance of the Income Summary account equals the net income or net loss for the period. A credit balance in the Income Summary account represents a net income (revenues exceed expenses), and a debit balance represents a net loss (expenses exceed revenues).

At this point, the balance of the Income Summary account, whatever its nature, is closed to the Retained Earnings account, as shown in Exhibit S3.1. Exhibit S3.4 shows how the closing entry is posted when a company has a net income. Notice the dual effect of closing the Income Summary account and transferring the balance to Retained Earnings.

Step 4: Closing the Dividends Account Balance

STUDY NOTE: Notice that the Dividends account is closed to the Retained Earnings account, not to the Income Summary account.

The Dividends account shows the amount by which cash dividends reduce retained earnings during an accounting period. The debit balance of the Dividends account is closed to the Retained Earnings account, as illustrated in Exhibit S3.1. Exhibit S3.5 shows the posting of the closing entry and the transfer of the balance of the Dividends account to the Retained Earnings account.

The Accounts After Closing

After all the steps in the closing process have been completed and all closing entries have been posted, everything is ready for the next accounting period. The revenue, expense, and Dividends accounts (temporary accounts) have zero balances. The Retained Earnings account has been increased or decreased to reflect net income or net loss (net income in our example) and has been decreased for dividends. The balance sheet accounts (permanent accounts) show the correct balances, which are carried forward to the next period, as shown in the post-closing trial balance in Exhibit S3.6 (p. 188).

EXHIBIT S3.5
Posting the Closing Entry of the Dividends Account Balance to the Retained Earnings Account

DIVIDENDS — ACCOUNT NO. 313

DATE	ITEM	POST. REF.	DEBIT	CREDIT	BALANCE DEBIT	BALANCE CREDIT
July 31		J2	2,800		2,800	
31	Closing	J4		2,800		—

RETAINED EARNINGS — ACCOUNT NO. 312

DATE	ITEM	POST. REF.	DEBIT	CREDIT	BALANCE DEBIT	BALANCE CREDIT
July 31	Closing	J4		3,160		3,160
31	Closing	J4	2,800			360

EXHIBIT S3.6
Post-Closing Trial Balance

Creative Designs, Inc. Post-Closing Trial Balance July 31, 2011		
Cash	$22,480	
Accounts Receivable	5,000	
Office Supplies	3,660	
Prepaid Rent	1,600	
Office Equipment	16,320	
Accumulated Depreciation—Office Equipment		$ 300
Accounts Payable		6,280
Unearned Design Revenue		600
Wages Payable		720
Income Taxes Payable		800
Common Stock		40,000
Retained Earnings		360
	$49,060	$49,060

THE WORK SHEET: AN ACCOUNTANT'S TOOL

Accountants must collect relevant data to determine what should be included in financial reports. For example, they must examine insurance policies to calculate how much prepaid insurance has expired, examine plant and equipment records to determine depreciation, and compute the amount of accrued wages. To organize such data and avoid omitting important information that might affect the financial statements, accountants use *working papers.* Because working papers provide evidence of past work, they also enable accountants to retrace their steps when they need to verify information in the financial statements.

The *work sheet* is a special kind of working paper. It often serves as a preliminary step in preparing financial statements. Using a work sheet lessens the possibility of leaving out an adjustment and helps the accountant check the arithmetical accuracy of the accounts. The work sheet is never published and is rarely seen by management. It is a tool for the accountant.

Because preparing a work sheet is a mechanical process, many accountants use a computer for this purpose. Some accountants use a spreadsheet program to prepare the work sheet. Others use a general ledger system to prepare financial statements from the adjusted trial balance.

Preparing the Work Sheet

A common form of work sheet has one column for account names and/or account numbers and multiple columns with headings like the ones shown in Exhibit S3.7. A heading that includes the name of the company and the period of time covered (as on the income statement) identifies the work sheet. As Exhibit S3.7 shows, preparation of a work sheet involves five steps.

STUDY NOTE: *The Trial Balance columns of a work sheet replace the trial balance.*

Step 1. Enter and total the account balances in the Trial Balance columns. The debit and credit balances of the accounts as of the last day of an accounting period are copied directly from the ledger into the Trial Balance columns, as shown in Exhibit S3.7. When accountants use a work sheet, they do not have to prepare a separate trial balance.

Step 2. Enter and total the adjustments in the Adjustments columns. The required adjustments are entered in the Adjustments columns of the work sheet. As each adjustment is entered, a letter is used to identify its debit and credit parts. For example, in Exhibit S3.7, the letter (a) identifies the adjustment made for the rent that Creative Designs, Inc., prepaid on July 3, which results in a debit to Rent Expense and a credit to Prepaid Rent. These identifying letters may be used to reference supporting computations or documentation for the related adjusting entries and can simplify the recording of adjusting entries in the journal.

A trial balance includes only accounts that have balances; if an adjustment involves an account that does not appear in the trial balance, the new account is added below the accounts listed on the work sheet. For example, Rent Expense has been added to Exhibit S3.7. Accumulated depreciation accounts, which have a zero balance only in the initial period of operation, are the only exception to this rule. They are listed immediately after their associated asset accounts.

When all the adjustments have been made, the two Adjustments columns must be totaled. This procedure proves that the debits and credits of the adjustments are equal, and it generally reduces errors in the work sheet.

EXHIBIT S3.7
The Work Sheet

Creative Designs, Inc.
Work Sheet
For the Month Ended July 31, 2011

	Trial Balance		Adjustments		Adjusted Trial Balance		Income Statement		Balance Sheet	
Account Name	**Debit**	**Credit**	**Debit**	**Credit**	**Debit**	**Credit**	**Debit**	**Credit**	**Debit**	**Credit**
Cash	22,480				22,480				22,480	
Accounts Receivable	4,600		(g) 400		5,000				5,000	
Office Supplies	5,200			(b) 1,540	3,660				3,660	
Prepaid Rent	3,200			(a) 1,600	1,600				1,600	
Office Equipment	16,320				16,320				16,320	
Accumulated Depreciation—Office Equipment		—		(c) 300		300				300
Accounts Payable		6,280				6,280				6,280
Unearned Design Revenue		1,400	(f) 800			600				600
Common Stock		40,000				40,000				40,000
Dividends	2,800				2,800				2,800	
Design Revenue		12,400		(f) 800 (g) 400		13,600		13,600		
Wages Expense	4,800		(d) 720		5,520		5,520			
Utilities Expense	680				680		680			
	60,080	60,080								
Rent Expense			(a) 1,600		1,600		1,600			
Office Supplies Expense			(b) 1,540		1,540		1,540			
Depreciation Expense—Office Equipment			(c) 300		300		300			
Wages Payable				(d) 720		720				720
Income Taxes Expense			(e) 800		800		800			
Income Taxes Payable				(e) 800		800				800
			6,160	6,160	62,300	62,300	10,440	13,600	51,860	48,700
Net Income							3,160			3,160
							13,600	13,600	51,860	51,860

Note: The columns of the work sheet are prepared in the following order: (1) Trial Balance, (2) Adjustments, (3) Adjusted Trial Balance, and (4) Income Statement and Balance Sheet columns. In the fifth step, the Income Statement and Balance Sheet columns are totaled.

Step 3. Enter and total the adjusted account balances in the Adjusted Trial Balance columns. The adjusted trial balance in the work sheet is prepared by combining the amount of each account in the Trial Balance columns with the corresponding amount in the Adjustments columns and entering each result in the Adjusted Trial Balance columns.

Exhibit S3.7 contains examples of *crossfooting*, or adding and subtracting a group of numbers horizontally.

- The first line shows Cash with a debit balance of $22,480. Because there are no adjustments to the Cash account, $22,480 is entered in the debit column of the Adjusted Trial Balance columns.
- On the second line, Accounts Receivable shows a debit of $4,600 in the Trial Balance columns. Because there is a debit of $400 from adjustment (g) in the Adjustments columns, it is added to the $4,600 and carried over to the debit column of the Adjusted Trial Balance columns as $5,000.
- On the next line, Office Supplies shows a debit of $5,200 in the Trial Balance columns and a credit of $1,540 from adjustment (b) in the Adjustments columns. Subtracting $1,540 from $5,200 results in a $3,660 debit balance in the Adjusted Trial Balance columns.

This process is followed for all the accounts, including those added below the trial balance totals. The Adjusted Trial Balance columns are then *footed* (totaled) to check the accuracy of the crossfooting.

Step 4. Extend the account balances from the Adjusted Trial Balance columns to the Income Statement or Balance Sheet columns. Every account in the adjusted trial balance is an income statement account or a balance sheet account. Each account is extended to its proper place as a debit or credit in either the Income Statement columns or the Balance Sheet columns. As shown in Exhibit S3.7, revenue and expense accounts are extended to the Income Statement columns, and asset, liability, and the Common Stock and Dividends accounts are extended to the Balance Sheet columns.

To avoid overlooking an account, the accounts are extended line by line, beginning with the first line (Cash) and not omitting any subsequent lines. For instance, the Cash debit balance of $22,480 is extended to the debit column of the Balance Sheet columns; then, the Accounts Receivable debit balance of $5,000 is extended to the debit column of the Balance Sheet columns; and so forth.

Step 5. Total the Income Statement columns and the Balance Sheet columns. Enter the net income or net loss in both pairs of columns as a balancing figure and recompute the column totals. This last step, shown in Exhibit S3.7, is necessary to compute net income or net loss and to prove the arithmetical accuracy of the work sheet.

Net income (or net loss) is equal to the difference between the total debits and credits of the Income Statement columns. It is also equal to the difference between the total debits and credits of the Balance Sheet columns.

Revenues (Income Statement credit column total)	$13,600
Expenses (Income Statement debit column total)	(10,440)
Net Income	$ 3,160

In this case, revenues (credit column) exceed expenses (debit column). Thus, Creative Designs, Inc., has a net income of $3,160. The same difference occurs between the total debits and credits of the Balance Sheet columns.

The $3,160 is entered in the debit side of the Income Statement columns and in the credit side of the Balance Sheet columns to balance the columns. Remember that the excess of revenues over expenses (net income) increases stockholders' equity and that increases in stockholders' equity are recorded by credits.

When a net loss occurs, the opposite rule applies. The excess of expenses over revenues—net loss—is placed in the credit side of the Income Statement columns as a balancing figure. It is then placed in the debit side of the Balance Sheet columns because a net loss decreases stockholders' equity, and decreases in stockholders' equity are recorded by debits.

As a final check, the four columns are totaled again. If the Income Statement columns and the Balance Sheet columns do not balance, an account may have been extended or sorted to the wrong column, or an error may have been made in adding the columns. Of course, equal totals in the two pairs of columns are not absolute proof of accuracy. If an asset has been carried to the Income Statement debit column (or an expense has been carried to the Balance Sheet debit column) or a similar error with revenues or liabilities has been made, the work sheet will balance, but the net income figure will be wrong.

Using the Work Sheet

Accountants use the completed work sheet in performing three principal tasks:

STUDY NOTE: Theoretically, adjusting entries can be recorded in the accounting records before the financial statements are prepared, or even before the work sheet is completed. However, they always precede the preparation of closing entries.

- **Recording the adjusting entries in the journal:** Because the information needed to record the adjusting entries can be copied from the work sheet, entering the adjustments in the journal is an easy step, as shown in Exhibit S3.8. The adjusting entries are then posted to the ledger.
- **Recording the closing entries in the journal:** The Income Statement columns of the work sheet show all the accounts that need to be closed, except for the Dividends account. Exhibits S3.1 through S3.5 show how the closing entries are entered in the journal and posted to the ledger.
- **Preparing the financial statements:** Once the work sheet has been completed, preparing the financial statements is simple because the account balances have been sorted into the Income Statement and Balance Sheet columns.

EXHIBIT S3.8
Adjustments from the Work Sheet Entered in the General Journal

General Journal **Page 3**

Date	Description	Post. Ref.	Debit	Credit
2011				
July 31	Rent Expense	514	1,600	
	Prepaid Rent	117		1,600
	To recognize expiration of one month's rent			
	Office Supplies Expense	517	1,540	
	Office Supplies	116		1,540
	To recognize office supplies used during the month			
	Depreciation Expense—Office Equipment	520	300	
	Accumulated Depreciation—Office Equipment	147		300
	To record depreciation of office equipment for a month			
	Wages Expense	511	720	
	Wages Payable	214		720
	To accrue unrecorded wages			
	Income Taxes Expense	521	800	
	Income Taxes Payable	215		800
	To accrue estimated income taxes			
	Unearned Design Revenue	213	800	
	Design Revenue	411		800
	To recognize performance of services paid for in advance			
	Accounts Receivable	113	400	
	Design Revenue	411		400
	To accrue website design fees earned but unrecorded			

Supplement Assignments

Review Questions

1. Can the work sheet be used as a substitute for the financial statements? Explain your answer.
2. Why should the Adjusted Trial Balance columns of the work sheet be totaled before the adjusted amounts are carried to the Income Statement and Balance Sheet columns?
3. What sequence should be followed in extending the amounts in the Adjusted Trial Balance columns to the Income Statement and Balance Sheet columns? Discuss your answer.
4. Do the Income Statement columns and the Balance Sheet columns of the work sheet balance after the amounts from the Adjusted Trial Balance columns are extended? Why or why not?
5. Do the totals of the Balance Sheet columns of the work sheet agree with the totals on the balance sheet? Explain your answer.
6. Should adjusting entries be posted to the ledger accounts before or after the closing entries? Explain your answer.
7. At the end of the accounting period, does the posting of adjusting entries to the ledger precede or follow preparation of the work sheet?

Exercises

Preparation of Closing Entries

E 1. The items below are from the Income Statement columns of the work sheet for Best Repair Shop, Inc., for the year ended December 31, 2011.

	Income Statement	
Account Name	**Debit**	**Credit**
Repair Revenue		25,620
Wages Expense	8,110	
Rent Expense	1,200	
Supplies Expense	4,260	
Insurance Expense	915	
Depreciation Expense—Repair Equipment	1,345	
Income Taxes Expense	1,000	
	16,830	25,620
Net Income	8,790	
	25,620	25,620

Prepare journal entries to close the revenue, expense, Income Summary, and Dividends accounts. Dividends of $5,000 were paid during the year.

Completion of a Work Sheet

E 2. The following is a highly simplified list of trial balance accounts and their normal balances for the month ended October 31, 2011, which was the company's first month of operation:

Trial Balance Accounts and Balances

Cash	$4	Unearned Service Revenue	$ 3
Accounts Receivable	7	Common Stock	5
Prepaid Insurance	2	Retained Earnings	7
Supplies	4	Dividends	6
Office Equipment	8	Service Revenue	23
Accumulated Depreciation—Office Equipment	1	Utilities Expense	2
Accounts Payable	4	Wages Expense	10

1. Prepare a work sheet, entering the trial balance accounts in the order they would normally appear and putting the balances in the correct columns.
2. Complete the work sheet using the following information: (a) expired insurance, $1; (b) of the Unearned Revenue balance, $2 has been earned by the end of the month; (c) estimated depreciation on office equipment, $1; (d) Accrued wages, $1; (e) unused supplies on hand, $1; and (f) estimated federal income taxes, $1.

Problems

Closing Entries Using T Accounts and Preparation of Financial Statements

P 1. The adjusted trial balance for Settles Tennis Club, Inc., at the end of the company's fiscal year appears below.

Settles Tennis Club, Inc.
Adjusted Trial Balance
June 30, 2011

	Debit	Credit
Cash	$ 26,200	
Prepaid Advertising	9,600	
Supplies	1,200	
Land	100,000	
Building	645,200	
Accumulated Depreciation—Building		$ 260,000
Equipment	156,000	
Accumulated Depreciation—Equipment		50,400
Accounts Payable		73,000
Wages Payable		9,000
Property Taxes Payable		22,500
Unearned Revenue—Locker Fees		3,000
Income Taxes Payable		20,000
Common Stock		200,000
Retained Earnings		271,150
Dividends	54,000	
Revenue from Court Fees		678,100
Revenue from Locker Fees		9,600
Wages Expense	351,000	
Maintenance Expense	51,600	
Advertising Expense	39,750	
Utilities Expense	64,800	
Supplies Expense	6,000	
Depreciation Expense—Building	30,000	
Depreciation Expense—Equipment	12,000	
Property Taxes Expense	22,500	
Miscellaneous Expense	6,900	
Income Taxes Expense	20,000	
	$1,596,750	$1,596,750

REQUIRED

1. Prepare T accounts and enter the balances for Retained Earnings, Dividends, Income Summary, and all revenue and expense accounts.
2. Enter the four required closing entries in the T accounts, labeling the components (a), (b), (c), and (d) as appropriate.
3. Prepare an income statement, a statement of retained earnings, and a balance sheet for Settles Tennis Club, Inc.

USER INSIGHT ▶ 4. Explain why it is necessary to make closing entries at the end of an accounting period.

The Complete Accounting Cycle Without a Work Sheet: Two Months *(second month optional)*

P 2. On May 1, 2011, Javier Munoz opened Javier's Repair Service, Inc. During the month, he completed the following transactions for the company:

May 1 Began business by depositing $5,000 in a bank account in the name of the company in exchange for 500 shares of $10 par value common stock.
1 Paid the rent for a store for current month, $425.
1 Paid the premium on a one-year insurance policy, $480.
2 Purchased repair equipment from Motley Company, $4,200. Terms were $600 down and $300 per month for one year. First payment is due June 1.
5 Purchased repair supplies from AWD Company on credit, $468.
8 Paid cash for an advertisement in a local newspaper, $60.
15 Received cash repair revenue for the first half of the month, $400.
21 Paid AWD Company on account, $225.
31 Received cash repair revenue for the second half of May, $975.
31 Declared and paid a cash dividend, $300.

REQUIRED FOR MAY

1. Prepare journal entries to record the May transactions.
2. Open the following accounts: Cash (111); Prepaid Insurance (117); Repair Supplies (119); Repair Equipment (144); Accumulated Depreciation—Repair Equipment (145); Accounts Payable (212); Income Taxes Payable (213); Common Stock (311); Retained Earnings (312); Dividends (313); Income Summary (314); Repair Revenue (411); Store Rent Expense (511); Advertising Expense (512); Insurance Expense (513); Repair Supplies Expense (514); Depreciation Expense—Repair Equipment (515); and Income Taxes Expense (516). Post the May entries to the ledger accounts.
3. Using the following information, record adjusting entries in the journal and post to the ledger accounts: (a) one month's insurance has expired; (b) remaining inventory of unused repair supplies, $169; (c) estimated depreciation on repair equipment, $70; and (d) estimated income taxes, $50.
4. From the accounts in the ledger, prepare an adjusted trial balance. (*Note*: Normally a trial balance is prepared before adjustments but is omitted here to save time.)
5. From the adjusted trial balance, prepare an income statement, a statement of retained earnings, and a balance sheet for May.
6. Prepare and post closing entries.
7. Prepare a post-closing trial balance.

(OPTIONAL)

During June, Javier Munoz completed these transactions for Javier's Repair Service, Inc.:

June 1 Paid the monthly rent, $425.
1 Made the monthly payment to Motley Company, $300.
6 Purchased additional repair supplies on credit from AWD Company, $863.
15 Received cash repair revenue for the first half of the month, $914.
20 Paid cash for an advertisement in the local newspaper, $60.
23 Paid AWD Company on account, $600.
30 Received cash repair revenue for the last half of the month, $817.
30 Declared and paid a cash dividend, $300.

8. Prepare and post journal entries to record the June transactions.
9. Using the following information, record adjusting entries in the journal and post to the ledger accounts: (a) one month's insurance has expired; (b) remaining inventory of unused repair supplies, $413; (c) estimated depreciation on repair equipment, $70; and (d) estimated income taxes, $50.
10. From the accounts in the ledger, prepare an adjusted trial balance.

11. From the adjusted trial balance, prepare the June income statement, statement of retained earnings, and balance sheet.
12. Prepare and post closing entries.
13. Prepare a post-closing trial balance.

Preparation of a Work Sheet, Financial Statements, and Adjusting and Closing Entries

P 3. Beauchamp Theater Corporation's trial balance at the end of its current fiscal year appears below.

Beauchamp Theater Corporation
Trial Balance
June 30, 2011

	Debits	Credits
Cash	$ 31,800	
Accounts Receivable	18,544	
Prepaid Insurance	19,600	
Office Supplies	780	
Cleaning Supplies	3,590	
Land	20,000	
Building	400,000	
Accumulated Depreciation—Building		$ 39,400
Theater Furnishings	370,000	
Accumulated Depreciation—Theater Furnishings		65,000
Office Equipment	31,600	
Accumulated Depreciation—Office Equipment		15,560
Accounts Payable		45,506
Gift Books Liability		41,900
Mortgage Payable		300,000
Common Stock		200,000
Retained Earnings		112,648
Dividends	60,000	
Ticket Sales Revenue		411,400
Theater Rental Revenue		45,200
Usher Wages Expense	157,000	
Office Wages Expense	24,000	
Utilities Expense	112,700	
Interest Expense	27,000	
	$1,276,614	$1,276,614

REQUIRED

1. Enter Beauchamp Theater Corporation's trial balance amounts in the Trial Balance columns of a work sheet and complete the work sheet using the following information: (a) expired insurance, $17,400; (b) inventory of unused office supplies, $244; (c) inventory of unused cleaning supplies, $468; (d) estimated depreciation on the building, $14,000; (e) estimated depreciation on the theater furnishings, $36,000; (f) estimated depreciation on the office equipment, $3,160; (g) The company credits all gift books sold during the year to the Gift Books Liability account. A gift book is a booklet of ticket coupons that is purchased in advance as a gift. The recipient redeems the coupons at some point in the future. On June 30, it was estimated that $37,800 worth of the gift books had been redeemed; (h) accrued but unpaid usher wages at the end of the accounting period, $860; and (i) estimated federal income taxes, $20,000.
2. Prepare an income statement, a statement of retained earnings, and a balance sheet.
3. Prepare adjusting and closing entries.

CHAPTER 4

DECISION POINT
A User's Focus Dell Computer Corporation

In a presentation to financial analysts, **Dell**'s management focused on its goals of liquidity, profitability, and growth.[1] In judging whether Dell or any other company has achieved its goals, investors, creditors, managers, and others analyze relationships between key numbers in the financial statements that appear in the company's annual report.

Dell's annual reports summarize the company's financial performance by condensing a tremendous amount of information into a few numbers that managers and external users of financial statements consider most important. As shown in the Financial Highlights that follow, Dell used five key elements in its 2010 annual report to summarize its operating results and the change in those results from one fiscal year to the next.

DELL'S FINANCIAL HIGHLIGHTS
OPERATING RESULTS (in millions, except earnings per share)

	2010	2009	Change*
Net revenue	$52,902	$61,101	(13)%
Gross margin	9,261	10,957	(15)%
Operating income	2,172	3,190	(32)%
Net income	1,433	2,478	(42)%
Diluted earnings per share	0.73	1.25	(42)%

*Parentheses indicate a negative percentage.

Russell Mills/Alamy

Questions

1. *How should financial statements be organized to provide the best information?*
2. *What key measures best capture a company's financial performance?*

Financial Reporting and Analysis

LEARNING OBJECTIVES

LO 1 Describe the objective of financial reporting and identify the qualitative characteristics, conventions, and ethical considerations of accounting information. (pp. 198–201)

LO 2 Define and describe the conventions of *consistency, full disclosure, materiality, conservatism*, and *cost-benefit*. (pp. 201–204)

LO 3 Identify and describe the basic components of a classified balance sheet. (pp. 204–210)

LO 4 Describe the features of multistep and single-step classified income statements. (pp. 210–215)

LO 5 Use financial ratios to evaluate a company's performance. (pp. 215–223)

Stockholders, investors, creditors, and other interested parties rely on the integrity of a company's financial reports. A company's managers and accountants therefore have a responsibility to act ethically in the reporting process. However, what is often overlooked is that the users of financial reports also have a responsibility to recognize and understand the types of judgments and estimates that underlie these reports.

FOCUS ON FINANCIAL STATEMENTS

INCOME STATEMENT

Revenues
− Expenses
= Net Income

STATEMENT OF RETAINED EARNINGS

Opening Balance
+ Net Income
− Dividends
= Retained Earnings

BALANCE SHEET

Assets	Liabilities
	Equity

A = L + E

STATEMENT OF CASH FLOWS

Operating Activities
+ Investing Activities
+ Financing Activities
= Change in Cash
+ Starting Balance
= Ending Cash Balance

Classifying accounts in groups on the financial statements facilitates financial analysis.

FOUNDATIONS OF FINANCIAL REPORTING

LO 1 Describe the objective of financial reporting and identify the qualitative characteristics, conventions, and ethical considerations of accounting information.

By issuing stocks and bonds that are traded in financial markets, corporations can raise the cash they need to carry out business activities. Investors in stocks expect increases in the firm's stock price and returns from dividends. Bondholders and other creditors want to know if the firm can repay the money it borrows plus interest in accordance with specified terms. Very importantly, both investors and creditors need to know if the firm can generate adequate cash flows to maintain its liquidity. Information pertaining to all these matters appears in the financial statements published in a company's annual report.

In the following sections, we describe the objective of financial reporting and the qualitative characteristics, accounting conventions, and ethical considerations that are involved. Exhibit 4.1 illustrates these factors.

Objective of Financial Reporting

The Financial Accounting Standards Board (FASB) emphasizes the information needs of capital providers and others when it defines the objective of financial reporting as follows:

> To provide financial information about the reporting entity that is useful to present and potential equity investors, lenders, and other creditors in making decisions in their capacity as capital providers. Information that is decision-useful to capital providers may also be useful to other users of financial reporting who are not capital providers.[2]

EXHIBIT 4.1
Factors Affecting Financial Reporting

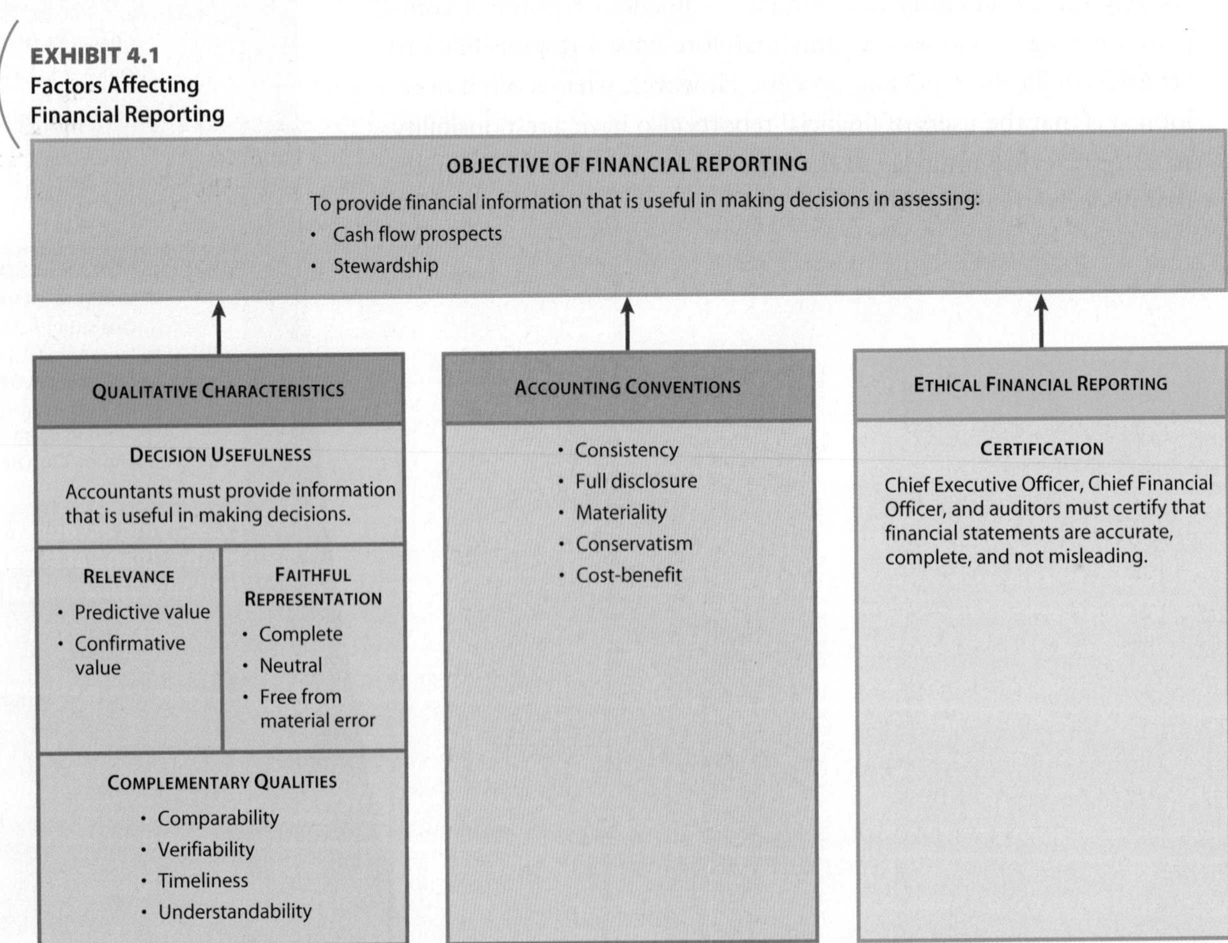

OBJECTIVE OF FINANCIAL REPORTING
To provide financial information that is useful in making decisions in assessing:
• Cash flow prospects
• Stewardship
QUALITATIVE CHARACTERISTICS
DECISION USEFULNESS
Accountants must provide information that is useful in making decisions.
RELEVANCE
• Predictive value
• Confirmative value
FAITHFUL REPRESENTATION
• Complete
• Neutral
• Free from material error
COMPLEMENTARY QUALITIES
• Comparability
• Verifiability
• Timeliness
• Understandability
ACCOUNTING CONVENTIONS
• Consistency
• Full disclosure
• Materiality
• Conservatism
• Cost-benefit
ETHICAL FINANCIAL REPORTING
CERTIFICATION
Chief Executive Officer, Chief Financial Officer, and auditors must certify that financial statements are accurate, complete, and not misleading.

STUDY NOTE: Reading financial reports requires some understanding of business, but it does not require the skills of a CPA.

To be useful for decision making, financial reporting must enable the user to do the following:

- **Assess cash flow prospects.** The ultimate value of a business and its ability to pay dividends, interest, or otherwise provide returns to capital providers depends on its ability to generate future cash flows. Capital providers and other users therefore need information that will help them make judgments about the business's ability to generate cash flows.
- **Assess management's stewardship.** Management is accountable for the custody and safekeeping of the business's economic resources and for their efficient and profitable use—a responsibility the FASB calls "stewardship." To assess the results of management's stewardship, capital providers and others need information about the business's resources (assets), claims against them (liabilities and stockholders' equity), and changes in these resources and claims resulting from transactions (earnings and cash flows) and other economic events.

Financial reporting includes the financial statements (the balance sheet, income statement, statement of retained earnings, and statement of cash flows) that are periodically presented to parties outside the business. Although these statements are very important outputs of the accounting system, they are not the only output. Management's explanations of underlying assumptions and significant uncertainties about methods and estimates used in preparing the financial statements are also important components of financial reporting. Because of a potential conflict of interest between managers, who must prepare the statements, and investors or creditors, who invest in or lend money to the business, financial statements usually are audited by outside accountants to ensure their reliability.

Qualitative Characteristics of Accounting Information

Introductory accounting textbooks present basic accounting concepts in a simple form to help students understand them. All the problems can be solved, and all the numbers add up, making accounting seem like mathematics in its precision. In practice, however, accounting information is neither simple nor precise. The FASB emphasizes this fact in the following statement:

> The information provided by financial reporting often results from approximate, rather than exact, measures. The measures commonly involve numerous estimates, classifications, summarizations, judgments and allocations. The outcome of economic activity in a dynamic economy is uncertain and results from combinations of many factors. Thus, despite the aura of precision that may seem to surround financial reporting in general and financial statements in particular, with few exceptions the measures are approximations, which may be based on rules and conventions, rather than exact amounts.[3]

The goal of generating accounting information is to provide data that different users need to make informed decisions for their unique situations. How this goal is achieved provides much of the interest and controversy in accounting. To facilitate interpretation of accounting information, the FASB has established standards, or **qualitative characteristics**, by which to judge the information.[4] The most important or fundamental of these characteristics are relevance and faithful representation.

Relevance **Relevance** means that information should have a direct bearing on a decision. In other words, if the information were not available, a different decision would be made. To be relevant, information must have predictive value, confirmative value, or both.

- **Predictive value:** Information has *predictive value* if it helps capital providers make decisions about the future. For example, the statement of cash flows can provide information about whether the company has sufficient funds to expand or if it will need to raise funds from capital providers.
- **Confirmative value:** Information has *confirmative value* if it helps determine whether expectations have been met. For example, the income statement provides information about whether the company met earnings expectations during the past accounting period.

The financial statements may provide information that is both predictive and confirmative. For example, the statement of cash flows not only helps to project future cash flows but also confirms expectations about various prior actions.

Faithful Representation **Faithful representation** means that financial information is complete, neutral, and free from material error.

- **Complete:** Complete information provides all the information necessary for a reliable decision.
- **Neutral:** Neutral information is free of any bias intended to achieve a certain result or bring about a particular behavior.
- **Free from material error:** To be free from material error means that information should meet a minimum level of accuracy so that the information does not distort what is being reported. It does not mean that information is absolutely accurate because most financial information is based on estimates and judgments.

If major uncertainties about faithful representation exist, they should be disclosed in a note to the financial statements.

Additional Qualitative Characteristics Other qualitative characteristics that the FASB has established for interpreting accounting information include comparability, verifiability, timeliness, and understandability.

- **Comparability:** **Comparability** is the quality that enables users to identify similarities and differences between two sets of financial data.
- **Verifiability:** **Verifiability** is the quality that assures users that information as presented can be substantiated.
- **Timeliness:** **Timeliness** is the quality that enables users to receive information in time to influence their decisions.
- **Understandability:** **Understandability** is the quality that enables users to comprehend the meaning of the information they receive.

Accounting Conventions

For accounting information to be understandable, accountants must prepare financial statements in accordance with accepted practices. But the decision maker also must know how to interpret the information; in making decisions, he or she must judge what information to use, how to use it, and what it means. Familiarity with the **accounting conventions**, or constraints, used in preparing financial statements enables the user to better understand accounting information. These conventions, which we discuss later in the chapter, affect how and what information is presented in financial statements.

Ethical Financial Reporting

As we noted earlier in the text, in 2002, in the wake of accounting scandals at **Enron** and **WorldCom,** Congress passed the Sarbanes-Oxley Act. One of the important outcomes of this legislation was that the Securities and Exchange Commission instituted rules requiring the chief executive officers and chief financial officers of all publicly traded companies to certify that, to their knowledge, the quarterly and annual statements that their companies file with the SEC are accurate and complete. After the passage of this legislation, an investigation by the audit committee of **Dell**'s board of directors and management disclosed weaknesses in the company's controls and led to restatements of the financial statements for the prior four years. After extensive improvements in control and the restatements, the company's chief executive officer, Michael S. Dell, made the following certifying statement in the company's annual report to the SEC:

> Based on my knowledge, the financial statements, and other financial information included in this report, fairly present in all material respects the financial condition, results of operations and cash flows . . . for the periods represented in this report.[5]

The chief financial officer may sign a similar certification.

As the Enron and WorldCom scandals demonstrated, fraudulent financial reporting can have high costs for investors, lenders, employees, and customers. It can also have high costs for the people who condone, authorize, or prepare misleading reports—even those at the highest corporate levels. In March 2005, Bernard J. Ebbers, former CEO of WorldCom, was convicted of seven counts of filing false reports with the SEC and one count each of securities fraud and conspiracy.[6] In 2006, both Kenneth Lay, former chairman of Enron Corporation, and Jeffrey Skilling, Enron's former CEO, were convicted on charges similar to the ones of which Ebbers was convicted.

Stop & Apply

The numbered items below are important concepts or terms in financial accounting. Match the number of each of these items to the letter of the category in which it belongs.

____ 1. Furnishing information that is useful in assessing cash flow prospects
____ 2. Verifiability
____ 3. Relevance
____ 4. Assess stewardship
____ 5. Faithful representation
____ 6. Recognition
____ 7. Investors
____ 8. Predictive value
____ 9. Management
____ 10. Valuation
____ 11. Internal accounting control
____ 12. Furnishing information that is useful to investors and creditors

a. Decision makers (users of accounting information)
b. Objective of accounting information
c. Accounting measurement considerations
d. Accounting recordkeeping considerations
e. Qualitative characteristics

SOLUTION

1. b; 2. e; 3. e; 4. b; 5. e; 6. c; 7. a; 8. e; 9. a; 10. c; 11. d; 12. b

iStock Photo

ACCOUNTING CONVENTIONS FOR PREPARING FINANCIAL STATEMENTS

Define and describe the conventions of *consistency, full disclosure, materiality, conservatism*, and *cost-benefit*.

Financial statements are based largely on estimates and the application of accounting rules for recognition and allocation. To deal with the natural difficulties in providing financial information, accountants depend on five conventions in recording transactions and preparing financial statements: consistency, full disclosure, materiality, conservatism, and cost-benefit.

Consistency

Consistency requires that once a company has adopted an accounting procedure, it must use it from one period to the next unless a note to the financial statements informs users of a change in procedure. Generally accepted accounting principles specify what the note must contain:

> The nature of and justification for a change in accounting principle and its effect on income should be disclosed in the financial statements of the period in which the change is made. The justification for the change should explain clearly why the newly adopted accounting principle is preferable.[7]

For example, in the notes to its financial statements, **Goodyear Tire & Rubber Company** disclosed that it had changed its method of accounting for inventories with the approval of its auditors because management felt the new method improved the matching of revenues and costs.[8] Without such an acknowledgment, users of financial statements can assume that the treatment of a particular transaction, account, or item has not changed since the last period.

Full Disclosure (Transparency)

Full disclosure (or *transparency*) requires that financial statements present all the information relevant to users' understanding of the statements. That is, the statements must be transparent so that they include any explanation needed to keep them from being misleading. Explanatory notes are therefore an integral part of the financial statements. For instance, as we have already mentioned, the notes should disclose any change that a company has made in its accounting procedures.

A company must also disclose significant events arising after the balance sheet date in the financial statements. For example, suppose that a firm has purchased a piece of land for a future subdivision. Shortly after the end of its fiscal year, the firm is served papers to halt construction because the Environmental Protection Agency asserts that the land was once a toxic waste dump. This information, which obviously affects the users of the financial statements, must be disclosed in the statements for the fiscal year just ended.

Additional note disclosures required by the FASB and other official bodies include the accounting procedures used in preparing the financial statements and important terms of a company's debt, commitments, and contingencies. However, the statements can become so cluttered with notes that they impede rather than help understanding. Beyond the required disclosures, the application of the full-disclosure convention is based on the judgment of management and of the accountants who prepare the financial statements.

In recent years, independent auditors, the stock exchanges, and the SEC have made more demands for disclosure by publicly owned companies. The SEC has pushed especially hard for the enforcement of full disclosure. As a result, more and better information about corporations is now available to investors and creditors than ever before.

Theoretically, a $10 stapler is a long-term asset and should therefore be capitalized and depreciated over its useful life. However, the conventions of materiality and cost benefit allow the stapler to be expensed entirely in the year of purchase because its cost is small and will have no effect on anyone's decision making.

CHEN PING-HUNG/iStockphoto

Materiality

Materiality refers to the relative importance of an item or event. In general, an item or event is material if there is a reasonable expectation that knowing about it would influence the decisions of users of financial statements. Some items or events are so small or insignificant that they would make little difference to decision makers no matter how they are handled. Thus, a large company like **Dell Computer** may decide that expenditures for durable items of less than $500 should be charged as expenses rather than recorded as long-term assets and depreciated.

The materiality of an item normally is determined by relating its dollar value to an element of the financial statements,

Focus on Business Practice

How Much Is Material? It's Not Only a Matter of Numbers.

The materiality issue was long a pet peeve of the SEC, which contended that companies were increasingly abusing the convention to protect their stocks from taking a pounding when earnings did not reach their targets. In consequence, the SEC issued a rule that put stricter requirements on the use of materiality. In addition to providing quantitative guides, the rule includes qualitative considerations. The percentage assessment of materiality—the rule of thumb of 5 percent or more of net income that accountants and companies have traditionally used—is acceptable as an initial screening. However, the rule states that companies cannot decline to book items in the interest of meeting earnings estimates, preserving a growing earnings trend, converting a loss to a profit, increasing management compensation, or hiding an illegal transaction, such as a bribe.[9]

iStock Photo

such as net income or total assets. As a rule, when an item is worth 5 percent or more of net income, accountants treat it as material. However, materiality depends not only on the value of an item but also on its nature. For example, in a multimillion-dollar company, a mistake of $5,000 in recording an item may not be important, but the discovery of even a small bribe or theft can be very important. Moreover, many small errors can add up to a material amount.

Conservatism

STUDY NOTE: *The purpose of conservatism is not to produce the lowest net income and lowest asset value. It is a guideline for choosing among GAAP alternatives, and it should be used with care.*

When accountants are uncertain about the judgments or estimates they must make, they look to the convention of **conservatism**. This convention holds that when faced with choosing between two equally acceptable procedures or estimates, accountants should choose the one that is least likely to overstate assets and income. One of the most common applications of the conservatism convention is the use of the lower-of-cost-or-market method in accounting for inventories. Under this method, if an item's market value is greater than its original cost, the more conservative cost figure is used. If the market value is below the original cost, the more conservative market value is used. The latter situation often occurs in the computer industry.

Conservatism can be a useful tool, but if abused, it can lead to incorrect and misleading financial statements. For example, there is no uncertainty about how a long-term asset of material cost should be treated. As explained in Chapter 3, the cost of such an asset should be spread over the asset's useful life. When conservatism is used to justify expensing a long-term asset in the period of purchase, income and assets for the current period will be understated, and income in future periods will be overstated. Accountants therefore apply the conservatism convention only when they are uncertain about which accounting procedure or estimate to use.

Cost-Benefit

The **cost-benefit** convention holds that the benefits to be gained from providing accounting information should be greater than the costs of providing it. Of course, minimum levels of relevance and faithful representation must be reached if accounting information is to be useful. Beyond the minimum levels, however, it is up to

Focus on International Practices

IFRS How Will Convergence of U.S. GAAP with IFRS Affect Accounting Conventions?

The FASB and the IASB are working toward merging U.S. generally accepted accounting principles (GAAP) with international financial reporting standards (IFRS). Their goal is "to increase the international comparability and the quality of standards used in the United States [which] is consistent with the FASB's obligation to its domestic constituents, who benefit from comparability across national borders."[10] If IFRS are merged with GAAP, the comparability convention may not be the only accounting convention affected. For instance, conservatism, which has been the bedrock of U.S. accounting practice for many decades, will no longer be part of the conceptual framework. The practice under IFRS of writing up the value of an asset, such as inventory or equipment, that has increased in fair value and recording it as income violates the conservatism convention under GAAP. Thus, the convergence of IFRS with GAAP may well influence the way accountants in the United States analyze financial statements.

iStock Photo

the FASB and the SEC, which stipulate the information that must be reported, and the accountant, who provides the information, to judge the costs and benefits in each case.

Firms use the cost-benefit convention for both accounting and non-accounting decisions. Department stores could almost completely eliminate shoplifting if they hired five times as many clerks as they now have and assigned them to watching customers. The benefit would be reduced shoplifting. The cost would be reduced sales (customers do not like being closely watched) and increased wages expense. Although shoplifting is a serious problem for department stores, the benefit of reducing shoplifting in this way does not outweigh the cost.

Cost-benefit is a question that the FASB, SEC, and all other regulators face. For instance, in considering a far-reaching and costly requirement for accounting disclosure, they have to weigh the final costs and benefits. Even though there are no definitive ways of measuring costs and benefits, much of an accountant's work deals with these concepts.

Stop & Apply

Match each item on the left below to the related accounting convention on the right.

____ 1. A note to the financial statements explains the company's method of revenue recognition.	a. Consistency
____ 2. Inventory is accounted for at its market value, which is less than its original cost.	b. Full disclosure
____ 3. A company uses the same method of revenue recognition year after year.	c. Materiality
____ 4. Several accounts are grouped into one category because the total amount of each account is small.	d. Conservatism
____ 5. A company does not keep detailed records of certain operations because the information gained from the detail is not deemed useful.	e. Cost-benefit

SOLUTION

1. b; 2. d; 3. a; 4. c; 5. e

iStock Photo

CLASSIFIED BALANCE SHEET

LO 3 Identify and describe the basic components of a classified balance sheet.

As you know, a balance sheet presents a company's financial position at a particular time. The balance sheets we have presented thus far categorize accounts as assets, liabilities, and stockholders' equity. Because even a fairly small company can have hundreds of accounts, simply listing accounts in these broad categories is not particularly helpful to a statement user. Setting up subcategories within the major categories can make financial statements much more useful. This format enables investors and creditors to study and evaluate relationships among the subcategories.

General-purpose external financial statements that are divided into subcategories are called **classified financial statements**. Exhibit 4.2 depicts the subcategories into which the principal elements of assets, liabilities, and stockholders' equity are broken down.

EXHIBIT 4.2
Classified Balance Sheet

ASSETS		LIABILITIES
• Current Assets • Investments • Property, Plant, and Equipment • Intangible Assets	=	• Current Liabilities • Long-Term Liabilities
		+
		STOCKHOLDERS' EQUITY
		• Contributed Capital • Retained Earnings

The subcategories of Martin Auto Parts' classified balance sheet, shown in Exhibit 4.3, are those used by most U.S. corporations. Stockholders' equity would, of course, not appear on the statement if Martin Auto Parts were a sole proprietorship or partnership rather than a corporation.

EXHIBIT 4.3
Classified Balance Sheet for Martin Auto Parts Corporation

Martin Auto Parts Corporation Balance Sheet December 31, 2011			
Assets			
Current assets			
Cash		$ 41,440	
Short-term investments		28,000	
Notes receivable		32,000	
Accounts receivable		141,200	
Merchandise inventory		191,600	
Prepaid insurance		26,400	
Supplies		6,784	
Total current assets			$467,424
Investments			
Land held for future use			50,000
Property, plant, and equipment			
Land		$ 18,000	
Building	$ 82,600		
Less accumulated depreciation	34,560	48,040	
Equipment	$108,000		
Less accumulated depreciation	57,800	50,200	
Total property, plant, and equipment			116,240
Intangible assets			
Trademark			2,000
Total assets			$635,664
Liabilities			
Current liabilities			
Notes payable		$ 60,000	
Accounts payable		102,732	
Salaries payable		8,000	
Total current liabilities			$ 170,732
Long-term liabilities			
Mortgage payable			71,200
Total liabilities			$241,932
Stockholders' Equity			
Contributed capital			
Common stock, $10 par value, 20,000 shares authorized, issued, and outstanding		$200,000	
Additional paid-in capital		40,000	
Total contributed capital		$240,000	
Retained earnings		153,732	
Total stockholders' equity			393,732
Total liabilities and stockholders' equity			$635,664

Assets

As you can see in Exhibit 4.3 (p. 205), the classified balance sheet of a U.S. company typically divides assets into current assets; investments; property, plant, and equipment; and intangible assets. These four categories are listed in the order of how easily they can be converted into cash. For example, current assets are usually more easily converted to cash than are property, plant, and equipment. For simplicity, some companies group investments, intangible assets, and other miscellaneous assets into a single category called **other assets**.

Current Assets **Current assets** include cash and other assets that a company can reasonably expect to convert to cash, sell, or consume within one year or its *normal operating cycle*, whichever is longer. A company's **normal operating cycle** is the average time it needs to go from spending cash to receiving cash. For example, suppose a company uses cash to buy inventory and sells the inventory to a customer on credit. To classify the resulting receivable as a current asset, there must be a reasonable expectation that it will be collected in cash before the normal operating cycle ends.

STUDY NOTE: *Investments classified as current must be readily marketable—i.e., management must expect to sell them within the next year or within the current operating cycle.*

We have already mentioned that cash is a current asset. Short-term investments, notes and accounts receivable, and inventory that a company expects to convert to cash (by selling it) within the next year or the normal operating cycle are also current assets. They are listed on the balance sheet in the order of how easily they can be converted to cash.

Prepaid expenses, such as rent and insurance paid in advance, and supplies bought for use by the company rather than for sale and already paid for should be classified as current assets. They are current in the sense that if they had not been paid for earlier, they would require a current outlay of cash.

Investments **Investments** include assets, usually long term, that are not used in normal business operations and that management does not plan to convert to cash within the next year. Items in this category are securities held as long-term investments, long-term notes receivable, land held for future use, plant or equipment not used in the business, and special funds established to pay off a debt or buy a building. Also included are large permanent investments (those a company does not intend to sell) made in another company for the purpose of controlling that company.

Property, Plant, and Equipment **Property, plant, and equipment** include tangible long-term assets used in a business's day-to-day operations. They represent a place to operate (land and buildings) and the equipment used to produce, sell, and deliver goods or services. They are therefore also called *operating assets*, *fixed assets*, *tangible assets*, *long-lived assets*, or *plant assets*. Through depreciation, the costs of these assets (except for the cost of land) are spread over the periods they benefit. Past depreciation of these assets is recorded in Accumulated Depreciation accounts and deducted from their related asset accounts on the balance sheet.

To reduce clutter on the balance sheet, property, plant, and equipment are often combined—for example:

Property, plant, and equipment (net) $116,240

Focus on Business Practice

Normal Operating Cycles Can Be Long

The normal operating cycle for most companies is less than one year, but there are exceptions. For example, because of the length of time it takes **The Boeing Company** to build aircraft, its normal operating cycle exceeds one year. The inventory used in building the planes is nonetheless considered a current asset because the planes will be sold within the normal operating cycle. Another example is a company that sells on an installment basis. The payments for a television set or a refrigerator can extend over 24 or 36 months, but these receivables are still considered current assets.

iStock Photo

The company provides the details in a note to the financial statements.

The property, plant, and equipment category also includes natural resources owned by the company, such as forest lands, oil and gas properties, and coal mines, if they are used in the regular course of business. If they are not, they are listed in the investments category.

Richard T Nowitz/PhotoLibrary

Intangible assets can be worth an enormous amount for some companies. Consider the value of Coca-Cola's trademark, which over the years has become a familiar and easily recognizable symbol worldwide.

Intangible Assets **Intangible assets** are long-term assets with no physical substance whose value stems from the rights or privileges accruing to their owners. Examples include patents, copyrights, franchises, and trademarks. These assets are recorded at cost, which is spread over the expected life of the right or privilege. Goodwill, which arises in the acquisition of another company, is another intangible asset that is recorded at cost, but the cost is not allocated, that is, amortized, over future accounting periods. Goodwill is reviewed each year for possible loss of value, or impairment.

Liabilities

Liabilities are divided into two categories that are based on when the liabilities fall due: current liabilities and long-term liabilities.

Current Liabilities **Current liabilities** are obligations that must be satisfied within one year or within the company's normal operating cycle, whichever is longer. These liabilities are typically paid out of current assets or by incurring new short-term liabilities. They include notes payable, accounts payable, the current portion of long-term debt, salaries and wages payable, taxes payable, and customer advances (unearned revenues).

Long-Term Liabilities **Long-term liabilities** are debts that fall due more than one year in the future or beyond the normal operating cycle and are thus paid out of noncurrent assets. Mortgages payable, long-term notes, bonds payable, employee pension obligations, and long-term lease liabilities generally fall into this category. Public corporations often include deferred income taxes as a separate category in the long-term liability section of their balance sheets. This liability arises because the rules for measuring income for tax purposes differ from those for financial reporting. The cumulative annual difference between the income taxes payable to governments and the income taxes expense reported on the income statement is included in the account Deferred Income Taxes.

STUDY NOTE: *The portion of a mortgage due during the next year or the current operating cycle is classified as a current liability; the portion due after the next year or the current operating cycle is classified as a long-term liability.*

Stockholders' Equity

As you know, corporations are owned by their stockholders and are separate legal entities. As shown in Exhibit 4.3 (p. 205), the stockholders' equity section of a corporation's balance sheet has two parts: contributed capital and retained earnings.

Contributed Capital **Contributed capital** is the amount that stockholders invest in the business. Generally, contributed capital is shown on a corporate balance sheet as two amounts: the par value of the issued stock and additional paid-in capital, which is the amount paid in above par value.

Retained Earnings **Retained earnings** are the earnings of the corporation less any losses, dividends, or transfers to contributed capital. The amount of retained earnings in the stockholders' equity section of the balance sheet comes from the ending balance of the statement of retained earnings.

Owner's Equity and Partners' Equity

Although the form of business organization does not usually affect the accounting treatment of assets and liabilities, the equity section of a sole proprietorship's or partnership's balance sheet is very different from the equity section of a corporation's balance sheet.

Focus on International Practices

IFRS IASB Proposes Change in Format of Financial Statements

In the United States, classified financial statements have been used for more than a century, and accountants and most people engaged in business are very familiar with their format. However, the format of financial statements may change in the near future. The International Accounting Standards Board (IABS) is considering reorganizing the balance sheet and income statement so that their formats resemble the one used in the statement of cash flows. Under the proposal, both statements would include the categories now found on the statement of cash flows: operating, investing, and financing activities. The balance sheet form that equates total assets with liabilities and stockholders' equity (A = L + SE) would be replaced by a form in which each category of liabilities is netted against its corresponding asset category. For example, current operating liabilities would be subtracted from current operating assets, and long-term debt would be subtracted from long-term assets on the asset side of the balance sheet.

iStock Photo

Sole Proprietorship The equity section of a sole proprietorship's balance sheet simply shows the capital in the owner's name at an amount equal to the net assets of the company. It might appear as follows:

Owner's Equity

Martin Wikar, Capital	$395,732

Because in a sole proprietorship, there is no legal separation between the owner and the business, there is no need to separate contributed capital from earnings retained for use in the business. The Capital account is increased by both the owner's investments and net income. It is decreased by net losses and withdrawals of assets from the business for personal use by the owner.

The terms *owner's equity*, *proprietorship*, *owner's capital*, and *net worth* are used interchangeably. All refer to the owner's interest, or equity, in the company. However, the first three terms are preferred to *net worth* because many assets are recorded at their original cost rather than at their current value.

STUDY NOTE: *Equity in a sole proprietorship and in a partnership differs only in the number of Capital accounts.*

Partnership The equity section of a partnership's balance sheet is called *partners' equity*. It is much like that in a sole proprietorship's balance sheet. It might appear as follows:

Partners' Equity

Steven Lall, Capital	$168,750	
Martin Wikar, Capital	224,982	
Total partners' equity		$393,732

Dell's Balance Sheets

Although balance sheets generally resemble the one shown in Exhibit 4.3 (p. 205) for Martin Auto Parts, no two companies have financial statements that are exactly alike. **Dell Computer**'s balance sheet provides a good example of some of the variations. As shown in Exhibit 4.4, it provides data for two years so that users can evaluate changes from one year to the next. Note that its major classifications are similar but not identical to those of Martin Auto Parts. For instance, Martin Auto Parts has asset categories for investments and intangible assets, and Dell has an asset category called "other non-current assets," which is a small amount of its total assets. Also note that Dell has a category called "other non-current liabilities." Because this category is listed after long-term debt, it represents longer-term liabilities, due more than one year after the balance sheet date. The components of Dell's stockholders' equity section include items that will be covered in later chapters.

EXHIBIT 4.4
Classified Balance Sheet for Dell Computer Corporation

Dell Computer Corporation
Consolidated Statement of Financial Position
(In millions)

	January 29, 2010	January 30, 2009
Assets		
Current assets:		
Cash and cash equivalents	$10,635	$ 8,352
Short-term investments	373	740
Accounts receivable, net	5,837	4,731
Financing receivables, net	2,706	1,712
Inventories, net	1,051	867
Other current assets	3,643	3,749
Total current assets	$24,245	$20,151
Property, plant, and equipment, net	2,181	2,277
Investments	781	454
Long-term financing receivables, net	332	500
Goodwill	4,074	1,737
Purchased intangible assets, net	1,694	724
Other non-current assets	345	657
Total assets	$33,652	$26,500
Liabilities and Stockholders' Equity		
Current liabilities:		
Short-term debt	$ 663	$ 113
Accounts payable	11,373	8,309
Accrued and other	3,884	3,736
Short-term deferred services revenue	3,040	2,701
Total current liabilities	$18,960	$14,859
Long-term debt	3,417	1,898
Long-term deferred services revenue	3,029	3,000
Other non-current liabilities	2,605	2,472
Total liabilities	$28,011	$22,229
Stockholders' equity:		
Preferred stock and capital in excess of $0.01 par value; shares issued and outstanding:	—	—
Common stock and capital in excess of $0.01 par value; shares authorized: 7,000; shares issued: 3,351 and 3,338, respectively; shares outstanding: 1,957 and 1,944, respectively	11,472	11,189
Treasury stock, at cost; 919 shares	(27,904)	(27,904)
Retained earnings	22,110	20,677
Other comprehensive loss	(37)	309
Total stockholders' equity	5,641	4,271
Total liabilities and stockholders' equity	$33,652	$26,500

Source: Adapted from Dell Computer Corporation, *Annual Report*, 2010.

Stop & Apply

The numbered items are account titles. The lettered items below are categories that appear on a balance sheet. Match each account to the letter of the appropriate category or indicate that it does not appear on the balance sheet.

___ 1. Trademark
___ 2. Marketable Securities
___ 3. Land Held for Future Use
___ 4. Taxes Payable
___ 5. Bond Payable in Five Years
___ 6. Common Stock
___ 7. Land Used in Operations
___ 8. Accumulated Depreciation
___ 9. Accounts Receivable
___ 10. Interest Expense
___ 11. Unearned Revenue
___ 12. Prepaid Rent

a. Current assets
b. Investments
c. Property, plant, and equipment
d. Intangible assets
e. Current liabilities
f. Long-term liabilities
g. Stockholders' equity
h. Not on balance sheet

SOLUTION

1. d; 2. a; 3. b; 4. e; 5. f; 6. g; 7. c; 8. c; 9. a; 10. h; 11. e; 12. a

iStock Photo

FORMS OF THE INCOME STATEMENT

LO 4 Describe the features of multistep and single-step classified income statements.

In the income statements we have presented thus far, expenses have been deducted from revenue in a single step to arrive at net income. Here, we look at a multistep income statement and a single-step format more complex than the one we presented in earlier chapters.

Multistep Income Statement

A **multistep income statement** goes through a series of steps, or subtotals, to arrive at net income. Exhibit 4.5 compares the multistep income statement of a service company (which provides services as opposed to products) with that of a **merchandising company** (which buys and sells products), and a **manufacturing company** (which makes and sells products). As you can see, in a service company's multistep income statement, the operating expenses are deducted from revenues in a single step to arrive at income from operations. In contrast, because manufacturing and merchandising companies make or buy goods for sale, their income statements include an additional step of calculating gross margin by subtracting the cost of goods from net sales.

The following sections describe the major parts of a merchandising or manufacturing company's multistep income statement. Refer to Exhibit 4.6 (p. 212), the multistep income statement for Martin Auto Parts to see how net income, "the bottom line in the income statement," is derived.

Net Sales (or Net Revenue) The first major part of a merchandising or manufacturing company's multistep income statement is **net sales**, which some companies, including **Dell Computer**, call *net revenue* and others refer to simply as *sales.* Net sales are gross sales less sales returns and allowances.

- **Gross sales** consist of the total revenue from cash and credit sales recorded during an accounting period. Under the revenue recognition rule, even when cash from a credit sale is not received during the current accounting period, it must be recorded if title to the merchandise has passed to the buyer.
- **Sales returns and allowances** include cash refunds and credits on account. They also include any discounts from selling prices made to customers who have returned defective products or products that are otherwise unsatisfactory. If other types of discounts are given to customers, they also should be deducted from gross sales.

EXHIBIT 4.5
A Comparison of the Components of Multistep Income Statements for Service and Merchandising or Manufacturing Companies

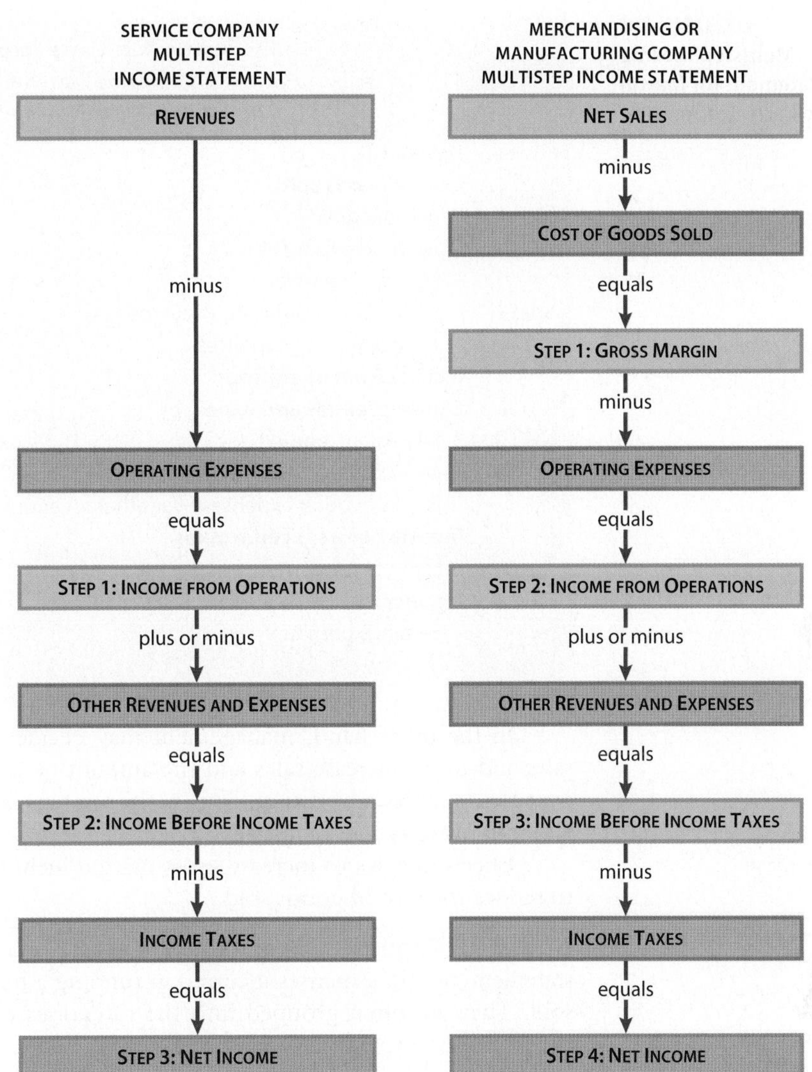

Cost of Goods Sold (or Cost of Sales) **Cost of goods sold**, which some companies call *cost of sales* or *cost of revenue*, is the second major part of a multistep income statement. It is the amount a merchandiser paid for the merchandise it sold during an accounting period. For a manufacturer, it is the cost of making the products it sold during an accounting period.

Gross Margin (or Gross Profit) The third major part of a multistep income statement is **gross margin**, which some companies call *gross profit*. It is the difference between net sales and the cost of goods sold, shown in Exhibit 4.6 as the subtotal in Step 1. A company's gross margin must be sufficient to cover operating expenses and provide an adequate after-tax income.

Managers and investors are interested in both the amount and percentage of gross margin. The percentage is computed by dividing the amount of gross margin by net sales. For Martin Auto Parts, the amount of gross margin is $433,584, and the percentage of gross margin is 34.7 percent, calculated as:

$$\text{Gross Margin} \div \text{Net Sales} = \text{Percentage of Gross Margin}$$
$$\$433{,}584 \div \$1{,}248{,}624 = 34.7\%$$

STUDY NOTE: Gross margin measures profitability. When it is less than operating expenses, the company suffers a net loss from operations.

This information is useful in planning business operations. For instance, management may try to increase total sales of a product by reducing the selling price. Although this strategy reduces the percentage of gross margin, it will work if the number of items sold increases enough to raise the absolute amount of gross margin. This is the strategy used by discount warehouse stores like **Sam's Club** and **Costco Wholesale Corporation**.

EXHIBIT 4.6
Multistep Income Statement for Martin Auto Parts Corporation

Martin Auto Parts Corporation
Income Statement
For the Year Ended December 31, 2011

Step 1	**Net sales**		$1,248,624
	Cost of goods sold		815,040
	Gross margin		$ 433,584
Step 2	**Operating expenses**		
	Selling expenses	$219,120	
	General and administrative expenses	138,016	
	Total operating expenses		357,136
	Income from operations		$ 76,448
Step 3	**Other revenues and expenses**		
	Interest income	$ 5,600	
	Less interest expense	10,524	
	Excess of other expenses over other revenues		4,924
	Income before income taxes		$ 71,524
Step 4	**Income taxes**		13,524
	Net income		$ 58,000
	Earnings per share		$ 2.90

On the other hand, management may decide to keep a high gross margin from sales and try to increase sales and the amount of gross margin by increasing operating expenses, such as advertising. This is the strategy used by upscale specialty stores like **Neiman Marcus** and **Tiffany & Co.**

Other strategies to increase gross margin include using better purchasing methods to reduce the cost of goods sold.

Operating Expenses **Operating expenses**, the next major part of a multistep income statement, are the expenses incurred in running a business other than the cost of goods sold. They are often grouped into the categories of selling expenses and general and administrative expenses.

- **Selling expenses** include the costs of storing goods and preparing them for sale; preparing displays, advertising, and otherwise promoting sales; and delivering goods to a buyer if the seller has agreed to pay the cost of delivery.
- **General and administrative expenses** include expenses for accounting, personnel, credit checking, collections, and any other expenses that apply to overall operations. Although occupancy expenses, such as expenses for rent, insurance expense, and utilities, are often classified as general and administrative expenses, they can be allocated between selling expenses and general and administrative expenses.

Careful planning and control of operating expenses can improve a company's profitability.

STUDY NOTE: Income from operations is a key measure of profitability for financial analysts.

Income from Operations (or Operating Income) **Income from operations**, also called *operating income*, is the income from a company's main business. As shown in Step 2 of Exhibit 4.6, it is derived by deducting operating expenses from gross margin. Income from operations is often used to compare the profitability of two or more companies or divisions within a company.

Other Revenues and Expenses (or Nonoperating Revenues and Expenses) **Other revenues and expenses**, also called *nonoperating revenues and expenses*, are not related to a company's operating activities. Among the items commonly included in this section of a multistep income statement are revenues from investments (such as dividends and interest on stocks, bonds, and savings accounts) and interest expense and other expenses that result from borrowing money. Because Martin Auto Parts' "other expenses" were more than its "other revenue," the total amount of these items, shown in Step 3 of Exhibit 4.6, is called "excess of other expenses over other revenues."

Income Before Income Taxes **Income before income taxes** is the amount a company has earned from all activities—operating and nonoperating—before taking into account the amount of income taxes it incurred. As shown in Step 3 of Exhibit 4.6, income before income taxes is derived by subtracting (or adding) the total of "other revenues and expenses" from "income from operations." Because companies are subject to different income tax rates, income before income taxes is often used to compare the profitability of companies.

Income Taxes (or Provision for Income Taxes) **Income taxes**, which some companies call *provision for income taxes*, represent the expense for federal, state, and local taxes on income. As shown in Exhibit 4.6, they appear as a separate item in a corporation's income statement (usually the word *expense* is not used in the statement). They do not appear on the income statements of sole proprietorships and partnerships because the individuals who own these businesses are the tax-paying units; they pay income taxes on their share of the business income.

Because federal, state, and local income taxes for corporations are substantial, they have a significant effect on business decisions. Current federal income tax rates for corporations vary from 15 percent to 35 percent depending on the amount of income before income taxes and other factors. Most other taxes, such as property and employment taxes, are included in operating expenses.

Net Income (or Net Earnings) **Net income**, also called *net earnings*, is the final figure, or "bottom line," of an income statement. As shown in Step 4 in Exhibit 4.6, it is what remains of gross margin ($433,584 for Martin Auto Parts) after operating expenses ($357,136) have been deducted, other revenues and expenses have been added or deducted (a deduction of $4,924 for Martin Auto Parts), and income taxes ($13,524) have been deducted. Net income for Martin Auto Parts is $58,000.

Net income is an important performance measure because it represents the amount of earnings that accrue to stockholders. It is the amount transferred to retained earnings from all the income that business operations have generated during an accounting period. Both managers and investors often use net income to measure a business's financial performance over the past accounting period.

STUDY NOTE: *Because it is a shorthand measure of profitability, earnings per share is the performance measure most commonly cited in the financial press.*

Earnings per Share (or Net Income per Share) **Earnings per share**, often called *net income per share*, is the net income earned on each share of common stock. It is reported immediately below net income on the income statement. In the simplest case, it is computed by dividing net income by the average number of shares of common stock outstanding during the year:

Earnings per Share = Net Income ÷ Average Shares of Common Stock Outstanding

Martin Auto Parts had 20,000 shares of common stock outstanding in 2011 (see the stockholders' equity section in Exhibit 4.3). Thus, its earnings per share is computed as follows:

$2.90 = $58,000 ÷ 20,000 shares

Investors find earnings per share a quick way of assessing both a company's profitability and its earnings in relation to the market price of its stock.

Dell's Income Statements

Like balance sheets, income statements vary among companies. You will rarely, if ever, find an income statement exactly like the one we have presented for Martin Auto Parts. Companies use both different terms and different structures. For example, as you can see in Exhibit 4.7 (p. 214), in its multistep income statement, **Dell Computer Corporation** provided three years of data for purposes of comparison.

EXHIBIT 4.7
Multistep Income Statement for Dell Computer Corporation

Dell Computer Corporation
Consolidated Statement of Income
(In millions, except per share amounts)

	Fiscal Year Ended		
	January 29, 2010	**January 30, 2009**	**February 1, 2008**
Net revenue	$52,902	$61,101	$61,133
Cost of revenue	43,641	50,144	49,462
Gross margin	9,261	10,957	11,671
Operating expenses:			
Selling, general, and administrative	6,465	7,102	7,538
In-process research and development	—	2	83
Research, development, and engineering	624	663	610
Total operating expenses	7,089	7,767	8,231
Operating income	2,172	3,190	3,440
Interest and other, net	(148)	134	387
Income before income taxes	2,024	3,324	3,827
Income tax provision	591	846	880
Net income	$ 1,433	$ 2,478	$ 2,947
Earnings per share*	$ 0.73	$ 1.25	$ 1.33

*Basic
Source: Dell Computer Corporation, *Annual Report*, 2010.

STUDY NOTE: *Analysts often convert a single-step statement to a multistep one because the latter separates operating sources of income from nonoperating ones. Investors want income to result primarily from operations, not from one-time gains or losses.*

Single-Step Income Statement

Exhibit 4.8 shows a **single-step income statement** for Martin Auto Parts. In this statement, income before income taxes is derived in a single step by putting the major categories of revenues in the first part of the statement and the major categories of costs and expenses in the second part. As on the multistep income statement, income taxes are shown as a separate item.

EXHIBIT 4.8
Single-Step Income Statement for Martin Auto Parts Corporation

Martin Auto Parts Corporation
Income Statement
For the Year Ended December 31, 2011

Revenues		
Net sales		$ 1,248,624
Interest income		5,600
Total revenues		$ 1,254,224
Costs and expenses		
Cost of goods sold	$815,040	
Selling expenses	219,120	
General and administrative expenses	138,016	
Interest expense	10,524	
Total costs and expenses		1,182,700
Income before income taxes		$ 71,524
Income taxes		13,524
Net income		$ 58,000
Earnings per share		$ 2.90

Both the multistep form and the single-step form of the income statement have advantages: the multistep form shows the components used in deriving net income, and the single-step form has the advantage of simplicity. About one-third of public companies use the single-step form. Analysts often convert a single-step statement to multistep form to get a better idea of a company's profitability from gross margin and income from operations.

Stop & Apply

The numbered items are account titles. The lettered items below are categories that appear on a multistep income statement. Match each account to the letter of the appropriate category or indicate that it is not on the income statement.

____ 1. Sales Returns and Allowances
____ 2. Cost of Goods Sold
____ 3. Dividend Income
____ 4. Delivery Expense
____ 5. Office Salaries Expense
____ 6. Wages Payable
____ 7. Sales Salaries Expense
____ 8. Advertising Expense
____ 9. Interest Expense
____ 10. Commissions Expense

a. Net sales
b. Cost of goods sold
c. Selling expenses
d. General and administrative expenses
e. Other revenues and expenses
f. Not on income statement

SOLUTION

1. a; 2. b; 3. e; 4. c; 5. d; 6. f; 7. c; 8. c; 9. e; 10. c

iStock Photo

USING FINANCIAL RATIOS FOR PERFORMANCE EVALUATION

Use financial ratios to evaluate a company's performance. 

STUDY NOTE: Accounts must be classified correctly before the ratios are computed. Otherwise, the ratios will be incorrect.

As discussed in Chapter 1, six elements of the financial statements and four financial ratios are critical in assessing whether a company is achieving its strategic objectives. A familiarity with these elements and ratios is the basis for making good business decisions.

In earlier chapters, we showed how profit margin, asset turnover, and cash flow yield are used to evaluate and predict a company's performance. Here, to emphasize the importance of these ratios, we provide a brief review. We also explain how the fourth critical ratio—the debt to equity ratio—shows whether companies are achieving their strategic objectives. In addition, we discuss other financial ratios that can have a bearing on a company's financial performance.

Critical Financial Ratios and Financial Statement Elements

As noted above, the four critical financial ratios are profit margin, asset turnover, cash flow yield, and the debt to equity ratio. Each of these uses various elements of the financial statements. These financial statement elements and financial ratios have been chosen because they are critical for companies achieving their strategic objectives. In other words, simply understanding how to find these elements in the financial statements and how to compute these ratios will allow you to analyze financial statements and determine how well or poorly a company is performing.

Financial Ratio: Profit Margin The **profit margin** shows the percentage of each sales dollar that results in net income. It is an indication of how well a company is controlling its costs: the lower its costs, the higher its profit margin. (Do not confuse this ratio with gross margin, which is the amount by which revenues exceed the cost of goods sold.)

The profit margin uses two elements of the income statement—net income and revenue (often called *net sales* or *net revenue*). For Martin Auto Parts, it is computed as shown below.

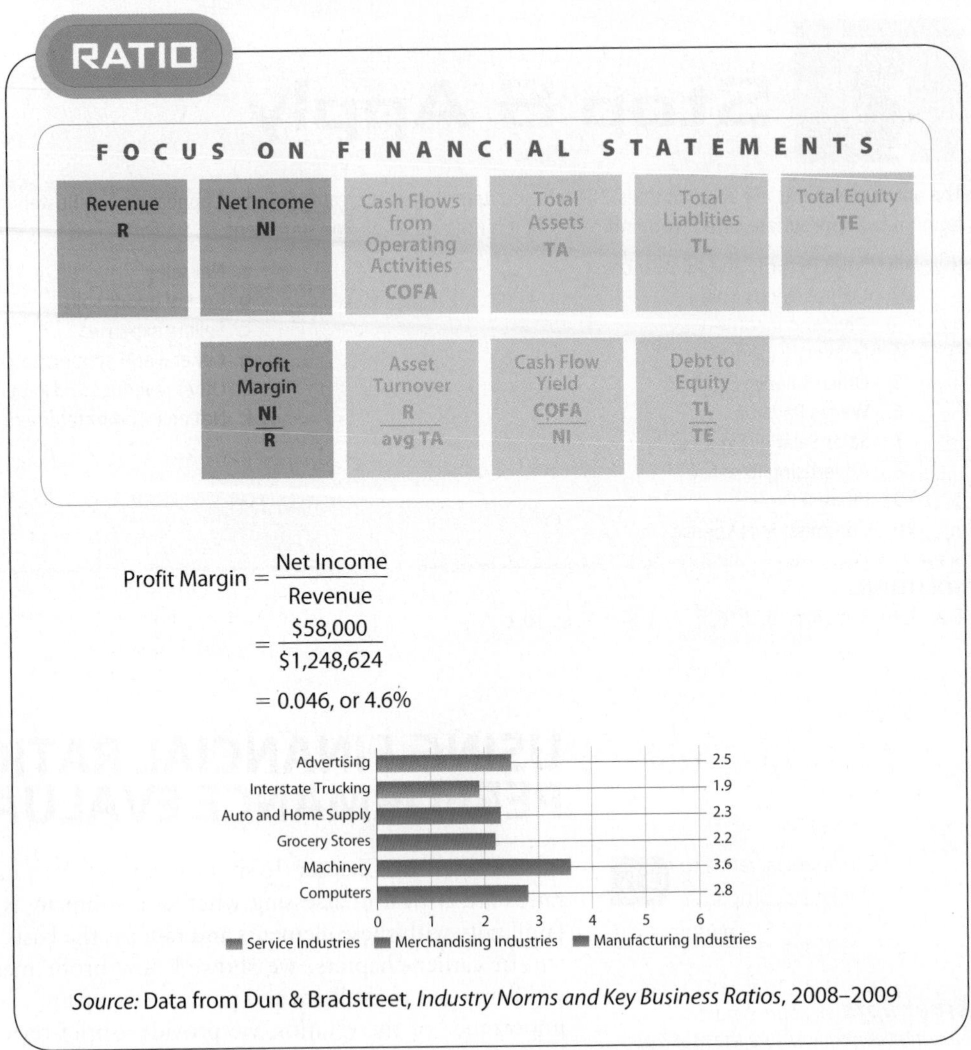

Source: Data from Dun & Bradstreet, *Industry Norms and Key Business Ratios*, 2008–2009

Martin Auto Parts' profit margin of 4.6 percent means that the company earns 4.6 cents on each dollar of sales. Is this a satisfactory profit? The answer requires a comparison with the profit margin ratios of other companies in the same industry. As shown in the graph above, the average profit margin for the auto and home supply industry is 2.3 percent. So, although a profit margin of 4.6 percent may not seem like much, it is double the industry average of 2.3 percent. A difference of 1 or 2 percent in a company's profit margin can be the difference between a fair year and a very profitable one.

Financial Ratio: Asset Turnover The **asset turnover** ratio measures how efficiently assets are used to produce sales. In other words, how much revenue is generated by each dollar of assets? A company with a high asset turnover uses its assets more productively than one with a low asset turnover.

The asset turnover ratio uses revenue from the income statement and total assets from the balance sheet. It is computed by dividing revenue by average total assets.

Average total assets are the sum of total assets at the beginning of an accounting period and total assets at the end of the period divided by 2. Since revenues take place over the year, they are compared with average total assets, which is intended to represent the usual level of assets over the year. For example, if Martin Auto Parts had assets of \$594,480 at the beginning of the year, its asset turnover would be computed as shown below.

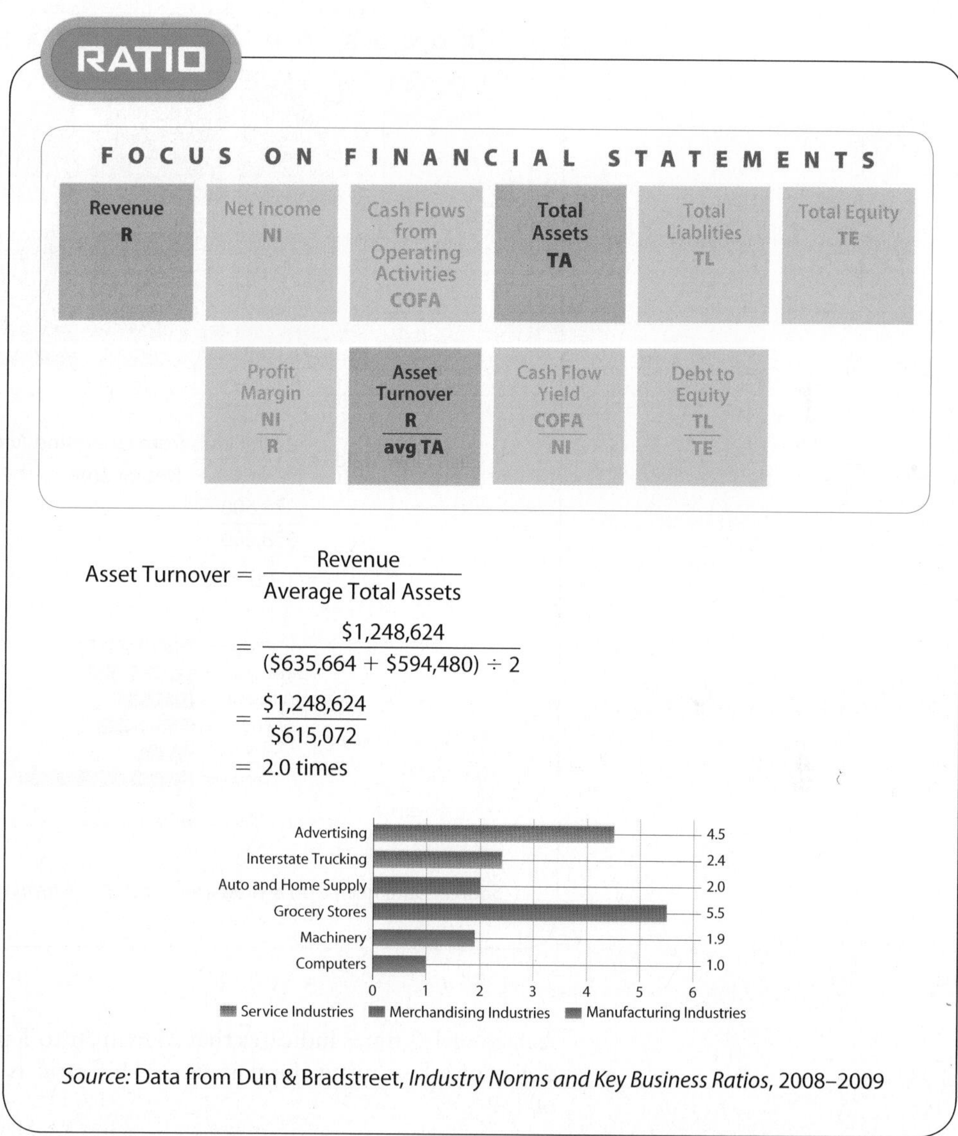

Source: Data from Dun & Bradstreet, *Industry Norms and Key Business Ratios*, 2008–2009

STUDY NOTE: *If revenue is twice the amount of average total assets, each dollar of assets will produce \$2.00 in revenue.*

Thus, Martin Auto Parts produces \$2.00 in sales for each dollar invested in assets. Its asset turnover of 2.0 times is the same as the industry average. In other words, the company is as productive in producing revenue as other companies in the auto and home supply industry.

Financial Ratio: Cash Flow Yield The **cash flow yield** ratio measures how much cash a company's operations generate in relation to its net income. It is critical that operations result in cash payments. For instance, Martin Auto Parts may increase sales by selling on credit, but credit sales do not benefit the company until the customers remit cash. If not collected, an account receivable becomes a loss.

The cash flow yield relates an element of the income statement—net income—to an element of the statement of cash flows—cash flows from operating activities. For example, if Martin Auto Parts' cash flow from operations is \$72,500, the cash flow yield would be computed as shown below.

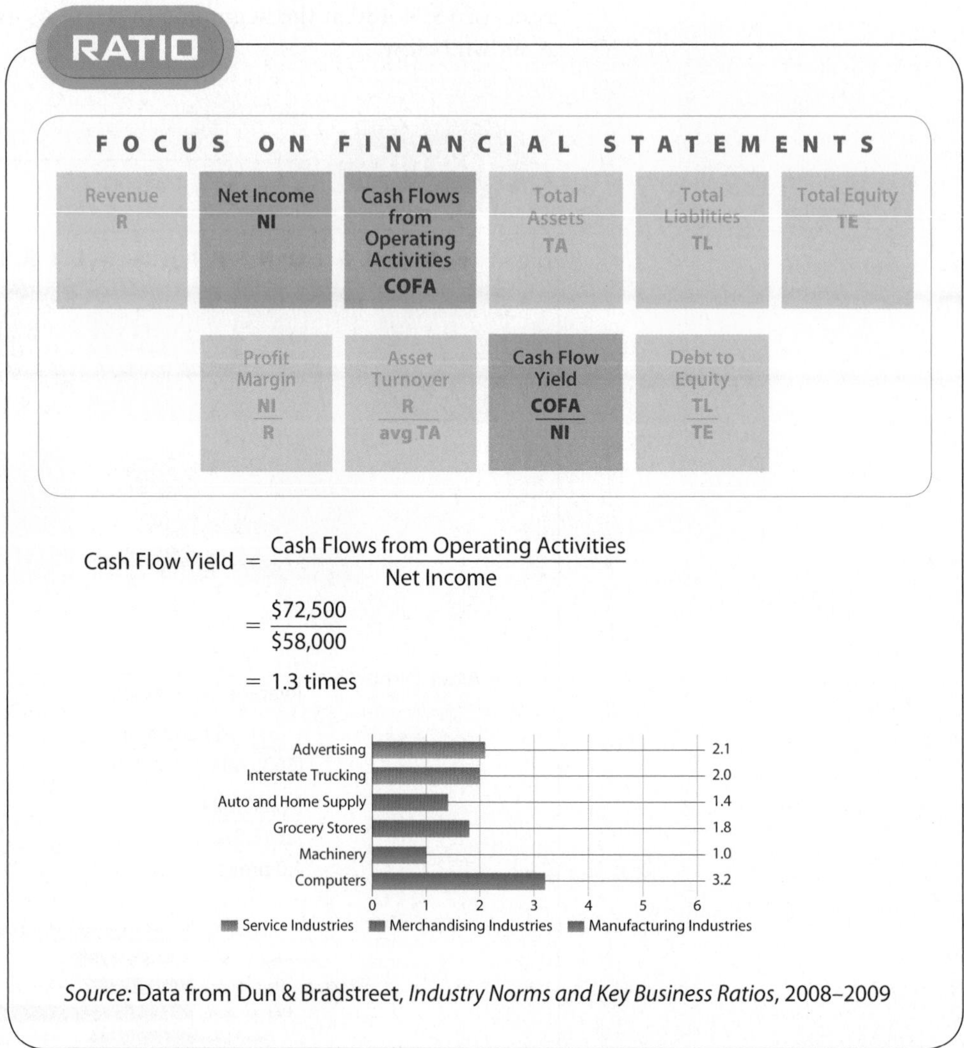

Source: Data from Dun & Bradstreet, *Industry Norms and Key Business Ratios*, 2008–2009

A ratio of 1.3 times indicates that Martin Auto Parts produced \$1.30 of cash for every dollar of sales during the past year. This ratio is slightly below the industry average of 1.4.

Financial Ratio: Debt to Equity Ratio The **debt to equity ratio** reflects a company's strategy for financing its operations. It shows the proportion of a company's assets that are financed by creditors and the proportion financed by stockholders. It is thus a measure of financial risk; the more debt a company has in relation to stockholders' equity, the greater its financial risk. Creditors and interest on debt must be paid on time regardless of how well or poorly a company is performing. Stockholders' investments, on the other hand, do not have to be repaid, and dividends can be deferred when a company's performance is poor.

__STUDY NOTE:__ The balance sheets of most public companies do not show total liabilities; a quick way of determining them is to deduct total equity from total assets.

The debt to equity ratio uses two elements of the balance sheet: total liabilities and total equity. For Martin Auto Parts, it is computed as shown on page 219.

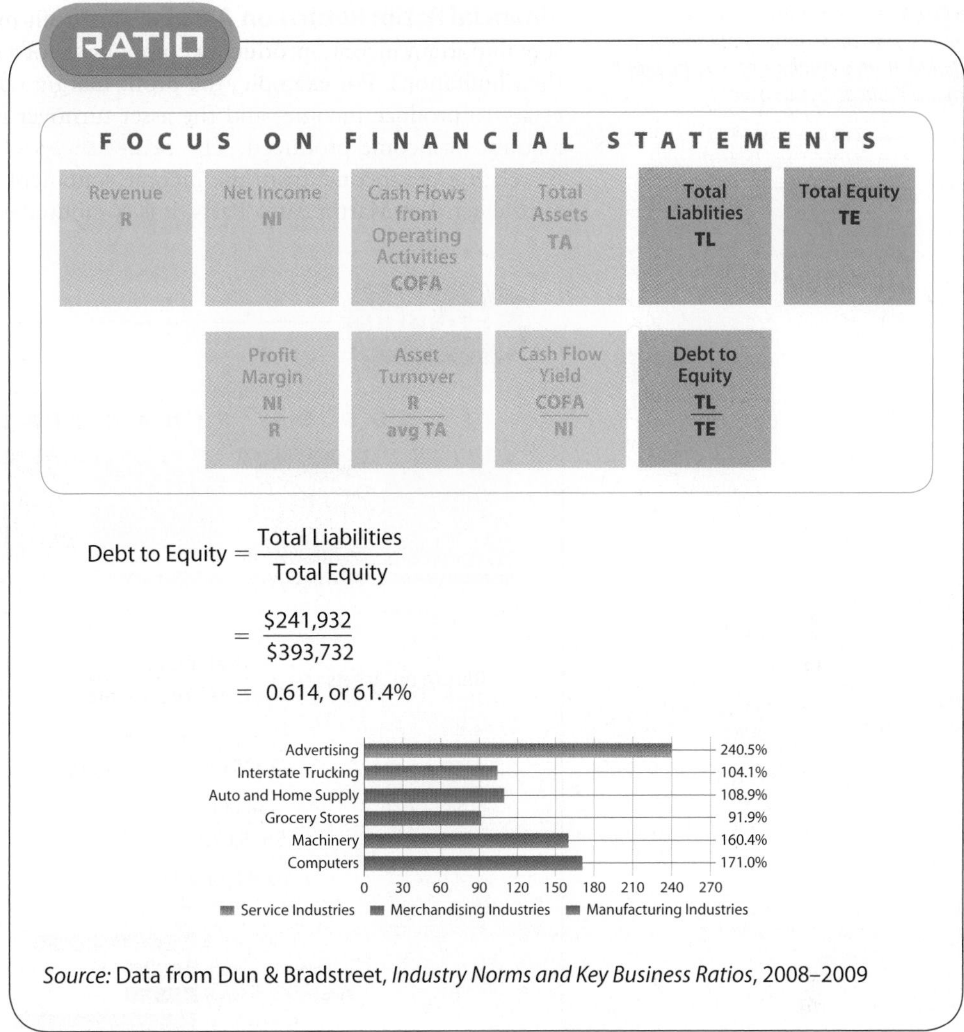

STUDY NOTE: *If liabilities are 50 cents and stockholders' equity is $1.00, then total assets are $1.50. Thus, liabilities are one-third of assets.*

A debt to equity ratio of 1.0 means that equal amounts of liabilities and stockholders' equity are used to finance the assets. A ratio of 0.5 means that if a company has 50 cents of liabilities for every dollar of equity, one-third of a company's total assets are financed by creditors. Martin Auto Parts' debt to equity ratio of 0.614, or 61.4 percent, indicates that the company relied more on investors than on creditors to finance its assets.

As shown in the graph of industry averages presented above, the average debt to equity ratio in the home and auto parts industry is 108.9 percent. The averages for all the selected industries vary from a low of 91.9 percent in the grocery industry to a high of 240.5 percent in the advertising industry. Thus, Martin Auto Parts has less financial risk than most other companies. In the future, the company might choose to expand by using additional long-term borrowing.

Beyond the Basics: Additional Financial Ratios

The four ratios discussed previously provide an excellent snapshot of a company's performance. However, when companies perform poorly on any of these ratios, other financial ratios either derived from these ratios or underlying them are also likely to indicate poor performance. Analyzing these derivative ratios is one way to find out what is causing the poor performance. Here, we introduce some of these ratios and discuss what additional information they can offer to businesses looking to improve their performance.

STUDY NOTE: *Return on assets is a widely used measure of profitability. It derives from a combination of the profit margin and asset turnover.*

Financial Ratio: Return on Assets The profit margin and asset turnover ratios measure important income-producing components of a company's operations, but they have their limitations. For example, the profit margin ratio does not consider the assets necessary to produce income, and the asset turnover ratio does not take into account the amount of income produced. The **return on assets** ratio overcomes these deficiencies by relating net income from the income statement to average total assets from the balance sheet. For Martin Auto Parts, it is computed as shown below.

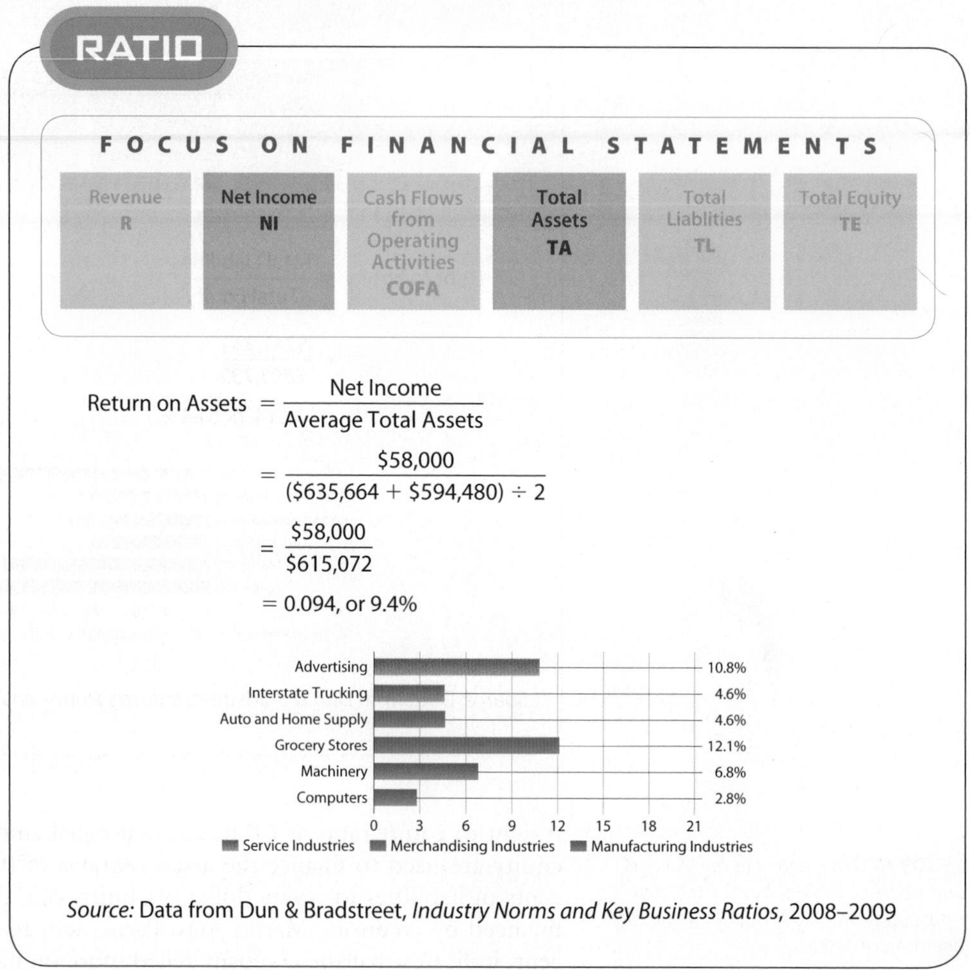

Source: Data from Dun & Bradstreet, *Industry Norms and Key Business Ratios*, 2008–2009

For each dollar of invested assets, Martin Auto Parts earned 9.4 cents of net income. This ratio combines the firm's income-generating strength (profit margin) and its revenue-generating effectiveness (asset turnover):

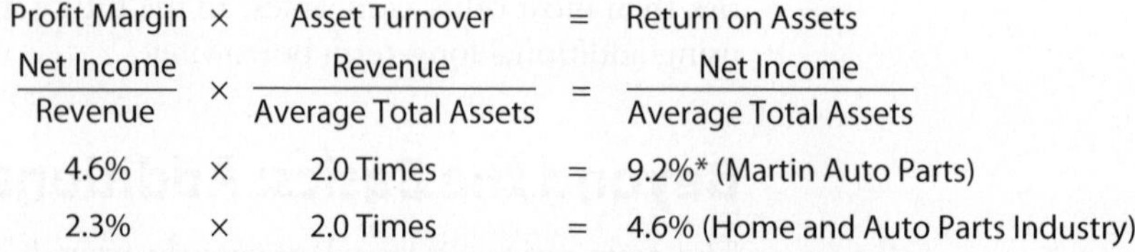

Profit Margin	×	Asset Turnover	=	Return on Assets
$\frac{\text{Net Income}}{\text{Revenue}}$	×	$\frac{\text{Revenue}}{\text{Average Total Assets}}$	=	$\frac{\text{Net Income}}{\text{Average Total Assets}}$
4.6%	×	2.0 Times	=	9.2%* (Martin Auto Parts)
2.3%	×	2.0 Times	=	4.6% (Home and Auto Parts Industry)

*The difference between 9.4 and 9.2 percent is due to rounding.

Martin Auto Parts' profit margin of 4.6 percent is well above the auto and home supply industry's average of 2.3 percent; its asset turnover of 2.0 times is the same as the industry average. Martin Auto Parts is able to achieve a higher profit margin than the industry norm without sacrificing asset turnover. Clearly, its strategy is working because the corporation's return on assets of 9.2 percent is twice the industry average of 4.6 percent.

Focus on Business Practice

What Performance Measures Do Top Companies Use to Compensate Executives?

The boards of directors of public companies often use financial ratios to judge the performance of their top executives and to determine annual bonuses. Public companies disclose the ratios or performance measures used for this purpose. Studies show that successful public companies use earnings goals combined with sales growth 61 percent of the time, compared to 43 percent of less successful companies. Among the most common earnings goals are return on assets and return on equity. Clearly, successful companies set objectives that provide management with performance incentives.[11]

iStock Photo

In sum, a company's management may improve overall profitability by increasing the profit margin, the asset turnover, or both. A financial statement user must consider how these two ratios interact to produce return on assets.

STUDY NOTE: Return on assets measures how much income a company is earning from its assets, whereas cash return on assets measures how much cash those assets are generating.

Financial Ratio: Cash Return on Assets **Cash return on assets** is another important measure of the productivity of a company's assets. It relates cash flows from operating activities from the statement of cash flows to average total assets from the balance sheet. If Martin Auto Parts had cash flows of $72,500 from operating activities during the year, its cash return on assets would be computed as shown below.

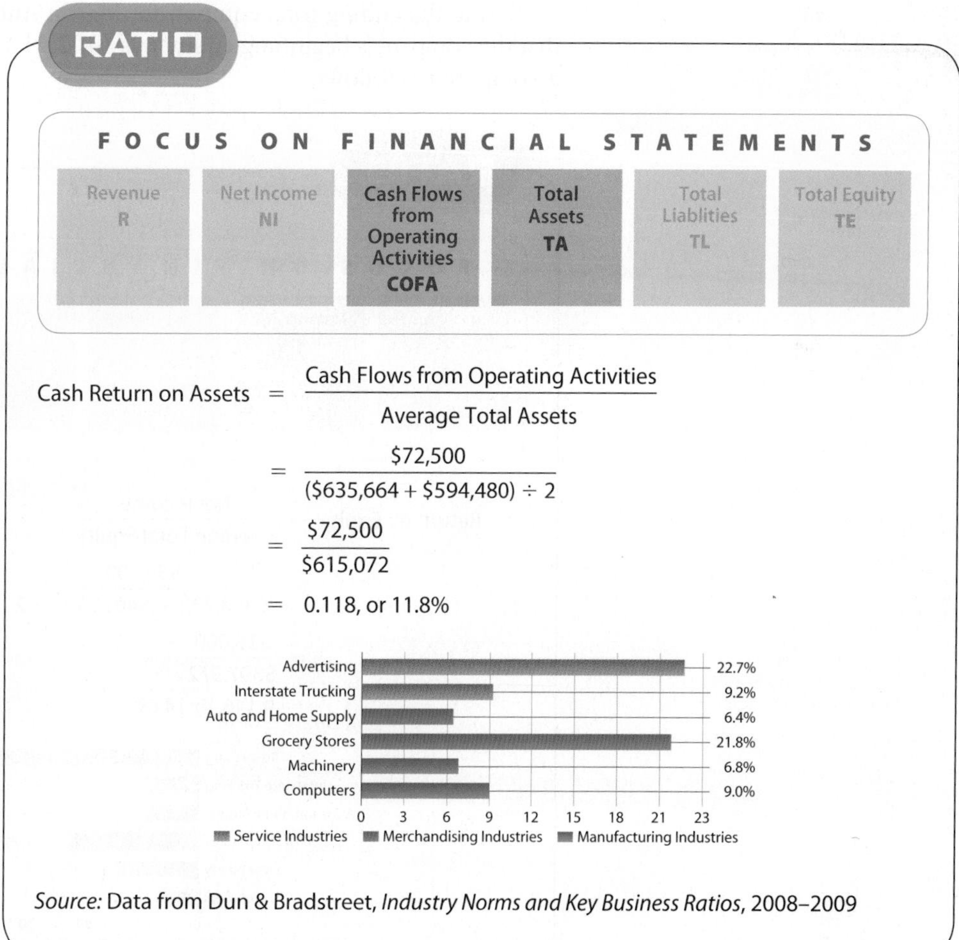

$$\text{Cash Return on Assets} = \frac{\text{Cash Flows from Operating Activities}}{\text{Average Total Assets}}$$

$$= \frac{\$72{,}500}{(\$635{,}664 + \$594{,}480) \div 2}$$

$$= \frac{\$72{,}500}{\$615{,}072}$$

$$= 0.118, \text{ or } 11.8\%$$

Source: Data from Dun & Bradstreet, *Industry Norms and Key Business Ratios*, 2008–2009

Martin Auto Parts' ratio of 11.8 percent means that the company generated 11.8 cents of cash for every dollar of average total assets during the past year. Its cash-generating ability is excellent in that its cash return on assets exceeds its return on assets of 9.4 percent and the industry average of 6.4 percent.

The relationship between return on assets and cash return on assets is expressed by the cash flow yield, as shown in the following calculation:

$$\text{Return on Assets} \times \text{Cash Flow Yield} = \text{Cash Return on Assets}$$

$$\frac{\text{Net Income}}{\text{Average Total Assets}} \times \frac{\text{Cash Flow from Operating Activities}}{\text{Net Income}} = \frac{\text{Cash Flow from Operating Activities}}{\text{Average Total Assets}}$$

$$9.4\% \times 1.25 \text{ times} = 11.8\% \text{ (Martin Auto Parts)}$$

$$4.6\% \times 1.4 \text{ times} = 6.4\% \text{ (Home and Auto Parts industry)}$$

The cash flow yield reflects the relationship between accrual accounting for income (as reflected by return on assets) and cash generated by operations (as reflected by cash return on assets).

Financial Ratio: Return on Equity **Return on equity** is the ratio of net income to average total equity. It indicates whether a company has earned a favorable return for stockholders. Return on equity will always be greater than return on assets because total equity will always be less than total assets. A greater return on assets is an advantage to stockholders, but as we noted in our discussion of the debt to equity ratio, the more debt a company has, the greater its financial risk. A company must carefully balance the amount of financial risk it assumes with its desire to increase its return to stockholders.

Using the ending total equity from Martin Auto Parts' balance sheet and assuming that the company's beginning equity was $402,212, Martin Auto Parts' return on equity is computed as follows.

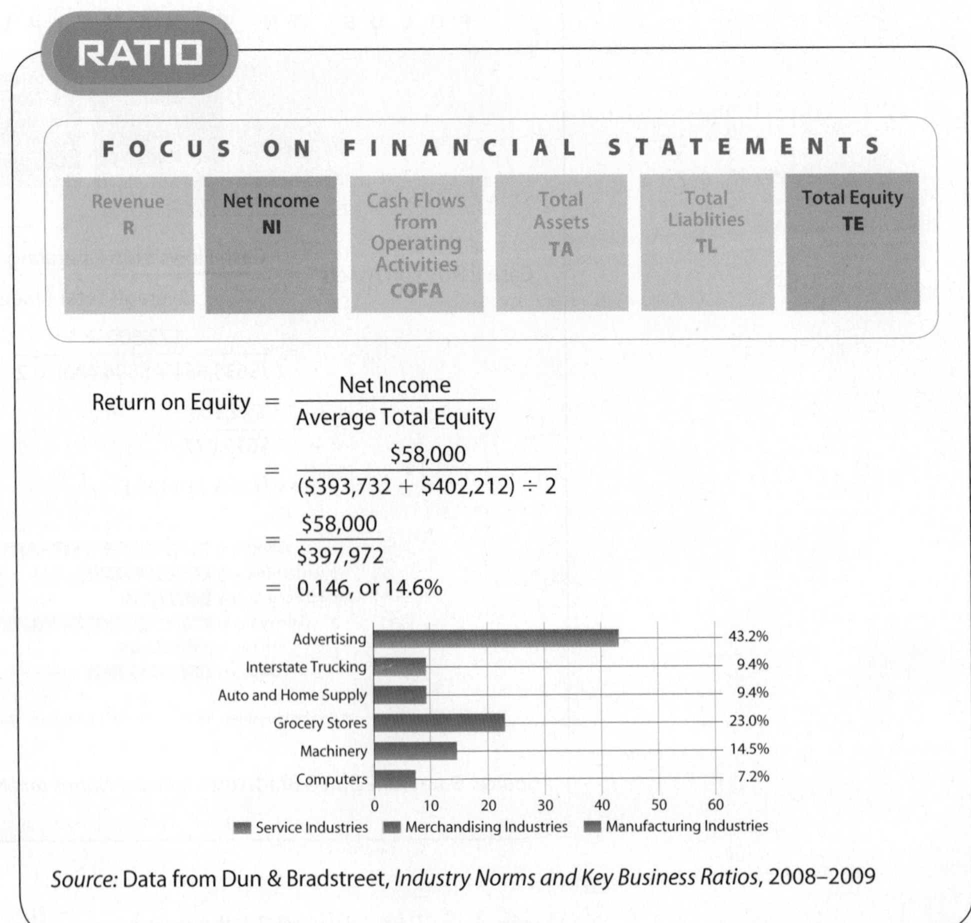

Source: Data from Dun & Bradstreet, *Industry Norms and Key Business Ratios*, 2008–2009

Thus, Martin Auto Parts earned 14.6 percent, or 14.6 cents, on every dollar of equity. Is this an acceptable return? Martin Auto Parts' average return on equity is higher than the average for the auto and home supply industry (9.4 percent). Although the advertising industry's return on equity of 43.2 percent is the highest of the selected industries, this industry also has the highest debt to equity ratio (240.5 percent); it is therefore financially the riskiest of all the selected industries.

Stop & Apply

The following end-of-year amounts are from the financial statements of Roth Company: total assets, $220,000; total liabilities, $80,000; stockholders' equity, $140,000; net sales, $300,000; net income, $18,000; and cash flows from operating activities, $24,000. One year ago, total assets were $180,000, and stockholders' equity was $122,000. Compute Roth's (1) profit margin, (2) asset turnover, (3) cash flow yield, (4) debt to equity ratio, (5) return on assets, (6) cash return on assets, and (7) return on equity. (*Note:* Round to one decimal place.)

SOLUTION

(1) Profit margin: $18,000 ÷ $300,000 = 0.06, or 6.0%

(2) Asset turnover: $300,000 ÷ [($180,000 + $220,000) ÷ 2)] = 1.5 times

(3) Cash flow yield: $24,000 ÷ $18,000 = 1.3 times

(4) Debt to equity ratio: $80,000 ÷ $140,000 = 0.571, or 57.1%

(5) Return on assets: $18,000 ÷ [($180,000 + $220,000) ÷ 2)] = 0.09, or 9.0%

(6) Cash return on assets: $24,000 ÷ [($180,000 + $220,000) ÷ 2) = 0.12, or 12.0%

(7) Return on equity: $18,000 ÷ [($122,000 + $140,000)] = 0.137, or 13.7%

iStock Photo

A look back at ▸ Dell Computer Corporation

As we noted in this chapter's Decision Point, **Dell**'s management focuses on the goals of liquidity, profitability, and growth. We also noted that in judging whether any company has achieved its objectives, investors, creditors, and others analyze relationships between key numbers in the company's financial statements. We asked these questions:

1. How should financial statements be organized to provide the best information?
2. What key measures best capture a company's financial performance?

Dell provides a classified balance sheet (Exhibit 4.4) and a multistep income statement (Exhibit 4.7) to communicate its financial results to users. The Financial Highlights derived from these statements and presented in the Decision Point show that between 2009 and 2010, Dell's net revenues decreased by 13 percent and that its operating income and net income decreased by 32 percent and 42 percent, respectively.

RATIO

Financial Ratios

Using key elements from the balance sheets and income statements in Dell's 2010 annual report, we can compute financial ratios that capture the financial performance for the company in 2009 and 2010 as follows (dollars are in millions):

	2010	2009
Profit Margin:		
Net Income ÷ Revenue	$1,433 ÷ $52,902 0.027, or 2.7%	$2,478 ÷ $61,101 0.041, or 4.1%

(continued)

	2010	2009
Asset Turnover:		
Revenue ÷ Average Total Assets	$52,902 ÷ [($33,652 + $26,500) ÷ 2]	$61,101 ÷ [($26,500 + $27,561) ÷ 2]
	$52,902 ÷ $30,076	$61,101 ÷ $27,031
	1.8 times	2.3 times
Return on Assets:		
Net Income ÷ Average Total Assets	$1,433 ÷ [($33,652 + $26,500) ÷ 2]	$2,478 ÷ [($26,500 + $27,561) ÷ 2]
	$1,433 ÷ $30,076	$2,478 ÷ $27,031
	0.048, or 4.8%	0.092, or 9.2%

The decrease in net income resulted from a decrease in profit margin and a decrease in the asset turnover. The result is a reduction in return on assets by almost half (from 9.2% to 4.8%). However, by comparing these results with averages for the computer industry, we can see that Dell was, in fact, among the more profitable computer companies:

	Profit Margin	×	Asset Turnover	=	Return on Assets
2010:	2.7%	×	1.8 times	=	4.8%
2009:	4.1%	×	2.3 times	=	9.2%
Industry Average:	2.8%	×	1.0 times	=	2.8%

	2010	2009
Cash Flow Yield:		
Cash Flow from Operating Activities ÷ Net Income	$3,906 ÷ $1,433	$1,894 ÷ $2,478
	2.7 times	0.8 times
Cash Return on Assets:		
Cash Flow from Operating Activities ÷ Average Total Assets	$3,906 ÷ $30,076	$1,894 ÷ $27,031
	0.130, or 13.0%	0.070, or 7.0%

The increases in cash flow yield and cash return on assets resulted primarily from the increase in cash flow from operating activities. Because cash flow yield was about 2.7 in 2010, cash return on assets of 13 percent was more than return on assets of 4.8 percent. This is a favorable situation compared with the one in 2009 when the cash flow yield was less than 1.0, which produces only a 7.0 percent cash return on assets.

Dell also took advantage of debt financing to increase its profitability into a very high return on equity, as shown by its debt to equity and return on equity ratios:

	2010	2009
Debt to Equity Ratio:		
Total Liabilities ÷ Total Equity	$28,011 ÷ $5,641	$22,229 ÷ $4,271
	4.97, or 497%	5.20, or 520%
Industry Average:	1.71, or 171%	1.09, or 109%
Return on Equity:		
Net Income ÷ Average Stockholders' Equity	$1,433 ÷ [($5,641 + $4,271) ÷ 2]	$2,478 ÷ [($4,271 + $3,735) ÷ 2]
	$1,433 ÷ $4,956	$2,478 ÷ $4,003
	0.289, or 28.9%	0.619, or 61.9%

Although Dell transformed a profit margin of 2.7 percent into a return to its stockholders of 28.9 percent—a performance much better than that of its competitors—the large amount of debt may cause Dell difficulty in the future.

Review Problem

Using Financial Ratios to Analyze Performance 

RATIO

Comfy Shoe Company has been facing increased competition from overseas shoemakers. Its total assets and stockholders' equity for 2009 were $690,000 and $590,000, respectively. A summary of the firm's data for 2010 and 2011 follows.

	2011	2010
Total assets	$ 880,000	$ 710,000
Current liabilities	90,000	50,000
Long-term liabilities	150,000	50,000
Stockholders' equity	640,000	610,000
Sales	1,200,000	1,050,000
Net income	60,000	80,000
Cash flows from operating activities	52,000	87,000

Required

1. Calculate the following financial ratios for Comfy Shoe Company for 2010 and 2011: profit margin, asset turnover, return on assets, and return on equity. (*Note:* Round to one decimal place.)
2. Comment on how these ratios document the company's declining financial performance.

ANSWERS TO REVIEW PROBLEM

1.

	A B C D	E	F G H	I	J	K	L	M	N
1		Net Income	Sales	Profit Margin	Average Total Assets	Asset Turnover	Return on Assets	Average Stockholders' Equity	Return on Equity
2	2010	$ 80,000	$1,050,000	7.6%	$700,000 [1]	1.5	11.4%	$600,000 [3]	13.3%
3	2011	60,000	1,200,000	5.0%	795,000 [2]	1.5	7.5%	625,000 [4]	9.6%
4	Increase (decrease)	$(20,000)	$ 150,000	-2.6%	$ 95,000	0.0	(3.9%)	$ 25,000	(3.7%)
5									
6	1 ($710,000 +	$690,000	) ÷	2					
7	2 ($880,000 +	$710,000	) ÷	2					
8	3 ($610,000 +	$590,000	) ÷	2					
9	4 ($640,000 +	$610,000	) ÷	2					
10									

		O	P	Q	R
1		Cash Flow From Operating Activities	Net Income	Cash Flow Yield	Cash Return on Assets
2	2010	$ 87,000	$ 80,000	1.09	12.4%
3	2011	52,000	60,000	0.87	6.5%
4	Increase (decrease)	$(35,000)	$(20,000)	(0.22)	(5.9%)

2. Net income decreased by $20,000 despite an increase in sales of $150,000 and an increase in average total assets of $95,000. Thus, the profit margin fell from 7.6 percent to 5.0 percent, and return on assets fell from 11.4 percent to 7.5 percent. Asset turnover

showed almost no change and so did not contribute to the decline in profitability. Cash flow from operating activities dropped more than net income, having an adverse effect on cash flow yield and cash return on assets. The decrease in return on equity, from 13.3 percent to 9.6 percent, was not as great as the decrease in return on assets because the growth in total assets was financed mainly by debt rather than by stockholders' equity, as shown in the capital structure analysis below.

	A	B	C	D
1		**Total Liabilities**	**Stockholders' Equity**	**Debt to Equity Ratio**
2	2010	$100,000	$610,000	16.4%
3	2011	240,000	640,000	37.5%
4	Increase	$140,000	$ 30,000	21.1%
5				

Total liabilities increased by $140,000, while stockholders' equity increased by $30,000. Thus, the amount of the business financed by debt in relation to the amount financed by stockholders' equity increased between 2010 and 2011.

Stop & Review

LO 1 Describe the objective of financial reporting and identify the qualitative characteristics, conventions, and ethical considerations of accounting information.

The objective of financial reporting is to provide information that is useful to present and potential equity investors, lenders, and other creditors in making decisions in their capacity as capital providers. To be useful for decision making, financial information must enable the reader to assess cash flow prospects and management's stewardship. Financial information must exhibit the qualitative characteristics of relevance and faithful representation. To be relevant, it must have predictive value, confirmative value, or both. To be faithfully represented, it must be complete, neutral, and free from material error. Other qualitative characteristics of financial information are comparability, verifiability, timeliness, and understandability. It is important for users to understand the accounting conventions, or constraints, used in preparing financial statements. Since the passage of the Sarbanes-Oxley Act in 2002, CEOs and CFOs have been required to certify that their companies' financial statements are accurate and complete.

LO 2 Define and describe the conventions of *consistency*, *full disclosure*, *materiality*, *conservatism*, and *cost-benefit*.

Because accountants' measurements are not exact, certain conventions are applied to help users interpret financial statements. The first of these conventions is consistency. Consistency requires the use of the same accounting procedures from period to period and enhances the comparability of financial statements. Full disclosure means including all relevant information in the financial statements. The materiality convention has to do with determining the relative importance of an item. Conservatism entails using the procedure that is least likely to overstate assets and income. The cost-benefit convention holds that the benefits to be gained from providing accounting information should be greater than the costs of providing it.

LO 3 Identify and describe the basic components of a classified balance sheet.

The basic components of a classified balance sheet are as follows:

Assets	**Liabilities**
Current assets	Current liabilities
Investments	Long-term liabilities
Property, plant, and equipment	**Stockholders' Equity**
Intangible assets	Contributed capital
(Other assets)	Retained earnings

Current assets are cash and other assets that a firm can reasonably expect to convert to cash or use up during the next year or the normal operating cycle, whichever is longer. Investments are assets, usually long term, that are not used in the normal operation of a business. Property, plant, and equipment are tangible long-term assets used in day-to-day operations. Intangible assets are long-term assets with no physical substance whose value stems from the rights or privileges accruing to their owners.

A current liability is an obligation that must be satisfied within the next year or the normal operating cycle, whichever is longer. Long-term liabilities are debts that fall due more than one year in the future or beyond the normal operating cycle.

The stockholders' equity section of a corporation's balance sheet differs from the balance sheet of a proprietorship or partnership in that it has subcategories for contributed capital (the amount invested by stockholders) and retained earnings (stockholders' claim to assets earned from operations and reinvested in operations).

LO4 Describe the features of multistep and single-step classified income statements.

Classified income statements for external reporting can be in multistep or single-step form. The multistep form arrives at income before income taxes through a series of steps; the single-step form arrives at income before income taxes in a single step. A multistep income statement usually has a separate section for other revenues and expenses.

LO5 Use financial ratios to evaluate a company's performance.

In evaluating a company's performance, investors and creditors rely on the data provided in financial statements. Seven key performance ratios are profit margin, asset turnover, cash flow yield, debt to equity ratio, return on assets, cash return on assets, and return on equity. Data from multiple years and industry averages are useful in interpreting these ratios.

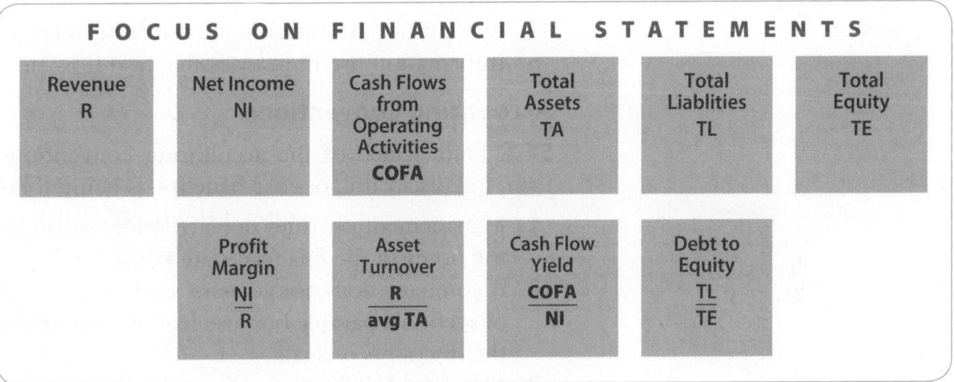

Key Terms and Ratios

Accounting conventions 200 (LO1)
Classified financial statements 204 (LO3)
Comparability 200 (LO1)
Conservatism 203 (LO2)
Consistency 202 (LO2)
Contributed capital 207 (LO3)
Cost-benefit 203 (LO2)
Cost of goods sold 211 (LO4)
Current assets 206 (LO3)
Current liabilities 207 (LO3)
Earnings per share 213 (LO4)
Faithful representation 200 (LO1)
Full disclosure 202 (LO2)
General and administrative expenses 212 (LO4)
Gross margin 211 (LO4)
Gross sales 210 (LO4)
Income before income taxes 213 (LO4)
Income from operations 212 (LO4)
Income taxes 213 (LO4)
Intangible assets 207 (LO3)
Investments 206 (LO3)
Long-term liabilities 207 (LO3)
Manufacturing company 210 (LO4)
Materiality 202 (LO2)
Merchandising company 210 (LO4)
Multistep income statement 210 (LO4)
Net income 213 (LO4)
Net sales 210 (LO4)
Normal operating cycle 206 (LO3)
Operating expenses 212 (LO4)
Other assets 206 (LO3)
Other revenues and expenses 212 (LO4)
Property, plant, and equipment 206 (LO3)
Qualitative characteristics 199 (LO1)
Relevance 199 (LO1)

Retained earnings 207 (LO3)
Sales returns and allowances 210 (LO4)
Selling expenses 212 (LO4)
Single-step income statement 214 (LO4)
Timeliness 200 (LO1)
Understandability 200 (LO1)
Verifiability 200 (LO1)

FINANCIAL RATIOS

Asset turnover 216 (LO5)
Cash return on assets 221 (LO5)
Cash flow yield 217 (LO5)
Debt to equity ratio 218 (LO5)
Profit margin 215 (LO5)
Return on assets 220 (LO5)
Return on equity 222 (LO5)

Chapter Assignments Building Your Basic Knowledge and Skills

Short Exercises

LO 1

Objectives and Qualitative Characteristics

SE 1. Identify each of the following statements as related to either the objective (O) of financial information or a qualitative (Q) characteristic of accounting information.

1. Information about business resources, claims to those resources, and changes in them should be provided.
2. Decision makers must be able to interpret accounting information.
3. Information that is useful in making investment and credit decisions should be furnished.
4. Accounting information must exhibit relevance and faithful representation.
5. Information useful in assessing cash flow prospects should be provided.

LO 2

Accounting Conventions

SE 2. State which of the accounting conventions—consistency, materiality, conservatism, full disclosure, or cost-benefit—is being followed in each of the cases listed below.

1. Management provides detailed information about the company's long-term debt in the notes to the financial statements.
2. A company does not account separately for discounts received for prompt payment of accounts payable because few of these transactions occur and the total amount of the discounts is small.
3. Management eliminates a weekly report on property, plant, and equipment acquisitions and disposals because no one finds it useful.
4. A company follows the policy of recognizing a loss on inventory when the market value of an item falls below its cost but does nothing if the market value rises.
5. When several accounting methods are acceptable, management chooses a single method and follows that method from year to year.

LO 3

Classification of Accounts: Balance Sheet

SE 3. Tell whether each of the following accounts is a current asset; an investment; property, plant, and equipment; an intangible asset; a current liability; a long-term liability; stockholders' equity; or not on the balance sheet.

1. Delivery Trucks
2. Accounts Payable
3. Note Payable (due in 90 days)
4. Delivery Expense
5. Common Stock
6. Prepaid Insurance
7. Trademark
8. Investment to Be Held Six Months
9. Income Taxes Payable
10. Factory Not Used in Business

LO 3

Classified Balance Sheet

SE 4. Using the following accounts, prepare a classified balance sheet at year-end, May 31, 2011: Accounts Payable, $800; Accounts Receivable, $1,100; Accumulated Depreciation—Equipment, $700; Cash, $200; Common Stock, $1,000; Equipment,

$3,000; Franchise, $200; Investments (long-term), $500; Merchandise Inventory, $600; Notes Payable (long-term), $400; Retained Earnings, ?; Wages Payable, $100.

LO 3

Classified Balance Sheet

SE 5. Using the following accounts, prepare a classified balance sheet at year-end, July 31, 2011: Accounts Payable, $1,200; Accounts Receivable, $1,650; Accumulated Depreciation—Equipment, $1,050; Cash, $300; Common Stock, $1,500; Equipment, $4,500; Franchise, $300; Investments (long-term), $750; Merchandise Inventory, $900; Notes Payable (long-term), $600; Retained Earnings, ?; Wages Payable, $150.

LO 4

Classification of Accounts: Income Statement

SE 6. Tell whether each of the following accounts is part of net sales, cost of goods sold, operating expenses, other revenues and expenses, or is not on the income statement.

1. Delivery Expense
2. Interest Expense
3. Unearned Revenue
4. Sales Returns and Allowances
5. Depreciation Expense
6. Investment Income
7. Retained Earnings

LO 4

Single-Step Income Statement

SE 7. Using the following accounts, prepare a single-step income statement at year-end May 31, 2011: Cost of Goods Sold, $840; General Expenses, $450; Income Taxes, $105; Interest Expense, $210; Interest Income, $90; Net Sales, $2,400; Selling Expenses, $555. (*Note:* Ignore earnings per share.)

LO 4

Multistep Income Statement

SE 8. Using the accounts presented in **SE** 7, prepare a multistep income statement.

LO 4

Single-Step Income Statement

SE 9. Using the following accounts, prepare a single-step income statement for the year ended July 31, 2011: Cost of Goods Sold, $1,260; General Expenses, $675; Income Taxes, $158; Interest Expense, $315; Interest Income, $135; Net Sales, $3,600; Selling Expenses, $833. (*Note:* Ignore earnings per share.)

LO 4

Multistep Income Statement

SE 10. Using the accounts presented in **SE** 9, prepare a multistep income statement.

LO 5

Financial Ratios: Performance Measures

SE 11. Using the following information from a balance sheet and an income statement, compute the (1) profit margin, (2) asset turnover, (3) cash flow yield, (4) debt to equity ratio, (5) return on assets, (6) cash return on assets, and (7) return on equity. (*Note:* Round to one decimal place.) (*Note:* The previous year's total assets were $200,000, and stockholders' equity was $140,000.)

Total assets	$240,000
Total liabilities	60,000
Total stockholders' equity	180,000
Net sales	260,000
Cost of goods sold	140,000
Operating expenses	80,000
Income taxes	10,000
Cash flow from operating activities	30,000

LO 5

Relationship of Financial Ratios

SE 12. Assume that a company has a profit margin of 8.0 percent, an asset turnover of 2.1 times, and a debt to equity ratio of 50 percent. What are the company's return on assets and return on equity?

Exercises

LO 1, 2, 3

Discussion Questions

E 1. Develop a brief answer to each of the following questions:

1. How do the four basic financial statements meet the stewardship objective of financial reporting?
2. What are some areas that require estimates to record transactions under the matching rule?
3. How can financial information be consistent but not comparable?
4. When might an amount be material to management but not to the CPA auditing the financial statements?

LO 4, 5

Discussion Questions

E 2. Develop a brief answer to each of the following questions:

1. Why is it that land held for future use and equipment not currently used are classified as investments rather than as property, plant, and equipment?
2. Which is the better measure of a company's performance—income from operations or net income?
3. Why is it important to compare a company's financial performance with industry standards?
4. Is the statement "Return on assets is a better measure of profitability than profit margin" true or false and why?

LO 1, 2

Financial Accounting Concepts

E 3. Match each of the lettered items, which represent a classification scheme for the concepts of financial accounting, with the numbered term.

a. Decision makers (users of accounting information)
b. Business activities or entities relevant to accounting measurement
c. Objective of accounting information
d. Accounting measurement considerations
e. Accounting processing considerations
f. Qualitative characteristics
g. Accounting conventions
h. Financial statements

1. Conservatism
2. Verifiability
3. Statement of cash flows
4. Materiality
5. Faithful representation
6. Recognition
7. Cost-benefit
8. Predictive value
9. Business transactions
10. Consistency
11. Full disclosure
12. Furnishing information that is useful to investors and creditors
13. Specific business entities
14. Classification
15. Management
16. Neutrality
17. Internal accounting control
18. Valuation
19. Investors
20. Completeness
21. Relevance
22. Furnishing information that is useful in assessing cash flow prospects

LO 2

Accounting Concepts and Conventions

E 4. Each of the statements below violates a convention in accounting. State which of the following accounting conventions is violated: comparability and consistency, materiality, conservatism, full disclosure, or cost-benefit.

1. Reports that are time-consuming and expensive to prepare are presented to the board of directors each month, even though the reports are never used.
2. A company changes its method of accounting for depreciation.

3. The company in **2** does not indicate in the financial statements that the method of depreciation was changed; nor does it specify the effect of the change on net income.
4. A company's new office building, which is built next to the company's existing factory, is debited to the Factory account because it represents a fairly small dollar amount in relation to the factory.
5. The asset account for a pickup truck still used in the business is written down to what the truck could be sold for, even though the carrying value under conventional depreciation methods is higher.

LO 3

Classification of Accounts: Balance Sheet

E 5. Match each of the lettered items, which represent a classification scheme for a balance sheet, with the numbered account titles.

a. Current assets
b. Investments
c. Property, plant, and equipment
d. Intangible assets
e. Current liabilities
f. Long-term liabilities
g. Stockholders' equity
h. Not on the balance sheet

1. Patent
2. Building Held for Sale
3. Prepaid Rent
4. Wages Payable
5. Note Payable in Five Years
6. Building Used in Operations
7. Fund Held to Pay Off Long-Term Debt
8. Inventory
9. Prepaid Insurance
10. Depreciation Expense
11. Accounts Receivable
12. Interest Expense
13. Unearned Revenue
14. Short-Term Investments
15. Accumulated Depreciation
16. Retained Earnings

LO 3

Classified Balance Sheet Preparation

E 6. The following data pertain to Mamba, Inc.: Accounts Payable, $20,400; Accounts Receivable, $15,200; Accumulated Depreciation—Building, $5,600; Accumulated Depreciation—Equipment, $6,800; Bonds Payable, $24,000; Building, $28,000; Cash, $12,480; Common Stock, $10 par, 4,000 shares authorized, issued, and outstanding, $40,000; Copyright, $2,480; Equipment, $60,800; Inventory, $16,000; Investment in Corporate Securities (long-term), $8,000; Investment in Six-Month Government Securities, $6,560; Land, $3,200; Paid-In Capital in Excess of Par Value, $20,000; Prepaid Rent, $480; Retained Earnings, $35,280; and Revenue Received in Advance, $1,120.

Prepare a classified balance sheet at December 31, 2011.

LO 4

Classification of Accounts: Income Statement

E 7. Using the classification scheme below for a multistep income statement, match each account with the letter of the category in which it belongs.

a. Net sales
b. Cost of goods sold
c. Selling expenses
d. General and administrative expenses
e. Other revenues and expenses
f. Not on the income statement

1. Sales Returns and Allowances
2. Cost of Goods Sold
3. Dividend Income
4. Advertising Expense
5. Office Salaries Expense
6. Freight Out Expense
7. Prepaid Insurance
8. Utilities Expense
9. Sales Salaries Expense
10. Rent Expense
11. Depreciation Expense—Delivery Equipment
12. Taxes Payable
13. Interest Expense

LO 4

Preparation of Income Statements

E 8. The following data pertain to a Kellman Corporation: net sales, $405,000; cost of goods sold, $220,000; selling expenses, $90,000; general and administrative expenses,

$60,000; income taxes, $7,500; interest expense, $4,000; interest income, $3,000; and common stock outstanding, 25,000 shares.

1. Prepare a single-step income statement.
2. Prepare a multistep income statement.

LO 4 **Multistep Income Statement**

E 9. A single-step income statement follows. Present the information in a multistep income statement and indicate what insights can be obtained from the multistep form as opposed to the single-step form.

Pasica, Inc.
Income Statement
For the Year Ended December 31, 2011

Revenues		
Net sales		$1,197,132
Interest income		5,720
Total revenues		$1,202,852
Costs and expenses		
Cost of goods sold	$777,080	
Selling expenses	203,740	
General and administrative expenses	100,688	
Interest expense	13,560	
Total costs and expenses		1,095,068
Income before income taxes		$ 107,784
Income taxes		24,000
Net income		$ 83,784
Earnings per share		$ 8.38

LO 5 RATIO **Financial Ratios: Performance Measures**

E 10. The following end-of-year amounts are from the financial statements of Kostas Corporation: total assets, $106,500; total liabilities, $43,000; stockholders' equity, $63,500; net sales, $195,500; cost of goods sold, $116,500; operating expenses, $47,000; income taxes, $8,500; and dividends, $10,000. Cash flows from operating activities were $35,000. During the past year, total assets increased by $18,750. Total stockholders' equity was affected only by net income and dividends. Compute the (1) profit margin, (2) asset turnover, (3) return on assets, (4) cash flow yield, (5) cash return on assets, (6) debt to equity ratio, and (7) return on equity. (*Note:* Round to one decimal place.)

LO 5 RATIO **Financial Ratios: Performance Measures**

E 11. The simplified balance sheet and income statement for a corporation appear below.

Balance Sheet
December 31, 2011

Assets		**Liabilities**	
Current assets	$110,000	Current liabilities	$ 50,000
Investments	20,000	Long-term liabilities	60,000
Property, plant, and equipment	293,000	Total liabilities	$110,000
Intangible assets	37,000	**Stockholders' Equity**	
		Common stock	$200,000
		Retained earnings	150,000
		Total stockholders' equity	$350,000
Total assets	$460,000	Total liabilities and stockholders equity	$460,000

Income Statement For the Year Ended December 31, 2011	
Net sales	$830,000
Cost of goods sold	500,000
Gross margin	$330,000
Operating expenses	260,000
Income before income taxes	$ 70,000
Income taxes	10,000
Net income	$ 60,000

Total assets and stockholders' equity at the beginning of 2011 were $360,000 and $280,000, respectively. Cash flows from operating activities were $72,000.

Compute the following profitability measures: (1) profit margin, (2) asset turnover, (3) return on assets, (4) cash flow yield, (5) cash return on assets, (6) debt to equity ratio, and (7) return on equity. (*Note:* Round to one decimal place.)

Problems

LO 2

Accounting Conventions

P 1. For each of the following cases, identify the accounting convention that applies, state whether or not the treatment is in accord with the convention and GAAP, and briefly explain why.

USER INSIGHT ▶

1. Dooley Manufacturing Company uses the cost method for computing the balance sheet amount of inventory unless the market value of the inventory is less than the cost, in which case the market value is used. At the end of the current year, the market value is $302,000 and the cost is $324,000. Dooley uses the $302,000 figure to compute current assets because management believes it is the more cautious approach.

USER INSIGHT ▶

2. Jasper Company has annual sales of $20,000,000. It follows the practice of recording any items costing less than $500 as expenses in the year purchased. During the current year, it purchased several chairs for the executive conference room at $490 each, including freight. Although the chairs were expected to last for at least 10 years, they were recorded as an expense in accordance with company policy.

USER INSIGHT ▶

3. Nogel Company closed its books on October 31, 2011, before preparing its annual report. On November 3, 2011, a fire destroyed one of the company's two factories. Although the company had fire insurance and would not suffer a loss on the building, a significant decrease in sales in 2011 was expected because of the fire. The fire damage was not reported in the 2011 financial statements because the fire had not affected the company's operations during that year.

USER INSIGHT ▶

4. Act Drug Company spends a substantial portion of its profits on research and development. The company had been reporting its $12,000,000 expenditure for research and development as a lump sum, but management recently decided to begin classifying the expenditures by project, even though its recordkeeping costs will increase.

USER INSIGHT ▶

5. During the current year, BRB Company changed from one generally accepted method of accounting for inventories to another method.

LO 4

✔ Income from operations, 2011: $33,213; income from operations, 2010: $55,314

Forms of the Income Statement

P 2. Elm Nursery Corporation's single-step income statements for 2011 and 2010 follow.

Elm Nursery Corporation
Income Statements
For the Years Ended April 30, 2011 and 2010

	2011	2010
Revenues		
Net sales	$262,966	$237,632
Interest income	900	425
Total revenues	$263,866	$238,057
Costs and expenses		
Cost of goods sold	$117,474	$ 85,925
Selling expenses	80,846	75,350
General and administrative expenses	31,433	21,043
Interest expense	1,800	850
Total costs and expenses	$231,553	$183,168
Income before income taxes	$ 32,313	$ 54,889
Income taxes	8,000	14,300
Net income	$ 24,313	$ 40,589
Earnings per share	$ 1.22	$ 2.03

Elm Nursery Corporation had 20,000 shares of common stock outstanding during both 2011 and 2010.

REQUIRED

1. From the information provided, prepare multistep income statements for 2011 and 2010 showing percentages of net sales for each component.

USER INSIGHT ▶ 2. Did income from operations increase or decrease from 2010 to 2011? Write a short explanation of why this change occurred.

USER INSIGHT ▶ 3. What effect did other revenues and expenses have on the change in income before income taxes? What action by management probably caused this change?

LO 3, 5

✔ Total assets: $1,195,200

Classified Balance Sheet

P 3. The following information is from the June 30, 2011, post-closing trial balance of Bissel Hardware Corporation.

Account Name	Debit	Credit
Cash	$ 64,000	
Short-Term Investments	66,000	
Notes Receivable	20,000	
Accounts Receivable	552,000	
Merchandise Inventory	290,000	
Prepaid Rent	3,200	
Prepaid Insurance	9,600	
Sales Supplies	2,560	
Office Supplies	880	
Deposit for Future Advertising	7,360	
Building, Not in Use	99,200	
Land	46,800	
Delivery Equipment	82,400	
Accumulated Depreciation—Delivery Equipment		$ 56,800
Trademark	8,000	
Accounts Payable		229,200
Salaries Payable		10,400

Interest Payable	$ 3,680
Long-Term Notes Payable	160,000
Common Stock ($1.10 par value)	44,000
Paid-In Capital in Excess of Par Value	320,000
Retained Earnings	427,920

REQUIRED

1. From the information provided, prepare a classified balance sheet for Bissel Hardware Corporation.

USER INSIGHT ▶ 2. As a user of the classified balance sheet, why would you want to know the debt to equity ratio?

LO 5

Liquidity and Profitability

RATIO

P 4. A summary of data from the income statements and balance sheets for Wesley Construction Supply, Inc., for 2011 and 2010 appears below.

	2011	2010
Total assets	$ 580,000	$435,000
Current liabilities	45,000	30,000
Long-term liabilities	200,000	145,000
Stockholders' equity	335,000	260,000
Net sales	1,150,000	870,000
Net income	75,000	51,000
Cash flows from operating activities	82,500	67,500

Total assets and stockholders' equity in 2009 were $340,000 and $210,000, respectively.

REQUIRED

1. Compute the following profitability measures: (a) profit margin, (b) asset turnover, (c) return on assets, (d) cash flow yield, (e) cash return on assets, (f) debt to equity ratio, and (g) return on equity. (*Note:* Round to one decimal place.)

USER INSIGHT ▶ 2. Comment on the change in performance from 2010 to 2011.

LO 3, 4, 5

Classified Financial Statement Preparation and Analysis

✔ Net income: $18,065; total assets: $270,950

P 5. Surosa Corporation sells outdoor furniture. At the December 31, 2011, year-end, the following financial information was available from the income statement: administrative expenses, $40,400; cost of goods sold, $175,210; income taxes, $3,500; interest expense, $11,320; interest income, $1,400; net sales, $357,195; and selling expenses, $110,100.

The following information was available from the balance sheet (after closing entries were made): accounts payable, $16,300; accounts receivable, $52,400; accumulated depreciation—delivery equipment, $8,550; accumulated depreciation—store fixtures, $21,110; cash, $14,200; common stock, $0.50 par value, 10,000 shares authorized, issued, and outstanding, $5,000; delivery equipment, $44,250; inventory, $68,270; investment in securities (long-term), $28,000; investment in U.S. government securities (short-term), $19,800; long-term notes payable, $50,000; paid-in capital in excess of par value, $45,000; prepaid expenses (short-term), $2,880; retained earnings, ending balance, $129,650, beginning balance, $141,585; notes payable (short-term), $25,000; prepaid expenses (short-term), $2,880; and store fixtures, $70,810.

Total assets and total stockholders' equity at December 31, 2010, were $262,200 and $191,585, respectively, cash flows from operating activities were $20,000, and dividends for the year were $30,000.

REQUIRED

1. From the information above, prepare (a) an income statement in single-step form, (b) a statement of retained earnings, and (c) a classified balance sheet.

RATIO

2. From the statements you have prepared, compute the following performance measures: (a) profit margin, (b) asset turnover, (c) cash flow yield, (d) debt to equity ratio, (e) return on assets, (f) cash return on assets, and (g) return on equity. (*Note:* Round to one decimal place.)

USER INSIGHT ▶ 3. Using the industry averages for the auto and home supply industries illustrated in the graphs in the ratio boxes throughout this chapter, determine whether Surosa Corporation needs to improve its performance. Explain your answer, making recommendations as to specific areas on which Surosa Corporation should concentrate.

Alternate Problems

LO 2

Accounting Conventions

P 6. In each of the following cases, identify the accounting convention that applies, state whether or not the treatment is in accord with the convention and generally accepted accounting principles, and briefly explain why.

USER INSIGHT ▶ 1. After careful study, Kepling Company, which has offices in 40 states, has determined that its method of depreciating office furniture should be changed. The new method is adopted for the current year, and the change is noted in the financial statements.

USER INSIGHT ▶ 2. In the past, Zumi Corporation has recorded operating expenses in general accounts (e.g., Salaries Expense and Utilities Expense). Management has determined that despite the additional recordkeeping costs, the company's income statement should break down each operating expense into its components of selling expense and administrative expense in order to provide better information for managing the business.

USER INSIGHT ▶ 3. Fuzesi Corporation's auditor discovered that a company official had authorized the payment of a $1,200 bribe to a local official. Management argued that because the item was so small in relation to the size of the company ($1,700,000 in sales), the illegal payment should not be disclosed.

USER INSIGHT ▶ 4. Glowaty Bookstore built a small addition to its main building to house a new computer games section. Because no one could be sure that the computer games section would succeed, the accountant took a conservative approach and recorded the addition as an expense.

USER INSIGHT ▶ 5. Since it began operations 10 years ago, Lam Company has used the same generally accepted inventory method. The company does not disclose in its financial statements what inventory method it uses.

LO 4

Forms of the Income Statement

✔ Income from operations, 2011: $34,320; income from operations, 2010: $84,748

P 7. The income statements that follow are for Kaluza Hardware Corporation.

Kaluza Hardware Corporation
Income Statements
For the Years Ended July 31, 2011 and 2010

	2011	**2010**
Revenues		
Net sales	$464,200	$388,466
Interest income	1,420	750
Total revenues	$465,620	$389,216
Costs and expenses		
Cost of goods sold	$243,880	$198,788
Selling expenses	95,160	55,644
General and administrative expenses	90,840	49,286
Interest expense	5,600	1,100
Total costs and expenses	$435,480	$304,818
Income before income taxes	$ 30,140	$ 84,398
Income taxes	8,000	21,250
Net income	$ 22,140	$ 63,148
Earnings per share	$ 2.21	$ 6.31

REQUIRED

1. From the information provided, prepare a multistep income statement for 2011 and 2010 showing percentages of net sales for each component.

USER INSIGHT ▶ 2. Did income from operations increase or decrease from 2010 to 2011? Write a short explanation of why this change occurred.

USER INSIGHT ▶ 3. What effect did other revenues and expenses have on the change in income before income taxes? What action by Kaluza Hardware's management probably accounted for this change?

LO 5

RATIO

Financial Ratios: Performance Measures

P 8. As the accountant for Collins Products Corporation, you have the following information available to you:

	2011	2010
Total assets	$ 72,500	$ 55,000
Current liabilities	10,000	5,000
Long-term liabilities	10,000	—
Stockholders' equity	52,500	50,000
Net sales	131,000	100,000
Net income	8,000	5,500
Cash flows from operating activities	12,000	7,500

Total assets and stockholders' equity in 2009 were $45,000 and $40,000, respectively.

REQUIRED

1. Compute the following profitability measures for 2010 and 2011: (a) profit margin, (b) asset turnover, (c) cash flow yield, (d) debt to equity ratio, (e) return on assets, (f) cash return on assets, and (g) return on equity. (*Note:* Round to one decimal place.)

USER INSIGHT ▶ 2. Comment on the change in performance from 2010 to 2011.

LO 3, 5

✔ Total assets: $298,800

Classified Balance Sheet

P 9. The following information is from the June 30, 2011, post-closing trial balance of Beauty Supplies Corporation.

Account Name	Debit	Credit
Cash	$ 16,000	
Short-Term Investments	16,500	
Notes Receivable	5,000	
Accounts Receivable	138,000	
Merchandise Inventory	72,500	
Prepaid Rent	800	
Prepaid Insurance	2,400	
Sales Supplies	640	
Office Supplies	220	
Deposit for Future Advertising	1,840	
Building, Not in Use	24,800	
Land	11,700	
Delivery Equipment	20,600	
Accumulated Depreciation—Delivery Equipment		$ 14,200
Trademark	2,000	
Accounts Payable		57,300
Salaries Payable		2,600
Interest Payable		920
Long-Term Notes Payable		40,000
Common Stock ($1.10 par value)		11,000
Paid-In Capital in Excess of Par Value		80,000
Retained Earnings		106,980

REQUIRED

1. From the information provided, prepare a classified balance sheet for Beauty Supplies Corporation.
2. As a user of the classified balance sheet, what key elements of other financial statements would be essential to understanding Beauty Supplies Corporation's performance?

USER INSIGHT ▶

Classified Financial Statement Preparation and Analysis

LO 3, 4, 5

✔ Net income: $72,260; total assets: $1,083,800

P 10. Cubicle Corporation is in the machinery business. At the December 31, 2011 year-end, the following financial information was available from the income statement: administrative expenses, $161,600; cost of goods sold, $700,840; income taxes, $14,000; interest expense, $45,280; interest income, $5,600; net sales, $1,428,780; and selling expenses, $440,400.

The following information was available from the balance sheet (after closing entries were made): accounts payable, $65,200; accounts receivable, $209,600; accumulated depreciation—delivery equipment, $34,200; accumulated depreciation—store fixtures, $84,440; cash, $56,800; common stock, $1.00 par value, 20,000 shares authorized, issued, and outstanding, $20,000; delivery equipment, $177,000; inventory, $273,080; investment in securities (long-term), $112,000; investment in U.S. government securities (short-term), $79,200; notes payable (long-term), $200,000; notes payable (short-term), $100,000; paid-in capital in excess of par value, $180,000; prepaid expenses (short-term), $11,520; retained earnings, ending balance, $518,600, beginning balance, $566,340; and store fixtures, $283,240.

Total assets and total stockholders' equity at December 31, 2010, were $1,048,800 and $766,340, respectively; cash flow from operating activities were $60,000; and dividends for the year were $120,000.

REQUIRED

1. From the preceding information, prepare (a) an income statement in single-step form, (b) a statement of retained earnings, and (c) a classified balance sheet.
2. From the statements you have prepared, compute the following ratios: (a) profit margin, (b) asset turnover, (c) cash flow yield, (d) debt to equity ratio, (e) return on assets, (f) cash return on assets, and (g) return on equity. (*Note:* Round to one decimal place.)
3. Using the industry averages for the machinery industry given in the graphs in the ratio boxes throughout this chapter, determine whether Cubicle Corporation needs to improve its performance. Explain your answer, making recommendations as to specific areas on which Cubicle Corporation should concentrate.

RATIO

USER INSIGHT ▶

Cases

Conceptual Understanding: Consistency, Full Disclosure, and Materiality

LO 2

C 1. Metro Parking, which operates a seven-story parking building, has a calendar year-end. It serves daily and hourly parkers, as well as monthly parkers who pay a fixed monthly rate in advance. The company traditionally has recorded all cash receipts as revenues when received. Most monthly parkers pay in full during the month prior to that in which they have the right to park. The company's auditors have said that beginning in 2011, the company should consider recording the cash receipts from monthly parking on an accrual basis, crediting Unearned Revenues. Total cash receipts for 2011 were $1,250,000, and the cash receipts received in 2011 and applicable to January 2012 were $62,500. Discuss the relevance of the accounting conventions of consistency, full disclosure, and materiality to the decision to record the monthly parking revenues on an accrual basis.

LO 2 **Conceptual Understanding: Materiality**

C 2. Laskowski, Inc., operates a chain of consumer electronics stores. This year, the company achieved annual sales of $75 million, on which it earned a net income of $3 million. At the beginning of the year, management implemented a new inventory system that enabled it to track all purchases and sales. At the end of the year, a physical inventory revealed that the actual inventory was $120,000 below what the new system indicated it should be. The inventory loss, which probably resulted from shoplifting, was reflected in a higher cost of goods sold. The problem concerns management but seems to be less important to the company's auditors. What is materiality? Why might the inventory loss concern management more than it does the auditors? Do you think the amount of inventory loss is material?

LO 5 **Interpreting Financial Reports: Comparison of Profitability**

C 3. Two of the largest chains of grocery stores in the United States are **Supervalu Inc.** and the **Great Atlantic & Pacific Tea Company (A&P)**. In fiscal 2009, Supervalu had a net loss of $2,855 million, and A&P had a net loss of $140 million. It is difficult to judge from these figures alone which company is more profitable because they do not take into account the relative sales, sizes, and investments of the companies. Data (in millions) needed for a complete financial analysis of the two companies follow:[12]

	Supervalu	A&P
Net sales	$44,564	$9,516
Beginning total assets	21,062	3,644
Ending total assets	17,604	3,546
Beginning total liabilities	15,109	3,226
Ending total liabilities	15,023	3,278
Beginning stockholders' equity	5,953	418
Ending stockholders' equity	2,581	268

RATIO

1. Determine which company was more profitable by computing profit margin, asset turnover, the debt to equity ratio, return on assets, and return on equity for the two companies. Comment on the relative profitability of the two companies.
2. What do the ratios tell you about the factors that go into achieving an adequate return on assets in the grocery industry? For industry data, refer to the graphs in the ratio boxes throughout the chapter.
3. How would you characterize the use of debt financing in the grocery industry and the use of debt by these two companies?

LO 5 **Interpreting Financial Reports: Evaluation of Performance**

RATIO

C 4. Monica Wish is the principal stockholder and president of Wish Linens, Inc., a wholesaler of fine linens. Because Wish was not satisfied with the company's earnings in 2010, she raised prices in 2011. As a result, gross margin from sales increased from 30 percent in 2010 to 35 percent in 2011. Wish is pleased that net income also increased between 2010 and 2011, as shown in the comparative income statements that follow.

	2011	2010
Revenues		
Net sales	$1,222,600	$1,386,400
Costs and expenses		
Cost of goods sold	$ 794,690	$ 970,480
Selling and administrative expenses	308,398	305,008
Total costs and expenses	$1,103,088	$1,275,488
Income before income taxes	$ 119,512	$ 110,912
Income taxes	30,000	28,000
Net income	$ 89,512	$ 82,912

Total assets for Wish Linens at the end of 2009, 2010, and 2011 were $1,246,780, $1,386,810, and $1,536,910, respectively.

1. Did Wish Linens' profitability really improve? (*Hint:* Compute profit margin and return on assets.)
2. What factors did Wish overlook in evaluating the profitability of the company? (*Hint*: Compute asset turnover and consider the role it plays in profitability.)

LO 3, 4, 5

Annual Report Case: Classified Balance Sheet and Multistep Income Statement

C 5. Refer to the **CVS** annual report in the Supplement to Chapter 1 to answer the following questions.

1. Consolidated balance sheets:
   a. Does CVS use a classified balance sheet?
   b. Did CVS's debt to equity ratio change from 2008 to 2009?
   c. What is the contributed capital for 2009? How does contributed capital compare with retained earnings?

RATIO

2. Consolidated statements of operations:
   a. Does CVS use a multistep or single-step income statement?
   b. Is it a comparative statement?
   c. What is the trend of net earnings?
   d. How significant are income taxes for CVS?

LO 5

Comparison Analysis: Financial Performance

RATIO

C 6. Compare the financial performance of **CVS** and **Southwest Airlines Co.** on the basis of profitability in 2009 and 2008. Use the following ratios: profit margin, asset turnover, cash flow yield, debt to equity ratio, return on assets, and return on equity. In 2007, total assets, total stockholders' equity, and cash flows from operating activities for CVS were $54,722 million, $31,322 million, and $3,230 million, respectively. Southwest's total assets were $16,772 million in 2007, and its total stockholders' equity and cash flow from operating activities were $6,941 million and negative $1,521, respectively. Comment on the relative performance of the two companies. In general, how does Southwest's performance compare to CVS's with respect to profitability? What distinguishes Southwest's profitability performance from that of CVS?

LO 1

Ethical Dilemma: Ethics and Financial Reporting

C 7. Beacon Systems develops computer software and licenses it to financial institutions. The firm records revenues from the software it has developed on a percentage of completion basis. For example, if a project is 50 percent complete, then 50 percent of the contracted revenue is recognized. Preliminary estimates for a $7 million project now in development are that the project is 75 percent complete. Estimates of completion are a matter of judgment, and management therefore feels justified in asking for a new report showing that the project is 90 percent complete. The change will enable senior managers to meet their financial goals for the year and thus receive substantial year-end bonuses. Do you think management's action is ethical? If you were the company controller and were asked to prepare the new report, would you do it? What action would you take?

SUPPLEMENT TO CHAPTER 4

The Annual Report Project

Many instructors assign a term project that requires reading and analyzing an annual report. The Annual Report Project described here has been successful in our classes. It may be used with the annual report of any company, including **CVS Caremark Corporation**'s annual report and the financial statements from **Southwest Airlines Co.**'s annual report that appear in the Supplement to Chapter 1.

The extent to which financial analysis is required depends on the point in the course at which the Annual Report Project is assigned. Instruction 3E, which follows, provides several options.

Instructions

1. Choose a company and obtain its most recent annual report online (use the search [*company name*] *Investor Relations*; then click on financial report or annual reports) or through your library or another source.
2. Use the Internet or your library to locate at least two articles about the company and the industry in which it operates. Read the articles as well as the annual report and summarize your findings. Review the company's products and services and its financial information. Summarize what you have learned.
3. Your analysis should consist of five or six double-spaced pages organized according to the following outline:

A. Introduction

Identify the company by writing a summary that includes the following elements:

- Name of the chief executive officer
- Location of the home office
- Ending date of latest fiscal year
- Description of the company's principal products or services
- Main geographic area of activity
- Name of the company's independent accountants (auditors). In your own words, explain what the accountants said about the company's financial statements.
- The most recent price of the company's stock and its dividend per share. Be sure to provide the date for this information.

B. Industry Situation and Company Plans

Describe the industry and its outlook. Then summarize the company's future plans based on what you learned from the annual report and your other research. Be sure to include any relevant information from management's letter to the stockholders.

C. Financial Statements

Income Statement: Decide whether the format most like a single-step or multistep format. Determine gross profit, income from operations, and net income for the last two years. Comment on the increases or decreases in these amounts.

Balance Sheet: Show that Assets = Liabilities + Stockholders' Equity for the past two years.

Statement of Cash Flows: Indicate whether the company's cash flows from operations for the past two years were more or less than net income. Also indicate whether the company is expanding through investing activities. Identify the company's most important source of financing. Overall, has cash increased or decreased over the past two years?

D. Accounting Policies

Describe the company's significant accounting policies, if any, relating to revenue recognition, cash, accounts receivable, short-term investments, merchandise inventories, and property and equipment. Identify the topics of the notes to the financial statements.

E. Financial Analysis

For the past two years, calculate and discuss the significance of the ratios below. In your discussion, focus on the interrelationships of the ratios and the broad picture as to whether the company is improving in each category.

Option a: Basic Financial Analysis (After Completing Chapter 4)

Financial Ratios
- Profit margin
- Asset turnover
- Cash flow yield
- Debt to equity
- Return on assets
- Return on equity

Option b: Basic with Enhanced Financial–Analysis and the Cash Cycle (After Completing Chapter 8)

Basic Financial Ratios
- Profit margin
- Asset turnover
- Cash flow yield
- Debt to equity
- Return on assets
- Return on equity

Operating Asset Management (Cash Cycle) Financial Ratios
- Receivable turnover
- Days' sales uncollected
- Inventory turnover
- Days' inventory on hand
- Payables turnover
- Days' payable
- Operating cycle
- Financing period

Supplemental Operating Asset Management Financial Ratios
- Working capital
- Current ratio

Option c: Comprehensive Financial Analysis (After Completing Chapter 12, 13, or 14)

Liquidity Ratios
- Working capital
- Current ratio
- Receivable turnover
- Days' sales uncollected
- Inventory turnover
- Days' inventory on hand
- Payables turnover
- Days' payable
- Operating cycle
- Financing period

Profitability and Total Asset Management Financial Ratios
- Profit margin
- Asset turnover
- Return on assets

Liquidity Financial Ratios
- Cash flow yield
- Cash return on sales
- Cash return on assets
- Free cash flow

Financial Risk Financial Ratios
- Debt to equity ratio
- Return on equity
- Interest coverage

Operating Asset Management (Cash Cycle) Financial Ratios
- Receivable turnover
- Days' sales uncollected
- Inventory turnover
- Days' inventory on hand
- Payables turnover
- Days' payable
- Operating cycle
- Financing period

Supplemental Operating Asset Management Financial Ratios
- Working capital
- Current ratio

Market Indicator Financial Ratios
- Price/earnings per share (P/E)
- Dividends yield

CHAPTER 5

DECISION POINT
A User's Focus Best Buy Co., Inc.

Best Buy is a highly successful electronics merchandising company. Like all other merchandisers, it has two key decisions to make: the price at which it will sell goods and the level of service it will provide. A department store may set the price of its merchandise at a relatively high level and provide a great deal of service. A discount store, on the other hand, may price its merchandise at a relatively low level and provide limited service. Best Buy does not precisely fit either of these categories. It purchases merchandise in large quantities from many suppliers, sells the merchandise to customers at the lowest prices it can afford, and provides good service.

As you can see in the company's Financial Highlights,[1] Best Buy is achieving success in controlling its expenses in that operating expenses are growing at a slower rate than gross margin, which leads to increased operating income.

BEST BUY'S FINANCIAL HIGHLIGHTS
OPERATING RESULTS (in millions)

Fiscal-Year Ended	February 27, 2010	February 28, 2009	Change
Net revenue	$49,694	$45,015	10.4%
Cost of sales	37,534	34,017	10.3
Gross margin	$12,160	$10,998	10.6
Operating expenses	9,925	9,128	8.7
Operating income	$ 2,235	$ 1,870	19.5

Questions

1. *How can Best Buy efficiently manage its cycle of merchandising operations?*
2. *How should merchandising transactions be recorded to reflect the company's performance?*
3. *How can the company maintain control over its merchandising operations?*

Justin Sullivan/Getty Images News/Getty Images

The Operating Cycle and Merchandising Operations

LEARNING OBJECTIVES

LO 1 Identify the management issues related to merchandising businesses. (pp. 246–251)

LO 2 Describe the terms of sale related to merchandising transactions. (pp. 252–254)

LO 3 Prepare an income statement and record merchandising transactions under the perpetual inventory system. (pp. 254–258)

LO 4 Prepare an income statement and record merchandising transactions under the periodic inventory system. (pp. 258–262)

LO 5 Describe the components of internal control, control activities, and limitations on internal control. (pp. 263–265)

LO 6 Apply internal control activities to common merchandising transactions. (pp. 265–270)

In the last chapter, we pointed out management's responsibility for ensuring the accuracy and fairness of financial statements. To fulfill all its responsibilities, management must see that transactions are properly recorded and that the company's assets are protected. That, in turn, requires a system of internal controls. In this chapter, we examine internal controls over the transactions of merchandising companies and the operating cycle in which such transactions take place. The internal controls and other issues that we describe here also apply to manufacturing companies.

FOCUS ON FINANCIAL STATEMENTS

INCOME STATEMENT

Revenues
− Expenses
= Net Income

STATEMENT OF RETAINED EARNINGS

(2)

Opening Balance
+ Net Income
− Dividends
= Retained Earnings

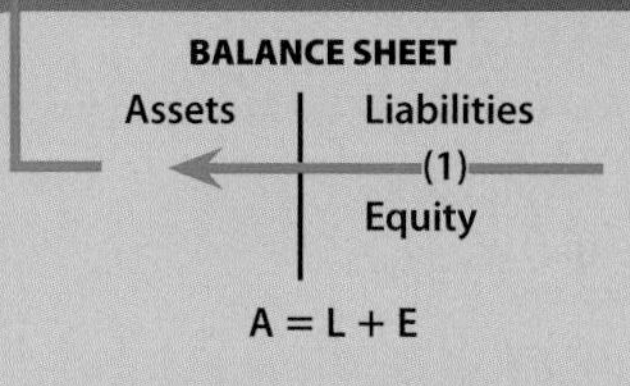

STATEMENT OF CASH FLOWS

Operating Activities
+ Investing Activities
+ Financing Activities
= Change in Cash
+ Starting Balance
= Ending Cash Balance

Under the perpetual inventory system, merchandise inventory is updated after every purchase (1) and sale (2).

MANAGING MERCHANDISING BUSINESSES

LO 1 Identify the management issues related to merchandising businesses.

A **merchandising business** earns income by buying and selling goods, which are called **merchandise inventory**. Whether a merchandiser is a wholesaler or a retailer, it uses the same basic accounting methods as a service company. However, the buying and selling of goods adds to the complexity of the business and of the accounting process.

Evaluation of Liquidity

One of the most important issues related to merchandising businesses is having adequate liquidity. As you know, *liquidity* means having enough money on hand to pay bills when they are due and to take care of unexpected needs for cash. A common measure of liquidity is working capital. **Working capital**, which uses two elements of the classified balance sheet, is the amount by which current assets exceed current liabilities. It is an important measure of liquidity because current liabilities must be satisfied within one year or one operating cycle, whichever is longer, and current assets are used to pay the current liabilities. Thus, the excess of current assets over current liabilities—the working capital—is what is on hand to continue business operations.

For Best Buy, working capital in 2010 is computed as follows:

Current assets	$10,566
Less current liabilities	8,978
Working capital	$ 1,588

Working capital can be used to buy inventory, obtain credit, and finance expanded sales. Lack of working capital can lead to a company's failure.

RATIO

Financial Ratio: Current Ratio The current ratio is closely related to working capital. Many bankers and other creditors believe it is a good indicator of a company's ability to pay its debts on time. The **current ratio** is the ratio of current assets to current liabilities, computed as follows for Best Buy:

$$\text{Current Ratio} = \frac{\text{Current Assets}}{\text{Current Liabilities}} = \frac{\$10,566}{\$\ 8,978} = 1.18$$

Industry	Current Ratio
Advertising	1.3
Interstate Trucking	1.7
Auto and Home Supply	2.1
Grocery Stores	1.9
Machinery	2.3
Computers	2.1

Service Industries · Merchandising Industries · Manufacturing Industries

Source: Data from Dun & Bradstreet, *Industry Norms and Key Business Ratios*, 2008–2009.

Most companies try to maintain a current ratio of between 1.0 and 2.0, as can be seen by the industries presented in the illustration, but Best Buy has only $1.18 of current assets for each $1.00 of current liabilities.

Operating Cycle

Merchandising businesses engage in a series of transactions called the **operating cycle**. Exhibit 5.1 shows the transactions that make up this cycle. Some companies buy merchandise for cash and sell it for cash, but these companies are usually small companies like a produce market or a hot dog stand. Most companies buy merchandise on credit and sell it on credit, thereby engaging in the following four transactions:

1. Purchase of merchandise inventory for cash or on credit
2. Payment for purchases made on credit
3. Sales of merchandise inventory for cash or on credit
4. Collection of cash from credit sales

The first three transactions represent the time it takes to purchase inventory, sell it, and collect for it. Merchandisers must be able to do without the cash for this period of time either by relying on cash flows from other sources within the company or by borrowing. If they lack the cash to pay bills when they come due, they can be forced out of business. Thus, managing cash flow is a critical concern.

The suppliers that sold the company the merchandise usually also sell on credit and thus help alleviate the cash flow problem by providing financing for a period of time before they require payment (transaction 4). However, this period is rarely as long as the operating cycle. The period between the time the supplier must be paid and the end of the operating cycle is called the *financing period*; it is also sometimes referred to as the *cash gap*.

STUDY NOTE: *A company must provide financing for the average days' inventory on hand plus the average number of days it needs to collect credit sales less the average number of days it is allowed to pay its suppliers.*

The **financing period**, illustrated in Exhibit 5.2 (p. 248), is the amount of time from the purchase of inventory until it is sold and payment is collected, less the amount of time creditors give the company to pay for the inventory. Thus, if it takes 60 days to sell the inventory, it takes 60 days to collect for the sale, and creditors' payment terms are 30 days, the financing period is 90 days [60 + (60 – 30)]. During the financing period, the company will be without cash from this series of transactions and will need either to have funds available internally or to borrow from a bank.

The way in which a merchandising company manages its inventories, receivables, and payables will affect its financing period. For example, compare **Best Buy**'s[2] financing period with that of a typical discount store chain, **Target Corporation**:[3]

	Target	Best Buy	Difference
Days' inventory on hand	58 days	50 days	(8) days
Days' receivable	42	14	(28)
Less days' payable	(53)	(49)	(4)
Financing period	**47 days**	**15 days**	**(32) days**

EXHIBIT 5.1
Cash Flows in the Operating Cycle

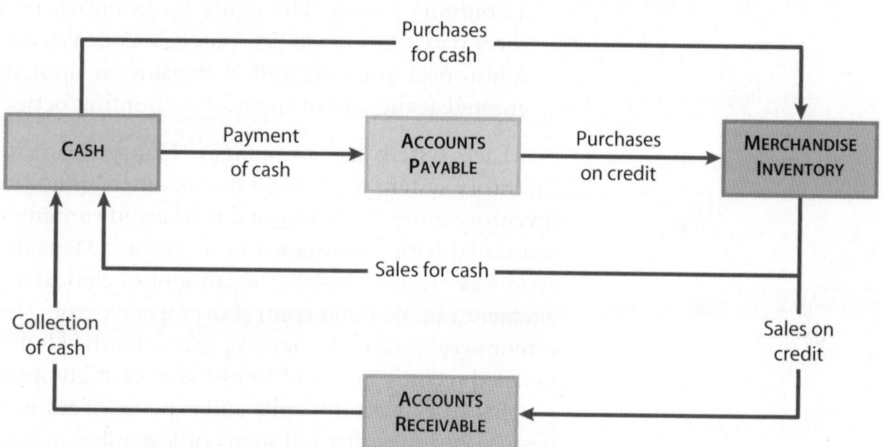

EXHIBIT 5.2
The Financing Period

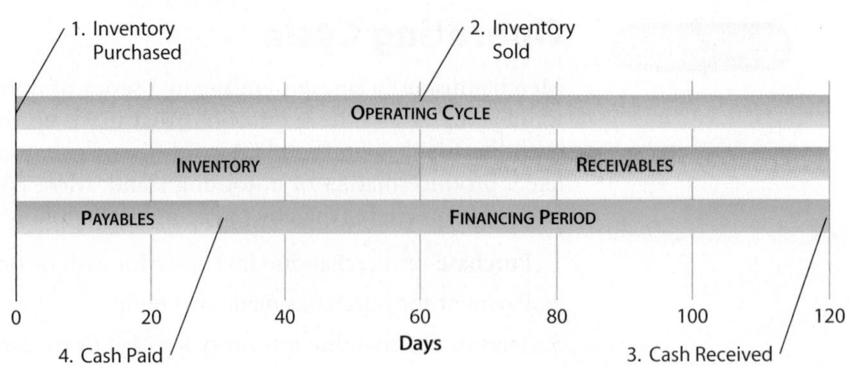

These companies are very comparable in terms of how long it takes to sell inventory and to pay creditors, but Best Buy has a distinct advantage over Target because it sells and collects receivables much faster. Its days' receivable is only 14 compared to 42 for Target, which results in a very short financing period of only 15 days.

By reducing its financing period, a company can improve its cash flow. Many merchandisers, including Best Buy, do this by selling as much as possible for cash. Cash sales include sales on bank *credit cards*, such as Visa or MasterCard, and on *debit cards*, which draw directly on the purchaser's bank account. They are considered cash sales because funds from them are available to the merchandiser immediately. Small retail stores may have mostly cash sales and very few credit sales, whereas large wholesale concerns may have almost all credit sales.

Choice of Inventory System

Another issue in managing a merchandising business is the choice of inventory system. Management must choose the system or combination of systems that best achieves the company's goals. The two basic systems of accounting for the many items in merchandise inventory are the perpetual inventory system and the periodic inventory system.

- Under the **perpetual inventory system**, continuous records are kept of the quantity and, usually, the cost of individual items as they are bought and sold. The cost of each item is recorded in the Merchandise Inventory account when it is purchased. As merchandise is sold, its cost is transferred from the Merchandise Inventory account to the Cost of Goods Sold account. Thus, at all times, the balance of the Merchandise Inventory account equals the cost of goods on hand, and the balance in Cost of Goods Sold equals the cost of merchandise sold to customers.
- Under the **periodic inventory system**, the inventory not yet sold, or on hand, is counted periodically. This physical count is usually taken at the end of the accounting period. No detailed records of the inventory on hand are maintained during the accounting period. The figure for inventory on hand is accurate only on the balance sheet date. As soon as any purchases or sales are made, the inventory figure becomes a historical amount, and it remains so until the new ending inventory amount is entered at the end of the next accounting period.

Each system has advantages. Managers use the detailed data from the perpetual inventory system to respond to customers' inquiries about product availability, to order inventory more effectively and thus avoid running out of stock, and to control the costs associated with investments in inventory. Managers may choose the periodic inventory system because it reduces the amount of clerical work. If a company is fairly small, management can maintain control over its inventory simply through observation or use of an offline system of cards or computer records. However, for larger companies, the lack of detailed records may lead to lost sales or high operating costs.

Because of the difficulty and expense of accounting for the purchase and sale of each item, companies that sell items of low value in high volume have traditionally used the periodic inventory system. Examples of such companies include small retailers, drugstores, and grocery stores. In contrast, companies that sell items that have a high unit value, such as appliances or automobiles, have tended to use the perpetual inventory system. As technology has improved with the use of bar codes, companies like Best Buy can use the perpetual method for all its inventory—both low cost and high cost.

STUDY NOTE: *The costs of an automated perpetual system are considerable. They include the costs of automating the system, maintaining the system, and taking a physical inventory.*

The distinction between high and low unit value for inventory systems has blurred considerably in recent years. Although the periodic inventory system is still widely used, computerization has led to a large increase in the use of the perpetual inventory system. It is important to note that the perpetual inventory system does not eliminate the need for a physical count of the inventory; one should be taken periodically to ensure that the actual number of goods on hand matches the quantity indicated by the computer records.

Foreign Business Transactions

Most large merchandising and manufacturing firms and even many small ones transact some of their business overseas. For example, a U.S. manufacturer may expand by selling its product to foreign customers, or it may lower its product cost by buying a less expensive part from a source in another country. Such sales and purchase transactions may take place in Japanese yen, British pounds, or some other foreign currency.

When an international transaction involves two different currencies, as most such transactions do, one currency has to be translated into another by using an exchange rate. As we noted earlier in the text, an *exchange rate* is the value of one currency stated in terms of another. We also noted that the values of other currencies in relation to the dollar rise and fall daily according to supply and demand. Thus, if there is a delay between the date of sale or purchase and the date of receipt of payment, the amount of cash involved in an international transaction may differ from the originally agreed-upon amount.

If the billing of an international sale and the payment for it are both in the domestic currency, no accounting problem arises. For example, if a U.S. maker of precision tools sells $160,000 worth of its products to a British company and bills the British company in dollars, the U.S. company will receive $160,000 when it collects payment. However, if the U.S. company bills the British company in British pounds and accepts payment in pounds, it will incur an **exchange gain or loss** if the exchange rate between dollars and pounds changes between the date of sale and the date of payment, as shown in the following examples:

- **Sale in foreign currency:** Assume that a U.S. company bills a sale of $200,000 at £125,000, reflecting an exchange rate of 1.6 (that is, $1.60 per pound) on the sale date. Now assume that by the date of payment, the exchange rate has fallen to 1.50. When the U.S. company receives its £125,000, it will be worth only $187,500 (£125,000 × $1.50 = $187,500). It will have incurred an exchange loss of $12,500 because it agreed to accept a fixed number of British pounds in payment for its products, and the value of each pound dropped before the payment was made. Had the value of the pound in relation to the dollar increased, the company would have made an exchange gain.
- **Purchase in foreign currency:** The same logic applies to purchases as to sales, except that the relationship of exchange gains and losses to changes in exchange rates is reversed. For example, assume that the U.S company purchases products from the British company for $200,000. If the payment is to be made in U.S. dollars, no accounting problem arises. However, if the British company expects to be paid in pounds, the U.S. company will have an exchange gain of $12,500 because it agreed to pay a fixed £125,000, and between the dates of purchase and payment, the exchange value of the pound decreased from $1.60 to $1.50. To make the £125,000 payment, the U.S. company has to expend only $187,500.

Exchange gains and losses are reported on the income statement. Because of their bearing on a company's financial performance, they are of considerable interest to managers and investors. Lack of uniformity in international accounting standards is another matter of which investors must be wary.

Focus on International Practices

IFRS Income Statements Under IFRS May Not Show Cost of Goods Sold

Under U.S. GAAP, the Cost of Good Sold account is needed because the income statement requires listing of costs and expense by function such as cost of goods sold, selling expenses, general and administrative expenses, and so forth. IFRS, on the other hand, give companies the option of listing by function like the U.S. GAAP or by nature, such as materials costs, labor costs, and so forth. Most European companies chose the latter option and thus have no cost of goods sold, gross margin, or operating income on their income statements.

iStock Photo

The Need for Internal Controls

Buying and selling, the principal transactions of merchandising businesses, involve assets—cash, accounts receivable, and merchandise inventory—that are vulnerable to theft and embezzlement. Cash and inventory can, of course, be fairly easy to steal. The reason the potential for embezzlement exists is that the large number of transactions that are usually involved in a merchandising business (e.g., cash receipts, receipts on account, payments for purchases, and receipts and shipments of inventory) makes monitoring the accounting records difficult.

If a merchandising company does not take steps to protect its assets, it can suffer high losses of both cash and inventory. Management's responsibility is to establish an environment, accounting systems, and control procedures that will protect the company's assets. These systems and procedures are called **internal controls**.

A company's merchandise inventory includes all goods intended for sale regardless of where they are located—on shelves, in storerooms, in warehouses, or in trucks between warehouses and stores. It also includes goods in transit from suppliers if title to the goods has passed to the merchandiser. Ending inventory does not include merchandise that a company has sold but not yet delivered to customers. Nor does it include goods that it cannot sell because they are damaged or obsolete. If damaged or obsolete goods can be sold at a reduced price, however, they should be included in ending inventory at their reduced value.

Taking a **physical inventory** facilitates control over merchandise inventory. This process involves an actual count of all merchandise on hand. It can be a difficult task because it is easy to accidentally omit items or count them twice. As we noted earlier, a physical inventory must be taken under both the periodic and the perpetual inventory systems.

Merchandise inventory includes all goods intended for sale wherever they are located—on store shelves, in warehouses, on car lots, or in transit from suppliers if title to the goods has passed to the merchandiser. To prevent a loss of inventory, a merchandiser must have an effective system of control.

Raymond Forbes/PhotoLibrary

Merchandisers usually take a physical inventory after the close of business on the last day of their fiscal year. To facilitate the process, they often end the fiscal year in a slow season, when inventories are at relatively low levels. For example, many department stores end their fiscal year in January or February. After hours—at night, on a weekend, or when the store closes for all or part of a day for taking inventory—employees count all items and record the results on numbered inventory tickets or sheets, following procedures to ensure that no items will be missed. Using bar coding to take inventory electronically has greatly facilitated the process in many companies.

Most companies experience losses of merchandise inventory from spoilage, shoplifting, and theft by employees. When such losses occur, the periodic inventory system provides no means of identifying them because the costs are automatically included in the cost of goods sold. For example, suppose a company has lost $1,250 in stolen merchandise during an accounting period. When the physical inventory is taken, the missing items are not in stock, so they cannot be counted. Because the ending inventory does not contain these items, the amount subtracted from goods available for sale is less than it would be if the goods were in stock. The cost of goods sold, then, is overstated by $1,250. In a sense, the cost of goods sold is inflated by the amount of merchandise that has been lost.

STUDY NOTE: An adjustment to the Merchandise Inventory account will be needed if the physical inventory reveals a difference between the actual inventory and the amount in the records.

The perpetual inventory system makes it easier to identify such losses. Because the Merchandise Inventory account is continuously updated for sales, purchases, and returns, the loss will show up as the difference between the inventory records and the physical inventory taken at the end of the accounting period. Once the amount of the loss has been identified, the ending inventory is updated by crediting the Merchandise Inventory account. The offsetting debit is usually an increase in Cost of Goods Sold because the loss is considered a cost that reduces the company's gross margin.

Management's Responsibility for Internal Control

Management is responsible for establishing a satisfactory system of internal controls. Such a system includes all the policies and procedures needed to ensure the reliability of financial reporting, compliance with laws and regulations, and the effectiveness and efficiency of operations. In other words, management must safeguard the firm's assets, ensure the reliability of its accounting records, and see that its employees comply with all legal requirements and operate the firm to the best advantage of its owners.

Section 404 of the Sarbanes-Oxley Act of 2002 requires that the chief executive officer, the chief financial officer, and the auditors of a public company fully document and certify the company's system of internal controls. For example, in its annual report, **Best Buy**'s management acknowledges its responsibility for internal control as follows:

> Our management is responsible for establishing and maintaining adequate internal control over financial reporting.[4]

iStock Photo

Focus on Business Practice

Will Sarbanes-Oxley Stop Fraud?

Although the Sarbanes-Oxley Act has heightened awareness of internal control and has required increased diligence, it will never stop fraud from occurring. For instance, a recent study of 350 alleged accounting fraud cases investigated by the SEC found that fraud affects companies of all sizes. The average fraud was $12.1 million, and more than 30 cases involved fraud over $500 million. Additional guidance with regard to internal controls are expected to be issued.[5]

iStock Photo

Stop & Apply

The management of SavRite Corporation made the following decisions. Indicate whether each decision pertains primarily to (a) cash flow management, (b) choice of inventory system, or (c) foreign transactions.

1. Decided to decrease the credit terms offered to customers from 30 days to 20 days to speed up collection of accounts.
2. Decided to purchase goods made by a supplier in India.
3. Decided to measure working capital monthly to ensure that there is an adequate reserve to maintain liquidity.
4. Decided that sales would increase if salespeople knew how much inventory was on hand at any one time.
5. Decided to try to negotiate a longer time to pay suppliers than had been previously granted.

SOLUTION 1. a; 2. c; 3. a; 4. b; 5. a

TERMS OF SALE

Describe the terms of sale related to merchandising transactions. LO 2

When goods are sold on credit, both parties should understand the amount and timing of payment as well as other terms of the purchase, such as who pays delivery charges and what warranties or rights of return apply. Sellers quote prices in different ways. Many merchants quote the price at which they expect to sell their goods. Others, particularly manufacturers and wholesalers, quote prices as a percentage (usually 30 percent or more) off their list or catalogue prices. Such a reduction is called a **trade discount**.

For example, if an article is listed at $1,000 with a trade discount of 40 percent, or $400, the seller records the sale at $600, and the buyer records the purchase at $600. The seller may raise or lower the trade discount depending on the quantity purchased. The list or catalogue price and related trade discount are used only to arrive at an agreed-upon price; they do not appear in the accounting records.

Sales and Purchases Discounts

The terms of sale are usually printed on the sales invoice and thus constitute part of the sales agreement. Terms differ from industry to industry. In some industries, payment is expected in a short period of time, such as 10 or 30 days. In these cases, the invoice is marked "n/10" ("net 10") or "n/30" ("net 30"), meaning that the amount of the invoice is due either 10 days or 30 days after the invoice date. If the invoice is due 10 days after the end of the month, it is marked "n/10 eom."

STUDY NOTE: *A trade discount applies to the list or catalogue price. A sales discount applies to the sales price.*

Sales Discount In some industries, it is customary to give a **sales discount** for early payment. An invoice that offers a sales discount might be labeled "2/10, n/30," which means that the buyer either can pay the invoice within 10 days of the invoice date and take a 2 percent discount or can wait 30 days and pay the full amount of the invoice. It is often advantageous for a buyer to take the discount because the saving of 2 percent over a period of 20 days (from the 11th day to the 30th day) represents an effective annual rate of 36.5 percent (365 days ÷ 20 days × 2% = 36.5%). Most companies would be better off borrowing money to take the discount.

STUDY NOTE: *Early collection also reduces the probability of a customer's defaulting.*

Because it is not possible to know at the time of a sale whether the customer will pay in time to take advantage of a sales discount, the discounts are recorded only at the time the customer pays. For example, suppose Wagon Sportswear Corporation sells merchandise to a customer on September 20 for $600 on terms of 2/10, n/30. Wagon Sportswear records the sale on September 20 for the full amount of $600. If the customer takes advantage of the discount by paying on or before September 30, Wagon Sportswear will receive $588 in cash and will reduce its Accounts Receivable by $600. The difference of $12 ($600 × 0.02) will be debited to an account called *Sales Discounts.* Sales Discounts is a contra-revenue account with a normal debit balance that is deducted from sales on the income statement.

Although sales discounts were intended to increase the seller's liquidity by reducing the amount of money tied up in accounts receivable, the practice of giving sales discounts has been declining. Sales discounts are costly to the seller, and from the buyer's viewpoint, the amount of the discount is usually very small in relation to the price of the purchase.

Purchases Discount **Purchases discounts** are discounts that a buyer takes for the early payment of merchandise. For example, the buyer that purchased the merchandise from Wagon Sportswear Corporation will record the purchase on September 20 at $600. If the buyer pays on or before September 30, it will record cash paid of $588 and reduce its Accounts Payable by $600. The difference of $12 is recorded as a credit to an account called *Purchases Discounts.* The Purchases Discounts account reduces Cost of Goods Sold or Purchases depending on the inventory method used. As a result of the decline in the use of sales discounts mentioned previously, the use of purchase discounts is also declining.

Transportation Costs

In some industries, the seller usually pays transportation costs and charges a price that includes those costs. In other industries, it is customary for the purchaser to pay transportation charges. The following special terms designate whether the seller or the purchaser pays the freight charges:

- **FOB shipping point** means that the seller places the merchandise "free on board" at the point of origin and the buyer bears the shipping costs. The title to the merchandise passes to the buyer at that point. For example, when the sales agreement for the purchase of a car says "FOB factory," the buyer must pay the freight from the factory where the car was made to wherever he or she is located, and the buyer owns the car from the time it leaves the factory.
- **FOB destination** means that the seller bears the transportation costs to the place where the merchandise is delivered. The seller retains title until the merchandise reaches its destination and usually prepays the shipping costs, in which case the buyer makes no accounting entry for freight.

The effects of these special shipping terms are summarized as follows:

Shipping Term	Where Title Passes	Who Pays the Cost of Transportation
FOB shipping point	At origin	Buyer
FOB destination	At destination	Seller

When the buyer pays the transportation charge, it is called **freight-in**, and it is added to the cost of merchandise purchased. Thus, freight-in increases the buyer's cost of merchandise inventory, as well as the cost of goods sold after they are sold. When freight-in is a relatively small amount, most companies include the cost in the cost of goods sold on the income statement rather than going to the trouble of allocating part of it to merchandise inventory.

When the seller pays the transportation charge, it is called **delivery expense**, or *freight-out.* Because the seller incurs this cost to facilitate the sale of its product, the cost is included in selling expenses on the income statement.

Terms of Debit and Credit Card Sales

Many retailers allow customers to use debit or credit cards to charge their purchases. Debit cards deduct directly from a person's bank account, whereas a credit card allows for payment later. Five of the most widely used credit cards are American Express, Discover Card, Diners Club, MasterCard, and Visa. The customer establishes credit with the lender (the credit card issuer) and receives a plastic card to use in making charges. If a seller accepts the card, the customer signs an invoice at the time of the sale. The sale is communicated to the seller's bank, resulting in a cash deposit in the seller's bank account. Thus, the seller does not have to establish the customer's credit, collect from the customer, or tie up money in accounts receivable. As payment, the lender, rather than paying the total amount of the credit card sales, takes a discount of 2 to 6 percent. The discount is a selling expense for the merchandiser. For example, if a restaurant makes sales of $1,000 on Visa credit cards and Visa takes a 4 percent discount on the sales, the restaurant would record Cash in the amount of $960 and Credit Card Expense in the amount of $40.

Stop & Apply

A local company sells refrigerators that it buys from the manufacturer.

a. The manufacturer sets a list or catalogue price of $1,200 for a refrigerator. The manufacturer offers its dealers a 40 percent trade discount and terms of FOB destination.

b. Assume the same terms as **a**, except the manufacturer sells the refrigerator under terms of FOB shipping point. The cost of shipping is $120.

c. Assume the same terms as **b**, except the manufacturer offers a sales discount of 2/10, n/30. Sales discounts do not apply to shipping costs.

What is the net cost of the refrigerator to the dealer in each case, assuming payment is made within 10 days of purchase?

SOLUTION

a. $1,200 – ($1,200 × 0.40) = $720 b. $720 + $120 = $840 c. $840 – ($720 × 0.02) = $825.60

iStock Photo

PERPETUAL INVENTORY SYSTEM

LO 3 Prepare an income statement and record merchandising transactions under the perpetual inventory system.

Exhibit 5.3 shows how an income statement appears when a company uses the perpetual inventory system. The focal point of the statement is cost of goods sold, which is deducted from net sales to arrive at gross margin. Under the perpetual inventory system, the Merchandise Inventory and Cost of Goods Sold accounts are continually updated during the accounting period as purchases, sales, and other inventory transactions that affect these accounts occur.

EXHIBIT 5.3
Income Statement Under the Perpetual Inventory System

STUDY NOTE: *On the income statement, freight-in is included as part of cost of goods sold, and delivery expense (freight-out) is included as an operating (selling) expense.*

Wagon Sportswear Corporation
Income Statement
For the Year Ended December 31, 2011

Net sales	$957,300
Cost of goods sold*	525,440
Gross margin	$431,860
Operating expenses	313,936
Income before income taxes	$117,924
Income taxes	20,000
Net income	$ 97,924

*Freight-in has been included in cost of goods sold.

Purchases of Merchandise

Exhibit 5.4 shows how transactions involving purchases of merchandise are recorded under the perpetual inventory system. As you can see, the focus of these entries is

EXHIBIT 5.4
Recording Purchase Transactions Under the Perpetual Inventory System

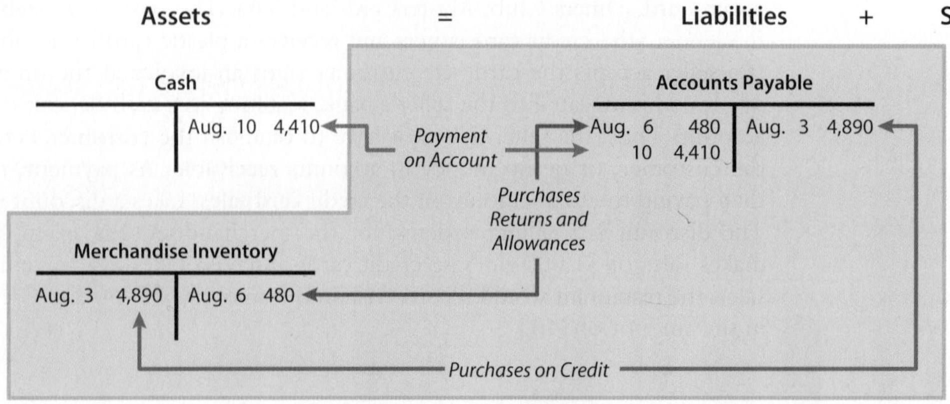

Accounts Payable In this section, we present a summary of the entries made for merchandise purchases.

Purchases on Credit

Aug. 3: Received merchandise purchased on credit, invoice dated August 1, terms n/10, $4,890.

Analysis: Under the perpetual inventory system, the cost of merchandise is recorded in the Merchandise Inventory account at the time of purchase, which

- ▲ *increases* the *Merchandise Inventory* account and
- ▲ *increases* the *Accounts Payable* account.

Journal Entry:

Aug. 3	Merchandise Inventory	4,890	
	Accounts Payable		4,890
	Purchases on credit		

Comment: In the transaction described here, payment is due 10 days from the invoice date. If an invoice includes a charge for shipping or if shipping is billed separately, it should be debited to Freight-In.

Purchases Returns and Allowances

Aug. 6: Returned part of merchandise received on August 3 for credit, $480.

Analysis: Under the perpetual inventory system, when a buyer is allowed to return all or part of a purchase or is given an allowance—a reduction in the amount to be paid—Merchandise Inventory is reduced, as is Accounts Payable. In other words, purchases returns and allowances

- ▼ *decrease* the *Accounts Payable* account and
- ▼ *decrease* the *Merchandise Inventory* account.

Journal Entry:

Aug. 6	Accounts Payable	480	
	Merchandise Inventory		480
	Returned merchandise from purchase		

Payments on Account

Aug. 10: Paid amount due in full for the purchase of August 3, part of which was returned on August 6, $4,410.

Analysis: Payment is made for the net amount due of $4,410 ($4,890 – $480), which

- ▼ *decreases* the *Accounts Payable* account and
- ▼ *decreases* the *Cash* account.

Journal Entry:

Aug. 10	Accounts Payable	4,410	
	Cash		4,410
	Made payment on account		

Sales of Merchandise

Exhibit 5.5 shows how transactions involving sales of merchandise are recorded under the perpetual inventory system. These transactions involve several accounts, including Cash, Accounts Receivable, Merchandise Inventory, Sales Returns and Allowances, and Cost of Goods Sold. The following sections present a summary of the entries made for sales of merchandise.

Sales on Credit

Aug. *7:* Sold merchandise on credit, terms n/30, FOB destination, $1,200; the cost of the merchandise was $720.

Analysis: Under the perpetual inventory system, sales always require two entries, as shown in Exhibit 5.5. First, the sale is recorded, which

- ▲ *increases* the *Accounts Receivable* account and
- ▲ *increases* the *Sales* account.

Second, Cost of Goods Sold is updated by a transfer from Merchandise Inventory, which

- ▲ *increases* the *Cost of Goods Sold* account and
- ▼ *decreases* the *Merchandise Inventory* account.

Journal Entry:

Aug. 7	Accounts Receivable	1,200	
	Sales		1,200
	Sold merchandise to Gonzales Distributors		
7	Cost of Goods Sold	720	
	Merchandise Inventory		720
	Transferred cost of merchandise inventory sold to Cost of Goods Sold		

Comment: In the case of cash sales, Cash rather than Accounts Receivable is debited for the amount of the sale. If the seller pays for the shipping, the shipping cost should be debited to Delivery Expense.

EXHIBIT 5.5
Recording Sales Transactions Under the Perpetual Inventory System

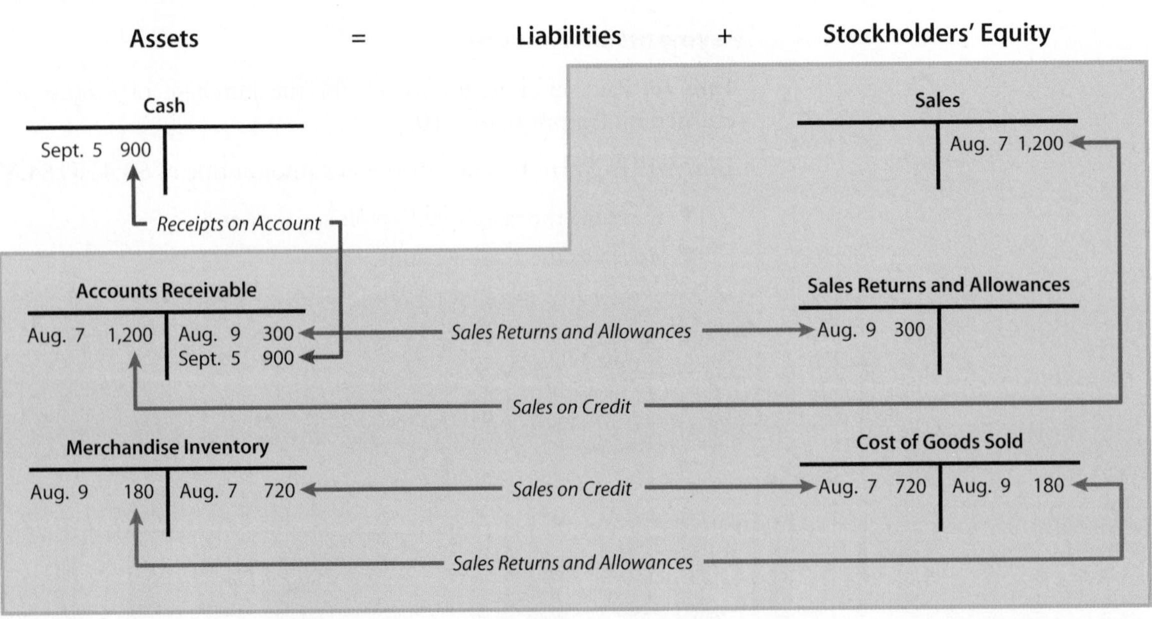

Sales Returns and Allowances

Aug. 9: Accepted return of part of merchandise sold on August 7 for full credit and returned it to merchandise inventory, $300; the cost of the merchandise was $180.

Analysis: Under the perpetual inventory system, when a seller allows the buyer to return all or part of a sale or gives an allowance—a reduction in amount—two entries are again necessary. First, the original sale is reversed, which

▲ *increases* the *Sales Returns and Allowances* account and
▼ *decreases* the *Accounts Receivable* account.

STUDY NOTE: *Because the Sales account is established with a credit, its contra account, Sales Returns and Allowances, is established with a debit.*

The **Sales Returns and Allowances account** gives management a readily available measure of unsatisfactory products and dissatisfied customers. This account is a contra-revenue account with a normal debit balance, and it is deducted from sales on the income statement. Second, the cost of the merchandise must also be transferred from the Cost of Goods Sold account back into the Merchandise Inventory account, which

▲ *increases* the *Merchandise Inventory* account and
▼ *decreases* the *Cost of Goods Sold* account.

Journal Entry:

Aug. 9	Sales Returns and Allowances	300	
	Accounts Receivable		300
	Accepted returns of merchandise		
9	Merchandise Inventory	180	
	Cost of Goods Sold		180
	Transferred cost of merchandise returned to Merchandise Inventory		

Comment: If the company makes an allowance instead of accepting a return or if the merchandise cannot be returned to inventory and resold, this transfer is not made.

Receipts on Account

Sept. 5: Collected in full for sale of merchandise on August 7, less the return on August 9, $900.

Analysis: Collection is made for the net amount due of $900 ($1,200 – $300), which

▲ *increases* the *Cash* account and
▼ *decreases* the *Accounts Receivable* account.

Journal Entry:

Sept. 5	Cash	900	
	Accounts Receivable		900
	Received on account		

Focus on Business Practice

How Are Web Sales Doing?

In spite of the demise of many Internet retailers, merchandise sales over the Internet continue to thrive. Internet sales increased 14.3 percent in the first quarter of 2010 and are expected to exceed $200 billion for the year.[6] The companies that have been most successful in using the Internet are established mail-order retailers like **Lands' End** and **L.L. Bean**. Other retailers have also used the Internet to enhance their operations. For example, **Office Depot**, which focuses primarily on business-to-business Internet sales, has set up customized web pages for tens of thousands of corporate clients. These web pages allow customers to make online purchases and check store inventories. Although Internet transactions are recorded in the same way as on-site transactions, the technology adds a level of complexity to the transactions.

iStock Photo

Stop & Apply

The numbered items below are account titles, and the lettered items that follow are types of merchandising transactions. For each transaction, indicate which accounts are debited or credited by placing the account numbers in the appropriate columns, assuming use of a perpetual inventory system.

1. Cash
2. Accounts Receivable
3. Merchandise Inventory
4. Accounts Payable
5. Sales
6. Sales Returns and Allowances
7. Cost of Goods Sold

	Account Debited	Account Credited		Account Debited	Account Credited
a. Purchase on credit	____	____	e. Sale for cash	____	____
b. Purchase return for credit	____	____	f. Sales return for credit	____	____
c. Purchase for cash	____	____	g. Payment on account	____	____
d. Sale on credit	____	____	h. Receipt on account	____	____

SOLUTION

	Account Debited	Account Credited		Account Debited	Account Credited
a. Purchase on credit	3	4	e. Sale for cash	1, 7	5, 3
b. Purchase return for credit	4	3	f. Sales return for credit	6, 3	2, 7
c. Purchase for cash	3	1	g. Payment on account	4	1
d. Sale on credit	2, 7	5, 3	h. Receipt on account	1	2

iStock Photo

PERIODIC INVENTORY SYSTEM

LO 4 Prepare an income statement and record merchandising transactions under the periodic inventory system.

Exhibit 5.6 shows how an income statement appears when a company uses the periodic inventory system. A major feature of this statement is the computation of cost of goods sold. *Cost of goods sold* must be computed on the income statement because it is not updated for purchases, sales, and other transactions during the accounting period, as it is under the perpetual inventory system.

It is important to distinguish between goods available for sale and cost of goods sold. **Cost of goods available for sale** is the total cost of merchandise that *could* be sold in

EXHIBIT 5.6
Income Statement Under the Periodic Inventory System

STUDY NOTE: Most published financial statements are condensed, eliminating the detail shown here under cost of goods sold.

Wagon Sportswear Corporation
Income Statement
For the Year Ended December 31, 2011

Net sales			$957,300
Cost of goods sold			
Merchandise inventory, December 31, 2010		$211,200	
Purchases	$505,600		
Less purchases returns and allowances	31,104		
Net purchases	$474,496		
Freight-in	32,944		
Net cost of purchases		507,440	
Cost of goods available for sale		$718,640	
Less merchandise inventory, December 31, 2011		193,200	
Cost of goods sold			525,440
Gross margin			$431,860
Operating expenses			313,936
Income before income taxes			$117,924
Income taxes			20,000
Net income			$ 97,924

the accounting period. Cost of goods sold is the cost of merchandise *actually* sold. The difference between the two numbers is the amount *not* sold, or the ending merchandise inventory. Cost of goods available for sale is the sum of the following two factors:

- The amount of merchandise on hand at the beginning of the accounting period or beginning inventory.
- The net purchases during the period. (**Net purchases** consist of total purchases plus any freight-in less any deductions such as purchases returns and allowances and discounts from suppliers for early payment.)

As you can see in Exhibit 5.6, Wagon Sportswear Corporation has cost of goods available for sale during the period of $718,640 ($211,200 + $507,440). The ending inventory of $193,200 is deducted from this figure to determine the cost of goods sold. Thus, the company's cost of goods sold is $525,440 ($718,640 – $193,200). Exhibit 5.7 illustrates these relationships.

EXHIBIT 5.7
The Components of Cost of Goods Sold

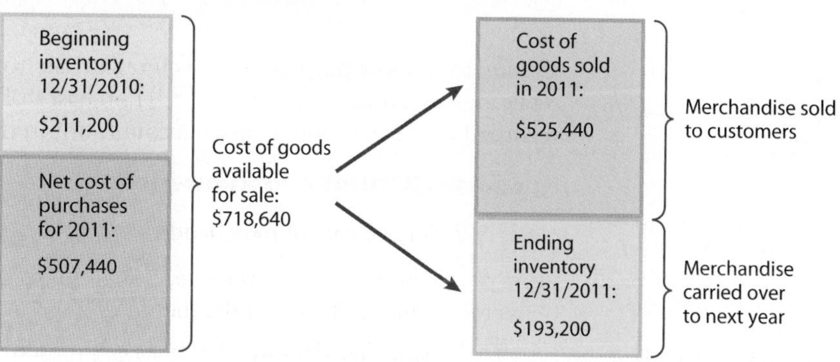

Purchases of Merchandise

STUDY NOTE: Purchases and Purchases Returns and Allowances accounts are used only in a periodic inventory system.

Exhibit 5.8 shows how transactions involving purchases of merchandise are recorded under the periodic inventory system. A primary difference between the perpetual and periodic inventory systems is that in the perpetual inventory system, the Merchandise Inventory account is adjusted each time a purchase, a sale, or another inventory transaction occurs, whereas in the periodic inventory system, the Merchandise Inventory account stays at its beginning balance until the physical inventory is recorded at the end of the period. The periodic system uses a Purchases account to accumulate purchases during an accounting period and a Purchases Returns and Allowances account to accumulate returns of and allowances on purchases.

The following examples show how Wagon Sportswear Corporation would record purchase transactions under the periodic inventory system.

EXHIBIT 5.8
Recording Purchase Transactions Under the Periodic Inventory System

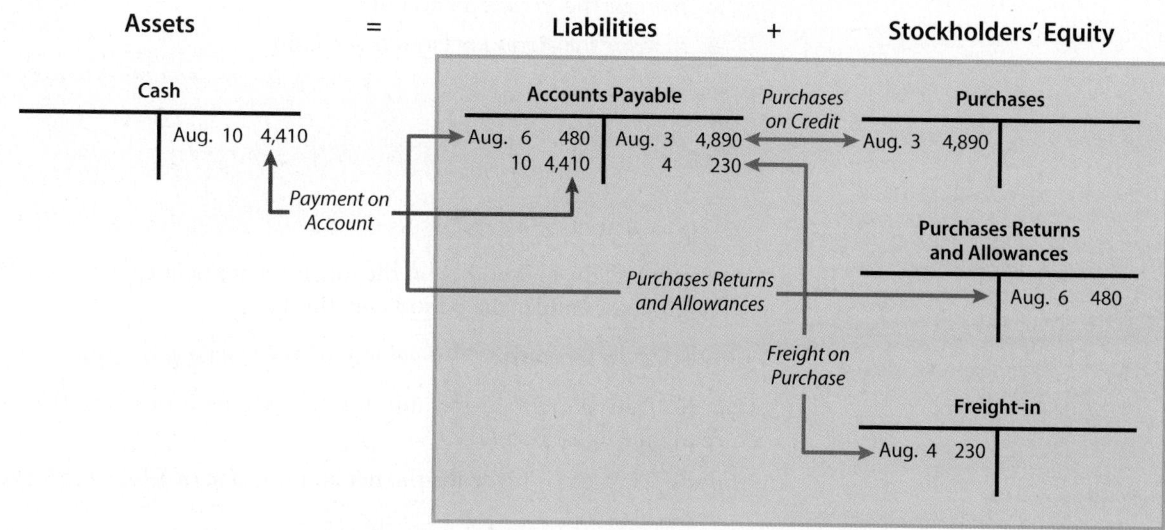

Purchases on Credit

Aug. 3: Received merchandise purchased on credit, invoice dated August 1, terms n/10, $4,890.

Analysis: Under the periodic inventory system, the cost of merchandise is recorded in the **Purchases account** at the time of purchase. This account is a temporary one used only with the periodic inventory system. The Purchases account does not indicate whether merchandise has been sold or is still on hand. Purchases made by a company

- ▲ *increase* the *Purchases* account and
- ▲ *increase* the *Accounts Payable* account.

Journal Entry:

Aug. 3	Purchases	4,890	
	Accounts Payable		4,890
	Purchases on credit		

Comment: Its sole purpose is to accumulate the total cost of merchandise purchased for resale during an accounting period. (Purchases of other assets, such as equipment, are recorded in the appropriate asset account, not in the Purchases account.)

Purchases Returns and Allowances

Aug. 6: Returned part of merchandise received on August 3 for credit, $480.

Analysis: This is a contra-purchases account with a normal credit balance, and it is deducted from purchases on the income statement to arrive at net purchases, which

- ▼ *decreases* the *Accounts Payable* account and
- ▲ *increases* the *Purchases Returns and Allowances* account.

STUDY NOTE: *Because debits establish the Purchases account, credits create its contra account, Purchases Returns and Allowances.*

Journal Entry:

Aug. 6	Accounts Payable	480	
	Purchases Returns and Allowances		480
	Returned merchandise from purchase		

Comment: Under the periodic inventory system, the amount of a return or an allowance is recorded in the **Purchases Returns and Allowances account**.

Freight-in

Aug. 7: Received a bill for freight costs of the purchases on Aug. 3, $230.

Analysis: Freight costs on purchases

- ▲ *increase* the *Freight-in* account
- ▲ *increase* the *Accounts Payable* account.

Journal Entry:

Aug. 7	Freight-in	230	
	Accounts Payable		230
	Freight costs on Aug.3 purchase		

Comment: Freight-in is added on the income statement to net purchases to arrive at net cost of purchases under the periodic method.

Payments on Account

Aug. 10: Paid amount in full due for the purchase of August 3, part of which was returned on August 6, $4,410.

Analysis: Payment is made for the net amount due of $4,410 ($4,890 − $480), which

▼ *decreases* the *Accounts Payable* account and
▼ *decreases* the *Cash* account.

Journal Entry:

Aug. 10	Accounts Payable	4,410	
	Cash		4,410
	Made payment on account		

Sales of Merchandise

EXHIBIT 5.9
Recording Sales Transactions Under the Periodic Inventory System

Exhibit 5.9 shows how transactions involving sales of merchandise are recorded under the periodic inventory system.

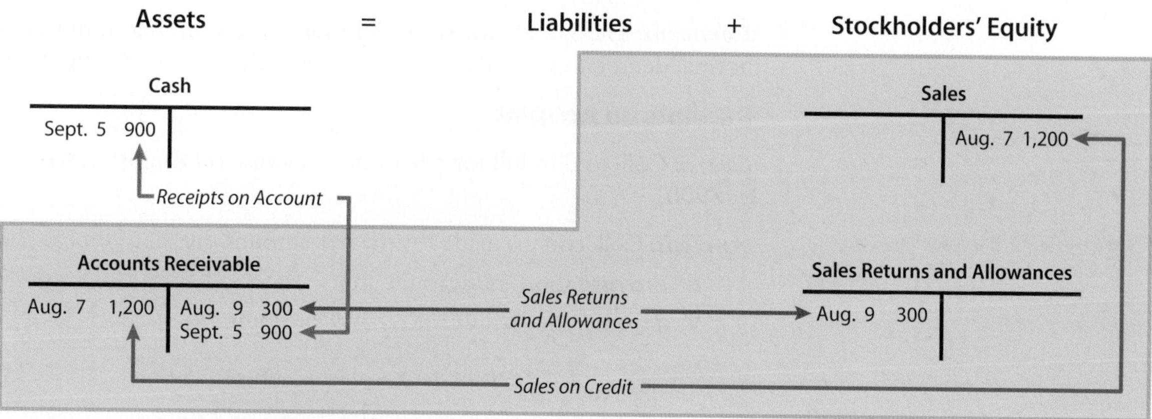

Sales on Credit

Aug. 7: Sold merchandise on credit, terms n/30, FOB destination, $1,200; the cost of the merchandise was $720.

Analysis: As shown in Exhibit 5.9, under the periodic inventory system, sales require only one entry, which

▲ *increases* the *Accounts Receivable* account and
▲ *increases* the *Sales* account.

Journal Entry:

Aug. 7	Accounts Receivable	1,200	
	Sales		1,200
	Sold merchandise on credit		

Comment: In the case of cash sales, Cash rather than Accounts Receivable is debited for the amount of the sale. If the seller pays for the shipping, the amount should be debited to Delivery Expense.

iStock Photo

Focus on Business Practice

Are Sales Returns Worth Accounting For?

Some industries routinely have a high percentage of sales returns. More than 6 percent of all nonfood items sold in stores are eventually returned to vendors. This amounts to over $100 billion a year, or more than the gross national product of two-thirds of the world's nations.[7] Book publishers like **Simon & Schuster** often have returns as high as 30 to 50 percent because to gain the attention of potential buyers, they must distribute large numbers of copies to many outlets. Magazine publishers like **AOL Time Warner** expect to sell no more than 35 to 38 percent of the magazines they send to newsstands and other outlets.[8] In all these businesses, it pays management to scrutinize the Sales Returns and Allowances account for ways to reduce returns and increase profitability.

Sales Returns and Allowances

Aug. 9: Accepted return of part of merchandise sold on August 7 for full credit and returned it to merchandise inventory, $300; the cost of the merchandise was $180.

Analysis: Under the periodic inventory system, when a seller allows the buyer to return all or part of a sale or gives an allowance, only one entry is needed, which

▲ *increases* the *Sales Returns and Allowances* account and

▼ *decreases* the *Accounts Receivable* account.

Journal Entry:

Aug. 9	Sales Returns and Allowances	300	
	Accounts Receivable		300
	Accepted return of merchandise		

Comment: The Sales Returns and Allowances account is a contra-revenue account with a normal debit balance and is deducted from sales on the income statement.

Receipts on Account

Sept. 5: Collected in full for sale of merchandise on August 7, less the return on August 9, $900.

Analysis: Collection is made for the net amount due of $900 ($1,200 − $300), which

▲ *increases* the *Cash* account and

▼ *decreases* the *Accounts Receivable* account.

Journal Entry:

Sept. 5	Cash	900	
	Accounts Receivable		900
	Received on account		

Stop & Apply

The numbered items below are account titles, and the lettered items that follow are types of merchandising transactions. For each transaction, indicate which accounts are debited or credited by placing the account numbers in the appropriate columns, assuming use of a periodic inventory system.

1. Cash
2. Accounts Receivable
3. Merchandise Inventory
4. Accounts Payable
5. Sales
6. Sales Returns and Allowances
7. Purchases
8. Purchases Returns and Allowances

	Account Debited	Account Credited		Account Debited	Account Credited
a. Purchase on credit	___	___	e. Sale for cash	___	___
b. Purchase return for credit	___	___	f. Sales return for credit	___	___
c. Purchase for cash	___	___	g. Payment on account	___	___
d. Sale on credit	___	___	h. Receipt on account	___	___

SOLUTION

	Account Debited	Account Credited		Account Debited	Account Credited
a. Purchase on credit	7	4	e. Sale for cash	1	5
b. Purchase return for credit	4	8	f. Sales return for credit	6	2
c. Purchase for cash	7	1	g. Payment on account	4	1
d. Sale on credit	2	5	h. Receipt on account	1	2

INTERNAL CONTROL: COMPONENTS, ACTIVITIES, AND LIMITATIONS

LO 5 Describe the components of internal control, control activities, and limitations on internal control.

As mentioned earlier, if a merchandising company does not take steps to protect its assets, it can suffer high losses of cash and inventory through embezzlement and theft. To avoid them, management must set up and maintain a good system of internal control.

STUDY NOTE: *The components of internal control are equally important to manual and computerized accounting systems.*

Components of Internal Control

An effective system of internal control has the following five interrelated components:[9]

- ***Control environment:*** The **control environment** is created by management's overall attitude, awareness, and actions. It encompasses a company's ethics, philosophy and operating style, organizational structure, method of assigning authority and responsibility, and personnel policies and practices. Personnel should be qualified to handle responsibilities, meaning that they must be trained and informed about what is expected of them. For example, the manager of a retail store should train employees to follow prescribed procedures for handling cash sales, credit card sales, and returns and refunds.
- ***Risk Assessment:*** This component involves identifying areas in which risks of loss of assets or inaccuracies in accounting records are high so that adequate controls can be implemented for **risk assessment**. Among the greater risks in a retail store are that employees may steal cash and customers may steal goods.
- ***Information and Communication:*** **Information and communication** pertains to the accounting system established by management—to the way the system gathers and treats information about the company's transactions and to how it communicates individual responsibilities within the system. Employees must understand exactly what their functions are.
- ***Control Activities:*** The policies and procedures management puts in place to see that its directives are carried out are called **control activities**.
- ***Monitoring:*** Management's regular assessment of the quality of internal control, including periodic review of compliance with all policies and procedures, is part of **monitoring**. Large companies often have a staff of internal auditors who review the company's system of internal control to determine if it is working properly and if procedures are being followed. In smaller businesses, owners and managers conduct these reviews.

Control Activities

Control activities are a very important way of implementing internal control. The goal of these activities is to safeguard a company's assets and ensure the reliability of its accounting records.

Focus on Business Practice

Which Frauds Are Most Common?

The frauds commonly facing retailers are credit card fraud, check fraud, false invoices and phantom vendors, and expense account abuse. The most common reasons for the occurrences of these frauds were poor internal controls, management override of internal controls, and collusion. The most common methods of detecting them were notification by an employee, internal controls, internal auditor review, notification by a customer, and accidental discovery. Companies that are successful in preventing fraud have a good system of internal control, a formal code of ethics, and a program to monitor compliance that includes a system for reporting incidents of fraud. These companies routinely communicate the existence of the program to their employees.[10]

iStock Photo

Control activities include the following:

- ***Authorization:*** **Authorization** means the approval of certain transactions and activities. In a retail store, for example, cashiers customarily authorize cash sales, but other transactions, such as issuing a refund, may require a manager's approval.
- ***Recording transactions:*** To establish accountability for assets, all transactions should be recorded. For example, if a retail store uses a cash register that records sales, refunds, and other transactions on a paper tape or computer disk, the cashier can be held accountable for the cash received and the merchandise removed during his or her shift.
- ***Documents and records:*** Well-designed documents help ensure that transactions are properly recorded. For example, using prenumbered invoices is a way of ensuring that all sales transactions are recorded.
- ***Physical controls:*** **Physical controls** are controls that limit access to assets. For example, in a retail store, only the person responsible for the cash register should have access to it. Other employees should not be able to open the cash drawer when the cashier is not present. Similarly, only authorized personnel should have access to warehouses, storerooms, and accounting records, including those stored in company computers.
- ***Periodic independent verification:*** **Periodic independent verification** means that someone other than the persons responsible for the accounting records and assets should periodically check the records against the assets. For example, at the end of each shift or day in a retail store, the owner or manager should count the cash in the cash drawer and compare the amount with the amount recorded on the tape or computer disk in the cash register. Other examples of independent verification are periodic counts of physical inventory and reconciliations of monthly bank statements.
- ***Separation of duties:*** **Separation of duties** means that no one person should authorize transactions, handle assets, or keep records of assets. For example, in a well-managed electronics store, each employee oversees only a single part of a transaction. A sales employee takes the order and creates an invoice. Another employee receives the customer's cash or credit card payment and issues a receipt. Once the customer has a receipt, and only then, a third employee obtains the item from the warehouse and gives it to the customer. A person in the accounting department subsequently compares all sales recorded on the tape or disk in the cash register with the sales invoices and updates the inventory in the accounting records. The separation of duties means that a mistake, careless or not, cannot be made without being seen by at least one other person.
- ***Sound personnel practices:*** Personnel practices that promote internal control include adequate supervision, rotation of key people among different jobs, insistence that employees take vacations, and bonding of personnel who handle cash or inventory. **Bonding** is the process of carefully checking an employee's background and insuring the company against theft by that person. Bonding does not guarantee against theft, but it does prevent or reduce loss if theft occurs. Prudent personnel practices help ensure that employees know their jobs, are honest, and will find it difficult to carry out and conceal embezzlement over time.

Limitations on Internal Control

STUDY NOTE: *While no control procedure guarantees the prevention of theft, the more that are in place, the less likely it is that theft will occur.*

No system of internal control is without weaknesses. As long as people perform control procedures, an internal control system will be vulnerable to human error. Errors can arise from misunderstandings, mistakes in judgment, carelessness, distraction, or fatigue. Separation of duties can be defeated through collusion by employees who secretly agree to deceive a company. In addition, established procedures may be ineffective against employees' errors or dishonesty, and controls that were initially effective may become ineffective when conditions change.

In some cases, the costs of establishing and maintaining elaborate control systems may exceed the benefits. In a small business, for example, active involvement on the part of the owner can be a practical substitute for the separation of some duties.

Stop & Apply

Match the internal control components on the right with the related statements on the left.

____ 1. Establishes separation of duties		a. Control environment
____ 2. Communicates appropriate information to employees		b. Risk assessment
____ 3. Has an internal audit department		c. Information and communication
____ 4. Performs periodic independent verification of employees' work		d. Control activities
____ 5. Assesses the possibility of losses		e. Monitoring
____ 6. Instructs and trains employees		
____ 7. Has well-designed documents and records		
____ 8. Limits physical access to authorized personnel		

iStock Photo

SOLUTION 1. d; 2. c; 3. e; 4. d; 5. b; 6. a; 7. d; 8. d

INTERNAL CONTROL OVER MERCHANDISING TRANSACTIONS

LO 6 Apply internal control activities to common merchandising transactions.

Sound internal control activities are needed in all aspects of a business, but particularly when assets are involved. Assets are especially vulnerable when they enter and leave a business. When sales are made, for example, cash or other assets enter the business, and goods or services leave. Controls must be set up to prevent theft during those transactions. Purchases of assets and payments of liabilities must also be controlled; adequate purchasing and payment systems can safeguard most such transactions. In addition, assets on hand, such as cash, investments, inventory, plant, and equipment, must be protected.

In this section of the text, you will see how merchandising companies apply internal control activities to such transactions as cash sales, receipts, purchases, and cash payments. Service and manufacturing businesses use similar procedures.

Internal Control and Management Goals

When a system of internal control is applied effectively to merchandising transactions, it can achieve important management goals. As we have noted, it can prevent losses of cash and inventory due to theft or fraud, and it can ensure that records of transactions and account balances are accurate. It can also help managers achieve the following three broader goals:

- Keep enough inventory on hand to sell to customers without overstocking merchandise.
- Keep sufficient cash on hand to pay for purchases in time to receive discounts.
- Keep credit losses as low as possible by making credit sales only to customers who are likely to pay on time.

STUDY NOTE: *Maintaining internal control is especially difficult for a merchandiser like* **Best Buy**. *Management must not only establish controls for cash sales, receipts, purchases, and cash payments, but also protect its inventory.*

One control that managers use to meet these broad goals is the cash budget, which projects future cash receipts and disbursements. By maintaining adequate cash balances, a company is able to take advantage of discounts on purchases, prepare to borrow money when necessary, and avoid the damaging effects of being unable to pay bills when they are due. By investing excess cash, the company can earn interest until the cash is needed.

A more specific control is the separation of duties that involve the handling of cash. Such separation makes theft without detection extremely unlikely unless two or more employees conspire. The separation of duties is easier in large businesses than in small ones, where one person may have to carry out several duties. The effectiveness of internal control over cash varies, based on the size and nature of the company. Most firms, however, should use the following procedures:

- Separate the functions of authorization, recordkeeping, and custodianship of cash.
- Limit the number of people who have access to cash and designate who those people are.
- Bond all employees who have access to cash.

- Keep the amount of cash on hand to a minimum by using banking facilities as much as possible.
- Physically protect cash on hand by using cash registers, cashiers' cages, and safes.
- Record and deposit all cash receipts promptly and make payments by check rather than by currency.
- Have a person who does not handle or record cash make unannounced audits of the cash on hand.
- Have a person who does not authorize, handle, or record cash transactions reconcile the Cash account each month.

Notice that each of these procedures helps safeguard cash by making it more difficult for any one individual who has access to cash to steal or misuse it without being detected.

Control of Cash Receipts

Cash payments for sales of goods and services can be received by mail or over the counter in the form of checks, credit or debit cards, or currency. Whatever the source of the payments, cash should be recorded immediately upon receipt. Such a journal establishes a written record of cash receipts that should prevent errors and make theft more difficult.

Control of Cash Received by Mail Cash received by mail is vulnerable to theft by the employees who handle it. For that reason, companies that deal in mail-order sales generally ask customers to pay by credit card, check, or money order instead of with currency.

When cash is received in the mail, two or more employees should handle it. The employee who opens the mail should make a list in triplicate of the money received. The list should contain each payer's name, the purpose for which the money was sent, and the amount. One copy goes with the cash to the cashier, who deposits the money. The second copy goes to the accounting department for recording. The person who opens the mail keeps the third copy. Errors can be easily caught because the amount deposited by the cashier must agree with the amount received and the amount recorded in the cash receipts journal.

STUDY NOTE: *The cashier should not be allowed to remove the cash register tape or to record the day's cash receipts.*

Control of Cash Received over the Counter Cash registers and prenumbered sales tickets are common tools for controlling cash received over the counter. The amount of a cash sale is rung up on the cash register at the time of the sale. The register should be placed so that the customer can see the amount recorded. Each cash register should have a locked-in tape on which it prints the day's transactions. At the end of the day, the cashier counts the cash in the register and turns it in to the cashier's office. Another employee takes the tape out of the cash register and records the cash receipts for the day in the cash receipts journal. The amount of cash turned in and the amount recorded on the tape should agree; if not, any differences must be explained.

Large retail chains like **Best Buy** commonly monitor cash receipts by having each cash register tied directly into a computer that records each transaction as it occurs. Whether the elements are performed manually or by computer, separating responsibility for cash receipts, cash deposits, and recordkeeping is necessary to ensure good internal control.

Focus on Business Practice

How Do Computers Promote Internal Control?

Building good internal controls into accounting programs is a difficult challenge for computer programmers. These programs must include controls that prevent unintentional errors, as well as unauthorized access and tampering. They prevent errors through reasonableness checks (such as not allowing any transactions over a specified amount), mathematical checks that verify the arithmetic of transactions, and sequence checks that require documents and transactions to be in proper order. They typically use passwords and questions about randomly selected personal data to prevent unauthorized access to computer records. They may also use firewalls, which are strong electronic barriers to unauthorized access, and data encryption, which is a way of coding data so that if they are stolen, they are useless to the thief.

iStock Photo

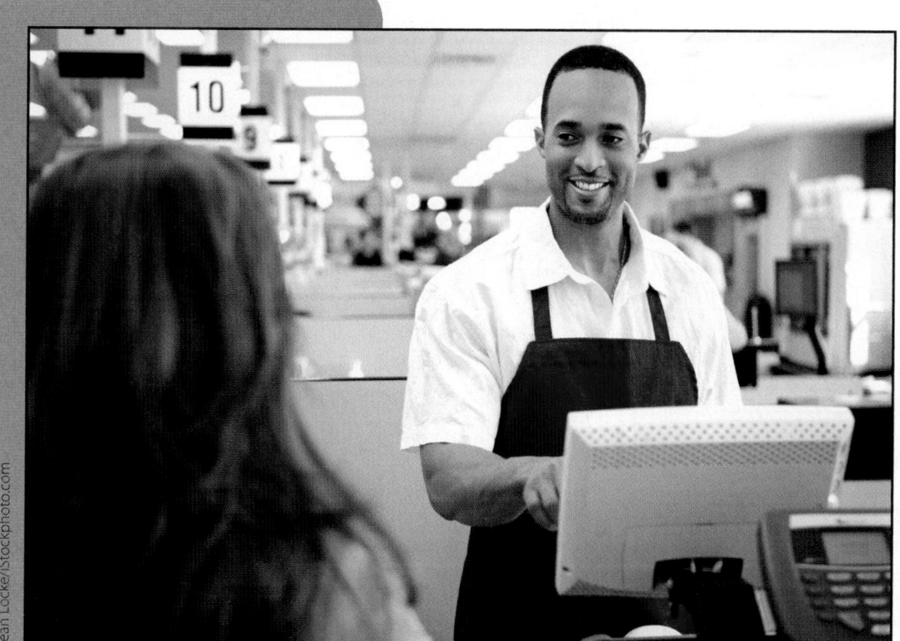

The cashier should not be allowed to remove the cash register tape or to record the day's cash receipts.

In some stores, internal control is further strengthened by the use of prenumbered sales tickets and a central cash register or cashier's office, where all sales are rung up and collected by a person who does not participate in the sale. The salesperson completes a prenumbered sales ticket at the time of the sale, giving one copy to the customer and keeping a copy. At the end of the day, all sales tickets must be accounted for, and the sales total computed from the sales tickets must equal the total sales recorded on the cash register.

Control of Purchases and Cash Disbursements

Cash disbursements are particularly vulnerable to fraud and embezzlement. In one case, the treasurer of one of the nation's largest jewelry retailers was charged with having stolen over $500,000 by systematically overpaying the company's federal income taxes and keeping the refund checks as they came back to the company.

To avoid this type of theft, cash payments should be made only after they have been specifically authorized and supported by documents that establish the validity and amount of the claims. A company should also separate the duties involved in purchasing goods and services and the duties involved in paying for them. The degree of separation that is possible varies, depending on the size of the business.

Exhibit 5.10 shows how a large company can maximize the separation of duties. Five internal units (the requesting department, the purchasing department, the accounting department, the receiving department, and the treasurer) and two firms outside the company (the vendor and the bank) play a role in this control plan. Notice that business documents are crucial components of the plan.

Exhibit 5.11 (pp. 268–269) illustrates the typical sequence in which documents are used in a company's internal control plan for purchases and cash disbursements.

As shown in Exhibit 5.11, every action is documented and verified by at least one other person. Thus, the requesting department cannot work out a kickback scheme to make

EXHIBIT 5.10
Internal Controls in a Large Company: Separation of Duties and Documentation

STUDY NOTE: Every business document must have a number for purposes of reference.

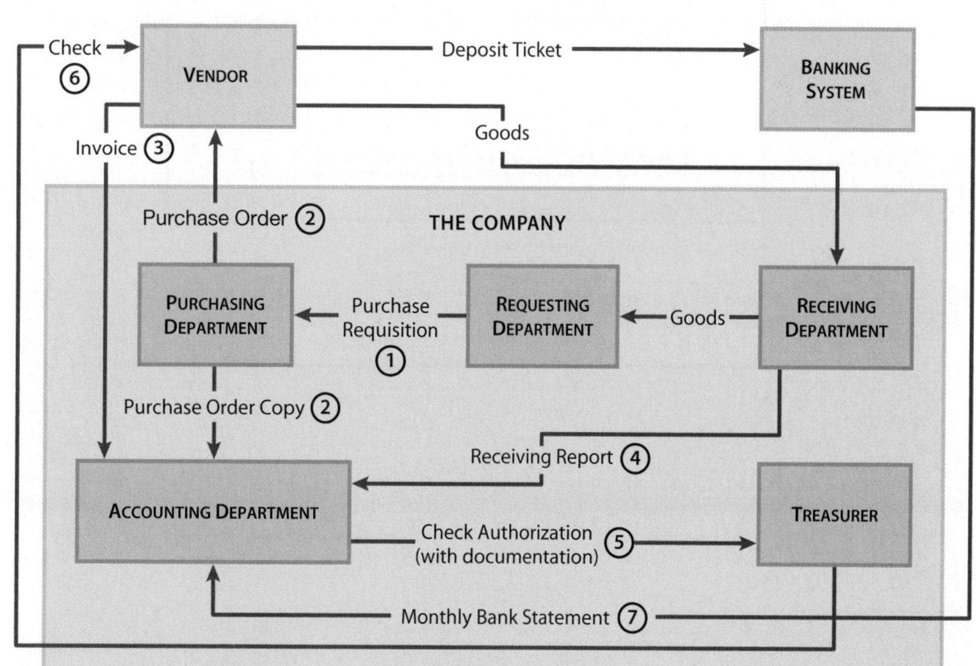

Note: Circled numbers refer to documents in Figure 5-11.

EXHIBIT 5.11
Internal Control Plan for Purchases and Cash Disbursements

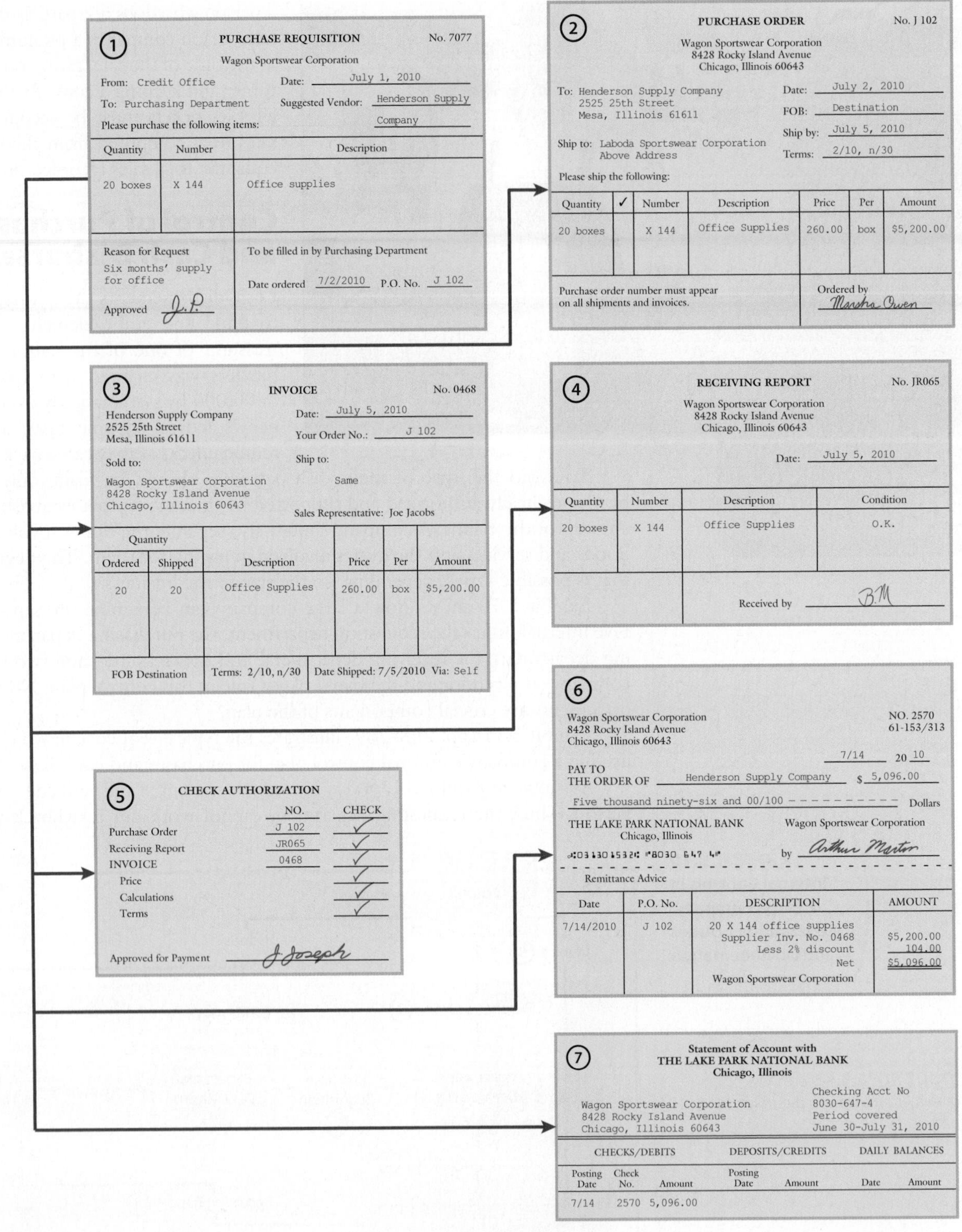

① **PURCHASE REQUISITION** No. 7077
Wagon Sportswear Corporation

From: Credit Office — Date: July 1, 2010
To: Purchasing Department — Suggested Vendor: Henderson Supply Company
Please purchase the following items:

Quantity	Number	Description
20 boxes	X 144	Office supplies

Reason for Request: Six months' supply for office
To be filled in by Purchasing Department
Date ordered 7/2/2010 P.O. No. J 102
Approved J.P.

② **PURCHASE ORDER** No. J 102
Wagon Sportswear Corporation
8428 Rocky Island Avenue
Chicago, Illinois 60643

To: Henderson Supply Company
2525 25th Street
Mesa, Illinois 61611
Date: July 2, 2010
FOB: Destination
Ship by: July 5, 2010
Terms: 2/10, n/30
Ship to: Laboda Sportswear Corporation
Above Address
Please ship the following:

Quantity	✓	Number	Description	Price	Per	Amount
20 boxes		X 144	Office Supplies	260.00	box	$5,200.00

Purchase order number must appear on all shipments and invoices.
Ordered by Marsha Owen

③ **INVOICE** No. 0468
Henderson Supply Company
2525 25th Street
Mesa, Illinois 61611
Date: July 5, 2010
Your Order No.: J 102
Sold to:
Wagon Sportswear Corporation
8428 Rocky Island Avenue
Chicago, Illinois 60643
Ship to: Same
Sales Representative: Joe Jacobs

Quantity		Description	Price	Per	Amount
Ordered	Shipped				
20	20	Office Supplies	260.00	box	$5,200.00

FOB Destination — Terms: 2/10, n/30 — Date Shipped: 7/5/2010 Via: Self

④ **RECEIVING REPORT** No. JR065
Wagon Sportswear Corporation
8428 Rocky Island Avenue
Chicago, Illinois 60643
Date: July 5, 2010

Quantity	Number	Description	Condition
20 boxes	X 144	Office Supplies	O.K.

Received by B.M.

⑤ **CHECK AUTHORIZATION**

	NO.	CHECK
Purchase Order	J 102	✓
Receiving Report	JR065	✓
INVOICE	0468	✓
Price		✓
Calculations		✓
Terms		✓

Approved for Payment J Joseph

⑥ Wagon Sportswear Corporation
8428 Rocky Island Avenue
Chicago, Illinois 60643
NO. 2570
61-153/313
7/14 20 10
PAY TO THE ORDER OF Henderson Supply Company $ 5,096.00
Five thousand ninety-six and 00/100 Dollars
THE LAKE PARK NATIONAL BANK
Chicago, Illinois
Wagon Sportswear Corporation
by Arthur Martin
⑆031301532⑆ ⑈8030 647 4⑈

Remittance Advice

Date	P.O. No.	DESCRIPTION	AMOUNT
7/14/2010	J 102	20 X 144 office supplies Supplier Inv. No. 0468 Less 2% discount Net	 $5,200.00 104.00 $5,096.00
		Wagon Sportswear Corporation	

⑦ **Statement of Account with**
THE LAKE PARK NATIONAL BANK
Chicago, Illinois

Wagon Sportswear Corporation
8428 Rocky Island Avenue
Chicago, Illinois 60643
Checking Acct No 8030-647-4
Period covered June 30-July 31, 2010

CHECKS/DEBITS			DEPOSITS/CREDITS		DAILY BALANCES	
Posting Date	Check No.	Amount	Posting Date	Amount	Date	Amount
7/14	2570	5,096.00				

Business Document	Description	Prepared by	Sent to	Verification and Related Procedures
(1) Purchase requisition	To begin, the credit office (requesting department) of Wagon Sportswear Corporation fills out a formal request for a purchase, or **purchase requisition**, for office supplies. The head of the requesting department approves it and forwards it to the purchasing department.	Requesting department	Purchasing department	Purchasing verifies authorization.
(2) Purchase order	The people in the purchasing department prepare a **purchase order**. The purchase order indicates that Wagon Sportswear will not pay any bill that does not include a purchase order number. The purchase order is addressed to the vendor (seller) and contains a description of the quantity and type of items ordered, the expected price, the shipping date and terms, and other instructions.	Purchasing department	Vendor	Vendor sends goods or services in accordance with purchase order.
(3) Invoice	After receiving the purchase order, the vendor, Henderson Supply Company, ships the goods and sends an **invoice** to Wagon Sportswear. The invoice shows the quantity of goods delivered, describes what they are, and lists the price and terms of payment. If all the goods cannot be shipped immediately, the invoice indicates the estimated date of shipment for the remaining goods.	Vendor	Accounting department	Accounting receives invoice from vendor.
(4) Receiving report	When the goods reach Wagon Sportswear's receiving department, an employee notes the quantity, type of goods, and their condition on a **receiving report**. The receiving department does not receive a copy of the purchase order or the invoice, so its employees don't know what should be received or its value. Thus, they are not tempted to steal any excess that may be delivered.	Receiving department	Accounting department	Accounting compares invoice, purchase order, and receiving report. Accounting verifies prices.
(5) Check authorization	The receiving report goes to the accounting department, where it is compared to the purchase order and the invoice. If everything is correct, the accounting department completes a **check authorization** and attaches it to the three supporting documents. The check authorization form shown in Exhibit 5.11 has a space for each item to be checked off as it is examined. Notice that the accounting department has all the documentary evidence for the transaction, but it does not have access to the assets purchased, nor does it write the check for payment. Thus, the people doing the accounting cannot conceal fraud by falsifying documents.	Accounting department	Treasurer	Accounting attaches check authorization to invoice, purchase order, and receiving report.
(6) Check	The treasurer examines all the documents. If the treasurer approves them, he or she signs or authorizes an electronic **check**, which is an authorization for the bank to pay the vendor in the amount of the invoice less any applicable discount. The check is then sent to the vendor or the vendor's bank, with a remittance advice showing what the check is for. A vendor that is not paid the proper amount will complain, of course, thus providing a form of outside control over the payment.	Treasurer	Vendor	Treasurer verifies all documents before preparing check.
(7) Bank statement	The vendor deposits the check in its bank, and the canceled check appears in Wagon Sportswear's monthly **bank statement**, which may be in either paper or electronic form. If the treasurer has made the check out for the wrong amount (or altered an amount that was already filled in), the problem will show up in the company's bank reconciliation.	Buyer's bank	Accounting department	Accounting compares amount and payee's name on returned check with check authorization.

illegal payments to the vendor because the receiving department independently records receipts and the accounting department verifies prices. The receiving department cannot steal goods because the receiving report must equal the invoice. For the same reason, the vendor cannot bill for more goods than it ships. The treasurer verifies the accounting department's work, and the accounting department ultimately checks the treasurer's work.

The system we have described is a simple one that provides adequate internal control. There are many variations on it.

Stop & Apply

Items (a)–(e) below are a company's departments. Items (f) and (g) are firms with which the company has transactions.

a. Requesting department
b. Purchasing department
c. Receiving department
d. Accounting department
e. Treasurer
f. Vendor
g. Bank

Use the letter of the department or firm to indicate which one prepares and sends the following business documents:

	Prepared by	Received by
1. Receiving report	___	___
2. Purchase order	___	___
3. Purchase requisition	___	___
4. Check	___	___
5. Invoice	___	___
6. Check authorization	___	___
7. Bank statement	___	___

SOLUTION

	Prepared by	Received by
1. Receiving report	c	d
2. Purchase order	b	f
3. Purchase requisition	a	b
4. Check	e	f
5. Invoice	f	d
6. Check authorization	d	e
7. Bank statement	g	d

iStock Photo

A look back at ▸ Best Buy Co., Inc.

In this chapter's Decision Point, we noted that **Best Buy**'s managers face many challenges. To ensure the company's success, they must address the following questions:

1. How can Best Buy efficiently manage its cycle of merchandising operations?
2. How should merchandising transactions be recorded to reflect the company's performance?
3. How can the company maintain control over its merchandising operations?

Best Buy is a very efficiently run organization as reflected by its operating cycle. It sells its inventory every 50 days on average and has few receivables. The Financial Highlights at the beginning of the chapter also demonstrate operating efficiency. They show that Best Buy's operating expenses increased by 8.7 percent, which is less than the increase of 10.4 percent in net revenue and the increase of 10.6 percent in gross margin. Because operating expenses grew slower than gross margin, Best Buy's operating income increased by 19.5 percent.

By buying and selling merchandise in bulk, providing limited service, and keeping its financing period to a minimum, Best Buy is able to offer its customers low prices. A comparison of gross margin with net revenue in fiscal year 2010 shows that Best Buy made 24.5 percent ($12,160 ÷ $49,694) of operating income on each dollar of sales.

To sell for less and still make a profit, Best Buy must have a system of recording sales and purchase transactions that accurately reflects its financial performance. It must also maintain a system of internal control that will not only ensure that these transactions are properly recorded, but also protect the company's assets.[11]

Review Problem

Merchandising Transactions: Perpetual and Periodic Inventory Systems

Gawlak Company engaged in the following transactions during July:

July 1 Sold merchandise to Hans Schmitt on credit, terms n/30, FOB shipping point, $2,100 (cost, $1,260).
2 Purchased merchandise on credit from Mango Company, terms n/30, FOB shipping point, $3,800.
2 Paid Custom Freight $290 for freight charges on merchandise received.
9 Purchased merchandise on credit from ABR Company, terms n/30, FOB shipping point, $3,600, including $200 freight costs paid by ABR Company.
11 Accepted from Hans Schmitt a return of merchandise, which was returned to inventory, $300 (cost, $180).
14 Returned for credit $600 of merchandise purchased on July 2.
16 Sold merchandise for cash, $1,000 (cost, $600).
22 Paid Mango Company for purchase of July 2 less return on July 14.
23 Received full payment from Hans Schmitt for his July 1 purchase, less return on July 11.

Required

1. Prepare journal entries for these transactions, assuming Gawlak Company uses the perpetual inventory system.
2. Prepare journal entries for these transactions, assuming Gawlak Company uses the periodic inventory system.

ANSWERS TO REVIEW PROBLEM

Accounts that differ under the two systems are shown in blue.

	A	B	C–F	G	H	J–L	M	N
1			**1. Perpetual Inventory System**			**2. Periodic Inventory System**		
2	July	1	Accounts Receivable	2,100		Accounts Receivable	2,100	
3			Sales		2,100	Sales		2,100
4			Sold merchandise on			Sold merchandise on		
5			account to Hans Schmitt,			account to Hans Schmitt,		
6			terms n/30, FOB shipping			terms n/30. FOB shipping		
7			point			point		
8		1	Cost of Goods Sold	1,260				
9			Merchandise Inventory		1,260			
10			Transferred cost of					
11			merchandise sold to Cost					
12			of Goods Sold account					
13		2	Merchandise Inventory	3,800		Purchases	3,800	
14			Accounts Payable		3,800	Accounts Payable		3,800
15			Purchased merchandise			Purchased merchandise		
16			on account from Mango			on account from Mango		
17			Company, terms n/30, FOB			Company, terms n/30, FOB		
18			shipping point			shipping point		
19		2	Freight-In	290		Freight-In	290	
20			Cash		290	Cash		290
21			Paid freight on previous			Paid freight on previous		
22			purchase			purchase		
23		9	Merchandise Inventory	3,400		Purchases	3,400	
24			Freight-In	200		Freight-In	200	
25			Accounts Payable		3,600	Accounts Payable		3,600
26			Purchased merchandise on			Purchased merchandise on		
27			account from ABR Company			account from ABR Company		
28			terms n/30, FOB shipping			terms n/30, FOB shipping		
29			point, freight paid by supplier			point, freight paid by supplier		

(continued)

	A	B	C	D	E	F	G	H	I	J	K	L	M	N
1						**1. Perpetual Inventory System**						**2. Periodic Inventory System**		
2	July	11	Sales Returns and Allowances				300			Sales Returns and Allowances			300	
3				Accounts Receivable				300			Accounts Receivable			300
4					Accepted return of							Accepted return of		
5					merchandise from Hans							merchandise from Hans		
6					Schmitt							Schmitt		
7		11	Merchandise Inventory				180							
8				Cost of Goods Sold				180						
9					Transferred cost of									
10					merchandise returned to									
11					Merchandise Inventory									
12					account									
13		14	Accounts Payable				600			Accounts Payable			600	
14				Merchandise Inventory				600			Purchases Returns and Allowances			600
15					Returned portion of							Returned portion of		
16					merchandise purchased							merchandise purchased		
17					from Mango Company							from Mango Company		
18		16	Cash				1,000			Cash			1,000	
19				Sales				1,000			Sales			1,000
20					Sold merchandise for cash							Sold merchandise for cash		
21		16	Cost of Goods Sold				600							
22				Merchandise Inventory				600						
23					Transferred cost of									
24					merchandise sold to Cost of									
25					Goods Sold account									
26		22	Accounts Payable				3,200			Accounts Payable			3,200	
27				Cash				3,200			Cash			3,200
28					Made payment on account to							Made payment on account to		
29					Mango Company							Mango Company		
30					$3,800 – $600 = $3,200							$3,800 – $600 = $3,200		
31		23	Cash				1,800			Cash			1,800	
32				Accounts Receivable				1,800			Accounts Receivable			1,800
33					Received payment on							Received payment on		
34					account from Hans Schmitt							account from Hans Schmitt		
35					$2,100 – $300 = $1,800							$2,100 – $300 = $1,800		

Stop & Review

Identify the management issues related to merchandising businesses. **LO1**

Merchandising companies differ from service companies in that they earn income by buying and selling goods. The buying and selling of goods adds to the complexity of the business and raises five issues that management must address. First, a company must have adequate liquidity to pay its bills; working capital and the current ratio are common measures of liquidity. Second, the series of transactions in which merchandising companies engage (the operating cycle) requires careful cash flow management. Third, management must choose whether to use the perpetual or the periodic inventory system. Fourth, if a company has international transactions, it must deal with changing exchange rates. Fifth, management must establish an internal control structure that protects the company's assets—its cash, merchandise inventory, and accounts receivable.

Describe the terms of sale related to merchandising transactions. 

A trade discount is a reduction from a product's list or catalogue price. A sales discount is a discount given for early payment of a sale on credit. Terms of 2/10, n/30 mean that the buyer can take a 2 percent discount if the invoice is paid within 10 days of the invoice date. Otherwise, the buyer is obligated to pay the full amount in 30 days. Discounts on sales are recorded in the Sales Discounts account, and discounts on purchases are recorded in the Purchases Discounts account. FOB shipping point means that the buyer bears the cost of transportation and that title to the goods passes to the buyer at the shipping origin. FOB destination means that the seller bears the cost of transportation and that title does not pass to the buyer until the goods reach their destination. Debit and credit card sales are considered cash sales and involve a fee paid by the seller for convenience.

Prepare an income statement and record merchandising transactions under the perpetual inventory system. LO 3

Under the perpetual inventory system, the Merchandise Inventory account is continuously adjusted by entering purchases, sales, and other inventory transactions as they occur. Purchases increase the Merchandise Inventory account, and purchases returns decrease it. As goods are sold, their cost is transferred from the Merchandise Inventory account to the Cost of Goods Sold account.

Prepare an income statement and record merchandising transactions under the periodic inventory system. LO 4

When the periodic inventory system is used, the cost of goods sold section of the income statement must include the following elements:

Purchases − Purchases Returns and Allowances + Freight-In = Net Cost of Purchases

Beginning Merchandise Inventory + Net Cost of Purchases = Cost of Goods Available for Sale

Cost of Goods Available for Sale − Ending Merchandise Inventory – Cost of Goods Sold

Under the periodic inventory system, the Merchandise Inventory account stays at the beginning level until the physical inventory is recorded at the end of the accounting period. A Purchases account is used to accumulate purchases of merchandise during the accounting period, and a Purchases Returns and Allowances account is used to accumulate returns of purchases and allowances on purchases.

Describe the components of internal control, control activities, and limitations on internal control. LO 5

Internal control consists of all the policies and procedures a company uses to ensure the reliability of financial reporting, compliance with laws and regulations, and the effectiveness and efficiency of operations. Internal control has five components: the control environment, risk assessment, information and communication, control activities, and monitoring. Control activities include having managers authorize certain transactions; recording all transactions to establish accountability for assets; using well-designed documents to ensure proper recording of transactions; instituting physical controls; periodically checking records and assets; separating duties; and using sound personnel practices. A system of internal control relies on the people who implement it. Thus, the effectiveness of internal control is limited by the people involved. Human error, collusion, and failure to recognize changed conditions can contribute to a system's failure.

Apply internal control activities to common merchandising transactions. LO 6

To implement internal control over cash sales, receipts, purchases, and disbursements, the functions of authorization, recordkeeping, and custodianship of cash should be kept separate. The people who have access to cash should be specifically designated and their number limited. Employees who have access to cash should be bonded. The control system should also provide for the use of banking services, physical protection of assets, prompt recording and deposit of cash receipts, and payment by check. A person who does not authorize, handle, or record cash transactions should make unannounced audits of the cash on hand, and the Cash account should be reconciled each month.

Key Terms and Ratios

Authorization 264 (LO5)
Bank statement 269 (LO6)
Bonding 264 (LO5)
Check 269 (LO6)
Check authorization 269 (LO6)
Control activities 263 (LO5)
Control environment 263 (LO5)
Cost of goods available for sale 258 (LO4)
Delivery expense 253 (LO2)
Exchange gain or loss 249 (LO1)
Financing period 247 (LO1)
FOB destination 253 (LO2)
FOB shipping point 253 (LO2)
Freight-in 253 (LO2)
Information and communication 263 (LO5)
Internal controls 250 (LO1)
Invoice 269 (LO6)
Merchandise inventory 246 (LO1)
Merchandising business 246 (LO1)
Monitoring 263 (LO5)
Net purchases 259 (LO4)
Operating cycle 247 (LO1)
Periodic independent verification 264 (LO5)
Periodic inventory system 248 (LO1)
Perpetual inventory system 248 (LO1)
Physical controls 264 (LO5)
Physical inventory 250 (LO1)
Purchase order 269 (LO6)
Purchase requisition 269 (LO6)
Purchases account 260 (LO4)
Purchases discounts 252 (LO2)
Purchases Returns and Allowances account 260 (LO4)
Receiving report 269 (LO6)
Risk assessment 263 (LO5)
Sales discount 252 (LO2)
Sales Returns and Allowances account 257 (LO3)
Separation of duties 264 (LO5)
Trade discount 252 (LO2)
Working capital 246 (LO1)

FINANCIAL RATIO

Current ratio 246 (LO1)

Chapter Assignments Building Your Basic Knowledge and Skills

Short Exercises

LO 1

Identification of Management Issues

SE 1. Identify each of the following decisions as most directly related to (a) liquidity and managing the operating cycle, (b) choice of inventory system, (c) foreign merchandising transactions, or (d) internal controls:

1. Determination of how to protect cash from theft or embezzlement
2. Determination of the effects of changes in exchange rates
3. Determination of policies governing sales of merchandise on credit
4. Determination of whether to use the periodic or the perpetual inventory system

LO 1

Working Capital and Current Ratio

SE 2. Using the following accounts and balances taken from a year-end balance sheet, compute working capital and the current ratio (*Note:* Round to one decimal place.):

Accounts Payable	$ 6,500
Accounts Receivable	5,000
Cash	2,000
Common Stock	10,000
Marketable Securities	1,000
Merchandise Inventory	6,000
Notes Payable in Three Years	6,500
Property, Plant, and Equipment	20,000
Retained Earnings	14,000

LO 1 **Operating Cycle**

SE 3. On average, Mason Company holds its inventory 40 days before it is sold, waits 25 days for customers' payments, and takes 33 days to pay suppliers. For how many days must it provide financing in its operating cycle?

LO 2 **Terms of Sale**

SE 4. A dealer buys tooling machines from a manufacturer and resells them.

a. The manufacturer sets a list or catalogue price of $12,000 for a machine. The manufacturer offers its dealers a 40 percent trade discount.
b. The manufacturer sells the machine under terms of FOB shipping point. The cost of shipping is $700.
c. The manufacturer offers a sales discount of 2/10, n/30. The sales discount does not apply to shipping costs.

What is the net cost of the tooling machine to the dealer, assuming it is paid for within 10 days of purchase?

LO 2 **Sales and Purchases Discounts**

SE 5. On April 15, Peach Company sold merchandise to Orange Company for $2,500 on terms of 2/10, n/30. Assume a return of merchandise on April 20 of $425 and payment in full on April 25. What is the payment by Orange to Peach on April 25?

LO 3 **Purchases of Merchandise: Perpetual Inventory System**

SE 6. Set up T accounts and post each of the following transactions, assuming the perpetual inventory system is used:

Aug. 2 Purchased merchandise on credit from Indio Company, invoice dated August 1, terms n/10, FOB shipping point, $1,150.
3 Received bill from Lee Shipping Company for transportation costs on August 2 shipment, invoice dated August 1, terms n/30, $105.
7 Returned damaged merchandise received from Indio Company on August 2 for credit, $180.
10 Paid in full the amount due to Indio Company for the purchase of August 2, part of which was returned on August 7.

LO 4 **Purchases of Merchandise: Periodic Inventory System**

SE 7. Set up T accounts and post the transactions in **SE 6**, assuming the periodic inventory system is used.

LO 3 **Purchases of Merchandise: Perpetual Inventory System**

SE 8. Set up T accounts and post each of the following transactions, assuming the perpetual inventory system is used:

May 2 Purchased merchandise on credit from Bindu Company, invoice dated May 1, terms n/10, FOB shipping point, $1,725.
3 Received bill from Go Shipping Company for transportation costs on May 2 shipment, invoice dated May 1, terms n/30, $158.
7 Returned damaged merchandise received from Bindu Company on May 2 for credit, $270.
10 Paid in full the amount due to Bindu Company for the purchase of May 2, part of which was returned on May 7.

LO 4 **Purchases of Merchandise: Periodic Inventory System**

SE 9. Set up T accounts and post the transactions in **SE 8**, assuming the periodic inventory system is used.

LO 4

Cost of Goods Sold: Periodic Inventory System

SE 10. Using the following data and assuming cost of goods sold is $273,700, prepare the cost of goods sold section of a merchandising income statement (periodic inventory system). Include the amount of purchases for the month of October.

Freight-in	$13,800
Merchandise inventory, September 30, 2011	37,950
Merchandise inventory, October 31, 2011	50,600
Purchases	?
Purchases returns and allowances	10,350

LO 4

Sales of Merchandise: Periodic Inventory System

SE 11. Set up T accounts and post the following transactions, assuming the periodic inventory system is used:

Aug. 4 Sold merchandise on credit to Jing Corporation, terms n/30, FOB destination, $2,520.
5 Paid transportation costs for sale of August 4, $231.
9 Part of the merchandise sold on August 4 was accepted back from Jing Corporation for full credit and returned to the merchandise inventory, $735.
Sept. 3 Received payment in full from Jing Corporation for merchandise sold on August 4, less the return on August 9.

LO 5, 6

Internal Control Activities

SE 12. Match the following check-writing policies for a small business with the associated control activities:

a. Authorization
b. Recording transactions
c. Documents and records
d. Physical controls
e. Periodic independent verification
f. Separation of duties
g. Sound personnel practices

____ 1. The person who writes the checks to pay bills is different from the people who authorize the payments and keep records of the payments.
____ 2. The checks are kept in a locked drawer. The only person who has the key writes the checks.
____ 3. The person who writes the checks is bonded.
____ 4. Once each month, the owner compares and reconciles the amount of money shown in the accounting records with the amount in the bank account.
____ 5. The owner of the business approves each check before it is mailed.
____ 6. Information pertaining to each check is recorded on the check stub.
____ 7. Every day, all checks are recorded in the accounting records, using the information on the check stubs.

LO 5

Limitations of Internal Control

SE 13. Internal control has several inherent limitations. Indicate whether each of the following situations is an example of (a) human error, (b) collusion among employees, (c) changed conditions, or (d) cost-benefit considerations:

1. Effective separation of duties in a restaurant is impractical because the business is too small.
2. The cashier and the manager of a retail shoe store work together to avoid the internal controls for the purpose of embezzling funds.
3. The cashier in a pizza shop does not understand the procedures for operating the cash register and thus fails to ring up all the sales and count the cash at the end of the day.
4. At a law firm, computer supplies are mistakenly delivered to the reception area instead of the receiving area because the supplier began using a different system of shipment. As a result, the receipt of supplies is not recorded.

Exercises

LO 1, 2

Discussion Questions

E 1. Develop a brief answer to each of the following questions:

1. Can a company have a "negative" financing period?
2. If you sell goods to a company in Europe and the exchange rate for the dollar is declining as it relates to the euro, do you want the eventual payment to be made in dollars or euros?
3. Who has ultimate responsibility for safeguarding a company's assets with a system of internal control?
4. Assume a large shipment of uninsured merchandise to your company is destroyed when the delivery truck has an accident and burns. Would you want the terms to be FOB shipping point or FOB destination?

LO 3, 4, 5, 6

Discussion Questions

E 2. Develop a brief answer to each of the following questions:

1. Under the perpetual inventory system, the Merchandise Inventory account is constantly updated. What would cause it to have the wrong balance?
2. Why is a physical inventory needed under both the periodic and perpetual inventory systems?
3. Which of the following accounts would be assigned a higher level of risk: Building or Merchandise Inventory?
4. Why is it important to write down the amount of cash received through the mail or over the counter?

LO 1

Management Issues and Decisions

E 3. The decisions that follow were made by the management of Walter Cotton Company. Indicate whether each decision pertains primarily to (a) cash flow management, (b) choice of inventory system, (c) foreign transactions, or (d) control of merchandising operations.

1. Decided to mark each item of inventory with a magnetic tag that sets off an alarm if the tag is removed from the store before being deactivated.
2. Decided to reduce the credit terms offered to customers from 30 days to 20 days to speed up collection of accounts.
3. Decided that the benefits of keeping track of each item of inventory as it is bought and sold would exceed the costs of such a system.
4. Decided to purchase goods made by a Chinese supplier.
5. Decided to purchase a new type of cash register that can be operated only by a person who knows a predetermined code.
6. Decided to switch to a new cleaning service that will provide the same service at a lower cost with payment due in 30 days instead of 20 days.

LO 1

Foreign Merchandising Transactions

E 4. King Corporation purchased a machine from Gutten Corporation on credit for €150,000. At the date of purchase, the exchange rate was $1.00 per euro. On the date of the payment, which was made in euros, the value of the euro was $1.25. Did King incur an exchange gain or loss? How much was it?

LO 1

Working Capital and Current Ratio

E 5. The accounts and balances that follow are from the general ledger of Charlton Corporation.

Accounts Payable	$13,280
Accounts Receivable	8,160
Cash	1,200
Current Portion of Long-Term Debt	8,000
Long-Term Investments	16,640
Marketable Securities	10,080
Merchandise Inventory	20,320
Notes Payable (90 days)	12,000
Notes Payable (2 years)	32,000
Notes Receivable (90 days)	20,800
Notes Receivable (2 years)	16,000
Prepaid Insurance	320
Property, Plant, and Equipment	96,000
Property Taxes Payable	1,000
Retained Earnings	45,280
Salaries Payable	680
Supplies	280
Unearned Revenue	600

1. Compute the working capital.
2. Compute the current ratio. (*Note:* Round to 2 decimal places.)

LO 2

Terms of Sale

E 6. A dealer buys aboveground pools from a manufacturer and resells them.

- The manufacturer sets a list or catalogue price of $5,000 for a pool. The manufacturer offers its dealers a 30 percent trade discount.
- The manufacturer sells the machine under terms of FOB destination. The cost of shipping is $480.
- The manufacturer offers a sales discount of 2/10, n/30. Sales discounts do not apply to shipping costs.

What is the net cost of the pool to the dealer, assuming it is paid for within 10 days of purchase?

LO 2, 4

Sales Involving Returns and Discounts: Periodic Inventory System

E 7. Prepare journal entries under the periodic inventory system for the following transactions of Sanford Company and determine the total amount received from Sun Company:

Mar. 1 Sold merchandise on credit to Sun Company, terms 2/10, n/30, FOB shipping point, $2,000.
3 Accepted a return from Sun Company for full credit, $800.
10 Received payment from Sun Company for the sale, less the return and discount.
11 Sold merchandise on credit to Sun Company, terms 2/10, n/30, FOB shipping point, $3,200.
31 Received payment from Sun Company for the sale of March 11.

LO 2, 3

Purchases Involving Returns and Discounts: Perpetual Inventory System

E 8. Milwaukee Company engaged in the following transactions:

July 2 Purchased merchandise on credit from Lucas Company, terms n/20, FOB destination, invoice dated July 1, $2,000.
6 Returned some merchandise to Lucas Company for full credit, $250.
11 Paid Lucas Company for purchase of July 2 less return and discount.
14 Purchased merchandise on credit from Lucas Company, terms n/20, FOB destination, invoice dated July 12, $2,250.
31 Paid amount owed Lucas Company for purchase of July 14.

Prepare journal entries for these transactions, assuming Milwaukee Company uses the perpetual inventory system, and determine the total amount paid to Lucas Company.

LO 3

Preparation of the Income Statement: Perpetual Inventory System

E 9. Using the selected account balances at December 31, 2011, for Parties, Etc. that follow, prepare an income statement for the year ended December 31, 2011. Show detail of net sales. The company uses the perpetual inventory system, and Freight-In has not been included in Cost of Goods Sold.

Account Name	Debit	Credit
Sales		$249,000
Sales Returns and Allowances	$ 11,750	
Cost of Goods Sold	142,000	
Freight-In	7,350	
Selling Expenses	21,500	
General and Administrative Expenses	43,500	
Income Taxes	6,000	

LO 3

Recording Purchases: Perpetual Inventory System

E 10. Prepare T accounts to record each of the following transactions under the perpetual inventory system:

a. Purchased merchandise on credit, terms n/30, FOB shipping point, $5,000.
b. Paid freight on the shipment in transaction **a**, $270.
c. Purchased merchandise on credit, terms n/30, FOB destination, $2,800.
d. Purchased merchandise on credit, terms n/30, FOB shipping point, $5,200, which includes freight paid by the supplier of $400.
e. Returned part of the merchandise purchased in transaction **c**, $1,000.
f. Paid the amount owed on the purchase in transaction **a**.
g. Paid the amount owed on the purchase in transaction **d**.
h. Paid the amount owed on the purchase in transaction **c** less the return in **e**.

LO 3

Recording Sales: Perpetual Inventory System

E 11. On June 15, Lama Company sold merchandise for $2,600 on terms of n/30 to Cat Company. On June 20, Cat Company returned some of the merchandise for a credit of $600, and on June 25, Cat paid the balance owed. Prepare T accounts to record the sale, return, and receipt of payment under the perpetual inventory system. The cost of the merchandise sold on June 15 was $1,500, and the cost of the merchandise returned to inventory on June 20 was $350.

LO 4

Preparation of the Income Statement: Periodic Inventory System

E 12. Using the selected year-end account balances at December 31, 2011, for Handy General Store shown below, prepare a 2011 income statement. Show detail of net sales and cost of goods sold. The company uses the periodic inventory system. Beginning merchandise inventory was $14,000; ending merchandise inventory is $10,500.

Account Name	Debit	Credit
Sales		$154,500
Sales Returns and Allowances	$ 7,600	
Purchases	57,400	
Purchases Returns and Allowances		3,500
Freight-In	2,800	
Selling Expenses	28,200	
General and Administrative Expenses	18,600	
Income Taxes	9,000	

LO 4

Merchandising Income Statement: Missing Data, Multiple Years

E 13. Determine the missing data for each letter in the following three income statements for Sampson Paper Company (amounts are in thousands):

	2011	2010	2009
Sales	$ p	$ h	$286
Sales returns and allowances	24	19	a
Net sales	q	317	b
Merchandise inventory, beginning	r	i	38
Purchases	192	169	c
Purchases returns and allowances	31	j	17
Freight-in	s	29	22
Net cost of purchases	189	k	d
Cost of goods available for sale	222	212	182
Merchandise inventory, ending	39	l	42
Cost of goods sold	t	179	e
Gross margin	142	m	126
Selling expenses	u	78	f
General and administrative expenses	39	n	33
Total operating expenses	130	128	g
Income before income taxes	v	o	27
Income taxes	3	2	5
Net income	w	8	22

LO 4

Recording Purchases: Periodic Inventory System

E 14. Using the data in **E 10**, prepare T accounts to record each of the transactions under the periodic inventory system.

LO 4

Recording Sales: Periodic Inventory System

E 15. Using the relevant data in **E 11**, prepare T accounts to record each of the transactions under the periodic inventory system.

LO 5

Use of Accounting Records in Internal Control

E 16. Careful scrutiny of accounting records and financial statements can lead to the discovery of fraud or embezzlement. Each situation described below may indicate a breakdown in internal control. Indicate the nature of the possible fraud or embezzlement in each of these situations.

1. Wages expense for a branch office was 30 percent higher in 2011 than in 2010, even though the office was authorized to employ only the same four employees and raises were only 5 percent in 2011.
2. Sales returns and allowances increased from 5 percent to 20 percent of sales in the first two months of 2011, after record sales in 2010 resulted in large bonuses for the sales staff.
3. Gross margin decreased from 40 percent of net sales in 2010 to 20 percent in 2011, even though there was no change in pricing. Ending inventory was 50 percent less at the end of 2011 than it was at the beginning of the year. There is no immediate explanation for the decrease in inventory.
4. A review of daily records of cash register receipts shows that one cashier consistently accepts more discount coupons for purchases than do the other cashiers.

LO 5, 6

Control Procedures

E 17. Grace Wielgus operates a small grocery store and has established the following policies for checkout cashiers:

a. Each cashier has his or her own cash drawer, to which no one else has access.
b. Cashiers may accept checks for purchases under $50 with proper identification. For checks over $50, they must receive approval from Wielgus.
c. Every sale must be rung up on the cash register and a receipt given to the customer. Each sale is recorded on a tape inside the cash register.
d. At the end of each day, Wielgus counts the cash in the drawer and compares it with the amount on the tape inside the cash register.

Match the following conditions for internal control to each of the policies listed above:

1. Transactions are executed in accordance with management's general or specific authorization.
2. Transactions are recorded as necessary to permit preparation of financial statements and maintain accountability for assets.
3. Access to assets is permitted only as allowed by management.
4. At reasonable intervals, the records of assets are compared with the existing assets.

LO 5, 6

Internal Control Procedures

E 18. Delfi Movie has established the following policies for purchases of new DVDs at each of its branch stores:

1. Employees are required to take vacations, and the duties of employees are rotated periodically.
2. Once each month a person from the home office visits each branch store to examine the receiving records and to compare the inventory of DVDs with the accounting records.
3. Purchases of new DVDs must be authorized by purchase order in the home office and paid for by the treasurer in the home office. Receiving reports are prepared in each branch and sent to the home office.
4. All new personnel receive one hour of training in how to receive and catalogue new DVDs.
5. The company maintains a perpetual inventory system that keeps track of all DVDs purchased, sold, and on hand.

Match the following control procedures to each of the above policies. (Some may have more than one answer.)

a. Authorization
b. Recording transactions
c. Documents and records
d. Limited access
e. Periodic independent verification
f. Separation of duties
g. Sound personnel policies

Problems

LO 1, 3

Merchandising Income Statement: Perpetual Inventory System

✔ Net income: $26,870

P 1. At the end of the fiscal year, August 31, 2011, selected accounts from the adjusted trial balance for Leonid's Delivery, Inc., appeared as follows:

Leonid's Delivery, Inc.
Partial Adjusted Trial Balance
August 31, 2011

Sales		$338,000
Sales Returns and Allowances	$ 18,000	
Cost of Goods Sold	127,400	
Store Salaries Expense	65,650	
Office Salaries Expense	25,750	
Advertising Expense	48,200	
Rent Expense	4,800	
Insurance Expense	2,400	
Utilities Expense	3,120	
Store Supplies Expense	5,360	
Office Supplies Expense	2,350	
Depreciation Expense—Store Equipment	2,500	
Depreciation Expense—Office Equipment	1,600	
Income Taxes	4,000	

REQUIRED

1. Using the information given, prepare an income statement for Leonid's Delivery, Inc. Store Salaries Expense, Advertising Expense, Stores Supplies Expense, and Depreciation Expense—Store Equipment are selling expenses. The other expenses are general and administrative expenses. Freight-in should be combined with Cost of Goods Sold. The company uses the perpetual inventory system. Show details of net sales and operating expenses.

USER INSIGHT ▶

2. Based on your knowledge at this point in the course, how would you use the income statement for Leonid's Delivery, Inc., to evaluate the company's profitability? What other financial statement should be considered and why?

LO 3

Merchandising Transactions: Perpetual Inventory System

P 2. Justyna Company engaged in the following transactions in July 2011:

July	1	Sold merchandise to Tina Lands on credit, terms n/30, FOB shipping point, $1,050 (cost, $630).
	3	Purchased merchandise on credit from Livomax Company, terms n/30, FOB shipping point, $1,900.
	5	Paid Team Freight for freight charges on merchandise received, $145.
	8	Purchased merchandise on credit from Arbor Supply Company, terms n/30, FOB shipping point, $1,800, which includes $100 freight costs paid by Arbor Supply Company.
	12	Returned some of the merchandise purchased on July 3 for credit, $300.
	15	Sold merchandise on credit to John Nuzzo, terms n/30, FOB shipping point, $600 (cost, $360).
	17	Sold merchandise for cash, $500 (cost, $300).
	18	Accepted for full credit a return from Tina Lands and returned merchandise to inventory, $100 (cost, $60).
	24	Paid Livomax Company for purchase of July 3 less return of July 12.
	25	Received check from Tina Lands for July 1 purchase less the return on July 18.

REQUIRED

1. Prepare journal entries to record these transactions, assuming the company uses the perpetual inventory system.

USER INSIGHT ▶

2. In their published financial statements, most companies call the first line on their income statements "net sales." Other companies call them "sales." Do you think these terms are equivalent and comparable? What would be the content of "net sales"? What might be the reason a company uses "sales" instead of "net sales"?

LO 1, 4

Merchandising Income Statement: Periodic Inventory System

✔ Net income: $9,470

P 3. Shown below are selected accounts from the adjusted trial balance of Hill Sporting Equipment, Inc., on September 30, 2011, the fiscal year-end. The company's beginning merchandise inventory was $40,611, and ending merchandise inventory was $38,332.

Hill Sporting Equipment, Inc.
Partial Adjusted Trial Balance
September 30, 2011

Sales		$220,456
Sales Returns and Allowances	$ 9,125	
Purchases	110,593	
Purchases Returns and Allowances		15,119
Freight-In	5,039	
Store Salaries Expense	52,775	
Office Salaries Expense	13,250	
Advertising Expense	10,100	
Rent Expense	7,500	
Insurance Expense	1,100	
Utilities Expense	9,380	
Store Supplies Expense	232	
Office Supplies Expense	407	
Depreciation Expense—Store Equipment	900	
Depreciation Expense—Office Equipment	925	
Income Taxes	2,500	

REQUIRED

1. Prepare a multistep income statement for Hill Sporting Equipment, Inc. Store Salaries Expense, Advertising Expense, Store Supplies Expense, and Depreciation Expense—Store Equipment are selling expenses. The other expenses are general and administrative expenses. Hill Sporting Equipment uses the periodic inventory system. Show details of net sales and operating expenses.

USER INSIGHT ▶

2. Based on your knowledge at this point in the course, how would you use the income statement for Hill Sporting Equipment to evaluate the company's profitability? What other financial statements should you consider and why?

LO 4

Merchandising Transactions: Periodic Inventory System

P 4. Use the data in **P 2** for this problem.

REQUIRED

1. Prepare journal entries to record the transactions, assuming the company uses the periodic inventory system.

USER INSIGHT ▶

2. In their published financial statements, most companies call the first line on the income statement "net sales." Other companies call them "sales." Do you think these terms are equivalent and comparable? What would be the content of "net sales"? What might be the reason a company uses "sales" instead of "net sales"?

LO 5, 6

Internal Control

P 5. Industrial Services Company provides maintenance services to factories. It buys a large amount of cleaning supplies, and it has consistently been over budget in its expenditures for these items. In the past, the warehouse has been left open in the evenings so that the onsite supervisors could take supplies as needed. A clerk in the accounting department periodically ordered additional supplies from a long-time supplier. No records were maintained other than to record purchases. Once a year, an inventory of supplies was made for the preparation of the financial statements.

To solve the budgetary problem, management has implemented a new system for purchasing and controlling supplies. It involves the following:

1. A supplies clerk is now in charge of a secured storeroom for cleaning supplies.
2. Supervisors use a purchase requisition to request supplies for the jobs they oversee.
3. Each job receives a predetermined amount of supplies based on a study of each job's needs.
4. In the storeroom, the supplies clerk notes the levels of supplies and completes the purchase requisition when new supplies are needed.
5. The purchase requisition goes to a purchasing clerk, a new position. The purchasing clerk is solely responsible for authorizing purchases and preparing the purchase orders.
6. The purchasing clerk continuously monitors suppliers' prices to ensure that the lowest price is obtained.
7. When supplies are received, the supplies clerk checks them in and prepares a receiving report. The supplies clerk sends the receiving report to accounting, where each payment to a supplier is documented by the purchase requisition, the purchase order, and the receiving report.
8. The accounting department also maintains a record of supplies inventory, supplies requisitioned by supervisors, and supplies received.
9. Once each month, the warehouse manager takes a physical inventory of cleaning supplies in the storeroom and compares it against the supplies inventory records that the accounting department maintains.

REQUIRED

1. Indicate which of the following control activities applies to each of the improvements in the internal control system (more than one may apply):

a. Authorization
b. Recording transactions
c. Documents and records
d. Physical controls
e. Periodic independent verification
f. Separation of duties
g. Sound personnel practices

USER INSIGHT ▶ 2. Explain why each new control activity is an improvement over the activities of the old system.

Alternate Problems

LO 1, 3

Merchandising Income Statement: Perpetual Inventory System

✔ Net income: $5,522

P 6. Shown below are selected accounts from the adjusted trial balance of Joseph's Video Store, Inc., at the end of the fiscal year, June 30, 2011.

Joseph's Video Store, Inc.
Partial Adjusted Trial Balance
June 30, 2011

Sales		$870,824
Sales Returns and Allowances	$ 25,500	
Cost of Goods Sold	442,370	
Freight-In	20,156	
Store Salaries Expense	216,700	
Office Salaries Expense	53,000	
Advertising Expense	36,400	
Rent Expense	28,000	
Insurance Expense	5,600	
Utilities Expense	18,320	
Store Supplies Expense	3,328	
Office Supplies Expense	3,628	
Depreciation Expense—Store Equipment	3,600	
Depreciation Expense—Office Equipment	3,700	
Income Taxes	5,000	

REQUIRED

1. Prepare a multistep income statement for Joseph's Video Store, Inc. Freight-In should be combined with Cost of Goods Sold. Store Salaries Expense, Advertising Expense, Store Supplies Expense, and Depreciation Expense—Store Equipment are selling expenses. The other expenses are general and administrative expenses. The company uses the perpetual inventory system. Show details of net sales and operating expenses.

USER INSIGHT ▶ 2. Based on your knowledge at this point in the course, how would you use the income statement for Joseph's Video Store to evaluate the company's profitability? What other financial statement should you consider and why?

LO 3

Merchandising Transactions: Perpetual Inventory System

P 7. Kitty Company engaged in the following transactions in October 2011:

Oct.	7	Sold merchandise on credit to Ron Moore, terms n/30, FOB shipping point, $3,000 (cost, $1,800).
	8	Purchased merchandise on credit from Lima Company, terms n/30, FOB shipping point, $6,000.
	9	Paid Warta Company for shipping charges on merchandise purchased on October 8, $254.
	10	Purchased merchandise on credit from Maria's Company, terms n/30, FOB shipping point, $9,600, including $600 freight costs paid by Maria's.
	14	Sold merchandise on credit to Kate Lang, terms n/30, FOB shipping point, $2,400 (cost, $1,440).
	14	Returned damaged merchandise received from Lima Company on October 8 for credit, $600.
	17	Received check from Ron Moore for his purchase of October 7.
	19	Sold merchandise for cash, $1,800 (cost, $1,080).
	20	Paid Maria's Company for purchase of October 10.
	21	Paid Lima Company the balance from the transactions of October 8 and October 14.
	24	Accepted from Kate Lang a return of merchandise, which was put back in inventory, $200 (cost, $120).

REQUIRED

1. Prepare journal entries to record these transactions, assuming the company uses the perpetual inventory system.

USER INSIGHT ▶ 2. Receiving cash rebates from suppliers based on the past year's purchases is a common practice in some industries. If at the end of the year Kitty Company receives rebates in cash from a supplier, should these cash rebates be reported as revenue? Why or why not?

LO 1, 4

Merchandising Income Statement: Periodic Inventory System

P 8. Following are selected accounts from the adjusted trial balance for Robert's Shop, Inc., as of March 31, 2011, the end of the fiscal year.

✔ Net income: $2,435

Robert's Shop, Inc.
Partial Adjusted Trial Balance
March 31, 2011

Sales		$168,700
Sales Returns and Allowances	$ 5,700	
Purchases	70,200	
Purchases Returns and Allowances		2,600
Freight-In	2,300	
Store Salaries Expense	33,125	

(continued)

Office Salaries Expense	$12,875
Advertising Expense	23,800
Rent Expense	2,400
Insurance Expense	1,300
Utilities Expense	1,560
Store Supplies Expense	2,880
Office Supplies Expense	1,075
Depreciation Expense—Store Equipment	1,050
Depreciation Expense—Office Equipment	800
Income Taxes	1,000

The merchandise inventory for Robert's Shop was $38,200 at the beginning of the year and $29,400 at the end of the year.

1. Using the information given, prepare an income statement for Robert's Shop, Inc. Store Salaries Expense, Advertising Expense, Store Supplies Expense, and Depreciation Expense—Store Equipment are selling expenses. The other expenses are general and administrative expenses. The company uses the periodic inventory system. Show details of net sales and operating expenses.

USER INSIGHT ▶ 2. Based on your knowledge at this point in the course, how would you use the income statement for Robert's Shop to evaluate the company's profitability? What other financial statements should you consider and why?

LO 4 **Merchandising Transactions: Periodic Inventory System**

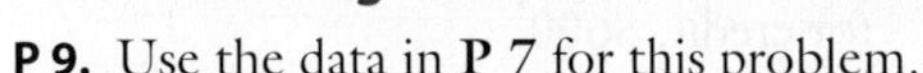

P 9. Use the data in **P** 7 for this problem.

REQUIRED

1. Prepare journal entries to record these transactions, assuming the company uses the periodic inventory system.

USER INSIGHT ▶ 2. Receiving cash rebates from suppliers based on the past year's purchases is common in some industries. If at the end of the year, Kitty Company receives rebates in cash from a supplier, should these cash rebates be reported as revenue? Why or why not?

LO 5, 6 **Internal Control Activities**

P 10. Veil is a retail store with several departments. Its internal control procedures for cash sales and purchases are as follows:

Cash sales. The salesclerk in each department rings up every cash sale on the department's cash register. The cash register produces a sales slip, which the clerk gives to the customer along with the merchandise. A continuous tape locked inside the cash register makes a carbon copy of the sales ticket. At the end of each day, the salesclerk presses a "total" key on the register, and it prints the total sales for the day on the continuous tape. The salesclerk then unlocks the tape, reads the total sales figure, and makes the entry in the accounting records for the day's cash sales. Next, she counts the cash in the drawer, places the $100 change fund back in the drawer, and gives the cash received to the cashier. Finally, she files the cash register tape and is ready for the next day's business.

Purchases. At the request of the various department heads, the purchasing agent orders all goods. When the goods arrive, the receiving clerk prepares a receiving report in triplicate. The receiving clerk keeps one copy; the other two copies go to the purchasing agent and the department head. Invoices are forwarded immediately to the accounting department to ensure payment before the discount period elapses. After payment, the invoice is forwarded to the purchasing agent for comparison with the purchase order and the receiving report and is then returned to the accounting office for filing.

REQUIRED

1. Identify the significant internal control weaknesses in the preceding situations.

USER INSIGHT ▶ 2. In each case identified in requirement 1, recommend changes that would improve the system.

Cases

LO 1

Conceptual Understanding: Cash Flow Management

C 1. Amazing Sound Source, Inc., has been in business for 30 years. It carries a large inventory so that it can offer customers a wide selection of merchandise and deliver purchases quickly. It accepts credit cards and checks but also provides 90 days' credit to reliable customers who have made purchases in the past. It maintains good relations with suppliers by paying invoices quickly.

To pay bills during the past year, the company has had to borrow from its bank. An analysis of the company's financial statements reveals that, on average, inventory is on hand for 70 days before being sold and that receivables are held for 90 days before being paid. Accounts payable are, on average, paid in 20 days.

What are the operating cycle and financing period? How long are Amazing Sound Source's operating cycle and financing period? Describe three ways in which this company can improve its cash flow management.

LO 1

Conceptual Understanding: Periodic versus Perpetual Inventory Systems

C 2. Books Unlimited is a well-established chain of 20 bookstores in western Ohio. In recent years, the company has grown rapidly, adding five new stores in regional malls. The manager of each store selects stock based on the market in his or her region. Managers select books from a master list of titles that the central office provides. Every six months, a physical inventory is taken, and financial statements are prepared using the periodic inventory system. At that time, books that have not sold well are placed on sale or, whenever possible, returned to the publisher.

Management has found that when selecting books, managers of the new stores are not judging the market as well as the managers of the older, more established stores. Management is therefore thinking of implementing a perpetual inventory system and carefully monitoring sales from the central office. Do you think Books Unlimited should switch to the perpetual inventory system or stay with the periodic inventory system it has used in the past? Discuss the advantages and disadvantages of each system.

LO 1

Conceptual Understanding: Effects of a Weak Dollar

C 3. In 2004, **McDonald**'s reported that its sales in Europe exceeded its sales in the United States for the first time. It reported the same result in subsequent years. This performance, while reflective of the company's phenomenal success in Europe, was also attributed to the weak dollar in relation to the euro. McDonald's reports its sales wherever they take place in U.S. dollars. Explain why a weak dollar relative to the euro would lead to an increase in McDonald's reported European sales. Why is a weak dollar not relevant to a discussion of McDonald's sales in the United States?

LO 5

Interpreting Financial Reports: Internal Control Lapse

C 4. Starbucks Corporation accused an employee and her husband of embezzling $3.7 million by billing the company for services from a fictitious consulting firm. The couple created a phony company called RAD Services Inc. and charged Starbucks for work they never provided. The employee worked in Starbucks' Information Technology Department. RAD Services Inc. charged Starbucks as much as $492,800 for consulting services in a single week.[12] For such a fraud to have taken place, certain control activities were likely not implemented. Identify and describe these activities.

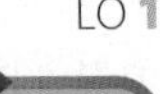

LO 1

Annual Report Case: The Operating Cycle and Financing Period

C 5. Write a brief memorandum to your instructor describing **CVS**'s operating cycle and financing period. To do this, refer to the **CVS** annual report in the Supplement to Chapter 1 and to Exhibits 5.1 and 5.2. Your memorandum should identify the most common transactions in the operating cycle as they apply to CVS. It should also refer to the importance of accounts receivable, accounts payable, and merchandise inventory in CVS's financial statements. Recall from previous chapters that CVS had inventory days on hand of about 45 days, days' receivable of 21 days, and days payable of 19 days. Complete the memorandum by explaining why CVS's operating cycle and financing period are favorable to the company.

LO 1

Comparison Analysis: Income Statement Analysis

C 6. Refer to the **CVS** annual report in the Supplement to Chapter 1 and to the following data (in millions) for **Walgreens** in 2009: net sales, $63,335; cost of sales, $45,722; total operating expenses, $14,366; and inventories, $6,789. Determine which company—CVS or Walgreens—had more profitable merchandising operations in 2009 by preparing a schedule that compares the companies based on net sales, cost of sales, gross margin, total operating expenses, and income from operations as a percentage of sales. (*Hint:* You should put the income statements in comparable formats.) In addition, for each company, compute inventories as a percentage of the cost of sales. Which company has the highest prices in relation to costs of sales? Which company is more efficient in its operating expenses? Which company manages its inventories better? Overall, on the basis of the income statement, which company is more profitable? Explain your answers.

LO 1, 3, 4, 5

Decision Analysis: Analysis of a Merchandising Income Statement

C 7. In 2010, Lisa Perry opened Lisa's Jeans Company, a small store that sold designer jeans in a suburban mall. Lisa Perry worked 14 hours a day and controlled all aspects of the operation. The company was such a success that in 2011, Perry opened a second store in another mall. Because the new shop needed her attention, she hired a manager for the original store.

During 2011, the new store was successful, but the original store's performance did not match its performance in 2010. Concerned about this, Perry compared the two years' results for the original store. Her analysis showed the following:

	2011	2010
Net sales	$325,000	$350,000
Cost of goods sold	225,000	225,000
Gross margin	$100,000	$125,000
Operating expenses	75,000	50,000
Income before income taxes	$ 25,000	$ 75,000

Perry's analysis also revealed that the cost and the selling price of the jeans were roughly the same in both years, as was the level of operating expenses, except for the new manager's $25,000 salary. The amount of sales returns and allowances was insignificant in both years.

Studying the situation further, Perry discovered the following about the cost of goods sold:

	2011	2010
Purchases	$200,000	$271,000
Total purchases allowances	15,000	20,000
Freight-in	19,000	27,000
Physical inventory, end of year	32,000	53,000

Still not satisfied, Perry went through all the individual sales and purchase records for 2011. She found that they were correct, but given the unit purchases and sales during the year, the 2011 ending inventory should have been $57,000. After puzzling over all this information, Perry has come to you for accounting help.

1. Using Perry's new information, compute the cost of goods sold for 2010 and 2011 and account for the difference in income before income taxes between 2010 and 2011.
2. Suggest at least two reasons for the discrepancy in the 2011 ending inventory. How might Perry improve the management of the original store?

CHAPTER 6

DECISION POINT
A User's Focus Cisco Systems, Inc.

Cisco Systems manufactures and sells networking and communications products. It is the world's leading producer of the switches, hubs, gateways, and firewalls that make the Internet possible. As you can see in Cisco's Financial Highlights,[1] inventory is an important component of the company's total assets.

CISCO'S FINANCIAL HIGHLIGHTS
(in millions)

	2009	2008	Change
Sales of products	$29,131	$33,099	(12.0%)
Cost of goods sold	10,481	11,660	(10.1)
Operating income (loss)	7,322	9,442	(22.5)
Inventories	890	997	(10.7)
Total current assets*	14,894	14,655	1.6

*Excluding investments

Questions

1. *What is the impact of inventory decisions on operating results?*
2. *How should inventory be valued?*
3. *How should the level of inventory be evaluated?*

Dan Krauss/Stringer/Getty Images News/Getty Images

Inventories

LEARNING OBJECTIVES

LO 1 Explain the management decisions related to inventory accounting, evaluation of inventory level, and the effects of inventory misstatements on income measurement. (pp. 292–297)

LO 2 Define *inventory cost*, contrast goods flow and cost flow, and explain the lower-of-cost-or-market (LCM) rule. (pp. 297–299)

LO 3 Calculate inventory cost under the periodic inventory system using various costing methods. (pp. 299–302)

LO 4 Explain the effects of inventory costing methods on income determination and income taxes. (pp. 302–305)

LO 5 Calculate inventory cost under the perpetual inventory system using various costing methods. (pp. 305–307)

LO 6 Use the retail method and gross profit method to estimate the cost of ending inventory. (pp. 308–309)

For any company that makes or sells merchandise, inventory is an extremely important asset. Managing this asset is a challenging task. It requires not only protecting goods from theft or loss, but also ensuring that operations are highly efficient. Further, as you will see in this chapter, proper accounting of inventory is essential because misstatements will affect net income in at least two years.

FOCUS ON FINANCIAL STATEMENTS

INCOME STATEMENT
Revenues
− Expenses
= Net Income

STATEMENT OF RETAINED EARNINGS
Opening Balance
+ Net Income
− Dividends
= Retained Earnings

BALANCE SHEET
Assets | Liabilities
Equity
A = L + E

STATEMENT OF CASH FLOWS
Operating Activities
+ Investing Activities
+ Financing Activities
= Change in Cash
+ Starting Balance
= Ending Cash Balance

Valuation of merchandise inventory on the balance sheet is linked to measurement of cost of goods sold on the income statement.

MANAGING INVENTORIES

LO 1 Explain the management decisions related to inventory accounting, evaluation of inventory level, and the effects of inventory misstatements on income measurement.

Inventory is considered a current asset because a company normally sells it within a year or within its operating cycle. For a merchandising company like **CVS** or **Walgreens**, inventory consists of all goods owned and held for sale in the regular course of business. Because manufacturing companies like **Cisco Systems** are engaged in making products, they have three kinds of inventory:

- Raw materials (goods used in making products)
- Work in process (partially completed products)
- Finished goods ready for sale

In a note to its financial statements, Cisco showed the following breakdown of its inventories (figures are in millions):[2]

Inventories	*2009*	*2008*
Raw materials (includes supplies)	$165	$111
Work in process	33	53
Finished goods	692	833
Total inventories	$890	$997

The work in process and finished goods inventories have three cost components:

- Cost of the raw materials that go into the product
- Cost of the labor used to convert the raw materials to finished goods
- Overhead costs that support the production process

Overhead costs include the costs of indirect materials (such as packing materials), indirect labor (such as the salaries of supervisors), factory rent, depreciation of plant assets, utilities, and insurance.

STUDY NOTE: *Management considers the behavior of inventory costs over time when selecting inventory costing methods.*

Inventory Decisions

The primary objective of inventory accounting is to determine income properly by matching costs of the period against revenues for the period. As you can see in Exhibit 6.1, in

EXHIBIT 6.1
Management Choices in Accounting for Inventories

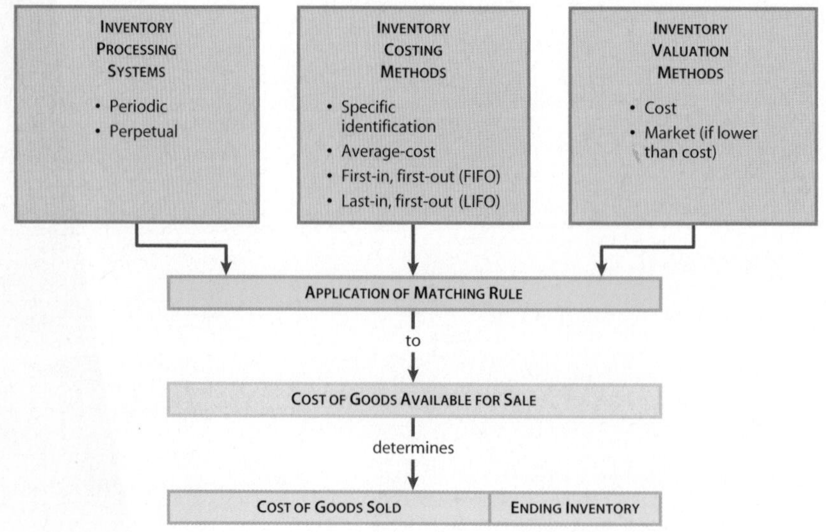

accounting for inventory, management must choose among different processing systems, costing methods, and valuation methods. These different systems and methods usually result in different amounts of reported net income. Thus, management's choices affect investors' and creditors' evaluations of a company, as well as internal evaluations, such as the performance reviews on which bonuses and executive compensation are based.

The consistency convention requires that once a company has decided on the systems and methods it will use in accounting for inventory, it must use them from one accounting period to the next unless management can justify a change. When a change is justifiable, the full disclosure convention requires that the company clearly describe the change and its effects in the notes to its financial statements.

Because the valuation of inventory affects income, it can have a considerable impact on the amount of income taxes a company pays—and the amount of taxes it pays can have a considerable impact on its cash flows. Federal income tax regulations are specific about the valuation methods a company may use. As a result, management is sometimes faced with the dilemma of how to apply GAAP to income determination and still minimize income taxes.

Financial Ratios: Inventory Turnover and Days' Inventory on Hand

STUDY NOTE: *Some of the costs of carrying inventory are insurance, property tax, and storage costs. Other costs may result from spoilage and employee theft.*

The level of inventory a company maintains has important economic consequences, and it involves conflicting goals. One goal is to have a great variety and quantity of goods on hand so that customers have a large choice and do not have to wait for an item to be restocked. But this goal conflicts with the goal of controlling costs, which favors keeping the level of inventory low. Handling and storage costs and the interest cost of the funds needed to maintain high inventory levels are usually substantial. However, low inventory levels can result in disgruntled customers and lost sales. Managers control inventory by closely observing two financial ratios: inventory turnover and days' inventory on hand.

Inventory Turnover **Inventory turnover** is the average number of times a company sells an amount equal to its average level of inventory during an accounting period. It is computed by dividing cost of goods sold by average inventory. Average inventory is used to put it on a comparable basis to cost of goods sold during the year. For example, using the data presented in this chapter's Decision Point, we can compute **Cisco System**'s inventory turnover for 2009 as follows (figures are in millions):

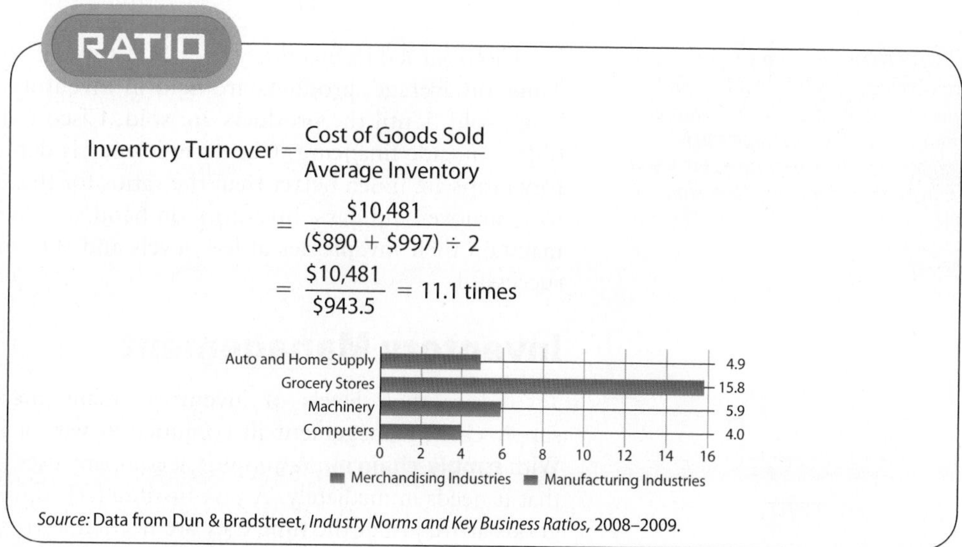

$$\text{Inventory Turnover} = \frac{\text{Cost of Goods Sold}}{\text{Average Inventory}} = \frac{\$10{,}481}{(\$890 + \$997) \div 2} = \frac{\$10{,}481}{\$943.5} = 11.1 \text{ times}$$

Source: Data from Dun & Bradstreet, *Industry Norms and Key Business Ratios*, 2008–2009.

Focus on Business Practice

A Whirlwind Inventory Turnover—How Does Dell Do It?

Dell Computer Corporation turns its inventory over every five days. How can it do this when other computer companies have inventory on hand for 60 days or even longer? Technology and good inventory management are a big part of the answer.

Dell's speed from order to delivery sets the standard for the computer industry. Consider that a computer ordered by 9 A.M. can be delivered the next day by 9 P.M. How can Dell do this when it does not start ordering components and assembling computers until a customer places an order? First, Dell's suppliers keep components warehoused just minutes from Dell's factories, making efficient, just-in-time (JIT) operations possible. Further, computer monitors are no longer shipped first to Dell and then on to buyers. Dell sends an email message to a shipper, such as **United Parcel Service**, and the shipper picks up a monitor from a supplier and schedules it to arrive with the PC. In addition to contributing to a high inventory turnover, this practice saves Dell about $30 per monitor in freight costs. Dell is showing the world how to run a business in the cyber age by selling more than $1 million worth of computers a day on its website.[3]

iStock Photo

Days' Inventory on Hand **Days' inventory on hand** is the average number of days it takes a company to sell an amount equal to its average inventory. It is computed using the inventory turnover. For Cisco Systems, it is computed as follows:

RATIO

$$\text{Days' Inventory on Hand} = \frac{365}{\text{Inventory Turnover}}$$

$$= \frac{365 \text{ days}}{11.1 \text{ times}}$$

$$= 32.9 \text{ days}$$

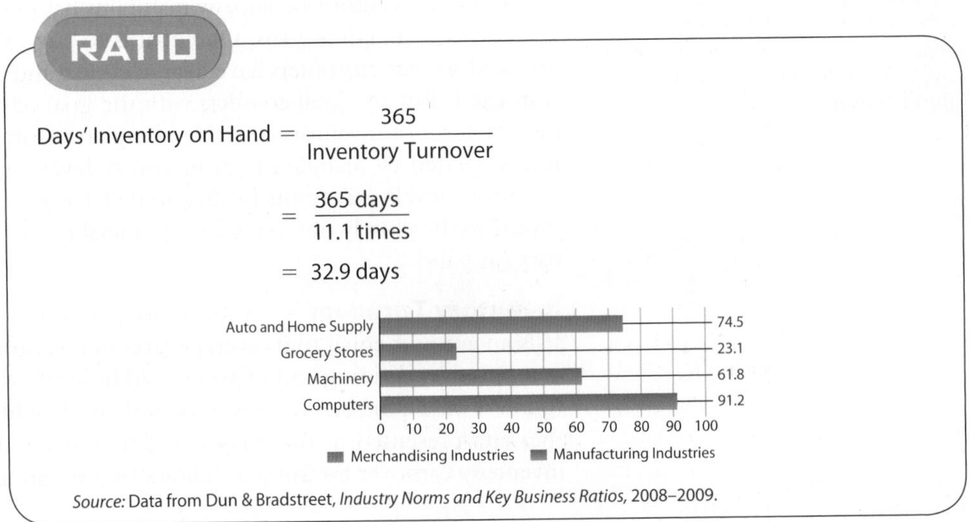

Source: Data from Dun & Bradstreet, *Industry Norms and Key Business Ratios*, 2008–2009.

STUDY NOTE: *Inventory turnover will be systematically higher if year-end inventory levels are low. For example, many merchandisers' year-end is January 31 when inventories are lower than at any other time of the year.*

Cisco turned its inventory over 11.1 times in 2009 or, on average, every 32.9 days. Thus, on average, products are held in inventory for a little over one month before being sold. Until the products are sold, Cisco either has to tie up its own money or obtain outside financing. Cisco's efficiency is demonstrated by the fact that its inventory ratios are much better than the ratios for the computer industry. Although inventory turnover and days' inventory on hand vary by industry, companies like Cisco that maintain their inventories at low levels and still satisfy customers' needs are the most successful.

Inventory Management

To reduce their levels of inventory, many merchandisers and manufacturers use supply-chain management in conjunction with a just-in-time operating environment. With **supply-chain management**, a company uses the Internet to order and track goods that it needs immediately. A **just-in-time (JIT) operating environment** is one in which goods arrive just at the time they are needed.

Cisco uses supply-chain management to increase inventory turnover. It manages its inventory purchases through business-to-business transactions that it conducts over

Jeff Greenberg/PhotoEdit

Harley Davidson uses a just-in-time operating environment when producing its legendary motorcycles—often with only 8 to10 hours of inventory on hand. A lack of supply can therefore shut down assembly lines, so the company is careful when considering where to source parts because of the longer lead times and customs delays that can occur.

the Internet. Cisco also uses a JIT operating environment in which it works closely with suppliers to coordinate and schedule shipments so that the shipments arrive exactly when they are needed. The major benefits of using supply-chain management in a JIT operating environment are that Cisco has less money tied up in inventory and its cost of carrying inventory is reduced.

Effects of Inventory Misstatements on Income Measurement

The reason inventory accounting is so important to income measurement is the way income is measured on the income statement. Recall that gross margin is the difference between net sales and cost of goods sold and that cost of goods sold depends on the portion of cost of goods available for sale assigned to ending inventory. These relationships lead to the following conclusions:

- The higher the value of ending inventory, the lower the cost of goods sold and the higher the gross margin.
- Conversely, the lower the value of ending inventory, the higher the cost of goods sold and the lower the gross margin.

Because the amount of gross margin has a direct effect on net income, the value assigned to ending inventory also affects net income. In effect, the value of ending inventory determines what portion of the cost of goods available for sale is assigned to cost of goods sold and what portion is assigned to the balance sheet (as inventory to be carried over into the next accounting period).

The basic issue in separating goods available for sale into two components—goods sold and goods not sold—is to assign a value to the goods not sold, the ending inventory. The portion of goods available for sale not assigned to the ending inventory is used to determine the cost of goods sold. Because the figures for ending inventory and cost of goods sold are related, a misstatement in the inventory figure at the end of an accounting period will cause an equal misstatement in gross margin and income before income taxes in the income statement. The amount of assets and stockholders' equity on the balance sheet will be misstated by the same amount.

Inventory Misstatements and Fraud

Inventory is particularly susceptible to fraudulent financial reporting. For example, it is easy to overstate or understate inventory by including end-of-the-year purchase and sales transactions in the wrong fiscal year or by simply misstating inventory. A misstatement can occur because of mistakes in the accounting process. It can also occur because of deliberate manipulation of operating results motivated by a desire to enhance the market's perception of the company, obtain bank financing, or achieve compensation incentives.

In one spectacular case of fraudulent financial reporting, **Rite Aid Corporation**, the large drugstore chain, falsified income by manipulating its computerized inventory system to cover losses it had sustained from shoplifting, employee theft, and spoilage.[4] In another case, bookkeepers at **RentWay, Inc.**, a company that rents furniture to apartment dwellers, boosted income artificially over several years by overstating inventory in small increments that were not noticed by top management.[5]

Inventory Misstatements Illustrated Whatever the causes of an overstatement or understatement of inventory, the three examples that follow illustrate the effects. In each case, beginning inventory, net cost of purchases, and cost of goods available for sale are stated correctly. In Example 1, ending inventory is correctly stated; in Example 2, it is overstated by $3,000; and in Example 3, it is understated by $3,000.

Example 1. Ending Inventory Correctly Stated at $5,000

Cost of Goods Sold for the Year		*Income Statement for the Year*	
Beginning inventory	$ 6,000	Net sales	$50,000
Net cost of purchases	29,000	Cost of goods sold	30,000
Cost of goods available for sale	$35,000	Gross margin	$20,000
Ending inventory	5,000	Operating expenses	16,000
Cost of goods sold	$30,000	Income before income taxes	$ 4,000

Example 2. Ending Inventory Overstated by $3,000

Cost of Goods Sold for the Year		*Income Statement for the Year*	
Beginning inventory	$ 6,000	Net sales	$50,000
Net cost of purchases	29,000	Cost of goods sold	27,000
Cost of goods available for sale	$35,000	Gross margin	$23,000
Ending inventory	8,000	Operating expenses	16,000
Cost of goods sold	$27,000	Income before income taxes	$ 7,000

Example 3. Ending Inventory Understated by $3,000

Cost of Goods Sold for the Year		*Income Statement for the Year*	
Beginning inventory	$ 6,000	Net sales	$50,000
Net cost of purchases	29,000	Cost of goods sold	33,000
Cost of goods available for sale	$35,000	Gross margin	$17,000
Ending inventory	2,000	Operating expenses	16,000
Cost of goods sold	$33,000	Income before income taxes	$ 1,000

In all three examples, the cost of goods available for sale was $35,000. The difference in income before income taxes resulted from how this $35,000 was divided between ending inventory and cost of goods sold.

STUDY NOTE: *A misstatement of inventory has the opposite effect in two successive accounting periods.*

Because the ending inventory in one period becomes the beginning inventory in the following period, a misstatement in inventory valuation affects not only the current period but the following period as well. Over two periods, the errors in income before income taxes will offset, or counterbalance, each other. For instance, in Example 2, the overstatement of ending inventory will cause a $3,000 overstatement of beginning inventory in the following year, which will result in a $3,000 understatement of income. Because the total income before income taxes for the two periods is the same, it may appear that one need not worry about inventory misstatements. However, the misstatements violate the matching rule. In addition, management, creditors, and investors base many decisions on the accountant's determination of net income. The accountant has an obligation to make the net income figure for each period as useful as possible.

The effects of inventory misstatements on income before income taxes are as follows:

Year 1	Year 2
Ending inventory overstated	**Beginning inventory overstated**
Cost of goods sold understated	Cost of goods sold overstated
Income before income taxes overstated	Income before income taxes understated
Ending inventory understated	**Beginning inventory understated**
Cost of goods sold overstated	Cost of goods sold understated
Income before income taxes understated	Income before income taxes overstated

Stop & Apply

During 2011, Max's Sporting Goods had beginning inventory of \$500,000, ending inventory of \$700,000, and cost of goods sold of \$2,100,000. Compute the inventory turnover and days' inventory on hand.

SOLUTION

$$\text{Inventory Turnover} = \frac{\text{Cost of Goods Sold}}{\text{Average Inventory}}$$

$$= \frac{\$2{,}100{,}000}{(\$700{,}000 + \$500{,}000) \div 2} = \frac{\$2{,}100{,}000}{\$600{,}000}$$

$$= 3.5 \text{ times}$$

$$\text{Days' Inventory on Hand} = \frac{365}{\text{Inventory Turnover}}$$

$$= 365 \div 3.5$$

$$= 104.3 \text{ days}$$

iStock Photo

INVENTORY COST AND VALUATION

LO 2 Define *inventory cost*, contrast goods flow and cost flow, and explain the lower-of-cost-or-market (LCM) rule.

The primary basis of accounting for inventories is cost, the price paid to acquire an asset. **Inventory cost** includes the following:

- Invoice price less purchases discounts
- Freight-in, including insurance in transit
- Applicable taxes and tariffs

Other costs—for ordering, receiving, and storing—should in principle be included in inventory cost. In practice, however, it is so difficult to allocate such costs to specific inventory items that they are usually considered expenses of the accounting period rather than inventory costs.

Inventory costing and valuation depend on the prices of the goods in inventory. The prices of most goods vary during the year. A company may have purchased identical lots of merchandise at different prices. Also, when a company deals in identical items, it is often impossible to tell which have been sold and which are still in inventory. When that is the case, it is necessary to make an assumption about the order in which items have been sold. Because the assumed order of sale may or may not be the same as the actual order of sale, the assumption is really about the *flow of costs* rather than the *flow of physical inventory.*

Goods Flows and Cost Flows

Goods flow refers to the actual physical movement of goods in the operations of a company. **Cost flow** refers to the association of costs with their assumed flow in the operations of a company. The assumed cost flow may or may not be the same as the actual goods flow. The possibility of a difference between cost flow and goods flow may seem strange at first, but it arises because several choices of assumed cost flow are available under generally accepted accounting principles. In fact, it is sometimes preferable to use an assumed cost flow that bears no relationship to goods flow because it gives a better estimate of income, which is the main goal of inventory valuation.

Merchandise in Transit Because merchandise inventory includes all items that a company owns and holds for sale, the status of any merchandise in transit, whether the company is selling it or buying it, must be evaluated to see if the merchandise should be included in the inventory count. Neither the seller nor the buyer has *physical* possession of merchandise in transit. As Exhibit 6.2 (p. 298) shows, ownership is determined by the terms of the shipping agreement, which indicate when title passes. Outgoing goods shipped FOB (free on board) destination are included in the seller's merchandise inventory, whereas those shipped FOB shipping point are not. Conversely, incoming goods shipped FOB shipping point are included in the buyer's merchandise inventory, but those shipped FOB destination are not.

EXHIBIT 6.2
Merchandise in Transit

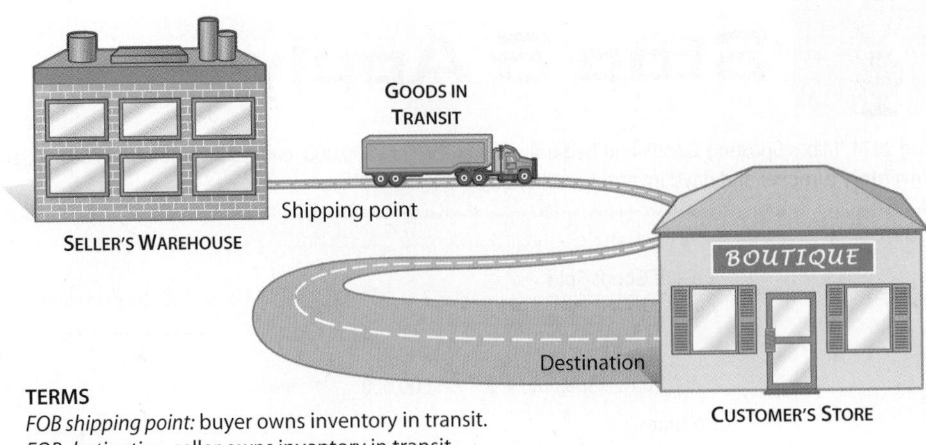

TERMS
FOB shipping point: buyer owns inventory in transit.
FOB destination: seller owns inventory in transit.

Merchandise on Hand Not Included in Inventory At the time a company takes a physical inventory, it may have merchandise on hand to which it does not hold title. For example, it may have sold goods but not yet delivered them to the buyer, but because the sale has been completed, title has passed to the buyer. Thus, the merchandise should be included in the buyer's inventory, not the seller's. Goods held on consignment also fall into this category. A **consignment** is merchandise that its owner (the consignor) places on the premises of another company (the consignee) with the understanding that payment is expected only when the merchandise is sold and that unsold items may be returned to the consignor. Title to consigned goods remains with the consignor until the consignee sells the goods. Consigned goods should not be included in the consignee's physical inventory because they still belong to the consignor.

When the lower-of-cost or market rule comes into play, it can be an indication of how bad things are for a company. For example, through poor management, a downturn in the economy, and underperforming stores, Kmart found itself with a huge amount of excess merchandise. The company had to mark down its inventory by $1 billion in order to sell it, which resulted in a debilitating loss.

Lower-of-Cost-or-Market (LCM) Rule

Although cost is usually the most appropriate basis for valuation of inventory, inventory may at times be properly shown in the financial statements at less than its historical, or original, cost. If the market value of inventory falls below its historical cost because of physical deterioration, obsolescence, or decline in price level, a loss has occurred. This loss is recognized by writing the inventory down to **market**—that is, to its current replacement cost. For a merchandising company, market is the amount that it would pay at the present time for the same goods, purchased from the usual suppliers and in the usual quantities.

Syracuse Newspapers/L. Long/The Image Works

When the replacement cost of inventory falls below its historical cost (as determined by an inventory costing method), the **lower-of-cost-or-market (LCM) rule** requires that the inventory be written down to the lower value and that a loss be recorded. This rule is an example of the application of the conservatism convention because the loss is recognized before an actual transaction takes place. Under historical cost accounting, the inventory would remain at cost until it is sold. According to an AICPA survey, approximately 80 percent of large companies apply the LCM rule to their inventories for financial reporting.[6]

Focus on International Practices

Is "Market" the Same as Fair Value Under IFRS?

When the lower-of-cost-or-market rule is used, what does "market" mean? Under international financial reporting standards (IFRS), market is considered fair value, which is defined as the amount at which an asset can be sold. However, in valuing inventory under U.S. standards, market is normally considered the replacement cost, or the amount at which the asset can be purchased. The two "market" values, selling price and purchasing price, can often be quite different for the same asset. This is an issue that will have to be addressed if the U.S. and international standards are to achieve convergence.

iStock Photo

Disclosure of Inventory Methods

The full disclosure convention requires that companies disclose their inventory methods, including the use of LCM, in the notes to their financial statements, and users should pay close attention to them. For example, **Cisco** discloses that it uses the lower-of-cost-or-market method in this note to its financial statements:

> Inventories are stated at the lower of cost or market. Cost is computed using standard cost, which approximates actual cost, on a first-in, first-out basis.[7]

Stop & Apply

Match the letter of each item on the right with the numbers of the related items on the left:

_____ 1. Cost of consigned goods held from suppliers	a. An inventory cost
_____ 2. A note to the financial statements explaining inventory policies	b. An assumption used in the valuation of inventory
_____ 3. Application of the LCM rule	c. Full disclosure convention
_____ 4. Goods flow	d. Conservatism convention
_____ 5. Transportation charge for merchandise shipped FOB shipping point	e. Consistency convention
_____ 6. Cost flow	f. Not an inventory cost or assumed flow
_____ 7. Choosing a method and sticking with it	
_____ 8. Transportation charge for merchandise shipped FOB destination	

SOLUTION

1\. f; 2. c; 3. d; 4. f; 5. a; 6. b; 7. e; 8. f

iStock Photo

INVENTORY COST UNDER THE PERIODIC INVENTORY SYSTEM

LO3 Calculate inventory cost under the periodic inventory system using various costing methods.

The value assigned to ending inventory is the result of two measurements: quantity and cost. Under the periodic inventory system, quantity is determined by taking a physical inventory; under the perpetual inventory system, quantities are updated as purchases and sales take place. Cost is determined by using one of the following methods, each based on a different assumption of cost flow:

- Specific identification method
- Average-cost method
- First-in, first-out (FIFO) method
- Last-in, first-out (LIFO) method

The choice of method depends on the nature of the business, the financial effects of the method, and the cost of implementing the method.

***STUDY NOTE:** If the prices of merchandise purchased never changed, inventory methods would be unnecessary. However, because prices do change, assumptions must be made about the order in which goods are sold.*

To illustrate how each method is used under the periodic inventory system, we use the following data for April, a month in which prices were rising:

April 1	Inventory	160 units @ $10.00	$ 1,600
6	Purchase	440 units @ $12.50	5,500
25	Purchase	400 units @ $14.00	5,600
Goods available for sale		1,000 units	$12,700
Sales		560 units	
On hand April 30		440 units	

The problem of inventory costing is to divide the cost of the goods available for sale ($12,700) between the 560 units sold and the 440 units on hand.

Specific Identification Method

The **specific identification method** identifies the cost of each item in ending inventory. It can be used only when it is possible to identify the units in ending inventory as coming from specific purchases. For instance, if the April 30 inventory consisted of 100 units from the April 1 inventory, 200 units from the April 6 purchase, and 140 units from the April 25 purchase, the specific identification method would assign the costs as follows:

Periodic Inventory System—Specific Identification Method

100 units @ $10.00	$1,000	Cost of goods available	
200 units @ $12.50	2,500	for sale	$12,700
140 units @ $14.00	1,960	Less April 30 inventory	5,460
440 units at a cost of	$5,460	Cost of goods sold	$ 7,240

Although the specific identification method may appear logical, most companies do not use it for the following reasons:

- It is usually impractical, if not impossible, to keep track of the purchase and sale of individual items.
- When a company deals in items that are identical but that it bought at different prices, deciding which items were sold becomes arbitrary. If the company were to use the specific identification method, it could raise or lower income by choosing the lower- or higher-priced items.

Average-Cost Method

Under the **average-cost method** (sometimes called *weighted average method*), inventory is priced at the average cost of the goods available for sale during the accounting period. Average cost is computed by dividing the total cost of goods available for sale by the total units available for sale. This gives an average unit cost that is applied to the units in ending inventory.

In our illustration, the ending inventory would be $5,588, or $12.70 per unit, determined as follows:

Periodic Inventory System—Average-Cost Method

Cost of Goods Available for Sale ÷ Units Available for Sale = Average Unit Cost

$12,700 ÷ 1,000 units = $12.70

Ending inventory: 440 units @ $12.70	= $ 5,588
Cost of goods available for sale	$12,700
Less April 30 inventory	5,588
Cost of goods sold	$ 7,112

The average-cost method tends to level out the effects of cost increases and decreases because the cost of the ending inventory is influenced by all the prices paid during the year and by the cost of beginning inventory. Some analysts, however, criticize this method because they believe recent costs are more relevant for income measurement and decision making.

First-In, First-Out (FIFO) Method

STUDY NOTE: Because of their perishable nature, some products, such as milk, require a physical flow of first-in, first-out. However, the inventory method used to account for them can be based on an assumed cost flow that differs from FIFO, such as average-cost or LIFO.

The **first-in, first-out (FIFO) method** assumes that the costs of the first items acquired should be assigned to the first items sold. The costs of the goods on hand at the end of a period are assumed to be from the most recent purchases, and the costs assigned to goods that have been sold are assumed to be from the earliest purchases. Any business, regardless of its goods flow, can use the FIFO method because the assumption underlying it is based on the flow of costs, not the flow of goods. In our illustration, the FIFO method would result in an ending inventory of $6,100, computed as follows:

Periodic Inventory System—FIFO Method	
400 units @ $14.00 from purchase of April 25	$ 5,600
40 units @ $12.50 from purchase of April 6	500
440 units at a cost of	$ 6,100
Cost of goods available for sale	$12,700
Less April 30 inventory	6,100
Cost of goods sold	$ 6,600

Thus, the FIFO method values ending inventory at the most recent costs and includes earlier costs in cost of goods sold. During periods of rising prices, FIFO yields the highest possible amount of net income because cost of goods sold shows the earliest costs incurred, which are lower during periods of inflation. Another reason for this is that businesses tend to raise selling prices as costs increase, even when they purchased the goods before the cost increase. In periods of declining prices, FIFO tends to charge the older and higher prices against revenues, thus reducing income. Consequently, a major criticism of FIFO is that it magnifies the effects of the business cycle on income.

Last-In, First-Out (LIFO) Method

STUDY NOTE: Physical flow under LIFO can be likened to the changes in a gravel pile as the gravel is sold. As the gravel on top leaves the pile, more is purchased and added to the top. The gravel on the bottom may never be sold. Although the physical flow is last-in, first-out, any acceptable cost flow assumption can be made.

The **last-in, first-out (LIFO) method** of costing inventories assumes that the costs of the last items purchased should be assigned to the first items sold and that the cost of ending inventory should reflect the cost of the goods purchased earliest. Under LIFO, the April 30 inventory would be $5,100:

Periodic Inventory System—LIFO Method	
160 units @ $10.00 from April 1 inventory	$ 1,600
280 units @ $12.50 from purchase of April 6	3,500
440 units at a cost of	$ 5,100
Cost of goods available for sale	$12,700
Less April 30 inventory	5,100
Cost of goods sold	$ 7,600

The effect of LIFO is to value inventory at the earliest prices and to include the cost of the most recently purchased goods in the cost of goods sold. This assumption, of course, does not agree with the actual physical movement of goods.

There is, however, a strong logical argument to support LIFO. A certain size of inventory is necessary in a going concern—that is, when inventory is sold, it must be replaced with more goods. The supporters of LIFO reason that the fairest determination of income occurs if the current costs of merchandise are matched against current sales prices, regardless of which physical units of merchandise are sold. When prices are moving either up or down, the cost of goods sold will, under LIFO, show costs closer to the price level at the time the goods are sold. Thus, the LIFO method tends to show a smaller net income during inflationary times and a larger net income during deflationary times than other methods of inventory valuation. The peaks and valleys of the business cycle tend to be smoothed out.

STUDY NOTE: In inventory valuation, the flow of costs—and hence income determination—is more important than the physical movement of goods and balance sheet valuation.

An argument can also be made against LIFO. Because the inventory valuation on the balance sheet reflects earlier prices, it often gives an unrealistic picture of the inventory's current value. Balance sheet measures like working capital and current ratio may be distorted and must be interpreted carefully.

Summary of Inventory Costing Methods

Exhibit 6.3 summarizes how the four inventory costing methods affect the cost of goods sold on the income statement and inventory on the balance sheet when a company uses the periodic inventory system. In periods of rising prices, FIFO yields the highest inventory valuation, the lowest cost of goods sold, and hence a higher net income; LIFO yields the lowest inventory valuation, the highest cost of goods sold, and thus a lower net income.

EXHIBIT 6.3
The Impact of Costing Methods on the Income Statement and Balance Sheet Under the Periodic Inventory System

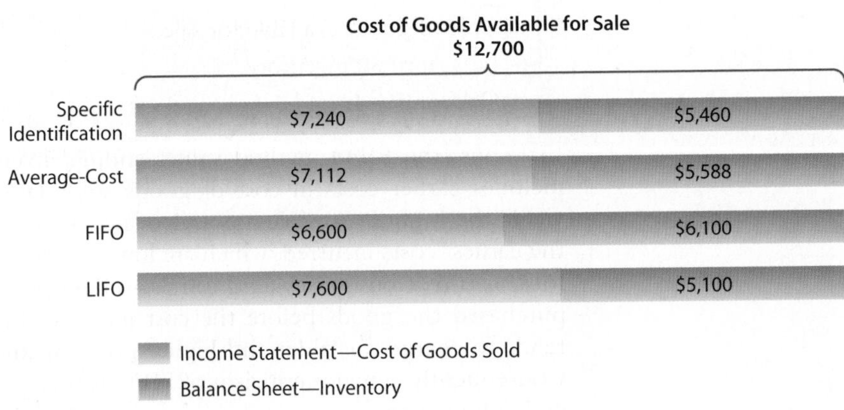

Stop & Apply

Match the following inventory costing methods with the related statements.

a. Average cost
b. FIFO
c. LIFO

___ 1. In periods of rising prices, this method results in the highest cost of goods sold.
___ 2. In periods of rising prices, this method results in the highest income.
___ 3. In periods of rising prices, this method results in the lowest ending inventory cost.
___ 4. In periods of decreasing prices, this method results in neither the highest inventory cost nor the lowest income.
___ 5. In periods of decreasing prices, this method results in the lowest income.
___ 6. In periods of decreasing prices, this method results in the highest cost of goods sold.

SOLUTION
1. c; 2. b; 3. c; 4. a; 5. b; 6. b

iStock Photo

IMPACT OF INVENTORY DECISIONS

LO 4 Explain the effects of inventory costing methods on income determination and income taxes.

Exhibit 6.4 shows how the specific identification, average-cost, FIFO, and LIFO methods of pricing inventory affect gross margin. Differences in gross margin will affect net income to the same extent. The table uses the same data as in the previous section and assumes April sales of $10,000.

EXHIBIT 6.4
Effects of Inventory Costing Methods on Gross Margin

	Specific Identification Method	Average-Cost Method	FIFO Method	LIFO Method
Sales	$10,000	$10,000	$10,000	$10,000
Cost of goods sold				
Beginning inventory	$ 1,600	$ 1,600	$ 1,600	$ 1,600
Purchases	11,100	11,100	11,100	11,100
Cost of goods available for sale	$12,700	$12,700	$12,700	$12,700
Less ending inventory	5,460	5,588	6,100	5,100
Cost of goods sold	$ 7,240	$ 7,112	$ 6,600	$ 7,600
Gross margin	$ 2,760	$ 2,888	$ 3,400	$ 2,400

Keeping in mind that April was a period of rising prices, you can see in Exhibit 6.4 that LIFO, which charges the most recent—and, in our example, the highest—prices to cost of goods sold, resulted in the lowest gross margin. Conversely, FIFO, which charges the earliest—and, in this case, the lowest—prices to cost of goods sold, produced the highest gross margin. The gross margin under the average-cost method falls between the gross margins produced by LIFO and FIFO, so this method clearly has a less pronounced effect.

During a period of declining prices, the LIFO method would produce a higher gross margin than the FIFO method. It is apparent that both these methods have the greatest impact on gross margin during prolonged periods of price changes, whether the changes are up or down. Because the specific identification method depends on the particular items sold, no generalization can be made about the effect of changing prices on gross margin.

Effects on the Financial Statements

As Exhibit 6.5 shows, the FIFO, LIFO, and average-cost methods of inventory costing are widely used. Each method has its advantages and disadvantages—none is perfect. Among the factors managers should consider in choosing an inventory costing method are the trend of prices and the effects of each method on financial statements, income taxes, and cash flows.

As we have pointed out, inventory costing methods have different effects on the income statement and balance sheet. The LIFO method is best suited for the income statement because it matches revenues and cost of goods sold. But it is not the best method for valuation of inventory on the balance sheet, particularly during a prolonged period of price increases or decreases. FIFO, on the other hand, is well suited to the balance sheet because the ending inventory is closest to current values and thus gives a more realistic view of a company's current assets. Readers of financial statements must be alert to the inventory methods a company uses and be able to assess their effects.

EXHIBIT 6.5
Inventory Costing Methods Used by 500 Large Companies

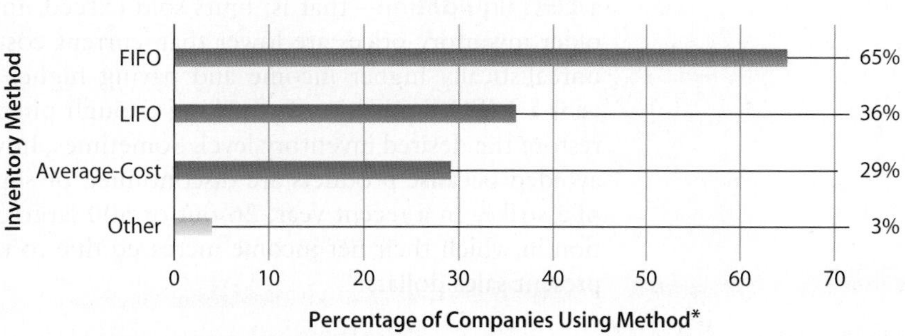

Totals more than 100% due to use of more than one method.

Source: "Industry Costing Methods Used by 500 Large Companies." Copyright © 2010 by AICPA. Reproduced with permission.

Focus on International Practices

Achieving Convergence of Inventory Methods Will Be Difficult

Achieving convergence in inventory methods between U.S. and international accounting standards will be difficult. As Exhibit 6.5 (p. 303) shows, LIFO is the second most popular inventory method in the United States. However, outside the United States, very few companies use LIFO because it is not allowed under international financial reporting standards (IFRS). Furthermore, U.S. companies may use different inventory methods for different portions of their inventory as long as there is proper disclosure, but international standards allow this practice only in very limited cases. Also, as noted earlier in the chapter, U.S. and international standards have different ways of measuring the "market" value of inventories. Because these differences are so significant, the FASB and IASB have decided not to pursue convergence with regard to inventories at this time.[8]

iStock Photo

Effects on Income Taxes

The Internal Revenue Service governs how inventories must be valued for federal income tax purposes. IRS regulations give companies a wide choice of inventory costing methods, including specific identification, average-cost, FIFO, and LIFO. Except when companies use the LIFO method, they may use the lower-of-cost-or-market rule. However, if a company wants to change the valuation method it uses for income tax purposes, it must have advance approval from the IRS.* This requirement conforms to the consistency convention. A company should change its inventory method only if there is a good reason to do so. The company must show the nature and effect of the change in its financial statements.

Many accountants believe that using the FIFO and average-cost methods in periods of rising prices causes businesses to report more than their actual profit, which results in excess payment of income tax. Profit is overstated because cost of goods sold is understated relative to current prices. Thus, a company must buy replacement inventory at higher prices and at the same time pay higher income taxes. During periods of rapid inflation, billions of dollars reported as profits and paid in income taxes were believed to be the result of poor matching of current costs and revenues under the FIFO and average-cost methods. Consequently, many companies, believing that prices would continue to rise, switched to the LIFO inventory method.

When a company uses the LIFO method to report income for tax purposes, the IRS requires that it use the same method in its accounting records, and, as we have noted, it disallows use of the LCM rule. The company may, however, use the LCM rule for financial reporting purposes.

Over a period of rising prices, a business that uses the LIFO method may find that for balance sheet purposes, its inventory is valued at a figure far below what it currently pays for the same items. Management must monitor such a situation carefully because if it lets the inventory quantity at year-end fall below the level at the beginning of the year, the company will find itself paying higher income taxes. Higher income before taxes results because the company expenses the historical costs of inventory, which are below current costs.

When sales have reduced inventories below the levels set in prior years, it is called a **LIFO liquidation**—that is, units sold exceed units purchased for the period. Since older inventory prices are lower than current costs, a company can end up reporting unrealistically higher income and paying higher income taxes. Managers can prevent a LIFO liquidation by making enough purchases before the end of the year to restore the desired inventory level. Sometimes, however, a LIFO liquidation cannot be avoided because products are discontinued or supplies are interrupted, as in the case of a strike. In a recent year, 26 out of 500 large companies reported a LIFO liquidation in which their net income increased due to the matching of historical costs with present sales dollars.[9]

*A single exception to this rule is that when companies change to LIFO from another method, they do not need advance approval from the IRS.

Effects on Cash Flows

CASH FLOW

Generally speaking, the choice of accounting methods does not affect cash flows. For example, a company's choice of average cost, FIFO, or LIFO does not affect what it pays for goods or the price at which it sells them. However, because income tax law requires a company to use the same method for income tax purposes and financial reporting, the choice of inventory method will affect the amount of income tax paid. Therefore, choosing a method that results in lower income will result in lower income taxes due. In most other cases in which there is a choice of accounting method, a company may choose different methods for income tax computations and financial reporting.

Stop & Apply

Match the inventory costing methods on the right with the descriptions on the left.

____ 1. Matches recent costs with recent revenues		a. Specific identification
____ 2. Assumes that each item of inventory is identifiable		b. Average-cost
____ 3. Results in the most realistic balance sheet valuation		c. First-in, first-out (FIFO)
____ 4. Results in the lowest net income in periods of deflation		d. Last-in, first-out (LIFO)
____ 5. Results in the lowest net income in periods of inflation		
____ 6. Matches the oldest costs with recent revenues		
____ 7. Results in the highest net income in periods of inflation		
____ 8. Results in the highest net income in periods of deflation		
____ 9. Tends to level out the effects of inflation		
____ 10. Is unpredictable as to the effects of inflation		

SOLUTION

1. d; 2. a; 3. c; 4. c; 5. d; 6. c; 7. c; 8. d; 9. b; 10. a

iStock Photo

INVENTORY COST UNDER THE PERPETUAL INVENTORY SYSTEM

LO 5 Calculate inventory cost under the perpetual inventory system using various costing methods.

Under the perpetual inventory system, cost of goods sold is accumulated as sales are made and costs are transferred from the Inventory account to the Cost of Goods Sold account. The cost of the ending inventory is the balance of the Inventory account. To illustrate costing methods under the perpetual inventory system, we use the following data:

Inventory Data—April 30

April 1	Inventory	160 units @ $10.00
6	Purchase	440 units @ $12.50
10	Sale	560 units
25	Purchase	400 units @ $14.00
30	Inventory	440 units

The specific identification method produces the same inventory cost and cost of goods sold under the perpetual system as under the periodic system because cost of goods sold and ending inventory are based on the cost of the identified items sold and on hand. The detailed records of purchases and sales maintained under the perpetual system facilitate the use of the specific identification method.

The average-cost method uses a different approach under the perpetual and periodic systems, and it produces different results. Under the periodic system, the average cost is computed for all goods available for sale during the period. Under the perpetual system, an average is computed after each purchase or series of purchases, as follows:

Perpetual Inventory System—Average-Cost Method

April	1	Inventory	160 units @ $10.00	$1,600
	6	Purchase	440 units @ $12.50	5,500
	6	Balance	600 units @ $11.83*	$7,100
				(new average computed)
	10	Sale	560 units @ $11.83*	(6,625)
	10	Balance	40 units @ $11.83*	$ 475
	25	Purchase	400 units @ $14.00	5,600
	30	Inventory	440 units @ $13.80*	$6,075
				(new average computed)
Cost of goods sold				$6,625

The costs applied to sales become the cost of goods sold, $6,625. The ending inventory is the balance, $6,075.

When costing inventory with the FIFO and LIFO methods, it is necessary to keep track of the components of inventory at each step of the way because as sales are made, the costs must be assigned in the proper order. The FIFO method is applied as follows:

Perpetual Inventory System—FIFO Method

April	1	Inventory	160 units @ $10.00		$1,600
	6	Purchase	440 units @ $12.50		5,500
	10	Sale	160 units @ $10.00	$(1,600)	
			400 units @ $12.50	(5,000)	(6,600)
	10	Balance	40 units @ $12.50		$ 500
	25	Purchase	400 units @ $14.00		5,600
	30	Inventory	40 units @ $12.50	$ 500	
			400 units @ $14.00	5,600	$6,100
Cost of goods sold					$6,600

*Rounded

Note that the ending inventory of $6,100 and the cost of goods sold of $6,600 are the same as the figures computed earlier under the periodic inventory system. This will always occur because the ending inventory under both systems consists of the last items purchased—in this case, the entire purchase of April 25 and 40 units from the purchase of April 6.

The LIFO method is applied as follows:

Perpetual Inventory System—LIFO Method

April	1	Inventory	160 units @ $10.00		$1,600
	6	Purchase	440 units @ $12.50		5,500
	10	Sale	440 units @ $12.50	$(5,500)	
			120 units @ $10.00	(1,200)	(6,700)
	10	Balance	40 units @ $10.00		$ 400
	25	Purchase	400 units @ $14.00		5,600
	30	Inventory	40 units @ $10.00	$ 400	
			400 units @ $14.00	5,600	$6,000
Cost of goods sold					$6,700

Notice that the ending inventory of $6,000 includes 40 units from the beginning inventory and 400 units from the April 25 purchase.

Focus on Business Practice

More Companies Enjoy LIFO!

The availability of better technology may partially account for the increasing use of LIFO in the United States. Using the LIFO method under the perpetual inventory system has always been a tedious process, especially if done manually. The development of faster and less expensive computer systems has made it easier for companies that use the perpetual inventory system to switch to LIFO and enjoy that method's economic benefits.

iStock Photo

Exhibit 6.6 compares the average-cost, FIFO, and LIFO methods under the perpetual inventory system. The rank of the results is the same as under the periodic inventory system, but some amounts have changed. For example, LIFO has the lowest balance sheet inventory valuation regardless of the inventory system used, but the amount is $6,000 using the perpetual system versus $5,100 using the periodic system.

EXHIBIT 6.6
The Impact of Costing Methods on the Income Statement and Balance Sheet Under the Perpetual Inventory System

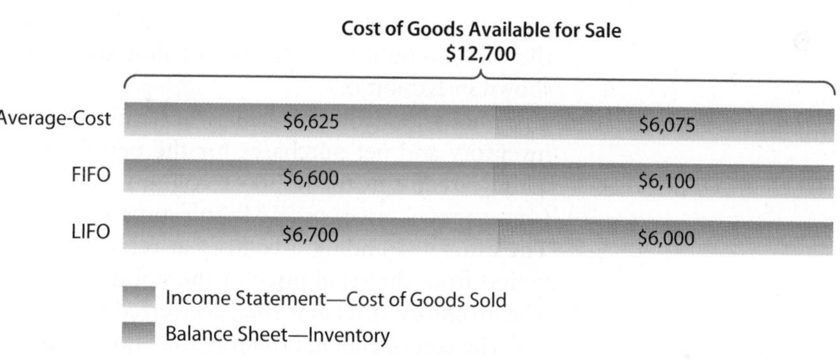

Stop & Apply

Make the calculations asked for below given the following data:

Inventory Data—April 30

May	1	Inventory	100 units @ $4.00
	5	Purchase	200 units @ $5.00
	6	Sale	250 units

Using the perpetual inventory system and (a) the average-cost method, (b) the FIFO method, and (c) the LIFO method, determine the cost of goods sold associated with the sale on May 6.

SOLUTION

a. Average-cost method:

100 units × $4.00	$ 400
200 units × $5.00	1,000
300 units	$1,400

$1,400 ÷ 300 = $4.67 per unit

Cost of goods sold = 250 units × $4.67 = $1,168*

*Rounded

b. FIFO method:

100 units × $4.00	$ 400
150 units × $5.00	750
Cost of goods sold =	$1,150

c. LIFO method:

200 units × $5.00	$1,000
50 units × $4.00	200
Cost of goods sold =	$1,200

iStock Photo

VALUING INVENTORY BY ESTIMATION

LO 6 Use the retail method and gross profit method to estimate the cost of ending inventory.

It is sometimes necessary or desirable to estimate the value of ending inventory. The retail method and gross profit method are most commonly used for this purpose.

Retail Method

The **retail method** estimates the cost of ending inventory by using the ratio of cost to retail price. Retail merchandising businesses use this method for two main reasons:

STUDY NOTE: When estimating inventory by the retail method, the inventory need not be counted.

- To prepare financial statements for each accounting period, one must know the cost of inventory; the retail method can be used to estimate the cost without taking the time or going to the expense of determining the cost of each item in the inventory.
- Because items in a retail store normally have a price tag or a universal product code, it is common practice to take the physical inventory "at retail" from these price tags or codes and to reduce the total value to cost by using the retail method. *At retail* means the amount of the inventory at the marked selling prices of the inventory items.

When the retail method is used to estimate ending inventory, the records must show the beginning inventory at cost and at retail. They must also show the amount of goods purchased during the period at cost and at retail. The net sales at retail is the balance of the Sales account less returns and allowances. A simple example of the retail method is shown in Exhibit 6.7.

Goods available for sale is determined at cost and at retail by listing beginning inventory and net purchases for the period at cost and at their expected selling price, adding freight-in to the Cost column, and totaling. The ratio of these two amounts (cost to retail price) provides an estimate of the cost of each dollar of retail sales value. The estimated ending inventory at retail is then determined by deducting sales for the period from the retail price of the goods that were available for sale during the period. The inventory at retail is then converted to cost on the basis of the ratio of cost to retail.

The cost of ending inventory can also be estimated by applying the ratio of cost to retail price to the total retail value of the physical count of the ending inventory. Applying the retail method in practice is often more difficult than this simple example because of such complications as changes in retail price during the period, different markups on different types of merchandise, and varying volumes of sales for different types of merchandise.

Gross Profit Method

The **gross profit method** (also known as the *gross margin method*) assumes that the ratio of gross margin for a business remains relatively stable from year to year. The gross profit method is used in place of the retail method when records of the retail prices of beginning inventory and purchases are not available. It is a useful way of estimating the amount of inventory lost or destroyed by theft, fire, or other hazards; insurance

EXHIBIT 6.7
Retail Method of Inventory Estimation

	Cost	Retail
Beginning inventory	$ 80,000	$110,000
Net purchases for the period (excluding freight-in)	214,000	290,000
Freight-in	6,000	
Goods available for sale	$300,000	$400,000
Ratio of cost to retail price: $\frac{\$300,000}{\$400,000} = 75\%$		
Net sales during the period		320,000
Estimated ending inventory at retail		$ 80,000
Ratio of cost to retail	75%	
Estimated cost of ending inventory	$ 60,000	

STUDY NOTE: Freight-in does not appear in the Retail column because retailers automatically price their goods high enough to cover freight charges.

companies often use it to verify loss claims. The gross profit method is acceptable for estimating the cost of inventory for interim reports, but it is not acceptable for valuing inventory in the annual financial statements.

As Exhibit 6.8 shows, the gross profit method is simple to use:

1. Calculate the cost of goods available for sale in the usual way (add purchases to beginning inventory).
2. Estimate the cost of goods sold by deducting the estimated gross margin of 30 percent from sales.
3. Deduct the estimated cost of goods sold from the goods available for sale to arrive at the estimated cost of ending inventory.

EXHIBIT 6.8
Gross Profit Method of Inventory Estimation

1.	Beginning inventory at cost		$100,000
	Purchases at cost (including freight-in)		580,000
	Cost of goods available for sale		$680,000
2.	Less estimated cost of goods sold		
	Sales at selling price	$800,000	
	Less estimated gross margin ($800,000 × 30%)	240,000	
	Estimated cost of goods sold		560,000
3.	Estimated cost of ending inventory		$120,000

Stop & Apply

Campus Jeans Shop had net retail sales of $195,000 during the current year. The following additional information was obtained from the company's accounting records:

	At Cost	At Retail
Beginning inventory	$ 40,000	$ 60,000
Net purchases (excluding freight-in)	130,000	210,000
Freight-in	10,000	

Using the retail method, estimate the company's ending inventory at cost. Assuming that a physical inventory taken at year-end revealed an inventory on hand of $66,000 at retail value, what is the estimated amount of inventory shrinkage (loss due to theft, damage, etc.) at cost using the retail method?

SOLUTION

	Cost	Retail
Beginning inventory	$ 40,000	$ 60,000
Net purchases for the period (excluding freight-in)	130,000	210,000
Freight-in	10,000	
Goods available for sale	$180,000	$270,000
Ratio of cost to retail price: $\frac{\$180,000}{\$270,000} = 66.7\%$		
Net sales during the period		195,000
Estimated ending inventory at retail		$ 75,000
Ratio of cost to retail	66.7%	
Estimated cost of ending inventory	$ 50,025	

Estimated Inventory Loss = Estimated Cost − (Retail Inventory Count × 66.7%)
= $50,025 − ($66,000 × 66.7%) = $50,025 − $44,022
= $6,003

A look back at ▸ Cisco Systems, Inc.

In this chapter's Decision Point, we posed the following questions:

1. What is the impact of inventory decisions on operating results?
2. How should inventory be valued?
3. How should the level of inventory be evaluated?

As we pointed out in the chapter, **Cisco** uses supply-chain management and a just-in-time operating environment to manage its inventory. By doing so, it reduces its operating costs. We also pointed out that a note in Cisco's annual report disclosed that the company uses the average costing method and applies the lower-of-cost-or-market rule to its inventories. Cisco's approach to valuation adheres to the conservatism convention because it may recognize losses in value before the products are sold if their value decreases.

RATIO

Financial Ratios: Inventory Turnover and Days' Inventory on Hand

Using data from Cisco's Financial Highlights, we can evaluate the company's success in managing its inventories by comparing its inventory turnover ratio and days' inventory on hand in 2009 and 2008 (dollar amounts are in millions; inventory in 2007 was $1,076):

	2009	**2008**
$\frac{\text{Cost of Goods Sold}}{\text{Average Inventory}}$	$\frac{\$10,481}{(\$890 + \$997)} \div 2$	$\frac{\$11,660}{(\$997 + \$1,076)} \div 2$
	$\frac{\$10,481}{\$943.5}$	$\frac{\$11,660}{\$1,036.5}$
Inventory Turnover:	11.1 times	11.2 times
$\frac{\text{Number of Days in a Year}}{\text{Inventory Turnover}}$	$\frac{365 \text{ Days}}{11.1 \text{ Times}}$	$\frac{365 \text{ Days}}{11.3 \text{ Times}}$
Days' Inventory on Hand:	32.9 days	32.3 days

Thus, in 2009, Cisco experienced only a very small decrease in its inventory turnover, which resulted in a small increase in the number of days it had inventory on hand. The company controlled its inventory level very well in a year in which both sales and cost of goods sold declined.

Review Problem

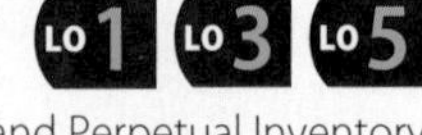

Periodic and Perpetual Inventory Systems

The following table summarizes the beginning inventory, purchases, and sales of Zeta Company's single product during May:

	A	B	C	D	E	F	G	H
1					Beginning Inventory and Purchases			
2	Date				Units	Cost	Total	Sales Units
3	May	1		Inventory	2,800	$20	$ 56,000	
4		8		Purchase	1,200	22	26,400	
5		10		Sale				3,200
6		24		Purchase	1,600	24	38,400	
7								
8	Totals				5,600		$120,800	3,200
9								

Required

1. Assuming that the company uses the periodic inventory system, compute the cost that should be assigned to ending inventory and to cost of goods sold using (a) the average-cost method, (b) the FIFO method, and (c) the LIFO method.
2. Assuming that the company uses the perpetual inventory system, compute the cost that should be assigned to ending inventory and to cost of goods sold using (a) the average-cost method, (b) the FIFO method, and (c) the LIFO method.
3. RATIO Compute inventory turnover and days' inventory on hand under each of the inventory cost flow assumptions in **1**. What conclusion can you draw from this comparison?

ANSWERS TO REVIEW PROBLEM

	Units	Amount
Beginning inventory	2,800	$ 56,000
Purchases	2,800	64,800
Available for sale	5,600	$120,800
Sale	3,200	
Ending inventory	2,400	

1. Periodic inventory system:

   a. Average-cost method

Cost of goods available for sale	$120,800
Less ending inventory consisting of 2,400 units at $21.57*	51,768
Cost of goods sold	$ 69,032

*$120,800 ÷ 5,600 units = $21.57 (rounded)

   b. FIFO method

Cost of goods available for sale		$120,800
Less ending inventory consisting of		
May 24 purchase (1,600 × $24)	$38,400	
May 8 purchase (800 × $22)	17,600	56,000
Cost of goods sold		$ 64,800

   c. LIFO method

Cost of goods available for sale	$120,800
Less ending inventory consisting of beginning inventory (2,400 × $20)	48,000
Cost of goods sold	$ 72,800

2. Perpetual inventory system:

   a. Average-cost method

Date			Units	Cost	Amount
May	1	Inventory	2,800	$20.00	$56,000
	8	Purchase	1,200	22.00	26,400
	8	Balance	4,000	20.60	$82,400
	10	Sale	(3,200)	20.60	(65,920)
	10	Balance	800	20.60	$16,480
	24	Purchase	1,600	24.00	38,400
	31	Inventory	2,400	22.87*	$54,880
Cost of goods sold					$65,920

*Rounded

b. FIFO method

Date			Units	Cost	Amount
May	1	Inventory	2,800	$20	$56,000
	8	Purchase	1,200	22	26,400
	8	Balance	2,800	20	
			1,200	22	$82,400
	10	Sale	(2,800)	20	
			(400)	22	(64,800)
	10	Balance	800	22	$17,600
	24	Purchase	1,600	24	38,400
	31	Inventory	800	22	
			1,600	24	$56,000
Cost of goods sold					$64,800

c. LIFO method

Date			Units	Cost	Amount
May	1	Inventory	2,800	$20	$56,000
	8	Purchase	1,200	22	26,400
	8	Balance	2,800	20	
			1,200	22	$82,400
	10	Sale	(1,200)	22	
			(2,000)	20	(66,400)
	10	Balance	800	20	$16,000
	24	Purchase	1,600	24	38,400
	31	Inventory	800	20	
			1,600	24	$54,400
Cost of goods sold					$66,400

3. Ratios computed:

	Average-Cost	FIFO	LIFO
Cost of Goods Sold / Average Inventory	$\frac{\$69{,}032}{\$53{,}884} = 1.3$	$\frac{\$64{,}800}{\$56{,}000} = 1.2$	$\frac{\$72{,}800}{\$52{,}000} = 1.4$
	($51,768 + $56,000) ÷ 2	($56,000 + $56,000) ÷ 2	($48,000 + $56,000) ÷ 2
Inventory Turnover:	1.3 times	1.2 times	1.4 times
Days' Inventory on Hand:	(365 Days ÷ 1.3 Times) 280.8 days	(365 Days ÷ 1.2 Times) 304.2 days	(365 Days ÷ 1.4 Times) 260.7 days

In periods of rising prices, the LIFO method will always result in a higher inventory turnover and lower days' inventory on hand than the other costing methods. When comparing companies' inventory ratios, their inventory methods should be considered.

Stop & Review

Explain the management decisions related to inventory accounting, evaluation of inventory level, and the effects of inventory misstatements on income measurement. LO 1

The objective of inventory accounting is the proper determination of income through the matching of costs and revenues. In accounting for inventories, management must choose the type of processing system, costing method, and valuation method the company will use. Because the value of inventory affects a company's net income, management's choices will affect not only external and internal evaluations of the company, but also the amount of income taxes the company pays and its cash flows.

The level of inventory a company maintains has important economic consequences. To evaluate inventory levels, managers commonly use inventory turnover and its related measure, days' inventory on hand. Supply-chain management and a just-in-time operating environment are a means of increasing inventory turnover and reducing inventory carrying costs. If the value of ending inventory is understated or overstated, a corresponding error—dollar for dollar—will be made in income before income taxes. Furthermore, because the ending inventory of one period is the beginning inventory of the next, the misstatement affects two accounting periods, although the effects are opposite.

Define *inventory cost*, contrast goods flow and cost flow, and explain the lower-of-cost-or-market (LCM) rule. LO 2

Inventory cost includes the invoice price less purchases discounts; freight-in, including insurance in transit; and applicable taxes and tariffs. Goods flow refers to the actual physical flow of merchandise in a business, whereas cost flow refers to the assumed flow of costs. The lower-of-cost-or-market rule states that if the replacement cost (market cost) of the inventory is lower than the original cost, the lower figure should be used.

Calculate inventory cost under the periodic inventory system using various costing methods. LO 3

The value assigned to ending inventory is the result of two measurements: quantity and cost. Under the periodic inventory system, quantity is determined by taking a physical inventory. Cost is determined by using one of four inventory methods, each based on a different assumption of cost flow. The specific identification method identifies the actual cost of each item in inventory. The average-cost method assumes that the cost of inventory is the average cost of goods available for sale during the period. The first-in, first-out (FIFO) method assumes that the costs of the first items acquired should be assigned to the first items sold. The last-in, first-out (LIFO) method assumes that the costs of the last items acquired should be assigned to the first items sold.

Explain the effects of inventory costing methods on income determination and income taxes. LO 4

During periods of rising prices, the LIFO method shows the lowest gross margin and thus net income; FIFO, the highest; and average-cost, somewhere in between. LIFO and FIFO have the opposite effects in periods of falling prices. No generalization can be made regarding the specific identification method. The Internal Revenue Service requires a company that uses LIFO for tax purposes to use LIFO in its accounting records. It also does not allow a company that uses LIFO to apply the lower-of-cost-or-market rule.

Calculate inventory cost under the perpetual inventory system using various costing methods. LO 5

Under the perpetual inventory system, cost of goods sold is accumulated as sales are made, and costs are transferred from the Inventory account to the Cost of Goods Sold account. The cost of the ending inventory is the balance of the Inventory account. The specific identification method and the FIFO method produce the same results under both the perpetual and periodic inventory systems. The results differ for the average-cost method because an average is calculated after each sale rather than at the end of the accounting period. Results also differ for the LIFO method because the cost components of inventory change constantly as goods are bought and sold.

Use the retail method and gross profit method to estimate the cost of ending inventory. LO 6

Two methods of estimating the value of inventory are the retail method and the gross profit method. Under the retail method, inventory is determined at retail prices and is then reduced to estimated cost by applying a ratio of cost to retail price. Under the gross profit method, cost of goods sold is estimated by reducing sales by estimated gross margin. The estimated cost of goods sold is then deducted from the cost of goods available for sale to estimate the cost of ending inventory.

Key Terms and Ratios

Average-cost method 300 (LO3)
Consignment 298 (LO2)
Cost flow 297 (LO2)
First-in, first-out (FIFO) method 301 (LO3)
Goods flow 297 (LO2)
Gross profit method 308 (LO6)
Inventory cost 297 (LO2)
Just-in-time (JIT) operating environment 294 (LO1)
Last-in, first-out (LIFO) method 301 (LO3)
LIFO liquidation 304 (LO4)
Lower-of-cost-or-market (LCM) rule 298 (LO2)
Market 298 (LO2)
Retail method 308 (LO6)
Specific identification method 300 (LO3)
Supply-chain management 294 (LO1)

FINANCIAL RATIOS

Days' inventory on hand 294 (LO1)
Inventory turnover 293 (LO1)

Chapter Assignments Building Your Basic Knowledge and Skills

Short Exercises

LO 1

Management Issues

SE 1. Indicate whether each of the following items is associated with (a) allocating the cost of inventories in accordance with the matching rule, (b) assessing the impact of inventory decisions, (c) evaluating the level of inventory, or (d) engaging in an unethical practice.

1. Calculating days' inventory on hand
2. Ordering a supply of inventory to satisfy customer needs
3. Valuing inventory at an amount to achieve a specific profit objective
4. Calculating the income tax effect of an inventory method
5. Deciding the cost to place on ending inventory

LO 1

Inventory Turnover and Days' Inventory on Hand

SE 2. During 2011, Chico Clothiers had beginning inventory of $480,000, ending inventory of $560,000, and cost of goods sold of $2,200,000. Compute the inventory turnover and days' inventory on hand.

LO 1

Inventory Turnover and Days' Inventory on Hand

SE 3. During 2011, Hank's Supplies had beginning inventory of $1,440,000, ending inventory of $1,780,000, and cost of goods sold of $6,500,000. Compute the inventory turnover and days' inventory on hand.

LO 3

Specific Identification Method

SE 4. Assume the following data with regard to inventory for Caciato Company:

Aug. 1	Inventory	40 units @ $10 per unit	$ 400
8	Purchase	50 units @ $11 per unit	550
22	Purchase	35 units @ $12 per unit	420
Goods available for sale		125 units	$1,370
Aug. 15	Sale	45 units	
28	Sale	25 units	
Inventory, Aug. 31		55 units	

Assuming that the inventory consists of 30 units from the August 8 purchase and 25 units from the purchase of August 22, calculate the cost of ending inventory and cost of goods sold.

LO 3 **Average-Cost Method: Periodic Inventory System**

SE 5. Using the data in SE 4, calculate the cost of ending inventory and cost of goods sold according to the average-cost method under the periodic inventory system. (*Note:* Round final answers to the nearest whole dollar.)

LO 3 **FIFO Method: Periodic Inventory System**

SE 6. Using the data in SE 4, calculate the cost of ending inventory and cost of goods sold according to the FIFO method under the periodic inventory system. (*Note:* Round inventory amounts and cost of goods sold to the nearest whole dollar.)

LO 3 **LIFO Method: Periodic Inventory System**

SE 7. Using the data in SE 4, calculate the cost of ending inventory and cost of goods sold according to the LIFO method under the periodic inventory system.

LO 4 **Effects of Inventory Costing Methods and Changing Prices**

SE 8. Using Exhibit 6.4 as an example, prepare a table with four columns that shows the ending inventory and cost of goods sold for each of the results of your calculations in SE 4 through SE 7. Which method(s) would result in the lowest income taxes?

LO 5 **Average-Cost Method: Perpetual Inventory System**

SE 9. Using the data in SE 4, calculate the cost of ending inventory and cost of goods sold according to the average-cost method under the perpetual inventory system.

LO 5 **FIFO Method: Perpetual Inventory System**

SE 10. Using the data in SE 4, calculate the cost of ending inventory and cost of goods sold according to the FIFO method under the perpetual inventory system.

LO 5 **LIFO Method: Perpetual Inventory System**

SE 11. Using the data in SE 4, calculate the cost of ending inventory and cost of goods sold according to the LIFO method under the perpetual inventory system.

LO 4 **Effects of Inventory Costing Methods and Changing Prices**

SE 12. Using Exhibit 6.4 as an example, prepare a table with four columns that shows the ending inventory and cost of goods sold for each of the results from your calculations in SE 9 through SE 11. Which method(s) would result in the lowest income taxes?

Exercises

LO 1, 2 **Discussion Questions**

E 1. Develop a brief answer to each of the following questions:

1. Is it good or bad for a retail store to have a large inventory?
2. Which is more important from the standpoint of inventory costing: the flow of goods or the flow of costs?
3. Why is misstatement of inventory one of the most common means of financial statement fraud?
4. Given that the LCM rule is an application of the conservatism convention in the current accounting period, is the effect of this application also conservative in the next period?

LO 4, 5, 6 **Discussion Questions**

E 2. Develop a brief answer to each of the following questions:

1. Under what condition would all four methods of inventory costing produce exactly the same results?
2. Under the perpetual inventory system, why is the cost of goods sold not determined by deducting the ending inventory from the cost of goods available for sale, as it is under the periodic inventory system?

3. Which of the following does not require a physical inventory: the periodic inventory system, perpetual inventory system, retail method, or gross profit method?

LO 1

Management Issues

E 3. Indicate whether each of the following items is associated with (a) allocating the cost of inventories in accordance with the matching rule, (b) assessing the impact of inventory decisions, (c) evaluating the level of inventory, or (d) engaging in an unethical action.

1. Computing inventory turnover
2. Valuing inventory at an amount to meet management's targeted net income
3. Using a just-in-time operating environment
4. Determining the effects of inventory decisions on cash flows
5. Apportioning the cost of goods available for sale to ending inventory and cost of goods sold
6. Determining the effects of inventory methods on income taxes
7. Determining the assumption about the flow of costs into and out of the company

LO 1

Inventory Ratios

E 4. Just a Buck Discount Stores is assessing its levels of inventory for 2010 and 2011 and has gathered the following data:

	2011	2010	2009
Ending inventory	$ 96,000	$ 81,000	$69,000
Cost of goods sold	480,000	450,000	

Compute the inventory turnover and days' inventory on hand for 2010 and 2011 and comment on the results. (*Note:* Round final answers to one decimal place.)

LO 1

Effects of Inventory Errors

E 5. Condensed income statements for Kozumel Company for two years are shown below.

	2011	2010
Sales	$252,000	$210,000
Cost of goods sold	150,000	108,000
Gross margin	$102,000	$102,000
Operating expenses	60,000	60,000
Income before income taxes	$ 42,000	$ 42,000

After the end of 2011, the company discovered that an error had resulted in an $18,000 understatement of the 2010 ending inventory.

Compute the corrected income before income taxes for 2010 and 2011. What effect will the error have on income before income taxes and stockholders' equity for 2012?

LO 1, 2, 3

Accounting Conventions and Inventory Valuation

E 6. For a number of years, Turnbow Company, a manufacturer of telecommunications equipment, has been using the LIFO method adjusted for lower of cost or market. Because the prices of its equipment have been falling, Turnbow has had to reduce the cost of inventory to market each year for two years. It is now considering changing its method to FIFO adjusted for lower of cost or market.

Explain how the accounting conventions of consistency, full disclosure, and conservatism apply to this decision. If the change were made, why would management expect fewer adjustments to market in the future?

LO 3

Periodic Inventory System and Inventory Costing Methods

E 7. Jola's Grain Shop recorded the following purchases and sales during the past year:

Jan.	1	Beginning inventory	125 cases @ $23	$2,875
Feb.	25	Purchase	100 cases @ $26	2,600
June	15	Purchase	200 cases @ $28	5,600

Oct. 15	Purchase	150 cases @ $28	$ 4,200
Dec. 15	Purchase	100 cases @ $30	3,000
Goods available for sale		675 cases	$18,275
Total sales		500 cases	
Dec. 31	Ending inventory	175 cases	

Assume that Jola's Grain Shop sold all of the June 15 purchase and 100 cases each from the January 1 beginning inventory, the October 15 purchase, and the December 15 purchase.

Determine the costs that should be assigned to ending inventory and cost of goods sold under each of the following assumptions: (1) costs are assigned by the specific identification method, (2) costs are assigned by the average-cost method, (3) costs are assigned by the FIFO method, (4) costs are assigned by the LIFO method. What conclusions can be drawn about the effect of each method on the company's income statement and balance sheet? Round your answers to the nearest whole number and assume the periodic inventory system.

LO 3

Periodic Inventory System and Inventory Costing Methods

E 8. During its first year of operation, Krempna Company purchased 2,800 units of a product at $42 per unit. During the second year, it purchased 3,000 units of the same product at $48 per unit. During the third year, it purchased 2,500 units at $60 per unit. In each year, it had an ending inventory of 500 units. Krempna uses the periodic inventory system.

Prepare cost of goods sold statements that compare the value of ending inventory and the cost of goods sold for each of the three years using (1) the FIFO inventory costing method and (2) the LIFO method. From the resulting data, what conclusions can you draw about the relationships between the changes in unit price and the changes in the value of ending inventory?

LO 3

Periodic Inventory System and Inventory Costing Methods

E 9. The inventory, purchases, and sales of a single product for the month of June are as follows:

		Units	Amount per Unit
June 1	Beginning inventory	150	$30
4	Purchase	400	33
12	Purchase	800	36
16	Sale	1,300	60
24	Purchase	300	39

Using the periodic inventory system, compute the cost of ending inventory, cost of goods sold, and gross margin. Use the following inventory costing methods: average cost, FIFO, and LIFO. Explain the reasons for the differences in gross margin produced by the three methods. (*Note:* Round unit costs to cents and totals to dollars.)

LO 4

Effects of Inventory Costing Methods on Cash Flows

E 10. Forever Products, Inc., sold 120,000 cases of glue at $20 per case during 2011. Its beginning inventory consisted of 20,000 cases at a cost of $12 per case. During 2011, it purchased 60,000 cases at $14 per case and 50,000 cases at $15 per case. Operating expenses were $550,000, and the applicable income tax rate was 30 percent.

Using the periodic inventory system, compute net income using the FIFO and LIFO methods for costing inventory. Which method produces the larger cash flow?

The company is considering a purchase of 10,000 cases at $15 per case just before the end of 2011. What effect on net income and on cash flow will this proposed purchase have under each method? (*Hint:* What are the income tax consequences?)

LO 5

Perpetual Inventory System and Inventory Costing Methods

E 11. Referring to the data in E 9 and using the perpetual inventory system, compute the cost of ending inventory, cost of goods sold, and gross margin. Use the average-cost, FIFO, and LIFO inventory costing methods. Explain the reasons for the differences in gross margin produced by the three methods. (*Note:* Round unit costs to cents and totals to dollars.)

LO 3, 5

Periodic and Perpetual Systems and Inventory Costing Methods

E 12. During July 2011, Fulton, Inc., sold 250 units of its product Cozy for $8,000. The following units were available:

	Units	Cost
Beginning inventory	100	$ 4
Purchase 1	40	8
Purchase 2	60	12
Purchase 3	150	18
Purchase 4	90	24

A sale of 250 units was made after purchase 3. Of the units sold, 100 came from beginning inventory, and 150 came from purchase 3.

Determine the goods available for sale in units and dollars and the ending inventory in units. Then determine the costs that should be assigned to cost of goods sold and ending inventory under each of the following assumptions: (1) Costs are assigned under the periodic inventory system using (a) the specific identification method, (b) the average-cost method, (c) the FIFO method, and (d) the LIFO method. (2) Costs are assigned under the perpetual inventory system using (a) the average-cost method, (b) the FIFO method, and (c) the LIFO method. In each case, show the gross margin. (*Note:* Round unit costs to cents and totals to dollars.)

LO 6

Retail Method

E 13. Joan's Dress Shop had net retail sales of $250,000 during the current year. The following additional information was obtained from the company's accounting records:

	At Cost	At Retail
Beginning inventory	$ 40,000	$ 60,000
Net purchases (excluding freight-in)	140,000	220,000
Freight-in	10,400	

1. Using the retail method, estimate the company's ending inventory at cost.
2. Assume that a physical inventory taken at year-end revealed an inventory on hand of $18,000 at retail value. What is the estimated amount of inventory shrinkage (loss due to theft, damage, etc.) at cost using the retail method?

LO 6

Gross Profit Method

E 14. Chen Mo-Wan was at home when he received a call from the fire department telling him his store had burned. His business was a total loss. The insurance company asked him to prove his inventory loss. For the year, until the date of the fire, Chen's company had sales of $900,000 and purchases of $560,000. Freight-in amounted to $27,400, and beginning inventory was $90,000. Chen always priced his goods to achieve a gross margin of 40 percent. Compute Chen's estimated inventory loss.

Problems

LO 1, 3

Periodic Inventory System and Inventory Costing Methods

✔ Cost of goods available for sale: $157,980

P 1. Eleni Cabinet Company sold 2,200 cabinets during 2011 at $160 per cabinet. Its beginning inventory on January 1 was 130 cabinets at $56. Purchases made during the year were as follows:

February	225 cabinets @ $62
April	350 cabinets @ $65
June	700 cabinets @ $70
August	300 cabinets @ $66
October	400 cabinets @ $68
November	250 cabinets @ $72

The company's selling and administrative expenses for the year were $101,000. Eleni uses the periodic inventory system.

REQUIRED

1. Prepare a schedule to compute the cost of goods available for sale. (*Note:* Round average cost per unit to two decimal places. Round amounts for inventory and cost of goods sold to the nearest whole dollar amount.)
2. Compute income before income taxes under each of the following inventory cost flow assumptions: (a) the average-cost method, (b) the FIFO method, and (c) the LIFO method.

USER INSIGHT ▶

3. Compute inventory turnover and days' inventory on hand under each of the inventory cost flow assumptions in requirement **2**. What conclusion can you draw from this comparison? (*Note:* Round ratios to one decimal place.)

LO 1, 3

✔ Cost of goods sold for average-cost method: March, $4,578; April, $10,660

Periodic Inventory System and Inventory Costing Methods

P 2. The inventory, purchases, and sales of Product SOL for March and April are listed below. The company closes its books at the end of each month. It uses the periodic inventory system.

Mar. 1	Beginning inventory	60 units @ $49	Apr. 4	Purchase	120 units @ $53
10	Purchase	100 units @ $52	15	Purchase	50 units @ $54
19	Sale	90 units	23	Sale	200 units
31	Ending inventory	70 units	25	Purchase	100 units @ $55
			30	Ending inventory	140 units

REQUIRED

1. Compute the cost of the ending inventory on March 31 and April 30 using the average-cost method. In addition, determine cost of goods sold for March and April. Round unit costs to cents and totals to dollars.
2. Compute the cost of the ending inventory on March 31 and April 30 using the FIFO method. Also determine cost of goods sold for March and April.
3. Compute the cost of the ending inventory on March 31 and April 30 using the LIFO method. Also determine cost of goods sold for March and April.

USER INSIGHT ▶

4. Do the cash flows from operations for March and April differ depending on which inventory costing method is used—average-cost, FIFO, or LIFO? Explain.

LO 4, 5

✔ Cost of goods sold for FIFO method: March, $4,500; April, $10,540

Perpetual Inventory System and Inventory Costing Methods

P 3. To prepare solutions to the requirements listed below, use the data provided in **P2**, but assume that the company uses the perpetual inventory system. (*Hint*: It is helpful to determine the balance of inventory after each transaction, as shown in the Review Problem in this chapter.)

REQUIRED

1. Determine the cost of ending inventory and cost of goods sold for March and April using the average-cost method. Round unit costs to cents and totals to dollars.
2. Determine the cost of ending inventory and cost of goods sold for March and April using the FIFO method.
3. Determine the cost of ending inventory and cost of goods sold for March and April using the LIFO method.

USER INSIGHT ▶

4. Assume that this company grows for many years in a long period of rising prices. How realistic do you think the balance sheet value for inventory would be, and what effect would it have on the inventory turnover ratio?

LO 6

Retail Method

✔ Estimated inventory shortage: at cost, $24,208; at retail, $35,600

P 4. Gonera Company operates a large discount store and uses the retail method to estimate the cost of ending inventory. Recently, the company has had unusually heavy inventory losses, which management suspects have been due to shoplifting or employee pilferage. To estimate the amount of the loss, the company has taken a physical inventory and will compare the results with the estimated cost of inventory. Data from Gonera's accounting records are as follows:

	At Cost	At Retail
October 1 beginning inventory	$205,952	$297,200
Purchases	286,932	434,000
Purchases returns and allowances	(8,172)	(12,800)
Freight-in	3,800	
Sales		436,732
Sales returns and allowances		(3,732)
October 31 physical inventory at retail		249,800

REQUIRED

1. Using the retail method, prepare a schedule to estimate the dollar amount of the store's month-end inventory at cost.
2. Use the store's cost to retail ratio to reduce the retail value of the physical inventory to cost.
3. Calculate the estimated amount of inventory shortage at cost and at retail.
4. Many retail chains use the retail method because they find it an efficient way to operate. Why do you think they find this method efficient?

USER INSIGHT ▶ (4)

LO 6

Gross Profit Method

✔ Estimated loss of inventory in fire: $163,258

P 5. Gonzo Furniture is a large retail furniture company that operates in two adjacent warehouses. One warehouse is a showroom, and the other is used to store merchandise. On the night of April 22, 2011, a fire broke out in the storage warehouse and destroyed the merchandise stored there. The fire did not reach the showroom, so all the merchandise on display was saved.

Although the company maintained a perpetual inventory system, its records were rather haphazard, and the last reliable physical inventory had been taken on December 31, 2010. In addition, there was no control of the flow of goods between the showroom and the warehouse. Thus, it was impossible to tell what goods would have been in either place. As a result, the insurance company required an independent estimate of the amount of loss. The insurance company examiners were satisfied when they received the following information:

Merchandise inventory on December 31, 2010	$181,850
Purchases, January 1 to April 22, 2011	301,525
Purchases returns, January 1 to April 22, 2011	(1,338)
Freight-in, January 1 to April 22, 2011	6,638
Sales, January 1 to April 22, 2011	494,881
Sales returns, January 1 to April 22, 2011	(3,725)
Merchandise inventory in showroom on April 22, 2011	50,370
Average gross margin	44%

REQUIRED

1. Prepare a schedule that estimates the amount of the inventory loss that Gonzo Furniture suffered in the fire.
2. What are some other reasons management might need to estimate the amount of inventory?

USER INSIGHT ▶ (2)

Alternate Problems

LO 1, 3

Periodic Inventory System and Inventory Costing Methods

✔ Cost of goods available for sale: $5,280,000

P 6. McRay Company merchandises a single product called Bright. The following data pertain to the beginning inventory and purchases of Bright during the past year:

January 1 inventory	34,000 units @ $11.00
February purchases	40,000 units @ $12.00
March purchases	80,000 units @ $12.40
May purchases	60,000 units @ $12.60
July purchases	100,000 units @ $12.80
September purchases	80,000 units @ $12.60
November purchases	30,000 units @ $13.00

Sales of Bright totaled 393,000 units at $20.00 per unit. Selling and administrative expenses totaled $2,551,000 for the year. McRay Company uses the periodic inventory system.

REQUIRED

1. Prepare a schedule to compute the cost of goods available for sale.
2. Compute income before income taxes under each of the following inventory cost flow assumptions: (a) the average-cost method, (b) the FIFO method, and (c) the LIFO method.

USER INSIGHT ▶

3. Compute inventory turnover and days' inventory on hand under each of the inventory cost flow assumptions listed in requirement 2. What conclusion can you draw?

LO 1, 3

Periodic Inventory System and Inventory Costing Methods

✔ Cost of goods sold for FIFO method: April, $19,000; May, $43,760

P 7. The inventory of Product A and data on purchases and sales for a two-month period follow. The company closes its books at the end of each month. It uses the periodic inventory system.

Apr. 1	Beginning inventory	50 units @ $204
10	Purchase	100 units @ $220
17	Sale	90 units
30	Ending inventory	60 units
May 2	Purchase	100 units @ $216
14	Purchase	50 units @ $224
22	Purchase	60 units @ $234
30	Sale	200 units
31	Ending inventory	70 units

REQUIRED

1. Compute the cost of ending inventory of Product A on April 30 and May 31 using the average-cost method. In addition, determine cost of goods sold for April and May. Round unit costs to cents and totals to dollars.
2. Compute the cost of the ending inventory on April 30 and May 31 using the FIFO method. In addition, determine cost of goods sold for April and May.
3. Compute the cost of the ending inventory on April 30 and May 31 using the LIFO method. In addition, determine cost of goods sold for April and May.

USER INSIGHT ▶

4. Do the cash flows from operations for April and May differ depending on which inventory costing method is used? Explain.

LO 4, 5

Perpetual Inventory System and Inventory Costing Methods

✔ Cost of goods sold for average-cost method: April, $19,320; May, $44,238

P 8. To prepare solutions to the following requirements, use the data provided in P 7, but assume that the company uses the perpetual inventory system. (*Hint*: It is helpful to determine the balance of inventory after each transaction, as shown in the Review Problem in this chapter.)

REQUIRED

1. Determine the cost of ending inventory and cost of goods sold for April and May using the average-cost method. Round unit costs to cents and totals to dollars.
2. Determine the cost of ending inventory and cost of goods sold for April and May using the FIFO method.
3. Determine the cost of ending inventory and cost of goods sold for April and May using the LIFO method.

USER INSIGHT ▶

4. Assume that this company grows for many years in a long period of rising prices. How realistic do you think the balance sheet value for inventory would be, and what effect would it have on the inventory turnover ratio?

LO 6

Retail Method

✔ Estimated cost of ending inventory: at cost, $48,518

P 9. Decent Company operates a large discount store and uses the retail method to estimate the cost of ending inventory. Recently, the company has had unusually heavy inventory losses, which management suspects have been due to shoplifting or employee pilferage. To estimate the amount of the loss, the company has taken a physical inventory and will compare the results with the estimated cost of inventory. Data from the company's accounting records are as follows:

	At Cost	At Retail
August 1 beginning inventory	$51,488	$ 74,300
Purchases	71,733	108,500
Purchases returns and allowances	(2,043)	(3,200)
Freight-in	950	
Sales		109,183
Sales returns and allowances		(933)
August 31 physical inventory at retail		62,450

REQUIRED

1. Using the retail method, prepare a schedule to estimate the dollar amount of the store's month-end inventory at cost.
2. Use the store's cost to retail ratio to reduce the retail value of the physical inventory to cost.
3. Calculate the estimated amount of inventory shortage at cost and at retail.

USER INSIGHT ▶

4. Many retail chains use the retail method because they find it an efficient way to operate. Why do you think they find this method efficient?

LO 6

Gross Profit Method

✔ Estimated loss of inventory in fire: $731,612

P 10. Pearly Tooth Corporation is a large retailer of medical equipment that operates in two adjacent warehouses. One warehouse is a showroom, and the other is used to store merchandise. On the night of May 5, 2011, a fire broke out in the storage warehouse and destroyed the merchandise stored there. The fire did not reach the showroom, so all the merchandise on display was saved.

Although the company maintained a perpetual inventory system, its records were rather haphazard, and the last reliable physical inventory had been taken on December 31, 2010. In addition, there was no control of the flow of goods between the showroom and the warehouse. Thus, it was impossible to tell what goods would have been in either place. As a result, the insurance company required an independent estimate of the amount of loss. The insurance company examiners were satisfied when they received the following information:

Merchandise inventory on December 31, 2010	$ 727,400
Purchases, January 1 to May 5, 2011	1,206,100
Purchases returns, January 1 to May 5, 2011	(5,353)
Freight-in, January 1 to May 5, 2011	26,550
Sales, January 1 to May 5, 2011	1,979,525
Sales returns, January 1 to May 5, 2011	(14,900)
Merchandise inventory in showroom on May 5, 2011	201,480
Average gross margin	48%

REQUIRED

1. Prepare a schedule that estimates the amount of the inventory lost in the fire.

USER INSIGHT ▶ 2. What are some other reasons management might need to estimate the amount of inventory?

Cases

LO 1

Conceptual Understanding: Evaluation of Inventory Levels

RATIO

C 1. JCPenney, a large retail company with many stores, has an inventory turnover of 3.4 times. **Dell Computer Corporation**, an Internet mail-order company, has an inventory turnover of 49.0. Dell achieves its high turnover through supply-chain management in a just-in-time operating environment. Why is inventory turnover important to companies like JCPenney and Dell? Why are comparisons among companies important? Are JCPenney and Dell a good match for comparison? Describe supply-chain management and a just-in-time operating environment. Why are they important to achieving a favorable inventory turnover?

LO 1

Conceptual Understanding: Misstatement of Inventory

C 2. Crazy Eddie, Inc., a discount consumer electronics chain, seemed to be missing $52 million in merchandise inventory. "It was a shock," the new management was quoted as saying. It was also a memorable swindle. Investors lost $145.6 million when the company declared bankruptcy. A count turned up only $75 million in inventory, compared with $126.7 million reported by former management. Net sales could account for only $6.7 million of the difference. At the time, it was not clear whether bookkeeping errors in prior years or an actual physical loss created the shortfall, although at least one store manager felt it was a bookkeeping error because security was strong. "It would be hard for someone to steal anything," he said. Former management was eventually fined $72.7 million.[10]

1. What is the effect of the misstatement of inventory on Crazy Eddie's reported earnings in prior accounting periods?
2. Is this a situation you would expect in a company that is experiencing financial difficulty? Explain.

LO 4

Conceptual Understanding: LIFO Inventory Method

C 3. Sixty-eight percent of chemical companies use the LIFO inventory method for the costing of inventories, whereas only 13 percent of computer equipment companies use LIFO.[11]

Describe the LIFO inventory method. What effects does it have on reported income, cash flows, and income taxes during periods of price changes? Why do you think so many chemical companies use LIFO and most companies in the computer industry do not?

LO 2

Interpreting Financial Reports: LCM and Conservatism

C 4. ExxonMobil Corporation, the world's second-largest company, uses the LIFO inventory method for most of its inventories. Its inventory costs are heavily dependent on the cost of oil. When the price of oil was down, ExxonMobil, following the lower-of-cost-or-market (LCM) rule, wrote down its inventory by $325 million. In the next year, when the price of oil recovered, the company reported that market price exceeded the LIFO carrying values by $6.8 billion.[12] Explain why the LCM rule resulted in a write-down in the first year. What is the inconsistency between the first- and second-year treatments of the change in the price of oil? How does the accounting convention of conservatism explain the inconsistency? If the price of oil declined substantially in a third year, what would be the likely consequence?

LO 1, 4

Interpreting Financial Reports: FIFO and LIFO

C 5. ExxonMobil Corporation had net income of $19.3 billion in 2009. Inventories under the LIFO method used by the company were $8.7 billion in 2009. Inventory would have been $17.1 billion higher if the company had used FIFO.[13] Why do you suppose ExxonMobil's management chooses to use the LIFO inventory method? On what economic conditions, if any, do those reasons depend?

LO 1, 4

Annual Report Case: Inventory Costing Methods and Ratios

RATIO

C 6. Refer to the note related to inventories in the **CVS** annual report in the Supplement to Chapter 1 to answer the following questions: What inventory method(s) does CVS use? If CVS's LIFO inventories had been valued at FIFO, they would have been the same. Explain why there is no difference between inventory valued at FIFO and inventory valued at LIFO? Do you think many of the company's inventories are valued at market? Why or why not? Few companies use the retail method, so why do you think CVS uses it? Compute and compare the inventory turnover and days' inventory on hand for CVS for 2009 and 2008. Ending inventories in 2007 were $8,008 million.

LO 1

Comparison Analysis: Inventory Efficiency

C 7. Refer to **CVS**'s annual report in the Supplement to Chapter 1 and to the following data (in millions) for **Walgreens**: cost of goods sold, $45,722 and $42,391 for 2009 and 2008, respectively; inventories, $6,789, $7,249, and $6,790 for 2009, 2008, and 2007, respectively. Ending inventories for 2007 for CVS were $8,008 million.

Calculate inventory turnover and days' inventory on hand for 2009 and 2008. If you did **C 6**, refer to your answer there for CVS. Has either company improved its performance in these areas over the past two years? If so, what advantage does this give the company? Which company appears to make the most efficient use of inventories? Explain your answers.

LO 1, 4

Ethical Dilemma: Inventories, Income Determination, and Ethics

C 8. Lady, Inc., whose fiscal year ends on December 31, designs and sells fashions for young professional women. Margaret Lutz, president of the company, fears that the forecasted profitability goals for 2011 will not be reached. She is pleased when Lady, Inc., receives a large order on December 30, 2011, from The Executive Woman, a retail chain of upscale stores for businesswomen. Lutz immediately directs the controller to record the sale, which represents 13 percent of Lady's annual sales. At the same time, she directs the inventory control department not to separate the goods for shipment until after January 1, 2012. Separated goods are not included in inventory because they have been sold.

On December 31, 2011, the company's auditors arrive to observe the year-end taking of the physical inventory under the periodic inventory system. How will Lutz's actions affect Lady's profitability in 2011? How will they affect Lady's profitability in 2012? Were Lutz's actions ethical? Why or why not?

LO 3, 4

Decision Analysis Using Excel: FIFO versus LIFO Analysis

C 9. Refrigerated Trucks (RT) Company buys large refrigerated trucks from the manufacturer and sells them to companies and independent truckers. Because of the high cost of financing its inventory, RT tries to maintain as small an inventory as possible. In fact, at the beginning of July, the company had no inventory or liabilities, as shown on the balance sheet that follows.

RT Company
Balance Sheet
July 1, 2011

Assets		Stockholders' Equity	
Cash	$400,000	Common stock	$400,000
Total assets	$400,000	Total stockholders' equity	$400,000

On July 9, 2011, RT took delivery of a truck, for which it paid $150,000. On July 19, it took delivery of an identical truck, for which it paid $160,000. On July 28, it sold one of the trucks for $195,000. During July, RT's expenses totaled $15,000. All transactions were paid in cash.

1. Assuming an income tax rate of 40 percent and using (a) the FIFO method of inventory valuation and (b) the LIFO method, prepare an income statement and balance sheet for RT on July 31. Explain the effects of each method on these financial statements.
2. Assume that RT's management has a policy of declaring a cash dividend each period exactly equal to net income. What effects does this policy have on the financial statements prepared in requirement 1? How do the balance sheets of July 31 compare with the balance sheet on July1? Which inventory method, if either, do you think is more realistic in representing RT's income?
3. Assume that RT receives notice of a price increase of $10,000 on trucks to take effect on August 1. How does this information relate to management's dividend policy, and how will it affect next month's operations?

CHAPTER 7

DECISION POINT
A User's Focus Hewlett-Packard Company

Hewlett-Packard (HP) is one of the largest and best-known companies in the computer industry. It sells its computers, printers, and related products to individual consumers; small and large businesses; and government, health, and education organizations. Like any company that sells on credit, HP must give its customers time to pay for their purchases, but at the same time, it must have enough cash on hand to pay its suppliers. As you can see in HP's Financial Highlights, cash and accounts receivable have made up over 50 percent of the company's current assets in recent years.[1] HP must therefore plan and control its cash flows very carefully.

HP'S FINANCIAL HIGHLIGHTS
(in millions)

	2009	2008	2007
Cash	$ 13,279	$ 10,153	$ 11,293
Accounts receivable, net	16,537	16,928	13,420
Total current assets	52,539	51,728	47,402
Net revenue	114,552	118,364	104,286

Questions

1. *How can the company control its cash needs?*
2. *How can the company evaluate its credit policies and the level of its receivables?*

Justin Sullivan/Getty Images News/Getty Images

Cash and Receivables

LEARNING OBJECTIVES

LO 1 Identify and explain the management and ethical issues related to cash and receivables. (pp. 328–333)

LO 2 Define *cash equivalents* and explain methods of controlling cash, including bank reconciliations. (pp. 334–337)

LO 3 Apply the allowance method of accounting for uncollectible accounts. (pp. 337–343)

LO 4 Define *promissory note* and make common calculations for promissory notes receivable. (pp. 343–347)

Cash and receivables require careful oversight to ensure that they are ethically handled. If cash is mismanaged or stolen, it can bring about the downfall of a business. Because accounts receivable and notes receivable require estimates of future losses, they can be easily manipulated to show improvement in reported earnings. Improved earnings can, of course, enhance a company's stock price, as well as the bonuses of its executives. In this chapter, we address the management of cash and demonstrate the importance of estimates in accounting for receivables.

FOCUS ON FINANCIAL STATEMENTS

INCOME STATEMENT
Revenues
– Expenses
= Net Income

STATEMENT OF RETAINED EARNINGS
Opening Balance
+ Net Income
– Dividends
= Retained Earnings

BALANCE SHEET
Assets | Liabilities
Equity
A = L + E

STATEMENT OF CASH FLOWS
Operating Activities
+ Investing Activities
+ Financing Activities
= Change in Cash
+ Starting Balance
= Ending Cash Balance

Valuation of accounts receivable on the balance sheet is linked to measurement of uncollectible accounts expense on the income statement.

MANAGEMENT ISSUES RELATED TO CASH AND RECEIVABLES

LO 1 Identify and explain the management and ethical issues related to cash and receivables.

The management of cash and accounts receivable and notes receivable is critical to maintaining adequate liquidity. These assets are important components of the operating cycle, which also includes inventories and accounts payable. In dealing with cash and receivables, management must address five key issues: managing cash needs, setting credit policies, evaluating the level of accounts receivable, financing receivables, and making ethical estimates of credit losses.

Cash Management

On the balance sheet, **cash** usually consists of

- currency and coins on hand,
- checks and money orders from customers, and
- deposits in checking and savings accounts.

Cash is the most liquid of all assets and the most readily available for use in paying debts. It is central to the operating cycle because all operating transactions eventually use or generate cash.

Cash may include a *compensating balance*, an amount that is not entirely free to be spent. A **compensating balance** is a minimum amount that a bank requires a company to keep in its bank account as part of a credit-granting arrangement. Such an arrangement restricts cash; in effect, it increases the interest on the loan and reduces a company's liquidity. The Securities and Exchange Commission therefore requires companies that have compensating balances to disclose the amounts involved.

Most companies experience seasonal cycles of business activity during the year. During some periods, sales are weak; during others, they are strong. There are also periods when expenditures are high and periods when they are low. For toy companies, college textbook publishers, amusement parks, construction companies, and manufacturers of sports equipment, the cycles are dramatic, but all companies, even computer companies like **Hewlett-Packard**, experience them to some degree.

Seasonal cycles require careful planning of cash inflows, cash outflows, borrowing, and investing. Exhibit 7.1 shows the seasonal cycles typical of an athletic sportswear company like **Nike**. As you can see, cash receipts from sales are highest in the late spring, summer, and fall because that is when most people engage in outdoor sports. Sales are relatively low in the winter months. On the other hand, cash expenditures are highest in late winter and spring as the company builds up inventory for spring and summer selling. During the late summer, fall, and winter, the company has excess cash on hand that it needs to invest in a way that will earn a return but still permit access to cash as needed. During late spring and early summer, the company needs to plan for short-term borrowing to tide it over until cash receipts pick up later in the year.

Focus on Business Practice

How Do Good Companies Deal with Bad Times?

Good companies manage their cash well even in bad times. During the recent financial crisis, companies are increasing their cash, reducing their debt, and putting their cash to good use. For instance, **Morgan Stanley** reported that companies increased their cash balances to 30 percent of their debt by the end of 2009 compared to 25 percent the year before. In spite of the decline in the housing market, strong home supplies companies like **Home Depot** have raised their quarterly dividend and **Lowe**'s has announced a large purchase of its own stock. Such actions signal to the market that investors should have confidence in these companies.[2]

iStock Photo

EXHIBIT 7.1
Seasonal Cycles and Cash Requirements for an Athletic Sportswear Company

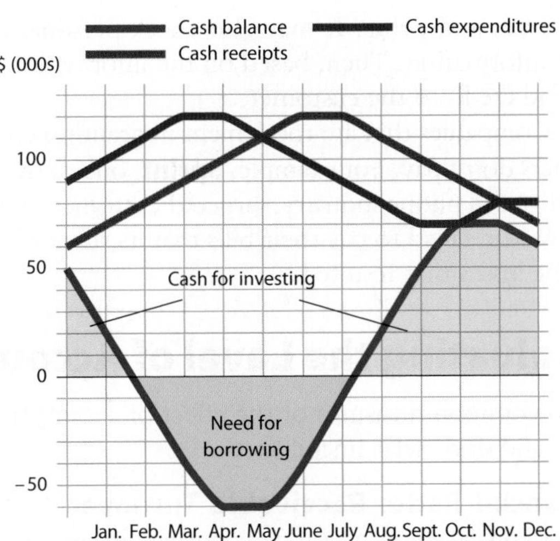

Accounts Receivable and Credit Policies

Like cash, accounts receivable and notes receivable are major types of **short-term financial assets**. Both kinds of receivables result from extending credit to individual customers or to other companies. Retailers like **Macy's** and **Target** have made credit available through their company credit cards to nearly every responsible person in the United States. Every field of retail trade has expanded by allowing customers to make payments a month or more after the date of sale. What is not so apparent is that credit has expanded even more among wholesalers and manufacturers like **HP** than at the retail level. Exhibit 7.2 shows the levels of accounts receivable in selected industries.

As we have indicated, **accounts receivable** are short-term financial assets that arise from credit sales made in the ordinary course of business. This type of credit is often called **trade credit**. Terms of trade credit usually range from 5 to 60 days, depending on industry practice, and may allow customers to pay in installments. Credit sales or loans not made in the ordinary course of business, such as those made to employees, officers, or owners, should appear separately on the balance sheet under asset titles like *receivables from employees*. Also, when accounts have credit balances due to overpayment and purchase returns, the company should show the total credits on its balance sheet as a current liability because it may have to grant refunds.

Companies that sell on credit do so to be competitive and to increase sales. In setting credit terms, a company must keep in mind the credit terms of its competitors and the needs of its customers. Obviously, any company that sells on credit wants customers who will pay their bills on time. To increase the likelihood of selling only to customers who will pay on time, most companies develop control procedures and maintain a credit department. The credit department's responsibilities include examining each person or company that applies for credit and approving or rejecting a credit sale to that customer. Typically, the credit department asks for information about the customer's financial

EXHIBIT 7.2
Accounts Receivable as a Percentage of Total Assets for Selected Industries

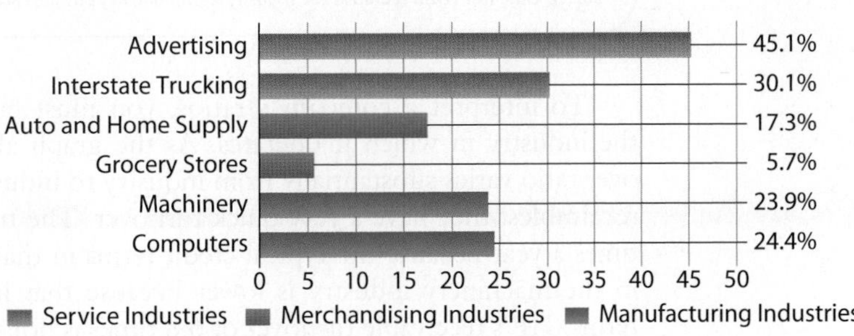

Source: Data from Dun & Bradstreet, *Industry Norms and Key Business Ratios*, 2008–2009.

resources and debts. It may also check personal references and credit bureaus for further information. Then, based on the information it has gathered, it decides whether to extend credit to the customer.

Companies that are too lenient in granting credit can run into difficulties when customers don't pay. For example, **Sprint**, one of the weaker companies in the highly competitive cell phone industry, targeted customers with poor credit histories. It attracted so many who failed to pay their bills that its stock dropped by 50 percent to $2.50 because of the losses that resulted.[3]

Evaluating the Level of Accounts Receivable

Two common measures of the effect of a company's credit policies are receivable turnover and days' sales uncollected.

Financial Ratio: Receivable Turnover **Receivable turnover** shows how many times, on average, a company turned its receivables into cash during an accounting period. This measure reflects the relative size of a company's accounts receivable and the success of its credit and collection policies. It may also be affected by external factors, such as seasonal conditions and interest rates.

The receivable turnover is computed by dividing net sales (net revenue) by average accounts receivable (net of allowances). Theoretically, the numerator should be net credit sales, but the amount of net credit sales is rarely available in public reports, so investors use total net sales. Using data from **HP**'s Financial Highlights at the beginning of the chapter, we can compute the company's receivable turnover in 2009 as follows (dollar amounts are in millions):

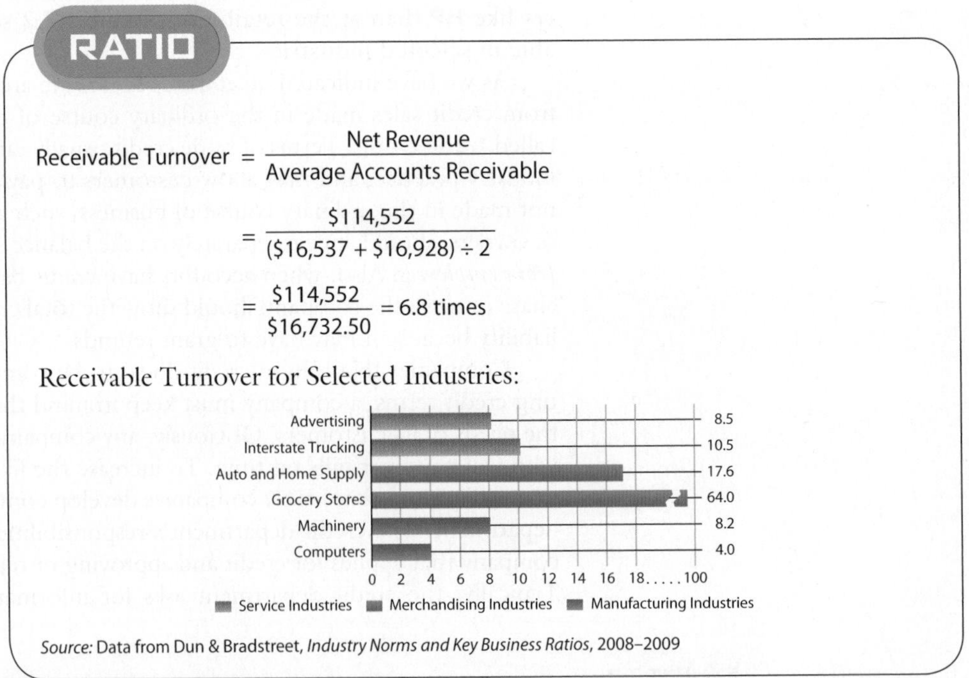

$$\text{Receivable Turnover} = \frac{\text{Net Revenue}}{\text{Average Accounts Receivable}}$$

$$= \frac{\$114{,}552}{(\$16{,}537 + \$16{,}928) \div 2}$$

$$= \frac{\$114{,}552}{\$16{,}732.50} = 6.8 \text{ times}$$

Source: Data from Dun & Bradstreet, *Industry Norms and Key Business Ratios*, 2008–2009

To interpret a company's ratios, you must take into consideration the norms of the industry in which it operates. As the graph above illustrates, the receivable turnover ratio varies substantially from industry to industry. Because grocery stores have few receivables, they have a very quick turnover. The turnover in interstate trucking is 10.5 times a year because the typical credit terms in that industry are 30 days. The turnover in the machinery industry is lower because that industry tends to have longer credit terms. HP's receivable turnover of 6.8 times is not unusual among computer companies because their credit terms typically allow customers 30 to 60 days to pay.

Financial Ratio: Days' Sales Uncollected **Days' sales uncollected** shows, on average, how long it takes to collect accounts receivable. To find days' sales uncollected, the number of days in a year is divided by the receivable turnover. For HP, it is computed as follows:

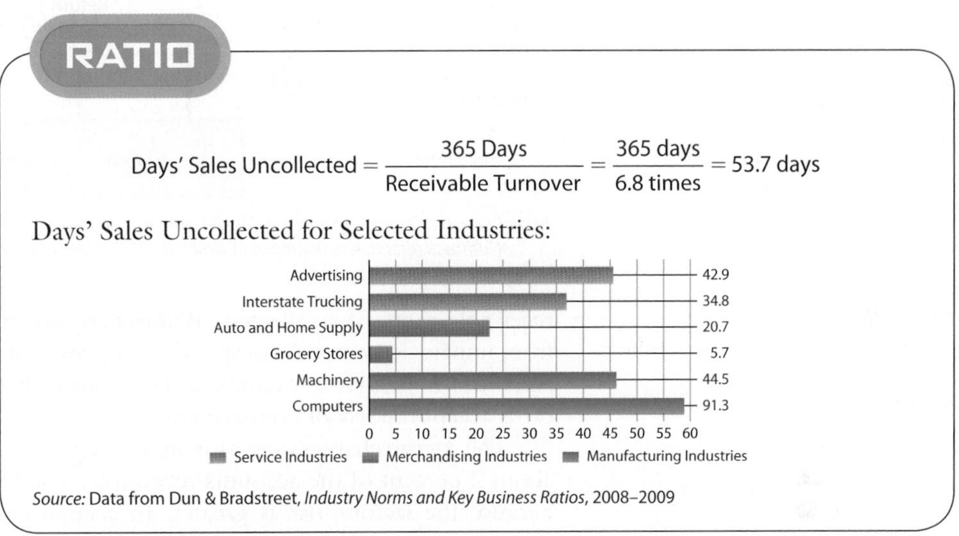

As you can see in the preceding graph, grocery stores have the lowest days' sales uncollected (5.7 days), and they therefore require the least amount of receivables financing; the computer industry, with days' sales uncollected of 91.3 days, requires the most. HP at only 53.7 days does a better job of managing its receivables than the average computer company.

For many businesses with seasonal sales activity, such as **Nordstrom**, **Dillard's**, and **Macy's**, receivables are highest at the balance sheet date, resulting in an artificially low receivable turnover and high days' sales uncollected.

Financing Receivables

Financial flexibility is important to most companies. Companies that have significant amounts of assets tied up in accounts receivable may be unwilling or unable to wait until they collect cash from their receivables. Many corporations have set up finance companies to help their customers pay for the purchase of their products. For example, **Ford** set up Ford Motor Credit Company (FMCC) and **Sears** set up Sears Roebuck Acceptance Corporation (SRAC). Other companies borrow funds by pledging their accounts receivable as collateral. If a company does not pay back its loan, the creditor can take the collateral (in this case, the accounts receivable) and convert it to cash to satisfy the loan.

AP Photo/Diane Bondareff

Companies can also finance their receivables by selling or transferring accounts receivable to another entity. Three methods of financing receivables in this way are factoring, securitization, and discounting.

Factoring As Exhibit 7.3 shows, **factoring** is the sale or transfer of accounts receivable to an entity called a **factor**. Factoring can be done with or without recourse. *With recourse* means that the seller of the receivables is liable to the factor (i.e., the purchaser) if a

EXHIBIT 7.3
How Factoring Works

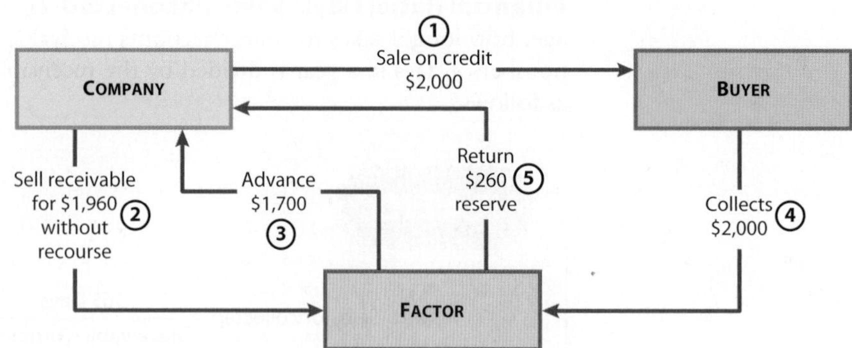

Note: Factor will keep $260 reserve if buyer does not pay. Numbers refer to the sequence in which transactions take place.

STUDY NOTE: *A company that factors its receivables will have a better receivable turnover and days' sales uncollected than a company that does not factor them.*

receivable cannot be collected. *Without recourse* means that the factor bears any losses from unpaid accounts. A company's acceptance of credit cards like Visa, MasterCard, or American Express is an example of factoring without recourse because the issuers of the cards accept the risk of nonpayment.

The factor charges a fee for its service. The fee for sales with recourse is usually about 2 percent of the accounts receivable. The fee is higher for sales without recourse because the factor's risk is greater. In accounting terminology, a seller of receivables with recourse is said to be contingently liable. A **contingent liability** is a potential liability that can develop into a real liability if a particular event occurs. In this case, the event would be a customer's nonpayment of a receivable. A contingent liability generally requires disclosure in the notes to the financial statements.

Securitization **Securitization** is a process in which a company groups its receivables in batches and sells them at a discount to other companies or investors. When the receivables are paid, the buyers get the full amount; their profit depends on the amount of the discount. **Circuit City** tried to avoid bankruptcy by selling all its receivables without recourse, which means that after selling them, it had no further liability, even if no customers were to pay. If Circuit City had sold its receivables with recourse and a customer did not pay, it would have had to make good on the debt.[4] However, by selling without recourse, it had to accept a lower price for its receivables. Unfortunately, this strategy did not prevent it from going bankrupt and out of business.

Discounting **Discounting** is a method of financing receivables by selling promissory notes held as notes receivable to a financial lender, usually a bank. The bank derives its profit by deducting or discounting the interest from the maturity value of the note. The holder of the note (usually the payee) endorses the note and turns it over it to the bank. The bank expects to collect the maturity value of the note (principal plus interest) on the maturity date, but it also has recourse against the note's endorser.

For example, if Vonnegut Company holds a $20,000 note from Hemingway Company and the note will pay $1,200 in interest, a bank may be willing to buy the note for $19,200. If Hemingway pays, the bank will receive $21,200 at maturity and realize a

Focus on Business Practice

Why Are Subprime Loans Bad?

Although subprime loans (home loans to individuals with poor credit ratings and low incomes) represent only a small portion of the mortgage loan market, they have caused huge problems in the real estate market in recent years. These loans are a form of securitization in that they are batched together and sold in units as safe investments, when in fact they are quite risky. As just one of many examples, when people by the thousands were unable to keep up with their mortgage payments, the investments were marked down to their fair value. This loss of value led to the demise of such venerable firms as **Lehman Brothers**, the sale of **Merrill Lynch**, and ultimately to a massive government bailout of several well-known financial institutions.[5]

iStock Photo

$2,000 profit. If it fails to pay, Vonnegut is liable to the bank for payment. In the meantime, Vonnegut has a contingent liability in the amount of the discounted note plus interest that it must disclose in the notes to its financial statements.

Ethics and Estimates in Accounting for Receivables

As we have noted, companies extend credit to customers because they expect that doing so will increase their sales and earnings, but they know they will always have some credit customers who cannot or will not pay. The accounts of such customers are called **uncollectible accounts**, or *bad debts*, and they are expenses of selling on credit. To match these expenses, or losses, to the revenues they help generate, they should be recognized at the time credit sales are made.

Of course, at the time a company makes credit sales, it cannot identify which customers will not pay their bills, nor can it predict the exact amount of money it will lose. Therefore, to adhere to the matching rule, it must estimate losses from uncollectible accounts. The estimate becomes an expense in the fiscal year in which the sales are made.

Because the amount of uncollectible accounts can only be estimated and the exact amount will not be known until later, a company's earnings can be easily manipulated. Earnings can be overstated by underestimating the amount of losses from uncollectible accounts and understated by overestimating the amount of the losses. Misstatements of earnings can occur simply because of a bad estimate. But, as we have noted, they can be deliberately made to meet analysts' estimates of earnings, reduce income taxes, or meet benchmarks for bonuses.

Examples of unethical or questionable practices in dealing with uncollectible accounts include the following cases investigated by the SEC:

- The policy of **Household International**, a large personal finance company, seems to be flexible about when to declare loans delinquent. As a result, the company can vary its estimates of uncollectible accounts from year to year.[6]
- By making large allowances for estimated uncollectible accounts and then gradually reducing them, **Bank One** improved its earnings over several years.[7]
- **HealthSouth** manipulated its income by varying its estimates of the difference between what it charged patients and what it could collect from insurance companies.[8]

Companies with high ethical standards try to be accurate in their estimates of uncollectible accounts, and they disclose the basis of their estimates. For example, **HP**'s management describes its estimates as follows:

> We maintain an allowance for doubtful accounts for all customers based on a variety of factors, including . . . the financial condition of customers, the length of time receivables are past due, . . . and historical experience.[9]

Stop & Apply

Ricotta Company has cash of $20,000, net accounts receivable of $60,000, and net sales of $500,000. Last year's net accounts receivable were $40,000. Compute Ricotta's receivable turnover and days' sales uncollected.

SOLUTION

$$\text{Receivable Turnover} = \frac{\text{Net Sales}}{\text{Average Accounts Receivable}}$$

$$= \frac{\$500{,}000}{(\$60{,}000 + \$40{,}000) \div 2} = \frac{\$500{,}000}{\$\ 50{,}000} = 10.0 \text{ times}$$

$$\text{Days' Sales Uncollected} = \frac{\text{365 Days}}{\text{Receivable Turnover}}$$

$$\frac{\text{365 days}}{\text{10.0 times}} = 36.5 \text{ days}$$

iStock Photo

CASH EQUIVALENTS AND CASH CONTROL

Cash Equivalents

Define *cash equivalents* and explain methods of controlling cash, including bank reconciliations. LO2

STUDY NOTE: *The statement of cash flows explains the change in the balance of cash and cash equivalents from one accounting period to the next.*

At times, a company may have more cash on hand than it needs to pay its debts. Excess cash should not remain idle, especially during periods of high interest rates. Management may decide to invest the excess cash in short-term interest-bearing accounts or certificates of deposit (CDs) at banks and other financial institutions, in government securities (such as U.S. Treasury notes), or in other securities. If these investments have a term of 90 days or less when they are purchased, they are called **cash equivalents** because the funds revert to cash so quickly that they are treated as cash on the balance sheet.

HP describes its treatment of cash equivalents as follows:

> HP classifies investments as cash equivalents if the original maturity of an investment is three months or less. . . . The carrying value of . . . cash equivalents approximates fair value due to the short period of time to maturity.[10]

Like HP, most companies record cash equivalents at their approximate fair value, that is, their market value.

According to a survey of large U.S. corporations, 2.5 percent use the term *cash* as the balance sheet caption, and 96 percent use either *cash and cash equivalents* or *cash and equivalents*. The rest either combine cash with marketable securities or have no cash.[11]

Cash Control Methods

In an earlier chapter, we discussed the concept of internal control and how it applies to cash transactions. Here, we address three additional ways of controlling cash: imprest systems; banking services, including electronic funds transfer; and bank reconciliations.

Imprest Systems Most companies need to keep some currency and coins on hand. Currency and coins are needed for cash registers, for payment of expenses that are impractical to pay by check, and for situations that require cash advances—for example, when sales representatives need cash for travel expenses. One way to control a cash fund and cash advances is by using an **imprest system**.

A common form of imprest system is a petty cash fund, which is established at a fixed amount. A receipt documents each cash payment made from the fund. The fund is periodically reimbursed, based on the documented expenditures, by the exact amount necessary to restore its original cash balance. The person responsible for the petty cash fund must always be able to account for its contents by showing that total cash and receipts equal the original fixed amount.

Banking Services Banks provide safe depositories for cash, negotiable instruments, and other valuable business documents such as stocks and bonds. The checking accounts

Focus on Business Practice

Are Money Market Funds Always a Safe Bet?

When companies have more cash than they need for current operations, they often earn interest on their excess cash by investing it in money market funds. Investments in money market funds have traditionally been considered safe because these funds have usually invested in very safe securities. However, in recent years, in an attempt to earn a slightly higher interest rate, a few money market funds invested in batches of subprime mortgages. This turned out to be a very poor decision. **Bank of America**, for instance, had to shut down its $34 billion money market fund—called Columbia Strategic Cash Portfolio—when investors pulled out $21 billion because the fund was losing a great deal of money due to its investment in subprime loans.[12]

iStock Photo

that they provide improve control by minimizing the amount of currency a company needs to keep on hand and by supplying permanent records of all cash payments. Banks also serve as agents in a variety of transactions, such as the collection and payment of certain kinds of debts and the exchange of foreign currencies.

Electronic funds transfer (EFT) is a method of conducting business transactions that does not involve the actual transfer of cash. With EFT, a company electronically transfers cash from its bank to another company's bank. For the banks, the electronic transfer is simply a bookkeeping entry. Companies today rely heavily on this method of payment. **Wal-Mart**, for example, makes 75 percent of its payments to suppliers through EFT.

Automated teller machines (ATMs) allow bank customers to make deposits, withdraw cash, transfer funds among accounts, and pay bills. Large consumer banks like **Citibank**, **Chase**, and **Bank of America** process hundreds of thousands of ATM transactions each week. Many banks also give customers the option of paying bills online or over the telephone with debit cards. In 2009, debit cards accounted for more than $1.5 trillion in transactions.[13] As we noted in an earlier chapter, when a customer makes a retail purchase using a debit card, the amount of the purchase is deducted directly from the customer's bank account. The bank usually documents debit card transactions for the retailer, but the retailer must develop new internal controls to ensure that the transactions are recorded properly and that unauthorized transfers do not occur.

***STUDY NOTE:** Bank reconciliations are an important factor in internal control. When done by someone who cannot access the company's bank account, they provide an independent check on people who do have access.*

Bank Reconciliations Rarely does the balance of a company's Cash account exactly equal the cash balance on its bank statement. The bank may not yet have recorded certain transactions that appear in the company's records, and the company may not yet have recorded certain bank transactions. A bank reconciliation is therefore a necessary step in internal control. A **bank reconciliation** is the process of accounting for the difference between the balance on a company's bank statement and the balance in its Cash account. This process involves making additions to and subtractions from both balances to arrive at the adjusted cash balance.

The following are the transactions that most commonly appear in a company's records but not on its bank statement:

- **Outstanding checks:** Checks that a company has issued and recorded but that do not yet appear on its bank statement.
- **Deposits in transit:** Deposits a company has sent to its bank but that the bank did not receive in time to enter on the bank statement.

Transactions that may appear on the bank statement but not in the company's records include the following:

- **Service charges (SC):** Banks often charge a fee, or service charge, for the use of a checking account. Many banks base the service charge on a number of factors, such as the average balance of the account during the month or the number of checks drawn.
- **NSF (nonsufficient funds) checks:** An NSF check is a check that a company has deposited but that is not paid when the bank presents it to the issuer's bank. The bank charges the company's account and returns the check so that the company can try to collect the amount due. If the bank has deducted the NSF check on the bank statement but the company has not deducted it from its book balance, an adjustment must be made in the bank reconciliation. The company usually reclassifies the NSF check from Cash to Accounts Receivable because it must now collect from the person or company that wrote the check.

***STUDY NOTE:** A credit memorandum means that an amount was added to the bank balance; a debit memorandum means that an amount was deducted.*

- **Miscellaneous debits and credits:** Banks also charge for other services, such as stopping payment on checks and printing checks. The bank notifies the depositor of each deduction by including a debit memorandum with the monthly statement. A bank also sometimes serves as an agent in collecting on promissory notes for the depositor.

When it does, it includes a credit memorandum in the bank statement, along with a debit memorandum for the service charge.

- **Interest income:** Banks commonly pay interest on a company's average balance. Accounts that pay interest are sometimes called NOW or money market accounts.

An error by either the bank or the depositor will, of course, require immediate correction.

To illustrate the preparation of a bank reconciliation, suppose that Julian Maintenance Company's bank statement for August shows a balance of $1,735.53 on August 31 and that on the same date, the company's records show a cash balance of $1,207.95. The purpose of a bank reconciliation is to identify the items that make up the difference between these amounts and to determine the correct cash balance. Exhibit 7.4 shows Julian Maintenance Company's bank reconciliation for August. The circled numbers in the exhibit refer to the following:

1. The bank has not recorded a deposit in the amount of $138.00 that the company mailed to the bank on August 31.
2. The bank has not paid the five checks that the company issued in July and August. Even though the July 14 check was deducted in the July 30 reconciliation, it must be deducted again in each subsequent month in which it remains outstanding.
3. The company incorrectly recorded a $150 deposit from cash sales as $165.00. On August 6, the bank received the deposit and corrected the amount.
4. Among the returned checks was a credit memorandum showing that the bank had collected a promissory note from K. Diaz in the amount of $140.00, plus $10.00 in interest on the note. A debit memorandum was also enclosed for the $2.50 collection fee. The company had not entered these amounts in its records.

EXHIBIT 7.4
Bank Reconciliation

Julian Maintenance Company
Bank Reconciliation
August 31, 2011

Balance per bank, August 31		$ 1,735.53
① Add deposit of August 31 in transit		138.00
		$ 1,873.53
② Less outstanding checks:		
No. 551, issued on July 14	$ 75.00	
No. 576, issued on Aug. 30	20.34	
No. 578, issued on Aug. 31	250.00	
No. 579, issued on Aug. 31	185.00	
No. 580, issued on Aug. 31	65.25	595.59
Adjusted bank balance, August 31		**$1,277.94**
Balance per books, August 31		$ 1,207.95
Add:		
④ Note receivable collected by bank	$140.00	
④ Interest income on note	10.00	
⑦ Interest income	7.81	157.81
		$ 1,365.76
Less:		
③ Overstatement of deposit of August 6	$ 15.00	
④ Collection fee	2.50	
⑤ NSF check of Austin Chase	64.07	
⑥ Service charge	6.25	87.82
Adjusted book balance, August 31		**$1,277.94**

STUDY NOTE: *It is possible to place an item in the wrong section of a bank reconciliation and still have it balance. The correct adjusted balance must be obtained.*

5. Also returned with the bank statement was an NSF check for $64.07 that the company had received from a customer named Austin Chase. The NSF check was not reflected in the company's records.
6. A debit memorandum was enclosed for the regular monthly service charge of $6.25. The company had not yet recorded this charge.
7. Interest earned on the company's average balance was $7.81.

As you can see in Exhibit 7.4, starting from their separate balances, both the bank and book amounts are adjusted to the amount of $1,277.94. This adjusted balance is the amount of cash the company owns on August 31 and thus is the amount that should appear on its August 31 balance sheet.

When outstanding checks are presented to the bank for payment and the bank receives and records the deposit in transit, the bank balance will automatically become correct. However, the company must update its book balance by recording all the items reported by the bank. Thus, Julian Maintenance Company would record an increase (debit) in Cash with the following items:

▼ *Decrease* (credit) in Notes Receivable, $140.00
▲ *Increase* (credit) in Interest Income, $10.00 (interest on note)
▲ *Increase* (credit) in Interest Income, $7.81 (interest on average bank balance)

The company would record a reduction (credit) in Cash with the following items:

▼ *Decrease* (debit) in Sales, $15.00 (error in recording deposit)
▲ *Increase* (debit) in Accounts Receivable, $64.07 (return of NSF check)
▲ *Increase* (debit) in Bank Service Charges, $8.75 ($6.25 + $2.50)

Stop & Apply

At year end, Tipi Company had currency and coins in cash registers of $1,100, money orders from customers of $2,000, deposits in checking accounts of $12,000, U.S. Treasury bills due in 80 days of $50,000, certificates of deposit at the bank that mature in six months of $200,000, and U.S. Treasury bonds due in one year of $100,000. Calculate the amount of cash and cash equivalents that will be shown on the company's year-end balance sheet.

SOLUTION

Currency and coins	$ 1,100
Money orders	2,000
Checking accounts	12,000
U.S. Treasury bills (due in 80 days)	50,000
Cash and cash equivalents	$65,100

The certificates of deposit and U.S. Treasury bonds mature in more than 90 days and thus are not cash equivalents.

iStock Photo

UNCOLLECTIBLE ACCOUNTS

LO3 Apply the allowance method of accounting for uncollectible accounts.

Some companies recognize a loss at the time they determine that an account is uncollectible by reducing Accounts Receivable and increasing Uncollectible Accounts Expense. Federal regulations require companies to use this method of recognizing a loss—called the **direct charge-off method**—in computing taxable income. However, because a direct charge-off is usually recorded in a different accounting period from the one in which the sale takes place, this method does not conform to the matching rule. Generally accepted accounting principles therefore prohibit its use in the preparation of financial statements.

The Allowance Method

STUDY NOTE: *The allowance method relies on an estimate of uncollectible accounts, but unlike the direct charge-off method, it is in accord with the matching rule.*

Under the **allowance method**, losses from bad debts are matched against the sales they help to produce. As mentioned earlier, when management extends credit to increase sales, it knows it will incur some losses from uncollectible accounts. Losses from credit sales should be recognized at the time the sales are made so that they are matched to the revenues they help generate. Of course, at the time a company makes credit sales, management cannot identify which customers will not pay their debts, nor can it predict the exact amount of money the company will lose. Therefore, to observe the matching rule, losses from uncollectible accounts must be estimated, and the estimate becomes an expense in the period in which the sales are made.

For example, suppose that Edwards Company made most of its sales on credit during its first year of operation, 2011. At the end of the year, accounts receivable amounted to $200,000. On December 31, 2011, management reviewed the collectible status of the accounts receivable. Approximately $12,000 of the $200,000 of accounts receivable were estimated to be uncollectible. This adjusting entry would be made on December 31 of that year:

A	= L +	SE
−12,000		−12,000

2011			
Dec. 31	Uncollectible Accounts Expense	12,000	
	Allowance for Uncollectible Accounts		12,000
	To record the estimated uncollectible accounts expense for the year		

Disclosure of Uncollectible Accounts

STUDY NOTE: *The allowance account often has other titles, such as* Allowance for Doubtful Accounts *and* Allowance for Bad Debts. Bad Debts Expense *is a title often used for Uncollectible Accounts Expense.*

Uncollectible Accounts Expense appears on the income statement as an operating expense. **Allowance for Uncollectible Accounts** appears on the balance sheet as a contra account that is deducted from accounts receivable. It reduces the accounts receivable to the amount of cash estimated to be collectible (net realizable value), as follows:

Current assets:		
Cash		$ 20,000
Short-term investments		30,000
Accounts receivable	$200,000	
Less allowance for uncollectible accounts	12,000	188,000
Inventory		112,000
Total current assets		$350,000

The allowance account is necessary because the specific uncollectible accounts will not be identified until later. Do not confuse it with another contra account, Accumulated Depreciation. The purpose of the latter is to show how much of the cost of the plant and equipment has been allocated as an expense to previous accounting periods.

Accounts receivable may also be shown on the balance sheet as follows:

Accounts receivable (net of allowance for uncollectible accounts of $12,000)	$188,000

Accounts receivable may also be shown at "net," with the amount of the allowance for uncollectible accounts identified in a note to the financial statements. For most companies, the "net" amount of accounts receivable approximates fair value. Fair value disclosures are not required for accounts receivable, but 56 percent of large companies made this disclosure voluntarily. Of those, 95 percent indicated that the net accounts receivable approximated fair value.[14]

Focus on International Practices

IFRS Can Users Depend on the Allowance for Uncollectible Accounts?

Financial statements contain many estimates, one of which is the allowance for uncollectible accounts. In their effort to converge U.S. GAAP and IFRS, the FASB and the IASB have agreed that estimates must be a faithful representation of what they purport to represent and that they be verifiable. Under their agreement, faithful information is unbiased and contains no errors or omissions. Further, verifiability means that two independent experts could reach agreement as to the estimate.[15] In other words, users can be assured that net accounts receivable (accounts receivable less the allowance) represent the best estimate of the future cash receipts from the receivables.

iStock Photo

Estimating Uncollectible Accounts Expense

As noted, expected losses from uncollectible accounts must be estimated. Of course, estimates can vary widely. If management takes an optimistic view and projects a small loss from uncollectible accounts, the resulting net accounts receivable will be larger than if management takes a pessimistic view. The net income will also be larger under the optimistic view because the estimated expense will be smaller. The company's accountant makes an estimate based on past experience and current economic conditions. For example, losses from uncollectible accounts are normally expected to be greater in a recession than during a period of economic growth. The final decision, made by management, on the amount of the expense will depend on objective information, such as the accountant's analyses, and on certain qualitative factors, such as how investors, bankers, creditors, and others view the performance of the debtor. Regardless of the qualitative considerations, the estimated losses from uncollectible accounts should be realistic.

Two common methods of estimating uncollectible accounts expense are the percentage of net sales method and the accounts receivable aging method.

STUDY NOTE: *Unlike the direct charge-off method, the percentage of net sales method matches revenues with expenses.*

Percentage of Net Sales Method The **percentage of net sales method** asks how much of this year's *net sales* will not be collected. The answer determines the amount of uncollectible accounts expense for the year. For example, the following balances represent Romeo Company's ending figures for 2013:

SALES			
		Dec. 31	322,500

SALES RETURNS AND ALLOWANCES			
Dec. 31	20,000		

SALES DISCOUNTS			
Dec. 31	2,500		

ALLOWANCE FOR UNCOLLECTIBLE ACCOUNTS			
		Dec. 31	1,800

The following are Romeo's actual losses from uncollectible accounts for the past three years:

Year	*Net Sales*	*Losses from Uncollectible Accounts*	*Percentage*
2010	$260,000	$ 5,100	1.96
2011	297,500	6,950	2.34
2012	292,500	4,950	1.69
Total	$850,000	$17,000	2.00

Romeo's management believes that its uncollectible accounts will continue to average about 2 percent of net sales. The uncollectible accounts expense for the year 2013 is therefore estimated as follows:

$$0.02 \times (\$322{,}500 - \$20{,}000 - \$2{,}500) = 0.02 \times \$300{,}000 = \$6{,}000$$

The following entry would be made to record the estimate:

A	= L +	SE
−6,000		−6,000

2013			
Dec. 31	Uncollectible Accounts Expense	6,000	
	Allowance for Uncollectible Accounts		6,000
	To record uncollectible accounts expense at 2 percent of $300,000 net sales		

Allowance for Uncollectible Accounts will now have a balance of $7,800:

ALLOWANCE FOR UNCOLLECTIBLE ACCOUNTS		
	Dec. 31	1,800
	Dec. 31 Adj.	6,000
	Dec. 31 Bal.	**7,800**

The balance consists of the $6,000 estimated uncollectible accounts receivable from 2013 sales and the $1,800 estimated uncollectible accounts receivable from previous years.

Accounts Receivable Aging Method The **accounts receivable aging method** asks how much of the *ending balance of accounts receivable* will not be collected. With this method, the ending balance of Allowance for Uncollectible Accounts is determined directly through an analysis of accounts receivable. The difference between the amount determined to be uncollectible and the actual balance of Allowance for Uncollectible Accounts is the expense for the period. In theory, this method should produce the same result as the percentage of net sales method, but in practice it rarely does.

STUDY NOTE: *An aging of accounts receivable is an important tool in cash management because it helps to determine what amounts are likely to be collected in the months ahead.*

The **aging of accounts receivable** is the process of listing each customer's receivable account according to the due date of the account. If the customer's account is past due, there is a possibility that the account will not be paid. And that possibility increases as the account extends further beyond the due date. The aging of accounts receivable helps management evaluate its credit and collection policies and alerts it to possible problems.

Exhibit 7.5 illustrates the aging of accounts receivable for Mayer Company. Each account receivable is classified as being not yet due or as being 1–30 days, 31–60 days, 61–90 days, or over 90 days past due. Based on past experience, the estimated percentage for each category is determined and multiplied by the amount in each category

EXHIBIT 7.5
Analysis of Accounts Receivable by Age

Mayer Company
Analysis of Accounts Receivable by Age
December 31, 2011

Customer	Total	Not Yet Due	1–30 Days Past Due	31–60 Days Past Due	61–90 Days Past Due	Over 90 Days Past Due
J. Lee	$ 300		$ 300			
F. Moll	800			$ 800		
A. Orr	2,000	$ 1,800	200			
S. Sovin	500				$ 500	
Others	85,200	42,000	28,000	7,600	4,400	$3,200
Totals	$88,800	$43,800	$28,500	$8,400	$4,900	$3,200
Estimated percentage uncollectible		1.0	2.0	10.0	30.0	50.0
Allowance for Uncollectible Accounts	$ 4,918	$ 438	$ 570	$ 840	$1,470	$1,600

to determine the estimated, or target, balance of Allowance for Uncollectible Accounts. In total, it is estimated that $4,918 of the $88,800 in accounts receivable will not be collected.

STUDY NOTE: When the write-offs in an accounting period exceed the amount of the allowance, a debit balance in Allowance for Uncollectible Accounts results.

Once the target balance for Allowance for Uncollectible Accounts has been found, it is necessary to determine the amount of the adjustment. The amount depends on the current balance of the allowance account. Let's assume two cases for the balance of Mayer Company's Allowance for Uncollectible Accounts on December 31: (1) a credit balance of $1,600 and (2) a debit balance of $1,600.

In the first case, an adjustment of $3,318 is needed to bring the balance of the allowance account to a $4,918 credit balance:

Targeted balance for allowance for uncollectible accounts	$4,918
Less current credit balance of allowance for uncollectible accounts	1,600
Uncollectible accounts expense	$3,318

The uncollectible accounts expense is recorded as follows:

A	= L +	SE
−3,318		−3,318

2011			
Dec. 31	Uncollectible Accounts Expense	3,318	
	Allowance for Uncollectible Accounts		3,318
	To bring the allowance for uncollectible accounts to the level of estimated losses		

The resulting balance of Allowance for Uncollectible Accounts is $4,918:

ALLOWANCE FOR UNCOLLECTIBLE ACCOUNTS

		Dec. 31	1,600
		Dec. 31 Adj.	3,318
		Dec. 31 Bal.	**4,918**

In the second case, because Allowance for Uncollectible Accounts has a debit balance of $1,600, the estimated uncollectible accounts expense for the year will have to be $6,518 to reach the targeted balance of $4,918. This calculation is as follows:

Targeted balance for allowance for uncollectible accounts	$4,918
Plus current debit balance of allowance for uncollectible accounts	1,600
Uncollectible accounts expense	$6,518

The uncollectible accounts expense is recorded as follows:

A	= L +	SE
−6,518		−6,518

2011			
Dec. 31	Uncollectible Accounts Expense	6,518	
	Allowance for Uncollectible Accounts		6,518
	To bring the allowance for uncollectible accounts to the level of estimated losses		

After this entry, Allowance for Uncollectible Accounts has a credit balance of $4,918:

ALLOWANCE FOR UNCOLLECTIBLE ACCOUNTS

Dec. 31	1,600	Dec. 31 Adj.	6,518
		Dec. 31 Bal.	**4,918**

Comparison of the Two Methods Both the percentage of net sales method and the accounts receivable aging method estimate the uncollectible accounts expense in accordance with the matching rule, but as shown in Exhibit 7.6 (p. 342), they do so in different

EXHIBIT 7.6
Two Methods of Estimating Uncollectible Accounts

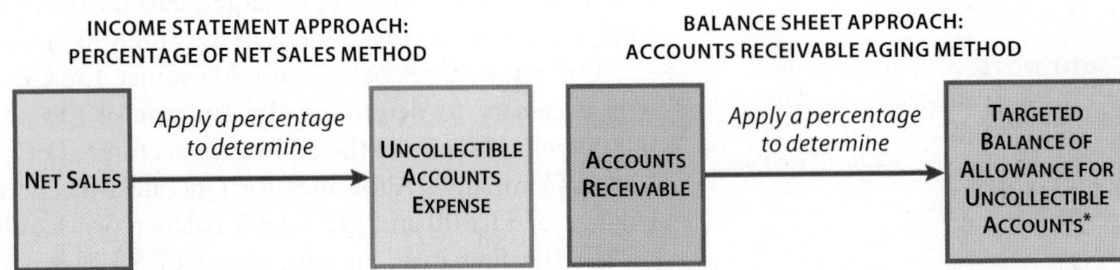

Add current debit balance or subtract current credit balance to determine uncollectible accounts expense.

STUDY NOTE: Describing the aging method as the balance sheet method emphasizes that the computation is based on ending accounts receivable rather than on net sales for the period.

ways. The percentage of net sales method is an income statement approach. It assumes that a certain proportion of sales will not be collected, and this proportion is the *amount of Uncollectible Accounts Expense* for the period. The accounts receivable aging method is a balance sheet approach. It assumes that a certain proportion of accounts receivable outstanding will not be collected. This proportion is the *targeted balance of the Allowance for Uncollectible Accounts account.* The expense for the accounting period is the difference between the targeted balance and the current balance of the allowance account.

Writing Off Uncollectible Accounts

Regardless of the method used to estimate uncollectible accounts, the total of accounts receivable written off in an accounting period will rarely equal the estimated uncollectible amount. The allowance account will show a credit balance when the total of accounts written off is less than the estimated uncollectible amount. It will show a debit balance when the total of accounts written off is greater than the estimated uncollectible amount.

STUDY NOTE: When writing off an individual account, debit Allowance for Uncollectible Accounts, not Uncollectible Accounts Expense.

When it becomes clear that a specific account receivable will not be collected, the amount should be written off to Allowance for Uncollectible Accounts. Remember that the uncollectible amount was already accounted for as an expense when the allowance was established. For example, assume that on January 15, 2012, S. Sovin, who owes Mayer Company $500, is declared bankrupt by a federal court. The journal entry to *write off* this account is as follows:

A	= L +	SE
+500		
−500		

2011			
Jan. 15	Allowance for Uncollectible Accounts	500	
	Accounts Receivable		500
	To write off receivable from S. Sovin as uncollectible because of his bankruptcy		

Although the write-off removes the uncollectible amount from Accounts Receivable, it does not affect the estimated net realizable value of accounts receivable. It simply reduces S. Sovin's account to zero and reduces Allowance for Uncollectible Accounts by $500, as follows:

	Balances Before Write-Off	*Balances After Write-Off*
Accounts receivable	$88,800	$88,300
Less allowance for uncollectible accounts	4,918	4,418
Estimated net realizable value of accounts receivable	$83,882	$83,882

Occasionally, a customer whose account has been written off as uncollectible will later be able to pay some or all of the amount owed. When that happens, two entries must be made: one to reverse the earlier write-off (which is now incorrect) and another to show the collection of the account.

Stop & Apply

Rock Instruments, Inc., sells its merchandise on credit. In the company's last fiscal year, which ended July 31, it had net sales of $7,000,000. At the end of the fiscal year, it had accounts receivable of $1,800,000 and a credit balance in Allowance for Uncollectible Accounts of $11,200. In the past, the company has been unable to collect on approximately 1 percent of its net sales. An aging analysis of accounts receivable has indicated that $80,000 of current receivables are uncollectible.

1. Calculate the amount of uncollectible accounts expense and use T accounts to determine the resulting balance of Allowance for Uncollectible Accounts under the percentage of net sales method and the accounts receivable aging method.
2. How would your answers change if Allowance for Uncollectible Accounts had a debit balance of $11,200 instead of a credit balance?

SOLUTION

1. Percentage of net sales method:

ALLOWANCE FOR UNCOLLECTIBLE ACCOUNTS

	July 31	11,200
	31 Uncollectible Accounts Expense	70,000*
	July 31 Bal.	**81,200**

*Uncollectible Accounts Expense = $7,000,000 × 0.01

Accounts receivable aging method:

ALLOWANCE FOR UNCOLLECTIBLE ACCOUNTS

	July 31	11,200
	31 Uncollectible Accounts Expense	68,800*
	July 31 Bal.	**80,000**

*Uncollectible Accounts Expense = $80,000 – $11,200

2. Under the percentage of net sales method, the amount of the expense is the same in (1) and (2), but the ending balance will be $58,800 ($70,000 – $11,200). Under the accounts receivable aging method, the ending balance is the same, but the amount of the expense will be $91,200 ($80,000 + $11,200).

iStock Photo

NOTES RECEIVABLE

Define *promissory note* and make common calculations for promissory notes receivable. **LO 4**

A **promissory note** is an unconditional promise to pay a definite sum of money on demand or at a future date. The person or company that signs the note and thereby promises to pay is the *maker* of the note. The entity to whom payment is to be made is the *payee*. The promissory note shown in Exhibit 7.7 is an unconditional promise by the maker, Samuel Mason, to pay a definite sum—or principal ($1,000)—to the payee, Cook County Bank & Trust, on August 18, 2011. As you can see, this promissory note is dated May 20, 2011, and bears an interest rate of 8 percent.

STUDY NOTE: *Notes receivable and notes payable are distinguished from accounts receivable and accounts payable because the latter were not created by a formal promissory note.*

A payee includes all the promissory notes it holds that are due in less than one year in **notes receivable** in the current assets section of its balance sheet. A maker

EXHIBIT 7.7
A Promissory Note

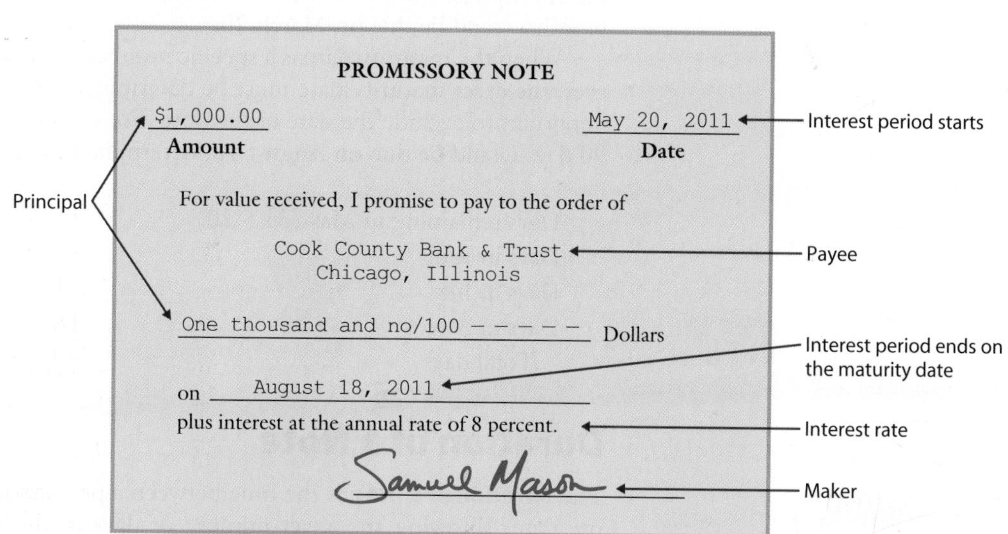
PROMISSORY NOTE

$1,000.00 — Amount

May 20, 2011 — Date

For value received, I promise to pay to the order of

Cook County Bank & Trust
Chicago, Illinois

One thousand and no/100 – – – – – Dollars

on August 18, 2011

plus interest at the annual rate of 8 percent.

Samuel Mason

You may already be familiar with promissory notes if you have taken out student loans or car loans. When you take out these loans, you sign a contract with a lender promising to repay the loan under certain terms.

Andres/iStockphoto.com

includes them in **notes payable** in the current liabilities section of its balance sheet. Because notes receivable and notes payable are financial instruments, companies may voluntarily disclose their fair value. In most cases, fair value approximates the amount in the account records, but sometimes the adjustments to fair value are significant, such as in the recent cases of subprime loans gone bad.

The nature of a company's business generally determines how frequently it receives promissory notes from customers. Firms that sell durable goods of high value, such as farm machinery and automobiles, often accept promissory notes. Among the advantages of these notes are that they produce interest income and represent a stronger legal claim against a debtor than accounts receivable do. In addition, selling—or discounting—promissory notes to banks is a common financing method. Almost all companies occasionally accept promissory notes, and many companies obtain them in settlement of past-due accounts.

Maturity Date

The **maturity date** is the date on which a promissory note must be paid. This date must be stated on the note or be determinable from the facts stated on the note. The following are among the most common statements of maturity date:

- A specific date, such as "November 14, 2011"
- A specific number of months after the date of the note, such as "three months after November 14, 2011"
- A specific number of days after the date of the note, such as "60 days after November 14, 2011"

The maturity date is obvious when a specific date is stated. And when the maturity date is a number of months from the date of the note, one simply uses the same day in the appropriate future month. For example, a note dated January 20 that is due in two months would be due on March 20.

When the maturity date is a specific number of days from the date of the note, however, the exact maturity date must be determined. In computing the maturity date, it is important to exclude the date of the note. For example, a note dated May 20 and due in 90 days would be due on August 18, determined as follows:

Days remaining in May (31 – 20)	11
Days in June	30
Days in July	31
Days in August	18
Total days	90

Duration of a Note

The **duration of a note** is the time between a promissory note's issue date and its maturity date. Knowing the exact number of days in the duration of a note is important because interest is calculated on that basis. Identifying the duration is easy when the maturity date is stated as a specific number of days from the date of the note because the two numbers are the same. However, when the maturity date is stated as a specific date, the exact number of days must be determined. Assume that a note issued on May 10 matures on August 10. The duration of the note is 92 days:

Days remaining in May (31 – 10)	21
Days in June	30
Days in July	31
Days in August	10
Total days	92

Another way to compute the duration of notes is to begin with the interest period, as follows:

90	Interest period
−11	days remaining in May (31 – 20)
79	
−30	days in June
49	
−31	days in July
18	due date in August

Interest and Interest Rate

Interest is the cost of borrowing money or the return on lending money, depending on whether one is the borrower or the lender. The amount of interest is based on three factors:

- Principal (the amount of money borrowed or lent)
- Rate of interest
- Loan's length of time

The formula used in computing interest is as follows:

Principal × Rate of Interest × Time = Interest

Interest rates are usually stated on an annual basis. For example, the interest on a one-year, 8 percent, $1,000 note would be $80, calculated as follows:

Principal × Rate of Interest × Time = Interest
$1,000 × 8/100 × 1 = $80

If the term, or time period, of the note is three months instead of a year, the interest charge would be $20, calculated as follows:

$1,000 × 8/100 × 3/12 = $20

When the term of a note is expressed in days, the exact number of days must be used in computing the interest. Thus, if the term of the note described above was 45 days, the interest would be $9.86, computed as follows:

$1,000 × 8/100 × 45/365 = $9.86

Maturity Value

The **maturity value** is the total proceeds of a promissory note—face value plus interest—at the maturity date. The maturity value of a 90-day, 8 percent, $1,000 note is computed as follows:

$$\begin{aligned} \text{Maturity Value} &= \text{Principal} + \text{Interest} \\ &= \$1{,}000 + (\$1{,}000 \times 8/100 \times 90/365) \\ &= \$1{,}000 + \$19.73 \\ &= \$1{,}019.73 \end{aligned}$$

There are also so-called *non-interest-bearing notes.* The maturity value is the face value, or principal amount. In this case, the principal includes an implied interest cost.

Accrued Interest

A promissory note received in one accounting period may not be due until a later period. The interest on a note accrues by a small amount each day of the note's duration. As we described in an earlier chapter, the matching rule requires that the accrued interest be apportioned to the periods in which it belongs. For example, assume that the $1,000, 90-day, 8 percent note discussed above was received on August 31 and that the fiscal year ended on September 30. In this case, 30 days' interest would be $6.58, calculated as follows:

$$\text{Principal} \times \text{Rate of Interest} \times \text{Time} = \text{Interest}$$

$$\$1{,}000 \times 8/100 \times 30/365 = \$6.58$$

The $6.58 of interest would be earned in the fiscal year that ends on September 30. An adjusting entry would be made to record the interest receivable as an asset and the interest income as revenue. The remainder of the interest income would be $13.15, calculated as follows:

$$\$1{,}000 \times 8/100 \times 60/365 = \$13.15$$

The remainder of the interest income ($13.15) would be recorded as income, and the interest receivable ($6.58) would be shown as received when the note is paid. Note that all the cash for the interest is received when the note is paid, but the interest income is apportioned to two fiscal years.

Dishonored Note

A note not paid at maturity is called a **dishonored note**. The holder, or payee, of a dishonored note should transfer the total amount due (including interest income) from Notes Receivable to an individual account receivable for the debtor. Doing so accomplishes two things:

- It leaves only notes that have not matured and are presumably collectible in the Notes Receivable account.
- It establishes a record showing that the customer has dishonored a note receivable, which may be helpful in deciding whether to extend credit to that customer in the future.

Stop & Apply

Assume that on December 1, 2011, a company receives a 90-day, 8 percent, $5,000 note and that the company prepares financial statements monthly.

1. What is the maturity date of the note?
2. How much interest will be earned on the note if it is paid when due?
3. What is the maturity value of the note?
4. If the company's fiscal year ends on December 31, describe the adjusting entry that would be made, including the amount.
5. How much interest will be earned on this note in 2011?

iStock Photo

(continued)

SOLUTION

1. Maturity date is February 29, 2012, determined as follows:

Days remaining in December (31 – 1)	30
Days in January	31
Days in February	28
Days in March	1
Total days	90

2. Interest: $5,000 × 8/100 × 90/365 = $98.63
3. Maturity value: $5,000.00 + $98.63 = $5,098.63
4. An adjusting entry to accrue 30 days of interest income in the amount of $32.88 ($5,000 × 8/100 × 30/365) would be needed to *debit* Interest Receivable and *credit* Interest Income.
5. Interest earned in 2012: $65.75 ($98.63 − $32.88)

A look back at ▸ Hewlett-Packard Company (HP)

In this chapter's Decision Point, we noted that **HP** must give its customers time to pay for their purchases, but at the same time, HP must have enough cash on hand to pay its suppliers. To plan the company's cash flows, HP's management must address the following questions:

1. How can the company control its cash needs?
2. How can the company evaluate its credit policies and the level of its receivables?

As we noted earlier in the chapter, all companies—even computer companies like HP—go through seasonal cycles that affect their cash flows. At times, HP may have excess cash available that it can invest in a way that earns a return but still permits ready access to cash. At other times, it may have to borrow funds. To ensure that it can borrow funds when needed, HP maintains good relations with its banks.

Financial Ratios: Receivables Turnover and Days' Receivable

To evaluate the company's credit policies and the level of its accounts receivable, management can compare the current year's receivable turnover and days' sales uncollected with those ratios in previous years. Using data from HP's Financial Highlights, we can compute these ratios for 2009 and 2008 as follows (dollars are in millions):

RATIO

		2009	2008
Receivable Turnover	=	$\frac{\text{Net Revenue}}{\text{Average Accounts Receivable}}$	$\frac{\text{Net Revenue}}{\text{Average Accounts Receivable}}$
	=	$\frac{\$114{,}552}{(\$16{,}537 + \$16{,}928)/2}$	$\frac{\$118{,}364}{(\$16{,}928 + \$13{,}420)/2}$
	=	$\frac{\$114{,}552}{\$16{,}732.50}$	$\frac{\$118{,}364}{\$15{,}174.00}$
		6.8 times	7.8 times
Days' Sales Uncollected	=	$\frac{\text{Number of Days in a Year}}{\text{Receivable Turnover}}$	$\frac{\text{Number of Days in a Year}}{\text{Receivable Turnover}}$
	=	$\frac{365 \text{ days}}{6.8 \text{ times}}$	$\frac{365 \text{ days}}{7.8 \text{ times}}$
	=	53.7 days	46.8 days

Thus, in 2009, HP had a decrease of 1.0 in its receivable turnover. This result increased the number of days it takes to collect accounts receivable by 6.9 days. This increase may not seem like much, but it represents about $2 billion in cash.

Review Problem

LO 1 LO 3

Estimating Uncollectible Accounts and Receivables Analysis

Farming Equipment Corporation sells merchandise on credit and also accepts notes as payment. During the year ended June 30, the company had net sales of $2,400,000. At the end of the year, it had accounts receivable of $800,000 and a debit balance in Allowance for Uncollectible Accounts of $4,200. In the past, approximately 1.5 percent of net sales has been uncollectible. Also, an aging analysis of accounts receivable reveals that $34,000 in accounts receivable appears to be uncollectible.

Required

1. Compute Uncollectible Accounts Expense and determine the ending balance of Allowance for Uncollectible Accounts and Accounts Receivable, net under (a) the percentage of net sales method and (b) the accounts receivable aging method.

RATIO

2. Compute the receivable turnover and days' sales uncollected using the data from the accounts receivable aging method in requirement 1 and assuming that the prior year's net accounts receivable were $706,000.

ANSWERS TO REVIEW PROBLEM

1. Uncollectible Accounts Expense and ending account balances
   a. Percentage of net sales method:

      Uncollectible Accounts Expense = $2,400,000 × 0.015 = $36,000
      Allowance for Uncollectible Accounts = $36,000 − $4,200 = $31,800
      Accounts Receivable, net = $800,000 − $31,800 = $768,200

   b. Accounts receivable aging method:

      Uncollectible Accounts Expense = $4,200 + $34,000 = $38,200
      Allowance for Uncollectible Accounts = $34,000
      Accounts Receivable, net = $800,000 − $34,000 = $766,000

2. Receivable turnover and days' sales uncollected

$$\text{Receivable Turnover} = \frac{\$2{,}400{,}000}{(\$766{,}000 + \$706{,}000) \div 2} = 3.3 \text{ times}$$

$$\text{Days' Sales Uncollected} = \frac{365 \text{ days}}{6.8 \text{ times}} = 110.6 \text{ days}$$

Stop & Review

LO 1 Identify and explain the management and ethical issues related to cash and receivables.

The management of cash and receivables is critical to maintaining adequate liquidity. In dealing with these assets, management must (1) consider the need for short-term investing and borrowing as the business's balance of cash fluctuates during seasonal cycles, (2) establish credit policies that balance the need for sales with the ability to collect, (3) evaluate the level of receivables using receivable turnover and days' sales uncollected, (4) assess the need to increase cash flows through the financing of receivables, and (5) understand the importance of ethics in estimating credit losses.

Define *cash equivalents* and explain methods of controlling cash, including bank reconciliations. **LO 2**

Cash equivalents are investments that have a term of 90 days or less. Most companies record cash equivalents at their approximate fair value. Methods of controlling cash include imprest systems; banking services, including electronic funds transfer; and bank reconciliations. A bank reconciliation accounts for the difference between the balance on a company's bank statement and the balance in its Cash account. It involves adjusting for outstanding checks, deposits in transit, service charges, NSF checks, miscellaneous debits and credits, and interest income.

Apply the allowance method of accounting for uncollectible accounts. **LO 3**

Because of the lag between the time credit sales are made and the time accounts are judged uncollectible, the allowance method is used to match the amount of uncollectible accounts against revenues in any given period. Uncollectible accounts expense is estimated by using either the percentage of net sales method or the accounts receivable aging method. When the first method is used, bad debts are judged to be a certain percentage of sales during the period. When the second method is used, certain percentages are applied to groups of accounts receivable that have been arranged by due dates.

Allowance for Uncollectible Accounts is a contra-asset account to Accounts Receivable. The estimate of uncollectible accounts is debited to Uncollectible Accounts Expense and credited to the allowance account. When an individual account is determined to be uncollectible, it is removed from Accounts Receivable by debiting the allowance account and crediting Accounts Receivable. If the written-off account is later collected, the earlier entry is reversed and the collection is recorded in the normal way.

Define *promissory note* and make common calculations for promissory notes receivable. **LO 4**

A promissory note is an unconditional promise to pay a definite sum of money on demand or at a future date. Companies that sell durable goods of high value, such as farm machinery and automobiles, often accept promissory notes. Selling these notes to banks is a common financing method. In accounting for promissory notes, it is important to know how to calculate the maturity date, duration of a note, interest and interest rate, and maturity value.

Key Terms and Ratios

Accounts receivable 329 (LO1)
Accounts receivable aging method 340 (LO3)
Aging of accounts receivable 340 (LO3)
Allowance for Uncollectible Accounts 338 (LO3)
Allowance method 338 (LO3)
Bank reconciliation 335 (LO2)
Cash 328 (LO1)
Cash equivalents 334 (LO2)
Compensating balance 328 (LO1)
Contingent liability 332 (LO1)
Direct charge-off method 337 (LO3)
Discounting 332 (LO1)
Dishonored note 346 (LO4)
Duration of a note 344 (LO4)
Electronic funds transfer (EFT) 335 (LO2)
Factor 331 (LO1)
Factoring 331 (LO1)
Imprest system 334 (LO2)
Interest 345 (LO4)
Maturity date 344 (LO4)
Maturity value 345 (LO4)
Notes payable 344 (LO4)
Notes receivable 343 (LO4)
Percentage of net sales method 339 (LO3)
Promissory note 343 (LO4)
Securitization 332 (LO1)
Short-term financial assets 329 (LO1)
Trade credit 329 (LO1)
Uncollectible accounts 333 (LO1)

FINANCIAL RATIOS

Days' sales uncollected 331 (LO1)
Receivable turnover 330 (LO1)

Chapter Assignments Building Your Basic Knowledge and Skills

Short Exercises

LO 1 **Management Issues**

SE 1. Indicate which of the management issues on the right is related to each action on the left.

1. Selling accounts receivable to a factor	a. Managing cash needs
2. Borrowing funds for short-term needs during slow periods	b. Setting credit policies
3. Conducting thorough checks of new customers' ability to pay	c. Financing receivables
4. Making every effort to reflect possible future losses accurately	d. Ethically reporting receivables

LO 1 **Financial Ratios**

SE 2. Graff Company has cash of $40,000, net accounts receivable of $90,000, and net sales of $720,000. Last year's net accounts receivable were $70,000. Compute the following ratios (*Note:* Round to one decimal place.):

a. Receivable turnover
b. Days' sales uncollected

LO 1 **Financial Ratios**

SE 3. Zebra Company has cash of $60,000, net accounts receivable of $135,000, and net sales of $1,080,000. Last year's net accounts receivable were $100,000. Compute the following ratios (*Note:* Round to one decimal place.):

a. Receivable turnover
b. Days' sales uncollected

LO 2 **Cash and Cash Equivalents**

SE 4. Compute the amount of cash and cash equivalents on Blazer Company's balance sheet if, on the balance sheet date, it has currency and coins on hand of $250, deposits in checking accounts of $1,500, U.S. Treasury bills due in 80 days of $15,000, and U.S. Treasury bonds due in 200 days of $25,000.

LO 2 **Bank Reconciliation**

SE 5. Prepare a bank reconciliation from the following information:

- Balance per bank statement as of April 30, $7,294.15
- Balance per books as of April 30, $3,719.22
- Deposits in transit, $981.36
- Outstanding checks, $4,543.33
- Interest on average balance, $12.96

LO 2 **Bank Reconciliation**

SE 6. Prepare a bank reconciliation from the following information:

- Balance per bank statement as of June 30, $4,862.77
- Balance per books as of June 30, $2,479.48
- Deposits in transit, $654.24
- Outstanding checks, $3,028.89
- Interest on average balance, $8.64

LO 3 **Percentage of Net Sales Method**

SE 7. At the end of October, Fanny Company's management estimates the uncollectible accounts expense to be 1 percent of net sales of $750,000. Prepare a journal entry to record the uncollectible accounts expense, assuming Allowance for Uncollectible Accounts has a debit balance of $3,500.

LO 3 **Accounts Receivable Aging Method**

SE 8. An aging analysis on September 30 of the accounts receivable of Kukiz Corporation indicates that uncollectible accounts amount to $129,000. Prepare a journal entry to record uncollectible accounts expense under each of the following independent assumptions:

a. Allowance for Uncollectible Accounts has a credit balance of $27,000 before adjustment.
b. Allowance for Uncollectible Accounts has a debit balance of $21,000 before adjustment.

LO 3 **Accounts Receivable Aging Method**

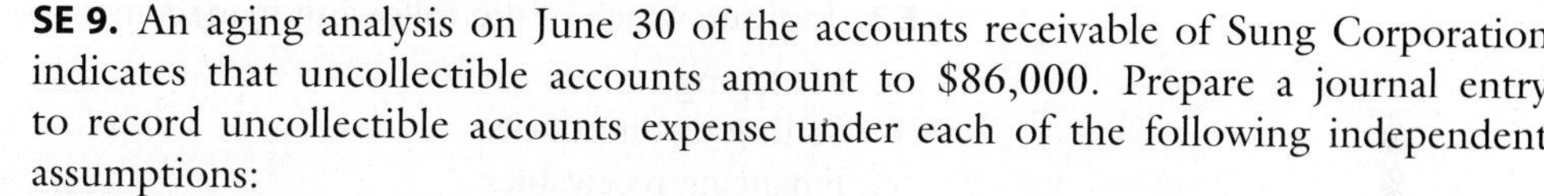

SE 9. An aging analysis on June 30 of the accounts receivable of Sung Corporation indicates that uncollectible accounts amount to $86,000. Prepare a journal entry to record uncollectible accounts expense under each of the following independent assumptions:

a. Allowance for Uncollectible Accounts has a credit balance of $18,000 before adjustment.
b. Allowance for Uncollectible Accounts has a debit balance of $14,000 before adjustment.

LO 3 **Write-Off of Accounts Receivable**

SE 10. Clod Corporation, which uses the allowance method, has accounts receivable of $25,400 and an allowance for uncollectible accounts of $4,900. An account receivable from Raphael Mazur of $2,200 is deemed to be uncollectible and is written off. What is the amount of net accounts receivable before and after the write-off?

LO 4 **Notes Receivable Calculations**

SE 11. On August 25, Champion Company received a 90-day, 9 percent note in settlement of an account receivable in the amount of $20,000. Determine the following:

a. Maturity date
b. Amount of interest on the note
c. Maturity value

LO 4 **Notes Receivable Calculations**

SE 12. On March 21, Dane Company received a 90-day, 7 percent note in settlement of an account receivable in the amount of $30,000. Determine the following:

a. Maturity date
b. Amount of interest on the note
c. Maturity value

Exercises

LO 1, 2 **Discussion Questions**

E 1. Develop a brief answer to each of the following questions:

1. Name some businesses whose needs for cash fluctuate during the year. Name some whose needs for cash are relatively stable over the year.
2. Why is it advantageous for a company to finance its receivables?

3. To increase its sales, a company decides to increase its credit terms from 15 to 30 days. What effect will this change in policy have on receivable turnover and days' sales uncollected?
4. How might the receivable turnover and days' sales uncollected reveal that management is consistently underestimating the amount of losses from uncollectible accounts? Is this action ethical? Explain your answer.

LO 3, 4

Discussion Questions

E 2. Develop a brief answer to each of the following questions:

1. What accounting rule is violated by the direct charge-off method of recognizing uncollectible accounts? Why?
2. In what ways is Allowance for Uncollectible Accounts similar to Accumulated Depreciation? In what ways is it different?
3. Under what circumstances would an accrual of interest income on an interest-bearing note receivable not be required at the end of an accounting period?

LO 1

Management Issues

E 3. Indicate which of the following management issues is related to each action below.

a. Managing cash needs
b. Setting credit policies
c. Financing receivables
d. Ethically reporting accounts receivable

_____ 1. Buying a U.S. Treasury bill with cash that is not needed for a few months
_____ 2. Comparing receivable turnover for two years
_____ 3. Setting a policy that allows customers to buy on credit
_____ 4. Selling notes receivable to a financing company
_____ 5. Making careful estimates of losses from uncollectible accounts
_____ 6. Borrowing funds for short-term needs in a period when sales are low
_____ 7. Changing the terms for credit sales in an effort to reduce the days' sales uncollected
_____ 8. Revising estimated credit losses in a timely manner when economic conditions change
_____ 9. Establishing a department whose responsibility is to approve customers' credit

LO 1

RATIO

Financial Ratios

E 4. The following data are from Gwelph Corporation's financial statements for the current year:

Current assets	
Cash	$ 70,000
Short-term investments	170,000
Notes receivable	240,000
Accounts receivable, net	400,000
Inventory	500,000
Prepaid assets	50,000
Total current assets	$1,430,000
Current liabilities	
Notes payable	$ 600,000
Accounts payable	150,000
Accrued liabilities	20,000
Total current liabilities	$ 770,000
Net sales	$3,200,000
Last year's accounts receivable, net	$ 360,000

a. Compute the receivable turnover.
b. Compute the days' sales uncollected.

LO 2 **Cash and Cash Equivalents**

E 5. At year end, Allel Company had currency and coins in cash registers of $5,600, money orders from customers of $10,000, deposits in checking accounts of $64,000, U.S. Treasury bills due in 80 days of $180,000, certificates of deposit at the bank that mature in six months of $200,000, and U.S. Treasury bonds due in one year of $100,000. Calculate the amount of cash and cash equivalents that will be shown on the company's year-end balance sheet.

LO 2 **Bank Reconciliation**

E 6. Prepare a bank reconciliation from the following information:

- Balance per bank statement as of May 31, $35,510.88
- Balance per books as of May 31, $24,423.88
- Deposits in transit, $4,509.62
- Outstanding checks,$15,636.32
- Bank service charge, $39.70

LO 3 **Percentage of Net Sales Method**

E 7. At the end of the year, Molly Enterprises estimates the uncollectible accounts expense to be 0.8 percent of net sales of $3,787,500. The current credit balance of Allowance for Uncollectible Accounts is $6,450. Prepare a journal entry to record the uncollectible accounts expense. What is the balance of Allowance for Uncollectible Accounts after this adjustment?

LO 3 **Accounts Receivable Aging Method**

E 8. The Accounts Receivable account of Roger Company shows a debit balance of $26,000 at the end of the year. An aging analysis of the individual accounts indicates estimated uncollectible accounts to be $1,675.

Prepare a journal entry to record the uncollectible accounts expense under each of the following independent assumptions:

a. Allowance for Uncollectible Accounts has a credit balance of $200 before adjustment.
b. Allowance for Uncollectible Accounts has a debit balance of $200 before adjustment.
c. What is the balance of Allowance for Uncollectible Accounts after each of these adjustments?

LO 3 **Aging Method and Net Sales Method Contrasted**

E 9. At the beginning of 2011, the balances for Accounts Receivable and Allowance for Uncollectible Accounts were $215,000 and $15,700 (credit), respectively. During the year, credit sales were $1,600,000, and collections on account were $1,475,000. In addition, $17,500 in uncollectible accounts was written off.

1. Using T accounts, determine the year-end balances of Accounts Receivable and Allowance for Uncollectible Accounts.
2. Prepare the year-end adjusting entry to record the uncollectible accounts expense under each of the following conditions. Also, show the year-end balance sheet presentation of accounts receivable and allowance for uncollectible accounts. Post the results of each of the entries to the T account for Allowance for Uncollectible Accounts.
   a. Management estimates the percentage of uncollectible credit sales to be 1.4 percent of total credit sales.
   b. Based on an aging of accounts receivable, management estimates the end-of-year uncollectible accounts receivable to be $19,350.

LO 3 **Aging Method and Net Sales Method Contrasted**

E 10. During 2011, Salmon Company had net sales of $5,700,000. Most of the sales were on credit. At the end of 2011, the balance of Accounts Receivable was $700,000, and Allowance for Uncollectible Accounts had a debit balance of $24,000.

Salmon's management uses two methods of estimating uncollectible accounts expense: the percentage of net sales method and the accounts receivable aging method.

The percentage of uncollectible sales is 1.5 percent of net sales, and based on an aging of accounts receivable, the end-of-year uncollectible accounts total $70,000.

a. Prepare the end-of-year adjusting entry to record the uncollectible accounts expense using the percentage of net sales method. What will the balance of Allowance for Uncollectible Accounts be after the adjustment?
b. Prepare the end-of-year adjusting entry to record the uncollectible accounts expense using the accounts receivable aging method. What will the balance of Allowance for Uncollectible Accounts be after the adjustment?
c. Why are the results different? Which method is likely to be more reliable? Why?

LO 3

Aging Method and Net Sales Method Contrasted

E 11. Anuk Company sells merchandise on credit. During the fiscal year ended July 31, the company had net sales of $2,300,000. At the end of the year, it had Accounts Receivable of $600,000 and a debit balance in Allowance for Uncollectible Accounts of $3,400. In the past, approximately 1.4 percent of net sales have been uncollectible. Also, an aging analysis of accounts receivable reveals that $30,000 of the receivables appears to be uncollectible.

a. Prepare journal entries to record uncollectible accounts expense using the percentage of net sales method. What is the resulting balance of Allowance for Uncollectible Accounts? How would your answer change if Allowance for Uncollectible Accounts had a credit balance of $3,400 instead of a debit balance?
b. Prepare journal entries to record uncollectible accounts expense using the accounts receivable aging method. What is the resulting balance of Allowance for Uncollectible Accounts? How would your answer change if Allowance for Uncollectible Accounts had a credit balance of $3,400 instead of a debit balance?
c. Why do the methods result in different balances?

LO 3

Write-Off of Accounts Receivable

E 12. Maxim Company, which uses the allowance method, has accounts receivable of $130,000 and Allowance for Uncollectible Accounts of $12,800 (credit). The company sold merchandise to Olga Boruc for $14,400 and later received $4,800 from Boruc. The rest of the amount due from Boruc had to be written off as uncollectible. Using T accounts, show the beginning balances and the effects of the Boruc transactions on Accounts Receivable and Allowance for Uncollectible Accounts. What is the amount of net accounts receivable before and after the write-off?

LO 4

Interest Computations

E 13. Determine the interest on the following notes:

a. $38,760 at 10 percent for 90 days
b. $27,200 at 12 percent for 60 days
c. $30,600 at 9 percent for 30 days
d. $51,000 at 15 percent for 120 days
e. $18,360 at 6 percent for 60 days

LO 4

Notes Receivable Calculations

E 14. Determine the maturity date, interest at maturity, and maturity value for a 90-day, 10 percent, $72,000 note from Stone Corporation dated February 15.

LO 4

Notes Receivable Calculations

E 15. Determine the maturity date, interest in 2011 and 2012, and maturity value for a 90-day, 12 percent, $15,000 note from a customer dated December 1, 2011, assuming a December 31 year-end.

LO 4

Notes Receivable Calculations

E 16. Determine the maturity date, interest at maturity, and maturity value for each of the following notes:

a. A 60-day, 10 percent, $2,400 note dated January 5 received from R. Stroll for granting a time extension on a past-due account
b. A 60-day, 12 percent, $1,500 note dated March 9 received from J. Collins for granting a time extension on a past-due account

Problems

LO 2

Bank Reconciliation

✔ Adjusted book balance: $296,928.56

P 1. The following information is available for Merry Corporation as of April 30, 2011:

- Cash on the books as of April 30 amounted to $226,350.56. Cash on the bank statement for the same date was $281,434.16.
- A deposit of $28,699.68, representing cash receipts of April 30, did not appear on the bank statement.
- Outstanding checks totaled $14,605.28.
- A check for $4,840.00 returned with the statement was recorded as $4,048.00. The check was for advertising.
- The bank service charge for April amounted to $70.00 and had not been recorded.
- The bank collected $72,600.00 for Merry on a note. The face value of the note was $72,000.00.
- An NSF check for $2,280.00 from a customer, Jim Hall, was returned with the statement.
- The bank mistakenly deducted a check for $1,400.00 that was drawn by Ice Corporation.
- The bank reported a credit of $1,120.00 for interest on the average balance.

REQUIRED

1. Prepare a bank reconciliation for Merry Corporation as of April 30, 2011.
2. Prepare the necessary journal entries from the reconciliation.
3. State the amount of cash that should appear on Merry's balance sheet as of April 30.
4. USER INSIGHT ▶ Why is a bank reconciliation a necessary internal control?

LO 1, 3

Methods of Estimating Uncollectible Accounts and Receivables Analysis

✔ Uncollectible accounts expense: percentage of net sales method, $4,488; accounts receivable aging method, $3,925

P 2. On December 31 of last year, the balance sheet of Union Company had accounts receivable of $74,500 and a credit balance in Allowance for Uncollectible Accounts of $5,075. During the current year, Union's financial records included the following selected activities:

- Sales on account, $298,750
- Sales returns and allowances, $18,250
- Collections from customers, $287,500
- Accounts written off as worthless, $4,000

In the past, 1.6 percent of Union's net sales have been uncollectible.

REQUIRED

1. Prepare T accounts for Accounts Receivable and Allowance for Uncollectible Accounts. Enter the beginning balances and show the effects on these accounts of the items listed above, summarizing the year's activity. Determine the ending balance of each account.
2. Compute the amount of uncollectible accounts expense and determine the ending balance of Allowance for Uncollectible Accounts under (a) the percentage of net sales method and (b) the accounts receivable aging method. Assume that an aging of the accounts receivable shows that $5,000 may be uncollectible.
3.  Compute the receivable turnover and days' sales uncollected using the data from the accounts receivable aging method in requirement 2.
4. USER INSIGHT ▶ How do you explain that the two methods used in requirement 2 result in different amounts for uncollectible accounts expense? What rationale underlies each method?

LO 3

Accounts Receivable Aging Method

✔ Amount of uncollectible accounts expense: $4,546

P 3. Thorn Company uses the accounts receivable aging method to estimate uncollectible accounts. At the beginning of the year, the balance of the Accounts Receivable account was a debit of $45,215, and the balance of Allowance for Uncollectible Accounts was a credit of $4,050. During the year, the store had sales on account of $237,500, sales returns and allowances of $3,100, worthless accounts written off of $4,400, and collections from customers of $226,363. At the end of the year (December

31, 2011), a junior accountant for Thorn was preparing an aging analysis of accounts receivable. At the top of page 6 of the report, the following totals appeared:

Customer Account	Total	Not Yet Due	1–30 Days Past Due	31–60 Days Past Due	61–90 Days Past Due	Over 90 Days Past Due
Balance Forward	$44,820	$24,515	$12,055	$4,605	$1,995	$1,650

To finish the analysis, the following accounts need to be classified:

Account	Amount	Due Date
S. Ballarin	$ 465	Jan. 14 (next year)
W. Czuma	323	Dec. 24
R. Edler	925	Sept. 28
C. Fuller	1,103	Aug. 16
N. Kotler	175	Dec. 14
P. Tent	893	Jan. 23 (next year)
M. Villas	148	Nov. 5
	$4,032	

From past experience, Thorn has found that the following rates are realistic for estimating uncollectible accounts:

Time	Percentage Considered Uncollectible
Not yet due	2
1–30 days past due	5
31–60 days past due	15
61–90 days past due	25
Over 90 days past due	50

REQUIRED

1. Complete the aging analysis of accounts receivable.
2. Compute the end-of-year balances (before adjustments) of Accounts Receivable and Allowance for Uncollectible Accounts.
3. Prepare an analysis computing the estimated uncollectible accounts.
4. Calculate Thorn's estimated uncollectible accounts expense for the year (round the amount to the nearest whole dollar).

USER INSIGHT ▶ 5. What role do estimates play in applying the aging analysis? What factors might affect these estimates?

LO 4

Notes Receivable Calculations

✔ Total accrued interest income as of June 30: $482.06

P 4. Hampton Importing Company engaged in the following transactions involving promissory notes:

May 3 Sold engines to Belca Company for $15,000 in exchange for a 90-day, 12 percent promissory note.

16 Sold engines to Weiss Company for $8,000 in exchange for a 60-day, 13 percent note.

31 Sold engines to Weiss Company for $7,500 in exchange for a 90-day, 11 percent note.

REQUIRED

1. For each of the notes, determine the maturity date, interest on the note, and maturity value.
2. Assume that the fiscal year for Hampton Importing ends on June 30. How much interest income should be recorded on that date?

USER INSIGHT ▶ 3. What are the effects of the transactions in May on cash flows for the year ended June 30?

Alternate Problems

LO 2

Bank Reconciliation

✔ Adjusted book balance: $55,485.60

P 5. The following information is available for Lotus Lake, Inc., as of May 31, 2011:

- Cash on the books as of May 31 amounted to $43,784.16. Cash on the bank statement for the same date was $53,451.46.
- A deposit of $5,220.94, representing cash receipts of May 31, did not appear on the bank statement.
- Outstanding checks totaled $3,936.80.
- A check for $1,920.00 returned with the statement was recorded incorrectly in the check register as $1,380.00. The check was for a cash purchase of equipment.
- The bank service charge for May amounted to $30.00.
- The bank collected $12,200.00 for Lotus Lake on a note. The face value of the note was $12,000.00.
- An NSF check for $178.56 from a customer, Justin Curtis, was returned with the statement.
- The bank mistakenly charged to the company account a check for $750.00 drawn by another company.
- The bank reported that it had credited the account for $250.00 in interest on the average balance for May.

REQUIRED

1. Prepare a bank reconciliation for Lotus Lake, Inc., as of May 31, 2011.
2. Prepare the journal entries necessary to adjust the accounts.
3. What amount of cash should appear on Lotus Lake's balance sheet as of May 31?
4. USER INSIGHT ▶ Why is a bank reconciliation considered an important control over cash?

LO 1, 3

Methods of Estimating Uncollectible Accounts and Receivables Analysis

✔ Uncollectible accounts expense: percentage of net sales method, $49,930; accounts receivable aging method, $54,200

P 6. Hernandez Company had an Accounts Receivable balance of $640,000 and a credit balance in Allowance for Uncollectible Accounts of $33,400 at January 1, 2011. During the year, Hernandez recorded the following transactions:

- Sales on account, $2,104,000
- Sales returns and allowances by credit customers, $106,800
- Collections from customers, $1,986,000
- Worthless accounts written off, $39,600

The company's past history indicates that 2.5 percent of its net credit sales will not be collected.

REQUIRED

1. Prepare T accounts for Accounts Receivable and Allowance for Uncollectible Accounts. Enter the beginning balances, and show the effects on these accounts of the items listed above, summarizing the year's activity. Determine the ending balance of each account.
2. Compute the amount of uncollectible accounts expense, and determine the ending balance of Allowance for Uncollectible Accounts under (a) the percentage of net sales method and (b) the accounts receivable aging method, assuming an aging of the accounts receivable shows that $48,000 may be uncollectible.
3. RATIO Compute the receivable turnover and days' sales uncollected, using the data from the accounts receivable aging method in requirement 2. (*Note:* Round to one decimal place.)
4. USER INSIGHT ▶ How do you explain that the two methods used in requirement 2 result in different amounts for Uncollectible Accounts Expense? What rationale underlies each method?

LO 3

Accounts Receivable Aging Method

✔ Amount of uncollectible accounts expense: $72,713

P 7. Fossella Fashions uses the accounts receivable aging method to estimate uncollectible accounts. On February 1, 2010, the balance of the Accounts Receivable account was a debit of $442,341, and the balance of Allowance for Uncollectible Accounts was a credit of $43,700. During the year, the store had sales on account of $3,722,000, sales returns and allowances of $60,000, worthless accounts written off of $44,300, and collections from customers of $3,211,000. As part of the end-of-year (January 31, 2011) procedures, an aging analysis of accounts receivable is prepared. The analysis, which is partially complete, is as follows:

Customer Account	Total	Not Yet Due	1–30 Days Past Due	31–60 Days Past Due	61–90 Days Past Due	Over 90 Days Past Due
Balance Forward	$793,791	$438,933	$149,614	$106,400	$57,442	$41,402

To finish the analysis, the following accounts need to be classified:

Account	Amount	Due Date
K. Baker	$11,077	Jan. 15
L. Dawson	9,314	Feb. 15 (next fiscal year)
Z. Kopara	8,664	Dec. 20
C. Mural	780	Oct. 1
R. Otis	14,710	Jan. 4
B. Softy	6,316	Nov. 15
T. Wilson	4,389	Mar. 1 (next fiscal year)
	$55,250	

From past experience, the company has found that the following rates are realistic for estimating uncollectible accounts:

Time	Percentage Considered Uncollectible
Not yet due	2
1–30 days past due	5
31–60 days past due	15
61–90 days past due	25
Over 90 days past due	50

REQUIRED

1. Complete the aging analysis of accounts receivable.
2. Compute the end-of-year balances (before adjustments) of Accounts Receivable and Allowance for Uncollectible Accounts.
3. Prepare an analysis computing the estimated uncollectible accounts.
4. How much is Fossella Fashions' estimated uncollectible accounts expense for the year? (*Note:* Round the adjustment to the nearest whole dollar.)

USER INSIGHT ▶ 5. What role do estimates play in applying the aging analysis? What factors might affect these estimates?

LO 4

Notes Receivable Calculations

✔ Total accrued interest income as of April 30: $1,609.31

P 8. Abraham Motor Company performed the following transactions involving promissory notes:

Mar. 3 Sold machines to Anton Company for $60,000 in exchange for a 90-day, 10 percent promissory note.

16 Sold machines to Yu Company for $32,000 in exchange for a 60-day, 11 percent note.

31 Sold machines to Yu Company for $30,000 in exchange for a 90-day, 9 percent note.

REQUIRED

1. For each of the notes, determine the maturity date, interest on the note, and maturity value.

2. Assume that the fiscal year for Abraham Motor ends on April 30. How much interest income should be recorded on that date?

USER INSIGHT ▶ 3. What are the effects of the transactions in March on cash flows for the year ended April 30?

Cases

LO 1

Conceptual Understanding: Role of Credit Sales

C 1. **Mitsubishi Corp.**, a broadly diversified Japanese company, instituted a credit plan called Three Diamonds for customers who buy its major electronic products, such as large-screen televisions, from specified retail dealers.[16] Under the plan, approved customers who make purchases in July of one year do not have to make any payments until September of the next year. Nor do they have to pay interest during the intervening months. Mitsubishi pays the dealer the full amount less a small fee, sends the customer a Mitsubishi credit card, and collects from the customer at the specified time.

What was Mitsubishi's motivation for establishing such generous credit terms? What costs are involved? What are the accounting implications?

LO 1, 3

Conceptual Understanding: Role of Estimates in Accounting for Receivables

C 2. **CompuCredit** is a credit card issuer in Atlanta. It prides itself on making credit cards available to almost anyone in a matter of seconds over the Internet. The cost to the consumer is an interest rate of 28 percent, about double that of companies that provide cards only to customers with good credit. Despite its high interest rate, CompuCredit was successful for many years. To calculate its income, the company estimated that 10 percent of its $1.3 billion in accounts receivable would not be paid; the industry average is 7 percent. Some analysts were critical of CompuCredit for being too optimistic in its projections of losses.[17] In fact, during the recent recession, CompuCredit losses from uncollectible accounts increased and exceeded its interest income and the company reported large operating losses.[18] Why are estimates necessary in accounting for receivables? If CompuCredit were to use the same estimate of losses as other companies in its industry, would it have been better or worse off? How would one determine if CompuCredit's estimate of losses is reasonable?

LO 1

Conceptual Understanding: Receivables Financing

C 3. Gerard Appliances, Inc., is a small manufacturer of washing machines and dryers. It sells its products to large, established discount retailers that market the appliances under their own names. Gerard generally sells the appliances on trade credit terms of n/60, but if a customer wants a longer term, it will accept a note with a term of up to nine months. At present, the company is having cash flow troubles and needs $10 million immediately. Its Cash balance is $400,000, its Accounts Receivable balance is $4.6 million, and its Notes Receivable balance is $7.4 million.

How might Gerard Appliances use its accounts receivable and notes receivable to raise the cash it needs? What are its prospects for raising the needed cash?

LO 1

Interpreting Financial Reports: Comparison and Interpretation of Ratios

RATIO

C 4. **Fosters Group Limited** and **Heineken N.V.** are two well-known breweries. Fosters is an Australian company; Heineken is Dutch. Fosters is about half the size of Heineken.

Ratios can help in comparing and understanding companies that differ in size and that use different currencies. For example, the receivable turnovers for Fosters and Heineken in 2009 and 2008 were as follows:[19]

	2009	2008
Fosters	4.5 times	3.9 times
Heineken	6.1 times	6.7 times

What do the ratios tell you about the credit policies of the two companies? How long does it take each, on average, to collect a receivable? What do the ratios tell you about the companies' relative needs for capital to finance receivables? Which company is improving? Can you tell which company has a better credit policy? Explain your answers.

LO 1, 3

Interpreting Financial Reports: Accounting for Accounts Receivable

C 5. Robinson Products Co., a major consumer goods company, sells more than 3,000 products in 135 countries. Its report to the Securities and Exchange Commission in 2011 presented the following data:

	2011	2010	2009
Net sales	$9,820,000	$9,730,000	$9,888,000
Accounts receivable	1,046,000	1,048,000	1,008,000
Allowance for uncollectible accounts	37,200	42,400	49,000
Uncollectible accounts expense	30,000	33,400	31,600
Uncollectible accounts written off	38,600	40,200	35,400
Recoveries of accounts previously written off	3,400	200	2,000

1. Compute the ratio of uncollectible accounts expense to net sales and to accounts receivable and the ratio of allowance for uncollectible accounts to accounts receivable for 2009, 2010, and 2011. (*Note:* Round to one decimal place.)
2. Compute the receivable turnover and days' sales uncollected for each year assuming that net accounts receivable in 2008 were $930,000. (*Note:* Round to one decimal place.)
3. What is your interpretation of the ratios? Describe management's attitude toward the collectability of accounts receivable over the three-year period.

LO 1, 2, 3

Annual Report Case: Cash and Receivables

C 6. Refer to the **CVS** annual report in the Supplement to Chapter 1 to answer the following questions:

1. What amount of cash and cash equivalents did CVS have in 2009? Do you suppose most of that amount is cash in the bank or cash equivalents?
2. What customers represent the main source of CVS's accounts receivable, and how much is CVS's allowance for uncollectible accounts?
3. What do you think CVS's seasonal needs for cash are? Where in CVS's financial statements is the seasonality of sales discussed?

LO 1

Comparison Analysis: Accounts Receivable Analysis

C 7. Refer to the **CVS** annual report in the Supplement to Chapter 1 and to the following data (in millions) for **Walgreens**: net sales, $63,335 and $59,034 for 2009 and 2008, respectively; accounts receivable, net, $2,496 and $2,527 for 2009 and 2008, respectively.[20]

1. Compute receivable turnover and days' sales uncollected for 2009 and 2008 for CVS and Walgreens. Accounts receivable in 2007 were $4,580 million for CVS and $2,237 million for Walgreens.
2. Do you discern any differences in the two companies' credit policies? Explain your answer.

LO 1, 3

Ethical Dilemma: Uncollectible Accounts

C 8. Mullin Interiors, a successful retailer of high-quality furniture, is located in an affluent suburb where a large insurance company has just announced that it will lay off 4,000 employees. Because most of Mullin Interiors' sales are made on credit, accounts receivable is one of its major assets. Although the company's annual losses from uncollectible accounts are not out of line, they represent a sizable amount. The company depends on bank loans for its financing. Sales and net income have declined in the past year, and some customers are falling behind in paying their accounts.

Veronica Mullin, the owner of the business, knows that the bank's loan officer likes to see a steady performance. She has therefore instructed the company's controller to underestimate the uncollectible accounts this year to show a small growth in earnings. Mullin believes this action is justified because earnings in future years will average out the losses. Since the company has a history of success, she believes the adjustments are meaningless accounting measures anyway.

Are Mullin's actions ethical? Would any parties be harmed by her actions? How important is it to try to be accurate in estimating losses from uncollectible accounts?

CHAPTER 8

DECISION POINT
A User's Focus Microsoft

Microsoft is the world's leading computer software company. It earns revenue by developing, manufacturing, licensing, and supporting a wide range of software products, such as Windows 7®, its latest operating system, and Xbox360®, its most recent game console. As you can see in Microsoft's Financial Highlights, the company's total current liabilities in 2009 were over $27.0 billion, which is about 68.2 percent of its stockholders' equity of $39.6 billion.[1]

Managing liabilities is obviously important to achieving profitability and liquidity. If a company has too few liabilities, it may not be earning up to its potential. If it has too many liabilities, it may be incurring excessive risks. A company that does not manage its debt carefully is vulnerable to failure.

MICROSOFT'S FINANCIAL HIGHLIGHTS (in millions)

Current Liabilities	2009	2008
Accounts payable	$ 3,324	$ 4,034
Short-term debt	2,000	—
Accrued compensation	3,156	2,934
Income taxes payable	725	3,248
Short-term unearned revenue	13,003	13,397
Securities lending payable and other	4,826	6,273
Total current liabilities	$27,034	$29,886
Long-term debt	3,746	—
Long-term unearned revenue and other long-term liabilities	7,550	6,621
Total liabilities	$38,330	$36,507

Questions

1. *How does Microsoft's decision to incur debt relate to the goals of the business?*
2. *Is the level of accounts payable in the operating cycle satisfactory?*
3. *Has the company properly identified and accounted for all its current liabilities?*

Jochen Tack/PhotoLibrary

Current Liabilities and Fair Value Accounting

LEARNING OBJECTIVES

LO 1 Identify the management issues related to current liabilities. (pp. 364–367)

LO 2 Identify, compute, and record definitely determinable and estimated current liabilities. (pp. 368–376)

LO 3 Distinguish *contingent liabilities* from *commitments*. (pp. 376–377)

LO 4 Identify the valuation approaches to fair value accounting and define *time value of money* and *interest* and apply them to present values. (pp. 377–382)

LO 5 Apply present value to simple valuation situations. (pp. 382–384)

Although some current liabilities, such as accounts payable, are recorded when a company makes a purchase, others accrue during an accounting period and are not recorded until adjusting entries are made at the end of the period. In addition, the value of some accruals must be estimated. If accrued liabilities are not recognized and valued properly, both liabilities and expenses will be understated on the financial statements, making the company's performance look better than it actually is.

FOCUS ON FINANCIAL STATEMENTS

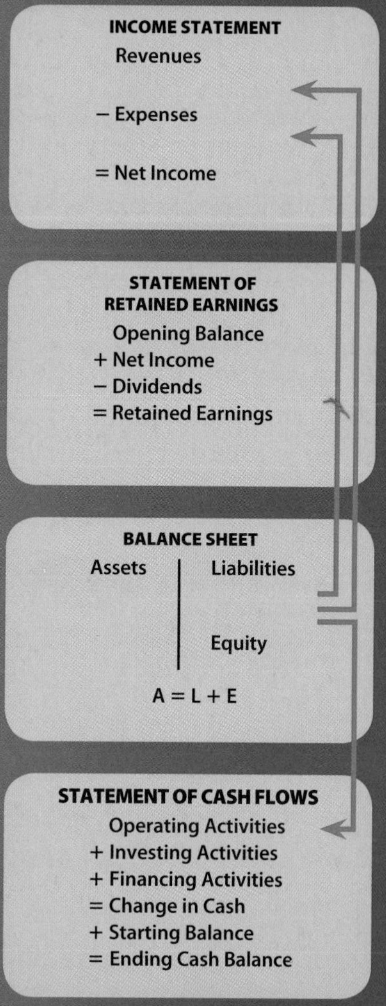

INCOME STATEMENT
Revenues
− Expenses
= Net Income

STATEMENT OF RETAINED EARNINGS
Opening Balance
+ Net Income
− Dividends
= Retained Earnings

BALANCE SHEET
Assets | Liabilities
Equity
A = L + E

STATEMENT OF CASH FLOWS
Operating Activities
+ Investing Activities
+ Financing Activities
= Change in Cash
+ Starting Balance
= Ending Cash Balance

Valuation of unearned revenues and accrued liabilities on the balance sheet is linked to measurement of revenues and expenses on the income statement.

MANAGEMENT ISSUES RELATED TO CURRENT LIABILITIES

LO 1 Identify the management issues related to current liabilities.

Current liabilities are debts and obligations that a company expects to satisfy within one year or within its normal operating cycle, whichever is longer. They require not only careful management of liquidity and cash flows, but also close monitoring of accounts payable. In reporting on current liabilities, managers must understand how they should be recognized, valued, classified, and disclosed.

Managing Liquidity and Cash Flows

The primary reason a company incurs current liabilities is to meet its needs for cash during the operating cycle. As explained in Chapter 5, the operating cycle is the length of time it takes to purchase inventory, sell the inventory, and collect payment. Most current liabilities arise in support of this cycle, as when accounts payable arise from purchases of inventory, accrued expenses arise from operating costs, and unearned revenues arise from customers' advance payments. Companies incur short-term debt to raise cash during periods of inventory build-up or while waiting for collection of receivables. They use the cash to pay the portion of long-term debt that is currently due and to pay liabilities arising from operations.

Failure to manage the cash flows related to current liabilities can have serious consequences for a business. For instance, if suppliers are not paid on time, they may withhold shipments that are vital to a company's operations. Continued failure to pay current liabilities can lead to bankruptcy.

To evaluate a company's ability to pay its current liabilities, analysts often use two measures of liquidity, both of which we discussed in an earlier chapter:

- Working Capital = Current Assets – Current Liabilities
- Current Ratio = Current Assets ÷ Current Liabilities

As shown below (in millions), **Microsoft**'s short-term liquidity as measured by working capital and the current ratio was positive in 2008 and increased quite a bit in 2009.

	Current Assets	–	Current Liabilities	=	Working Capital	Current Ratio
2008	$43,242	–	$29,886	=	$13,356	1.45*
2009	$49,280	–	$27,034	=	$22,246	1.82*

*Rounded

Focus on Business Practice

Debt Problems Can Plague Even Well-Known Companies

In a Wall Street horror story that illustrates the importance of managing current liabilities, **Xerox Corporation**, one of the most storied names in American business, found itself combating rumors that it was facing bankruptcy. Following a statement by Xerox's CEO that the company's financial model was "unsustainable," management was forced to defend the company's liquidity by saying it had adequate funds to continue operations. But in a report filed with the SEC, management acknowledged that it had tapped into its $7 billion bank credit for more than $3 billion to pay off short-term debt that was coming due. Unable to secure more money from any other source to pay these debts, Xerox had no choice but to turn to the line of credit from its bank. Had it run out, the company might well have gone bankrupt.[2] Fortunately, Xerox was able to restructure its line of credit and stay in business.

iStock Photo

Obviously, Microsoft had no problem in 2009 with liquidity and cash flow. Note the large amounts of both short- and long-term unearned revenue in the Financial Highlights presented at the beginning of the chapter. These revenues are fees that customers pay in advance for licenses and services, which increases the cash flow.

Evaluating Accounts Payable

Another consideration in managing liquidity and cash flows is the time suppliers give a company to pay for purchases. Measurements commonly used to assess a company's ability to pay within a certain time frame are payables turnover and days' payable.

Financial Ratio: Payables Turnover **Payables turnover** is the number of times, on average, that a company pays its accounts payable in an accounting period. This measure reflects the relative size of accounts payable, the credit terms offered by suppliers, and a company's diligence in paying its suppliers.

To measure payables turnover for **Microsoft**, we must first calculate purchases by adjusting cost of goods sold for the change in inventory. An increase in inventory means purchases were more than cost of goods sold; a decrease means purchases were less than cost of goods sold. Microsoft's cost of goods sold in 2009 was $12,155 million, and its inventory decreased by $268 million. Using these data, we can compute Microsoft's payables turnover as follows (in millions):

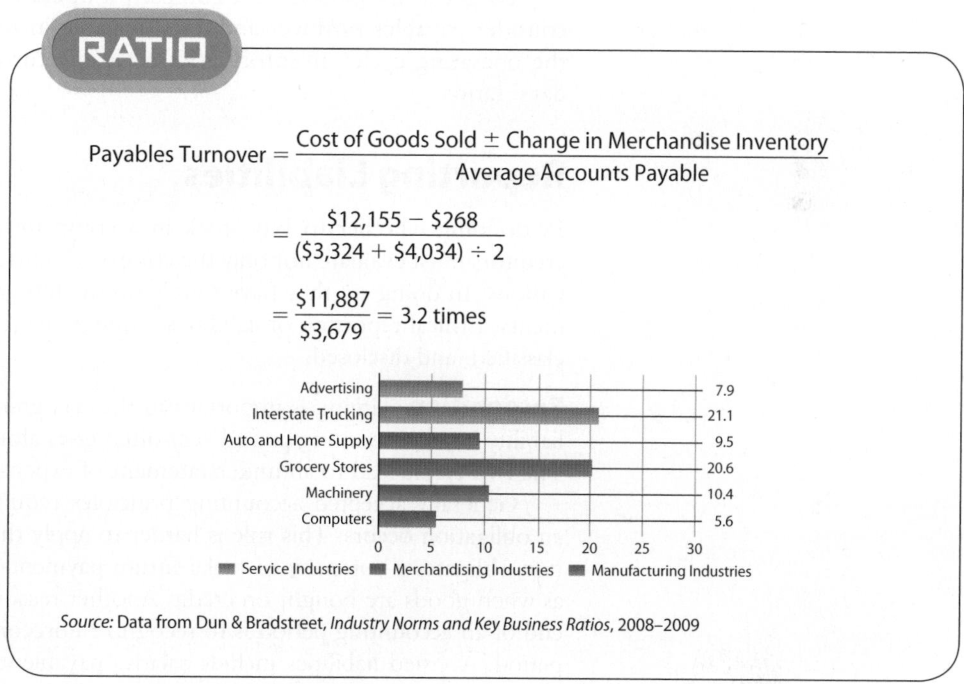

RATIO
Payables Turnover = Cost of Goods Sold ± Change in Merchandise Inventory / Average Accounts Payable
= $12,155 − $268 / ($3,324 + $4,034) ÷ 2
= $11,887 / $3,679 = 3.2 times
Advertising 7.9
Interstate Trucking 21.1
Auto and Home Supply 9.5
Grocery Stores 20.6
Machinery 10.4
Computers 5.6
0 5 10 15 20 25 30
Service Industries
Merchandising Industries
Manufacturing Industries
Source: Data from Dun & Bradstreet, Industry Norms and Key Business Ratios, 2008–2009

As you can see in the graph above, companies in the computer industry have lower payables turnover than those in other industries. This indicates that the terms they receive from suppliers are less favorable than the terms granted to Microsoft and other computer-related companies.

Financial Ratio: Days' Payable **Days' payable** shows how long, on average, a company takes to pay its accounts payable. It is computed by dividing the number of days in a year by the payables turnover. For Microsoft, it is computed as follows:

RATIO

$$\text{Days' Payable} = \frac{365 \text{ Days}}{\text{Payables Turnover}} = \frac{365 \text{ days}}{3.2 \text{ times}} = 114.1 \text{ days}$$

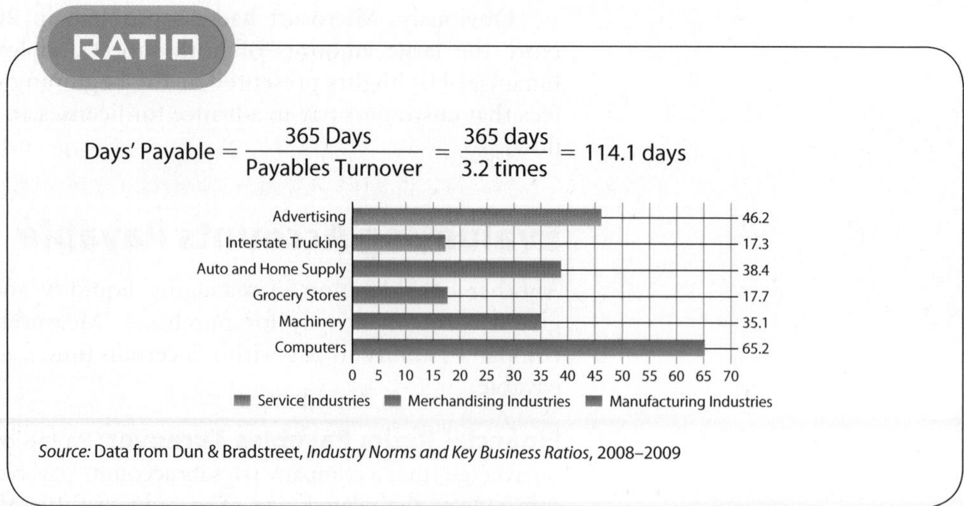

Source: Data from Dun & Bradstreet, *Industry Norms and Key Business Ratios*, 2008–2009

Like Microsoft's payables turnover of 3.2 times, its 114.1 days' payable indicates that the credit terms the company receives from its suppliers are excellent. Although both payables turnover and days' payable have been major factors in Microsoft's success in maintaining liquidity, another factor is that some product costs, aside from the cost of development, are small relative to sales price. For example, after a product like Windows 7 has been developed, it can be sold and delivered online, thus requiring no physical product.

To get a full picture of a company's operating cycle and liquidity, analysts also consider payables turnover and days' payable in relation to the other components of the operating cycle: inventory and receivable turnovers and their related number of days' ratios.

Reporting Liabilities

In deciding whether to buy stock in a company or lend money to it, investors and creditors must evaluate not only the company's current liabilities, but also its future obligations. In doing so, they have to rely on the integrity of the company's financial statements. Ethical reporting of liabilities requires that they be properly recognized, valued, classified, and disclosed.

Recognition Timing is important in the recognition of liabilities. Failure to record a liability in an accounting period very often goes along with failure to record an expense. The two errors lead to an understatement of expense and an overstatement of income.

Generally accepted accounting principles require that a liability be recorded when an obligation occurs. This rule is harder to apply than it might appear. When a transaction obligates a company to make future payments, a liability arises and is recognized, as when goods are bought on credit. Another reason for making adjusting entries at the end of an accounting period is to recognize unrecorded liabilities that accrue during the period. Accrued liabilities include salaries payable and interest payable. Other liabilities that can only be estimated, such as taxes payable, must also be recognized through adjusting entries.

Agreements for future transactions do not have to be recognized. For instance, **Microsoft** might agree to pay an executive $250,000 a year for a period of three years, or it might agree to buy an unspecified amount of advertising at a certain price over the next five years. Such contracts, though they are definite commitments, are not considered liabilities because they are for future—not past—transactions. Because there is no current obligation, no liability is recognized. However, if the amounts involved are material, these commitments would be mentioned in the notes to the financial statements and SEC filings.

STUDY NOTE: Disclosure of the fair value and the bases for estimating the fair value of short-term notes payable, loans payable, and other short-term debt are required unless it is not practical to estimate the value. Fair value accounting is covered later in this chapter.

Valuation On the balance sheet, a liability is generally valued at the amount of money needed to pay the debt or at the fair market value of the goods or services to be delivered.

The amount of most liabilities is definitely known. For example, **Amazon.com** sells a large number of gift certificates that are redeemable in the future. The amount of the liability (unearned revenue) is known, but the exact timing is not known.

Some companies, however, must estimate future liabilities. For example, if an automobile dealer sells a car with a one-year warranty on parts and service, the obligation is definite because the sale has occurred, but the amount of the obligation can only be estimated. Such estimates are usually based on past experience and anticipated changes in the business environment.

Classification As noted earlier, current liabilities are liabilities due in the next year or within the normal operating cycle, whichever is longer, and are normally paid out of current assets or with cash generated by operations. They contrast with **long-term liabilities**, which are liabilities due beyond one year or beyond the normal operating cycle. For example, Microsoft incurs long-term liabilities to finance its software development and to accomplish other objectives. The distinction between current and long-term liabilities is important because it affects the evaluation of a company's liquidity. Microsoft carefully distinguishes between short-term unearned revenues, which represent services to be performed in the next year, and long-term unearned revenues, which represent services that will be performed in future years.

Disclosure A company may have to include additional explanation of some liability accounts in the notes to its financial statements. For example, if a company's Notes Payable account is large, it should disclose the balances, maturity dates, interest rates, and other features of the debts in an explanatory note. Any special credit arrangements should also be disclosed. In this note to its 2009 financial statements, **Hershey Foods Corporation**, the famous candy company, discloses the nature of its credit arrangements:

> **Short-Term Debt and Financing Arrangements**
>
> As a source of short-term financing, we utilize commercial paper, or bank loans with an original maturity of 3 months or less . . . [In addition], we maintain lines of credit with domestic and international commercial banks.[3]

Unused lines of credit allow a company to borrow on short notice up to the credit limit, with little or no negotiation. Thus, the type of disclosure in Hershey's note is helpful in assessing whether a company has additional borrowing power.

Stop & Apply

RATIO

Kate's Cookie Company has current assets of $30,000 and current liabilities of $20,000, of which accounts payable are $15,000. Kate's cost of goods sold is $125,000, its merchandise inventory increased by $5,000, and accounts payable were $11,000 the prior year. Calculate Kate's current ratio, payables turnover, and days' payable.

SOLUTION

Current Ratio = Current Assets ÷ Current Liabilities
= $30,000 ÷ $20,000
= 1.50 times

Payables Turnover = $\frac{\text{Cost of Goods Sold} \pm \text{Change in Inventory}}{\text{Average Accounts Payable}}$

$= \frac{\$125{,}000 + \$5{,}000}{(\$15{,}000 + \$11{,}000) \div 2} = \frac{\$130{,}000}{\$13{,}000}$

= 10.0 times

Days' Payable = 365 Days ÷ Payables Turnover

$= \frac{365 \text{ days}}{10.0 \text{ times}} = 36.5 \text{ days}$

iStock Photo

COMMON TYPES OF CURRENT LIABILITIES

Identify, compute, and record definitely determinable and estimated current liabilities. LO2

As noted earlier, a company incurs current liabilities to meet its needs for cash during the operating cycle. These liabilities fall into two major groups: definitely determinable liabilities and estimated liabilities.

Definitely Determinable Liabilities

Current liabilities that are set by contract or statute and that can be measured exactly are called **definitely determinable liabilities**. The problems in accounting for these liabilities are to determine their existence and amount and to see that they are recorded properly. The most common definitely determinable liabilities are described in the following sections.

STUDY NOTE: *On the balance sheet, the order of presentation for current liabilities is not as strict as for current assets. Generally, accounts payable or notes payable appear first, and the rest of current liabilities follow.*

Accounts Payable Accounts payable (sometimes called *trade accounts payable*) are short-term obligations to suppliers for goods and services. The amount in the Accounts Payable account is generally supported by an accounts payable subsidiary ledger, which contains an individual account for each person or company to which money is owed. As shown in the Financial Highlights at the beginning of the chapter, accounts payable made up more than 12 percent of **Microsoft**'s current liabilities in 2009.

Notes Payable Short-term notes payable are obligations represented by promissory notes. A company may sign promissory notes to obtain bank loans, pay suppliers for goods and services, or secure credit from other sources. The interest rate is usually stated on the face of the note, as shown in Exhibit 8.1.

The journal entry to record the note in Exhibit 8.1 is as follows:

ISSUANCE

A	=	L	+ SE
+10,000.00		+10,000.00	

Aug. 31	Cash	10,000.00	
	Notes Payable		10,000.00
	Issued 60-day, 12% promissory note		

The entry to record the payment of the note with interest after 60 days is as follows:

PAYMENT

A	=	L	+ SE
−10,197.26		−10,000.00	−197.26

Oct. 30	Notes Payable	10,000.00	
	Interest Expense	197.26	
	Cash		10,197.26
	Payment of promissory note with interest		

$$\$10{,}000 \times \frac{12}{100} \times \frac{60}{365} = \$197.26^{*}$$

*Rounded

Bank Loans and Commercial Paper Management often establishes a **line of credit** with a bank. This arrangement allows the company to borrow funds when they are needed to finance current operations. In a note to its financial statements, **Goodyear Tire & Rubber Company** describes its lines of credit as follows: "In aggregate, we had total credit arrangements of $7,579 million available at December 31, 2009, of which $2,567 million were unused."[4]

EXHIBIT 8.1
Promissory Note

Chicago, Illinois August 31, 2010

Sixty days after date I promise to pay First Federal Bank the sum of $10,000 with interest at the rate of 12% per annum.

Sandra Caron
Caron Corporation

Although a company signs a promissory note for the full amount of a line of credit, it has great flexibility in using the available funds. It can increase its borrowing up to the limit when it needs cash and reduce the amount borrowed when it generates enough cash of its own. Both the amount borrowed and the interest rate charged by the bank may change daily. The bank may require the company to meet certain financial goals (such as maintaining specific profit margins, current ratios, or debt to equity ratios) to retain its line of credit.

Companies with excellent credit ratings can borrow short-term funds by issuing *commercial paper*. **Commercial paper** refers to unsecured loans (i.e., loans not backed by any specific assets) that are sold to the public, usually through professionally managed investment firms. Highly rated companies rely heavily on commercial paper to raise short-term funds, but they can quickly lose access to this means of borrowing if their credit rating drops. Because of disappointing operating results in recent years, well-known companies like **DaimlerChrysler**, **Lucent Technologies**, and **Motorola** have lost some or all of their ability to issue commercial paper.

STUDY NOTE: *Only the used portion of a line of credit is recognized as a liability in the financial statements.*

The portion of a line of credit currently borrowed and the amount of commercial paper issued are usually combined with notes payable in the current liabilities section of the balance sheet. Details are disclosed in a note to the financial statements.

Accrued Liabilities As we noted earlier, a key reason for making adjusting entries at the end of an accounting period is to recognize liabilities that are not already in the accounting records. This practice applies to any type of liability. As you will see, accrued liabilities (also called *accrued expenses*) can include estimated liabilities. For example, as can be seen in **Microsoft**'s Financial Highlights, the company had accrued compensation of $3,156 million in 2009.

Here, we focus on interest payable, a definitely determinable liability. Interest accrues daily on interest-bearing notes. In accordance with the matching rule, an adjusting entry is made at the end of each accounting period to record the interest obligation up to that point. For example, if the accounting period of the issuer of the note in Exhibit 8.1 ends on September 30, or 30 days after the issuance of the 60-day note, the adjusting entry would be as follows:

A	=	L	+ SE
		+98.63	−98.63

Sept. 30	Interest Expense	98.63	
	Interest Payable		98.63
	To record 30 days' interest expense on promissory note		
	$\$10{,}000 \times \frac{12}{100} \times \frac{30}{365} = \$98.63^{*}$		

*Rounded

Dividends Payable Cash dividends are a distribution of earnings to a corporation's stockholders, and a corporation's board of directors has the sole authority to declare them. The corporation has no liability for dividends until the date of declaration. The time between that date and the date of payment of dividends is usually short. During this brief interval, the dividends declared are considered current liabilities of the corporation.

Sales and Excise Taxes Payable Most states and many cities levy a sales tax on retail transactions, and the federal government imposes an excise tax on some products, such as gasoline. A merchant that sells goods subject to these taxes must collect the taxes and forward them periodically to the appropriate government agency. Until the merchant remits the amount it has collected to the government, that amount represents a current liability.

For example, suppose a merchant makes a $200 sale that is subject to a 5 percent sales tax and a 10 percent excise tax. If the sale takes place on June 1, the journal entry to record it is as follows:

A	=	L	+ SE
+230		+10	+200
		+20	

June 1	Cash	230	
	Sales		200
	Sales Tax Payable		10
	Excise Tax Payable		20
	Sale of merchandise and collection of sales and excise tax		

The sale is properly recorded at $200, and the taxes collected are recorded as liabilities to be remitted to the appropriate government agencies.

Companies that have a physical presence in many cities and states require a complex accounting system for sales taxes because the rates vary from state to state and city to city. For Internet companies, the sales tax situation is simpler. For example, **Amazon.com** is an Internet company without a physical presence in most states and thus does not always have to collect sales tax from its customers. This situation may change in the future, but so far Congress has exempted most Internet sales from sales tax.

Current Portion of Long-Term Debt If a portion of long-term debt is due within the next year and is to be paid from current assets, that portion is classified as a current liability. Companies commonly have portions of long-term debt, such as notes or mortgages, due in the next year. No entry is necessary when this is the case. The total debt is simply reclassified or divided into two categories—short-term and long-term—when the company prepares its balance sheet and other financial statements.

Payroll Liabilities For most organizations, the cost of labor and payroll taxes is a major expense. In the banking and airlines industries, payroll costs represent more than half of all operating costs. Payroll accounting is important because complex laws and significant liabilities are involved. The employer is liable to employees for wages and salaries and to various agencies for amounts withheld from wages and salaries and for related taxes. **Wages** are compensation of employees at an hourly rate; **salaries** are compensation of employees at a monthly or yearly rate.

Because payroll accounting applies only to an organization's employees, it is important to distinguish between employees and independent contractors, as follows:

- An **employee** is a person who is paid a wage or salary by the organization and is under its direct supervision and control.
- An **independent contractor** is a person who is not an employee of the organization and so is not accounted for under the payroll system. Independent contractors offer services to the organization for a fee, but they are not under its direct control or supervision. Certified public accountants, advertising agencies, and lawyers, for example, often act as independent contractors.

Exhibit 8.2 shows how payroll liabilities relate to employee earnings and employer taxes and other costs. When accounting for payroll liabilities, it is important to keep the following in mind:

- The amount payable to employees is less than the amount of their earnings. This occurs because employers are required by law or are requested by employees to withhold certain amounts from wages and send them directly to government agencies or other organizations.

EXHIBIT 8.2
Illustration of Payroll Costs

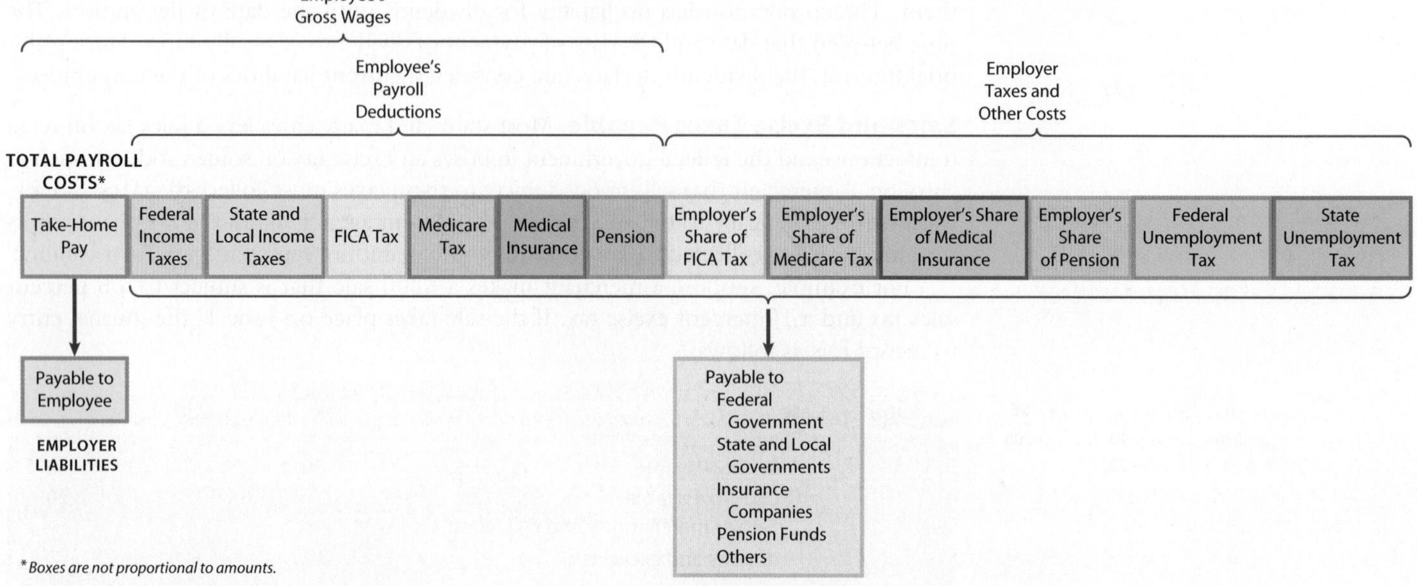

iStock Photo

Focus on Business Practice

Small and Mid-Sized Businesses Offer Benefits, Too

A national survey of small and mid-sized businesses focused on the employee benefits that these companies offer. The graph at the right presents the results. As you can see, 75 percent of respondents provided paid vacation and 61 percent provided health/medical benefits.[5]

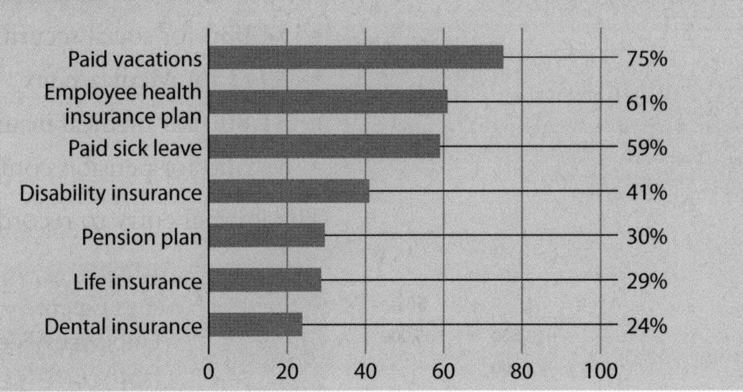

- An employer's total liabilities exceed employees' earnings because the employer must pay additional taxes and make other contributions (e.g., for pensions and medical care) that increase the cost and liabilities.

STUDY NOTE: *Vacation pay, sick pay, personal days, health insurance, life insurance, and pensions are additional costs that may be negotiated between employers and employees.*

The most common withholdings, taxes, and other payroll costs are described below.

- **Federal income taxes:** Employers are required to withhold federal income taxes from employees' paychecks and pay them to the U.S. Treasury. These taxes are collected each time an employee is paid.
- **State and local income taxes:** Most states and some local governments levy income taxes. In most cases, the procedures for withholding are similar to those for federal income taxes.
- **Social security (FICA) tax:** The social security program (the Federal Insurance Contribution Act) provides retirement and disability benefits and survivor's benefits. About 90 percent of the people working in the United States fall under the provisions of this program. The 2010 social security tax rate of 6.2 percent was paid by *both* employee and employer on the first $106,800 earned by an employee during the calendar year. Both the rate and the base to which it applies are subject to change in future years.
- **Medicare tax:** A major extension of the social security program is Medicare, which provides hospitalization and medical insurance for persons over age 65. In 2010, the Medicare tax rate was 1.45 percent of gross income, with no limit, paid by *both* employee and employer.
- **Medical insurance:** Many organizations provide medical benefits to employees. Often, the employee contributes a portion of the cost through withholdings from income and the employer pays the rest—usually a greater amount—to the insurance company.
- **Pension contributions:** Many organizations also provide pension benefits to employees. A portion of the pension contribution is withheld from the employee's income, and the organization pays the rest of the amount into the pension fund.
- **Federal unemployment insurance (FUTA) tax:** This tax pays for programs for unemployed workers. It is paid *only* by employers and recently was 6.2 percent of the first $7,000 earned by each employee (this amount may vary from state to state). The employer is allowed a credit for unemployment taxes it pays to the state. The maximum credit is 5.4 percent of the first $7,000 earned by each employee. Most states set their rate at this maximum. Thus, the FUTA tax most often paid is 0.8 percent (6.2 percent – 5.4 percent) of the taxable wages.
- **State unemployment insurance tax:** State unemployment programs provide compensation to eligible unemployed workers. The compensation is paid out of the fund provided by the 5.4 percent of the first $7,000 (or the amount the state sets) earned by each employee. In some states, employers with favorable employment records may be entitled to pay less than 5.4 percent.

STUDY NOTE: *The employee pays all federal, state, and local taxes on income. The employer and employee share FICA and Medicare taxes. The employer bears FUTA and state unemployment taxes.*

To illustrate the recording of a payroll, suppose that on February 15, a company's wages for employees are $65,000 and withholdings for employees are as follows:

- $10,800 for federal income taxes
- $2,400 for state income taxes
- $4,030 for social security tax
- $942 for Medicare tax
- $1,800 for medical insurance
- $2,600 for pension contributions

The journal entry to record this payroll is as follows:

A =	L +	SE
	+10,800	−65,000
	+2,400	
	+4,030	
	+942	
	+1,800	
	+2,600	
	+42,428	

Feb. 15	Wages Expense	65,000	
	Employees' Federal Income Taxes Payable		10,800
	Employees' State Income Taxes Payable		2,400
	Social Security Tax Payable		4,030
	Medicare Tax Payable		942
	Medical Insurance Premiums Payable		1,800
	Pension Contributions Payable		2,600
	Wages Payable		42,428
	To record the payroll		

Note that although the employees earned $65,000, their take-home pay was only $42,428.

Using the same data but assuming that the employer pays 80 percent of the medical insurance premiums and half of the pension contributions, the employer's taxes and benefit costs would be recorded as follows:

A =	L +	SE
	+4,030	−18,802
	+942	
	+7,200	
	+2,600	
	+520	
	+3,510	

Feb. 15	Payroll Taxes and Benefits Expense	18,802	
	Social Security Tax Payable		4,030
	Medicare Tax Payable		942
	Medical Insurance Premiums Payable		7,200
	Pension Contributions Payable		2,600
	Federal Unemployment Tax Payable		520
	State Unemployment Tax Payable		3,510
	To record payroll taxes and other costs		

Note that the payroll taxes and benefits expense increase the total cost of the payroll to $83,802 ($18,802 + $65,000), which exceeds the amount earned by employees by almost 29 percent. This is a typical situation. **Microsoft** has all these payroll liabilities in its internal records, but for simplicity combines them all into a single account called Accrued Compensation, as shown in the Financial Highlights at the beginning of this chapter.

Unearned Revenues **Unearned revenues** are advance payments for goods or services that a company must provide in a future accounting period. The company recognizes the revenue over the period in which it provides the products or services. Microsoft, for example, states in its annual report that unearned revenue represents advance customer billings, which it accounts for as subscriptions with revenue recognized over the period covered by the billing. Assume that Microsoft bills a customer in advance for a one-year subscription. The following entry would be made:

A =	L +	SE
+3,600	+3,600	

Accounts Receivable	3,600	
Unearned Revenue		3,600
Subscriptions billed in advance		

Microsoft will soon receive cash in the amount of $3,600, but it also has a liability of $3,600 that will slowly be reduced over the year as it provides the service. After the first month, the company records the recognition of revenue as follows:

A	=	L	+	SE
		−300		+300

Unearned Revenue	300	
Revenue		300
Recognition of revenue for services provided		

Many businesses, including special-order firms, repair companies, and construction companies, ask for a deposit before they will deliver goods or services. Until they do deliver the goods or services, these deposits are current liabilities.

Estimated Liabilities

STUDY NOTE: *Estimated liabilities are recorded and presented in the financial statements in the same way as definitely determinable liabilities. The only difference is that the computation of estimated liabilities involves some uncertainty.*

Estimated liabilities are definite debts or obligations whose exact dollar amount cannot be known until a later date. Because there is no doubt that a legal obligation exists, the primary accounting problem is to estimate and record the amount of the liability. The following are examples of estimated liabilities.

Income Taxes Payable The federal government, most state governments, and some cities and towns levy a tax on a corporation's income. The amount of the liability depends on the results of a corporation's operations, which are often not known until after the end of the corporation's fiscal year. However, because income taxes are an expense in the year in which income is earned, an adjusting entry is necessary to record the estimated tax liability. **Microsoft**, for example, had income taxes payable of $725 million in 2009, as shown in the Financial Highlights at the beginning of the chapter.

Sole proprietorships and partnerships do *not* pay income taxes. However, their owners must report their share of the firm's income on their individual tax returns.

Property Taxes Payable Property taxes are a main source of revenue for local governments. They are levied annually on real property, such as land and buildings, and on personal property, such as inventory and equipment. Because the fiscal years of local governments rarely correspond to a company's fiscal year, it is necessary to estimate the amount of property taxes that applies to each month of the year.

Promotional Costs You are no doubt familiar with the coupons and rebates that are part of many companies' marketing programs. Because of frequent flyer programs, for example, U.S. airline companies today have more than 10 trillion "free miles" outstanding. What are the accounting implications of these promotional programs? Companies usually record the costs as a reduction in sales (a contra-sales account) rather than as an expense with a corresponding current liability.

As **Hershey Foods Corporation** acknowledged in one of its recent annual reports, promotional costs are hard to estimate:

> Accrued liabilities requiring the most difficult or subjective judgments include liabilities associated with marketing promotion programs. . . . We recognize the costs

Focus on Business Practice

What Is the Cost of Frequent Flyer Miles?

In the early 1980s, **American Airlines** developed a frequent flyer program that awards free trips and other bonuses to customers based on the number of miles they fly on the airline. Since then, many other airlines have instituted similar programs, and it is estimated that 180 million people now participate in them. Today, U.S. airlines have more than 10 trillion "free miles" outstanding, and 8 percent of passengers travel on "free" tickets. Estimated liabilities for these tickets have become an important consideration in evaluating an airline's financial position. Complicating the estimate is that almost half the miles have been earned through purchases from hotels, car rental and telephone companies, Internet service providers like **AOL**, and bank credit cards.[6]

iStock Photo

Focus on Business Practice

Those Little Coupons Can Add Up

Many companies promote their products by issuing coupons that offer "cents off" or other enticements. Because four out of five shoppers use coupons, companies are forced by competition to distribute them. The total value of unredeemed coupons, each of which represents a potential liability for the issuing company, is staggering. In 2009, marketers distributed approximately 500 billion coupons, of which about 1 billion were Internet coupons. In total, the coupons were worth about $500 billion, but consumers redeemed only 4.2 billion coupons worth an estimated $6 billion. Thus, a big advertiser can issue millions of coupons and expect less than 1 percent to be redeemed.[7]

iStock Photo

> of marketing promotion programs as a reduction to net sales along with a corresponding accrued liability based on estimates at the time of revenue recognition. . . . We determine the amount of the accrued liability by analysis of programs offered; historical trends; expectations regarding customer and consumer participation; sales and payment trends; and experience . . . with similar, previously offered programs.[8]

Hershey accrues over $720 million in promotional costs each year and reports that its estimates are usually accurate within about 2 percent, or $14.4 million.

STUDY NOTE: Recording a product warranty expense in the period of the sale is an application of the matching rule.

Product Warranty Liability When a company sells a product or service with a warranty, it has a liability for the length of the warranty. The warranty is a feature of the product and is included in the selling price; its cost should therefore be debited to an expense account in the period of the sale. Based on past experience, it should be possible to estimate the amount that the warranty will cost the company in the future. Warranties on some products will cost the company very little; others may cost a lot. Thus, there will be an average cost per product.

For example, suppose a muffler company like **Midas** guarantees that it will replace free of charge any muffler it sells that fails during the time the buyer owns the car. The company charges a small service fee for replacing the muffler. In the past, 6 percent of the mufflers sold have been returned for replacement under the warranty. The average cost of a muffler is $50. If the company sold 700 mufflers during July, the accrued liability would be recorded as an adjustment at the end of July, as shown in the following journal entry:

A	=	L	+	SE
		+2,100		−2,100

July 31	Product Warranty Expense	2,100	
	Estimated Product Warranty Liability		2,100
	To record estimated product warranty expense:		
	Number of units sold	700	
	Rate of replacement under warranty	× 0.06	
	Estimated units to be replaced	42	
	Estimated cost per unit	× $50	
	Estimated liability for product warranty	$2,100	

When a muffler is returned for replacement under the warranty, the cost of the muffler is charged against the Estimated Product Warranty Liability account. For example, suppose that on December 5, a customer returns a defective muffler, which cost $50, and pays a $30 service fee to have it replaced. The journal entry is:

A	=	L	+	SE
+30		−50		+30
−50				

Dec. 5	Cash	30	
	Estimated Product Warranty Liability	50	
	Service Revenue		30
	Merchandise Inventory		50
	Replacement of muffler under warranty		

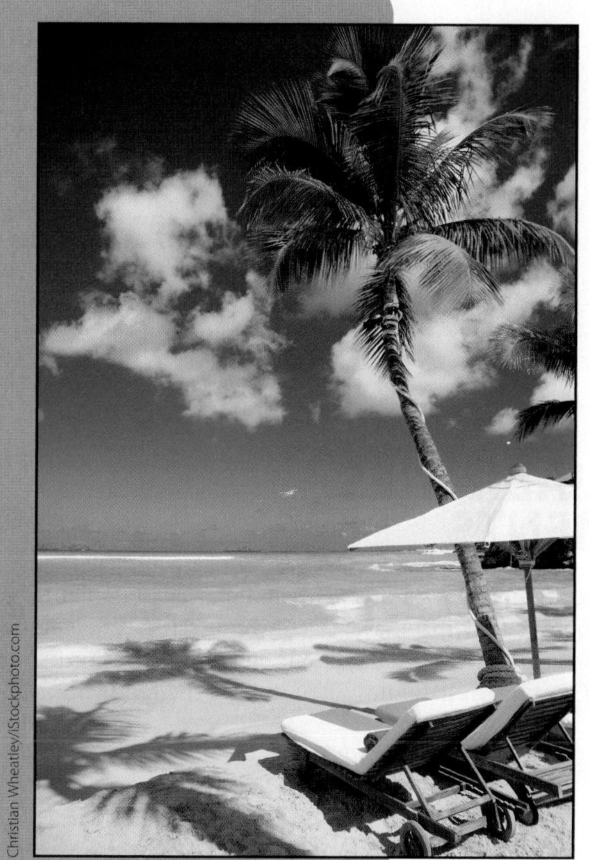

Just as employees earn paid vacation days and holidays when working, employers incur expenses and liabilities for those paid days off.

Vacation Pay Liability In most companies, employees accrue paid vacation as they work during the year. For example, an employee may earn two weeks of paid vacation for each 50 weeks of work. Thus, the employee is paid 52 weeks' salary for 50 weeks' work. The cost of the two weeks' vacation should be allocated as an expense over the year so that month-to-month costs will not be distorted. The vacation pay represents 4 percent (two weeks' vacation divided by 50 weeks) of the employee's pay. Every week worked earns the employee a small fraction (2 percent) of vacation pay, which is 4 percent of that person's annual salary.

Vacation pay liability can represent a substantial amount of money. As an example, in the 10-K form that **US Airways** submitted to the SEC for 2009, the airline reported accrued salaries, wages, and vacation liabilities of $178 million.

Suppose that a company with a vacation policy of two weeks of paid vacation for each 50 weeks of work has a payroll of $42,000 and that it paid $2,000 of that amount to employees on vacation for the week ended April 20. Because of past experience with employee turnover, the company assumes that only 75 percent of employees will ultimately collect vacation pay. The computation of vacation pay expense based on the payroll of employees not on vacation ($42,000 − $2,000) is as follows:

$$\$40{,}000 \times 0.04 \times 0.75 = \$1{,}200$$

The company would make the following journal entry to record vacation pay expense for the week ended April 20:

A	=	L	+	SE
		+1,200		−1,200

Apr. 20	Vacation Pay Expense	1,200	
	Estimated Liability for Vacation Pay		1,200
	Estimated vacation pay expense		

At the time employees receive their vacation pay, an entry is made debiting Estimated Liability for Vacation Pay and crediting Cash or Wages Payable. The following entry records the $2,000 paid to employees on vacation during the month of August:

A*	=	L	+	SE
−2,000		−2,000		

*Assumes cash paid

Aug. 31	Estimated Liability for Vacation Pay	2,000	
	Cash (or Wages Payable)		2,000
	Wages of employees on vacation		

The treatment of vacation pay presented here can also be applied to other payroll costs, such as bonus plans and contributions to pension plans.

Stop & Apply

Identify each of the following as either (a) a definitely determinable liability or (b) an estimated liability.

____ 1. Bank loan
____ 2. Dividends payable
____ 3. Product warranty liabilities
____ 4. Interest payable
____ 5. Income taxes payable
____ 6. Vacation pay liability
____ 7. Notes payable
____ 8. Property taxes payable
____ 9. Commercial paper
____ 10. Gift certificate liability

SOLUTION

1. a; 2. a; 3. b; 4. a; 5. b; 6. b; 7. a; 8. b; 9. a; 10. b

iStock Photo

CONTINGENT LIABILITIES AND COMMITMENTS

Distinguish *contingent liabilities* from *commitments*. LO 3

The FASB requires companies to disclose in a note to their financial statements any contingent liabilities and commitments they may have. A **contingent liability** is not an *existing* obligation. Rather, it is a *potential* liability because it depends on a future event arising out of a past transaction. Contingent liabilities often involve the following:

- Lawsuits
- Income tax disputes
- Discounted notes receivable
- Guarantees of debt
- Failure to follow government regulations

For instance, a construction company that signed a contract with a state to build a bridge may be sued by the state for using poor materials. The past transaction is the contract for building the bridge. The future event is the outcome of the lawsuit, which is not yet known.

***STUDY NOTE:** Contingencies are recorded when they are probable and can be reasonably estimated.*

The FASB has established two conditions for determining when a contingency should be entered in the accounting records:

- The liability must be probable.
- The liability can be reasonably estimated.[9]

Estimated liabilities like those for income tax, warranty, and vacation pay that we described earlier meet these conditions. They are therefore accrued in the accounting records.

In a survey of large companies, lawsuits involving many different issues and environmental concerns, including toxic waste cleanup, were among the most common types of contingencies reported.[10] In a note to its 2009 financial statements, **Microsoft** described its contingent liabilities as lawsuits involving infringement of European competition law, antitrust and overcharge actions, and patent and intellectual property claims, among other matters. Microsoft's management stated:

> While we intend to vigorously defend these matters, there exists the possibility of adverse outcomes that we estimate could be up to $2.2 billion in aggregate beyond recorded amounts.[11]

CASH FLOW

A **commitment** is a legal obligation that does not meet the technical requirements for recognition as a liability and so is not recorded. The most common examples are purchase agreements and leases.[12] For example, Microsoft reported in the notes to its financial statements that it had construction commitments in the amount of $621 million and purchase commitments in the amount of $3,672 million. Knowledge of these amounts is very important in planning cash flows for the coming year.

Focus on International Practices

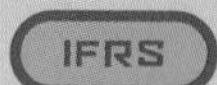

Balance Sheet Liabilities Are Often Greater Under IFRS

iStock Photo

U.S. GAAP do not record commitments, such as purchase agreements, as liabilities even though they are a *legal* obligation since they do not meet the technical definition of a liability. Disclosure in a note to the financial statements is required. Under IFRS, however, these agreements are recognized when an entity has a demonstrable commitment.

Stop & Apply

iStock Photo

Identify each of the following as (a) a contingent liability or (b) a commitment.

____ 1. A tax dispute with the IRS

____ 2. A long-term lease agreement

____ 3. An agreement to purchase goods in the future

____ 4. A potential lawsuit over a defective product

SOLUTION

1. a; 2. b; 3. b; 4. a

VALUATION APPROACHES TO FAIR VALUE ACCOUNTING

LO 4 Identify the valuation approaches to fair value accounting and define *time value of money* and *interest* and apply them to present values.

Recall that fair value is the price for which an asset or a liability could be sold, or exit the company, as opposed to the price for which the company could buy the asset or liability. As pointed out previously, the concept of fair value applies to some financial assets, such as cash equivalents and investments, and to some liabilities, such as notes payable. Fair value is also applicable to determining whether tangible assets such as inventories and long-term assets have sustained a permanent decline in value below their cost. The FASB identifies three approaches to measurement of fair value:[13]

- **Market approach:** When available, external market transactions involving identical or comparable assets or liabilities are ideal. For example, the market approach is good for valuing investments and liabilities for which there is an active market in which quoted prices are available for the specific asset or liability. However, an active market or a quoted price is not always available. For example, there may not be an active market for special-purpose equipment. In these cases, it may be possible to observe quoted prices for comparable types of equipment.
- **Income (or cash flow) approach:** The income approach, as defined by the FASB, converts future cash flows to a single present value. This approach is used when the market approach cannot be used because there are no identical or comparable quoted prices available. This approach is based on management's best determination of the future cash amounts generated by an asset or payments that will be made for a liability. It is often based on internally generated information, which should be reasonable for the circumstances. For instance, management may estimate the cash flows or cost savings expected to be generated by the special-purpose equipment.
- **Cost approach:** The cost approach is based on the amount that currently would be required to replace an asset with the same or a comparable asset. For example, inventory is usually valued at lower of cost or market, where market is the replacement cost. For plant assets like special-purpose equipment, the replacement cost of a new asset must be adjusted to take into account the asset's age, condition, depreciation, and obsolescence.

Focus on International Practices

IFRS How Does the IASB Define Fair Value?

In contrast to U.S. GAAP, the IASB defines *fair value* as a single concept based on exit value. Specifically, fair value is the amount an asset may be exchanged for, or a liability settled, between knowledgeable parties in an arm's length transaction. The best evidence of fair value is quoted prices in an active market. If the market for a financial instrument is not active, a valuation technique must be used. The objective of a valuation technique is to establish what the transaction price is on the measurement date in an arm's length exchange motivated by normal business considerations. Valuation techniques include using arm's length market transactions between knowledgeable, willing parties, if available; reference to the current fair value of another instrument that is substantially the same; discounted cash flow analysis; and options pricing models.[14]

iStock Photo

The following sections, which focus on the income or cash flow approach, require knowledge of interest and the time value of money and present value techniques.

Interest, the Time Value of Money, and Future Value

"Time is money" is a common expression. It derives from the concept of the **time value of money**, which refers to the costs or benefits of holding or not holding money over time. **Interest** is the cost of using money for a specific period.

The interest associated with the time value of money is an important consideration in any kind of business decision. For example, if you have $100 and hold that amount for one year without putting it in a savings account, you have forgone the interest that the money would have earned. However, if you put the $100 in an interest-bearing checking account, you will have the $100 plus the interest at the end of the year.

The amount of principle plus interest after one or more periods is known as **future value.** Future value may be computed using either simple interest or compound interest.

- **Simple interest** is the interest cost for one or more periods when the principal sum—the amount on which interest is computed—stays the same from period to period.
- **Compound interest** is the interest cost for two or more periods when, after each period, the interest earned in that period is added to the amount on which interest is computed in future periods. In other words, the principal sum is increased at the end of each period by the interest earned in that period.

STUDY NOTE: *Compound interest is useful in business because it helps decision makers choose among alternative courses of action.*

The following examples illustrate these concepts.

Example of Future Value Using Simple Interest Erin Burns accepts an 8 percent, $15,000 note due in 90 days. How much will she receive at that time? The interest is calculated as follows:

$$\begin{aligned} \text{Interest} &= \text{Principal} \times \text{Rate} \times \text{Time} \\ &= \$15,000 \times 8/100 \times 90/365 \\ &= \$295.89 \end{aligned}$$

Therefore, the future value that Burns will receive is $15,295.89, calculated as follows:

$$\begin{aligned} \text{Total} &= \text{Principal} + \text{Interest} \\ &= \$15,000.00 + \$295.89 \\ &= \$15,295.89 \end{aligned}$$

Example of Future Value Using Compound Interest Jake Laverne deposits $10,000 in an account that pays 6 percent interest. He expects to leave the principal and accumulated interest in the account for three years. If the interest is paid at the end of each year and is then added to the principal and this amount in turn earns interest, how much will Laverne's account total at the end of three years? The amount is computed as follows:

Year	*Principal Amount at Beginning of Year*	*Annual Amount of Interest (Principal at Beginning of Year × 6%)*	*Accumulated Amount at End of Year (Principal at Beginning of Year + Annual Amount of Interest)*
1	$10,000.00	$600.00	$10,600.00
2	10,600.00	636.00	11,236.00
3	11,236.00	674.16	11,910.16

Laverne will have a future value of $11,910.16 in his account at the end of three years. Note that the amount of interest increases each year by the interest rate times the interest of the previous year. For example, between year 1 and year 2, the interest increased by $36, which equals 6 percent times $600.

Calculating Present Value

STUDY NOTE: *Present value is a method of determining today the value of future cash flows. Financial analysts commonly compute present value to determine the value of potential investments.*

Suppose you had the choice of receiving $100 today or one year from today. No doubt you would choose to receive it today. Why? If you have the money today, you can put it in a savings account to earn interest so you will have more than $100 a year from today. In other words, an amount to be received in the future (future value) is not worth as much today as an amount received today (present value). **Present value** is the amount that must be invested today at a given rate of interest to produce a given future value. Thus, present value and future value are closely related.

For example, suppose Debra Shield needs $10,000 one year from now. How much does she have to invest today to achieve that goal if the interest rate is 5 percent? From earlier examples, we can establish the following equation:

Present Value × (1.0 + Interest Rate)	=	Future Value
Present Value × 1.05	=	$10,000.00
Present Value	=	$10,000.00 ÷ 1.05
Present Value	=	$9,523.81

To achieve a future value of $10,000, Shield must invest a present value of $9,523.81. Interest of 5 percent on $9,523.81 for one year equals $476.19, and these two amounts added together equal $10,000.

Present Value of a Single Sum Due in the Future When more than one period is involved, the calculation of present value is more complicated. For example, suppose Ken Morris wants to be sure of having $8,000 at the end of three years. How much must he invest today in a 5 percent savings account to achieve this goal? We can compute the present value of $8,000 at compound interest of 5 percent for three years by adapting the above equation:

Year	*Amount at End of Year*		*Divide by*		*Present Value at Beginning of Year*
3	$8,000.00	÷	1.05	=	$7,619.05
2	7,619.05	÷	1.05	=	7,256.24
1	7,256.24	÷	1.05	=	6,910.70

Ken Morris must invest $6,910.70 today to achieve a value of $8,000 in three years.

We can simplify the calculation by using a table of present values. In the table in Exhibit 8.3 (p. 380), the point at which the 5 percent column and the row for period 3

EXHIBIT 8.3
Present Value of $1 to Be Received at the End of a Given Number of Periods

Period	1%	2%	3%	4%	5%	6%	7%	8%	9%	10%
1	0.990	0.980	0.971	0.962	0.952	0.943	0.935	0.926	0.917	0.909
2	0.980	0.961	0.943	0.925	0.907	0.890	0.873	0.857	0.842	0.826
3	0.971	0.942	0.915	0.889	0.864	0.840	0.816	0.794	0.772	0.751
4	0.961	0.924	0.888	0.855	0.823	0.792	0.763	0.735	0.708	0.683
5	0.951	0.906	0.863	0.822	0.784	0.747	0.713	0.681	0.650	0.621
6	0.942	0.888	0.837	0.790	0.746	0.705	0.666	0.630	0.596	0.564
7	0.933	0.871	0.813	0.760	0.711	0.665	0.623	0.583	0.547	0.513
8	0.923	0.853	0.789	0.731	0.677	0.627	0.582	0.540	0.502	0.467
9	0.914	0.837	0.766	0.703	0.645	0.592	0.544	0.500	0.460	0.424
10	0.905	0.820	0.744	0.676	0.614	0.558	0.508	0.463	0.422	0.386

intersect shows a factor of 0.864. This factor, when multiplied by $1, gives the present value of $1 to be received three years from now at 5 percent interest. Thus, we solve the problem as follows:

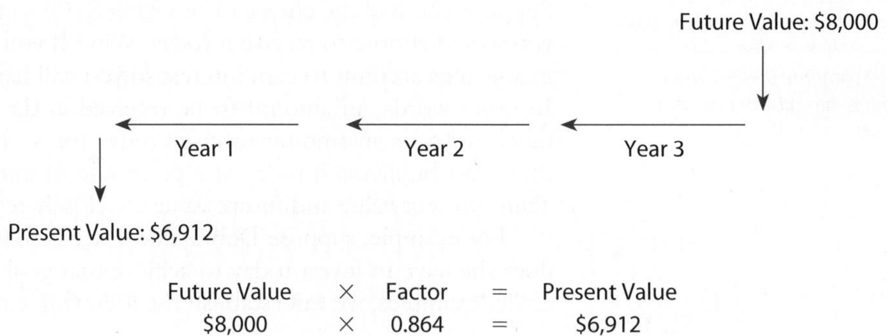

Future Value	×	Factor	=	Present Value
$8,000	×	0.864	=	$6,912

Except for a rounding difference of $1.30, this result is the same as our earlier one.

Present Value of an Ordinary Annuity It is often necessary to compute the present value of a series of receipts or payments equally spaced over time, with compound interest—in other words, the present value of an **ordinary annuity**. For example, suppose Vickie Long has sold a piece of property and is to receive $18,000 in three equal annual payments of $6,000 beginning one year from today. What is the present value of this sale if the current interest rate is 5 percent?

Using Exhibit 8.3, we can compute the present value by calculating a separate value for each of the three payments and summing the results, as follows:

Future Receipts (Annuity)				*Present Value Factor at 5%*		*Present*
Year 1	*Year 2*	*Year 3*		*(from Exhibit 8.3)*		*Value*
$6,000			×	0.952	=	$ 5,712
	$6,000		×	0.907	=	5,442
		$6,000	×	0.864	=	5,184
Total Present Value						$16,338

The present value of the sale is $16,338. Thus, there is an implied interest cost (given the 5 percent rate) of $1,662 associated with the payment plan that allows the purchaser to pay in three installments.

We can make this calculation more easily by using the table in Exhibit 8.4. The point at which the 5 percent column intersects the row for period 3 shows a factor

EXHIBIT 8.4
Present Value of an Ordinary $1 Annuity Received in Each Period for a Given Number of Periods

Period	1%	2%	3%	4%	5%	6%	7%	8%	9%	10%
1	0.990	0.980	0.971	0.962	0.952	0.943	0.935	0.926	0.917	0.909
2	1.970	1.942	1.913	1.886	1.859	1.833	1.808	1.783	1.759	1.736
3	2.941	2.884	2.829	2.775	2.723	2.673	2.624	2.577	2.531	2.487
4	3.902	3.808	3.717	3.630	3.546	3.465	3.387	3.312	3.240	3.170
5	4.853	4.713	4.580	4.452	4.329	4.212	4.100	3.993	3.890	3.791
6	5.795	5.601	5.417	5.242	5.076	4.917	4.767	4.623	4.486	4.355
7	6.728	6.472	6.230	6.002	5.786	5.582	5.389	5.206	5.033	4.868
8	7.652	7.325	7.020	6.733	6.463	6.210	5.971	5.747	5.535	5.335
9	8.566	8.162	7.786	7.435	7.108	6.802	6.515	6.247	5.995	5.759
10	9.471	8.983	8.530	8.111	7.722	7.360	7.024	6.710	6.418	6.145

of 2.723. When multiplied by $1, this factor gives the present value of a series of three $1 payments (spaced one year apart) at compound interest of 5 percent. Thus, we solve the problem as follows:

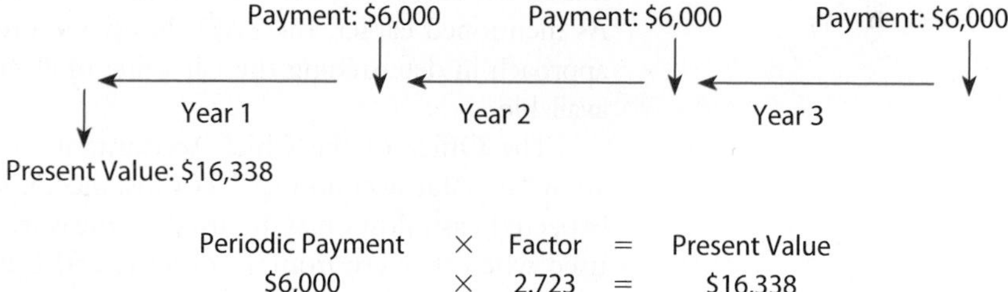

Periodic Payment	×	Factor	=	Present Value
$6,000	×	2.723	=	$16,338

This result is the same as the one we computed earlier.

STUDY NOTE: The interest rate used when compounding interest for less than one year is the annual rate divided by the number of periods in a year.

Time Periods As in all our examples, the compounding period is in most cases one year, and the interest rate is stated on an annual basis. However, in Exhibits 8.3 and 8.4, the far left columns refer not to years but to periods. This wording accommodates compounding periods of less than one year. Savings accounts that record interest quarterly and bonds that pay interest semiannually are cases in which the compounding period is less than one year. To use Exhibits 8.3 and 8.4 in these cases, you must divide the annual interest rate by the number of periods in the year and multiply the number of periods in one year by the number of years,

For example, suppose we want to compute the present value of a $6,000 payment that is to be received in two years and that the annual interest rate is 8 percent and the compounding period is semiannual. Before using Exhibit 8.3 in this computation, we must compute the interest rate that applies to each compounding period and the total number of compounding periods.

- The interest rate is 4 percent (8% annual rate ÷ 2 periods per year).
- The total number of compounding periods is 4 (2 periods per year × 2 years).

We can then use Exhibit 8.3 to compute the present value of the payment as follows:

Principal	×	Factor	=	Present Value
$6,000	×	0.855	=	$5,130

This procedure is used whenever the corresponding period is less than one year. For example, a monthly compounding requires dividing the annual interest rate by 12 and multiplying the number of years by 12 to use the tables.

This method of determining the interest rate and the number of periods when the compounding period is less than one year can be used with Exhibits 8.3 and 8.4 or with Tables 1 and 2 in Appendix B.

Stop & Apply

Use Exhibits 8.3 (p. 380) and 8.4 (p. 381) to determine the present value of the following:

1. A single payment of $10,000 at 5 percent for 10 years
2. 10 annual payments of $1,000 at 5 percent
3. A single payment of $10,000 at 7 percent for 5 years
4. 10 annual payments of $1,000 at 9 percent

SOLUTION

1. From Exhibit 8.3: $10,000 × 0.614 = $6,140
2. From Exhibit 8.4: $1,000 × 7.722 = $7,722
3. From Exhibit 8.3: $10,000 × 0.713 = $7,130
4. From Exhibit 8.4: $1,000 × 6.418 = $6,418

APPLICATIONS USING PRESENT VALUE

Apply present value to simple valuation situations.

The concept of present value is widely used in business decision making and financial reporting. For example, the value of a long-term note receivable or payable can be determined by calculating the present value of the future interest payments and repayment. As mentioned earlier, the FASB has made present value an important component of its approach in determining the fair value of assets and liabilities when a market price is not available.

The Office of the Chief Accountant of the SEC has issued guidance on how to apply fair value accounting.[15] For instance, it says that management's assumptions about expected cash flows may be used to measure fair value and that market quotes may be used when they are from an orderly, active market as opposed to a distressed, inactive market. Thus, **Microsoft** may determine the expected present value of the future cash flows of an investment by using its internal cash flow projections and a market rate of interest. By comparing the result to the current value of the investment, Microsoft can determine if an adjustment needs to be made to record a gain or loss.

In the sections that follow, we illustrate two simple, useful applications of present value. These applications will be helpful in understanding the uses of present value that we discuss in later chapters.

Valuing an Asset

An asset is something that will provide future benefits to the company that owns it. Usually, the purchase price of an asset represents the present value of those future benefits. It is possible to evaluate a proposed purchase price by comparing it with the present value of the asset to the company.

For example, suppose Daniel Lutz is thinking of buying a new machine that will reduce his annual labor cost by $1,400 per year. The machine will last eight years. The interest rate that Lutz assumes for making equipment purchases is 10 percent. What is the maximum amount (present value) that Lutz should pay for the machine?

The present value of the machine to Lutz is equal to the present value of an ordinary annuity of $1,400 per year for eight years at compound interest of 10 percent. Using the factor from the table in Exhibit 8.4, we compute the value as follows:

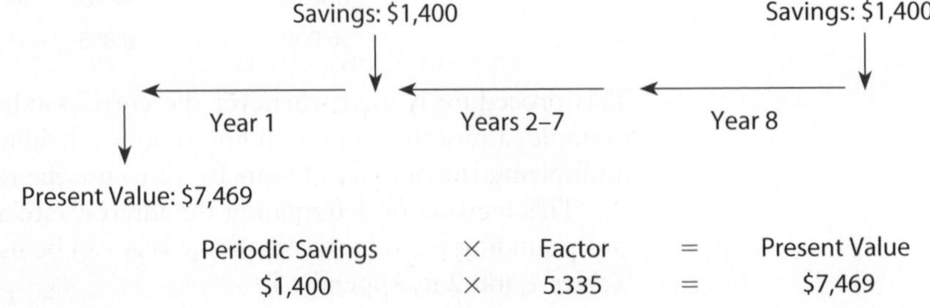

Periodic Savings	×	Factor	=	Present Value
$1,400	×	5.335	=	$7,469

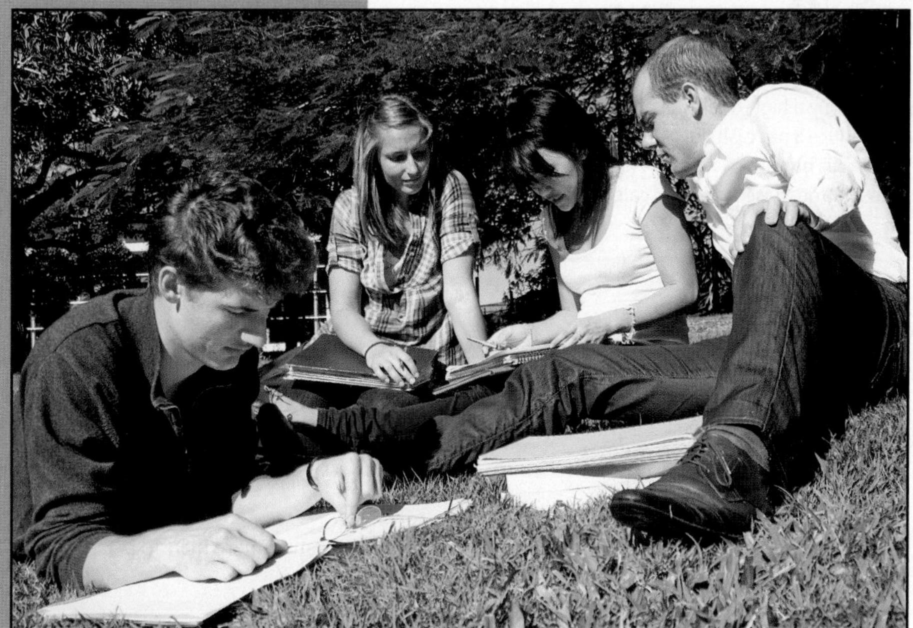

Colleges that offer student loans often allow students to defer payment until after graduation because students often cannot pay full tuition prices until they have a full-time job.

Lutz should not pay more than $7,469 for the machine because this amount equals the present value of the benefits he would receive from owning it.

Deferred Payment

To encourage buyers to make a purchase, sellers sometimes agree to defer payment for a sale. This practice is common among companies that sell agricultural equipment to farmers who need new equipment in the spring but cannot pay for it until they sell their crops in the fall.

Suppose Plains Implement Corporation sells a tractor to Ivana Popov for $100,000 on February 1 and agrees to receive payment 10 months later, on December 1. With such an agreement, the future payment includes not only the selling price, but also an implied (imputed) interest cost. If the prevailing annual interest rate is 12 percent compounded monthly, the actual price of the tractor would be the present value of the future payment, computed using the factor from the table in Exhibit 8.3 [10 periods, 1 percent (12 percent divided by 12 months)], as follows:

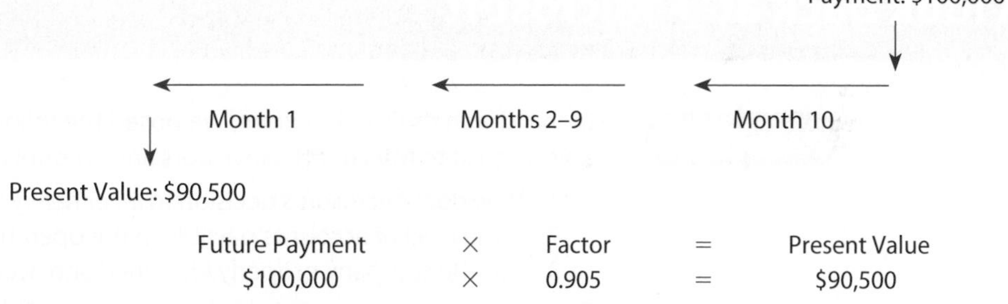

Future Payment	×	Factor	=	Present Value
$100,000	×	0.905	=	$90,500

Popov records the present value, $90,500, in his purchase records, and Plains Implement Corporation records it in its sales records. The balance consists of interest expense or interest income.

Other Applications

Other applications of present value in accounting include the following:

- Computing imputed interest on non-interest-bearing notes
- Accounting for installment notes
- Valuing a bond
- Recording lease obligations
- Accounting for pension obligations
- Valuing debt
- Depreciating property, plant, and equipment
- Making capital expenditure decisions
- Accounting for any item in which time is a factor

Stop & Apply

George owns a restaurant and has the opportunity to buy a high-quality espresso coffee machine for $5,000. After carefully studying projected costs and revenues, George estimates that the machine will produce a net cash flow of $1,600 annually and will last for five years. He determines that an interest rate of 10 percent is an adequate return on investment for his business.

Calculate the present value of the machine to George. Based on your calculation, do you think George would be wise to purchase the machine? Explain your answer.

SOLUTION

Calculation of the present value:

Annual cash flow	$ 1,600.00
Factor from Exhibit 8.4 (5 years at 10%)	× 3.791
Present value of net cash flows	$ 6,065.60
Less purchase price	−5,000.00
Net present value	$ 1,065.60

The present value of the net cash flows from the machine exceeds the purchase price. Thus, the investment will return more than 10 percent to George's business. A decision to purchase the machine would therefore be wise.

iStock Photo

A look back at ▸ Microsoft

In this chapter's Decision Point, we posed the following questions, which are of considerable interest to **Microsoft**'s investors and creditors:

1. How does Microsoft's decision to incur heavy debt relate to the goals of the business?
2. Is the level of accounts payable in the operating cycle satisfactory?
3. Has the company properly identified and accounted for all its current liabilities?

To maintain its position as the world's leading software company, Microsoft must continue introducing new products and services. Doing that requires research and development, which, in turn, requires a lot of capital; for example, in 2009, Microsoft invested $9 billion in research and development. The company raises much of the capital needed for this purpose by borrowing money. This accounts for the hefty size of its current liabilities ($27 billion, or over 68 percent of its stockholders' equity, in 2009).

Microsoft analyzes its future cash flows in terms of present value and carefully plans its cash needs by making very good use of the operating cycle. By using advance billings, keeping inventories low, and making maximum use of credit from its suppliers, it keeps its cash needs to a minimum. The list of current liabilities in Microsoft's 2009 annual report gives readers a clear picture of the company's short-term obligations.

RATIO

Financial Ratios: Payables Turnover and Days' Payable

Microsoft's skill at cash management is particularly evident when we compare its payables turnover and days' payable for 2008 and 2009. In 2007, Microsoft's merchandise inventory was $1,127 million, and its accounts payable were $3,247 million. (Dollar amounts shown below are in millions.)

		2009	2008
Payables Turnover = (Cost of Goods Sold ± Change in Merchandise Inventory) / Average Accounts Payable	=	$12,155 − $268 / ($3,324 + $4,034) ÷ 2	$11,598 − $142 / ($4,034 + $3,247) ÷ 2
	=	$11,887 / $3,679	$11,456 / $3,641
	=	3.2 times	3.1 times
Days' Payable = 365 Days / Payables Turnover	=	365 days / 3.2 times	365 days / 3.1 times
	=	114.1 days	117.7 days

Clearly, Microsoft maintained a favorable payables turnover and days' payable ratio over the two-year period.

Review Problem

Identification and Evaluation of Current Liabilities 

Teresa Madej started a fitness business, Teresa's Fitness Center, in 2010. In addition to offering exercise classes, the center sells nutritional supplements. Teresa Madej has not yet filed any tax reports for her business and therefore owes taxes. Because she has limited experience in running a business, she has brought you all her business records—a checkbook, canceled checks, deposit slips, suppliers' invoices, a notice of annual property taxes of $3,600 due to the city, and a promissory note to her bank for $16,000. She wants you to determine what her business owes the government and other parties.

You analyze all her records and determine the following as of December 31, 2011:

Unpaid invoices for nutritional supplements	$12,000
Sales of nutritional supplements (excluding sales tax)	57,000
Cost of supplements sold	33,600
Exercise instructors' salaries	22,800
Exercise revenues	81,400
Current assets	40,000
Supplements inventory, December 31, 2011	27,000
Supplements inventory, December 31, 2010	21,000

You learn that the company has sold gift certificates in the amount of $700 that have not been redeemed and that it has deducted $1,374 from its two employees' salaries for federal income taxes owed to the government. The current social security tax is 6.2 percent on maximum earnings of $106,800 for each employee, and the current Medicare tax is 1.45 percent (no maximum earnings). The FUTA tax is 5.4 percent to the state and 0.8 percent to the federal government on the first $7,000 earned by each employee; both employees earned more than $7,000. Madej has not filed a sales tax report to the state (6 percent of supplements sales).

Required

1. Given these facts, determine the company's current liabilities as of December 31, 2011.
2. Your analysis of the company's current liabilities has been based on documents that the owner showed you. What liabilities may be missing from your analysis?

3. Evaluate the company's liquidity by calculating working capital, payables turnover, and days' payable. Comment on the results. (*Note:* Assume average accounts payable were the same as year-end accounts payable.)

ANSWERS TO REVIEW PROBLEM

1. Current liabilities of Teresa's Fitness Center as of December 31, 2011:

	A	B	C	D	E	F	G
1	Accounts payable						$12,000.00
2	Notes payable						16,000.00
3	Property taxes payable						3,600.00
4	Sales tax payable	(	$57,000	x	0.06	)	3,420.00
5	Social security tax payable	(	$22,800	x	0.062	)	1,413.60
6	Medicare tax payable	(	$22,800	x	0.0145	)	330.60
7	State unemployment tax payable	(	$ 7,000	x	0.054	)	378.00
8	Federal unemployment tax payable	(	$ 7,000	x	0.008	)	56.00
9	Employees' federal income taxes payable						1,374.00
10	Unearned revenues						700.00
11	Total current liabilities						$39,272.20
12							

2. The company may have current liabilities for which you have not seen any documentary evidence. For instance, invoices for accounts payable could be missing. In addition, the company may have accrued liabilities, such as vacation pay for its two employees, which would require establishing an estimated liability. If the promissory note to Madej's bank is interest-bearing, it also would require an adjustment to accrue interest payable, and the company could have other loans outstanding for which you have not seen documentary evidence. Moreover, the company may have to pay penalties and interest to the federal and state governments because of its failure to remit tax payments on a timely basis. State and federal income tax withholdings for the employees could be other overlooked liabilities.

3. Working capital, payables turnover, and days' payable computed and evaluated:

	A	B	C	D	E	F	G
1	Working Capital	=	Current Assets		–	Current Liabilities	
2		=	$40,000.00		–	$39,272.20	
3		=	$727.80				
4							
5	Payables Turnover	=	Cost of Goods Sold		+/–	Change in Merchandise Inventory	
6						Accounts Payable	
7							
8		=	$33,600		+	$6,000	
9					$12,000		
10							
11		=	$39,600				
12			$12,000				
13							
14		=	3.3	times			
15							
16	Days' Payable	=	365	Days			
17			Payables Turnover				
18							
19		=	365	days			
20			3.3	times			
21							
22		=	110.6	days*			
23							

Teresa's Fitness Center has negligible working capital of $727.80, its payables turnover is only 3.3 times, and it takes an average of 110.6 days to pay its accounts payable. Its liquidity is therefore highly questionable. Many of its current assets are inventory, which it must sell to generate cash, and it must pay most of its current liabilities sooner than the 110.6 days would indicate.

Stop & Review

LO1 Identify the management issues related to current liabilities.

Current liabilities are an important consideration in managing a company's liquidity and cash flows. Key measures of liquidity are working capital, payables turnover, and days' payable. Liabilities result from past transactions and should be recognized at the time a transaction obligates a company to make future payments. They are valued at the amount of money necessary to satisfy the obligation or at the fair value of the goods or services to be delivered. Liabilities are classified as current or long term. Companies are required to provide supplemental disclosure when the nature or details of the obligations would help in understanding the liability.

LO2 Identify, compute, and record definitely determinable and estimated current liabilities.

The two major categories of current liabilities are definitely determinable liabilities and estimated liabilities. Definitely determinable liabilities can be measured exactly. These liabilities include accounts payable, bank loans and commercial paper, notes payable, accrued liabilities, dividends payable, sales and excise taxes payable, the current portion of long-term debt, payroll liabilities, and unearned revenues. Estimated liabilities definitely exist, but their amounts are uncertain and must be estimated. They include liabilities for income taxes, property taxes, promotional costs, product warranties, and vacation pay.

LO3 Distinguish *contingent liabilities* from *commitments*.

A contingent liability is a potential liability that arises from a past transaction and is dependent on a future event. Contingent liabilities often involve lawsuits, income tax disputes, discounted notes receivable, guarantees of debt, and failure to follow government regulations. A commitment is a legal obligation, such as a purchase agreement, that is not recorded as a liability.

LO 4 Identify the valuation approaches to fair value accounting and define *time value of money* and *interest* and apply them to present values.

The FASB identifies three approaches to measuring fair value. The *market approach* is useful when there is an active market in which quoted prices are available for the specific asset or liability. The *income* (or *cash flow*) *approach* converts future cash flows to a single present value. The *cost approach* is based on the amount that currently would be required to replace an asset with a comparable one.

The time value of money refers to the costs or benefits derived from holding or not holding money over time. Interest is the cost of using money for a specific period. In the computation of simple interest, the amount on which the interest is computed stays the same from period to period. In the computation of compound interest, the interest for a period is added to the principal amount before the interest for the next period is computed.

Future value is the amount an investment will be worth at a future date if invested at compound interest. Present value is the amount that must be invested today at a given rate of interest to produce a given future value. An ordinary annuity is a series of equal payments made at the end of equal intervals of time, with compound interest on the payments. The present value of an ordinary annuity is the present value of a series of payments. Calculations of present values are simplified by using the appropriate tables, which appear in Appendix B.

LO 5 Apply present value to simple valuation situations.

Present value is commonly used in determining fair value and may be used in determining the value of an asset, in computing the present value of deferred payments, and in establishing a fund for loan repayment. Present value also can be applied to numerous other accounting situations in which time is a factor.

Key Terms and Ratios

Commercial paper 369 (LO2)
Commitment 376 (LO3)
Compound interest 378 (LO4)
Contingent liability 376 (LO3)
Current liabilities 364 (LO1)
Definitely determinable liabilities 368 (LO2)
Employee 370 (LO2)
Estimated liabilities 373 (LO2)
Future value 378 (LO4)
Independent contractor 370 (LO2)
Interest 378 (LO4)
Line of credit 368 (LO2)
Long-term liabilities 367 (LO1)
Ordinary annuity 380 (LO4)
Present value 379 (LO4)
Salaries 370 (LO2)
Simple interest 378 (LO4)
Time value of money 378 (LO4)
Unearned revenues 372 (LO2)
Wages 370 (LO2)

FINANCIAL RATIOS
Days' payable 365 (LO1)
Payables turnover 365 (LO1)

Chapter Assignments Building Your Basic Knowledge and Skills

Short Exercises

LO 1 **Issues in Accounting for Liabilities**

SE 1. Indicate whether each of the following actions relates to (a) management of liquidity and cash flow, (b) recognition of liabilities, (c) valuation of liabilities, (d) classification of liabilities, or (e) disclosure of liabilities.

1. Determining that a liability will be paid in less than one year
2. Estimating the amount of a liability

3. Providing information about when liabilities are due and their interest rates
4. Determining when a liability arises
5. Assessing working capital and payables turnover

LO 1

Measuring Short-Term Liquidity

SE 2. Robinson Company has current assets of $65,000 and current liabilities of $40,000, of which accounts payable are $35,000. Robinson's cost of goods sold is $230,000, its merchandise inventory increased by $10,000, and accounts payable were $25,000 the prior year. Calculate Robinson's working capital, payables turnover, and days' payable.

LO 1

Measuring Short-Term Liquidity

SE 3. Angels Corporation has current assets of $87,000 and current liabilities of $56,000, of which accounts payable are $48,000. Angels' cost of goods sold is $274,000, its merchandise inventory increased by $16,000, and accounts payable were $32,000 the prior year. Calculate Angels' working capital, payables turnover, and days' payable.

LO 2, 3

Types of Liabilities

SE 4. Indicate whether each of the following is (a) a definitely determinable liability, (b) an estimated liability, (c) a commitment, or (d) a contingent liability.

1. Dividends payable
2. Pending litigation
3. Income taxes payable
4. Current portion of long-term debt
5. Vacation pay liability
6. Guaranteed loans of another company
7. Purchase agreement

LO 2

Interest Expense on Note Payable

SE 5. On the last day of August, Murcio Company borrowed $480,000 on a bank note for 60 days at 12 percent interest. (*Note:* Assume that interest is stated separately.) Prepare the following journal entries: (1) August 31, recording of note, and (2) October 30, payment of note plus interest.

LO 2

Payroll Expenses

SE 6. The following payroll totals for the month of April are from the payroll register of Hall Corporation: salaries, $446,000; federal income taxes withheld, $62,880; social security tax withheld, $27,652; Medicare tax withheld, $6,468; medical insurance deductions, $13,160; and salaries subject to unemployment taxes, $313,200.

Determine the total and components of (1) the monthly payroll and (2) employer's payroll expense, assuming social security and Medicare taxes equal to the amounts for employees, a federal unemployment insurance tax of 0.8 percent, a state unemployment tax of 5.4 percent, and medical insurance premiums for which the employer pays 80 percent of the cost.

LO 2

Product Warranty Liability

SE 7. Harper Corp. manufactures and sells travel clocks. Each clock costs $12.50 to produce and sells for $25. In addition, each clock carries a warranty that provides for free replacement if it fails during the two years following the sale. In the past, 5 percent of the clocks sold have had to be replaced under the warranty. During October, Harper sold 52,000 clocks, and 2,800 clocks were replaced under the warranty. Prepare journal entries to record the estimated liability for product warranties during the month and the clocks replaced under warranty during the month.

LO 2

Interest Expense on Note Payable

SE 8. On the last day of March, Brunswick Corporation borrowed $360,000 on a bank note for 60 days at 10 percent interest. Assume that interest is stated separately. Prepare the following journal entries: (1) March 31, recording of note, and (2) May 30, payment of note plus interest.

LO 2 **Product Warranty Liability**

SE 9. Geek Company manufactures and sells financial calculators. Each calculator costs $18.50 to produce and sells for $37. In addition, each calculator carries a warranty that provides for free replacement if it fails during the two years following the sale. In the past, 6 percent of the calculators sold have had to be replaced under the warranty. During July, Geek sold 78,000 calculators, and 4,900 calculators were replaced under the warranty. Prepare journal entries to record the estimated liability for product warranties during the month and the calculators replaced under warranty during the month.

LO 4 **Present Value Calculations**

SE 10. Find the present value of (1) a single payment of $36,000 at 4 percent made 12 years from now, (2) 12 annual payments of $3,000 at 4 percent, (3) a single payment of $7,000 at 8 percent made 5 years from now, and (4) five annual payments of $7,000 at 8 percent. (*Note:* Tables 1 and 2 in Appendix B may be used where appropriate.)

LO 5 **Valuing an Asset for the Purpose of Making a Purchasing Decision**

SE 11. Hogan Whitner owns a machine shop and has the opportunity to purchase a new machine for $30,000. After carefully studying projected costs and revenues, Whitner estimates that the new machine will produce a net cash flow of $7,200 annually and will last for eight years. Whitner believes that an interest rate of 10 percent is adequate for his business.

Calculate the present value of the machine to Whitner. (*Note:* Tables 1 and 2 in Appendix B may be used where appropriate.) Does the purchase appear to be a smart business decision? Explain your answer.

LO 5 **Valuing an Asset for the Purpose of Making a Purchasing Decision**

SE 12. Arnold Jones owns a carpentry shop and has the opportunity to purchase a new machine for $45,000. After carefully studying projected costs and revenues, Jones estimates that the new machine will produce a net cash flow of $10,800 annually and will last for seven years. Jones believes that an interest rate of 9 percent is adequate for his business.

Calculate the present value of the machine to Jones. (*Note:* Tables 1 and 2 in Appendix B may be used where appropriate.) Does the purchase appear to be a smart business decision? Explain your answer.

Exercises

LO 1, 2, 3 **Discussion Questions**

E 1. Develop a brief answer to each of the following questions:

1. Nate Livio, a star college basketball player, received a contract from the Eastern Blazers to play professional basketball. The contract calls for a salary of $210,000 per year for four years, dependent on his making the team in each of those years. Should this contract be considered a liability and recorded on the books of the basketball team? Why or why not?
2. Is an increasing payables turnover good or bad for a company? Why?
3. Do adjusting entries involving estimated liabilities and accruals ever affect cash flows?
4. When would a commitment be recognized in the accounting records?

LO 4 **Discussion Questions**

E 2. Develop a brief answer to each of the following questions:

1. A friend borrows money from you for three years and agrees to pay you interest after each year. Is the friend paying you simple or compound interest?
2. Ordinary annuities assume that the first payment is made at the end of each year. In a transaction, who is better off in this arrangement, the payer or the receiver? Why?

3. Why are three methods (levels) of computing fair value needed?
4. Why is present value one of the most useful concepts in making business decisions?

LO 1

Issues in Accounting for Liabilities

E 3. Indicate whether each of the following actions relates to (a) management of liquidity and cash flow, (b) recognition of liabilities, (c) valuation of liabilities, (d) classification of liabilities, or (e) disclosure of liabilities.

1. Setting a liability at the fair market value of goods to be delivered
2. Arranging the payment date of a liability to the length of the operating cycle
3. Recording a liability in accordance with the matching rule
4. Providing information about financial instruments on the balance sheet
5. Estimating the amount of "cents-off" coupons that will be redeemed
6. Categorizing a liability as long-term debt
7. Measuring working capital
8. Comparing this year's days' payable with last year's

LO 1

Measuring Short-Term Liquidity

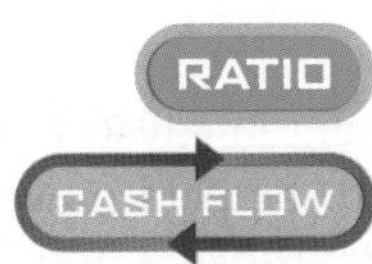

E 4. In 2010, Ronaldo Company had current assets of $620,000 and current liabilities of $400,000, of which accounts payable were $260,000. Cost of goods sold was $1,700,000, merchandise inventory increased by $160,000, and accounts payable were $220,000 in the prior year. In 2011, Ronaldo had current assets of $840,000 and current liabilities of $640,000, of which accounts payable were $300,000. Cost of goods sold was $1,900,000, and merchandise inventory decreased by $60,000. Calculate Ronaldo's working capital, payables turnover, and days' payable for 2010 and 2011. (*Note:* Round to one decimal place.) Assess Ronaldo's liquidity and cash flows in relation to the change in the payables turnover from 2010 to 2011.

LO 2

Interest Expense on Note Payable

E 5. On the last day of October, Thornton Company borrows $240,000 on a bank note for 60 days at 11 percent interest. Interest is not included in the face amount. Prepare the following journal entries: (1) October 31, recording of note; (2) November 30, accrual of interest expense; and (3) December 30, payment of note plus interest.

LO 2

Sales and Excise Taxes

E 6. Web Design Services billed its customers a total of $490,200 for the month of August, including 9 percent federal excise tax and 5 percent sales tax.

1. Determine the proper amount of service revenue to report for the month.
2. Prepare a journal entry to record the revenue and related liabilities for the month.

LO 2

Payroll Expenses

E 7. At the end of October, the payroll register for Symphony Die Corporation contained the following totals: wages, $371,000; federal income taxes withheld, $94,884; state income taxes withheld, $15,636; social security tax withheld, $23,002; Medicare tax withheld, $5,380; medical insurance deductions, $12,870; and wages subject to unemployment taxes, $57,240.

Determine the total and components of the (1) monthly payroll and (2) employer payroll expenses, assuming social security and Medicare taxes equal to the amount for employees, a federal unemployment insurance tax of 0.8 percent, a state unemployment tax of 5.4 percent, and medical insurance premiums for which the employer pays 80 percent of the cost.

LO 2

Product Warranty Liability

E 8. Nap Company manufactures and sells electronic games. Each game costs $100 to produce, sells for $180, and carries a warranty that provides for free replacement if it fails during the two years following the sale. In the past, 7 percent of the games sold had to be replaced under the warranty. During July, Nap sold 13,000 games, and 1,400 games were replaced under the warranty.

1. Prepare a journal entry to record the estimated liability for product warranties during the month.
2. Prepare a journal entry to record the games replaced under warranty during the month.

LO 2

Vacation Pay Liability

E 9. Beaver Corporation gives three weeks' paid vacation to each employee who has worked at the company for one year. Based on studies of employee turnover and previous experience, management estimates that 65 percent of the employees will qualify for vacation pay this year.

1. Assume that Beaver's July payroll is $300,000, of which $20,000 is paid to employees on vacation. Calculate the estimated employee vacation benefit for the month.
2. Prepare a journal entry to record the employee benefit for July.
3. Prepare a journal entry to record the pay to employees on vacation.

LO 4, 5

Determining an Advance Payment

E 10. Laura Daniels is contemplating paying five years' rent in advance. Her annual rent is $12,600. Calculate the single sum that would have to be paid now for the advance rent if we assume compound interest of 8 percent. (*Note:* Tables 1 and 2 in Appendix B may be used where appropriate.)

LO 4

Present Value Calculations

E 11. Find the present value of (1) a single payment of $24,000 at 6 percent made 12 years from now, (2) 12 annual payments of $2,000 at 6 percent, (3) a single payment of $5,000 at 9 percent made 5 years from now, and (4) five annual payments of $5,000 at 9 percent. (*Note:* Tables 1 and 2 in Appendix B may be used where appropriate.)

LO 4, 5

Present Value of a Lump-Sum Contract

E 12. A contract calls for a lump-sum payment of $30,000. Find the present value of the contract, assuming that (1) the payment is due in 5 years and the current interest rate is 9 percent, (2) the payment is due in 10 years and the current interest rate is 9 percent, (3) the payment is due in 5 years and the current interest rate is 5 percent, and (4) the payment is due in 10 years and the current interest rate is 5 percent. (*Note:* Tables 1 and 2 in Appendix B may be used where appropriate.)

LO 4, 5

Present Value of an Annuity Contract

E 13. A contract calls for annual payments of $600. Find the present value of the contract, assuming (1) the number of payments is 7 and the current interest rate is 6 percent, (2) the number of payments is 14 and the current interest rate is 6 percent, (3) the number of payments is 7 and the current interest rate is 8 percent, and (4) the number of payments is 14 and the current interest rate is 8 percent. (*Note:* Tables 1 and 2 in Appendix B may be used where appropriate.)

LO 4, 5

Valuing an Asset for the Purpose of Making a Purchasing Decision

E 14. Edwin Ogden owns a service station and has the opportunity to purchase a car wash machine for $15,000. After carefully studying projected costs and revenues, Ogden estimates that the car wash machine will produce a net cash flow of $2,600 annually and will last for eight years. He determines that an interest rate of 14 percent is adequate for his business. Calculate the present value of the machine to Ogden. (*Note:* Tables 1 and 2 in Appendix B may be used where appropriate.) Does the purchase appear to be a smart business decision? Explain your answer.

LO 4, 5 **Deferred Payment**

E 15. Antoine Equipment Corporation sold a precision tool machine with computer controls to Roma Corporation for $400,000 on January 2 and agreed to take payment nine months later on October 2. Assuming that the prevailing annual interest rate for such a transaction is 16 percent compounded quarterly, what is the actual sale (purchase) price of the machine tool? (*Note:* Tables 1 and 2 in Appendix B may be used where appropriate.)

LO 4, 5 **Negotiating the Sale of a Business**

E 16. Marta Otis is attempting to sell her business to Hubert Betley. The company has assets of $1,800,000, liabilities of $1,600,000, and stockholders' equity of $200,000. Both parties agree that the proper rate of return to expect is 12 percent; however, they differ on other assumptions. Otis believes that the business will generate at least $200,000 per year of cash flows for 20 years. Betley thinks that $160,000 in cash flows per year is more reasonable and that only 10 years in the future should be considered. Using Table 2 in Appendix B, determine the range for negotiation by computing the present value of Otis's offer to sell and of Betley's offer to buy.

Problems

LO 1, 2, 3 **Identification of Current Liabilities, Contingencies, and Commitments**

P 1. Listed below are common types of current liabilities, contingencies, and commitments.

a. Accounts payable
b. Bank loans and commercial paper
c. Notes payable
d. Dividends payable
e. Sales and excise taxes payable
f. Current portion of long-term debt
g. Payroll liabilities
h. Unearned revenues
i. Income taxes payable
j. Property taxes payable
k. Promotional costs
l. Product warranty liability
m. Vacation pay liability
n. Contingent liability
o. Commitment

REQUIRED

1. For each of the following statements, identify the category (**a** through **o**) with which it is most closely associated.
   1. A company agrees to replace parts of a product if they fail.
   2. An employee earns one day off for each month worked.
   3. A company signs a contract to lease a building for five years.
   4. A company puts discount coupons in the newspaper.
   5. A company agrees to pay insurance costs for employees.
   6. A portion of a mortgage on a building is due this year.
   7. The board of directors declares a dividend.
   8. A company has trade payables.
   9. A company has a lawsuit pending against it.
   10. A company uses a line of credit.
   11. A company signs a note due in 60 days.
   12. A company operates in a state that has a sales tax.
   13. A company earns a profit that is taxable.
   14. A company owns buildings that are subject to property taxes.

USER INSIGHT ▶ 2. Of the items listed from **a** to **o**, which would you not expect to see listed on the balance sheet with a dollar amount? Of the items that would be listed on the balance sheet with a dollar amount, which do you think involve the most judgment or discretion on the part of management?

LO 2

Notes Payable

✔ June 30 interest expense: $138.08

P 2. Lazur Corporation, whose fiscal year ended June 30, 2011, completed the following transactions involving notes payable:

May 21	Obtained a 60-day extension on a $9,000 trade account payable owed to a supplier by signing a 60-day, $9,000 note. Interest is in addition to the face value, at the rate of 14 percent.
June 30	Made the end-of-year adjusting entry to accrue interest expense.
July 20	Paid off the note plus interest due the supplier.

REQUIRED

1. Prepare journal entries for the notes payable transactions.
2. USER INSIGHT ▶ When notes payable appears on the balance sheet, what other current liability would you expect to be associated with the notes? What would it mean if this other current liability did not appear?

LO 2

Wages Payable

✔ July 31 Payroll Taxes and Benefits Expense, $17,583.66

P 3. The payroll register for Lazur Corporation contained the following totals at the end of July 2011: wages, $69,623; federal income taxes withheld, $17,791; state income taxes withheld, $2,923; social security tax withheld, $4,313; Medicare tax withheld, $1,009; medical insurance deductions, $2,400; and wages subject to unemployment taxes, $42,930.

REQUIRED

1. Prepare journal entries to record the (a) monthly payroll and (b) employer payroll expenses, assuming social security and Medicare taxes equal to the amount for employees, a federal unemployment insurance tax of 0.8 percent, a state unemployment tax of 5.4 percent, and medical insurance premiums for which the employer pays 80 percent of the cost.
2. USER INSIGHT ▶ If Lazur is planning to hire a new employee for a salary of $1,000 per month, approximately how should the company budget per month for the total cost of this new employee?

LO 2

Product Warranty Liability

✔ (b). Estimated product warranty liability: $10,800

P 4. Vision Company sells high-definition televisions (HDTVs). Each HDTV has a 24-month warranty on parts. If a repair under warranty is required, the company charges for the labor. Management has found that 20 percent of the HDTVs sold require some work before the warranty expires. Furthermore, the average cost of replacement parts has been $120 per repair. At the beginning of January, the account for the estimated liability for product warranties had a credit balance of $28,600. During January, 112 HDTVs were returned under the warranty. The cost of the parts used in repairing the HDTVs was $17,530, and $18,884 was collected as service revenue for the labor involved. During January, the month before the Super Bowl, Vision Company sold 450 HDTVs.

REQUIRED

1. Prepare journal entries to record (a) the warranty work completed during January, including related revenue, and (b) the estimated liability for product warranties for HDTVs sold during the month.
2. Compute the balance of the Estimated Product Warranty Liability account at the end of the month.
3. USER INSIGHT ▶ If the company's product warranty liability is overestimated, what are the effects on current and future years' income?

LO 1, 2

Identification and Evaluation of Current Liabilities

✔ Total current liabilities: $39,436.20

P 5. Jorge Gundy opened a small motorcycle repair shop, Gundy Cycle Repair, on January 2, 2011. The shop also sells a limited number of motorcycle parts. In January 2012, Gundy realized he had never filed any tax reports for his business and therefore probably owes a considerable amount of taxes. Since he has limited experience in running a business, he has brought you all his business records, including a checkbook, canceled checks, deposit slips, suppliers' invoices, a notice of annual property taxes of $4,620 due to the city, and a promissory note to his father-in-law for $5,000. He wants you to determine what his business owes the government and other parties.

You analyze all his records and determine the following as of December 31, 2011:

Unpaid invoices for motorcycle parts	$ 18,000
Parts sales (excluding sales tax)	88,540
Cost of parts sold	62,250
Workers' salaries	36,400
Repair revenues	120,600
Current assets	32,600
Motorcycle parts inventory	23,500

You learn that the company has deducted $952 from the two employees' salaries for federal income taxes owed to the government. The current social security tax is 6.2 percent on maximum earnings of $106,800 for each employee, and the current Medicare tax is 1.45 percent (no maximum earnings). The FUTA tax is 5.4 percent to the state and 0.8 percent to the federal government on the first $7,000 earned by each employee, and both employees earned more than $7,000. Gundy has not filed a sales tax report to the state (5 percent of sales).

REQUIRED

1. Given these limited facts, determine Gundy Cycle Repair's current liabilities as of December 31, 2011.

USER INSIGHT ▶

2. What additional information would you want from Gundy to ensure that all current liabilities have been identified?

USER INSIGHT ▶

3. Evaluate Gundy's liquidity by calculating working capital, payables turnover, and days' payable. Comment on the results. (*Note:* Assume average accounts payable were the same as year-end accounts payable.)

LO 4, 5

✔ (a). Initial deposit: $27,563
(b). Purchase price: $99,825

Applications of Present Value

P 6. The management of LAS, Inc., took the following actions, which went into effect on May 2, 2011. Each action involved an application of present value.

a. Asked for a fund to be established by a single payment to accumulate to $37,500 in four years.
b. Approved the purchase of a parcel of land for future plant expansion. Payments are to start May 2, 2012, at $25,000 per year for five years.

REQUIRED

1. Assuming an annual interest rate of 8 percent and using Tables 1 and 2 in Appendix B, answer the following questions:
   a. In action **a**, how much will need to be deposited initially to accumulate the desired amount?
   b. In action **b**, what is the purchase price (present value) of the land?

USER INSIGHT ▶

2. What is the fundamental reason present value analysis is a useful tool in making business decisions?

Alternate Problems

LO 2

GL GENERAL LEDGER

✔ December 31 interest expense: $852.16

Notes Payable

P 7. Hammer Company, whose fiscal year ends December 31, completed the following transactions involving notes payable:

2011
Nov. 25 Purchased a new loading cart by issuing a 60-day, 10 percent note for $86,400.
Dec. 31 Made the end-of-year adjusting entry to accrue interest expense.

2012
Jan. 24 Paid off the loading cart note.

REQUIRED

1. Prepare journal entries for Hammer's notes payable transactions.
2. When notes payable appears on the balance sheet, what other current liability would you expect to be associated with the notes? What would it mean if this other current liability did not appear? **USER INSIGHT ▶**

LO 2

Wages Payable

✔ Oct. 31 Payroll Taxes and Benefits Expense, $46,888.76

P 8. At the end of October 2011, the payroll register for Hammer Company in **P 7** contained the following totals: wages, $185,500; federal income taxes withheld, $47,442; state income taxes withheld, $7,818; social security tax withheld, $11,501; Medicare tax withheld, $2,690; medical insurance deductions, $6,400; and wages subject to unemployment taxes, $114,480.

REQUIRED

1. Prepare journal entries to record the (1) monthly payroll and (2) employer payroll expenses, assuming social security and Medicare taxes equal to the amount for employees, a federal unemployment insurance tax of 0.8 percent, a state unemployment tax of 5.4 percent, and medical insurance premiums for which the employer pays 80 percent of the cost.
2. If Hammer is planning to hire a new employee for a salary of $2,000 per month, approximately how should the company budget per month for the total cost of this new employee? **USER INSIGHT ▶**

LO 2

Product Warranty Liability

✔ (b). Estimated product warranty liability: $10,080

P 9. Yuppie Products Company manufactures and sells cell phones, and it guarantees them for five years. If a cell phone fails, it is replaced free, but the customer is charged a service fee for handling. In the past, management has found that only 3 percent of the cell phones sold required replacement under the warranty. The average cell phone costs the company $120. At the beginning of September, the account for estimated liability for product warranties had a credit balance of $104,000. During September, 250 cell phones were returned under the warranty. The company collected $4,930 of service fees for handling. During the month, the company sold 2,800 cell phones.

REQUIRED

1. Prepare journal entries to record (a) the cost of cell phones replaced under warranty and (b) the estimated liability for product warranties for cell phones sold during the month.
2. Compute the balance of the Estimated Product Warranty Liability account at the end of the month.
3. If the product warranty liability is underestimated, what are the effects on the company's current and future years' income? **USER INSIGHT ▶**

LO 1, 2

Identification and Evaluation of Current Liabilities

✔ Total current liabilities: $18,541.25

P 10. Linda Lopez opened a beauty studio, Linda's Salon, on January 2, 2011. The salon also sells beauty supplies. In January 2012, Lopez realized she had never filed any tax reports for her business and therefore probably owes a considerable amount of taxes. Since she has limited experience in running a business, she has brought you all her business records, including a checkbook, canceled checks, deposit slips, suppliers' invoices, a notice of annual property taxes of $1,970 due to the city, and a promissory note to her father-in-law for $3,000. She wants you to determine what her business owes the government and other parties.

You analyze all her records and determine the following as of December 31, 2011:

Unpaid invoices for beauty supplies	$ 7,500
Beauty supplies sales (excluding sales tax)	39,430
Cost of beauty supplies sold	27,631
Workers' salaries	17,750
Service revenues	51,900
Current assets	15,800
Beauty supplies inventory	9,980

You learn that the company has deducted $516 from the two employees' salaries for federal income taxes owed to the government. The current social security tax is 6.2 percent on maximum earnings of $106,800 for each employee, and the current Medicare tax is 1.45 percent (no maximum earnings). The FUTA tax is 5.4 percent to the state and 0.8 percent to the federal government on the first $7,000 earned by each employee, and both employees earned more than $7,000. Lopez has not filed a sales tax report to the state (5 percent of sales).

REQUIRED

1. Given these limited facts, determine Linda's Salon's current liabilities as of December 31, 2011.

USER INSIGHT ▶

2. What additional information would you want from Lopez to be sure that all current liabilities have been identified?

3. Evaluate Lopez's liquidity by calculating working capital, payables turnover, and days' payable. Comment on the results. (*Note:* Assume average accounts payable were the same as year-end accounts payable.)

LO 4, 5

Applications of Present Value

✔ (a). Present value of liability: $375,500
(b). Cost of buyout: $158,500

P 11. Bergson Corporation's management took the following actions, which went into effect on March 2, 2011. Each action involved an application of present value.

a. Entered into a purchase agreement that calls for a payment of $500,000 three years from now.
b. Bought out the contract of a member of top management for a payment of $50,000 per year for four years beginning March 2, 2012.

REQUIRED

1. Assuming an annual interest rate of 10 percent and using Tables 1 and 2 in Appendix B, answer the following questions:
   a. In action **a**, what is the present value of the liability for the purchase agreement?
   b. In action **b**, what is the cost (present value) of the buyout?

2. Many businesses analyze present value extensively when making decisions about investing in long-term assets. Why is this type of analysis particularly appropriate for such decisions?

LO 4, 5

Applications of Present Value

✔ (a). Present value of liability: $366,600
(b). Cost of buyout: $265,370

P 12. Kowalski Corporation's management took the following actions, which went into effect on January 2, 2011. Each action involved an application of present value.

a. Entered into a purchase agreement that calls for a payment of $650,000 six years from now.
b. Bought out the contract of a member of top management for a payment of $70,000 per year for five years beginning January 2, 2012.

REQUIRED

1. Assuming an annual interest rate of 10 percent and using Tables 1 and 2 from Appendix B, answer the following questions:
   a. In action **a**, what is the present value of the liability for the purchase agreement?
   b. In action **b**, what is the cost (present value) of the buyout?

USER INSIGHT ▶

2. Many businesses analyze present value extensively when making decisions about investing in long-term assets. Why is this type of analysis particularly appropriate for such decisions?

Cases

LO 2

Conceptual Understanding: Frequent Flyer Plan

C 1. FlyJet Airways instituted a frequent flyer program in which passengers accumulate points toward a free flight based on the number of miles they fly on the airline. One point was awarded for each mile flown, and a minimum of 750 miles was awarded for any one flight. Because of competition in 2011, the company began a bonus plan in which passengers receive triple the normal mileage points. In the past, about 1.5 percent of passenger miles were flown by passengers who had converted points to free flights; with the triple mileage program, FlyJet expects that the rate will increase to 2.5 percent.

During 2011, the company had passenger revenues of $966.3 million and passenger transportation operating expenses of $802.8 million before depreciation and amortization. Operating income was $86.1 million. What is the appropriate rate to use to estimate free miles? What effect would the estimated liability for free travel by frequent flyers have on 2011 net income? Describe several ways to estimate the amount of this liability. Be prepared to discuss the arguments for and against recognizing this liability.

LO **3**

Conceptual Understanding: Lawsuits and Contingent Liabilities

C 2. When faced with lawsuits, many companies recognize a loss and therefore credit a liability or reserve account for any future losses that may result. For instance, in the famous **WorldCom** case, **Citibank**, one of the world's largest financial services firms, announced it was setting up reserves or liabilities of $5.6 billion because of pending lawsuits due to its relationship with WorldCom.[16] Were these pending lawsuits contingent liabilities? According to the FASB, what conditions must exist before a liability related to a pending lawsuit can be entered in the accounting records?

LO **4, 5**

Conceptual Understanding: Present Value

C 3. In its "Year-End Countdown Sale," a local Cadillac car dealer advertised "0% interest for 60 months!"[17] What role does the time value of money play in this promotion? Assuming that the car dealer is able to borrow funds at 8 percent interest, what is the cost to the dealer of every customer who takes advantage of this offer? If you could borrow money to buy a car from this dealer, which rate would be more relevant in determining how much you might offer for the car: the rate at which you borrow money or the rate at which the dealer borrows money?

LO **1**

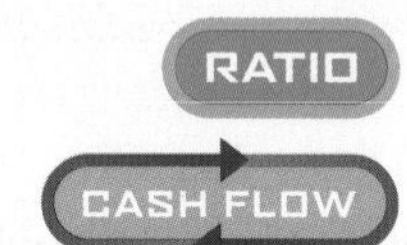

Interpreting Financial Reports: Comparison of Two Companies' Ratios with Industry Ratios

C 4. Both **Sun Microsystems Inc.** and **Cisco Systems** are in the computer industry. These data (in millions) are from the end of their fiscal years 2009:[18]

	Sun	Cisco
Accounts payable	$1,027	$ 675
Cost of goods sold	6,718	13,023
Increase (decrease) in inventory	(114)	(161)

Compare the payables turnover and days' payable for both companies. How are cash flows affected by days' payable? How do Sun Microsystems' and Cisco Systems' ratios compare with the computer industry ratios shown on pages 365 and 366? (Use year-end amounts for ratios.)

LO **2**

Interpreting Financial Reports: Nature and Recognition of an Estimated Liability

C 5. The decision to recognize and record a liability is sometimes a matter of judgment. People who use **General Motors (GM)** credit cards earn rebates toward the purchase or lease of GM vehicles in relation to the amount of purchases they make with their cards. In 2008, GM treated these outstanding rebates as a commitment in the notes to its financial statements:

> GM sponsors a credit card program . . . which offers rebates that can be applied primarily against the purchase or lease of GM vehicles. The amount of rebates available to qualified cardholders (net of deferred program income) was $3.1 billion and $3.4 billion at December 31, 2009, and 2008, respectively.[19]

Using the two criteria established by the FASB for recording a contingency, explain GM's reasoning in treating this liability as a commitment in the notes, where it would likely receive less attention by analysts, rather than including it on the income statement as an expense and on the balance sheet as an estimated liability. Do you agree with this position? (*Hint:* Apply the matching rule.)

LO 1, 3 Annual Report Case: Commitments and Contingencies

C 6. Read **CVS**'s note on commitments and contingencies in the Supplement to Chapter 1. What commitments and contingencies does the company have? Why is it important to consider this information when analyzing accounts payable?

LO 1 Comparison Analysis: Payables Analysis

RATIO

C 7. Refer to **CVS**'s financial statements in the Supplement to Chapter 1 and to the following data for **Walgreens**:

	2009	2008	2007
Cost of goods sold	$45,722	$42,391	$38,518
Accounts payable	4,308	4,289	3,734
Increase (decrease) in merchandise inventory	(460)	459	740

Compute the payables turnover and days' payable for CVS and Walgreens in 2008 and 2009. In 2007, CVS had accounts payable of $3,593 million, and in 2008, its merchandise inventory increased by $1,144. Which company do you think made the most use of financing from creditors during the operating cycle?

LO 2 Ethical Dilemma: Known Legal Violations

C 8. Surf and Turf is a large restaurant in the suburbs of Chicago. Ronald Swift, an accounting student at a nearby college, recently secured a full-time accounting job there. He felt fortunate to have a good job that accommodated his class schedule. After a few weeks on the job, Swift realized that his boss, the owner of the business, was paying the kitchen workers in cash and not withholding federal and state income taxes or social security and Medicare taxes. Swift knows that federal and state laws require these taxes to be withheld and paid to the appropriate agency in a timely manner. He also realizes that if he raises this issue, he could lose his job. What alternatives are available to Swift? What action would you take if you were in his position? Why did you make this choice?

LO 4, 5 Business Communication: Baseball Contract

C 9. Devon Turner, who has been playing shortstop for the St. Louis Titans for five years, made the All-Star team in 2011. He has three years left on a contract that pays him $2.4 million a year. He wants to renegotiate his contract because other players with records similar to his are receiving as much as $10.5 million per year for five years.

Titans' management has a policy of never renegotiating a current contract but is willing to consider extending Turner's contract to additional years. In fact, the Titans have offered Turner an additional three years at $6.0 million, $9.0 million, and $12.0 million. They have also added an option year at $15.0 million. Management points out that this package is worth $42.0 million, or $10.5 million per year on average. Turner is considering this offer and is also thinking of asking for a bonus if and when he signs the contract.

Write a memorandum to Turner that comments on management's position and evaluates the offer, assuming a current interest rate of 10 percent. (*Hint:* Use present values.) Propose a range for the signing bonus. Finally, include other considerations that may affect the value of the offer.

CHAPTER 9

DECISION POINT
A User's Focus Apple Computer, Inc.

Long known for its innovative technology and design, **Apple Computer** revolutionized the music industry with its iPod, and it hopes to do the same in the computer industry with its new iPad tablet. The company's success stems from its willingness to invest in research and development and long-term assets to create new products. In 2009, it spent almost $1,333 million on research and development and about $1,144 million on new long-term assets. About 34 percent of its assets are long-term. You can get an idea of the extent and importance of Apple's long-term assets by looking at the Financial Highlights from the company's balance sheet.[1]

Apple Computer's Financial Highlights
(in millions)

	2009	2008
Long-term marketable securities	$10,528	$2,379
Property, Plant, and Equipment:		
Land and buildings	$ 955	$ 810
Machinery, equipment, and internal-use software	1,932	1,491
Office furniture and equipment	115	122
Leasehold improvements	1,665	1,324
	4,667	3,747
Less accumulated depreciation and amortization	1,713	1,292
Total property, plant, and equipment, net	$ 2,954	$2,455
Other Noncurrent Assets:		
Goodwill	$ 206	$ 207
Acquired intangible assets	247	285
Capitalized software development costs	106	67
Other noncurrent assets	1,905	772
Total other noncurrent assets	$ 2,464	$1,331

Questions

1. *What are Apple's long-term assets?*
2. *What are its policies in accounting for long-term assets?*
3. *Does the company generate enough cash flow to finance its continued growth?*

Justin Sullivan/Getty Images News/Getty Images

Long-Term Assets

LEARNING OBJECTIVES

LO 1 Define *long-term assets* and explain the management issues related to them. (pp. 402–407)

LO 2 Distinguish between *capital expenditures* and *revenue expenditures* and account for the cost of property, plant, and equipment. (pp. 407–410)

LO 3 Compute depreciation under the straight-line, production, and declining-balance methods. (pp. 411–417)

LO 4 Account for the disposal of depreciable assets. (pp. 417–419)

LO 5 Identify the issues related to accounting for natural resources and compute depletion. (pp. 419–421)

LO 6 Identify the issues related to accounting for intangible assets, including research and development costs and goodwill. (pp. 422–426)

Long-term assets include tangible assets, such as land, buildings, and equipment; natural resources, such as timberland and oil fields; and intangible assets, such as patents and copyrights. These assets represent a company's strategic commitments well into the future. The judgments related to their acquisition, operation, and disposal and to the allocation of their costs will affect a company's performance for years to come. Investors and creditors rely on accurate and full reporting of the assumptions and judgments that underlie the measurement of long-term assets.

FOCUS ON FINANCIAL STATEMENTS

INCOME STATEMENT
Revenues
− Expenses
= Net Income

STATEMENT OF RETAINED EARNINGS
Opening Balance
+ Net Income
− Dividends
= Retained Earnings

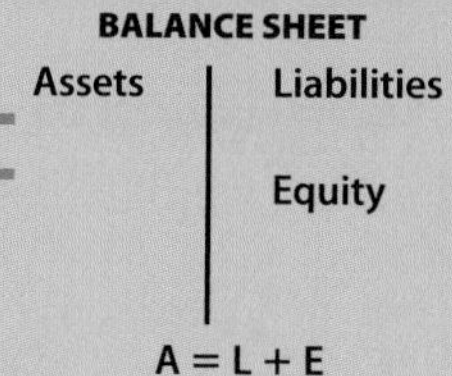

STATEMENT OF CASH FLOWS
Operating Activities
+ Investing Activities
+ Financing Activities
= Change in Cash
+ Starting Balance
= Ending Cash Balance

Allocating the cost of long-term assets on the balance sheet affects the income statement. Buying/disposing of long-term assets affects the statement of cash flows.

MANAGEMENT ISSUES RELATED TO LONG-TERM ASSETS

Define *long-term assets* and explain the management issues related to them. LO 1

Long-term assets were once called fixed assets, but this term has fallen out of favor because it implies that the assets last forever, which they do not. Long-term assets have the following characteristics:

STUDY NOTE: To be classified as property, plant, and equipment, an asset must be used for its intended purpose in operating the business. If an asset is taken out of service, such as a closed retail outlet, it should be reclassified as Other Assets.

- **They have a useful life of more than one year.** This distinguishes them from current assets, which a company expects to use up or convert to cash within one year or during its operating cycle, whichever is longer. They also differ from current assets in that they support the operating cycle, rather than being part of it. Although there is no strict rule for defining the useful life of a long-term asset, the most common criterion is that the asset be capable of repeated use for at least a year. Included in this category is equipment used only in peak or emergency periods, such as electric generators.
- **They are used in the operation of a business.** Assets not used in the normal course of business, such as land held for speculative reasons or buildings no longer used in ordinary business operations, should be classified as long-term investments, not as long-term assets.
- **They are not intended for resale to customers.** An asset that a company intends to resell to customers should be classified as inventory—not as a long-term asset—no matter how durable it is. For example, a printing press that a manufacturer offers for sale is part of the manufacturer's inventory, but it is a long-term asset for a printing company that buys it to use in its operations.

Exhibit 9.1 shows the relative importance of long-term assets in various industries.

Long-term assets include *tangible assets*, *natural resources*, and *intangible assets* (see Exhibit 9.2). They appear as assets on the balance sheet and are accounted for as expenses on the income statement.

- **Tangible assets** have physical substance. They include buildings, equipment, and land. Most tangible assets are accounted for through **depreciation**—the periodic allocation of the cost of a tangible long-lived asset over its estimated useful life. Land is not depreciated because it has an unlimited life.
- **Natural resources** are assets that are extracted from the land and purchased for their economic value—for example, coal, oil, and lumber. Although they are tangible assets, they are accounted for, not through depreciation, but through **depletion**—the proportional allocation of the cost of a natural resource to the units extracted.
- **Intangible assets** are assets, such as copyrights and trademarks, that have no physical substance. Their value is based on legal rights or advantages accruing to their owners. Most intangible assets are accounted for through **amortization**—the periodic allocation of the cost of the asset to the periods it benefits. However, some intangible assets, including goodwill, are not subject to amortization if their fair value is below their carrying value.

STUDY NOTE: To be classified as intangible, an asset must lack physical substance, be long-term, and represent a legal right or advantage.

EXHIBIT 9.1
Long-Term Assets as a Percentage of Total Assets for Selected Industries

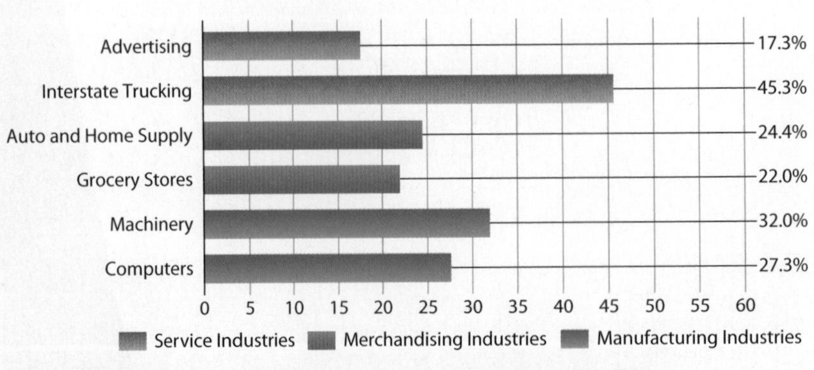

Source: Data from Dun & Bradstreet, *Industry Norms and Key Business Ratios*, 2008–2009.

EXHIBIT 9.2
Classification of Long-Term Assets and Methods of Accounting for Them

BALANCE SHEET
Long-Term Assets

INCOME STATEMENT
Expenses

Tangible Assets: long-term assets that have physical substance

- Land
- Plant Assets
  - Plant
  - Buildings
  - Equipment

Land is not expensed because it has an unlimited life.

Depreciation: periodic allocation of the cost of a tangible long-lived asset (other than land and natural resources) over its estimated useful life

Natural Resources: long-term assets purchased for the economic value that can be taken from the land and used up, as with ore, lumber, oil, and gas or other resources contained in the land

- Mines
- Timberland
- Oil and Gas Fields

Depletion: exhaustion of a natural resource through mining, cutting, pumping, or other extraction and the way in which the cost is allocated

Intangible Assets: long-term assets that have no physical substance but have a value based on rights or advantages accruing to the owner

Subject to Amortization and Impairment Test	*Subject Only to Annual Impairment Test*
• Copyrights	• Brand names
• Customer lists	• Franchises
• Leaseholds	• Goodwill
• Noncompete covenants	• Licenses
• Patents	• Trademarks
• Software	

Amortization: periodic allocation of the cost of an intangible asset to the periods it benefits

Impairment: occurs when the fair value of the asset falls below the carrying value; all long-term assets are subject to an annual test for impairment

Carrying value (also called *book value*) is the unexpired part of an asset's cost (see Exhibit 9.3). Long-term assets are generally reported at carrying value. If a long-term asset loses any of its potential to generate revenue before the end of its useful life, it is deemed *impaired*, and its carrying value is reduced.

All long-term assets, including intangible assets that are not subject to amortization, are subject to an annual impairment evaluation. **Asset impairment** occurs when the carrying value of a long-term asset exceeds its fair value.[2] *Fair value* is the amount for which the asset could be bought or sold in a current transaction. Under GAAP, testing for impairment of long-lived assets is as follows:

1. If the total *undiscounted*, or total, future cash flows of a long-lived asset are greater than its carrying value, then no impairment exists and no further step is required.
2. If the carrying value of the long-term asset is less than the total *undiscounted* future cash flows, then the *discounted*, or present value, of the future cash flows has to be computed. The impairment loss equals the carrying value minus the *discounted* cash flows.

Reducing carrying value to fair value, as measured by the present value of future cash flows, is an application of conservatism. A reduction in carrying value as the result of impairment is recorded as a loss. When the market prices used to establish fair value are not available, the amount of impairment must be estimated from the best available information.

EXHIBIT 9.3
Carrying Value of Long-Term Assets on the Balance Sheet

Plant Assets	Natural Resources	Intangible Assets
Less Accumulated Depreciation	Less Accumulated Depletion	Less Accumulated Amortization
Carrying Value	Carrying Value	Carrying Value

Focus on International Practices

IFRS Asset Impairment Under IFRS

In contrast to the GAAP method of evaluating asset impairment, the IFRS method does not consider undiscounted cash flows. Instead, it compares the carrying value with the recoverable amount. The recoverable amount is the greater of either *net selling price* (the market value of the asset less disposal costs) or of *value in use* (the discounted value of the future net cash flows—i.e., present value).

Because discounted cash flows are always less than undiscounted cash flows, the IFRS method is much more likely than the GAAP method to result in write-offs due to impairment. The IFRS method also allows reversals of impairment write-offs if the value later increases because of revaluation, whereas the GAAP method prohibits future impairment reversals. One exception under IFRS is that goodwill impairments cannot be reversed.

iStock Photo

In 2004, **Apple** recognized losses of $5.5 million in asset impairments, but it recognized none in subsequent years. A few years earlier, in the midst of an economic slowdown in the telecommunications industry, **WorldCom** recorded asset impairments that totaled $79.8 billion, the largest impairment write-down in history. Since then, other telecommunications companies, including **AT&T** and **Qwest Communications**, have taken large impairment write-downs. Due to these companies' declining revenues, the carrying value of some of their long-term assets no longer exceeded the cash flows that they were meant to help generate.[3] Because of the write-downs, these companies reported large operating losses.

Taking a large write-down in a bad year is often called "taking a big bath" because it "cleans" future years of the bad year's costs and thus can help a company return to a profitable status. In other words, by taking the largest possible loss on a long-term asset in a bad year, companies hope to reduce the costs of depreciation or amortization on the asset in subsequent years.[4]

Acquiring Long-Term Assets

The decision to acquire a long-term asset is a complex process. For example, **Apple**'s decision to invest capital in establishing its own retail stores required very careful analysis. Evaluating data to make sound decisions about acquiring long-term assets is part of the capital budgeting process, a topic covered in detail in managerial accounting texts. However, a general awareness of how acquisition decisions are made is helpful in understanding the management issues related to long-term assets.

To illustrate an acquisition decision, suppose that Apple's management is considering buying a $100,000 customer-relations software package. Management estimates that the new software will reduce cash outflows by $40,000 per year over a period of four years, the usual life of new software, and that the software will be worth $20,000 at the end of that period. These data are shown in Exhibit 9.4.

EXHIBIT 9.4
Illustration of an Acquisition Decision

	Year 1	Year 2	Year 3	Year 4
Acquisition cost	$(100,000)			
Net annual savings in cash flows	40,000	$40,000	$40,000	$40,000
Disposal price				20,000
Net cash flows	$ (60,000)	$40,000	$40,000	$60,000

To put the cash flows on a comparable basis, it is helpful to use present value tables, such as Tables 1 and 2 in Appendix B. If the interest rate set by management as a desirable return on its investments is 10 percent compounded annually, the purchase decision would be evaluated as follows:

		Present Value
Acquisition cost	Present value factor = 1.000 1.000 × $100,000	$(100,000)
Net annual savings in cash flows	Present value factor = 3.170 (Table 2: 4 periods, 10%) 3.170 × $40,000	126,800
Disposal value	Present value factor = 0.683 (Table 1: 4 periods, 10%) 0.683 × $20,000	13,660
Net present value		$ 40,460

As long as the net present value is positive, Apple will earn at least 10 percent on the investment. In this example, however, the return would be greater than 10 percent because the net present value is a positive $40,460. Moreover, the net present value is large relative to the acquisition cost. Based on this analysis, Apple's management should purchase the software. However, in making its decision, it should take other considerations into account, including the costs of training personnel to use the new software and the possibility that because of unforeseen circumstances, the savings may not be as great as expected.

Information about acquisitions of long-term assets appears in the investing activities section of the statement of cash flows. In referring to this section of its 2009 annual report, Apple's management made the following statement:

> The Company's cash payments for capital asset purchases were $1.1 billion during [fiscal] 2009. . . . The Company anticipates utilizing approximately $1.9 billion for capital asset purchases during 2010, including approximately $400 million for Retail facilities and approximately $1.5 billion for corporate facilities, infrastructure, and product tooling and manufacturing process equipment.

Financing Long-Term Assets

When management decides to acquire a long-term asset, it must also decide how to finance the purchase. Many financing arrangements are based on the life of the asset. For example, an automobile loan generally spans four or five years, whereas a mortgage on a house may span 30 years. To finance a major long-term acquisition, a company may issue stock, long-term notes, or bonds. Some companies are profitable enough to pay for long-term assets out of cash flows from operations. A good place to study a company's financing activities is its statement of cash flows, and a good measure of its ability to finance long-term assets is free cash flow.

Free Cash Flow Although not a financial ratio, **free cash flow** is an important and commonly cited measure of a company's financial strength. It is the amount of cash that remains after deducting the funds a company must commit to continue operating at its planned level. These commitments include current or continuing operations, interest, income taxes, dividends, and net capital expenditures (purchases of plant assets minus sales of plant assets).

If a company fails to pay for current or continuing operations, interest, and income taxes, its creditors or the government may take legal action. Although the payment of dividends is not required, dividends represent a commitment to stockholders. If they are reduced or eliminated, stockholders may be unhappy, which could cause the price of the company's stock to fall.

A positive free cash flow means that a company has met all its cash commitments and has cash available to reduce debt or to expand operations. A negative free cash flow means that it will have to sell investments, borrow money, or issue stock to continue at its planned level. If its free cash flow remains negative for several years, a company may not be able to raise cash by issuing stock or bonds.

Computing Free Cash Flow Using data from **Apple**'s statement of cash flows in its 2009 annual report, we can compute the company's free cash flow as follows (in millions):

$$\begin{aligned}\text{Free Cash Flow} &= \text{Net Cash Flows from Operating Activities} - \text{Dividends}\\ &\quad - \text{Purchases of Plant Assets} + \text{Sales of Plant Assets}\\ &= \$10{,}159 - \$0 - \$1{,}144 + \$0\\ &= \$9{,}015\end{aligned}$$

This analysis confirms Apple's strong financial position. Its cash flow from operating activities far exceeded its net capital expenditures of $1,144 million. A factor in its positive free cash flow of $9,015 million is that the company pays no dividends. In addition, the financing activities section of Apple's statement of cash flows indicates that the company, rather than incurring debt for expansion, actually made net investments of $16,147 million.

Applying the Matching Rule

When a company records an expenditure as a long-term asset, it defers some of the asset's cost to later periods. Thus, the current period's profitability looks better than it would have if the asset's total cost had been expensed immediately. Management has considerable latitude in making the judgments and estimates necessary to account for long-term assets, and this latitude has sometimes been used unethically. For example, in the **WorldCom** accounting fraud, management ordered that expenditures that should have been recorded as operating expenses be recorded as long-term assets and written off over several years. The result was an overstatement of income by about $10 billion, which ultimately led to one of the largest bankruptcies in the history of U.S. business.

To avoid fraudulent reporting of long-term assets, a company's management must apply the matching rule in resolving two important issues. The first is how much of the total cost of a long-term asset to allocate to expense in the current accounting period. The second is how much to retain on the balance sheet as an asset that will benefit future periods. To resolve these issues, management must answer four important questions about the acquisition, use, and disposal of each long-term asset (see Exhibit 9.5):

1. How is the cost of the long-term asset determined?
2. How should the expired portion of the cost of the long-term asset be allocated against revenues over time?
3. How should subsequent expenditures, such as repairs and additions, be treated?
4. How should disposal of the long-term asset be recorded?

Management's answers to these questions can be found in the company's annual report under management's discussion and analysis and in the notes to the financial statements.

EXHIBIT 9.5
Issues in Accounting for Long-Term Assets

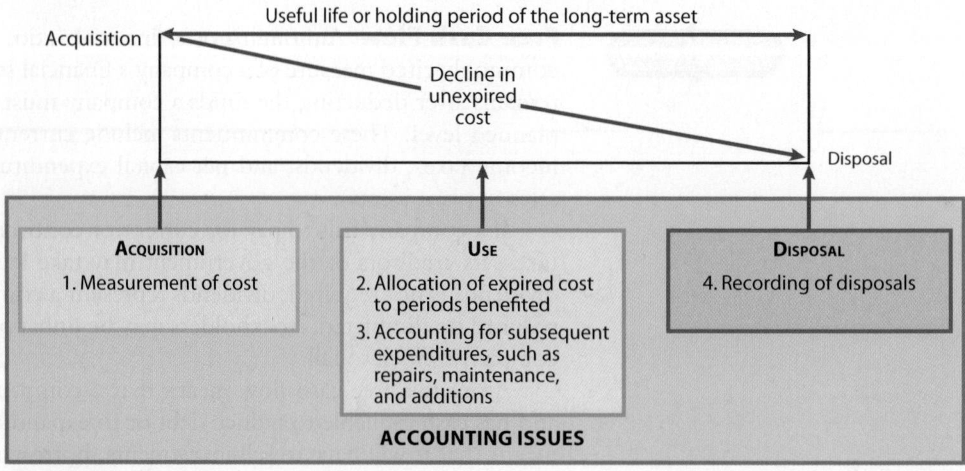

Stop & Apply

In the past year, Himera Company had cash flows from operating activities of $133,000. During the year, it expended $61,000 on property, plant, and equipment; sold property, plant, and equipment for $14,000; and paid dividends of $20,000. Calculate the company's free cash flow. What does the result tell you about the company?

SOLUTION

Net cash flows from operating activities	$133,000
Purchases of property, plant, and equipment	(61,000)
Sales of property, plant, and equipment	14,000
Dividends	(20,000)
Free cash flow	$ 66,000

Himera's operations provide sufficient cash flows to fund its current expansion and its payment of dividends without raising additional capital.

iStock Photo

ACQUISITION COST OF PROPERTY, PLANT, AND EQUIPMENT

LO2 Distinguish between *capital expenditures* and *revenue expenditures* and account for the cost of property, plant, and equipment.

Expenditure refers to a payment or an obligation to make a future payment for an asset, such as a truck, or for a service, such as a repair. Expenditures are classified as capital expenditures or revenue expenditures.

- **Capital expenditure:** An expenditure for the purchase or expansion of a long-term asset. Capital expenditures are recorded in asset accounts because they benefit several future accounting periods.
- **Revenue expenditure:** An expenditure made for ordinary repairs and maintenance needed to keep a long-term asset in good operating condition. For example, trucks, machines, and other equipment require periodic tune-ups and routine repairs. Expenditures of this type are recorded in expense accounts because their benefits are realized in the current period.

Capital expenditures include outlays for plant assets, natural resources, and intangible assets. They also include expenditures for the following:

- **Additions:** Enlargements of a plant asset's physical layout. For example, if a new wing is added to a building, the benefits from the expenditure will be received over several years, and the amount paid should be debited to an asset account.
- **Betterments:** Improvements to a plant asset that do not add to the plant's physical layout. Installation of an air-conditioning system is an example. Because betterments provide benefits over a period of years, their costs should be debited to an asset account.
- **Extraordinary repairs:** Repairs that significantly enhance a plant asset's estimated useful life or residual value. For example, a complete overhaul of a building's heating and cooling system may extend the system's useful life by five years. Extraordinary repairs are typically recorded by reducing the Accumulated Depreciation account; the assumption in doing so is that some of the depreciation previously recorded on the asset has now been eliminated. The effect of the reduction is to increase the asset's carrying value by the cost of the extraordinary repair. The new carrying value should be depreciated over the asset's new estimated useful life.

The distinction between capital and revenue expenditures is important in applying the matching rule, as illustrated in the examples below.

	Asset Incorrectly Recorded as Revenue Expenditure	*Revenue Expenditure Incorrectly Recorded as Asset*
Example	The purchase of a machine that will benefit a company for several years is mistakenly recorded as a revenue expenditure.	A revenue expenditure, such as the routine overhaul of a piece of machinery, is charged to an asset account.
Result	The total cost of the machine becomes an expense on the income statement in the current period. ▼ Current net income will be reported at a lower amount *(understated)*. ▲ In future periods, net income will be reported at a higher amount *(overstated)*.	▼ The expense of the current period will be *understated*. ▲ Current net income will be *overstated* by the same amount. ▼ The net income of future periods will be *understated*.

General Approach to Acquisition Costs

STUDY NOTE: *Expenditures necessary to prepare an asset for its intended use are a cost of the asset.*

The acquisition cost of property, plant, and equipment includes all expenditures reasonable and necessary to get an asset in place and ready for use. For example, the cost of installing and testing a machine is a legitimate cost of acquiring the machine. However, if the machine is damaged during installation, the cost of repairs is an operating expense, not an acquisition cost.

Acquisition cost is easiest to determine when a purchase is made for cash. In that case, the cost of the asset is equal to the cash paid for it plus expenditures for freight, insurance while in transit, installation, and other necessary related costs:

Cost of Asset = Cash + Additional Expenditures (freight, installation, etc.)

Thus, expenditures for freight, insurance while in transit, and installation are included in the cost of the asset because they are necessary if the asset is to function. In accordance with the matching rule, these expenditures are allocated over the asset's useful life rather than charged as expenses in the current period.

Any interest charges incurred in purchasing an asset are not a cost of the asset; they are a cost of borrowing the money to buy the asset and are therefore an operating expense. An exception to this rule is that interest costs incurred during the construction of an asset are properly included as a cost of the asset.[5]

As a matter of practicality, many companies establish policies that define when an expenditure should be recorded as an expense or as an asset. For example, small expenditures for items that qualify as long-term assets may be treated as expenses because the amounts involved are not material in relation to net income. Thus, although a wastebasket may last for years, it would be recorded as supplies expense rather than as a depreciable asset.

Specific Applications

The sections that follow discuss some of the problems in determining the cost of long-term plant assets.

Land The purchase price of land should be debited to the Land account. Other expenditures that should be debited to the Land account include commissions to real estate agents; lawyers' fees; accrued taxes paid by the purchaser; costs of preparing the land to build on, such as the costs of tearing down old buildings and grading the land; and

Focus on International Practices

Depreciation of Buildings Under IFRS

iStock Photo

Under GAAP, the costs of a building and its components, such as a heating and air conditioning system, are usually lumped together as one asset and are depreciated over the life of the building. Under IFRS, however, a building and its components are depreciated on an individual basis. In other words, each component of a building—each property, plant, and equipment asset—is considered to have its own useful life and fair value and is depreciated on that basis. Because many of a building's assets often have shorter useful lives than the building itself, IFRS tend to increase depreciation expense. These standards also require more precise record keeping.

assessments for local improvements, such as putting in streets and sewage systems. The cost of landscaping is usually debited to the Land account because such improvements are relatively permanent. Land is not subject to depreciation because it has an unlimited useful life.

Assume that a company buys land for a new retail operation. The net purchase price is $340,000. The company also pays brokerage fees of $12,000, legal fees of $4,000, $20,000 to have an old building on the site torn down, and $2,000 to have the site graded. It receives $8,000 in salvage from the old building. The cost of the land is $370,000, calculated as follows:

Net purchase price		$340,000
Brokerage fees		12,000
Legal fees		4,000
Tearing down old building	$20,000	
Less salvage	8,000	12,000
Grading		2,000
Total cost		$370,000

When **Dow Chemical** donated the former **Union Carbine** headquarters to the University of Charleston, the university planned to convert it to classrooms and faculty offices. To determine the costs involved in preparing the land for use, accountants estimated the purchase price of the land, brokerage and legal fees involved in the purchase, taxes paid by the purchaser, and landscaping, which would all be debited to the Land account. When these costs were estimated at $10 million, the university decided to implode the building and sell the seven-acre site.

Land Improvements Some improvements to real estate, such as driveways, parking lots, and fences, have a limited life and thus are subject to depreciation. They should be recorded in an account called Land Improvements rather than in the Land account.

Buildings When a company buys a building, the cost includes the purchase price of the building and all repairs and other expenditures required to put the building in usable condition. When a company uses a contractor to construct a building, the cost includes the net contract price plus other expenditures necessary to put the building in usable condition. When a company constructs its own building, the cost includes all reasonable and necessary expenditures. Reasonable and necessary expenditures include the costs of materials, labor, part of the overhead and other indirect costs, architects' fees, insurance during construction, interest on construction loans during the period of construction, lawyers' fees, and building permits. Because buildings have a limited useful life, they are subject to depreciation.

Bob Krist/Corbis

Leasehold Improvements Improvements to leased property that become the property of the lessor (the owner of the property) at the end of the lease are called **leasehold improvements**. For example, a tenant's installation of light fixtures, carpets, or walls would be considered a leasehold improvement. These improvements are usually classified as tangible assets in the property, plant, and equipment section of the balance sheet. Sometimes, they are included in the intangible assets section; the theory in reporting them as intangibles is that because they revert to the lessor at the end of the lease, they are more of a right than a tangible asset. The cost of a leasehold improvement is depreciated or amortized over the remaining term of the lease or the useful life of the improvement, whichever is shorter.

Leasehold improvements are fairly common in large businesses. A study of large companies showed that 22 percent report leasehold improvements.[6] The percentage is likely to be much higher for small businesses because they generally operate in leased premises.

STUDY NOTE: The wiring and plumbing of a dental chair are included in the cost of the asset because they are a necessary cost of preparing the asset for use.

Equipment The cost of equipment includes all expenditures connected with purchasing the equipment and preparing it for use. Among these expenditures are the invoice price less cash discounts; freight, including insurance; excise taxes and tariffs; buying expenses; installation costs; and test runs to ready the equipment for operation. Equipment is subject to depreciation.

Group Purchases Companies sometimes purchase land and other assets for a lump sum. Because land has an unlimited life and is a nondepreciable asset, it must have a separate ledger account, and the lump-sum purchase price must be apportioned between the land and the other assets. Suppose, for example, that a company buys a building and the land on which it is situated for a lump sum of $170,000. The company can apportion the costs by determining what it would have paid for the building and for the land if it had purchased them separately and applying the appropriate percentages to the lump-sum price. Assume that appraisals yield estimates of $20,000 for the land and $180,000 for the building if purchased separately. In that case, 10 percent of the lump-sum price, or $17,000, would be allocated to the land, and 90 percent, or $153,000, would be allocated to the building. The allocation would be as follows:

	Appraisal	*Percentage*		*Apportionment*	
Land	$ 20,000	10%	($20,000 ÷ $200,000)	$ 17,000	($170,000 × 10%)
Building	180,000	90%	($180,000 ÷ $200,000)	153,000	($170,000 × 90%)
Totals	$200,000	100%		$170,000	

Stop & Apply

Match each term on the left with the corresponding action on the right by writing the appropriate letters in the blanks.

_____ 1. Addition
_____ 2. Betterment
_____ 3. Extraordinary repair
_____ 4. Land
_____ 5. Land improvement
_____ 6. Leasehold improvement
_____ 7. Buildings
_____ 8. Equipment
_____ 9. Not a capital expenditure

a. Purchase of a computer
b. Purchase of a lighting system for a parking lot
c. Repainting of an existing building
d. Installation of a new roof that extends an existing building's useful life
e. Construction of a foundation for a new building
f. Erection of a new storage facility at the back of an existing building
g. Installation of partitions and shelves in a leased space
h. Clearing of land in preparation for construction of a new building
i. Installation of an improved heating system in an existing building

SOLUTION
1. f; 2. i; 3. d; 4. h; 5. b; 6. g; 7. e; 8. a; 9. c

iStock Photo

DEPRECIATION

Compute depreciation under the straight-line, production, and declining-balance methods. **LO 3**

As we noted earlier, *depreciation* is the periodic allocation of the cost of a tangible asset (other than land and natural resources) over the asset's estimated useful life. In accounting for depreciation, it is important to keep the following in mind:

- All tangible assets except for land have a limited useful life, and the costs of these assets must be distributed as expenses over the years they benefit. *Physical deterioration* and *obsolescence* are the major factors in limiting a depreciable asset's useful life.
- **Physical deterioration:** The result of use or exposure to the elements, such as wind and sun. Periodic repairs and a sound maintenance policy may keep buildings and equipment in good operating order and prolong their useful lives, but every machine or building must at some point be discarded. Repairs do not eliminate the need for depreciation.
- **Obsolescence:** The process of going out of date. Because of fast-changing technology and fast-changing demands, machinery and even buildings often become obsolete before they wear out.

STUDY NOTE: *A computer may function just as well as it did when purchased four years ago, but because faster and more efficient computers are now available, it is today obsolete.*

Accountants do not distinguish between physical deterioration and obsolescence because they are interested in the length of an asset's useful life, not in what limits its useful life.

- Depreciation refers to the allocation of the cost of a plant asset to the periods that benefit from the asset, not to the asset's physical deterioration or decrease in market value. The term *depreciation* describes the gradual conversion of the cost of the asset into an expense.
- Depreciation is not a process of valuation. Accounting records are not indicators of changing price levels; they are kept in accordance with the cost principle. Because of an advantageous purchase price and market conditions, the value of a building may increase. Nevertheless, because depreciation is a process of allocation, not valuation, depreciation on the building must continue to be recorded. Eventually, the building will wear out or become obsolete regardless of interim fluctuations in market value.

STUDY NOTE: *Depreciation is the allocation of the acquisition cost of a plant asset. Any similarity between carrying value and current market value is pure coincidence.*

Factors in Computing Depreciation

Four factors affect the computation of depreciation:

- **Cost**: As explained earlier, cost is the net purchase price of an asset plus all reasonable and necessary expenditures to get it in place and ready for use.
- **Residual value: Residual value** is the portion of an asset's acquisition cost that a company expects to recover when it disposes of the asset. Other terms used to describe residual value are *salvage value, disposal value*, and *trade-in value.*

STUDY NOTE: *Estimates of residual value and useful life are, at best, educated guesses.*

Focus on Business Practice

How Long Is the Useful Life of an Airplane?

Most airlines depreciate their planes over an estimated useful life of 10 to 20 years. But how long will a properly maintained plane really last? **Western Airlines** paid $3.3 million for a new Boeing 737 in July 1968. More than 78,000 flights and 30 years later, this aircraft was still flying for **Vanguard Airlines**, a no-frills airline. Among the other airlines that have owned this plane are **Piedmont**, **Delta**, and **US Airways**. Virtually every part of the plane has been replaced over the years. **Boeing** believes the plane could theoretically make double the number of flights before it is retired.

The useful lives of many types of assets can be extended indefinitely if the assets are correctly maintained, but proper accounting in accordance with the matching rule requires depreciation over a "reasonable" useful life. Each airline that owned the plane would have accounted for the plane in this way.

iStock Photo

STUDY NOTE: *It is depreciable cost, not acquisition cost, that is allocated over a plant asset's useful life*

- **Depreciable cost: Depreciable cost** is an asset's cost less its residual value. For example, a truck that cost $24,000 and that has a residual value of $6,000 would have a depreciable cost of $18,000. Depreciable cost must be allocated over the useful life of the asset.
- **Estimated useful life: Estimated useful life** is the total number of service units expected from a long-term asset. Service units may be measured in terms of the years an asset is expected to be used, the units it is expected to produce, the miles it is expected to be driven, or similar measures. In computing an asset's estimated useful life, an accountant should consider all relevant information, including past experience with similar assets, the asset's present condition, the company's repair and maintenance policy, and current technological and industry trends.

Depreciation is recorded at the end of an accounting period with an adjusting entry that takes the following form:

A	= L +	SE
−XXX		−XXX

Depreciation Expense—Asset Name	XXX	
Accumulated Depreciation—Asset Name		XXX
To record depreciation for the period		

Methods of Computing Depreciation

Many methods are used to allocate the cost of plant assets to accounting periods through depreciation. Each is appropriate in certain circumstances. The most common methods are the straight-line method, the production method, and an accelerated method known as the declining-balance method.

Straight-Line Method When the **straight-line method** is used to calculate depreciation, the asset's depreciable cost is spread evenly over the estimated useful life of the asset. The straight-line method is based on the assumption that depreciation depends only on the passage of time. The depreciation expense for each period is computed by dividing the depreciable cost (the cost of the depreciating asset less its estimated residual value) by the number of accounting periods in the asset's estimated useful life:

$$\text{Depreciation Expense} = \text{Cost} - \text{Residual Value} \div \text{Estimated Useful Life}$$

The rate of depreciation is the same in each year.

Suppose, for example, that a delivery truck cost $20,000 and has an estimated residual value of $2,000 at the end of its estimated useful life of five years. Under the straight-line method, the annual depreciation would be $3,600, calculated as follows:

$$\text{Depreciation Expense} = \frac{\text{Cost} - \text{Residual Value}}{\text{Estimated Useful Life}} = \frac{\$20{,}000 - \$2{,}000}{5\text{ Years}} = \$3{,}600\text{ per Year}$$

Exhibit 9.6 shows the depreciation schedule for the five years. Note that in addition to annual depreciation's being the same each year, the accumulated depreciation increases uniformly, and the carrying value decreases uniformly until it reaches the estimated residual value.

EXHIBIT 9.6
Depreciation Schedule, Straight-Line Method

	Cost	Annual Depreciation	Accumulated Depreciation	Carrying Value
Date of purchase	$20,000	—	—	$20,000
End of first year	20,000	$3,600	$ 3,600	16,400
End of second year	20,000	3,600	7,200	12,800
End of third year	20,000	3,600	10,800	9,200
End of fourth year	20,000	3,600	14,400	5,600
End of fifth year	20,000	3,600	18,000	2,000

STUDY NOTE: *The production method is appropriate when a company has widely fluctuating rates of production. For example, carpet mills often close during the first two weeks in July but may run double shifts in September. With the production method, depreciation would be in direct relation to a mill's units of output.*

Production Method The **production method** (also called *units of production method*) is based on the assumption that depreciation is solely the result of use and that the passage of time plays no role in the process. If we assume that the delivery truck in the previous example has an estimated useful life of 90,000 miles, the depreciation cost per mile would be determined as follows:

$$\text{Depreciation Expense} = \frac{\text{Cost} - \text{Residual Value}}{\text{Estimated Units of Useful Life}} = \frac{\$20{,}000 - \$2{,}000}{90{,}000} = \$0.20 \text{ per Mile}$$

If the truck were driven 20,000 miles in the first year, 30,000 miles in the second, 10,000 miles in the third, 20,000 miles in the fourth, and 10,000 miles in the fifth, the depreciation schedule for the truck would be as shown in Exhibit 9.7. As you can see, the amount of depreciation each year is directly related to the units of use. The accumulated depreciation increases annually in direct relation to these units, and the carrying value decreases each year until it reaches the estimated residual value.

In considering whether to use the production method, it is important to keep the following points in mind:

- It must be possible to estimate with reasonable accuracy the output of an asset over its useful life.
- The unit used to measure the estimated useful life of an asset must be appropriate for the asset. For example, the number of items produced may be an appropriate measure for one machine, but the number of hours of use may be a better measure for another.

Declining-Balance Method An **accelerated method** of depreciation results in relatively large amounts of depreciation in the early years of an asset's life and smaller amounts in later years. This type of method, which is based on the passage of time, assumes that many plant assets are most efficient when new and so provide the greatest benefits in their first years. It is consistent with the matching rule to allocate more depreciation to an asset in its earlier years than to later ones if the benefits it provides in its early years are greater than those it provides later on.

Under an accelerated method, depreciation charges will be highest in years when revenue generation from the asset is highest. For example, fast-changing technologies often cause equipment to become outdated and lose service value rapidly. In such cases, using an accelerated method is appropriate because it allocates more depreciation to earlier years than to later ones. Another argument in favor of using an accelerated method is that repair expense is likely to increase as an asset ages. Thus, the total of repair and depreciation expense will remain fairly constant over the years. This result naturally assumes that the services received from the asset are roughly equal from year to year.

The **declining-balance method** is the most common accelerated method of depreciation. With this method, depreciation is computed by applying a fixed rate to the carrying value (the declining balance) of a tangible long-term asset. It therefore results in higher depreciation charges in the early years of the asset's life. Though any fixed

EXHIBIT 9.7
Depreciation Schedule, Production Method

	Cost	Miles	Annual Depreciation	Accumulated Depreciation	Carrying Value
Date of purchase	$20,000	—	—	—	$20,000
End of first year	20,000	20,000	$4,000	$ 4,000	16,000
End of second year	20,000	30,000	6,000	10,000	10,000
End of third year	20,000	10,000	2,000	12,000	8,000
End of fourth year	20,000	20,000	4,000	16,000	4,000
End of fifth year	20,000	10,000	2,000	18,000	2,000

rate can be used, the most common rate is a percentage equal to twice the straight-line depreciation percentage. When twice the straight-line rate is used, the method is usually called the **double-declining-balance method**.

In our example of the straight-line method, the delivery truck had an estimated useful life of five years, and the annual depreciation rate for the truck was therefore 20 percent:

$$\text{Annual Depreciation Rate} = \frac{\text{Percent of Useful Life}}{\text{Estimated Useful Life}}$$

$$= \frac{100\%}{5 \text{ Years}}$$

$$= 20\%$$

STUDY NOTE: In the double-declining-balance method, the annual rate for straight-line depreciation is doubled.

Under the double-declining-balance method, the fixed rate would be 40 percent, or "double" the straight-line rate.

$$\text{Annual Depreciation Rate} = 2 \times 20\% = 40\%$$

This fixed rate is applied to the carrying value that remains at the end of each year. With the double-declining-balance method, the depreciation schedule would be as shown in Exhibit 9.8.

STUDY NOTE: The double-declining-balance method is the only method presented here in which the residual value is not deducted before calculating depreciation.

Note that the fixed rate is always applied to the carrying value at the end of the previous year. Depreciation is greatest in the first year and declines each year after that. The depreciation in the last year is limited to the amount necessary to reduce carrying value to residual value.

Comparison of the Three Methods Exhibit 9.9 compares yearly depreciation and carrying value under the three methods. The graph on the left shows yearly depreciation. As you can see, straight-line depreciation is uniform at $3,600 per year over the five-year period. The double-declining-balance method begins at $8,000 and decreases each year to amounts that are less than straight-line (ultimately, $592). The production method does not generate a regular pattern because of the random fluctuation of the depreciation from year to year.

The graph on the right side of Exhibit 9.9 shows the carrying value under the three methods. Each method starts in the same place (cost of $20,000) and ends at the same place (residual value of $2,000). However, the patterns of carrying value during the asset's useful life differ. For instance, the carrying value under the straight-line method is always greater than under the double-declining-balance method, except at the beginning and end of the asset's useful life.

EXHIBIT 9.8
Depreciation Schedule, Double-Declining-Balance Method

	Cost	Annual Depreciation	Accumulated Depreciation	Carrying Value
Date of purchase	$20,000	—	—	$20,000
End of first year	20,000	(40% × $20,000) = $8,000	$ 8,000	12,000
End of second year	20,000	(40% × $12,000) = 4,800	12,800	7,200
End of third year	20,000	(40% × $7,200) = 2,880	15,680	4,320
End of fourth year	20,000	40% × $4,320) = 1,728	17,408	2,592
End of fifth year	20,000	592*	18,000	2,000

*Depreciation is limited to the amount necessary to reduce carrying value to residual value: $2,592 (previous carrying value) – $2,000 (residual value) = $592.

EXHIBIT 9.9
Graphic Comparison of Three Methods of Determining Depreciation

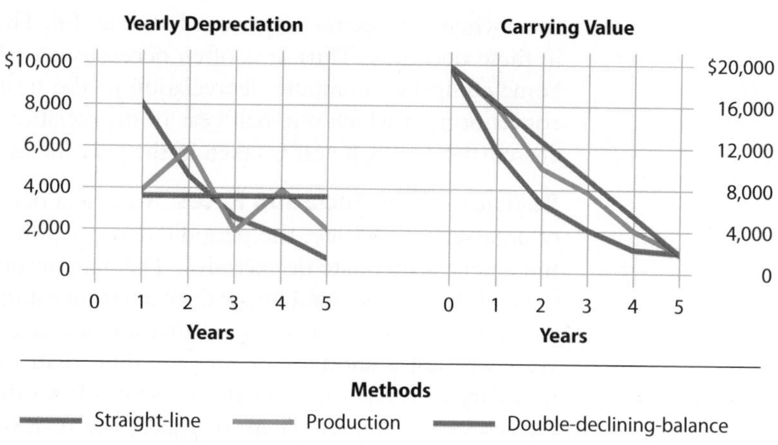

Special Issues in Depreciation

Other issues in depreciating assets include group depreciation, depreciation for partial years, revision of depreciation rates, and accelerated cost recovery for tax purposes.

Group Depreciation The estimated useful life of an asset is the average length of time assets of the same type are expected to last. For example, the average useful life of a particular type of machine may be six years, but some machines in this category may last only two or three years, while others may last eight or nine years or longer. For this reason, and for convenience, large companies group similar assets, such as machines, trucks, and pieces of office equipment, to calculate depreciation. This method, called **group depreciation**, is widely used in all fields of industry and business. A survey of large businesses indicated that 65 percent used group depreciation for all or part of their plant assets.[7]

Depreciation for Partial Years To simplify our examples of depreciation, we have assumed that plant assets were purchased at the beginning or end of an accounting period. Usually, however, businesses buy assets when they are needed and sell or discard

Focus on Business Practice

Accelerated Methods Save Money!

As shown in the graph below, an AICPA study of large companies found that the overwhelming majority used the straight-line method of depreciation for financial reporting. Only about 7 percent used some type of accelerated method, and 3 percent used the production method. However, these figures tend to be misleading about the importance of accelerated depreciation methods, especially when it comes to income taxes. Federal income tax laws allow either the straight-line method or an accelerated method, and for tax purposes, about 75 percent of the companies studied preferred an accelerated method.

Companies use different methods of depreciation for good reason. The straight-line method can be advantageous for financial reporting because it can produce the highest net income, and an accelerated method can be beneficial for tax purposes because it can result in lower income taxes.

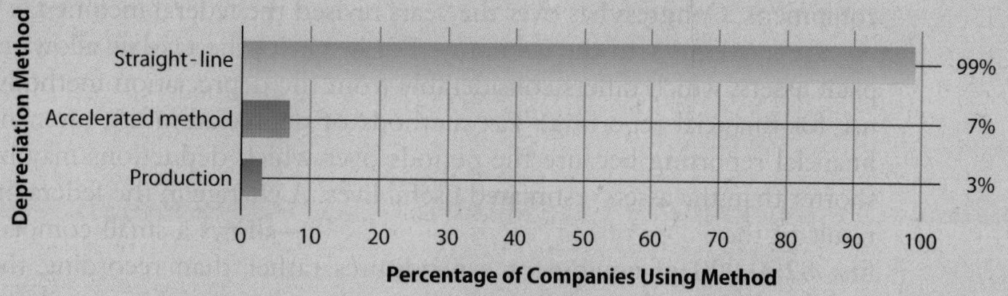

Note: Total percentage exceeds 100 because some companies used different methods for different types of depreciable assets.
Source: "Depreciation Methods Used by 500 Large Companies." Copyright © 2009 by AICPA. Reproduced with permission.

iStock Photo

them when they are no longer needed or useful. The time of year is normally not a factor in these decisions. Thus, it is often necessary to calculate depreciation for partial years. Some companies compute depreciation to the nearest month. Others use the half-year convention, in which one-half year of depreciation is taken in the year the asset is purchased and one-half year is taken in the year the asset is sold.

Revision of Depreciation Rates Because a depreciation rate is based on an estimate of an asset's useful life, the periodic depreciation charge is seldom precise. It is sometimes very inadequate or excessive. This may result from an underestimate or overestimate of the asset's useful life or from a wrong estimate of its residual value. What should a company do when it discovers that a piece of equipment that it has used for several years will last a shorter—or longer—time than originally estimated? Sometimes, it is necessary to revise the estimate of useful life so that the periodic depreciation expense increases or decreases. Then, to reflect the revision, the remaining depreciable cost of the asset is spread over the remaining years of useful life.

With this technique, the annual depreciation expense is increased or decreased to reduce the asset's carrying value to its residual value at the end of its remaining useful life. For example, suppose a delivery truck cost $14,000 and has a residual value of $2,000. At the time of the purchase, the truck was expected to last six years, and it was depreciated on the straight-line basis. However, after two years of intensive use, it is determined that the truck will last only two more years, but its residual value at the end of the two years will still be $2,000. In other words, at the end of the second year, the truck's estimated useful life is reduced from six years to four years. At that time, the asset account and its related accumulated depreciation account would be as follows:

DELIVERY TRUCK			ACCUMULATED DEPRECIATION—DELIVERY TRUCK	
Cost	14,000			
			Depreciation, Year 1	2,000
			Depreciation, Year 2	2,000

The remaining depreciable cost is computed as follows:

Cost	–	Depreciation Already Taken	–	Residual Value	
$14,000	–	$4,000	–	$2,000	= $8,000

The new annual periodic depreciation charge is computed by dividing the remaining depreciable cost of $8,000 by the remaining useful life of two years. Therefore, the new periodic depreciation charge is $4,000. This method of revising depreciation is used widely in industry. It is also supported by *Opinion No. 9* and *Opinion No. 20* of the Accounting Principles Board of the AICPA.

Special Rules for Tax Purposes To encourage businesses to invest in new plant and equipment, Congress has over the years revised the federal income tax law to provide an economic stimulus to the economy. For instance, the tax law allows rapid write-offs of plant assets, which differs considerably from the depreciation methods most companies use for financial reporting. Tax methods of depreciation are often not acceptable for financial reporting because the periods over which deductions may be taken are often shorter than the assets' estimated useful lives. A change in the federal income tax law—a result of the **Economic Stimulus Act of 2008**—allows a small company to expense the first $250,000 of equipment expenditures rather than recording them as assets and depreciating them over their useful lives. Also, for assets that are subject to depreciation, there is a bonus first-year deduction. These rules are quite complex and are the subject of more advanced courses.

Stop & Apply

On January 13, 2010, Louise Company purchased a company car for $47,500. Louise expects the car to last five years or 120,000 miles, with an estimated residual value of $7,500 at the end of that time. During 2011, the car is driven 24,000 miles. Louise's year-end is December 31. Compute the depreciation for 2011 under each of the following methods: (1) straight-line, (2) production, and (3) double-declining-balance. Using the amount computed in (3), prepare the journal entry to record depreciation expense for the second year and show how the company car account would appear on the balance sheet.

SOLUTION

Depreciation computed:

1. Straight-line method: ($47,500 − $7,500) ÷ 5 years = $8,000
2. Production method: ($47,500 − $7,500) ÷ 120,000 miles = $0.33 1/3 per mile

   24,000 miles × $0.33 1/3 = $8,000
3. Double-declining-balance method: 1/5 × 2 = 40%

   Year 1: $47,500 × 0.40 = $19,000

   Year 2: ($47,500 − $19,000) × 0.40 = $11,400

Journal entry:

Depreciation Expense	11,400	
Accumulated Depreciation		11,400
Depreciation of car: ($47,500 − $19,000) × 0.40		
Balance sheet presentation:		
Company car	$47,500	
Less accumulated depreciation	30,400	$17,100

iStock Photo

DISPOSAL OF DEPRECIABLE ASSETS

Account for the disposal of depreciable assets. 

STUDY NOTE: When a company disposes of an asset, it must bring the depreciation up to date and remove all evidence of ownership of the asset, including the contra account Accumulated Depreciation.

When plant assets like plant, buildings, and equipment are no longer useful because they have physically deteriorated or become obsolete, a company can dispose of them by discarding them, selling them for cash, or trading them in on the purchase of a new asset. Regardless of how a company disposes of a plant asset, it must record depreciation expense for the partial year up to the date of disposal. This step is required because the company used the asset until that date and, under the matching rule, the accounting period should receive the proper allocation of depreciation expense.

In the next sections, we show how to record each type of disposal. As our example, we assume that DOT Company buys a machine on January 2, 2010, for $13,000 and plans to depreciate it on a straight-line basis over an estimated useful life of eight years. The machine's residual value at the end of eight years is estimated to be $600. On December 31, 2015, the balances of the relevant accounts are as shown below, and on January 2, 2016, management disposes of the asset.

MACHINERY		ACCUMULATED DEPRECIATION—MACHINERY	
13,000			9,300

Discarded Plant Assets

A plant asset rarely lasts exactly as long as its estimated life. If it lasts longer, it is not depreciated past the point at which its carrying value equals its residual value. The purpose of depreciation is to spread the depreciable cost of an asset over its estimated life. Thus, the total accumulated depreciation should never exceed the total depreciable cost.

If an asset remains in use beyond the end of its estimated life, its cost and accumulated depreciation remain in the ledger accounts. Proper records will thus be available for maintaining control over plant assets. If the residual value is zero, the carrying value of a fully depreciated asset is zero until the asset is disposed of. If such an asset is discarded, no gain or loss results. In our example, however, the discarded equipment has a carrying value of $3,700 at the time of its disposal. The carrying value is computed from the T accounts as machinery of $13,000 less accumulated depreciation of $9,300. A loss equal to the carrying value should be recorded when the machine is discarded, as follows:

A	= L +	SE
+9,300		−3,700
−13,000		

Date	Account	Debit	Credit
2016			
Jan. 2	Accumulated Depreciation—Machinery	9,300	
	Loss on Disposal of Machinery	3,700	
	Machinery		13,000
	Disposal of machine no longer in use		

Gains and losses on disposals of plant assets are classified as other revenues and expenses on the income statement.

Plant Assets Sold for Cash

STUDY NOTE: *When an asset is sold for cash, the gain or loss equals cash received minus the carrying value.*

The entry to record a plant asset sold for cash is similar to the one just illustrated, except that the receipt of cash should also be recorded. The following journal entries show how to record the sale of a machine under three assumptions about the selling price.

Cash Received Equal to Carrying Value Assume that $3,700 cash is received and is exactly equal to the $3,700 carrying value of the machine; therefore, no gain or loss occurs:

A	= L +	SE
+3,700		
+9,300		
−13,000		

Date	Account	Debit	Credit
2016			
Jan. 2	Cash	3,700	
	Accumulated Depreciation—Machinery	9,300	
	Machinery		13,000
	Sale of machine for carrying value; no gain or loss		

Cash Received Less Than Carrying Value Assume that $2,000 cash is received, which is less than the carrying value of $3,700, resulting in a loss of $1,700.

A	= L +	SE
+2,000		−1,700
+9,300		
−13,000		

Date	Account	Debit	Credit
2016			
Jan. 2	Cash	2,000	
	Accumulated Depreciation—Machinery	9,300	
	Loss on Sale of Machinery	1,700	
	Machinery		13,000
	Sale of machine at less than carrying value; loss of $1,700 ($3,700 − $2,000) recorded		

Cash Received More Than Carrying Value Assume that $4,000 cash is received, which exceeds the carrying value of $3,700, resulting in a gain of $300.

A	= L +	SE
+4,000		+300
+9,300		
−13,000		

Date	Account	Debit	Credit
2016			
Jan. 2	Cash	4,000	
	Accumulated Depreciation—Machinery	9,300	
	Machinery		13,000
	Gain on Sale of Machinery		300
	Sale of machine at more than the carrying value; gain of $300 ($4,000 – $3,700) recorded		

Exchanges of Plant Assets

As we have noted, businesses can dispose of plant assets by trading them in on the purchase of other plant assets. Exchanges may involve similar assets, such as an old machine traded in on a newer model, or dissimilar assets, such as a cement mixer traded in on a truck. In either case, the purchase price is reduced by the amount of the trade-in allowance.

Basically, accounting for exchanges of plant assets is similar to accounting for sales of plant assets for cash. If the trade-in allowance is greater than the asset's carrying value, the company realizes a gain. If the allowance is less, it suffers a loss. (Some special rules apply and are addressed in more advanced courses.)

Stop & Apply

Louise Company sold a company car that cost $47,500 and on which $30,400 of accumulated depreciation had been recorded on January 2, the first day of business of the current year. For each of the following assumptions, prepare the journal entry (without explanation) for the disposal. (1) The car was sold for $17,100 cash. (2) The car was sold for $15,000 cash. (3) The car was sold for $20,000 cash.

SOLUTION

	Debit	Credit
(1) Cash	17,100	
Accumulated Depreciation—Company Car	30,400	
Company Car		47,500
(2) Cash	15,000	
Accumulated Depreciation—Company Car	30,400	
Loss on Sale of Company Car	2,100	
Company Car		47,500
(3) Cash	20,000	
Accumulated Depreciation—Company Car	30,400	
Company Car		47,500
Gain on Sale of Company Car		2,900

iStock Photo

NATURAL RESOURCES

LO 5 Identify the issues related to accounting for natural resources and compute depletion.

Natural resources are long-term assets that appear on a balance sheet with descriptive titles like "Timberlands," "Oil and gas reserves," and "Mineral deposits." Their distinguishing characteristic is that they are converted to inventory by cutting, pumping, mining, or other extraction methods.

Natural resources are recorded at acquisition cost, which may include some costs of development. As these resources are extracted and converted to inventory, their asset accounts must be proportionally reduced. For example, the carrying value of oil reserves on the balance sheet is reduced by the proportional cost of the barrels pumped during the period. The original cost of the oil reserves is thus gradually reduced, and depletion is recognized in the amount of the decrease.

Depletion

Depletion refers not only to the exhaustion of a natural resource, but also to the proportional allocation of the cost of a natural resource to the units extracted. The way in which the cost of a natural resource is allocated closely resembles the production method of calculating depreciation. When a natural resource is purchased or developed, the total units that will be available, such as barrels of oil, tons of coal, or board-feet of lumber, must be estimated. The depletion cost per unit is determined by dividing the cost of the natural resource (less residual value, if any) by the estimated number of units available.

For example, suppose a mine was purchased for $3,600,000 and it has an estimated residual value of $600,000 and contains an estimated 3,000,000 tons of coal. The depletion charge per ton of coal is $1, calculated as follows:

$$\text{Depletion Cost per Unit} = \frac{\text{Cost} - \text{Residual Value}}{\text{Estimated Number of Units}}$$

$$\frac{\$3{,}600{,}000 - \$600{,}000}{3{,}000{,}000 \text{ Tons}} = \$1 \text{ per Ton}$$

The amount of the depletion cost for each accounting period is then computed by multiplying the depletion cost per unit by the number of units extracted and sold. Thus, if 230,000 tons of coal are mined and sold during the first year, the depletion charge for the year is $230,000. This charge would be recorded as follows:

A	=	L	+	SE
−230,000				−230,000

Dec. 31	Depletion Expense—Coal Deposits	230,000	
	Accumulated Depletion—Coal Deposits		230,000
	To record depletion of coal mine: $1 per ton for 230,000 tons mined and sold		

On the balance sheet, data for the mine would be presented as follows:

Coal deposits	$3,600,000	
Less accumulated depletion	230,000	$3,370,000

Often, a portion of a natural resource is not sold in the year it is extracted. In this case, only the portion sold in the current year would be recorded as depletion *expense* in the year. The cost of the unsold portion is recorded as inventory.

Depreciation of Related Plant Assets

The extraction of natural resources generally requires special on-site buildings and equipment (e.g., conveyors, drills, and pumps). The useful life of these plant assets may be longer than the estimated time it will take to deplete the resources. However, a company may plan to abandon these assets after all the resources have been extracted because they no longer serve a useful purpose and it is too expensive to move them to another site. In this case, they should be depreciated on the same basis as the depletion.

Environmental laws often require companies to put land back in its original condition after a natural resource has been extracted.

For example, suppose machinery with a useful life of 10 years is installed on an oil field that is expected to be depleted in 8 years. The machinery should be depreciated over the eight-year period using the production method. That way, each year's depreciation will be proportional to the year's depletion. If one-sixth of the oil field's total reserves is pumped in one year, then the depreciation should be one-sixth of the machinery's cost minus the residual value.

If the useful life of a long-term plant asset is less than the expected life of the resource, the shorter life should be used to compute depreciation. In such cases, or when an asset will not be abandoned after all reserves have been depleted, other depreciation methods, such as the straight-line or declining-balance method, are appropriate.

Focus on Business Practice

How Do You Measure What's Underground? With a Good Guess

iStock Photo

Accounting standards require publicly traded energy companies to disclose in their annual reports their production activities, estimates of their proven oil and gas reserves, and estimates of the present value of the future cash flows that those reserves are expected to generate. The figures are not easy to estimate. After all, the reserves are often miles underground or beneath deep water. These figures are therefore considered "supplementary" and not reliable enough to be audited independently. As a result, some companies have overestimated their reserves and thus overestimated their future prospects. Apparently, some managers at **Royal Dutch/Shell Group** were receiving bonuses based on the amount of new reserves added to the annual report. When the company announced that it was reducing its reported reserves by 20 percent, the price of its stock dropped.[8]

Development and Exploration Costs in the Oil and Gas Industry

The costs of exploring and developing oil and gas resources can be accounted for under one of two methods. Under **successful efforts accounting**, the cost of a successful exploration—for example, an exploration that produces an oil well—is a cost of the resource. It should be recorded as an asset and depleted over the resource's estimated life. The cost of an unsuccessful exploration—such as one that produces a dry well—is written off immediately as a loss. Because of these immediate write-offs, successful efforts accounting is considered the more conservative method and is used by most large oil companies.

On the other hand, small, independent oil companies argue that the cost of dry wells is part of the overall cost of the systematic development of an oil field and is thus a part of the cost of producing wells. Under the **full-costing method**, all costs, including the cost of dry wells, are recorded as assets and depleted over the estimated life of the resources. This method tends to improve a company's earnings performance in its early years.

The Financial Accounting Standards Board permits the use of either method.[9]

Stop & Apply

Romero Mining Company paid \$8,800,000 for land containing an estimated 40 million tons of ore. The land without the ore is estimated to be worth \$2,000,000. The company spent \$1,380,000 to erect buildings on the site and \$2,400,000 on installing equipment. The buildings have an estimated useful life of 30 years, and the equipment has an estimated useful life of 10 years. Because of the remote location, neither the buildings nor the equipment has a residual value. The company expects that it can mine all the usable ore in 10 years. During its first year of operation, it mined and sold 2,800,000 tons of ore.

1. Compute the depletion charge per ton.
2. Compute the depletion expense that Romero Mining should record for its first year of operation.
3. Determine the depreciation expense for the year for the buildings, making it proportional to the depletion.
4. Determine the depreciation expense for the year for the equipment under two alternatives: (a) making the expense proportional to the depletion and (b) using the straight-line method.

SOLUTION

1. $\frac{\$8{,}800{,}000 - \$2{,}000{,}000}{40{,}000{,}000 \text{ Tons}} = \$0.17 \text{ per Ton}$
2. 2,800,000 Tons × \$0.17 per Ton = \$476,000
3. $\frac{2{,}800{,}000 \text{ Tons}}{40{,}000{,}000 \text{ Tons}} \times \$1{,}380{,}000 = \$96{,}600$
4. a. $\frac{2{,}800{,}000 \text{ Tons}}{40{,}000{,}000 \text{ Tons}} \times \$2{,}400{,}000 = \$168{,}000$

   b. $\frac{\$2{,}400{,}000}{10 \text{ Years}} \times 1 \text{ Year} = \$240{,}000$

iStock Photo

INTANGIBLE ASSETS

LO 6 Identify the issues related to accounting for intangible assets, including research and development costs and goodwill.

An intangible asset is both long-term and nonphysical. Its value comes from the long-term rights or advantages it affords its owner. Exhibit 9.10 describes the most common types of intangible assets—copyrights, patents, leaseholds, software, noncompete covenants, customer lists, goodwill, trademarks and brand names, and franchises and licenses—and their accounting treatment. Like intangible assets, some current assets—for example, accounts receivable and certain prepaid expenses—have no physical substance, but because they are short-term, they are not classified as intangible assets.

Exhibit 9.11 shows the percentage of companies (out of companies surveyed) that report the various types of intangible assets. For some companies, intangible assets make up a substantial portion of total assets. As noted in this chapter's Decision Point, **Apple Computer**'s goodwill, other acquired intangible assets, and capitalized software costs amounted to $559 million in 2009. How these assets are accounted for has a major effect on Apple's performance. For example, acquired software costs are amortized over three years and amortization expenses for these costs amounted to $25 million in 2009.

EXHIBIT 9.10
Accounting for Intangible Assets

Type	Description	Usual Accounting Treatment
	Subject to Amortization and Annual Impairment Test	
Copyright	An exclusive right granted by the federal government to reproduce and sell literary, musical, and other artistic materials and computer programs for a period of the author's life plus 70 years	Record at acquisition cost and amortize over the asset's useful life, which is often much shorter than its legal life. For example, the cost of paperback rights to a popular novel would typically be amortized over a useful life of two to four years.
Patent	An exclusive right granted by the federal government for a period of 20 years to make a particular product or use a specific process. A design may be granted a patent for 14 years.	The cost of successfully defending a patent in a patent infringement suit is added to the acquisition cost of the patent. Amortize over the asset's useful life, which may be less than its legal life.
Leasehold	A right to occupy land or buildings under a long-term rental contract. For example, if Company A sells or subleases its right to use a retail location to Company B for 10 years in return for one or more rental payments, Company B has purchased a leasehold.	The lessor (Company A) debits Leasehold for the amount of the rental payment and amortizes it over the remaining life of the lease. The lessee (Company B) debits payments to Lease Expense.
Software	Capitalized costs of computer programs developed for sale, lease, or internal use	Record the amount of capitalizable production costs and amortize over the estimated economic life of the product.
Noncompete covenant	A contract limiting the rights of others to compete in a specific industry or line of business for a specified period	Record at acquisition cost and amortize over the contract period.
Customer list	A list of customers or subscribers	Debit Customer Lists for amount paid and amortize over the asset's expected life.
	Subject to Annual Impairment Test Only	
Goodwill	The excess of the amount paid for a business over the fair market value of the business's net assets	Debit Goodwill for the acquisition cost and review impairment annually.
Trademark, Brand name	A registered symbol or name that can be used only by its owner to identify a product or service	Debit Trademark or Brand Name for the acquisition cost and amortize it over a reasonable life.
Franchise, License	A right to an exclusive territory or market or the right to use a formula, technique, process, or design	Debit Franchise or License for the acquisition cost and amortize it over a reasonable life.

EXHIBIT 9.11
Intangible Assets Reported Large Companies

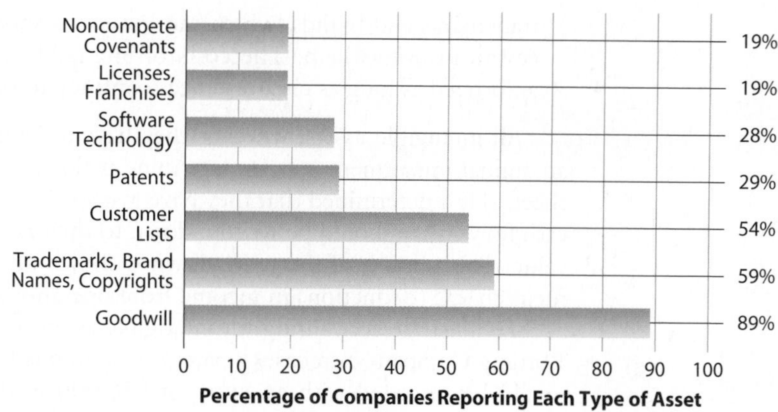

Source: Data from American Institute of Certified Public Accountants, *Accounting Trends & Techniques* (New York: AICPA, 2009).

The purchase of an intangible asset is a special kind of capital expenditure. Such assets are accounted for at acquisition cost—that is, the amount that a company paid for them. Some intangible assets, such as goodwill and trademarks, may be acquired at little or no cost. Even though these assets may have great value and be needed for profitable operations, a company should include them on its balance sheet only if it purchased them from another party at a price established in the marketplace. When a company develops its own intangible assets, it should record the costs of development as expenses. An exception to this is the cost of internally developed computer software after a working prototype of the software has been developed.

Purchased intangible assets are recorded at cost or at fair value when purchased as part of a group of assets. The useful life of an intangible asset is the period over which the asset is expected to contribute to the company's future cash flows. The useful life may be definite or indefinite:[10]

- **Definite useful life:** A *definite useful life* means that the useful life of the asset is subject to a legal limit or can be reasonably estimated. Examples of assets with definite useful lives include patents, copyrights, and leaseholds. The estimated useful lives of these assets are often less than their legal limits. The cost of an intangible asset with a definite useful life should be allocated to expense through periodic amortization over the asset's useful life in much the same way that a building is depreciated.
- **Indefinite useful life:** An *indefinite useful life* means that the useful life of the asset is not limited by legal, regulatory, contractual, competitive, economic, or other factors. This definition does not imply that these assets last forever. Examples can include

Focus on Business Practice

Who's Number One in Brands?

Brands are intangible assets that often do not appear on a company's balance sheet because rather than purchasing them, the company has developed them over time. A recent report attempted to value brands by the discounted present value of future cash flows.[11] According to the report, the 10 most valuable brands in the world were as follows:

Coca-Cola	**Nokia**	**Intel**
IBM	**McDonald's**	**Disney**
Microsoft	**Google**	
GE	**Toyota**	

Coca-Cola's brand was valued at almost $68.7 billion, whereas Disney's brand was valued at $28.4 billion. Where did **Apple Computer** stand? It was number 20 at $15.4 billion, up from number 24 one year before, which reflects the increased brand power from the great success of the iPod, iPhone, and iPad.

iStock Photo

trademarks and brands, which can last for as short or as long as the company is successful in using them. The costs of intangible assets with an indefinite life are not amortized as long as circumstances continue to support an indefinite life.

All intangible assets, whether they have a definite or indefinite life, are subject to an annual impairment test to determine if the assets justify their value on the balance sheet. If it is determined that they have lost some or all of their value in producing future cash flows, they should be written down to their fair value or to zero if they have no fair value. The amount of the write-down is shown on the income statement as an impairment charge (deduction) in income from operations.

To illustrate accounting for intangible assets with limited useful lives, suppose WIT Bottling Company purchases a patent on a unique bottle cap for $36,000. The purchase would be recorded with an entry of $36,000 in the asset account Patents. Although the patent for the bottle cap will last for 20 years, WIT determines that it will sell the product that uses the cap for only six years. Thus, the annual amortization expense is for $6,000 ($36,000 ÷ 6 years). When the expense is recorded, the Patents account is reduced directly by the amount of the amortization expense (in contrast to the treatment of other long-term asset accounts, for which depreciation or depletion is accumulated in separate contra accounts). The entry would be as follows:

A	=	L	+	SE
−6,000				−6,000

Dec. 31	Amortization Expense—Patents	6,000	
	Patents		6,000
	To record amortization of patent		

Research and Development Costs

Most successful companies carry out research and development (R&D) activities, often within a separate department. Among these activities are development of new products, testing of existing and proposed products, and pure research. The costs of these activities are substantial for many companies. As noted in this chapter's Decision Point, **Apple** spent $1.3 billion, or about 3.6 percent of its revenues, on R&D in 2009.[12] R&D costs can be even greater in other high-tech fields like pharmaceuticals. For example, **Abbott Laboratories** recently spent $2.7 billion, or 8.9 percent of its revenues, on R&D.[13]

The Financial Accounting Standards Board requires that all R&D costs be treated as revenue expenditures and charged to expense in the period in which they are incurred.[14] The reasoning behind this requirement is that it is too hard to trace specific costs to specific profitable developments. Also, the costs of research and development are continuous and necessary for the success of a business and so should be treated as current expenses. To support this conclusion, the FASB cited studies showing that 30 to 90 percent of all new products fail and that 75 percent of new-product expenses go to unsuccessful products. Thus, their costs do not represent future benefits.

Focus on International Practices

IFRS R&D Costs Under IFRS

In contrast to GAAP, under which all research and development costs are expensed, IFRS require that research costs be expensed and that development costs be capitalized and amortized. This requires a judgment about what constitutes research and what constitutes development. These differences in accounting treatments—immediate expensing versus amortization over time—can have considerable impact on reported income over many years.

iStock Photo

Computer Software Costs

The costs that companies incur in developing computer software for sale or lease or for their own internal use are considered research and development costs until the product has proved technologically feasible. Thus, costs incurred before that point should be charged to expense as they are incurred. A product is deemed technologically feasible when a detailed working program has been designed. Once that occurs, all software production costs are recorded as assets and are amortized over the software's estimated economic life using the straight-line method.

Capitalized software costs are becoming more prevalent, as shown in Exhibit 9.11 (p. 423). They appear on the balance sheets of 28 percent of the large companies surveyed. In 2009, **Apple**'s capitalized software development costs amounted to $106 million (see the Financial Highlights in the this chapter's Decision Point). If at any time a company cannot expect to realize from the software the amount of the unamortized costs on the balance sheet, the asset should be written down to the amount expected to be realized.[15]

Goodwill

Goodwill means different things to different people. Generally, it refers to a company's good reputation. From an accounting standpoint, goodwill exists when a purchaser pays more for a business than the fair market value of the business's net assets. In other words, the purchaser would pay less if it bought the assets separately. Most businesses are worth more as going concerns than as collections of assets.

When the purchase price of a business is more than the fair market value of its physical assets, the business must have intangible assets. If it does not have patents, copyrights, trademarks, or other identifiable intangible assets of value, the excess payment is assumed to be for goodwill. Goodwill reflects all the factors that allow a company to earn a higher-than-market rate of return on its assets, including customer satisfaction, good management, manufacturing efficiency, the advantages of having a monopoly, good locations, and good employee relations. The payment above and beyond the fair market value of the tangible assets and other specific intangible assets is properly recorded in the Goodwill account.

The FASB requires that purchased goodwill be reported as a separate line item on the balance sheet and that it be reviewed annually for impairment. If the fair value of goodwill is less than its carrying value on the balance sheet, goodwill is considered impaired. In that case, goodwill is reduced to its fair value, and the impairment charge is reported on the income statement. A company can perform the fair value measurement for each reporting unit at any time as long as the measurement date is consistent from year to year.[16]

A company should record goodwill only when it acquires a controlling interest in another business. The amount to be recorded as goodwill can be determined by writing the identifiable net assets up to their fair market values at the time of purchase and subtracting the total from the purchase price. For example, suppose a company pays $11,400,000 to purchase another business.

- If the net assets of the business (total assets – total liabilities) are *fairly valued* at $10,000,000, then the amount of the goodwill is $1,400,000 ($11,400,000 – $10,000,000).
- If the fair market value of the net assets is more or less than $10,000,000, an entry is made in the accounting records to adjust the assets to the fair market value. The goodwill would then represent the difference between the adjusted net assets and the purchase price of $11,400,000.

Stop & Apply

For each of the following intangible assets, indicate (a) if the asset is to be amortized over its useful life or (b) if the asset is not amortized but only subject to an annual impairment test:

1. Goodwill
2. Copyright
3. Brand
4. Patent
5. Trademark

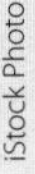

SOLUTION

1. b; 2. a; 3. b; 4. a; 5. b

A look back at ▸ Apple Computer, Inc.

We began the chapter by emphasizing that **Apple**'s success as an innovator and marketer is a result of its wise and steady investments in research and development and long-term assets. In evaluating Apple's performance, investors and creditors look for answers to the following questions:

1. What are Apple's long-term assets?
2. What are its policies in accounting for long-term assets?
3. Does the company generate enough cash flow to finance its continued growth?

Apple's tangible long-term assets include land, buildings, machinery, equipment, and leasehold improvements to its retail stores. Its balance sheet includes goodwill and acquired intangible assets. Because internally developed intangible assets are not recorded as assets, the value of Apple's own brand name is not reflected on the balance sheet. Clearly, however, it far exceeds the value of the intangible assets that are listed.

In accordance with GAAP, Apple's accounting policies include using the straight-line depreciation method for tangible assets, amortizing intangible assets over a reasonable useful life, and expensing research and development costs. In addition, it evaluates its long-term assets for impairment each year to ensure that it is not carrying assets on its balance sheet at amounts that exceed their value.

Free Cash Flow

A good measure of the funds that Apple has available for growth is its free cash flow, which for 2008 and 2009 is calculated as follows:

Free Cash Flow = Net Cash Flows from Operating Activities − Dividends − Purchases of Plant Assets + Sales of Plant Assets

		2009		2008
Free Cash Flow	=	\$10,159 − \$0 − \$1,144 + \$0		\$9,596 − \$0 − \$1,091 + \$0
	=	\$9,015	=	\$8,505

The improvement in Apple's free cash flow in 2009 was due to the success of its iPod and iPhone and excitement about the iPad. The company obviously generated enough cash to finance its continued growth. Its policy of not paying dividends contributes to the amount of cash it has available for this purpose. Although Apple may have sold some plant assets, the amounts were sufficiently immaterial that it did not report them separately.

Review Problem

Comparison of Depreciation Methods **LO 3**

Hubert Building Company purchased a cement mixer on January 2, 2011, for $29,000. The mixer was expected to have a useful life of five years and a residual value of $2,000. The company's engineers estimated that the mixer would have a useful life of 15,000 hours. It was used for 3,000 hours in 2011, 5,250 hours in 2012, 4,500 hours in 2013, 1,500 hours in 2014, and 750 hours in 2015. The company's fiscal year ends on December 31.

Required

1. Compute the depreciation expense and carrying value for each year from 2011 to 2015 using the following methods: (a) straight-line, (b) production, and (c) double-declining-balance.
2. Show the balance sheet presentation for the cement mixer on December 31, 2011. Assume the company uses the straight-line method.
3. What conclusions can you draw from the patterns of yearly depreciation?

ANSWERS TO REVIEW PROBLEM

1. Depreciation computed:

	Depreciation Method	Year	Computation			Depreciation	Carrying Value
a.	Straight-line	2011	$27,000	÷	5	$ 5,400	$23,600
		2012	27,000	÷	5	5,400	18,200
		2013	27,000	÷	5	5,400	12,800
		2014	27,000	÷	5	5,400	7,400
		2015	27,000	÷	5	5,400	2,000
b.	Production	2011	$27,000	x	3,000/15,000	$ 5,400	$23,600
		2012	27,000	x	5,250/15,000	9,450	14,150
		2013	27,000	x	4,500/15,000	8,100	6,050
		2014	27,000	x	1,500/15,000	2,700	3,350
		2015	27,000	x	750/15,000	1,350	2,000
c.	Double-declining-balance	2011	$29,000	x	0.40	$11,600	$17,400
		2012	17,400	x	0.40	6,960	10,440
		2013	10,440	x	0.40	4,176	6,264
		2014	6,264	x	0.40	2,506	3,758
		2015	3,758	–	2,000	1,758*	2,000

* Remaining depreciation to reduce carrying value to residual value ($3,758 – $2,000)

2. Balance sheet presentation on December 31, 2011:

Property, plant, and equipment	
Cement mixer	$29,000
Less accumulated depreciation	5,400
	$23,600

3. The pattern of depreciation for the straight-line method differs significantly from the pattern for the double-declining-balance method. In the earlier years, the amount of depreciation under the double-declining-balance method is significantly greater than the amount under the straight-line method. In the later years, the opposite is true. The carrying value under the straight-line method is greater than the amount under the double-declining-balance method at the end of all years except the fifth year. Depreciation under the production method differs from depreciation under the other methods in that it follows no regular pattern. It varies with the amount of use. Consequently, depreciation is greatest in 2012 and 2013, which are the years of greatest use. Use declined significantly in the last two years.

Stop & Review

LO 1 Define *long-term assets* and explain the management issues related to them.

Long-term assets have a useful life of more than one year, are used in the operation of a business, and are not intended for resale. They can be tangible or intangible. In the former category are land, plant assets, and natural resources. In the latter are patents, trademarks, franchises, and other rights, as well as goodwill. The management issues related to long-term assets include decisions about whether to acquire the assets, how to finance them, and how to account for them.

LO 2 Distinguish between *capital expenditures* and *revenue expenditures* and account for the cost of property, plant, and equipment.

Capital expenditures are recorded as assets, whereas revenue expenditures are recorded as expenses of the current period. Capital expenditures include not only outlays for plant assets, natural resources, and intangible assets, but also expenditures for additions, betterments, and extraordinary repairs that increase an asset's residual value or extend its useful life. Revenue expenditures are made for ordinary repairs and maintenance. The error of classifying a capital expenditure as a revenue expenditure, or vice versa, has an important effect on net income.

The acquisition cost of property, plant, and equipment includes all expenditures reasonable and necessary to get the asset in place and ready for use. Among these expenditures are purchase price, installation cost, freight charges, and insurance during transit. The acquisition cost of a plant asset is allocated over the asset's useful life.

LO 3 Compute depreciation under the straight-line, production, and declining-balance methods.

Depreciation—the periodic allocation of the cost of a plant asset over its estimated useful life—is commonly computed by using the straight-line method, the production method, or an accelerated method. The straight-line method is related directly to the passage of time, whereas the production method is related directly to use or output. An accelerated method, which results in relatively large amounts of depreciation in earlier years and reduced amounts in later years, is based on the assumption that plant assets provide greater economic benefits in their earlier years than in later ones. The most common accelerated method is the declining-balance method.

LO 4 Account for the disposal of depreciable assets.

A company can dispose of a long-term plant asset by discarding or selling it or exchanging it for another asset. Regardless of the way in which a company disposes of such an asset, it must record depreciation up to the date of disposal. To do so, it must remove the carrying value from the asset account and the depreciation to date from the accumulated depreciation account. When a company sells a depreciable long-term asset at a price that differs from its carrying value, it should report the gain or loss on its income statement. In recording exchanges of similar plant assets, a gain or loss may arise.

LO 5 Identify the issues related to accounting for natural resources and compute depletion.

Natural resources are depletable assets that are converted to inventory by cutting, pumping, mining, or other forms of extraction. They are recorded at cost as long-term assets. As natural resources are sold, their costs are allocated as expenses through depletion charges. The depletion charge is based on the ratio of the resource extracted to the total estimated resource. A major issue related to this subject is accounting for oil and gas reserves.

LO 6 Identify the issues related to accounting for intangible assets, including research and development costs and goodwill.

The purchase of an intangible asset should be treated as a capital expenditure and recorded at acquisition cost. All intangible assets are subject to annual tests for impairment of value. Intangible assets with a definite life are also amortized annually. The FASB requires that research and development costs be treated as revenue expenditures and charged as expenses in the periods of expenditure. Software costs are treated as research and development costs and expensed until a feasible working program is developed, after which time the costs may be capitalized and amortized over a reasonable estimated life. Goodwill is the excess of the amount paid for a business over the fair market value of the net assets and is usually related to the business's superior earning potential. It should be recorded only when a company purchases an entire business, and it should be reviewed annually for possible impairment.

Key Terms

Accelerated method 413 (LO3)
Additions 407 (LO2)
Amortization 402 (LO1)
Asset impairment 403 (LO1)
Betterments 407 (LO2)
Brand name 422 (LO6)
Capital expenditure 407 (LO2)
Carrying value 403 (LO1)
Copyright 422 (LO6)
Customer list 422 (LO6)
Declining-balance method 413 (LO3)
Depletion 402 (LO1)
Depreciable cost 412 (LO3)
Depreciation 402 (LO1)
Double-declining-balance method 414 (LO3)
Economic Stimulus Act of 2008 416 (LO3)
Estimated useful life 412 (LO3)
Expenditure 407 (LO2)
Extraordinary repairs 407 (LO2)
Franchise 422 (LO6)
Free cash flow 405 (LO1)
Full-costing method 421 (LO5)
Goodwill 422 (LO6)
Group depreciation 415 (LO3)
Intangible assets 402 (LO1)
Leasehold 422 (LO6)
Leasehold improvements 410 (LO2)
License 422 (LO6)
Long-term assets 402 (LO1)
Natural resources 402 (LO1)
Noncompete covenant 422 (LO6)
Obsolescence 411 (LO3)
Patent 422 (LO6)
Physical deterioration 411 (LO3)
Production method 413 (LO3)
Residual value 411 (LO3)
Revenue expenditure 407 (LO2)
Software 422 (LO6)
Straight-line method 412 (LO3)
Successful efforts accounting 421 (LO5)
Tangible assets 402 (LO1)
Trademark 422 (LO6)

Chapter Assignments Building Your Basic Knowledge and Skills

Short Exercises

LO 1

Management Issues

SE 1. Indicate whether each of the following actions is primarily related to (a) acquiring long-term assets, (b) evaluating the adequacy of financing of long-term assets, or (c) applying the matching rule to long-term assets.

1. Deciding between common stock and long-term notes for the raising of funds
2. Relating the acquisition cost of a long-term asset to the cash flows generated by the asset

3. Determining how long an asset will benefit the company
4. Deciding to use cash flows from operations to purchase long-term assets
5. Determining how much an asset will sell for when it is no longer useful to the company
6. Calculating free cash flow

LO 1 **Free Cash Flow**

SE 2. Sun Corporation had cash flows from operating activities during the past year of $194,000. During the year, the company expended $25,000 for dividends; expended $158,000 for property, plant, and equipment; and sold property, plant, and equipment for $12,000. Calculate the company's free cash flow. What does the result tell you about the company?

LO 2 **Determining Cost of Long-Term Assets**

SE 3. Randy Auto purchased a neighboring lot for a new building and parking lot. Indicate whether each of the following expenditures is properly charged to (a) Land, (b) Land Improvements, or (c) Buildings.

1. Paving costs
2. Architects' fee for building design
3. Cost of clearing the property
4. Cost of the property
5. Building construction costs
6. Lights around the property
7. Building permit
8. Interest on the construction loan

LO 2 **Group Purchase**

SE 4. Lian Company purchased property with a warehouse and parking lot for $1,500,000. An appraiser valued the components of the property if purchased separately as follows:

Land	$ 400,000
Land improvements	200,000
Building	1,000,000
Total	$1,600,000

Determine the cost to be assigned to each component.

LO 2 **Group Purchase**

SE 5. Chris Deli purchased property with a building and parking lot for $1,700,000. An appraiser valued the components of the property if purchased separately as follows:

Land	$ 600,000
Land improvements	300,000
Building	900,000
Total	$1,800,000

Determine the cost to be assigned to each component.

LO 3 **Straight-Line Method**

SE 6. Dora's Fitness Center purchased a new step machine for $8,250. The apparatus is expected to last four years and have a residual value of $750. What will the depreciation expense be for each year under the straight-line method?

LO 3 **Production Method**

SE 7. Assume that the step machine in **SE 6** has an estimated useful life of 8,000 hours and was used for 2,400 hours in year 1, 2,000 hours in year 2, 2,200 hours in year 3, and 1,400 hours in year 4. How much would depreciation expense be in each year?

LO 3 **Double-Declining-Balance Method**

SE 8. Assume that the step machine in **SE 6** is depreciated using the double-declining-balance method. How much would depreciation expense be in each year?

LO 3 **Double-Declining-Balance Method**

SE 9. Park Company purchased a recycle processor for $11,200. It has an estimated useful life of four years and an estimated residual value of $1,200. Compute the depreciation charge for each of the four years using the double-declining-balance method.

LO 4 **Disposal of Plant Assets: No Trade-In**

SE 10. Alarico Printing owned a piece of equipment that cost $16,200 and on which it had recorded $9,000 of accumulated depreciation. The company disposed of the equipment on January 2, the first day of business of the current year.

1. Calculate the carrying value of the equipment.
2. Calculate the gain or loss on the disposal under each of the following assumptions:
   a. The equipment was discarded as having no value.
   b. The equipment was sold for $3,000 cash.
   c. The equipment was sold for $8,000 cash.

LO 4 **Disposal of Plant Assets: No Trade-In**

SE 11. Rola Manufacturing owned a piece of equipment that cost $24,300 and on which it had recorded $13,500 of accumulated depreciation. The company disposed of the equipment on January 2, the first day of business of the current year.

1. Calculate the carrying value of the equipment.
2. Calculate the gain or loss on the disposal under each of the following assumptions:
   a. The equipment was discarded as having no value.
   b. The equipment was sold for $4,500 cash.
   c. The equipment was sold for $12,000 cash.

LO 5 **Natural Resources**

SE 12. Wiert Company purchased land containing an estimated 8,000,000 tons of iron ore for $24,000,000. The land will be worth $3,600,000 without the ore after eight years of active mining. Although the equipment needed for the mining will have a useful life of 20 years, it is not expected to be usable and will have no value after the mining on this site is complete. Compute the depletion charge per ton and the amount of depletion expense for the first year of operation, assuming that 900,000 tons of ore are mined and sold. Also, compute the first-year depreciation on the mining equipment using the production method, assuming a cost of $28,800,000 with no residual value.

LO 5 **Natural Resources**

SE 13. Narda Company purchased land containing an estimated 4,000,000 tons of ore for $16,000,000. The land will be worth $2,400,000 without the ore after eight years of active mining. Although the equipment needed for the mining will have a useful life of 20 years, it is not expected to be usable and will have no value after the mining on this site is complete. Compute the depletion charge per ton and the amount of depletion expense for the first year of operation, assuming that 600,000 tons of ore are mined and sold. Also, compute the first-year depreciation on the mining equipment using the production method, assuming a cost of $19,200,000 with no residual value.

LO 6 **Intangible Assets: Computer Software**

SE 14. Danya Company has created a new software application for PCs. Its costs during research and development were $250,000. Its costs after the working program was developed were $175,000. Although the company's copyright may be amortized over 40 years, management believes that the product will be viable for only five years. How should the costs be accounted for? At what value will the software appear on the balance sheet after one year?

LO 6 **Intangible Assets: Computer Software**

SE 15. Rocco Company has created new apps for mobile phones. Its costs during research and development were $375,000. Its costs after the working program was developed were $264,000. Although the company's copyright may be amortized over 40 years, management believes that the product will be viable for only six years. How should the costs be accounted for? At what value will the apps appear on the balance sheet after one year?

Exercises

LO 1, 2, 3 **Discussion Questions**

E 1. Develop a brief answer for each of the following questions:

1. Is carrying value ever the same as market value? Explain your answer.
2. What major advantage does a company that has positive free cash flow have over a company that has negative free cash flow?
3. What incentive does a company have to allocate more of a group purchase price to land than to building?
4. Which depreciation method would best reflect the risk of obsolescence from rapid technological changes?

LO 4, 5, 6 **Discussion Questions**

E 2. Develop a brief answer for each of the following questions:

1. When would the disposal of a long-term asset result in no gain or loss?
2. When would annual depletion not equal depletion expense?
3. Why would a firm amortize a patent over fewer years than the patent's life?
4. Why would a company spend millions of dollars on goodwill?

LO 1 **Management Issues**

E 3. Indicate whether each of the following actions is primarily related to (a) acquiring long-term assets, (b) evaluating the financing of long-term assets, or (c) applying the matching rule to long-term assets.

1. Deciding to use the production method of depreciation
2. Allocating costs on a group purchase
3. Determining the total units a machine will produce
4. Deciding to borrow funds to purchase equipment
5. Estimating the savings a new machine will produce and comparing that amount to cost
6. Examining the trend of free cash flow over several years
7. Deciding whether to rent or buy a piece of equipment

LO 1 **Purchase Decision—Present Value Analysis**

E 4. Management is considering the purchase of a new machine for a cost of $24,000. It is estimated that the machine will generate positive net cash flows of $6,000 per year for five years and will have a disposal price at the end of that time of $2,000. Assuming an interest rate of 9 percent, determine if management should purchase the machine. Use Tables 1 and 2 in Appendix B to determine the net present value of the new machine.

LO 1 **Free Cash Flow**

E 5. Zedek Corporation had cash flows from operating activities during the past year of $216,000. During the year, the company expended $462,000 for property, plant, and equipment; sold property, plant, and equipment for $54,000; and paid dividends of $50,000. Calculate the company's free cash flow. What does the result tell you about the company?

LO 2 **Special Types of Capital Expenditures**

E 6. Tell whether each of the following transactions related to an office building is a revenue expenditure (RE) or a capital expenditure (CE). In addition, indicate whether each transaction is an ordinary repair (OR), an extraordinary repair (ER), an addition (A), a betterment (B), or none of these (N).

1. The hallways and ceilings in the building are repainted at a cost of $8,145.
2. The hallways, which have tile floors, are carpeted at a cost of $31,000.
3. A new wing is added to the building at a cost of $123,378.
4. Furniture is purchased for the entrance to the building at a cost of $17,489.
5. The air-conditioning system is overhauled at a cost of $26,215. The overhaul extends the useful life of the air-conditioning system by 10 years.
6. A cleaning firm is paid $185 per week to clean the newly installed carpets.

LO 2 **Determining Cost of Long-Term Assets**

E 7. Kay Manufacturing purchased land next to its factory to be used as a parking lot. The expenditures incurred by the company were as follows: purchase price, $300,000; broker's fees, $24,000; title search and other fees, $2,200; demolition of a cottage on the property, $8,000; general grading of property, $4,200; paving parking lots, $40,000; lighting for parking lots, $32,000; and signs for parking lots, $6,400. Determine the amounts that should be debited to the Land account and the Land Improvements account.

LO 2 **Group Purchase**

E 8. Daria Dzik purchased a car wash for $240,000. If purchased separately, the land would have cost $60,000, the building $135,000, and the equipment $105,000. Determine the amount that should be recorded in the new business's records for land, building, and equipment.

Cost of Long-Term Asset and Depreciation

LO 2, 3 **E 9.** Ebra Allen purchased a used tractor for $70,000. Before the tractor could be used, it required new tires, which cost $4,400, and an overhaul, which cost $5,600. Its first tank of fuel cost $300. The tractor is expected to last six years and have a residual value of $8,000. Determine the cost and depreciable cost of the tractor and calculate the first year's depreciation under the straight-line method.

LO 3 **Depreciation Methods**

E 10. On January 13, 2011, Silverio Oil Company purchased a drilling truck for $45,000. Silverio expects the truck to last five years or 200,000 miles, with an estimated residual value of $7,500 at the end of that time. During 2012, the truck is driven 48,000 miles. Silverio's year-end is December 31. Compute the depreciation for 2012 under the following methods: (1) straight-line, (2) production, and (3) double-declining-balance. Using the amount computed in **3**, prepare the journal entry to record depreciation expense for the second year and show how the Drilling Truck account would appear on the balance sheet.

LO 3 **Double-Declining-Balance Method**

E 11. Prevention Alarm Systems Company purchased a computer for $1,120. It has an estimated useful life of four years and an estimated residual value of $120. Compute the depreciation charge for each of the four years using the double-declining-balance method.

LO 3 **Revision of Depreciation Rates**

E 12. Mercy Hospital purchased a special x-ray machine. The machine, which cost $623,120, was expected to last 10 years, with an estimated residual value of $63,120. After two years of operation (and depreciation charges using the straight-line method), it became evident that the x-ray machine would last a total of only seven years. The estimated residual value, however, would remain the same. Given this information, determine the new depreciation charge for the third year on the basis of the revised estimated useful life.

LO 4 **Disposal of Plant Assets**

E 13. A piece of equipment that cost $16,200 and on which $9,000 of accumulated depreciation had been recorded was disposed of on January 2, the first day of business of the current year. For each of the following assumptions, compute the gain or loss on the disposal.

1. The equipment was discarded as having no value.
2. The equipment was sold for $3,000 cash.
3. The equipment was sold for $9,000 cash.

LO 4 **Disposal of Plant Assets**

E 14. Lila Company purchased a computer on January 2, 2011, at a cost of $2,500. The computer is expected to have a useful life of five years and a residual value of $250. Assume that the computer is disposed of on July 1, 2014. Record the depreciation expense for half a year and the disposal under the straight-line method under each of the following assumptions:

1. The computer is discarded.
2. The computer is sold for $400.
3. The computer is sold for $1,100.

LO 5 **Natural Resource Depletion and Depreciation of Related Plant Assets**

E 15. Okram Company purchased land containing an estimated 5.0 million tons of ore for a cost of $8,800,000. The land without the ore is estimated to be worth $600,000. During its first year of operation, the company mined and sold 750,000 tons of ore. Compute the depletion charge per ton. Compute the depletion expense that Okram should record for the year.

LO 6 **Copyrights and Trademarks**

E 16. The following exercise is about amortizing copyrights and trademarks.

1. King Publishing Company purchased the copyright to a basic computer textbook for $40,000. The usual life of a textbook is about four years. However, the copyright will remain in effect for another 50 years. Calculate the annual amortization of the copyright.
2. Cooby Company purchased a trademark from a well-known supermarket for $320,000.

LO 6 **Accounting for a Patent**

E 17. At the beginning of the fiscal year, Natalie Company purchased for $1,030,000 a patent that applies to the manufacture of a unique tamperproof lid for medicine bottles. Natalie incurred legal costs of $450,000 in successfully defending use of the lid by a competitor. Natalie estimated that the patent would be valuable for at least 10 years. During the first two years of operations, Natalie successfully marketed the lid. At the beginning of the third year, a study appeared in a consumer magazine showing that children could in fact remove the lid. As a result, all orders for the lids were canceled, and the patent was rendered worthless.

Prepare journal entries to record the following: (a) purchase of the patent; (b) successful defense of the patent; (c) amortization expense for the first year; and (d) write-off of the patent as worthless.

Problems

LO 1, 2 **Identification of Long-Term Assets Terminology**

CASH FLOW

P 1. Listed below are common terms associated with long-term assets:

a. Tangible assets
b. Natural resources
c. Intangible assets
d. Additions
e. Betterments
f. Extraordinary repair
g. Depreciation
h. Depletion
i. Amortization
j. Revenue expenditure
k. Free cash flow

REQUIRED

1. For each of the following statements, identify the term on the preceding page with which the statement is associated. (If two terms apply, choose the one that is most closely associated.)
   1. Periodic cost associated with intangible assets
   2. Cost of constructing a new wing on a building
   3. A measure of funds available for expansion
   4. A group of assets encompassing property, plant, and equipment
   5. Cost associated with enhancing a building but not expanding it
   6. Periodic cost associated with tangible assets
   7. A group of assets that gain their value from contracts or rights
   8. Cost of normal repairs to a building
   9. Assets whose value derives from what can be extracted from them
   10. Periodic cost associated with natural resources
   11. Cost of a repair that extends the useful life of a building

USER INSIGHT ▶

2. Assuming the company uses cash for all its expenditures, which of the items listed above would you expect to see on the income statement? Which ones would not result in an outlay of cash?

LO 2

Determining Cost of Assets

✔ Totals: Land, $213,706; Land Improvements, $83,520; Buildings, $420,680; Machinery, $633,070; Expense, $9,140

P 2. Lake Company was formed on January 1, 2011, and began constructing a new plant. At the end of 2011, its auditor discovered that all expenditures involving long-term assets had been debited to an account called Fixed Assets. An analysis of the Fixed Assets account, which had a year-end balance of $1,329,866, disclosed that it contained the following items:

Cost of land	$ 160,300
Surveying costs	2,050
Transfer of title and other fees required by the county	460
Broker's fees for land	10,572
Attorney's fees associated with land acquisition	3,524
Cost of removing timber from land	24,800
Cost of grading land	2,100
Cost of digging building foundation	17,550
Architect's fee for building and land improvements (80 percent building)	33,600
Cost of building construction	357,500
Cost of sidewalks	5,700
Cost of parking lots	27,200
Cost of lighting for grounds	40,150
Cost of landscaping	5,900
Cost of machinery	496,500
Shipping cost on machinery	27,650
Cost of installing machinery	88,100
Cost of testing machinery	10,800
Cost of changes in building to comply with safety regulations pertaining to machinery	6,270
Cost of repairing building that was damaged in the installation of machinery	4,450
Cost of medical bill for injury received by employee while installing machinery	1,280
Cost of water damage to building during heavy rains prior to opening the plant for operation	3,410
Account balance	$1,329,866

Lake Company sold the timber it cleared from the land to a firewood dealer for $3,500. This amount was credited to Miscellaneous Income.

During the construction period, two of Lake's supervisors worked part-time on the construction project. A portion of their total annual salaries of $45,000 should be allocated to parts the project based on the amount of time spent. They spent two months on the purchase and preparation of the land, six months on the construction of the building (approximately one-sixth of which was devoted to improvements on the grounds), and one month on machinery installation. When the plant began operation on October 1, the supervisors returned to their regular duties. Their salaries were debited to Factory Salaries Expense.

REQUIRED

1. Prepare a schedule with the following column headings: Land, Land Improvements, Buildings, Machinery, and Expense. Place each of the above expenditures in the appropriate column. Negative amounts should be shown in parentheses. Total the columns.

USER INSIGHT ▶

2. What impact does the classification of the items among several accounts have on evaluating the profitability performance of the company?

LO 3, 4

Comparison of Depreciation Methods

✔ Depreciation, year 3: a. $20,000; b. $32,000; c. $11,250

P 3. Modern Designs, Inc., purchased a computerized blueprint printer that will assist in the design and display of plans for factory layouts. The cost of the printer was $90,000, and its expected useful life is four years. The company can probably sell the printer for $10,000 at the end of four years. The printer is expected to last 12,000 hours. It was used 2,400 hours in year 1, 3,600 hours in year 2, 4,800 hours in year 3, and 1,200 hours in year 4.

REQUIRED

1. Compute the annual depreciation and carrying value for the new blueprint printer for each of the four years (round to the nearest dollar where necessary) under each of the following methods: (a) straight-line, (b) production, and (c) double-declining-balance.
2. If the printer is sold for $48,000 after year 2, what would be the gain or loss under each method?

USER INSIGHT ▶

3. What conclusions can you draw from the patterns of yearly depreciation and carrying value in requirement 1? Do the three methods differ in their impact on profitability? Do they differ in their effect on the company's operating cash flows? Explain.

LO 3, 4

Comparison of Depreciation Methods

✔ Depreciation, year 3: a. $217,000; b. $325,500; c. $213,630

P 4. Miles Construction Company purchased a new crane for $1,442,000 at the beginning of year 1. The crane has an estimated residual value of $140,000 and an estimated useful life of six years. The crane is expected to last 20,000 hours. It was used 3,600 hours in year 1, 4,000 in year 2, 5,000 in year 3, 3,000 in year 4, 2,400 in year 5, and 2,000 in year 6.

REQUIRED

1. Compute the annual depreciation and carrying value for the new crane for each of the six years (round to the nearest dollar where necessary) under each of the following methods: (a) straight-line, (b) production, and (c) double-declining-balance.
2. If the crane is sold for $1,000,000 after year 3, what would be the amount of gain or loss under each method? (*Note:* Round depreciation rate to two decimal places.)

USER INSIGHT ▶

3. Do the three methods differ in their effect on the company's profitability? Do they differ in their effect on the company's operating cash flows? Explain.

LO 5

Natural Resource Depletion and Depreciation of Related Plant Assets

CASH FLOW

✔ Depletion expense: $288,000

P 5. Kantor Mining Company purchased land containing an estimated 10 million tons of ore for a cost of $4,400,000. The land without the ore is estimated to be worth $800,000. The company expects that all the usable ore can be mined in 10 years. Buildings costing $400,000 with an estimated useful life of 30 years were erected on the site. Equipment costing $480,000 with an estimated useful life of 10 years was installed. Because of the remote location, neither the buildings nor the equipment has an estimated residual value. During its first year of operation, the company mined and sold 800,000 tons of ore.

REQUIRED

1. Compute the depletion charge per ton.
2. Compute the depletion expense that should be recorded for the year.
3. Determine the depreciation expense for the year for the buildings, making it proportional to the depletion.
4. Determine the depreciation expense for the year for the equipment under two alternatives: (a) making the expense proportional to the depletion and (b) using the straight-line method.
5. USER INSIGHT ▶ Suppose the company mined and sold 1,000,000 tons of ore (instead of 800,000) during the first year. Would the change in the results in requirements 2 or 3 affect earnings or cash flows? Explain.

Alternate Problems

LO 2

Determining Cost of Assets

✔ Totals: Land, $724,500; Land Improvements, $142,800; Building, $1,396,900; Equipment, $209,200

P 6. Pappas Computers constructed a new training center in 2011. You have been hired to manage the training center. A review of the accounting records shows the following expenditures debited to an asset account called Training Center:

Attorney's fee, land acquisition	$ 35,200
Cost of land	597,000
Architect's fee, building design	102,000
Building	1,025,000
Parking lot and sidewalk	135,600
Electrical wiring, building	168,000
Landscaping	55,000
Cost of surveying land	8,900
Training equipment, tables, and chairs	136,400
Installation of training equipment	65,600
Cost of grading the land	14,000
Cost of changes in building to soundproof rooms	58,700
Total account balance	$2,401,400

An employee of Pappas Computers worked full-time overseeing the construction project. He spent two months on the purchase and preparation of the site, six months on the construction, one month on land improvements, and one month on equipment installation and training room furniture purchase and setup. His salary of $72,000 during these 10 months was charged to Administrative Expense. The training center was placed in operation on November 1.

REQUIRED

1. Prepare a schedule with the following four column (account) headings: Land, Land Improvements, Building, and Equipment. Place each of the above expenditures in the appropriate column. Total the columns.
2. USER INSIGHT ▶ What impact does the classification of the items among several accounts have on evaluating the profitability performance of the company?

LO 3, 4

Comparison of Depreciation Methods

CASH FLOW

✔ Depreciation, year 3: a. $82,500; b. $66,000; c. $45,000

P 7. Champ Manufacturing Company purchased a robot for $360,000 at the beginning of year 1. The robot has an estimated useful life of four years and an estimated residual value of $30,000. The robot, which should last 20,000 hours, was operated 6,000 hours in year 1; 8,000 hours in year 2; 4,000 hours in year 3; and 2,000 hours in year 4.

REQUIRED

1. Compute the annual depreciation and carrying value for the robot for each year assuming the following depreciation methods: (a) straight-line, (b) production, and (c) double-declining-balance.
2. If the robot is sold for $375,000 after year 2, what would be the amount of gain or loss under each method?

USER INSIGHT ▶ 3. What conclusions can you draw from the patterns of yearly depreciation and carrying value in requirement 1? Do the three methods differ in their effect on the company's profitability? Do they differ in their effect on the company's operating cash flows? Explain.

LO 5

Natural Resource Depletion and Depreciation of Related Plant Assets

✔ Depletion expense: $121,500

P 8. Szot Company purchased land containing an estimated 10 million tons of ore for a cost of $3,300,000. The land without the ore is estimated to be worth $600,000. The company expects that all the usable ore can be mined in 10 years. Buildings costing $300,000 with an estimated useful life of 20 years were erected on the site. Equipment costing $360,000 with an estimated useful life of 10 years was installed. Because of the remote location, neither the buildings nor the equipment has an estimated residual value. During its first year of operation, the company mined and sold 450,000 tons of ore.

REQUIRED

1. Compute the depletion charge per ton.
2. Compute the depletion expense that Szot should record for the year.
3. Determine the depreciation expense for the year for the buildings, making it proportional to the depletion.
4. Determine the depreciation expense for the year for the equipment under two alternatives: (a) making the expense proportional to the depletion and (b) using the straight-line method.

USER INSIGHT ▶ 5. Suppose the company mined and sold 250,000 tons of ore (instead of 450,000) during the first year. Would the change in the results in requirement 2 or 3 affect earnings or cash flows? Explain.

LO 3, 4

Comparison of Depreciation Methods

✔ Depreciation, year 3: a. $93,000; b. $129,167; c. $74,160

P 9. Diego Corporation purchased a new truck for $515,000 at the beginning of year 1. The truck has an estimated residual value of $50,000 and an estimated useful life of five years. The truck is expected to last 18,000 hours. It was used 3,600 hours in year 1, 4,000 in year 2, 5,000 in year 3, 3,000 in year 4, and 2,400 in year 5.

REQUIRED

1. Compute the annual depreciation and carrying value for the new truck for each of the five years (round to the nearest dollar where necessary) under each of the following methods: (a) straight-line, (b) production, and (c) double-declining-balance.
2. If the truck is sold for $300,000 after year 3, what would be the amount of gain or loss under each method?

USER INSIGHT ▶ 3. Do the three methods differ in their effect on the company's profitability? Do they differ in their effect on the company's operating cash flows? Explain.

Cases

LO 1

Conceptual Understanding: Effect of Change in Estimates

C 1. The airline industry was hit particularly hard after the 9/11 attacks on the World Trade Center in 2001. In 2002, **Southwest Airlines**, one of the healthier airline companies, decided to lengthen the useful lives of its aircraft from 22 to 27 years. Shortly thereafter, following Southwest's lead, other airlines made the same move.[17] What advantage, if any, did the airlines gain by making this change in estimate? Would it have changed earnings or cash flows, and if it did, would the change have been favorable or negative?

Some people argue that the useful lives and depreciation of airplanes are irrelevant. They claim that because of the extensive maintenance and testing that airline companies are required by law to perform, the planes theoretically can be in service for an indefinite future period. What is wrong with this argument?

LO 1

Conceptual Understanding: Impairment Test

C 2. An annual report of **Costco Wholesale Corporation**, the large discount company, contained the following statement:

> The Company periodically evaluates long-lived assets for impairment when . . . circumstances occur that may indicate the carrying amount of the asset group . . . may not be fully recoverable.[18]

What does the concept of impairment mean in accounting? What effect does impairment have on profitability and cash flows? Why would the concept of impairment be referred to as a conservative accounting approach?

LO 3

Conceptual Understanding: Accounting Policies

C 3. IBM, the large computer equipment and services company, stated in one of its annual reports that "[p]lant, rental machines and other property are carried at cost and depreciated over their estimated useful lives using the straight-line method."[19] What estimates are necessary to carry out this policy? What factors should be considered in making each of the estimates?

LO 6

Interpreting Financial Reports: Brands

C 4. Hilton Hotels Corporation and **Marriott International** provide hospitality services. Hilton Hotels' well-known brands include Hilton, Doubletree, Conrad Hotels, Hampton Inn, Hampton Inns & Suits, Embassy Suites Hotels, Hilton Grand Vacations, Hilton Garden Inn, Waldorf-Astoria Collection, and Homewood Suites by Hilton. Marriott also owns or manages properties with recognizable brand names, such as Marriott Hotels & Resorts, Ritz-Carlton Hotel Company and Destination Club, Marriott ExecuStay, Marriott Executive Apartments, Marriott Vacation Club, SpringHill Suits by Marriott, Renaissance Hotels & Resorts, JW Marriott Hotels & Resorts, EDITION Hotels, Autograph Collection, Courtyard by Marriott, Residence Inn by Marriott, Fairfield Inn & Suites by Marriott, TownePlace Suites by Marriott, and Marriott Conference Centers.

On its balance sheet, Hilton Hotels Corporation includes brands of $6.4 billion, or 17 percent of total assets. Marriott International, however, does not list brands among its intangible assets.[20] The value of the brands was more than justified when the Blackstone Group purchased the company for $20 billion more than the company's net tangible assets.[21] What principles of accounting for intangibles require Hilton to record brands as an asset while Marriott does not? How do these differences in accounting for brands generally affect the net income and return on assets of these two competitors?

LO 1, 2, 3, 6

Annual Report Case: Long-Term Assets

C 5. To answer the following questions, refer to the **CVS** annual report in the Supplement to Chapter 1. Examine the balance sheets, as well as the summary of significant accounting policies on property and equipment in the notes to the financial statements.

1. What percentage of total assets in 2009 was property and equipment, net? Identify the major categories of CVS's property and equipment. Which types of property and equipment are most significant? What are leasehold improvements? How significant are these items, and what are their effects on CVS's earnings?
2. What method of depreciation does CVS use? How long does management estimate its buildings will last as compared with furniture and equipment? What does this say about the company's need to remodel its stores?
3. How does the company determine if it has impaired assets?

LO 1

Comparison Analysis: Long-Term Assets and Free Cash Flows

C 6. To complete the assignments listed below, refer to the **CVS** annual report and the financial statements of **Southwest Airlines Co.** in the Supplement to Chapter 1.

1. Prepare a table that shows the net amount each company spent on property and equipment (from the statement of cash flows), the net amount of its property and equipment (from the balance sheet), and the percentage of net amount spent to the net amount of property and equipment for each of the past two years. In which company did the amount of property and equipment grow more rapidly?
2. Calculate free cash flow for both companies for the past two years. What conclusions can you draw about each company's need to raise funds from debt and equity and its ability to grow?

LO 2

Ethical Dilemma: Ethics and Allocation of Acquisition Costs

C 7. Hamlin Company has purchased land and a warehouse for $18,000,000. The warehouse is expected to last 20 years and to have a residual value equal to 10 percent of its cost. The chief financial officer (CFO) and the controller are discussing the allocation of the purchase price. The CFO believes that the largest amount possible should be assigned to the land because that would improve reported net income in the future. Depreciation expense would be lower because land is not depreciated. He suggests allocating one-third, or $6,000,000, of the cost to the land. This would result in depreciation expense each year of $540,000 [($12,000,000 − $1,200,000) ÷ 20 years].

The controller disagrees. She argues that the smallest amount possible, say one-fifth of the purchase price, should be allocated to the land because the depreciation of the warehouse, which is tax-deductible, would be greater and thus reduce income taxes. Under this plan, annual depreciation would be $648,000 [($14,400,000 − $1,440,000) ÷ 20 years]. The annual tax savings at a 30 percent tax rate is $32,400 [($648,000 − $540,000) × 0.30].

How would each decision affect the company's cash flows? Ethically, how should the purchase cost be allocated? Who would be affected by the decision?

LO 1

Decision Analysis Using Excel: Purchase Decision and Time Value of Money

C 8. Morning Machine Works has obtained a contract from the government to manufacture special parts for a new military aircraft. The parts are to be delivered over the next five years, and the company will be paid as the parts are delivered.

To make the parts, Morning Machine Works will have to purchase new equipment. Two types are available. Type A is conventional equipment that can be put into service immediately; it requires an immediate cash investment of $1,000,000 and will produce enough parts to provide net cash receipts of $340,000 in each of the five years specified in the contract. Type B requires one year to be put into service but is more efficient than Type A. The company can purchase Type B by signing a two-year non-interest-bearing note for $1,346,000. Type B is projected to produce net cash receipts of zero in year 1, $500,000 in year 2, $600,000 in year 3, $600,000 in year 4, and $200,000 in year 5.

Morning Machine Works will not be able to use either type of equipment on other contracts, and neither type will have any useful life remaining at the end of the contract. The company currently pays an interest rate of 16 percent to borrow money.

1. What is the present value of the investment required for each type of equipment? (Use Table 1 in Appendix B.)
2. Compute the net present value of each type of equipment based on your answer to **1** and the present value of the net cash receipts projected to be received. (Use Tables 1 and 2 in Appendix B.)
3. Write a memorandum to the board of directors recommending the best option for Morning Machine Works. Explain your reasoning and include your answers to **1** and **2** as attachments.

CHAPTER 10

DECISION POINT
A User's Focus McDonald's Corporation

McDonald's, the world's largest restaurant chain, passed a milestone in 2004 when it earned more revenues in Europe than in the United States. To finance its continued global expansion, the company raises funds by issuing both debt and capital stock. As you can see in its Financial Highlights, McDonald's relies heavily on debt financing. In 2009, its total long-term liabilities were 94 percent of total stockholders' equity, and its total current and long-term liabilities amounted to over 115 percent of stockholders' equity. McDonald's long-term debt includes bonds and notes payable. Among its other long-term obligations are numerous leases on real estate and employee pension and health plans.[1]

MCDONALD'S FINANCIAL HIGHLIGHTS
(in millions)

	2009	2008
Total current liabilities	$ 2,988.7	$ 2,537.9
Long-term debt	$10,560.3	$10,186.0
Other long-term liabilities	1,363.1	1,410.1
Deferred income taxes	1,278.9	944.9
Total long-term liabilities	$13,202.3	$12,541.0
Total stockholders' equity	$14,033.9	$13,382.6
Total liabilities and stockholders' equity	$30,224.9	$28,461.5

Questions

1. *What are McDonald's most important long-term debts?*
2. *What are its considerations in deciding to take on long-term debt?*
3. *How does one evaluate whether a company has too much debt?*

Mary Kate Denny/PhotoEdit

Long-Term Liabilities

LEARNING OBJECTIVES

LO 1 Identify the management issues related to long-term debt. (pp. 444–452)

LO 2 Describe the features of a bond issue and the major characteristics of bonds. (pp. 452–455)

LO 3 Record bonds issued at face value and at a discount or premium. (pp. 455–457)

LO 4 Use present values to determine the value of bonds. (pp. 457–459)

LO 5 Amortize bond discounts and bond premiums using the straight-line and effective interest methods. (pp. 459–467)

LO 6 Account for the retirement of bonds and the conversion of bonds into stock. (pp. 468–469)

Long-term liabilities can be an attractive means of financing the expansion of a business. By incurring long-term debt to fund growth, a company may be able to earn a return that exceeds the interest it pays on the debt. When it does, it increases earnings for stockholders—that is, return on equity. Many companies reward top managers with bonuses for improving return on equity. This incentive provides a temptation to incur too much debt, which increases a company's financial risk. Thus, in deciding on an appropriate level of debt, as in so many other management issues, ethics is a major concern.

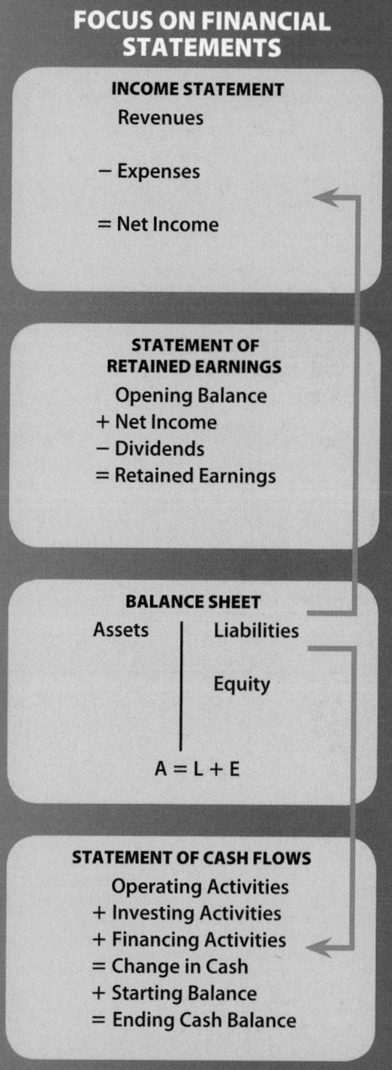

FOCUS ON FINANCIAL STATEMENTS

INCOME STATEMENT
Revenues
− Expenses
= Net Income

STATEMENT OF RETAINED EARNINGS
Opening Balance
+ Net Income
− Dividends
= Retained Earnings

BALANCE SHEET
Assets | Liabilities
Equity
A = L + E

STATEMENT OF CASH FLOWS
Operating Activities
+ Investing Activities
+ Financing Activities
= Change in Cash
+ Starting Balance
= Ending Cash Balance

Interest on long-term liabilities on the balance sheet is an expense on the income statement. Borrowing/repaying long-term liabilities affects the statement of cash flows.

MANAGEMENT ISSUES RELATED TO LONG-TERM DEBT FINANCING

LO 1 Identify the management issues related to long-term debt.

Profitable operations and short-term credit seldom provide sufficient cash for a growing business. Growth usually requires investment in long-term assets and in research and development and other activities that will produce income in future years. To finance these assets and activities, a company needs funds that will be available for long periods. Two key sources of long-term funds are the issuance of capital stock and the incurrence of long-term debt. The management issues related to long-term debt financing are whether to take on long-term debt, how much long-term debt to carry, and what types of long-term debt to incur.

Deciding to Issue Long-Term Debt

A key decision for management is whether to rely solely on stockholders' equity—capital stock issued and retained earnings—for long-term funds or to rely partially on long-term debt. Some companies, such as **Microsoft** and **Apple Computer**, do not issue long-term debt, but like **McDonald's**, most companies find it useful to do so.

Because long-term debt must be paid at maturity and because it usually requires periodic payments of interest, issuing common stock has two advantages over issuing long-term debt:

- ***Permanent financing:*** Common stock does not have to be paid back.
- ***Dividend payout optional:*** Dividends on common stock are normally paid only if the company earns sufficient income.

Issuing long-term debt, however, does have the following advantages over issuing common stock:

- ***Stockholder control:*** When a corporation issues long-term debt, common stockholders do not relinquish any of their control over the company because bondholders and other creditors do not have voting rights. In contrast, when a corporation issues additional shares of common stock, the votes of the new stockholders may force current stockholders and management to give up some control.
- ***Tax advantage:*** The interest on debt is tax-deductible, whereas dividends on common stock are not. For example, if a corporation pays $100,000 in interest and its income tax rate is 30 percent, its net cost will be $70,000 because it will save $30,000 on income taxes. To pay $100,000 in dividends on common stock, the corporation would have to earn $142,857 before income taxes [($100,000 ÷ (1 − 0.30)].
- ***Financial leverage:*** If a corporation earns more from the funds it raises by incurring long-term debt than it pays in interest on the debt, the excess will increase its earnings for the stockholders. This concept is called **financial leverage**, or *trading on equity*. For example, if a company earns 10 percent on a $1,000,000 investment financed by long-term 8 percent notes, it will earn $20,000 before income taxes ($100,000 − $80,000).

Despite these advantages, debt financing is not always in a company's best interest. It may entail the following:

- ***Financial risk:*** A high level of debt exposes a company to financial risk. A company whose plans for earnings do not pan out, whose operations are subject to the ups and downs of the economy, or whose cash flow is weak may be unable to pay the principal amount of its debt at the maturity date or even to make periodic interest payments. Creditors can then force the company into bankruptcy—something that has occurred often in the heavily debt-financed airline industry. **TWA**, **Continental Airlines**, and **United Airlines** filed for bankruptcy protection because they could not make payments on their long-term debt and other liabilities. (While in bankruptcy, they restructured their debt and interest payments: TWA sold off its assets, Continental survived, and United subsequently came out of bankruptcy. The latter two airlines have since merged.)

- ***Negative financial leverage:*** Financial leverage can work against a company if the earnings from its investments do not exceed its interest payments. For example, many small retail companies failed in recent years because they relied too heavily on debt financing before developing sufficient resources to ensure their survival.

Evaluating Long-Term Debt

Financial leverage—using long-term debt to fund investments or operations that increase return on equity—is advantageous as long as a company is able to make timely interest payments and repay the debt at maturity. Because failure to do so can force a company into bankruptcy, companies must assess the financial risk involved. Financial risk is measured by the debt to equity ratio and the interest coverage ratio.

Financial Ratio: Debt to Equity Ratio To assess how much debt to carry, managers compute the **debt to equity ratio**, which, as noted earlier in the text, shows the amount of debt a company carries in relation to its stockholders' equity. The higher this ratio, the greater the company's financial risk. Using data from **McDonald's** Financial Highlights, we can compute its debt to equity ratio in 2009 as shown below (in millions).

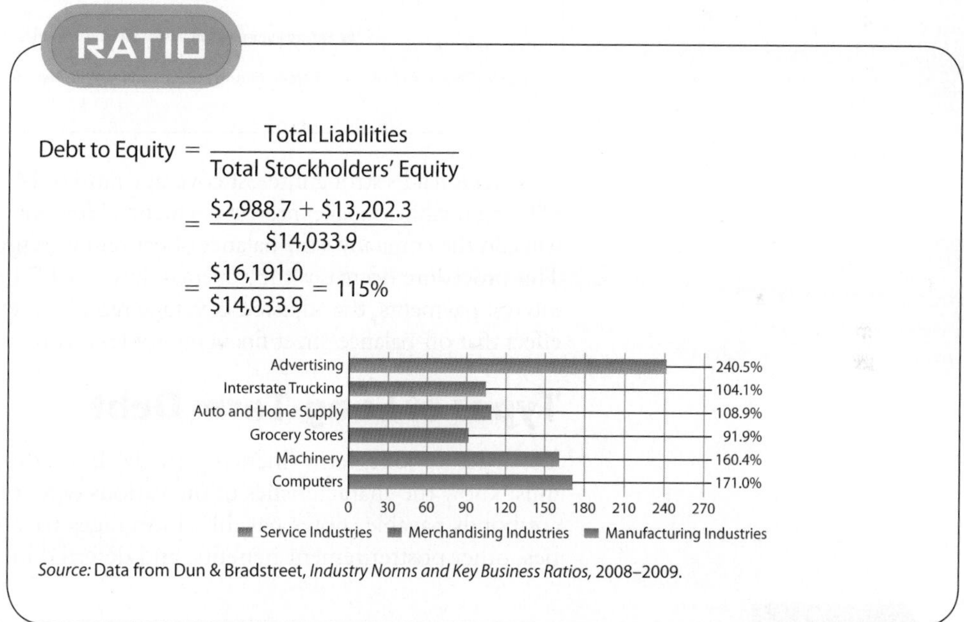

RATIO

$$\text{Debt to Equity} = \frac{\text{Total Liabilities}}{\text{Total Stockholders' Equity}}$$

$$= \frac{\$2{,}988.7 + \$13{,}202.3}{\$14{,}033.9}$$

$$= \frac{\$16{,}191.0}{\$14{,}033.9} = 115\%$$

Source: Data from Dun & Bradstreet, *Industry Norms and Key Business Ratios,* 2008–2009.

McDonald's debt to equity ratio of 115 percent is not large compared with the range of percentages (91.9 to 240.5 percent) shown in the graph of averages for selected industries presented above. However, it does not tell the whole story. McDonald's also has long-term leases on property at more than 13,850 locations, but it structures these leases in such a way that they do not appear as liabilities on its balance sheet. This practice is called **off-balance-sheet financing** and, as used by McDonald's, is entirely legal. The leases are, however, long-term commitments of cash payments and so have the effect of long-term liabilities. McDonald's total commitment for its leases, which are generally for 20 years, is $10,717.5 million.[2] If we add the discounted present value of these lease obligations to McDonald's balance sheet debt, it brings the total debt to about $20,000 million.

Financial Ratio: Interest Coverage Ratio The **interest coverage ratio** measures the degree of protection a company has from default on interest payments. The lower this ratio, the greater the financial risk.

Most analysts want to see an interest coverage ratio of at least 3 or 4 times. Lower interest coverage would mean the company is at risk from a downturn in the economy. McDonald's 2009 annual report shows that the company had income before taxes of $6,487.0 million and interest expense of $473.2 million. Using these figures, we can compute McDonald's interest coverage ratio as follows:

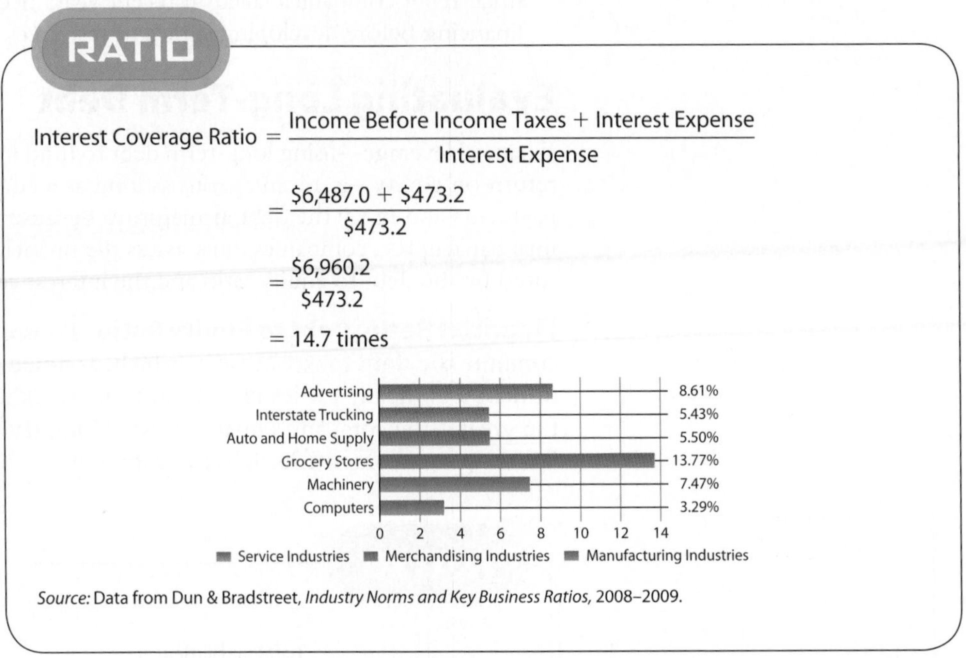

RATIO
Interest Coverage Ratio = Income Before Income Taxes + Interest Expense / Interest Expense
= $6,487.0 + $473.2 / $473.2
= $6,960.2 / $473.2
= 14.7 times
Advertising 8.61%
Interstate Trucking 5.43%
Auto and Home Supply 5.50%
Grocery Stores 13.77%
Machinery 7.47%
Computers 3.29%
0 2 4 6 8 10 12 14
Service Industries
Merchandising Industries
Manufacturing Industries
Source: Data from Dun & Bradstreet, Industry Norms and Key Business Ratios, 2008–2009.

McDonald's strong interest coverage ratio of 14.7 times shows that it was in no danger of being unable to make interest payments. However, in computing this ratio, management will add the company's off-balance-sheet rent expense of $1,301.70 to its interest expense. This procedure decreases the coverage ratio to 4.7 times. Although still adequate to cover interest payments, the adjusted coverage ratio is far less robust, which shows the significant effect that off-balance-sheet financing for leases can have on a company's financial situation.

Types of Long-Term Debt

To structure long-term financing to the best advantage of their companies, managers must know the characteristics of the various types of long-term debt. The most common are bonds payable, notes payable, mortgages payable, long-term leases, pension liabilities, other postretirement benefits, and deferred income taxes.

Focus on Business Practice

How Does Debt Affect a Company's Ability to Borrow?

Credit ratings by agencies like **Standard & Poor's (S&P)** reflect the fact that the greater a company's debt, the greater its financial risk. S&P rates companies from AAA (best) to CCC (worst) based on various factors, including a company's debt to equity ratio, as shown in the table below.

Rating	AAA	AA	A	BBB	BB	B	CCC
Debt to Equity Ratio*	4.5%	34.1%	42.9%	47.9%	59.8%	76.0%	75.7%

*Averages of companies with similar ratings. Ratings also take into effect other factors such as the companies' profitability, interest coverage, and stability.

These ratings affect not only how much a company can borrow, but also what the interest will cost. The lower its rating, the more a company must pay in interest, and vice versa.

For a company in a heavily debt-laden industry such as the auto industry, a change in credit rating can mean millions of dollars. For instance, when S&P lowered **General Motors'** credit ratings to "junk status" (i.e., BB), it meant that GM had to pay 1 or more percentage points in additional interest. On GM's $291 billion debt, this amounted to about $2–3 billion.[3] S&P proved to be correct in its downgrade, as GM subsequently went bankrupt and had to be bailed out by the federal government. **McDonald's** solid credit is reflected in an A rating.

iStock Photo

Bonds Payable Long-term bonds are the most common type of long-term debt. They can have many different characteristics, including the amount of interest, whether the company can elect to repay them before their maturity date, and whether they can be converted to common stock. We cover bonds in detail in later sections of this chapter.

Notes Payable Long-term notes payable, those that come due in more than one year, are also very common. They differ from bonds mainly in the way the contract with the creditor is structured. A long-term note is a promissory note that represents a loan from a bank or another creditor, whereas a bond is a more complex financial instrument that usually involves debt to many creditors. Analysts often do not distinguish between long-term notes and bonds because they have similar effects on the financial statements.

Mortgages Payable A **mortgage** is a long-term debt secured by real property. It is usually paid in equal monthly installments. Each monthly payment includes interest on the debt and a reduction in the debt. Exhibit 10.1 shows the first three monthly payments on a $100,000, 12 percent mortgage.

EXHIBIT 10.1
Monthly Payment Schedule on a $100,000, 12 Percent Mortgage

	A	B	C	D	E
Payment Date	Unpaid Balance at Beginning of Period	Monthly Payment	Interest for 1 Month at 1% on Unpaid Balance* (1% × A)	Reduction in Debt (B − C)	Unpaid Balance at End of Period (A − D)
June 1					$100,000
July 1	$100,000	$1,600	$1,000	$600	99,400
Aug. 1	99,400	1,600	994	606	98,794
Sept. 1	98,794	1,600	988	612	98,182

*Rounded to the nearest dollar.

Mortgage Payment The mortgage was obtained on June 1, and the monthly payments are $1,600.

Analysis: The journal entry to record the mortgage payments

▼ *decreases* Mortgage Payable with a debit of $600,
▲ *increases* Mortgage Interest Expense with a debit of $1,000, and
▼ *decreases* Cash with a credit of $1,600.

A	=	L	+	SE
−1,600		−600		−1,000

Journal Entry:

July 1	Mortgage Payable	600	
	Mortgage Interest Expense	1,000	
	Cash		1,600
	Made monthly mortgage payment		

Comment: Notice from the entry and from Exhibit 10.1 that the July 1 payment represents the following:

- Interest expense: $100,000 × 0.12 × 1/12 = $1,000
- Reduction in debt: $1,600 − $1,000 = $600

Therefore, the July payment reduces the unpaid balance to $99,400. August's interest expense is slightly less than July's because of the decrease in the debt.

Long-Term Leases A company can obtain a plant or equipment asset in three ways:

- ***By borrowing money and buying the asset:*** When a company uses this method, it records the asset and liability at the amount paid, and the asset is subject to periodic depreciation.
- ***By renting the asset on a short-term lease:*** When a company uses this method, the risks of ownership of the asset remain with the lessor, and the lease is shorter than the asset's useful life. This type of agreement is called an **operating lease**. Payments on operating leases are properly treated as rent expense.

Capital leases are long-term leases that resemble a purchase or sale on installment. At the end of a capital lease, ownership transfers to the lessee. Some common examples of plant assets that fall under this category are heavy machinery or equipment and real estate.

- ***By obtaining the asset on a long-term lease:*** This is one of the fastest-growing ways of financing plant assets in the United States today. A long-term lease on a plant asset has several advantages. It requires no immediate cash payment, the rental payment is deducted in full for tax purposes, and it costs less than a short-term lease. Acquiring the use of plant assets under long-term leases does create several accounting challenges, however.

Capital Leases: Long-term leases may be carefully structured, as they are by **McDonald's**, so that they can be accounted for as operating leases. Accounting standards require, however, that a long-term lease be treated as a **capital lease** when it meets the following conditions:

- It cannot be canceled.
- Its duration is about the same as the useful life of the asset.
- It stipulates that the lessee has the option to buy the asset at a nominal price at the end of the lease.

A capital lease is thus more like a purchase or sale on installment than a rental. The lessee in a capital lease should record an asset, depreciation on the asset, and a long-term liability equal to the present value of the total lease payments during the lease term.[4] Much like a mortgage payment, each lease payment consists partly of interest expense and partly of repayment of debt.

Suppose, for example, that Karma Manufacturing Company enters into a long-term lease for a machine. The lease terms call for an annual payment of $8,000 for six years, which approximates the useful life of the machine. At the end of the lease period, the title to the machine passes to Karma. This lease is clearly a capital lease and should be recorded as an asset and a liability. Present value techniques can be used to place a value on the asset and on the corresponding liability in a capital lease.

STUDY NOTE: *A capital lease is in substance an installment purchase, and the leased asset and related liability must be recognized at their present value.*

Capital Lease Recognition Suppose Karma's interest cost on the unpaid part of its obligation is 16 percent. Using the factor for 16 percent and six periods in Table 2 in Appendix B, we can compute the present value of the lease payments as follows:

Periodic Payment × Factor = Present Value

$8,000 × 3.685 = $29,480

$29,480 ÷ 6 years = $4,913

Analysis: The journal entry to record the lease

▲ *increases* the asset Capital Lease Equipment with a debit and

▲ *increases* the liability Capital Lease Obligations with a credit.

A	=	L	+	SE
+29,480		+29,480		

Journal Entry:

	Debit	Credit
Capital Lease Equipment	29,480	
Capital Lease Obligations		29,480
To record capital lease on machinery		

Comment: Capital Lease Equipment is classified as a long-term asset. Capital Lease Obligations is classified as a long-term liability.

Depreciation Recorded Each year, Karma must record depreciation on the leased asset. Straight-line depreciation, a six-year life, and no residual value is assumed.

Analysis: The journal entry to record depreciation

▲ *increases* Depreciation Expense, Capital Lease Equipment with a debit and

▲ *increases* the contra-asset account Accumulated Depreciation, Capital Lease Equipment with a credit.

Adivin/iStockphoto

A	=	L	+	SE
−4,913				−4,913

Journal Entry:

Depreciation Expense, Capital Lease Equipment	4,913	
Accumulated Depreciation, Capital Lease Equipment		4,913
To record depreciation expense on capital lease		

Comment: The interest expense for each year is computed by multiplying the interest rate (16 percent) by the amount of the remaining lease obligation. Exhibit 10.2 shows these calculations.

EXHIBIT 10.2
Payment Schedule on a 16 Percent Capital Lease

Year	A Lease Payment	B Interest (16%) on Unpaid Obligation* (D × 16%)	C Reduction of Lease Obligation (A − B)	D Balance of Lease Obligation (D − C)
Beginning				$29,480
1	$ 8,000	$ 4,717	$ 3,283	26,197
2	8,000	4,192	3,808	22,389
3	8,000	3,582	4,418	17,971
4	8,000	2,875	5,125	12,846
5	8,000	2,055	5,945	6,901
6	8,000	1,099†	6,901	—
	$48,000	$18,520	$29,480	

*Rounded to the nearest dollar.

†The last year's interest equals $1,099 ($8,000 − $6,901); it does not exactly equal $1,104 $\left(\$6,901 \times \frac{16}{100} \times 1\right)$ because of the cumulative effect of rounding.

Lease Payment Refer to the data in Exhibit 10.2.

Analysis: The journal entry to record the first lease payment

▲ *increases* Interest Expense with a debit,
▼ *decreases* Capital Lease Obligations with credit, and
▼ *decreases* Cash with a credit.

A	=	L	+	SE
−8,000		−3,283		−4,717

Journal Entry:

Interest Expense (Column B)	4,717	
Capital Lease Obligations (Column C)	3,283	
Cash (Column A)		8,000
Made payment on capital lease		

Comment: This example suggests why companies are motivated to engage in off-balance-sheet financing for leases. By structuring long-term leases so that they can be accounted for as operating leases, companies avoid recording them on the balance sheet as long-term assets and liabilities. This practice, which is legal and which **McDonald's**

Focus on International Practices

IFRS Recording Liabilities and Assets Will Not Look the Same Under IFRS

Under U.S. GAAP, most leases are accounted for as operating expenses. Current lease payments are generally recorded as operating expenses, and future lease obligations appear as described in the footnotes to the financial statements. Under International Financial Reporting Standards (IFRS), lease obligations are recorded at fair value as a liability, and the related debit is recorded as an asset. Fair value is usually measured at the discounted present value of the future lease payments. The result is that more assets and liabilities will appear to be greater under IFRS than under GAAP.

uses with skill, not only improves the debt to equity ratio by showing less debt on the balance sheet, but also improves the return on assets by reducing the total assets.

Pension Liabilities Most employees of medium-sized and large companies are covered by a **pension plan**, a contract that requires a company to pay benefits to its employees after they retire. Some companies pay the full cost of the pension plan, but in many companies, employees share the cost by contributing part of their salaries or wages. The contributions from employer and employees are usually paid into a **pension fund**, which is invested on behalf of the employees and from which benefits are paid to retirees. Pension benefits typically consist of monthly payments to retired employees and other payments upon disability or death.

Employers whose pension plans do not have sufficient assets to cover the present value of their pension obligations must record the amount of the shortfall as a liability on their balance sheets. If a pension plan has sufficient assets to cover its obligations, no balance sheet reporting is required or permitted.

There are two kinds of pension plans:

- ***Defined contribution plan:*** Under a defined contribution plan, the employer makes a fixed annual contribution, usually a percentage of the employee's gross pay; the amount of the contribution is specified in an agreement between the company and the employees. Retirement payments vary depending on how much the employee's retirement account earns. Employees usually control their own investment accounts, can make additional contributions of their own, and can transfer the funds if they leave the company. Examples of defined contribution plans include 401(k) plans, profit-sharing plans, and employee stock ownership plans (ESOPs). Companies prefer defined contribution plans because the employees assume the risk that their pension assets will earn a sufficient return to meet their retirement needs.
- ***Defined benefit plan:*** Under a defined benefit plan, the employer contributes an amount annually required to fund estimated future pension liability arising from employment in the current year. The exact amount of the liability will not be known until the retirement and death of the current employees. Although the amount of future benefits is fixed, the annual contributions vary depending on assumptions about how much the pension fund will earn.

Annual pension expense under a defined contribution plan is simple and predictable. Pension expense equals the fixed amount of the annual contribution. In contrast, annual expense under a defined benefit plan is one of the most complex topics in accounting. The intricacies are reserved for advanced courses, but in concept, the procedure is simple. Computation of the annual expense takes into account the estimation of many factors, such as the average remaining service life of active employees, the long-run return on pension plan assets, and future salary increases. A recent accounting standard requires companies and other entities with defined benefit plans not backed by a fund sufficient to pay them to record the unfunded portion as a liability.[5] For many companies, this can amount to millions or even billions of dollars.

Because pension expense under a defined benefit plan is not predictable and can vary from year to year, many companies are adopting the more predictable defined contribution plans. For example, in its 2009 annual report, **McDonald's** states that its plan

Focus on Business Practice

Postretirement Liabilities Affect Everyone

The rule requiring recognition of unfunded pension plans as liabilities impacts even government entities. Most government entities have defined benefit pension plans and provide postretirement medical benefits. As a result, states, school districts, and municipalities are all encountering previously ignored pension and health care liabilities. For example, the state of New Jersey actually stopped setting aside funds to pay for health care in order to give a tax cut. No one added up the cost until the new accounting rule required it. The estimated cost to provide the health care promised to New Jersey's current and future retirees is $58 billion, or twice the state's annual budget.[8] These cases, while extreme, are not unusual, especially in light of the decrease in government tax collections during the recent recession. Citizens across the country will likely face tax increases to pay for these liabilities.

iStock Photo

includes a "401(k) feature, an ESOP feature . . . and profit sharing." McDonald's, for example, has a pension liability exceeding $500 million.[6]

STUDY NOTE: Other postretirement benefits should be expensed as the employee earns them, in accordance with the matching rule, not when they are paid after the employee retires.

Other Postretirement Benefits Many companies provide retired employees not only with pensions, but also with health care and other benefits. In the past, these **other postretirement benefits** were accounted for on a cash basis—that is, they were expensed when the benefits were paid, after an employee had retired. However, because postretirement benefits such as health care are a type of long-term debt for the company that provides them, accounting standards now hold that employees earn these benefits during their employment and that the benefits should therefore be estimated and accrued during the time the employee is working.[7]

The estimates must take into account assumptions about retirement age; mortality; and, most significantly, future trends in health care benefits. Like pension benefits, such future benefits should be discounted to the current period. **General Motors**, the nation's largest private purchaser of health care, recently reported that its future health care liabilities for retirees were almost $37 billion in 2009.[9]

STUDY NOTE: Differences between GAAP-based tax expense and Internal Revenue code-based tax liability create the need for the Deferred Income Taxes account.

Deferred Income Taxes Among the long-term liabilities on the balance sheets of many companies, including **McDonald's**, is an account called **Deferred Income Taxes**. Deferred income taxes are the result of using different accounting methods to calculate income taxes on the income statement and income tax liability on the income tax return. For instance, companies often use straight-line depreciation for financial reporting and an accelerated method to calculate income tax liability. Because straight-line depreciation is less than accelerated depreciation in the early years of an asset's life, the assumption is that the income taxes will eventually have to be paid. Thus, the difference is listed as a long-term liability, called deferred income taxes. Because companies try to manage their affairs to minimize income taxes paid, deferred income taxes can become quite large. In McDonald's case, as shown in the company's Financial Highlights, they amounted to almost $1.3 billion in 2009.

Income Tax Expense Vistula Corporation has income taxes expense of $289,000. Vistula's actual income taxes payable are $184,000.

Analysis: The journal entry to record income taxes expense when it differs from the actual income taxes payable

▲ *increases* the Income Taxes Expense account with a debit for the amount of the expense,

▲ *increases* the Income Taxes Payable account with a credit for the amount owed the government, and

▲▼ *increases* (*decreases*) the Deferred Income taxes account with a credit (debit) to balance the entry.

A	=	L	+	SE
		+184,000		−289,000
		+105,000		

Journal Entry:

Dec. 31	Income Taxes Expense	289,000	
	Income Taxes Payable		184,000
	Deferred Income Taxes		105,000
	To record estimated current and deferred income taxes		

Comment: Deferred Income Taxes is classified as a liability when it has a credit balance and as an asset when it has a debit balance. It may also be classified as current or noncurrent, depending on the classification of the asset or liability that created the temporary difference. A survey of the financial statements of 600 large companies indicates that deferred income taxes is most often classified as a long-term liability. About 68 percent reported deferred income taxes with a credit balance in the long-term liability section of their balance sheets.[10]

Cash Flow Information

The best source of information concerning cash flows related to short-term and long-term debt is the financing activities section of the statement of cash flows. For instance,

McDonald's cash flows are clearly revealed in this excerpt from its 2009 statement of cash flows (in millions):

	2009	2008	2007
Financing Activities			
Net short-term borrowings	$ (285.4)	$ 266.7	$ 101.3
Long-term financing issuances	1,169.3	3,477.5	2,116.8
Long-term financing repayments	(664.6)	(2,698.5)	(1,645.5)

Note that McDonald's has little short-term borrowing and that the company's cash outflows for long-term borrowing for the three years exceeded cash inflows by $1,755.0 million.

Stop & Apply

Match each type of long-term liability listed below with the statement to which it applies.

1. Bonds payable
2. Long-term notes payable
3. Mortgage payable
4. Long-term lease
5. Pension liabilities
6. Other postretirement benefits
7. Deferred income taxes

_____ a. Cost of health care after employees' retirement
_____ b. The most common type of long-term debt
_____ c. The result of differences between accounting income and taxable income
_____ d. Debt that is secured by real estate
_____ e. Promissory notes that are due in more than one year
_____ f. May be based on a percentage of employees' wages or on future benefits
_____ g. Can be similar in form to an installment purchase

SOLUTION a. 6; b. 1; c. 7; d. 3; e. 2; f. 5; g. 4

iStock Photo

THE NATURE OF BONDS

LO 2 Describe the features of a bond issue and the major characteristics of bonds.

A **bond** is a security, usually long term, representing money that a corporation borrows from the investing public. (The federal, state, and local governments also issue bonds to raise money, as do foreign countries.) A bond entails a promise to repay the amount borrowed, called the *principal*, on a specified date and to pay interest at a specified rate at specified times—usually semiannually. In contrast to stockholders, who are the owners of a corporation, bondholders are a corporation's creditors.

When a public corporation decides to issue bonds, it must submit the appropriate legal documents to the Securities and Exchange Commission (SEC) for permission to borrow the funds. The SEC reviews the corporation's financial health and the specific terms of the **bond indenture**, which is a contract that defines the rights, privileges, and limitations of the bondholders. The bond indenture generally describes such things as:

- the maturity date of the bonds,
- interest payment dates, and
- the interest rate.

It may also cover repayment plans and restrictions.

Once the bond issue is approved, the corporation has a limited time in which to issue the authorized bonds. As evidence of its debt to the bondholders, the corporation provides each of them with a **bond certificate**.

Bond Issue: Prices and Interest Rates

A **bond issue** is the total value of bonds issued at one time. For example, a $1,000,000 bond issue could consist of a thousand $1,000 bonds. The prices of bonds are stated in terms of a percentage of the face value, or principal, of the bonds. A bond issue quoted at 103½ means that a $1,000 bond costs $1,035 ($1,000 × 1.035). When a bond sells at exactly 100, it is said to sell at face (or par) value. When it sells below 100, it is said to sell at a discount; above 100, at a premium. For instance, a $1,000 bond quoted at 87.62 would be selling at a discount and would cost the buyer $876.20.

Face Interest Rate and Market Interest Rate Two interest rates relevant to bond prices are the face interest rate and market interest rate:

- *Face interest rate:* The **face interest rate** is the fixed rate of interest paid to bondholders based on the face value of the bonds. The rate and amount are fixed over the life of the bond. To allow time to file with the SEC, publicize the bond issue, and print the bond certificates, a company must decide in advance what the face interest rate will be. Most companies try to set the face interest rate as close as possible to the market interest rate.
- *Market interest rate:* The **market interest rate** (also called the *effective interest rate*) is the rate of interest paid in the market on bonds of similar risk.* The market interest rate fluctuates daily. Because a company has no control over it, the market interest rate often differs from the face interest rate on the issue date.

STUDY NOTE: *A bond sells at face value when the face interest rate of the bond is identical to the market interest rate for similar bonds on the date of issue. When the face interest and market interest rates are different, a premium or discount arises.*

Discounts and Premiums If the market interest rate fluctuates from the face interest rate before the issue date, the issue price of bonds will not equal their face value. This fluctuation in market interest rate causes the bonds to sell at either a discount or premium:

- *Discount*: A **discount** equals the excess of the face value over the issue price. The issue price will be less than the face value when the market interest rate is higher than the face interest rate.
- *Premium*: A **premium** equals the excess of the issue price over the face value. The issue price will be more than the face value when the market interest rate is lower than the face interest rate.

Discounts or premiums are contra-accounts that are subtracted from or added to bonds payable on the balance sheet.

Characteristics of Bonds

STUDY NOTE: *Do not confuse the terms* indenture *and* debenture. *They sound alike, but an indenture is a bond contract, whereas a debenture is an unsecured bond. A debenture bond of a stable company actually might be a less risky investment than a secured bond of an unstable company.*

A bond indenture can be written to fit an organization's financing needs. As a result, the bonds issued in today's financial markets have many different features. We describe several of the more important features of bonds in the following sections.

Unsecured and Secured Bonds Bonds can be either unsecured or secured. **Unsecured bonds** (also called *debenture bonds*) are issued on the basis of a corporation's general credit. **Secured bonds** carry a pledge of certain corporate assets as a guarantee of repayment. A pledged asset may be a specific asset, such as a truck, or a general category of asset, such as property, plant, or equipment.

STUDY NOTE: *An advantage of issuing serial bonds is that the organization retires the bonds over a period of years, rather than all at once.*

Term and Serial Bonds When all the bonds of an issue mature at the same time, they are called **term bonds**. For instance, a company may decide to issue $1,000,000 worth of bonds, all due 20 years from the date of issue.

When the bonds of an issue mature on different dates, they are called **serial bonds**. For example, suppose that a $1,000,000 bond issue calls for paying $200,000 of the principal every five years. This arrangement means that after the issuing company makes the

Focus on Business Practice

Check Out Those Bond Prices!

The price of many bonds can be found daily on the Internet at sites such as finance.Yahoo.com. Quotations for the bonds of **Ford Motor Company** and **Abbott Laboratories**, two very active corporate bond traders, are shown below:[11]

	Face Rate	Maturity	Last Price	Last Yield
Ford Motor	8.125	1/20	108.00	7.523
Abbott	6.000	4/39	112.19	5.348

Abbott is one of the strongest companies financially, while Ford Motor is one of the weaker ones. Note that the face rate on Abbott's bond is lower than the face rate on Ford Motor's (6.000 percent versus 8.125 percent). Both bonds sell for more than 100 (108.00 and 112.19), which means that investors are willing to accept a market rate (7.523% and 5.348%) that is even less than the bond's face rate. The prices of bonds vary daily as companies' fortunes and interest rates change.

*At the time this chapter was written, the market interest rates on corporate bonds were volatile. Therefore, we use a variety of interest rates in our examples.

Because callable bonds can be bought back by the issuing corporation before their maturity dates, they are riskier for investors. However, to compensate for the risk, issuers will often offer bonds at a premium (a value exceeding face value). In 2009, the Agricultural Bank of China sold 20 billion yuan of 10-year callable bonds to help boost capital.

Imaginechina via AP Images

first $200,000 payment, $800,000 of the bonds would remain outstanding for the next five years, $600,000 for the next five years, and so on. A company may issue serial bonds to ease the task of retiring its debt—that is, paying off what it owes on the bonds.

Callable and Convertible Bonds When bonds are callable and convertible, a company may be able to retire them before their maturity dates. When a company does retire a bond issue before its maturity date, it is called **early extinguishment of debt**. Doing so can be to a company's advantage.

Callable bonds give the issuer the right to buy back and retire the bonds before maturity at a specified **call price**, which is usually above face value. Callable bonds give a company flexibility in financing its operations. For example, if bond interest rates drop, the company can call the bonds and reissue debt at a lower interest rate. A company might also call its bonds if it has earned enough to pay off the debt, if the reason for having the debt no longer exists, or if it wants to restructure its debt to equity ratio. The bond indenture states the time period and the prices at which the bonds can be redeemed.

Convertible bonds allow the bondholder to exchange a bond for a specified number of shares of common stock. The face value of a convertible bond when issued is greater than the market value of the shares to which it can be converted. However, if the market price of the common stock rises above a certain level, the value of the bond rises in relation to the value of the common stock. Even if the stock price does not rise, the investor still holds the bond and receives both the periodic interest payments and the face value at the maturity date.

One advantage of issuing convertible bonds is that the interest rate is usually lower because investors are willing to give up some current interest in the hope that the value of the stock will increase and the value of the bonds will therefore also increase. In addition, if the bonds are both callable and convertible and the market value of the stock rises to a level at which the bond is worth more than face value, management can avoid repaying the bonds by calling them for redemption, thereby forcing the bondholders to convert their bonds into common stock. The bondholders will agree to convert because no gain or loss results from the transaction.

Registered and Coupon Bonds **Registered bonds** are issued in the names of the bondholders. The issuing organization keeps a record of the bondholders' names and addresses and pays them interest by check on the interest payment date. Most bonds today are registered.

Stop & Apply

Match each term below with the related term.

1. Face interest rate	_____	a. Secured
2. Discount	_____	b. Coupon
3. Unsecured	_____	c. Convertible
4. Term	_____	d. Premium
5. Registered	_____	e. Market interest rate
6. Callable	_____	f. Serial
7. Non-convertible	_____	g. Non-callable
8. Deferred income taxes		

SOLUTION a. 3; b. 5; c. 7; d. 2; e. 1; f. 4; g. 6

iStock Photo

Coupon bonds are not registered with the organization. Instead, they bear coupons stating the amount of interest due and the payment date. The bondholder removes the coupons from the bonds on the interest payment dates and presents them at a bank for collection.

ACCOUNTING FOR THE ISSUANCE OF BONDS

LO 3 Record bonds issued at face value and at a discount or premium.

When the board of directors of a public corporation decides to issue bonds, the company must submit the appropriate legal documents to the Securities and Exchange Commission for authorization to borrow the funds. It is not necessary to make a journal entry to record the SEC's authorization of a bond issue. However, most companies disclose the authorization in the notes to their financial statements. The note lists the number and value of bonds authorized, the interest rate, the interest payment dates, and the life of the bonds.

In the sections that follow, we show how to record bonds issued at face value, at a discount, and at a premium.

Bonds Issued at Face Value

Bond: Zumi Corporation issues $200,000 of 9 percent, five-year bonds on January 1, 2011, and sells them on the same date for their face value. The bond indenture states that interest is to be paid on January 1 and July 1 of each year.

Analysis: The journal entry to record the issuance of bonds at face value

▲ *increases* Cash with a debit and

▲ *increases* Bonds Payable with a credit.

A	=	L	+	SE
+200,000		+200,000		

Journal Entry:

2011			
Jan. 1	Cash	200,000	
	Bonds Payable		200,000
	Sold $200,000 of 9%, 5-year bonds at face value		

STUDY NOTE: *When calculating semiannual interest, use half the annual rate.*

Interest Expense: As noted earlier, once a corporation issues bonds, it must pay interest to the bondholders over the life of the bonds, usually semiannually, and the principal of the bonds at maturity. For Zumi, interest is paid on January 1 and July 1 of each year. Thus, Zumi would owe the bondholders $9,000 interest on July 1, 2011:

$$\text{Interest} = \text{Principal} \times \text{Rate} \times \text{Time}$$
$$= \$200{,}000 \times \frac{9}{100} \times 6/12 \text{ year}$$
$$= \$9{,}000$$

Analysis: The journal entry to record the interest paid to the bondholders on each semiannual interest payment date (January 1 or July 1)

▲ *increases* Bond Interest Expense with a debit and

▼ *decreases* Cash with a credit (or *increases* Interest Payable with a credit).

A*	=	L	+	SE
−9,000				−9,000

*Assumes cash paid.

Journal Entry:

Jan. 1	Bond Interest Expense	9,000	
	Cash (or Interest Payable)		9,000
	Paid (or accrued) semiannual interest to bondholders of 9%, 5-year bonds		

Bonds Issued at a Discount

Bond: Zumi issues $200,000 of 9 percent, five-year bonds at 96.149 on January 1, 2011, when the market interest rate is 10 percent. In this case, the bonds are being issued at a discount because the market interest rate exceeds the face interest rate.

Analysis: The entry to record the issuance of the bonds at a discount

- ▲ *increases* Cash with a debit for the amount of the bond issue less the discount,
- ▲ *increases* Unamortized Bond Discount with a debit for the amount of discount, and
- ▲ *increases* Bonds Payable with a credit for the amount of the bond issued.

A	=	L	+	SE
+192,298		−7,702		
		+200,000		

Journal Entry:

2011				
Jan. 1	Cash		192,298	
	Unamortized Bond Discount		7,702	
	Bonds Payable			200,000
	Sold $200,000 of 9%, 5-year bonds at 96.149			
	Face amount of bonds	$200,000		
	Less purchase price of bonds ($200,000 × 0.96149)	192,298		
	Unamortized bond discount	$ 7,702		

Comment: If a balance sheet is prepared immediately after the bonds are issued at a discount, the liability for bonds payable is reported as follows:

Long-term liabilities		
9% bonds payable, due 1/1/2016	$200,000	
Less unamortized bond discount	7,702	$192,298

Unamortized Bond Discount is a contra-liability account. Its balance is deducted from the face amount of the bonds to arrive at the carrying value, or present value, of the bonds. The bond discount is described as unamortized because it will be amortized (written off) over the life of the bonds.

Bonds Issued at a Premium

Bond: Zumi issues $200,000 of 9 percent, five-year bonds for $208,200 on January 1, 2011, when the market interest rate is 8 percent. This means that investors will purchase the bonds at 104.1 percent of their face value. In this case, the bonds are being issued at a premium because the face interest rate exceeds the market rate for similar investments.

Analysis: The journal entry to record the bond issue at a premium

- ▲ *increases* the Cash account for the amount of the bond issue plus the premium,
- ▲ *increases* the Unamortized Bond Premium account for the amount of the premium, and
- ▲ *increases* the Bonds Payable account for the amount of the bond issue.

A	=	L	+	SE
+208,200		+8,200		
		+200,000		

Journal Entry:

2011			
Jan. 1	Cash	208,200	
	Unamortized Bond Premium		8,200
	Bonds Payable		200,000
	Sold $200,000 of 9%, 5-year bonds at 104.1 ($200,000 × 1.041)		

Comment: Immediately after this entry is made, bonds payable would be presented on the balance sheet as follows:

Long-term liabilities		
9% bonds payable, due 1/1/2016	$200,000	
Unamortized bond premium	8,200	$208,200

STUDY NOTE: *The carrying amount is always the face value of the bonds less the unamortized discount or plus the unamortized premium. The carrying amount always approaches the face value over the life of the bond.*

Here, the carrying value of the bonds payable is $208,200, which equals the face value of the bonds plus the unamortized bond premium. This means that the purchasers were willing to pay a premium of $8,200 to buy these bonds because their face interest rate was higher than the market interest rate.

Focus on Business Practice

100-Year Bonds Are Not for Everyone

When interest rates on long-term debt are at historically low levels, some companies attempt to lock in those low costs for long periods. In 1993, in a classic case example, **The Walt Disney Company** aggressively issued $150 million of 100-year bonds at a yield of only 7.5 percent in 1993. Among the others that followed Walt Disney's lead by issuing 100-year bonds were the **Coca-Cola Company, Columbia HCA Healthcare, Bell South, IBM,** and even the People's Republic of China. Some analysts wondered if even Mickey Mouse could survive 100 years. In fact, in 2010, interest rates had dropped so far that Disney is now paying more than the market rate of only 6.2 percent. Investors who purchased the bonds have had a gain because the bonds are now selling at a premium at 124.[12]

iStock Photo

Bond Issue Costs

The costs of issuing bonds can amount to as much as 5 percent of a bond issue. These costs often include the fees of underwriters, whom corporations hire to take care of the details of marketing a bond issue. Because the issue costs benefit the whole life of a bond issue, it makes sense to spread them over that period. It is generally accepted practice to establish a separate account for these costs and to amortize them over the life of the bonds.

Because issue costs decrease the amount of money a company receives from a bond issue, they have the effect of raising the discount or lowering the premium on the issue. Thus, bond issue costs can be spread over the life of the bonds through the amortization of a discount or premium. This method simplifies recordkeeping. In the rest of our discussion, we assume that all bond issue costs increase the discounts or decrease the premiums on bond issues.

Stop & Apply

Gill Foods is planning to issue $1,000,000 in long-term bonds. Depending on market conditions, Gill's CPA advises that the bonds could be issued at (a) 99, (b) 100, or (c) 101. Calculate the amount that Gill would receive under each alternative. Indicate whether it is at face value, a discount, or a premium and include the amount of the discount or premium of each.

SOLUTION

(a) $1,000,000 × 0.99 = $990,000; a discount of $10,000
(b) $1,000,000 × 1.00 = $1,000,000; at face value; no discount or premium
(c) $1,000,000 × 1.01 = $1,010,000; a premium of $10,000

iStock Photo

USING PRESENT VALUE TO VALUE A BOND

Use present values to determine the value of bonds.

A bond's value is determined by summing the following two present value concepts presented previously in Chapter 8:

- a series of fixed interest payments
- a single payment at maturity.

As we have noted, the amount of interest a bond pays is fixed over the life of the bond. The market interest rate, on the other hand, varies from day to day and is the rate used to determine the bond's present value. Thus, the amount investors are willing to pay for a bond varies because the bond's present value changes as the market interest rate changes. In the next sections, we show how to calculate the present value of a bond when the market rate is above the face value and when it is below the face value.

Market Rate Above Face Rate

Suppose a bond has a face value of $20,000 and pays fixed interest of $900 every six months (a 9 percent annual rate). The bond is due in five years. If the market interest rate today is 12 percent, what is the present value of the bond?

To answer this question, we use Table 2 in Appendix B to calculate the present value of the periodic interest payments of $900, and we use Table 1 in the same appendix to calculate the present value of the single payment of $20,000 at maturity. Because interest payments are made every six months, the compounding period is half a year. Thus, we have to convert the annual rate to a semiannual rate of 6 percent (12 percent divided by two 6-month periods per year) and use 10 periods (five years multiplied by two 6-month periods per year). With this information, we can compute the present value of the bond as follows:

Present value of 10 periodic payments at 6%: $900 × 7.360 (Table 2, Appendix B)	$ 6,624
Present value of a single payment at the end of 10 periods at 6%: $20,000 × 0.558 (Table 1, Appendix B):	11,160
Present value of $20,000 bond	$17,784

The market interest rate has increased so much since the bond was issued—from 9 percent to 12 percent—that the value of the bond today is only $17,784. That amount is all investors would be willing to pay at this time for a bond that provides income of $900 every six months and a return of the $20,000 principal in five years.

Market Rate Below Face Rate

As Exhibit 10.3 shows, if the market interest rate on the bond described above falls below the face interest rate, say to 8 percent (4 percent semiannually), the present value of the bond will be greater than the face value of $20,000:

Present value of 10 periodic payments at 4%: $900 × 8.111 (Table 2, Appendix B)	$ 7,300
Present value of a single payment at the end of 10 periods at 4%: $20,000 × 0.676 (Table 1, Appendix B)	13,520
Present value of $20,000 bond	$20,820

EXHIBIT 10.3
Using Present Value to Value a $20,000, 9 Percent, Five-Year Bond

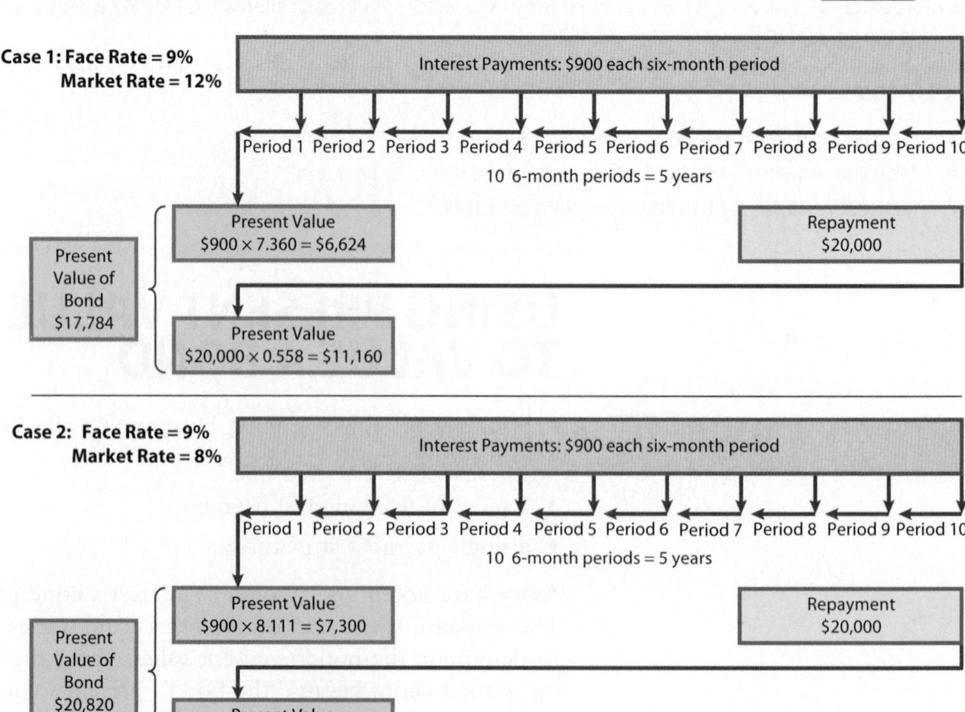

Stop & Apply

Tyler Company's $500,000 bond issue pays semiannual interest of $16,000 and is due in 20 years. Assume that the market interest rate is 6 percent. Calculate the present value of the bond issue.

SOLUTION

Present value of 40 periodic payments of 3% (Table 2, Appendix B):

$16,000 × 23.115 (Table 2, Appendix B) = $369,840 (Table 2, Appendix B)

Present value of a single payment at the end of 40 years (40 periods) at 3% (Table 1, Appendix B):

$500,000 × 0.307 (Table 1, Appendix B) = $153,500 (Table 1, Appendix B)

Present value of the bond issue = $523,340

iStock Photo

AMORTIZATION OF BOND DISCOUNTS AND PREMIUMS

LO 5 Amortize bond discounts and bond premiums using the straight-line and effective interest methods.

A bond discount or premium represents the amount by which the total interest expense is higher or lower than the total interest payments. To record interest expense properly and ensure that the carrying value of bonds payable at maturity equals face value, it is necessary to systematically reduce the bond discount or premium—that is, to amortize them—over the life of the bonds. This can be accomplished by using either the straight-line method or the effective interest method.

Amortizing a Bond Discount

Because a bond discount affects interest expense in each year of a bond issue, the bond discount should be amortized over the life of the bond issue. In this way, the unamortized bond discount will decrease gradually over time, and the carrying value of the bond issue (face value less unamortized discount) will gradually increase. By the maturity date, the carrying value of the bond issue will equal its face value, and the unamortized bond discount will be zero.

In the following sections, we calculate Zumi Corporation's total interest expense and amortize its bond discount using the straight-line and the effective interest methods.

Calculating Total Interest Expense When a corporation issues bonds at a discount, the market (or effective) interest rate that it pays is greater than the face interest rate on the bonds. The reason is that the interest expense is the stated interest payments *plus* the amount of the bond discount. That is, although the company does not receive the full face value of the bonds on issue, it still must pay back the full face value at maturity. The difference between the issue price and the face value must be added to the total interest payments to arrive at the actual interest expense.

Bond Issue: On January 1, 2011, Zumi issued $200,000 of five-year bonds at a time when the market interest rate of 10 percent exceeded the face interest rate of 9 percent. The bonds sold for $192,298, resulting in an unamortized bond discount of $7,702.

Analysis: The journal entry to record the bond issue

- ▲ *increases* the Cash account with a debit for $192,298,
- ▲ *increases* the Unamortized Bond Discount account with a debit for $7,702, and
- ▲ *increases* the Bonds Payable account with a credit for $200,000.

Journal Entry:

2011			
Jan. 1	Cash	192,298	
	Unamortized Bond Discount		7,702
	Bonds Payable		200,000
	Sold $200,000 of 9%, 5-year bond issue at discount of $7,702		

Comment: The total expense to Zumi of issuing its bonds at a discount is as follows:

Cash to be paid to bondholders	
Face value at maturity	$200,000
Interest payments ($200,000 × 0.09 × 5 years)	90,000
Total cash paid to bondholders	$290,000
Less cash received from bondholders	192,298
Total interest expense	$ 97,702

Or alternatively:

Interest payments ($200,000 × 0.09 × 5 years)	$ 90,000
Bond discount	7,702
Total interest expense	$ 97,702

The total interest expense of $97,702 is made up of $90,000 in interest payments and the $7,702 bond discount. Thus, the bond discount *increases* the interest paid on the bonds from the face interest rate to the market interest rate. The market (or effective) interest rate is the real interest expense of the bond over its life.

To have each year's interest expense reflect the market interest rate, the discount must be allocated over the remaining life of the bonds as an increase in the interest expense each period. Thus, the interest expense for each period will exceed the actual payment of interest by the amount of the bond discount that is amortized over the period. This process of allocation is called *amortization of the bond discount.*

STUDY NOTE: *The discount on a zero coupon bond represents the interest that will be paid (in its entirety) on the maturity date.*

Some bonds do not require periodic interest payments. These bonds, called **zero coupon bonds**, are simply a promise to pay a fixed amount at the maturity date. They are issued at a large discount because the only interest that the buyer earns or the issuer pays is the discount. For example, a five-year, $200,000 zero coupon bond issued when the market rate is 8 percent, compounded semiannually, would sell for only $136,200. That amount is the present value of a single payment of $200,000 at the end of five years. The discount of $63,800 ($200,000 – $136,200) is the total interest expense, which is amortized over the life of the bond.

Straight-Line Method The **straight-line method** equalizes amortization of a bond discount for each interest period in the life of the bonds.

Bond Issue: Using the Zumi Corporation example, the interest payment dates of the bond issue are January 1 and July 1 of each year, and the bonds mature in five years.

STUDY NOTE: *The bond interest expense recorded exceeds the amount of interest paid because of the amortization of the bond discount. The matching rule dictates that the discount be amortized over the life of the bond.*

Bond Discount Amortized and Interest Expense: With the straight-line method, the amount of the bond discount amortized and the interest expense for each semiannual period are calculated in four steps:

Step 1: Determine the total number of interest payments:

$$\text{Total Interest Payments} = \text{Interest Payments per Year} \times \text{Life of Bonds}$$
$$= 2 \times 5 = 10$$

Step 2: Determine the amount of bond discount amortization per period:

$$\text{Amortization of Bond Discount per Interest Period} = \frac{\text{Bond Discount}}{\text{Total Interest Payments}}$$
$$= \frac{\$7,702}{10}$$
$$= \$770^{*}$$

*Rounded.

Step 3: Determine the cash interest payment:

Cash Interest Payment = Face Value × Face Interest Rate × Time

= $200,000 × 0.09 × 6/12 = $9,000

Step 4: Determine the interest expense per period:

Interest Expense per Interest Period = Interest Payment + Amortization of Bond Discount

= $9,000 – $770 = $9,770

Analysis: The journal entry to record the bond discount amortized and interest expense

▲ *increases* the Bond Interest Expense account with a debit for the amount calculated in Step 4,

▼ *decreases* the Unamortized Bond Discount account with a credit for the amount calculated in Step 2, and

▼▲ *decreases* the Cash account (or *increases* the Interest Payable account with a credit) for the amount in Step 3.

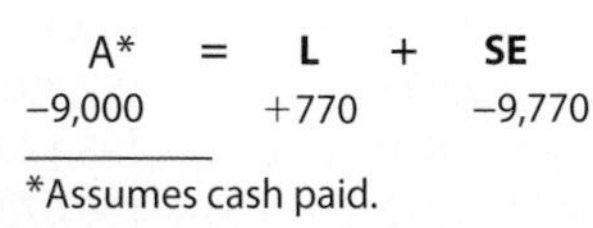

A*	=	L	+	SE
−9,000		+770		−9,770

*Assumes cash paid.

Journal Entry:

2011			
July 1	Bond Interest Expense	9,770	
	Unamortized Bond Discount		770
	Cash (or Interest Payable)		9,000
	Paid (or accrued) semiannual interest to bondholders and amortized the discount on 9%, 5-year bonds		

STUDY NOTE: *Whether a bond is sold at a discount or a premium, its carrying value will equal its face value on the maturity date.*

Comment: Notice that the bond interest expense is $9,770, but the amount paid to the bondholders is the $9,000 face interest payment. The difference of $770 is the credit to Unamortized Bond Discount. This lowers the debit balance of Unamortized Bond Discount and raises the carrying value of the bonds payable by $770 each interest period. If no changes occur in the bond issue, this entry will be made every six months during the life of the bonds. When the bond issue matures, the Unamortized Bond Discount account will have a zero balance, and the carrying value of the bonds will be $200,000—exactly equal to the amount due the bondholders.

Although the straight-line method has long been used, it has a certain weakness. When it is used to amortize a discount, the carrying value goes up each period, but the bond interest expense stays the same; thus, the rate of interest falls over time. Conversely, when this method is used to amortize a premium, the rate of interest rises over time. The Accounting Principles Board therefore holds that the straight-line method should be used only when it does not lead to a *material difference* from the effective interest method.[13] A material difference is one that affects the evaluation of a company.

Effective Interest Method When the **effective interest method** is used to compute the interest and amortization of a bond discount, a constant interest rate is applied to the carrying value of the bonds at the beginning of each interest period. This constant rate is the market rate (i.e., the effective rate) at the time the bonds were issued. The amount amortized each period is the difference between the interest computed by using the market rate and the actual interest paid to bondholders.

Bond Issue: Use the same facts for Zumi that we used earlier—a $200,000 bond issue at 9 percent, with a five-year maturity and interest to be paid twice a year. The market rate at the time the bonds were issued was 10 percent, so the bonds sold for $192,298, a discount of $7,702. Exhibit 10.4 (p. 462) shows the interest and amortization of the bond discount.

EXHIBIT 10.4
Interest and Amortization of a Bond Discount: Effective Interest Method

Semiannual Interest Period	A Carrying Value at Beginning of Period	B Semiannual Interest Expense at 10% to Be Recorded* (5% × A)	C Semiannual Interest Payment to Bondholders ($4\frac{1}{2}$% × $200,000)	D Amortization of Bond Discount (B − C)	E Unamortized Bond Discount at End of Period (E − D)	F Carrying Value at End of Period (A + D)
0					$7,702	$192,298
1	$192,298	$9,615	$9,000	$615	7,087	192,913
2	192,913	9,646	9,000	646	6,441	193,559
3	193,559	9,678	9,000	678	5,763	194,237
4	194,237	9,712	9,000	712	5,051	194,949
5	194,949	9,747	9,000	747	4,304	195,696
6	195,696	9,785	9,000	785	3,519	196,481
7	196,481	9,824	9,000	824	2,695	197,305
8	197,305	9,865	9,000	865	1,830	198,170
9	198,170	9,908	9,000	908	922	199,078
10	199,078	9,922†	9,000	922	—	200,000

*Rounded to the nearest dollar.
†Last period's interest expense equals $9,922 ($9,000 + $922); it does not equal $9,954 ($199,078 × 0.05) because of the cumulative effect of rounding.

Carrying Value, Interest Expense, Discount Amortized, and Discount Unamortized

The amounts in Exhibit 10.4 for period 1 were computed as follows:

Column A: The carrying value of the bonds is computed as:

Face Value − Unamortized Discount = Carrying Value
$200,000 − $7,702 = $192,298

Column B: The interest expense to be recorded is the effective interest, computed as:

Carrying Value × Market Interest Rate × Interest Time Period = Interest Expense
$192,298 × 0.10 × 6/12 = $9,615

Column C: The interest paid in the period is a constant amount, computed as:

Face Value × Face Interest Rate × Interest Time Period = Interest Payments
$200,000 × 0.09 × 6/12 = $9,000

Column D: The discount amortized is computed as:

Interest Expense − Interest Payment = Amortized Discount
$9,615 − $9,000 = $615

Column E: The unamortized bond discount is computed as:

Discount at the Beginning of the Period − Current Period Amortization = Unamortized Discount
$7,702 − $615 = $7,087

The unamortized discount decreases in each interest payment period because it is amortized as a portion of interest expense.

Column F: The carrying value of the bonds at the end of the period is computed as:

Carrying Value at Beginning of Period + Amortization During Period = Carrying Value at End of Period

$192,298 + $615 = $192,913

Notice that the sum of the carrying value and the unamortized discount (Column F + Column E) always equals the face value of the bonds (for example, $192,913 + $7,087 = $200,000).

Analysis: The journal entry to record the bond discount amortized and interest expense is exactly like the one when the straight-line method is used. However, the amounts debited and credited to the various accounts are different. The journal entry to record the bond discount amortized and interest expense under the effective interest method

- ▲ *increases* the Bond Interest Expense account with a debit for the amount calculated in Column B,
- ▼ *decreases* the Unamortized Bond Discount account with a credit for the amount calculated in Column D, and
- ▼▲ *decreases* the Cash account (or *increases* the Interest Payable account) with a credit for the amount in Column C.

A*	=	L	+	SE
−9,000		+615		−9,615

*Assumes cash paid.

Journal Entry:

2011			
July 1	Bond Interest Expense	9,615	
	Unamortized Bond Discount		615
	Cash (or Interest Payable)		9,000
	Paid (or accrued) semiannual interest to bondholders and amortized the discount on 9%, 5-year bonds		

Comment: Although an interest and amortization table is useful because it can be prepared in advance for all periods, it is not necessary to have one to determine the amortization of a discount for any one interest payment period. It is necessary only to multiply the carrying value by the effective interest rate and subtract the interest payment from the result. For example, the amount of discount to be amortized in the seventh interest payment period is $824, calculated as:

(Carrying Value × Interest Rate) − Interest Payment = Amortized Discount

($196,481 × 0.05) − $9,000 = $824

STUDY NOTE: *The bond interest increases each period because the carrying value of the bonds (the principal on which the interest is calculated) increases each period.*

Exhibit 10.5, which is based on the data in Exhibit 10.4, shows how the effective interest method affects the amortization of a bond discount. Notice that the carrying value (the issue price) is initially less than the face value but that it gradually increases toward the face value over the life of the bond issue. Notice also that interest expense exceeds interest payments by the amount of the bond discount amortized. Interest expense increases gradually over the life of the bond because it is based on the gradually increasing carrying value (multiplied by the market interest rate).

EXHIBIT 10.5
Carrying Value and Interest Expense—Bonds Issued at a Discount

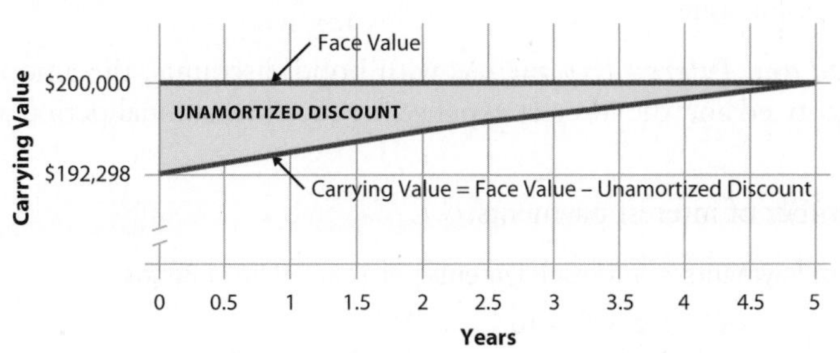

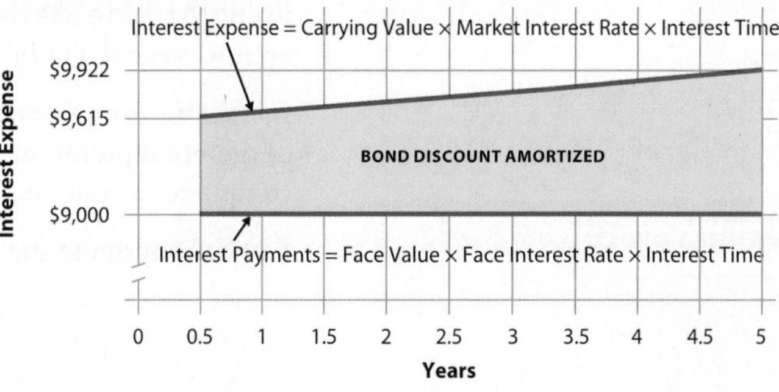

Amortizing a Bond Premium

Like a bond discount, a bond premium must be amortized over the life of the bonds so that it can be matched to its effects on interest expense during that period. In the following sections, we calculate Zumi Corporation's total interest expense and amortize its bond premium using the straight-line and effective interest methods.

STUDY NOTE: A bond premium is deducted from interest payments in calculating total interest expense because a bond premium represents an amount over the face value of a bond that the corporation never has to return to bondholders. In effect, it reduces the higher-than-market interest the corporation is paying on the bond.

Calculating Total Interest Expense When bondholders pay more than face value for the bonds, the premium represents an amount that the bondholders will not receive at maturity. The premium is in effect a reduction, in advance, of the total interest paid on the bonds over the life of the bond issue. The total interest expense over the issue's life therefore needs to be determined.

Bond Issue: In our earlier example of bonds issued at a premium, Zumi issued $200,000 of five-year bonds at a time when the market interest rate was 8 percent and the face interest rate was 9 percent. The bonds sold for $208,200, which resulted in an unamortized bond premium of $8,200 ($208,200 − $200,000).

Analysis: The journal entry to record the bond issue

- ▲ *increases* the Cash account with a debit for $192,298,
- ▲ *increases* the Unamortized Bond Discount account with a debit for $7,702, and
- ▲ *increases* the Bonds Payable account with a credit for $200,000.

Journal Entry:

2011			
Jan 1	Cash	208,200	
	Unamortized Bond Premium		8,200
	Bonds Payable		200,000
	Sold $200,000 of 9%, 5-year bond issue at premium of $8,200		

STUDY NOTE: The bond interest expense recorded is less than the amount of interest paid because of the amortization of the bond premium. The matching rule dictates that the premium be amortized over the life of the bond.

Comment: The total interest expense over the bond issue's life is computed as follows:

Cash to be paid to bondholders	
Face value at maturity	$200,000
Interest payments ($200,000 × 0.09 × 5 years)	90,000
Total cash paid to bondholders	$290,000
Less cash received from bondholders	208,200
Total interest expense	$ 81,800

Alternatively, the total interest expense can be computed as follows:

Interest payments ($200,000 × 0.09 × 5 years)	$90,000
Less bond premium	8,200
Total interest expense	$81,800

Notice that the total interest payments of $90,000 exceed the total interest expense of $81,800 by $8,200, the amount of the bond premium.

Straight-Line Method Under the straight-line method, the bond premium is spread evenly over the life of the bond issue.

Bond Discount Amortized and Interest Expense: As with bond discounts, the amount of the bond premium amortized and the interest expense for each semiannual period are computed in four steps:

Step 1: Determine the number of interest payments:

$$\text{Total Interest Payments} = \text{Interest Payments per Year} \times \text{Life of Bonds}$$
$$= 2 \times 5 = 10$$

Step 2: Determine the amount of bond discount amortization per period bond interest amortization:

$$\text{Amortization of Bond Premium per Interest Period} = \frac{\text{Bond Premium}}{\text{Total Interest Payments}}$$

$$= \frac{\$8{,}200}{10}$$

$$= \$820$$

Step 3: Determine the cash interest payment:

$$\text{Cash Interest Payment} = \text{Face Value} \times \text{Face Interest Rate} \times \text{Time}$$

$$= \$200{,}000 \times 0.09 \times 6/12 = \$9{,}000$$

Step 4: Determine the interest expense per period:

$$\text{Interest Expense per Interest Period} = \text{Interest Payment} - \text{Amortization of Bond Premium}$$

$$= \$9{,}000 - \$820 = \$8{,}180$$

Analysis: The journal entry to record the bond premium amortized and interest expense

- ▲ *increases* the Bond Interest Expense account with a debit for the amount calculated in Step 4,
- ▼ *decreases* the Unamortized Bond Premium account with a debit for the amount calculated in Step 2, and
- ▼▲ *decreases* the Cash account (or *increases* the Interest Payable account) with a credit for the amount in Step 3.

A*	=	L	+	SE
−9,000		−820		−8,180

*Assumes cash paid.

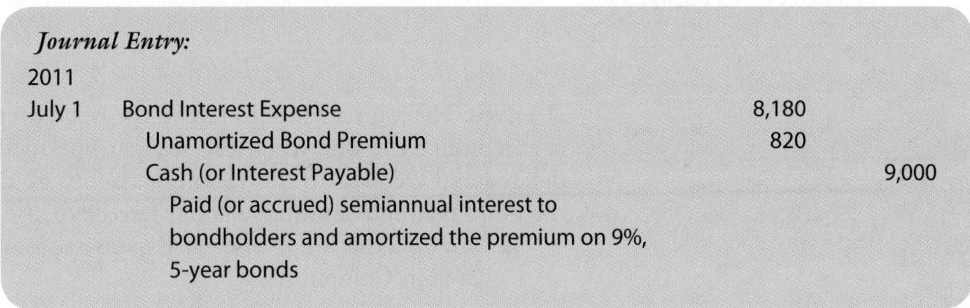

Journal Entry:

2011			
July 1	Bond Interest Expense	8,180	
	Unamortized Bond Premium	820	
	Cash (or Interest Payable)		9,000
	Paid (or accrued) semiannual interest to bondholders and amortized the premium on 9%, 5-year bonds		

Comment: Note that the bond interest expense is $8,180, but the amount that bondholders receive is the $9,000 face interest payment. The difference of $820 is the debit to Unamortized Bond Premium. This lowers the credit balance of the Unamortized Bond Premium account and the carrying value of the bonds payable by $820 each interest period. If the bond issue remains unchanged, the same entry will be made on every semiannual interest date over the life of the bond issue. When the bond issue matures, the balance in the Unamortized Bond Premium account will be zero, and the carrying value of the bonds payable will be $200,000—exactly equal to the amount due the bondholders.

As we pointed out earlier, the straight-line method should be used only when it does not lead to a material difference from the effective interest method.

Effective Interest Method Under the straight-line method, the effective interest rate changes constantly, even though the interest expense is fixed, because the effective interest rate is determined by comparing the fixed interest expense with a carrying value that changes as a result of amortizing the discount or premium. To apply a fixed interest rate over the life of the bonds based on the actual market rate at the time of the bond issue, one must use the effective interest method. With this method, the interest expense decreases slightly each period (Exhibit 10.6, Column B, p. 466) because the amount of the bond premium amortized increases slightly (Column D). This occurs because a fixed rate is applied each period to the gradually decreasing carrying value (Column A).

EXHIBIT 10.6
Interest and Amortization of a Bond Premium: Effective Interest Method

Semiannual Interest Period	A Carrying Value at Beginning of Period	B Semiannual Interest Expense at 8% to Be Recorded* (4% × A)	C Semiannual Interest Payment to Bondholders (4½% × $200,000)	D Amortization of Bond Premium (C − B)	E Unamortized Bond Premium at End of Period (E − D)	F Carrying Value at End of Period (A − D)
0					$8,200	$208,200
1	$208,200	$8,328	$9,000	$ 672	7,528	207,528
2	207,528	8,301	9,000	699	6,829	206,829
3	206,829	8,273	9,000	727	6,102	206,102
4	206,102	8,244	9,000	756	5,346	205,346
5	205,346	8,214	9,000	786	4,560	204,560
6	204,560	8,182	9,000	818	3,742	203,742
7	203,742	8,150	9,000	850	2,892	202,892
8	202,892	8,116	9,000	884	2,008	202,008
9	202,008	8,080	9,000	920	1,088	201,088
10	201,088	7,912†	9,000	1,088	—	200,000

*Rounded to the nearest dollar.
†Last period's interest expense equals $7,912 ($9,000 − $1,088); it does not equal $8,044 ($201,088 × 0.04) because of the cumulative effect of rounding.

Analysis: The journal entry to record the bond premium amortized and interest expense is exactly like the one when the straight-line method is used. However, the amounts debited and credited to the various accounts are different. The journal entry to record the bond premium amortized and interest expense using the effective interest method

▲ *increases* the Bond Interest Expense account with a debit for the amount calculated in Column B,

▼ *decreases* the Unamortized Bond Discount account with a debit for the amount calculated in Column D, and

▲▼ *decreases* the Cash account (or *increases* the Interest Payable account) with a credit for the amount in Column C.

A*	=	L	+	SE
−9,000		−672		−8,328

*Assumes cash paid.

Journal Entry:

2011			
July 1	Bond Interest Expense	8,328	
	Unamortized Bond Premium	672	
	Cash (or Interest Payable)		9,000
	Paid (or accrued) semiannual interest to bondholders and amortized the premium on 9%, 5-year bonds		

Comment: Note that the unamortized bond premium (Column E) decreases gradually to zero as the carrying value decreases to the face value (Column F). To find the amount of premium amortized in any one interest payment period, subtract the effective interest expense (the carrying value times the effective interest rate, Column B) from the interest payment (Column C). In semiannual interest period 5, for example, the amortization of premium is $786, which is calculated as follows:

Interest Payment − (Carrying Value × Interest Rate) = Amortized Premium
$9,000 − ($205,346 × 0.04) = $786

EXHIBIT 10.7
Carrying Value and Interest Expense—Bonds Issued at a Premium

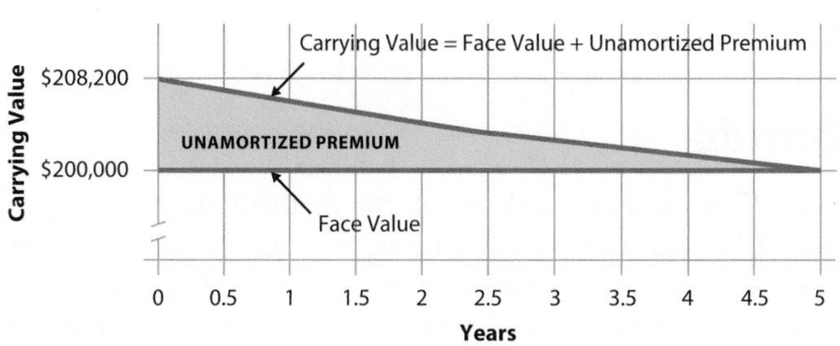

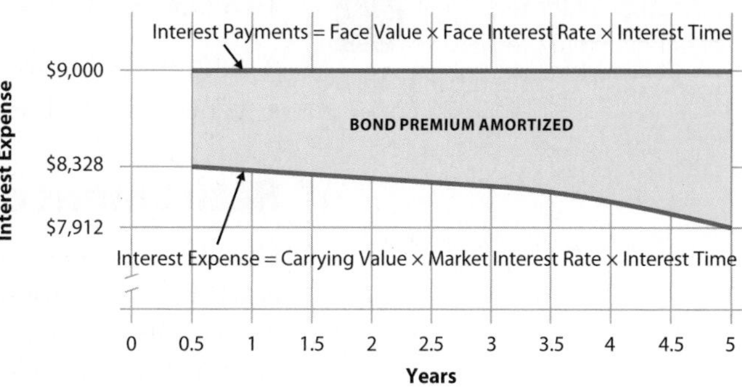

Exhibit 10.7, which is based on the data in Exhibit 10.6, shows how the effective interest method affects the amortization of a bond premium. Note that the carrying value (issue price) is initially greater than the face value, but it gradually decreases toward the face value over the bond issue's life. Note also that interest payments exceed interest expense by the amount of the premium amortized. Interest expense decreases gradually over the life of the bond because it is based on the gradually decreasing carrying value (multiplied by the market interest rate).

Stop & Apply

On June 1, Rola Corporation issues $4,000,000 of 8 percent, 20-year bonds at 97. Interest is payable semiannually, on May 31 and November 30. Rola's fiscal year ends on November 30.

1. Using the straight-line method of amortization, prepare journal entries for June 1 and November 30.
2. Using the effective interest method and assuming the same facts as above except that the market rate of interest is 8.5 percent, prepare the journal entry for November 30.

SOLUTION

1. Straight-line method

June 1	Cash	3,880,000	
	Unamortized Bond Discount	120,000	
	Bonds Payable		4,000,000
	Issue of $4,000,000 of 8%, 20-year bonds at 97 $4,000,000 × 0.97 = $3,880,000		
Nov. 30	Bond Interest Expense	163,000	
	Unamortized Bond Discount		3,000
	Cash		160,000
	Paid bondholders semiannual interest and amortized the discount on 8%, 20-year bonds $120,000 ÷ 40 periods = $3,000 $4,000,000 × 0.04 = $160,000		

2. Effective interest method

Nov. 30	Bond Interest Expense	164,900	
	Unamortized Bond Discount		4,900
	Cash		160,000
	Paid bondholders semiannual interest and amortized the discount on 8%, 20-year bonds $3,880,000 × 0.0425 = $164,900 $4,000,000 × 0.04 = $160,000		

RETIREMENT AND CONVERSION OF BONDS

Account for the retirement of bonds and the conversion of bonds into stock. LO 6

Two ways in which a company can reduce its bond debt are by:

- retiring the bonds or
- converting the bonds into common stock.

Retirement of Bonds

Usually, companies repay bonds when they are due—on the maturity date. However, as noted in our discussion of callable and convertible bonds, retiring a bond issue before its maturity date can be to a company's advantage. For example, when interest rates drop, many companies refinance their bonds at the lower rate, much like homeowners who refinance their mortgage loans when interest rates go down. Although companies usually pay a premium for early extinguishment of bond debt, what they save on interest can make the refinancing cost effective. Bonds may be retired either by calling the bonds or by buying them back from the bondholders on the open market. In either case, the transaction analysis is the same.

Bond Issue: Suppose Zumi can call, or retire, at 105 the $200,000 of bonds it issued at a premium (104.1) on January 1, 2011, and it decides to do so on July 1, 2014. The retirement thus takes place on the seventh interest payment date. Assume the entry for the required interest payment and the amortization of the premium has been made.

Analysis: The journal entry to record the retirement of bonds

- ▼ *decreases* the Bonds Payable account with a debit for the face amount to remove the bonds from the balance sheet,
- ▼ *decreases* the Unamortized Bond Premium account with a debit (or the Unamortized Bond Discount account with a credit) to remove the related premium (or discount) with a credit from the records,
- ▼ *decreases* cash for the amount required to call the bonds, and
- ▲ *increases* loss (or gain) on Retirement of Bonds with a debit (or credit) for the net amount.

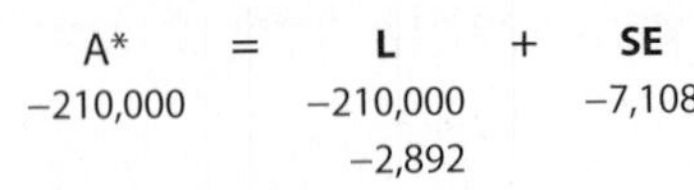

A*	=	L	+	SE
−210,000		−210,000		−7,108
		−2,892		

*Assumes cash paid.

Journal Entry:

2014			
July 1	Bonds Payable	200,000	
	Unamortized Bond Premium	2,892	
	Loss on Retirement of Bonds	7,108	
	Cash		210,000
	Retired 9% bonds at 105		

Comment: In this entry, the cash paid is the face value times the call price ($200,000 × 1.05 = $210,000). The unamortized bond premium can be found in Column E of Exhibit 10.6 (p. 466). The loss on retirement of bonds occurs because the call price of the bonds is greater than the carrying value ($210,000 − $202,892 = $7,108).

Sometimes, a rise in the market interest rate can cause the market value of bonds to fall considerably below their face value. If it has the cash to do so, the company may find it advantageous to purchase the bonds on the open market and retire them, rather than wait and pay them off at face value. For example, if Zumi were able to purchase the above bonds on the open market at 85, a gain would be recognized for the difference between the purchase price of the bonds and the carrying value of the retired bonds.

Conversion of Bonds

When a bondholder converts bonds to common stock, the company records the common stock at the carrying value of the bonds. The bond liability and the unamortized discount or premium are written off the books. For this reason, no gain or loss on the transaction is recorded.

Bond Issue: Suppose that Zumi does not call its bonds on July 1, 2014. Instead, the corporation's bondholders decide to convert all their bonds to $8 par value common stock under a convertible provision of 40 shares of common stock for each $1,000 bond.

Analysis: The journal entry to record the conversion of bonds to common stock

- ▼ *decreases* the Bonds Payable account with a debit for the face amount to remove the bonds from the balance sheet,
- ▼ *decreases* the Unamortized Bond Premium account with a debit (or the Unamortized Bond Discount account with a credit) to remove the related premium (or discount) from the records,
- ▲ *increases* the Common Stock account for the par value of the shares, and
- ▲ *increases* the Additional Paid-In Capital account for the amount required to balance the entry.

A	=	L	+	SE
		−200,000		+64,000
		−2,892		+138,892

Journal Entry:

2014			
July 1	Bonds Payable	200,000	
	Unamortized Bond Premium	2,892	
	Common Stock		64,000
	Additional Paid-In Capital		138,892
	Converted 9% bonds payable into $8 par value common stock at a rate of 40 shares for each $1,000 bond		

Comment: The unamortized bond premium is found in Column E of Exhibit 10.6 (p. 466). At a rate of 40 shares for each $1,000 bond, 8,000 shares will be issued, with a total par value of $64,000 (8,000 × $8). The Common Stock account is credited for the amount of the par value of the stock issued. In addition, Additional Paid-In Capital is credited for the difference between the carrying value of the bonds and the par value of the stock issued ($202,892 − $64,000 = $138,892). No gain or loss is recorded.

Stop & Apply

Assume that in the Zumi example of retirement above, the company is able to buy the $200,000 in bonds on the open market at 95 and retire them. The Unamortized Bond Premium remains at $2,892. Prepare the entry to record the purchase and retirement on July 1, 2014.

SOLUTION

2014			
July 1	Bonds Payable	200,000	
	Unamortized Bond Premium	2,892	
	Gain on Retirement of Bonds		12,892
	Cash		190,000
	Retired 9% bonds at 95		

iStock Photo

A look back at ▸ McDonald's Corporation

As we noted in this chapter's Decision Point, McDonald's relies on both debt and equity financing to support its continued global expansion. Because of the extent of the company's long-term debt liabilities, potential investors and creditors need to address the following questions:

1. What are McDonald's most important long-term debts?
2. What are its considerations in deciding to take on long-term debt?
3. How does one evaluate whether a company has too much debt?

In addition to bonds, notes payable, and mortgages, it is important to consider McDonald's numerous leases on properties in evaluating the company's long-term debt. The company also has deferred income taxes and pension and health plans. Its purpose in taking on long-term debt is to foster growth and increase earnings. By using financial leverage in this way, McDonald's, like any other company, assumes financial risk. In McDonald's case, the risk is partially offset because much of its long-term debt relates to leases on real estate, an area in which the company has long experience and great expertise. McDonald's management commits the company to long-term leases not only because it believes the company will stay in the leased locations for a long time, but also because it is a way of financing expansion.

McDonald's 2009 annual report includes a detailed description of management's approach to debt financing. It points out that Standard & Poor's gives the company an "A" credit rating and that management carefully monitors critical credit ratios that "incorporate capitalized operating leases to estimate total adjusted debt."

We can evaluate whether McDonald's maintains an appropriate level of debt by computing its debt to equity and interest coverage ratios over a two-year period, as follows:

RATIO

$$\text{Debt to Equity} = \frac{\text{Total Liabilities}}{\text{Total Stockholders' Equity}}$$

	2009	2008
Debt to Equity =	$\frac{\$2,988.7 + \$13,202.3}{14,033.9}$	$\frac{\$2,537.9 + \$12,541.0}{\$13,382.6}$
=	$\frac{\$16,191.0}{\$14,033.9}$	$\frac{\$15,078.9}{\$13,382.6}$
=	115%	113%

+

RATIO

$$\text{Interest Coverage Ratio} = \frac{\text{Income Before Income Taxes} + \text{Interest Expense}}{\text{Interest Expense}}$$

	2009	2008
Interest Coverage Ratio =	$\frac{\$6,487.0 + \$473.2}{\$473.2}$	$\frac{\$6,158.0 + \$522.6}{\$522.6}$
=	$\frac{\$6,960.2}{\$473.2}$	$\frac{\$6,680.6}{\$522.6}$
=	14.7 times	12.8 times

This analysis shows that McDonald's maintains a steady level of debt and can easily cover its interest payments. There is plenty of cushion in the latter ratio to cover all of McDonald's balance sheet commitments, including long-term leases.

Review Problem

Accounting for a Bond Discount, Bond Retirement, and Bond Conversion.

When Oketo Company wanted to expand its metal window division, it did not have enough capital to finance the project. To fund it, management sought and received approval from the board of directors to issue bonds. The bond indenture stated that the company would issue $2,500,000 of 8 percent, five-year bonds on January 1, 2011, and would pay interest semiannually, on June 30 and December 31 of each of the five years. It also stated that the bonds would be callable at 104 and that each $1,000 bond would be convertible to 30 shares of $10 par value common stock. Oketo sold the bonds on January 1, 2011, at 96 because the market rate of interest for similar investments was 9 percent. It decided to amortize the bond discount by using the effective interest method. On July 1, 2013, management called and retired half the bonds, and investors converted the other half to common stock.

Required

1. Prepare an interest and amortization schedule for the first five interest periods.
2. Prepare journal entries to record the sale of the bonds, the first two interest payments, the bond retirement, and the bond conversion.

ANSWERS TO REVIEW PROBLEM

1. Schedule for the first five interest periods:

	A	B	C–F	G–L	M	N	O
1			Interest and Amortization of Bond Discount				
2–3	Semiannual Interest Payment Date	Carrying Value at Beginning of Period	Semiannual Interest Expense* (9% x 1/2)	Semiannual Interest Expense (8% x 1/2)	Amortization of Discount	Unamortized Bond Discount at End of Period	Carrying Value at End of Period
4	Jan. 1, 2011					$100,000	$2,400,000
5	June 30, 2011	$2,400,000	$108,000	$100,000	$8,000	92,000	2,408,000
6	Dec. 31, 2011	2,408,000	108,360	100,000	8,360	83,640	2,416,360
7	June 30, 2012	2,416,360	108,736	100,000	8,736	74,904	2,425,096
8	Dec. 31, 2012	2,425,096	109,129	100,000	9,129	65,774†	2,434,226
9	June 30, 2013	2,434,226	109,540	100,000	9,540	56,234	2,443,766
10							
11	*Rounded to the nearest dollar.						
12	†Rounded.						

2. Journal entries:

	A	B–C	D–E	F	G
1	2011				
2	Jan.	1	Cash	2,400,000	
3			Unamortized Bond Discount	100,000	
4			Bonds Payable		2,500,000
5			Sold $2,500,000 of 8%, 5-year bonds at 96		
6	June	30	Bond Interest Expense	108,000	
7			Unamortized Bond Discount		8,000
8			Cash		100,000
9			Paid semiannual interest and amortized		
10			the discount on 8%, 5-year bonds		
11	2011				
12	Dec.	31	Bond Interest Expense	108,360	
13			Unamortized Bond Discount		8,360
14			Cash		100,000
15			To record accrued semiannual interest and		
16			amortize the discount on 8%, 5-year bonds		

(continued)

	A	B	C	D	E	F	G
17	2013						
18	July	1	Bonds Payable			1,250,000	
19			Loss on Retirement of Bonds			78,117	
20				Unamortized Bond Discount			28,117
21				Cash			1,300,000
22					Called $1,250,000 of 8% bonds and retired		
23					them at 104 ($56,234 x 1/2 = $28,117*)		
24			Bonds Payable			1,250,000	
25				Unamortized Bond Discount			28,117
26				Common Stock			375,000
27				Additional Paid-In Capital			846,883
28					Converted $1,250,000 of 8% bonds into		
29					common stock		
30					1,250 x 30 shares = 37,500 shares		
31					37,500 shares x $10 = $375,000		
32					$56,235 – $28,118 = $28,117		
33					$1,250,000 – ($28,117 + $375,000) = $846,883		

Stop & Review

LO 1 Identify the management issues related to long-term debt.

Long-term debt is used to finance assets and business activities, such as research and development, that will produce income in future years. The management issues related to long-term debt are whether to take on long-term debt, how much debt to carry, and what types of debt to incur. The advantages of issuing long-term debt are that common stockholders do not relinquish any control, interest on debt is tax-deductible, and financial leverage can increase earnings. The disadvantages are that interest and principal must be paid on time and financial leverage can work against a company if an investment is not successful. The level of debt can be evaluated using the debt to equity ratio and the interest coverage ratio. Common types of long-term debt are bonds payable, notes payable, mortgages payable, long-term leases, pension liabilities, other postretirement benefits, and deferred income taxes.

LO 2 Describe the features of a bond issue and the major characteristics of bonds.

A bond is a security that represents money borrowed from the investing public. When a corporation issues bonds, it enters into a contract, called a bond indenture, with the bondholders. The bond indenture defines the terms of the bond issue. A bond issue is the total value of bonds issued at one time. The prices of bonds are stated in terms of a percentage of the face value, or principal, of the bonds. The face interest rate is the fixed rate of interest paid to bondholders based on the face value. The market interest rate is the rate of interest paid in the market on bonds of similar risk. If the market rate fluctuates from the face interest rate before the bond issue date, the bonds will sell at either a discount or a premium.

A corporation can issue several types of bonds, each having different characteristics. For example, a bond issue may or may not require security (secured versus unsecured bonds). It may be payable at a single time (term bonds) or at several times (serial bonds). And the holder may receive interest automatically (registered bonds) or may have to return coupons to receive interest payable (coupon bonds). Bonds may also be callable and convertible.

LO 3 Record bonds issued at face value and at a discount or premium.

Bondholders pay face value for bonds when the interest rate on the bonds approximates the market rate for similar investments. The issuing corporation records the bond issue at face value as a long-term liability in the Bonds Payable account. Bonds are issued at a discount when their face interest rate is lower than the market rate for similar investments. The difference between the face value and the issue price is debited to Unamortized Bond Discount. Bonds are issued at a premium when their face interest rate is greater than the market interest rate on similar investments. The difference between the issue price and the face value is credited to Unamortized Bond Premium.

Use present values to determine the value of bonds. 

The value of a bond is determined by summing the present values of (1) the series of fixed interest payments of the bond issue and (2) the single payment of the face value at maturity. Tables 1 and 2 in Appendix B on present value tables should be used in making these computations.

Amortize bond discounts and bond premiums using the straight-line and effective interest methods. LO 5

The straight-line method allocates a fixed portion of a bond discount or premium each interest period to adjust the interest payment to interest expense. The effective interest method, which is used when the effects of amortization are material, applies a constant rate of interest to the carrying value of the bonds. To find interest and the amortization of discounts or premiums, the effective interest rate is applied to the carrying value of the bonds (face value minus the discount or plus the premium) at the beginning of the interest period. The amount of the discount or premium to be amortized is the difference between the interest figured by using the effective rate and that obtained by using the face rate. The results of using the effective interest method on bonds issued at a discount or a premium are summarized below and compared with issuance at face value:

	Bonds Issued at		
	Face Value	**Discount**	**Premium**
Trend in carrying value over bond term	Constant	Increasing	Decreasing
Trend in interest expense over bond term	Constant	Increasing	Decreasing
Interest expense versus interest payments	Interest expense = interest payments	Interest expense > interest payments	Interest expense < interest payments
Classification of bond discount or premium	Not applicable	Contra-liability (deducted from Bonds Payable)	Adjunct-liability (added to Bonds Payable)

Account for the retirement of bonds and the conversion of bonds into stock. LO 6

Callable bonds can be retired before maturity at the option of the issuing corporation. The call price is usually an amount greater than the face value of the bonds, in which case the corporation recognizes a loss on the retirement of the bonds. Sometimes, a rise in the market interest rate causes the market value of the bonds to fall below face value. If a company purchases its bonds on the open market at a price below carrying value, it recognizes a gain on the transaction.

Convertible bonds allow the bondholder to convert bonds to the issuing corporation's common stock. When bondholders exercise this option, the common stock issued is recorded at the carrying value of the bonds being converted. No gain or loss is recognized.

Key Terms and Ratios

Bond 452 (LO2)
Bond certificate 452 (LO2)
Bond indenture 452 (LO2)
Bond issue 452 (LO2)
Callable bonds 454 (LO2)
Call price 454 (LO2)
Capital lease 448 (LO1)
Convertible bonds 454 (LO2)
Coupon bonds 455 (LO2)
Deferred Income Taxes 451 (LO1)
Discount 453 (LO2)
Early extinguishment of debt 454 (LO2)
Effective interest method 461 (LO5)
Face interest rate 453 (LO2)
Financial leverage 444 (LO1)
Market interest rate 453 (LO2)
Mortgage 447 (LO1)
Off-balance-sheet financing 445 (LO1)
Operating lease 447 (LO1)
Other postretirement benefits 451 (LO1)
Pension fund 450 (LO1)
Pension plan 450 (LO1)
Premium 453 (LO2)
Registered bonds 454 (LO2)
Secured bonds 453 (LO2)
Serial bonds 453 (LO2)
Straight-line method 460 (LO5)
Term bonds 453 (LO2)
Unsecured bonds 453 (LO2)
Zero coupon bonds 460 (LO5)

FINANCIAL RATIOS
Debt to equity ratio 445 (LO1)
Interest coverage ratio 445 (LO1)

Chapter Assignments Building Your Basic Knowledge and Skills

Short Exercises

LO 1

Bond Versus Common Stock Financing

SE 1. Indicate whether each of the following is an advantage or a disadvantage of using long-term bond financing rather than issuing common stock.

1. Interest paid on bonds is tax-deductible.
2. Investments are sometimes not as successful as planned.
3. Financial leverage can have a negative effect when investments do not earn as much as the interest payments on the related debt.
4. Bondholders do not have voting rights in a corporation.
5. Positive financial leverage may be achieved.

LO 1

Types of Long-Term Liabilities

SE 2. Place the number of the liability next to the statement to which it applies.

1. Bonds payable
2. Long-term notes payable
3. Mortgage payable
4. Long-term lease
5. Pension liabilities
6. Other postretirement benefits
7. Deferred income taxes

___ a. May result in a capital lease
___ b. Differences in income taxes on accounting income and taxable income
___ c. The most popular form of long-term financing
___ d. Often used to purchase land and buildings
___ e. Often used interchangeably with bonds payable
___ f. Future health care costs are a major component
___ g. May include 401(k), ESOPs, or profit-sharing

LO 1

Mortgage Payable

SE 3. Karib Corporation purchased a building by signing a $150,000 long-term mortgage with monthly payments of $1,200. The mortgage carries an interest rate of 8 percent. Prepare a monthly payment schedule showing the monthly payment, the interest for the month, the reduction in debt, and the unpaid balance for the first three months. (*Note:* Round amounts to the nearest dollar.)

LO 1

Mortgage Payable

SE 4. Birma Corporation purchased an office building by signing a $225,000 long-term mortgage with monthly payments of $1,800. The mortgage carries an interest rate of 9 percent. Prepare a monthly payment schedule showing the monthly payment, the interest for the month, the reduction in debt, and the unpaid balance for the first three months. (*Note:* Round amounts to the nearest dollar.)

LO 1

Deferred Income Taxes

SE 5. Prepare the journal entry to record income taxes on December 31, 2011, assuming that Turner Corporation's income tax expense is $35,000 and that it owes $30,000 in income taxes to the government. Prepare the journal entry to record income taxes on December 31, 2011. Tell where each of the accounts in your entry will appear in the financial statements assuming that the difference between income tax expense and income taxes owed is due to differences in depreciation on buildings for financial reporting and for income tax calculation.

LO 4 **Valuing Bonds Using Present Value**

SE 6. Rogers Paints, Inc., is considering the sale of two bond issues. Choice A is a $600,000 bond issue that pays semiannual interest of $32,000 and is due in 20 years. Choice B is a $600,000 bond issue that pays semiannual interest of $30,000 and is due in 15 years. Assume that the market interest rate for each bond is 12 percent. Calculate the amount that Rogers Paints will receive if both bond issues occur. (Calculate the present value of each bond issue and sum.)

LO 3, 5 **Straight-Line Method**

SE 7. On April 1, 2011, Morimoto Corporation issued $8,000,000 in 8.5 percent, five-year bonds at 98. The semiannual interest payment dates are April 1 and October 1. Prepare journal entries for the issue of the bonds by Morimoto on April 1, 2011, and the first two interest payments on October 1, 2011, and April 1, 2012. Use the straight-line method and ignore year-end accruals.

LO 3, 5 **Straight-Line Method**

SE 8. On April 1, 2011, Castile Corporation issued $10,000,000 in 8.0 percent, five-year bonds at 102. The semiannual interest payment dates are April 1 and October 1. Prepare journal entries for the issue of the bonds by Castile on April 1, 2011, and the first two interest payments on October 1, 2011, and April 1, 2012. Use the straight-line method and ignore year-end accruals.

LO 3, 5, 6 **Effective Interest Method**

SE 9. On March 1, 2011, Speedy Freight Company sold $200,000 of its 9.5 percent, 20-year bonds at 106. The semiannual interest payment dates are March 1 and September 1. The market interest rate is 8.9 percent. The firm's fiscal year ends August 31. Prepare journal entries to record the sale of the bonds on March 1, the accrual of interest and amortization of premium on August 31, and the first interest payment on September 1. Use the effective interest method to amortize the premium.

LO 6 **Bond Retirement**

SE 10. The Velvet Corporation has outstanding $400,000 of 8 percent bonds callable at 104. On December 1, immediately after the payment of the semiannual interest and the amortization of the bond discount were recorded, the unamortized bond discount equaled $10,500. On that date, $240,000 of the bonds were called and retired. Prepare the journal entry to record the retirement of the bonds on December 1.

LO 6 **Bond Retirement**

SE 11. Schiff Stores has outstanding $100,000 of 7 percent bonds callable at 103. On July 1, immediately after recording the payment of the semiannual interest and the amortization of the premium, the unamortized bond premium equaled $2,500. On that date, all of the bonds were called and retired.

a. How much cash must be paid to retire the bonds?
b. Is there a gain or loss on retirement? If so, how much is it?

LO 6 **Bond Conversion**

SE 12. The Tramot Corporation has $2,000,000 of 6 percent, $1,000 bonds outstanding. There is $40,000 of unamortized discount remaining on the bonds after the March 1, 2011, semiannual interest payment. The bonds are convertible at the rate of 20 shares of $10 par value common stock for each $1,000 bond. On March 1, 2011, bondholders presented $1,200,000 of the bonds for conversion. Prepare the journal entry to record the conversion of the bonds.

LO 6 **Bond Conversion**

SE 13. Bear Corporation has $3,000,000 of 8 percent, $1,000 bonds outstanding. There is $60,000 of unamortized discount remaining on the bonds after the June 1,

2011, semiannual interest payment. The bonds are convertible at the rate of 30 shares of $10 par value common stock for each $1,000 bond. On June 1, 2011, bondholders presented $1,800,000 of the bonds for conversion. Prepare the journal entry to record the conversion of the bonds.

Exercises

LO 1, 2, 6

Discussion Questions

E 1. Develop brief answers to each of the following questions:

1. How does a lender assess the risk that a borrower may default—that is, not pay interest and principal when due?
2. If a company with a high debt to equity ratio wants to increase its debt when the economy is weak, what kind of bond might it issue? (RATIO)
3. Why might a company lease a long-term asset rather than buy it and issue long-term bonds?
4. Why are callable and convertible bonds considered to add to management's future flexibility in financing a business?

LO 3, 4, 5, 6

Discussion Questions

E 2. Develop brief answers to each of the following questions:

1. What determines whether bonds are issued at a discount, premium, or face value?
2. Why does the market price of a bond vary over time?
3. When is it acceptable to use the straight-line method to amortize a bond discount or premium?
4. Why must the accrual of bond interest be recorded at the end of an accounting period?

RATIO LO 1

Interest Coverage Ratio

E 3. Compute the interest coverage ratios for 2011 and 2012 from the partial income statements of Rozmus Company that appear below. State whether the ratio improved or worsened over time.

	2012	2011
Income from operations	$11,945	$9,230
Interest expense	2,900	1,650
Income before income taxes	$ 9,045	$7,580
Income taxes	2,700	2,225
Net income	$ 6,345	$5,355

LO 1

Mortgage Payable

E 4. Tobby Corporation purchased a building by signing a $300,000 long-term mortgage with monthly payments of $4,000. The mortgage carries an interest rate of 12 percent.

1. Prepare a monthly payment schedule showing the monthly payment, the interest for the month, the reduction in debt, and the unpaid balance for the first three months. (*Note:* Round amounts to the nearest dollar.)
2. Prepare journal entries to record the purchase and the first two monthly payments.

LO 1

Recording Lease Obligations

E 5. Velocity Corporation has leased a piece of equipment that has a useful life of 12 years. The terms of the lease are payments of $86,000 per year for 12 years. Velocity currently is able to borrow money at a long-term interest rate of 15 percent. (*Note:* Round amounts to the nearest dollar.)

1. Calculate the present value of the lease.
2. Prepare the journal entry to record the lease agreement.

3. Prepare the journal entry to record depreciation of the equipment for the first year using the straight-line method.
4. Prepare the journal entries to record the lease payments for the first two years.

LO 1

Deferred Income Taxes

E 6. Prepare the entry to record income taxes on December 31, 2011, assuming that Jason Corporation's income tax expense is $120,000 and that it owes $80,000 in income taxes to the government. Prepare the journal entry to record income taxes on December 31, 2011. Tell where each of the accounts in your entry will appear in the financial statements assuming that the difference between income tax expense and income taxes owed is due to differences in depreciation on equipment for financial reporting and for income tax calculation.

LO 4

Valuing Bonds Using Present Value

E 7. Boris, Inc., is considering the sale of two bond issues. Choice A is a $400,000 bond issue that pays semiannual interest of $32,000 and is due in 20 years. Choice B is a $400,000 bond issue that pays semiannual interest of $30,000 and is due in 15 years. Assume that the market interest rate for each bond is 12 percent. Calculate the amount that Boris will receive if both bond issues are made. (*Hint:* Calculate the present value of each bond issue and sum.)

LO 4

Valuing Bonds Using Present Value

E 8. Use Tables 1 and 2 in Appendix B to calculate the issue price of a $150,000 bond issue in each of the following independent cases. Assume interest is paid semiannually.

a. A 10-year, 8 percent bond issue; the market interest rate is 10 percent.
b. A 10-year, 8 percent bond issue; the market interest rate is 6 percent.
c. A 10-year, 10 percent bond issue; the market interest rate is 8 percent.
d. A 20-year, 10 percent bond issue; the market interest rate is 12 percent.
e. A 20-year, 10 percent bond issue; the market interest rate is 6 percent.

LO 4

Zero Coupon Bonds

E 9. The state of Idaho needs to raise $50,000,000 for highway repairs. Officials are considering issuing zero coupon bonds, which do not require periodic interest payments. The current market interest rate for the bonds is 10 percent. What face value of bonds must be issued to raise the needed funds assuming that the bonds will be due in 30 years and compounded annually? How would your answer change if the bonds were due in 50 years? How would both answers change if the market interest rate were 8 percent instead of 10 percent?

LO 3, 5

Straight-Line Method

E 10. Kinga Corporation issued $8,000,000 in 10.5 percent, 10-year bonds on February 1, 2011, at 104. Semiannual interest payment dates are January 31 and July 31. Use the straight-line method and ignore year-end accruals.

1. With regard to the bond issue on February 1, 2011:
   a. How much cash is received?
   b. How much is Bonds Payable?
   c. What is the difference between **a** and **b** called, and how much is it?
2. With regard to the bond interest payment on July 31, 2011:
   a. How much cash is paid in interest?
   b. How much is the amortization?
   c. How much is interest expense?
3. With regard to the bond interest payment on January 31, 2012:
   a. How much cash is paid in interest?
   b. How much is the amortization?
   c. How much is interest expense?

LO 3, 5 **Straight-Line Method**

E 11. Lori Corporation issued $4,000,000 in 8.5 percent, five-year bonds on March 1, 2011, at 96. The semiannual interest payment dates are September 1 and March 1. Prepare journal entries for the issue of the bonds by Lori on March 1, 2011, and the first two interest payments on September 1, 2011, and March 1, 2012. Use the straight-line method and ignore year-end accruals.

LO 3, 5 **Straight-Line Method**

E 12. Sari Corporation issued $5,000,000 in 7.0 percent, five-year bonds on March 1, 2011, at 103. The semiannual interest payment dates are September 1 and March 1. Prepare journal entries for the issue of the bonds by Sari on March 1, 2011, and the first two interest payments on September 1, 2011, and March 1, 2012. Use the straight-line method and ignore year-end accruals.

LO 3, 5 **Effective Interest Method**

E 13. Cute Toy Company sold $250,000 of 9.5 percent, 20-year bonds on April 1, 2011, at 106. The semiannual interest payment dates are March 31 and September 30. The market interest rate is 8.9 percent. The company's fiscal year ends September 30. Use the effective interest method to calculate the amortization. (*Note:* Round amounts to the nearest dollar.)

1. With regard to the bond issue on April 1, 2011:
   a. How much cash is received?
   b. How much is Bonds Payable?
   c. What is the difference between **a** and **b** called, and how much is it?
2. With regard to the bond interest payment on September 30, 2011:
   a. How much cash is paid in interest?
   b. How much is the amortization?
   c. How much is interest expense?
3. With regard to the bond interest payment on March 31, 2012:
   a. How much cash is paid in interest?
   b. How much is the amortization?
   c. How much is interest expense?

LO 3, 5 **Effective Interest Method**

E 14. On March 1, 2011, Wurt Corporation issued $2,400,000 of 10 percent, five-year bonds. The semiannual interest payment dates are February 28 and August 31. Because the market rate for similar investments was 11 percent, the bonds had to be issued at a discount. The discount on the issuance of the bonds was $97,340. The company's fiscal year ends February 28. Prepare journal entries to record the bond issue on March 1, 2011, and the payment of interest and the amortization of the discount on August 31, 2011 and on February 28, 2012. Use the effective interest method. (*Note:* Round amounts to the nearest dollar.)

LO 6 **Bond Retirement**

E 15. The Maruska Corporation has outstanding $800,000 of 8 percent bonds callable at 104. On September 1, immediately after recording the payment of the semiannual interest and the amortization of the discount, the unamortized bond discount equaled $21,000. On that date, $480,000 of the bonds was called and retired.

1. How much cash must be paid to retire the bonds?
2. Is there a gain or loss on retirement? If so, how much is it?

LO 6 **Bond Conversion**

E 16. The Monaco Corporation has $800,000 of 6 percent, $1,000 bonds outstanding. There is $40,000 of unamortized discount remaining on these bonds after the July 1, 2011, semiannual interest payment. The bonds are convertible at the rate of 20 shares of $10 par value common stock for each $1,000 bond. On July 1, 2011, bondholders presented $600,000 of the bonds for conversion.

1. Is there a gain or loss on conversion? If so, how much is it?
2. How many shares of common stock are issued in exchange for the bonds?
3. In dollar amounts, how does this transaction affect the total liabilities and the total stockholders' equity of the company? In your answer, show the effects on four accounts.

LO 4, 6

Time Value of Money and Early Extinguishment of Debt

E 17. Jolanta's, Inc., has a $700,000, 8 percent bond issue that was issued a number of years ago at face value. There are now 10 years left on the bond issue, and the market interest rate is 16 percent. Interest is paid semiannually. The company purchases the bonds on the open market at the calculated current market value and retires the bonds.

1. Using present value tables in Appendix B, calculate the current market value of the bond issue.
2. Is there a gain or loss on retirement of bonds? If so, how much is it?

Problems

LO 1

Lease Versus Purchase

✔ 1. a. Present value of lease: $171,864; 2. a. Unpaid balance at the end of third month: $157,582

P 1. Kabura Corporation can either lease or buy a small garage next to its business that will provide parking for its customers. The company can lease the building for a period of 12 years, which approximates the useful life of the facility and thus qualifies as a capital lease. The terms of the lease are payments of $24,000 per year for 12 years. Kabura currently is able to borrow money at a long-term interest rate of 9 percent. The company can purchase the building by signing a $160,000 long-term mortgage with monthly payments of $2,000. The 12-year mortgage also carries an interest rate of 9 percent.

REQUIRED

1. With regard to the lease option:
   a. Calculate the present value of the lease. (*Note:* Round amounts to the nearest dollar.)
   b. Prepare the journal entry to record the lease agreement.
   c. Prepare the journal entry to record depreciation of the equipment for the first year using the straight-line method.
   d. Prepare the journal entries to record the lease payments for the first two years.
2. With regard to the purchase option:
   a. Prepare a monthly payment schedule showing the monthly payment, the interest for the month, the reduction in debt, and the unpaid balance for the first three months. (*Note:* Round amounts to the nearest dollar.)
   b. Prepare the journal entries to record the purchase and the first two monthly payments.

USER INSIGHT ▶

3. Based on your calculations, which option seems to be best? Aside from cost, name an advantage and a disadvantage of each option.

LO 1, 2, 3

Bond Terminology

P 2. Listed below are common terms associated with bonds:

a. Bond certificate
b. Bond issue
c. Bond indenture
d. Unsecured bonds
e. Debenture bonds
f. Secured bonds
g. Term bonds
h. Serial bonds
i. Registered bonds
j. Coupon bonds
k. Callable bonds
l. Convertible bonds
m. Face interest rate
n. Market interest rate
o. Effective interest rate
p. Bond premium
q. Bond discount

REQUIRED

1. For each of the statements on p. 480, identify the term with which it is associated. (If more than one statement applies, choose the term with which it is most closely associated.)

1. Occurs when bonds are sold at more than face value
2. Rate of interest that will vary depending on economic conditions
3. Bonds that may be exchanged for common stock
4. Bonds that are not registered
5. A bond issue in which all bonds are due on the same date
6. Occurs when bonds are sold at less than face value
7. Rate of interest that will be paid regardless of market conditions
8. Bonds that may be retired at management's option
9. A document that is evidence of a company's debt
10. Same as market rate of interest
11. Bonds for which the company knows who owns them
12. A bond issue for which bonds are due at different dates
13. The total value of bonds issued at one time
14. Bonds whose payment involves a pledge of certain assets
15. Same as debenture bonds
16. Contains the terms of the bond issue
17. Bonds issued on the general credit of the company

USER INSIGHT ▶ 2. What effect will a decrease in interest rates below the face interest rate and before a bond is issued have on the cash received from the bond issue? What effect will the decrease have on interest expense? What effect will the decrease have on the amount of cash paid for interest?

LO 3, 5, 6

Bond Basics—Straight-Line Method, Retirement, and Conversion

✔ 1. d. Interest expense: $517,500; 2. d. Interest Expense: $532,500

P 3. Delicious Corporation has $10,000,000 of 10.5 percent, $1,000 20-year bonds dated June 1, 2011, with interest payment dates of May 31 and November 30. After 10 years, the bonds are callable at 104, and each $1,000 bond is convertible into 25 shares of $10 par value common stock. The company's fiscal year ends on December 31. It uses the straight-line method to amortize bond premiums or discounts.

REQUIRED

1. Assume the bonds are issued at 103 on June 1, 2011.
   a. How much cash is received?
   b. How much is Bonds Payable?
   c. What is the difference between **a** and **b** called, and how much is it?
   d. With regard to the bond interest payment on November 30, 2011:
      (1) How much cash is paid in interest?
      (2) How much is the amortization?
      (3) How much is interest expense?
2. Assume the bonds are issued at 97 on June 1, 2011.
   a. How much cash is received?
   b. How much is Bonds Payable?
   c. What is the difference between **a** and **b** called, and how much is it?
   d. With regard to the bond interest payment on November 30, 2011:
      (1) How much cash is paid in interest?
      (2) How much is the amortization?
      (3) How much is interest expense?
3. Assume the issue price in requirement 1 and assume that the bonds are called and retired 10 years later.
   a. How much cash will have to be paid to retire the bonds?
   b. Is there a gain or loss on retirement? If so, how much is it?
4. Assume the issue price in requirement 2 and assume that the bonds are converted to common stock 10 years later.
   a. Is there a gain or loss on conversion? If so, how much is it?
   b. How many shares of common stock are issued in exchange for the bonds?
   c. In dollar amounts, how does this transaction affect the total liabilities and the total stockholders' equity of the company? In your answer, show the effects on four accounts.

USER INSIGHT ▶

5. Assume that after 10 years, market interest rates have dropped significantly and that the price of the company's common stock has risen significantly. Also assume that management wants to improve its credit rating by reducing its debt to equity ratio and that it needs what cash it has for expansion. Which approach would management prefer—the approach and result in requirement 3 or 4? Explain your answer. What would be a disadvantage of the approach you chose?

LO 3, 5

Bond Transactions—Straight-Line Method

✔ 1. Feb. 28, Bond Interest Expense: $94,000; 2. Feb. 28, Bond Interest Expense: $96,000

P 4. Waxman Corporation has $2,000,000 of 9.5 percent, 25-year bonds dated March 1, 20101, with interest payable on February 28 and August 31. The company's fiscal year-end is February 28. It uses the straight-line method to amortize bond premiums or discounts. (*Note:* Round amounts to the nearest dollar.)

REQUIRED

1. Assume the bonds are issued at 102.5 on March 1, 2011. Prepare journal entries for March 1, 2011; August 31, 2011; and February 28, 2012.
2. Assume the bonds are issued at 97.5 on March 1, 2011. Prepare journal entries for March 1, 2011; August 31, 2011; and February 28, 2012.

USER INSIGHT ▶

3. Explain the role that market interest rates play in causing a premium in requirement 1 and a discount in requirement 2.

LO 3, 5

Bond Transactions—Effective Interest Method

✔ 1. Feb. 28, Bond Interest Expense: $94,268; 2. Feb. 28, Bond Interest Expense: $95,577

P 5. Waxman Corporation has $2,000,000 of 9.5 percent, 25-year bonds dated March 1, 2011, with interest payable on February 28 and August 31. The company's fiscal year-end is February 28. It uses the effective interest method to amortize bond premiums or discounts. (*Note:* Round amounts to the nearest dollar.)

REQUIRED

1. Assume the bonds are issued at 102.5 on March 1, 2011, to yield an effective interest rate of 9.2 percent. Prepare journal entries for March 1, 2011; August 31, 2011; and February 28, 2012.
2. Assume the bonds are issued at 97.5 on March 1, 2011, to yield an effective interest rate of 9.8 percent. Prepare journal entries for March 1, 2011; August 31, 2011; and February 28, 2012.

USER INSIGHT ▶

3. Explain the role that market interest rates play in causing a premium in requirement 1 and a discount in requirement 2.

Alternate Problems

LO 1

Lease Versus Purchase

✔ 1. a. Present value of lease: $154,062; 2. a. Unpaid balance at the end of third month: $117,898

P 6. Fender Corporation can either lease or buy a specialized piece of equipment. The company can lease the equipment for a period of 15 years, which approximates the useful life of the facility and thus qualifies as a capital lease. The terms of the lease are payments of $18,000 per year for 15 years. Fender currently is able to borrow money at a long-term interest rate of 8 percent. The company can purchase the equipment by signing a $120,000 long-term note with monthly payments of $1,500. The note also carries an interest rate of 8 percent.

REQUIRED

1. With regard to the lease option:
   a. Calculate the present value of the lease. (*Note:* Round amounts to the nearest dollar.)
   b. Prepare the journal entry to record the lease agreement.
   c. Prepare the journal entry to record depreciation of the equipment for the first year using the straight-line method.
   d. Prepare the journal entries to record the lease payments for the first two years.

2. With regard to the purchase option:
   a. Prepare a monthly payment schedule showing the monthly payment, the interest for the month, the reduction in debt, and the unpaid balance for the first three months. (*Note:* Round amounts to the nearest dollar and round interest rate to two decimal places.)
   b. Prepare the journal entries to record the purchase and the first two monthly payments.

USER INSIGHT ▶

3. Based on your calculations, which option seems to be best? Aside from cost, name an advantage and a disadvantage of each option.

LO 3, 5, 6

Bond Basics—Straight-Line Method, Retirement, and Conversion

✔ 1. d. Interest expense: $187,200; 2. d. Interest expense: $192,800

P 7. Abellan Corporation has $4,000,000 of 9.5 percent, 25-year, $1,000 bonds dated May 1, 2011, with interest payable on April 30 and October 31. The company's fiscal year ends on December 31, and it uses the straight-line method to amortize bond premiums or discounts. The bonds are callable after 10 years at 103 or convertible into 40 shares of $10 par value common stock.

REQUIRED

1. Assume the bonds are issued at 103.5 on May 1, 2011.
   a. How much cash is received?
   b. How much is Bonds Payable?
   c. What is the difference between **a** and **b** called, and how much is it?
   d. With regard to the bond interest payment on October 31, 2011:
      (1) How much cash is paid in interest?
      (2) How much is the amortization?
      (3) How much is interest expense?
2. Assume the bonds are issued at 96.5 on May 1, 2011.
   a. How much cash is received?
   b. How much is Bonds Payable?
   c. What is the difference between **a** and **b** called, and how much is it?
   d. With regard to the bond interest payment on October 31, 2011:
      (1) How much cash is paid in interest?
      (2) How much is the amortization?
      (3) How much is interest expense?
3. Assume the issue price in requirement 1 and assume that the bonds are called and retired 10 years later.
   a. How much cash will have to be paid to retire the bonds?
   b. Is there a gain or loss on retirement? If so, how much is it?
4. Assume the issue price in requirement 2 and assume that the bonds are converted to common stock 10 years later.
   a. Is there a gain or loss on conversion? If so, how much is it?
   b. How many shares of common stock are issued in exchange for the bonds?
   c. In dollar amounts, how does this transaction affect the total liabilities and the total stockholders' equity of the company? In your answer, show the effects on four accounts.

USER INSIGHT ▶

5. Assume that after 10 years, market interest rates have dropped significantly and that the price of the company's common stock has risen significantly. Also assume that management wants to improve its credit rating by reducing its debt to equity ratio and that it needs what cash it currently has for expansion. Would management prefer the approach and result in requirement 3 or 4? Explain your answer. What would be a disadvantage of the approach you chose?

LO 3, 5

Bonds Transaction—Straight-Line Method

✔ 1. Nov. 30, Bond Interest Expense: $517,500; 2. Nov. 30, Bond Interest Expense: $532,500

P 8. Romero Corporation has $10,000,000 of 10.5 percent, 20-year bonds dated June 1, 2011, with interest payment dates of May 31 and November 30. The company's fiscal year ends November 30. It uses the straight-line method to amortize bond premiums or discounts.

REQUIRED

1. Assume the bonds are issued at 103 on June 1. Prepare journal entries for June 1, 2011; November 30, 2011; and May 31, 2012. (*Note:* Round amounts to the nearest dollar.)

2. Assume the bonds are issued at 97 on June 1. Prepare journal entries for June 1, 2011; November 30, 2011; and May 31, 2012. (*Note:* Round amounts to the nearest dollar.)

USER INSIGHT ▶ 3. Explain the role that market interest rates play in causing a premium in requirement 1 and a discount in requirement 2.

LO 3, 5

Bond Transactions—Straight-Line Method

✔ 1. Nov. 30, Bond Interest Expense: $394,000; 2. Nov. 30, Bond Interest Expense: $406,000

P 9. Romero Corporation has $10,000,000 of 8 percent, 25-year bonds dated June 1, 2011, with interest payment dates of May 31 and November 30. The company's fiscal year ends November 30. It uses the straight-line method to amortize bond premiums or discounts.

REQUIRED

1. Assume the bonds are issued at 103 on June 1. Prepare journal entries for June 1, 2011; November 30, 2011; and May 31, 2012. (*Note:* Round amounts to the nearest dollar.)
2. Assume the bonds are issued at 97 on June 1. Prepare journal entries for June 1, 2011; November 30, 2011; and May 31, 2012. (*Note:* Round amounts to the nearest dollar.)

USER INSIGHT ▶ 3. Explain the role that market interest rates play in causing a premium in requirement 1 and a discount in requirement 2.

LO 3, 5

Bond Transactions—Effective Interest Method

GL GENERAL LEDGER

✔ 1. Sept. 30, Bond Interest Expense: $711,450; 2. Sept. 30, Bond Interest Expense: $734,400

P 10. Angel Corporation has $15,000,000 of 9.6 percent, 10-year bonds dated April 1, 2011, with interest payment dates of March 31 and September 30. The company's fiscal year ends September 30. It uses the effective interest method to amortize bond premiums or discounts.

REQUIRED

1. Assume the bonds are issued at 102 on April 1 to yield an effective interest rate of 9.3 percent. Prepare journal entries for April 1, 2011; September 30, 2011; and March 31, 2012. (*Note:* Round amounts to the nearest dollar.)
2. Assume the bonds are issued at 96 on April 1 to yield an effective interest rate of 10.2 percent. Prepare journal entries for April 1, 2011; September 30, 2011; and March 31, 2012. (*Note:* Round amounts to the nearest dollar.)

3. Explain the role that market interest rates play in causing a premium in requirement 1 and a discount in requirement 2.

Cases

LO 1

Conceptual Understanding: Effect of Long-Term Leases

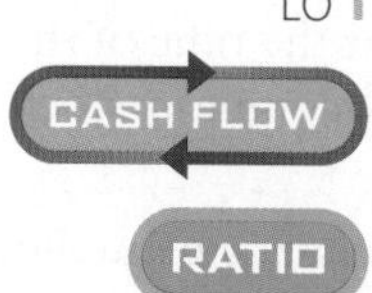

C 1. Many companies use long-term leases to finance long-term assets. Although these leases are similar to mortgage payments, they can be structured in such a way that they qualify as operating leases. As a result, the lease commitments do not appear on the companies' balance sheets.

At the end of 2009, **Walgreens,** one of the largest drugstore chains, had almost $35 billion in total operating lease commitments, of which almost $2.0 billion was due in 2010. Further, the firm had total assets of $12.8 billion and total liabilities of $12.2 billion. Capital leases and related liabilities were less than 1 percent of these numbers. Because of heavy losses in previous years, its stockholders' equity was only $0.6 billion.[14]

What effect, if any, do these types of leases have on the balance sheet? Why would the use of these long-term leases make a company's debt to equity ratio, interest coverage ratio, and free cash flow look better than they really are? What is a capital lease? How does the application of capital lease accounting provide insight into a company's financial health?

LO 2, 6

Conceptual Understanding: Bond Issue

C 2. In 2003, **Eastman Kodak**, the imaging company, issued a $1 billion bond issue. Even though the company's credit rating was low, the bond issue was well received by the investment community because the company offered attractive terms. The offering comprised $500 million of 10-year unsecured notes and $500 million of 30-year convertible bonds. The convertible bonds were callable after seven years and would be convertible into common stock at about 40 to 45 percent higher than the current price.[15]

What are unsecured notes? Why would they carry a relatively high interest rate? What are convertible securities? Why are they good for the investor and for the company? Why would they carry a relatively low interest rate? What does *callable* mean? What advantage does this feature give the company?

LO 2, 3

Conceptual Understanding: Bond Interest Rates and Market Prices

C 3. Among the long-term liabilities of **Wal-Mart Stores**, the world's largest discount company, is a bond due in 2040 that carries a face interest rate of 4.87 percent.[16] In 2010, this bond sold on the New York Stock Exchange at 108.[17]

Did this bond sell at a discount or a premium? Assuming the bond was originally issued at face value, did interest rates rise or decline after the date of issue? Would you have expected the market rate of interest on this bond to be more or less than 4.875 percent? Did the current market price affect either the amount that the company paid in semiannual interest or the amount of interest expense for the same period? Explain your answers.

LO 1

Interpreting Financial Reports: Leverage, Debt to Equity, and Financial Risk

RATIO

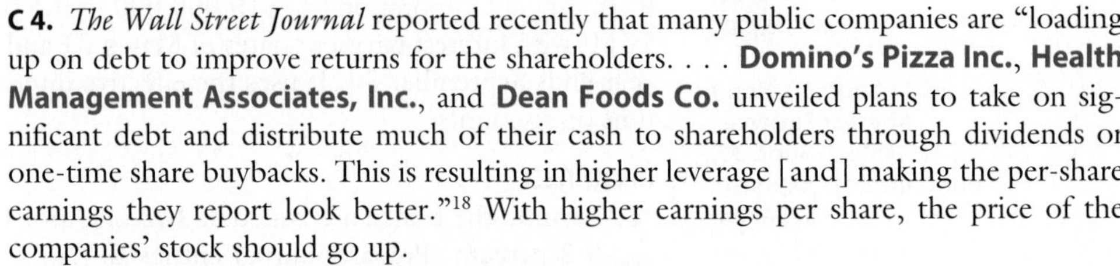

C 4. *The Wall Street Journal* reported recently that many public companies are "loading up on debt to improve returns for the shareholders. . . . **Domino's Pizza Inc., Health Management Associates, Inc.**, and **Dean Foods Co.** unveiled plans to take on significant debt and distribute much of their cash to shareholders through dividends or one-time share buybacks. This is resulting in higher leverage [and] making the per-share earnings they report look better."[18] With higher earnings per share, the price of the companies' stock should go up.

What is leverage? Why does this plan result in higher leverage, and what ratio reflects the higher leverage? Will the companies have more or less financial risk after these transactions? Why will this plan make earnings per share look better?

LO 2

Interpreting Financial Reports: Characteristics of Convertible Debt

RATIO

C 5. Amazon.com, Inc., is well known today as an online marketplace for books, music, and other products. Although the increase in its stock price was initially meteoric, it was some years before the company began to earn a profit. To support its enormous growth, Amazon.com issued $500,000,000 in 6.875 percent convertible notes due in 2010 at face value. Interest is payable on February 1 and August 1. The notes are convertible into common stock at a price of $112 per share, which at the time of the issue was above the market price. The market value of Amazon.com's common stock has been quite volatile, ranging from $48 to $146 in 2009.[19]

What reasons can you suggest for Amazon.com's management choosing notes that are convertible into common stock rather than simply issuing nonconvertible notes or issuing common stock directly? Are there any disadvantages to this approach? Based on the fact that the price of the company's common stock is over $100 per share, what would be the total theoretical value of the notes? If the holders of the notes were to elect to convert the notes into common stock, what would be the effect on the company's debt to equity ratio, and what would be the effect on the percentage ownership of the company by other stockholders?

LO 1

Annual Report Case: Business Practice, Long-Term Debt, Leases, Pensions, and Other Postretirement Benefits

C 6. To answer the following questions, refer to the financial statements and the notes to the financial statements in the **CVS** annual report in the Supplement to Chapter 1:

1. Does CVS own or lease most of its buildings?
2. The note on leases in CVS 2009 annual report indicates that CVS has future obligations under capital leases of only $324 million as compared to future obligations under operating leases of $26,913 million. What is the difference between capital

and operating leases and why would CVS be careful to structure most of its leases to be operating leases?

3. At the end of 2009, CVS has a defined benefit plan with an obligation of $612 million of which $372 million is funded. What is a defined benefit plan and what is the implication of the funding?

LO 1

Comparison Case: Use of Debt Financing

RATIO

C 7. Refer to the **CVS** annual report and the financial statements of **Southwest Airlines Co.** in the Supplement to Chapter 1. Calculate the debt to equity ratio and the interest coverage ratio for both companies' two most recent years. CVS has total lease commitments of $26,913 million including $1,724 million in 2008 and $1,899 in 2009. Southwest's lease expenses were $527 million and $596 million in 2008 and 2009, respectively, and its total lease commitments for future years were $2,634 million. What effect do the total lease commitments and lease expense have on your assessment of the ratios you calculated? Evaluate and comment on the relative performance of the two companies with regard to debt financing. Which company has more risk of not being able to meet its interest obligations? How does leasing affect the analysis? Explain.

LO 2

Ethical Dilemma: Bond Indenture and Ethical Reporting

C 8. Cell-Works Technology, Inc., a biotech company, has a $24,000,000 bond issue outstanding. The bond indenture has several restrictive provisions, including requirements that current assets exceed current liabilities by a ratio of 2 to 1 and that income before income taxes exceed the annual interest on the bonds by a ratio of 3 to 1. If those requirements are not met, the bondholders can force the company into bankruptcy. The company is still awaiting Food and Drug Administration (FDA) approval of its new product, CMZ-12, a cancer treatment drug. Management has been counting on sales of CMZ-12 this year to meet the provisions of the bond indenture. As the end of the fiscal year approaches, the company does not have sufficient current assets or income before income taxes to meet the requirements.

Barry Kwak, the chief financial officer, proposes, "Because we can assume that FDA approval will occur early next year, I suggest we book sales and receivables from our major customers now in anticipation of next year's sales. This action will increase our current assets and our income before income taxes. It is essential that we do this to save the company. Look at all the people who will be hurt if we don't do it."

Is Kwak's proposal acceptable accounting? Is it ethical? Who could be harmed by it? What steps might management take?

LO 1, 2

Decision Analysis Using Excel: Issuance of Long-Term Bonds Versus Leasing

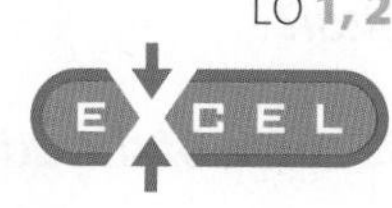

C 9. Atom Chemical Corporation plans to build or lease a new plant that will produce liquid fertilizer for the agricultural market. The plant is expected to cost $800,000,000 and will be located in the southwestern United States. The company's chief financial officer, Megan Russ, has spent the last several weeks studying different means of financing the plant, which is expected to cost $800,000,000. After talking with bankers and other financiers, she has decided that there are two basic choices: the plant can be financed through the issuance of a long-term bond or through a long-term lease. Details for the two options are as follows:

1. Issue $800,000,000 of 25-year, 16 percent bonds secured by the new plant. Interest on the bonds would be payable semiannually.
2. Sign a 25-year lease for an existing plant that calls for lease payments of $65,400,000 on a semiannual basis.

Russ wants to know what effect each choice would have on the company's financial statements. She estimates that the useful life of the plant is 25 years, at which time the plant is expected to have an estimated residual value of $80,000,000.

Russ is planning a meeting to discuss the alternatives. Write a short memorandum to her identifying the issues that should be considered at this meeting. (*Note:* You are not asked to make any calculations, discuss the factors, or recommend an action.)

CHAPTER 11

DECISION POINT
A User's Focus Google, Inc.

When a company issues stock to the public for the first time, it is called an **initial public offering (IPO)**. There are many initial public offerings in any given year, but when **Google**, the popular Internet search engine company, went to market with its IPO in August 2004, it created a national sensation for two reasons. First, it was the largest IPO by an Internet company after the tech bust in 2001 and 2002. Second, Google provides a very well-known and widely used search service. Those who were fortunate enough to buy shares at $85 each saw the price per share soar to $135 in a few days and reach $700 in 2008. The price per share later dropped to below $300 but rose to almost $600 in early 2010. Google's Financial Highlights show the components of Google's stockholders' equity.[1]

GOOGLE'S FINANCIAL HIGHLIGHTS
(in thousands)

	Dec. 31, 2009	Dec. 31, 2008
Stockholders' equity		
Preferred stock	$ —	$ —
Common stock ($0.0001 par value)	318	315
Additional paid-in capital	15,816,738	14,450,338
Retained earnings	20,082,078	13,561,630
Accumulated other comprehensive income	105,090	226,579
Total stockholders' equity	$36,004,224	$28,238,862
Total assets	$40,496,778	$31,767,575

Questions

1. *Why did Google's management choose to issue common stock to satisfy the company's need for new capital?*
2. *What are some of the advantages and disadvantages of this approach to financing a business?*
3. *What measures should investors use in evaluating management's performance?*

Jochen Tack/Alamy

Stockholders' Equity

LEARNING OBJECTIVES

LO1 Identify and explain the management issues related to contributed capital. (pp. 488–496)

LO2 Identify the components of stockholders' equity and their characteristics. (pp. 497–501)

LO3 Account for the issuance of stock for cash and other assets. (pp. 501–504)

LO4 Account for treasury stock. (pp. 505–508)

LO5 Account for stock dividends and stock splits. (pp. 508–512)

LO6 Describe the statement of stockholders' equity and compute book value per share. (pp. 512–515)

In the last chapter, we focused on long-term *debt* financing. Here, we focus on long-term *equity* financing—that is, on the capital that stockholders contribute to a corporation. Ethics is a major concern here as it was with debt financing. Management's decisions must be based not on personal gain, but on the value created for the corporation's owners. Equity financing—including the type of stock a corporation issues, the dividends it pays, and the treasury stock it purchases—can significantly affect return on equity and other measures on which management's compensation is based. Special transactions such as stock dividends and stock splits also affect stockholders' equity. All these transactions are reflected in the statement of stockholders' equity.

FOCUS ON FINANCIAL STATEMENTS

INCOME STATEMENT
Revenues
− Expenses
= Net Income

STATEMENT OF RETAINED EARNINGS
Opening Balance
+ Net Income
− Dividends
= Retained Earnings

BALANCE SHEET
Assets | Liabilities
Equity
A = L + E

STATEMENT OF CASH FLOWS
Operating Activities
+ Investing Activities
+ Financing Activities
= Change in Cash
+ Starting Balance
= Ending Cash Balance

Sale and/or repurchase of capital stock and payment of cash dividends on the balance sheet are financing activities on the statement of cash flows.

MANAGEMENT ISSUES RELATED TO CONTRIBUTED CAPITAL

Identify and explain the management issues related to contributed capital. LO 1

In Chapter 1, we defined a *corporation* as a business unit chartered by the state and legally separate from its owners—that is, its stockholders. *Contributed capital,* which refers to stockholders' investments in a corporation, is a major means of financing a corporation. Managing contributed capital requires an understanding of the advantages and disadvantages of the corporate form of business and of the issues involved in equity financing. It also requires familiarity with dividend policies, with how to use return on equity to evaluate performance, and with stock option plans.

The Corporate Form of Business

The corporate form of business is well suited to today's trends toward large organizations, international trade, and professional management. Although fewer in number than sole proprietorships and partnerships, corporations dominate the U.S. economy in part because of their ability to raise large amounts of capital. Exhibit 11.1 shows the amount

EXHIBIT 11.1
Sources of Capital Raised by U.S. Corporations

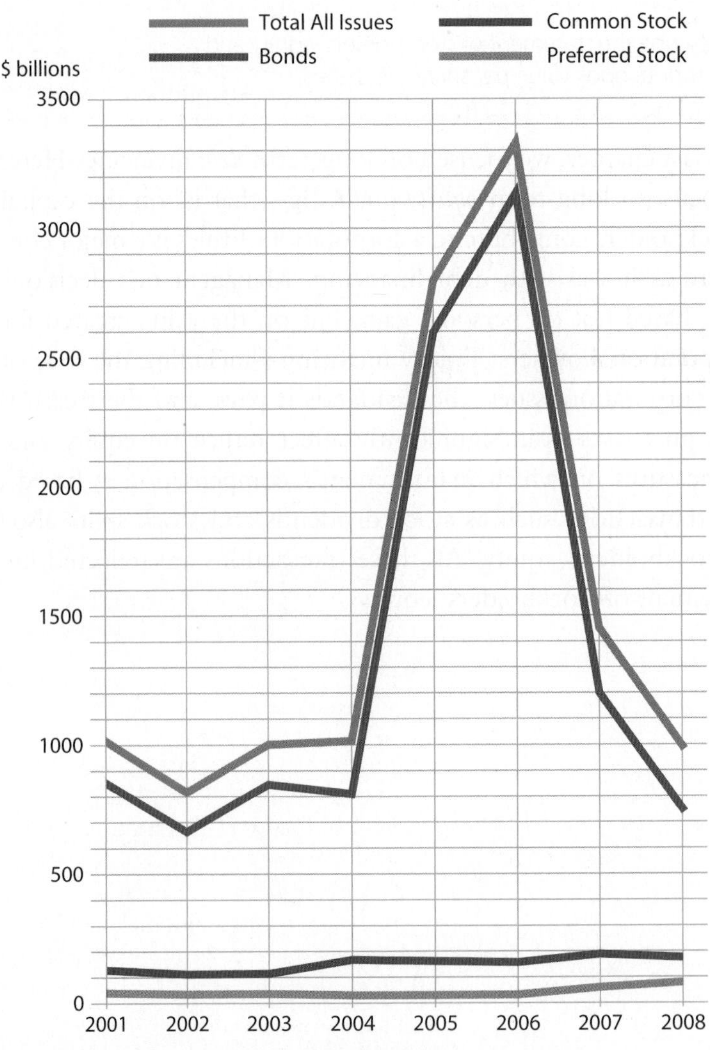

Source: "US Key Stats," Securities Industry and Financial Markets Association.

and sources of capital that U.S. corporations have raised in recent years. As you can see, the total amount of funds raised increased in most years during the last decade, but dropped during the financial crisis of 2008. Nevertheless, nearly $1 trillion was raised. Of this amount, $748 billion, or about 75.5 percent, was from bond issues; $164.9 billion, or 16.7 percent, from common stock; and 77.9 billion, or 7.9 percent, from preferred stock.

Advantages of Incorporation Managers of a corporation must be familiar with the advantages and disadvantages of this form of business. Some of the advantages are as follows:

- **Separate legal entity:** As a separate legal entity, a corporation can buy and sell property, sue other parties, enter into contracts, hire and fire employees, and be taxed.
- **Limited liability:** Because a corporation is a legal entity, separate from its owners, its creditors can satisfy their claims only against the assets of the corporation, not against the personal property of the corporation's owners. Because the owners are not responsible for the corporation's debts, their liability is limited to the amount of their investment. In contrast, the personal property of sole proprietors and partners generally is available to creditors.
- **Ease of capital generation:** It is fairly easy for a corporation to raise capital because shares of ownership in the business are available to a great number of potential investors for a small amount of money. As a result, a single corporation can have many owners.
- **Ease of transfer of ownership:** A **share of stock**, a unit of ownership in a corporation, is easily transferable. A stockholder can normally buy and sell shares without affecting the corporation's activities or needing the approval of other owners.
- **Lack of mutual agency:** If a stockholder tries to enter into a contract for a corporation, the corporation is not bound by the contract. But in a partnership, because of what is called *mutual agency*, all the partners can be bound by one partner's actions.
- **Continuous existence:** Because a corporation is a separate legal entity, an owner's death, incapacity, or withdrawal does not affect the life of the corporation. A corporation's life is set by its charter and regulated by state laws.
- **Centralized authority and responsibility:** A corporation's board of directors represents the stockholders and delegates the responsibility and authority for day-to-day operations to a single person, usually the president. Operating power is thus centralized rather than being divided among multiple owners of the business. The president may delegate authority over certain segments of the business to others, but he or she is held accountable to the board of directors. If the board is dissatisfied with the performance of the president, it can replace that person.
- **Professional management:** Large corporations have many owners, the vast majority of whom are not able to make timely decisions about business operations. So, in most large corporations, management and ownership are separate. This allows management to hire the best talent available to run the business.

Disadvantages of Incorporation The disadvantages of corporations include the following:

- **Government regulation:** Corporations must meet the requirements of state laws. As "creatures of the state," they are subject to greater state control and regulation than are other forms of business. They must file many reports with the state in which they are chartered. Publicly held corporations must also file reports with the Securities and Exchange Commission and with the stock exchanges on which they are listed. They must also maintain internal controls and have audits conducted in compliance with regulations set by the Public Company Accounting Oversight Board (PCAOB). Meeting these requirements is very costly.
- **Double taxation:** A major disadvantage of the corporate form of business is **double taxation**. Because a corporation is a separate legal entity, its earnings are subject to

STUDY NOTE: *Lenders to a small corporation may require the corporation's officers to sign a promissory note, which makes them personally liable for the debt.*

federal and state income taxes, which may be as much as 35 percent of corporate earnings. If any of a corporation's after-tax earnings are paid out as dividends, the earnings are taxed again as income to the stockholders. In contrast, the earnings of sole proprietorships and partnerships are taxed only once, as personal income to the owners.

- **Limited liability:** Although limited liability is an advantage of incorporation, it can also be a disadvantage. Limited liability restricts the ability of a small corporation to borrow money. Because creditors can lay claim only to the assets of a corporation, they may limit their loans to the level secured by those assets or require stockholders to guarantee the loans personally.
- **Separation of ownership and control:** Just as limited liability can be a drawback, so can the separation of ownership and control. Management sometimes makes decisions that are not good for the corporation as a whole. Poor communication can also make it hard for stockholders to exercise control over the corporation or even to recognize that management's decisions are harmful.

Equity Financing

Equity financing is accomplished by issuing stock to investors in exchange for assets, usually cash. Once the stock has been issued to them, the stockholders can transfer their ownership at will. In large corporations that are listed on the stock exchanges, stockholders' records are hard to maintain. Such companies can have millions of shares of stock, thousands of which change ownership every day. They therefore often appoint independent registrars and transfer agents (usually banks and trust companies) to help perform the transfer duties. The outside agents are responsible for transferring the corporation's stock, maintaining stockholders' records, preparing a list of stockholders for stockholders' meetings, and paying dividends.

Two important terms in equity financing are *par value* and *legal capital*:

- **Par value** is an arbitrary amount assigned to each share of stock. It must be recorded in the capital stock accounts. Par value usually bears little, if any, relationship to the market price of the shares. For example, although **Google**'s stock initially sold for $85 per share and the market price is now much higher, its par value per share is only $0.001.
- **Legal capital** is the number of shares issued times the par value. It is the minimum amount that a corporation can report as contributed capital. For example, even though the total market value of Google's shares now exceeds $150 billion, Google's legal capital is only about $318,000 (318 million shares × $0.001).

To help with its initial public offering (IPO), a corporation often uses an **underwriter**—an intermediary between the corporation and the investing public. For a fee—usually less than 1 percent of the selling price—the underwriter guarantees the sale of the stock. The corporation records the amount of the net proceeds of the offering—what the public paid less the underwriter's fees, legal expenses, and any other direct costs of the offering—in its Capital Stock and Additional Paid-In Capital accounts. Because of the size of its IPO, **Google** used a group of investment banks headed by two well-known investment bankers, **Morgan Stanley** and **Credit Suisse First Boston**.

The costs of forming a corporation are called **start-up and organization costs**. These costs, which are incurred before a corporation begins operations, include state incorporation fees and attorneys' fees for drawing up the articles of incorporation. They also include the cost of printing various legal documents, accountants' fees for registering the firm's initial stock, and other expenditures necessary for the formation of the corporation. Because Google's IPO was so large, the fees of the lawyers, accountants, and underwriters who helped arrange the IPO amounted to millions of dollars.

Theoretically, start-up and organization costs benefit the entire life of a corporation. For that reason, a case can be made for recording them as intangible assets and amortizing

STUDY NOTE: Start-up and organization costs are expensed as they are incurred.

them over the life of the corporation. However, a corporation's life normally is not known, so accountants expense start-up and organization costs as they are incurred.

Advantages of Equity Financing Financing a business by issuing common stock has several advantages:

- **Decreased financial risk:** Issuing common stock is less risky than financing with bonds because a company does not pay dividends on common stock unless the board of directors decides to pay them. In contrast, if a company does not pay interest on bonds, it can be forced into bankruptcy.
- **Increased cash for company operations:** When a company does not pay a cash dividend, it can shift the cash generated by profitable operations back into the company's operations. **Google**, for instance, does not currently pay any dividends, and its issuance of common stock provides it with funds for expansion.
- **Better debt to equity ratio:** A company can use the proceeds of a common stock issue to maintain or improve its debt to equity ratio.

Disadvantages of Equity Financing Issuing common stock also has certain disadvantages:

- **Increased tax liability:** Whereas the interest paid on bonds is tax-deductible, the dividends paid on stock are not tax-deductible.
- **Decreased stockholder control:** When a corporation issues more stock, it dilutes its ownership. Thus, the current stockholders must yield some control to the new stockholders.

Dividend Policies

A **dividend** is a distribution among stockholders of the assets that a corporation's earnings have generated. Stockholders receive these assets, usually cash, in proportion to the number of shares they own. A corporation's board of directors has sole authority to declare dividends, but senior managers, who usually serve as members of the board, influence dividend policies. Receiving dividends is one of two ways in which stockholders can earn a return on their investment in a corporation. The other way is to sell their shares for more than they paid for them.

Although a corporation may have sufficient cash and retained earnings to pay a dividend, its board of directors may not declare one for several reasons. The corporation may need the cash for expansion; it may want to improve its overall financial position by liquidating debt; or it may be facing major uncertainties, such as a pending lawsuit, a strike, or a projected decline in the economy, that make it prudent to preserve resources.

A corporation pays dividends quarterly, semiannually, annually, or at other times declared by its board of directors. Most states do not allow a corporation to declare a dividend that exceeds its retained earnings. When a corporation does declare a dividend that exceeds retained earnings, it is, in essence, returning to the stockholders part of their contributed capital. This is called a **liquidating dividend**. A corporation usually pays a liquidating dividend only when it is going out of business or reducing its operations.

Having sufficient retained earnings in itself does not justify the declaration of a dividend. If a corporation does not have cash or other assets readily available for distribution, it might have to borrow money to pay the dividend—an action most boards of directors want to avoid.

Companies usually pay dividends only when they have had profitable operations. For example, **Apple Computer** began paying dividends in 1987, but it stopped those payments in 1996 to conserve cash after it suffered large operating losses in 1995. Now that Apple is profitable again, it may resume paying dividends. However, factors other than earnings affect the decision to pay dividends. Among them are the following:

- **Industry policies:** A company may change its dividend policy to bring it in line with the prevailing policy in its industry. For example, despite positive earnings, **AT&T Corporation** slashed its dividends by 83 percent in 2002. This action put AT&T's policy more in line with the policies of its peers in the telecommunications industry, most of which do not pay dividends.[2]
- **Volatility of earnings:** If a company has years of good earnings followed by years of poor earnings, it may want to keep dividends low to avoid giving a false impression of sustained high earnings. For example, for many years, **General Motors** paid a fairly low but stable dividend and declared a bonus dividend in especially good years.

- **Effect on cash flows:** A company may not pay dividends because its operations do not generate enough cash to do so or because it wants to invest cash in future operations. **McDonald's** increases its dividends per share each year to reward its stockholders but also keeps back a portion of its earnings to spend for other purposes, such as researching and developing new drugs that will generate revenue in the future. In a recent year, for example, the company paid $2.05 per share dividend on earnings per share of $4.11.[3]

In recent years, because of a 15 percent reduction in the tax rate on dividends, attitudes toward dividends have changed. Many companies have either increased their dividends or started to pay dividends for the first time.

Dividend Dates Three important dates are associated with dividends: the declaration date, the record date, and the payment date.

- **Declaration Date:** The **declaration date** is the date on which the board of directors formally declares that the corporation is going to pay a dividend. The legal obligation to pay the dividend arises at this time.
- **Record Date:** The **record date** is the date on which ownership of stock, and therefore the right to receive a dividend, is determined. Persons who own the stock on the record date will receive the dividend. No journal entry is made on this date. Between the record date and the date of payment, the stock is said to be **ex-dividend**. If the owner on the date of record sells the shares of stock before the date of payment, the right to the dividend remains with that person; it does not transfer with the shares to the second owner.
- **Payment Date:** The **payment date** is the date on which the dividend is paid to the stockholders of record.

Companies usually pay dividends only when they have had profitable operations. In 2010, after a catastrophic oil spill in the Gulf of Mexico, British Petroleum (BP) considered suspending dividend payouts.

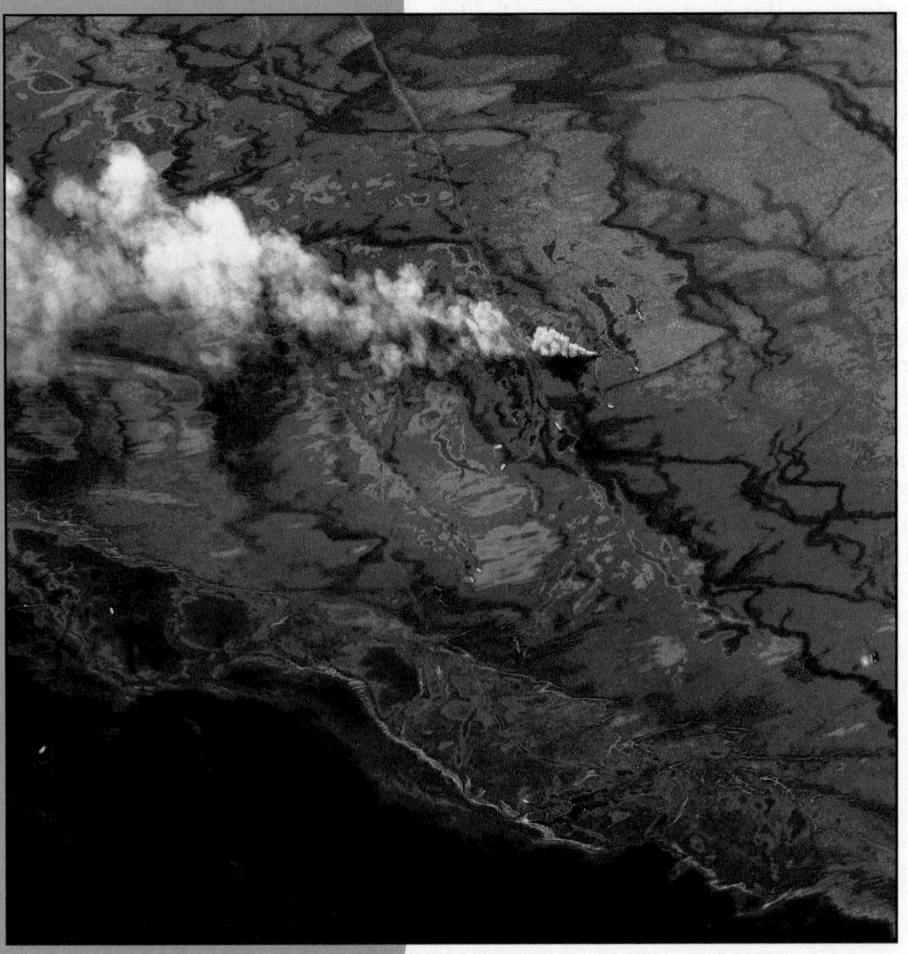

DigitalGlobe/Getty Images

Dividend Transactions

Declaration Date

Assume a board of directors declares a cash dividend of $28,000 on December 21. The record date is December 31, which is also the end of the company's accounting period. The dividend payment date is January 11.

Analysis: The journal entry to record the dividend on the declaration date (December 21)

▲ *increases* the equity account Dividends with a debit on the declaration date and

▲ *increases* the liability account Dividends Payable with a credit in the amount of the total dividends declared.

A	=	L	+	SE
		+28,000		−28,000

Journal Entry:

Dec. 21	Dividends	28,000	
	Dividends Payable		28,000
	Declaration of dividends		

Comment: The Dividends account reduces equity by appearing as a deduction on the statement of retained earnings, and Dividends Payable appears as a liability on the balance sheet.

STUDY NOTE: *Journal entries for dividends are made only on the declaration date and the payment date.*

Record Date

As we have noted, no journal entry is made on the record date (December 31).

Payment Date

Analysis: The journal entry to record the dividend on the payment date (January 11)

▼ *decreases* the liability account Dividends Payable with a debit in the amount of the total dividends declared and

▼ *decreases* the asset account Cash with a credit.

A	=	L	+	SE
−28,000		−28,000		

Journal Entry:

Jan. 11	Dividends Payable	28,000	
	Cash		28,000
	Payment of dividends		

Comment: When the date of declaration and the payment date occur in the same accounting period, the amount of dividends on the statement of retained earnings and on the statement of cash flows will be equal. In this example, however, the accounting period ended between the dates of declaration and payment. Thus, dividends declared during the period ending December 31 exceed the amount paid for dividends. As a result,

- The statement of retained earnings for the accounting period will show a *decrease* in the amount of the dividends declared of $28,000.
- The statement of cash flows will not show the dividends because the cash has not yet been paid out.

RATIO

Measuring Performance Using Financial Ratios

Among the most commonly cited ratios by financial analysts in evaluating a company's performance for investors are dividends yield, return on equity, and price earnings ratio.

Financial Ratio: Dividends Yield To evaluate the amount of dividends they receive, investors use the **dividends yield** ratio. This ratio is computed by dividing the dividends per share by the market price per share. **Microsoft**'s history of dividend payments provides an interesting example. Having built up a large cash balance through years of profitable operations with no dividends, the company paid a large dividend of $3.40 per share in 2005 and then began paying regular dividends thereafter ($0.35 per share in 2006) with annual increases. By 2009, Microsoft's annual dividend increased to $4.5 billion ($0.52 per share) in 2009.[4] The information in Exhibit 11.2 (p. 494) shows how Microsoft's dividends yield and last price are quoted on NASDAQ. Because the yield on corporate bonds exceeds 7 percent, Microsoft shareholders must expect some of their return to come from increases in the price of the shares.

Exhibit 11.2
Stock Quotations on NASDAQ

NASDAQ STOCK EXCHANGE

YTD % CHG	STOCK	SYM	YLD	DIV	PE	LAST	NET CHG
3.5	♣ Micros Systems	MCRS	...	...	27	32.11	0.23
−10.4	Microsemi Corp.	MSCC	...	...	dd	15.92	−0.07
− 2.9	♣ Microsoft Corp.	MSFT	1.8	0.52	18	29.60	0.01
− 5.2	MicroStrategy Inc.	MSTR	...	...	18	89.12	−0.15
7.5	Microtune Inc.	TUNE	...	...	dd	2.43	0.01
−15.1	MicroVision Inc.	MVIS	...	...	dd	2.69	0.12

Source: Stock quotes on the NASDAQ from *The Wall Street Journal*, March 22, 2010. Copyright © 2010 Dow Jones & Co., Inc. Reprinted by permission of Dow Jones & Company via Copyright Clearance Center.

Microsoft's dividends yield is computed as follows:

RATIO

$$\text{Dividends Yield} = \frac{\text{Dividends per Share}}{\text{Market Price per Share}} = \frac{\$0.52}{\$29.60} = 1.8\%$$

Although dividends yield is a helpful ratio for investors in assessing their potential return from owning the stock, they will also want to evaluate a firm's past and future financial performance to determine how secure the dividends are and to determine the potential for future stock price increases Two financial ratios can help them with this decision: the return on equity ratio and the price/earnings ratio.

Financial Ratio: Return on Equity **Return on equity** is the most important financial ratio associated with stockholders' equity. It is also a common measure of management's performance. For instance, when *BusinessWeek* and *Forbes* rate companies on their success, return on equity is the major basis of their evaluations. In addition, the compensation of top executives is often tied to return on equity benchmarks.

As noted in Chapter 4, return on equity is the ratio of net income to average total stockholders' equity. Microsoft's return on equity in 2009 is computed as follows:[5]

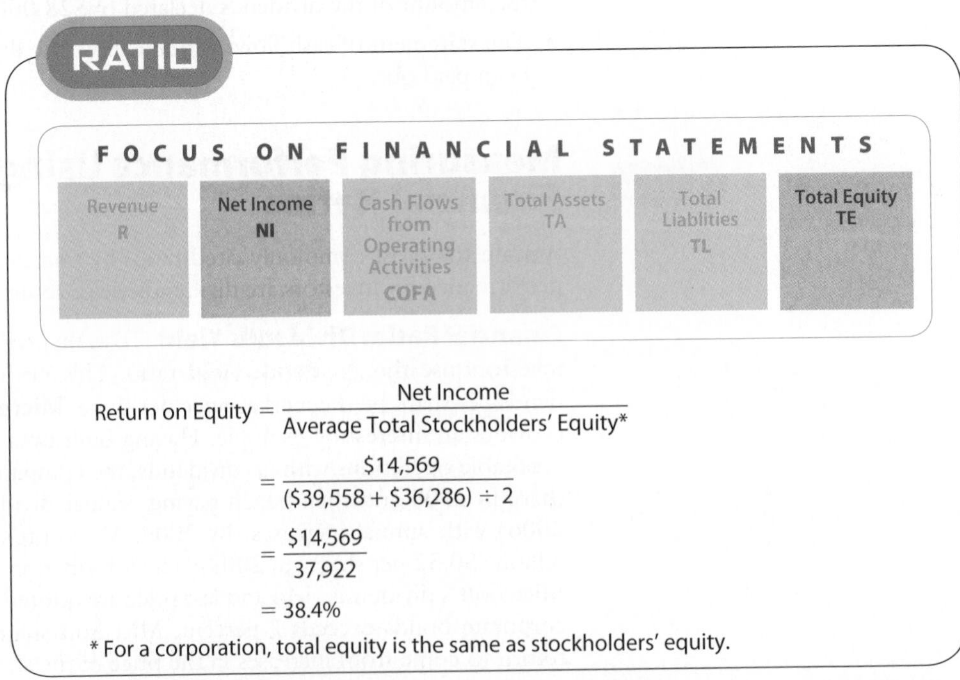

$$\text{Return on Equity} = \frac{\text{Net Income}}{\text{Average Total Stockholders' Equity*}}$$

$$= \frac{\$14{,}569}{(\$39{,}558 + \$36{,}286) \div 2}$$

$$= \frac{\$14{,}569}{37{,}922}$$

$$= 38.4\%$$

* For a corporation, total equity is the same as stockholders' equity.

Microsoft's's superb return on equity of 38.4 percent depends, of course, on the amount of net income the company earns. However, it also depends on the level of stockholders' equity, which in turn depends on management's decisions about the amount of stock the company sells to the public. As a company sells more shares,

▲ stockholders' equity *increases* and

▼ return on equity *decreases.*

Since it is advantageous to increase return on equity, management can keep stockholders' equity at a minimum, thereby increasing return on equity, by financing the business with cash flows from operations and by issuing debt instead of stock. However, as we have pointed out, issuing bonds and other types of debt increases a company's financial risk because the interest and principal of the debt must be paid in a timely manner.

Management can also reduce stockholder's equity, thereby increasing return on equity, by buying back the company's shares on the open market. The cost of these shares, which are called treasury stock, has the following effect:

▼ Stockholders' equity *decreases* and

▲ Return on equity *increases.*

Many companies buy back their own stock instead of paying or increasing dividends. Their reason for doing so is that it puts money into the hands of stockholders in the form of market price appreciation without creating a commitment to higher dividends in the future. For instance, in 2009, **Microsoft** purchased $9.4 billion of its common stock on the open market.[6] Microsoft's stock repurchases will improve the company's return on equity, increase its earnings per share, and lower its price/earnings ratio.

Financial Ratio: Price/Earnings Ratio The **price/earnings (P/E) ratio** is a measure of investors' confidence in a company's future. It is calculated by dividing the market price per share by the earnings per share. The price/earnings ratio will vary as market price per share fluctuates daily and the amount of earnings per share changes. If you look back at Exhibit 11.2, you will see that it shows a P/E ratio of 18 (rounded) for **Microsoft**. It was computed using the annual earnings per share from Microsoft's 2009 income statement, as follows:

RATIO

$$\text{Price/Earnings (P/E) Ratio} = \frac{\text{Market Price per Share}}{\text{Earnings per Share}} = \frac{\$29.60}{\$1.62} = 18.3 \text{ times}$$

Because the market price is 18.3 times earnings, investors are paying a high price in relation to earnings. They do so in the expectation that Microsoft will continue to be successful.

Stock Options as Compensation

More than 98 percent of public companies encourage employees to invest in their common stock through **stock option plans**.[7] Most such plans give employees the right to purchase stock in the future at a fixed price. Some companies offer stock option plans only to management personnel, but others, including **Google**, make them available to all employees. Because the market value of a company's stock is tied to a company's performance, these plans are a means of both motivating and compensating employees. As the market value of the stock goes up, the difference between the option price and the market price grows, which increases the amount of compensation. Another key benefit of stock option plans is that compensation expense is tax-deductible.

Focus on Business Practice

Politics and Accounting Don't Mix

The FASB has long held that stock options should be treated as an expense, but in trying to pass this rule, it has encountered heavy opposition from the technology industry, which is the largest user of stock options. Industry technology leaders have maintained that expensing stock options would hurt their companies' profits and growth. The FASB argued that stock options are a form of compensation and therefore have value. The U.S. Congress got involved and pressured the FASB to back down, using the companies' reasoning that stock options essentially have no value and thus are not an expense on the income statement, although they should be mentioned in a note to the financial statements. Many stock options were being granted, and the companies granting them were very loose in how they accounted for them. Many of the stock transactions were back-dated so that the exercise price would be most advantageous to the executives who were benefiting. By 2010, the SEC had settled more than 60 criminal investigations, usually resulting in settlements and significant fines.[8]

iStock Photo

In one example of how firms value stock options, **Google** recognized $1,164,054 of stock-based compensation expense in 2009. This amount represented about 7.6 percent of the company's total expenses and almost 17.9 percent of its net income.

Cash Flow Information

The best source of information concerning cash flows related to stock transactions and dividends is the financing activities section of the statement of cash flows. For instance, **Microsoft**'s cash flows from these activities are clearly revealed in this partial section of the company's 2009 statement of cash flows (in millions):

	2009	2008	2007
Financing Activities			
Common stock issued	$ 579	$ 3,494	$ 6,782
Common stock repurchased	(9,353)	(12,533)	(27,575)
Common stock cash dividend	(4,468)	(4,015)	(3,805)

Note the decreasing amounts of common stock repurchased (treasury stock) and the small amount of new common stock issued by the company in 2009. Both actions are a reflection of the company's success.

Stop & Apply

Match each item on the left with the topic on the right to which it pertains.

a. Advantage of the corporate form of business
b. Disadvantage of the corporate form of business
c. Dividend policies
d. Performance evaluation
e. Stock option

_____ 1. U.S. tax policies
_____ 2. Return on equity
_____ 3. Separate legal entity
_____ 4. Employee's right to purchase shares at a given price
_____ 5. Ease of ownership transfer
_____ 6. Distributing cash to stockholders
_____ 7. Need to deal with government regulation

iStock Photo

SOLUTION 1. b; 2. d; 3. a; 4. e; 5. a; 6. c; 7. b

COMPONENTS OF STOCKHOLDERS' EQUITY

LO 2 Identify the components of stockholders' equity and their characteristics.

In a corporation's balance sheet, the owners' claims to the business are called *stockholders' equity*. As shown in Exhibit 11.3, this section of a corporate balance sheet usually has *at least* three components:

- **Contributed capital**: The stockholders' investments in the corporation.
- **Retained earnings**: The earnings of the corporation since its inception, less any losses, dividends, or transfers to contributed capital. Retained earnings are reinvested in the business. They are not a pool of funds to be distributed to the stockholders; instead, they represent the stockholders' claim to assets resulting from profitable operations.
- **Treasury stock**: Shares of the corporation's own stock that it has bought back on the open market. The cost of these shares is treated *not* as an investment, but as a reduction in stockholders' equity. By buying back the shares, the corporation reduces the ownership of the business.

Less frequently, stockholders' equity can contain other items such as other comprehensive income. **Other comprehensive income** (or **loss**) includes a variety of items, such as the effect of foreign exchange adjustment and unrealized gains and losses, that do not appear on the income statement but go directly to stockholders' equity. When use of the phrase *accumulated other comprehensive income* is used, it means that there are various items from previous years included in the amount. For example, in the financial highlights at the beginning of the chapter, Google has other comprehensive income. When a company has other comprehensive income, the items that constitute it will appear on the statement of stockholders' equity.

In keeping with the convention of full disclosure, the stockholders' equity section of a corporate balance sheet gives a great deal of information about the corporation's stock. Under contributed capital, it lists the kinds of stock; their par value; and the number of shares authorized, issued, and outstanding.

A corporation can issue two kinds of stock: common stock and preferred stock.

- **Common stock** is the basic form of stock that a corporation issues; that is, if a corporation issues only one type of stock, it is common stock. Because shares of common stock carry voting rights, they generally provide their owners with a means of controlling the corporation. Common stock is also called **residual equity**, which means that if the corporation is liquidated, the claims of all creditors and usually those of preferred stockholders rank ahead of the claims of common stockholders.

EXHIBIT 11.3
Stockholders' Equity Section of a Balance Sheet

Stockholders' Equity		
Contributed capital		
Preferred stock, $50 par value, 2,000 shares authorized, issued, and outstanding		$100,000
Common stock, $5 par value, 60,000 shares authorized, 40,000 shares issued, 36,000 shares outstanding	$200,000	
Additional paid-in capital	100,000	300,000
Total contributed capital		$400,000
Retained earnings		120,000
Total contributed capital and retained earnings		$520,000
Less: Treasury stock, common (4,000 shares at cost)		40,000
Total stockholders' equity		$480,000

Focus on Business Practice

Are You a First-Class or Second-Class Stockholder?

When companies go public, insiders—usually the founders of the company or top management—often get first-class shares with extra votes, whereas outsiders get second-class shares with fewer votes. The class A and class B shares of **Adolph Coors Company**, the large brewing firm, are an extreme example. The company's class B shares, owned by the public, have no votes except in the case of a merger. Its class A shares, held by the Coors family trust, have all the votes on other issues.

Google also has two classes of common shares. Both classes are identical except that each class B share is entitled to 10 votes and each class A share is entitled to only one vote. Class A shares are the ones that Google offered to the public in its IPO. As a result, Class B shareholders control 78 percent of the company.[9]

Shareholder advocates denounce the class division of shares as undemocratic. They maintain that this practice gives a privileged few shareholders all or most of the control of a company and that it denies other shareholders voting power consistent with the risk they are taking. Defenders of the practice argue that it shields top executives from the market's obsession with short-term results and allows them to make better long-term decisions. They also point out that many investors don't care about voting rights as long as the stock performs well.

iStock Photo

- **Preferred stock** is stock that a corporation may issue to attract investors whose goals differ from those of common stockholders. Preferred stock gives its owners preference over common stockholders, usually in terms of receiving dividends and in terms of claims to assets if the corporation is liquidated.

As noted earlier, par value is an arbitrary amount assigned to each share of stock. In addition to identifying the kind of stock and its par value, the description of contributed capital in Exhibit 11.3 (p. 497) specifies the number of shares authorized, issued, and outstanding.

- **Authorized shares** are the maximum number of shares that a corporation's state charter allows it to issue. Most corporations are authorized to issue more shares than they need to issue at the time they are formed. Thus, they are able to raise more capital in the future by issuing additional shares. When a corporation issues all of its authorized shares, it cannot issue more without a change in its state charter.
- **Issued shares** are those that a corporation sells or otherwise transfers to stockholders. The owners of a corporation's issued shares own 100 percent of the business. Unissued shares have no rights or privileges until they are issued.
- **Outstanding shares** are shares that a corporation has issued and that are still in circulation. Treasury stock is not outstanding because it consists of shares that a corporation has issued but that it has bought back and thereby put out of circulation. Thus, a corporation can have more shares issued than are currently outstanding.

Exhibit 11.4 shows the relationship of authorized shares to issued, unissued, outstanding, and treasury shares. In this regard, **Google** is an interesting example. The company has 9 billion authorized shares of stock and only about 318 million shares issued. With its excess of authorized issues, Google obviously has plenty of flexibility for future stock transactions.

Characteristics of Preferred Stock

Most preferred stock has one or more of the following characteristics: preference as to dividends, preference as to assets if a corporation is liquidated, convertibility, and a callable option. A corporation may offer several different classes of preferred stock, each with distinctive characteristics to attract different investors.

EXHIBIT 11.4
Relationship of Authorized Shares to Unissued, Issued, Outstanding, and Treasury Shares

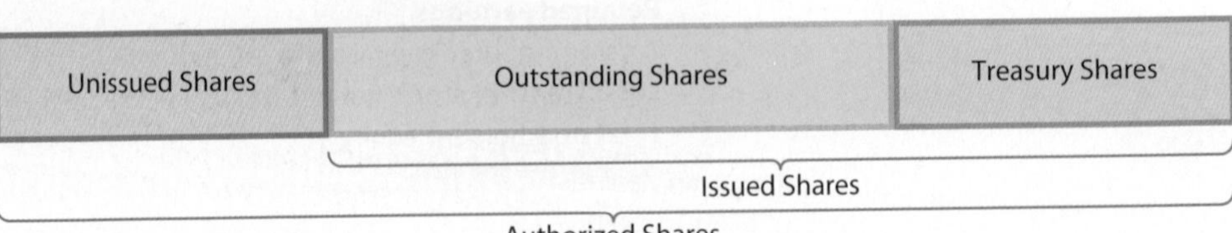

Preference as to Dividends Preferred stockholders ordinarily must receive a certain amount of dividends before common stockholders receive anything. The amount that preferred stockholders must be paid before common stockholders can be paid is usually stated in dollars per share or as a percentage of the par value of the preferred shares. For example, a company might pay an annual dividend of $4 per share on preferred stock, or it might issue preferred stock at $50 par value and pay an annual dividend of 8 percent of par value, which would also be $4 per share.

Preferred stockholders have no guarantee of ever receiving dividends. A company's board of directors must declare dividends on preferred stock before any liability arises. The consequences of not granting an annual dividend on preferred stock vary according to whether the stock is noncumulative or cumulative:

- If the stock is **noncumulative preferred stock** and the board of directors fails to declare a dividend on it in any given year, the company is under no obligation to make up the missed dividend in future years.
- If the stock is **cumulative preferred stock**, the dividend amount per share accumulates from year to year, and the company must pay the whole amount before it pays any dividends on common stock.

Dividends not paid on cumulative preferred stock in the year they are due are called **dividends in arrears**. If a corporation has dividends in arrears, it should report the amount either in the body of its financial statements or in a note to its financial statements. The following note is typical of one that might appear in a corporation's annual report:

> On December 31, 2010, the company was in arrears by $37,851,000 ($1.25 per share) on dividends to its preferred stockholders. The company must pay all dividends in arrears to preferred stockholders before paying any dividends to common stockholders.

Suppose that a corporation has 20,000 outstanding shares of $10 par value, 6 percent cumulative preferred stock. Operations in 2011 produced income of only $8,000. However, in 2011, the corporation's board of directors declared a $6,000 cash dividend to the preferred stockholders. Dividends in arrears are calculated as follows:

2011 dividends due preferred stockholders	
[(20,000 × $10) × 0.06]	$12,000
Less 2011 dividends declared to preferred stockholders	6,000
2011 preferred stock dividends in arrears	$ 6,000

Before the corporation can pay a dividend of $12,000 in 2012 to common stockholders, it must pay the preferred stockholders the $6,000 in arrears from 2011, plus $12,000 for 2012 for a total of $18,000.

Now suppose that in 2012, the corporation earns income of $60,000 and wants to pay dividends to both preferred and common stockholders. The corporation's board of directors declares a $24,000 dividend and distributes it as follows:

2012 declaration of dividends	$24,000
Less 2011 preferred stock dividends in arrears	6,000
Amount available for 2012 dividends	$18,000
Less 2012 dividends due preferred stockholders	
[(20,000 × $10) × 0.06]	12,000
Remainder available to common stockholders	$ 6,000

Preference as to Assets Preferred stockholders often have preference in terms of their claims to a corporation's assets if the corporation goes out of business. If a corporation is liquidated, these preferred stockholders have a right to receive the par value of their stock or a larger stated liquidation value per share before the common stockholders receive any share of the corporation's assets. This preference can also extend to any dividends in arrears owed to the preferred stockholders.

STUDY NOTE: When preferred stockholders convert their shares to common stock, they gain voting rights but lose the dividend and liquidation preference. Conversion back to preferred stock is not an option.

Convertible Preferred Stock Like all preferred stockholders, owners of **convertible preferred stock** are more likely than common stockholders to receive regular dividends. In addition, they can exchange their shares of preferred stock for shares of common stock at a ratio stated in the company's preferred stock contract. If the market value of the company's common stock increases, the conversion feature allows these stockholders to share in the increase by converting their stock to common stock. For example, if you look back at **Google**'s Financial Highlights at the beginning of the chapter, you will see that Google has preferred stock but none is outstanding. The reason for this is that early investors who bought the company's convertible preferred stock took advantage of the steep increase in the price of the common stock by converting their shares to common stock. The preferred stock is still authorized, and Google may decide to issue it again in the future.

As another example of the conversion of preferred stock to common stock, suppose that a company issues 1,000 shares of 8 percent, $100 par value convertible preferred stock for $100 per share. Each share of preferred stock can be converted to five shares of the company's common stock at any time. The market price of the common stock when the company issues the convertible preferred stock is $15 per share. The owner of one share of preferred stock therefore has an investment with a market value of about $75.

Now suppose that in the next few years, the market price of a share of the company's common stock increases from $15 to $30. By converting each of their shares to five common shares, preferred stockholders can realize a gain of $150 (5 shares × $30 per share).

Callable Preferred Stock Most preferred stock is **callable preferred stock**—that is, the issuing corporation can redeem it at a price stated in the preferred stock contract. An owner of callable preferred stock that is not convertible must surrender it to the issuing corporation when asked to do so. If the preferred stock is convertible, the stockholder can either surrender the stock to the corporation or convert it to common stock when the corporation calls the stock. The *call price*, or redemption price, is usually higher than the stock's par value. For example, preferred stock that has a $100 par value might be callable at $103 per share.

When preferred stock is called and surrendered, the stockholder is entitled to the following:

- The par value of the stock
- The call premium
- Any dividends in arrears
- The current period's dividend prorated by the proportion of the year to the call date

A corporation may decide to call its preferred stock for any of the following reasons:

- It may want to force conversion of the preferred stock to common stock because the dividend that it pays on preferred shares is higher than the dividend that it pays on the equivalent number of common shares.
- It may be able to replace the outstanding preferred stock with a preferred stock at a lower dividend rate or with long-term debt, which can have a lower after-tax cost.
- It may simply be profitable enough to retire the preferred stock.

Focus on International Practices

IFRS How Does a Stock Become a Debt Under IFRS?

An important difference between International Financial Reporting Standards (IFRS) and U.S. GAAP is the issue of what constitutes stockholders' equity. This issue is important because it affects financial ratios such as return on assets, requirements under loan agreements, and the capital requirements of banks. Under U.S. GAAP, most preferred stocks are classified as stockholders' equity. In contrast, under IFRS, most preferred stocks are classified as liabilities because they resemble debt in that they have fixed dividends rates and are often cumulative.

Some companies have issued preferred stock that is "mandatorily redeemable," which means that the issuing companies are required to buy back the stock at fixed future dates or under predetermined conditions. These preferred stocks are therefore similar to bonds in that they have a fixed maturity date.[10] The FASB is considering a proposal that would require these special preferred stocks to be classified as a liability on the balance sheet, which would be more in line with IFRS.[11]

iStock Photo

Stop & Apply

Nicea Corporation has 2,000 shares of $100 par value, 7 percent cumulative preferred stock outstanding and 200,000 shares of $1 par value common stock outstanding. In the corporation's first three years of operation, its board of directors declared cash dividends as follows. (*Note:* No dividends were declared in Nicea's first year of operation.)

2011: $20,000
2012: $30,000

Determine the total cash dividends paid to the preferred and common stockholders during each of the three years.

SOLUTION

2011:	Preferred dividends in arrears (2,000 shares × $100 × 0.07)	$14,000
	Current year remainder to preferred ($20,000 − $14,000)	6,000
	Total to preferred stockholders	$20,000
2012:	Preferred dividends in arrears ($14,000 − $6,000)	$ 8,000
	Current year to preferred (2,000 shares × $100 × 0.07)	14,000
	Total to preferred stockholders	$22,000
	Total to common stockholders ($30,000 − $22,000)	8,000
	Total dividends in 2012	$30,000

iStock Photo

ISSUANCE OF STOCK FOR CASH AND OTHER ASSETS

Account for the issuance of stock for cash and other assets. 

A share of capital stock may be either par or no par. The value of par stock is stated in the corporate charter. It can be $0.01, $1, $5, $100, or any other amount established by the organizers of the corporation. For instance, the par value of **Google**'s common stock is $0.001. The par values of common stock tend to be lower than those of preferred stock.

STUDY NOTE: *Legal capital is the minimum amount a corporation can report as contributed capital. To protect creditors, a corporation cannot declare a dividend that would reduce capital below the amount of legal capital.*

As noted earlier, par value is the amount per share that when multiplied times the number of shares issued is recorded in a corporation's Capital Stock accounts, and it constitutes a corporation's legal capital. A corporation cannot declare a dividend that would cause stockholders' equity to fall below the firm's legal capital. Par value is thus a minimum cushion of capital that protects a corporation's creditors. Any amount in excess of par value that a corporation receives from a stock issue is recorded in its Additional Paid-In Capital account and represents a portion of its contributed capital.

No-par stock does not have a par value. A corporation may issue stock without a par value for several reasons. For one thing, rather than recognizing par value as an arbitrary figure, investors may confuse it with the stock's market value. For another, most states do not allow a stock issue below par value, and this limits a corporation's flexibility in obtaining capital.

State laws often require corporations to place a **stated value** on each share of stock that they issue, but even when this is not required, a corporation's board of directors may do so as a matter of convenience. The stated value can be any value set by the board unless the state specifies a minimum amount, which is sometimes the case. The stated value can be set before or after the shares are issued if the state law is not specific.

Par Value Stock

When a corporation issues par value stock, the appropriate Capital Stock account (usually Common Stock or Preferred Stock) is credited for the par value regardless of whether the proceeds are more or less than the par value. When a corporation issues stock at a price greater than par value, as is usually the case, the proceeds in excess of par are credited to Additional Paid-In Capital. Consider the following example:

Issuing Stock Above Par Value

Stock: Winter Corporation is authorized to issue 10,000 shares of $10 par value common stock. On January 1, 2011, it issues 5,000 shares at $12 each.

Analysis: The journal entry to record this issuance of stock above par value

- ▲ *increases* Cash with a debit for the proceeds of $60,000 (5,000 shares × $12),
- ▲ *increases* Common Stock with a credit for the total par value of $50,000 (5,000 shares × $10), and
- ▲ *increases* Additional Paid-In Capital with a credit for the difference of $10,000 (5,000 shares × $2).

A	= L +	SE
+60,000		+50,000
		+10,000

Journal Entry:

Jan. 1	Cash	60,000	
	Common Stock		50,000
	Additional Paid-In Capital		10,000
	Issued 5,000 shares of $10 par value common stock for $12 per share		

The amount in excess of par value is part of Winter's contributed capital and will be included in the stockholders' equity section of its balance sheet. Immediately after the stock issue, that section of Winter's balance sheet would appear as follows:

Contributed capital	
Common stock, $10 par value, 10,000 shares authorized, 5,000 shares issued and outstanding	$50,000
Additional paid-in capital	10,000
Total contributed capital	$60,000
Retained earnings	—
Total stockholders' equity	$60,000

Comment: If a corporation issues stock for less than par value, an account called Discount on Capital Stock is debited for the difference. The issuance of stock at a discount rarely occurs; it is illegal in many states.

No-Par Stock

STUDY NOTE: *When no-par stock has a stated value, the stated value serves the same purpose as par value in that it represents the minimum legal capital.*

Most states require that all or part of the proceeds from a corporation's issuance of no-par stock be designated as legal capital, which cannot be used unless the corporation is liquidated. The purpose of this requirement is to protect the corporation's assets for creditors. Consider the following examples, again using Winter Corporation.

Issuing No-Par Stock with No Stated Value

Stock: On January 1, 2011, Winter issues 5,000 shares of no-par common stock at $15 per share.

Analysis: The journal entry to record this no-par stock with no stated value

- ▲ *increases* Cash with a debit of $75,000 (5,000 shares x $15) and
- ▲ *increases* Common stock with a credit of $75,000.

A	= L +	SE
+75,000		+75,000

Journal Entry:

Jan. 1	Cash	75,000	
	Common Stock		75,000
	Issued 5,000 shares of no-par common stock for $15 per share		

Comment: Because the stock does not have a stated or par value, all proceeds of the issue ($75,000) are *credited* to Common Stock and are part of the company's legal capital.

Issuing No-Par Stock with a Stated Value

Stock: As noted earlier, state laws may require corporations to put a stated value on each share of stock that they issue. Assume the same facts as were provided previously except that Winter puts a $10 stated value on each share of its no-par stock.

Analysis: The journal entry to record this no-par stock with a stated value

- ▲ *increases* Cash with a debit of $75,000 (5,000 shares × $10),
- ▲ *increases* Common Stock with a credit of $50,000 (the stated value decided by Winter's board of directors), and
- ▲ *increases* Additional Paid-In Capital with a credit of $25,000, which is the difference between the proceeds ($75,000) and the total stated value ($50,000).

A	= L +	SE
+75,000		+50,000
		+25,000

Journal Entry:

Jan. 1	Cash	75,000	
	Common Stock		50,000
	Additional Paid-In Capital		25,000
	Issued 5,000 shares of no-par common stock with $10 stated value for $15 per share		

Start-up companies commonly exchange services or intellectual property in exchange for stock in the company because they have little money and need people with a wealth of expertise in specific areas. For example, Mark Zuckerberg and Adam D'Angelo, the founders of Facebook, essentially traded the intellectual property involved in creating programming language and their time investment for stock in the company.

Comment: In this case, the company's legal capital is $50,000 because the no-par common stock has a stated value.

Issuance of Stock for Noncash Assets

A corporation may issue stock in return for assets or services other than cash. Transactions of this kind usually involve a corporation's exchange of stock for land or buildings or for the services of attorneys and others who help organize the corporation. Generally, this kind of transaction is recorded at the fair market value of the stock that the corporation is giving up. If the stock's fair market value cannot be determined, the fair market value of the assets or services received can be used. A corporation's board of directors has the right to determine the fair market value of the assets or services that the corporation receives in exchange for its stock.

AP Photo/Eric Risberg

Issuing Stock for Noncash Assets When No Market Value for the Stock Exists

Stock: When Winter was formed on January 1, 2011, its attorney agreed to accept 200 shares of its $10 par value common stock for services rendered. At that time, the market value of the stock could not be determined. However, for similar services, the attorney would have charged Winter $3,000.

Analysis: The journal entry to record stock for noncash assets when no market value for the stock exists

- ▲ *increases* Legal Expenses with a debit of $3,000 (estimated cost for attorney services),
- ▲ *increases* Common Stock with a credit for the total par value of $2,000 (200 shares × $10), and

▲ *increases* Additional Paid-In Capital with a credit for the difference of the proceeds ($3,000) and the total stated value ($2,000).

A	=	L	+	SE
				−3,000
				+2,000
				+1,000

Journal Entry:

Jan. 1	Legal Expenses	3,000	
	Common Stock		2,000
	Additional Paid-In Capital		1,000
	Issued 200 shares of $10 par value common stock for attorney's services		

STUDY NOTE: *In establishing the fair market value of property that a corporation exchanges for stock, a board of directors cannot be arbitrary; it must use all the information at its disposal.*

Issuance of Stock for Noncash Assets When Market Value for the Stock Exists

Stock: Two years later, Winter exchanged 500 shares of its $10 par value common stock for a piece of land. At the time of the exchange, Winter's stock was selling on the market for $16 per share.

Analysis: In this case, the market value of the land is irrelevant because the value of the stock is known. The journal entry to record stock for noncash assets when market value for the stock exists

▲ *increases* Land with a debit of $8,000 (500 shares × $16),

▲ *increases* Common Stock with a credit of $5,000 (500 shares × $10), and

▲ *increases* Additional Paid-In Capital with a credit for $3,000 ($8,000 − $5,000).

A	=	L	+	SE
+8,000				+5,000
				+3,000

Journal Entry:

Jan. 1	Land	8,000	
	Common Stock		5,000
	Additional Paid-In Capital		3,000
	Issued 500 shares of $10 par value common stock with a market value of $16 per share for a piece of land		

Stop & Apply

Omron Company is authorized to issue 10,000 shares of common stock. The company sold 1,000 shares at $10 per share. Prepare the journal entries to record the sale of stock for cash under each of the following alternatives: (1) The stock has a par value of $2, and (2) the stock has a no-par value but a stated value of $1 per share.

SOLUTION

1. The stock has a par value of $2.

Cash	10,000	
Common Stock		2,000
Additional Paid-In Capital		8,000
Issued $2 par value common stock at $10 per share		

2. The stock has a no-par value but has a stated value of $1.

Cash	10,000	
Common Stock		1,000
Additional Paid-In Capital		9,000
Issued no-par value common stock with a stated value of $1 at $10 per share		

iStock Photo

ACCOUNTING FOR TREASURY STOCK

Account for treasury stock. 

As we noted earlier, treasury stock is stock that the issuing company has reacquired, usually by purchasing shares on the open market. Although repurchasing its own stock can be a severe drain on a corporation's cash, it is a common practice. In a recent year, for example, 350, or 70 percent, of 500 large companies held treasury stock.[12]

A company may want to buy back its own stock for any of the following reasons:

- To distribute stock to employees through stock option plans
- To maintain a favorable market for its stock
- To increase its earnings per share or stock price per share
- To have additional shares of stock available for purchasing other companies
- To prevent a hostile takeover

STUDY NOTE: *Treasury stock is not the same as unissued stock. Treasury stock represents shares that have been issued but are no longer outstanding. Unissued shares, on the other hand, have never been in circulation.*

A purchase of treasury stock reduces a company's assets and stockholders' equity. Because treasury stock *reduces* stockholder's equity—the denominator of the return on equity ratio—the return on equity will *increase* when treasury shares are purchased even though there is no increase in earnings. Treasury stock is not considered a purchase of assets, as the purchase of shares in another company would be. A company can hold treasury shares for an indefinite period or reissue or retire them. Treasury shares have no rights until they are reissued. Like unissued shares, they do not have voting rights, rights to dividends, or rights to assets during liquidation of the company. However, there is one major difference between unissued shares and treasury shares: A share of stock issued at par value or greater and reacquired as treasury stock can be reissued at less than par value.

Purchase of Treasury Stock

When a firm purchases treasury stock, the purchase is recorded at cost. The par value, stated value, or original issue price of the stock is ignored. Consider the following example.

Purchase of Treasury Stock

Stock: On September 15, Marble Corporation purchases 2,000 shares of its $5 par value common stock on the market at a price of $50 per share.

Analysis: The journal entry to record this purchase of treasury stock

▲ *increases* Treasury Stock, Common with a debit of $100,000 (2,000 shares × $50) and

▼ *decreases* Cash with a credit of $100,000 (2,000 shares × $50).

A	= L +	SE
−100,000		−100,000

Journal Entry:

		Debit	Credit
Sept. 15	Treasury Stock, Common	100,000	
	Cash		100,000
	Acquired 2,000 shares of the company's common stock for $50 per share		

Comment: In the stockholders' equity section of Marble Corporation's balance sheet, $100,000 would be deducted from total contributed capital and retained earnings, as shown below.

Contributed capital	
Common stock, $5 par value, 200,000 shares authorized, 60,000 shares issued, 58,000 shares outstanding	$ 300,000
Additional paid-in capital	60,000
Total contributed capital	$ 360,000
Retained earnings	1,800,000
Total contributed capital and retained earnings	$2,160,000
Less: Treasury stock, common (2,000 shares at cost)	**100,000**
Total stockholders' equity	$2,060,000

Focus on Business Practice

Are Share Buybacks Really Good?

Corporate America has increased share buybacks significantly in the last two decades: from $10 billion in 1991 to an estimated $500 billion in 2007 when the market was experiencing record highs. **The Home Depot**, **Wal-Mart**, **General Electric**, **Johnson & Johnson**, and **Microsoft**, along with many other companies, spent billions to boost their stock prices. The stated aim was to increase stock prices and earnings per share by reducing the supply of stock in public hands. These companies had suffered declines in their stock prices in 2008 and 2009.

According to renowned investor Warren Buffett and others, share buybacks are ill-advised. What is often not stated publicly is that many shares do not stay out of public hands because the companies recycle the stock into generous stock options for management and thus do not achieve the desired goal of reducing outstanding shares. An estimated half of the stock purchased is little more than "backdoor compensation" for employees. Furthermore, many companies have borrowed money to repurchase stock, thereby increasing their debt to equity ratios.[13]

iStock Photo

Note that the number of shares issued, and therefore the legal capital, has not changed. However, the number of shares outstanding has *decreased* as a result of the transaction.

Sale of Treasury Stock

Treasury shares can be sold at cost, above cost, or below cost.

Sale of Treasury Shares at Cost

Stock: On September 15, Marble sold 2,000 shares of its $5 par value common stock on the market at a price of $50 per share.

Analysis: When treasury shares are sold at cost, the entry is the reverse of the previous transaction for the purchase of the shares. The journal entry to record this sale of treasury stock at cost

- ▲ *increases* Cash with a debit for the sales amount and
- ▼ *decreases* Treasury Stock and Common Stock with a credit for the same amount.

A	= L +	SE
−100,000		−100,000

Journal Entry:

		Debit	Credit
Sept. 15	Cash	100,000	
	Treasury Stock, Common		100,000
	Sold 2,000 shares of the company's common stock for $50 per share		

Sale of Treasury Shares at Above Cost

Stock: On October 15, Marble sold for $60 per share 1,000 of the treasury shares that it repurchased at $50 per share.

***Analysis*:** Even though the treasury stock was sold at above cost, no gain is recorded. The journal entry to record this sale of treasury stock above cost

- ▲ *increases* Cash with a debit of $60,000 (1,000 shares × $60),
- ▼ *decreases* Treasury Stock, Common with a credit of $50,000 (1,000 shares × $50), and
- ▲ *increases* Paid-In Capital, Treasury Stock with a credit of $10,000 ($60,000 − $50,000).

A	= L +	SE
+60,000		+50,000
		+10,000

Journal Entry:

		Debit	Credit
Oct. 15	Cash	60,000	
	Treasury Stock, Common		50,000
	Paid-In Capital, Treasury Stock		10,000
	Sold 1,000 shares of treasury stock for $60 per share; cost was $50 per share		

Comment: Note that when treasury shares are sold for an amount greater than their cost, the excess of the sales price over the cost is not considered a gain but is credited to Paid-In Capital, Treasury Stock.

Sale of Treasury Shares at Below Cost

Stock: On December 15, Marble sells its remaining 1,000 treasury shares for $38 per share.

Analysis: When treasury shares are sold below their cost, the difference is deducted from Paid-In Capital, Treasury Stock. If this account does not exist or if its balance is insufficient to cover the excess of the cost over the reissue price, Retained Earnings absorbs the excess. The journal entry to record the sale of treasury stock below cost

- ▲ *increases* Cash with a debit of $38,000 (1,000 shares × $38),
- ▼ *decreases* Paid-In Capital, Treasury Stock with a debit of $10,000 [$50,000 – ($38,000 + $2,000)],
- ▼ *decreases* Retained Earnings with a debit for the remaining $2,000 by which the shares were sold below their cost ($50,000 – $38,000 – $10,000), and
- ▼ *decreases* Treasury Stock, Common with a credit of $50,000 ($38,000 + $10,000 + $2,000).

A	= L +	SE
+38,000		−10,000
		−2,000
		+50,000

Journal Entry:

Dec. 15	Cash	38,000	
	Paid-In Capital, Treasury Stock	10,000	
	Retained Earnings	2,000	
	Treasury Stock, Common		50,000
	Sold 1,000 shares of treasury stock for $38 per share; cost was $50 per share		

Comment: Note that the *decrease* in Treasury Stock, Common *increases* stockholders' equity. Also, note that no loss is recorded. Further, Retained Earnings is debited only when the Paid-In Capital, Treasury Stock account does not exist or has been depleted.

Retirement of Treasury Stock

If a company decides not to reissue treasury stock, it can retire the stock. All items related to those shares are then removed from the associated capital accounts. If the cost of buying back the treasury stock is less than the company received when it issued the stock, the difference is recorded in Paid-In Capital, Retirement of Stock. If the cost is more than was received when the stock was first issued, the difference is a reduction in stockholders' equity and is debited to Retained Earnings. Consider the following example.

Retiring Treasury Stock

Stock: On November 15, Marble decides to retire the 2,000 shares of stock that it bought back for $100,000. The $5 par value common stock was originally issued at $6 per share.

Analysis: The journal entry to record this retirement of treasury stock

- ▼ *decreases* Common Stock with a debit of $10,000 (2,000 shares × $5),
- ▼ *decreases* Additional Paid-In Capital with a debit of $2,000 [$100,000 – ($10,000 + $88,000)],
- ▼ *decreases* Retained Earnings with a debit of $88,000 ($100,000 – $10,000 – $2,000), and
- ▼ *decreases* Treasury Stock, Common with a credit of $100,000 (2,000 shares × $50).

A	=	L	+	SE
				−10,000
				−2,000
				−88,000
				+100,000

Journal Entry:

Nov. 15	Common Stock	10,000	
	Additional Paid-In Capital	2,000	
	Retained Earnings	88,000	
	Treasury Stock, Common		100,000
	Retired 2,000 shares that cost \$50 per share and were issued originally at \$6 per share		

Comment: Note that this transaction does not change the total stockholders' equity because all accounts are in stockholders' equity.

Stop & Apply

Prepare journal entries to record the following stock transactions for Paulo Company during 2011:

May 1 Purchased 5,000 shares of its own \$1 par value common stock for \$10 per share, the current market price.

17 Sold 1,000 shares of treasury stock purchased on May 1 for \$11 per share.

SOLUTION

May 1	Treasury Stock, Common	50,000	
	Cash		50,000
	Purchased 5,000 shares of Paulo Company's common stock at \$10 per share		
17	Cash	11,000	
	Treasury Stock, Common		10,000
	Paid-In Capital, Treasury Stock		1,000
	Sold 1,000 shares of treasury stock for \$11 per share		

iStock Photo

STOCK DIVIDENDS AND STOCK SPLITS

Account for stock dividends and stock splits. 

Two transactions that commonly modify the content of stockholders' equity are stock dividends and stock splits. In the sections that follow, we describe how to account for both kinds of transactions.

Stock Dividends

A **stock dividend** is a proportional distribution of shares among a corporation's stockholders. Unlike a cash dividend, a stock dividend involves no distribution of assets, and so it has no effect on a firm's assets or liabilities. A board of directors may declare a stock dividend for the following reasons:

- To give stockholders some evidence of the company's success without affecting working capital (which would be the case if it paid a cash dividend)
- To reduce the stock's market price by increasing the number of shares outstanding (This goal is, however, more often met by a stock split.)
- To make a nontaxable distribution to stockholders (Stock dividends that meet certain conditions are not considered income and are thus not taxed.)
- To increase the company's permanent capital by transferring an amount from retained earnings to contributed capital

STUDY NOTE: *The declaration of a stock dividend results in a reshuffling of stockholders' equity—that is, a portion of retained earnings is converted to contributed capital (by closing the Stock Dividends account). Total stockholders' equity is not affected.*

A stock dividend does not affect total stockholders' equity. Basically, it transfers a dollar amount from retained earnings to contributed capital. The amount transferred is the fair market value (usually, the market price) of the additional shares that the company issues. When stock distributions are small—less than 20 to 25 percent of a company's outstanding common stock—generally accepted accounting principles require that the market price be used to account for the stock dividends.[14]

Stock Dividends Transactions To illustrate how to account for stock dividends, suppose that stockholders' equity in Wing Corporation is as follows:

Contributed capital	
Common stock, \$5 par value, 50,000 shares authorized, 15,000 shares issued and outstanding	\$ 75,000
Additional paid-in capital	15,000
Total contributed capital	\$ 90,000
Retained earnings	450,000
Total stockholders' equity	\$540,000

Declaration Date

Stock Dividend: On February 24, when the market price of Wing's \$5 par value common stock is \$20 per share, the corporation's board of directors declares a 10 percent stock dividend to be distributed on March 31 to stockholders of record on March 15.

STUDY NOTE: *For a small stock dividend, the portion of retained earnings transferred is determined by multiplying the number of shares to be distributed by the stock's market price on the declaration date.*

Analysis: The journal entry to record this stock dividend on the declaration date (February 24)

- ▲ *increases* the Stock Dividends account with a debit of \$30,000 (0.10 × 15,000 × \$20), the total market value of the stock dividend,
- ▲ *increases* Common Stock Distributable (a temporary account until the 1,500 shares are distributed on March 31) with a credit at total par value of \$7,500 (1,500 × \$5), and
- ▲ *increases* Additional Paid-In Capital with a credit of \$22,500 (\$30,000 − \$7,500), the amount by which the total market value of the stock to be issued exceeds its total par value.

A	=	L	+	SE
				−30,000
				+7,500
				−22,500

Journal Entry:

Feb. 24	Stock Dividends	30,000	
	Common Stock Distributable		7,500
	Additional Paid-In Capital		22,500
	Declared a 10 percent stock dividend on common stock, distributable on March 31 to stockholders of record on March 15: 15,000 shares × 0.10 = 1,500 shares 1,500 shares × \$20 per share = \$30,000 1,500 shares × \$5 per share = \$7,500		

Comment: Because Common Stock Distributable represents an obligation to distribute additional shares of capital stock, it is a stockholders' equity account, not a liability account, as Cash Dividends Payable is. Also, the Stock Dividends account appears as a deduction on the statement of retained earnings.

Record Date

Analysis: No entry is needed on the date of record (March 15).

Payment Date

Analysis: The journal entry to record the stock dividend on the distribution, or payment, date (March 31)

▼ *decreases* Common Stock Distributable to zero with debit of $7,500 (1,500 shares × $5) and

▲ *increases* Common Stock with a credit of $7,500 (5,000 shares × $15).

A	=	L	+	SE
				−7,500
				+7,500

Journal Entry:

Mar. 31	Common Stock Distributable	7,500	
	Common Stock		7,500
	Distributed a stock dividend of 1,500 shares of common stock		

Effect of a Stock Dividend on Stockholders' Equity If financial statements are prepared between the declaration date and the date of distribution, Common Stock Distributable should be reported as part of contributed capital.

Contributed capital	
Common stock, $5 par value, 50,000 shares authorized, 15,000 shares issued and outstanding	$ 75,000
Common stock distributable, 1,500 shares	7,500
Additional paid-in capital	37,500
Total contributed capital	$120,000
Retained earnings	420,000
Total stockholders' equity	$540,000

Note that after the stock dividend has been distributed,

- total stockholders' equity is the same before and after the stock dividend.
- the assets of the corporation are not reduced, as they would be by a cash dividend.
- the proportionate ownership in the corporation of any individual stockholder is the same before and after the stock dividend.

Large Stock Dividends All stock dividends have some effect on the market price of a company's stock, but some are so large that they have a material effect. For example, a 50 percent stock dividend would cause the market price of a stock to drop about 33 percent because the increase would be one-third of the shares outstanding. The AICPA has ruled that large stock dividends—those greater than 20 to 25 percent—should be accounted for by transferring the par or stated value of the stock on the declaration date from retained earnings to contributed capital.[15]

Stock Splits

STUDY NOTE: Stock splits and stock dividends reduce earnings per share because they increase the number of shares issued and outstanding. Cash dividends have no effect on earnings per share.

A **stock split** occurs when a corporation increases the number of shares of stock issued and outstanding and reduces the par or stated value proportionally. A company may plan a stock split for the following reasons:

- To lower its stock's market price per share and thereby increase the demand and volume of trading for its stock at this lower price
- To signal to the market its success in achieving its operating goals

Nike achieved these strategic objectives in fiscal year 2009 by increasing its cash dividend and declaring a 2-for-1 stock split in fiscal 2007 and increasing its cash dividend.[16] After the stock split, the number of the company's outstanding shares doubled, thereby cutting the share price from about $80 per share to $40 per share. The stock split left each stockholder's total wealth unchanged but increased the income stockholders received from dividends. The stock split was a sign that Nike has continued to do well. However, stock splits tend to follow the market. There is no fundamental reason why a stock should go up because of a stock split. Research shows that stock splits have no long-term effect on stock prices. Long-term effects depend on the company's performance and the overall stock market environment.

Focus on Business Practice

Do Stock Splits Help Increase a Company's Market Price?

When **General Mills**, the cereal company, completed a 2-for-1 split in May 2010, its stock dropped from about $70 per share to about $35 per share. Since then, the price has trended upward with the market to $38 per share.[17]

Stock Split

Stock: Suppose that Wing Corporation has 15,000 shares of $5 par value stock outstanding and that the market value is $70 per share. The corporation plans a 2-for-1 split.

Analysis: The journal entry to record this split

▼ *decreases* the par value to $2.50 per share ($5.00 ÷ 2) and

▲ *increases* the number of shares outstanding to 30,000 (15,000 shares × 2).

After the split, a stockholder who previously owned 200 shares of the $5 par value stock will own

- 400 shares of the $2.50 par value stock in outstanding shares of stock.
- the same proportionate share of the company as before the split.
- approximately the same total market value of stock because the 2-for-1 stock split will cause the price of the stock to drop by approximately 50 percent, to about $35.

Journal Entry: A stock split does not increase the number of shares authorized, nor does it change the balances in the stockholders' equity section of the balance sheet. It simply changes the par value and number of shares issued for both shares outstanding and treasury stock. Thus, a journal entry is unnecessary.

However, it is appropriate to document the change with a memorandum entry in the general journal. For example:

July 15	The 15,000 shares of $5 par value common stock issued and outstanding were split 2 for 1, resulting in 30,000 shares of $2.50 par value common stock issued and outstanding.

Stockholders' equity before and after the stock split follow:

Before Stock Split		After Stock Split	
Contributed capital		Contributed capital	
Common stock, $5 par value, 50,000 shares authorized; 15,000 shares issued and outstanding	$ 75,000	Common stock, $2.50 par value, 50,000 shares authorized, 30,000 shares issued and outstanding	$ 75,000
Additional paid-in capital	15,000	Additional paid-in capital	15,000
Total contributed capital	$ 90,000	Total contributed capital	$ 90,000
Retained earnings	450,000	Retained earnings	450,000
Total stockholders' equity	$540,000	Total stockholders' equity	$540,000

Comment: The balances of all accounts remain the same. Only the par value and number of shares issued and outstanding change. If the number of split shares exceeds the number of authorized shares, the corporation's board of directors must secure state and stockholders' approval before it can issue the additional shares.

Stop & Apply

Kelly Corporation's board of directors declared a 2 percent stock dividend applicable to the outstanding shares of its $10 par value common stock, of which 1,000,000 shares are authorized, 300,000 are issued, and 100,000 are held in the treasury. It then declared a 2-for-1 stock split on issued shares. How many authorized, issued, and treasury shares existed after each of these transactions? What is the par value per share?

SOLUTION

Stock dividend applies to outstanding shares:

(300,000 shares − 100,000 shares) × 0.02 = 4,000 shares

Stock split applies to all issued shares:

304,000 shares × 2 = 608,000 shares

Authorized shares are unchanged (1,000,000, but par value is now $5 per share); issued shares are 608,000; and outstanding shares are 408,000 (400,000 + 8,000).

iStock Photo

THE STATEMENT OF STOCKHOLDERS' EQUITY AND BOOK VALUE PER SHARE

LO 6 Describe the statement of stockholders' equity and compute book value per share.

The following sections describe the statement of stockholder's equity and show how to calculate book value per share.

Statement of Stockholders' Equity

STUDY NOTE: *The statement of stockholders' equity is a labeled calculation of the change in each stockholder's equity account over an accounting period.*

The **statement of stockholders' equity**, also called the *statement of changes in stockholders' equity*, summarizes changes in the components of the stockholders' equity section of the balance sheet. Most companies use this statement in place of the statement of retained earnings because it reveals much more about the stockholders' equity transactions that took place during the accounting period. For example, in the statement of stockholders' equity in Exhibit 11.5, the first line shows the beginning balance of each account in the stockholders' equity section of Snow Corporation's balance sheet. Each subsequent line discloses the effects of transactions on those accounts.

As shown in Exhibit 11.5, Snow had the following:

- Net income of $540,000
- A foreign currency translation loss of $20,000, which it reported as accumulated other comprehensive income (loss). Recall that this is an item that does not appear on the income statement.
- 10,000 shares of common stock issued for $500,000
- Conversion of $200,000 of preferred stock to common stock
- A 10 percent stock dividend on common stock
- Treasury stock purchases of $48,000
- Cash dividends on both preferred and common stock

The ending balances of the accounts appear at the bottom of the statement. Those accounts and balances make up the stockholders' equity section of Snow's balance sheet on December 31, 2011, as shown in Exhibit 11.6.

EXHIBIT 11.5
Statement of Stockholders' Equity

Snow Corporation
Statement of Stockholders' Equity
For the Year Ended December 31, 2011

	Preferred Stock $100 Par Value 8% Convertible	Common Stock $10 Par Value	Additional Paid-In Capital	Retained Earnings	Treasury Stock	Accumulated Other Comprehensive Income (loss)	Total
Balance, December 31, 2010	$800,000	$600,000	$ 600,000	$1,200,000			$3,200,000
Net income				540,000			540,000
Foreign currency translation adjustment						$(20,000)	(20,000)
Issuance of 10,000 shares of common stock		100,000	400,000				500,000
Conversion of 2,000 shares of preferred stock to 6,000 shares of common stock	(200,000)	60,000	140,000				—
10 percent stock dividend on common stock, 7,600 shares		76,000	304,000	(380,000)			—
Purchase of 1,000 shares of treasury stock					$(48,000)		(48,000)
Cash dividends							
Preferred stock				(48,000)			(48,000)
Common stock				(95,200)			(95,200)
Balance, December 31, 2011	$600,000	$836,000	$1,444,000	$1,216,800	$(48,000)	$(20,000)	$4,028,800

EXHIBIT 11.6
Stockholders' Equity Section of a Balance Sheet

STUDY NOTE: *The ending balances on the statement of stockholders' equity appear in the stockholders' equity section of the balance sheet.*

Snow Corporation
Balance Sheet December 31, 2011
Stockholders' Equity

Contributed capital		
Preferred stock, $100 par value, 8 percent convertible, 20,000 shares authorized, 6,000 shares issued and outstanding		$ 600,000
Common stock, $10 par value, 200,000 shares authorized, 83,600 shares issued, 82,600 shares outstanding	$ 836,000	
Additional paid-in capital	1,444,000	2,280,000
Total contributed capital		$2,880,000
Retained earnings		1,216,800
Total contributed capital and retained earnings		$4,096,800
Less: Treasury stock, common (1,000 shares, at cost)	$ 48,000	
Accumulated other comprehensive loss	20,000	68,000
Total stockholders' equity		$4,028,800

Focus on International Practices

IFRS Comprehensive Income Under IFRS Versus GAAP

One must be careful when comparing the "bottom line" of IFRS statements with U.S. GAAP statements. Instead of the traditional GAAP income statement, IFRS require a statement of comprehensive income. This statement is similar to the income statement under GAAP except for a section at the bottom that includes what under U.S. GAAP would appear in a separate statement or in the column for "other comprehensive income" in the statement of stockholders' equity. In Exhibit 11.6 (p. 513), this would be the foreign currency translation adjustment. In other words, under GAAP, this negative amount would not appear on the income statement, but under IFRS, it would be deducted on the statement of comprehensive income. This difference affects financial ratios such as profit margin, return on assets, and return on equity.

iStock Photo

Book Value per Share

The word *value* is associated with shares of stock in several ways. Par value or stated value is set when the stock is authorized, and it establishes a company's legal capital. Neither par value nor stated value has any relationship to a stock's book value or market value. The **book value** of stock represents a company's total assets less its liabilities. It is simply the stockholders' equity in a company or, to put it another way, it represents a company's net assets. The **book value per share** is therefore the equity of the owner of one share of stock in the net assets of a company. That value, of course, generally does not equal the amount a stockholder receives if the company is sold or liquidated because in most cases, assets are recorded at historical cost, not at their current market value.

Book Value Per Share of Common Stock If a company has only common stock outstanding, book value per share is calculated by dividing stockholders' equity by the number of common shares outstanding. Common stock distributable is included in the number of shares outstanding, but treasury stock is not. For example, if a firm has total stockholders' equity of $2,060,000 and 58,000 shares outstanding, the book value per share of its common stock would be calculated as follows:

Stockholders' Equity ÷ Common Shares Outstanding = Book Value per Share
$2,060,000 ÷ 58,000 Shares = $35.52

Book Value for Common and Preferred Stock If a company has both preferred and common stock, determining the book value per share is not so simple. Generally, the preferred stock's call value (or par value, if a call value is not specified) and any dividends in arrears are subtracted from stockholders' equity to determine the equity pertaining to common stock. Refer to the stockholders' equity section of Snow Corporation's balance sheet in Exhibit 11.6 (p. 513). If Snow has no dividends in arrears and its preferred stock is callable at $105, the equity pertaining to its common stock would be calculated as follows:

Total stockholders' equity	$4,028,800
Less equity allocated to preferred stockholders (6,000 shares × $105)	630,000
Equity pertaining to common stockholders	$3,398,800

As indicated in Exhibit 11.6, Snow has 82,600 shares of common stock outstanding (83,600 shares issued less 1,000 shares of treasury stock). Its book values per share are computed as follows:

Preferred stock: $630,000 ÷ 6,000 Shares = $105 per Share
Common stock: $3,398,800 ÷ 82,600 Shares = $41.15 per Share

Book Value for Dividends in Arrears Assume the same facts except that Snow's preferred stock is 8 percent cumulative and that one year of dividends is in arrears. The stockholders' equity would be allocated as follows:

Total stockholders' equity		$4,028,800
Less call value of outstanding preferred shares	$630,000	
Dividends in arrears ($600,000 × 0.08)	48,000	
Equity allocated to preferred stockholders		678,000
Equity pertaining to common stockholders		$3,350,800

The book values per share would then be as follows:

Preferred stock: $678,000 ÷ 6,000 Shares = $113 per Share
Common stock: $3,350,800 ÷ 82,600 Shares = $40.57 per Share

Stop & Apply

Using the data from the stockholders' equity section of Pskov Corporation's balance sheet shown below, compute the book value per share for both the preferred and common stock.

Contributed capital	
Preferred stock, $100 par value, 6 percent cumulative, 20,000 shares authorized, 2,000 shares issued and outstanding*	$ 200,000
Common stock, $5 par value, 200,000 shares authorized, 100,000 shares issued and outstanding	500,000
Additional paid-in capital	300,000
Total contributed capital	$1,000,000
Retained earnings	500,000
Total stockholders' equity	$1,500,000

*The preferred stock is callable at $104 per share, and one year's dividends are in arrears.

SOLUTION

Preferred stock book value per share: $104 + $6 = $110
Common stock book value per share: [$1,500,000 − (2,000 preferred shares × $110)] ÷ 100,000 common shares = $12.80

iStock Photo

A look back at ▸ Google, Inc.

In this chapter's Decision Point, we focused on one of the most exciting financing events in recent history, **Google's** IPO. We asked the following questions:

1. Why did Google's management choose to issue common stock to satisfy the company's need for new capital?
2. What are some of the advantages and disadvantages of this approach to financing a business?
3. What measures should investors use in evaluating management's performance?

As a relatively new company, Google needed to raise capital so that it could expand its operations. The company's management decided to do so by issuing common stock. This approach to financing does not burden a company with debt or interest payments. In addition, a company that issues common stock has the option of paying or not paying dividends. If, like Google, it does not pay dividends, it can invest cash from its earnings to expand the company. Issuing stock does, however, dilute the ownership of a company's current owners, and if the company pays dividends, they are not tax-deductible, as interest on debt is.

Return on equity is, of course, a critical measure of management's performance. Using data from Google's 2008 and 2009 annual reports, we can compute the company's return on equity in those years as shown below (in thousands). (Google's stockholders' equity in 2007 was $22,689,679 thousand.)

RATIO

$$\text{Return on Equity} = \frac{\text{Net Income}}{\text{Average Total Stockholders' Equity}}$$

	2009	2008
Return on Equity =	$6,520,448 / (($36,004,224 + $28,238,862) ÷ 2)	$4,226,858 / (($28,238,862 + $22,689,679) ÷ 2)
=	20.3%	16.6%

Google's return on equity increased from 16.6 percent to 20.3 percent, indicating that Google's management is successful growing the company's earnings faster than the increase in stockholders' equity.

At the time of Google's IPO, when its stock sold for $85 per share, its P/E ratio was 74.6 times. In 2008 and 2009, its P/E ratios were as follows:

RATIO

$$\text{P/E Ratio} = \frac{\text{Market Price per Share}}{\text{Earnings per Share}}$$

	2009	2008
P/E Ratio =	$554 / $20.41	$332 / $13.31
=	27.1 Times	24.9 Times

These are very high P/E ratios. At the beginning of 2010, when Google's stock price had risen from below $300 per share to almost $600, the average P/E ratio for S&P 500 stocks was only about 17. Evidently, despite Google's not paying dividends, investors were rewarding the company's high return on equity and thinking the company's future was very bright.

Google's book value per share may be computed using the information in the financial highlights, as follows:

$$\text{Book Value per Share} = \frac{\text{Total Stockholders' Equity}}{\text{Common Shares Outstanding}}$$

	2009	2008
Book Value per Share =	$36,004,224 / 318,000,000 shares*	$28,238,862 / 315,000,000 shares**
=	$0.11 per share	$0.09 per share

*$318,000/$0.0001 par value = 318,000,000 shares

**$315,000/$0.0001 par value = 315,000,000 shares

This result illustrates that there is no relationship between Google's book value per share of $0.11 and $0.09 per share in 2008 and 2009, respectfully, and market prices per share of $554 and $332.

Review Problem

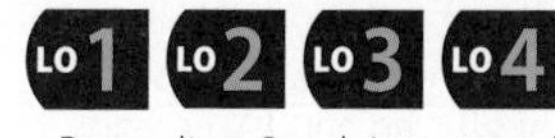

Recording Stock Issues and Calculating Related Financial Ratios

Dingo Corporation was organized in 2011 in Arizona. Its state charter authorized it to issue 2 million shares of $1 par value common stock and 50,000 shares of 4 percent, $20 par value cumulative and convertible preferred stock. Dingo's stock transactions during 2011 were as follows:

Feb.	1	Issued 200,000 shares of common stock for $250,000.
	15	Issued 6,000 shares of common stock for accounting and legal services. The bills for these services totaled $7,200.
Mar.	15	Issued 240,000 shares of common stock to Tom Lee in exchange for a building and land appraised at $200,000 and $50,000, respectively.
Apr.	2	Purchased 40,000 shares of common stock for the treasury at $1.25 per share from a person who changed her mind about investing in the company.
July	1	Issued 50,000 shares of preferred stock for $1,000,000.
Sept.	30	Sold 20,000 of the shares in the treasury for $1.50 per share.
Dec.	31	Dingo's board of directors declared dividends of $49,820 payable on January 15, 2012, to stockholders of record on January 7. Dividends included preferred stock dividends of $20,000 for one-half year.

For the period ended December 31, 2011, Dingo reported net income of $80,000 and earnings per common share of $0.14. At that time, the market price per common share was $1.60.

Required

1. Record Dingo's stock transactions in T accounts.
2. Prepare the stockholders' equity section of Dingo's balance sheet as of December 31, 2011. (*Hint:* Use net income and dividends to calculate retained earnings.)
3. Calculate Dingo's dividends yield on common stock, price/earnings ratio of common stock, book value per share, and return on equity.

ANSWERS TO REVIEW PROBLEM

1. Entries in T accounts:

	A	B	C	D	E	F	G	H	I	J	K	L	M	N	O	P	Q	R	S	T
1			Assets				=			Liabilities				+			Stockholders' Equity			
2																				
3			Cash							Dividends Payable							Preferred Stock			
4	Feb.	1	250,000	Apr.	2	50,000					Dec.	31	49,820					July	1	1,000,000
5	July	1	1,000,000																	
6	Sept	30	30,000														Common Stock			
7																		Feb.	1	200,000
8			Building																15	6,000
9	Mar.	15	200,000															Mar.	15	240,000
10																		Bal.		446,000
11			Land																	
12	Mar.	15	50,000														Additional Paid-In Capital			
13																		Feb.	1	50,000
14																			15	1,200
15																		Mar.	15	10,000
16																		Bal.		61,200
17																				
18																	Paid-In Capital, Treasury Stock			
19																		Sept.	30	5,000
20																				

Assets	=	Liabilities	+	Stockholders' Equity					
				Dividends					
				Dec.	31	49,820			
				Treasury Stock					
				Apr.	2	50,000	Sept.	30	25,000
				Bal.		25,000			
				Start-up and Organization Costs					
				Feb.	15	7,200			

2. Stockholders' equity section of the balance sheet:

Dingo Corporation		
Balance Sheet		
December 31, 2011		
Stockholders' Equity		
Contributed capital		
Preferred stock, 4 percent cumulative and convertible, $20 par value, 50,000 shares authorized, issued, and outstanding		$1,000,000
Common stock, $1 par value, 2,000,000 shares authorized, 446,000 shares issued, and 426,000 shares outstanding*	$446,000	
Additional paid-in capital	61,200	
Paid-in capital, treasury stock	5,000	512,200
Total contributed capital		$1,512,200
Retained earnings		30,180*
Total contributed capital and retained earnings		$1,542,380
Less: Treasurystock (20,000 shares, at cost)		25,000
Total stockholders' equity		$1,517,380
* Retained Earnings = Net Income − Cash Dividends Declared		
Retained Earnings = $80,000 − $49,820 = $30,180		

*200,000 + 6,000 + 240,000 – 40,000 + 20,000 = 426,000 outstanding shares

3. Dividends yield on common stock, price/earnings ratio of common stock, book value per share, and return on equity:

$$\text{Dividends per Share} = \frac{\text{Common Stock Dividend}}{\text{Common Shares Outstanding}} = \frac{\$29{,}820}{426{,}000} = \$0.07$$

$$\text{Dividends Yield} = \frac{\text{Dividends per Share}}{\text{Market Price per Share}} = \frac{\$0.07}{\$1.60} = 4.4\%$$

$$\text{Price/Earnings Ratio} = \frac{\text{Market Price per Share}}{\text{Earnings per Share}} = \frac{\$1.60}{\$0.14} = 11.4\text{ Times}$$

$$\text{Book Value per Share} = \frac{\text{Total Stockholders' Equity}}{\text{Common Shares Outstanding}} - \text{Preferred Stock} = \frac{\$1{,}517{,}380 - \$1{,}000{,}000}{426{,}000} = \frac{\$517{,}880}{426{,}000} = \$1.22$$

The opening balance of stockholders' equity on February 1, 2011, was $250,000.

$$\text{Return on Equity} = \frac{\text{Net Income}}{\text{Average Stockholders' Equity}}$$

$$= \frac{\$80{,}000}{(\$1{,}517{,}380 + \$250{,}000) \div 2}$$

$$= \frac{\$80{,}000}{\$883{,}690}$$

$$= 9.1\%$$

Stop & Review

LO1 Identify and explain the management issues related to contributed capital.

Contributed capital is a critical component in corporate financing. Managing contributed capital requires an understanding of the advantages and disadvantages of the corporate form of business and of the issues involved in using equity financing. Managers must also know how to determine dividend policies and how to evaluate these policies using dividends yield, return on equity, and the price/earnings ratio. The liability for payment of dividends arises on the date the board of directors declares a dividend. The declaration is recorded with a debit to Dividends and a credit to Dividends Payable. The record date—the date on which ownership of the stock, and thus of the right to receive a dividend, is determined—requires no entry. On the payment date, the Dividends Payable account is eliminated, and the Cash account is reduced. Another issue involved in managing contributed capital is using stock options as compensation. Information concerning cash flows related to stock transactions and dividends is found in the financing activities section of the statement of cash flows.

LO2 Identify the components of stockholders' equity and their characteristics.

The stockholders' equity section of a corporate balance sheet usually has at least three components: contributed capital, retained earnings, and treasury stock. Contributed capital consists of money raised through stock issues. A corporation can issue two types of stock: common stock and preferred stock. Common stockholders have voting rights; they also share in the corporation's earnings. Preferred stockholders usually have preference over common stockholders in one or more areas. Retained earnings are reinvested in the corporation; they represent stockholders' claims to assets resulting from profitable operations. Treasury stock is stock that the issuing corporation has reacquired. It is treated as a deduction from stockholders' equity.

Preferred stock generally gives its owners first right to dividend payments. Only after these stockholders have been paid can common stockholders receive any portion of a dividend. If the preferred stock is cumulative and dividends are in arrears, a corporation must pay the amount in arrears to preferred stockholders before it pays any dividends to common stockholders. Preferred stockholders also usually have preference over common stockholders in terms of their claims to corporate assets if the corporation is liquidated. In addition, preferred stock may be convertible to common stock, and it is often callable at the option of the corporation.

LO3 Account for the issuance of stock for cash and other assets.

Corporations normally issue their stock in exchange for cash or other assets. Most states require corporations to issue stock at a minimum value called *legal capital*. Legal capital is represented by the stock's par or stated value.

When stock is issued for cash at par or stated value, Cash is debited and Common Stock or Preferred Stock is credited. When stock is sold at an amount greater than par or stated value, the excess is recorded in Additional Paid-In Capital.

When stock is issued for noncash assets, the general rule is to record the stock at its market value. If this value cannot be determined, the fair market value of the asset received is used to record the transaction.

Account for treasury stock. 

Treasury stock is stock that the issuing company has reacquired. A company may buy back its own stock for several reasons, including a desire to create stock option plans, maintain a favorable market for the stock, increase earnings per share, or purchase other companies. The purchase of treasury stock is recorded at cost and is deducted from stockholders' equity. Treasury stock can be reissued or retired. It is similar to unissued stock in that it does not have rights until it is reissued.

Account for stock dividends and stock splits. 

A stock dividend is a proportional distribution of shares among a corporation's stockholders. The following is a summary of the key dates and accounting treatments of stock dividends:

Key Date	Stock Dividend
Declaration date	Debit Stock Dividends for the market value of the stock to be distributed (if the stock dividend is small) and credit Common Stock Distributable for the stock's par value and Additional Paid-In Capital for the excess of the market value over the stock's par value.
Record date	No entry is needed.
Date of distribution	Debit Common Stock Distributable and credit Common Stock for the par value of the stock

A company usually declares a stock split to reduce the market value of its stock and thereby increase the demand for the stock. Because the par value of the stock normally decreases in proportion to the number of additional shares issued, a stock split has no effect on the dollar amount in stockholders' equity. A stock split does not require a journal entry, but a memorandum entry in the general journal is appropriate.

Describe the statement of stockholders' equity and compute book value per share. **LO 6**

The statement of stockholders' equity summarizes changes during an accounting period in each component of the stockholders' equity section of the balance sheet. This statement reveals much more than the statement of retained earnings does about the transactions that affect stockholders' equity.

Book value per share is stockholders' equity per share. Book value per share of common stock is calculated by dividing stockholders' equity by the number of common shares outstanding. If a company has both preferred and common stock, the call or par value of the preferred stock and any dividends in arrears are deducted from stockholders' equity before dividing by the common shares outstanding.

Key Terms and Ratios

Authorized shares 498 (LO2)
Book value 514 (LO6)
Book value per share 514 (LO6)
Callable preferred stock 500 (LO2)
Common stock 497 (LO2)
Contributed capital 497 (LO2)
Convertible preferred stock 500 (LO2)
Cumulative preferred stock 499 (LO2)
Declaration date 492 (LO1)
Dividend 491 (LO1)
Dividends in arrears 499 (LO2)
Double taxation 489 (LO1)
Ex-dividend 492 (LO1)
Initial public offering (IPO) 486 *(Decision Point)*
Issued shares 498 (LO2)
Legal capital 490 (LO1)
Liquidating dividend 491 (LO1)
Noncumulative preferred stock 499 (LO2)
No-par stock 501 (LO3)
Other comprehensive income (loss) 497 (LO2)
Outstanding shares 498 (LO2)
Par value 490 (LO1)
Payment date 492 (LO1)
Preferred stock 498 (LO2)
Record date 492 (LO1)
Residual equity 497 (LO2)
Retained earnings 497 (LO2)
Share of stock 489 (LO1)
Start-up and organization costs 490 (LO1)
Stated value 501 (LO3)
Statement of stockholders' equity 512 (LO6)
Stock dividend 508 (LO5)
Stock option plans 495 (LO1)
Stock split 510 (LO5)
Treasury stock 497 (LO2)
Underwriter 490 (LO1)

FINANCIAL RATIOS
Dividends yield 493 (LO1)
Price/earnings (P/E) ratio 495 (LO1)
Return on equity 494 (LO1)

Chapter Assignments Building Your Basic Knowledge and Skills

Short Exercises

LO 1 **Management Issues**

SE 1. Indicate whether each of the following actions is related to (a) managing under the corporate form of business, (b) using equity financing, (c) determining dividend policies, (d) evaluating performance using return on equity, or (e) issuing stock options:

1. Considering whether to make a distribution to stockholders
2. Controlling day-to-day operations
3. Determining whether to issue preferred or common stock
4. Compensating management based on the company's meeting or exceeding the targeted return on equity
5. Compensating employees by giving them the right to purchase shares at a given price
6. Transferring shares without the approval of other owners

LO 1 **Advantages and Disadvantages of a Corporation**

SE 2. Identify whether each of the following characteristics is an advantage or a disadvantage of the corporate form of business:

1. Ease of transfer of ownership
2. Taxation
3. Separate legal entity
4. Lack of mutual agency
5. Government regulation
6. Continuous existence

LO 1 **Cash Dividends**

SE 3. Tone Corporation has authorized 200,000 shares of $1 par value common stock, of which 160,000 are issued and 140,000 are outstanding. On May 15, the board of directors declared a cash dividend of $0.20 per share, payable on June 15 to stockholders of record on June 1. Prepare the journal entries, as necessary, for each of the three dates.

LO 2 **Effect of Start-up and Organization Costs**

SE 4. At the beginning of 2011, Domino Company incurred the following start-up and organization costs: (1) attorneys' fees with a market value of $40,000, paid with 24,000 shares of $1 par value common stock, and (2) incorporation fees of $24,000. Calculate total start-up and organization costs. What will be the effect of these costs on the income statement and balance sheet?

LO 2 **Stockholders' Equity**

SE 5. Prepare the stockholders' equity section of Fina Corporation's balance sheet from the following accounts and balances on December 31, 2011:

Common Stock, $10 par value, 30,000 shares authorized, 20,000 shares issued, and 19,500 shares outstanding	$200,000
Additional Paid-In Capital	100,000
Retained Earnings	15,000
Treasury Stock, Common (500 shares, at cost)	7,500

LO 2 **Preferred Stock Dividends with Dividends in Arrears**

SE 6. Ferris Corporation has 2,000 shares of $100, 8 percent cumulative preferred stock outstanding and 40,000 shares of $1 par value common stock outstanding. In the company's first three years of operation, its board of directors paid cash dividends as follows: 2010, none; 2011, $40,000; and 2012, $80,000. Determine the total cash dividends and dividends per share paid to the preferred and common stockholders during each of the three years.

LO 3 **Issuance of Stock**

SE 7. Rattich Company is authorized to issue 50,000 shares of common stock. The company sold 2,500 shares at $12 per share. Prepare journal entries to record the sale of stock for cash under each of the following independent alternatives: (1) The stock has a par value of $5, and (2) the stock has no par value but a stated value of $1 per share.

LO 3 **Issuance of Stock for Noncash Assets**

SE 8. Linear Corporation issued 16,000 shares of its $1 par value common stock in exchange for land that had a fair market value of $100,000. Prepare the journal entries necessary to record the issuance of the stock for the land under each of these conditions: (1) The stock was selling for $7 per share on the day of the transaction, and (2) management attempted to place a value on the common stock but could not do so.

LO 4 **Treasury Stock Transactions**

SE 9. Prepare the journal entries necessary to record the following stock transactions of Seoul Company during 2011:

Oct. 1 Purchased 2,000 shares of its own $2 par value common stock for $20 per share, the current market price.

17 Sold 500 shares of treasury stock purchased on October 1 for $25 per share.

LO 4 **Retirement of Treasury Stock**

SE 10. On October 28, 2011, Seoul Company (**SE 9**) retired the remaining 1,500 shares of treasury stock. The shares were originally issued at $5 per share. Prepare the necessary journal entry.

LO 5 **Stock Dividends**

SE 11. On February 15, Asher Corporation's board of directors declared a 2 percent stock dividend applicable to the outstanding shares of its $10 par value common stock, of which 400,000 shares are authorized, 260,000 are issued, and 40,000 are held in the treasury. The stock dividend was distributed on March 15 to stockholders of record on March 1. On February 15, the market value of the common stock was $15 per share. On March 30, the board of directors declared a $0.50 per share cash dividend. No other stock transactions have occurred. Record, as necessary, the transactions of February 15, March 1, March 15, and March 30.

LO 5 **Stock Split**

SE 12. On August 10, 2011, the board of directors of Pearl International declared a 3-for-1 stock split of its $9 par value common stock, of which 400,000 shares were authorized and 125,000 were issued and outstanding. The market value on that date was $60 per share, the balance of additional paid-in capital was $3,000,000, and the balance of retained earnings was $3,250,000. Prepare the stockholders' equity section of the company's balance sheet after the stock split. What entry, if any, is needed to record the stock split?

LO 6 **Statement of Stockholders' Equity**

SE 13. Refer to the statement of stockholders' equity for Snow Corporation in Exhibit 11.5 (p. 513) to answer the following questions: (1) At what price per share were the 10,000 shares of common stock sold? (2) What was the conversion price per share of the common stock? (3) At what price was the common stock selling on the date of the stock dividend? (4) At what price per share was the treasury stock purchased?

LO 5, 6

Effects of Stockholders' Equity Actions

SE 14. Tell whether the following actions will increase, decrease, or have no effect on total assets, total liabilities, and total stockholders' equity: (1) declaration of a stock dividend, (2) declaration of a cash dividend, (3) stock split, and (4) purchase of treasury stock.

LO 6

Book Value for Preferred and Common Stock

SE 15. Using data from Soong Corporation's partial balance sheet below, compute the book value per share for both the preferred and the common stock.

Contributed capital	
Preferred stock, $100 par value, 8 percent cumulative, 20,000 shares authorized, 1,000 shares issued and outstanding*	$ 100,000
Common stock, $10 par value, 200,000 shares authorized, 80,000 shares issued and outstanding	800,000
Additional paid-in capital	1,032,000
Total contributed capital	$1,932,000
Retained earnings	550,000
Total stockholders' equity	$2,482,000

*The preferred stock is callable at $108 per share, and one year's dividends are in arrears.

Exercises

LO 1, 2

Discussion Questions

E 1. Develop a brief answer to each of the following questions:

1. Why are most large companies established as corporations rather than partnerships?
2. Why do many companies like to give stock options as compensation?
3. If an investor sells shares after the declaration date but before the date of record, does the seller still receive the dividend?
4. Why does a company usually not want to issue all of its authorized shares?

LO 3, 4

Discussion Questions

E 2. Develop a brief answer to each of the following questions:

1. Why would a company want to issue callable preferred stock?
2. What arguments can you give for treating preferred stock as debt rather than equity when carrying out financial analysis?
3. What relevance does par value or stated value have to a financial ratio such as return on equity or debt to equity?
4. Why is treasury stock not considered an investment or an asset?

RATIO

LO 1

Dividends Yield and Price/Earnings Ratio

RATIO

E 3. In 2011, Fly Corporation earned $4.40 per share and paid a dividend of $2.00 per share. At year-end, the price of its stock was $66.00 per share. Calculate the dividends yield and the price/earnings ratio. (*Note:* Round ratios to one decimal place.)

LO 1

Cash Dividends

E 4. Elm Corporation secured authorization from the state for 200,000 shares of $10 par value common stock. It has 80,000 shares issued and 70,000 shares outstanding. On June 5, the board of directors declared a $0.25 per share cash dividend to be paid on June 25 to stockholders of record on June 15. Prepare journal entries to record these events.

LO 1, 4

Cash Dividends

E 5. Nova Corporation has 500,000 authorized shares of $1 par value common stock, of which 200,000 are issued, including 20,000 shares of treasury stock. On October 15, the corporation's board of directors declared a cash dividend of $0.50 per share payable on November 15 to stockholders of record on November 1. Prepare journal entries for each of the three dates.

LO 2

Stockholders' Equity

E 6. The following accounts and balances are from the records of Quest Corporation on December 31, 2011:

Preferred Stock, $100 par value, 9 percent cumulative, 20,000 shares authorized, 6,000 shares issued and outstanding	$600,000
Common Stock, $12 par value, 90,000 shares authorized, 30,000 shares issued, and 28,500 shares outstanding	360,000
Additional Paid-In Capital	194,000
Retained Earnings	23,000
Treasury Stock, Common (1,500 shares, at cost)	30,000

Prepare the stockholders' equity section for Quest's balance sheet as of December 31, 2011.

LO 2

Characteristics of Common and Preferred Stock

E 7. Indicate whether each of the following characteristics is more closely associated with common stock (C) or preferred stock (P):

1. Often receives dividends at a set rate
2. Is considered the residual equity of a company
3. Can be callable
4. Can be convertible
5. More likely to have dividends that vary in amount from year to year
6. Can be entitled to receive dividends not paid in past years
7. Likely to have full voting rights
8. Receives assets first in liquidation
9. Generally receives dividends before other classes of stock

LO 2, 3

Stock Entries Using T Accounts; Stockholders' Equity

E 8. Rich Supply Corporation was organized in 2011. It was authorized to issue 100,000 shares of no-par common stock with a stated value of $5 per share and 20,000 shares of $100 par value, 6 percent noncumulative preferred stock. On March 1, the company issued 30,000 shares of its common stock for $15 per share and 4,000 shares of its preferred stock for $100 per share.

1. Record the issuance of the stock in T accounts.
2. Prepare the stockholders' equity section of Rich Supply's balance sheet as it would appear immediately after the company issued the common and preferred stock.

LO 2

Cash Dividends with Dividends in Arrears

E 9. Rim Corporation has 5,000 shares of its $100 par value, 7 percent cumulative preferred stock outstanding, and 25,000 shares of its $1 par value common stock outstanding. In Rim's first four years of operation, its board of directors paid cash dividends as follows: 2009, none; 2010, $60,000; 2011, $70,000; 2012, $70,000. Determine the dividends per share and total cash dividends paid to the preferred and common stockholders during each of the four years.

LO 2

Cash Dividends on Preferred and Common Stock

E 10. Oblinger Corporation pays dividends at the end of each year. The dividends that it paid for 2009, 2010, and 2011 were $40,000, $30,000, and $90,000, respectively. Calculate the total amount of dividends Oblinger paid in each of these years to its common and preferred stockholders under both of the following capital structures: (1) 10,000 shares of $100 par, 6 percent noncumulative preferred stock and 30,000 shares of $10 par common stock and (2) 5,000 shares of $100 par, 7 percent cumulative preferred stock and 30,000 shares of $10 par common stock. Oblinger had no dividends in arrears at the beginning of 2009.

LO 3 **Issuance of Stock**

E 11. Blue Moon Company is authorized to issue 100,000 shares of common stock. On August 1, the company issued 5,000 shares at $25 per share. Prepare journal entries to record the issuance of stock for cash under each of the following alternatives: (1) the stock has a par value of $25, (2) the stock has a par value of $10, (3) the stock has no par value, and (4) the stock has a stated value of $1 per share.

LO 3 **Issuance of Stock for Noncash Assets**

E 12. On July 1, 2011, Salas Inc., a new corporation, issued 40,000 shares of its common stock to finance a corporate headquarters building. The building has a fair market value of $1,200,000 and a book value of $800,000. Because Salas is a new corporation, it is not possible to establish a market value for its common stock. Record the issuance of stock for the building, assuming the following conditions: (1) the par value of the stock is $10 per share, (2) the stock is no-par stock, and (3) the stock has a stated value of $4 per share.

LO 4 **Treasury Stock Transactions**

E 13. Record in T accounts the following stock transactions of Gorce Company, which represent all of the company's treasury stock transactions for the year:

May 5	Purchased 3,200 shares of its own $2 par value common stock for $40 per share, the current market price.
17	Sold 1,200 shares of treasury stock purchased on May 5 for $44 per share.
21	Sold 800 shares of treasury stock purchased on May 5 for $40 per share.
28	Sold the remaining 1,200 shares of treasury stock purchased on May 5 for $38 per share.

LO 4 **Treasury Stock Transactions Including Retirement**

E 14. Record in T accounts the following stock transactions of Santiago Corporation, which represent all its treasury stock transactions for the year:

June 1	Purchased 1,000 shares of its own $15 par value common stock for $35 per share, the current market price.
10	Sold 250 shares of treasury stock purchased on June 1 for $40 per share.
20	Sold 350 shares of treasury stock purchased on June 1 for $29 per share.
30	Retired the remaining shares purchased on June 1. The original issue price was $21 per share.

LO 5 **Stock Dividends**

E 15. Tusk Company has 60,000 shares of its $1 par value common stock outstanding. Prepare journal entries for the following transactions as they relate to the company's common stock:

July 17	Declared a 10 percent stock dividend on common stock to be distributed on August 10 to stockholders of record on July 31. Market value of the stock was $5 per share on this date.
31	Date of record.
Aug. 10	Distributed the stock dividend declared on July 17.
Sept. 1	Declared a $0.50 per share cash dividend on common stock to be paid on September 16 to stockholders of record on September 10.

LO 5 **Stock Split**

E 16. Agat Company currently has 250,000 shares of $1 par value common stock authorized with 100,000 shares outstanding. The board of directors declared a 2-for-1 split on May 15, 2011, when the market value of the common stock was $2.50 per share. The retained earnings balance on May 15 was $350,000. Additional paid-in capital on this date was $10,000. Prepare the stockholders' equity section of the company's balance sheet before and after the stock split. What entry, if any, would be necessary to record the stock split?

LO 5 **Stock Split**

E 17. On January 15, 2011, the board of directors of Mendoza International declared a 3-for-1 stock split of its $12 par value common stock, of which 1,600,000 shares were authorized and 400,000 were issued and outstanding. The market value on that date was $45 per share. On the same date, the balance of additional paid-in capital was $8,000,000, and the balance of retained earnings was $16,000,000. Prepare the stockholders' equity section of the company's balance sheet before and after the stock split. What entry, if any, is needed to record the stock split?

LO 6 **Statement of Stockholders' Equity**

E 18. The stockholders' equity section of Ruff Corporation's balance sheet on December 31, 2011, follows.

Contributed capital	
Common stock, $2 par value, 250,000 shares authorized, 200,000 shares issued and outstanding	$ 400,000
Additional paid-in capital	600,000
Total contributed capital	$1,000,000
Retained earnings	2,100,000
Total stockholders' equity	$3,100,000

Prepare a statement of stockholders' equity for the year ended December 31, 2012, assuming the following transactions occurred in sequence in 2012:

a. Issued 5,000 shares of $100 par value, 9 percent cumulative preferred stock at par after obtaining authorization from the state.
b. Issued 20,000 shares of common stock in connection with the conversion of bonds having a carrying value of $300,000.
c. Declared and issued a 2 percent common stock dividend. The market value on the date of declaration was $14 per share.
d. Purchased 5,000 shares of common stock for the treasury at a cost of $16 per share.
e. Earned net income of $230,000.
f. Declared and paid the full year's dividend on preferred stock and a dividend of $0.40 per share on common stock outstanding at the end of the year.
g. Had foreign currency translation adjustment of minus $50,000.

LO 6 **Book Value for Preferred and Common Stock**

E 19. Below is the stockholders' equity section of Picado Corporation's balance sheet. Determine the book value per share for both the preferred and the common stock.

Contributed capital	
Preferred stock, $100 per share, 6 percent cumulative, 20,000 shares authorized, 400 shares issued and outstanding*	$ 40,000
Common stock, $5 par value, 200,000 shares authorized, 20,000 shares issued, 18,000 shares outstanding	100,000
Additional paid-in capital	56,000
Total contributed capital	$196,000
Retained earnings	190,000
Total contributed capital and retained earnings	$386,000
Less: Treasury stock, common (2,000 shares at cost)	30,000
Total stockholders' equity	$356,000

*The preferred stock is callable at $105 per share, and one year's dividends are in arrears.

Problems

LO 1, 2, 3, 4

✔ 2. Total stockholders' equity: $1,342,000

Common Stock Transactions and Stockholders' Equity

P 1. Dewey Corporation began operations on September 1, 2011. The corporation's charter authorized 300,000 shares of $8 par value common stock. Dewey engaged in the following transactions during its first quarter:

Sept. 1	Issued 50,000 shares of common stock, $500,000.
1	Paid an attorney $32,000 to help start up and organize the corporation and obtain a corporate charter from the state.
Oct. 2	Issued 80,000 shares of common stock, $960,000.
15	Purchased 10,000 shares of common stock for $150,000.
Nov. 30	Declared a cash dividend of $0.40 per share to be paid on December 15 to stockholders of record on December 10.

REQUIRED

1. Record the above transactions in T accounts.
2. Prepare the stockholders' equity section of Dewey's balance sheet on November 30, 2011. Net income for the quarter was $80,000.

3. What effect, if any, will the cash dividend declaration on November 30 have on net income, retained earnings, and cash flows?

LO 1, 2

✔ 1. Total dividends in 2013: preferred, $70,000; common, $205,000

Preferred and Common Stock Dividends and Dividends Yield

P 2. DeMono Corporation had both common stock and preferred stock outstanding from 2011 through 2013. Information about each stock for the three years is as follows:

Type	Par Value	Shares Outstanding	Other
Preferred	$100	10,000	7% cumulative
Common	20	150,000	

The company paid $35,000, $200,000, and $275,000 in dividends for 2011 through 2013, respectively. The market price per common share was $15 and $17 per share at the end of 2012 and 2013, respectively.

REQUIRED

1. Determine the dividends per share and total dividends paid to the common and preferred stockholders each year.
2. Assuming that the preferred stock was noncumulative, repeat the computations performed in **1**.

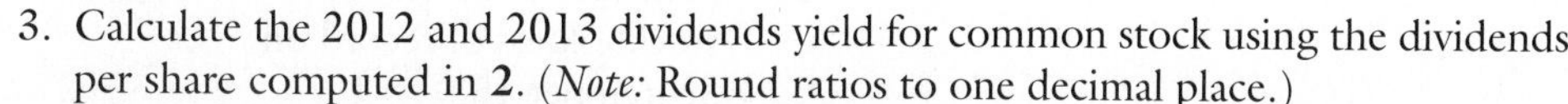

3. Calculate the 2012 and 2013 dividends yield for common stock using the dividends per share computed in **2**. (*Note:* Round ratios to one decimal place.)

USER INSIGHT

4. How are cumulative preferred stock and noncumulative preferred stock similar to long-term bonds? How do they differ from long-term bonds?

LO 1, 2, 3, 4

Comprehensive Stockholders' Equity Transactions

P 3. In January 2011, Delgado Corporation was organized and authorized to issue 2,000,000 shares of no-par common stock and 50,000 shares of 5 percent, $50 par value, noncumulative preferred stock. The stock-related transactions for the first year's operations were as follows:

		Account			
		Debited		Credited	
		Account Number	Dollar Amount	Account Number	Dollar Amount
Jan. 19	Sold 15,000 shares of common stock for $31,500. State law requires a minimum of $1 stated value per share.	110	$31,500	310 312	$15,000 $16,500

(Continued)

		Account			
		Debited		Credited	
		Account Number	Dollar Amount	Account Number	Dollar Amount
Jan. 21	Issued 5,000 shares of common stock to attorneys and accountants for services valued at $11,000 and provided during the organization of the corporation.				
Feb. 7	Issued 30,000 shares of common stock for a building that had an appraised value of $78,000.				
Mar. 22	Purchased 10,000 shares of its common stock at $3 per share.				
July 15	Issued 5,000 shares of common stock to employees under a stock option plan that allows any employee to buy shares at the current market price, which is now $3 per share.				
Aug. 1	Sold 2,500 shares of treasury stock for $4 per share.				
Sept. 1	Declared a cash dividend of $0.15 per common share to be paid on September 25 to stockholders of record on September 15.				
15	Date of record for cash dividends.				
25	Paid cash dividends to stockholders of record on September 15.				
Oct. 30	Issued 4,000 shares of common stock for a piece of land. The stock was selling for $3 per share, and the land had a fair market value of $12,000.				
Dec. 15	Issued 2,200 shares of preferred stock for $50 per share.				

REQUIRED

1. For each of the preceding transactions, enter in the blanks provided the account numbers and dollar amounts (as shown in the example) for the account(s) debited and credited. The account numbers are as follows: 110, Cash; 120, Land; 121, Building; 220, Dividends Payable; 305, Preferred Stock; 310, Common Stock; 312, Additional Paid-In Capital; 313, Paid-In Capital, Treasury Stock; 340, Retained Earnings; 341, Dividends; 350, Treasury Stock, Common; 510, Start-up and Organization Costs.

USER INSIGHT ▶

2. Why is the stockholders' equity section of the balance sheet an important consideration in analyzing the performance of a company?

LO 1, 2, 3, 4

Comprehensive Stockholders' Equity Transactions and Financial Ratios

✔ 2. Total stockholders' equity: $441,475

P 4. Stas Corporation was chartered in the state of California. The company was authorized to issue 5,000 shares of $100 par value, 6 percent preferred stock and 25,000 shares of no-par common stock. The common stock has a $2 stated value. The stock-related transactions for the quarter ended October 31, 2011, were as follows:

Aug.	3	Issued 5,000 shares of common stock at $22 per share.
	15	Issued 4,000 shares of common stock for land. Asking price for the land was $50,000. Common stock's market value was $12 per share.
	22	Issued 2,500 shares of preferred stock for $250,000.
Oct.	4	Issued 2,500 shares of common stock for $30,000.
	10	Purchased 1,250 shares of common stock for the treasury for $3,250.
	15	Declared a quarterly cash dividend on the outstanding preferred stock and $0.10 per share on common stock outstanding, payable on October 31 to stockholders of record on October 25.
	25	Date of record for cash dividends.
	31	Paid cash dividends.

REQUIRED

1. Record transactions for the quarter ended October 31, 2011, in T accounts.
2. Prepare the stockholders' equity section of the balance sheet as of October 31, 2011. Net income for the quarter was $11,500.

3. Calculate quarterly performance: dividends yield, price/earnings ratio, and return on equity. Assume earnings per common share are $1.97 and market price per common share is $25. For beginning stockholders' equity, use the balance after the August transactions. (*Note:* Round ratios to one decimal place.)

USER INSIGHT ▶

4. Discuss the results in 3, including the effect on investors' returns and the firm's profitability as it relates to stockholders' equity.

LO 5, 6

Dividends, Stock Splits, and Stockholders' Equity

✔ 2. Total stockholders' equity: $1,049,000

P 5. The stockholders' equity section of Rigby Storage, Inc., as of December 31, 2011, was as follows:

Contributed capital	
Common stock, $3 par value, 1,000,000 shares authorized, 80,000 shares issued and outstanding	$240,000
Additional paid-in capital	75,000
Total contributed capital	$315,000
Retained earnings	240,000
Total stockholders' equity	$555,000

A review of the stockholders' equity records of Rigby Storage, Inc., disclosed the following transactions during 2012:

Mar.	25	The board of directors declared a 5 percent stock dividend to stockholders of record on April 20 to be distributed on May 1. The market value of the common stock was $21 per share.
Apr.	20	Date of record for stock dividend.
May	1	Issued stock dividend.
Sept.	10	Declared a 3-for-1 stock split.
Dec.	15	Declared a 10 percent stock dividend to stockholders of record on January 15 to be distributed on February 15. The market price on this date is $9 per share.

REQUIRED

1. Record the stockholders' equity components of the transactions for Rigby Storage in T accounts.
2. Prepare the stockholders' equity section of the company's balance sheet as of December 31, 2012. Assume net income for 2012 is $494,000.

USER INSIGHT ▶

3. If you owned 2,000 shares of Rigby Storage stock on March 1, 2012, how many shares would you own on February 15, 2013? Would your proportionate share of the ownership of the company be different on the latter date than it was on the former date? Explain your answer.

Alternate Problems

LO 1, 2, 3

Common Stock Transactions and Stockholders' Equity

✔ 2. Total stockholders' equity: $151,200

P 6. On March 1, 2011, Algae Corporation began operations with a charter it received from the state that authorized 50,000 shares of $4 par value common stock. Over the next quarter, the company engaged in the transactions that follow.

Mar.	1	Issued 15,000 shares of common stock, $100,000.
	2	Paid legal fees associated with obtaining the charter and starting up and organizing the corporation, $12,000.
Apr.	10	Issued 6,500 shares of common stock, $65,000.
	15	Purchased 2,500 shares of common stock, $25,000.
May	31	The board of directors declared a $0.20 per share cash dividend to be paid on June 15 to shareholders of record on June 10.

REQUIRED

1. Record the above transactions in T accounts.
2. Prepare the stockholders' equity section of Algae's balance sheet on May 31, 2011. Net income earned during the first quarter was $15,000.

USER INSIGHT ▶

3. What effect, if any, will the cash dividend declaration on May 31 have on Algae's net income, retained earnings, and cash flows?

LO 1, 2

Preferred and Common Stock Dividends and Dividends Yield

✔ 1. Total dividends in 2013: preferred, $40,000; common, $90,000

P 7. Morris Corporation had the following stock outstanding from 2010 through 2013:

Preferred stock: $100 par value, 8 percent cumulative, 5,000 shares authorized, issued, and outstanding

Common stock: $10 par value, 100,000 shares authorized, issued, and outstanding

The company paid $30,000, $30,000, $94,000, and $130,000 in dividends during 2010, 2011, 2012, and 2013, respectively. The market price per common share was $7.25 and $8.00 per share at the end of 2012 and 2013, respectively.

REQUIRED

1. Determine the dividends per share and the total dividends paid to common stockholders and preferred stockholders in 2010, 2011, 2012, and 2013.
2. Perform the same computations, with the assumption that the preferred stock was noncumulative.

RATIO

3. Calculate the 2012 and 2013 dividends yield for common stock using the dividends per share computed in 2. (*Note:* Round ratios to one decimal place.)

USER INSIGHT ▶

4. How are cumulative preferred stock and noncumulative preferred stock similar to long-term bonds? How do they differ from long-term bonds?

LO 1, 2, 3, 4

Comprehensive Stockholders' Equity Transactions and Stockholders' Equity

✔ 2. Total stockholders' equity: $236,520

P 8. Java, Inc., was organized and authorized to issue 5,000 shares of $100 par value, 9 percent preferred stock and 50,000 shares of no-par, $5 stated value common stock on July 1, 2011. Stock-related transactions for Java are as follows:

July	1	Issued 10,000 shares of common stock at $11 per share.
	1	Issued 500 shares of common stock at $11 per share for legal services rendered in connection with the organization of the company.
	2	Issued 1,000 shares of preferred stock at par value for cash.
	10	Issued 2,500 shares of common stock for land on which the asking price was $35,000. Market value of the stock was $12. Management wishes to record the land at full market value of the stock.
Aug.	2	Purchased 1,500 shares of its common stock at $13 per share.
	10	Declared a cash dividend for one month on the outstanding preferred stock and $0.02 per share on common stock outstanding, payable on August 22 to stockholders of record on August 12.
	12	Date of record for cash dividends.
	22	Paid cash dividends.

REQUIRED

1. Prepare journal entries to record the transactions.
2. Prepare the stockholders' equity section of the balance sheet as it would appear on August 31, 2011. The company's net income for July and August was $11,500.

RATIO

3. Calculate quarterly performance measures: dividends yield, price/earnings ratio, and return on equity. Assume earnings per common share are $1 and market price per common share is $20. For beginning stockholders' equity, use the balance after the July transactions. (*Note:* Round ratios to one decimal place.)

USER INSIGHT ▶

4. Discuss the results in **3**, including the effect on investors' returns and the company's profitability as it relates to stockholders' equity.

LO 5, 6

Comprehensive Stockholders' Equity Transactions

✔ 2. Retained earnings: $297,600; total stockholders' equity: $5,605,600

P 9. On December 31, 2011, the stockholders' equity section of Sophia Company's balance sheet appeared as follows:

Contributed capital	
Common stock, $8 par value, 400,000 shares authorized, 120,000 shares issued and outstanding	$ 960,000
Additional paid-in capital	2,560,000
Total contributed capital	$3,520,000
Retained earnings	1,648,000
Total stockholders' equity	$5,168,000

The following are selected transactions involving stockholders' equity in 2012:

Jan.	4	The board of directors obtained authorization for 40,000 shares of $40 par value noncumulative preferred stock that carried an indicated dividend rate of $4 per share and was callable at $42 per share.
	14	The company sold 24,000 shares of the preferred stock at $40 per share and issued another 4,000 in exchange for a building valued at $160,000.
Mar.	8	The board of directors declared a 2-for-1 stock split on the common stock.
Apr.	20	After the stock split, the company purchased 6,000 shares of common stock for the treasury at an average price of $12 per share.
May	4	The company sold 2,000 of the shares purchased on April 20, at an average price of $16 per share.
July	15	The board of directors declared a cash dividend of $4 per share on the preferred stock and $0.40 per share on the common stock.
July	25	Date of record.
Aug.	15	Paid the cash dividend.
Nov.	28	The board of directors declared a 15 percent stock dividend when the common stock was selling for $20 per share to be distributed on January 5 to stockholders of record on December 15.
Dec.	15	Date of record for the stock dividend.

REQUIRED

1. Prepare the journal entries to record the transactions.
2. Prepare the stockholders' equity section of the company's balance sheet as of December 31, 2012. Net loss for 2012 was $436,000. (*Hint:* Use T accounts to keep track of transactions.)
3. Compute the book value per share for preferred and common stock (including common stock distributable) on December 31, 2011 and 2012, using end-of-year shares outstanding. What effect would you expect the change in book value to have on the market price per share of the company's stock?

USER INSIGHT ▶

LO 5, 6

Dividends and Stock Split Transactions and Stockholder's Equity

✔ 2. Retained earnings: $720,000; total stockholders' equity: $4,920,000

P 10. The stockholders' equity section of Jet Moving Company's balance sheet as of December 31, 2011, appears below.

Contributed capital	
Common stock, $2 par value, 6,000,000 shares authorized,	
1,000,000 shares issued and outstanding	$2,000,000
Additional paid-in capital	800,000
Total contributed capital	$2,800,000
Retained earnings	2,160,000
Total stockholders' equity	$4,960,000

The company engaged in the following stockholders' equity transactions during 2012:

Mar.	5	Declared a $0.40 per share cash dividend to be paid on April 6 to stockholders of record on March 20.
	20	Date of record.
Apr.	6	Paid the cash dividend.
June	17	Declared a 10 percent stock dividend to be distributed August 17 to stockholders of record on August 5. The market value of the stock was $14 per share.
Aug.	5	Date of record for the stock dividend.
	17	Distributed the stock dividend.
Oct.	2	Split its stock 2 for 1.
Dec.	27	Declared a cash dividend of $0.20 payable January 27, 2013, to stockholders of record on January 14, 2013.

REQUIRED

1. Prepare journal entries to record the 2012 transactions.
2. Prepare the stockholders' equity section of Jet Moving Company's balance sheet as of December 31, 2012. Assume net income for the year is $800,000.
3. If you owned some shares of Jet, would you expect the total value of your shares to go up or down as a result of the stock dividends and stock split? What intangibles might affect the stock value?

USER INSIGHT ▶

Cases

LO 1

Conceptual Understanding: Reasons for Issuing Common Stock

C 1. When **DreamWorks Animation**, led by billionaire Microsoft founder Paul Allen, went public in 2004 with its class A common stock at $28 per share, it raised $650 million. By the end of the first day, its stock was up 36 percent to $38 per share, giving the company a value of almost $1 billion. The initial enthusiasm did not last. By June 2010, the price was only around $28 per share.[18] As a growing company that had produced such animated hits as *Shrek* and *Shrek II*, DreamWorks could have borrowed significant funds by issuing long-term debt. What are some advantages that issuing common stock has over issuing bonds? What are some disadvantages?

LO 2

Conceptual Understanding: Reasons for Issuing Preferred Stock

C 2. Preferred stock is a hybrid security; it has some of the characteristics of stock and some of the characteristics of bonds. Historically, preferred stock has not been a popular means of financing. In the past few years, however, it has become more attractive to companies and individual investors alike, and investors are buying large amounts because of high yields. Large preferred stock issues have been made by such banks as **Citibank, J.P. Morgan**, and **Wells Fargo**, as well as by other companies. The dividends yields on these stocks are over 6 percent, higher than the interest rates on bonds of comparable risk.[19] Especially popular are preferred equity redemption convertible stocks, or PERCs, which are automatically convertible into common stock after three years if the company does not call them first and retire them. What reasons can you give for the popularity of preferred stock, and of PERCs in particular, when the tax-deductible interest on bonds is lower? Discuss from both the company's and the investor's standpoint.

LO 4

Conceptual Understanding: Purposes of Treasury Stock

RATIO

C 3. Many companies in recent years have bought back their common stock. For example, **IBM**, with large cash holdings, spent almost $350 billion over three years repurchasing its stock.[20] What are the reasons companies buy back their own shares? What is the effect of common stock buybacks on earnings per share, return on equity, return on assets, debt to equity, and the current ratio?

LO 5

Conceptual Understanding: Stock Split

C 4. When **General Mills, Inc.,** the cereal company, rose from about $55 per share to above $70 per share on improved earnings in 2010, the company announced a 2-for-1 stock split.[21] What is a stock split, and what effect does it have on the company's stockholders' equity? What effect will it likely have on the market value of the company's stock? In light of your answers, do you think the stock split is positive for the company and for its stockholders?

LO 3

Interpreting Financial Reports: Effect of Stock Issue

C 5. When **Google, Inc.,** went public with an IPO, it used an auction system that allowed everyone to participate rather than allocating shares of stock to a few insiders. As mentioned in this chapter's Decision Point, the company's IPO drew widespread attention. Announcements of the IPO would have been similar to the following:

22,500,000 Shares
GOOGLE, INC.
$0.001 Par Value Common Stock
Price $85 a share

The gross proceeds of the IPO before issue costs were $1.9 billion.

Shown below is a portion of the stockholders' equity section of the balance sheet adapted from Google's annual report, which was issued prior to this stock offering:

Stockholders' Equity (in thousands)	
Common stock, $0.001 par value, 700,000,000 shares authorized; 161,000,000 shares issued and outstanding	$ 161
Additional paid-in capital	725,219
Retained earnings	191,352

1. Assume that the net proceeds to Google after issue costs were $1.8 billion. Prepare journal entries to record the stock issuance on Google's accounting records.
2. Prepare the portion of the stockholders' equity section of the balance sheet shown above after the issue of the common stock, based on the information given. (*Note:* Round all answers to the nearest thousand.)

3. Based on your answer to **2**, did Google have to increase its authorized shares to undertake this stock issue?
4. What amount per share did Google receive, and how much did Google's underwriters receive to help in issuing the stock? What do underwriters do to earn their fees?

LO 6 **Interpreting Financial Reports: Statement of Stockholders' Equity**

C 6. The consolidated statement of stockholders' equity for Spencer Electronics, Inc., a manufacturer of a broad line of electrical components, follows. It has nine summary transactions.

Spencer Electronics, Inc.
Consolidated Statement of Stockholders' Equity
For the Year Ended September 30, 2011
(in thousands)

	Preferred Stock	Common Stock	Additional Paid-In Capital	Retained Earnings	Treasury Stock, Common	Accumulated Other Comprehensive Income	Total
Balance at September 30, 2010	$2,756	$3,902	$14,149	$119,312	$ (942)		$139,177
(1) Net income				18,753			18,753
(2) Unrealized gain on available for sale securities						$12,000	12,000
(3) Redemption and retirement of preferred stock (27,560 shares)	(2,756)						(2,756)
(4) Stock options exercised (89,000 shares)		89	847				936
(5) Purchases of common stock for treasury (501,412 shares)					(12,552)		(12,552)
(6) Issuance of common stock (148,000 shares) in exchange for convertible subordinated debentures		148	3,635				3,783
(7) Issuance of common stock (715,000 shares) for cash		715	24,535				25,250
(8) Issuance of 500,000 shares of common stock in exchange for investment in Miti Company shares		500	17,263				17,763
(9) Cash dividends—common stock ($0.80 per share)				(3,086)			(3,086)
Balance at September 30, 2011	$ —	$5,354	$60,429	$134,979	$(13,494)	$12,000	$199,268

1. Show that you understand this statement by writing an explanation of each transaction. Determine the average price per common share wherever applicable. For some transactions, you will have to make assumptions about an offsetting part of the entry. For example, assume debentures (long-term bonds) are recorded at face value and that employees pay cash for stock purchased under company incentive plans.
2. Define other comprehensive income and determine the amount for Spencer Electronics.

LO 1, 2, 6

Annual Report Case: Stockholders' Equity

C 7. Refer to the **CVS** annual report in the Supplement to Chapter 1 to answer the following questions:

1. What type of capital stock does CVS have? What is the par value? How many shares were authorized, issued, and outstanding at the end of fiscal 2009?

RATIO

2. What is the dividends yield for CVS and its relationship to the investors' total return? (*Note:* Use the average price of stock in the last quarter and round calculation to one decimal place.) Does the company rely mostly on stock or on earnings for its stockholders' equity?
3. Does the company have a stock option plan? If so, do the stock options apply to all employees, and given the market price of the stock shown in the report, are these options of significant value?
4. What transactions most often affect the stockholders' equity section of the CVS balance sheet? (*Hint:* Examine CVS's statements of shareholders' equity.)

LO 1, 4, 6

Comparison Analysis: Return on Equity, Treasury Stock, Dividends Policy, Book Value, and Market Prices

C 8. Refer to the **CVS** annual report and the financial statements of **Southwest Airlines Co.** in the Supplement to Chapter 1. (*Note:* Round calculations to one decimal place.)

RATIO

1. Compute the return on equity for both companies in fiscal 2009 and 2008. Total stockholders' equity for CVS and Southwest in 2007 was $31,322 million and $6,941 million, respectively.
2. Did either company purchase treasury stock during these years? How does the purchase of treasury stock affect return on equity and earnings per share?
3. Did either company issue stock during these years? If so, what are the details?
4. Compare the two companies' dividend policies.

RATIO

5. Compute the 2009 and 2008 book value per share for both companies and compare the results to the average stock price of each one in the fourth quarter of 2009 (shown in the notes to the financial statements). Southwest's average price per share was $9.94 in 2009 and $11.01 in 2008.
6. How do you explain the differences in book value per share, and how do you interpret their relationship to market prices?

LO 1, 4

Ethical Dilemma: Ethics, Management Compensation, and Treasury Stock

C 9. Compensation of senior management is often tied to earnings per share or return on equity. Treasury stock purchases have a favorable impact on both these measures because treasury stock reduces the denominator in both calculations. In the recent buyback boom, many companies borrowed money to purchase treasury shares. In some cases, the motivation for the borrowing and repurchase of shares was the desire of executives to secure their year-end cash bonuses. Did these executives act ethically? Were their actions in the best interests of stockholders? Why or why not? How might such behavior be avoided in the future?

CHAPTER 12

DECISION POINT
A User's Focus Amazon.com, Inc.

Founded in 1995, **Amazon.com, Inc.**, is now the largest online merchandising company in the world and one of the 500 largest companies in the United States. The company's financial focus is on "long-term sustainable growth" in cash flows.

Strong cash flows are critical to achieving and maintaining liquidity. If cash flows exceed the amount a company needs for operations and expansion, it will not have to borrow additional funds. It can use its excess cash to reduce debt, thereby lowering its debt to equity ratio and improving its financial position. That, in turn, can increase the market value of its stock, which will increase shareholders' value.

Amazon.com's Financial Highlights summarize key components of the company's statement of cash flows.[1]

AMAZON.COM'S FINANCIAL HIGHLIGHTS: Consolidated Statement of Cash Flows
(in millions)

	2009	2008	2007
Net cash provided by operating activities	$3,293	$1,697	$1,405
Net cash provided by (used in) investing activities	(2,337)	(1,199)	42
Net cash provided by (used in) financing activities	(280)	(198)	50
Foreign currency effects	(1)	(70)	20
Increase (decrease) in cash and equivalents	$ 675	$ 230	$1,517

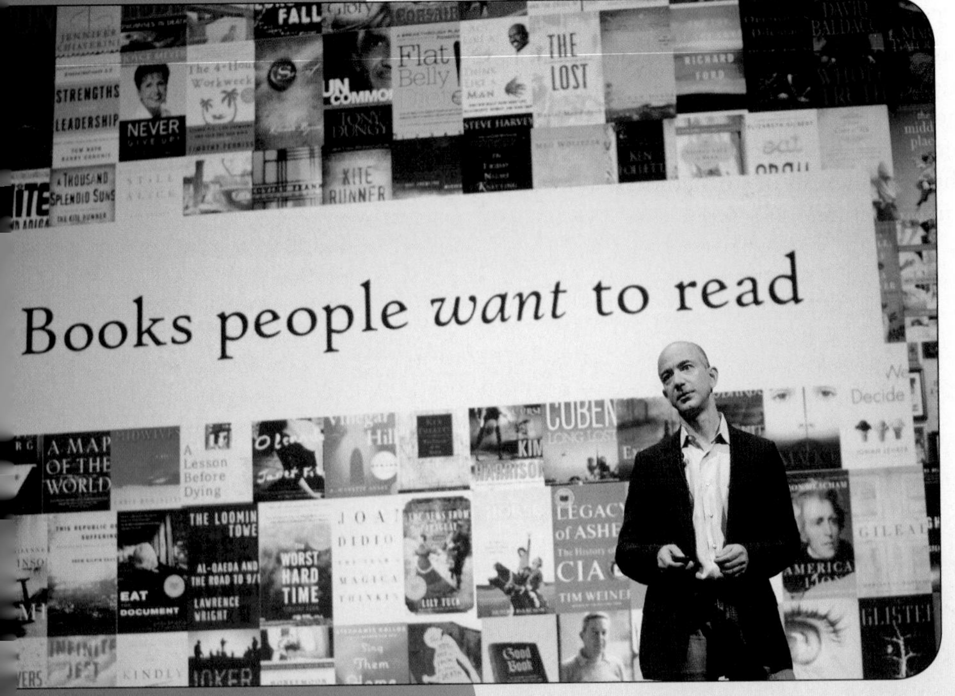

© James Leynse/Corbis

Questions

1. ***Are Amazon.com's operations generating sufficient operating cash flows?***

2. ***Is the company growing by investing in long-term assets?***

3. ***Has the company had to borrow money or issue stock to finance its growth?***

The Statement of Cash Flows

LEARNING OBJECTIVES

LO1 Describe the principal purposes and uses of the statement of cash flows and identify its components. (pp. 538–542)

LO2 Analyze the statement of cash flows. (pp. 542–546)

LO3 Use the indirect method to determine cash flows from operating activities. (pp. 546–553)

LO4 Determine cash flows from investing activities. (pp. 553–556)

LO5 Determine cash flows from financing activities. (pp. 556–560)

Cash flows are the lifeblood of a business. They enable a company to pay expenses, debts, employees' wages, and taxes and to invest in the assets it needs for its operations. Without sufficient cash flows, a company cannot grow and prosper. Because of the importance of cash flows, one must be alert to the possibility that items may be incorrectly classified in a statement of cash flows and that the statement may not fully disclose all pertinent information. This chapter identifies the classifications used in a statement of cash flows and explains how to analyze the statement.

FOCUS ON FINANCIAL STATEMENTS

INCOME STATEMENT
Revenues
− Expenses
= Net Income

STATEMENT OF RETAINED EARNINGS
Opening Balance
+ Net Income
− Dividends
= Retained Earnings

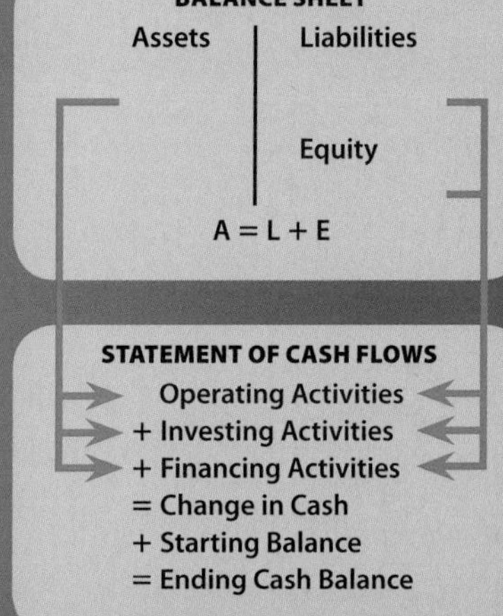

BALANCE SHEET
Assets
Liabilities
Equity
A = L + E
STATEMENT OF CASH FLOWS
Operating Activities
+ Investing Activities
+ Financing Activities
= Change in Cash
+ Starting Balance
= Ending Cash Balance

Changes in all noncash balance sheet accounts are used to explain changes in cash.

OVERVIEW OF THE STATEMENT OF CASH FLOWS

LO 1 Describe the principal purposes and uses of the statement of cash flows and identify its components.

The **statement of cash flows** shows how a company's operating, investing, and financing activities have affected cash during an accounting period. It explains the net increase (or decrease) in cash during the period. For purposes of preparing this statement, **cash** is defined as including both cash and cash equivalents. **Cash equivalents** are investments that can be quickly converted to cash; they have a maturity of 90 days or less when they are purchased. Cash equivalents include the following:

- Money market accounts
- Commercial paper (short-term corporate notes)
- U.S. Treasury bills

A company invests in cash equivalents to earn interest on cash that would otherwise be temporarily idle. Suppose, for example, that a company has $1,000,000 that it will not need for 30 days. To earn a return on this amount, the company could place the cash in an account that earns interest (such as a money market account), lend the cash to another corporation by purchasing that corporation's short-term notes (commercial paper), or purchase a short-term obligation of the U.S. government (a Treasury bill).

Because cash includes cash equivalents, transfers between the Cash account and cash equivalents are not treated as cash receipts or cash payments. On the statement of cash flows, cash equivalents are combined with the Cash account. Cash equivalents should not be confused with short-term investments or marketable securities. These items are not combined with the Cash account on the statement of cash flows; rather, purchases of marketable securities are treated as cash outflows, and sales of marketable securities are treated as cash inflows.

Purposes and Uses of the Statement of Cash Flows

The statement of cash flows provides information about a company's cash receipts and cash payments during an accounting period, as well as about the company's operating, investing, and financing activities. Some information about those activities may be inferred from other financial statements, but the statement of cash flows summarizes *all* transactions that affect cash.

The statement of cash flows is useful to management, as well as to investors and creditors. Management uses the statement of cash flows to

- assess liquidity (e.g., to determine whether short-term financing is needed to pay current liabilities).
- determine the company's dividend policy.
- evaluate the effects of major policy decisions involving investments and financing needs.

Investors and creditors use the statement of cash flows to assess a company's ability to

- manage cash flows.
- generate positive future cash flows.
- pay its liabilities, dividends, and interest.
- anticipate the need for additional financing.

Classification of Cash Flows

Exhibit 12.1 shows **Amazon.com**'s consolidated statements of cash flows. As you can see, this statement, like all statements of cash flows, has three major classifications: operating, investing, and financing activities. A reconciliation of the beginning and ending balances of cash appears at the bottom of the statement; these balances will tie into the cash balances on the balance sheet.

EXHIBIT 12.1
Consolidated Statements of Cash Flows

Amazon.com, Inc.
Consolidated Statements of Cash Flows

	For the Years Ended		
(In millions)	**2009**	**2008**	**2007**
Operating Activities			
Net income	$ 902	$ 645	$ 476
Adjustments to reconcile net income to net cash from operating activities:			
Depreciation and amortization	378	287	246
Stock-based compensation	341	275	185
Deferred income taxes	81	(5)	(99)
Excess tax benefits from stock-based compensation	(105)	(159)	(257)
Other	84	(60)	22
Cumulative effect of change in accounting principle	—	—	—
Changes in operating assets and liabilities:			
Inventories	(531)	(232)	(303)
Accounts receivable, net and other	(481)	(218)	(255)
Accounts payable	1,859	812	928
Accrued expenses and other	300	247	429
Additions to unearned revenue and other	465	105	33
Net cash provided by operating activities	$ 3,293	$ 1,697	$1,405
Investing Activities			
Purchases of fixed assets, including software and website development	$ (373)	$ (333)	$ (224)
Acquisitions, net of cash received and other	(40)	(494)	(75)
Sales and maturities of marketable securities and other investments	1,966	1,305	1,271
Purchases of marketable securities and other investments	(3,890)	(1,677)	(930)
Net cash provided by (used in) investing activities	$(2,337)	$(1,199)	$ 42
Financing Activities			
Excess tax benefits from exercises of stock options	$ 105	$ 159	$ 257
Common stock repurchased (treasury stock)	—	(100)	(248)
Proceeds from long-term debt and other	87	98	115
Repayments of long-term debt and capital lease obligations	(472)	(355)	(74)
Net cash provided by (used in) financing activities	$ (280)	$ (198)	$ 50
Foreign-currency effect on cash and cash equivalents	$ (1)	$ (70)	$ 20
Net Increase in Cash and Cash Equivalents	$ 675	$ 230	$1,517
Cash and Cash Equivalents, beginning of year	2,769	2,539	1,022
Cash and Cash Equivalents, end of year	$ 3,444	$ 2,769	$2,539

Source: Amazon.com, Inc., *Annual Report*, 2009 (adapted).

The components of operating, investing, and financing activities are illustrated in Exhibit 12.2 (p. 540) and summarized next.

Operating Activities The first section of the statement of cash flows is *cash flows from operating activities*. **Operating activities** involve the cash inflows and outflows from activities that enter into the determination of net income. Cash inflows in this category include cash receipts from the sale of goods and services and from the sale of trading securities. **Trading securities** are a type of marketable security that a company buys and sells for the purpose of making a profit in the near term as opposed to holding them indefinitely for investment purposes. Cash inflows also include interest and dividends received on loans and investments. Cash outflows include cash payments for wages, inventory, expenses, interest, taxes, and the purchase of trading securities.

Exhibit 12.2
Classification of Cash Inflows and Cash Outflows

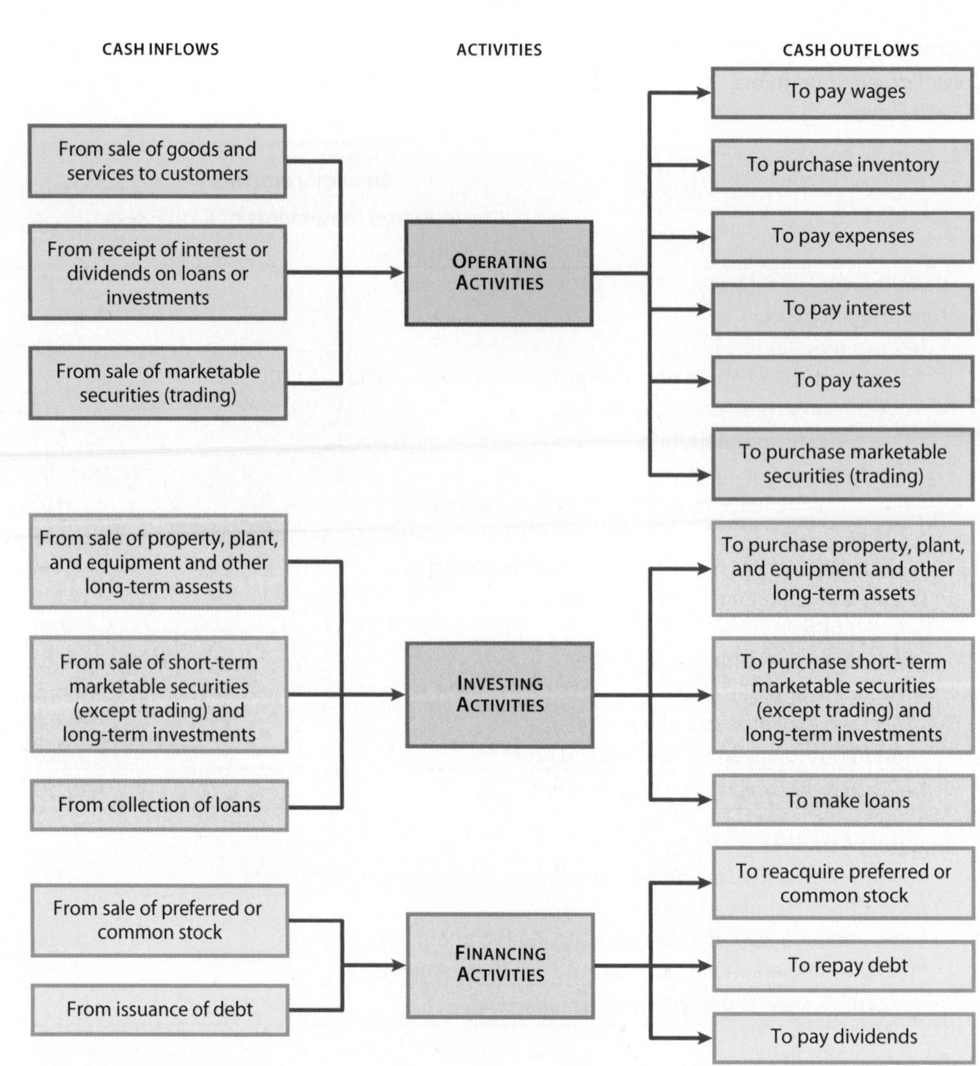

Investing Activities The second section of the statement of cash flows is *cash flows from investing activities.* **Investing activities** involve the purchase and sale of property, plant, and equipment and other long-term assets, including long-term investments. They also involve the purchase and sale of short-term marketable securities, other than trading securities, and the making and collecting of loans. Cash flows provided by investing activities include the cash received from selling marketable securities and long-term assets and from collecting on loans. Cash flows used by investing activities include the cash expended on purchasing these securities and assets and the cash lent to borrowers. Cash outflows for property, plant, equipment, or capital expenditures are usually shown separately from cash inflows from sales of these assets, as they are in Amazon.com's statement in Exhibit 12.1 (p. 539). However, when the inflows are not material, some companies combine these two lines to show the net amount of outflow.

STUDY NOTE: *Operating activities involve the day-to-day sale of goods and services, investing activities involve long-term assets and investments, and financing activities deal with stockholders' equity accounts and debt (borrowing).*

Financing Activities The third section of the statement of cash flows is *cash flows from financing activities.* **Financing activities** involve obtaining resources from stockholders and providing them with a return on their investments and obtaining resources from creditors and repaying the amounts borrowed or otherwise settling the obligations. Cash inflows include the proceeds from stock issues and from short- and long-term borrowing. Cash outflows include the repayments of loans (excluding interest) and payments to owners, including cash dividends. Treasury stock transactions are also considered financing activities. Repayments of accounts payable or accrued liabilities are not considered repayments of loans; they are classified as cash outflows under operating activities.

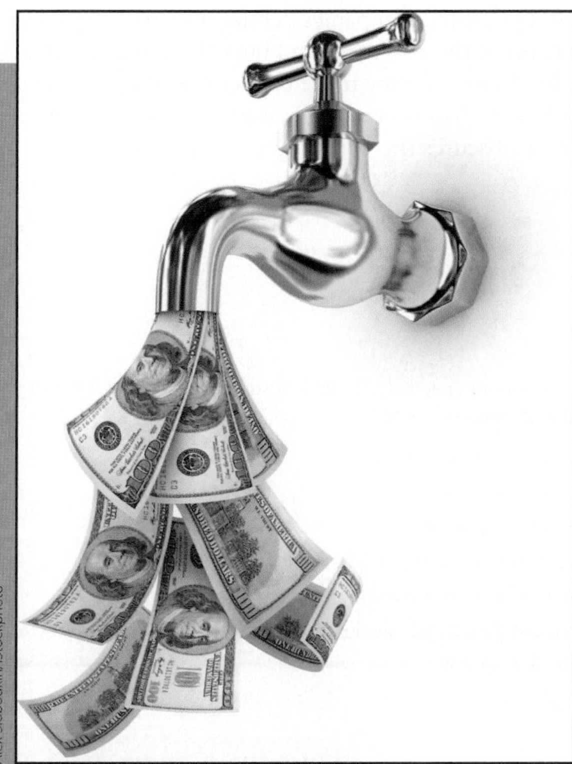

Alex Slobodkin/iStockphoto

The statement of cash flows is a financial statement that shows how a company's operating, investing, and financing activities have affected cash during an accounting period.

Cash Balances A reconciliation of the beginning and ending balances of cash appears at the bottom of the statement of cash flows. The cash balances will tie into the cash balances of the balance sheet.

Required Disclosure of Noncash Investing and Financing Transactions

Companies occasionally engage in significant **noncash investing and financing transactions**. These transactions involve *only* long-term assets, long-term liabilities, or stockholders' equity. For instance, a company might exchange a long-term asset for a long-term liability, settle a debt by issuing capital stock, or take out a long-term mortgage to purchase real estate. Although noncash transactions represent significant investing and financing activities, they are not reflected in the body of the statement of cash flows because they do not affect current cash inflows or outflows. They will, however, affect future cash flows. For this reason, they must be disclosed in a separate schedule, usually following the statement of cash flows.

Ethical Considerations and the Statement of Cash Flows

Although cash inflows and outflows are not as subject to manipulation as earnings are, managers are acutely aware of users' emphasis on cash flows from operations as an important measure of performance. Thus, an incentive exists to overstate these cash flows.

In earlier chapters, we cited an egregious example of earnings management. As you may recall, by treating operating expenses of about $10 billion over several years as purchases of equipment, **WorldCom** reduced reported expenses and improved reported earnings. In addition, by classifying payments of operating expenses as investments on the statement of cash flows, it was able to show an improvement in cash flows from operations. The inclusion of the expenditures in the investing activities section did not draw special attention because the company normally had large capital expenditures.

Another way a company can show an apparent improvement in its performance is through lack of transparency, or lack of full disclosure, in its financial statements. For instance, securitization—the sale of batches of accounts receivable—is clearly a means of financing, and the proceeds from it should be shown in the financing section of the statement of cash flows. However, because the accounting standards are somewhat

Focus on International Practices

How Universal Is the Statement of Cash Flows?

Despite the importance of the statement of cash flows in assessing the liquidity of companies in the United States, there has been considerable variation in its use and format in other countries. For example, in many countries, the statement shows the change in working capital rather than the change in cash and cash equivalents. Although the European Union's principal directives for financial reporting do not address the statement of cash flows, international accounting standards require it, and international financial markets expect it to be presented. As a result, most multinational companies include the statement in their financial reports. Most European countries adopted the statement of cash flows when the European Union adopted international accounting standards.

iStock Photo

vague about where these proceeds should go, some companies deduct the proceeds from accounts receivable in the operating section of the statement and bury the explanation in the notes to the financial statements. By doing so, they make collections of receivables in the operating activities section look better than they actually were. It is not illegal to do this, but from an ethical standpoint, it obscures the company's true performance.

Stop & Apply

Filip Corporation engaged in the transactions listed below. Identify each transaction as (a) an operating activity, (b) an investing activity, (c) a financing activity, (d) a noncash transaction, or (e) not on the statement of cash flows. (Assume the indirect method is used.)

1. Purchased office equipment.
2. Decreased accounts receivable.
3. Sold land at cost.
4. Issued long-term bonds for plant assets.
5. Increased inventory.
6. Issued common stock.
7. Repurchased common stock.
8. Issued notes payable.
9. Increased taxes payable.
10. Purchased a 60-day Treasury bill.
11. Purchased a long-term investment.
12. Declared and paid a cash dividend.

SOLUTION

1. b; 2. a; 3. b; 4. d; 5. a; 6. c; 7. c; 8. c; 9. a; 10. e (cash equivalent); 11. b; 12. c

iStock Photo

Analyze the statement of cash flows.

ANALYZING CASH FLOWS

Like the analysis of other financial statements, an analysis of the statement of cash flows can reveal significant relationships. One area on which analysts focus is the inflow and outflow of cash from operating activities, the first section on the statement of cash flows. Analysts use the information in this section to compute cash flow yield, cash flows to sales, cash flows to assets, and free cash flow. These performance measures reveal a company's degree of liquidity and how management spends the company's cash.

Cash Flow Ratios

The focal point of cash flow analysis is the inflow and outflow of cash from operating activities. These cash flows represent a company's ability to generate cash from its current or continuing operations and are a measure of its liquidity—its ability to pay its bills on time and to meet unexpected needs for cash.

Focus on Business Practice

Can a Company Have Too Much Cash?

Having a surplus of cash on hand can be a benefit or a risk. Many companies put their excess cash to good use by investing in productive assets, conducting research and development, paying off debt, buying back stock, or paying dividends. Of course, companies must also keep enough cash on hand for emergencies, but when companies like **ExxonMobil**, **Microsoft**, and **Cisco Systems** accumulated large amounts of cash before the market crash in 2008, some commentators argued that this was poor management. They pointed out that shareholders suffer when executives are too conservative and keep the money in low-paying money market accounts or make unwise acquisitions.[2] However, these companies and others, like **Ford** and **Google**, that had cash reserves not only survived the down years, but also were prospering by 2010.[3] For financial statement users, the lesson is that it is important to look closely at the components of the statement of cash flows to see how management is spending the company's cash.

iStock Photo

Analysts use data from the operating activities section of the statement of cash flows to compute cash flow ratios. In this section, we compute cash flow ratios for **Amazon.com** using data from Exhibit 12.1 (p. 539), as well as the following information from Amazon.com's 2009 annual report (amounts are in millions):

	2009	2008
Net sales	$24,509	$19,166
Total assets	13,813	8,314

Financial Ratio: Cash Flow Yield **Cash flow yield** is the ratio of net cash flows from operating activities to net income. For Amazon.com, it is calculated as follows:

RATIO

$$\text{Cash Flow Yield} = \frac{\text{Net Cash Flows from Operating Activities}}{\text{Net Income}}$$

$$= \frac{\$3{,}293}{\$902} = 3.7 \text{ Times*}$$

*Rounded

Cash flow yield is an important financial ratio because it shows whether a company is generating sufficient cash flow in relation to its net income or profitability. For most companies, the cash flow yield should exceed 1.0. Amazon.com's cash flow yield in 2009 was much better than that. With a cash flow yield of 3.7 times, Amazon.com was generating about $3.70 of cash for every dollar of net income.

The cash flow yield needs to be examined carefully. Keep in mind, for instance, that a firm with significant depreciable assets should have a cash flow yield greater than 1.0 because depreciation expense is added back to net income to arrive at cash flows from operating activities. If special items, such as discontinued operations, appear on the income statement and are material, income from continuing operations (from the income statement) should be used as the denominator. Also, an artificially high cash flow yield may result because a firm has very low net income, which is the denominator in the ratio.

Financial Ratio: Cash Flows to Sales **Cash flows to sales** is the ratio of net cash flows from operating activities to net sales. It is calculated as follows:

RATIO

$$\text{Cash Flows to Sales} = \frac{\text{Net Cash Flows from Operating Activities}}{\text{Net Sales}}$$

$$= \frac{\$3{,}293}{\$24{,}509} = 13.4\%\text{*}$$

*Rounded

Thus, Amazon.com generated positive cash flows to sales of 13.4 percent. Another way to state this result is that every dollar of sales generates 13.4 cents in cash.

Financial Ratio: Cash Flows to Assets **Cash flows to assets** is the ratio of net cash flows from operating activities to average total assets. It is calculated as follows:

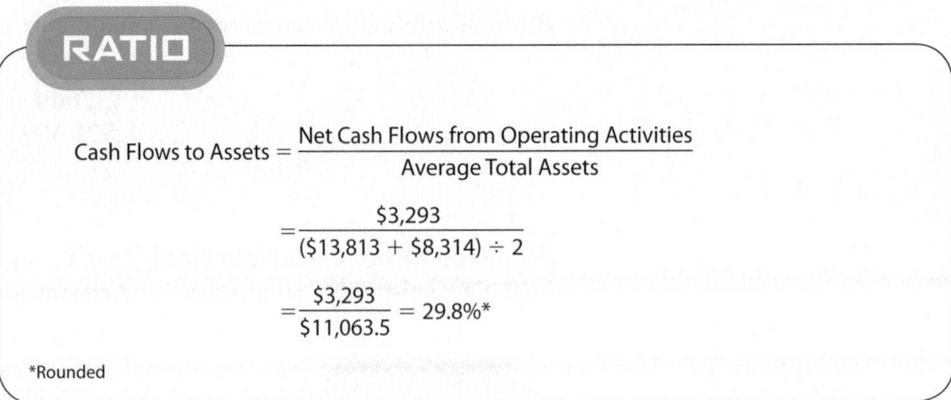

RATIO
Cash Flows to Assets = Net Cash Flows from Operating Activities / Average Total Assets
= $3,293 / ($13,813 + $8,314) ÷ 2
= $3,293 / $11,063.5 = 29.8%*
*Rounded

At 29.8 percent, Amazon.com's ratio of cash flows to assets indicates that for every dollar of assets, the company generated almost 30 cents. This excellent result is higher than its cash flows to sales ratio because of its good asset turnover ratio:

Asset Turnover = Sales ÷ Average Total Assets
2.2 Times = 29.8% ÷ 13.4%

Cash flows to sales and cash flows to assets are closely related to the profitability measures of profit margin and return on assets. They exceed those measures by the amount of the cash flow yield ratio because cash flow yield is the ratio of net cash flows from operating activities to net income.

Free Cash Flow

As we noted in an earlier chapter, **free cash flow** is the amount of cash that remains after deducting the funds a company must commit to continue operating at its planned level. Free cash flow is a very useful analytic tool; a study of 100 different measures showed it to be the best predictor of future increases in stock price.[4]

Free cash flow can be positive or negative:

- *Positive free cash flow* means that the company has met all of its planned cash commitments and has cash available to reduce debt or to expand.
- *Negative free cash flow* means that the company will have to sell investments, borrow money, or issue stock in the short term to continue at its planned level. If a company's free cash flow remains negative for several years, it may not be able to raise cash by issuing stocks or bonds.

Amazon.com has a stated primary financial objective of "long-term sustainable growth in free cash flow."[5] The company definitely achieved this objective in 2009, as shown in the following computation (in millions):

STUDY NOTE: *The computation for free cash flow sometimes uses net capital expenditures in place of (Purchases of Plant Assets + Sales of Plant Assets).*

Free Cash Flow = Net Cash Flows from Operating Activities − Dividends − Purchases of Plant Assets + Sales of Plant Assets
= $3,293 − $0 − $373 + $0
= $2,920

Purchases of plant assets (capital expenditures) and sales (dispositions) of plant assets, if any, appear in the investing activities section of the statement of cash flows. Dividends, if any, appear in the financing activities section. Amazon.com is a growing company and does not have material sales of plant assets and does not pay dividends. The company's positive free cash flow of $2,920 million is due primarily to its strong operating cash flow of $3,293 million. Consequently, the company does not have to borrow money to expand.

Focus on Business Practice

What Do You Mean, "Free Cash Flow"?

Because the statement of cash flows has been around for less than 25 years, no generally accepted analyses have yet been developed. For example, the term *free cash flow* is commonly used in the business press, but there is no agreement on its definition. An article in *Forbes* defines *free cash flow* as "cash available after paying out capital expenditures and dividends, but *before taxes and interest*"[6] [emphasis added]. An article in *The Wall Street Journal* defines it as "operating income less maintenance-level capital expenditures."[7] The definition with which we are most in agreement is the one used in *BusinessWeek*: free cash flow is net cash flows from operating activities less net capital expenditures and dividends. This "measures truly discretionary funds—company money that an owner could pocket without harming the business."[8]

iStock Photo

Asking the Right Questions About the Statement of Cash Flows

Most readers of financial statements are accustomed to looking at the "bottom line" to get an overview of a company's financial status. They look at total assets on the balance sheet and net income on the income statement. However, the statement of cash flows requires a different approach because the bottom line of cash on hand does not tell the reader very much; changes in the components of the statement during the year are far more revealing.

In interpreting a statement of cash flows, it pays to know the right questions to ask. To illustrate, let's use **Amazon.com** as an example (Exhibit 12.1, p. 539).

Cash Flows and Net Income *What are the primary reasons that Amazon.com's cash flows from operating activities differed from net income in 2009?*

For Amazon.com, among the largest positive items in 2009 were accounts payable and depreciation. They are added to net income for different reasons. Accounts payable represents an increase in the amount owed to creditors, whereas depreciation represents a noncash expense that is deducted in arriving at net income. Amazon.com's two largest negative items were increases in inventories and receivables. As a growing company, Amazon.com was managing its operating cycle by generating cash from creditors to pay for increases in inventories and receivables.

Investing Activities *What were Amazon.com's most important investing activities other than capital expenditures?*

Amazon.com had a large decrease in cash from investing activities in 2009. The company was managing its investing activities by making active use of investments. Sales of marketable securities and other investments were not sufficient to offset the purchase of marketable securities and other investments and the purchase of various assets; therefore, the cash flow from investing activities was negative.

Financing Activities *How did Amazon.com manage its financing activities during 2009?*

Amazon.com's financing activities showed a small decrease in cash in 2009. Excess tax benefits from stock-based compensation and proceeds from long-term debt provided funds to buy back treasury stock and pay off some long-term debt, but the inflows were less than the outflows. Because of its good cash flow from operations, Amazon.com did not need long-term financing.

Cash Flow Trends *What has been the trend of cash flows for Amazon.com?*

Because cash flows can vary from year to year, analysts should look at trends in cash flow measures over several years. For example, Amazon.com's management states:

> Because of our model we are able to turn our inventory quickly and have a cash-generating operating cycle. On average our high inventory velocity means we generally collect from our customers before our payments to suppliers come due. . . . We expect some variability in inventory turnover over time since it is affected by several

factors, including our product mix, the mix of sales by us and by other sellers, our continuing focus on in-stock inventory availability, our investment in new geographies and product lines, and the extent to which we choose to utilize outsource fulfillment providers. . . . We [also] expect some variability in accounts payable days over time since they are affected by several factors, including the mix of product sales, the mix of sales by other sellers, the mix of suppliers, seasonality, and changes in payment terms over time, including the effect of balancing pricing and timing of payment terms with suppliers.[9]

Stop & Apply

In 2011, Marthy Corporation had year-end assets of $2,400,000, sales of $2,000,000, net income of $400,000, net cash flows from operating activities of $360,000, dividends of $100,000, purchases of plant assets of $200,000, and sales of plant assets of $50,000. In 2010, year-end assets were $2,200,000. Calculate cash flow yield, cash flows to sales, cash flows to assets, and free cash flow.

SOLUTION

$$\text{Cash Flow Yield} = \frac{\$360{,}000}{\$400{,}000} = 0.9 \text{ Times}$$

$$\text{Cash Flows to Sales} = \frac{\$360{,}000}{\$2{,}000{,}000} = 0.18, \text{ or } 18\%$$

$$\text{Cash Flows to Assets} = \frac{\$360{,}000}{(\$2{,}400{,}000 + \$2{,}200{,}000) \div 2} = 0.16, \text{ or } 16\% \text{ (rounded)}$$

$$\text{Free Cash Flow} = \$360{,}000 - \$100{,}000 - \$200{,}000 + \$50{,}000 = \$110{,}000$$

iStock Photo

STEP ONE: DETERMINING CASH FLOWS FROM OPERATING ACTIVITIES

LO 3 Use the indirect method to determine cash flows from operating activities.

As shown in Exhibit 12.3, preparing a statement of cash flows involves four steps:

Step 1: Determine cash flows from operating activities.

Step 2: Determine cash flows from investing activities.

Step 3: Determine cash flows from financing activities.

Step 4: Prepare the statement of cash flows.

In this section, we begin with determining cash flows from operating activities.

To demonstrate the preparation of the statement of cash flows, we will use data for Zebra Corporation. Zebra's income statement for 2011 is presented in Exhibit 12.4, and its balance sheets for December 31, 2011 and 2010 appear in Exhibit 12.5. Exhibit 12.5 also shows the balance sheet accounts that we use for analysis and whether the change in each account is an increase or a decrease.

EXHIBIT 12.3
Preparation of the Statement of Cash Flows

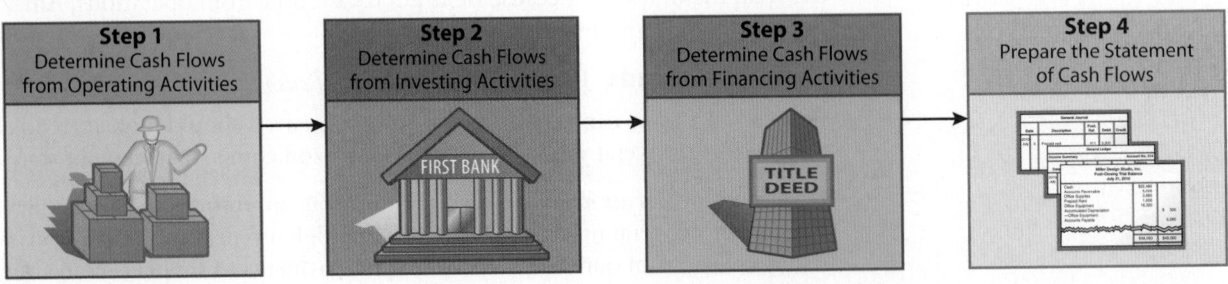

EXHIBIT 12.4
Income Statement

Zebra Corporation Income Statement For the Year Ended December 31, 2011		
Sales		$698,000
Cost of goods sold		520,000
Gross margin		$178,000
Operating expenses (including depreciation expense of $37,000)		147,000
Operating income		$ 31,000
Other income (expenses)		
Interest expense	$(23,000)	
Interest income	6,000	
Gain on sale of investments	12,000	
Loss on sale of plant assets	(3,000)	(8,000)
Income before income taxes		$ 23,000
Income taxes expense		7,000
Net income		$ 16,000

EXHIBIT 12.5
Comparative Balance Sheets Showing Changes in Accounts

Zebra Corporation Comparative Balance Sheets December 31, 2011 and 2010	2011	2010	Change	Increase or Decrease
Assets				
Current assets				
Cash	$ 46,000	$ 15,000	$ 31,000	Increase
Accounts receivable (net)	47,000	55,000	(8,000)	Decrease
Inventory	144,000	110,000	34,000	Increase
Prepaid expenses	1,000	5,000	(4,000)	Decrease
Total current assets	$238,000	$185,000	$ 53,000	
Investments	$115,000	$127,000	$ (12,000)	Decrease
Plant assets	$715,000	$505,000	$210,000	Increase
Less accumulated depreciation	(103,000)	(68,000)	(35,000)	Increase
Total plant assets	$612,000	$437,000	$175,000	
Total assets	$965,000	$749,000	$216,000	
Liabilities				
Current liabilities				
Accounts payable	$ 50,000	$ 43,000	$ 7,000	Increase
Accrued liabilities	12,000	9,000	3,000	Increase
Income taxes payable	3,000	5,000	(2,000)	Decrease
Total current liabilities	$ 65,000	$ 57,000	$ 8,000	
Long-term liabilities				
Bonds payable	295,000	245,000	50,000	Increase
Total liabilities	$360,000	$302,000	$ 58,000	
Stockholders' Equity				
Common stock, $5 par value	$276,000	$200,000	$ 76,000	Increase
Additional paid-in capital	214,000	115,000	99,000	Increase
Retained earnings	140,000	132,000	8,000	Increase
Treasury stock	(25,000)	0	(25,000)	Increase
Total stockholders' equity	$605,000	$447,000	$158,000	
Total liabilities and stockholders' equity	$965,000	$749,000	$216,000	

The income statement indicates how successful a company has been in earning an income from its operating activities, but because that statement is prepared on an accrual basis, it does not reflect the inflow and outflow of cash related to operating activities. Revenues are recorded even though the company may not yet have received the cash, and expenses are recorded even though the company may not yet have expended the cash. Thus, to ascertain cash flows from operations in step 1 in the preparation of the statement of cash flows, the figures on the income statement must be converted from an accrual basis to a cash basis.

There are two methods of accomplishing this:

- *Direct method:* The **direct method** adjusts each item on the income statement from the accrual basis to the cash basis. The result is a statement that begins with cash receipts from sales and interest and deducts cash payments for purchases, operating expenses, interest payments, and income taxes to arrive at net cash flows from operating activities.
- *Indirect method*: The **indirect method** does not require the adjustment of each item on the income statement. It lists only the adjustments necessary to convert net income to cash flows from operations.

STUDY NOTE: *The direct and indirect methods relate only to the operating activities section of the statement of cash flows. They are both acceptable for financial reporting purposes.*

The direct and indirect methods always produce the same net figure. The average person finds the direct method easier to understand because its presentation of operating cash flows is more straightforward than that of the indirect method. The indirect method is, however, the overwhelming choice of most companies and accountants. A survey of large companies shows that 99 percent use this method.[10] (For an example of the indirect method, see **Southwest Airlines**' statement of cash flows in the supplement to Chapter 1; **CVS**'s statement of cash flows in the same supplement provides an excellent example of the direct method.)

From an analyst's perspective, the indirect method is superior to the direct method because it begins with net income and derives cash flows from operations; the analyst can readily identify the factors that create cash flows from operations. From a company's standpoint, the indirect method is easier and less expensive to prepare. For these reasons, we use the indirect method in our example.

As Exhibit 12.6 shows, the indirect method focuses on adjusting items on the income statement to reconcile net income to net cash flows from operating activities. These items include the following:

- Depreciation, amortization, and depletion
- Gains and losses
- Changes in the balances of current asset and current liability accounts

These adjusting items can be seen in Exhibit 12.7, which shows the reconciliation of Zebra's net income to net cash flows from operating activities. Each adjusting item requires a different type of analysis as illustrated in the sections that follow.

Focus on International Practices

IFRS The Direct Method May Become More Important Under IFRS

At present, the direct method of preparing the operating section of the statement of cash flows is not used by many companies, but this may change if the International Accounting Standards Board (IASB) has its way. In the interest of converging U.S. GAAP with international financial reporting standards (IFRS), the IASB is promoting the use of the direct method, even though it is more costly for companies to prepare. IFRS will continue to require a reconciliation of net income and net cash flows from operating activities similar to what is now done with the indirect method. **CVS** is one of the few U.S. companies to use the direct method with a reconciliation. Thus, its approach is very similar to what all companies may do if the United States adopts IFRS.

iStock Photo

EXHIBIT 12.6
Indirect Method of Determining Net Cash Flows from Operating Activities

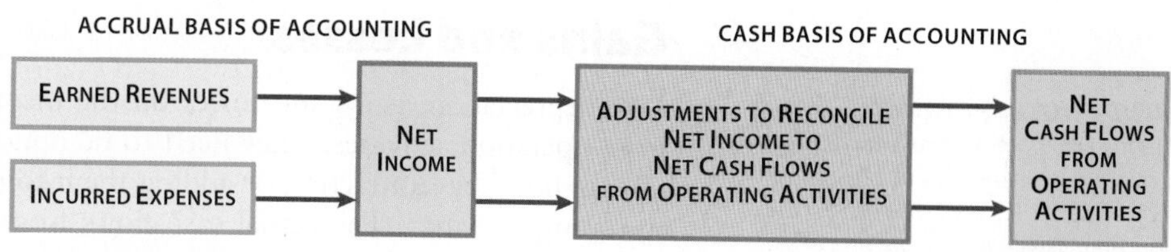

EXHIBIT 12.7
Schedule of Cash Flows from Operating Activities: Indirect Method

Zebra Corporation
Schedule of Cash Flows from Operating Activities
For the Year Ended December 31, 2011

Cash flows from operating activities		
Net income		$16,000
Adjustments to reconcile net income to net cash flows from operating activities		
Depreciation	$ 37,000	
Loss on sale of plant assets	3,000	
Gain on sale of investments	(12,000)	
Changes in current assets and current liabilities		
Decrease in accounts receivable	8,000	
Increase in inventory	(34,000)	
Decrease in prepaid expenses	4,000	
Increase in accounts payable	7,000	
Increase in accrued liabilities	3,000	
Decrease in income taxes payable	(2,000)	14,000
Net cash flows from operating activities		$30,000

Depreciation, Amortization, and Depletion

STUDY NOTE: *Operating expenses on the income statement include depreciation expense, which does not require a cash outlay.*

Although the cash payments made for plant assets, intangible assets, and natural resources appear in the investing activities section of the statement of cash flows, the depreciation expense, amortization expense, and depletion expense associated with these assets appear in the operating activities section. The amount of these expenses can usually be found in the income statement or in a note to the financial statements.

Financial Statement Information: Zebra's income statement (Exhibit 12.4, p. 547) shows *$37,000 of depreciation expense.*

A	=	L	+	SE
−37,000				−37,000

Journal Entry:

Depreciation Expense	37,000	
Accumulated Depreciation		37,000
To record annual depreciation on plant assets		

Operating Cash Flow Analysis:

Depreciation $37,000

Note that when depreciation expense is recorded, the Cash account is not affected. Thus, net income needs to be adjusted upward by the amount of depreciation, or $37,000, because depreciation expense involves no current outlay of cash even though it appears on the income statement.

Amortization and depletion expenses are handled in exactly the same way as depreciation expense.

Gains and Losses

STUDY NOTE: *Gains and losses by themselves do not represent cash flows; they are merely bookkeeping adjustments. For example, when a long-term asset is sold, the proceeds (cash received), not the gain or loss, constitute cash flow.*

Like depreciation, gains and losses on the income statement do not affect cash flows from operating activities. They need to be removed from this section of the statement of cash flows by subtracting or adding them to net income to arrive at cash flows from operating activities. The actual cash flows from these transactions are reflected in the investing and financing activities sections of the statement of cash flows.

Financial Statement Information: Zebra's income statement (Exhibit 12.4, p. 547) shows a *$12,000 gain on the sale of investments.*

Operating Cash Flow Analysis:

Gain on sale of investments ($12,000)

This amount is subtracted from net income to reconcile net income to net cash flows from operating activities. The reason for doing this is that the $12,000 is included in the investing activities section of the statement of cash flows as part of the cash from the sale of the investment. Because the gain has already been included in the calculation of net income, the $12,000 gain must be subtracted to prevent double counting.

Financial Statement Information: Zebra's income statement (Exhibit 12.4, p. 547) shows a *$3,000 loss on the sale of plant assets.*

Operating Cash Flow Analysis:

Loss on sale of plant assets $3,000

As was the case with depreciation expense, a loss on sale of assets is added to net income to reconcile net income to net cash flows from operating activities. The cash received associated with the transaction that resulted in this loss is reflected in the investing activities section of the statement of cash flows.

Changes in Current Assets

As explained in this section and the next, changes in current assets and current liabilities require a different approach to reconcile net income to cash flows from operating activities.

Decreases in current assets other than cash have positive effects on cash flows, and increases in current assets have negative effects on cash flows:

▼ A *decrease* in a current asset frees up invested cash, thereby increasing cash flow.

▲ An *increase* in a current asset consumes cash, thereby decreasing cash flow.

For example, consider the following examples from Zebra.

Financial Statement Information: Zebra's balance sheet (Exhibit 12.5, p. 547) shows an *$8,000 decrease in accounts receivable.* We can conclude that collections were $8,000 more than sales recorded for the year.

Operating Cash Flow Analysis:

Decrease in account receivable $8,000

Because net sales in 2011 were $698,000, the total cash received from sales can be calculated as follows:

Net Sales + Additional Cash Collections = Total Cash Collections Received
$698,000 + $8,000 = $706,000

The effect on Accounts Receivable can be illustrated as follows:

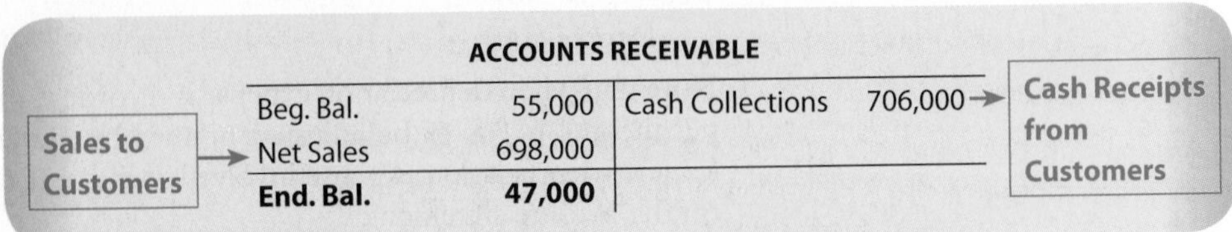

ACCOUNTS RECEIVABLE

Beg. Bal.	55,000	Cash Collections	706,000
Net Sales	698,000		
End. Bal.	**47,000**		

To reconcile net income to net cash flows from operating activities, the $8,000 decrease in Accounts Receivable is added to net income.

Inventory can be analyzed in the same way.

Financial Statement Information: Zebra's balance sheet (Exhibit 12.5, p. 547) shows a *$34,000 increase in inventory.*

Operating Cash Flow Analysis:

Increase in inventory ($34,000)

Because cost of goods sold in 2011 was $520,000, the total cash paid for inventory can be calculated as follows, as was done with accounts receivable:

Cost of Goods Sold + Additional Purchases = Total Purchases
$520,000 + $34,000 = $554,000

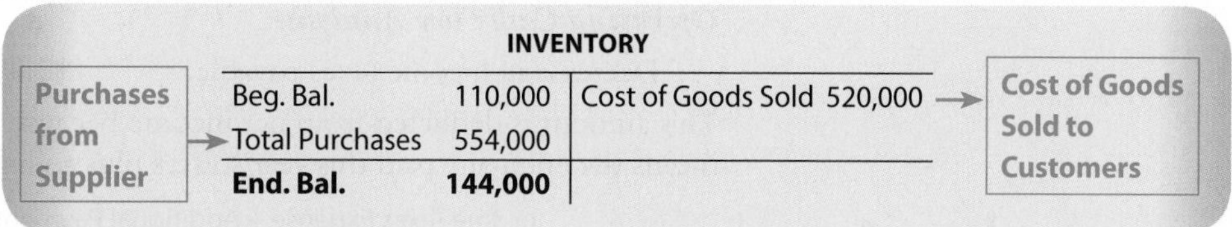

Thus, Zebra expended $34,000 more in cash for purchases than it included in cost of goods sold on its income statement. Because of this expenditure, net income is higher than net cash flows from operating activities; so $34,000 must be deducted from net income.

Financial Statement Information: Continuing with current assets, Zebra's balance sheet (Exhibit 12.5, p. 547) shows a *$4,000 decrease in prepaid expenses.*

Operating Cash Flow Analysis:

Decrease in prepaid expenses $4,000

Using the same logic, the decrease shown on the balance sheet is added to net income because Zebra expended less cash on prepaid expenses than was included on the income statement.

Changes in Current Liabilities

The effect that changes in current liabilities have on cash flows is the opposite of the effect of changes in current assets:

- ▲ An *increase* in a current liability represents a postponement of a cash payment, which frees up cash and *increases* cash flow in the current period; thus, it is added to net income.
- ▼ A *decrease* in a current liability consumes cash, which decreases cash flow; thus, it is *deducted* from net income.

Financial Statement Information: Zebra's balance sheet (Exhibit 12.5, p. 547) shows a *$7,000 increase in accounts payable.*

Operating Cash Flow Analysis:

Increase in accounts payable $7,000

This means that Zebra paid $7,000 less to creditors than the amount indicated in the cost of goods sold on its income statement, illustrated as follows:

Purchases on Account* − Amount Unpaid = Total Cash Payments
$554,000 − $7,000 = $547,000

The following T account illustrates this relationship:

ACCOUNTS PAYABLE

	Debit		Credit		
Cash Payments to Suppliers ←	Payments on Account 547,000	Beg. Bal.	43,000		
		Purchases on Account	554,000*	←	Purchases
		End. Bal.	**50,000**		

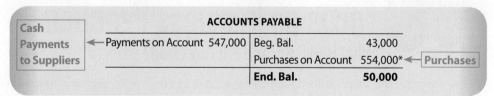

*Purchases = Cost of Goods Sold ($520,000) + Increase in Inventory ($34,000)

Thus, $7,000 must be added to net income to reconcile net income to net cash flows from operating activities.

The same logic can be applied to the other current liabilities in Exhibit 12.5.

Financial Statement Information:

Zebra's balance sheet (Exhibit 12.5, p. 547) shows a *$3,000 increase in accrued liabilities.*

Operating Cash Flow Analysis:

Increase in accrued liabilities	$3,000

Using the same logic as with the increase in accounts payable, this amount is added to net income. The increase in accrued liabilities was created by an adjusting entry that also increases expenses but does not use cash in the current period. Since expenses decrease net income, the increase in accrued expenses needs to be added to net income.

Financial Statement Information: Zebra's balance sheet (Exhibit 12.5, p. 547) shows a *$2,000 decrease in income taxes payable.*

Operating Cash Flow Analysis:

Decrease in income taxes payable	($2,000)

This amount is deducted from net income because the decrease in income taxes payable means the company paid this year's taxes plus an amount from the prior year, as follows:

Income Taxes Expense + Additional Payment = Total Income Taxes Payments
$7,000 + $2,000 = $9,000

INCOME TAXES PAYABLE

Cash Paid for Income Taxes ←	Income Taxes Payments	9,000	Beg. Bal.	5,000	
			Income Taxes Expense	7,000	← Income Taxes Expense for the Year
			End. Bal.	**3,000**	

Schedule of Cash Flows from Operating Activities

In summary, Exhibit 12.7 (p. 549) shows that by using the indirect method, net income of $16,000 has been adjusted by reconciling items totaling $14,000 to arrive at net cash flows from operating activities of $30,000:

Net Income +/− Reconciling Items = Cash Flows from Operating Activities
$16,000 + $14,000 = $30,000

Although Zebra's net income was $16,000, the company actually had net cash flows of $30,000 available from operating activities to use for purchasing assets, reducing debts, and paying dividends. The rules for reconciling items from the income statement that do not affect cash flows can be summarized as follows:

	Add to or Deduct from Net Income
Depreciation expense	+ Add
Amortization expense	+ Add
Depletion expense	+ Add
Losses	+ Add
Gains	− Deduct

Focus on Business Practice

What Is EBITDA, and Is It Any Good?

Some companies and analysts like to use EBITDA (an acronym for Earnings Before Interest, Taxes, Depreciation, and Amortization) as a shortcut measure of cash flows from operations. But experiences of the last decade have caused many analysts to reconsider this measure of performance. For instance, when **WorldCom** transferred $3.8 billion from expenses to capital expenditures in one year, it touted its EBITDA; at the time, the firm was, in fact, nearly bankrupt. The demise of **Vivendi**, the big French company that imploded when it did not have enough cash to pay its debts and that also touted its EBIDTA, is another reason that analysts have had second thoughts about relying on this measure of performance.

Some analysts are now saying that EBITDA is "to a great extent misleading" and that it "is a confusing metric. . . . Some take it for a proxy for profits and some take it for a proxy for cash flow, and it's neither."[11] Cash flows from operations and free cash flow, both of which take into account interest, taxes, and depreciation, are better and more comprehensive measures of a company's ability to generate sufficient cash flow.

iStock Photo

STUDY NOTE: *It is important to know these rules because many companies, including* **CVS** *and* **Southwest Airlines**, *do not use the terms* increase *or* decrease. *They expect the reader to understand the change in a current asset or current liability based on whether it is added or subtracted in the statement of cash flows.*

The following summarizes the adjustments from the balance sheet for increases and decreases in current assets and current liabilities:

	Add to Net Income +	*Deduct from Net Income* −
Current assets		
Accounts receivable (net)	▼ Decrease	▲ Increase
Inventory	▼ Decrease	▲ Increase
Prepaid expenses	▼ Decrease	▲ Increase
Current liabilities		
Accounts payable	▲ Increase	▼ Decrease
Accrued liabilities	▲ Increase	▼ Decrease
Income taxes payable	▲ Increase	▼ Decrease

Stop & Apply

For the year ended June 30, 2011, Saturn Corporation's net income was $7,400. Its depreciation expense was $2,000. During the year, its accounts receivable increased by $4,400, inventories increased by $7,000, prepaid rent decreased by $1,400, accounts payable increased by $14,000, salaries payable increased by $1,000, and income taxes payable decreased by $600. The company also had a gain on the sale of investments of $1,800. Use the indirect method to prepare a schedule of cash flows from operating activities.

SOLUTION

Saturn Corporation
Schedule of Cash Flows from Operating Activities
For the Year Ended June 30, 2011

Cash flows from operating activities		
Net income		$ 7,400
Adjustments to reconcile net income to net cash flows from operating activities		
Depreciation	$ 2,000	
Gain on sale of investments	(1,800)	
Changes in current assets and current liabilities		
Increase in accounts receivable	(4,400)	
Increase in inventories	(7,000)	
Decrease in prepaid rent	1,400	
Increase in accounts payable	14,000	
Increase in salaries payable	1,000	
Decrease in income taxes payable	(600)	4,600
Net cash flows from operating activities		$12,000

iStock Photo

STEP TWO: DETERMINING CASH FLOWS FROM INVESTING ACTIVITIES

Determine cash flows from investing activities.

STUDY NOTE: *Investing activities involve long-term assets and short- and long-term investments. Inflows and outflows of cash are shown in the investing activities section of the statement of cash flows.*

Determining cash flows from investing activities is step 2 in preparing the statement of cash flows. In this step, accounts involving cash receipts and cash payments from investing activities are examined individually. The objective is to explain the change in each account balance from one accounting period to the next.

Although investing activities relate mainly to the long-term assets shown on the balance sheet, they also include any short-term investments under current assets on the balance sheet and any investment gains and losses on the income statement. The balance sheets in Exhibit 12.5 (p. 547) show that Zebra had no short-term investments and that its long-term assets consisted of investments and plant assets. The income statement in Exhibit 12.4 (p. 547) shows that Zebra had a gain on the sale of investments and a loss on the sale of plant assets.

The following transactions pertain to Zebra's investing activities in 2011:

1. Purchased investments in the amount of $78,000.
2. Sold for $102,000 investments that cost $90,000.
3. Purchased plant assets in the amount of $120,000.
4. Sold for $5,000 plant assets that cost $10,000 and that had accumulated depreciation of $2,000.
5. Issued $100,000 of bonds at face value in a noncash exchange for plant assets.

In the following sections, we explain the effects of these transactions on Zebra's cash flows by analyzing their impact on the accounts related to investing activities.

Investments

Zebra's balance sheet (Exhibit 12.5, p. 547) shows a *$12,000 decrease in investments.* Our objective is to explain this decrease and its effects on the statement of cash flows by analyzing the increases and decreases in Zebra's Investments account.

Transaction 1 Purchased investments in the amount of $78,000.

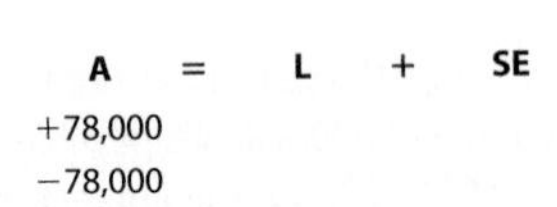
A	=	L	+	SE
+78,000				
−78,000				

Journal Entry:

Investments	78,000	
Cash		78,000
Purchase of investments		

Cash Flow Analysis:

Purchase of investments ($78,000)

Transaction 2 Sold for $102,000 investments that cost $90,000.

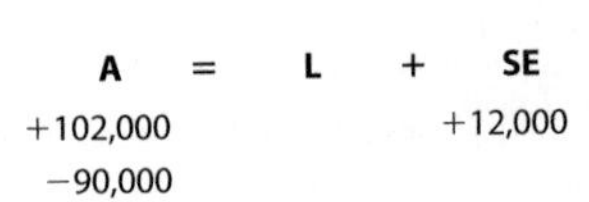
A	=	L	+	SE
+102,000				+12,000
−90,000				

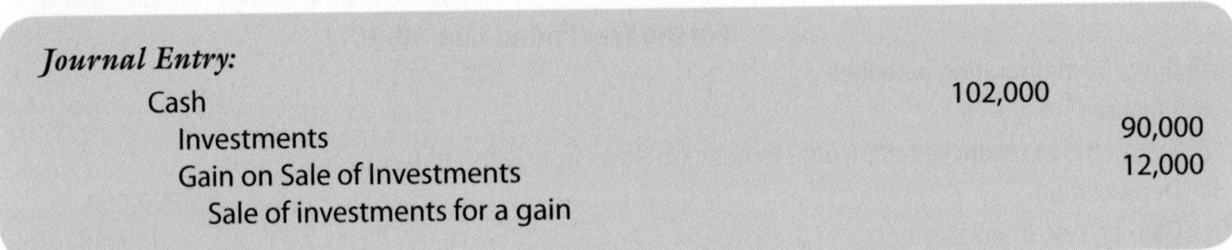
Journal Entry:

Cash	102,000	
Investments		90,000
Gain on Sale of Investments		12,000
Sale of investments for a gain		

Cash Flow Analysis:

Sale of investments $102,000

STUDY NOTE: The $102,000 price obtained, not the $12,000 gained, constitutes the cash flow.

Note that the gain on the sale is included in the $102,000. This is the reason we excluded it in computing cash flows from operations. If it had been not been excluded in that section, it would have been counted twice.

Reconciliation: We have now explained the $12,000 decrease in the Investments account, as illustrated in the following T account:

INVESTMENTS			
Beg. Bal.	127,000	Sales	90,000
Purchases	78,000		
End. Bal.	**115,000**		

Purchases and sales are listed separately as cash outflows and inflows to give analysts a complete view of investing activity. However, some companies prefer to list them as a single net amount. If Zebra had short-term investments or marketable securities, the analysis of cash flows would be the same.

Plant Assets

Zebra's balance sheet (Exhibit 12.5, p. 547) shows the following:

- *$210,000 increase in plant assets*
- *$35,000 increase in accumulated depreciation*

Our objective is to explain these changes and their effects on the statement of cash flows.

Transaction 3 Purchased plant assets in the amount of $120,000.

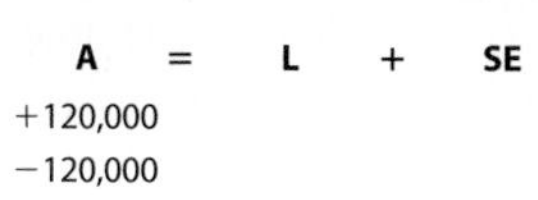

Journal Entry:

Plant Assets	120,000	
Cash		120,000
Purchase of plant assets		

STUDY NOTE: *Cash outflows and cash inflows related to plant assets are listed separately, but companies sometimes combine them into a single net amount, called capital expenditure, when the cash inflows from sales are immaterial.*

Cash Flow Analysis:

Purchase of plant assets ($120,000)

Transaction 4 Sold for $5,000 plant assets that cost $10,000 and that had accumulated depreciation of $2,000.

A	=	L	+	SE
+ 5,000				−3,000
+ 2,000				
−10,000				

Journal Entry:

Cash	5,000	
Accumulated Depreciation	2,000	
Loss on Sale of Plant Assets	3,000	
Plant Assets		10,000
Sale of plant assets at a loss		

Cash Flow Analysis:

Sale of plant assets $5,000

STUDY NOTE: *The amount of a loss or gain on the sale of an asset is determined by the amount of cash received and does not represent a cash outflow or inflow.*

Note that this transaction results in a positive cash flow of $5,000, even though the plant assets were sold at a loss of $3,000. As noted in our analysis of operating activities, the loss on the sale of plant assets is added back to net income. This action avoids counting the loss in two sections of the statement of cash flows.

Transaction 5 Issued $100,000 of bonds at face value in a noncash exchange for plant assets.

A	=	L	+	SE
+100,000				+100,000

Journal Entry:

Plant Assets	100,000	
Bonds Payable		100,000
Issued bonds at face value for plant assets		

Cash Flow Analysis:

Schedule of Noncash Investing and Financing Transactions

Issue of bonds payable for plant assets $100,000

Although this transaction does *not* involve an inflow or outflow of cash, it is a significant transaction involving both an investing activity (the purchase of plant assets) and a financing activity (the issue of bonds payable). Because one purpose of the statement of cash flows is to show important investing and financing activities, the transaction is listed at the bottom of the statement of cash flows or in a separate schedule.

Reconciliation: We have now explained all the changes related to Zebra's Plant Assets account. The following T accounts summarize these changes:

PLANT ASSETS

Beg. Bal.	505,000	Sales	10,000
Cash Purchase	120,000		
Noncash Purchase	100,000		
End. Bal.	**715,000**		

ACCUMULATED DEPRECIATION

Sale	2,000	Beg. Bal.	68,000
		Depreciation Expense	37,000
		End. Bal.	**103,000**

Had the balance sheet included specific plant asset accounts (e.g., Equipment and the related accumulated depreciation account) or other long-term asset accounts (e.g., Intangibles), the analysis would have been the same.

Stop & Apply

The following T accounts show Nadia Company's plant assets and accumulated depreciation at the end of 2011:

PLANT ASSETS

Beg. Bal.	65,000	Disposals	23,000
Purchases	33,600		
End. Bal.	**75,600**		

ACCUMULATED DEPRECIATION

Disposals	14,700	Beg. Bal.	34,500
		Depreciation	10,200
		End. Bal.	**30,000**

Nadia's income statement shows a gain on the sale of plant assets of $4,400. Compute the amounts that should be shown as cash flows from investing activities and show how they should appear on Nadia's 2011statement of cash flows.

SOLUTION

Cash flows from investing activities:

Purchase of plant assets	$(33,600)
Sale of plant assets	12,700

The T accounts show total purchases of plant assets of $33,600, which is an outflow of cash, and disposal of plant assets that cost $23,000 and that had accumulated depreciation of $14,700. The income statement shows a $4,400 gain on the sale of the plant assets. The cash inflow from the disposal was as follows:

Plant assets	$23,000
Less accumulated depreciation	14,700
Book value	$ 8,300
Add gain on sale	4,400
Cash inflow from sale of plant assets	$12,700

Because the gain on the sale is included in the $12,700 in the investing activities section of the statement of cash flows, it should be deducted from net income in the operating activities section.

iStock Photo

STEP THREE: DETERMINING CASH FLOWS FROM FINANCING ACTIVITIES

Determine cash flows from financing activities.

Determining cash flows from financing activities is step 3 in preparing the statement of cash flows. It is very similar to determining cash flows from investing activities, but the accounts analyzed relate to short-term borrowings, long-term liabilities, and stockholders' equity. Because Zebra does not have short-term borrowings, we deal only with long-term liabilities and stockholders' equity accounts.

The following transactions pertain to Zebra's financing activities in 2011:

1. Issued $100,000 of bonds at face value in a noncash exchange for plant assets.
2. Repaid $50,000 of bonds at face value at maturity.
3. Issued 15,200 shares of $5 par value common stock for $175,000.

4. Paid cash dividends in the amount of $8,000.
5. Purchased treasury stock for $25,000.

Bonds Payable

Zebra's balance sheet (Exhibit 12.5, p. 547) shows a *$50,000 increase in bonds payable.* Our objective is to explain this change and its effects on the statement of cash flows.

Transaction 1 Issued $100,000 of bonds at face value in a noncash exchange for plant assets. We have already analyzed Transaction 1 in connection with plant assets, but we also need to account for the difference in the Bonds Payable account. As we noted, this transaction is reported on the schedule of noncash investing and financing transactions.

Transaction 2 Repaid $50,000 of bonds at face value at maturity.

Journal Entry:

Bonds Payable	50,000	
Cash		50,000
Repayment of bonds at face value at maturity		

Cash Flow Analysis:

Repayment of bonds ($50,000)

Reconciliation: The following T account explains the change in Bonds Payable:

BONDS PAYABLE			
Repayment	50,000	Beg. Bal.	245,000
		Noncash Issue	100,000
		End. Bal.	**295,000**

If Zebra had any notes payable, the analysis would be the same.

Common Stock

Zebra's balance sheet (Exhibit 12.5, p. 547) shows a *$76,000 increase in common stock and a $99,000 increase in additional paid-in capital.* Our objective is to explain these changes and their effects on the statement of cash flows.

Transaction 3 Issued 15,200 shares of $5 par value common stock for $175,000.

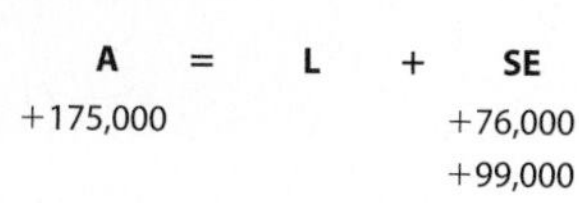

Journal Entry:

Cash	175,000	
Common Stock		76,000
Additional Paid-In Capital		99,000
Issued 15,200 shares of $5 par value common stock		

Cash Flow Analysis:

Issuance of common stock $175,000

Reconciliation: The following analysis of this transaction is all that is needed to explain the changes in the two accounts during 2011:

COMMON STOCK		
	Beg. Bal.	200,000
	Issue	76,000
	End. Bal.	**276,000**

ADDITIONAL PAID-IN CAPITAL		
	Beg. Bal.	115,000
	Issue	99,000
	End. Bal.	**214,000**

Retained Earnings

Zebra's balance sheet (Exhibit 12.5, p. 547) shows an *$8,000 increase in retained earnings.* Our objective is to explain this change and its effects on the statement of cash flows.

Transaction 4 Paid cash dividends in the amount of $8,000.

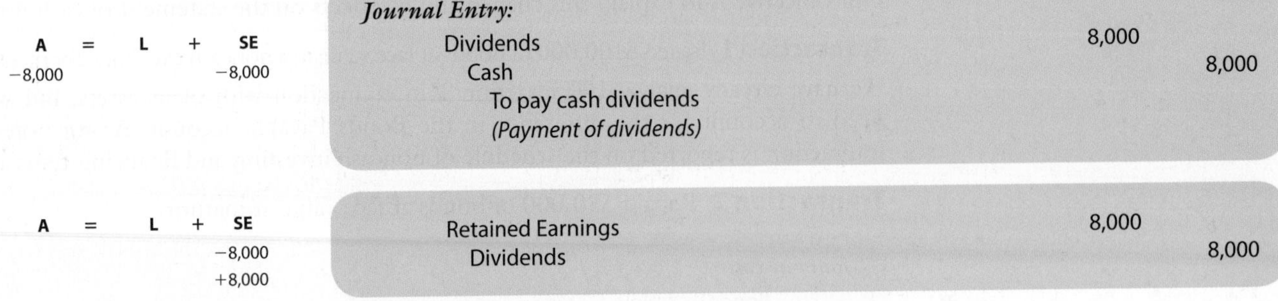

A	=	L	+	SE
−8,000				−8,000

Journal Entry:

Dividends	8,000	
Cash		8,000
To pay cash dividends		
(Payment of dividends)		

A	=	L	+	SE
				−8,000
				+8,000

Retained Earnings	8,000	
Dividends		8,000

Cash Flow Analysis:

Payment of dividends ($8,000)

STUDY NOTE: Dividends paid, not dividends declared, appear on the statement of cash flows.

Reconciliation: Recall that dividends will reduce Retained Earnings and that net income appears in the operating activities section of the statement of cash flows. Thus, we have now explained all the changes related to Zebra's Retained Earnings account. This T account shows the change in the Retained Earnings account:

RETAINED EARNINGS

Dividends	8,000	Beg. Bal.	132,000
		Net Income	16,000
		End. Bal.	**140,000**

Treasury Stock

Zebra's balance sheet (Exhibit 12.5, p. 547) shows a *$25,000 increase in treasury stock.* Our objective is to explain this change and its effects on the statement of cash flows.

Transaction 5 Purchased treasury stock for $25,000.

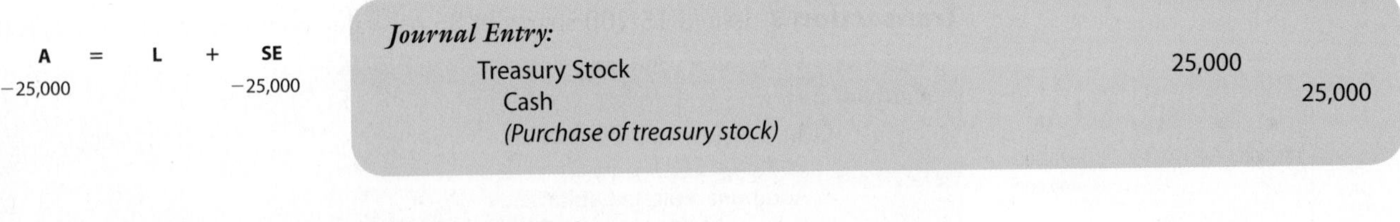

A	=	L	+	SE
−25,000				−25,000

Journal Entry:

Treasury Stock	25,000	
Cash		25,000
(Purchase of treasury stock)		

Cash Flow Analysis:

Purchase of treasury stock ($25,000)

Reconciliation: The following T account explains the change in Treasury Stock:

TREASURY STOCK

Purchase	25,000		

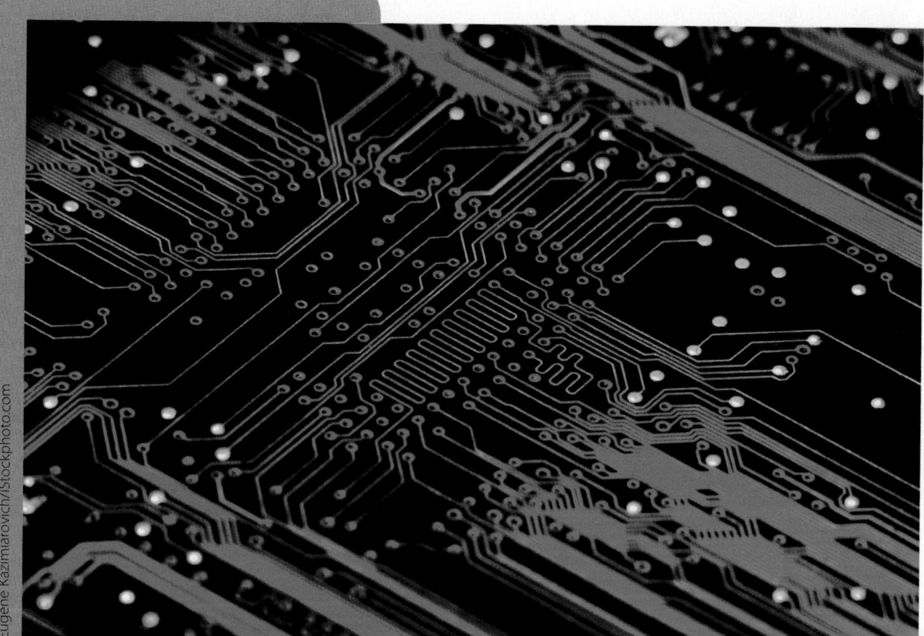

Eugene Kazimirovich/iStockphoto.com

High-tech companies with large amounts of intangible assets can lose up to 8 percent of their value in times of financial stress. As a hedge against economic downturns, these companies need to build cash reserves and may therefore choose to hoard cash rather than pay dividends.

STEP FOUR: PREPARING THE STATEMENT OF CASH FLOWS

We have now analyzed all of Zebra Corporation's income statement items, explained all balance sheet changes, and taken all additional information into account. Exhibit 12.8 shows how these data are assembled in Zebra's statement of cash flows.

EXHIBIT 12.8
Statement of Cash Flows: Indirect Method

Zebra Corporation
Statement of Cash Flows
For the Year Ended December 31, 2011

Cash flows from operating activities		
Net income		$ 16,000
Adjustments to reconcile net income to net cash flows from operating activities		
Depreciation	$ 37,000	
Loss on sale of plant assets	3,000	
Gain on sale of investments	(12,000)	
Changes in current assets and current liabilities		
Decrease in accounts receivable	8,000	
Increase in inventory	(34,000)	
Decrease in prepaid expenses	4,000	
Increase in accounts payable	7,000	
Increase in accrued liabilities	3,000	
Decrease in income taxes payable	(2,000)	14,000
Net cash flows from operating activities		$ 30,000
Cash flows from investing activities		
Purchase of investments	$ (78,000)	
Sale of investments	102,000	
Purchase of plant assets	(120,000)	
Sale of plant assets	5,000	
Net cash flows from investing activities		(91,000)
Cash flows from financing activities		
Repayment of bonds	$ (50,000)	
Issuance of common stock	175,000	
Payment of dividends	(8,000)	
Purchase of treasury stock	(25,000)	
Net cash flows from financing activities		92,000
Net increase in cash		$ 31,000
Cash at beginning of year		15,000
Cash at end of year		$ 46,000

Schedule of Noncash Investing and Financing Transactions

Issue of bonds payable for plant assets		$100,000

Stop & Apply

During 2011, Robinson Company issued $1,000,000 in long-term bonds at par, repaid $200,000 of notes payable at face value, issued notes payable of $40,000 for equipment, paid interest of $40,000, paid dividends of $25,000, and repurchased common stock in the amount of $50,000. Prepare the cash flows from financing activities section of the statement of cash flows.

SOLUTION

Cash flows from financing activities	
Issuance of long-term bonds	$1,000,000
Repayment of notes payable	(200,000)
Payment of dividends	(25,000)
Purchase of treasury stock	(50,000)
Net cash flows from financing activities	$ 725,000

Note: Interest is an operating activity. The exchange of the notes payable for equipment is a noncash investing and financing transaction.

iStock Photo

A look back at ▸ Amazon.com, Inc.

As we pointed out in this chapter's Decision Point, strong cash flows are a basic ingredient in **Amazon.com**'s plans for the future. Strong cash flows enable a company to achieve and maintain liquidity, to expand, and to increase the value of its shareholders' investments. A company's statement of cash flows provides information essential to evaluating the strength of its cash flows and its liquidity.

A user of Amazon.com's statement of cash flows would want answers to the following questions:

1. Are Amazon.com's operations generating sufficient operating cash flows?
2. Is the company growing by investing in long-term assets?
3. Has the company had to borrow money or issue stock to finance its growth?

Using data from Exhibit 12.1, which presents Amazon.com's statements of cash flows, we can answer these questions. We can gauge Amazon.com's ability to generate cash flows from operations by calculating its cash flow yields in 2009 and 2008:

RATIO

Cash Flow Yield		2009	2008
$\frac{\text{Net Cash Flows from Operating Activities}}{\text{Net Income}}$	=	$\frac{\$3,293}{\$902}$	$\frac{\$1,697}{\$645}$
	=	3.7 Times	2.6 Times

As you can see, Amazon.com's cash flow yield increased over the two years, from 2.6 to 3.7 times, and both years easily exceeded the 1.0 level normally considered the minimum acceptable cash flow yield. Although both net cash flows from operating activities and net income increased significantly from 2008 to 2009, net cash flows from operating activities grew more rapidly.

Free cash flow measures the sufficiency of cash flows in a different way, and as mentioned earlier in the chapter, it is a key financial objective of Amazon.com's management.

The computations below show that the company is meeting its objectives. Its free cash flow grew by $1,556 million between 2008 and 2009:

RATIO

Free Cash Flow		2009	2008
Net Cash Flows from Operating Activities − Dividends − Purchases of Plant Assets + Sales of Plant Assets	=	$3,293 − $0 − $373 + $0	$1,697 − $0 − $333 + $0
	=	$2,920	$1,364

An examination of Amazon.com's statement of cash flows in Exhibit 12.1 shows how the company is investing its free cash flow. In addition to investing in long-term assets ($373 million in 2009 and $333 million in 2008), the company increased its investment in marketable securities because purchases exceeded sales each year. Thus, the company did not have to rely on borrowing money (because repayments exceeded proceeds from debt) or issuing stock to finance its growth. Although it did not pay a cash dividend, Amazon.com did repurchase common stock in the amount of $100 million in 2008. Finally, it increased its balance of cash and cash equivalents from $2,769 million in 2008 to $3,444 million in 2009. One must conclude that Amazon.com is a very successful and growing company. It will be interesting to see if it can maintain its success.

Review Problem

The Statement of Cash Flows

Titan Corporation's income statement for 2011 and its comparative balance sheets for 2011 and 2010 appear below.

	A	B	C	D	E
1			**Titan Corporation**		
2			**Income Statement**		
3			**For the Year Ended December 31, 2011**		
4					
5	Net sales				$825,000
6	Cost of goods sold				460,000
7	Gross margin				$365,000
8	Operating expenses (including depreciation expense of $6,000				
9	on buildings and $11,550 on equipment and amortization				
10	expense of $2,400)				235,000
11	Operating income				$130,000
12	Other income				
13		Interest expense		$(27,500)	
14		Dividend income		1,700	
15		Gain on sale of investments		6,250	
16		Loss on disposal of equipment		(1,150)	(20,700)
17	Income before income taxes				$109,300
18	Income taxes expense				26,100
19	Net income				$ 83,200

	Titan Corporation Comparative Balance Sheets December 31, 2011 and 2010			
	2011	2010	Change	Increase or Decrease
Assets				
Cash	$ 52,925	$ 60,925	$ (8,000)	Decrease
Accounts receivable (net)	148,000	157,250	(9,250)	Decrease
Inventory	161,000	150,500	10,500	Increase
Prepaid expenses	3,900	2,900	1,000	Increase
Long-term investments	18,000	43,000	(25,000)	Decrease
Land	75,000	62,500	12,500	Increase
Buildings	231,000	231,000	—	—
Accumulated depreciation–buildings	(45,500)	(39,500)	(6,000)	Increase
Equipment	79,865	83,615	(3,750)	Decrease
Accumulated depreciation–equipment	(21,700)	(22,800)	1,100	Decrease
Intangible assets	9,600	12,000	(2,400)	Decrease
Total assets	$712,090	$741,390	$(29,300)	
Liabilities and Stockholders' Equity				
Accounts payable	$ 66,875	$116,875	$(50,000)	Decrease
Notes payable (current)	37,850	72,850	(35,000)	Decrease
Accrued liabilities	2,500	—	2,500	Increase
Income taxes payable	10,000	—	10,000	Increase
Bonds payable	105,000	155,000	(50,000)	Decrease
Mortgage payable	165,000	175,000	(10,000)	Decrease
Common stock, $10 par value	200,000	170,000	30,000	Increase
Additional paid-in capital	45,000	25,000	20,000	Increase
Retained earnings	104,865	46,665	58,200	Increase
Treasury stock	(25,000)	(20,000)	(5,000)	Increase
Total liabilities and stockholders' equity	$712,090	$741,390	$(29,300)	

The company's records for 2011 provide this additional information:

a. Sold long-term investments that cost $35,000 for a gain of $6,250; made other long-term investments in the amount of $10,000.

b. Purchased five acres of land to build a parking lot for $12,500.

c. Sold equipment that cost $18,750 and that had accumulated depreciation of $12,650 at a loss of $1,150; purchased new equipment for $15,000.

d. Repaid notes payable in the amount of $50,000; borrowed $15,000 by signing new notes payable.

e. Converted $50,000 of bonds payable into 3,000 shares of common stock.

f. Reduced the Mortgage Payable account by $10,000.

g. Declared and paid cash dividends of $25,000.

h. Purchased treasury stock for $5,000.

Required

1. Prepare a statement of cash flows using the indirect method.

RATIO

2. Compute cash flow yield, cash flows to sales, cash flows to assets, and free cash flow for 2011. (*Note:* Round ratios to the nearest decimal point.)

ANSWERS TO REVIEW PROBLEM

1. Statement of cash flows using the indirect method:

	A	B	C	D	E
1			**Titan Corporation**		
2			**Statement of Cash Flows**		
3			**For the Year Ended December 31, 2011**		
4					
5	**Cash flows from operating activities**				
6	Net income				$83,200
7	Adjustments to reconcile net income to net cash flows				
8	from operating activities				
9		Depreciation expense–buildings		$ 6,000	
10		Depreciation expense–equipment		11,550	
11		Amortization expense–intangible assets		2,400	
12		Gain on sale of investments		(6,250)	
13		Loss on disposal of equipment		1,150	
14		Changes in current assets and current liabilities			
15			Decrease in accounts receivable	9,250	
16			Increase in inventory	(10,500)	
17			Increase in prepaid expenses	(1,000)	
18			Decrease in accounts payable	(50,000)	
19			Increase in accrued liabilities	2,500	
20			Increase in income taxes payable	10,000	(24,900)
21	Net cash flows from operating activities				$58,300
22	**Cash flows from investing activities**				
23	Sale of long-term investments			$ 41,250[a]	
24	Purchase of long-term investments			(10,000)	
25	Purchase of land			(12,500)	
26	Sale of equipment			4,950[b]	
27	Purchase of equipment			(15,000)	
28	Net cash flows from investing activities				8,700
29	**Cash flows from financing activities**				
30	Repayment of notes payable			$(50,000)	
31	Issuance of notes payable			15,000	
32	Reduction in mortgage			(10,000)	
33	Dividends paid			(25,000)	
34	Purchase of treasury stock			(5,000)	
35	Net cash flows from financing activities				(75,000)
36	Net (decrease) in cash				$ (8,000)
37	Cash at beginning of year				60,925
38	Cash at end of year				$52,925
39					
40			**Schedule of Noncash Investing and Financing Transactions**		
41	Conversion of bonds payable into common stock				$50,000
42					
43	a	$35,000 + $6,250 (gain) = $41,250			
44	b	$18,750 − $12,650 = $6,100 (book value) − $1,150 (loss) = $4,950			

2. Cash flow yield, cash flows to sales, cash flows to assets, and free cash flow for 2011:

$$\text{Cash Flow Yield} = \frac{\$58,300}{\$83,200} = 0.7 \text{ Times}$$

$$\text{Cash Flows to Sales} = \frac{\$58,300}{\$825,000} = 7.1\%$$

$$\text{Cash Flows to Assets} = \frac{\$58,300}{(\$712,090 + \$741,390) \div 2} = 8.0\%$$

$$\text{Free Cash Flow} = \$58,300 - \$25,000 - \$12,500 - \$15,000 + \$4,950 = \$10,750$$

Stop & Review

LO 1 Describe the principal purposes and uses of the statement of cash flows and identify its components.

The statement of cash flows shows how a company's operating, investing, and financing activities have affected cash during an accounting period. For the statement of cash flows, *cash* is defined as including both cash and cash equivalents. The statement of cash flows provides information about a company's cash receipts and cash payments during an accounting period, as well as about the company's operating, investing, and financing activities. Management uses the statement to assess liquidity, determine dividend policy, and plan investing and financing activities. Investors and creditors use it to assess the company's cash-generating ability.

The statement of cash flows has three major classifications: (1) operating activities, which involve the cash effects of transactions and other events that enter into the determination of net income; (2) investing activities, which involve the acquisition and sale of marketable securities and long-term assets and the making and collecting of loans; and (3) financing activities, which involve obtaining resources from stockholders and creditors and providing the former with a return on their investments and the latter with repayment. Noncash investing and financing transactions are also important because they affect future cash flows; these exchanges of long-term assets or liabilities are of interest to potential investors and creditors.

LO 2 Analyze the statement of cash flows.

In examining a company's statement of cash flows, analysts tend to focus on the firm's degree of liquidity, which is determined by cash inflows and outflows from operating activities. The financial ratios used to measure a firm's ability to generate sufficient cash from its current or continuing operations are cash flow yield, cash flows to sales, and cash flows to assets. Free cash flow—the cash that remains after deducting the funds a firm must commit to continue operating at its planned level—is another important measure of the adequacy of cash flow.

LO 3 Use the indirect method to determine cash flows from operating activities.

The indirect method adjusts net income for all items in the income statement that do not have cash flow effects (such as depreciation, amortization, and gains and losses on sales of assets) and for changes in liabilities that affect operating cash flows. Generally, increases in current assets have a negative effect on cash flows, and decreases have a positive effect. Conversely, increases in current liabilities have a positive effect on cash flows, and decreases have a negative effect.

LO 4 Determine cash flows from investing activities.

Investing activities involve the acquisition and sale of property, plant, and equipment and other long-term assets, including long-term investments. They also involve the acquisition and sale of short-term marketable securities, other than trading securities, and the making and collecting of loans. Cash flows from investing activities are determined by analyzing the cash flow effects of changes in each account related to investing activities. The effects of gains and losses reported on the income statement must also be considered.

Determine cash flows from financing activities. 

Determining cash flows from financing activities is almost identical to determining cash flows from investing activities. The difference is that the accounts analyzed relate to short-term borrowings, long-term liabilities, and stockholders' equity. After the changes in the balance sheet accounts from one accounting period to the next have been explained, all the cash flow effects should have been identified, and the statement of cash flows can be prepared.

Key Terms and Ratios

Cash 538 (LO1)
Cash equivalents 538 (LO1)
Direct method 548 (LO3)
Financing activities 540 (LO1)
Free cash flow 544 (LO2)
Indirect method 548 (LO3)
Investing activities 540 (LO1)
Noncash investing and financing transactions 541 (LO1)
Operating activities 539 (LO1)
Statement of cash flows 538 (LO1)
Trading securities 539 (LO1)

FINANCIAL RATIOS
Cash flow yield 543 (LO2)
Cash flows to sales 543 (LO2)
Cash flows to assets 544 (LO2)

Chapter Assignments Building Your Basic Knowledge and Skills

Short Exercises

LO 1

Classification of Cash Flow Transactions

SE 1. The list that follows itemizes Swoboda Corporation's transactions. Identify each as (a) an operating activity, (b) an investing activity, (c) a financing activity, (d) a noncash transaction, or (e) none of the above.

1. Sold land.
2. Declared and paid a cash dividend.
3. Paid interest.
4. Issued common stock for plant assets.
5. Issued preferred stock.
6. Borrowed cash on a bank loan.

LO 2

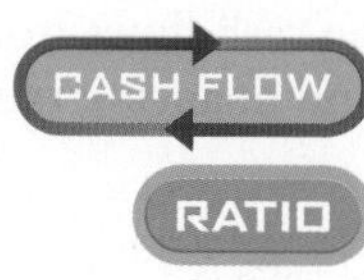

Cash Flow Ratios and Free Cash Flow

SE 2. In 2011, Coral Corporation had year-end assets of $275,000, sales of $395,000, net income of $45,000, net cash flows from operating activities of $90,000, purchases of plant assets of $60,000, and sales of plant assets of $10,000, and it paid dividends of $20,000. In 2010, year-end assets were $250,000. Calculate cash flow yield, cash flows to sales, cash flows to assets, and free cash flow. (*Note:* Round ratios to the nearest decimal point.)

LO 2

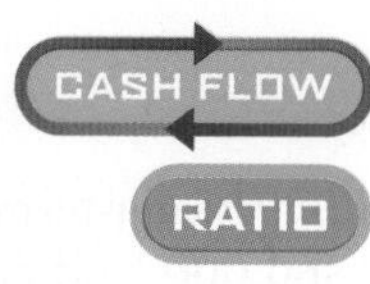

Cash Flow Ratios and Free Cash Flow

SE 3. In 2011, Mira Corporation had year-end assets of $825,000, sales of $1,185,000, net income of $135,000, net cash flows from operating activities of $270,000, purchases of plant assets of $180,000, and sales of plant assets of $30,000, and it paid dividends of $60,000. In 2010, year-end assets were $750,000. Calculate cash flow yield, cash flows to sales, cash flows to assets, and free cash flow. (*Note:* Round ratios to the nearest decimal point.)

LO 2

Cash Flow Ratios and Free Cash Flow

SE 4. Examine the cash flow performance measures in requirement 2 of the Review Problem in this chapter. Discuss the meaning of the cash flow ratios and free cash flow.

LO 3

Computing Cash Flows from Operating Activities: Indirect Method

SE 5. Express Corporation had a net income of $66,000 during 2011. During the year, the company had depreciation expense of $28,000. Accounts receivable increased by $22,000, and accounts payable increased by $10,000. Those were the company's only current assets and current liabilities. Use the indirect method to determine net cash flows from operating activities.

LO 3

Computing Cash Flows from Operating Activities: Indirect Method

SE 6. During 2011, Minh Corporation had a net income of $144,000. Included on its income statement were depreciation expense of $16,000 and amortization expense of $1,800. During the year, accounts receivable decreased by $8,200, inventories increased by $5,400, prepaid expenses decreased by $1,000, accounts payable decreased by $14,000, and accrued liabilities decreased by $1,700. Use the indirect method to determine net cash flows from operating activities.

LO 3

Computing Cash Flows from Operating Activities: Indirect Method

SE 7. During 2011, Pilch Corporation had a net income of $216,000. Included on its income statement were depreciation expense of $24,000 and amortization expense of $2,700. During the year, accounts receivable decreased by $12,300, inventories increased by $8,100, prepaid expenses decreased by $1,500, accounts payable decreased by $21,000, and accrued liabilities decreased by $2,550. Use the indirect method to determine net cash flows from operating activities.

LO 4

Cash Flows from Investing Activities and Noncash Transactions

SE 8. During 2011, Randy, Inc., purchased land for $563,000. It paid $188,000 in cash and signed a $375,000 mortgage for the rest. The company also sold equipment that originally cost $135,000, on which it had $105,000 of accumulated depreciation, for $143,000 cash, making a gain of $113,000. Prepare the cash flows from the investing activities section and the schedule of noncash investing and financing transactions of the statement of cash flows.

LO 4

Cash Flows from Investing Activities and Noncash Transactions

SE 9. During 2011, Howard Company purchased land for $375,000. It paid $125,000 in cash and signed a $250,000 mortgage for the rest. The company also sold a building that originally cost $90,000, on which it had $70,000 of accumulated depreciation, for $95,000 cash, making a gain of $75,000. Prepare the cash flows from the investing activities section and the schedule of noncash investing and financing transactions of the statement of cash flows.

LO 5

Cash Flows from Financing Activities

SE 10. During 2011, Arizona Company issued $500,000 in long-term bonds at 96, repaid $75,000 of bonds at face value, paid interest of $40,000, and paid dividends of $25,000. Prepare the cash flows from the financing activities section of the statement of cash flows.

LO 5

Cash Flows from Financing Activities

SE 11. During 2011, Neba Company issued $750,000 in long-term bonds at 98, repaid $113,000 of bonds at face value, paid interest of $60,000, and paid dividends of $38,000. Prepare the cash flows from the financing activities section of the statement of cash flows.

LO 1, 3, 4, 5

Identifying Components of the Statement of Cash Flows

SE 12. Assuming the indirect method is used to prepare the statement of cash flows, tell whether each of the following items would appear (a) in cash flows from operating activities, (b) in cash flows from investing activities, (c) in cash flows from financing activities, (d) in the schedule of noncash investing and financing transactions, or (e) not on the statement of cash flows at all:

1. Dividends paid
2. Cash receipts from customers
3. Decrease in accounts receivable
4. Sale of plant assets
5. Gain on sale of investments
6. Issue of stock for plant assets
7. Issue of common stock
8. Net income

Exercises

LO 1, 2

Discussion Questions

E 1. Develop brief answers to each of the following questions:

1. Which statement is more useful—the income statement or the statement of cash flows?
2. How would you respond to someone who says that the most important item on the statement of cash flows is the change in the cash balance for the year?
3. If a company's cash flow yield is less than 1.0, would its cash flows to sales and cash flows to assets be greater or less than profit margin and return on assets, respectively?

LO 3, 4, 5

Discussion Questions

E 2. Develop brief answers to each of the following questions:

1. If a company has positive earnings, can cash flows from operating activities ever be negative?
2. Which adjustments to net income in the operating activities section of the statement of cash flows are directly related to cash flows in other sections?
3. In computing free cash flow, what is an argument for treating the purchases of treasury stock like dividend payments?

LO 1

Classification of Cash Flow Transactions

E 3. Anit Corporation engaged in the transactions listed below. Identify each transaction as (a) an operating activity, (b) an investing activity, (c) a financing activity, (d) a noncash transaction, or (e) not on the statement of cash flows. (*Note:* Assume the indirect method is used.)

1. Declared and paid a cash dividend.
2. Purchased a long-term investment.
3. Increased interest payable.
4. Paid interest.
5. Sold equipment at a loss.
6. Issued long-term bonds for plant assets.
7. Increased dividends receivable.
8. Issued common stock.
9. Declared and issued a stock dividend.
10. Repaid notes payable.
11. Decreased wages payable.
12. Purchased a 60-day Treasury bill.
13. Purchased land.

LO 2

Cash Flow Ratios and Free Cash Flow

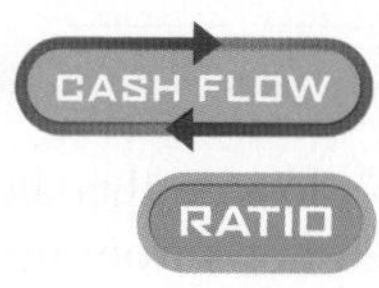

E 4. In 2011, Hnat Corporation had year-end assets of $600,000, sales of $825,000, net income of $70,000, net cash flows from operating activities of $98,000, dividends of $30,000, purchases of plant assets of $125,000, and sales of plant assets of $23,000. In 2010, year-end assets were $525,000. Calculate cash flow yield, cash flows to sales, cash flows to assets, and free cash flow. (*Note:* Round ratios to the nearest decimal point.)

LO 3 **Cash Flows from Operating Activities: Indirect Method**

E 5. The condensed single-step income statement for the year ended December 31, 2011, of Sunderland Chemical Company, a distributor of farm fertilizers and herbicides, appears as follows:

Sales		$13,000,000
Less: Cost of goods sold	$7,600,000	
Operating expenses (including depreciation of $820,000)	3,800,000	
Income taxes expense	400,000	11,800,000
Net income		$ 1,200,000

Selected accounts from Sunderland Chemical Company's balance sheets for 2011 and 2010 are as follows:

	2011	2010
Accounts receivable (net)	$2,400,000	$1,700,000
Inventory	840,000	1,020,000
Prepaid expenses	260,000	180,000
Accounts payable	960,000	720,000
Accrued liabilities	60,000	100,000
Income taxes payable	140,000	120,000

Prepare a schedule of cash flows from operating activities using the indirect method.

LO 3 **Computing Cash Flows from Operating Activities: Indirect Method**

E 6. During 2011, Lambda Corporation had net income of $82,000. Included on its income statement were depreciation expense of $4,600 and amortization expense of $600. During the year, accounts receivable increased by $6,800, inventories decreased by $3,800, prepaid expenses decreased by $400, accounts payable increased by $10,000, and accrued liabilities decreased by $900. Determine net cash flows from operating activities using the indirect method.

LO 3 **Preparing a Schedule of Cash Flows from Operating Activities: Indirect Method**

E 7. For the year ended June 30, 2011, net income for Freed Corporation was $14,800. Depreciation expense was $4,000. During the year, accounts receivable increased by $8,800, inventories increased by $14,000, prepaid rent decreased by $2,800, accounts payable increased by $28,000, salaries payable increased by $2,000, and income taxes payable decreased by $1,200. Use the indirect method to prepare a schedule of cash flows from operating activities.

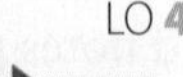

LO 4 **Computing Cash Flows from Investing Activities: Investments**

E 8. DOT Company's T account for long-term available-for-sale investments at the end of 2011 is as follows:

INVESTMENTS			
Beg. Bal.	76,000	Sales	78,000
Purchases	116,000		
End. Bal.	**114,000**		

In addition, DOT Company's income statement shows a loss on the sale of investments of $13,000. Compute the amounts to be shown as cash flows from investing activities and show how they are to appear in the statement of cash flows.

LO 4

Computing Cash Flows from Investing Activities: Plant Assets

E 9. The T accounts for Plant Assets and Accumulated Depreciation for DOT Company at the end of 2011 are as follows:

PLANT ASSETS				ACCUMULATED DEPRECIATION			
Beg. Bal.	130,000	Disposals	46,000	Disposals	29,400	Beg. Bal.	69,000
Purchases	67,200					Depreciation	20,400
End. Bal.	**151,200**					**End. Bal.**	**60,000**

In addition, DOT Company's income statement shows a gain on sale of plant assets of $8,800. Compute the amounts to be shown as cash flows from investing activities and show how they are to appear on the statement of cash flows.

LO 5

Determining Cash Flows from Financing Activities: Notes Payable

E 10. All transactions involving notes payable and related accounts of Rek Company during 2011 are recorded as follows:

Cash	36,000	
Notes Payable		36,000
Bank loan		
Patent	60,000	
Notes Payable		60,000
Purchase of patent by issuing note payable		
Notes Payable	10,000	
Interest Expense	1,000	
Cash		11,000
Repayment of note payable at maturity		

Determine the amounts of the transactions affecting financing activities and show how they are to appear on the statement of cash flows for 2011.

LO 3, 4, 5

Preparing the Statement of Cash Flows: Indirect Method

E 11. Bristol Corporation's income statement for the year ended June 30, 2011, and its comparative balance sheets for June 30, 2011 and 2010 follow.

Bristol Corporation
Income Statement
For the Year Ended June 30, 2011

Sales	$234,000
Cost of goods sold	156,000
Gross margin	$ 78,000
Operating expenses	45,000
Operating income	$ 33,000
Interest expense	2,800
Income before income taxes	$ 30,200
Income taxes expense	12,300
Net income	$ 17,900

Bristol Corporation
Comparative Balance Sheets
June 30, 2011 and 2010

	2011	2010
Assets		
Cash	$ 69,900	$ 12,500
Accounts receivable (net)	21,000	26,000
Inventory	43,400	48,400
Prepaid expenses	3,200	2,600
Furniture	55,000	60,000
Accumulated depreciation–furniture	(9,000)	(5,000)
Total assets	$183,500	$144,500
Liabilities and Stockholders' Equity		
Accounts payable	$ 13,000	$ 14,000
Income taxes payable	1,200	1,800
Notes payable (long term)	37,000	35,000
Common stock, $10 par value	115,000	90,000
Retained earnings	17,300	3,700
Total liabilities and stockholders' equity	$183,500	$144,500

Bristol issued a $22,000 note payable for purchase of furniture; sold furniture that cost $27,000 with accumulated depreciation of $15,300 at carrying value; recorded depreciation on the furniture for the year, $19,300; repaid a note in the amount of $20,000; issued $25,000 of common stock at par value; and paid dividends of $4,300. Prepare Bristol's statement of cash flows for the year ended June 30, 2011, using the indirect method.

Problems

LO 1

Classification of Cash Flow Transactions

P 1. Analyze each transaction listed below using the following header for formatting. Place Xs in the appropriate columns to indicate the transaction's classification and its effect on cash flows using the indirect method.

	Cash Flow Classification				Effect on Cash Flows		
Transaction	**Operating Activity**	**Investing Activity**	**Financing Activity**	**Noncash Transaction**	**Increase**	**Decrease**	**No Effect**
1. Increased accounts payable.							
2. Decreased inventory.							
3. Increased prepaid insurance.							
4. Earned a net income.							
5. Declared and paid a cash dividend.							
6. Issued stock for cash.							
7. Retired long-term debt by issuing stock.							
8. Purchased a long-term investment with cash.							
9. Sold trading securities at a gain.							
10. Sold a machine at a loss.							
11. Retired fully depreciated equipment.							
12. Decreased interest payable.							
13. Purchased available-for-sale securities (long-term).							
14. Decreased dividends receivable.							
15. Decreased accounts receivable.							
16. Converted bonds to common stock.							
17. Purchased 90-day Treasury bill.							

LO 1

✔ Free cash flow, 2010: ($171,976); free cash flow, 2011: $287,700

Interpreting and Analyzing the Statement of Cash Flows

P 2. The comparative statements of cash flows for Cole Corporation, a manufacturer of high-quality suits for men, follow. To expand its markets and familiarity with its brand, the company attempted a new strategic diversification in 2011 by acquiring a chain of retail men's stores in outlet malls. Its plan was to expand in malls around the country, but department stores viewed the action as infringing on their territory.

Cole Corporation
Statement of Cash Flows
For the Years Ended December 31, 2011 and 2010
(in thousands)

	2011	2010
Cash flows from operating activities		
Net income (loss)	$ (42,050)	$ 74,200
Adjustments to reconcile net income to net cash flows from operating activities		
Depreciation	$ 71,150	$ 49,100
Loss on closure of retail outlets	70,000	—
Changes in current assets and current liabilities		
Decrease (increase) in accounts receivable	98,700	(86,250)
Decrease (increase) in inventory	119,300	(98,475)
Decrease (increase) in prepaid expenses	2,570	4,200
Increase (decrease) in accounts payable	57,630	2,500
Increase (decrease) in accrued liabilities	3,000	(5,360)
Increase (decrease) in income taxes payable	(16,000)	(11,361)
	$ 406,350	$(145,646)
Net cash flows from operating activities	$ 364,300	$ (71,446)
Cash flows from investing activities		
Capital expenditures, net	$ (31,200)	$ (60,890)
Purchase of Retail Division, cash portion	—	(395,000)
Net cash flows from investing activities	$ (31,200)	$(455,890)
Cash flows from financing activities		
Increase (decrease) in notes payable to banks	$(247,000)	$ 453,500
Reduction in long-term debt	(18,050)	(21,500)
Payment of dividends	(45,400)	(39,640)
Purchase of treasury stock	—	(25,000)
Net cash flows from financing activities	$(310,450)	$ 367,360
Net increase (decrease) in cash	$ 22,650	$(159,976)
Cash at beginning of year	44,524	204,500
Cash at end of year	$ 67,174	$ 44,524
Schedule of Noncash Investing and Financing Transactions		
Issue of bonds payable for retail acquisition		$ 102,000

REQUIRED

Evaluate the success of the company's strategy by answering the questions that follow.

USER INSIGHT ▶ 1. What are the primary reasons cash flows from operating activities differ from net income? What is the effect of the acquisition in 2010? What conclusions can you draw from the changes in 2011?

2. Compute free cash flow for both years. What was the total cost of the acquisition? Is the company able to finance expansion in 2010 by generating internal cash flow? What was the situation in 2011?

USER INSIGHT ▶ 3. What are the most significant financing activities in 2010? How did the company finance the acquisition? Do you think this is a good strategy? What other issues might you question in financing activities?

USER INSIGHT ▶ 4. Based on results in 2011, what actions was the company forced to take, and what is your overall assessment of the company's diversification strategy?

LO 2, 3, 4, 5

Statement of Cash Flows: Indirect Method

✔ Net cash flows from operating activities: $137,000; from investing activities: $1,500; from financing activities: ($65,000)

P 3. Bronek Corporation's income statement for the year ended June 30, 2011, and its comparative balance sheets as of June 30, 2011 and 2010 follow. During 2011, the corporation sold at a loss of $2,000 equipment that cost $12,000, on which it had accumulated depreciation of $8,500. It also purchased land and a building for $50,000 through an increase of $50,000 in mortgage payable, made a $10,000 payment on the mortgage, repaid notes ($40,000) but borrowed an additional $15,000 through the issuance of a new note payable of $40,000, and declared and paid a $30,000 cash dividend.

Bronek Corporation
Income Statement
For the Year Ended June 30, 2011

Sales		$2,020,450
Cost of goods sold		1,828,150
Gross margin		$ 192,300
Operating expenses (including depreciation expense of $30,000)		94,600
Income from operations		$ 97,700
Other income (expenses)		
Loss on sale of equipment	$ (2,000)	
Interest expense	(18,800)	(20,800)
Income before income taxes		$ 76,900
Income taxes expense		17,100
Net income		$ 59,800

Bronek Corporation
Comparative Balance Sheets
June 30, 2011 and 2010

	2011	2010
Assets		
Cash	$ 83,500	$ 10,000
Accounts receivable (net)	50,000	60,000
Inventory	90,000	110,000
Prepaid expenses	300	500
Property, plant, and equipment	314,000	276,000
Accumulated depreciation–property, plant, and equipment	(91,500)	(70,000)
Total assets	$446,300	$386,500
Liabilities and Stockholders' Equity		
Accounts payable	$ 32,000	$ 21,000
Notes payable (due in 90 days)	15,000	40,000
Income taxes payable	13,000	9,000
Mortgage payable	180,000	140,000
Common stock, $5 par value	100,000	100,000
Retained earnings	106,300	76,500
Total liabilities and stockholders' equity	$446,300	$386,500

REQUIRED

1. Using the indirect method, prepare a statement of cash flows. Include a supporting schedule of noncash investing and financing transactions.

2. What are the primary reasons for Bronek Corporation's large increase in cash from 2010 to 2011?

3. Compute and assess cash flow yield and free cash flow for 2011. (*Note:* Round cash flow yield to one decimal place.) How would you assess the corporation's ability to generate sufficient cash flow?

LO 2, 3, 4, 5

CASH FLOW

Statement of Cash Flows: Indirect Method

✔ Net cash flows from operating activities: $126,600; from investing activities: ($25,800); from financing activities: $14,000

P 4. Brick Corporation's comparative balance sheets as of December 31, 2011 and 2010 and its income statement for the year ended December 31, 2011, follow.

Brick Corporation
Comparative Balance Sheets
December 31, 2011 and 2010

	2011	2010
Assets		
Cash	$164,800	$ 50,000
Accounts receivable (net)	165,200	200,000
Merchandise inventory	350,000	450,000
Prepaid rent	2,000	3,000
Furniture and fixtures	148,000	144,000
Accumulated depreciation–furniture and fixtures	(42,000)	(24,000)
Total assets	$788,000	$823,000
Liabilities and Stockholders' Equity		
Accounts payable	$143,400	$200,400
Income taxes payable	1,400	4,400
Notes payable (long-term)	40,000	20,000
Bonds payable	100,000	200,000
Common stock, $20 par value	240,000	200,000
Additional paid-in capital	181,440	121,440
Retained earnings	81,760	76,760
Total liabilities and stockholders' equity	$788,000	$823,000

Brick Corporation
Income Statement
For the Year Ended December 31, 2011

Sales		$1,609,000
Cost of goods sold		1,127,800
Gross margin		$ 481,200
Operating expenses (including depreciation expense of $46,800)		449,400
Income from operations		$ 31,800
Other income (expenses)		
Gain on sale of furniture and fixtures	$ 7,000	
Interest expense	(23,200)	(16,200)
Income before income taxes		$ 15,600
Income taxes expense		4,600
Net income		$ 11,000

During 2011, Brick Corporation engaged in the following transactions:

a. Sold at a gain of $7,000 furniture and fixtures that cost $35,600, on which it had accumulated depreciation of $28,800.
b. Purchased furniture and fixtures in the amount of $39,600.
c. Paid a $20,000 note payable and borrowed $40,000 on a new note.
d. Converted bonds payable in the amount of $100,000 into 4,000 shares of common stock.
e. Declared and paid $6,000 in cash dividends.

REQUIRED

1. Using the indirect method, prepare a statement of cash flows for Brick Corporation. Include a supporting schedule of noncash investing transactions and financing transactions.

2. What are the primary reasons for Brick Corporation's large increase in cash from 2010 to 2011, despite its low net income?

RATIO

3. Compute and assess cash flow yield and free cash flow for 2011. (*Note:* Round cash flow yield to one decimal place.) Compare and contrast what these two performance measures tell you about Brick's ability to generate sufficient cash flow.

LO 2, 3, 4, 5

Statement of Cash Flows: Indirect Method

✔ Net cash flows from operating activities: ($26,500); from investing activities: $8,500; from financing activities: $6,000

P 5. The comparative balance sheets for Carmelita Vases, Inc., for December 31, 2011 and 2010 follow. During 2011, the company had net income of $24,000 and building and equipment depreciation expenses of $20,000 and $15,000, respectively. It amortized intangible assets in the amount of $5,000; purchased investments for $29,000; sold investments for $37,500, on which it recorded a gain of $8,500; issued $60,000 of long-term bonds at face value; purchased land and a warehouse through an $80,000 mortgage; paid $10,000 to reduce the mortgage; borrowed $15,000 by issuing notes payable; repaid notes payable in the amount of $45,000; declared and paid cash dividends in the amount of $9,000; and purchased treasury stock in the amount of $5,000.

Carmelita Vases, Inc.
Comparative Balance Sheets
December 31, 2011 and 2010

	2011	2010
Assets		
Cash	$ 64,400	$ 76,400
Accounts receivable (net)	184,700	189,700
Inventory	240,000	200,000
Prepaid expenses	3,700	6,700
Long-term investments	110,000	110,000
Land	90,300	80,300
Building	300,000	230,000
Accumulated depreciation–building	(60,000)	(40,000)
Equipment	120,000	120,000
Accumulated depreciation–equipment	(29,000)	(14,000)
Intangible assets	5,000	10,000
Total assets	$1,029,100	$969,100
Liabilities and Stockholders' Equity		
Accounts payable	$ 117,700	$165,200
Notes payable (current)	10,000	40,000
Accrued liabilities	2,700	5,200
Mortgage payable	270,000	200,000
Bonds payable	250,000	190,000
Common stock	325,000	325,000
Additional paid-in capital	20,000	20,000
Retained earnings	63,700	48,700
Treasury stock	(30,000)	(25,000)
Total liabilities and stockholders' equity	$1,029,100	$969,100

REQUIRED

1. Using the indirect method, prepare a statement of cash flows for Carmelita Vases.

2. Why did Carmelita Vases experience a decrease in cash in a year in which it had a net income of $24,000? Discuss and interpret.

3. Compute and assess cash flow yield and free cash flow for 2011. (*Note:* Round cash flow yield to one decimal place.) Why is each of these measures important in assessing a company's ability to generate sufficient cash flow?

Alternate Problems

LO 1

CASH FLOW

Classification of Cash Flow Transactions

P 6. Analyze each transaction listed below using the following header for formatting. Place Xs in the appropriate columns to indicate the transaction's classification and its effect on cash flows using the indirect method.

	Cash Flow Classification				Effect on Cash Flows		
Transaction	**Operating Activity**	**Investing Activity**	**Financing Activity**	**Noncash Transaction**	**Increase**	**Decrease**	**No Effect**
1. Paid a cash dividend.							
2. Decreased accounts receivable.							
3. Increased inventory.							
4. Incurred a net loss.							
5. Declared and issued a stock dividend.							
6. Retired long-term debt with cash.							
7. Sold available-for-sale securities at a loss.							
8. Issued stock for equipment.							
9. Decreased prepaid insurance.							
10. Purchased treasury stock with cash.							
11. Retired a fully depreciated truck (no gain or loss).							
12. Increased interest payable.							
13. Decreased dividends receivable on investment.							
14. Sold treasury stock.							
15. Increased income taxes payable.							
16. Transferred cash to money market account.							
17. Purchased land and building with a mortgage.							

LO 2, 3, 4, 5

✔ Net cash flows from operating activities: $23,400; from investing activities: ($7,200); from financing activities: $51,000

Statement of Cash Flows: Indirect Method

P 7. The comparative balance sheets for Zagloba Materials, Inc., for December 31, 2011 and 2010 follow. Additional information about Zagloba Materials' operations during 2011 is as follows: (a) net income, $28,000; (b) building and equipment depreciation expense amounts, $15,000 and $3,000, respectively; (c) equipment that cost $13,500 with accumulated depreciation of $12,500 sold at a gain of $5,300; (d) equipment purchases, $12,500; (e) patent amortization, $3,000; purchase of patent, $1,000; (f) funds borrowed by issuing notes payable, $25,000; notes payable repaid, $15,000; (g) land and building purchased for $162,000 by signing a mortgage for the total cost; (h) 1,500 shares of $20 par value common stock issued for a total of $50,000; and (i) paid cash dividend, $9,000.

Zagloba Materials, Inc.
Comparative Balance Sheets
December 31, 2011 and 2010

	2011	2010
Assets		
Cash	$ 94,560	$ 27,360
Accounts receivable (net)	102,430	75,430
Inventory	112,890	137,890
Prepaid expenses	—	20,000
Land	25,000	—
Building	137,000	—
Accumulated depreciation–building	(15,000)	—
Equipment	33,000	34,000
Accumulated depreciation–equipment	(14,500)	(24,000)
Patents	4,000	6,000
Total assets	$479,380	$276,680
Liabilities and Stockholders' Equity		
Accounts payable	$ 10,750	$ 36,750
Notes payable (current)	10,000	—
Accrued liabilities	—	12,300
Mortgage payable	162,000	—
Common stock, $10 par value	180,000	150,000
Additional paid-in capital	57,200	37,200
Retained earnings	59,430	40,430
Total liabilities and stockholders' equity	$479,380	$276,680

REQUIRED

1. Using the indirect method, prepare a statement of cash flows for Zagloba Materials.
2. USER INSIGHT ▶ Why did Zagloba Materials have an increase in cash of $67,200 when it recorded net income of only $28,000? Discuss and interpret.
3.  Compute and assess cash flow yield and free cash flow for 2011. (*Note:* Round cash flow yield to one decimal place.) What is your assessment of Zagloba's ability to generate sufficient cash flow?

LO 2, 3, 4, 5

Statement of Cash Flows: Indirect Method

✔ Net cash flows from operating activities: $46,800; from investing activities: ($14,400); from financing activities: $102,000

P 8. The comparative balance sheets for Sharma Fabrics, Inc., for December 31, 2011 and 2010 follow.

Sharma Fabrics, Inc.
Comparative Balance Sheets
December 31, 2011 and 2010

	2011	2010
Assets		
Cash	$189,120	$ 54,720
Accounts receivable (net)	204,860	150,860
Inventory	225,780	275,780
Prepaid expenses	—	40,000
Land	50,000	—
Building	274,000	—
Accumulated depreciation–building	(30,000)	—
Equipment	66,000	68,000
Accumulated depreciation–equipment	(29,000)	(48,000)
Patents	8,000	12,000
Total assets	$958,760	$553,360

(continued)

	2011	2010
Liabilities and Stockholders' Equity		
Accounts payable	$ 21,500	$ 73,500
Notes payable (current)	20,000	—
Accrued liabilities	—	24,600
Mortgage payable	324,000	—
Common stock, $10 par value	360,000	300,000
Additional paid-in capital	114,400	74,400
Retained earnings	118,860	80,860
Total liabilities and stockholders' equity	$958,760	$553,360

Additional information about Sharma Fabrics' operations during 2011 is as follows: (a) net income, $56,000; (b) building and equipment depreciation expense amounts, $30,000 and $6,000, respectively; (c) equipment that cost $27,000 with accumulated depreciation of $25,000 sold at a gain of $10,600; (d) equipment purchases, $25,000; (e) patent amortization, $6,000; purchase of patent, $2,000; (f) funds borrowed by issuing notes payable, $50,000; notes payable repaid, $30,000; (g) land and building purchased for $324,000 by signing a mortgage for the total cost; (h) 3,000 shares of $20 par value common stock issued for a total of $100,000; and (i) paid cash dividend, $18,000.

REQUIRED

1. Using the indirect method, prepare a statement of cash flows for Sharma Fabrics.
2. Why did Sharma Fabrics have an increase in cash of $134,400 when it recorded net income of only $56,000? Discuss and interpret. (USER INSIGHT)
3. Compute and assess cash flow yield and free cash flow for 2011. (*Note:* Round cash flow yield to one decimal place.) What is your assessment of Sharma's ability to generate sufficient cash flow? (RATIO)

LO 2, 3, 4, 5 — CASH FLOW

Statement of Cash Flows: Indirect Method

✔ Net cash flows from operating activities: ($106,000); from investing activities: $34,000; from financing activities: $24,000

P 9. The comparative balance sheets for Karidis Ceramics, Inc., for December 31, 2012 and 2011 follow.

Karidis Ceramics, Inc.
Comparative Balance Sheets
December 31, 2012 and 2011

	2012	2011
Assets		
Cash	$ 257,600	$ 305,600
Accounts receivable (net)	738,800	758,800
Inventory	960,000	800,000
Prepaid expenses	14,800	26,800
Long-term investments	440,000	440,000
Land	361,200	321,200
Building	1,200,000	920,000
Accumulated depreciation–building	(240,000)	(160,000)
Equipment	480,000	480,000
Accumulated depreciation–equipment	(116,000)	(56,000)
Intangible assets	20,000	40,000
Total assets	$4,116,400	$3,876,400
Liabilities and Stockholders' Equity		
Accounts payable	$ 470,800	$ 660,800
Notes payable (current)	40,000	160,000
Accrued liabilities	10,800	20,800

(continued)

	2012	2011
Mortgage payable	$1,080,000	$ 800,000
Bonds payable	1,000,000	760,000
Common stock	1,300,000	1,300,000
Additional paid-in capital	80,000	80,000
Retained earnings	254,800	194,800
Treasury stock	(120,000)	(100,000)
Total liabilities and stockholders' equity	$4,116,400	$3,876,400

During 2012, the company had net income of $96,000 and building and equipment depreciation expenses of $80,000 and $60,000, respectively. It amortized intangible assets in the amount of $20,000; purchased investments for $116,000; sold investments for $150,000, on which it recorded a gain of $34,000; issued $240,000 of long-term bonds at face value; purchased land and a warehouse through a $320,000 mortgage; paid $40,000 to reduce the mortgage; borrowed $60,000 by issuing notes payable; repaid notes payable in the amount of $180,000; declared and paid cash dividends in the amount of $36,000; and purchased treasury stock in the amount of $20,000.

REQUIRED

1. Using the indirect method, prepare a statement of cash flows for Karidis Ceramics.
2. USER INSIGHT ▶ Why did Karidis Ceramics experience a decrease in cash in a year in which it had a net income of $96,000? Discuss and interpret.
3.  Compute and assess cash flow yield and free cash flow for 2012. (*Note:* Round cash flow yield to one decimal place.) Why is each of these measures important in assessing a company's ability to generate sufficient cash flow?

LO 1

Interpreting and Analyzing the Statement of Cash Flows

✔ Free cash flow, 2010: ($91,557); free cash flow, 2011: $145,158

P 10. Active Corporation markets sports fashions and equipment primarily to young adults through sports retailers. In 2010, it attempted to expand its market by buying a retail chain of sports stores. The comparative statements of cash flows for 2010 and 2011 for Active Corporation follow.

Active Corporation
Statement of Cash Flows
For the Years Ended December 31, 2011 and 2010
(In thousands)

	2011	2010
Cash flows from operating activities		
Net income (loss)	$ (21,545)	$ 38,015
Adjustments to reconcile net income to net cash flows from operating activities		
Depreciation	$ 35,219	$ 25,018
Loss on closure of retail outlets	35,000	—
Changes in current assets and current liabilities		
Decrease (increase) in accounts receivable	50,000	(44,803)
Decrease (increase) in inventory	60,407	(51,145)
Decrease (increase) in prepaid expenses	1,367	2,246
Increase (decrease) in accounts payable	30,579	1,266
Increase (decrease) in accrued liabilities	1,500	(2,788)
Increase (decrease) in income taxes payable	(8,300)	(6,281)
	$205,772	$ (76,487)
Net cash flows from operating activities	$184,227	$ (38,472)
Cash flows from investing activities		
Capital expenditures, net	$ (16,145)	$ (33,112)
Purchase of Retail Division, cash portion	—	(201,000)
Net cash flows from investing activities	$ (16,145)	$(234,112)

(continued)

	2011	2010
Cash flows from financing activities		
Increase (decrease) in notes payable to banks	$(123,500)	$228,400
Reduction in long-term debt	(9,238)	(10,811)
Payment of dividends	(22,924)	(19,973)
Purchase of treasury stock	—	(12,500)
Net cash flows from financing activities	$(155,662)	$185,116
Net increase (decrease) in cash	$ 12,420	$ (87,468)
Cash at beginning of year	16,032	103,500
Cash at end of year	$ 28,452	$ 16,032
Schedule of Noncash Investing and Financing Transactions		
Issue of bonds payable for retail acquisition		$ 50,000

REQUIRED

Evaluate the success of the company's strategy by answering the questions that follow.

USER INSIGHT ▶ 1. What are the primary reasons cash flows from operating activities differ from net income? What is the effect on the acquisition in 2010? What conclusions can you draw from the changes in 2011?

2. Compute free cash flow for both years. What was the total cost of the acquisition? Is the company able to finance expansion in 2010 by generating internal cash flow? What was the situation in 2011?

USER INSIGHT ▶ 3. What are the most significant financing activities in 2010? How did the company finance the acquisition? Do you think this is a good strategy? What other issues might you question in financing activities?

USER INSIGHT ▶ 4. Based on results in 2011, what actions was the company forced to take, and what is your overall assessment of the company's diversification strategy?

Cases

LO 1, 2

Conceptual Understanding: EBITDA and the Statement of Cash Flows

C 1. When **Fleetwood Enterprises, Inc.**, a large producer of recreational vehicles and manufactured housing, warned that it might not be able to generate enough cash to satisfy debt requirements and could be in default of a loan agreement, its cash flow, defined in the financial press as "EBITDA" (earnings before interest, taxes, depreciation, and amortization), was a negative $2.7 million. The company would have had to generate $17.7 million in the next accounting period to comply with the loan terms.[12] To what section of the statement of cash flows does EBITDA most closely relate? Is EBITDA a good approximation for this section of the statement of cash flows? Explain your answer, which should include an identification of the major differences between EBITDA and the section of the statement of cash flows you chose.

LO 

Interpreting Financial Reports: Anatomy of a Disaster

C 2. On October 16, 2001, Kenneth Lay, then chairman and CEO of **Enron Corporation**, announced the company's earnings for the first nine months of 2001 as follows:

> Our 26 percent increase in recurring earnings per diluted share shows the very strong results of our core wholesale and retail energy businesses and our natural gas pipelines. The continued excellent prospects in these businesses and Enron's leading market position make us very confident in our strong earnings outlook.[13]

Less than six months later, the company filed for the biggest bankruptcy in U.S. history. Its stock dropped to less than $1 per share, and a major financial scandal was underway.

Presented on the next page is Enron's statement of cash flows for the first nine months of 2001 and 2000 (restated to correct the previous accounting errors). Assume you report to an investment analyst who has asked you to analyze this statement for clues as to why the company went under.

RATIO

1. For the two time periods shown, calculate cash flow yield, cash flows to sales (Enron's revenues were $133,762 million in 2001 and $55,494 million in 2000), cash flows to assets (use total assets of $61,783 million for 2001 and $64,926 million for 2000), and free cash flow. (*Note:* Round ratios to one decimal place.)
2. Write a memorandum to the investment analyst that assesses Enron's ability to generate sufficient cash flow, taking into account the chairman's remarks, and that evaluates the company's available free cash flow, taking into account its financing activities. Identify significant changes in Enron's operating items and any special operating items that should be considered. Include your computations as an attachment.

Enron Corporation
Statement of Cash Flows
For the Nine Months Ended September 30, 2001 and 2000
(in millions)

	2001	**2000**
Cash flows from operating activities		
Reconciliation of net income to net cash provided by operating activities		
Net income	$ 225	$ 797
Cumulative effect of accounting changes, net of tax	(19)	0
Depreciation, depletion and amortization	746	617
Deferred income taxes	(134)	8
Gains on sales of non-trading assets	(49)	(135)
Investment losses	768	0
Changes in components of working capital		
Receivables	987	(3,363)
Inventories	1	339
Payables	(1,764)	2,899
Other	464	(455)
Trading investments		
Net margin deposit activity	(2,349)	541
Other trading activities	173	(555)
Other, net	198	(566)
Net cash provided by (used in) operating activities	$ (753)	$ 127
Cash flows from investing activities		
Capital expenditures	$(1,584)	$(1,539)
Equity investments	(1,172)	(858)
Proceeds from sales of non-trading investments	1,711	222
Acquisition of subsidiary stock	0	(485)
Business acquisitions, net of cash acquired	(82)	(773)
Other investing activities	(239)	(147)
Net cash used in investing activities	$(1,366)	$(3,580)
Cash flows from financing activities		
Issuance of long-term debt	$ 4,060	$ 2,725
Repayment of long-term debt	(3,903)	(579)
Net increase in short-term borrowings	2,365	1,694
Issuance of common stock	199	182
Net redemption of company-obligated preferred securities of subsidiaries	0	(95)
Dividends paid	(394)	(396)
Net (acquisition) disposition of treasury stock	(398)	354
Other financing activities	(49)	(12)
Net cash provided by financing activities	$ 1,880	$ 3,873
Increase (decrease) in cash and cash equivalents	$ (239)	$ 420
Cash and cash equivalents, beginning of period	1,240	333
Cash and cash equivalents, end of period	$ 1,001	$ 753

Source: Adapted from Enron Corporation, SEC filings, 2001.

RATIO

LO 2

Interpreting Financial Reports: Cash Flow Ratios and Free Cash Flow

C 3. The data that follow pertain to two of Japan's best-known and most successful companies, **Sony Corporation** and **Panasonic, Inc.**[14] (Numbers are in billions of yen.)

	Sony Corporation		Panasonic, Inc.	
	2009	**2008**	**2009**	**2008**
Sales	¥ 7,730	¥ 8,871	¥7,766	¥9,069
Net income	(99)	369	(379)	282
Average total assets	12,284	12,135	6,924	7,671
Net cash flows from operating activities	407	758	117	466
Dividends paid	43	25	83	69
Purchases of plant assets	496	475	522	419
Sales of plant assets	153	145	40	151

Calculate cash flow yield, cash flows to sales, cash flows to assets, and free cash flow for the two years for both Sony Corporation and Panasonic, Inc. (*Note:* Round cash flow yield to one decimal place.) Which company is better able to generate sufficient cash flow? Which company has the best year-to-year trend? Which company do you think will probably need external financing?

LO 2, 3, 4, 5

Interpreting Financial Reports: Analysis of Cash Flow Difficulty

C 4. Jerry Mak, a certified public accountant, has just given his employer Kevin Roll, the president of Roll Print Gallery, Inc., the following income statement.

Roll Print Gallery, Inc.
Income Statement
For the Year Ended December 31, 2011

Sales	$884,000
Cost of goods sold	508,000
Gross margin	$376,000
Operating expenses (including depreciation expense of $20,000)	204,000
Operating income	$172,000
Interest expense	24,000
Income before income taxes	$148,000
Income taxes expense	28,000
Net income	$120,000

After examining the statement, Roll said to Mak, "Jerry, the statement seems to be well done, but what I need to know is why I don't have enough cash to pay my bills this month. You show that I earned $120,000 in 2011, but I have only $24,000 in the bank. I know I bought a building on a mortgage and paid a cash dividend of $48,000, but what else is going on?"

Mak replied, "To answer your question, we have to look at comparative balance sheets and prepare another type of statement. Take a look at these balance sheets." The statement handed to Roll follows.

Roll Print Gallery, Inc.
Comparative Balance Sheets
December 31, 2011 and 2010

	2011	2010
Assets		
Cash	$ 24,000	$ 40,000
Accounts receivable (net)	178,000	146,000
Inventory	240,000	180,000
Prepaid expenses	10,000	14,000
Building	400,000	—
Accumulated depreciation	(20,000)	—
Total assets	$832,000	$380,000
Liabilities and Stockholders' Equity		
Accounts payable	$ 74,000	$ 96,000
Income taxes payable	6,000	4,000
Mortgage payable	400,000	—
Common stock	200,000	200,000
Retained earnings	152,000	80,000
Total liabilities and stockholders' equity	$832,000	$380,000

1. To what other statement is Mak referring? From the information given, prepare the additional statement using the indirect method.
2. Roll Print Gallery has a cash problem despite profitable operations. Explain why.

Annual Report Case: The Statement of Cash Flows

C 5. Refer to the statement of cash flows in the **CVS** annual report to answer the following questions:

1. Does CVS use the indirect method of reporting cash flows from operating activities? Other than net earnings, what are the most important factors affecting the company's cash flows from operating activities? Explain the trend of each of these factors.
2. Based on the cash flows from investing activities in 2008 and 2009, would you say that CVS is a diminishing or growing company? Explain your answer.
3. Did CVS use external financing in 2008 and 2009? If so, where did it come from?

LO 1, 2, 3, 4, 5

Comparison Case: Cash Flow Ratios

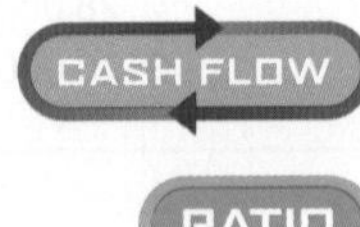

C 6. Refer to the **CVS** annual report and the financial statements of **Southwest Airlines Co.** in the Supplement to Chapter 1. Calculate for two years each company's cash flow yield, cash flows to sales, cash flows to assets, and free cash flow. (*Note:* Round cash flow yield to one decimal place.) At the end of 2007, Southwest's total assets were $16,772 million, and CVS's total assets were $54,722 million.

Discuss and compare the trends of the cash-generating ability of CVS and Southwest. Comment on each company's change in cash and cash equivalents over the two-year period.

LO 2

Ethical Dilemma: Ethics and Cash Flow Classifications

C 7. Toxic Waste Treatment, Inc., a fast-growing company that disposes of toxic wastes, has an $800,000 line of credit at its bank. One section in the credit agreement says that the ratio of cash flows from operations to interest expense must exceed 3.0. If this ratio falls below 3.0, the company must reduce the balance outstanding on its line of credit to one-half the total line if the funds borrowed against the line of credit exceed one-half of the total line.

After the end of the fiscal year, during a meeting with the president of the company, the controller made the following statement: "We will not meet the ratio requirements on our line of credit in 2012 because interest expense was $1.2 million and cash flows from operations were $3.2 million. Also, we have borrowed 100 percent of our line of credit. We do not have the cash to reduce the credit line by $400,000."

The president replied, "This is a serious situation. To pay our ongoing bills, we need our bank to increase our line of credit, not decrease it. What can we do about this?"

"Do you recall the $500,000 two-year note payable for equipment?" answered the controller. "It is now classified as 'Proceeds from Notes Payable' in cash flows provided from financing activities in the statement of cash flows. If we moved it to cash flows from operations and called it 'Increase in Payables,' it would increase cash flows from operations to $3.7 million and put us over the limit."

"Well, do it," ordered the president. "It surely doesn't make any difference where it appears on the statement. It is an increase in both places. It would be much worse for our company in the long term if we failed to meet this ratio requirement."

What is your opinion of the controller's and president's reasoning? Is the president's order ethical? Who benefits and who is harmed if the controller follows the president's order? What alternatives are available to management? What would you do?

CHAPTER 13

DECISION POINT
A User's Focus Starbucks Corporation

Formed in 1985, **Starbucks** is today a well-known specialty retailer. The company purchases and roasts whole coffee beans and sells them, along with a variety of freshly brewed coffees and other beverages and food items, in its retail shops. It also produces and sells bottled coffee drinks and a line of premium ice creams.

Like many other companies, Starbucks uses financial performance measures, primarily earnings per share, in determining compensation for top management. Earnings per share and the six financial measures used in computing the most critical financial ratios appear in the company's Financial Highlights.[1] By linking compensation to financial performance, Starbucks provides its executives with incentive to improve the company's performance. Compensation and financial performance are thus linked to increasing shareholders' value.

STARBUCKS' FINANCIAL HIGHLIGHTS
(in millions, except earnings per share)

	2009	2008	2007
Net revenues	$9,774.6	$10,383.0	$9,411.5
Net earnings	390.8	315.5	672.6
Total assets	5,576.8	5,672.6	5,343.9
Total debt	2,531.1	3,181.7	3,059.8
Total Equity	3,045.7	2,490.9	22,84.1
Cash flows from operating activities	1,389.0	1,258.7	1,331.2
Earnings per share—basic	$ 0.53	$ 0.43	$ 0.90

Questions

1. ***What standards should be used to evaluate Starbucks' performance?***
2. ***What analytical tools are available to measure performance?***
3. ***How successful has the company been in creating value for shareholders?***

Keith Dannemiller/Alamy

Financial Performance Measurement

LEARNING OBJECTIVES

LO 1 Describe the objectives, standards of comparison, sources of information, and compensation issues in measuring financial performance. (pp. 586–590)

LO 2 Define *quality of earnings* and identify the factors that affect quality of earnings. (pp. 590–594)

LO 3 Apply horizontal analysis, trend analysis, vertical analysis, and ratio analysis to financial statements. (pp. 594–600)

LO 4 Apply financial ratio analysis in a comprehensive evaluation of a company's financial performance. (pp. 600–611)

The ultimate purpose of financial reporting is to enable managers, creditors, investors, and other interested parties to evaluate a company's financial performance. In earlier chapters, we discussed the various measures used in assessing a company's financial performance; here, we provide a comprehensive summary of those measures. Because these measures play a key role in executive compensation, there is always the risk that they will be manipulated. Users of financial statements therefore need to be familiar with the analytical tools and techniques used in performance measurement and the assumptions that underlie them.

FOCUS ON FINANCIAL STATEMENTS

INCOME STATEMENT
Revenues
− Expenses
= Net Income

STATEMENT OF RETAINED EARNINGS
Opening Balance
+ Net Income
− Dividends
= Retained Earnings

BALANCE SHEET
Assets | Liabilities
Equity
A = L + E

STATEMENT OF CASH FLOWS
Operating Activities
+ Investing Activities
+ Financing Activities
= Change in Cash
+ Starting Balance
= Ending Cash Balance

Users of financial statements assess a company's performance by comparing categories within and across the statements.

FOUNDATIONS OF FINANCIAL PERFORMANCE MEASUREMENT

LO 1 Describe the objectives, standards of comparison, sources of information, and compensation issues in measuring financial performance.

Financial performance measurement, also called *financial statement analysis*, uses all the techniques available to show how important items in a company's financial statements relate to the company's financial objectives. Persons with a strong interest in measuring a company's financial performance fall into two groups:

- A company's top managers, who set and strive to achieve financial performance objectives; middle-level managers of business processes; and lower-level employees who own stock in the company
- Creditors and investors, as well as customers who have cooperative agreements with the company

Financial Performance Measurement: Management's Objectives

All the plans that management formulates to achieve a company's goals must eventually be stated in terms of financial objectives and related performance objectives. A complete financial plan should have objectives in all of the following categories:[2]

Financial Objective	Performance Objective
Profitability	To earn a satisfactory net income
Total asset management	To use all of the company's assets in a way that maximizes revenues while minimizing investment
Liquidity	To be able to pay bills when due and meet unexpected needs for cash
Financial risk	To use debt effectively without jeopardizing the company's future
Operating asset management	To use current assets and current liabilities in a way that supports growth in revenues with minimum investment

Management's main responsibility is to carry out its plan to achieve the company's financial objectives. This requires constant monitoring of key financial performance measures for each objective listed above, determining the cause of any deviations from the measures, and proposing ways of correcting the deviations. Management compares actual performance with the key performance measures in monthly, quarterly, and annual reports. The information in management's annual reports provides data for long-term trend analyses.

Management Compensation

As we noted earlier, one intent of the Sarbanes-Oxley Act of 2002 was to strengthen the corporate governance of public corporations. Under this act, a public corporation's board of directors must establish a **compensation committee** made up of independent directors to determine how the company's top executives will be compensated. The company must disclose the components of compensation and the criteria it uses to remunerate top executives in documents that it files with the SEC.

The components of **Starbucks**' compensation of executive officers are typical of those used by many companies. They include the following:

- Annual base salary
- Incentive bonuses
- Stock option awards[3]

Incentive bonuses are based on financial performance measures that the compensation committee identifies as important to the company's long-term success, especially in terms of increasing the value of shareholders' investments in the company. Many companies tie incentive bonuses to measures like growth in revenues and return on assets or return on equity. Starbucks bases 80 percent of its incentive bonus on an "earnings per share target approved by the compensation committee" and 20 percent on the executive's "specific individual performance." The Financial Highlights at the beginning of the chapter show the variation in Starbucks' earnings per share.

Stock option awards are usually based on how well the company is achieving its long-term strategic goals. In 2009, a challenging year for Starbucks, the company's CEO received a base salary of $643,954 and an incentive bonus of $1,000,000. He also received a stock option award of 9,530,162 shares of common stock.[4]

From one vantage point, earnings per share is a "bottom-line" number that encompasses all the other performance measures. However, using a single performance measure as the basis for determining compensation has the potential of leading to practices that are not in the best interests of a company or its stockholders. For instance, management could boost earnings per share by reducing the number of shares outstanding (the denominator in the earnings per share equation) while not improving earnings. It could accomplish this by using cash to repurchase shares of the company's stock (treasury stock), rather than investing the cash in more profitable operations.

As you study the comprehensive financial analysis of Starbucks later in this chapter, consider that knowledge of performance measurement not only is important for evaluating a company, but also leads to an understanding of the criteria by which a board of directors evaluates and compensates management.

Financial Performance Measurement: Creditors' and Investors' Objectives

Creditors and investors use financial performance evaluation to judge a company's past performance and present position. They also use it to assess a company's future potential and the risk connected with acting on that potential.

- *Investors* focus on a company's potential earnings ability because that ability will affect the market price of the company's stock and the amount of dividends the company will pay.
- *Creditors* focus on a company's potential debt-paying ability.

Past performance is often a good indicator of future performance. To evaluate a company's past performance, creditors and investors look at trends in past sales, expenses, net income, cash flow, and return on investment. To evaluate its current position, they look at its assets, liabilities, cash position, debt in relation to equity, and levels of inventories and receivables. Knowing a company's past performance and current position can be important in judging its future potential and the risk involved in making an investment or loan. The risk depends on how easy it is to predict future profitability or liquidity. If an investor can predict with confidence that a company's earnings per share will be between $2.50 and $2.60 in the next year, the investment is less risky than if the earnings per share are expected to fall between $2.00 and $3.00. For instance, the earnings of an electric utility may be more predictable within a tighter range and therefore less risky than a small Internet company whose earnings can be predicted only within a broader range.

In return for taking a greater risk, investors often look for a higher expected return (an increase in market price and/or dividends). Creditors who take a greater risk by advancing funds to a company may demand a higher interest rate and more assurance of repayment (e.g., a secured loan). The higher interest rate reimburses them for assuming the higher risk.

Standards of Comparison

When analyzing financial statements, decision makers must judge whether the relationships they find in the statements are favorable or unfavorable. Three standards of comparison that they commonly use are rule-of-thumb measures, a company's past performance, and industry norms.

Rule-of-Thumb Measures Many financial analysts, investors, and lenders apply general standards, or rule-of-thumb measures, to key financial ratios. For example, in its *Industry Norms and Key Business Ratios,* the credit-rating firm of **Dun & Bradstreet** offers the following rules of thumb:

- *Current debt to tangible net worth*: A business is usually in trouble when this relationship exceeds 80 percent.
- *Inventory to net working capital*: Ordinarily, this relationship should not exceed 80 percent.

Past Performance Comparing financial measures or ratios of the same company over time is an improvement over using rule-of-thumb measures. Such a comparison gives the analyst some basis for judging whether the measure or ratio is getting better or worse. Thus, it may be helpful in showing future trends. However, such projections must be made with care. Trends reverse over time, and a company's needs may change. For example, even if a company improves its return on investment from 3 percent in one year to 4 percent the next year, the 4 percent return may not be adequate for the company's current needs. In addition, using a company's past performance as a standard of comparison is not helpful in judging its performance relative to that of other companies.

Industry Norms Using industry norms as a standard of comparison overcomes some of the limitations of comparing a company's measures or ratios over time. Industry norms show how a company compares with other companies in the same industry. For example, if companies in a particular industry have an average rate of return on investment of 8 percent, a 3 or 4 percent rate of return is probably inadequate. Using industry norms as standards has three limitations:

- *Comparability:* Companies in the same industry may not be strictly comparable. Consider two companies in the oil industry. One purchases oil products and markets them through service stations. The other, an international company, discovers, produces, refines, and markets its own oil products. Because of the disparity in their operations, these two companies cannot be directly compared.
- *Accounting differences:* Companies in the same industry with similar operations may not use the same accounting procedures. For example, they may use different methods of valuing inventories and of depreciating assets.
- *Diversity:* **Diversified companies** are large companies that have multiple segments and operate in more than one industry (also called *conglomerates*). They may not be comparable to any other company.

The FASB provides a partial solution to the limitation posed by diversified companies. It requires a diversified company to report profit or loss, certain revenue and expense items, and assets for each of its segments. Segment information may be reported for operations in different industries

The FASB requires diversified companies like Goodyear to report financial information for each of their segments. Goodyear has four segments: North American Tire; Europe, Middle East, and Africa Tire; Latin American Tire; and Asia Pacific Tire.

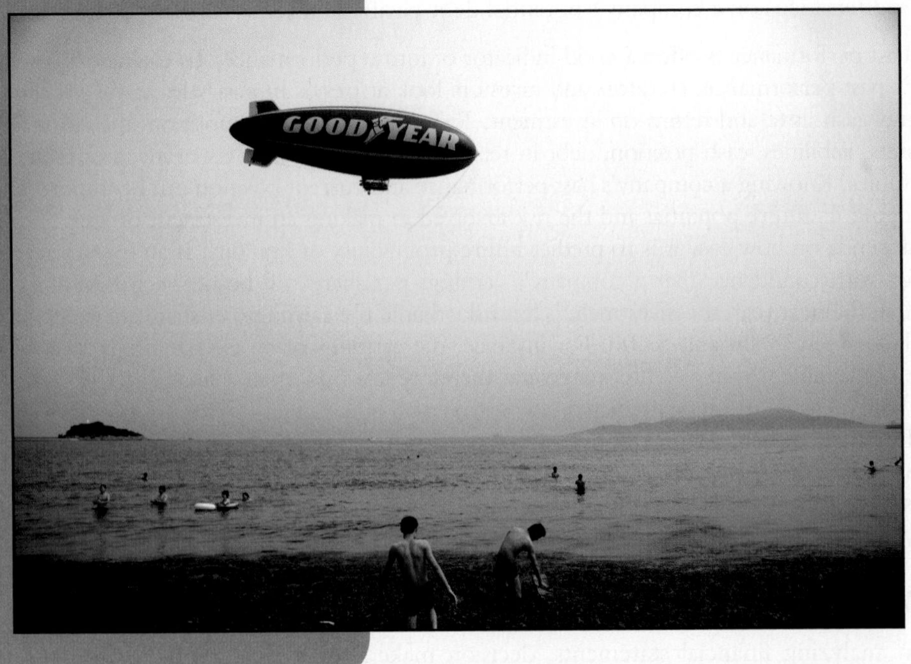

M. Scott Brauer/Alamy

EXHIBIT 13.1
Selected Segment Information for Goodyear Tire & Rubber Company

(in millions)	2009	2008	2007
Sales			
North American Tire	$ 6,977	$ 8,255	$ 8,862
Europe, Middle East, and Africa Tire	5,801	7,316	7,217
Latin American Tire	1,814	2,088	1,872
Asia Pacific Tire	1,709	1,829	1,693
Net Sales	**$16,301**	**$19,488**	**$19,644**
Segment Operating Income (Loss)			
North American Tire	$ (305)	$ (156)	$ 139
Europe, Middle East, and Africa Tire	166	425	582
Latin American Tire	301	367	359
Asia Pacific Tire	210	168	150
Total Segment Operating Income	**$ 372**	**$ 804**	**$ 1,230**
Assets			
North American Tire	$ 4,836	$ 5,514	$ 5,307
Europe, Middle East, and Africa Tire	5,144	5,707	6,020
Latin American Tire	1,672	1,278	1,265
Asia Pacific Tire	1,548	1,408	1,394
Total Segment Assets	**$13,200**	**$13,907**	**$13,986**

Sources: Goodyear Tire & Rubber Company, *Annual Report*, 2009, and *Annual Report*, 2008.

STUDY NOTE: *Each segment of a diversified company represents an investment that the home office or parent company evaluates and reviews frequently.*

or different geographical areas or for major customers.[5] Exhibit 13.1 shows how **Goodyear Tire & Rubber Company** reports data on sales, income, and assets for its tire products segments. These data allow the analyst to compute important measures of profitability, such as profit margin, asset turnover, and return on assets, for each segment and to compare them with the industry norms.

Despite these limitations, if little information about a company's past performance is available, industry norms probably offer the best available standards for judging current performance—as long as they are used with care.

Sources of Information

The major sources of information about public corporations are reports published by the corporations themselves, reports filed with the SEC, business periodicals, and credit and investment advisory services.

- *Reports published by a corporation:* A public corporation's annual report is an important source of financial information. Most public corporations also publish **interim financial statements** each quarter and sometimes each month. These reports, which present limited information in the form of condensed financial statements, are not subject to a full audit by an independent auditor. The financial community watches interim statements closely for early signs of change in a company's earnings trend.
- *Reports filed with the Securities and Exchange Commission (SEC):* Public corporations in the United States must file annual reports (**Form 10-K**), quarterly reports (**Form 10-Q**), and current reports (**Form 8-K**) with the SEC. If they have more than $10 million in assets and more than 500 shareholders, they must file these reports electronically at *www.sec.gov/edgar.shtml*, where anyone can access them free of charge.

- *Business periodicals and credit and investment advisory services:* Financial analysts must keep up with current events in the financial world. For example, a leading source of financial news is *The Wall Street Journal.* It is the most complete financial newspaper in the United States and is published every business day. Credit and investment advisory services such as **Moody's Investor Services**, **Standard & Poor**'s, and Dun & Bradstreet provide useful information including details about a company's financial history, industry data, and credit ratings.

Stop & Apply

Identify each of the following as (a) an objective of financial statement analysis, (b) a standard for financial statement analysis, (c) a source of information for financial statement analysis, or (d) an executive compensation issue:

1. A company's past performance
2. Investment advisory services
3. Assessment of a company's future potential
4. Incentive bonuses
5. Industry norms
6. Annual report
7. Creating shareholders' value
8. Form 10-K

SOLUTION

1. b
2. c
3. a
4. d
5. b
6. c
7. d
8. c

iStock Photo

EVALUATING QUALITY OF EARNINGS

Define *quality of earnings* and identify the factors that affect quality of earnings. LO 2

Net income (net earnings) is the measure most commonly used to evaluate a company's profitability. In fact, a survey of 2,000 members of the Association for Investment Management and Research indicated that the two important measures in evaluating common stocks were expected changes in earnings per share and return on assets.[6] Net income is a key component of both measures.

STUDY NOTE: *Although companies in the same industry may have comparable earnings, their quality of earnings may not be comparable. To assess the quality of a company's reported earnings, you must know the estimates and methods it uses to compute income.*

Because of the importance of net income, or the "bottom line," in measuring a company's prospects, there is significant interest in evaluating the quality of the net income figure, or the **quality of earnings**. The quality of a company's earnings refers to the substance of earnings and their sustainability into future accounting periods. Quality of earnings is affected by the following:

- Accounting methods
- Accounting estimates
- One-time items

Accounting Methods

The accounting methods a firm uses affect its operating income. Generally accepted accounting methods include uncollectible receivable methods (percentage of net sales and aging of accounts receivable), inventory methods (LIFO, FIFO, and average cost), depreciation methods (accelerated, production, and straight-line), and revenue recognition methods. All these methods are designed to match revenues and expenses. However, the expenses are estimates, and the period or periods benefited cannot be demonstrated conclusively. In practice, it is hard to justify one method of estimation over another.

Different accounting methods have different effects on net income. Some methods are more conservative than others because they tend to produce a lower net income in the current period. For example, suppose that Purdy Company and Isakov Company have similar operations, but Purdy uses FIFO for inventory costing and the straight-line

EXHIBIT 13.2
Effects of Different Accounting Methods

	Purdy Company (FIFO and SL)	*Isakov Company (LIFO and DDB)*
Net sales	$462,500	$462,500
Cost of goods available for sale	$200,000	$200,000
Less ending inventory	30,000	25,000
Cost of goods sold	$170,000	$175,000
Gross margin	$292,500	$287,500
Less depreciation expense	$ 20,000	$ 40,000
Less other expenses	85,000	85,000
Total operating expenses	$105,000	$125,000
Income from continuing operations before income taxes	$187,500	$162,500

(SL) method for computing depreciation, whereas Isakov uses LIFO for inventory costing and the double-declining-balance (DDB) method for computing depreciation. The income statements of the two companies might appear as shown in Exhibit 13.2.

Impact of Different Accounting Methods on Income The income from continuing operations before income taxes for the firm that uses LIFO and DDB is lower because in periods of rising prices, the LIFO method produces a higher cost of goods sold, and in the early years of an asset's useful life, accelerated depreciation yields a higher depreciation expense. The result is lower operating income. However, future operating income should be higher.

Impact of Different Accounting Methods on Cash Flows Although the choice of accounting method does not affect cash flows except for possible differences in income taxes, the $25,000 difference in operating income stems solely from the choice of accounting methods. Estimates of the useful lives and residual values of plant assets could lead to an even greater difference. In practice, of course, differences in net income occur for many reasons, but the user of financial statements must be aware of the discrepancies that can occur as a result of the accounting methods used in preparing the statements. In general, an accounting method or estimate that results in lower current earnings produces a better quality of operating income.

Impact of Different Accounting Methods on Financial Statements The latitude that companies have in their choice of accounting methods could cause problems in the interpretation of financial statements were it not for the conventions of full disclosure and consistency. As noted in an earlier chapter, full disclosure requires management to explain significant accounting policies used in preparing the financial statements in a note to the statement. For instance, in a note to its financial statements, **Starbucks** discloses that it uses the straight-line method for depreciation of property, plant, and equipment.[7] Consistency requires that the same accounting procedures be used from year to year. If a company changes its accounting procedure, it must explain the nature of the change and its monetary effect in a note to its financial statements.

Accounting Estimates

Users of financial statements also need to be aware of the impact that accounting estimates have on reported income. As you know, to comply with the matching rule, accountants must assign revenues and expenses to the periods in which they occur. If they cannot establish a direct relationship between revenues and expenses, they systematically allocate the expenses among the accounting periods that benefit from them, and in doing so, they must make estimates and exercise judgment. An accounting estimate should be based on realistic assumptions, but there is latitude in making the estimate, and the final judgment will affect the net income that appears on a company's income statement.

For example, when a company acquires an asset, the accountant must estimate the asset's useful life. Technological obsolescence could shorten the asset's expected useful life, and regular maintenance and repairs could lengthen it. Although the actual useful life cannot be known with certainty until some future date, the accountant's estimate of it affects both current and future operating income. Other areas that require accounting estimates include the residual value of assets, uncollectible accounts receivable, sales returns, total units of production, total recoverable units of natural resources, amortization periods, warranty claims, and environmental cleanup costs.

The importance of accounting estimates depends on the industry in which a firm operates. For example, estimated uncollectible receivables for a credit card firm such as **American Express** or for a financial services firm such as **Bank of America** can have a material impact on earnings, but estimated useful life may be less important because depreciable assets represent a small percentage of the firm's total assets. **Starbucks** has few receivables, but it has major investments in depreciable assets. Thus, estimates of useful life and residual value are more important to Starbucks than an estimate of uncollectible accounts receivable. The company depreciates its equipment over 2 to 7 years and its buildings over 30 to 40 years.[8]

One-Time Items

If earnings increase because of one-time items, that portion of earnings will not be sustained in the future. In contrast, one-time decreases in earnings may not indicate that earnings will be poor in the future. Examples of one-time items include the following:

- Gains and losses
- Write-downs and restructurings
- Nonoperating items

Because management has choices in the content and positioning of these income statement components, there is a potential for managing earnings to achieve specific income targets. It is therefore critical for users of income statements to understand these factors and take them into consideration when evaluating a company's performance.

Exhibit 13.3 shows the components of a typical corporate income statement. Net income or loss (the "bottom line" of the income statement) includes all revenues,

EXHIBIT 13.3
Corporate Income Statement

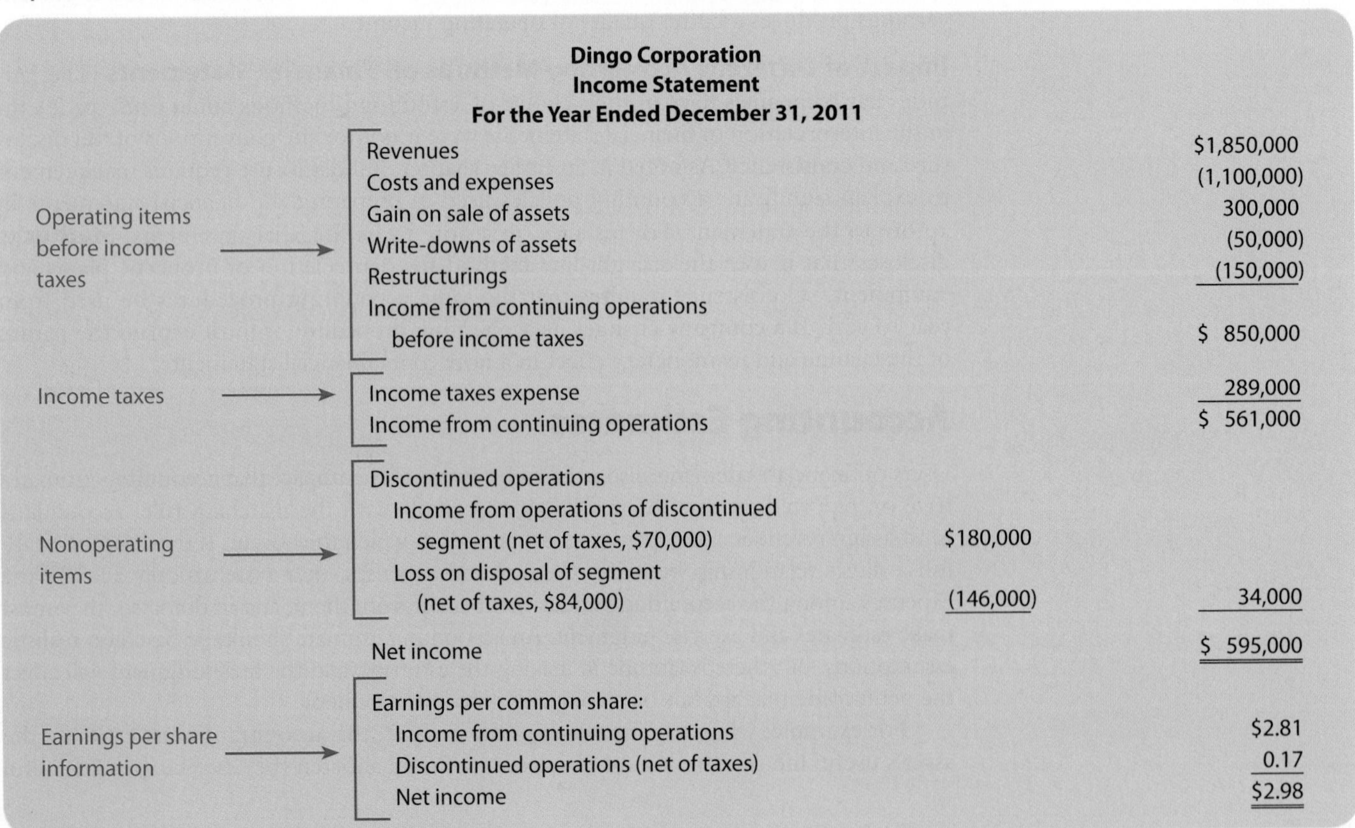

Dingo Corporation
Income Statement
For the Year Ended December 31, 2011

Operating items before income taxes	Revenues		$1,850,000
	Costs and expenses		(1,100,000)
	Gain on sale of assets		300,000
	Write-downs of assets		(50,000)
	Restructurings		(150,000)
	Income from continuing operations before income taxes		$ 850,000
Income taxes	Income taxes expense		289,000
	Income from continuing operations		$ 561,000
Nonoperating items	Discontinued operations		
	Income from operations of discontinued segment (net of taxes, $70,000)	$180,000	
	Loss on disposal of segment (net of taxes, $84,000)	(146,000)	34,000
	Net income		$ 595,000
Earnings per share information	Earnings per common share:		
	Income from continuing operations		$2.81
	Discontinued operations (net of taxes)		0.17
	Net income		$2.98

expenses, gains, and losses over the accounting period. When a company has both continuing and discontinued operations, the operating income section is called *income from continuing operations.* Income from continuing operations before income taxes may include gains or losses on the sale of assets, write-downs, and restructurings.

As you can see in Exhibit 13.3, the section of a corporate income statement that follows income taxes may contain such nonoperating items as **discontinued operations**—segments that are no longer part of a company's operations—and gains (or losses) on the sale or disposal of these segments. Another item that may appear in this section is the write-off of goodwill when its value has been impaired. Earnings per share information appears at the bottom of the statement

Gains and Losses When a company sells or otherwise disposes of operating assets or marketable securities, a gain or loss generally results. Although these gains or losses appear in the operating section of the income statement, they usually represent one-time events. They are not sustainable, ongoing operations, and management often has some choice as to their timing. Thus, from an analyst's point of view, they should be ignored when considering operating income.

Write-Downs and Restructurings When management decides that an asset is no longer of value to the company, a write-down or restructuring occurs.

- A **write-down**, also called a *write-off,* is a reduction in the value of an asset below its carrying value on the balance sheet.
- A **restructuring** is the estimated cost of a change in a company's operations. It usually involves the closing of facilities and the laying off of personnel.

Both write-downs and restructurings reduce current operating income and boost future income by shifting future costs to the current accounting period. They are often an indication of poor management decisions in the past, such as paying too much for the assets of another company or making operational changes that do not work out. Companies sometimes take all possible losses in the current year so that future years will be "clean" of these costs. Such "big baths," as they are called, commonly occur when a company is having a bad year. They also often occur in years when there is a change in management. The new management takes a "big bath" in the current year so it can show improved results in future years.

In a recent year, 46 percent of 500 large companies had write-downs of tangible assets, and 45 percent had restructurings. Another 31 percent had write-downs or charges related to intangible assets, often involving goodwill. In 2009, Starbucks had restructuring costs of $332.4 million (compared with net income of only $390.8 million) in connection with the closing of a number of its stores.[9]

Nonoperating Items The nonoperating items that appear on the income statement include discontinued operations and gains or losses on the sale or disposal of these segments. These items can significantly affect net income. For example, in Exhibit 13.3, earnings per common share for income from continuing operations are $2.81, but when

Focus on Business Practice

Beware of the "Bottom Line!"

In the second quarter of 2007, **McDonald's** posted its second-ever loss: $711.7 million. Should this have been cause for concern? The answer is no because the loss resulted from a one-time noncash impairment (decline in value) of $1.6 billion related to investments in Latin America; the company was actually in a period of rapidly growing revenues and profits. In another example, **Campbell Soup** showed unrealistically positive results. Its income jumped by 31 percent due to a tax settlement and an accounting restatement. Without these items, its revenue and income would have been up less than 1 percent; soup sales—its main product—actually dropped by 6 percent. The lesson to be learned is to look beyond the "bottom line" to the components of the income statement when evaluating a company's performance.[10]

iStock Photo

all the nonoperating items are taken into consideration, net income per share is $2.98. To make it easier to evaluate a company's ongoing operations, generally accepted accounting principles require that gains and losses from discontinued operations be reported separately on the income statement.

In Exhibit 13.3 (p. 592), the disclosure of discontinued operations has two parts:

- One part shows that after the decision to discontinue, the income from operations of the disposed segment was $180,000 (net of $70,000 taxes).
- The other part shows that the loss from the disposal of the segment was $146,000 (net of $84,000 tax savings). (The computation of the gains or losses involved in discontinued operations is covered in more advanced accounting courses.)

Stop & Apply

The following data apply to Bocian, Inc.: net sales, $180,000; cost of goods sold, $87,500; loss from discontinued operations (net of income tax benefit of $17,500), $50,000; loss on disposal of discontinued operations (net of income tax benefit of $4,000), $12,500; operating expenses, $32,500; income taxes expense on continuing operations, $18,000. From this information, prepare the company's income statement for the year ended December 31, 2011. (*Note:* Ignore earnings per share information.)

SOLUTION

Bocian, Inc.
Income Statement
For the Year Ended December 31, 2011

Net sales		$180,000
Cost of goods sold		87,500
Gross margin		$ 92,500
Operating expenses		32,500
Income from continuing operations before income taxes		$ 60,000
Income taxes expense		18,000
Income from continuing operations		$ 42,000
Discontinued operations		
Loss from discontinued operations (net of income tax benefit of $17,500)	$(50,000)	
Loss on disposal of discontinued operations (net of income tax benefit of $4,000)	(12,500)	(62,500)
Net Loss		$ (20,500)

iStock Photo

TOOLS AND TECHNIQUES OF FINANCIAL ANALYSIS

LO3 Apply horizontal analysis, trend analysis, vertical analysis, and ratio analysis to financial statements.

To gain insight into a company's financial performance, one must look beyond the individual numbers to the relationship between the numbers and their change from one period to another. The tools of financial analysis—horizontal analysis, trend analysis, vertical analysis, and ratio analysis—are intended to show these relationships and changes. To illustrate how these tools are used, we devote the rest of this chapter to a comprehensive financial analysis of **Starbucks Corporation**.

Horizontal Analysis

STUDY NOTE: *It is important to ascertain the base amount used when a percentage describes an item. For example, inventory may be 50 percent of total current assets but only 10 percent of total assets.*

Comparative financial statements provide financial information for the current year and the previous year. To gain insight into year-to-year changes, analysts use **horizontal analysis**, in which changes from the previous year to the current year are computed in both dollar amounts and percentages. The percentage change relates the size of the change to the size of the dollar amounts involved.

Exhibits 13.4 and 13.5 (p. 596) present **Starbucks Corporation**'s comparative balance sheets and income statements and show both the dollar and percentage changes. The percentage change is computed as follows:

$$\text{Percentage Change} = 100 \times \left(\frac{\text{Amount of Change}}{\text{Base Year Amount}}\right)$$

The **base year** is the first year considered in any set of data. For example, when comparing data for 2008 and 2009, 2008 is the base year. As the balance sheets in Exhibit 13.4 show, between 2008 and 2009, Starbucks' total current assets increased by $287.8 million, from $1,748.0 million to $2,035.8 million, or by 16.5 percent. This is computed as follows:

$$\text{Percentage Change} = 100 \times \left(\frac{\$287.8\text{ Million}}{\$1,748.0\text{ Million}}\right) = 16.5\%$$

EXHIBIT 13.4
Comparative Balance Sheets with Horizontal Analysis

Starbucks Corporation
Consolidated Balance Sheets
September 27, 2009, and September 28, 2008

(Dollar amounts in millions)	2009	2008	Increase (Decrease) Amount	Increase (Decrease) Percentage
	Assets			
Current assets:				
Cash and cash equivalents	$ 599.8	$ 269.8	$ 330.0	122.3
Short-term investments	66.3	52.5	13.8	26.3
Accounts receivable, net	271.0	329.5	(58.5)	(17.8)
Inventories	664.9	692.8	(27.9)	(4.0)
Prepaid expenses and other current assets	147.2	169.2	(22.0)	(13.0)
Deferred income taxes, net	286.6	234.2	52.4	22.4
Total current assets	$2,035.8	$1,748.0	$ 287.8	16.5
Property, plant, and equipment, net	2,536.4	2,956.4	(420.0)	(14.2)
Long-term investments	423.5	374.0	49.5	13.2
Other assets	253.8	261.1	(7.3)	(2.8)
Goodwill	259.1	266.5	(7.4)	(2.8)
Other intangible assets	68.2	66.6	1.6	2.4
Total assets	$5,576.8	$5,672.6	$ (95.8)	(1.7)
	Liabilities and Shareholders' Equity			
Current liabilities:				
Commercial paper and short-term borrowings	$ —	$ 713.0	$(713.0)	100.0
Accounts payable	267.1	324.9	(57.8)	(17.8)
Accrued compensation and related costs	307.5	253.6	53.9	21.3
Accrued occupancy costs	188.1	136.1	52.0	38.2
Accrued taxes	127.8	76.1	51.7	67.9
Other accrued expenses	301.6	316.9	(15.3)	(4.8)
Deferred revenue	388.7	368.4	20.3	5.5
Current portion of long-term debt	0.2	0.7	(0.5)	(71.4)
Total current liabilities	$1,581.0	$2,189.7	$ 608.7	27.8
Long-term debt and other liabilities	950.1	992.0	(41.9)	(4.2)
Shareholders' equity	3,045.7	2,490.9	554.8	22.3
Total liabilities and shareholders' equity	$5,576.8	$5,672.6	$ (95.8)	(1.7)

Source: Starbucks Corporation, *Form 10-K*, 2009.

EXHIBIT 13.5
Comparative Income Statements with Horizontal Analysis

Starbucks Corporation
Consolidated Income Statements
For the Years Ended September 27, 2009, and September 28, 2008

(Dollar amounts in millions, except per share amounts)	2009	2008	Increase (Decrease) Amount	Increase (Decrease) Percentage
Net revenues	$9,774.6	$10,383.0	$(608.4)	(5.9)
Cost of sales, including occupancy costs	4,324.9	4,645.3	(320.4)	(6.9)
Gross margin	$5,449.7	$ 5,737.7	$(288.0)	(5.0)
Operating expenses				
Store operating expenses	$3,425.1	$ 3,745.1	$(320.0)	(8.5)
Other operating expenses	264.4	330.1	(65.7)	(19.9)
Depreciation and amortization expenses	534.7	549.3	(14.6)	(2.7)
General and administrative expenses	453.0	456.0	(3.0)	(0.7)
Restructuring charges	332.4	266.9	65.5	24.5
Total operating expenses	$5,009.6	$ 5,347.4	$(337.8)	(6.3)
Operating income	$ 440.1	$ 390.3	$ 49.8	12.8
Interest income and other, net	158.2	122.6	35.6	29.0
Interest expense	39.1	53.4	(14.3)	(26.8)
Income before taxes	$ 559.2	$ 459.5	$ 99.7	21.7
Provision for income taxes	168.4	144.0	24.4	16.9
Net income	$ 390.8	$ 315.5	$ 75.3	23.9
Per common share:				
Net income per common share—basic	$ 0.53	$ 0.43	$ 0.1	23.3
Net income per common share—diluted	$ 0.52	$ 0.43	$ 0.09	20.9
Shares used in calculation of net income per common share—basic	738.7	731.5	7.2	1.0
Shares used in calculation of net income per common share—diluted	745.9	741.7	4.2	0.6

Source: Starbucks Corporation, *Form 10-K*, 2009.

When examining such changes, it is important to consider both the dollar amount of the change and the percentage change in each component. For example, the difference between the percentage increase in short-term investments (26.3 percent) and deferred income taxes (22.4 percent) is not great. However, the dollar increase in deferred income taxes is more than three times the dollar increase in short-term investments ($52.4 million vs. $13.8 million). Thus, even though the percentage changes are not very different, deferred income taxes require much more cash than short-term investments.

Starbucks' balance sheets for 2008 and 2009 also show a slight decrease in total assets of $95.8 million, or 1.7 percent. In addition, they show that stockholders' equity increased by $554.8 million, or 22.3 percent. All of this indicates that Starbucks was holding its own after the economic downturn in 2008.

Starbucks' income statements in Exhibit 13.5 show that net revenues decreased by $608.4 million, or 5.9 percent, while gross margin decreased by $288.0 million, or 5.0 percent. This indicates that cost of sales fell faster than net revenues. In fact, cost of sales decreased by 6.9 percent compared with the 5.9 percent decrease in net revenues.

Starbucks' total operating expenses decreased by $337.8 million, or 6.3 percent, faster than the 5.9 percent decrease in net revenues. As a result, operating income increased by $49.8 million, or 12.8 percent, and net income increased by $75.3 million, or 23.9 percent. The primary reason for the increases in operating income and net income is that total operating expenses decreased at a faster rate (6.3 percent) than net revenues (5.9 percent).

Trend Analysis

Trend analysis is a variation of horizontal analysis. With this tool, the analyst calculates percentage changes for several successive years instead of for just two years. Because of its long-term view, trend analysis can highlight basic changes in the nature of a business.

STUDY NOTE: To reflect the general five-year economic cycle of the U.S. economy, trend analysis usually covers a five-year period.

In addition to presenting comparative financial statements, many companies present a summary of key data for five or more years. Exhibit 13.6 shows a trend analysis of **Starbucks'** five-year summary of net revenues and operating income.

EXHIBIT 13.6
Trend Analysis

Starbucks Corporation
Net Revenues and Operating Income
Trend Analysis

	2009	2008	2007	2006	2005
Dollar values (in millions)					
Net revenues	$9,774.6	$10,383.0	$9,411.5	$7,786.9	$6,369.3
Operating income	440.1	390.3	945.9	800.0	703.9
Trend analysis (in percentages)					
Net revenues	153.5	163.0	147.8	122.3	100.0
Operating income	62.5	55.4	134.4	113.7	100.0

Source: Starbucks Corporation, *Form 10-K*, 2009.

Trend analysis uses an **index number** to show changes in related items over time. For an index number, the base year is set at 100 percent. Other years are measured in relation to that amount. For example, the 2009 index for Starbucks' net revenues is computed as follows (dollar amounts are in millions):

$$\text{Index} = 100 \times \left(\frac{\text{Index Year Amount}}{\text{Base Year Amount}}\right)$$

$$= 100 \times \left(\frac{\$9{,}774.6}{\$6{,}369.3}\right) = 153.5\%$$

The trend analysis in Exhibit 13.6 shows worrisome opposing trends. Although Starbucks' net revenues increased over the five-year period with a peak in 2008, operating income peaked a year earlier in 2007 and then declined below the 2005 level. Management is addressing this situation by closing unprofitable stores and controlling costs. Exhibit 13.7 illustrates these trends.

EXHIBIT 13.7
Graph of Trend Analysis Shown in Exhibit 13.6

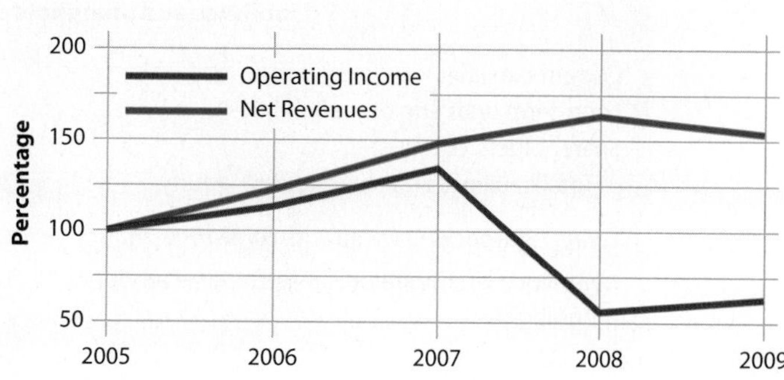

EXHIBIT 13.8
Common-Size Balance Sheets Presented Graphically

2009* **2008**

Assets = 100% **Liabilities and Shareholders' Equity = 100%**

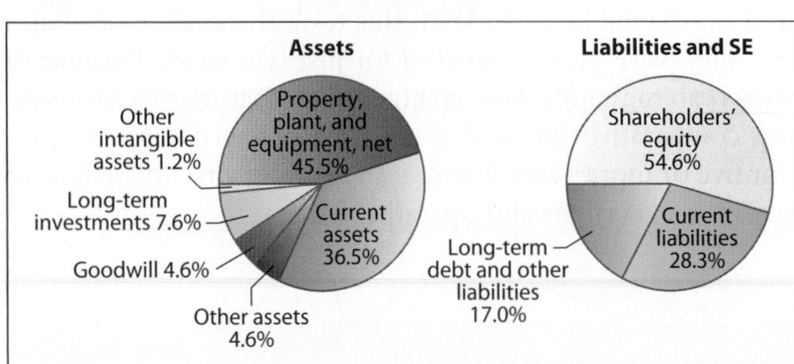

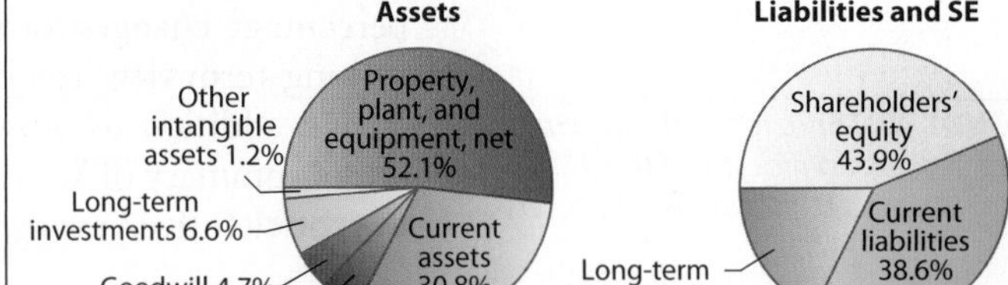

** Rounding causes some additions not to total precisely.*

Vertical Analysis

Vertical analysis shows how the different components of a financial statement relate to a total figure in the statement. The analyst sets the total figure at 100 percent and computes each component's percentage of that total. The resulting financial statement, which is expressed entirely in percentages, is called a **common-size statement**. Common-size balance sheets and common-size income statements for **Starbucks** are shown in pie-chart form in Exhibits 13.8 and 13.10 and in financial statement form in Exhibits 13.9 and 13.11. (On the balance sheet, the total figures are total assets and total liabilities and shareholders' equity, and on the income statement, the total figure is net revenues or net sales.)

Vertical analysis and common-size statements are useful in comparing the importance of specific components in the operation of a business and in identifying important

EXHIBIT 13.9
Common-Size Balance Sheets

Starbucks Corporation
Common-Size Balance Sheets
September 27, 2009, and September 28, 2008

	2009	2008
Assets		
Current assets	36.5%	30.8%
Property, plant, and equipment, net	45.5	52.1
Long-term investments	7.6	6.6
Other assets	4.6	4.6
Goodwill	4.6	4.7
Other intangible assets	1.2	1.2
Total assets	100.0%	100.0%
Liabilities and Shareholders' Equity		
Current liabilities	28.3%	38.6%
Long-term debt and other liabilities	17.0	17.5
Shareholders' equity	54.6	43.9
Total liabilities and shareholders' equity	100.0%	100.0%

Source: Starbucks Corporation, *Form 10-K*, 2009.

Note: Not all items are presented, and all amounts do not precisely total 100 percent due to rounding.

EXHIBIT 13.10
Common-Size Income Statements Presented Graphically

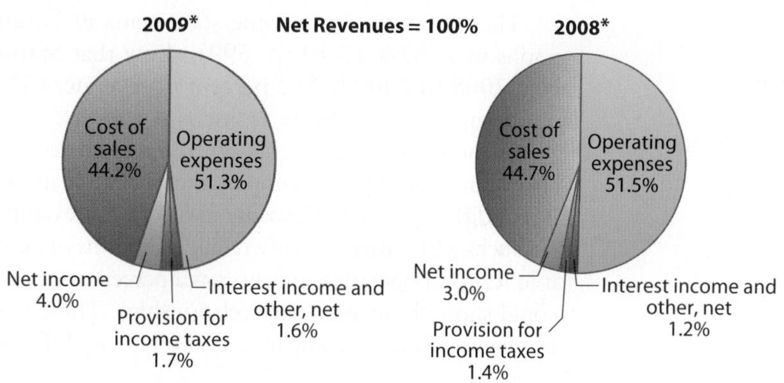

**Rounding causes some additions not to total precisely.*
Note: Not all items are presented.

changes in components from one year to the next. The main conclusions to be drawn from our analysis of Starbucks are as follows:

- Starbucks' assets consist largely of current assets and property, plant, and equipment.
- Starbucks finances assets primarily through equity and current liabilities.
- Starbucks has few long-term liabilities.

Looking at the pie charts in Exhibit 13.8 and the common-size balance sheets in Exhibit 13.9, you can see the following:

- The composition of Starbucks' assets shifted from property, plant, and equipment (declined from 52.1% to 45.5%) to current assets (increased from 30.8% to 36.5 %).
- The relationship of liabilities and equity shifted from current liabilities (declined from 38.6% to 28.3%) to shareholders' equity (increased from 43.9% to 54.6 %).

EXHIBIT 13.11
Common-Size Income Statements

Starbucks Corporation
Common-Size Income Statements
For the Years Ended September 27, 2009, and September 28, 2008

	2009	2008
Net revenues	100.0%	100.0%
Cost of sales, including occupancy costs	44.2	44.7
Gross margin	55.8%	55.3%
Operating expenses:		
Store operating expenses	35.0%	36.1%
Other operating expenses	2.7	3.2
Depreciation and amortization expenses	5.5	5.3
General and administrative expenses	4.6	4.4
Restructuring charges	3.4	2.6
Total operating expenses	51.3%	51.5%
Operating income	4.5%	3.8%
Interest income and other, net	1.6	1.2
Interest expense	0.4	0.5
Income before taxes	5.7%	4.4%
Provision for income taxes	1.7	1.4
Net income	4.0%	3.0%

Source: Starbucks Corporation, *Form 10-K*, 2009.

Note: All amounts do not precisely total 100 percent due to rounding.

The common-size income statements in Exhibit 13.11 (p. 599), illustrated as pie graphs in Exhibit 13.10 (p. 599), show that Starbucks reduced its operating expenses from 2008 to 2009 by 0.2 percent of revenues (51.5%–51.3%). In other words, operating expenses did not grow as fast as revenues.

Common-size statements are often used to make comparisons between companies. They allow an analyst to compare the operating and financing characteristics of two companies of different size in the same industry. For example, the analyst might want to compare Starbucks with other specialty retailers in terms of percentage of total assets financed by debt or in terms of operating expenses as a percentage of net revenues. Common-size statements would show those and other relationships. These statements can also be used to compare the characteristics of companies that report in different currencies.

RATIO

Financial Ratio Analysis

Financial ratio analysis identifies key relationships between the components of the financial statements. Financial ratios are useful tools for evaluating a company's financial position and operations and may reveal areas that need further investigation. To interpret ratios correctly, one must have a general understanding of the company and its environment, financial data for several years or for several companies, and an understanding of the data underlying the numerator and denominator.

Ratios can be expressed in several ways. For example, a ratio of net income of $100,000 to sales of $1,000,000 can be stated as follows:

- Net income is 1/10, or 10 percent, of sales.
- The ratio of sales to net income is 10 to 1 (10:1), or sales are 10 times net income.
- For every dollar of sales, the company has an average net income of 10 cents.

Stop & Apply

Joy Corporation's net sales and accounts receivable follow. Using 2009 as the base year, prepare a trend analysis. State whether the results suggest a favorable or unfavorable trend and explain why. (*Note:* Round your answers to one decimal place.)

	2011	2010	2009
Net sales	$123,000	$117,000	$105,000
Accounts receivable (net)	32,000	22,000	10,000

SOLUTION

	2011	2010	2009
Net sales	117.1%	111.4%	100.0%
Accounts receivable (net)	320.0%	220.0%	100.0%

These results show an unfavorable trend because the company is tying up increasing amounts of resources in accounts receivable without a correspondingly high increase in sales.

iStock Photo

COMPREHENSIVE ILLUSTRATION OF FINANCIAL RATIO ANALYSIS

LO 4 Apply financial ratio analysis in a comprehensive evaluation of a company's financial performance.

In this section, to illustrate how analysts use financial ratios in evaluating a company's financial performance, we perform a comprehensive ratio analysis of **Starbucks**' performance in 2008 and 2009. The following excerpt from the discussion and analysis section of Starbucks' 2009 annual report provides the context for our evaluation:

> Fiscal 2009 was a challenging year for Starbucks. The Company was confronted with extraordinary economic and operating challenges in addition to

Focus on International Practices

IFRS The Use and Evaluation of Performance Measures Must Change When Using IFRS

Financial statement users must carefully consider evaluations and comparisons of historical performance under IFRS for a variety of reasons. When a company switches from U.S. GAAP to IFRS, prior years' performance measures will not likely be comparable. In fact, 80 percent of companies surveyed in a research study of European companies reported higher net income for the same operations under IFRS than under U.S. GAAP. When this occurs, an IFRS profit margin will likely provide a more optimistic evaluation when compared with pre-IFRS results or with a U.S. GAAP based competitor. Further, the definitions of assets, liabilities, and equity differ under IFRS. The combined effect is that debt to equity, return on equity, and return on assets ratios may not exhibit historical trends. Contracts and management compensation based on these IFRS measures also require a closer look.

iStock Photo

facing an increasingly competitive landscape. Although the global economy has shown some signs of improvement recently, management recognizes the difficult economic situation that many consumers are still facing and does not expect that to significantly change over the course of fiscal 2010. . . . Starbucks responded to this difficult environment with a more disciplined focus on operations and the introduction of initiatives to permanently improve the Company's cost structure. The result is an underlying business model that is less reliant on high revenue growth to drive profitability, and that still preserves the fundamental strengths and values of the Starbucks brand. The primary initiatives in this strategy include . . . reducing the Company's cost structure, while renewing the focus on service excellence in the stores and delivering relevant innovation.

Starbucks' actions to rationalize its global store portfolio have included the planned closure of nearly 1,000 Company-operated stores globally.

STUDY NOTE: *Publishers often redefine the content of the ratios that companies provide. While the general content is similar, variations occur. Be sure to ascertain and evaluate the information that a published source uses to calculate ratios.*

We will use the key financial ratios introduced earlier in the text, as well as some commonly used supplemental financial ratios, to evaluate Starbucks' performance in relation to the five financial objectives: profitability, total asset management, liquidity, financial risk, and operating asset management. We will also evaluate Starbucks' market strength. The data that we use in computing all ratios are from Starbucks' Form 10-K, 2009, and Form 10-K, 2008. All dollar amounts shown in the computations are in millions.

Evaluating Profitability and Total Asset Management

Investors and creditors use profit margin to evaluate a company's ability to earn a satisfactory income (profitability). They use asset turnover to determine whether the company uses assets in a way that maximizes revenue (total asset management). These two ratios require only three numbers: revenue (or net sales),* net income, and average total assets. Their combined effect is overall earning power—that is, return on assets).

Financial Ratio: Profit Margin **Profit margin** measures the net income produced by each dollar of sales. Starbucks' profit margins in 2008 and 2009 are computed as follows.

*Starbucks refers to revenue as *net sales,* and we use that term throughout our examples.

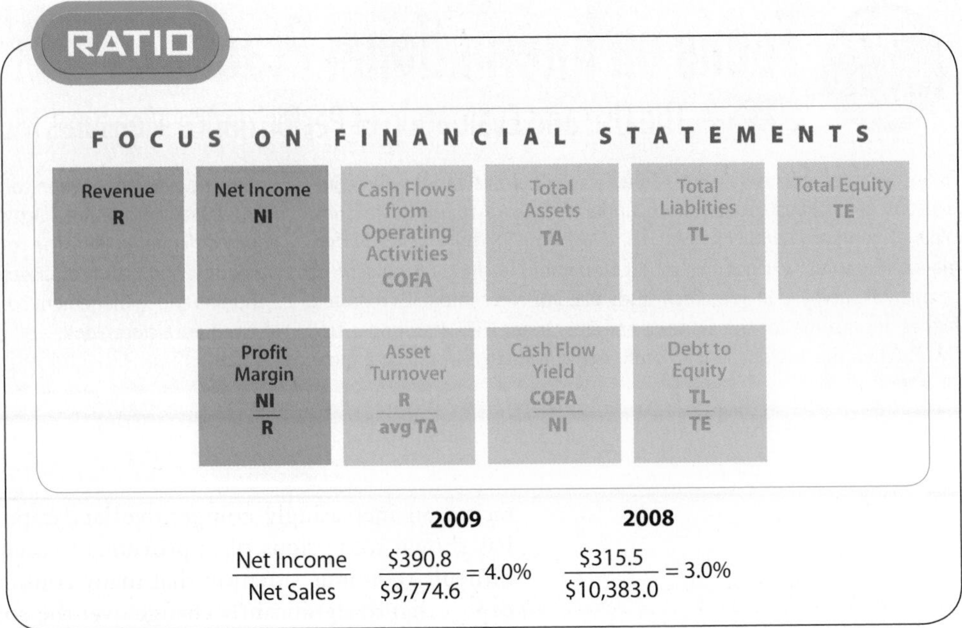

Starbucks' profit margin increased from 3.0 to 4.0 percent between 2008 and 2009 because net income increased while net sales declined.

Financial Ratio: Asset Turnover **Asset turnover** measures how efficiently assets are used to produce sales. Starbucks' asset turnover ratios in 2008 and 2009 are computed below.

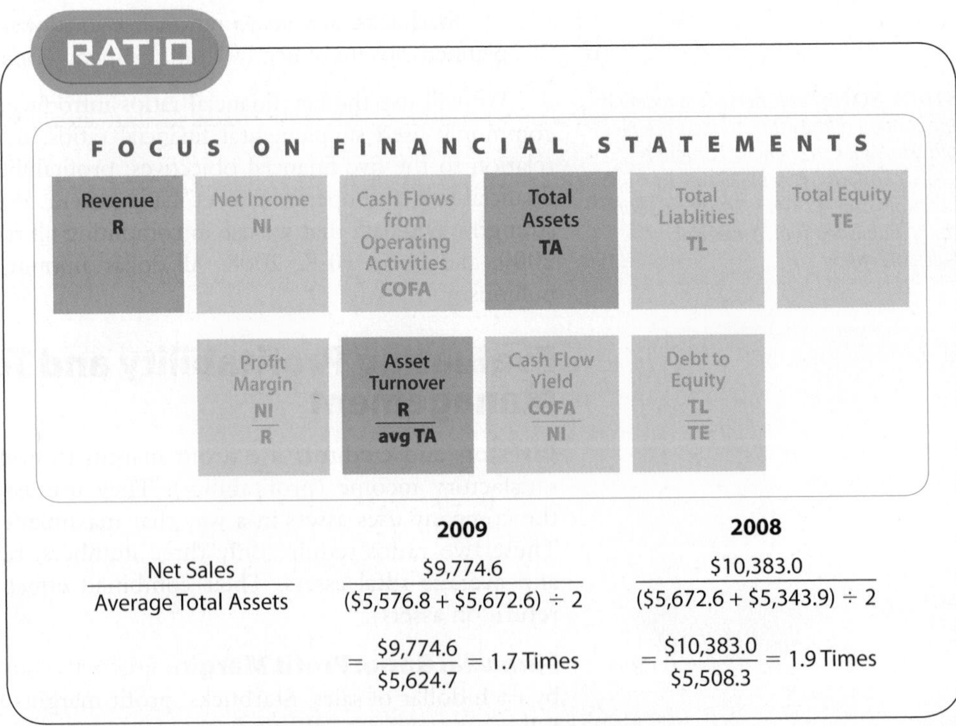

Starbucks' asset turnover decreased from 1.9 to 1.7 times because average total assets increased while net sales declined.

Financial Ratio: Return on Assets **Return on assets** measures a company's overall earning power, or profitability. Starbucks' return on assets ratios in 2008 and 2009 are computed as follows.

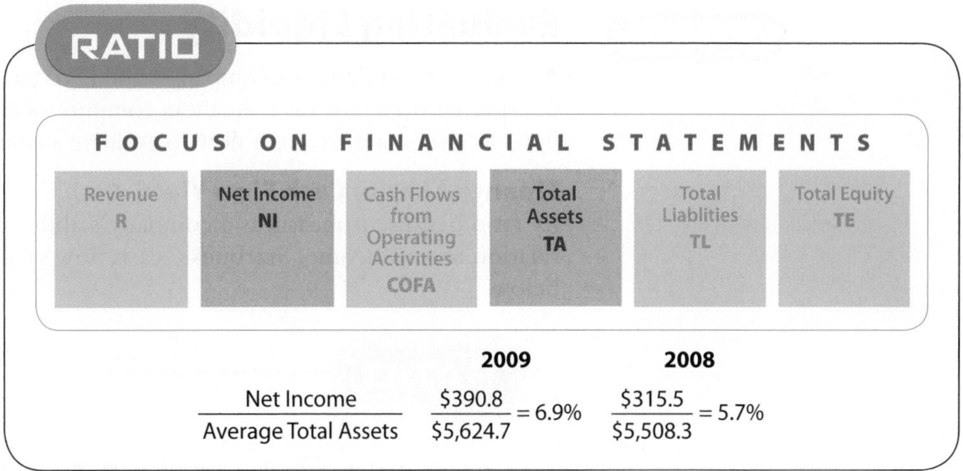

Starbucks' return on assets increased from 5.7 percent in 2008 to 6.9 percent in 2009 because net income increased proportionally more than average total assets.

Profitability Ratio Relationships The relationships of the three financial ratios for profitability are as follows:

	Profit Margin		*Asset Turnover*		*Return on Assets*
	Net Income / Net Sales	×	Net Sales / Average Total Assets	=	Net Income / Average Total Assets
2008	3.0%	×	1.9	=	5.7%
2009	4.0%	×	1.7	=	6.8%

Starbucks' return on assets improved in 2009 because of an increase in profit margin, but that was partially offset by a small decline in the asset turnover ratio. Although Starbucks' profitability and total asset management were relatively low, as you will see in the next section, Starbucks is very good at generating cash from these returns on assets.

__STUDY NOTE:__ The analysis of both asset turnover and return on assets is improved if only productive assets are used in the calculations. For example, when investments in unfinished new plant construction or in nonoperating plants are removed from the asset base, the result is a better picture of the productivity of assets.

It is important to note that net income is sometimes not as useful in computing profitability ratios as it is for Starbucks. If a company has one-time items on its income statement, such as gains, or losses on the sale or disposal of discontinued operations, income from operations before these items may be a better measure of sustainable earnings than net income. Some analysts like to use earnings before interest and taxes (EBIT) for the earnings measure because it excludes the effects of the company's borrowings and the tax rates from the analysis. Whatever figure one uses for earnings, it is important to determine the effects of various components on future operations.

Focus on Business Practice

Look Carefully at the Numbers

In recent years, companies have increasingly used pro forma statements—statements as they would appear without certain items—as a way of presenting a better picture of their operations than would be the case in reports prepared under GAAP. In one quarter, **Amazon.com** reported a "pro forma net" loss of $76 million; under GAAP, its net loss was $234 million. In addition, a common practice used by such companies as **Google**, **eBay**, and **Starbucks** is to provide in the notes to the financial statements income as it would be without the expense related to compensation for stock options.[11] Pro forma statements, which are unaudited, have come to mean whatever a company's management wants them to mean. As a result, the SEC issued new rules that prohibit companies from giving more prominence to non-GAAP measures and from using terms that are similar to GAAP measures.[12] Nevertheless, companies still report pro forma results.[13] Analysts should rely exclusively on financial statements that are prepared using GAAP and that are audited by an independent CPA.

iStock Photo

Evaluating Liquidity

As you know, liquidity is a company's ability to pay bills when they are due and to meet unexpected needs for cash. Analysts compute cash flow yield, cash flows to sales, cash flows to assets, and free cash flow to evaluate a company's liquidity.

Financial Ratio: Cash Flow Yield **Cash flow yield** is the most important liquidity ratio because it measures a company's ability to generate operating cash flows in relation to net income. Starbucks' cash flow yields in 2008 and 2009 are computed below.

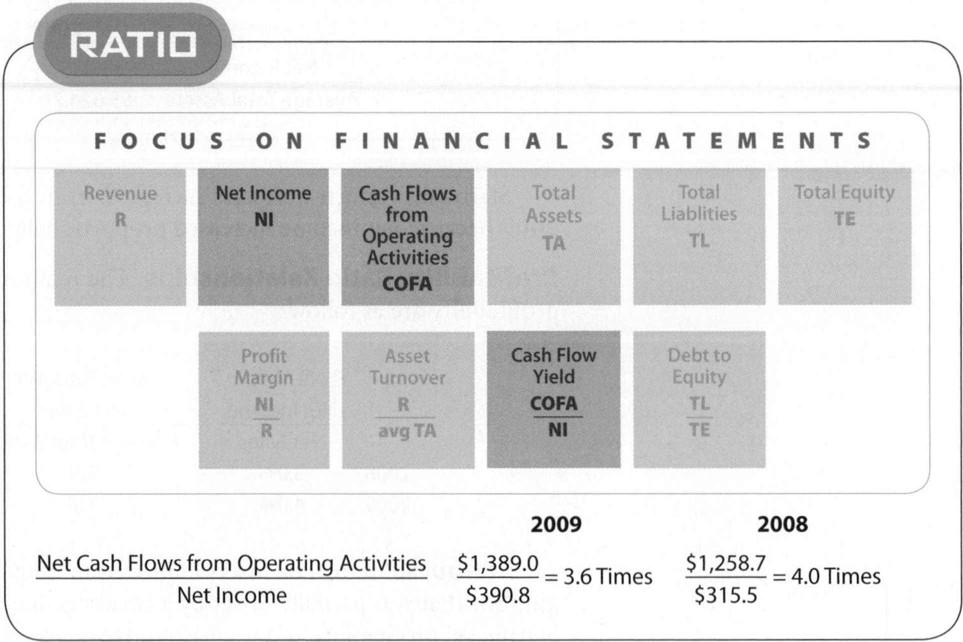

Starbucks' cash flow yield declined from 4.0 times in 2008 to 3.6 times in 2009 because net income increased proportionally more than net cash flows from operating activities. However, the company is still very proficient at generating cash flows from operations.

Financial Ratio: Cash Flows to Sales **Cash flows to sales** refers to the ability of sales to generate operating cash flows. Starbucks' cash flows to sales ratios in 2008 and 2009 are computed below.

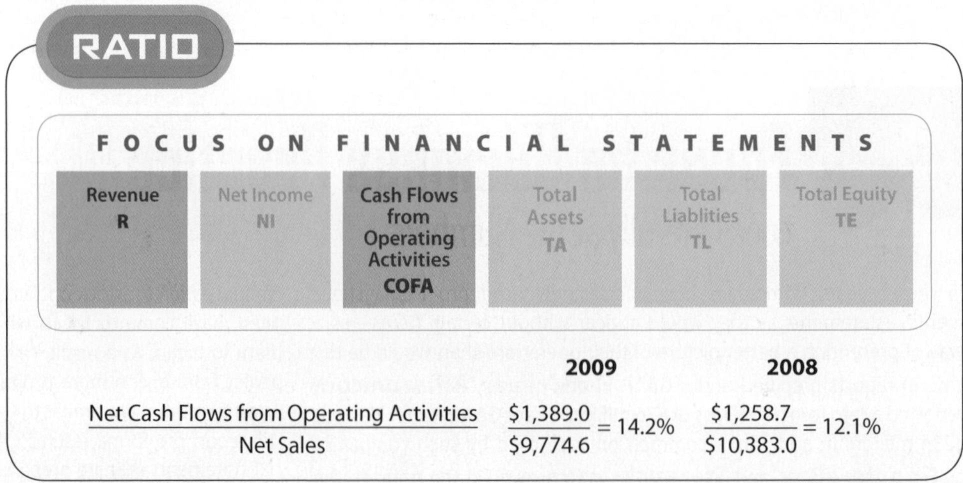

Starbucks' cash flows to sales increased from 12.1 to 14.2 percent because the company's net sales decreased while the cash flows provided by its operations increased.

Financial Ratio: Cash Flows to Assets **Cash flows to assets** measures the ability of assets to generate operating cash flows. Starbucks' cash flows to assets ratios in 2008 and 2009 are computed below.

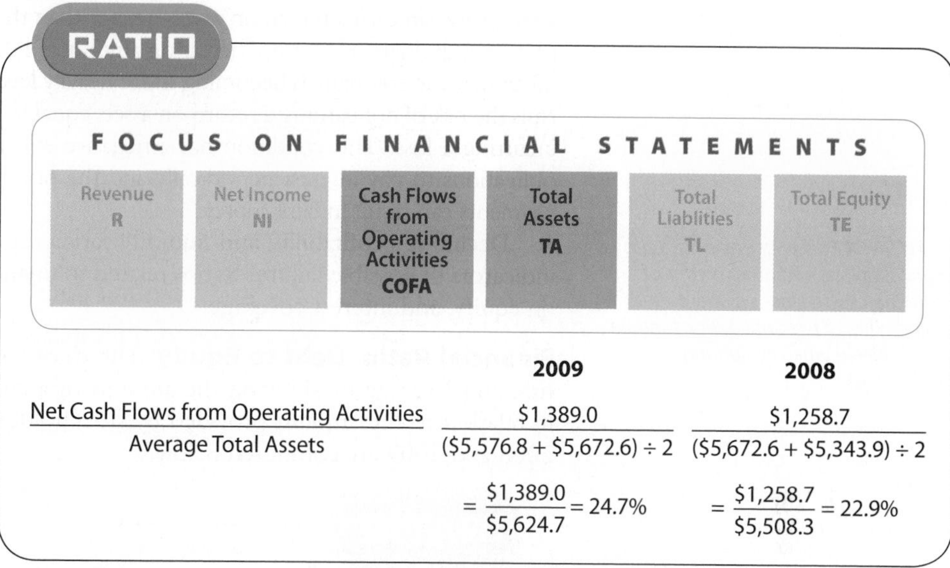

Starbucks' cash flows to assets increased from 22.9 to 24.7 percent. The cash flows provided by the company's operations increased proportionally faster than the average total assets.

Free Cash Flow **Free cash flow** is a measure of the cash remaining after providing for commitments. Starbucks' free cash flows in 2008 and 2009 are computed below.

	2009	2008
Net Cash Flows from Operating Activities – Dividends – Net Capital Expenditures	$1,389.0 – $0 – $445.6	$1,258.7 – $0 – $984.5
	= $943.4	= $274.2

Like its cash flows to sales and assets, Starbucks' free cash flow increased. While the company's net capital expenditures (the difference between purchases and sales of plant assets) decreased by $538.9 million, the net cash provided by operating activities increased by $130.3 million. Another favorable factor in Starbucks' free cash flow is that the company pays no dividends. In sum, Starbucks is very proficient in turning its income into cash. It has very good cash flow returns and strong free cash flow. Note management's comment regarding future liquidity and cash flows:

> Despite limited access to the commercial paper markets, management believes that cash flow from operations and its existing cash and liquid investments, supplemented as needed by the $1 billion in short-term borrowing capacity under the Company's revolving credit facility, will be sufficient to finance capital requirements for its core businesses for the foreseeable future, as well as to fund the cost of lease termination and related costs from the remaining international store closures. . . . The Company expects to use its cash and liquid investments, including any borrowings under its credit facility and commercial paper program, to invest in its core businesses, including new beverage and product innovations, as well as other new business opportunities related to its core businesses.[14]

Evaluating Financial Risk

Financial risk refers to a company's ability to survive in good times and bad. The aim of evaluating financial risk is to detect early signs that a company is headed for financial difficulty through its use of debt, or *financial leverage*, to finance part of the company. Many companies use financial leverage positively. They take advantage of the fact that interest paid on debt is tax-deductible, whereas dividends on stock are not. Because debt usually carries a fixed interest charge and the cost of financing can be limited, leverage can be used to advantage. If a company can earn a return on assets greater than the cost of interest, it increases the return to its stockholders. However, increasing amounts of debt in a company's capital structure can mean that the company is becoming more heavily leveraged. When this occurs, the company runs the risk of not earning a return on assets equal to the cost of financing the assets, thereby incurring a loss. This condition has a negative effect because it represents increasing legal obligations to pay interest periodically and the principal at maturity. Failure to make those payments can result in bankruptcy.

STUDY NOTE: *Because of innovative financing plans and other means of acquiring assets, lease payments and similar types of fixed obligations should be considered when evaluating financial risk.*

Declining profitability and liquidity ratios together with increased leverage are key indicators of possible failure. Ratios related to financial risk include debt to equity, return on equity, and interest coverage.

Financial Ratio: Debt to Equity The **debt to equity ratio** measures capital structure and leverage by showing the amount of a company's assets provided by creditors in relation to the amount provided by stockholders. Starbucks' debt to equity ratios in 2008 and 2009 are computed below.

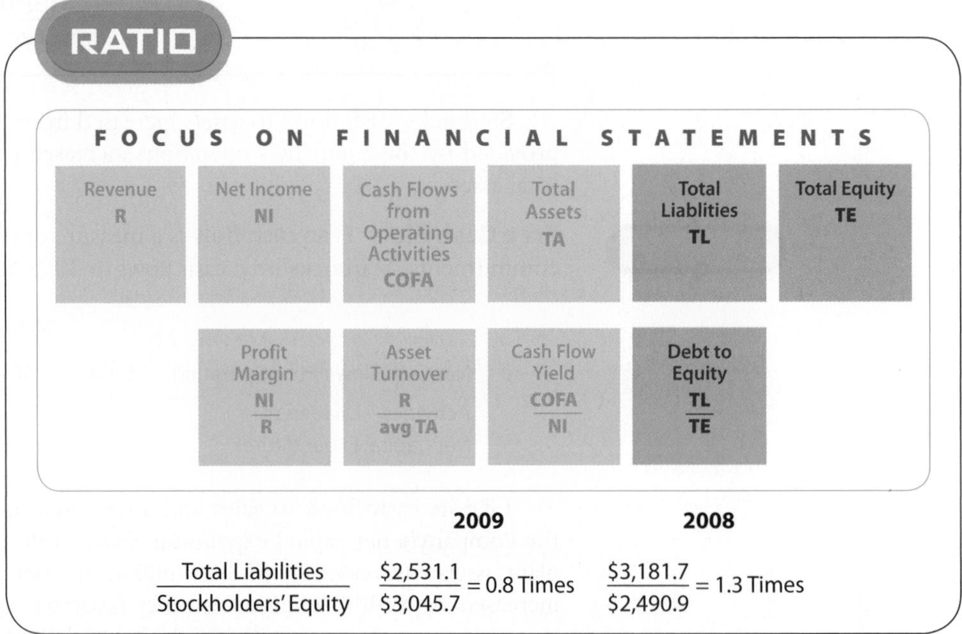

Starbucks' debt to equity ratio decreased from 1.3 times in 2008 to 0.8 times in 2009, which indicates an increased reliance on equity financing. Recall from Exhibit 13.9 that Starbucks' long-term debt and other liabilities decreased from 2008 to 2009 while stockholders' equity increased.

Financial Ratio: Return on Equity **Return on equity** measures the return to stockholders, or the profitability of stockholders' investments. Starbucks' return on equity ratios in 2008 and 2009 are computed as follows.

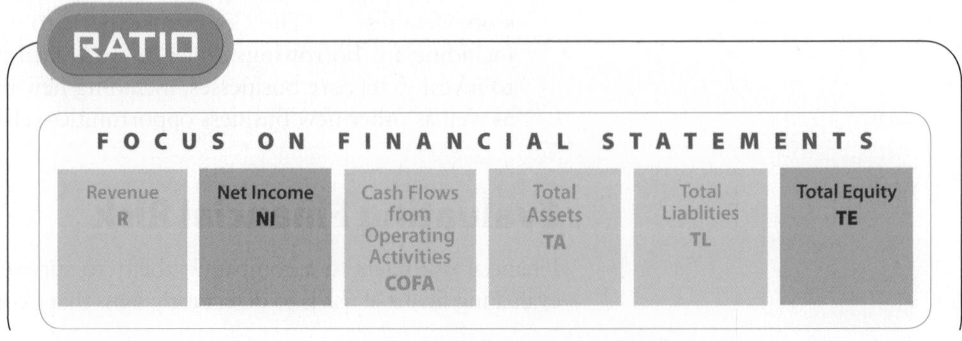

	2009	2008
$\frac{\text{Net Income}}{\text{Average Stockholders' Equity}}$	$\frac{\$390.8}{(\$3{,}045.7 + \$2{,}490.9) \div 2}$	$\frac{\$315.5}{(\$2{,}490.9 + \$2{,}284.1) \div 2}$
	$= \frac{\$390.8}{\$2{,}768.3} = 14.1\%$	$= \frac{\$315.5}{\$2{,}387.5} = 13.2\%$

Starbucks' return on equity increased from 13.2 percent in 2008 to 14.1 percent in 2009. These are excellent returns compared to return on assets of 5.7 percent in 2008 and 6.9 percent in 2009. Note that both the overall profitability (return on assets) and the return to stockholders (return on equity) increased. The reason for this is that Starbucks' net income increased proportionally more than average stockholders' equity.

Financial Ratio: Interest Coverage The **interest coverage ratio** is a supplementary ratio that measures the degree of protection creditors have from default on interest payments. Analysts use this ratio to determine whether a company's interest payments are in peril. Starbucks' interest coverage ratios in 2008 and 2009 are computed below.

RATIO

	2009	2008
$\frac{\text{Income Before Income Taxes + Interest Expense}}{\text{Interest Expense}}$	$\frac{\$559.2 + \$39.1}{\$39.1}$	$\frac{\$459.5 + \$53.4}{\$53.4}$
	$= \frac{\$598.3}{\$39.1} = 15.3 \text{ Times}$	$= \frac{\$512.9}{\$53.4} = 9.6 \text{ Times}$

Starbucks' interest coverage increased from 9.6 times in 2008 to 15.3 times in 2009 due to a decrease in interest expense. Thus, interest coverage is at a very safe level.

Evaluating Operating Asset Management

Research has shown that successful companies carefully manage the operating assets and payables in the **operating cycle**.[15] As we noted in Chapter 5, the operating cycle involves inventories, accounts receivable, and accounts payable. It spans the time it takes to purchase inventory, sell it, and collect for it. The **financing period**—the period between the time a supplier must be paid and the end of the operating cycle—defines how much additional financing the company must have to support its operations. Because additional debt increases a company's financial risk, it is important to keep the financing period at a manageable level.

The financial ratios that measure operating asset management include inventory turnover, days' inventory on hand, receivable turnover, days' sales uncollected, payables turnover, and days' payable. To determine the days in each component of the cash cycle, the turnover must first be computed by relating the average for each balance sheet account—inventory, accounts receivable, and accounts payable—to the respective income statement account for the period—cost of goods sold and net sales or revenues. The average number of days of each component is then determined by dividing the turnover into 365 days in a year.

Financial Ratio: Inventory Turnover Inventory turnover measures the relative size of inventories. Starbucks' inventory turnover ratios in 2008 and 2009 are computed as follows.

RATIO

	2009	2008
Costs of Goods Sold / Average Inventory	$4,324.9 / ($664.9 + $692.8) ÷ 2	$4,645.3 / ($692.8 + $691.7) ÷ 2
	= $4,324.9 / $678.9 = 6.4 Times	= $4,645.3 / $692.3 = 6.7 Times

Starbucks' inventory turnover decreased from 6.7 times in 2008 to 6.4 times in 2009 because cost of goods sold decreased proportionally more than did average inventory.

Financial Ratio: Days' Inventory on Hand **Days' inventory on hand** measures the average number of days that it takes to sell inventory. Starbucks' days' inventory on hand ratios in 2008 and 2009 are computed below.

RATIO

	2009	2008
Days in Year / Inventory Turnover	365 Days / 6.4 Times = 57.0 Days	365 Days / 6.7 Times = 54.5 Days

Starbucks' days' inventory on hand increased from 54.5 days in 2008 to 57.0 days in 2009 due to the decrease in inventory turnover.

Financial Ratio: Receivable Turnover **Receivable turnover** measures the relative size of accounts receivable and the effectiveness of credit policies. Starbucks' receivable turnover ratios in 2008 and 2009 are computed below.

RATIO

	2009	2008
Net Sales / Average Accounts Receivable	$9,774.6 / ($271.0 + $329.5) ÷ 2	$10,383.0 / ($329.5 + $287.9) ÷ 2
	= $9,774.6 / $300.3 = 32.5 Times	= $10,383.0 / $308.7 = 33.6 Times

Because most of Starbucks' sales are for cash or credit card, receivables are not a significant asset for Starbucks. Thus, its receivable turnover is very high. However, it declined slightly between 2008 and 2009, from 33.6 times in 2008 to 32.5 times in 2009.

Financial Ratio: Days' Sales Uncollected **Days' sales uncollected** measures the average number of days it takes to collect receivables. Starbucks' days' sales uncollected ratios in 2008 and 2009 are computed below.

RATIO

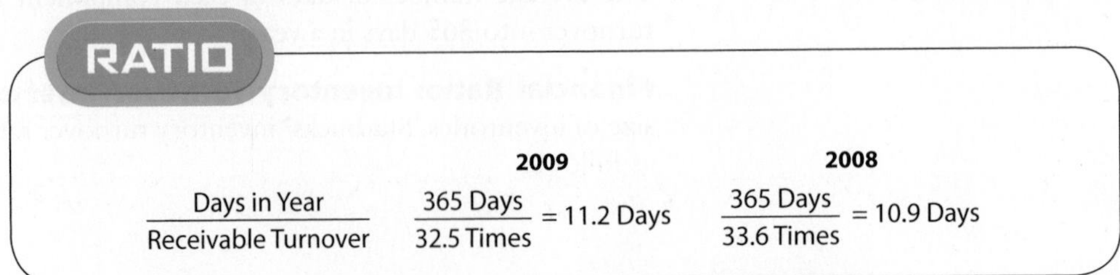

	2009	2008
Days in Year / Receivable Turnover	365 Days / 32.5 Times = 11.2 Days	365 Days / 33.6 Times = 10.9 Days

The high receivable turnover ratios resulted in an increase in days' sales uncollected from 10.9 days in 2008 to 11.2 days in 2009.

Financial Ratio: Payables Turnover **Payables turnover** measures the relative size of accounts payable and the credit terms creditors extend to a company. Starbucks' payables turnover ratios in 2008 and 2009 are computed below.

RATIO

	2009	2008
$\frac{\text{Costs of Goods Sold +/– Change in Inventory}}{\text{Average Accounts Payable}}$	$\frac{\$4,324.9 - \$27.9}{(\$267.1 + \$324.9) \div 2}$	$\frac{\$4,645.3 + \$1.1}{(\$324.9 + \$390.8) \div 2}$
	$= \frac{\$4,297.0}{\$296.0} = 14.5 \text{ Times}$	$= \frac{\$4,646.4}{\$357.9} = 13.0 \text{ Times}$

Starbucks' payables turnover increased from 13.0 times in 2008 to 14.5 times in 2009.

Financial Ratio: Days' Payable **Days' payable** measures the average number of days it takes to pay accounts payable. Starbucks' days' payable ratios in 2008 and 2009 are computed below.

RATIO

	2009	2008
$\frac{\text{Days in Year}}{\text{Payables Turnover}}$	$\frac{365 \text{ Days}}{14.5 \text{ Times}} = 25.2 \text{ Days}$	$\frac{365 \text{ Days}}{13.0 \text{ Times}} = 28.1 \text{ Days}$

The increase in payables turnover resulted in a decrease in days' payable from 28.1 days in 2008 to 25.2 days in 2009.

Financing Period We can now assess Starbucks' overall operating asset management by computing the financing period, the number of days of financing that must be provided. The financing period is computed by deducting the days' payable from the operating cycle (days' inventory on hand + days' sales uncollected). Starbucks' financing periods in 2008 and 2009 are computed as follows:

2009: 57.0 Days + 11.2 Days – 25.2 Days = 43.0 Days
2008: 54.5 Days + 10.9 Days – 28.1 Days = 37.3 Days

Since both days' inventory on hand and days' sales uncollected increased and days payable decreased, Starbucks had to provide 5.7 (43.0 – 37.3) more days of financing for its operating assets in 2009 than in 2008.

Supplemental Financial Ratios for Assessing Operating Asset Management and Liquidity

In evaluating operating asset management and liquidity, many analysts also consider two supplemental financial ratios: the current ratio and the quick ratio.

Financial Ratio: Current Ratio The **current ratio** measures short-term debt-paying ability by comparing current assets with current liabilities. Starbucks' current ratios in 2008 and 2009 are computed as follows.

RATIO

	2009	2008
$\frac{\text{Current Assets}}{\text{Current Liabilities}}$	$\frac{\$2{,}035.8}{\$1{,}581.0} = 1.3 \text{ Times}$	$\frac{\$1{,}748.0}{\$2{,}189.7} = 0.8 \text{ Times}$

Starbucks' current ratio increased from 0.8 times in 2008 to 1.3 times in 2009. From 2008 to 2009, its current assets grew while current liabilities declined.

Financial Ratio: Quick Ratio The **quick ratio**, another measure of short-term debt-paying ability, differs from the current ratio in that the numerator of the quick ratio excludes inventories and prepaid expenses. Inventories and prepaid expenses take longer to convert to cash than the current assets included in the numerator of the quick ratio. Starbucks' quick ratios in 2008 and 2009 are computed below.

RATIO

	2009	2008
$\frac{\text{Cash + Marketable Securities + Receivables}}{\text{Current Liabilities}}$	$\frac{\$599.8 + \$66.3 + \$271.0}{\$1{,}581.0}$	$\frac{\$269.8 + \$52.5 + \$329.5}{\$2{,}189.7}$
	$= \frac{\$937.1}{\$1{,}581.0} = 0.6 \text{ Times}$	$= \frac{\$651.8}{\$2{,}189.7} = 0.3 \text{ Times}$

Starbucks' quick ratio increased from 0.3 times in 2008 to 0.6 times in 2009.

Evaluating Market Strength with Financial Ratios

Market price is the price at which a company's stock is bought and sold. It indicates how investors view the potential return and risk connected with owning the stock. Market price by itself is not very informative, however, because companies have different numbers of shares outstanding, different earnings, and different dividend policies. Thus, market price must be related to earnings by considering the price/earnings (P/E) ratio and the dividends yield.

Financial Ratio: Price/earnings (P/E) **Price/earnings (P/E)** measures investors' confidence in a company and is the ratio of the market price per share to earnings per share. The P/E ratio is useful in comparing the earnings of different companies and the value of a company's shares in relation to values in the overall market. With a higher P/E ratio, the investor obtains less earnings per dollar invested. Starbucks' P/E ratios in 2008 and 2009 are computed below.

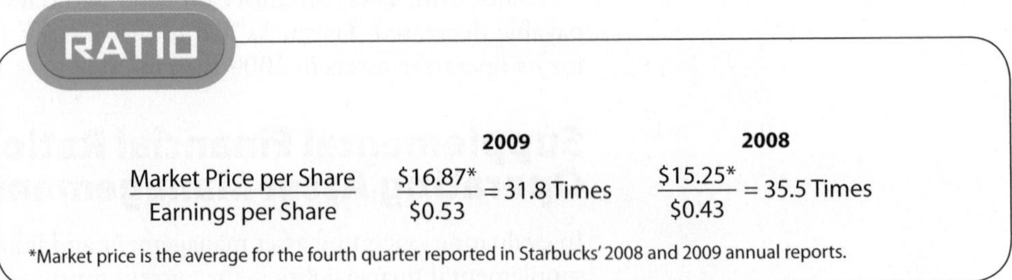

RATIO

	2009	2008
$\frac{\text{Market Price per Share}}{\text{Earnings per Share}}$	$\frac{\$16.87^{*}}{\$0.53} = 31.8 \text{ Times}$	$\frac{\$15.25^{*}}{\$0.43} = 35.5 \text{ Times}$

*Market price is the average for the fourth quarter reported in Starbucks' 2008 and 2009 annual reports.

Despite an increase in earnings per share from $0.43 in 2008 to $0.53 in 2009, Starbucks' P/E ratio declined from 35.5 times to 31.8 times because the market value of its stock increased less proportionally, or from about $15 to about $17. Earnings per share grew faster than market stock price. The implication is that investors are not as confident that Starbucks' earnings will continue to grow as fast in the future as it did in the past year.

Financial Ratio: Dividends Yield **Dividends yield** measures a stock's current return to an investor in the form of dividends.

RATIO

	2009	2008
$\frac{\text{Dividends per Share}}{\text{Market Price per Share}}$	Starbucks does not pay a dividend.	

Because Starbucks pays no dividends, we can conclude that those who invest in the company expect their return to come from increases in the stock's market value.

Stop & Apply

Lena's, a retail company, engaged in the transactions listed in the first column of the table below. Opposite each transaction is a ratio and space to mark the effect of each transaction on the ratio. Show that you understand the effect of business activities on performance measures by placing an X in the appropriate column to show whether the transaction increased, decreased, or had no effect on the ratio.

			Effect		
	Transaction	**Measure**	**Increase**	**Decrease**	**None**
a.	Sold treasury stock.	Profit margin			
b.	Borrowed cash by issuing bond payable.	Asset turnover			
c.	Paid wages expense.	Return on assets			
d.	Recorded depreciation expense.	Cash flow yield			
e.	Sold equipment.	Free cash flow			
f.	Repaid bond payable.	Debt to equity			
g.	Sold merchandise on account.	Return on equity			
h.	Accrued interest expense.	Interest coverage			
i.	Increased allowance for uncollectible accounts.	Receivable turnover			
j.	Purchased inventory on credit.	Payables turnover			
k.	Accrued salaries.	Current ratio			
l.	Purchased inventory.	Quick ratio			

SOLUTION

			Effect		
	Transaction	**Measure**	**Increase**	**Decrease**	**None**
a.	Sold treasury stock.	Profit margin			X
b.	Borrowed cash by issuing bond payable.	Asset turnover		X	
c.	Paid wages expense.	Return on assets		X	
d.	Recorded depreciation expense.	Cash flow yield	X		
e.	Sold equipment.	Free cash flow	X		
f.	Repaid bond payable.	Debt to equity		X	
g.	Sold merchandise on account.	Return on equity	X		
h.	Accrued interest expense.	Interest coverage		X	
i.	Increased allowance for uncollectible accounts.	Receivable turnover	X		
j.	Purchased inventory on credit.	Payables turnover		X	
k.	Accrued salaries.	Current ratio		X	
l.	Purchased inventory.	Quick ratio		X	

iStock Photo

A look back at Starbucks Corporation

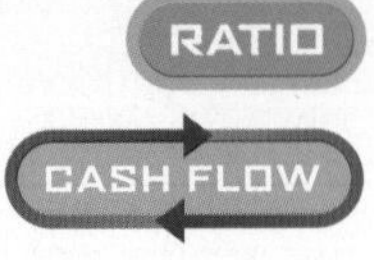

To assess a company's financial performance, managers, stockholders, creditors, and other interested parties use measures that are linked to creating value for shareholders. The financial highlights at the beginning of the chapter show that **Starbuck**'s record of growth in net earnings and cash flows from operating activities halted in 2008 due to the recession in that year, but began to recover in 2009, but for a comprehensive view of the company's performance, users of its financial statements must consider the following questions:

1. What standards should be used to evaluate Starbucks' performance?
2. What analytical tools are available to measure performance?
3. How successful has the company been in creating value for shareholders?

Starbucks' performance should be compared with the performance of other companies in the same industry—the specialty retail business. In addition, Starbucks' performance in the current year should be compared with its performance in past years. To make this comparison, users of Starbucks' financial statements employ such techniques as horizontal or trend analysis, vertical analysis, and ratio analysis.

Our comprehensive ratio analysis of Starbucks shows that the company was successfully dealing with the economic downturn that began in 2008. Its financial condition improved from 2008 to 2009, as measured by its profitability, total asset management, liquidity, financial risk, and operating asset management ratios. This performance resulted in an increase in earnings per share from $0.43 to $0.53, but it was not accompanied by a corresponding increase in shareholders' value due to an increase in share price from $15 to $17 that was slower than the increase in earnings per share.

Review Problem

Comparative Analysis of Two Companies

Debra Wright is considering investing in a fast-food restaurant chain. She has narrowed her choice to Slim Burger or Tasty Steak. The balance sheets and income statements of Slim Burger and Tasty Steak are presented on next page.

The following information pertaining to 2011 is also available to Debra Wright:

1. Slim Burger's statement of cash flows shows that it had net cash flows from operations of $2,200,000. Tasty Steak's statement of cash flows shows that its net cash flows from operations were $3,000,000.
2. Net capital expenditures were $2,100,000 for Slim Burger and $1,800,000 for Tasty Steak.
3. Slim Burger paid dividends of $500,000, and Tasty Steak paid dividends of $600,000.
4. The market prices of the stocks of Slim Burger and Tasty Steak were $30 and $20, respectively.

Financial information pertaining to prior years is not readily available to Debra Wright.

Required

Perform a comprehensive ratio analysis of both Slim Burger and Tasty Steak using the following steps. Assume that all notes payable of these two companies are current liabilities and that all their bonds payable are long-term liabilities. Show dollar amounts in thousands, use end-of-year balances for averages, assume no change in inventory, and round all ratios and percentages to one decimal place.

1. Prepare an analysis of profitability and total asset management.
2. Prepare an analysis of liquidity.

3. Prepare an analysis of financial risk.
4. Prepare an analysis of operating asset management.
5. Prepare an analysis of market strength.
6. In each analysis, indicate which company apparently had the more favorable ratio. (*Note:* Consider differences of 0.1 or less to be neutral.)
7. In what ways would having access to prior years' information aid in this analysis?

	A	B	C	D	E
1			**Balance Sheets**		
2			**December 31, 2011**		
3			(in thousands)		
4				**Slim Burger**	**Tasty Steak**
5			**Assets**		
6	Cash			$ 2,000	$ 4,500
7	Accounts receivable (net)			2,000	6,500
8	Inventory			2,000	5,000
9	Property, plant, and equipment (net)			20,000	35,000
10	Other assets			4,000	5,000
11		Total assets		$30,000	$56,000
12					
13			**Liabilities and Stockholders' Equity**		
14	Accounts payable			$ 2,500	$ 3,000
15	Notes payable			1,500	4,000
16	Bonds payable			10,000	30,000
17	Common stock, $1 par value			1,000	3,000
18	Additional paid-in capital			9,000	9,000
19	Retained earnings			6,000	7,000
20		Total liabilities and stockholders' equity		$30,000	$56,000

	A	B	C	D	E
1			**Income Statements**		
2			**For the Year Ended December 31, 2011**		
3			(in thousands, except per share amounts)		
4				**Slim Burger**	**Tasty Steak**
5	Net sales			$53,000	$86,000
6	Costs and expenses				
7		Cost of goods sold		$37,000	$61,000
8		Selling expenses		7,000	10,000
9		Administrative expenses		4,000	5,000
10			Total costs and expenses	$48,000	$76,000
11	Income from operations			$ 5,000	$10,000
12	Interest expense			1,400	3,200
13	Income before income taxes			$ 3,600	$ 6,800
14	Income taxes expense			1,800	3,400
15	Net income			$ 1,800	$ 3,400
16	Earnings per share			$ 1.80	$ 1.13

ANSWERS TO REVIEW PROBLEM

Ratio Name	Slim Burger	Tasty Steak	6. Company with More Favorable Ratio
1. Profitability and total asset management analysis			
a. Profit margin	$1,800 / $53,000 = 3.4%	$3,400 / $86,000 = 4.0%	Tasty Steak
b. Asset turnover	$53,000 / $30,000 = 1.8 Times	$86,000 / $56,000 = 1.5 Times	Slim Burger
c. Return on assets	$1,800 / $30,000 = 6.0%	$3,400 / $56,000 = 6.1%	Neutral

Ratio Name	Slim Burger	Tasty Steak	6. Company with More Favorable Ratio
2. Liquidity analysis			
a. Cash flow yield	$2,200 / $1,800 = 1.2 Times	$3,000 / $3,400 = 0.9 Times	Slim Burger
b. Cash flows to sales	$2,200 / $53,000 = 4.2%	$3,000 / $86,000 = 3.5%	Slim Burger
c. Cash flows to assets	$2,200 / $30,000 = 7.3%	$3,000 / $56,000 = 5.4%	Slim Burger
d. Free cash flow	$2,200 – $500 – $2,100 = ($400)	$3,000 – $600 – $1,800 = $600	Tasty Steak

Ratio Name	Slim Burger	Tasty Steak	6. Company with More Favorable Ratio
3. Financial risk analysis			
a. Debt to equity ratio	($2,500 + $1,500 + $10,000) / ($1,000 + $9,000 + $6,000) = $14,000 / $16,000 = 0.9 Times	($3,000 + $4,000 + $30,000) / ($3,000 + $9,000 + $7,000) = $37,000 / $19,000 = 1.9 Times	Slim Burger
b. Return on equity	$1,800 / ($1,000 + $9,000 + $6,000) = $1,800 / $16,000 = 11.3 Times	$3,400 / ($3,000 + $9,000 + $7,000) = $3,400 / $19,000 = 17.9 Times	Tasty Steak
c. Interest coverage ratio	($3,600 + $1,400) / $1,400 = $5,000 / $1,400 = 3.6 Times	($6,800 + $3,200) / $3,200 = $10,000 / $3,200 = 3.1 Times	Slim Burger

Ratio Name	Slim Burger	Tasty Steak	6. Company with More Favorable Ratio
4. Operating asset management analysis			
a. Inventory turnover	$37,000 / $2,000 = 18.5 Times	$61,000 / $5,000 = 12.2 Times	Slim Burger
b. Days' inventory on hand	365 Days / 18.5 Times = 19.7 Days	365 Days / 12.2 Times = 29.9 Days	Slim Burger
c. Receivable turnover	$53,000 / $2,000 = 26.5 Times	$86,000 / $6,500 = 13.2 Times	Slim Burger
d. Days' sales uncollected	365 Days / 26.5 Times = 13.8 Days	365 Days / 13.2 Times = 27.7 Days	Slim Burger
e. Payables turnover	$37,000 / $2,500 = 14.8 Times	$61,000 / $3,000 = 20.3 Times	Tasty Steak
f. Days' payable	365 Days / 14.8 Times = 24.7 Days	365 Days / 20.3 Times = 18.0 Days	Tasty Steak
g. Current ratio	($2,000 + $2,000 + $2,000) / ($2,500 + $1,500) = $6,000 / $4,000 = 1.5 Times	($4,500 + $6,500 + $5,000) / ($3,000 + $4,000) = $16,000 / $7,000 = 2.3 Times	Tasty Steak
h. Quick ratio	($2,000 + $2,000) / ($2,500 + $1,500) = $4,000 / $4,000 = 1.0 Times	($4,500 + $6,500) / ($3,000 + $4,000) = $11,000 / $7,000 = 1.6 Times	Tasty Steak

Note: This analysis indicates the company with the apparently more favorable ratio.
Class discussion may focus on conditions under which different conclusions may be drawn.

Ratio Name	Slim Burger	Tasty Steak	6. Company with More Favorable Ratio
5. Market strength analysis			
a. Price/earnings ratio	$30 / $1.80 = 16.7 Times	$20 / $1.13 = 17.7 Times	Tasty Steak
b. Dividends yield	($500,000 ÷ 1,000,000) / $30 = $0.50 / $30 = 1.7%	($600,000 ÷ 3,000,000) / $20 = $0.20 / $20 = 1.0%	Slim Burger

7. Prior years' information would be helpful in two ways. First, turnover, return on assets, and cash flows to assets ratios could be based on average amounts. Second, a trend analysis could be performed for each company.

Stop & Review

LO1 Describe the objectives, standards of comparison, sources of information, and compensation issues in measuring financial performance.

Management's main responsibility is to develop and carry out a financial plan that addresses the five financial objectives of profitability, total asset management, liquidity, financial risk, and operating asset management. Creditors and investors use financial performance measurement to judge a company's past performance and current position as well as its future potential and the risk associated with it. Creditors use the information gained from their analyses to make reliable loans that will be repaid with interest. Investors use the information to make investments that will provide a return that is worth the risk.

Three standards of comparison commonly used in evaluating financial performance are rule-of-thumb measures, a company's past performance, and industry norms. Rule-of-thumb measures are weak because of a lack of evidence that they can be widely applied. A company's past performance can offer a guideline for measuring improvement, but it is not helpful in judging performance relative to the performance of other companies. Although the use of industry norms overcomes this last problem, its disadvantage is that firms are not always comparable, even in the same industry.

The main sources of information about public corporations are reports that the corporations publish themselves, such as annual reports and interim financial statements, reports filed with the SEC, business periodicals, and credit and investment advisory services.

In public corporations, a committee made up of independent directors appointed by the board of directors determines the compensation of top executives. Although earnings per share can be regarded as a "bottom-line" number that encompasses all the other performance measures, using it as the sole basis for determining executive compensation may lead to management practices that are not in the best interests of the company or its stockholders.

LO2 Define *quality of earnings* and identify the factors that affect quality of earnings.

The quality of earnings refers to the substance of earnings and their sustainability into future accounting periods. The quality of a company's earnings may be affected by the accounting methods and estimates it uses and by one-time items that it reports on its income statement. One-time items include gains and losses, write-downs and restructurings, and nonoperating items.

When a company has both continuing and discontinued operations, the operating income section of its income statement is called *income from continuing operations*. Income from continuing operations before income taxes is affected by choices of accounting methods and estimates and may contain gains and losses on the sale of assets, write-downs, and restructurings. The lower part of the income statement may contain such nonoperating items as discontinued operations. Earnings per share information appears at the bottom of the statement.

LO3 Apply horizontal analysis, trend analysis, vertical analysis, and ratio analysis to financial statements.

Horizontal analysis involves the computation of changes in both dollar amounts and percentages from year to year.

Trend analysis is an extension of horizontal analysis in that it calculates percentage changes for several years. The analyst computes the changes by setting a base year equal to 100 and calculating the results for subsequent years as percentages of the base year.

Vertical analysis uses percentages to show the relationship of the component parts of a financial statement to a total figure in the statement. The resulting financial statements, which are expressed entirely in percentages, are called common-size statements.

Ratio analysis is a technique of financial performance evaluation that identifies key relationships between the components of the financial statements. To interpret ratios correctly, the analyst must have a general understanding of the company and its environment, financial data for several years or for several companies, and an understanding of the data underlying the numerators and denominators.

Apply financial ratio analysis in a comprehensive evaluation of a company's financial performance. **LO 4**

A comprehensive ratio analysis includes the evaluation of a company's profitability, total asset management, liquidity, financial risk, operating asset management, and market strength.

Key Terms and Ratios

Base year 595 (LO3)
Common-size statement 598 (LO3)
Compensation committee 586 (LO1)
Discontinued operations 593 (LO2)
Diversified companies 588 (LO1)
Financial performance measurement 586 (LO1)
Financing period 607 (LO4)
Form 8-K 589 (LO1)
Form 10-K 589 (LO1)
Form 10-Q 589 (LO1)
Free cash flow 605 (LO4)
Horizontal analysis 594 (LO3)
Index number 597 (LO3)
Interim financial statements 589 (LO1)
Operating cycle 607 (LO4)
Quality of earnings 590 (LO2)
Restructuring 593 (LO2)
Trend analysis 597 (LO3)
Vertical analysis 598 (LO3)
Write-down 593 (LO2)

FINANCIAL RATIOS
Asset turnover 602 (LO4)
Cash flow yield 604 (LO4)
Cash flows to assets 605 (LO4)
Cash flows to sales 604 (LO)
Current ratio 609 (LO4)
Days' inventory on hand 608 (LO4)
Days' payable 609 (LO4)
Days' sales uncollected 608 (LO4)
Debt to equity ratio 606 (LO4)
Dividends yield 611 (LO4)
Financial Ratio analysis 600 (LO3)
Interest coverage ratio 607 (LO4)
Inventory turnover 607 (LO4)
Payables turnover 609 (LO4)
Price/earnings (P/E) 610 (LO4)
Profit margin 601 (LO4)
Quick ratio 610 (LO4)
Receivable turnover 608 (LO4)
Return on assets 602 (LO4)
Return on equity 606 (LO)

Chapter Assignments Building Your Basic Knowledge and Skills

Short Exercises

LO 1

Objectives and Standards of Financial Performance Evaluation

SE 1. Indicate whether each of the following items is (a) an objective or (b) a standard of comparison of financial statement analysis:

1. Industry norms
2. Assessment of a company's past performance
3. The company's past performance
4. Assessment of future potential and related risk
5. Rule-of-thumb measures

LO 1

Sources of Information

SE 2. For each piece of information in the list that follows, indicate whether the best source would be (a) reports published by the company, (b) SEC reports, (c) business periodicals, or (d) credit and investment advisory services.

1. Current market value of a company's stock
2. Management's analysis of the past year's operations
3. Objective assessment of a company's financial performance
4. Most complete body of financial disclosures
5. Current events affecting the company

LO 2 **Quality of Earnings**

SE 3. Each of the items listed below is a quality of earnings issue. Indicate whether the item is (a) an accounting method, (b) an accounting estimate, or (c) a one-time item. For any item for which the answer is (a) or (b), indicate which alternative is usually the more conservative choice.

1. LIFO versus FIFO
2. Restructuring costs
3. 10-year useful life versus 15-year useful life
4. Straight-line versus accelerated method
5. Discontinued operations
6. Gain on sale of investments
7. Increase versus decrease in percentage of uncollectible accounts

LO 2 **Corporate Income Statement**

SE 4. Assume that Lincoln Company's chief financial officer gave you the following information: net sales, $720,000; cost of goods sold, $350,000; loss from discontinued operations (net of income tax benefit of $70,000), $200,000; loss on disposal of discontinued operations (net of income tax benefit of $16,000), $50,000; operating expenses, $130,000; income taxes expense on continuing operations, $60,000. From this information, prepare the company's income statement for the year ended June 30, 2012. (*Note:* Ignore earnings per share information.)

LO 3 **Trend Analysis**

SE 5. Using 2011 as the base year, prepare a trend analysis for the following data and tell whether the results suggest a favorable or unfavorable trend. (*Note:* Round your answers to one decimal place.)

	2013	2012	2011
Net sales	$316,000	$272,000	$224,000
Accounts receivable (net)	86,000	64,000	42,000

LO 3 **Horizontal Analysis**

SE 6. The comparative income statements and balance sheets of Otis, Inc., appear below. Compute the amount and percentage changes for the income statements and comment on the changes from 2011 to 2012. (*Note:* Round the percentage changes to one decimal place.)

Otis, Inc.
Comparative Income Statements
For the Years Ended December 31, 2012 and 2011

	2012	2011
Net sales	$360,000	$290,000
Cost of goods sold	224,000	176,000
Gross margin	$136,000	$114,000
Operating expenses	80,000	60,000
Operating income	$ 56,000	$ 54,000
Interest expense	14,000	10,000
Income before income taxes	$ 42,000	$ 44,000
Income taxes expense	14,000	16,000
Net income	$ 28,000	$ 28,000
Earnings per share	$ 2.80	$ 2.80

Otis, Inc.
Comparative Balance Sheets
December 31, 2012 and 2011

	2012	2011
Assets		
Current assets	$ 48,000	$ 40,000
Property, plant, and equipment (net)	260,000	200,000
Total assets	$308,000	$240,000
Liabilities and Stockholders' Equity		
Current liabilities	$ 36,000	$ 44,000
Long-term liabilities	180,000	120,000
Stockholders' equity	92,000	76,000
Total liabilities and stockholders' equity	$308,000	$240,000

LO 3 Vertical Analysis

SE 7. Express the comparative balance sheets of Otis, Inc., from **SE 6** as common-size statements and comment on the changes from 2011 to 2012. (*Note:* Round computations to one decimal place.)

LO 4 Operating Asset Management Analysis

RATIO

SE 8. Using the information for Otis, Inc., in **SE 6** and **SE 7**, compute current ratio, quick ratio, receivable turnover, days' sales uncollected, inventory turnover, days' inventory on hand, payables turnover, and days' payable for 2011 and 2012. Inventories were $8,000 in 2010, $10,000 in 2011, and $14,000 in 2012. Accounts receivable were $12,000 in 2010, $16,000 in 2011, and $20,000 in 2012. Accounts payable were $18,000 in 2010, $20,000 in 2011, and $24,000 in 2012. The company had no marketable securities or prepaid assets. Comment on the results. (*Note:* Round computations to one decimal place.)

LO 4 Profitability and Total Asset Management Analysis

SE 9. Using the information for Otis, Inc., in **SE 6** and **SE 7**, compute profit margin, asset turnover, and return on assets for 2011 and 2012. In 2010, total assets were $200,000. Comment on the results. (*Note:* Round computations to one decimal place.)

LO 4 Financial Risk Analysis

SE 10. Using the information for Otis, Inc., in **SE 6** and **SE 7**, compute the debt to equity ratio, return on equity, and the interest coverage ratio for 2011 and 2012. In 2010, total stockholders' equity was $60,000. Comment on the results. (*Note:* Round computations to one decimal place.)

LO 4 Liquidity Analysis

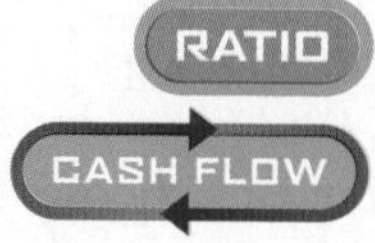

SE 11. Using the information for Otis, Inc., in **SE 6**, **SE 7**, and **SE 9**, compute cash flow yield, cash flows to sales, cash flows to assets, and free cash flow for 2011 and 2012. Net cash flows from operating activities were $42,000 in 2011 and $32,000 in 2012. Net capital expenditures were $60,000 in 2011 and $80,000 in 2012. Cash dividends were $12,000 in both years. Comment on the results. (*Note:* Round computations to one decimal place.)

LO 4

Market Strength Analysis

SE 12. Using the information for Otis, Inc., in **SE 6**, **SE 7**, and **SE 11**, compute the price/earnings (P/E) ratio and dividends yield for 2011 and 2012. The company had 10,000 shares of common stock outstanding in both years. The price of Otis's common stock was $30 in 2011 and $20 in 2012. Comment on the results. (*Note:* Round computations to one decimal place.)

Exercises

LO 1, 3

Discussion Questions

E 1. Develop brief answers to each of the following questions:

1. Why is it essential that management compensation, including bonuses, be linked to financial goals and strategies that achieve shareholder value?
2. How are past performance and industry norms useful in evaluating a company's performance? What are their limitations?
3. In a five-year trend analysis, why do the dollar values remain the same for their respective years while the percentages usually change when a new five-year period is chosen?

LO 4

Discussion Questions

E 2. Develop brief answers to each of the following questions:

1. Why does a decrease in receivable turnover create the need for cash from operating activities?
2. Why would ratios that include one balance sheet account and one income statement account, such as receivable turnover or return on assets, be questionable if they came from quarterly or other interim financial reports?
3. What is a limitation of free cash flow in comparing one company to another?

LO 1

Issues in Financial Performance Evaluation

E 3. Identify each of the following as (a) an objective of financial statement analysis, (b) a standard for financial statement analysis, (c) a source of information for financial statement analysis, or (d) an executive compensation issue:

1. Average ratios of other companies in the same industry
2. Assessment of the future potential of an investment
3. Interim financial statements
4. Past ratios of the company
5. SEC Form 10-K
6. Assessment of risk
7. A company's annual report
8. Linking performance to shareholder value

LO 2

Effect of Alternative Accounting Methods

E 4. At the end of its first year of operations, a company calculated its ending merchandise inventory according to three different accounting methods, as follows: FIFO, $190,000; average cost, $180,000; LIFO, $172,000. If the company used the average cost method, its net income for the year would be $68,000.

1. Determine net income if the company used the FIFO method.
2. Determine net income if the company used the LIFO method.
3. Which method is more conservative?
4. Will the consistency convention be violated if the company chooses to use the LIFO method? Why or why not?
5. Does the full-disclosure convention require disclosure of the inventory method used in the financial statements?

LO 2

Corporate Income Statement

E 5. Assume that Hugo Corporation's chief financial officer gave you the following information: net sales, $950,000; cost of goods sold, $525,000; gain on sale of equipment, $6,250;

loss from discontinued operations (net of income tax benefit of $15,000), $25,000; loss on disposal of discontinued operations (net of income tax benefit of $6,500), $17,500; selling expenses, $25,000; administrative expenses, $40,000; income taxes expense on continuing operations, $150,000. From this information, prepare the company's income statement for the year ended June 30, 2011. (*Note:* Ignore earnings per share information.)

LO 3

Trend Analysis

E 6. Using 2008 as the base year, prepare a trend analysis of the following data and tell whether the situation shown by the trends is favorable or unfavorable. (*Note:* Round your answers to one decimal place.)

	2012	2011	2010	2009	2008
Net sales	$50,040	$47,960	$48,400	$45,760	$44,000
Cost of goods sold	34,440	30,800	31,080	29,400	28,000
General and administrative expenses	10,560	10,368	10,176	9,792	9,600
Operating income	6,040	6,792	7,144	6,568	6,400

LO 3

Horizontal Analysis

E 7. Compute the amount and percentage changes for the following balance sheets for Davis Company and comment on the changes from 2011 to 2012. (*Note:* Round the percentage changes to one decimal place.)

Davis Company
Comparative Balance Sheets
December 31, 2012 and 2011

	2012	2011
Assets		
Current assets	$ 18,600	$ 12,800
Property, plant, and equipment (net)	109,464	97,200
Total assets	$128,064	$110,000
Liabilities and Stockholders' Equity		
Current liabilities	$ 11,200	$ 3,200
Long-term liabilities	35,000	40,000
Stockholders' equity	81,864	66,800
Total liabilities and stockholders' equity	$128,064	$110,000

LO 3

Vertical Analysis

E 8. Express the partial comparative income statements for Davis Company that follow as common-size statements and comment on the changes from 2011 to 2012. (*Note:* Round computations to one decimal place.)

Davis Company
Partial Comparative Income Statements
For the Years Ended December 31, 2012 and 2011

	2012	2011
Net sales	$212,000	$184,000
Cost of goods sold	127,200	119,600
Gross margin	$ 84,800	$ 64,400
Selling expenses	$ 53,000	$ 36,800
General expenses	25,440	18,400
Total operating expenses	$ 78,440	$ 55,200
Operating income	$ 6,360	$ 9,200

LO 4

RATIO

Operating Asset Management Analysis

E 9. Partial comparative balance sheet and income statement information for Sople Company is as follows:

	2012	2011
Cash	$ 13,600	$ 10,400
Marketable securities	7,200	17,200
Accounts receivable (net)	44,800	35,600
Inventory	54,400	49,600
Total current assets	$120,000	$112,800
Accounts payable	$ 40,000	$ 28,200
Net sales	$322,560	$220,720
Cost of goods sold	217,600	203,360
Gross margin	$104,960	$ 17,360

In 2010, the year-end balances for Accounts Receivable and Inventory were $32,400 and $51,200, respectively. Accounts Payable was $30,600 in 2010 and is the only current liability. Compute current ratio, quick ratio, receivable turnover, days' sales uncollected, inventory turnover, days' inventory on hand, payables turnover, and days' payable for each year. (*Note:* Round computations to one decimal place.) Comment on the change in the company's operating asset management, including its operating cycle and required days of financing from 2011 to 2012.

LO 4

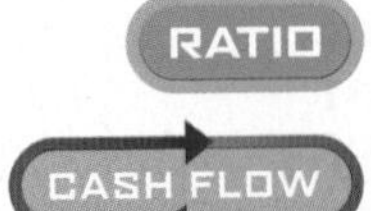

Turnover Analysis

E 10. Ike Tuxedo Rental has been in business for four years. Because the company has recently had a cash flow problem, management wonders whether there is a problem with receivables or inventories. Here are selected figures from the company's financial statements (in thousands):

	2012	2011	2010	2009
Net sales	$144	$112	$96	$80
Cost of goods sold	90	72	60	48
Accounts receivable (net)	24	20	16	12
Merchandise inventory	28	22	16	10
Accounts payable	13	10	8	5

Compute the receivable turnover, inventory turnover, and payables turnover for each of the four years and comment on the results relative to the cash flow problem that the firm has been experiencing. Merchandise inventory was $11,000, accounts receivable were $11,000, and accounts payable were $4,000 in 2008. (*Note:* Round computations to one decimal place.)

LO 4

Profitability and Total Asset Management Analysis

E 11. Barr Company had total assets of $320,000 in 2010, $340,000 in 2011, and $380,000 in 2012. The company's debt to equity ratio was 0.67 times in all three years. In 2011, Barr had net income of $38,556 on revenues of $612,000. In 2012, it had net income of $49,476 on revenues of $798,000. Compute the profit margin, asset turnover, return on assets, and return on equity for 2011 and 2012. Comment on the apparent cause of the increase or decrease in profitability. (*Note:* Round the percentages and other ratios to one decimal place.)

LO 4

Financial Risk and Market Strength Ratios

E 12. An investor is trying to decide whether to invest in the long-term bonds and common stock of Mayer Company and Matthews Company. Both companies operate in the same industry. Both also pay a dividend per share of $8 and have a yield of 10 percent on their long-term bonds. Other data for the two companies are as follows:

	Mayer Company	Matthews Company
Total assets	$4,800,000	$2,160,000
Total liabilities	2,160,000	1,188,000
Income before income taxes	576,000	259,200
Interest expense	194,400	106,920
Earnings per share	6.40	10.00
Market price of common stock	80.00	95.00

Compute the debt to equity, interest coverage, and price/earnings (P/E) ratios as well as the dividends yield and comment on the results. (*Note:* Round computations to one decimal place.)

LO 4

Liquidity Analysis

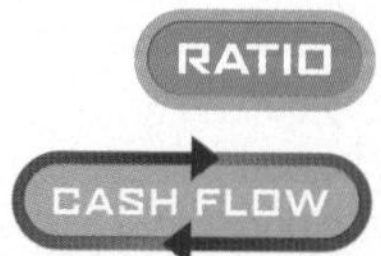

E 13. Using the data below from the financial statements of Coat, Inc., compute the company's cash flow yield, cash flows to sales, cash flows to assets, and free cash flow. (*Note:* Round computations to one decimal place.)

Net sales	$3,200,000
Net income	352,000
Net cash flows from operating activities	456,000
Total assets, beginning of year	2,890,000
Total assets, end of year	3,120,000
Cash dividends	120,000
Net capital expenditures	298,000

Problems

LO 2

Effect of Alternative Accounting Methods

✔ Difference in net income: $97,600

P 1. Dot Company began operations in 2012. At the beginning of the year, the company purchased plant assets of $900,000, with an estimated useful life of 10 years and no residual value. During the year, the company had net sales of $1,300,000, salaries expense of $200,000, and other expenses of $80,000, excluding depreciation. In addition, Dot purchased inventory as follows:

Jan. 15	400 units at $400	$160,000
Mar. 20	200 units at $408	81,600
June 15	800 units at $416	332,800
Sept. 18	600 units at $412	247,200
Dec. 9	300 units at $420	126,000
Total	2,300 units	$947,600

At the end of the year, a physical inventory disclosed 500 units still on hand. The managers of Dot know they have a choice of accounting methods, but they are unsure how those methods will affect net income. They have heard of the FIFO and LIFO inventory methods and the straight-line and double-declining-balance depreciation methods.

REQUIRED

1. Prepare two income statements for Dot Company, one using the FIFO and straight-line methods and the other using the LIFO and double-declining-balance methods. Ignore income taxes.
2. Prepare a schedule accounting for the difference in the two net income figures obtained in **1**.

USER INSIGHT ▶

3. What effect does the choice of accounting method have on Dot's inventory turnover? (*Note:* Round to one decimal place.) What conclusions can you draw? Use the year-end balance to compute the ratio.

USER INSIGHT ▶

4. How does the choice of accounting methods affect Dot's return on assets? Assume the company's only assets are cash of $80,000, inventory, and plant assets. Use year-end balances to compute the ratios. Is your evaluation of Dot's profitability affected by the choice of accounting methods? Explain your answer.

LO 3

Horizontal and Vertical Analysis

P 2. Whale Corporation's condensed comparative balance sheets and condensed comparative income statements for 2012 and 2011 follow.

Whale Corporation
Comparative Balance Sheets
December 31, 2012 and 2011

	2012	2011
Assets		
Cash	$ 81,200	$ 40,800
Accounts receivable (net)	235,600	229,200
Inventory	574,800	594,800
Property, plant, and equipment (net)	750,000	720,000
Total assets	$1,641,600	$1,584,800
Liabilities and Stockholders' Equity		
Accounts payable	$ 267,600	$ 477,200
Notes payable (short-term)	200,000	400,000
Bonds payable	400,000	—
Common stock, $10 par value	400,000	400,000
Retained earnings	374,000	307,600
Total liabilities and stockholders' equity	$1,641,600	$1,584,800

Whale Corporation
Comparative Income Statements
For the Years Ended December 31, 2012 and 2011

	2012	2011
Net sales	$3,276,800	$3,146,400
Cost of goods sold	2,088,800	2,008,400
Gross margin	$1,188,000	$1,138,000
Operating expenses		
Selling expenses	$ 476,800	$ 518,000
Administrative expenses	447,200	423,200
Total operating expenses	$ 924,000	$ 941,200
Income from operations	$ 264,000	$ 196,800
Interest expense	65,600	39,200
Income before income taxes	$ 198,400	$ 157,600
Income taxes expense	62,400	56,800
Net income	$ 136,000	$ 100,800
Earnings per share	$ 3.40	$ 2.52

REQUIRED

1. Prepare schedules showing the amount and percentage changes from 2011 to 2012 for the comparative income statements and the balance sheets.
2. Prepare common-size income statements and balance sheets for 2011 and 2012.

USER INSIGHT ▶

3. Comment on the results in **1** and **2** by identifying favorable and unfavorable changes in the components and composition of the statements.

LO 4

✔ Increase: a, b, e, f, l, m

Effects of Transactions on Ratios

P 3. Avalon Corporation engaged in the transactions listed in the first column of the following table. Opposite each transaction is a ratio and space to indicate the effect of each transaction on the ratio.

Transaction	Ratio	Effect: Increase	Effect: Decrease	Effect: None
a. Sold merchandise on account.	Current ratio			
b. Sold merchandise on account.	Inventory turnover			
c. Collected on accounts receivable.	Quick ratio			
d. Wrote off an uncollectible account.	Receivable turnover			
e. Paid on accounts payable.	Current ratio			
f. Declared cash dividend.	Return on equity			
g. Incurred advertising expense.	Profit margin			
h. Issued stock dividend.	Debt to equity ratio			
i. Issued bonds payable.	Asset turnover			
j. Accrued interest expense.	Current ratio			
k. Paid previously declared cash dividend.	Dividends yield			
l. Purchased treasury stock.	Return on assets			
m. Recorded depreciation expense.	Cash flow yield			

REQUIRED

USER INSIGHT ▶ Show that you understand the effect of business activities on performance measures by placing an X in the appropriate column to show whether the transaction increased, decreased, or had no effect on the indicated ratio.

LO 4

RATIO

CASH FLOW

✔ Profit margin, 2012: 4.2%; 2011: 3.2%

✔ Debt to equity, 2012: 1.1 times; 2011: 1.2 times

Comprehensive Ratio Analysis

P 4. Data for Whale Corporation in 2012 and 2011 follow. These data should be used in conjunction with the data in **P 2**.

	2012	2011
Net cash flows from operating activities	$(196,000)	$144,000
Net capital expenditures	$ 40,000	$ 65,000
Dividends paid	$ 44,000	$ 34,400
Number of common shares	40,000	40,000
Market price per share	$ 36.00	$ 60.00

Selected balances at the end of 2010 were accounts receivable (net), $206,800; inventory, $547,200; total assets, $1,465,600; accounts payable, $384,600; and stockholders' equity, $641,200. All of Whale's notes payable were current liabilities; all of its bonds payable were long-term liabilities.

REQUIRED

Perform a comprehensive ratio analysis for 2012 and 2011 following the steps outlined below. (*Note:* Round all answers to one decimal place.)

1. Prepare a profitability and total asset management analysis by calculating for each year the (a) profit margin, (b) asset turnover, and (c) return on assets.
2. Prepare a liquidity analysis by calculating for each year the (a) cash flow yield, (b) cash flows to sales, (c) cash flows to assets, and (d) free cash flow.
3. Prepare a financial risk analysis by calculating for each year the (a) debt to equity ratio, (b) return on equity, and (c) interest coverage ratio.
4. Prepare an operating asset management analysis by calculating for each year the (a) inventory turnover, (b) days' inventory on hand, (c) receivable turnover, (d) days' sales uncollected, (e) payables turnover, (f) days' payable, (g) current ratio, and (h) quick ratio.

5. Prepare a market strength analysis by calculating for each year the (a) price/earnings (P/E) ratio and (b) dividends yield.

USER INSIGHT ▶ 6. After making the calculations, indicate whether each ratio improved or deteriorated from 2011 to 2012. (Use *F* for favorable and *U* for unfavorable and consider changes of 0.1 or less to be neutral.)

LO 4

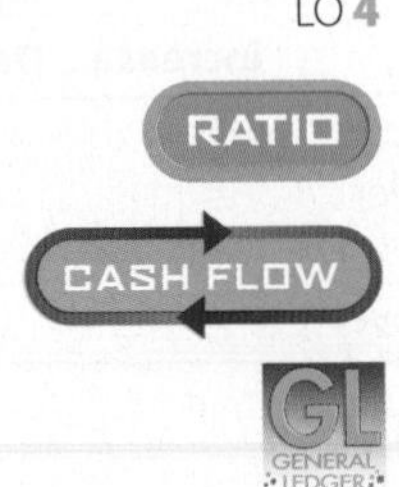

✔ Asset turnover, Roma: 2.5 times; Lima: 2.7 times

✔ Free cash flow, Roma: ($403,500); Lima: ($671,500)

Comprehensive Ratio Analysis of Two Companies

P 5. Kevin Wolfer is considering an investment in the common stock of a chain of retail department stores. He has narrowed his choice to two retail companies, Roma Corporation and Lima Corporation, whose income statements and balance sheets follow.

During the year, Roma Corporation paid a total of $50,000 in dividends. The market price per share of its stock is currently $60. In comparison, Lima Corporation paid a total of $114,000 in dividends, and the current market price of its stock is $76 per share. Roma Corporation had net cash flows from operations of $271,500 and net capital expenditures of $625,000. Lima Corporation had net cash flows from operations of $492,500 and net capital expenditures of $1,050,000. Information for prior years is not readily available. Assume that all notes payable are current liabilities and all bonds payable are long-term liabilities and that there is no change in inventory.

Income Statements

	Roma	Lima
Net sales	$12,560,000	$25,210,000
Costs and expenses		
Cost of goods sold	$ 6,142,000	$14,834,000
Selling expenses	4,822,600	7,108,200
Administrative expenses	986,000	2,434,000
Total costs and expenses	$11,950,600	$24,376,200
Income from operations	$ 609,400	$ 833,800
Interest expense	194,000	228,000
Income before income taxes	$ 415,400	$ 605,800
Income taxes expense	200,000	300,000
Net income	$ 215,400	$ 305,800
Earnings per share	$ 4.31	$ 10.19

Balance Sheets

	Roma	Lima
Assets		
Cash	$ 80,000	$ 192,400
Marketable securities (at cost)	203,400	84,600
Accounts receivable (net)	552,800	985,400
Inventory	629,800	1,253,400
Prepaid expenses	54,400	114,000
Property, plant, and equipment (net)	2,913,600	6,552,000
Intangibles and other assets	553,200	144,800
Total assets	$4,987,200	$9,326,600
Liabilities and Stockholders' Equity		
Accounts payable	$ 344,000	$ 572,600
Notes payable	150,000	400,000
Income taxes payable	50,200	73,400
Bonds payable	2,000,000	2,000,000
Common stock, $20 par value	1,000,000	600,000
Additional paid-in capital	609,800	3,568,600
Retained earnings	833,200	2,112,000
Total liabilities and stockholders' equity	$4,987,200	$9,326,600

REQUIRED

Conduct a comprehensive ratio analysis for each company, following the steps outlined below. Compare the results. (*Note:* Round percentages and ratios to one decimal place and consider changes of 0.1 or less to be indeterminate.)

1. Prepare a profitability and total asset management analysis by calculating for each company the (a) profit margin, (b) asset turnover, and (c) return on assets.
2. Prepare a liquidity analysis by calculating for each company the (a) cash flow yield, (b) cash flows to sales, (c) cash flows to assets, and (d) free cash flow.
3. Prepare a financial risk analysis by calculating for each company the (a) debt to equity ratio, (b) return on equity, and (c) interest coverage ratio.
4. Prepare an operating asset management analysis by calculating for each company (a) inventory turnover, (b) days' inventory on hand, (c) receivable turnover, (d) days' sales uncollected, (e) payables turnover, (f) days' payable, (g) current ratio, and (h) quick ratio.
5. Prepare a market strength analysis by calculating for each company the (a) price/earnings (P/E) ratio and (b) dividends yield.

USER INSIGHT ▶

6. Compare the two companies by inserting the ratio calculations from **1** through **5** in a table with the following column headings: Ratio Name, Roma, Lima, and Company with More Favorable Ratio. Indicate in the last column which company had the more favorable ratio in each case. (*Note:* Consider changes of 0.1 or less to be neutral.)

USER INSIGHT ▶

7. How could the analysis be improved if information about these companies' prior years were available?

Alternate Problems

LO 2

Effect of Alternative Accounting Methods

✔ Difference in net income: $30,950

P 6. Zeigler Corporation began operations in 2012. At the beginning of the year, the company purchased plant assets of $300,000, with an estimated useful life of 10 years and no residual value. During the year, the company had net sales of $450,000, salaries expense of $70,000, and other expenses of $25,000, excluding depreciation. In addition, Zeigler purchased inventory as follows:

Jan. 15	200	units at $100	$ 20,000
Mar. 20	100	units at $102	10,200
June 15	400	units at $104	41,600
Sept. 18	300	units at $103	30,900
Dec. 9	150	units at $105	15,750
Total	1,150	units	$118,450

At the end of the year, a physical inventory disclosed 250 units still on hand. The managers of Zeigler know they have a choice of accounting methods, but they are unsure how those methods will affect net income. They have heard of the FIFO and LIFO inventory methods and the straight-line and double-declining-balance depreciation methods.

REQUIRED

1. Prepare two income statements for Zeigler, one using the FIFO and straight-line methods and the other using the LIFO and double-declining-balance methods. Ignore income taxes.
2. Prepare a schedule accounting for the difference in the two net income figures obtained in **1**.

USER INSIGHT ▶

3. What effect does the choice of accounting method have on Zeigler's inventory turnover? (*Note:* Round to one decimal place.) What conclusions can you draw? Use the year-end balance to compute the ratio.

USER INSIGHT ▶

4. How does the choice of accounting methods affect Zeigler's return on assets? Assume the company's only assets are cash of $25,000, inventory, and plant assets. Use year-end balances to compute the ratios. Is your evaluation of Zeigler's profitability affected by the choice of accounting methods? Explain your answer.

LO 4

Effects of Transactions on Ratios

✔ Increase: d, h, i

P 7. Cozy Corporation, a clothing retailer, engaged in the transactions listed in the first column of the table that follows. Opposite each transaction is a ratio and space to mark the effect of each transaction on the ratio.

Transaction	Ratio	Effect		
		Increase	Decrease	None
a. Issued common stock for cash.	Asset turnover			
b. Declared cash dividend.	Current ratio			
c. Sold treasury stock.	Return on equity			
d. Borrowed cash by issuing note payable.	Debt to equity ratio			
e. Paid salaries expense.	Inventory turnover			
f. Purchased merchandise for cash.	Current ratio			
g. Sold equipment for cash.	Receivable turnover			
h. Sold merchandise on account.	Quick ratio			
i. Paid current portion of long-term debt.	Return on assets			
j. Gave sales discount.	Profit margin			
k. Purchased marketable securities for cash.	Quick ratio			
l. Declared 5% stock dividend.	Current ratio			
m. Purchased a building.	Free cash flow			

REQUIRED

USER INSIGHT ▶ Show that you understand the effect of business activities on performance measures by placing an X in the appropriate column to show whether the transaction increased, decreased, or had no effect on the indicated ratio.

LO 4

Comprehensive Ratio Analysis

CASH FLOW

✔ Return on assets, 2012: 5.0%; 2011: 10.7%
✔ Return on equity, 2012: 8.2%; 2011: 17.2%

P 8. The condensed comparative income statements of Ada Corporation appear below. The corporation's condensed comparative balance sheets follow. All figures are given in thousands of dollars except earnings per share and market price per share.

Additional data for Ada in 2012 and 2011 are as follows:

	2012	2011
Net cash flows from operating activities	$ 64,000	$99,000
Net capital expenditures	$119,000	$38,000
Dividends paid	$ 31,400	$35,000
Number of common shares	30,000	30,000
Market price per share	$ 80.00	$120.00

Balances of selected accounts at the end of 2010 were accounts receivable (net), $52,700; inventory, $99,400; accounts payable, $64,800; total assets, $647,800; and stockholders' equity, $376,600. All of the bonds payable were long-term liabilities.

Ada Corporation
Comparative Income Statements
For the Years Ended December 31, 2012 and 2011

	2012	2011
Net sales	$800,400	$742,600
Cost of goods sold	454,100	396,200
Gross margin	$346,300	$346,400
Operating expenses		
Selling expenses	$130,100	$104,600
Administrative expenses	140,300	115,500
Total operating expenses	$270,400	$220,100
Income from operations	$ 75,900	$126,300
Interest expense	25,000	20,000
Income before income taxes	$ 50,900	$106,300
Income taxes expense	14,000	35,000
Net income	$ 36,900	$ 71,300
Earnings per share	$ 1.23	$ 2.38

Ada Corporation
Comparative Balance Sheets
December 31, 2012 and 2011

	2012	2011
Assets		
Cash	$ 31,100	$ 27,200
Accounts receivable (net)	72,500	42,700
Inventory	122,600	107,800
Property, plant, and equipment (net)	577,700	507,500
Total assets	$803,900	$685,200
Liabilities and Stockholders' Equity		
Accounts payable	$104,700	$ 72,300
Notes payable	50,000	50,000
Bonds payable	200,000	110,000
Common stock, $10 par value	300,000	300,000
Retained earnings	149,200	152,900
Total liabilities and stockholders' equity	$803,900	$685,200

REQUIRED

Perform the following analyses for 2012 and 2011. (*Note:* Round percentages and ratios to one decimal place.)

1. Prepare a profitability and total asset management analysis by calculating for each year the (a) profit margin, (b) asset turnover, and (c) return on assets.
2. Prepare a liquidity analysis by calculating for each year the (a) cash flow yield, (b) cash flows to sales, (c) cash flows to assets, and (d) free cash flow.
3. Prepare a financial risk analysis by calculating for each year the (a) debt to equity ratio, (b) return on equity, and (c) interest coverage ratio.
4. Prepare an operating asset management analysis by calculating for each year the (a) inventory turnover, (b) days' inventory on hand, (c) receivable turnover, (d) days' sales uncollected, (e) payables turnover, (f) days' payable (g) current ratio, and (h) quick ratio.

5. Prepare a market strength analysis by calculating for each year the (a) price/earnings (P/E) ratio and (b) dividends yield.

USER INSIGHT ▶ 6. After making the calculations, indicate whether each ratio improved or deteriorated from 2011 to 2012. (Use *F* for favorable and *U* for unfavorable and consider changes of 0.1 or less to be neutral.)

Cases

LO 1 Conceptual Understanding: Using Segment Information

C 1. Refer to Exhibit 13.1, which shows segment information for **Goodyear Tire & Rubber Company**. In what business segments does Goodyear operate? What is the relative size of its business segments in terms of sales and income in the most recent year shown? Which segment is most profitable in terms of return on assets? In which region of the world is the tires segment largest, and which tire segment is most profitable in terms of return on assets?

LO 2 Interpreting Financial Reports: Corporate Income Statement and Evaluation of Business Operations

C 2. During 2012, Dash Corporation engaged in two transactions to improve the business—selling off a division and sale of investments. The company has always issued a simple single-step income statement, and the accountant has accordingly prepared the December 31 year-end income statements for 2011 and 2012, as shown below.

Dash Corporation
Income Statements
For the Years Ended December 31, 2012 and 2011

	2012	2011
Net sales	$2,000,000	$2,400,000
Cost of goods sold	(1,100,000)	(1,200,000)
Operating expenses	(450,000)	(300,000)
Income taxes expense	(358,200)	(270,000)
Income from operations of a discontinued segment	320,000	
Gain on disposal of discontinued segment	280,000	
Gain on retirement of bonds	144,000	
Net income	$ 835,800	$ 630,000
Earnings per share	$ 2.09	$ 1.58

Henry Dash, the president of Dash Corporation, is pleased that both net income and earnings per share increased by almost 33 percent from 2011 to 2012, and he intends to announce to the company's stockholders that the plan to improve the business has been successful.

1. Recast the 2012 and 2011 income statements in proper multistep form, including allocating income taxes to appropriate items (assume a 30 percent income tax rate) and showing earnings per share figures (400,000 shares outstanding).

USER INSIGHT ▶ 2. What is your assessment of Dash Corporation's plan and business operations in 2012?

LO 3 Interpreting Financial Reports: Trend Analysis

C 3. H. J. Heinz Company is a global company engaged in several lines of business, including food service, infant foods, condiments, pet foods, and weight-control food products. A five-year summary of operations and other related data for Heinz follows.[16] (Amounts are in thousands.)

H. J. Heinz Company and Subsidiaries
Five-Year Summary of Operations and Other Related Data

	2010	2009	2008	2007	2006
Summary of operations					
Sales	$10,494,983	$10,011,311	$ 9,885,556	$ 9,001,630	$8,643,438
Cost of products sold	6,700,677	6,442,075	6,233,420	5,608,730	5,550,364
Interest expense	295,711	339,635	364,808	333,270	316,296
Provision for income taxes	358,514	375,483	372,587	332,797	250,700
Net income (before special items)	931,940	944,400	858,176	791,602	442,761
Other related data					
Dividends paid: common	533,543	525,281	485,234	461,224	408,137
Total assets	10,075,711	9,664,184	10,565,043	10,033,026	9,737,767
Total debt	4,559,152	5,076,186	4,730,946	4,413,641	4,357,013
Shareholders' equity	1,948,496	1,279,105	1,887,820	1,841,683	2,048,823

Prepare a trend analysis for Heinz with 2006 as the base year and discuss the results. Identify important trends and state whether the trends are favorable or unfavorable. Discuss significant relationships among the trends.

LO 4

Interpreting Financial Reports: Comparison of International Companies' Operating Cycles

C 4. Ratio analysis enables one to compare the performance of companies whose financial statements are presented in different currencies. Selected data from 2009 for two large pharmaceutical companies—one American, **Pfizer, Inc.**, and one Swiss, **Roche**—are presented below (in millions).[17]

	Pfizer, Inc. (U.S.)	Roche (Swiss)
Net sales	$50,009	SF 49,051
Cost of goods sold	8,888	14,615
Accounts receivable	14,645	10,461
Inventories	12,403	5,648
Accounts payable	4,370	2,300

For each company, calculate receivable turnover, days' sales uncollected, inventory turnover, days' inventory on hand, payables turnover, and days' payable. Then determine the operating cycle and days of financing required for each company. (Accounts receivable in 2008 were $8,958 for Pfizer and SF 9,755 for Roche. Inventories in 2008 were $4,381 for Pfizer and SF 5,830 for Roche. Accounts payable in 2008 were $1,751 for Pfizer and SF 2,017 for Roche.) Describe your analysis of the operating cycles of these companies.

LO 4

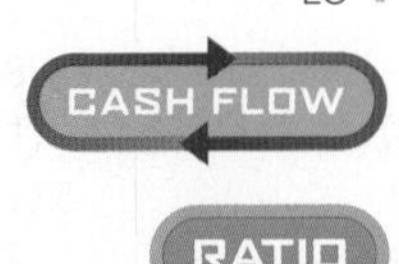

Annual Report Case: Comprehensive Ratio Analysis

RATIO

C 5. Using data from the **CVS** annual report in the Supplement to Chapter 1, conduct a comprehensive ratio analysis that compares the company's performance in 2009 and 2008. If you have computed ratios for CVS in previous chapters, you may prepare a table that summarizes the ratios and show calculations only for the ratios you have not previously calculated. If this is the first ratio analysis you have done for CVS, show all of your computations. In either case, after each group of ratios, comment on the performance of CVS. (*Note:* Round your calculations to one decimal place.) Prepare and comment on the following categories of ratios:

Profitability and total asset management analysis: profit margin, asset turnover, and return on assets. [Total assets were (in millions) $54,722 in 2007.]

Liquidity analysis: cash flow yield, cash flows to sales, cash flows to assets, and free cash flow.

Operating asset management analysis: inventory turnover, days' inventory on hand, receivable turnover, days' sales uncollected, payables turnover, days' payable, current ratio, and quick ratio. [Accounts Receivable, Inventories, and Accounts Payable were (in millions) $4,580, $8,008, and $3,593, respectively, in 2007.]

Financial risk analysis: debt to equity ratio, return on equity, and interest coverage ratio. [Total shareholders' equity was (in millions) $31,322 in 2007.]

Market strength analysis: price/earnings (P/E) ratio and dividends yield.

LO 4

Comparison Analysis: Key Financial Performance Measures

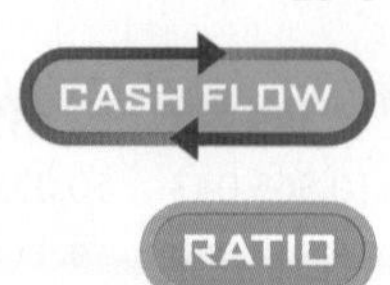

C 6. Refer to the annual report of **CVS** and the financial statements of **Southwest Airlines Co.** in the Supplement to Chapter 1. Prepare a table showing the following key financial performance measures for the two most recent years for both companies. (Use your computations in **C 5** or perform those computations if you have not already done so. Total assets for Southwest in 2007 were $16,772 million.)

Profitability and total asset management:	Profit margin
	Asset turnover
	Return on assets
Liquidity:	Cash flow yield
	Free cash flow
Financial risk:	Debt to equity ratio

Evaluate and comment on the relative performance of the two companies with respect to each of the above categories.

LO 3, 4

Decision Analysis Using Excel: Effect of a One-Time Item on a Loan Decision

C 7. Apple a Day, Inc., and Unforgettable Edibles, Inc., are food catering businesses that operate in the same metropolitan area. Their customers include Fortune 500 companies, regional firms, and individuals. The two firms reported similar profit margins for the current year, and both base bonuses for managers on the achievement of a target profit margin and return on equity. Each firm has submitted a loan request to you, a loan officer for City National Bank. The companies have provided you with the following information:

	Apple a Day	Unforgettable Edibles
Net sales	$625,348	$717,900
Cost of goods sold	225,125	287,080
Gross margin	$400,223	$430,820
Operating expenses	281,300	371,565
Operating income	$118,923	$ 59,255
Gain on sale of real estate	—	81,923
Interest expense	(9,333)	(15,338)
Income before income taxes	$109,590	$125,840
Income taxes expense	25,990	29,525
Net income	$ 83,600	$ 96,315
Average stockholders' equity	$312,700	$390,560

1. Perform a vertical analysis and prepare a common-size income statement for each firm. Compute profit margin and return on equity.
2. Discuss these results, the bonus plan for management, and loan considerations. Identify the company that is the better loan risk.

CHAPTER 14

DECISION POINT
A User's Focus Intel Corporation

Intel Corporation is the world's largest manufacturer of processors, which are the "brains" of all electronic devices. In 1971, Intel made computer history when it introduced the microprocessor to the market. Originally intended for use in scientific calculators, the microprocessor, which integrated the central processing functions of a computer on a single chip, was soon used in many other applications. Intel's processors are today used in everything from servers, workstations, desktops, and laptops to handheld devices.

Because Intel is highly profitable, it has a considerable amount of cash available for investments. As you can see in the company's Financial Highlights, these investments and the related accounts are important components of its financial statements.[1]

AP Photo/Paul Sakuma

INTEL'S FINANCIAL HIGHLIGHTS
(in millions)

	2009	2008
Balance Sheet		
Short-term investments	$ 5,285	$ 5,331
Long-term investments	4,952	3,276
Goodwill	4,421	3,932
Total assets	53,095	50,472
Income Statement		
Interest and other income, net	$ 163	$ 488
Net income	4,369	5,292
Statement of Cash Flows		
Cash flows from investing activities		
Purchases of available-for-sale investments	$ (8,655)	$ (6,479)
Maturities and sales of available-for-sale investments	7,756	7,993
Investments in equity investment	(250)	(1,691)
Purchases of trading assets	(4,186)	(2,676)
Maturities and sales of trading assets	2,543	1,766

Questions

1. *What types of investments are identified in Intel's financial statements?*
2. *How do Intel's investments affect its financial performance?*

Investments

LEARNING OBJECTIVES

LO 1 Identify and explain the management issues related to investments. (pp. 636–639)

LO 2 Explain the financial reporting implications of short-term investments. (pp. 639–643)

LO 3 Explain the financial reporting implications of long-term investments in stock and the cost-adjusted-to-market and equity methods used to account for them. (pp. 643–649)

LO 4 Explain the financial reporting implications of consolidated financial statements. (pp. 649–656)

LO 5 Explain the financial reporting implications of debt investments. (pp. 656–658)

Many companies invest in the stock or debt securities of other firms. They may do so for several reasons. For example, a company may temporarily have excess funds on which it can earn a return, or investments may be an integral part of its business, as in the case of a bank. A company may also invest in other firms for the purpose of partnering with or controlling them. This chapter presents an overview of both short- and long-term investments, including the importance of avoiding unethical trading in securities.

FOCUS ON FINANCIAL STATEMENTS

INCOME STATEMENT
Revenues
− Expenses
= Net Income

STATEMENT OF RETAINED EARNINGS
Opening Balance
+ Net Income
− Dividends
= Retained Earnings

BALANCE SHEET
Assets | Liabilities
Equity
A = L + E

STATEMENT OF CASH FLOWS
Operating Activities
+ Investing Activities
+ Financing Activities
= Change in Cash
+ Starting Balance
= Ending Cash Balance

Sales of investments at a gain or loss will affect operating as well as financing activities on the statement of cash flows.

MANAGEMENT ISSUES RELATED TO INVESTMENTS

Identify and explain the management issues related to investments. LO 1

In making investments, **Intel**'s management, like the management of any company, must understand issues related to the recognition, valuation, classification, disclosure, and ethics of investments.

Recognition

Recognition of investments as assets follows the general rule for recording transactions that we described earlier in the text—that is, purchases of investments are recorded on the date on which they are made, and sales of investments are reported on the date of sale. At the time of the transaction, there is either a transfer of funds or a definite obligation to pay. Income from investments is reported as other income on the income statement. Any gains or losses on investments are also reported on the income statement. Gains and losses appear as adjustments in the operating activities section of the statement of cash flows. The cash amounts of purchases and sales of investments appear in the investing activities section of the statement of cash flows.

Valuation

Like other purchase transactions, investments are valued according to the *cost principle*—that is, they are valued in terms of their cost at the time they are purchased. The cost, or purchase price, includes any commissions or fees. However, after the purchase, the value of investments on the balance sheet is adjusted to reflect subsequent conditions, including the following:

- Changes in the market value or fair value of the investments
- Changes caused by the passage of time (as in amortization)
- Changes in the operations of the investee companies

Long-term investments must be evaluated annually for any impairment or decline in value that is more than temporary. If impairment exists, a loss on the investment must be recorded.

Under certain conditions, companies are required to measure investments at fair value. Recall that **fair value** is the *exchange price* associated with an actual or potential business transaction between market participants. This requirement applies to all investments discussed in this chapter, except in the case of an investment in a subsidiary that is consolidated with the parent's financial statements. Fair value is not difficult to determine when there is a ready market in which there are buyers and sellers for an asset, but its determination becomes more problematic when there is no ready market. If a ready market for an investment does not exist, another valuation technique must be used, such as reference to the current fair value of another investment that is substantially the same, or if that option is not available, through discounted cash flow analysis.[2] Through the convergence project of the FASB and IASB, valuation practices under GAAP have come more in line with international financial reporting standards (IFRS).

Classification

Investments in debt and equity securities are classified as either short term or long term. **Short-term investments**, also called **marketable securities**, have a maturity of more than 90 days but are intended to be held only until cash is needed for current operations. (As we pointed out in an earlier chapter, investments with a maturity of *less* than 90 days are classified as cash equivalents.) **Long-term investments** are intended to be held for

Focus on Business Practice

What Role Did Fair Value Accounting Play in the Subprime Mortgage Collapse?

Investment banks and brokers experienced spectacular losses related to subprime mortgage securities during the economic decline that began in 2008. **UBS**, the large Swiss bank, had write-offs of $18.4 billion. When **Bear Stearns**, the large U.S. brokerage company, was bailed out by the Federal Reserve and **J.P. Morgan**, its stock price dropped from more than $90 per share to $2 per share in less than a week. What was the cause of all this? When interest rates rose and home prices fell, the fair value of the mortgages that backed up securities held by these companies declined. Under accounting standards, the companies were required to write down the securities to their fair value, which was substantially below the carrying value. The accounting rules that brought these losses to light were challenged in an editorial in *The Wall Street Journal*, which called fair value accounting a "fabulous failure" and predicted substantial write-ups once the crisis was over.[3] The supporters of fair value argued that the write-offs were not caused by accounting practices but reflected a real decline in value and that investors should have been able to act on this information quickly.

iStock Photo

more than one year. Long-term investments are reported in the investments section of the balance sheet, not in the current assets section. Although long-term investments may be just as marketable as short-term assets, management intends to hold them for an indefinite time.

Short- and long-term investments must be further classified as trading securities, available-for-sale securities, or held-to-maturity securities.[4]

- **Trading securities** are debt or equity securities bought and held principally for the purpose of being sold in the near term.
- **Available-for-sale securities** are debt or equity securities that do not meet the criteria for either trading or held-to-maturity securities. They may be short-term or long-term depending on what management intends to do with them.
- **Held-to-maturity securities** are debt securities that management intends to hold until their maturity date.

Exhibit 14.1 illustrates the classification of short- and long-term investments. Exhibit 14.2 (p. 638) shows the accounting treatment of various levels of equity investments, that is, ownership of another company's stock. It shows the relationship between the percentage of ownership in a company's stock and the investing company's level of control, as well as the classifications and accounting treatments of these stock investments. These classifications are important because each one requires a different accounting treatment. We discuss the accounting treatments later in this chapter.

In general, the percentage of ownership in another company's stock has the following effects:

- ***Noninfluential and noncontrolling investment:*** A firm that owns less than 20 percent of the stock of another company has no influence on the other company's operations.
- ***Influential but noncontrolling investment:*** A firm that owns between 20 to 50 percent of another company's stock can exercise significant influence over that company's

EXHIBIT 14.1
Classification of Investments

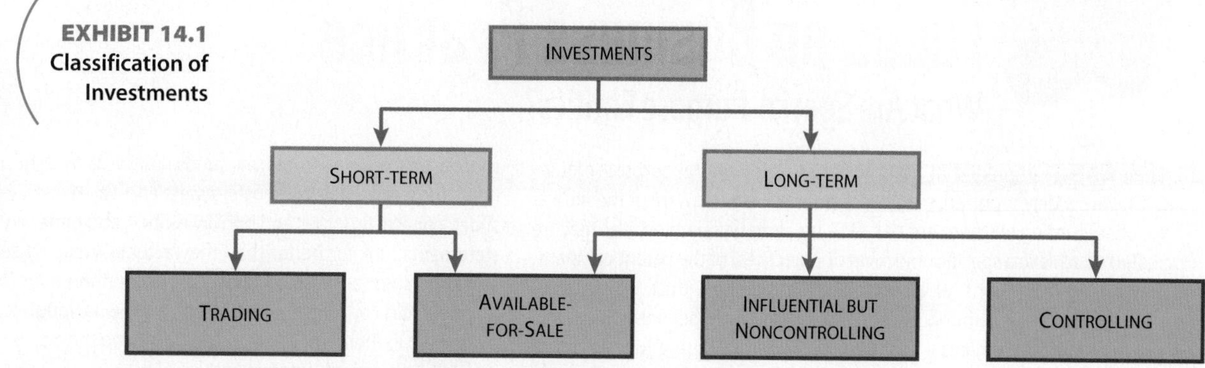

EXHIBIT 14.2
Accounting for Equity Investments

Level of Control	Percentage of Ownership	Classification	Accounting Treatment
Noninfluential and noncontrolling	Less than 20%	Short-term investments—trading securities	Recorded at cost initially; cost adjusted after purchase for changes in market value; unrealized gains and losses reported on the income statement
		Short- or long-term investments—available-for-sale securities	Recorded at cost initially; cost adjusted for changes in market value; unrealized gains and losses reported in stockholders' equity
Influential but noncontrolling	Between 20% and 50%	Long-term investments	Equity method: recorded at cost initially; cost subsequently adjusted for investor's share of net income or loss and for dividends received
Controlling	More than 50%	Long-term investments	Financial statements consolidated

operating and financial policies even though it holds 50 percent or less of the voting stock. Indications of significant influence include representation on the board of directors, participation in policymaking, exchange of managerial personnel, and technological dependency between the two companies.

STUDY NOTE: *Significant influence and control are related specifically to equity holdings, not debt holdings.*

- ***Controlling investment:*** A firm that owns more than 50 percent of another company's stock can exercise **control** over that company's operating and financial policies.

Disclosure

Companies provide detailed information about their investments and how they account for them in the notes to their financial statements. For instance, in 2009, in a note summarizing its significant accounting policies, **Intel** made this disclosure:

> We consider all liquid available-for-sale debt instruments with original maturities from the date of purchase of approximately three months or less to be cash and

Focus on Business Practice
What Are Special-Purpose Entities?

When **Enron** imploded in 2001 and its use of special-purpose entities (SPEs) was widely reported, many accountants were unaware of the intricacies of accounting for these entities. SPEs are firms with limited lives that are created to achieve a specific objective (or objectives) of the parent company. They may take the form of a partnership, corporation, trust, or joint venture. SPEs have been around since the 1970s and have been used primarily by banks and other financial institutions as a way of raising funds by bundling together receivables and other loans into packages that can be sold to investors or used to borrow funds. Enron turned this use of SPEs on its head. It used its SPEs to transfer assets and any related debt off its balance sheet, conceal its losses and borrow money, and generally make its financial statements look far better than they actually were. By setting up the SPEs as partnerships and using the obscure accounting rules for SPEs, Enron was able to avoid consolidating these entities even though it kept a 97 percent ownership in them. The FASB has since clarified the accounting rules for SPEs, which it calls variable interest entities (VIEs).[5]

iStock Photo

One of the most widely publicized insider trading cases in recent years involved Martha Stewart. In 2004, Stewart and her broker were found guilty of insider trading. Stewart was sentenced to the minimum of five months in prison and fined $30,000.

cash equivalents. Available-for-sale debt instruments with original maturities at the date of purchase greater than approximately three months and remaining maturities of less than one year are classified as short-term investments. Available-for-sale debt instruments with remaining maturities beyond one year are classified as other long-term investments.[6]

Intel's notes also provide detailed information about the company's other investments and acquisitions.

Ethics of Investing

When a company engages in investment transactions, there is always the possibility that its employees may use their knowledge about the transactions for personal gain. In the United States, **insider trading**, or making use of inside information for personal gain, is unethical and illegal. Before a publicly held company releases significant information about an investment to its stockholders and the general public, its officers and employees are not allowed to buy or sell stock in the company or in the firm whose shares the company is buying. Only after the information is released to the public can insiders engage in such trading. The Securities and Exchange Commission vigorously prosecutes any individual, whether employed by the company in question or not, who buys or sells shares of a publicly held company based on information not yet available to the public.

Not all countries prohibit insider trading. Until recently, insider trading was legal in Germany, but with the goal of expanding its securities markets, that country reformed its securities laws. It established the Federal Authority for Securities Trading (FAST), in part to oversee insider trading. However, historically, FAST devotes few staff members to investigations of insider trading, whereas the SEC has a much larger staff for these types of investigations.[7] Other countries continue to permit insider trading.

Stop & Apply

Indicate whether each phrase listed below is most closely related to (a) trading securities, (b) available-for-sale securities, (c) held-to-maturity securities, (d) noninfluential and noncontrolling ownership, (e) influential but noncontrolling ownership, or (f) controlling ownership:

1. No significant influence over investee
2. Securities bought and sold for short-term profit
3. Ability to make decisions for investee
4. Significant influence over investee
5. Securities that may be sold at any time
6. Debt securities that will be held until they are repaid

iStock Photo

SOLUTION

1. d; 2. a; 3. f; 4. e; 5. b; 6. c

SHORT-TERM INVESTMENTS IN EQUITY SECURITIES

LO2 Explain the financial reporting implications of short-term investments.

As we pointed out earlier, all trading securities are short-term investments, while available-for-sale securities may be either short-term or long-term.

Trading Securities

Trading securities are frequently bought and sold to generate profits on short-term changes in their prices. They are classified as current assets on the balance sheet and are valued at fair value, which is usually the same as market value. An increase or decrease in the fair value of a company's total trading portfolio (the group of securities it holds for trading purposes) is included in net income in the accounting period in which the increase or decrease occurs. For instance, **Intel** has substantial trading securities and describes its accounting for these securities as follows:

> Investments designated as trading assets are reported at fair value.[8]

In the sections that follow, we use Ralf Company's investments in **IBM** and **Microsoft** to show how to account for the purchase and sale of short-term investments in equity securities.

Purchase of Trading Securities Ralf Company buys 5,000 shares of **IBM** for $450,000 ($90 per share) and 5,000 shares of **Microsoft** for $150,000 ($30 per share) on October 25, 2011. The purchase is made for trading purposes—that is, Ralf's management intends to realize a gain by holding the shares for only a short period.

Analysis: The journal entry to record the investment at cost

- ▲ *increases* Short-Term Investments with a debit for the cost of $600,000 ($450,000 + $150,000) and
- ▼ *decreases* Cash with a credit for $600,000.

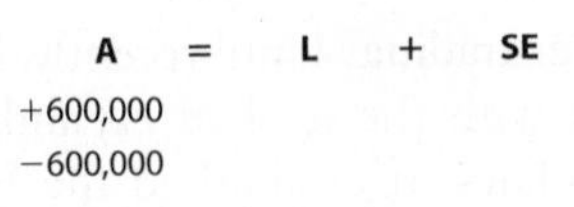

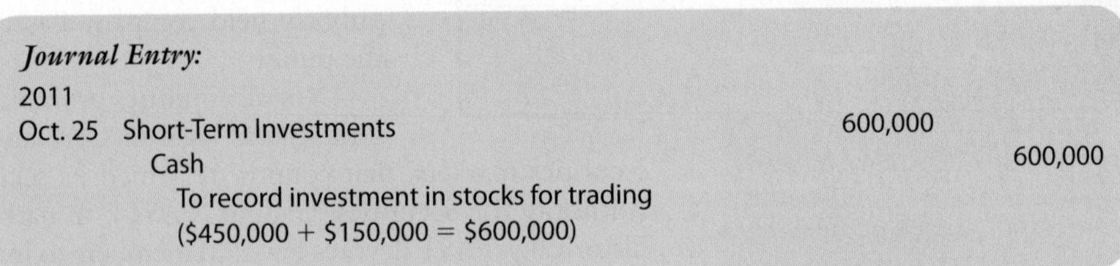

Journal Entry:

2011			
Oct. 25	Short-Term Investments	600,000	
	Cash		600,000
	To record investment in stocks for trading ($450,000 + $150,000 = $600,000)		

Year-End Valuation and Adjustment At year-end, IBM's stock price has decreased to $80 per share, and Microsoft's has risen to $32 per share. The trading portfolio is now valued at $560,000:

Security	*Market Value*	*Cost*	*Gain (Loss)*
IBM (5,000 shares)	$400,000	$450,000	
Microsoft (5,000 shares)	160,000	150,000	
Totals	$560,000	$600,000	$(40,000)

Analysis: Because the current fair value of the portfolio is $40,000 less than the original cost of $600,000, an *unrealized* loss has occurred. The journal entry to record the year-end adjustment

- ▲ *increases* Unrealized Loss on Short-Term Investments with a debit for the cost of $40,000 and
- ▲ *increases* Allowance to Adjust Short-Term Investments to Market with a credit of $40,000.

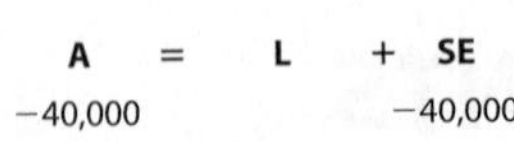

Journal Entry:

2011			
Dec. 31	Unrealized Loss on Short-Term Investments	40,000	
	Allowance to Adjust Short-Term Investments to Market		40,000
	To record unrealized loss on trading portfolio		

Focus on International Practices

IFRS Should Gains or Losses Be Reported Twice?

Under U.S. GAAP, an increase or a decrease in the value of a trading security can be reported twice on the income statement: first as an unrealized gain or loss when it is valued at the end of the accounting period and second as a realized gain or loss if the security is sold later while the value is still up or down. This practice is called *recycling* and is not allowed under international financial reporting standards (IFRS). Under IFRS, a gain or loss on a trading security is reported on the income statement only once, either at the time it is sold during the accounting period or when it is valued at the end of the period.

iStock Photo

STUDY NOTE: *The Allowance to Adjust Short-Term Investments to Market account is never changed when securities are sold. It changes only when an adjusting entry is made at year-end.*

Comment: The unrealized loss will appear on the income statement as a reduction in income. The loss is unrealized because the securities have not been sold. If unrealized gains occur due to an increase in the value of the portfolio, they are treated in the same way.

The Allowance to Adjust Short-Term Investments to Market account appears on the balance sheet as a contra-asset, as follows:

Short-term investments (at cost)	$600,000
Less allowance to adjust short-term investments to market	40,000
Short-term investments (at market)	$560,000
or, more simply, as	
Short-term investments (at market value, cost is $600,000)	$560,000

Sale of Trading Securities Ralf sells its 5,000 shares of Microsoft for $35 per share on March 2, 2012.

Analysis: The journal entry to record a ***realized*** gain on trading securities

▲ *increases* Cash with a debit for the selling price of $175,000,
▼ *decreases* Short-Term Investments with a credit of $150,000, and
▲ *increases* Gain on Sale of Investments with a credit for the difference of $25,000.

A	=	L	+	SE
+175,000				25,000
−150,000				

Journal Entry:

2012			
Mar. 2	Cash	175,000	
	Short-Term Investments		150,000
	Gain on Sale of Investments		25,000
	To record sale of 5,000 shares of Microsoft for $35 per share; cost was $30 per share		

Comment: The realized gain will appear on the income statement. Note that the realized gain is unaffected by the adjustment for the unrealized loss at the end of 2011. The two transactions are treated independently. If the stock had been sold for less than cost, a realized loss on investments would have been recorded. Realized losses also appear on the income statement.

Focus on Business Practice

How Can Even a Big Company Make an Accounting Mistake?

Like many companies, **General Electric**, one of America's largest corporations, protects itself against future increases in interest rates on debt by hedging its debt transactions with *derivatives*, which are agreements to buy or sell stocks, bonds, or other securities in the future. A derivative can be set up in such a way that it has no value and therefore entails no gain or loss. But when a derivative has value, it is considered a trading security and a money-making (or money-losing) tool rather than a true hedge; in this case, any gain or loss that results from valuing the derivative at fair value must be reported on the income statement. General Electric thought it had no gains or losses on its derivatives, but when it recalculated their value over a two-year period, it found that it had gains amounting to about $0.02 per share in each year. In a press release reporting the error, the company's CFO stated that "there are no exceptions to hedge accounting. . . . At the end of the day, the standard is the standard."[9]

iStock Photo

Subsequent Year-End Valuation and Adjustment During 2012, Ralf buys 1,000 shares of **Apple Computer** at $232 per share and has no transactions involving its shares of **IBM**. By December 31, 2012, the price of IBM's stock has risen to $95 per share, or $5 per share more than the original cost, and Apple's stock price has fallen to $222, or $10 less than the original cost. We can now analyze Ralf's trading portfolio as follows:

Security	*Market Value*	*Cost*	*Gain (Loss)*
IBM (5,000 shares)	$475,000	$450,000	
Apple (1,000 shares)	222,000	232,000	
Totals	$697,000	$682,000	$15,000

Analysis: The market value of Ralf's trading portfolio now exceeds the cost by $15,000 ($697,000 – $682,000). This amount represents the targeted ending balance for the Allowance to Adjust Short-Term Investments to Market account. Recall that at the end of 2011, that account had a credit balance of $40,000, meaning that the market value of the trading portfolio was less than the cost. Because no entries are made to the account during 2012, it retains its balance until adjusting entries are made at the end of the year. The adjustment for 2012 must be $55,000—enough to result in a debit balance of $15,000 in the allowance account. The journal entry to record the year-end adjustment

▼ *decreases* Allowance to Adjust Short-Term Investments to Market with a debit of $55,000 and

▲ *increases* Unrealized Gain on Short-Term Investments with a credit of $55,000.

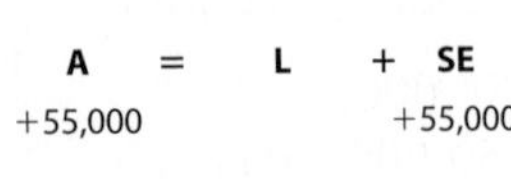

Journal Entry:

2012			
Dec. 31	Allowance to Adjust Short-Term Investments to Market	55,000	
	Unrealized Gain on Short-Term Investments		55,000
	To record unrealized gain on trading portfolio ($40,000 + $15,000 = $55,000)		

Comment: The 2012 ending balance of Ralf's allowance account can be determined as follows:

STUDY NOTE: *The entry in the Allowance to Adjust Short-Term Investments to Market account is equal to the change in the market value. Compute the new allowance and then compute the amount needed to change the account. The unrealized loss or gain is the other half of the entry.*

ALLOWANCE TO ADJUST SHORT-TERM INVESTMENTS TO MARKET

Dec. 31, 2012 Adj.	55,000	Dec. 31, 2011 Bal.	40,000
Dec. 31, 2012 Bal.	15,000		

Short-term investments are presented on the balance sheet as follows:

Short-term investments (at cost)	$582,000
Plus allowance to adjust short-term investments to market	15,000
Short-term investments (at market)	$597,000

or, more simply, as

Short-term investments (at market value, cost is $582,000)	$597,000

Available-for-Sale Securities

Short-term available-for-sale securities are accounted for in the same way as trading securities with the following two exceptions:

- An unrealized gain or loss is reported as other comprehensive income (loss) and is disclosed on the statement of stockholders' equity and listed as a separate item in the stockholders' equity section of the balance sheet. It does not appear as a gain or loss on the income statement.

- If a decline in the value of a security is considered permanent, it is charged as a loss on the income statement.

For example, **Intel**'s summary of significant accounting policies contains the following statement: "[U]nrealized gains and losses [on available-for-sale securities], net of tax, [are] recorded in accumulated other comprehensive income (loss)." The company's notes to the financial statements show unrealized gains on investments of $336 million in 2009 and unrealized losses on investments of $463 million in 2008. In addition, Intel's income statement shows losses on equity method investments, net of $147 million in 2009 and $1,380 million in 2008; and losses on other equity investments, net of $23 million in 2009 and $376 million in 2008.[10]

Stop & Apply

Kora Corporation began investing in trading securities in 2011. At the end of 2011, it had the following trading portfolio:

Security	*Cost*	*Market Value*
Apple (1,000 shares)	$100,000	$200,000
Delta Air Lines (20,000 shares)	240,000	160,000
Totals	$340,000	$360,000

Prepare the necessary year-end adjusting entry on December 31 and the journal entry for the sale of all the Delta shares on the following May 1 for $200,000.

SOLUTION

2011			
Dec. 31	Allowance to Adjust Short-Term Investments to Market	20,000	
	Unrealized Gain on Short-Term Investments		20,000
	To record unrealized gain on trading securities		
2012			
May 1	Cash	200,000	
	Loss on Sale of Investments	40,000	
	Short-Term Investments		240,000
	To record sales of 20,000 shares of Delta Air Lines at less than cost		

iStock Photo

LONG-TERM INVESTMENTS IN EQUITY SECURITIES

LO3 Explain the financial reporting implications of long-term investments in stock and the cost-adjusted-to-market and equity methods used to account for them.

The accounting treatment of long-term investments in equity securities, such as common stock, depends on the extent to which the investing company can exercise control over the other company.

Noninfluential and Noncontrolling Investment

As noted earlier, available-for-sale securities are debt or equity securities that cannot be classified as trading or held-to-maturity securities. When long-term equity securities are involved, a further criterion for classifying them as available for sale is that they be noninfluential and noncontrolling investments of less than 20 percent of the voting stock. Accounting for long-term available-for-sale securities requires using the **cost-adjusted-to-market method**. With this method, the securities are initially recorded at cost and are thereafter adjusted periodically for changes in market value by using an allowance account.[11]

Available-for-sale securities are classified as long term if management *intends* to hold them for more than one year. When accounting for long-term available-for-sale securities, the unrealized gain or loss resulting from the adjustment is not reported on the income statement. Instead, the gain or loss is reported as other comprehensive income (loss) on the statement of stockholders' equity and listed as a separate item in the stockholders' equity section of the balance sheet.

At the end of each accounting period, the total cost and the total market value of these long-term stock investments must be determined. If the total market value is less than the total cost, the difference must be credited to a contra-asset account called Allowance to Adjust Long-Term Investments to Market. Because of the long-term nature of the investment, the debit part of the entry, which represents a decrease in value below cost, is treated as a temporary decrease and does not appear as a loss on the income statement. It is shown in a contra-stockholders' equity account called Unrealized Loss on Long-Term Investments.* Thus, both of these accounts are balance sheet accounts. If the market value exceeds the cost, the allowance account is added to Long-Term Investments, and the unrealized gain appears as an addition to stockholders' equity.

When a company sells its long-term investments in stock, the difference between the sales price and the cost of the stock is recorded as a realized gain or loss on the income statement. Dividend income from such investments is recorded by a debit to Cash and a credit to Dividend Income.

In the sections that follow, we show how to account for the purchase and sale of long-term investments in equity securities using three corporations—Bell, Topez, and Norka—as examples.

Purchase of a Long-Term Investment On June 1, 2011, Bell Corporation paid cash for the following long-term investments: 5,000 shares of Topez Corporation's common stock (representing 2 percent of outstanding stock) at $25 per share and 2,500 shares of Norka Corporation's common stock (representing 3 percent of outstanding stock) at $15 per share.

Analysis: The journal entry to record the investment at cost

▲ *increases* Long-Term Investments with a debit of $162,500 and
▼ *decreases* Cash with a credit of $162,500.

A	=	L	+	SE
+162,500				
−162,500				

Journal Entry:

2011			
June 1	Long-Term Investments	162,500	
	Cash		162,500
	To record investments in Topez common stock (5,000 shares × $25 = $125,000) and Norka common stock (2,500 shares × $15 = $37,500)		

Comment: These investments are classified as long term because of management's intent to hold them more than one year.

Year-End Adjustment At the end of 2011, the market price of Topez's common stock is $21; the market price of Norka's is $17.

Analysis: Bell Corporation's trading portfolio is now valued at $147,500:

Company	*Shares*	*Market Price*	*Total Market Value*	*Total Cost*
Topez	5,000	$21	$105,000	$125,000
Norka	2,500	17	42,500	37,500
			$147,500	$162,500

Because the current fair value of the portfolio is $15,000 less than the original cost of $162,500, an *unrealized* loss has occurred. The journal entry to record the year-end adjustment

*If the decrease in market value of a long-term investment is deemed permanent or if the investment is deemed impaired, the decline or impairment is recorded by debiting a loss account on the income statement instead of the Unrealized Loss account.

▲ *increases* Unrealized Loss on Long-Term Investments with a debit of $15,000 and
▲ *increases* Allowance to Adjust Long-Term Investments to Market with a credit of $15,000.

A	=	L	+ SE
−15,000			−15,000

Journal Entry:

		Dr.	Cr.
2011			
Dec. 31	Unrealized Loss on Long-Term Investments	15,000	
	Allowance to Adjust Long-Term Investments to Market		15,000
	To record reduction of long-term investment to market		

STUDY NOTE: *A major difference between accounting for trading securities and accounting for long-term available-for-sale securities is that unrealized gains and losses appear on the income statement in the former case and on the statement of stockholders' equity in the latter case.*

Comment: As noted previously, the Unrealized Loss on Long-Term Investments does not appear on the income statement but appears on the statement of stockholders' equity as other comprehensive income (loss) and as a separate item in the stockholders' equity section of the balance sheet. The Allowance to Adjust Long-Term Investments to Market is a contra-asset account that reduces investments on the balance sheet.

Sale of a Long-Term Investment On April 1, 2012, a change in policy required the sale of 1,000 shares of Topez common stock at $23.

Analysis: The journal entry to record this sale

▲ *increases* Cash with a debit for the selling price of $23,000,
▲ *increases* Loss on Sale of Investments with a debit of $2,000, and
▼ *decreases* Long-Term Investments with a credit of $25,000.

A	=	L	+ SE
+23,000			−2,000
−25,000			

Journal Entry:

		Dr.	Cr.
2012			
Apr. 1	Cash	23,000	
	Loss on Sale of Investments	2,000	
	Long-Term Investments		25,000
	Sale of 1,000 shares of Topez's common stock		
	1,000 × $23 = $23,000		
	1,000 × $25 = 25,000		
	Loss $ 2,000		

Comment: Bell's sale of stock was the result of a change in policy. This illustrates that *intent* is often the only difference between long-term investments and short-term investments.

Cash Dividend Received On July 1, 2012, Bell received a cash dividend from Norka equal to $0.20 per share.

Analysis: The journal entry to record the cash dividend received

▲ *increases* Cash with a debit of $500 ($0.20 × 2,500 shares) and
▲ *increases* Dividend Income with a credit of $500.

A	=	L	+ SE
+500			+500

Journal Entry:

		Dr.	Cr.
2012			
July 1	Cash	500	
	Dividend Income		500
	To record receipt of cash dividend from Norka		

Year-End Adjustment At the end of 2012, the market price of Topez's common stock was $24; the market price of Norka's was $13.

Analysis: The trading portfolio is now valued at $128,500:

Company	*Shares*	*Market Price*	*Total Market Value*	*Total Cost*
Topez	4,000	$24	$ 96,000	$100,000
Norka	2,500	13	32,500	37,500
			$128,500	$137,500

The adjustment will equal the previous balance ($15,000 from the December 31, 2011, entry) minus the new balance ($9,000), or $6,000. The new balance of $9,000 is the difference at the present time between the total market value ($128,500) and the total cost of all investments ($137,500). The journal entry to record the year-end adjustment

▲ *increases* Allowance to Adjust Long-Term Investments to Market with a debit of $6,000 and

▼ *decreases* Unrealized Loss on Long-Term Investments with a credit of $6,000.

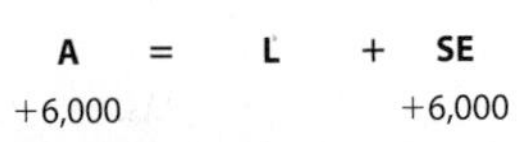

Journal Entry:

2012			
Dec. 31	Allowance to Adjust Long-Term Investments to Market	6,000	
	Unrealized Loss on Long-Term Investments		6,000
	To record the adjustment in long-term investments so it is reported at market		

Comment: Note that even though the portfolio increased in value from last year, it did not result in a credit to unrealized gain. It reduced the unrealized loss from last year. Only if the entire unrealized loss had been eliminated would an unrealized gain be recorded for the difference.

Also note that the Allowance to Adjust Long-Term Investments to Market and the Unrealized Loss on Long-Term Investments are reciprocal contra accounts, each with the same dollar balance:

▼ The Allowance account *reduces* long-term investments by the amount by which the cost of the investments exceeds market.

▼ The Unrealized Loss account *reduces* stockholders' equity by a similar amount.

The effects of these transactions on the T accounts are as follows:

CONTRA-ASSET ACCOUNT

ALLOWANCE TO ADJUST LONG-TERM INVESTMENTS

Dec. 31, 2012 Adj.	6,000	Dec. 31, 2011 Bal.	15,000
		Dec. 31, 2012 Bal.	9,000

CONTRA-STOCKHOLDERS' EQUITY ACCOUNT

UNREALIZED LOSS ON LONG-TERM INVESTMENTS TO MARKET

Dec. 31, 2011 Bal.	15,000	Dec. 31, 2012 Adj.	6,000
Dec. 31, 2012 Bal.	9,000		

The opposite effects will exist if market value exceeds cost, resulting in an unrealized gain.

An Influential but Noncontrolling Investment

As we have noted, ownership of 20 percent or more of a company's voting stock is considered sufficient to influence the company's operations. When that is the case, the **equity method** should be used to account for the stock investment. The equity method presumes that an investment of 20 percent or more is not a passive investment and that the investor should therefore share proportionately in the success or failure of the company. The main features of this method are as follows:

- The investor records the original purchase of the stock at cost.
- The investor records its share of the company's periodic net income as an increase in the Investment account, with a corresponding credit to an income account. Similarly,

Songquan Deng/Shutterstock.com

The equity method is a method of accounting for influential but noncontrolling long-term investments in which the investment is initially recorded at cost and is then adjusted for the investor's share of the company's net income or loss and for the dividends.

it records its share of a periodic loss as a decrease in the Investment account, with a corresponding debit to a loss account.

- When the investor receives a cash dividend, the asset account Cash is increased, and the Investment account is decreased.

Intel applies the equity method when it has "the ability to exercise significant influence, but not control, over the investee."[12]

In the sections that follow, we use the equity method to account for Opal Corporation's purchase and sale of long-term investments in equity securities.

Purchase of an Equity Investment On January 1 of the current year, Opal Corporation acquired 40 percent of Viva Corporation's voting common stock for $90,000.

Analysis: The journal entry to record the investment at cost

▲ *increases* Investment in Viva Corporation with a debit of $90,000 and
▼ *decreases* Cash with a credit of $90,000.

A	=	L	+	SE
+90,000				
−90,000				

Journal Entry:

Jan. 1	Investment in Viva Corporation	90,000	
	Cash		90,000
	To record investment in Viva Corporation common stock for a 40 percent ownership		

Comment: This entry is similar to the entries made for other investments, but note that with a 40 percent share of ownership, Opal can exert significant influence over Viva's operations.

Recognition of Income Assume that on December 31, Viva reported net income of $40,000.

Analysis: Because Opal can exert significant influence over Viva, 40 percent of Viva's earnings, or $16,000 (40% × $40,000), is considered to be Opal's. The journal entry to recognize income

▲ *increases* Investment in Viva Corporation with a debit of $16,000 and
▲ *increases* Income, Viva Corporation Investment with a credit of $16,000.

iStock Photo

Focus on Business Practice

Accounting for International Joint Ventures

When U.S. companies make investments abroad, they often find it wise or necessary to partner with a local company or with the government of the country. Some countries require that their citizens own a minimum percentage of each business. In other countries—among them, Brazil, China, India, and the former United Soviet Socialist Republics—the government has traditionally had a share of ownership. Such business arrangements are usually called *joint ventures*. Because the resulting enterprise is jointly owned, it is appropriate to treat the U.S. company's status as "influential but noncontrolling." Thus, the most appropriate accounting method for these arrangements is the equity method.

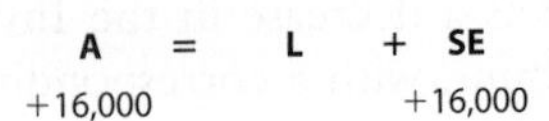

Journal Entry:

Investment in Viva Corporation	16,000	
Income, Viva Corporation Investment		16,000
To record 40% of income reported by Viva Corporation (40% × $40,000 = $16,000)		

Comment: Note that Opal's share of Viva's income will appear on Opal's income statement.

Receipt of a Cash Dividend Viva paid cash dividends for the year on December 31 of $10,000.

Analysis: Because Opal can exert significant influence over Viva, the amount of the cash dividend, or $4,000 (40% × $10,000), received from Viva is considered a reduction of Opal's investment in Viva. The journal entry to record the dividend

▲ *increases* Cash with a debit of $4,000 and
▼ *decreases* Investment in Viva Corporation with a credit of $4,000.

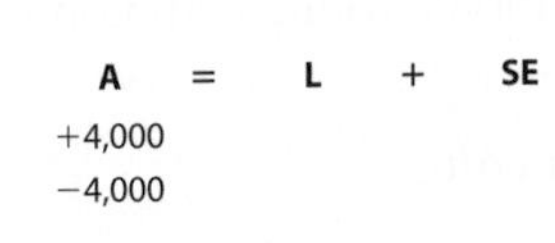

Journal Entry:

Cash	4,000	
Investment in Viva Corporation		4,000
To record cash dividend from Viva Corporation (40% × $10,000 = $4,000)		

Comment: The balance of the Investment in Viva Corporation account after these transactions is $102,000, as shown here:

INVESTMENT IN VIVA CORPORATION

Investment	90,000	Dividend Received	4,000
Share of Income	16,000		
Bal.	102,000		

STUDY NOTE: *Under the equity method, dividends received is not considered income; rather, it represents a return on investment and decreases the Investment account with a credit entry.*

The share of income is reported as a separate line item on the income statement as a part of income from operations. The dividends received affect cash flows from operating activities on the statement of cash flows. The reported income exceeds the cash received by $12,000 ($16,000 – $4,000).

A Controlling Investment

Some firms that own less than 50 percent of another company's voting stock exercise such powerful influence that for all practical purposes, they control the other company's policies. Nevertheless, ownership of more than 50 percent of the voting stock is required for accounting recognition of control. When a firm has a controlling interest in another company, a parent-subsidiary relationship is said to exist. The investing company is the **parent company**; the other company is a **subsidiary**.

STUDY NOTE: *Parents and subsidiaries are separate legal entities even though they combine their financial reports at year-end.*

Because a parent company and its subsidiaries are separate legal entities, each prepares separate financial statements. However, because of their special relationship, they are viewed for external financial reporting purposes as a single economic entity. For this reason, the FASB requires that they combine their financial statements into a single set of statements called **consolidated financial statements**.[13] For example, in its summary of significant accounting policies, **Intel** states that "our consolidated financial statements include the accounts of Intel Corporation and our wholly owned subsidiaries. Intercompany accounts and transactions have been eliminated."[14]

Stop & Apply

Laboda Corporation has the following long-term investments:

1. 40 percent of the common stock of Fastrak Corporation
2. 16 percent of the common stock of Pepper, Inc.
3. 80 percent of the nonvoting preferred stock of Sanddex Corporation
4. 100 percent of the common stock of its financing subsidiary, LP, Inc.
5. 75 percent of the common stock of the Canadian company Canoil Company
6. 40 percent of the common stock of the Mexican company Border Assembly Company

For each of these investments, tell which of the following methods should be used for external financial reporting:

a. Cost-adjusted-to-market method
b. Equity method
c. Consolidation of parent and subsidiary financial statements

iStock Photo

SOLUTION

1. b; 2. a; 3. a; 4. c; 5. c; 6. b

CONSOLIDATED FINANCIAL STATEMENTS

LO 4 Explain the financial reporting implications of consolidated financial statements.

All major corporations find it convenient for economic, legal, tax, or other reasons to operate in parent-subsidiary relationships. When we speak of a large company such as **PepsiCo** or **IBM**, we generally think of the parent company, not of its many subsidiaries. Potential investors, however, want a clear financial picture of the total economic entity. The main purpose of consolidated financial statements is to give such a view of the parent and subsidiary firms by treating them as if they were one combined company. On a consolidated balance sheet, the Inventory account includes the inventory held by the parent and all its subsidiaries. Similarly, on the consolidated income statement, the Sales account is the total revenue from sales by the parent and all its subsidiaries. This overview helps management, stockholders, and creditors of the parent company judge the company's progress in meeting its goals.

Consolidated Balance Sheet

__STUDY NOTE:__ As separate entities, the parent and subsidiary maintain individual accounting records. Work sheet eliminations remove only duplications that occur in consolidation and the effects of intercompany transactions.

The **purchase method** of preparing consolidated financial statements combines similar accounts from the separate statements of the parent and the subsidiaries. Some accounts result from transactions between the parent and the subsidiary—for example, sales and purchases between the two entities and debt owed by one of the entities to the other. It is not appropriate to include these accounts in the consolidated financial statements; the sales and purchases are only transfers between different parts of the business, and the payables and receivables do not represent amounts due to or receivable from outside parties. For this reason, it is important that certain **eliminations** be made. These eliminations avoid the duplication of accounts and reflect the financial position and operations from the standpoint of a single entity. Eliminations appear only on the work sheets used in preparing consolidated financial statements. They are never shown in the accounting records of either the parent or the subsidiary.

Focus on International Practices

IFRS Progress in the Convergence of U.S. GAAP and IFRS

For many decades, U.S. GAAP permitted two very different methods of accounting for consolidated companies. It was therefore often difficult to compare the financial performance of these companies and even sometimes to understand the differences between them. In 2009, the FASB issued a standard that "requires that all business combinations be accounted for by a single method—the purchase method."[15] It also requires better accounting for intangible assets in consolidated businesses. For example, certain intangible assets must be shown separately from goodwill on the balance sheet. This standard brings U.S. GAAP much closer to international financial reporting standards (IFRS) and helps achieve the stated goal of the FASB and the IASB for convergence—that is, bringing their standards closer together.

iStock Photo

Another good example of accounts that result from transactions between a parent and its subsidiary is the Investment in Subsidiary account on the parent's balance sheet and the stockholders' equity accounts of the subsidiary. When the balance sheets of the two companies are combined, these accounts must be eliminated to avoid duplicating them in the consolidated financial statements.

To illustrate the preparation of a consolidated balance sheet under the purchase method, we use the following balance sheet data for Parent Company and Subsidiary Company:

Accounts	*Parent Company*	*Subsidiary Company*
Cash	$ 50,000	$12,500
Other assets	380,000	30,000
Total assets	$430,000	$42,500
Liabilities	$ 30,000	$ 5,000
Common stock	300,000	27,500
Retained earnings	100,000	10,000
Total liabilities and stockholders' equity	$430,000	$42,500

100 Percent Purchase at Book Value Suppose that on July 1, Parent Company purchases 100 percent of the stock of Subsidiary Company for an amount exactly equal to Subsidiary Company's book value. The book value of Subsidiary Company is $37,500 ($42,500 – $5,000).

Analysis: Parent Company would record the purchase much as it would any other investment; thus, the journal entry

▼ *decreases* Cash with a credit of $37,500 and
▲ *increases* Investment in Subsidiary Company with a debit of $37,500.

Journal Entry:

July 1	Investment in Subsidiary Company	37,500	
	Cash		37,500
	To record purchase of 100 percent of Subsidiary Company at book value		

A	=	L	+	SE
+37,500				
−37,500				

STUDY NOTE: Eliminating entries appear only on the work sheet. They never appear in the accounting records.

Eliminating Entry When preparing a consolidated financial statement, it is helpful to use a work sheet like the one shown in Exhibit 14.3. Note that the balance of Parent Company's Cash account is now $12,500 and that its investment in Subsidiary Company is listed as an asset, reflecting the purchase of the subsidiary. To prepare a

EXHIBIT 14.3
Work Sheet for Preparing a Consolidated Balance Sheet

Parent and Subsidiary Companies
Work Sheet for Consolidated Balance Sheet
As of Acquisition Date

Accounts	Balance Sheet, Parent Company	Balance Sheet, Subsidiary Company	Eliminations Debit	Eliminations Credit	Consolidated Balance Sheet
Cash	12,500	12,500			25,000
Investment in Subsidiary Company	37,500			37,500*	
Other assets	380,000	30,000			410,000
Total assets	430,000	42,500			435,000
Liabilities	30,000	5,000			35,000
Common stock	300,000	27,500	27,500*		300,000
Retained earnings	100,000	10,000	10,000*		100,000
Total liabilities and stockholders' equity	430,000	42,500	37,500	37,500	435,000

*Elimination of intercompany investment

consolidated balance sheet, it is necessary to eliminate the investment in the subsidiary, as shown in Exhibit 14.3. This accomplishes two objectives:

- It eliminates the double counting that would take place when the net assets of the two companies are combined.
- It eliminates the stockholders' equity section of Subsidiary Company.

As we have pointed out, the theory underlying consolidated financial statements is that parent and subsidiary are a single entity. Thus, the stockholders' equity section of the consolidated balance sheet is the same for Parent Company and Subsidiary Company.

So, after eliminating the Investment in Subsidiary Company account and the stockholders' equity accounts of the subsidiary, we can take the information from the Consolidated Balance Sheet column in Exhibit 14.3 and present it in the following form:

Parent and Subsidiary Companies
Consolidated Balance Sheet
As of Acquisition Date

Cash	$ 25,000	Liabilities	$ 35,000
Other assets	410,000	Common stock	300,000
		Retained earnings	100,000
Total assets	$435,000	Total liabilities and stockholders' equity	$435,000

STUDY NOTE: When the elimination entry is made, all of the subsidiary's stockholders' equity accounts are eliminated.

Less Than 100 Percent Purchase at Book Value When a parent company purchases less than 100 percent but more than 50 percent of a subsidiary's voting stock, it will have control over the subsidiary, and it must prepare consolidated financial statements. It must also account for the interests of the subsidiary's stockholders who own less than 50 percent of the voting stock. These are the minority stockholders, and their **minority interest** must appear on the consolidated balance sheet (as part of stockholders' equity) as an amount equal to their percentage of ownership times the subsidiary's net assets.[16]

Suppose that Parent Company buys 90 percent of Subsidiary Company's voting stock for $33,750. In this case, the portion of the company purchased has a book value of $33,750 (90% × $37,500). The work sheet used to prepare the consolidated balance sheet appears in Exhibit 14.4 (p. 652). The elimination is made just as in Exhibit 14.3,

EXHIBIT 14.4
Work Sheet Showing Elimination When Purchase Is for Less Than 100 Percent Ownership

Parent and Subsidiary Companies
Work Sheet for Consolidated Balance Sheet
As of Acquisition Date

Accounts	Balance Sheet, Parent Company	Balance Sheet, Subsidiary Company	Eliminations Debit	Eliminations Credit	Consolidated Balance Sheet
Cash	16,250	12,500			28,750
Investment in Subsidiary Company	33,750			33,750*	
Other assets	380,000	30,000			410,000
Total assets	430,000	42,500			438,750
Liabilities	30,000	5,000			35,000
Common stock	300,000	27,500	27,500*		300,000
Retained earnings	100,000	10,000	10,000*	3,750*	100,000
Minority interest	—	—	—	—	3,750
Total liabilities and stockholders' equity	430,000	42,500	37,500	37,500	438,750

*Elimination of intercompany investment. Minority interest equals 10 percent of subsidiary's total stockholders' equity.

except that the minority interest must be accounted for. All the investment in Subsidiary Company ($33,750) is eliminated against all of Subsidiary Company's stockholders' equity accounts (totaling $37,500). The difference ($3,750, or 10% × $37,500) is the minority interest.

There are two ways to classify minority interest (the percentage not owned by the parent company) on a consolidated balance sheet. One way is to place the entry between long-term liabilities and stockholders' equity. The other way is to consider the stockholders' equity section as consisting of minority interest and the parent company's stockholders' equity, as shown here:

Minority interest	$ 3,750
Common stock	300,000
Retained earnings	100,000
Total stockholders' equity	$403,750

Purchase at More or Less Than Book Value The purchase price of a business depends on many factors, such as the current market price, the relative strength of the buyer's and seller's bargaining positions, and the prospects for future earnings. Thus, it is only by chance that the purchase price of a subsidiary equals the book value of its equity. Usually, it does not.

A parent company may pay more than the subsidiary's book value for a controlling interest for the following reasons:

- The subsidiary's assets are understated. This happens when the historical cost less depreciation of the subsidiary's assets does not reflect current market values.
- The subsidiary has something the parent wants, such as an important technical process, a new and different product, or a new market.

STUDY NOTE: *Regardless of the circumstances, the Investment in Subsidiary Company account must be eliminated completely and should not appear on the consolidated balance sheet.*

On the other hand, the parent may pay less than book value for these reasons:

- The subsidiary's assets are not worth their depreciated cost.
- Heavy losses suffered by the subsidiary have caused its stock price to drop.

When a parent company pays more than book value for its interest in a subsidiary, the Accounting Principles Board's guidelines are as follows:

> First, all identifiable assets acquired . . . and liabilities assumed in a business combination . . . should be assigned a portion of the cost of the acquired company, normally equal to their fair values at date of acquisition.
>
> Second, the excess of the cost of the acquired company over the sum of the amounts assigned to identifiable assets acquired less liabilities assumed should be recorded as goodwill.[17]

As explained in Chapter 9, goodwill is carried on the balance sheet at cost and is subject to an annual impairment test. **Intel** describes its treatment of goodwill as follows:

> We record goodwill when the purchase price of an acquisition exceeds the fair value of the net tangible and intangible assets as of the date of acquisition. We perform a quarterly review of goodwill for indicators of impairment.[18]

***STUDY NOTE:** Goodwill is recorded when the purchase price of a business exceeds the fair market value of the net assets purchased.*

To illustrate the application of these principles, suppose that Parent Company purchases 100 percent of Subsidiary Company's voting stock for $46,250, which is $8,750 more than book value. Parent Company is willing to pay $8,750 more than book value because it believes that the subsidiary's assets are understated by $5,000 and that the strength the subsidiary would bring to the organization is worth at least $3,750. The work sheet used to prepare the consolidated balance sheet appears in Exhibit 14.5. All of the investment in Subsidiary Company ($46,250) has been eliminated against all of its stockholders' equity ($37,500). The excess of cost over book value ($8,750) has been debited in the amount of $5,000 to other assets and in the amount of $3,750 to goodwill.

The amount of goodwill is determined as follows:

Cost of investment in subsidiary	$46,250
Book value of subsidiary	37,500
Excess of cost over book value	$ 8,750
Portion of excess attributable to undervalued other assets of subsidiary	5,000
Portion of excess attributable to goodwill	$ 3,750

EXHIBIT 14.5
Work Sheet Showing Elimination When Purchase Cost Is Greater Than Book Value

Parent and Subsidiary Companies
Work Sheet for Consolidated Balance Sheet
As of Acquisition Date

Accounts	Balance Sheet, Parent Company	Balance Sheet, Subsidiary Company	Eliminations Debit	Eliminations Credit	Consolidated Balance Sheet
Cash	3,750	12,500			16,250
Investment in Subsidiary Company	46,250			46,250*	—
Other assets	380,000	30,000	5,000*		415,000
Goodwill	—	—	3,750*		3,750
Total assets	430,000	42,500			435,000
Liabilities	30,000	5,000			35,000
Common stock	300,000	27,500	27,500*		300,000
Retained earnings	100,000	10,000	10,000*		100,000
Total liabilities and stockholders' equity	430,000	42,500	46,250	46,250	435,000

*Elimination of intercompany investment. Excess of cost over book value ($46,250 – $37,500 = $8,750) is allocated to other assets ($5,000) and goodwill ($3,750).

STUDY NOTE: In this example, neither company has goodwill on its balance sheet. Goodwill is "created" when consolidated statements are prepared.

On the consolidated balance sheet, goodwill appears as an asset representing the portion of the excess of the cost of the investment over book value that cannot be allocated to any specific asset. The combined total for other assets is $415,000 ($380,000 + $30,000 + $5,000).

When a parent company pays less than book value for its investment in a subsidiary, the excess of book value over the cost of the investment must be used to lower the carrying value of the subsidiary's long-term assets. The reasoning behind this requirement is that a ready market does not usually exist for long-term assets (other than marketable securities) and estimates of the market values of these assets are therefore generally not very reliable.

Intercompany Receivables and Payables If a subsidiary owes money to the parent company, there will be a receivable on the parent company's individual balance sheet and a payable on the subsidiary company's individual balance sheet. Conversely, if a parent owes money to a subsidiary, there will be a receivable on the subsidiary's balance sheet and a payable on the parent's balance sheet. When a consolidated balance sheet is prepared, both the receivable and the payable should be eliminated because from the viewpoint of the consolidated entity, neither the asset nor the liability exists. In other words, it does not make sense for a company to owe money to itself. The eliminating entry is made on the work sheet by debiting the payable and crediting the receivable for the amount of the intercompany loan.

Consolidated Income Statement

A consolidated income statement is prepared by combining the revenues and expenses of the parent and subsidiary companies. The procedure is the same as the one used to prepare a consolidated balance sheet—that is, intercompany transactions are eliminated to prevent double counting of revenues and expenses. The following intercompany transactions affect the consolidated income statement:

- Sales and purchases of goods and services between parent and subsidiary
- Income and expenses related to loans, receivables, or bond indebtedness between parent and subsidiary
- Other income and expenses from intercompany transactions

STUDY NOTE: Intercompany sales or purchases are not revenues or expenses of the consolidated entity. True revenues and expenses occur only when transactions are with parties outside the firm.

To illustrate the eliminating entries, suppose that Parent Company sold $60,000 of goods to Subsidiary Company, which in turn sold all the goods to others, and that Subsidiary Company paid Parent Company $1,000 interest on a loan. The work sheet in Exhibit 14.6 shows how to prepare a consolidated income statement for these two companies.

Because the purpose of the eliminating entries is to treat the two companies as a single entity, it is important to include only sales made to outsiders and to include in cost of goods sold only purchases made from outsiders. This goal is met with the first eliminating entry, which eliminates the $60,000 of intercompany sales and purchases by a debit of that amount to sales and a credit of that amount to cost of goods sold. Thus, only sales to outsiders ($255,000) and purchases from outsiders ($120,000) are included in the Consolidated Income Statement column. The intercompany interest income and expense are eliminated by a debit to other revenues and a credit to other expenses.

Public corporations also prepare consolidated statements of stockholders' equity and consolidated statements of cash flows. For examples of these statements, see the **CVS** annual report in the Supplement to Chapter 1.

Restatement of Foreign Subsidiary Financial Statements

Companies often expand by establishing or buying foreign subsidiaries. Such companies are called **multinational** or **transnational corporations**. If a company owns more than

EXHIBIT 14.6
Work Sheet for Preparing a Consolidated Income Statement

Parent and Subsidiary Companies
Work Sheet for Consolidated Income Statement
For the Year Ended December 31, 2011

Accounts	Income Statement, Parent Company	Income Statement, Subsidiary Company	Eliminations Debit	Eliminations Credit	Consolidated Income Statement
Sales	215,000	100,000	60,000*		255,000
Other revenues	30,000	5,000	1,000**		34,000
Total revenues	245,000	105,000			289,000
Cost of goods sold	105,000	75,000		60,000*	120,000
Other expenses	70,000	25,000		1,000**	94,000
Total costs and expenses	175,000	100,000			214,000
Net income	70,000	5,000	61,000	61,000	75,000

*Elimination of intercompany sales and purchases
**Elimination of intercompany interest income and interest expense

50 percent of a foreign subsidiary and thus exercises control, the foreign subsidiary should be included in the consolidated financial statements. The consolidation procedure is the same as the one for domestic subsidiaries, except that the foreign subsidiary's statements must be restated in the reporting currency before consolidation takes place. The **reporting currency** is the currency in which the consolidated financial statements are presented, which for U.S. companies is usually the U.S. dollar. For example, **Intel** states that "the U.S. dollar is the functional currency for Intel and our subsidiaries."[19] Thus, **restatement** of Intel's subsidiaries' statements into the currency of the parent company is necessary. After restatement, a parent's and subsidiaries' statements can be consolidated in the usual way.

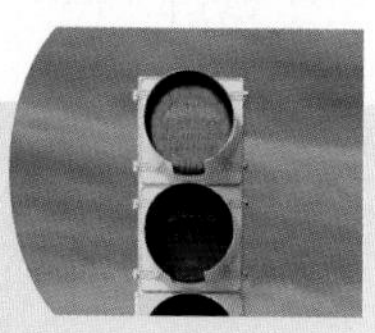

Stop & Apply

S Company has total stockholders' equity of $50,000. Fill in the dollar amounts for each of the following investments by P Company in S Company's common stock:

	Goodwill	Minority Interest
1. P Company pays $50,000 for 100% of S Company's common stock. S Company's net assets are fairly valued at $50,000.	________	________
2. P Company pays $60,000 for 100% of S Company's common stock. S Company's net assets are fairly valued at $50,000.	________	________
3. P Company pays $60,000 for 100% of S Company's common stock. S Company's net assets are fairly valued at $60,000.	________	________
4. P Company pays $40,000 for 80% of S Company's common stock. S Company's net assets are fairly valued at $50,000.	________	________
5. P Company pays $50,000 for 80% of S Company's common stock. S Company's net assets are fairly valued at $62,500.	________	________

iStock Photo

(continued)

SOLUTION

	Goodwill	Minority Interest
1.	0	0
2.	$10,000	0
3.	0	0
4.	0	$10,000
5.	0	$12,500

INVESTMENTS IN DEBT SECURITIES

LO 5 Explain the financial reporting implications of debt investments.

As noted in previous chapters, debt securities are considered financial instruments because they are claims that will be paid in cash. When a company purchases debt securities, it records them at cost plus any commissions and fees. Like investments in equity securities, short-term investments in debt securities are valued at fair value at the end of the accounting period and are accounted for as trading securities or available-for-sale securities. However, the accounting treatment is different if they qualify as held-to-maturity securities.

STUDY NOTE: *Any brokerage costs or other costs involved in acquiring securities are part of the cost of the securities.*

Held-to-Maturity Securities

As we noted earlier, held-to-maturity securities are debt securities that management intends to hold to their maturity date. Such securities are recorded at cost and are valued on the balance sheet at cost adjusted for the effects of interest. In the sections that follow, we show how to account for the purchase and sale of investments in debt securities for Roll Company.

Purchase of Held-to-Maturity Securities On December 1, 2011, Roll Company pays $48,500 for U.S. Treasury bills, which are short-term debt of the federal government. The bills will mature in 120 days at $50,000.

Analysis: Roll Company would record the purchase much as it would other short-term investments; thus, the journal entry to record the investment at cost

▲ *increases* Short-Term Investments with a debit for the cost of $48,500 and
▼ *decreases* Cash with a credit for $48,500.

A	=	L	+	SE
+48,500				
−48,500				

Journal Entry:

2011			
Dec. 1	Short-Term Investments	48,500	
	Cash		48,500
	To record purchase of U.S. Treasury bills that mature in 120 days		

Year-End Accrual of Interest At Roll's year-end on December 31, 2011, the interest income earned to date must be accrued in an adjusting entry.

Analysis: The journal entry to record the year-end adjustment

▲ *increases* Short-Term Investments with a debit for the accrued interest of $375 ($1,500 × 30/120) and
▲ *increases* Interest Income with a credit for $375.

A	=	L	+	SE
+375				+375

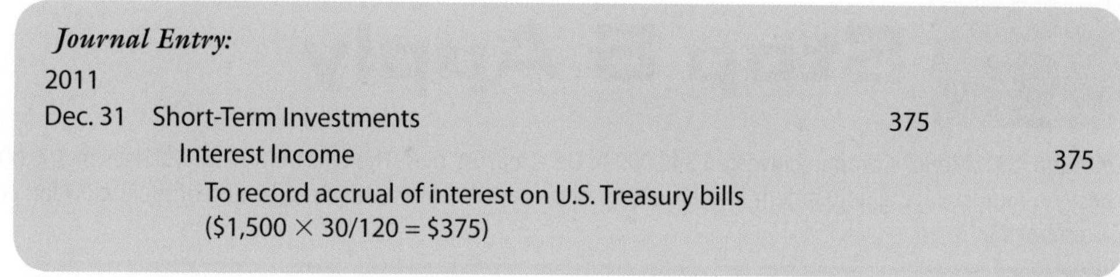

Journal Entry:

2011			
Dec. 31	Short-Term Investments	375	
	Interest Income		375
	To record accrual of interest on U.S. Treasury bills ($1,500 × 30/120 = $375)		

Comment: On December 31, the U.S. Treasury bills would be shown on the balance sheet as a short-term investment at their amortized cost of $48,875 ($48,500 + $375). The market value of the investment is ignored.

Receipt of Interest On March 31, 2012, Rolls Company receives the maturity value of the treasury notes.

Analysis: The journal entry to record the receipt of interest

▲ *increases* Cash with a debit for the maturity value of $50,000,
▼ *decreases* Short-Term Investments with a credit for $48,875, and
▲ *increases* Interest Income by a credit of the difference of $1,125.

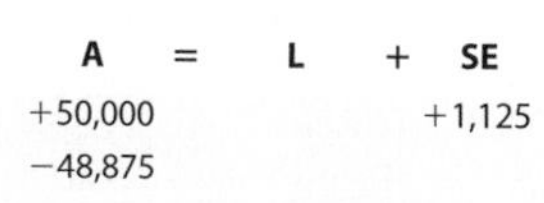

A	=	L	+	SE
+50,000				+1,125
−48,875				

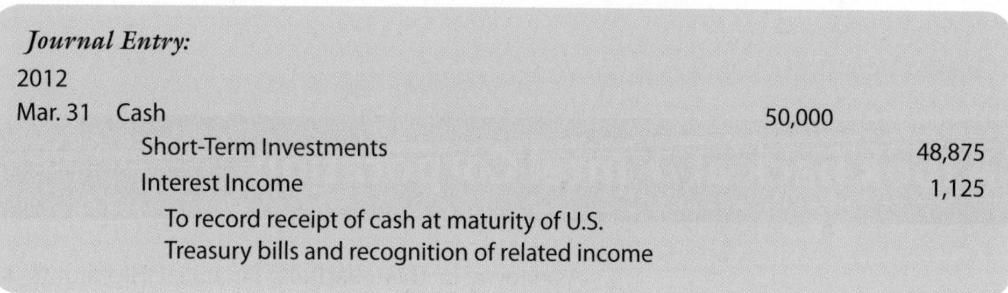

Journal Entry:

2012			
Mar. 31	Cash	50,000	
	Short-Term Investments		48,875
	Interest Income		1,125
	To record receipt of cash at maturity of U.S. Treasury bills and recognition of related income		

Comment: Note that the total interest income of $1,500 has been divided into the amount earned in 2011 ($375) and the amount earned in 2012 ($1,125). There is no gain or loss on the transaction.

Long-Term Investments in Bonds

Like all investments, investments in bonds are recorded at cost, which, in this case, is the price of the bonds plus the broker's commission. When bonds are purchased between interest payment dates, the purchaser must also pay an amount equal to the interest that has accrued on the bonds since the last interest payment date. Then, on the next interest payment date, the purchaser receives an interest payment for the whole period. The payment for accrued interest should be recorded as a debit to Interest Income, which will be offset by a credit to Interest Income when the semiannual interest is received.

STUDY NOTE: *The fair value of bonds is closely related to interest rates. An increase in interest rates lowers the fair value of bonds, and vice versa.*

Subsequent accounting for a corporation's long-term bond investments depends on the classification of the bonds. If the company plans to hold the bonds until they are paid off on their maturity date, they are considered held-to-maturity securities. Except in industries like insurance and banking, it is unusual for companies to buy the bonds of other companies with the express purpose of holding them until they mature, which can be in 10 to 30 years. Thus, most long-term bond investments are classified as available-for-sale securities, meaning that the company plans to sell them at some point before their maturity date. Such bonds are accounted for at fair value, much as equity or stock investments are; fair value is usually the market value. When bonds are intended to be held to maturity, they are accounted for not at fair value but at cost, adjusted for the amortization of their discount or premium. The procedure is similar to accounting for long-term bond liabilities, except that separate accounts for discounts and premiums are not used.

Stop & Apply

On August 31, Merick Company invested $49,000 in U.S. Treasury bills. The bills mature in 120 days at $50,000. Prepare journal entries to record the purchase on August 31; the adjustment to accrue interest on September 30, which is the end of the fiscal year; and the receipt of cash at the maturity date of December 29.

SOLUTION

Aug. 31	Short-Term Investments	49,000	
	Cash		49,000
	To record investment in 120-day U.S. Treasury bills		
Sept. 30	Short-Term Investments	250	
	Interest Income		250
	To record accrual of interest on U.S. Treasury bills ($1,000 × 30/120 = $250)		
Dec. 29	Cash	50,000	
	Short-Term Investments		49,250
	Interest Income		750
	To record receipt of cash at maturity of U.S. Treasury bills and recognition of related interest income		

iStock Photo

A look back at ▸ Intel Corporation

As shown in this chapter's Financial Highlights, short- and long-term investments and goodwill constitute a significant portion of the total assets on **Intel**'s balance sheet. These items have important effects on a company's income statement and statement of cash flows. To fully evaluate Intel's performance, users of its financial statements must address the following questions:

1. What types of investments are identified in Intel's financial statements?
2. How do Intel's investments affect its financial performance?

As indicated in this chapter, Intel has the following significant investments:

- Trading securities (short-term investments) that are reported at fair value on the balance sheet. Any gains or losses appear on the income statement.
- Available-for-sale securities, which are classified as both short- and long-term investments and reported at fair value on the balance sheet. Any unrealized gains and losses appear on the balance sheet under other comprehensive income, a component of stockholders' equity.
- Long-term equity investments in which the company has a significant but not controlling interest in another company appear on the balance sheet. If a decline in an investment's value is deemed permanent, it appears as a loss on the income statement.

Over $4 billion in goodwill from acquisitions appears on Intel's balance sheet and is subject to an annual impairment test. Interest income from investments in debt securities is reported on the income statement. The investing section of its statement of cash flows reveals significant purchase and sales of various types of investments.

In short, investments are an important part of Intel's business, and it is not possible to fully evaluate the company's performance without understanding how investments and acquisitions affect that performance.

Review Problem

LO 4

Consolidated Balance Sheet: Less Than 100 Percent Ownership.

In a cash transaction on June 30, 2011, Sava Company purchased 90 percent of the outstanding stock of Orion Company for $381,600. Right after the acquisition, the balance sheets of the two companies were as follows:

	A	B	C	D	E
1				Sava	Orion
2			**Assets**	**Company**	**Company**
3	Cash			$ 200,000	$ 24,000
4	Accounts receivable			325,000	120,000
5	Inventory			500,000	260,000
6	Investment in Orion Company			381,600	—
7	Plant and equipment (net)			750,000	440,000
8	Other assets			25,000	80,000
9	Total assets			$2,181,600	$924,000
10					
11			**Liabilities and Stockholders' Equity**		
12	Accounts payable			$ 400,000	$200,000
13	Long-term debt			500,000	300,000
14	Common stock			1,000,000	400,000
15	Retained earnings			281,600	24,000
16	Total liabilities and stockholders' equity			$2,181,600	$924,000
17					

The following information was also available:

1. Orion Company's other assets represented a long-term investment in Sava Company's long-term debt. Orion purchased the debt for an amount equal to Sava's carrying value of the debt.
2. Sava Company owed Orion Company $50,000 for services rendered.

Required

Prepare a work sheet for a consolidated balance sheet as of the acquisition date.

ANSWERS TO REVIEW PROBLEM

Sava and Orion Companies
Work Sheet for Consolidated Balance Sheet
June 30, 2011

Accounts	Balance Sheet: Sava Company	Balance Sheet: Orion Company	Eliminations: Debit	Eliminations: Credit	Consolidated Balance Sheet
Cash	200,000	24,000			224,000
Accounts receivable	325,000	120,000		*** 50,000	395,000
Inventory	500,000	260,000			760,000
Investment in Orion Company	381,600	—		* 381,600	—
Plant and equipment (net)	750,000	440,000			1,190,000
Other assets	25,000	80,000		** 80,000	25,000
Total assets	2,181,600	924,000			2,594,000
Accounts payable	400,000	200,000	*** 50,000		550,000
Long-term debt	500,000	300,000	** 80,000		720,000
Common stock	1,000,000	400,000	* 400,000		1,000,000
Retained earnings	281,600	24,000	* 24,000		281,600
Minority interest	—	—		* 42,400	42,400
Total liabilities and stockholders' equity	2,181,600	924,000	554,000	554,000	2,594,000

* Elimination of intercompany investment. Minority interest equals 10 percent of Orion Company's stockholders' equity [10% × ($400,000 + $24,000) = $42,400]

** Elimination of intercompany long-term debt

*** Elimination of intercompany receivables and payables

Stop & Review

Identify and explain the management issues related to investments.

Investments are recorded on the date on which the transaction occurs, at which time there is either a transfer of funds or a definite obligation to pay. Investments are recorded at cost, or purchase price, including any commissions or fees. After the purchase, the balance sheet value of investments is adjusted to reflect subsequent conditions, including changes in fair value.

Investments are classified as short term or long term; as trading, available-for-sale, or held-to-maturity securities; and as noninfluential and noncontrolling, influential but noncontrolling, or controlling investments. These classifications play an important role in accounting for investments. Noninfluential and noncontrolling investments represent less than 20 percent ownership of a company; influential but noncontrolling investments represent 20 percent to 50 percent ownership; and controlling investments represent more than 50 percent ownership.

A company should disclose its accounting policies for investments and related details in the notes to its financial statements.

Managers and other employees must avoid using their knowledge of their company's planned investment transactions for personal gain.

Explain the financial reporting implications of short-term investments. **LO2**

Short-term investments in stocks are classified as trading securities or available-for-sale securities. Trading securities are debt or equity securities that are bought and held principally for the purpose of being sold in the near term. They are classified as current assets on the balance sheet and are valued at fair value. Unrealized gains or losses on trading securities appear on the income statement.

Available-for-sale securities are debt or equity securities that do not meet the criteria for either trading or held-to-maturity securities. They are accounted for in the same way as trading securities with two exceptions: (1) an unrealized gain or loss is reported as a special item in the stockholders' equity section of the balance sheet; (2) if a decline in the value of a security is considered permanent, it is charged as a loss on the income statement.

Explain the financial reporting implications of long-term investments in stock and the cost-adjusted-to-market and equity methods used to account for them. **LO3**

The cost-adjusted-to-market method is used to account for noninfluential and noncontrolling investments in stock. With this method, investments are initially recorded at cost and are then adjusted to market value by using an allowance account. The equity method is used to account for influential but noncontrolling investments. With this method, the investment is initially recorded at cost and is then adjusted for the investor's share of the company's net income or loss and subsequent dividends.

Consolidated financial statements are required when an investing company has legal and effective control over another company. Control exists when the parent company owns more than 50 percent of the voting stock of the subsidiary company.

Explain the financial reporting implications of consolidated financial statements. **LO4**

Consolidated financial statements are useful to investors and others because they treat the parent company and its subsidiaries as an integrated economic unit. When a consolidated balance sheet is prepared at the date of acquisition, a work sheet entry is made to eliminate the investment from the parent company's financial statements and from the stockholders' equity section of the subsidiary's financial statements. The assets and liabilities of the two companies are combined. If the parent owns less than 100 percent of the subsidiary, minority interest equal to the percentage of the subsidiary owned by minority stockholders multiplied by the subsidiary's net assets appears on the consolidated balance sheet. If the cost of the parent's investment in the subsidiary is greater than the subsidiary's book value, an amount equal to the excess of cost over book value is allocated to undervalued subsidiary assets and to goodwill. If the cost of the parent's investment in the subsidiary is less than book value, the excess of book value over cost should be used to reduce the book value of the subsidiary's long-term assets (other than long-term marketable securities).

When consolidated income statements are prepared, intercompany sales, purchases, interest income, interest expense, and other income and expenses from intercompany transactions must be eliminated to avoid double counting of these items.

The financial statements of foreign subsidiaries must be restated in terms of the parent company's reporting currency before consolidated financial statements can be prepared.

Explain the financial reporting implications of debt investments. 

Held-to-maturity securities are debt securities that management intends to hold to their maturity date. They are valued on the balance sheet at cost adjusted for the effects of interest. Long-term investments in bonds fall into two categories: available-for-sale securities, which are recorded at cost and subsequently accounted for at fair value, and held-to-maturity securities.

Key Terms

Available-for-sale securities 637 (LO1)
Consolidated financial statements 648 (LO3)
Control 638 (LO1)
Cost-adjusted-to-market method 643 (LO3)
Eliminations 649 (LO4)
Equity method 646 (LO3)
Fair value 636 (LO1)
Held-to-maturity securities 637 (LO1)
Insider trading 639 (LO1)
Long-term investments 636 (LO1)
Marketable securities 636 (LO1)
Minority interest 651 (LO4)
Multinational or **transnational corporations** 654 (LO4)
Parent company 648 (LO3)
Purchase method 649 (LO4)
Reporting currency 655 (LO4)
Restatement 655 (LO4)
Short-term investments 636 (LO1)
Subsidiary 648 (LO3)
Trading securities 637 (LO1)

Chapter Assignments Building Your Basic Knowledge and Skills

Short Exercises

LO 2 **Trading Securities**

SE 1. Murray Corporation began investing in trading securities in 2011. At the end of 2011, it had the following trading portfolio:

Security	Cost	Market Value
Google (10,000 shares)	$220,000	$330,000
FedEx (5,000 shares)	100,000	75,000
Totals	$320,000	$405,000

Prepare the necessary year-end adjusting entry on December 31 and the journal entry for the sale of all the FedEx shares on the following March 23 for $95,000.

LO 3 **Cost-Adjusted-to-Market Method**

SE 2. On December 31, 2011, the market value of Pirat Tech Company's portfolio of long-term available-for-sale securities was $640,000. The cost of these securities was $570,000. Prepare the journal entry to adjust the portfolio to market at year-end, assuming that the company did not have any long-term investments prior to 2011.

LO 3 **Cost-Adjusted-to-Market Method**

SE 3. Refer to your answer to **SE 2**. Assume that on December 31, 2012, the cost of Pirat Tech Company's portfolio of long-term available-for-sale securities was $570,000 and that its market value was $490,000. Prepare the journal entry to record the 2012 year-end adjustment.

LO 3 **Equity Method**

SE 4. Bianka Company owns 30 percent of Bargain Company. In 2011, Bargain earned $60,000 and paid $40,000 in dividends. Prepare journal entries for Bianka's records on December 31 to record this information. Assume that the dividends are received on December 31.

LO 3 **Methods of Accounting for Long-Term Investments**

SE 5. For each of the investments listed below, tell which of the following methods should be used for external financial reporting: (a) cost-adjusted-to-market method, (b) equity method, (c) consolidation of parent and subsidiary financial statements.

1. 49 percent investment in Miraz Corporation
2. 51 percent investment in Roof Corporation
3. 5 percent investment in Rek Corporation

LO 3 **Equity Method**

SE 6. Perk Company owns 25 percent of Storm Company. During 2011, Storm earned $100,000 and paid $72,000 in dividends. Prepare journal entries for Perk's records on December 31 to record this information. Assume that the dividends are received on December 31.

LO 4 **Purchase of 100 Percent at Book Value**

SE 7. Vira Corporation buys 100 percent ownership of Ferguson Corporation for $100,000. At the time of the purchase, Ferguson's stockholders' equity consisted of $20,000 in common stock and $80,000 in retained earnings. Vira's stockholders' equity consisted of $200,000 in common stock and $400,000 in retained earnings. After the purchase, what would be the amount, if any, of the following accounts on the consolidated balance sheet: goodwill, minority interest, common stock, and retained earnings?

LO 4

Purchase of Less Than 100 Percent at Book Value

SE 8. Assume the same facts as in **SE** 7 except that Vira purchased 80 percent of Ferguson for $80,000. After the purchase, what would be the amount, if any, of the following accounts on the consolidated balance sheet: goodwill, minority interest, common stock, and retained earnings?

LO 4

Purchase of 100 Percent at More Than Book Value

SE 9. Assume the same facts as in **SE** 7 except that the purchase of 100 percent of Ferguson was for $120,000. After the purchase, what would be the amount, if any, of the following accounts on the consolidated balance sheet: goodwill, minority interest, common stock, and retained earnings? Assume that the fair value of Ferguson's net assets equals their book value.

LO 4

Intercompany Transactions

SE 10. P Company owns 100 percent of S Company. The following are accounts from the balance sheets and income statements of both companies:

	P Company	S Company
Accounts receivable	$ 460,000	$ 300,000
Accounts payable	360,000	180,000
Sales	2,400,000	1,780,000
Cost of goods sold	1,420,000	1,080,000

What would be the combined amount of each of the above accounts on the consolidated financial statements assuming the following additional information? (1) S Company sold to P Company merchandise at cost in the amount of $540,000; (2) P Company sold all the merchandise it bought from S Company to customers, but it still owes S Company $120,000 for the merchandise.

LO 5

Held-to-Maturity Securities

SE 11. On May 31, Fournier Company invested $98,000 in U.S. Treasury bills. The bills mature in 120 days at $100,000. Prepare journal entries to record the purchase on May 31; the adjustment to accrue interest on June 30, which is the end of the fiscal year; and the receipt of cash at the maturity date of September 28.

LO 5

Held-to-Maturity Securities

SE 12. On March 31, Logan Company invested $129,000 in U.S. Treasury bills. The bills mature in 90 days at $130,000. Prepare journal entries to record the purchase on March 31; the adjustment to accrue interest on April 30, which is the end of the fiscal year; and the receipt of cash at the maturity date of June 29.

Exercises

LO 1, 2, 3

Discussion Questions

E 1. Develop brief answers to each of the following questions:

1. Where in the financial statements are investment transactions reported?
2. What would cause an Allowance to Adjust Short-Term Investments to Market account that has a negative (credit) balance at the beginning of the year to have a positive (debit) balance at the end of the year?
3. When a company uses the equity method to record its proportionate share of the income and dividends of a company in which it has invested, what are the cash flow effects?

LO 4, 5 **Discussion Questions**

E 2. Develop brief answers to each of the following questions:

1. Under what conditions would a company have both minority interest and goodwill in a consolidation?
2. Why must the financial statements of foreign subsidiaries be restated?
3. What is the logic behind treating held-to-maturity securities different from any other investment?

LO 2 **Trading Securities**

E 3. Vela Corporation, which has begun investing in trading securities, engaged in the following transactions:

Jan. 6 Purchased 7,000 shares of IBM stock, $30 per share.
Feb. 15 Purchased 9,000 shares of Quaker Oats, $22 per share.

At year-end on June 30, IBM was trading at $40 per share, and Quaker Oats was trading at $18 per share.

Prepare the journal entries to record the purchases. Then prepare the journal entry to record the necessary year-end adjustment. Include a schedule of the trading portfolio cost and market value in the explanation. Also prepare the journal entry to record the sale of all the Quaker Oats shares on August 20 for $16 per share. Is the last entry affected by the June 30 adjustment? Explain.

LO 3 **Long-Term Investments**

E 4. Nelin Corporation has the following portfolio of long-term available-for-sale securities at year-end, December 31, 2011:

Company	Percentage of Voting Stock Held	Cost	Year-End Market Value
A Corporation	4	$ 80,000	$ 95,000
B Corporation	12	375,000	275,000
C Corporation	5	30,000	55,000
Total		$485,000	$425,000

Both the Unrealized Loss on Long-Term Investments account and the Allowance to Adjust Long-Term Investments to Market account currently have a balance of $40,000 from the last accounting period. Prepare T accounts with a beginning balance for each of these accounts. Record the effects of the above information on the accounts and determine the ending balances.

LO 3 **Long-Term Investments: Cost-Adjusted-to-Market and Equity Methods**

E 5. On January 1, Rurk Corporation purchased, as long-term investments, 8 percent of the voting stock of Star Corporation for $1,000,000 and 45 percent of the voting stock of Mit Corporation for $8,000,000. During the year, Star had earnings of $400,000 and paid dividends of $160,000. Mit Corporation had earnings of $1,200,000 and paid dividends of $800,000. The market value did not change for either investment during the year. Which of these investments should be accounted for using the cost-adjusted-to-market method? Which should be accounted for using the equity method? At what amount should each investment be carried on the balance sheet at year-end? Give a reason for each choice.

LO 3 **Long-Term Investments: Equity Method**

E 6. On January 1, 2011, Gong Corporation acquired 40 percent of the voting stock of Blue Corporation, an amount sufficient to exercise significant influence over Blue's activities, for $4,800,000 in cash. On December 31, Gong determined that Blue paid dividends of $800,000 but incurred a net loss of $400,000 for 2011. Prepare T accounts to record this information.

LO 3

Methods of Accounting for Long-Term Investments

E 7. Roland Corporation has the following long-term investments:

1. 60 percent of the common stock of Ariel Corporation
2. 13 percent of the common stock of Copper, Inc.
3. 50 percent of the nonvoting preferred stock of Taurus Corporation
4. 100 percent of the common stock of its financing subsidiary, PR, Inc.
5. 35 percent of the common stock of the French company Rue de le Brasseur
6. 70 percent of the common stock of the Canadian company Nova Scotia

For each of these investments, tell which of the following methods should be used for external financial reporting and why:

a. Cost-adjusted-to-market method
b. Equity method
c. Consolidation of parent and subsidiary financial statements

LO 4

Elimination Entry for a Purchase at Book Value

E 8. Sonic Manufacturing Company purchased 100 percent of the common stock of Pool Manufacturing Company for $600,000. Pool's stockholders' equity included common stock of $400,000 and retained earnings of $200,000. Prepare the eliminating journal entry that would appear on the work sheet for consolidating the balance sheets of these two entities as of the acquisition date.

LO 4

Elimination Entry and Minority Interest

E 9. The stockholders' equity section of East Corporation's balance sheet appeared as follows on December 31:

Common stock, $10 par value, 80,000 shares authorized and issued	$800,000
Retained earnings	96,000
Total stockholders' equity	$896,000

Danny Manufacturing Company owns 80 percent of East's voting stock and paid $11.20 per share. Prepare the journal entry (including minority interest) to eliminate Danny's investment and East's stockholders' equity that would appear on the work sheet used in preparing the consolidated balance sheet for the two firms.

LO 4

Consolidated Balance Sheet with Goodwill

E 10. On September 1, 2011, A Company purchased 100 percent of the voting stock of B Company for $480,000 in cash. The separate condensed balance sheets immediately after the purchase were as follows:

	A Company	B Company
Other assets	$1,103,000	$544,500
Investment in B Company	480,000	—
Total assets	$1,583,000	$544,500
Liabilities	$ 435,500	$ 94,500
Common stock	500,000	150,000
Retained earnings	647,500	300,000
Total liabilities and stockholders' equity	$1,583,000	$544,500

Prepare a work sheet for preparing the consolidated balance sheet immediately after A Company acquired control of B Company. Assume that any excess cost of A Company's investment in the subsidiary over book value is attributable to goodwill from consolidation.

LO 4
Preparation of Consolidated Income Statement

E 11. Lion Company has owned 100 percent of Fish Company since 2010. The income statements of these two companies for the year ended December 31, 2011, follow.

	Lion Company	Fish Company
Net sales	$1,500,000	$600,000
Cost of goods sold	750,000	400,000
Gross margin	$ 750,000	$200,000
Less: Selling expenses	$ 250,000	$ 50,000
General and administrative expenses	300,000	100,000
Total operating expenses	$ 550,000	$150,000
Income from operations	$ 200,000	$ 50,000
Other income	60,000	—
Net income	$ 260,000	$ 50,000

The following is additional information: (1) Fish purchased $280,000 of inventory from Lion, which it had sold to Fish customers by the end of the year. (2) Fish leased its building from Lion for $60,000 per year. Prepare a consolidated income statement work sheet for the two companies for the year ended December 31, 2011. Income taxes have been ignored.

LO 5
Held-to-Maturity Securities

E 12. Date Company experiences heavy sales in the summer and early fall, after which time it has excess cash to invest until the next spring. On November 1, 2011, the company invested $776,000 in U.S. Treasury bills. The bills mature in 180 days at $800,000. Prepare journal entries to record the purchase on November 1; the adjustment to accrue interest on December 31, which is the end of the fiscal year; and the receipt of cash at the maturity date of April 30.

Problems

LO 1, 2
Accounting for Investments

P 1. Dioda Gas Corporation is a successful oil and gas exploration business in the southwestern United States. At the beginning of 2011, the company made investments in three companies that perform services in the oil and gas industry. The details of each of these long-term investments follow.

Dioda purchased 100,000 shares of Ink Service Corporation at a cost of $16 per share. Ink has 1.5 million shares outstanding and during 2011 paid dividends of $0.80 per share on earnings of $1.60 per share. At the end of the year, Ink's shares were selling for $24 per share.

Dioda also purchased 2 million shares of Reef Drilling Company at $8 per share. Reef has 10 million shares outstanding. In 2011, Reef paid a dividend of $0.40 per share on earnings of $0.80 per share. During the year, the president of Dioda was appointed to Reef's board of directors. At the end of the year, Reef's stock was selling for $12 per share.

In another action, Dioda purchased 1 million shares of Bloom Oil Field Supplies Company's 5 million outstanding shares at $12 per share. The president of Dioda sought membership on Bloom's board of directors but was rebuffed when a majority of shareholders stated they did not want to be associated with Dioda. Bloom paid a dividend of $0.80 per share and reported a net income of only $0.40 per share for the year. By the end of the year, its stock price had dropped to $4 per share.

REQUIRED

1. For each investment, prepare journal entries to record the (a) initial investment, (b) receipt of cash dividend, and (c) recognition of income (if appropriate).
2. What adjusting entry (if any) is required at the end of the year?

3. Assume that Dioda sells its investment in Bloom after the first of the year for $6 per share. Prepare the appropriate journal entry.
4. Assume that no other transactions occur and that the market value of Dioda's investment in Ink exceeds cost by $2,400,000 at the end of the second year. What adjusting entry (if any) would be required?

USER INSIGHT ▶

5. What principal factors should be considered in determining how to account for Dioda's investments? Should Dioda's investments be shown on the balance sheet as short- or long-term investments? Why?

LO 3

Long-Term Investments: Equity Method

✔ Investment in Windson Corporation, Ending Balance: $367,000

P 2. Lander Corporation owns 35 percent of the voting stock of Windson Corporation. The balance of the Investment account on Lander's books as of January 1, 2011, was $360,000. During 2011, Windson reported the following quarterly earnings and dividends:

Quarter	Earnings	Dividends Paid
1	$ 80,000	$ 50,000
2	120,000	50,000
3	60,000	50,000
4	(40,000)	50,000
	$220,000	$200,000

Because of the percentage of voting shares Lander owns, it can exercise significant influence over the operations of Windson. Therefore, Lander must account for the investment using the equity method.

REQUIRED

1. Prepare a T account for Lander's investment in Windson and enter the beginning balance, the relevant transactions for the year in total, and the ending balance.

USER INSIGHT ▶

2. What is the effect and placement of the transactions in **1** on Lander's earnings as reported on the income statement?

CASH FLOW

3. What is the effect and placement of the transactions in **1** on the statement of cash flows?

USER INSIGHT ▶

4. How would the effects on the statements differ if Lander's ownership represented only a 15 percent share of Windson?

LO 4

Consolidated Balance Sheet: Cost Exceeding Book Value

✔ Consolidated Balance Sheet, Total assets: $640,000

P 3. The balance sheets of Arrak Company and Bivak Company as of December 31, 2011, appear below.

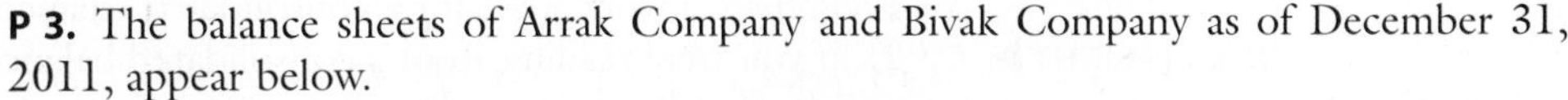

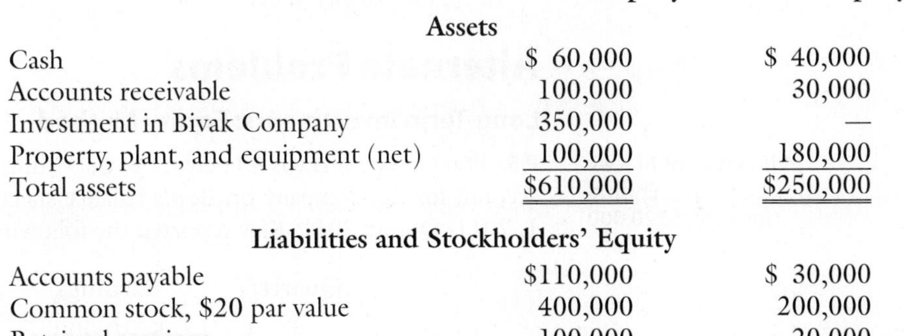

	Arrak Company	Bivak Company
Assets		
Cash	$ 60,000	$ 40,000
Accounts receivable	100,000	30,000
Investment in Bivak Company	350,000	—
Property, plant, and equipment (net)	100,000	180,000
Total assets	$610,000	$250,000
Liabilities and Stockholders' Equity		
Accounts payable	$110,000	$ 30,000
Common stock, $20 par value	400,000	200,000
Retained earnings	100,000	20,000
Total liabilities and stockholders' equity	$610,000	$250,000

Assume that Arrak purchased 100 percent of Bivak's common stock for $350,000 immediately prior to December 31, 2011. Also assume that $80,000 of the excess of cost over book value is attributable to the increased value of Bivak's property, plant, and equipment. The rest of the excess is considered by Arrak to be goodwill.

REQUIRED

1. Prepare a work sheet for preparing a consolidated balance sheet as of the acquisition date.

USER INSIGHT ▶ 2. If you were reading Arrak's consolidated balance sheet, what account would indicate that Arrak paid more than fair value for Bivak, and where would you find it on the balance sheet? Also, would you expect the amount of this account to change from year to year? What would cause it to change?

LO 4

Consolidated Balance Sheet: Less Than 100 Percent Ownership

✔ Consolidated Balance Sheet, Total assets: $4,488,000

P 4. In a cash transaction, Root Company purchased 70 percent of the outstanding stock of Mandela Company for $593,600 cash on June 30, 2011. Immediately after the acquisition, the separate balance sheets of the companies appeared as follows.

	Root Company	Mandela Company
Assets		
Cash	$ 320,000	$ 48,000
Accounts receivable	520,000	240,000
Inventory	800,000	520,000
Investment in Mandela Company	593,600	—
Property, plant, and equipment (net)	1,200,000	880,000
Other assets	40,000	160,000
Total assets	$3,473,600	$1,848,000
Liabilities and Stockholders' Equity		
Accounts payable	$ 640,000	$ 400,000
Long-term debt	800,000	600,000
Common stock, $10 par value	1,600,000	800,000
Retained earnings	433,600	48,000
Total liabilities and stockholders' equity	$3,473,600	$1,848,000

Additional information: (a) Mandela's other assets represent a long-term investment in Root's long-term debt. The debt was purchased for an amount equal to Root's carrying value of the debt. (b) Root owes Mandela $80,000 for services rendered.

REQUIRED

1. Prepare a work sheet for a consolidated balance sheet as of the acquisition date.

USER INSIGHT ▶ 2. If you were reading Root's consolidated balance sheet, what account would indicate that Root owned less than 100 percent of Mandela, and where would you find it on the balance sheet?

Alternate Problems

LO 3

Long-Term Investments: Equity Method

✔ Investment in Kiev Company, Ending Balance: $320,000

P 5. Bon Company owns 40 percent of the voting stock of Kiev Company. The investment account for this company on Bon's balance sheet had a balance of $300,000 on January 1, 2011. During 2011, Kiev reported the following quarterly earnings and dividends paid:

Quarter	Earnings	Dividends Paid
1	$ 40,000	$20,000
2	30,000	20,000
3	80,000	20,000
4	(20,000)	20,000
	$130,000	$80,000

Bon exercises a significant influence over Kiev's operations and therefore uses the equity method to account for its investment.

REQUIRED

1. Prepare a T account for Bon's investment in Kiev. Enter the beginning balance, the transactions entries for the year in total, and the ending balance.

USER INSIGHT ▶ 2. What is the effect and placement of the transactions in **1** on Bon's earnings as reported on the income statement?

USER INSIGHT ▶ CASH FLOW 3. What is the effect and placement of the transactions in **1** on the statement of cash flows?

USER INSIGHT ▶ 4. How would the effects on the statements differ if Bon's ownership represented only a 10 percent share of Kiev?

LO 4

Consolidated Balance Sheet: Cost Exceeding Book Value

✔ Consolidated Balance Sheet, Total assets: $4,790,000

P 6. The balance sheets of Cheese Company and Ham Company as of December 31, 2011, follow.

	Cheese Company	Ham Company
Assets		
Cash	$ 400,000	$ 120,000
Accounts receivable	550,000	1,200,000
Investment in Ham Company	1,400,000	—
Property, plant, and equipment (net)	1,370,000	900,000
Total assets	$3,720,000	$2,220,000
Liabilities and Stockholders' Equity		
Accounts payable	$ 950,000	$1,070,000
Common stock, $20 par value	1,850,000	1,000,000
Retained earnings	920,000	150,000
Total liabilities and stockholders' equity	$3,720,000	$2,220,000

Assume that Cheese purchased 100 percent of Ham's common stock for $1,400,000 immediately prior to December 31, 2011. Also assume that $100,000 of the excess of cost over book value is attributable to the increased value of Ham's property, plant, and equipment. Cheese considers the rest of the excess to be goodwill.

REQUIRED

1. Prepare a work sheet for a consolidated balance sheet as of the acquisition date.

USER INSIGHT ▶ 2. If you were reading Cheese's consolidated balance sheet, what account would indicate that Cheese paid more than fair value for Ham, and where would you find it on the balance sheet? Also, would you expect the amount of this account to change from year to year? If so, what would cause it to change?

LO 3

Long-Term Investment Transactions

✔ Dec. 31, 2011 Portfolio total cost: $212,000

P 7. On January 2, 2011, Healey Company made several long-term investments in the voting stock of various companies. It purchased 10,000 shares of Zima at $4.00 a share, 15,000 shares of Kane at $6.00 a share, and 6,000 shares of Rodriguez at $9.00 a share. Each investment represents less than 20 percent of the voting stock of the company. The remaining securities transactions of Healey during 2011 were as follows:

May 5	Purchased with cash 6,000 shares of Drennan stock for $6.00 per share. This investment represents less than 20 percent of the Drennan voting stock.
July 16	Sold the 10,000 shares of Zima stock for $3.60 per share.
Sept. 30	Purchased with cash 5,000 additional shares of Kane for $6.40 per share. This investment still represents less than 20 percent of the voting stock.
Dec. 31	The market values per share of the stock in the Long-Term Investments account were as follows: Kane, $6.50; Rodriguez, $8.00; and Drennan, $4.00.

Healey's transactions in securities during 2012 were as follows:

Feb. 1	Received a cash dividend from Kane of $0.20 per share.
July 15	Sold the 6,000 Rodriguez shares for $8.00 per share.
Aug. 1	Received a cash dividend from Kane of $0.20 per share.
Sept. 10	Purchased 3,000 shares of Parmet Company for $14.00 per share. This investment represents less than 20 percent of the voting stock of the company.
Dec. 31	The market values per share of the stock in the Long-Term Investments account were as follows: Kane, $6.50; Drennan, $5.00; and Parmet, $13.00.

REQUIRED

1. Prepare journal entries to record all of Healey's transactions in long-term investments during 2011 and 2012.

USER INSIGHT ▶ 2. Assume that Healey increased its ownership in Kane to 25 percent and its ownership in Parmet to 60 percent in 2013. How would these actions affect the methods used to account for the investments?

LO 2, 5

Held-to-Maturity and Trading Securities

✔ June 30, 2011 Portfolio total market value: $495,000

P 8. During certain periods, Yang Company invests its excess cash until it is needed. During 2011 and 2012, Yang engaged in these transactions:

2011

Jan. 16	Invested $146,000 in 120-day U.S. Treasury bills that had a maturity value of $150,000.
Apr. 15	Purchased 10,000 shares of King Tools common stock at $40 per share and 5,000 shares of Mellon Gas common stock at $30 per share as trading securities.
May 16	Received maturity value of U.S. Treasury bills in cash.
June 2	Received dividends of $2.00 per share from King Tools and $1.50 per share from Mellon Gas.
30	Made year-end adjusting entry for trading securities. Market price per share for King Tools is $32; for Mellon Gas, it is $35.
Nov. 14	Sold all the shares of King Tools for $42 per share.

2012

Feb. 15	Purchased 9,000 shares of MKD Communications for $50 per share as a trading security investment.
Apr. 1	Invested $195,500 in 120-day U.S. Treasury bills that had a maturity value of $200,000.
June 1	Received dividends of $2.20 per share from Mellon Gas.
30	Made year-end adjusting entry for held-to-maturity securities.
30	Made year-end adjusting entry for trading securities. Market price per share for Mellon Gas is $35; for MKD Communications, it is $60.

REQUIRED

1. Prepare journal entries to record the preceding transactions, assuming that Yang's fiscal year ends on June 30.
2. Show the balance sheet presentation of short-term investments on June 30, 2012.

USER INSIGHT ▶ 3. Explain the following statement: Held-to-maturity and trading securities are opposites in terms of investment strategy and thus require opposite accounting treatments.

Cases

LO 2, 3

Conceptual Understanding: Accounting for Investments

C 1. Dell Computer Corporation has significant investment activities. The following items are from Dell's 2010 financial statements (amounts are in millions):[20]

Short-term investments	$ 373
Long-term investments	781
Investment income	134
Purchase of investments	1,383
Sales of investments	1,538
Change in unrealized gains (losses) on long-term investments, net	6

Dell states that all debt and equity securities are classified as available-for-sale and are subject to an annual impairment test.

1. Where would you find each of the above items in Dell's financial statements?
2. What value (cost or fair value) would you expect the first two items on Dell's balance sheet to represent?
3. What are impairments, and how do they differ from unrealized losses on long-term investments?

LO 4

Conceptual Understanding: Goodwill and Minority Interest

C 2. DreamWorks Animation has made such well-known animated films as *Shrek, Monsters vs. Aliens,* and *How to Train Your Dragon.* Two items on the company's 2009 and 2008 consolidated balance sheets are as follows:[21]

	2009	2008
Goodwill	$34,216	$34,216
Minority interest	—	2,941

1. What is the difference between goodwill and minority interest, and where do these items appear on the balance sheet?
2. The amount of goodwill did not change from 2008 to 2009. Assuming no new acquisitions or sales, what would cause the amount of goodwill to change from year to year? Would it increase or decrease?

LO 4

Annual Report Case: Major Acquisitions

C 3. In the past several years, CVS has made major acquisitions of **Caremark Rx, Inc.**; **Longs Drug Stores; and Generation Health**. Refer to the annual report of **CVS** in the Supplement to Chapter 1. Which account in CVS's balance sheet would lead you to believe that CVS paid substantially more in total than the aggregate fair value of the net tangible and intangible assets of these companies? Explain your answer.

LO 2

Comparison Analysis: Investments in Derivatives

C 4. Refer to the annual report of **CVS** and the financial statements of **Southwest Airlines Co.** in the Supplement to Chapter 1. Look at comprehensive income (loss) in each company's statement of shareholders' equity. Which company has substantial unrealized gains or losses? What causes either an unrealized gain or loss to occur? (*Note:* Derivative instrument are a type of investment.)

LO 1

Ethical Dilemma: Insider Trading

C 5. Refer to the discussion about insider trading in this chapter to answer the following questions:

1. What does *insider trading* mean?
2. Why do you think insider trading is illegal in the United States and in Germany?

3. Why do you think insider trading is permissible in some other countries?
4. For what, if any, reasons should insider trading be permitted in the United States?

LO 1

Decision Analysis: Accounting for Short-Term Investments

C 6. Malam Christmas Tree Company's business—the growing and selling of Christmas trees—is seasonal. By January 1, its heavy selling season is over, and it has cash on hand that will not be needed for several months. It has minimal expenses from January to October and heavy expenses during the harvest and shipping months of November and December. The company believes in investing idle cash in marketable securities, which can be sold when funds are needed for operations. Its fiscal year ends on June 30.

On January 10 of the current year, Malam has cash of $597,300 on hand. It keeps $20,000 on hand for operating expenses and invests the rest as follows:

$100,000 three-month Treasury bills	$ 97,800
5,000 shares of Ford Motor Co. ($10 per share)	50,000
5,000 shares of McDonald's ($25 per share)	125,000
4,350 shares of IBM ($70 per share)	304,500
Total short-term investments	$577,300

On February 10 and May 10, Malam receives quarterly cash dividends from each company in which it has invested: $0.10 per share from Ford Motor Co., $0.14 per share from McDonald's, and $0.20 per share from IBM. It redeems the Treasury bills at face value on April 10. On June 1, it sells 1,000 shares of McDonald's at $28 per share.

On June 30, the market values of the investments are as follows:

Ford Motor Co.	$11 per share
McDonald's	$23 per share
IBM	$65 per share

Malam receives another quarterly dividend from each company on August 10. It sells all its remaining shares on November 1 at the following prices:

Ford Motor Co.	$ 9 per share
McDonald's	$22 per share
IBM	$80 per share

1. Record the investment transactions that occurred on January 10, February 10, April 10, May 10, and June 1. The Treasury bills are accounted for as held-to-maturity securities, and the stocks are trading securities. Prepare the required adjusting entry on June 30 and record the investment transactions on August 10 and November 1.
2. Explain how the short-term investments would be shown on the balance sheet on June 30.
3. After November 1, what is the balance of Allowance to Adjust Short-Term Investments to Market, and what will happen to this account next June?

4. What is your assessment of Malam's strategy with regard to idle cash?

APPENDIX A

Accounting for Unincorporated Businesses

Throughout the book, we have focused on accounting for the corporate form of business. In this appendix, our focus is on accounting for sole proprietorships and partnerships.

ACCOUNTING FOR SOLE PROPRIETORSHIPS

A *sole proprietorship* is a business owned by one person. For the individual, this business form can be a convenient way of separating business activities from personal interests. Legally, however, the proprietorship is the same economic unit as the individual. The sole proprietor receives all the profits or losses and is liable for all the obligations of the business. Proprietorships represent the largest number of businesses in the United States, but typically they are the smallest in size. The life of a proprietorship ends when the owner wishes it to or at the owner's death or incapacity.

When someone invests in his or her own company, the amount of the investment is recorded in that person's Capital account. For example, the journal entry to record the initial investment of $10,000 by Hyun Hooper in her new mail-order business would be a debit to the Cash account for $10,000 and a credit to the Hyun Hooper, Capital account for $10,000.

During the period, Hooper will probably withdraw assets from the business for personal living expenses. Because there is no legal separation between the owner and the sole proprietorship, it is not necessary to make a formal declaration of a withdrawal, as would be required in the case of corporate dividends. The withdrawal of $500 by Hooper is recorded as a debit to the Hyun Hooper, Withdrawals account for $500 and a credit to the Cash account for $500.

Revenue and expense accounts for sole proprietorships are closed out to Income Summary in the same way they are for corporations. Income Summary, however, is closed to the Capital account instead of to Retained Earnings. For example, the closing entries that follow assume a net income of $1,000 and withdrawals of $500:

Income Summary	1,000	
Hyun Hooper, Capital		1,000
To close Income Summary in a sole proprietorship		
Hyun Hooper, Capital	500	
Hyun Hooper, Withdrawals		500
To close Withdrawals		

ACCOUNTING FOR PARTNERSHIPS

The Uniform Partnership Act, which has been adopted by a majority of the states, defines a *partnership* as "an association of two or more persons to carry on as co-owners of a business for profit." Normally, partnerships are formed when owners of small businesses wish to combine capital or managerial talents for some common business purpose. Partnerships are treated as separate entities in accounting, but legally there is no economic separation between them and their owners. They differ in many ways from the other forms of business. The following are some of their important characteristics:

Voluntary Association A partnership is a voluntary association of individuals rather than a legal entity in itself. Therefore, a partner is responsible under the law for his or her partners' actions within the scope of the business. A partner also has unlimited liability for the debts of the partnership. Because of these potential liabilities, a partner must be allowed to choose the people who join the partnership.

Partnership Agreement A partnership is easy to form. Two or more people simply agree to be partners in a business enterprise. This agreement is known as a *partnership agreement*. The partnership agreement does not have to be in writing. However, it is good business practice to have a written document that clearly states the details of the partnership, including the name, location, and purpose of the business; the partners' names and their respective duties; the investments of each partner; the method of distributing income and losses; and procedures for the admission and withdrawal of partners, the withdrawal of assets allowed each partner, and the liquidation (termination) of the business.

Limited Life Because a partnership is formed by an agreement between partners, it has a *limited life*. It may be dissolved when a new partner is admitted; when a partner withdraws, goes bankrupt, is incapacitated (to the point that he or she cannot perform as obligated), retires, or dies; or when the terms of the partnership agreement are met (e.g., when the project for which the partnership was formed is completed). The partnership agreement can be written to cover each of these situations, thus allowing the partnership to continue legally.

Mutual Agency Each partner is an agent of the partnership within the scope of the business. Because of this *mutual agency*, any partner can bind the partnership to a business agreement as long as he or she acts within the scope of the company's normal operations. For example, a partner in a used-car business can bind the partnership through the purchase or sale of used cars. But this partner cannot bind the partnership to a contract for buying men's clothing or any other goods that are not related to the used-car business.

Unlimited Liability Each partner has personal *unlimited liability* for all the debts of the partnership. If a partnership cannot pay its debts, creditors must first satisfy their claims from the assets of the business. If these assets are not enough to pay all debts, the creditors can seek payment from the personal assets of each partner. If a partner's personal assets are used up before the debts are paid, the creditors can claim additional assets from the remaining partners who are able to pay. Each partner, then, can be required by law to pay all the debts of the partnership.

Co-ownership of Partnership Property When individuals invest property in a partnership, they give up the right to their separate use of the property. The property becomes an asset of the partnership and is owned jointly by the partners.

Participation in Partnership Income Each partner has the right to share in the company's income and the responsibility to share in its losses. The partnership agreement should state the method of distributing income and losses to each partner. If the agreement describes how income should be shared but does not mention losses, losses are distributed in the same way as income. If the agreement does not describe the method of income and loss distribution, the partners must by law share income and losses equally.

Accounting for Partners' Equity

The owners' equity of a partnership is called *partners' equity*. In accounting for partners' equity, it is necessary to maintain separate Capital and Withdrawals accounts for each partner and to divide the income and losses of the company among the partners. In the partners' equity section of the balance sheet, the balance of each partner's Capital account is listed separately:

Liabilities and Partners' Equity		
Total liabilities		$28,000
Partners' equity		
Desmond, capital	$25,000	
Frank, capital	34,000	
Total partners' equity		59,000
Total liabilities and partners' equity		$87,000

Each partner invests cash, other assets, or both in the partnership according to the partnership agreement. Noncash assets should be valued at their fair market value on the date they are transferred to the partnership. The assets invested by a partner are debited to the proper account, and the total amount is credited to the partner's Capital account.

To show how partners' investments are recorded, let's assume that Jack Haddock and Pilar Villamer have agreed to combine their capital and equipment in a partnership to operate a jewelry store. According to their partnership agreement, Haddock will invest $28,000 cash and $47,000 of equipment, and the partnership will assume a note payable on the equipment of $10,000. The journal entry to record one partner's initial investment is as follows:

July 1	Cash	28,000	
	Equipment	47,000	
	Note Payable		10,000
	Jack Haddock, Capital		65,000
	Initial investment of Jack Haddock in Haddock and Villamer		

Distribution of Partnership Income and Losses

A partnership's income and losses can be distributed according to whatever method the partners specify in the partnership agreement. Income in this form of business normally has three components: return to the partners for the use of their capital (called *interest on partners' capital*), compensation for services the partners have rendered (partners' salaries), and other income for any special contributions individual partners may make to the partnership or for risks they may take. The breakdown of total income into its three components helps clarify how much each partner has contributed to the firm.

Distributing income and losses among partners can be accomplished by using stated ratios or capital balance ratios or by paying the partners salaries and interest on their capital and sharing the remaining income according to stated ratios. *Salaries* and *interest here* are not *salaries expense* or *interest expense* in the ordinary sense of the terms. They do not affect the amount of reported net income. Instead, they refer to ways of determining each partner's share of net income or loss based on the time the partner spends on the business and the money he or she invests in it.

Stated Ratios One method of distributing income and losses is to give each partner a stated ratio of the total income or loss. If each partner is making an equal contribution to the firm, each can assume the same share of income and losses. It is important to understand that an equal contribution to the firm does not necessarily mean an equal capital investment in the firm. One partner may be devoting more time and talent to the firm, whereas another may have made a larger capital investment. And if the partners contribute unequally to the firm, unequal stated ratios can be appropriate. Let's assume that Haddock and Villamer had a net income last year of $140,000 and that the stated ratio is 60 percent for Haddock and 40 percent for Villamer. The computation of each partner's share of the income and the journal entry to show the distribution based on these ratios are as follows:

Haddock ($140,000 × 0.60)	$ 84,000
Villamer ($140,000 × 0.40)	56,000
Net income	$140,000

June 30	Income Summary	140,000	
	Jack Haddock, Capital		84,000
	Pilar Villamer, Capital		56,000
	Distribution of income for the year to the partners' Capital accounts		

Capital Balance Ratios If invested capital produces the most income for the partnership, then income and losses may be distributed according to *capital balance.* One way of distributing income and losses here is to use a ratio based on each partner's capital balance at the beginning of the year.

For example, suppose that at the start of the fiscal year, July 1, 2011, Jack Haddock's Capital account showed a $65,000 balance and Pilar Villamer's Capital account showed a $60,000 balance. The total partners' equity in the firm, then, was $125,000. Each partner's capital balance at the beginning of the year divided by the total partners' equity at the beginning of the year is that partner's beginning capital balance ratio:

	Beginning Capital Balance	Beginning Capital Balance Ratio
Jack Haddock	$ 65,000	65 ÷ 125 = 0.52 = 52%
Pilar Villamer	60,000	60 ÷ 125 = 0.48 = 48%
	$125,000	

The income that each partner should receive when distribution is based on beginning capital balance ratios is figured by multiplying the total income by each partner's capital ratio. If we assume that income for the year was $140,000, Jack Haddock's share of that income was $72,800, and Pilar Villamer's share was $67,200:

Jack Haddock	$140,000 × 0.52 =	$ 72,800
Pilar Villamer	$140,000 × 0.48 =	67,200
		$ 140,000

Salaries, Interest, and Stated Ratios Partners generally do not contribute equally to a firm. To make up for unequal contributions, a partnership agreement can allow for partners' salaries, interest on partners' capital balances, or a combination of both in the distribution of income. Again, salaries and interest of this kind are not deducted as expenses before the partnership income is determined. They represent a method of arriving at an equitable distribution of income or loss.

Salaries allow for differences in the services that partners provide the business. However, they do not take into account differences in invested capital. To allow for capital differences, each partner can receive, in addition to salary, a stated interest on his or her invested capital. Suppose that Jack Haddock and Pilar Villamer agree to annual salaries of $8,000 and $7,000, respectively, as well as 10 percent interest on their beginning capital balances. They also agreed to share any remaining income equally. The calculations for Haddock and Villamer, assuming income of $140,000, appear on the next page.

	Income of Partner		Income
	Haddock	Villamer	Distributed
Total income for distribution			$ 140,000
Distribution of salaries			
Haddock	$ 8,000		
Villamer		$ 7,000	(15,000)
Remaining income after salaries			$ 125,000
Distribution of interest			
Haddock ($65,000 × 0.10)	6,500		
Villamer ($60,000 × 0.10)		6,000	(12,500)
Remaining income after salaries and interest			$ 112,500
Equal distribution of remaining income			
Haddock ($112,500 × 0.50)	56,250		
Villamer ($112,500 × 0.50)		56,250	(112,500)
Remaining income			—
Income of partners	$70,750	$69,250	$ 140,000

If the partnership agreement allows for the distribution of salaries or interest or both, the amounts must be allocated to the partners even if profits are not enough to cover the salaries and interest. In fact, even if the company has a loss, these allocations must nonetheless be made. After the allocation of salaries and interest, the negative balance, or loss, must be distributed according to the stated ratio in the partnership agreement or equally if the agreement does not mention a ratio.

For example, let's assume that Haddock and Villamer agreed to the following conditions, with much higher annual salaries, for the distribution of income and losses:

	Salaries	Interest	Beginning Capital Balance
Haddock	$70,000	10% of beginning	$65,000
Villamer	60,000	capital balances	60,000

The computations for the distribution of the income and loss, again assuming income of $140,000, are as follows:

	Income of Partner		Income
	Haddock	Villamer	Distributed
Total income for distribution			$ 140,000
Distribution of salaries			
Haddock	$70,000		
Villamer		$60,000	(130,000)
Remaining income after salaries			$ 10,000
Distribution of interest			
Haddock ($65,000 × 0.10)	6,500		
Villamer ($60,000 × 0.10)		6,000	(12,500)
Remaining income after salaries and interest			$ (2,500)
Equal distribution of negative balance*			
Haddock ($2,500 × 0.50)	1,250		
Villamer ($2,500 × 0.50)		1,250	2,500
Remaining income			—
Income of partners	$75,250	$64,750	$ 140,000

*Notice that the negative balance is distributed equally because the partnership agreement does not indicate how income and losses should be distributed after salaries and interest are paid.

Dissolution of a Partnership

Dissolution of a partnership occurs whenever there is a change in the original association of partners. When a partnership is dissolved, the partners lose their authority to continue the business as a going concern. This does not mean that the business operation necessarily is ended or interrupted, but it does mean—from a legal and accounting standpoint—that the separate entity ceases to exist. The remaining partners can act for the partnership in finishing the affairs of the business or in forming a new partnership that will be a new accounting entity. The dissolution of a partnership takes place through, among other events, the admission of a new partner, the withdrawal of a partner, or the death of a partner.

Admission of a New Partner The admission of a new partner dissolves the old partnership because a new association has been formed. Dissolving the old partnership and creating a new one requires the consent of all the original partners and the ratification of a new partnership agreement. An individual can be admitted to a partnership in one of two ways: by purchasing an interest in the partnership from one or more of the original partners or by investing assets in the partnership.

Purchasing an Interest from a Partner When a person purchases an interest in a partnership from an original partner, the transaction is a personal one between these two people. However, the interest purchased must be transferred from the Capital account of the selling partner to the Capital account of the new partner.

Suppose that Jack Haddock decides to sell his interest of $70,000 in Haddock and Villamer to Richard Davis for $100,000 on August 31 and that Pilar Villamer agrees to the sale. The journal entry to record the sale on the partnership books would be as follows:

Aug. 31	Jack Haddock, Capital	70,000	
	Richard Davis, Capital		70,000
	Transfer of Jack Haddock's equity to Richard Davis		

Notice that the entry records the book value of the equity, not the amount Davis pays. The amount Davis pays is a personal matter between Davis and Haddock.

Investing Assets in a Partnership When a new partner is admitted through an investment in the partnership, both the assets and the partners' equity in the firm increase. This is because the assets the new partner invests become partnership assets, and as partnership assets increase, partners' equity increases.

For example, assume that Richard Davis wants to invest $75,000 for a one-third interest in the partnership of Haddock and Villamer. The Capital accounts of Jack Haddock and Pilar Villamer are $70,000 and $80,000, respectively. The assets of the firm are valued correctly. So, the partners agree to sell Davis a one-third interest in the firm for $75,000. Davis's $75,000 investment equals a one-third interest in the firm after the investment is added to the previously existing capital of the partnership:

Jack Haddock, Capital	$ 70,000
Pilar Villamer, Capital	80,000
Davis's investment	75,000
Total capital after Davis's investment	$225,000
One-third interest = $225,000 ÷ 3 =	$ 75,000

The journal entry to record Davis's investment would be as follows:

Aug. 31	Cash	75,000	
	Richard Davis, Capital		75,000
	Admission of Richard Davis for a one-third interest in the company		

Bonus to the Old Partners A partnership is sometimes so profitable or otherwise advantageous that a new investor is willing to pay more than the actual dollar interest he or she receives in the partnership. Suppose an individual pays \$100,000 for an \$80,000 interest in a partnership. The \$20,000 excess of the payment over the interest purchased is a *bonus to* the original partners. The bonus must be distributed to the original partners according to the partnership agreement. When the agreement does not cover the distribution of bonuses, it should be distributed to the original partners in accordance with the method of distributing income and losses.

Assume that Haddock and Villamer's firm has operated for several years and that the partners' capital balances and the stated ratios for distribution of income and loss are as follows:

Partners	Capital Balances	Stated Ratios
Haddock	\$160,000	55%
Villamer	140,000	45
	\$300,000	100%

Richard Davis wants to join the firm. He offers to invest \$100,000 on December 1 for a one-fifth interest in the business and income. The original partners agree to the offer. This is the computation of the bonus to the original partners:

Partners' equity in the original partnership		\$300,000
Cash investment by Richard Davis		100,000
Partners' equity in the new partnership		\$400,000
Partners' equity assigned to Richard Davis (\$400,000 × 1/5)		\$ 80,000
Bonus to the original partners		
Investment by Richard Davis	\$100,000	
Less equity assigned to Richard Davis	80,000	\$ 20,000
Distribution of bonus to original partners		
Jack Haddock (\$20,000 × 0.55)	\$ 11,000	
Pilar Villamer (\$20,000 × 0.45)	9,000	\$ 20,000

The journal entry that records Davis's admission to the partnership would be as follows:

Dec. 1	Cash	100,000	
	Jack Haddock, Capital		11,000
	Pilar Villamer, Capital		9,000
	Richard Davis, Capital		80,000
	Investment by Richard Davis for a one-fifth interest in the firm, and the bonus distributed to the original partners		

Bonus to the New Partner A partnership might want a new partner for several reasons. A partnership in financial trouble might need additional cash. Or the partners might want to expand the firm's markets and need more capital for this purpose than they themselves can provide. Also, the partners might know a person who would bring a unique talent to the firm. Under these conditions, a new partner may be admitted to the partnership with the understanding that part of the original partners' capital will be transferred (credited) to the new partner's Capital account as a bonus.

Withdrawal of a Partner Generally, a partner has the right to withdraw from a partnership in accord with legal requirements. However, to avoid disputes when a partner does decide to withdraw or retire from the firm, the partnership agreement should describe the procedures that are to be followed. The agreement should specify (1) whether an audit will be performed, (2) how the assets will be reappraised, (3) how a bonus will be determined, and (4) by what method the withdrawing partner will be paid.

A partner who wants to withdraw from a partnership can do so in one of several ways. The partner can sell his or her interest to another partner or to an outsider with the consent of the remaining partners, or the partner can withdraw assets equal to his or her capital balance, less than his or her capital balance (in this case, the remaining partners receive a bonus) or greater than his or her capital balance (in this case, the withdrawing partner receives a bonus). Bonuses upon withdrawal of a partner are allocated in much the same way as bonuses that arise when a new partner is admitted.

Death of a Partner When a partner dies, the partnership is dissolved because the original association has changed. The partnership agreement should state the actions to be taken. Normally, the books are closed, and financial statements are prepared. These actions are necessary to determine the capital balance of each partner on the date of the death. The agreement also may indicate whether an audit should be conducted, assets appraised, and a bonus recorded, as well as what procedures have been established for settling with the deceased partner's heirs. The remaining partners may purchase the deceased's equity, sell it to outsiders, or deliver certain business assets to the estate. If the firm intends to continue, a new partnership must be formed.

Liquidation of a Partnership

Liquidation of a partnership is the process of ending the business—of selling enough assets to pay the partnership's liabilities and distributing any remaining assets among the partners. Liquidation is a special form of dissolution. When a partnership is liquidated, the business will not continue. As the assets of the business are sold, any gain or loss should be distributed to the partners according to the stated ratios. As cash becomes available, it must be applied first to outside creditors, then to loans from partners, and finally to the partners' capital balances. Any deficits in partners' capital accounts must be made up from personal assets.

Short Exercises

Partnership Formation

SE 1. On January 1, Bob contributed cash of $12,000 and Kim contributed office equipment that cost $10,000 but was valued at $8,000 to the formation of a new partnership. Prepare the journal entry to form the partnership.

Distribution of Partnership Income: Stated Ratio

SE 2. During the first year, the Bob and Kim partnership (see **SE 1**) earned an income of $5,000. Assume the partners agreed to share income and losses in the ratio of the beginning balances of their capital accounts. How much income should be transferred to each Capital account on December 31?

Distribution of Partnership Income: Salary and Stated Ratio

SE 3. During the first year, the Bob and Kim partnership (see **SE 1**) earned an income of $5,000. Assume the partners agreed to share income and losses by figuring interest on the beginning capital balances at 10 percent and dividing the remainder equally. How much income should be transferred to each Capital account on December 31?

Distribution of Partnership Income: Interest on Capital and Stated Ratio

SE 4. During the first year, the Bob and Kim partnership (see **SE 1**) earned an income of $5,000. Assume the partners agreed to share income and losses by figuring interest on the beginning capital balances at 10 percent, allowing a salary of $6,000 to Bob, and dividing the remainder equally. How much income (or loss) should be transferred to each Capital account on December 31?

Withdrawal of a Partner

SE 5. After the partnership had been operating for a year, the Capital accounts of Bob and Kim were $15,000 and $10,000, respectively. Kim withdrew from the partnership by selling her interest in the business to Sonia for $8,000. What would be the Capital account balances of the partners in the new Bob and Sonia partnership? Prepare the journal entry on December 31 to record the transfer of ownership on the partnership books.

Admission of a New Partner: Bonus to Old Partners

SE 6. After the partnership had been operating for a year, the Capital accounts of Bob and Kim were $15,000 and $10,000, respectively. Sonia bought a one-sixth interest in the partnership by investing cash of $11,000. What would be the Capital account balances of the partners in the new Bob, Kim, and Sonia partnership, assuming a bonus to the old partners, who share income and losses equally? Prepare the journal entry on December 31 to record the transfer of ownership on the partnership books.

Admission of a New Partner: Bonus to New Partner

SE 7. After the partnership had been operating for a year, the Capital accounts of Bob and Kim were $15,000 and $10,000, respectively. Sonia bought a one-fourth interest in the partnership by investing cash of $5,000. What would be the Capital account balances of the partners in the new Bob, Kim, and Sonia partnership, assuming that the new partner received a bonus and that Bob and Kim share income and losses equally? Prepare the journal entry on December 31 to record the transfer of ownership on the partnership books.

Problems

Partnership Formation and Distribution of Income

P 1. In January 2011, Ed Rivers and Bob Bascomb agreed to produce and sell chocolate candies. Rivers contributed $240,000 in cash to the business. Bascomb contributed the building and equipment valued at $220,000 and $140,000, respectively. The partnership had an income of $84,000 during 2011 but was less successful during 2012, when income was only $40,000.

REQUIRED

1. Prepare the journal entry to record the investment of both partners in the partnership.
2. Determine the share of income for each partner in 2011 and 2012 under each of the following conditions (*Note:* Each of the following situations is independent.):
   a. The partners agreed to share income equally.
   b. The partners failed to agree on an income-sharing arrangement.
   c. The partners agreed to share income according to the ratio of their original investments.
   d. The partners agreed to share income by allowing interest of 10 percent on their original investments and dividing the remainder equally.

e. The partners agreed to share income by allowing salaries of $40,000 for Rivers and $28,000 for Bascomb and dividing the remainder equally.
f. The partners agreed to share income by paying salaries of $40,000 to Rivers and $28,000 to Bascomb, allowing interest of 9 percent on their original investments, and dividing the remainder equally.

Admission and Withdrawal of a Partner

P 2. Margaret, Tracy, and Lou are partners in Woodwork Company. Their capital balances as of July 31, 2011, are as follows:

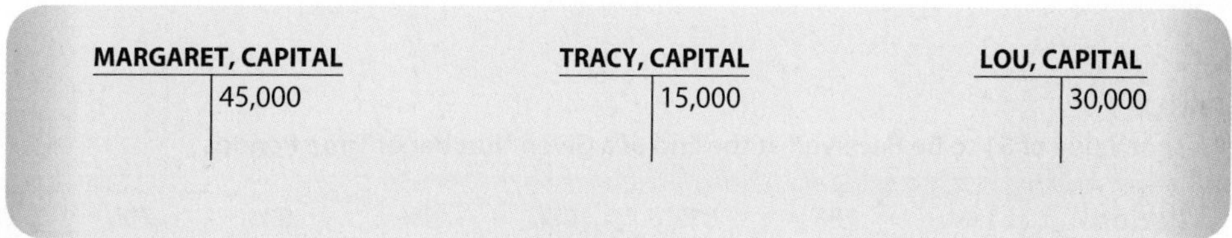

MARGARET, CAPITAL
45,000
TRACY, CAPITAL
15,000
LOU, CAPITAL
30,000

Each partner has agreed to admit Vonice to the partnership.

REQUIRED

Prepare the entries to record Vonice's admission to or Margaret's withdrawal from the partnership under each of the following conditions (*Note:* Each of the following situations is independent.):

a. Vonice pays Margaret $12,500 for 20 percent of Margaret's interest in the partnership.
b. Vonice invests $20,000 cash in the partnership and receives an interest equal to her investment.
c. Vonice invests $30,000 cash in the partnership for a 20 percent interest in the business. A bonus is to be recorded for the original partners on the basis of their capital balances.
d. Vonice invests $30,000 cash in the partnership for a 40 percent interest in the business. The original partners give Vonice a bonus according to the ratio of their capital balances on July 31, 2011.
e. Margaret withdraws from the partnership, taking $52,500. The excess of withdrawn assets over Margaret's partnership interest is distributed according to the balances of the Capital accounts.
f. Margaret withdraws by selling her interest directly to Vonice for $60,000.

APPENDIX B

Present Value Tables

TABLE 1
Present Value of $1 to Be Received at the End of a Given Number of Time Periods

Periods	1%	2%	3%	4%	5%	6%	7%	8%	9%	10%	12%
1	0.990	0.980	0.971	0.962	0.952	0.943	0.935	0.926	0.917	0.909	0.893
2	0.980	0.961	0.943	0.925	0.907	0.890	0.873	0.857	0.842	0.826	0.797
3	0.971	0.942	0.915	0.889	0.864	0.840	0.816	0.794	0.772	0.751	0.712
4	0.961	0.924	0.888	0.855	0.823	0.792	0.763	0.735	0.708	0.683	0.636
5	0.951	0.906	0.883	0.822	0.784	0.747	0.713	0.681	0.650	0.621	0.567
6	0.942	0.888	0.837	0.790	0.746	0.705	0.666	0.630	0.596	0.564	0.507
7	0.933	0.871	0.813	0.760	0.711	0.665	0.623	0.583	0.547	0.513	0.452
8	0.923	0.853	0.789	0.731	0.677	0.627	0.582	0.540	0.502	0.467	0.404
9	0.914	0.837	0.766	0.703	0.645	0.592	0.544	0.500	0.460	0.424	0.361
10	0.905	0.820	0.744	0.676	0.614	0.558	0.508	0.463	0.422	0.386	0.322
11	0.896	0.804	0.722	0.650	0.585	0.527	0.475	0.429	0.388	0.350	0.287
12	0.887	0.788	0.701	0.625	0.557	0.497	0.444	0.397	0.356	0.319	0.257
13	0.879	0.773	0.681	0.601	0.530	0.469	0.415	0.368	0.326	0.290	0.229
14	0.870	0.758	0.661	0.577	0.505	0.442	0.388	0.340	0.299	0.263	0.205
15	0.861	0.743	0.642	0.555	0.481	0.417	0.362	0.315	0.275	0.239	0.183
16	0.853	0.728	0.623	0.534	0.458	0.394	0.339	0.292	0.252	0.218	0.163
17	0.844	0.714	0.605	0.513	0.436	0.371	0.317	0.270	0.231	0.198	0.146
18	0.836	0.700	0.587	0.494	0.416	0.350	0.296	0.250	0.212	0.180	0.130
19	0.828	0.686	0.570	0.475	0.396	0.331	0.277	0.232	0.194	0.164	0.116
20	0.820	0.673	0.554	0.456	0.377	0.312	0.258	0.215	0.178	0.149	0.104
21	0.811	0.660	0.538	0.439	0.359	0.294	0.242	0.199	0.164	0.135	0.093
22	0.803	0.647	0.522	0.422	0.342	0.278	0.226	0.184	0.150	0.123	0.083
23	0.795	0.634	0.507	0.406	0.326	0.262	0.211	0.170	0.138	0.112	0.074
24	0.788	0.622	0.492	0.390	0.310	0.247	0.197	0.158	0.126	0.102	0.066
25	0.780	0.610	0.478	0.375	0.295	0.233	0.184	0.146	0.116	0.092	0.059
26	0.772	0.598	0.464	0.361	0.281	0.220	0.172	0.135	0.106	0.084	0.053
27	0.764	0.586	0.450	0.347	0.268	0.207	0.161	0.125	0.098	0.076	0.047
28	0.757	0.574	0.437	0.333	0.255	0.196	0.150	0.116	0.090	0.069	0.042
29	0.749	0.563	0.424	0.321	0.243	0.185	0.141	0.107	0.082	0.063	0.037
30	0.742	0.552	0.412	0.308	0.231	0.174	0.131	0.099	0.075	0.057	0.033
40	0.672	0.453	0.307	0.208	0.142	0.097	0.067	0.046	0.032	0.022	0.011
50	0.608	0.372	0.228	0.141	0.087	0.054	0.034	0.021	0.013	0.009	0.003

Table 1 is used to compute the value today of a single amount of cash to be received sometime in the future. To use Table 1, you must first know (1) the time period in years until funds will be received, (2) the stated annual rate of interest, and (3) the dollar amount to be received at the end of the time period.

Example—Table 1. What is the present value of $30,000 to be received 25 years from now, assuming a 14 percent interest rate? From Table 1, the required multiplier is 0.038, and the answer is:

$$\$30{,}000 \times 0.038 = \$1{,}140$$

The factor values for Table 1 are:

$$\text{PV Factor} = (1 + r)^{-n}$$

14%	15%	16%	18%	20%	25%	30%	35%	40%	45%	50%	Periods
0.877	0.870	0.862	0.847	0.833	0.800	0.769	0.741	0.714	0.690	0.667	1
0.769	0.756	0.743	0.718	0.694	0.640	0.592	0.549	0.510	0.476	0.444	2
0.675	0.658	0.641	0.609	0.579	0.512	0.455	0.406	0.364	0.328	0.296	3
0.592	0.572	0.552	0.516	0.482	0.410	0.350	0.301	0.260	0.226	0.198	4
0.519	0.497	0.476	0.437	0.402	0.328	0.269	0.223	0.186	0.156	0.132	5
0.456	0.432	0.410	0.370	0.335	0.262	0.207	0.165	0.133	0.108	0.088	6
0.400	0.376	0.354	0.314	0.279	0.210	0.159	0.122	0.095	0.074	0.059	7
0.351	0.327	0.305	0.266	0.233	0.168	0.123	0.091	0.068	0.051	0.039	8
0.308	0.284	0.263	0.225	0.194	0.134	0.094	0.067	0.048	0.035	0.026	9
0.270	0.247	0.227	0.191	0.162	0.107	0.073	0.050	0.035	0.024	0.017	10
0.237	0.215	0.195	0.162	0.135	0.086	0.056	0.037	0.025	0.017	0.012	11
0.208	0.187	0.168	0.137	0.112	0.069	0.043	0.027	0.018	0.012	0.008	12
0.182	0.163	0.145	0.116	0.093	0.055	0.033	0.020	0.013	0.008	0.005	13
0.160	0.141	0.125	0.099	0.078	0.044	0.025	0.015	0.009	0.006	0.003	14
0.140	0.123	0.108	0.084	0.065	0.035	0.020	0.011	0.006	0.004	0.002	15
0.123	0.107	0.093	0.071	0.054	0.028	0.015	0.008	0.005	0.003	0.002	16
0.108	0.093	0.080	0.060	0.045	0.023	0.012	0.006	0.003	0.002	0.001	17
0.095	0.081	0.069	0.051	0.038	0.018	0.009	0.005	0.002	0.001	0.001	18
0.083	0.070	0.060	0.043	0.031	0.014	0.007	0.003	0.002	0.001		19
0.073	0.061	0.051	0.037	0.026	0.012	0.005	0.002	0.001	0.001		20
0.064	0.053	0.044	0.031	0.022	0.009	0.004	0.002	0.001			21
0.056	0.046	0.038	0.026	0.018	0.007	0.003	0.001	0.001			22
0.049	0.040	0.033	0.022	0.015	0.006	0.002	0.001				23
0.043	0.035	0.028	0.019	0.013	0.005	0.002	0.001				24
0.038	0.030	0.024	0.016	0.010	0.004	0.001	0.001				25
0.033	0.026	0.021	0.014	0.009	0.003	0.001					26
0.029	0.023	0.018	0.011	0.007	0.002	0.001					27
0.026	0.020	0.016	0.010	0.006	0.002	0.001					28
0.022	0.017	0.014	0.008	0.005	0.002						29
0.020	0.015	0.012	0.007	0.004	0.001						30
0.005	0.004	0.003	0.001	0.001							40
0.001	0.001	0.001									50

TABLE 2
Present Value of $1 Received Each Period for a Given Number of Time Periods

Periods	1%	2%	3%	4%	5%	6%	7%	8%	9%	10%	12%
1	0.990	0.980	0.971	0.962	0.952	0.943	0.935	0.926	0.917	0.909	0.893
2	1.970	1.942	1.913	1.886	1.859	1.833	1.808	1.783	1.759	1.736	1.690
3	2.941	2.884	2.829	2.775	2.723	2.673	2.624	2.577	2.531	2.487	2.402
4	3.902	3.808	3.717	3.630	3.546	3.465	3.387	3.312	3.240	3.170	3.037
5	4.853	4.713	4.580	4.452	4.329	4.212	4.100	3.993	3.890	3.791	3.605
6	5.795	5.601	5.417	5.242	5.076	4.917	4.767	4.623	4.486	4.355	4.111
7	6.728	6.472	6.230	6.002	5.786	5.582	5.389	5.206	5.033	4.868	4.564
8	7.652	7.325	7.020	6.733	6.463	6.210	5.971	5.747	5.535	5.335	4.968
9	8.566	8.162	7.786	7.435	7.108	6.802	6.515	6.247	5.995	5.759	5.328
10	9.471	8.983	8.530	8.111	7.722	7.360	7.024	6.710	6.418	6.145	5.650
11	10.368	9.787	9.253	8.760	8.306	7.887	7.499	7.139	6.805	6.495	5.938
12	11.255	10.575	9.954	9.385	8.863	8.384	7.943	7.536	7.161	6.814	6.194
13	12.134	11.348	10.635	9.986	9.394	8.853	8.358	7.904	7.487	7.103	6.424
14	13.004	12.106	11.296	10.563	9.899	9.295	8.745	8.244	7.786	7.367	6.628
15	13.865	12.849	11.938	11.118	10.380	9.712	9.108	8.559	8.061	7.606	6.811
16	14.718	13.578	12.561	11.652	10.838	10.106	9.447	8.851	8.313	7.824	6.974
17	15.562	14.292	13.166	12.166	11.274	10.477	9.763	9.122	8.544	8.022	7.120
18	16.398	14.992	13.754	12.659	11.690	10.828	10.059	9.372	8.756	8.201	7.250
19	17.226	15.678	14.324	13.134	12.085	11.158	10.336	9.604	8.950	8.365	7.366
20	18.046	16.351	14.878	13.590	12.462	11.470	10.594	9.818	9.129	8.514	7.469
21	18.857	17.011	15.415	14.029	12.821	11.764	10.836	10.017	9.292	8.649	7.562
22	19.660	17.658	15.937	14.451	13.163	12.042	11.061	10.201	9.442	8.772	7.645
23	20.456	18.292	16.444	14.857	13.489	12.303	11.272	10.371	9.580	8.883	7.718
24	21.243	18.914	16.936	15.247	13.799	12.550	11.469	10.529	9.707	8.985	7.784
25	22.023	19.523	17.413	15.622	14.094	12.783	11.654	10.675	9.823	9.077	7.843
26	22.795	20.121	17.877	15.983	14.375	13.003	11.826	10.810	9.929	9.161	7.896
27	23.560	20.707	18.327	16.330	14.643	13.211	11.987	10.935	10.027	9.237	7.943
28	24.316	21.281	18.764	16.663	14.898	13.406	12.137	11.051	10.116	9.307	7.984
29	25.066	21.844	19.189	16.984	15.141	13.591	12.278	11.158	10.198	9.370	8.022
30	25.808	22.396	19.600	17.292	15.373	13.765	12.409	11.258	10.274	9.427	8.055
40	32.835	27.355	23.115	19.793	17.159	15.046	13.332	11.925	10.757	9.779	8.244
50	39.196	31.424	25.730	21.482	18.256	15.762	13.801	12.234	10.962	9.915	8.305

Table 2 is used to compute the present value of a *series* of *equal* annual cash flows.

Example—Table 2. Arthur Howard won a contest on January 1, 2010, in which the prize was $30,000, payable in 15 annual installments of $2,000 each December 31, beginning in 2010. Assuming a 9 percent interest rate, what is the present value of Howard's prize on January 1, 2010? From Table 2, the required multiplier is 8.061, and the answer is:

$$\$2{,}000 \times 8.061 = \$16{,}122$$

The factor values for Table 2 are:

$$\text{PVa Factor} = \frac{1 - (1 + r)^{-n}}{r}$$

14%	15%	16%	18%	20%	25%	30%	35%	40%	45%	50%	Periods
0.877	0.870	0.862	0.847	0.833	0.800	0.769	0.741	0.714	0.690	0.667	1
1.647	1.626	1.605	1.566	1.528	1.440	1.361	1.289	1.224	1.165	1.111	2
2.322	2.283	2.246	2.174	2.106	1.952	1.816	1.696	1.589	1.493	1.407	3
2.914	2.855	2.798	2.690	2.589	2.362	2.166	1.997	1.849	1.720	1.605	4
3.433	3.352	3.274	3.127	2.991	2.689	2.436	2.220	2.035	1.876	1.737	5
3.889	3.784	3.685	3.498	3.326	2.951	2.643	2.385	2.168	1.983	1.824	6
4.288	4.160	4.039	3.812	3.605	3.161	2.802	2.508	2.263	2.057	1.883	7
4.639	4.487	4.344	4.078	3.837	3.329	2.925	2.598	2.331	2.109	1.922	8
4.946	4.772	4.607	4.303	4.031	3.463	3.019	2.665	2.379	2.144	1.948	9
5.216	5.019	4.833	4.494	4.192	3.571	3.092	2.715	2.414	2.168	1.965	10
5.453	5.234	5.029	4.656	4.327	3.656	3.147	2.752	2.438	2.185	1.977	11
5.660	5.421	5.197	4.793	4.439	3.725	3.190	2.779	2.456	2.197	1.985	12
5.842	5.583	5.342	4.910	4.533	3.780	3.223	2.799	2.469	2.204	1.990	13
6.002	5.724	5.468	5.008	4.611	3.824	3.249	2.814	2.478	2.210	1.993	14
6.142	5.847	5.575	5.092	4.675	3.859	3.268	2.825	2.484	2.214	1.995	15
6.265	5.954	5.669	5.162	4.730	3.887	3.283	2.834	2.489	2.216	1.997	16
6.373	6.047	5.749	5.222	4.775	3.910	3.295	2.840	2.492	2.218	1.998	17
6.467	6.128	5.818	5.273	4.812	3.928	3.304	2.844	2.494	2.219	1.999	18
6.550	6.198	5.877	5.316	4.844	3.942	3.311	2.848	2.496	2.220	1.999	19
6.623	6.259	5.929	5.353	4.870	3.954	3.316	2.850	2.497	2.221	1.999	20
6.687	6.312	5.973	5.384	4.891	3.963	3.320	2.852	2.498	2.221	2.000	21
6.743	6.359	6.011	5.410	4.909	3.970	3.323	2.853	2.498	2.222	2.000	22
6.792	6.399	6.044	5.432	4.925	3.976	3.325	2.854	2.499	2.222	2.000	23
6.835	6.434	6.073	5.451	4.973	3.981	3.327	2.855	2.499	2.222	2.000	24
6.873	6.464	6.097	5.467	4.948	3.985	3.329	2.856	2.499	2.222	2.000	25
6.906	6.491	6.118	5.480	4.956	3.988	3.330	2.856	2.500	2.222	2.000	26
6.935	6.514	6.136	5.492	4.964	3.990	3.331	2.856	2.500	2.222	2.000	27
6.961	6.534	6.152	5.502	4.970	3.992	3.331	2.857	2.500	2.222	2.000	28
6.983	6.551	6.166	5.510	4.975	3.994	3.332	2.857	2.500	2.222	2.000	29
7.003	6.566	6.177	5.517	4.979	3.995	3.332	2.857	2.500	2.222	2.000	30
7.105	6.642	6.234	5.548	4.997	3.999	3.333	2.857	2.500	2.222	2.000	40
7.133	6.661	6.246	5.554	4.999	4.000	3.333	2.857	2.500	2.222	2.000	50

Table 2 is the columnar sum of Table 1. Table 2 applies to *ordinary annuities,* in which the first cash flow occurs one time period beyond the date for which the present value is computed.

An *annuity due* is a series of equal cash flows for N time periods, but the first payment occurs immediately. The present value of the first payment equals the face value of the cash flow; Table 2 then is used to measure the present value of N − 1 remaining cash flows.

Example—Table 2. Determine the present value on January 1, 2010, of 20 lease payments; each payment of $10,000 is due on January 1, beginning in 2010. Assume an interest rate of 8 percent.

Present Value = Immediate Payment + Present Value of 19 Subsequent Payments at 8%

= $10,000 + ($10,000 × 9.604) = $106,040

ENDNOTES

Chapter 1

1 *Statement of Financial Accounting Concepts No. 1*, "Objectives of Financial Reporting by Business Enterprises" (Norwalk, Conn.: Financial Accounting Standards Board, 1978), par. 9.
2 Ibid.
3 CVS Caremark Corporation, *Annual Report*, 2009.
4 National Commission on Fraudulent Financial Reporting, *Report of the National Commission on Fraudulent Financial Reporting* (Washington, D.C.: 1987), p. 2.
5 Target Corporation, *Annual Report*, 2009.
6 Robert Johnson, "The New CFO," *Crain's Chicago Business*, July 19, 2004.
7 Belverd E. Needles, Jr., Anton Shigaev, Marian Powers, and Mark Frigo, "Strategy and Integrated Financial Ratio Performance Measures: A Longitudinal Multi-Country Study of High Performance Companies," *Studies in Managerial and Financial Accounting*, vol. 20, 211–252. Copyright 2010 by Emerald Group Publishing Limited.
8 *Accounting Principles Board Statement No. 4*, "Basic Concepts and Accounting Principles Underlying Financial Statements of Business Enterprises" (New York: AICPA, 1970), par. 138.
9 John D. McKinnon, "US-EU Deal Paves Way for Accounting-Rule Shift," *The Wall Street Journal*, May 1, 2007.
10 "Brand Research Shows CPAs Viewed Positively in Marketplace," *AICPA News Update,* October 20, 2008.
11 *Statement Number 1C*, "Standards of Ethical Conduct for Management Accountants" (Montvale, N.J.: Institute of Management Accountants, 1983; revised 1997).
12 Costco Wholesale Corporation, *Annual Report*, 2009.
13 Southwest Airlines Co., *Annual Report*, 1996.
14 Queen Sook Kim, "Lechters Inc. Files for Chapter 11, Arranges Financing," *The Wall Street Journal*, May 22, 2001.
15 RIM Limited, *Annual Report*, 2009.

Chapter 2

1 "United Orders Boeing 787, Airbus Planes," *MSNBC.com,* December 8, 2009.
2 "Boeing Finalizes 787 Order," HeraldNet, April 17, 2010.
3 The Boeing Company, *Annual Report*, 2009.
4 *Statement of Financial Accounting Standards No. 157*, "Fair Value Measurements" (Norwalk, Conn.: Financial Accounting Standards Board, 2007).
5 The Boeing Company, *Annual Report*, 2009.
6 Gary McWilliams, "EDS Accounting Change Cuts Past Earnings by \$2.24 Billion," *The Wall Street Journal*, October 28, 2003.
7 The Boeing Company, *Annual Report*, 2009.
8 Ibid.
9 Mellon Bank, *Annual Report*, 2009.

Chapter 3

1 Netflix, Inc., *Annual Report*, 2009.
2 Ibid.
3 "Microsoft Settles with SEC," *CBSNews.com*, June 5, 2002.
4 Christopher Lawton and Don Clark, "Dell to Restate 4 Years of Results," *The Wall Street Journal*, August 17, 2007.
5 Securities and Exchange Commission, *Staff Accounting Bulletin No. 10*, 1999.
6 Ken Brown, "Wall Street Plays Numbers Games with Savings, Despite Reforms," *The Wall Street Journal*, July 22, 2003.
7 Netflix, Inc., *Annual Report*, 2009.
8 Ibid.
9 Lyric Opera of Chicago, *Annual Report*, 2009.
10 The Walt Disney Company, *Annual Report*, 2009.

Chapter 4

1 Dell Computer Corporation, Presentation to Financial Analysts, February 28, 2008.
2 *Financial Accounting Series No. 1570-100*, "Conceptual Framework for Financial Reporting: The Objective of Financial Reporting and Qualitative Characteristics and Constraints of Decision-Useful Financial Reporting Information" (Norwalk, Conn.: Financial Accounting Standards Board, May 29, 2008), p. 1.
3 *Statement of Financial Accounting Concepts No. 2*, "Qualitative Characteristics of Accounting Information" (Norwalk, Conn.: Financial Accounting Standards Board, 1980), par. 20.
4 *Financial Accounting Series No. 1570-100*, "Conceptual Framework for Financial Reporting: The Objective of Financial Reporting and Qualitative Characteristics and Constraints of Decision-Useful Financial Reporting Information" (Norwalk, Conn.: Financial Accounting Standards Board, May 29, 2008), chapters 1 and 2.
5 Dell Computer Corporation, *Annual Report*, 2010.
6 "Ex-Chief of WorldCom Is Found Guilty in \$11 Billion Fraud," *The New York Times*, March 16, 2005.
7 *Accounting Principles Board Opinion No. 20*, "Accounting Changes" (New York: AICPA, 1971), par. 17.
8 Securities and Exchange Commission, *Staff Accounting Bulletin No. 99*, 1999.
9 www.fasb.org, July 12, 2008.
10 Belverd E. Needles, Jr., Mark Frigo, and Marian Powers, "Performance Measures and Executive Compensation: Practices of High-Performance Companies," *Studies in Financial and Managerial Accounting* (London: JAI Elsevier Science Ltd.), vol. 18, 2008.
11 www.accountancy age.com/2197689.
12 Supervalu Inc., *Annual Report*, 2009; Great Atlantic & Pacific Tea Company, *Annual Report*, 2009.

Chapter 5

1 Best Buy Co., Inc., *Annual Report*, FY 2010.
2 Ibid.
3 Target Corporation, *Annual Report*, 2009.
4 Best Buy Co., Inc., *Annual Report*, FY 2010.
5 Committee of Sponsoring Organizations of the Treadway Commission, "Press Release: Financial Fraud at U.S. Public Companies, May 20, 2010."
6 Dan Davis, "E-Commerce Surges 14.3% in the First Quarter as Web Sales Grow Four Times Faster Than Stores." *Internet Retailer.com*, May 27, 2010.
7 Joel Millman, "Here's What Happens to Many Lovely Gifts After Santa Rides Off," *The Wall Street Journal*, December 26, 2001.

8 Matthew Rose, "Magazine Revenue at Newsstands Falls in Worst Year Ever," *The Wall Street Journal*, May 15, 2001.
9 American Institute of Certified Public Accountants, *Professional Standards*, vol. 1 (New York: AICPA June 1, 1999), Sec. AU 322.07.
10 KPMG Peat Marwick, "1998 Fraud Survey," 1998.
11 Best Buy Co., Inc., *Annual Report*, FY 2010.
12 Amy Merrick, "Starbucks Accuses Employee, Husband of Embezzling $3.7 Million from Firm," *The Wall Street Journal*, November 20, 2000.

Chapter 6

1 Cisco Systems, Inc., *Annual Report*, 2009.
2 Ibid.
3 Gary McWilliams, "Whirlwind on the Web," *BusinessWeek*, April 7, 1997.
4 Securities and Exchange Commission, SEC Announces Fraud Charges Against Former Rite Aid Senior Management, June 21, 2002.
5 Highbeam Research, "Former Rent-Way Executive Gets Prison, Fine in Fraud Case," November 23, 2003.
6 American Institute of Certified Public Accountants, *Accounting Trends & Techniques* (New York: AICPA, 2008).
7 Cisco Systems, Inc., 2009.
8 Ernst & Young, *U.S. GAAP vs. IFRS: The Basics*, 2007.
9 American Institute of Certified Public Accountants, *Accounting Trends & Techniques* (New York: AICPA, 2008).
10 "SEC Case Judge Rules Crazy Eddie Principals Must Pay $72.7 Million," *The Wall Street Journal*, May 11, 2000.
11 American Institute of Certified Public Accountants, *Accounting Trends & Techniques* (New York: AICPA, 2008).
12 ExxonMobil Corporation, *Annual Report*, 2006.
13 Ibid., 2009.

Chapter 7

1 Hewlett-Packard Company, *Annual Report*, 2009.
2 Morgan Stanley Optimistic on Home Depot's Prospects as Housing Recovers, mysmarthtrends.com, February 8, 2010.
3 Jesse Drucker, "Sprint Expects Loss of Subscribers," *The Wall Street Journal*, September 24, 2002.
4 Deborah Solomon and Damian Paletta, "U.S. Drafts Sweeping Plans to Fight Crisis as Turmoil Worsens in Credit Markets," *The Wall Street Journal*, September 19, 2008.
5 Circuit City Stores, Inc., *Annual Report*, 2004.
6 Heather Timmons, "Do Household's Numbers Add Up?" *BusinessWeek*, December 10, 2001.
7 Steve Daniels, "Bank One Reserves Feed Earnings," *Crain's Chicago Business*, December 15, 2003.
8 Jonathon Weil, "Accounting Scheme Was Straightforward but Hard to Detect," *The Wall Street Journal*, March 20, 2003.
9 Hewlett-Packard Company, *Annual Report*, 2009.
10 Ibid.
11 American Institute of Certified Public Accountants, *Accounting Trends & Techniques* (New York: AICPA, 2009).
12 Tom Lauricella, Shefali Anand, and Valerie Bauerlein, "A $34 Billion Cash Fund to Close Up," *The Wall Street Journal*, December 11, 2007.
13 www.creditcard.com, 2010.
14 American Institute of Certified Public Accountants, *Accounting Trends & Techniques* (New York: AICPA, 2009).
15 "Bad Loans Rattle Telecom Vendors," *BusinessWeek*, February 19, 2001.
16 Scott Thurm, "Better Debt Bolsters Bottom Lines," *The Wall Street Journal*, August 18, 2003.
17 Information based on promotional brochures of Mitsubishi Corp.
18 Elizabeth McDonald, "Unhatched Chickens," *Forbes*, February 19, 2001.
19 CompuCredit Holdings Corporation, *Annual Reports*, 2009.
20 Fosters Group Limited, *Annual Report*, 2009; Fosters Group Limited, *Annual Report*, 2008; Heineken N.V., *Annual Report*, 2009; Heineken N.V., *Annual Report*, 2008.
21 Walgreen's, *Annual Report*, 2009.

Chapter 8

1 Microsoft Corporation, *Annual Report*, 2009.
2 Pamela L. Moore, "How Xerox Ran Short of Black Ink," *BusinessWeek*, October 30, 2000.
3 Hershey Foods Corporation, *Annual Report*, 2009.
4 Goodyear Tire & Rubber Company, *Annual Report*, 2009.
5 "Small Business Poll on Compensating Employees," quoted on sbinformation.about.com, June 6, 2010.
6 "Press Room," www.webfyer.com, January 4, 2010.
7 "Online Coupons that Double as Marketing Databases," Internet Marketing, April 19, 2010.
8 Hershey Foods Corporation, *Annual Report*, 2009.
9 *Statement of Financial Accounting Standards No. 5*, "Accounting for Contingencies" (Norwalk, Conn.: Financial Accounting Standards Board, 1975).
10 American Institute of Certified Public Accountants, *Accounting Trends & Techniques* (New York: AICPA, 2009).
11 Microsoft Corporation, *Annual Report*, 2009.
12 American Institute of Certified Public Accountants, *Accounting Trends & Techniques* (New York: AICPA, 2009).
13 IASB Expert Advisory Panel, "Measuring and Disclosing the Fair Value of Financial Instruments in Markets That Are No Longer Active," October 2008.
14 *Statement of Financial Accounting Standards No. 157*, "Fair Value Measures" (Norwalk, Conn.: Financial Accounting Standards Board, 1975).
15 "Clarifications on Fair Value Accounting," U.S. Securities and Exchange Commission, *Release 2008-234*, October 1, 2008.
16 WorldCom (MCI), *Annual Report*, 2004.
17 Advertisement, *Chicago Tribune*, December 2007.
18 Sun Microsystems Inc., *Annual Report*, 2009; Cisco Systems, Inc., *Annual Report*, 2009.
19 General Motors Corporation, *Annual Report*, 2009.

Chapter 9

1 Apple Computer, Inc., *Annual Report*, 2009.
2 *Statement of Financial Accounting Standards No. 144*, "Accounting for the Impairment or Disposal of Long-Lived Assets" (Norwalk, Conn.: Financial Accounting Standards Board, 2001).
3 Sharon Young, "Large Telecom Firms, After WorldCom Moves, Consider Writedowns," *The Wall Street Journal*, March 18, 2003.
4 Edward J. Riedl, "An Examination of Long-Lived Asset Impairments," *The Accounting Review*, vol. 79, No. 3, pp. 823–852.
5 *Statement of Financial Accounting Standards No. 34*, "Capitalization of Interest Cost" (Norwalk, Conn.: Financial Accounting Standards Board, 1979).
6 American Institute of Certified Public Accountants, *Accounting Trends & Techniques* (New York: AICPA, 2009).
7 Ibid.
8 Jonathan Weil, "Oil Reserves Can Sure Be Slick," *The Wall Street Journal*, March 11, 2004.
9 *Statement of Financial Accounting Standards No. 25*, "Suspension of Certain Accounting Requirements for Oil and Gas Producing Companies" (Norwalk, Conn.: Financial Accounting Standards Board, 1979).
10 *Statement of Financial Accounting Standards No. 142*, "Goodwill and Other Intangible Assets" (Norwalk, Conn.: Financial Accounting Standards Board, 2001), par. 11–17.
11 "100 Best Global Brands 2009," *BusinessWeek Online*, 2009.
12 Apple Computer, Inc., *Annual Report*, 2009.
13 Abbott Laboratories, *Annual Report*, 2009.
14 *Statement of Financial Accounting Standards No. 2*, "Accounting for Research and Development Costs" (Norwalk, Conn.: Financial Accounting Standards Board, 1974), par. 12.

15 *Statement of Financial Accounting Standards No. 86*, "Accounting for the Costs of Computer Software to Be Sold, Leased, or Otherwise Marketed" (Norwalk, Conn.: Financial Accounting Standards Board, 1985).
16 *Statement of Financial Accounting Standards No. 142*, "Goodwill and Other Intangible Assets" (Norwalk, Conn.: Financial Accounting Standards Board, 2001), par. 11–17.
17 Southwest Airlines Co., *Annual Report*, 2002.
18 Costco Wholesale Corporation, *Annual Report*, 2009.
19 IBM Corporation, *Annual Report*, 2009.
20 Hilton Hotels Corporation, *Annual Report*, 2006; Marriott International, Inc., *Annual Report*, 2009.
21 "Hilton Hotels Corporation to Be Acquired by Blackstone Investment Funds," *Business Wire.com*, July 3, 2007.

Chapter 10

1 McDonald's Corporation, *Annual Report*, 2009.
2 Ibid.
3 Lee Hawkins, Jr., "S&P Cuts Rating on GM and Ford to Junk Status," *The Wall Street Journal*, May 6, 2005.
4 *Statement of Financial Accounting Standards No. 13*, "Accounting for Leases" (Norwalk, Conn.: Financial Accounting Standards Board, 1976), par. 10.
5 *Statement of Financial Accounting Standards No. 158*, "Employers' Accounting for Defined Benefit Pension and Other Postretirement Plans" (Norwalk, Conn.: Financial Accounting Standards Board, 2007).
6 McDonald's Corporation, *Annual Report*, 2009.
7 *Statement of Financial Accounting Standards No. 106*, "Employers' Accounting for Postretirement Benefits Other Than Pensions" (Norwalk, Conn.: Financial Accounting Standards Board, 1990).
8 Mary Williams Walsh, "$58 Billion Shortfall for New Jersey Retiree Care," *The New York Times*, July 25, 2007.
9 General Motors Corporation, *Annual Report*, 2009.
10 American Institute of Certified Public Accountants, *Accounting Trends & Techniques* (New York: AICPA, 2009).
11 www.reportsfinance.yahoo.com, April 18, 2010.
12 Ibid.
13 Accounting Principles Board, *Opinion No. 21*, "Interest on Receivables and Payables" (New York: AICPA, 1971), par. 15.
14 Walgreens, *Annual Report*, 2009.
15 Tom Sullivan and Sonia Ryst, "Kodak $1 Billion Issue Draws Crowds," *The Wall Street Journal*, October 8, 2003.
16 www.wallstreetjournal.com, July 13, 2010.
17 "How Borrowing Yields Dividends at Many Firms," *The Wall Street Journal*, March 27, 2007.
18 Amazon.com, *Annual Report*, 2009.

Chapter 11

1 Google, Inc., *Form S-1* (Registration Statement), 2004; *Annual Report*, 2009.
2 Deborah Solomon, "AT&T Slashes Dividends 83%, Cuts Forecasts," *The Wall Street Journal*, December 21, 2002.
3 McDonald's Corporation, *Annual Report*, 2009.
4 Microsoft Corporation, *Annual Report*, 2009.
5 Ibid.
6 Ibid.
7 American Institute of Certified Public Accountants, *Accounting Trends & Techniques* (New York: AICPA, 2009).
8 "Spotlight on Stock Options Backdating," www.sec.org, 2010.
9 Joseph Weber, "One Share, Many Votes," *BusinessWeek*, March 29, 2004; "A Class (B) Act," *BusinessWeek*, May 28, 2007.
10 Michael Rapoport and Jonathan Weil, "More Truth-in-Labeling for Accounting Carries Liabilities," *The Wall Street Journal*, August 23, 2003.
11 "The FASB's Basic Ownership Approach and a Reclassification of Preferred Stock as a Liability," www.cfo.com, July 18, 2008.
12 American Institute of Certified Public Accountants, *Accounting Trends & Techniques* (New York: AICPA, 2009).
13 David Henry, "The Dirty Little Secret About Buybacks," *BusinessWeek*, January 23, 2006; Peter A. McKay and Justin Lahart, "Boom in Buybacks Helps Lift Stocks to Record Heights," *The Wall Street Journal*, July 18, 2007.
14 American Institute of Certified Public Accountants, *Accounting Research Bulletin No. 43* (New York: AICPA, 1953), chap. 7, sec. B, par. 10.
15 Ibid., par. 13.
16 Nike, Inc., *Annual Report*, 2009.
17 "General Mills Declares Two-for-One Stock Split," MarketWatch.com, May 3, 2010.
18 Marissa Marr, "DreamWorks Shares Rise 38% on First Day," *The Wall Street Journal*, October 10, 2004; Yahoo Finance, December 26, 2007.
19 "Market Data Center," *The Wall Street Journal*, June 21, 2010.
20 IBM Corporation, *Annual Report*, 2009; "IBM Board Approves $5 Billion for Stock Repurchase," www.wopular.com, June 17, 2010.
21 INO Markets, www.ino.com, June 21, 2010.

Chapter 12

1 Amazon.com, Inc., *Form 10-K*, 2009.
2 Ian McDonald, "Companies Are Rolling in Cash. Too Bad," *The Wall Street Journal*, August 20, 2006; Justin Lahart, "U.S. Firms Build Up Record Cash Piles," *The Wall Street Journal*, June 11, 2010.
3 Lulu Chang, "Companies Hoarding Cash," CNBC, July 19, 2010.
4 "Free Cash Flow Standouts," *Upside Newsletter*, October 3, 2005.
5 Amazon.com, Inc., *Form 10-K*, 2009.
6 Gary Slutsker, "Look at the Birdie and Say: 'Cash Flow,'" *Forbes*, October 25, 1993.
7 Jonathan Clements, "Yacktman Fund Is Bloodied but Unbowed," *The Wall Street Journal*, November 8, 1993.
8 Jeffery Laderman, "Earnings, Schmearnings—Look at the Cash," *BusinessWeek*, July 24, 1989.
9 Amazon.com, Inc., *Form 10-K*, 2009.
10 American Institute of Certified Public Accountants, *Accounting Trends & Techniques* (New York: AICPA, 2009).
11 Martin Peers and Robin Sidel, "WorldCom Causes Analysts to Evaluate EBITDA's Role," *The Wall Street Journal*, July 15, 2002.
12 "Cash Flow Shortfall in Quarter May Lead to Default on Loan," *The Wall Street Journal*, September 4, 2001.
13 Enron Corporation, *Press Release*, October 16, 2001.
14 Sony Corporation, *Annual Report*, 2009; Panasonic, *Annual Report*, 2009.

Chapter 13

1 Starbucks Corporation, *Annual Report*, 2009.
2 Belverd E. Needles, Jr., Anton Shigaev, Marian Powers, and Mark L. Frigo, "Strategy and Integrated Financial Ratio Performance Measures: A Longitudinal Multi-Country Study of High Performance Companies," in *Studies in Financial and Managerial Accounting*, vol. 20, edited by Marc Epstein and Jean-Francois Manzoni (London: JAI Elsevier Science Ltd., 2010), pp. 211–252.
3 Starbucks Corporation, *Proxy*, January 22, 2010.
4 Ibid.
5 *Statement of Financial Accounting Standards No. 131*, "Segment Disclosures" (Norwalk, Conn.: Financial Accounting Standards Board, 1997).
6 Belverd E. Needles, Jr., Marian Powers, and Mark Frigo, "Performance Measurement and Executive Compensation: Practices of High Performance Companies," in *Studies in Financial and Managerial Accounting*, (Marc Epstein and Jean-Francois Manzoni, eds.), (London: JAI Elsevier Science Ltd.), *18*, 2008.

7 Starbucks Corporation, *Annual Report*, 2009.
8 Ibid.
9 American Institute of Certified Public Accountants, *Accounting Trends & Techniques*, (New York: AICPA, 2009); Starbucks Corporation, *Form 10-K*, 2009.
10 "After Charge for Licensing, McDonald's Posts a Record Loss," *The New York Times*, July 25, 2007; Christina Cheddar Berk, "Campbell's Profit Jumps 31 Percent," *The Wall Street Journal*, November 22, 2005.
11 David Henry, "The Numbers Game," *BusinessWeek*, May 13, 2001.
12 Craig Schneider, "Stock Options, Meet Pro Forma," *CFO.com*, October 31, 2005.
13 Gary M. Entwistle, Glenn D. Felham, and Chima Mbagwu, "Financial Reporting Regulation and the Reporting of Pro Forma Earnings," *Accounting Horizons*, March 2006.
14 Starbucks Corporation, *Annual Report*, 2009.
15 Belverd E. Needles, Jr., Anton Shigaev, Marian Powers, and Mark L. Frigo, "Strategy and Integrated Financial Ratio Performance Measures: A Longitudinal Multi-Country Study of High Performance Companies," in *Studies in Financial and Managerial Accounting*, vol. 20, edited by Marc Epstein and Jean-Francois Manzoni (London: JAI Elsevier Science Ltd., 2010), pp. 211–252.
16 H. J. Heinz Company, *Annual Reports*, 2006–2010.
17 Pfizer, Inc., *Annual Report*, 2009; Roche Group, *Annual Report*, 2009.

Chapter 14

1 Intel Corporation, *Annual Report*, 2009.
2 *Statement of Financial Accounting Standards No. 157*, "Fair Value Measurements" (Norwalk, Conn.: Financial Accounting Standards Board, 2007); *Statement of Financial Accounting Standards No. 159*, "The Fair Value Option for Financial Assets and Financial Liabilities" (Norwalk, Conn.: Financial Accounting Standards Board, 2007).
3 Holman W. Jenkins, Jr., "Anatomy of a Meltdown," *The Wall Street Journal*, March 3, 2008.
4 *Statement of Financial Accounting Standards No. 115*, "Accounting for Certain Investments in Debt and Equity Securities" (Norwalk, Conn.: Financial Accounting Standards Board, 1993).
5 Jalal Soroosh and Jack T. Ciesielski, "Accounting for Special Purpose Entities Revised, FASB Interpretation (46R)," *The CPA Journal*, July 2004.
6 Intel Corporation, *Annual Report*, 2009.
7 Greg Steinmetz and Cacilie Rohwedder, "SAP Insider Probe Points to Reforms Needed in Germany," *The Wall Street Journal*, May 8, 1997.
8 Intel Corporation, *Annual Report*, 2009.
9 Kathryn Kranhold and Deborah Solomon, "GE Restates Several Years of Earnings," *The Wall Street Journal*, May 9, 2005.
10 Intel Corporation, *Annual Report*, 2009.
11 *Statement of Financial Accounting Standards No. 115*, "Accounting for Certain Investments in Debt and Equity Securities" (Norwalk, Conn.: Financial Accounting Standards Board, 1993).
12 Intel Corporation, *Annual Report*, 2009.
13 *Statement of Financial Accounting Standards No. 94*, "Consolidation of All Majority-Owned Subsidiaries" (Norwalk, Conn.: Financial Accounting Standards Board, 1987).
14 Intel Corporation, *Annual Report*, 2009.
15 Financial Accounting Standards Board, "Summary of Statement No. 141: Business Combinations," www.fasb.org, 2009.
16 *Statement of Financial Accounting Standards No. 160*, "Noncontrolling Interest in Consolidated Financial Statements" (Norwalk, Conn.: Financial Accounting Standards Board, 2007).
17 *Accounting Principles Board, Opinion No. 16*, "Business Combinations" (New York: AICPA, 1970).
18 Intel Corporation, *Annual Report*, 2009.
19 Ibid.
20 Dell, Inc., *Annual Report*, 2010.
21 DreamWorks Animation SKG, Inc., *Annual Report*, 2009.

COMPANY NAME INDEX

Abbott Laboratories, 424, 453
Adolph Coors Company, 498
Amazon.com, Inc., 367, 370, 484, 536, 538–539, 543, 545, 560–561, 603
America Online (AOL), 180, 373
American Airlines, 373
American Express, 592
AOL Time Warner, 261
Apple Computer, Inc., 139, 400, 404, 406, 422, 423, 424, 425, 426, 444, 491, 641
AT&T Corporation, 404, 492
Bank of America, 334, 335, 592
Bank One, 333
Bear Stearns, 637
Bed Bath & Beyond, 42
Bell South, 457
Best Buy Co., 4, 244, 247–248, 251, 265, 266, 270
Boeing Company, 88, 91, 92, 113, 114–115, 206, 411
British Petroleum (BP), 492
Burger King Holdings, Inc., 4
Caesars World, 139
Campbell Soup, 593
Caremark Rx, Inc., 671
Chase, 335
Circuit City, 332
Cisco Systems, Inc., 290, 292, 293–295, 299, 310, 339, 398, 542
Citibank, 335, 398, 533
Coca-Cola Company, 23, 207, 423, 457
Columbia HCA Healthcare, 457
CompuCredit, 359
Computer Associates, 92
Continental Airlines, 444–445
Costco Wholesale Corporation, 4, 42, 211, 439
Crazy Eddie, Inc., 323
Credit Suisse First Boston, 490
CVS Caremark Corporation, 2, 5, 6, 7, 9, 11, 12, 15, 26, 33, 43, 44, 46–76, 92, 133, 134, 181, 240, 242, 288, 292, 324, 360, 399, 439, 440, 484, 485, 535, 548, 553, 582, 631, 632, 654, 671
DaimlerChrysler, 369
Dean Foods Co., 484
Dell Computer Corporation, 141, 196, 201, 202, 208–209, 210, 213–214, 223–224, 294, 323, 671
Deloitte & Touché, 23
Dillard's, 331
Disney, 423
Domino's Pizza, Inc., 484
Dow Chemical, 409
DreamWorks Animation, 532, 671
Dun & Bradstreet, 590
Eastman Kodak, 483
eBay, 603
Eclipsys, 180
Electronic Data Systems Corporation (EDS), 113
Enron Corporation, 7, 14, 93, 200–201, 579, 639
Ernst & Young, 23
ExxonMobil Corporation, 13, 23, 323, 323–324, 542
Facebook, 503
Fidelity Investments Company, 42
Fleetwood Enterprises, Inc., 139, 579
Ford Motor Company, 23, 331, 542, 453
Fosters Group Limited, 359
Gap Inc., 7
General Electric (GE), 23, 423, 506, 641
General Mill, Inc., 533, 511
General Motors (GM), 6, 23, 398, 446, 451, 492
Generation Health, 671
Goodyear Tire & Rubber Company, 202, 368, 588–589, 630
Google, Inc., 423, 486, 490, 491, 495, 496, 498, 500, 501, 515–516, 533, 542, 603
Great Atlantic & Pacific Tea Company (A&P), 239
H. J. Heinz Company, 139, 630
Harley Davidson, 295
Health Management Associates, Inc., 484
HealthSouth, 333
Heineken N.V., 359
Hershey Foods Corporation, 367, 373
Hewlett-Packard (HP), 326, 328, 329–330, 333, 334, 347–348
Hilton Hotels Corporation, 439
Home Depot, The, 328, 506
Honda, 5
Household International, 333
IBM, 23, 423, 457, 533, 640, 641, 649
Intel Corporation, 423, 634, 636, 638, 639, 642, 647, 648, 653, 655, 658
JCPenney, 323
Johnson & Johnson, 506
J.P. Morgan, 533, 637
Kelly Services, 139
Kmart, 298
KnowledgeWare, 180
KPMG, 23
Kraft Foods, 133
Lands' End, 257
Lechters, Inc., 42
Lehman Brothers, 332
L.L. Bean, 257
Longs Drug Stores, 671
Lowe's, 328
Lucent Technologies, 180, 339, 369
Lyric Opera of Chicago, 180–181
Macy's, 329, 331
Marriott International, 439
McDonald's Corporation, 23, 112, 287, 423, 442, 444, 445, 446, 448, 449, 450, 451, 470, 492, 593
MCI, 93
Mellon Bank, 133
Merrill Lynch, 332
MGM-UA Communications, 139
Microsoft, 141, 362, 364, 365, 366, 368, 369, 372, 373, 376, 382, 384–385, 423, 444, 493, 494, 495, 496, 506, 542, 640
Midas, 374
Mitsubishi Corp., 359
Moody's Investor Services, 590
Morgan Stanley, 328, 490
Motorola, 369
Neiman Marcus, 212
Nestlé, 133
Netflix, Inc., 136, 138, 148–149, 151–152, 155, 158
Nike, Inc., 4, 328, 510
Nokia, 423
Nordstrom, 331
Nortel Networks, 339
Office Depot, 257
Panasonic, Inc., 581
PepsiCo, 649
Pfizer, Inc., 631
Piedmont Delta, 411
PricewaterhouseCoopers, 23
Procter & Gamble, 23
Qwest Communications, 404
RentWay, Inc., 295

Research in Motion Limited (RIM), 42–43
Rite Aid Corporation, 295
Roche, 631
Royal Dutch/Shell Group, 421
Sam's Club, 211
Sara Lee, 133
Sears, 331
Simon & Schuster, 261
Sony Corporation, 581
Southwest Airlines Co., 33, 42, 44, 46, 77–87, 134, 181, 240, 242, 438, 440, 485, 535, 548, 553, 582, 632, 671
Sprint, 330
Standard & Poor's (S&P), 446, 590
Starbucks Corporation, 4, 287, 584, 586, 591, 592, 594–599, 600–611, 612
Sun Microsystems Inc., 398
Supervalu Inc., 239
Target Corporation, 8, 247–248, 329, 601
Tiffany & Co., 212
Toyota, 423
Toys "R" Us, 139
TWA, 444–445
UAL (United Airlines) Corp., 4, 88, 91, 92, 114, 444–445
UBS, 637
Union Carbine, 409
United Parcel Service, 294
US Airways, 375, 411
Vanguard Airlines, 411
Vivendi, 552
Walgreens, 288, 292, 324, 360, 399, 483, 601
Wal-Mart Stores, 335, 484, 506
Walt Disney Company, The, 181, 457
Wells Fargo, 533
Western Airlines, 411
WorldCom, 7, 8, 14, 93, 200–201, 398, 404, 406, 541, 552
Xerox Corporation, 2, 180, 364

SUBJECT INDEX

Note: **Boldface** type indicate key terms.

Accelerated method, 413
Account(s), 93, 93–94
- adjusting, 143
- after closing, 187
- chart of, 108
- collection on, 102–103
- contra, 147
- expense, 184
- nominal, 154
- payments on, 255, 260
- permanent, 154
- real, 154
- receipts on, 257, 262
- revenue, 184
- temporary uncollectible, 337–342

Account balance, 94
Accounting, 4
- accrual, 141–143
- and politics don't mix, 496
- as an information system, 4–8, 4 (exh.)
- cash basis of, 140
- development of, 7
- financial and management, 6–7
- rules of double-entry, 94–95

Accounting conventions, 200, 201–204
Accounting cycle, 96, 96–97, 97 (exh.)
Accounting differences, industry norms standard, 588
Accounting equation, 17, 17 (exh.)
Accounting estimates, 591–592
Accounting information
- qualitative characteristics of, 199–200
- users of, 8–11, 9 (exh.)

Accounting measurement, 11–12
Accounting methods, 590–591, 591 (exh.)
Accounting mistake, 641
Accounting policies, 91
- in annual report, 50

Accounting Principles Board's Opinion No. 9 and No. 20, 416
Accounting standards
- organizations that issue, 24
- publicly traded energy companies and, 421

Accounts payable, 17, 368
- evaluating, 365–366
- in general ledger, 110 (exh.)

Accounts receivable, 17, **329**
- analysis of by age, 340 (exh.)
- as percentage of total assets for selected industries, 329 (exh.)
- credit policies and, 329–330
- evaluating level of, 330–331

Accounts receivable aging method, 340, 340–341
- percentage of net sales method compared with, 341–342

Accrual, 145
Accrual accounting, 141, 141–143
Accrued expenses, 148, 148 (exh.), 148–149
Accrued interest, 346
Accrued liabilities, 369
Accrued revenues, 151, 151–152
Accumulated Depreciation accounts, 147
Accumulated other comprehensive income, 497
Acquisition cost of property, plant, and equipment, 407–410
Acquisition decision, 404 (exh.)
Additional paid-in capital, 18
Additions, 407
Adjusted trial balance, 152
Adjusting entries, 144
- prepaid (deferred) expenses, 145 (exh.)
- recording in journal, 191
- unearned revenues, 150 (exh.)
- unrecorded expenses, 148 (exh.)
- unrecorded revenues, 151 (exh.)

Adjustments, 191 (exh.), 143, 144 (exh.), 144–152
Aging of accounts receivable, 340
AICPA. *See* American Institute of Certified Public Accountants
Allowance for Uncollectible Accounts, 338
Allowance method, 338
American Institute of Certified Public Accountants (AICPA), 24, 25
- APB Opinions No. 9 and No 20, 416

Amortization, 402, 403, 549
- of bond discounts, 459–464
- of bond premiums, 464–467

Annual report, 46–54, 50, 55–76, 77–87, 242–243
Annuity. *See* Ordinary annuity
Articles of incorporation, 14
Asset impairment, 403, 404
Asset management, evaluating operating, 607–609
Asset turnover, 115, 216, 216–217, **602**
Assets, 17, 206–207
- cash flows to, 544, 605
- cash return on, 221–222
- current, 206, 550–551
- disposal of depreciable, 417–419
- evaluating total management of, 601–611
- fixed, 206
- intangible, 207, 402, 422 (exh.), 422–425, 423 (exh.)
- investing in partnership, 679–680
- issuance of stock for cash and other, 501–504
- issuance of stock for noncash, 503–504
- long-lived, 206
- long-term, 402 (exh.), 402–406, 403 (exh.), 406 (exh.)
- operating, 206
- other, 206
- plant, 206, 417–418, 419, 420, 554–556
- purchase of, 100–101
- recording under IFRS, 479
- return on, 220–221, 602–603
- short-term financial, 329
- stockholders preference as to, 499
- tangible, 206, 402
- valuing, 382–383

Audit, 23
Audit committee, 14
Auditor's report, 53, 54 (exh.)
- opinion section of, 54
- scope section of, 54

Authorization, 264
Authorized shares, 498, 498 (exh.)
Available-for-sale debt instruments, 638
Available-for-sale securities, 637, 642
Average-cost method, 300, 300–301
Bad debts, 333
Bad times, how companies deal with, 328
Balance, 94
- account, 94
- cash, 541
- compensating, 328
- credit, 184
- debit, 184
- normal, 95
- trial. *See* trial balance

Balance sheet, 16, 16–18, 18 (exh.), 20 (exh.), 153 (exh.)
- classified, 204 (exh.), 204–209, 205 (exh.)
- common-size, 598 (exh.)
- comparative, 547 (exh.), 595 (exh.)
- consolidated, 63, 78, 649–654, 651 (exh.)
- in annual report, 48, 49 (exh.)
- liabilities, greater under IFRS, 377
- stockholders' equity section of, 497 (exh.), 513 (exh.)

Bank loans, 368–369
Bank reconciliation, 335, 335–337, 336 (exh.)
Bank statement, 269
Banking services, 334–335
Barter transactions, 92
Base year, 595
Benefits offered by small and mid-sized businesses, 371
Betterments, 407
Board of directors, 14
Bond(s), 452
accounting for issuance of, 455–457
callable, 454
characteristics of, 453–455
convertible, 454
coupon, 455–456
debenture, 453
issued at discount, 455–456, 463 (exh.)
issued at face value, 455
issued at premium, 456, 467 (exh.)
long-term investment in, 657
nature of, 452–455
100-year, 457
payable, 447, 557
registered, 454
retirement and conversion of, 468–469
secured, 453
serial, 453–454
term, 453
unsecured, 453
valuing using present value, 457–458
zero coupon, 460
Bond certificate, 452
Bond discount, amortizing, 459–463, 462 (exh.)
Bond indenture, 452
Bond issue, 452, 452–453
costs, 457
Bond premium, amortizing, 464–467, 466 (exh.)
Bond prices, 453
Bonding, 264
Bonus,partner, 680–681
Book of original entry, 98
Book value, 403, **514**
for common and preferred stock, 514
for dividends in arrears, 514–515
less than 100 percent purchase at, 651–652
100 percent purchase at, 650
purchase at more or less than, 652–654
Book value per share, 514, 514–515
Bookkeeping, 7
Bottom line, 593
Brand name, 422
Brands, 423
Buildings, 409
See also Property, plant, and equipment
Business(es), 4
accounting for unincorporated, 674–681
corporate form of, 13–15, 14 (exh.), 488–490
forms of, 13
goals and activities, 4–6, 5(exh.)
owner's investment in, 98–99
small and mid-sized offer benefits, 371
Business periodicals, 590
Business transactions, 11, 11–12
analysis, 98–105
economic event that is not, 99
foreign, 249
See also Transactions
Business Week, 494
definition of free cash flow, 545
Call price, 454, 500
Callable bonds, 454
Callable preferred stock, 500
Capital
additional paid-in, 18
contributed, 18, 207, 488–496, 497
ease of generation of, 489
interest on partners', 676
legal, 490
owner's, 208
sources of, raised by U.S. corporations, 488 (exh.)
working, 246
Capital balance ratios, 677
Capital expenditure, 407
Capital lease, 448, 449 (exh.)
Carrying value, 147, 403, 462–463
cash received equal to, 418
cash received less than, 418
cash received more than, 418
of long-term assets on balance sheet, 403 (exh.)
Cash, 328, 538
balances, 541
bonuses, 6
can a company have too much, 542
collections can be hard to estimate, 339
control methods, 334–337
disbursements, control of, 267–270, 268–269 (exh.)
expense paid in, 103
gap, 247
issuance of stock for, 501–504
management, 328–333
plant assets sold for, 418
prepayment of expenses in, 99
purchase of asset partly on credit and partly in, 100–101
requirements and seasonal cycles, 329 (exh.)
revenue in, 101
See also Cash receipts
Cash basis of accounting, 140
Cash dividend received, 645, 648
Cash equivalents, 334, 538
Cash flow ratios, 542–544
Cash flow trends, 545–546
Cash flow yield, 158, 217, 217–218, **543, 604**
Cash flows, 18
analyzing, 542–546
assess prospects, 199
classification of, 538–541
effect on, 492
free, 405, 406, 426
from accrual-based information, 156–157, 157 (exh.)
from financing activities, 18, 540, 556–558
from investing activities, 18, 540, 553–556
from operating activities, 18, 546–553, 539, 549 (exh.)
impact of different accounting methods on, 591
in operating cycle, 247 (exh.)
information, 451–452, 496
inventory decisions effects on, 305
managing, 364–365
net income and, 545
should earnings be aligned with, 113
timing of transactions and, 112–113
See also Statement of cash flows
Cash flows to assets, 544, 605
Cash flows to sales, 543, 604
Cash inflows and outflows, classification of, 540 (exh.)
Cash receipts
by mail, 266
control of, 266–267
equal to carrying value, 418
less than carrying value, 418
more than carrying value, 418
over the counter, 266–267
Cash return on assets, 221, 221–222
Centralized authority and responsibility, 489
Certified public accountant (CPA), 23
reports of, 53–54
Chart of accounts, 108, 109 (exh.)
Check, 269
NSF, 335
outstanding, 335
Check authorization, 269
Chief executive officer (CEO), 9
Chief financial officer (CFO), 9
Classification, 92, 367, 636–637
issue, 90
of investments, 637 (exh.)
of long-term assets and methods of accounting for them, 403 (exh.)
Classified balance sheet, 204 (exh.), 204–209, 205 (exh.), 209 (exh.)
Classified financial statements, 204
Closely held corporations, 46

Closing
credit balances, 184
debit balances, 184
dividends account balance, 187
income summary account balance, 187
overview of process, 155 (exh.)
Closing entries, 154, 154–155, 186 (exh.), 187 (exh.)
preparing, 184–187, 185 (exh.)
recording in journal, 191
work sheet and, 184–191
Collection on account, 102–103
Commercial paper, 368–369, **369**
Commitment, 376
Common stock, 14, 497, 557
book value per share of, 514
Common-size balance sheets, 598 (exh.)
Common-size income statements, 599 (exh.)
Common-size statement, 598
Compact Disclosure, 46
Company description, in annual report, 47
Company operations, increased cash for, 491
Comparability, 200
industry norms standard, 588
Compensating balance, 328
Compensation
executive, 221
management, 586–590, 601
stock options as, 495–496
Compensation committee, 586
Compound entry, 101
Compound interest, 378, 378–379
Comprehensive income under IFRS vs. GAAP, 514
Computers
internal control and, 266
software costs, 425
Confirmative value, 200
Conglomerates, 588
Conservatism, 203
Consignment, 298
Consistency, 202
Consolidated financial statements, 62, 63, 64, 65–66, 67–74, 78, 79, 80, 81, 539 (exh.), **648**, 649–655, 651 (exh.), 655 (exh.)
in annual report, 47
Consumer groups, 10
Contingent liability, 332, 376
Continuity, 139
Continuous existence, 489
Contra account, 147
Contributed capital, 18, 207, 488–496, **497**
Control, 637
of cash receipts, 266–267
of purchases and cash disbursements, 267–270
separation of ownership and, 490
See also Internal control
Control activities, 263, 263–264
Control environment, 263
Controlling investment, 637, 648
Conversion of bonds, 469
Convertible bonds, 454
Convertible preferred stock, 500
Copyright, 422
Corporate form of business, 13–15, 14 (exh.), 488–490
Corporate governance, 14
Corporate income statement, 592 (exh.)
Corporation(s), 14, 488
big or small business, 15
formation and organization of, 14–15
reports published by, 589
multinational or transnational, 654
number and receipts of U.S., 13 (exh.)
private or closely held, 46
Cost(s), 411
bond issue, 457
expired, 138
of doing business, 138
of frequent flyer miles, 373
of revenue, 211
of sales, 211
transportation, 253
Cost approach, 377–378
Cost flow, 297, 297–298
Cost of goods available for sale, 258
Cost of goods sold, 211, 250, 258 (exh.), 259
Cost principle, 91, 636
Cost-adjusted-to-market method, 643
Cost-benefit, 203, 203–204
Council of Economic Advisers, 10
Coupon bonds, 455–456, **456**
Coupons, 374
Credit(s), 94
and investment advisory services, 590
miscellaneous, 335–336
purchase of asset on, 100–101
purchases on, 255, 260
revenue on, 102
sales on, 256, 261
Credit balances, 184, 186 (exh.)
closing, 184
Credit cards, 248
terms of sales, 253
Creditors, 10
advisors of, 10
equities, 17
focus, 587
objectives, financial performance measurement, 587
Crossfooting, 190
Cumulative preferred stock, 499
Current assets, 206
changes in, 550–551
Current debt to tangible net worth relationship, 588
Current liabilities, 207, 364
changes in, 551–552
common types of, 368–375
management issues related to, 364–367
Current ratio, 246, 609, 609–610
Customer list, 422
Customers, 10
D'Angelo, Adam, 503
Day's inventory on hand, 310, 294, 608
Days' payable, 365, 365–366, **385, 609**
Days' sales uncollected, 331, 347–348, 608, 608–609
Death of partners, 681
Debenture bonds, 453
Debit(s), 94
balances, 184, 186 (exh.)
miscellaneous, 335–336
Debit cards, 248
terms of sales, 253
Debt
early extinguishment of, 454
how does it affect a company's ability to borrow, 446
long-term, 444–445, 445–446, 446–451
problems, 364
Debt instruments, available-for sale, 638
Debt securities, investments in, 656–657
Debt to equity ratio, 218, 218–219, **445**, 491, **606**
Decision makers, 8–11
Declaration date, 492, 492–493, 509
Declining-balance method, 413, 413–414, 415 (exh.)
Deferral, 145
Deferred expenses, 145–148
Deferred income taxes, 451
Deferred payment, 383
Deferred revenues, 150–151
Defined benefit plan, 450
Defined contribution plan, 450
Definite useful life, 423
Definitely determinable liabilities, 368, 368–373
Delivery expense, 253
Dell, Michael S., 201
Depletion, 402, 403, 419–420, 549
Deposits in transit, 335
Depreciable assets, disposal of, 417–419
Depreciable cost, 412
Depreciation, 147, 402, 403, 411–416, 549
accelerated methods save money, 415
comparison of methods, 414, 415 (exh.)
factors in computing, 411–412
for partial years, 415–416

group, 415
methods of computing, 412–415
of buildings under IFRS, 409
of plant and equipment, 146–147
of related plant assets, 420
special issues in, 415–416
Depreciation expense, 147
Depreciation rates, revision of, 416
Depreciation schedule
double-declining-balance method, 414 (exh.)
production method, 413 (exh.)
straight-line method, 412 (exh.)
Derivatives, 641
Development and exploration costs in oil and gas industry, 421
Direct charge-off method, 337
Direct method, 548
Discarded plant assets, 417–418
Disclosure, 367, 638
of inventory methods, 299
of uncollectible accounts, 338
Discontinued operations, 593
Discount, 453
amortized, 462–463
bonds issued at, 455–456
sales and purchases, 252–253
unamortized, 462–463
Discounting, 332, 332–333
Dishonored note, 346
Disposal of depreciable assets, 417–419
Dissolution of partnership, 679–681
Distribution date, 509
Distribution of partnership income and losses, 676–678
Diversified companies, 588
Diversity, industry norms standard, 588
Dividend(s), 16, 104, **491**
dates, 492
liquidating, 491
payout optional, 444
policies, 491–493
stockholders preference as to, 499
transactions, 492–493
Dividends account balance, closing, 187, 187 (exh.)
Dividends in arrears, 499, 514–515
Dividends payable, 369
Dividends yield ratio, 493, 493–494, **611**
Documents and records, 264
Double taxation, 489, 489–490
Double-declining-balance method, 414
Double-entry system, 93, 93–97
rules of, 94–95
Due care, 25
Duration of a note, 344, 344–345
Duties, separation of, 264
Early extinguishment of debt, 454
Earnings
aligned with cash flows, 113
EBIT, 603
EBITDA, 552
evaluating quality of, 590–594
misstatements and overstatements of, 141
net, 213
retained, 16, 207, 497, 558
volatility of, 492
Earnings management, 140
Earnings per share, 213
Ebbers, Bernard J., 8, 201
EBIT, 603
EBITDA (earnings before interest, taxes, depreciation, and amortization), 552
Economic planners, 10
Economic Stimulus Act of 2008, 416
Economic value added (EVA), 601
Effective interest method, 461
amortizing bond premium, 465–467
Effective interest rate, 453
Electronic funds transfer (EFT), 335
Eliminations, 652 (exh.), 653 (exh.), **949**
entry for, 650–651
Employee, 370
Employee stock ownership plans (ESOPs), 450
Environmental Protection Agency, 202
Equipment, 410
See also Property, plant, and equipment
Equity
accounting for partners', 676
owner's, 17, 207–208
partners', 207–208
ratio of debt to, 218–219, 445, 491, 606
residual, 497
return on, 222–223, 494–495, 606–607
stockholders', 17–18, 207
trading on, 444
Equity financing, 490–491
Equity investment
accounting for, 638
purchase of, 647
Equity method, 646
Equity securities
long-term investments in, 643–648
short-term investments in, 639–642
Estimated liabilities, 373, 373–375
Estimated useful life, 412
Estimation
of uncollectible accounts expense, 339–342, 342 (exh.)
valuing inventory by, 308–309
Ethics, 7, 92–93
adjustments and, 143
and estimates in account for receivables, 333
in financial reporting, 7–8, 200–201
matching rule and, 140–141
of investing, 638–639
profitability measurement issues and, 138–141
statements of cash flows and, 541–542
Evaluation of liquidity, 246
Exchange gain or loss, 249
Exchange price, 91, 636
Exchange rate, 12, 249
Ex-dividend, 492
Executive compensation, performance measures and, 221
Expenditure, 407
capital, 407
revenue, 407
Expense(s), 16, 138
accounts, 184
accrued, 148–149
deferred, 145–149
delivery, 253
depreciation, 147
general and administrative, 212
nonoperating, 212
operating, 212
other revenues and, 212–213
paid in cash, 103
prepaid, 145–146
prepayment of in cash, 99
recognition of, 142
selling, 212
to be paid later, 103–104
Expenses, nonoperating, 212
Expired costs, 138
Explanatory notes, 50–53
External decision makers, 7
Extraordinary repairs, 407
Face interest rate, 453
Face value, bonds issued at, 455
Factor, 331
in computing depreciation, 411–412
Factoring, 331, 332 (exh.)
Fair value, 91, 403, **636**
defined by FASB, 378
Fair value accounting
challenge of, 92
subprime mortgages and, 637
valuation approaches to, 377–381
Faithful representation, 200
FASB. *See* Financial Accounting Standards Board
Federal Authority for Securities Trading (FAST), 639
Federal income taxes, 371
Federal Reserve Board, 10
Federal unemployment insurance (FUTA) tax, 371
Financial accounting, 6–7, 7

Financial Accounting Standards Board (FASB), 23, **24**, 53, 92, 198, 424, 588
rules vs. GAAP principles, 142
valuation and, 636
Financial analysis, 5
tools and techniques of, 594–600
Financial highlights in annual report, 56, 47
Financial leverage, 444, 606
negative, 445
Financial performance measurement, 586
creditors' and investors' objectives, 587
management's objectives, 586
Financial ratio(s), 6, 19–22, 26, 215–219, 223–224
additional, 219–223
cash flow yield, 158, 217–218, 543, 604
cash flows to assets, 544, 605
cash flows to sales, 543, 604
cash return on assets, 221–222
current ratio, 246, 609–610
days' inventory on hand, 293–294, 310, 608
days' payable, 365–366, 385, 609
days' receivable, 347–348
days' sales uncollected, 331, 608–609
debt to equity ratio, 218–219, 445, 606
dividends yield, 493–494, 611
evaluating market strength with, 610–611
interest coverage ratio, 445–446, 607
inventory turnover, 293–294, 310, 607–608
measuring performance using, 493–495
payables turnover, 365, 385, 609
price/earnings (P/E), 495, 610–611
profit margin, 215–216, 601–602
quick ratio, 610
receivable turnover, 330, 347–348, 608
return on assets, 220–221, 602–603
return on equity, 222–223, 494–495, 606–607
supplemental, 609–610
using for performance evaluations, 215–223
Financial ratio analysis, 600, 600–601
Financial reporting
ethical, 200–201
factors affecting, 198 (exh.)
foundations of, 198–201
objective, 198–199
Financial risk, 444–445
decreased, 491
evaluating, 605–607
Financial statement analysis, 586
standards of comparison, 587–589
Financial statement elements
critical financial ratios and, 215–219
focus on, 19–22, 21 (exh.)
Financial statements, 7, 15–22
accounting conventions for preparing, 201–204
consolidated, 649–655
IASB proposes change in format of, 208
impact of different accounting methods on, 591
in annual report, 47–50
inventory decisions effects on, 303
preparing, 191
relationships among, 19
restatement of foreign subsidiary, 654–655
using adjusted trial balance to prepare, 152–154
See also Notes to financial statements
Financial summary, five-year, CVS's annual report, 75
Financing activities, 5, 540, 545
cash flows from, 18, 556–558
Financing period, 247, 248 (exh.), **607**, 609
Financing receivables, 331–333
Financing transactions, required disclosure of noncash, 541
First-in, first-out (FIFO) method, 301
Fiscal year, 139
Fixed assets, 206
Flow of costs, 297
Flow of physical inventory, 297
FOB destination, 253, 297
FOB shipping point, 253, 297
Footed, 190
Footings, 94
Forbes, 494
definition of free cash flow, 545
Foreign business transactions, 249
Foreign currency, purchase or sale in, 249
Foreign exchange rates, examples of, 12 (exh.)
Foreign subsidiary financial statements, restatement of, 654–655
Form 8-K, 589
Form 10-K, 46, **589**
Form 10-Q, 589
Formatting guidelines, 112 (exh.)
401 (k) plans, 450
Franchise, 422
Fraud, 263
inventory misstatements and, 295–296
Sarbanes-Oxley Act and, 251
Fraudulent financial reporting, 7
Free cash flow, 405, 426, **544, 605**
computing, 406
definition of, 545
Freight-in, 253, 260
Freight-out, 253
Full disclosure, 202
Full-costing method, 421
Future value, 378, 378–379
GAAP. *See* generally accepted accounting principles
Gains, 550, 593, 641
exchange, 249
General and administrative expenses, 212
General journal, 108, 108–110, 110 (exh.)
adjustments from work sheet entered in, 191 (exh.)
posting from, to ledger, 111 (exh.)
General ledger, 108, **110**, 110–111, 110 (exh.)
General public, 10
Generally accepted accounting principles (GAAP), 22, 22–25, 90, 92, 548
convergence of IFRS and, 203, 650
independent CPA's report and, 23–24
other organizations that influence, 24–25
principles vs. FASB rules, 142
recycling and, 641
valuation practices under, 636
vs. IFRS, comprehensive income under, 514
Goethe, 93
Going concern, 139
Goods flow, 297, 297–298
Goodwill, 422, 425
Government regulation, 489
Governmental Accounting Standards Board (GASB), 24
Governmental organizations, 10–11
Gross margin, 211, 211–212
effects of inventory costing methods on, 303 (exh.)
method, 308
Gross profit, 211–212
Gross profit method, 308, 308–309, 309 (exh.)
Gross sales, 210
Group depreciation, 415
Group purchases, 410
Held-to-maturity securities, 637, 656–657
purchase of, 656
Horizontal analysis, 594, 594–597, 595 (exh.), 596 (exh.)
IASB. *See* International Accounting Standards Board
IFRS. *See* International financial reporting standards
Impairment, 403
Imprest systems, 334
In balance, 106

Income
accumulated other comprehensive, 497
comprehensive, 514
distribution of partnership, 676–678
from continuing operations, 593
impact of different accounting methods on, 591
interest, 336
net, 16, 213, 438, 545
operating, 212
other comprehensive, 497
participation in partnership, 675
recognition of, 647–648
Income (or cash flow) approach, 377
Income before income taxes, 213
Income from operations, 212
Income measurement
assumptions, 138–140
effects of inventory misstatements on, 295
Income statement, 15, 15–16, 16 (exh.), 20 (exh.), 48 (exh.), 153 (exh.), 213–214, 547 (exh.)
common-size, 599 (exh.)
comparative, 596 (exh.)
consolidated, 654, 655 (exh.)
corporate, 592 (exh.)
forms of, 210–215
in annual report, 48
multistep, 210–213, 211 (exh.), 212 (exh.), 214 (exh.)
single-step, 214–215, 214 (exh.)
under IFRS, 250
under periodic inventory system, 258 (exh.), 302 (exh.)
under perpetual inventory system, 254 (exh.), 307 (exh.)
Income Summary account, 154, 186 (exh.)
balance, closing, 187, 187 (exh.)
Income taxes, 213
deferred, 451
federal, 371
inventory decisions effects on, 304
payable, 373
state and local, 371
Incorporation
advantages of, 489
disadvantages of, 489–490
Indefinite useful life, 423
Independence, 25
Independent contractor, 370
Independent CPA's report, GAAP and, 23–24
Independent directors, 14
Index number, 597
Indirect method, 548
Industry norms, 588
Industry policies, 492
Influential but noncontrolling investment, 637, 646–648
Information and communication, 263
Information sources, 589–590
Information system, accounting as, 4–8
Initial public offering (IPO), 486
Insider trading, 638
Institute of Management Accountants (IMA), 25
Intangible assets, 207, 402, 422–425, 422 (exh.), 423 (exh.)
Integrity, 25
Intercompany receivables and payables, 654
Interest, 345, 378, 378–379, 677–678
on partners' capital, 676
purchasing from partner, 679
receipt of, 657
users with direct financial, 9–10
users with indirect financial, 10
year-end accrual of, 656–657
Interest coverage ratio, 445, 445–446, **607**
Interest expense, 462–463
calculation of total, 459–460, 464
Interest income, 336
Interest rate, 345
bond issue, 452–453
Interim financial statements, 53, **589**
Interim periods, 139
Internal control(s), 250, 263–264
components of, 263
computers and, 266
in large company, 267 (exh.)
limitations of, 264
management goals and, 265–266
management's responsibility for, 251
need for, 250–251
over merchandising transactions, 265–270
plan for purchases and cash disbursements, 268–269 (exh.)
See also Control
Internal decision makers, 6
Internal Revenue Service (IRS), 24, 304
International Accounting Standards Board (IASB), 23, **24**, 92, 208, 548
valuation and, 636
International certified public accounting firms, 23 (exh.)
International financial reporting standards (IFRS), 23, **24**, 92
asset impairment under, 404
convergence of GAAP and, 203, 650
depreciation of buildings under, 409
direct method and, 548
how does a stock become a debt under, 500
recording liabilities and assets will not look the same under, 449
recycling and, 641
research development costs under, 424
valuation and, 636
vs. GAAP, comprehensive income under, 514
International joint ventures, accounting for, 647
Inventory
costing methods, 302, 303 (exh.)
managing of, 292–296, 292 (exh.)
system, choice of, 248–249
to net working capital relationship, 588
valuing by estimation, 308–309
Inventory cost, 297
under periodic inventory system, 299–302
under perpetual inventory system, 305–307
valuation and, 297–299
Inventory decisions, 292–293
impact of, 302–305
Inventory estimation
gross profit method of, 309 (exh.)
retail method of, 308 (exh.)
Inventory methods
achieving convergence of, 304
disclosure of, 299
Inventory misstatements
effects of on income measurement, 295
fraud and, 295–296
illustrated, 296
Inventory turnover, 293, 294, **310**, **607**, 607–608
Investing activities, 5, 540, 545
cash flows from, 18, 553–556
Investing, ethics of, 638–639
Investing transactions, required disclosure of noncash, 541
Investment(s), 206, 554
accounting for equity, 638
classification of, 637 (exh.)
controlling, 637, 648
in business by owner, 98–99
in debt securities, 656–657
influential but noncontrolling, 637, 646–648
long-term, 645, 657
management issues related to, 636–639
noninfluential and noncontrolling, 637, 643–646
short-term, 639–642
Investors, 9, 9–10
advisors of, 10
focus, 587
objectives, financial performance measurement, 587
Invoice, 269
Issued shares, 498
Issues in accounting for long-term assets, 406 (exh.)

Joint ventures, accounting for international, 647
Journal, 98, 108
recording adjusting and closing entries in, 191
Journal entry, 98, 152
Just-in-time (JIT) operating environment, 294
Labor unions, 10
Lack of mutual agency, 489
Land, 408–409
improvements, 409
See also Property, plant, and equipment
Last-in, first-out (LIFO) method, 301, 301–302, 307
Lay, Kenneth, 201
Leasehold, 422
Leasehold improvements, 409–410, **410**
Leases
capital, 448
long-term, 447–450
operating, 447
Ledger, 108, 111 (exh.)
Ledger account form, 110
Legal capital, 490
Letter to stockholders (shareholders), 46–47, 58–61
Liabilities, 17, 207
accrued, 369
balance sheet, 377
current, 207, 364–367, 368–375, 551–552
definitely determinable, 368–373
estimated, 373–375
long-term, 207, 367
payroll, 370–372
pension, 450–451
postretirement, 450
recording will not look the same under IFRS, 449
reporting, 366–367
Liability
contingent, 332
limited, 489, 490
partnerships unlimited, 675
payment of, 101
vacation pay, 375
License, 422
LIFO liquidation, 304
Limited liability, 489, 490
Limited life, partnerships, 675
Line of credit, 368
Liquidating dividend, 491
Liquidation of partnership, 681
Liquidity, 5, 6, 246
evaluation of, 246, 604–605
managing, 364–365
supplemental financial ratios for assessing, 609–610
Long-term assets, 206, **402**
acquiring, 404–405
as a percentage of total assets for selected industries, 402 (exh.)
carrying value of, on balance sheet, 403 (exh.)
classification of and methods of accounting for them, 403 (exh.)
financing, 405–406
management issues related to, 402–406
Long-term debt
current portion of, 370
deciding to issue, 444–445
evaluating, 445–446
financing, management issues related to, 444–452
types of, 446–451
Long-term investments, 636
in bonds, 657
in equity securities, 643–648
purchase of, 644
sale of, 645
Long-term leases, 447–450
Long-term liabilities, 207, 367
Losses
distribution of partnership, 676–678
exchange, 249
gains and, 550, 593, 641
net, 16, 438
other comprehensive, 497
Lower-of-cost-or-market (LCM) rule, 298
Maker, 343
Management, 9, 14–15
compensation, 586–590, 601
discussion and analysis, 47
internal control and, 251, 265–266
objectives, financial performance measurement, 586
reports of responsibilities, 53
stewardship, assessment of, 199
Management accounting, 6, 6–7
Management information systems (MIS), 7
Management issues
related to cash and receivables, 328–333
related to contributed capital, 488–496
related to current liabilities, 364–367
related to investments, 636–639
related to long-term assets, 402–406
related to long-term debt financing, 444–452
Manufacturing company, 210
Market, 298
same as fair value under IFRS, 299
Market approach, 377
Market interest rate, 453
Market price, do stock splits help increase, 511
Market rate, 458
Market strength, evaluating with financial ratios, 610–611
Marketable securities, 636
Matching rule, 140
applying, 406
assumptions and, 140 (exh.)
ethics and, 140–141
Material difference, 461
Materiality, 202, 202–203
Maturity date, 344
Maturity value, 345, 345–346
Measurement
accounting, 11–12
assumptions of income, 138–140
effects of inventory misstatements on income, 295
financial performance, 586, 587
issues, 90–93, 90 (exh.), 138–141
Medical insurance, 371
Medicare tax, 371
Merchandise
in transit, 297, 298 (exh.)
on hand not included in inventory, 298
purchases of, 254–255
sales of, 256–257, 261–262
Merchandise inventory, 246
Merchandising business, 246, 246–251
Merchandising company, 210
transactions, internal control over, 265–270
Minority interest, 651
Money market funds, 334
Money measure, 12
Monitoring, 263
Mortgage, 447, 447 (exh.)
Mortgages payable, 447
Multinational or transnational corporations, 654
Multistep income statement, 210, 210–213, 211 (exh.), 212 (exh.), 214 (exh.)
Mutual agency
lack of, 489
partnerships, 675
Natural resources, 402, 419–421
Negative financial leverage, 445
Negative free cash flows, 544
Net assets, 17
Net earnings, 213
Net income, 16, 138, 213
cash flows and, 545
per share, 213
Net loss, 16, 138
Net purchases, 259
Net revenue, 210, 216
Net sales, 210, 216, 601
Net selling price, 404
Net worth, 17, 208
Nominal accounts, 154

Noncash assets, issuance of stock for, 503–504
Noncash investing and financing transactions, 541
Noncompete covenant, 422
Noncontrolling investment
 influential but, 637, 646–648
 noninfluential and, 637, 643–646
Noncumulative preferred stock, 499
Noninfluential and noncontrolling investment, 637, 643–646
Nonoperating items, 593–594
Nonoperating revenues and expenses, 212
No-par stock, 501, 502–503
Normal balance, 95, 95 (exh.)
Normal operating cycle, 206
Note, duration of, 344–345
Notes on presentation, 111
Notes payable, 344, 368, 447
Notes receivable, 343, 343–346
Notes to the financial statements, 50–53
 annual report, 67–74, 82–87
Not-for-profit organizations, 10–11
NSF (nonsufficient funds) checks, 335
Numbers, look carefully at, 603
Objectivity, 25
Obsolescence, 411
Off-balance-sheet financing, 445
Oil and gas industry, development and exploration costs in, 421
100-year bonds, 457
One-time items, 592–594
Operating activities, 5, 539
 cash flows from, 546–533, 549 (exh.), 552–553
Operating asset management
 evaluating, 607–609
 supplemental financial ratios for assessing, 609–610
Operating assets, 206
Operating cycle, 247, 247–248, 247 (exh.), **607**
Operating expenses, 212
Operating income, 212
Operating lease, 447
Ordinary annuity, 380
 present value of, 380–381
Organizations
 governmental and not-for-profit, 10–11
 that influence GAAP, 24–25
 that issue accounting standards, 24
Other assets, 206
Other comprehensive income or loss, 497
Other postretirement benefits, 451
Other revenues and expenses, 212, 212–213
Outstanding checks, 335
Outstanding shares, 498
Owner's capital, 208
Owner's equity, 17, 207–208
Owner's investment in business, 98–99
Ownership
 ease of transfer of, 489
 separation of control and, 490
Pacioli, Fra Luca, 93
Par value, 18, 490
Par value stock, 501–502
Parent company, 648
Partner
 admission of, 679
 bonus to, 680–681
 capital, interest on, 676
 death of, 681
 equity, 207–208, 676
 purchasing an interest from, 679
 withdrawal of, 681
Partnership, 13, 208
 accounting for, 675–681
 co-ownership of property, 675
 defined, 675
 dissolution of, 679–681
 distribution of income and losses of, 676–678
 investing assets in, 679–680
 liquidation of, 681
 number and receipts of U.S., 13 (exh.)
Partnership agreement, 675
Partnership income, participation in, 675
Patent, 422
Payables, intercompany, 654
Payables turnover, 365, 385, 609
Payee, 343
Payment
 deferred, 383
 of liability, 101
 on account, 255, 260
Payment date, 492, 493
Payroll costs, illustrations of, 370 (exh.)
Payroll liabilities, 370–372
Pension contributions, 371
Pension fund, 450
Pension liabilities, 450–451
Pension plan, 450
Percentage of net sales method, 339, 339–340
 compared with accounts receivable aging method, 341–342
Performance measures, 5
 executive compensation and, 221
 standards of comparison for past, 588
 using financial ratios for, 215–223, 493–495
Periodic independent verification, 264
Periodic inventory system, 248, 258–262
 income statement under, 258 (exh.), 302 (exh.)
 inventory cost under, 299–302
 recording purchase transactions under, 259 (exh.)
 recording sales transactions under, 261 (exh.)
Periodicity, 139
Permanent accounts, 154
Permanent financing, 444
Perpetual inventory system, 248, 254–257
 income statement under, 254 (exh.), 307 (exh.)
 inventory cost under, 305–307
 recording purchase transactions under, 254 (exh.)
 recording sales transactions under, 256 (exh.)
Physical controls, 264
Physical deterioration, 411
Physical inventory, 250
Plant assets, 206, 554–556
 depreciation of related, 420
 discarded, 417–418
 exchanges of, 419
 sold for cash, 418
Politics and accounting don't mix, 496
Positive free cash flows, 544
Post-closing trial balance, 155, 188 (exh.)
Posting, 110, 110–111, 186 (exh.), 187 (exh.)
 from general journal to ledger, 111 (exh.)
 recording of transactions and, 108–112
Postretirement liabilities affect everyone, 450
Predictive value, 200
Preferred stock, 498
 book value for, 514
 callable, 500
 characteristics of, 498–500
 convertible, 500
 noncumulative, 499
Premium, 453
 bonds issued at, 456
Prepaid expenses, 145, 145–146, 145 (exh.)
Prepayment of expenses in cash, 99
Present value, 379, 380 (exh.), 381 (exh.)
 applications using, 382–383
 calculating, 379–381
 of an ordinary annuity, 380–381
 of single sum due in future, 379–380
 tables, 684–687
 value a bond using, 457–458, 458 (exh.)
Presentation, notes on, 111
Price
 bond issue, 452–453
 call, 454

Price/earnings (P/E) ratio, 495, 610, 610–611
Principal, 452
Principle of duality, 93
Private Company Financial Reporting Committee, 24
Private corporations, 46
Product warranty liability, 374
Production method, 413
comparison of straight-line method, declining-balance method, and, 414, 415 (exh.)
Professional conduct, 25
Professional management, 489
Profit, 138
Profit margin, 22, 26, **215**, 215–216, **601**, 601–602
Profitability, 5, 6
evaluating, 601–611
measurement issues and ethics, 138–141
ratio relationships, 603
Profit-sharing plans, 450
Promissory note, 343, 343 (exh.), 368 (exh.)
Promotional costs, 373–374
Property taxes payable, 373
Property, plant, and equipment, 206, 206–207
acquisition cost of, 407–410
Proprietorships, 208
number and receipts of U.S., 13 (exh.)
Provision for income taxes, 213
Public companies, 46
Public Company Accounting Oversight Board (PCAOB), 24, 54, 489
Publicly held corporations, 489
Publicly traded energy companies and accounting standards, 421
Purchase(s)
control of, 267–270, 268–269 (exh.)
group, 410
in foreign currency, 249
net, 259
of assets, 100–101
of equity investment, 647
of held-to-maturity securities, 656
of long-term investment, 644
of merchandise, 254–255, 259–261
of trading securities, 640
of treasury stock, 505–506
on credit, 255, 260
Purchase method, 649, 650
Purchase order, 269
Purchase requisition, 269
Purchase transactions
recording under periodic inventory system, 259 (exh.)
recording under perpetual inventory system, 254 (exh.)
Purchases account, 260
Purchases discount, 252, 252–253
Purchases returns and allowances, 255, 260
Purchases Returns and Allowances account, 260
Qualitative characteristics, 199, 200
Quality of earnings, 590, 590–594
Quick ratio, 610
Ratios
capital balance, 677
cash flow, 542–544
financial, 6, 19–22, 26, 115, 158, 215–223, 223–224, 246, 293–294, 310, 330, 331, 347–348, 365–366, 385, 445–446, 493–495, 543, 544, 601–602, 602–603, 604, 605, 606–607, 607–608, 608–609, 609–610, 610–611
financial analysis, 600–601
stated, 676–677, 677–678
Real accounts, 154
Receipt of cash dividend, 648
Receipt of interest, 657
Receipts on account, 257, 262
Receivables
intercompany, 654
management issues related to, 328–333
Receivable(s) turnover, 330, 347–348, 608
Receiving report, 269
Recognition, 90, 90–91, 366, 636
of income, 647–648
Recognition point, 91
Record date, 492, 493, 509
Recycling, 641
Registered bonds, 454
Registered independent auditors' report, 53
See also Auditor's report
Regulatory agencies, 10
Relevance, 199, 199–200
Reporting currency, 655
Reports
filed with SEC, 589
of certified public accountants, 53–54
of management's responsibilities, 53
published by corporation, 589
Research and development costs, 424
Residual equity, 497
Residual value, 411
Restatement, 655
of foreign subsidiary financial statements, 654–655
Restructurings, 593
Retail method, 308, 308 (exh.)
Retail pharmacy segment, 50
Retained earnings, 16, 207, 497, 558
account, 187 (exh.)
Retirement of
bonds, 468
treasury stock, 507–508
Return on assets, 220, 220–221, **602**, 602–603
Return on equity, 222, 222–223, **494**, 494–495, **606**, 606–607
Revenue(s), 15, 138
accrued, 151–152
and expenses, other, 212–213
cost of, 211
deferred, 150–151
earned, 151–152
in cash, 101
net, 210, 216
nonoperating, 212
on credit, 102
received in advance, 102
unearned, 150–151, 150 (exh.), 372–373
Revenue accounts, 184
Revenue expenditure, 407
Revenue recognition, 142
Risk assessment, 263
Rule of thumb measures, 588
Rules for double-entry accounting, 94–95
Ryan, Thomas M., 58–61
Salaries, 370, 677–678
Sale(s), 210
and excise taxes payable, 369–370
in foreign currency, 249
of long-term investment, 645
of merchandise, 256–257, 261–262
of trading securities, 641
of treasury shares, 506–507
of treasury stock, 506
on credit, 256, 261
terms of, 252–253
Sales discounts, 252
Sales returns, accounting for, 261
Sales returns and allowances, 210, 257, 262
Sales Returns and Allowances account, 257
Sales transactions
recording under periodic inventory system, 261 (exh.)
recording under perpetual inventory system, 256 (exh.)
Sarbanes-Oxley Act, 8, 14, 53, 200, 251, 586
Scope section of auditor's report, 54
SEC. *See* Securities and Exchange Commission
Secured bonds, 453
Securities and Exchange Commission (SEC), 8, **10**, 23, **24**, 46, 53, 141, 142, 452, 489, 638
reports filed with, 589
Securitization, 332

Segment information, 589 (exh.)
Selling expenses, 212
Separate entity, 12
Separate legal entity, 489
Separation of duties, 264
Separation of ownership and control, 490
Serial bonds, 453, 453–454
Service charges (SC), 335
Share buybacks, 506
Share of stock, 14, 489
Shareholders, 46
Shareholders' equity, 17
  See also Statement of shareholders' equity
Short-term financial assets, 329
Short-term investments, 636
  in equity securities, 639–642
Significant influence, 637
Simple interest, 378
  example of future value using, 378
Single-step income statement, 214, 214–215, 214 (exh.)
Skilling, Jeffrey, 201
Social security (FICA) tax, 371
Software, 422
Sole proprietorship, 13, 208, 674
Sombart, Werner, 93
Sound personnel practices, 264
Source documents, 98
Special-purpose entities (SPEs), 639
Specific identification method, 300
Standards of comparison, financial statement analysis, 587–589
Start-up and organization costs, 490
State and local income taxes, 371
State unemployment insurance tax, 371
Stated ratios, 676–677, 677–678
Stated value, 501
Statement of cash flows, 18, 18–19, 19 (exh.), 20 (exh.), 51 (exh.), **538**
  asking right questions about, 545–546
  consolidated, 64, 81, 539 (exh.)
  ethical considerations and, 541–542
  how universal is, 541
  in annual report, 50
  indirect method, 559 (exh.)
  overview of, 538–542
  preparing, 559, 546 (exh.)
  purposes and uses of, 538
Statement of changes in stockholders' equity, 512
Statement of financial position, 16
Statement of operations, 15
  consolidated, 62
Statement of retained earnings, 16, 17 (exh.), 20 (exh.), 153 (exh.)
Statement of stockholders' equity, 52–53 (exh.), **512**, 512–513, 513 (exh.)
  consolidated, 80
Statements of Financial Accounting Standards, 24
Statements of shareholders' equity
  consolidated, 65–66
  in annual report, 50
Statement of income, consolidated, 79
Stewardship, 199
Stewart, Martha, 638
Stock
  becomes debt under IFRS, 500
  issuance of, for cash and other assets, 501–504
  issuance of, for noncash assets, 503–504
  issuing above par value, 502
  issuing no-par with a stated value, 503
  issuing no-par with no stated value, 502–503
  share of, 489
  See also Common stock; Preferred stock
Stock dividends, 508, 508–510
  effect of on stockholders' equity, 510
  transactions, 509
Stock option plans, 495
Stock options as compensation, 495–496
Stock quotations on NASDAQ, 494 (exh.)
Stock splits, 510, 510–511
Stockholder control, 444
  decreased, 491
Stockholders, 7, 14
  first-class or second-class, 498
  letter to, 46–47
Stockholders' equity, 17, 17–18, 207
  accounts, 96, 96 (exh.)
  components of, 497–500
  effect of stock dividend on, 510
  section of balance sheet, 497 (exh.), 513 (exh.)
  statement of, 512–513
Straight-line method, 412, 460, 460–461
  amortizing bond premium, 464–465
  comparison of production method, declining-balance method, and, 414, 415 (exh.)
Subprime loans, 332
Subprime mortgage, fair value accounting and, 637
Subsidiary, 648
Successful efforts accounting, 421
Supplemental financial ratios for assessing operating asset management and liquidity, 609–610
Supplementary information notes, 53
Supply-chain management, 294
T-account, 94
Tangible assets, 206, **402**
Tax
  advantage, 444
  authorities, 10
  double taxation, 489–490
  FUTA, 371
  liability, increased, 491
  Medicare, 371
  purposes, special rules for, 416
  social security, 371
  SUTA, 371
  See also Income taxes
Taxes payable, sales and excise, 369–370
Temporary accounts, 154
Term bonds, 453
Terms of sale, 252–253
  debit and credit card sales, 253
Time periods, 381
Time value of money, 378, 378–379
Timeliness, 200
Total asset management, evaluating, 601–611
Trade accounts payable, 368
Trade credit, 329
Trade discount, 252
Trademark, 422
Trading on equity, 444
Trading securities, 539, 637, 639–642
  purchase of, 640
  sale of, 641
Transactions, 113 (exh.)
  cash flows and timing of, 112–113
  dividend, 492–493
  merchandising, 265–270
  noncash investing and financing, 541
  posting of, 108–112
  purchase, 254 (exh.), 259 (exh.)
  recording, 108–112, 264
  sales, 256 (exh.), 261 (exh.)
  stock dividends, 509
  summary of, 104, 105 (exh.)
  See also Business transactions
Transfer of ownership, ease of, 489
Transnational corporations, 654
Transparency, 202
Transportation costs, 253
Treasury shares, 506–507
Treasury stock, 495, **497**, 558
  accounting for, 505–508
  purchase of, 505–506
  retirement of, 507–508
  sale of, 506
Trend analysis, 597, 597 (exh.)
Trial balance, 106, 106–107, 106 (exh.), 143 (exh.), 153 (exh.), 185 (exh.)
  adjusted, 152–154
  errors, 107
  post-closing, 155, 188 (exh.)
U.S. GAAP. *See* Generally accepted accounting principles (GAAP)
Uncollectible accounts, 333, 337–342
  disclosure of, 338
  estimating expense, 339–342, 342 (exh.)
  writing off, 342

Understandability, 200
Underwriter, 490
Unearned revenues, 150, 150–151, 150 (exh.), **372**, 372–373
Uniform Partnership Act, 675
Units of production method, 413
Unlimited liability, partnerships, 675
Unrecorded revenues, adjustment for, 151 (exh.)
Unsecured bonds, 453
Useful life
  definite, 423
  estimated, 412
  indefinite, 423
  of airplanes, 411
Vacation pay liability, 375
Valuation, 91, 91–92, 367, 636
  and adjustment, year-end, 640, 641
  approaches to fair value accounting, 377–381
  issue, 90
  of an asset, 382–383
  of inventory by estimation, 308–309
Value, 514
  in use, 404
Variable interest entities (VIEs), 639
Verifiability, 200
Vertical analysis, 598, 598–600
Voluntary association, partnerships as, 675
Wages, 370
Wall Street Journal, 590, 637
  definition of free cash flow, 545
Web sales, 257
Weighted average method, 300
With recourse, 331
Withdrawal of partner, 681
Without recourse, 332
Work sheet, 188–191, 189 (exh.), 191 (exh.), 651 (exh.), 652 (exh.), 653 (exh.), 655 (exh.)
  closing entries and, 184–191
  preparing, 188–191
  using, 191
Working capital, 246
Working papers, 188
Write-downs, 593
Write-off, 593
  uncollectible accounts, 342
Year-end accrual of interest, 656–657
Year-end adjustment, 644–645, 645–646
Year-end valuation and adjustment, 640, 641
Zero coupon bonds, 460
Zuckerberg, Mark, 503